WRITERS' & ARTISTS'
YEARBOOK 1997

Writers' & Artists' Yearbook 1997

NINETIETH YEAR OF ISSUE

A directory for writers, artists, playwrights, writers for film, radio and television, photographers and composers

A&C BLACK · LONDON

The publishers make no representation,
express or implied, with regard to the
accuracy of the information contained
in this book and cannot accept any
legal responsibility for any errors
or omissions that may take place.

A CIP catalogue record for this book
is available from the British Library.

ISBN 0-7136-4427-3

Typeset by Page Bros., Norwich, England
Printed and bound in Great Britain by
BPC Paperbacks Ltd.

Contents

Part One: Markets

Articles, Reports and Short Stories

Books

Photography

Picture Research

Music

Agents

Part Two: General Information

Preparation of Materials, Resources

Publishing Practice

Copyright and Libel

Finance

Societies, Prizes and Festivals

Index – page *678*

Preface

Writers' & Artists' Yearbook is constantly changing. This 90th annual edition has been rigorously revised and updated. New articles are included and all sections of the book have been carefully checked, many thousands of changes being made to the directory entries. Improvements, amendments and additions have been made throughout the book. As a consequence *Writers' & Artists' Yearbook* maintains its pre-eminent position as the essential guide to all areas of the media.

New features of this edition include: a detailed list of literature festivals; advice on stereotyping in *Sexism, Racism, Ageism and other Isms* by Karen Judd; an updated survey on *Writing for Broadcasting*, focusing on markets in the changing face of broadcasting, by Jocelyn Hay of Voice of the Listener; and details of the latest changes to UK copyright law as a result of EC harmonisation in the article on *UK Copyright*. The introduction of self-assessment for tax purposes is covered in the *Income Tax* article, and authors' agents have listed, in their entries, their leading authors. Also included is a checklist of publishers specialising in multimedia, and a *Journalists' Calendar* for 1997.

Writers' & Artists' Yearbook is arranged in two main parts with fourteen clearly defined sections.

Part One provides *Markets* for articles, books, scripts, poetry, illustrations, photographs, music and includes articles on picture research and self-publishing.

Part Two offers *General Information*, with articles on many practical and legal matters of importance to writers and artists, together with lists of resources and useful addresses. This part also provides details of societies, associations and clubs, as well as a list of prizes, awards and competitions.

Vanity publishing Every edition of the *Yearbook* contains a strong warning that authors who pay for the publication of their work are almost invariably making an expensive mistake. It has been suggested that several distinguished poets have found it necessary to underwrite their first books in order to establish themselves, and in this respect the cautionary note on 'vanity publishing' on page 267 has been mildly modified; but unhappily there is still ample evidence that an emphatic general warning is necessary. Writers who cannot resist the temptation of seeing their work in print should read the advice given in the article on self-publishing which begins on page 263.

It should be repeated, too, that the publishers of the *Yearbook* cannot provide an advisory service, and that to rely on an out-of-date edition is to invite inevitable difficulties and disappointments.

PART ONE
Markets

Articles, reports and short stories

Newspapers and Magazines

SUBMITTING MATERIAL

Over a thousand titles are included in the newspapers and magazines section of the *Yearbook*, almost all of them offering opportunities to the writer. Some overseas titles have little space for freelance contributions, but many of them will always consider outstanding work. Many do not appear in our lists because the market they offer for the freelance writer is either too small or too specialised, or both. Those who wish to offer contributions to technical, specialist or local journals are likely to know their names and can find their addresses; before submitting a manuscript to any such periodical it is advisable to write a preliminary letter to its editor.

Magazine editors frequently complain to us about the unsuitability of many manuscripts submitted to them. Not only are these unsuitable, but no postage is sent for their return. In their own interests, writers and others are advised to *enclose postage for the return of unsuitable material*. It is also advisable to send the material to the correct person. Each section of the main newspapers and magazines nowadays has its own commissioning editor. A telephone call to the main switchboard will establish the name of the editor in question.

Before submitting manuscripts, writers should study carefully the editorial requirements of a magazine; not only for the subjects dealt with, but for the approach, treatment, style and length. Obvious though these comments may be to the practised writer, the beginner would be spared much disappointment by studying the market more carefully (but should not expect editors to send free specimen copies of their magazines). An article or short story suitable for *Woman's Weekly* is unlikely to appeal to the readers of *The Literary Review*. The importance of studying the market cannot be overemphasised. It is an editor's job to know what readers want, and to see that they get it. Thus freelance contributions must be tailored to fit a specific market; subject, theme, treatment, length, etc., must meet the editor's requirements.

Editors also prefer, and expect, material to be well presented. Neatly typed, double-spaced, with good margins, on A4 paper is the standard to aim at – see *Preparing and submitting a manuscript* on page 460 and Randall McMullan's article, *Word Processing*, on page 475.

When submitting illustrations, be they colour or b&w prints or transparencies, line drawings or cartoons, it is advisable not to send these 'on spec', but to check with the editor first. See also page 120.

It has always been our aim to obtain and publish the rates of payment offered for contributions by newspapers and magazines. Many journals, however, are reluctant to state a standard rate, since the value of a contribution may be

3

dependent not upon length but upon the standing of the writer or of the information given. Many other periodicals, in spite of efforts to extract more precise information from them, prefer to state 'by negotiation'.

A number of magazines and newspapers will accept and pay for letters to the editor, brief fillers and gossip paragraphs, as well as puzzles and quizzes. For a list of these see the **Classified index** on page 127. This index provides only a rough guide to markets and must be used with discrimination. For lists of recent mergers, changes of title, and terminations, see page 126. For a list of magazines and newspapers willing to pay for cartoons, see page 339.

Readers are reminded that potential contributors living outside the UK should always enclose return postage in the form of International Reply Coupons when submitting queries or MSS. They might also consider approaching an agent to syndicate their material. Most agents operate on an international basis and are more aware of current market requirements. Again, return postage should always be included. See **Syndicates, news and press agencies** on page 141.

MARKETS

See Jill Dick's article, **Writing for newspapers**, on page 114, John Hines' article, **Writing magazine articles**, on page 117 and Barbara Wood-Kaczmar's article, **Writing for the European Union**, on page 122.

The lists of overseas newspapers and magazines contain only a selection of those journals which offer some market for the freelance (*Willings Press Guide Volume 2 Overseas* provides fuller listings). The overseas market for stories and articles is small and editors often prefer their fiction to have a local setting.

The larger newspapers and magazines buy many of their stories, as the smaller papers buy general articles, through one or other of the well-known syndicates, and a writer may be well advised to send printed copies of stories he/she has had published at home to an agent for syndication overseas.

Most of the big newspapers depend for news on their own staffs and the press agencies. The most important papers have permanent representatives in Britain who keep them supplied, not only with news of especial interest to the country concerned, but also with regular summaries of British news and with articles on events of particular importance. While many overseas newspapers and magazines have a London office, it is usual for MSS from freelance contributors to be submitted to the headquarters' editorial office overseas.

When sending MSS abroad it is important to remember to enclose International Reply Coupons; these can be exchanged in any foreign country for stamps representing the minimum postage payable on a letter sent from that country to this country.

See also Journalists' Calendar of
selected anniversaries
(page 444)

UNITED KINGDOM

(For Northern Ireland publications, see under Irish listings, page 104.)

Aberdeen Evening Express, Moreen Simpson, Aberdeen Journals Ltd, PO Box 43, Lang Stracht, Mastrick, Aberdeen AB9 8AF   *tel* (01224) 690222   *telex* 739244 JNLSAB G   *fax* (01224) 699575.
24p. D. Lively evening paper reading. *Illustrations:* colour and b&w, cartoons. *Payment:* by arrangement.

Accountancy (1889), Brian Singleton-Green, 40 Bernard Street, London WC1N 1LD   *tel* 0171-833 3291   *fax* 0171-833 2085.
£3.60. M. Articles on accounting, taxation, financial, legal and other subjects likely to be of professional interest to accountants in practice or industry, and to top management generally; cartoons. *Payment:* £110 per page.

Accountancy Age (1969), Robert Outram, VNU Business Publications, VNU House, 32-34 Broadwick Street, London W1A 2HG   *tel* 0171-396 9000   *fax* 0171-396 9008.
£1.50. W. Articles of accounting, financial and business interest. *Illustrations:* colour photos; freelance assignments commissioned. *Payment:* by arrangement.

Achievement, World Trade Magazines Ltd, World Trade House, 49 Dartford Road, Sevenoaks, Kent TN13 3TE   *tel* (01732) 458144   *fax* (01732) 456295.
£2.00. Q. Lively articles relating to British business achievements in international project management. *Illustrations:* first-class photos. *Payment:* by arrangement.

Active Life (1989), Helene Hodge, Aspen Specialist Media, Christ Church, Cosway Street, London NW1 5NJ   *tel* 0171-262 2622.
£1.75. Bi-M. Lifestyle advice for the over 50s, including holidays and health, fashion and food, finance and fiction, hobbies and home, plus personality profiles. *Submit ideas in writing. Length:* 600-1200 words. *Illustrations:* colour. *Payment:* £100 per 1000 words; photos by negotiation.

Acumen (1985), Patricia Oxley, 6 The Mount, Higher Furzeham, Brixham, South Devon TQ5 8QY   *tel* (01803) 851098.
£10.00 p.a. Tri-annual (Jan/May/Sept) Poetry, literary and critical articles, reviews, literary memoirs, etc., 100pp or more. Send sae with submissions. *Payment:* by negotiation.

Administrator (1971), 16 Park Crescent, London W1N 4AH   *tel* 0171-580 4741   *fax* 0171-323 1132.
£4.00. M. (£37.00 p.a. post free UK) Official Journal of The Institute of Chartered Secretaries and Administrators. Practical and topical articles (750-1600 words) on law, finance and management affecting company secretaries and other senior administrators in business, nationalised industries, local and central government and other institutions in Britain and overseas. Most articles commissioned from leading administrators. *Payment:* by arrangement.

Aeromodeller (1935), John Stroud, Nexus Special Interests, Nexus House, Boundary Way, Hemel Hempstead, Herts. HP2 7ST   *tel* (01442) 66551   *fax* (01442) 66998.
£2.25. M. Articles and news concerning model aircraft. Suitable articles and first-class photos by outside contributors are always considered. *Length:* 750-2000 words, or by arrangement. *Illustrations:* photos and line drawings to scale. *Payment:* by negotiation.

Aeroplane Monthly (1973), Richard T. Riding, IPC Magazines Ltd, King's Reach Tower, Stamford Street, London SE1 9LS   *tel* 0171-261 5551   *fax* 0171-261 7851.
£2.50. M. Articles and photos relating to historical aviation. *Length:* up to 3000 words. *Illustrations:* line, half-tone, colour, cartoons. *Payment:* £45 per 1000 words, payable on publication; photos £10; colour £80 per page.

Africa Confidential (1960), Patrick Smith, Blackwell Publishing Ltd, 73 Farringdon Road, London EC1M 3JB   *tel* 0171-831 3511   *fax* 0171-831 6778.
£180.00 p.a. F. News and analysis of political and economic developments in Africa. Unsolicited contributions welcomed, but must be exclusive and not published elsewhere. *Length:* 1200-word features, 200-word pointers. *Payment:* £200 per 1000 words. *No* illustrations or advertising.

African Business (1978), Anver Versi, IC Publications Ltd, 7 Coldbath Square, London EC1R 4LQ   *tel* 0171-713 7711   *telex* 8811757 ARABY G   *fax* 0171-713 7970.
£1.90. M. Articles on business, economic and financial topics of interest to businessmen, ministers, officials concerned with African affairs. *Length:* 400-750 words; shorter coverage 100-400 words. *Illustrations:* line, half-tone. *Payment:* £70 per 1000 words; £1 per column cm for illustrations.

Agenda, William Cookson and Peter Dale, 5 Cranbourne Court, Albert Bridge Road, London SW11 4PE   *tel/fax* 0171-228 0700.
£20.00 p.a. Q. (libraries, institutions and overseas: rates on application) Poetry and criticism. Contributors should study the journal before submitting MSS with an sae. *Illustrations:* half-tone. *Payment:* variable – depending on finances.

Air International (1971), Malcolm English, Key Publishing Ltd, PO Box 100, Stamford, Lincs. PE9 1XQ   *tel* (01780) 55131   *fax* (01780) 57261.
£2.55. M. Technical articles on aircraft; features on topical aviation subjects – civil and military; historical aviation subjects. *Length:* up to 5000 words. *Illustrations:* colour transparencies/prints, b&w prints/line drawings, cartoons. *Payment:* £50 per 1000 words or by negotiation; £25 colour, £10 b&w.

Air Pictorial International, Barry C. Wheeler, HPC Publishing, Drury Lane, St Leonards-on-Sea, East Sussex TN38 9BJ   *tel* (01424) 720477   *fax* (01424) 443693/434086.
£2.15. M. Covers all aspects of aviation. Many articles commissioned, and the editor is glad to consider competent articles exploring fresh ground or presenting an individual point of view on technical matters. All articles are *illustrated*, mainly with photos. *Payment:* by arrangement.

Amateur Gardening (1884), G. Clarke, IPC Magazines Ltd, Westover House, West Quay Road, Poole, Dorset BH15 1JG   *tel* (01202) 680586   *fax* (01202) 674335.
87p. W. Articles up to 700 words about any aspect of gardening. *Payment:* by arrangement. *Illustrations:* colour.

Amateur Photographer (1884), Keith Wilson, IPC Magazines Ltd, King's Reach Tower, Stamford Street, London SE1 9LS   *tel* 0171-261 5100   *fax* 0171-261 5404.
£1.50. W. Original articles of pictorial or technical interest, preferably illustrated with either photos or diagrams. Good instructional features especially sought. *Length preferred:* (unillustrated) 400-800 words; articles up to 1500 words; (illustrated) 2 to 4 pages. *Payment:* weekly, at rates according to usage. *Illustrations* unaccompanied by text considered for covers or feature illustrations – please indicate if we can hold on file; cartoons.

Amateur Stage (1946), Charles Vance, Platform Publications Ltd, 83 George Street, London W1H 5PL   *tel* 0171-486 1732/7930   *fax* 0171-224 2215.
£1.80. M. Articles on all aspects of the amateur theatre, preferably practical and factual. *Length:* 600-2000 words. *Illustrations:* photos and line drawings. *Payment:* none.

Ambit (1959), Dr Martin Bax, 17 Priory Gardens, Highgate, London N6 5QY   *tel* 0181-340 3566.
£5.50. Q. (£22.00 p.a.) Poems, short stories, criticism. *Payment:* by arrangement. *Illustrations:* line, half-tone, colour.

Angler's Mail, Roy Westwood, IPC Magazines Ltd, King's Reach Tower, Stamford Street, London SE1 9LS   *tel* 0171-261 5778   *fax* 0171-261 6016.
80p. W. News items about coarse and sea fishing. *Payment:* by agreement.

Angling Times (1953), Keith Higginbottom, EMAP Pursuit Publishing Ltd, PO Box 231, Bretton Court, Bretton, Peterborough PE3 8EN   *tel* (01733) 266222/264666   *fax* (01733) 265515/263294.
70p. W. Articles, pictures, news stories, on all forms of angling. *Illustrations:* line, half-tone, colour. *Payment:* by arrangement.

The Antique Collector (1930), Susan Morris, Orpheus Publications Ltd, 7 St John's Road, Harrow-on-the-Hill, Middlesex HA1 2EE   *tel* 0181-863 2020   *fax* 0181-863 2444.
£4.00. 6 p.a. Authoritative, topical and fully illustrated information for those interested in extending their knowledge and enjoyment of all aspects of antiques and the fine and decorative arts. *Illustrations:* fine b&w photos or colour transparencies. *Payment:* £250 per feature; illustrations at cost.

The Antique Dealer & Collectors Guide, Philip Bartlam, PO Box 805, Greenwich, London SE10 8TD   *tel* 0181-691 4820.
£2.75. M. Articles on antique collecting and art. *Length:* 1500-2000 words. *Payment:* £76 per 1000 words. *Illustrations:* half-tone, colour.

Apollo (1925), Robin Simon, 1-2 Castle Lane, London SW1E 6DR   *tel* 0171-233 6640   *fax* 0171-630 7791.
£7.80. M. Knowledgeable articles of about 2500 words on art, architecture, ceramics, furniture, armour, glass, sculpture, and any subject connected with art and collecting. *Payment:* by arrangement. *Illustrations:* half-tone, colour.

The Aquarist and Pondkeeper (1924), Dick Mills, M&J Publications Ltd, Caxton House, Wellesley Road, Ashford, Kent TN24 8ET   *tel* (01233) 636349   *fax* (01233) 631239.
£2.25. M. Illustrated authoritative articles by professional and amateur biologists, naturalists and aquarium hobbyists on all matters concerning life in and near water, conservation and herpetology. *Length:* about 1500 words. *Illustrations:* line, half-tone, colour, cartoons. *Payment:* by arrangement.

The Architects' Journal (1895), Paul Finch, EMAP Construct, 151 Rosebery Avenue, London EC1R 4QX   *tel* 0171-505 6700   *fax* 0171-505 6701.
£1.60. W. Articles (mainly technical) on architecture, planning and building accepted only with prior agreement of synopsis. *Illustrations:* photos and drawings. *Payment:* by arrangement.

Architectural Design (1930), Maggie Toy, Academy Group Ltd, 42 Leinster Gardens, London W2 3AN   *tel* 0171-402 2141   *fax* 0171-723 9540.
£68.00 p.a. 6 double issues (£50.00 p.a. students) International magazine comprising an extensively illustrated thematic profile presenting architecture and critical interpretations of architectural history, theory and practice. Uncommissioned articles not accepted. *Illustrations:* drawings and photos, colour, half-tone, line (colour preferred). *Payment:* by arrangement.

Architectural Review (1896), Peter Davey, EMAP Construct, 151 Rosebery Avenue, London EC1R 4QX   *tel* 0171-505 6725   *fax* 0171-505 6701.
£5.95. M. Articles on architecture and the allied arts. Writers must be thoroughly qualified. *Length:* up to 3000 words. *Payment:* by arrangement. *Illustrations:* photos, drawings, etc.

Architecture Today (1989), Ian Latham and Mark Swenarton, 161 Rosebery Avenue, London EC1R 4QX   *tel* 0171-837 0143   *fax* 0171-837 0155.
Free to architects. £3.00. 10 p.a. 'The independent architectural magazine.' *Mostly commissioned* articles and features on today's European architecture. *Length:* 200-800 words. *Illustrations:* colour. *Payment:* by negotiation.

Arena (1986), Peter Howarth, 3rd Floor Block A, Exmouth House, Pine Street, London EC1R 0JL   *tel* 0171-837 7270   *fax* 0171-837 3906.
£2.00. 10 p.a. Profiles, articles on a wide range of subjects intelligently treated; art, architecture, politics, sport, business, music, film, design, media, fashion. *Length:* up to 3000 words. *Illustrations:* b&w and colour photos. *Payment:* £200 per 1000 words; varies for illustrations.

Army Quarterly & Defence Journal (1829), T.D. Bridge, 1 West Street, Tavistock, Devon PL19 8DS   *tel* (01822) 613577/612785   *fax* (01822) 612785.
£49.80 p.a. Q. (£132.00 3-yr saver contract) Articles on a wide range of British, UN, Commonwealth and worldwide defence issues, historical and current; also Quarterly Diary, Defence Contracts, International Defence Reports, book and video reviews. *Preliminary letter with synopsis preferred. Length:* 1000-4800 words. *Illustrations:* b&w photos, line drawings, maps. *Payment:* by arrangement.

Aromatherapy Quarterly (1983), Séza Eccles, 5 Ranelagh Avenue, Barnes, London SW13 0BY   *tel/fax* 0181-392 1691.
£4.00. Q. (£16.00 p.a.) Specialist articles and case studies on aromatherapy and related issues. Potential contributors should have read the magazine and have a significant knowledge of the subject matter. *Length:* 1500-3000 words. *Illustrations:* b&w photos and line. *Payment:* none; complimentary copy.

Art & Craft (1936), Siân Morgan, Scholastic Ltd, Villiers House, Clarendon Avenue, Leamington Spa, Warks. CV32 5PR   *tel* (01926) 887799   *fax* (01926) 883331.
£1.95. M. Articles offering fresh, creative ideas of a practical nature, based on teaching art, design and technology in the National Curriculum, for the infant/junior school teacher. Articles by teachers for teachers. *Illustrations:* colour and b&w line drawings. *Payment:* by arrangement.

Art & Design (1985), Nicola Kearton, Academy Group Ltd, 42 Leinster Gardens, London W2 3AN   *tel* 0171-402 2141   *fax* 0171-723 9540.
£65.00 p.a. 6 double issues (£50.00 p.a. students) International magazine covering the whole spectrum of the arts, with particular emphasis on Contemporary Art. Each issue comprises extensively illustrated thematic features together with critical articles from well-known writers. Feature articles, exhibition reviews and previews, book reviews. Uncommissioned articles not accepted. *Illustrations:* line, half-tone, colour (colour preferred). *Payment:* by arrangement.

Art Business Today (1991), Annabelle Ruston, The Fine Art Trade Guild, 16-18 Empress Place, London SW6 1TT   *tel* 0171-381 6616   *fax* 0171-381 2596.
£15.00 p.a. Q. Distributed to the fine art and framing industry. Covers essential information on new products and technology, market trends and business analysis. *Length:* 800-1600 words. *Illustrations:* colour photos, cartoons. *Payment:* by arrangement.

Art Monthly (1976), Patricia Bickers, Britannia Art Publications Ltd, Suite 17, 26 Charing Cross Road, London WC2H 0DG   *tel* 0171-240 0389   *fax* 0171-240 0389.
£2.75. 10 p.a. Features on modern and contemporary visual artists and art history, art theory and art-related issues; exhibition and book reviews. *All material commissioned. Length:* 1000-2000 words. *Illustrations:* b&w photos. *Payment:* features £100-£150; none for photos.

The Art Newspaper (1990), Laura Suffield, 27-29 Vauxhall Grove, London SW8 1SY   *tel* 0171-735 3331   *fax* 0171-735 3332.
£4.50. 11 p.a. (£45.00 p.a.) International, up-to-date coverage of the art market, news, commentary. *Length:* 200-1000 words. *Illustrations:* b&w photos. *Payment:* £120 per 1000 words; negotiable.

Art Review (1949), David Lee, Art Review Ltd, Hereford House, 23-24 Smithfield Street, London EC1A 9LB   *tel* 0171-236 4880   *fax* 0171-236 4881.
£3.50. M. Art news and features. Commissioned work only. *Payment:* from £150 per 1000 words. *Illustrations:* line, half-tone, colour.

The Artist (1931), Sally Bulgin, The Artists' Publishing Co. Ltd, Caxton House, 63-65 High Street, Tenterden, Kent TN30 6BD   *tel* (01580) 763673.
£2.05. M. Practical, instructional articles on painting for all amateur and professional artists. *Payment:* by arrangement. *Illustrations:* line, half-tone, colour.

Artists and Illustrators (1986), Laura Gascoigne, 4th Floor, The Fitzpatrick Building, 188-194 York Way, London N7 9QR   *tel* 0171-700 8500   *fax* 0171-700 4985.
£2.25. M. Technical and practical articles for amateur and professional artists. *Length:* 1500 words. *Illustrations:* colour transparencies. *Payment:* variable.

Artists Newsletter (1983), Hannah Firth, AN Publications, PO Box 23, Sunderland SR4 6DG   *tel* (0191) 567 3589   *fax* (0191) 564 1600   *e-mail* anpubs@gn.apc.org
£2.50; £22.50 p.a. M. Articles, news and features for practising artists and makers. *Illustrations:* transparencies, colour and b&w photos. *Payment:* £90 per 1000 words.

The Asda Magazine (1986), Jacqueline Keelan, River Publishing, 55 Greek Street, London W1H 5LR   *tel* 0171-306 0304   *fax* 0171-306 0314.
Free. M. General features on food, health and nutrition; consumer stories. *Length:* 200-1500 words *Payment:* £100-£500.

The Asian Age (1994), M.J. Akbar, Suite No. 4, 55 Park Lane, London W1Y 3DB   *tel* 0171-304 4028   *fax* 0171-304 4029.
50p. D. Articles and features of interest to the Asian community; *material mostly commissioned. Length:* 200-1500 words. *Illustrations:* b&w photos. *Payment:* £50 per 1000 words; £40 per photo.

Asian Times (1983), Arif Ali, Hansib Publishing Ltd, Third Floor, Tower House, 141/149 Fonthill Road, London N4 3HF   *tel* 0171-281 1191   *fax* 0171-263 9656.
50p. W. News stories, articles and features of interest to Britain's Asian community.

Astronomy Now (1987), Steven Young, Pole Star Publications, PO Box 175, Tonbridge, Kent TN10 4ZY   *tel* (01732) 367542   *fax* (01732) 356230.
£1.95. M. Aimed at amateur astronomers. Interested in news items and longer features on astronomy and some space-related activities. Writers' guidelines available (send sae). *Length:* 1500-3000 words. *Illustrations:* line, half-tone, colour. *Payment:* 5p per word; from £10 per photo.

Athletics Weekly (1946), Nigel Walsh, EMAP Pursuit Publishing Ltd, Bretton Court, Bretton, Peterborough PE3 8DZ *tel* (01733) 261144 *fax* (01733) 465206/267198.
£1.10. W. News and features on track and field athletics, road running, cross country, fell and race walking. Material *mostly commissioned*. *Length:* 1000-3000 words. *Illustrations:* colour and b&w action and head/shoulder photos, line, cartoons. *Payment:* varies.

Attitude (1994), Pas Paschali, Northern & Shell plc, Northern & Shell Tower, City Harbour, London E14 9GL *tel* 0171-987 5090 *fax* 0171-538 3690.
£2.95. M. Men's magazine aimed primarily but not exclusively at gay men. Covers style/fashion, interviews, reviews, news, art and leisure. *Illustrations:* colour transparencies and b&w prints. *Payment:* £150 per 1000 words; £100 per full page illustration.

The Author (1890), Derek Parker, 84 Drayton Gardens, London SW10 9SB *tel* 0171-373 6642.
£7.00. Q. Organ of The Society of Authors. Commissioned articles from 1000-2000 words on any subject connected with the legal, commercial or technical side of authorship. Little scope for the freelance writer: *preliminary letter* advisable. *Illustrations:* line, occasional cartoons. *Payment:* by arrangement.

Auto Express (1988), David Johns, Express Newspapers, Ludgate House, 245 Blackfriars Road, London SE1 9UX *tel* 0171-928 8000 *fax* 0171-928 2847.
£1.20. W. News stories, and general interest features about drivers as well as cars. *Illustrations:* colour photos. *Payment:* features £250 per 1000 words; photos, varies.

Autocar (1895), Michael Harvey, Haymarket Publishing Ltd, 38-42 Hampton Road, Teddington, Middlesex TW11 0JE *tel* 0181-943 5851 *fax* 0181-943 5853 *e-mail* compuserve 100020.2017
£1.65. W. Articles on all aspects of cars, motoring and the motor industry: general, practical, competition and technical. *Illustrations:* line (litho), colour and electronic (Illustrator). Press day news: Thursday. *Payment:* varies; mid-month following publication.

Back Street Heroes (1983), Karen Tait, PO Box 28, Altrincham, Cheshire WA15 8SH *tel* 0161-928 3480 *fax* 0161-941 6897.
£2.40. M. Custom motorcycle features plus informed lifestyle pieces; biker fiction. *Illustrations:* colour, cartoons. *Payment:* by arrangement.

Bad Attitude (1992), 121 Railton Road, London SE24 0LR *tel* 0171-978 9057 *fax* 0171-326 0353.
£1.00. Q. Feminist newspaper. News, features, reviews, short stories – feminist/relating to women. *Length:* up to 3000 words. *Illustrations:* b&w photos, line, cartoons. *Payment:* expenses (maximum £3 per article/photo).

Balance (1935), Maggie Gibbons, British Diabetic Association, 10 Queen Anne Street, London W1M 0BD *tel* 0171-323 1531 *fax* 0171-637 3644.
£1.85. Bi-M. Articles on diabetes or related topics. *Length:* 1000-2000 words. *Payment:* by arrangement. *Illustrations:* colour.

Ballroom Dancing Times (1956), Editor: Mary Clarke, Executive Editor: Bronya Siefert, The Dancing Times Ltd, Clerkenwell House, 45-47 Clerkenwell Green, London EC1R 0EB *tel* 0171-250 3006 *fax* 0171-253 6679.
80p. M. Ballroom and social dancing from every aspect, but chiefly from the serious competitive, teaching and medal test angles. Well-informed freelance articles are occasionally used, but only after preliminary arrangements.

Payment: by arrangement. *Illustrations:* action photos preferred, b&w or colour.

The Banker (1926), Stephen Timewell, Greystoke Place, Fetter Lane, London EC4A 1ND   *tel* 0171-405 6969   *telex* 23700 FINBI G   *fax* 0171-831 9136. £4.00. M. Articles on capital markets, trade finance, bank analysis and top 1000 listings. *Illustrations:* half-tones of people, charts, tables. *Payment:* by negotiation.

Baptist Times (1855), John Capon, PO Box 54, Didcot, Oxon OX11 8XB   *tel* (01235) 512012   *fax* (01235) 512013. 40p. W. Religious or social affairs material, up to 1000 words. *Payment:* by arrangement. *Illustrations:* half-tone, cartoons.

The Bath Chronicle (1770), David Gledhill, Westminster Press Ltd, Media in Wessex, 33-34 Westgate Street, Bath BA1 1EW   *tel* (01225) 444044   *fax* (01225) 445969. 30p. Mon.-Sat. Welcomes local news and features. *Length:* 200-500 words. *Illustrations:* colour photos. *Payment:* 8p-15.7p per printed line; £5 per photo where commissioned.

BBC Gardeners' World Magazine (1991), Adam Pasco, BBC Worldwide Publishing, Woodlands, 80 Wood Lane, London W12 0TT   *tel* 0181-576 3959   *fax* 0181-576 3986. £1.95. M. Features and ideas on plants, garden design and garden visits. *All material commissioned.* Study of magazine essential before submitting ideas. *Length:* varies, mainly 800-1000 words. *Illustrations:* colour transparencies; all artwork commissioned. *Payment:* by negotiation.

BBC GoodFood (1989), Mitzie Wilson, BBC Worldwide Publishing, Woodlands, 80 Wood Lane, London W12 0TT   *tel* 0181-576 2000   *fax* 0181-576 3825. £1.55. M. Recipes from TV and radio, cookery features, food and wine news. *No* unsolicited material. *Length:* 700-1400 words. *Illustrations:* colour photos and line. *Payment:* by arrangement.

BBC Homes & Antiques (1993), Judith Hall, BBC Worldwide Publishing, Woodlands, 80 Wood Lane, London W12 0TT   *tel* 0181-576 3490   *fax* 0181-576 3867. £1.95. M. Features on homes and antiques-related subjects. *Length:* 850-1500 words. *Illustrations:* colour. *Payment:* by arrangement.

BBC Music Magazine (1992), Fiona Maddocks, BBC Worldwide Publishing, Room A1004, Woodlands, 80 Wood Lane, London W12 0TT   *tel* 0181-576 3283   *fax* 0181-576 3292. £3.95. M. Articles, features, news and reviews on classical music. *All material commissioned. Length:* up to 2000 words. *Illustrations:* line, half-tone, colour. *Payment:* £150 per 1000 words; varies for illustrations.

BBC Top Gear Magazine (1993), Kevin Blick, BBC Worldwide Publishing, Woodlands, 80 Wood Lane, London W12 0TT   *tel* 0181-576 2000   *fax* 0181-576 3754. £2.70. M. Features on *any* aspect of cars and motoring; car tests. *Material mostly commissioned. Length:* 1500-3000 words. *Illustrations:* colour photos and line drawings. *Payment:* £200 per 1000 words; by agreement for illustrations.

BBC Vegetarian GoodFood (1992), Mary Gwynn, BBC Worldwide Publishing, Woodlands, 80 Wood Lane, London W12 0TT   *tel* 0181-576 2000   *fax* 0181-749 0538.

£1.65. M. Cooking, nutrition, environmental issues. Accepts only single-page feature outlines; *no* unsolicited material. *Illustrated*, including cartoons. *Payment:* by arrangement.

BBC Wildlife Magazine, Rosamund Kidman Cox, Broadcasting House, White-ladies Road, Bristol BS8 2LR *tel* (0117) 973 8402 *fax* (0117) 946 7075.
£2.30. M. Popular but scientifically accurate articles about wildlife and conservation (national and international), some linked by subject to TV and radio programmes. Two news sections for short, topical biological and environmental stories. *Length of articles:* 3000 words. *Illustrations:* top-quality colour photos. *Payment:* £200-£350 per article; photos according to reproduction size, £45-£150.

The Beano, D.C. Thomson & Co. Ltd, Albert Square, Dundee DD1 9QJ *tel* (01382) 223131 *fax* (01382) 322214; and 185 Fleet Street, London EC4A 2HS *tel* 0171-242 5086 *fax* 0171-404 5694.
40p. W. Comic strips for children. Series, 11-22 pictures. *Payment:* on acceptance.

Beano Comic Library, D.C. Thomson & Co. Ltd, Albert Square, Dundee DD1 9QJ *tel* (01382) 223131 *fax* (01382) 322214; and 185 Fleet Street, London EC4A 2HS *tel* 0171-242 5086 *fax* 0171-404 5694.
50p. 2 p.m. Extra-long comic adventure stories featuring well-known characters from the weekly Beano publication.

Bedfordshire Magazine (1947), Betty Chambers, White Crescent Press, 50 Shefford Road, Meppershall, Shefford SG17 5LL *tel* (01462) 813363.
£2.25. Q. Articles of Bedfordshire interest, especially history and biography. *Length:* up to 1500 words. *Illustrations:* line, half-tone. *Payment:* nominal, plus complimentary copy.

Bella (1987), Jackie Highe, Shirley House, 25 Camden Road, London NW1 9LL *tel* 0171-284 0909 *fax* 0171-485 3774.
50p. W. General interest magazine for women: practical articles on fashion and beauty, health, cooking, home, travel; real life stories, plus fiction up to 2000 words. *Payment:* by arrangement. *Illustrations:* line including cartoons, half-tone, colour.

Best (1987), Maire Fahey, 10th Floor, Portland House, Stag Place, London SW1E 5AU *tel* 0171-245 8700 *fax* 0171-245 8825.
55p. W. Short stories. No other uncommissioned work accepted, but always willing to look at ideas/outlines. *Length:* 1300 words for short stories, variable for other work. *Illustrations:* line, half-tone, colour, cartoons. *Payment:* by agreement.

Big! (1989), Dominic Smith, EMAP Metro, Mappin House, 4 Winsley Street, London W1N 7AR *tel* 0171-436 1515 *fax* 0171-631 0781.
90p. F. Teenage entertainment, aimed at 11-17-year-olds, covering pop, video, and film and soap stars. Approach features editor (Richard Galpin) by phone with ideas for celebrity interviews, and gossip. *All material commissioned. Length:* features, 800 words. *Illustrations:* colour and b&w photos, cartoons. *Payment:* features £80-£250, illustrations £80-£250.

The Big Issue (1991), Joanne Mallabar, 57-61 Clerkenwell Road, London EC1M 5NP *tel* 0171-418 0427.
70p. W. Features, news, reviews, interviews – of general interest and on social issues, especially homelessness. *Length:* features 1200-2000 words. *Illustrations:* colour and b&w photos and line. *Payment:* £150 per 1000 words.

Bike (1971), Phil West, EMAP Nationals, Bushfield House, Orton Centre, Peterborough PE2 5UW *tel* (01733) 237111 *fax* (01733) 370283.

£2.40. M. 'Britain's biggest motorcycle magazine.' Interested in articles, features, news, short stories. *Length:* articles/features 1000-3000 words. *Illustrations:* colour and b&w photos, line, cartoons. *Payment:* £120 per 1000 words; illustrations per size/position.

Bird Keeper (1988), Peter Moss, IPC Magazines Ltd, King's Reach Tower, Stamford Street, London SE1 9LS   *tel* 0171-261 6201   *fax* 0171-261 7851.
£2.10. M. Articles on the care, health and breeding of birds, beginner bird keepers and how-to. Send synopsis of ideas. *Length:* up to 1200 words. *Illustrations:* colour photos and transparencies of birds in collections, or how-to. *Payment:* £65-£85 per 1000 words; £20-£45 per illustration.

Bird Watching (1986), David Cromack, EMAP Pursuit Publishing Ltd, Bretton Court, Bretton, Peterborough PE3 8DZ   *tel* (01733) 264666   *fax* (01773) 261984.
£2.25. M. Practical advice articles on birdwatching techniques or places to visit. Send synopsis first. *Length:* 850 words. *Illustrations:* colour and b&w photos, cartoons. *Payment:* by negotiation.

Birdwatch (1991), Dominic Mitchell, Solo Publishing Ltd, 310 Bow House, 153-159 Bow Road, London E3 2SE   *tel* 0181-983 1855   *fax* 0181-983 0246.
£2.25. M. Topical articles on all aspects of birds and birding, including conservation, identification, sites and habitats, equipment, overseas expeditions. *Length:* 700-1500 words. *Illustrations:* colour slides, b&w photos, colour and b&w line. *Payment:* from £40 per 1000 words; colour: photos £15-£40, cover £70, line by negotiation; b&w: photos £10, line £10-£40.

Birmingham Evening Mail (1870), I. Dowell, 28 Colmore Circus, Queensway, Birmingham B4 6AX   *tel* 0121-236 3366   *fax* 0121-625 1105; *London office:* 11 Buckingham Street, WC2N 6DF   *tel* 0171-409 7409   *fax* 0171-495 2742.
27p. D. Ind. Features of topical Midland interest considered. *Length:* 400-800 words. *Payment:* by arrangement.

The Birmingham Post, N. Hastilow, PO Box 18, 28 Colmore Circus, Birmingham B4 6AX   *tel* 0121-236 3366   *fax* 0121-625 1105; *London office:* 11 Buckingham Street, WC2N 6DF   *tel* 0171-409 7409   *fax* 0171-495 2742.
35p. D. Authoritative and well-written articles of industrial, political or general interest are considered, especially if they have relevance to the Midlands. *Length:* up to 1000 words. *Payment:* by arrangement.

Black Beauty & Hair (1982), Irene Shelley, Hawker Publications, 13 Park House, 140 Battersea Park Road, London SW11 4NB   *tel* 0171-720 2108   *fax* 0171-498 3023.
£2.00. Q. Beauty and style articles relating specifically to the black woman; celebrity features. *No* short stories. *Length:* approx. 1000 words. *Illustrations:* colour and b&w photos. *Payment:* £85 per 1000 words; photos £50-£100.

Blueprint (1983), Rowan Moore, Christ Church, 35 Cosway Street, London NW1 5NJ   *tel* 0171-262 2622   *fax* 0171-706 4811.
£3.50. 11 p.a. The magazine of modern architecture and design. Interested in articles, features and reviews. *Length:* up to 2500 words. *Illustrations:* colour and b&w photos and line. *Payment:* negotiable.

Boards (1982), Bill Dawes, Yachting Press Ltd, 196 Eastern Esplanade, Southend-on-Sea, Essex SS1 3AB   *tel* (01702) 582245   *fax* (01702) 588434.
£2.50. 10 p.a. (M. during summer, Bi-M. during winter) Articles, photos and reports on all aspects of windsurfing and boardsailing. *Payment:* by arrangement. *Illustrations:* line, half-tone, colour, cartoons.

The Boatman (1992), Pete Greenfield, Waterside Publications Ltd, PO Box 1992, Falmouth, Cornwall TR11 3RU   *tel* (01326) 375757   *fax* (01326) 378551.

£2.95. 10 p.a. 'The world of traditional boats and boat craftsmanship.' Articles and news items on practical and historical aspects of traditional boats; reports of regattas and rallies – subject knowledge *essential. Length:* articles 1000-3000 words. *Illustrations:* colour prints and transparencies, b&w photos, line art and diagrams. *Payment:* £100 per 1000 words (or 500 words + pix); illustrations £100 per full page, smaller sizes pro rata.

Bolton Evening News (1867), Newspaper House, Churchgate, Bolton, Lancs. BL1 1DE   *tel* (01204) 522345   *fax* (01204) 365068.
28p. D. Articles, particularly those with South Lancashire appeal. *Length:* up to 500 words. *Illustrations:* photos; considered at usual rates. *Payment:* by arrangement.

The Book Collector (1952) (incorporating **Bibliographical Notes and Queries**), Editorial Board: Nicolas Barker (Editor), A. Bell, J. Commander, J. Fergusson, T. Hofmann, D. McKitterick, The Collector Ltd, 43 Gordon Square, London WC1H 0PD   *tel* 0171-388 0846   *fax* 0171-388 0854.
£34.00 p.a. ($60.00). Q. Articles, biographical and bibliographical, on the collection and study of printed books and MSS. *Payment:* for reviews only.

Books in Wales—see **Llais Llyfrau.**

Books Magazine (1987), Liz Thomson, 43 Museum Street, London WC1A 1LY   *tel* 0171-404 0304   *fax* 0171-242 0762.
£1.50. Bi-M. Reviews, features, interviews with authors. *Payment:* negotiable but little bought in.

The Bookseller (1858), Louis Baum, J. Whitaker and Sons Ltd, 12 Dyott Street, London WC1A 1DF   *tel* 0171-420 6000   *fax* 0171-420 6103.
£115.00 p.a. W. Journal of the publishing and bookselling trades. While outside contributions are welcomed, most of the journal's contents are commissioned. *Length:* about 1000-1500 words. *Payment:* by arrangement.

Bowls International (1981), Melvyn Beck, Key Publishing Ltd, PO Box 100, Stamford, Lincs. PE9 1XQ   *tel* (01780) 55131   *fax* (01780) 57261.
£1.80. M. Sport and news items and features; occasional, bowls-oriented short stories. *Illustrations:* colour transparencies, b&w photos, occasional line, cartoons. *Payment:* sport/news approx. 25p per line, features approx. £50 per page; colour £25, b&w £10.

Brewing & Distilling International (1865), Bruce Stevens, 52 Glenhouse Road, Eltham, London SE9 1JQ   *tel* 0181-859 4300   *fax* 0181-859 5813.
£44.00 p.a. M. (£75.00 p.a. overseas airmail) Journal for brewers, maltsters, hop merchants, distillers, soft drinks manufacturers, bottlers and allied traders, circulating in over 80 countries. Technical and marketing articles (average 1000 words) accepted, by prior arrangement, from authors with specialist knowledge. *Illustrations:* line drawings, photos. *Payment:* by prior agreement with editor.

Bridge (formerly **Bridge International**) (1926), Mark Horton, Chess & Bridge Ltd, 369 Euston Road, London NW1 3AR   *tel* 0171-388 2404   *fax* 0171-388 2407.
£2.95. M. Articles on bidding and play; instruction, competitions, tournament reports and humour. *Payment:* by arrangement. *Illustrations:* line, half-tone.

Bristol Evening Post (1932), A. King, Temple Way, Bristol BS99 7HD   *tel* (0117) 926 0080.
27p. D. Takes freelance news and articles. *Payment:* by arrangement.

British Birds (1907), Dr J.T.R. Sharrock, Fountains, Park Lane, Blunham, Bedford MK44 3NJ   *tel/fax* (01767) 640025.

£48.50 p.a. M. Original observations relating to birds of Britain, Europe and North Africa. *Illustrations:* line, half-tone, colour. *Payment:* none for articles, nominal for illustrations.

British Chess Magazine (1881), M. Chandler, BCM Chess Shop, 69 Masbro Road, London W14 0LS.
£2.50. M. (£26.00 p.a. post free) Commisioned articles, 800-2500 words, on historical and cultural aspects of chess. *Illustrations:* colour, b&w, line, cartoons. *Payment:* by arrangement.

The British Deaf News (1955), Mrs Irene Hall, The British Deaf Association, 38 Victoria Place, Carlisle CA1 1HU *tel* (01228) 48844 (Voice), (01228) 48844 (DCT) *fax* (01228) 41420.
85p. M. (£12.00 p.a., members £10.00 p.a.) Articles, news items, letters dealing with deafness. *Payment:* by arrangement. *Illustrations:* line, half-tone.

British Journal of General Practice (formerly **Journal of the Royal College of General Practitioners**), Dr A.F. Wright MBE. MD. FRCGP, 12 Queen Street, Edinburgh EH2 1JE *tel* 0131-225 7629 *fax* 0131-220 6750.
£124.00 p.a. M. (£140 overseas, £158.55 by airmail) Articles relevant to general medical practice. *Illustrations:* half-tone, colour. *Payment:* none.

The British Journal of Photography (1854), Reuel Golden, Timothy Benn Publishing, 58 Fleet Street, London EC4Y 1JU *tel* 0171-583 8000 *fax* 0171-583 8001.
£1.20. W. Articles on professional, commercial and press photography, and on the more advanced aspects of amateur, technical, industrial, medical, scientific and colour photography. *Illustrations:* line, half-tone, colour. *Payment:* by arrangement.

British Journal of Special Education, Christina Tilstone, The University of Birmingham, School of Education, Edgbaston, Birmingham B15 2TT *tel* 0121-414 4805 *fax* 0121-414 4865.
Q. (non-member institutions/individuals Europe £52.50 p.a., rest of the world £74.00 p.a.) Official Journal of the National Association for Special Educational Needs. Articles by specialists on the education of children and young people with a range of special educational needs; plus research findings, and examples of good practice in associated areas: medical, psychological, therapeutic and sociological. *Length:* about 3000 words. *Payment:* none. *Illustrations:* line, half-tone.

British Journalism Review (1989), Geoffrey Goodman, BJR Publishing Ltd, c/o John Libbey Media, Faculty of Humanities, University of Luton, 75 Castle Street, Luton, Beds. LU1 3AJ *tel* (01582) 743297 *fax* (01582) 743298.
£25.00 p.a. Q. (other rates on application) Comment/criticism/review of matters published by, or of interest to, the media. *Length:* 1000-3000 words. *Illustrations:* b&w photos. *Payment:* by arrangement.

British Medical Journal (1840), Richard Smith BSc, MB, ChBEd, MSc, MFPHM, FRCPE, British Medical Association House, Tavistock Square, London WC1H 9JR *tel* 0171-387 4499 *fax* 0171-383 6418.
£6.70. W. Medical and related articles. *Payment:* by arrangement.

British Printer (1888), Jane Ellis, Miller Freeman Publishers Ltd, Sovereign Way, Tonbridge, Kent TN9 1RW *tel* (01732) 364422 *fax* (01732) 377362.
£66.00 p.a. M. Articles on technical and aesthetic aspects of printing processes and graphic reproduction. *Payment:* by arrangement. *Illustrations:* offset litho from photos, line drawings and diagrams, cartoons.

Broadcast, Mike Jones, EMAP Media, 33-39 Bowling Green Lane, London EC1R 0DA *tel* 0171-505 8014 *fax* 0171-505 8050.

£1.90. W. News and authoritative articles designed for all concerned with the UK and international television and radio industry, and with programmes and advertising on television, radio, video, cable, satellite, business. *Illustrations:* colour, b&w, line, cartoons. *Payment:* by arrangement.

Brownie, Marion Thompson, The Guide Association, 17-19 Buckingham Palace Road, London SW1W 0PT   *tel* 0171-834 6242.
£1.10. M. Official Magazine of The Guide Association. Short articles for Brownies (girls 7-10 years); fiction with Brownie background (500-800 words); puzzles; 'things to make', etc. *Illustrations:* line, colour. *Payment:* £40 per 1000 words; varies for illustrations.

Budgerigar World (1982), The County Press, Bala, Gwynedd LL23 7PG   *tel* (01678) 520262   *fax* (01678) 521262; *editor:* Terry A. Tuxford, 145 Western Way, Basingstoke, Hants RG22 6EX   *tel* (01256) 28898.
£30.00 p.a. M. Articles about exhibition budgerigars. *Payment:* by arrangement. *Illustrations:* half-tone, colour.

Building (1842), Peter Bill, The Builder Group, Builder House, 1 Millharbour, London E14 9RA   *tel* 0171-560 4141   *fax* 0171-560 4004.
£2.20. W. Covers the entire professional, industrial and manufacturing aspects of the building industry. Articles on architecture and techniques at home and abroad considered, also news and photos. *Payment:* by arrangement.

Building Design (1970), Lee Mallett, 30 Calderwood Street, Woolwich, London SE18 6QH   *tel* 0181-855 7777   *fax* 0181-854 8058.
Controlled circulation. W. (£65.00 p.a.) News and features on all aspects of building design. *All material commissioned. Length:* up to 1500 words. *Illustrations:* colour and b&w photos, line, cartoons. *Payment:* £120 per 1000 words; illustrations by negotiation.

Built Environment, Prof Peter Hall and Prof David Banister, Alexandrine Press, PO Box 15, 51 Cornmarket Street, Oxford OX1 3EB   *tel* (01865) 724627   *fax* (01865) 792309.
£67.50 p.a. Q. Articles about architecture, planning and the environment. *Preliminary letter* advisable. *Length:* 1000-5000 words. *Payment:* by arrangement. *Illustrations:* photos and line.

Bunty, D.C. Thomson & Co. Ltd, Albert Square, Dundee DD1 9QJ   *tel* (01382) 223131   *fax* (01382) 322214; and 185 Fleet Street, London EC4A 2HS   *tel* 0171-242 5086   *fax* 0171-404 5694.
55p. W. Vividly told picture-story serials for young girls of school age: 16-18 frames in each 2-page instalment; 23-24 frames in each 3-page instalment. Comic strips and features. *Payment:* on acceptance.

Bunty Library, D.C. Thomson & Co. Ltd, Albert Square, Dundee DD1 9QJ   *tel* (01382) 223131   *fax* (01382) 322214; and 185 Fleet Street, London EC4A 2HS   *tel* 0171-242 5086   *fax* 0171-404 5694.
50p. F. Picture-stories for schoolgirls, 64 pages (about 140 line drawings): ballet, school, adventure, theatre, sport. Scripts considered; promising artists and scriptwriters encouraged. *Payment:* on acceptance.

Burlington Magazine (1903), Caroline Elam, 14-16 Duke's Road, London WC1H 9AD   *tel* 0171-388 1228   *fax* 0171-388 1230.
£10.40. M. Deals with the history and criticism of art. Average *length* of article, 500-3000 words. The editor can use only articles by those who have special knowledge of the subjects treated and cannot accept MSS compiled from works of reference. Book and exhibition reviews and an illustrated monthly Calendar section. No verse. *Payment:* up to £100. *Illustrations:* almost invariably made from photos.

Burton Mail (1898), Brian J. Vertigen, Burton Daily Mail Ltd, 65-68 High Street, Burton on Trent DE14 1LE   *tel* (01283) 512345   *fax* (01283) 515351.
24p. D. Features, news and articles of interest to Burton and south Derbyshire readers. *Length:* 400-500 words. *Illustrations:* colour and b&w. *Payment:* by negotiation.

Buses (1949), Stephen Morris, Coombelands House, Coombelands Lane, Addlestone, Surrey KT15 1HY   *tel* (01932) 855909   *fax* (01932) 854750.
£2.40. M. Articles of interest to both road passenger transport operators and bus enthusiasts. *Preliminary enquiry* essential. *Illustrations:* colour transparencies, half-tone, line maps. *Payment:* on application.

Business Life (1985), Sandra Harris, Premier Magazines, Haymarket House, 1 Oxenden Street, London SW1Y 4EE   *tel* 0171-925 2544   *fax* 0171-839 4508.
Free. M. Inflight magazine for British Airways. Articles and features of interest to the European business traveller. *All material commissioned*; approach in writing with ideas. *Length:* 850-1500 words. *Illustrations:* colour photos and line. *Payment:* £300 per 1000 words; £100-£400 for illustrations.

BusinessAge (1992), Peter Kirwan, VNU Business Publications Ltd, 32-34 Broadwick Street, London W1A 2HG   *tel* 0171-316 9605   *fax* 0171-316 9612.
£2.20. M. News and features reviewing management performance and challenging conventional business thinking. *Illustrations:* colour and b&w. *Payment:* £100-£150 per 1000 words.

BusinessMatters (1992), Elly Donovan, GMC Publications, Castle Place, 166 High Street, Lewes, East Sussex BN7 1XU   *tel* (01273) 477374   *fax* (01273) 486300.
£2.50. Bi-M. How to run and market small- to medium-sized businesses. Articles based on case studies; relevant news. *Length:* 400-2400 words. *Illustrations:* colour and b&w photos, cartoons. *Payment:* £50 per 500 words; £50 per illustration.

Business Scotland (1947), Graham Lironi, Peebles Publishing Group, Bergius House, Clifton Street, Glasgow G3 7LA   *tel* 0141-331 1022   *fax* 0141-331 1395.
Controlled circulation. M. Features, profiles and news items of interest to business and finance in Scotland. *Payment:* by arrangement.

Buster (1960), Fleetway Editions Ltd, Egmont House, 25/31 Tavistock Place, London WC1H 9SU   *tel* 0171-344 6400   *fax* 0171-388 4020.
£1.00. F. Juvenile comic. Comedy characters in picture strips, for children aged 6 to 12. Full colour. *Payment:* by arrangement.

Cage and Aviary Birds (1902), Peter Moss, IPC Magazines Ltd, King's Reach Tower, Stamford Street, London SE1 9LS   *tel* 0171-261 6116   *fax* 0171-261 6095.
85p. W. Practical articles on bird-keeping. First-hand knowledge only. *Illustrations:* line, half-tone, colour, cartoons. *Payment:* by arrangement.

Cambridge Evening News (1888), Robert Satchwell, 51 Newmarket Road, Cambridge CB5 8EJ   *tel* (01223) 358877   *fax* (01223) 460846.
28p. Mon.-Sat. The voice of Mid-Anglia – news, views and sport. *Illustrations:* colour prints, b&w graphics. *Payment:* by negotiation.

Camcorder User (incorporating **Video Editing** and **Desktop Video**) (1988), Christine Morgan, WV Publications, 57-59 Rochester Place, London NW1 9JU   *tel* 0171-485 0011   *fax* 0171-482 6269/284 2145.
£2.40. M. Features on film/video-making techniques, specifically tailored to the amateur enthusiast. *Material mostly commissioned. Length:* 1000-2500

words. *Illustrations:* colour and b&w; contact editor for details. *Payment:* by arrangement.

Campaign, Dominic Mills, Haymarket Business Publications Ltd, 174 Hammersmith Road, London W6 7JP   *tel* 0171-413 4036   *fax* 0171-413 4507.
£1.85. W. News and articles covering the whole of the mass communications field, particularly advertising in all its forms, marketing and the media. Features should not exceed 2000 words. News items also welcome. Press day, Wednesday. *Payment:* by arrangement.

Camping Magazine (1961), John Lloyd, Garnett Dickinson Publishing, Fitzwilliam Road, Rotherham S65 1JU   *tel/fax* (editorial) (01273) 477421.
£2.20. M. Covers the spectrum of camping and related activities in all shapes and forms – camping is more than a tent on a site! Lively, anecdotal articles and photos are welcome, but call to discuss your ideas with the editor first. *Length:* 500-1500 words on average. *Illustrations:* line, half-tone, colour. *Payment:* by arrangement.

Car (1962), Rob Munro-Hall, EMAP National Publications Ltd, Abbots Court, 34 Farringdon Lane, London EC1R 3AV   *tel* 0171-216 6200   *fax* 0171-216 6259.
£2.75. M. Top-grade journalistic features on car driving, car people and cars. *Length:* 1000-2500 words. *Payment:* minimum £260 per 1000 words. *Illustrations:* b&w and colour photos to professional standards.

Car Mechanics, Peter Simpson, Kelsey House, 77 High Street, Beckenham, Kent BR3 1AN   *tel* 0181-658 3531 or (01733) 203749   *fax* 0181-650 8035.
£2.20. M. Practical articles on maintaining, repairing and uprating modern cars for the DIY and enthusiast market. *Preliminary letter* outlining feature necessary. *Payment:* by arrangement. *Illustrations:* line drawings, colour prints or transparencies.

Caravan Magazine (1933), Barry Williams, Link House, Dingwall Avenue, Croydon CR9 2TA   *tel* 0181-686 2599   *fax* 0181-781 6044/760 0973.
£2.10. M. Lively articles based on real experience of touring caravanning, especially if well illustrated by photos. General countryside or motoring material not wanted. *Payment:* by arrangement.

Carers World (1993), Jennie Davidson, 4 Larch Way, Haywards Heath, West Sussex RH16 3TY   *tel/fax* (01444) 416866.
£1.50. Bi-M. Factual and informative articles aimed at carers, the disabled and the elderly. *Length:* up to 1200 words. *Illustrations:* line, half-tone. *Payment:* by arrangement.

Caribbean Times, incorporating African Times (1981), Arif Ali, Hansib Publishing Ltd, Third Floor, Tower House, 141/149 Fonthill Road, London N4 3HF   *tel* 0171-281 1191   *fax* 0171-263 9656.
50p. W. News stories, articles and features of interest to Britain's African-Caribbean community.

Cat World (1981), Joan Moore, 10 Western Road, Shoreham-by-Sea, West Sussex BN43 5WD   *tel* (01273) 462000   *fax* (01273) 455994.
£1.50. M. Bright, lively articles on any aspect of cat ownership. Articles on breeds of cats and veterinary articles by acknowledged experts only. No unsolicited fiction. *Illustrations:* b&w and colour photos, cartoons. *Payment:* by arrangement; £7.50 per illustration.

Catch, D.C. Thomson & Co. Ltd, Albert Square, Dundee DD1 9QJ   *tel* (01382) 223131   *fax* (01382) 200880; and 185 Fleet Street, London EC4A 2HS   *tel* 0171-242 5086   *fax* 0171-404 5694.
£1.30. M. 92-page gravure monthly for 17-21-year-old women. Fiction (up to

1500 words), fashion, beauty, features. *Illustrations:* art illustrations in full colour, colour photos, cartoons. *Payment:* on acceptance.

Caterer & Hotelkeeper (1893), Gary Crossley, Reed Business Publishing, Quadrant House, The Quadrant, Sutton, Surrey SM2 5AS *tel* 0181-652 8680 *telex* 892084 REEDBP G *fax* 0181-652 8973/8947.
£1.50. W. Articles on all aspects of the hotel and catering industries. *Length:* up to 1500 words. *Illustrations:* line, half-tone, colour. *Payment:* by arrangement.

Catholic Gazette (1910), Fr. John Breen, The Chase Centre, 114 West Heath Road, London NW3 7TX *tel* 0181-458 3316 *fax* 0181-905 5780.
95p. M. Articles on evangelisation and the Christian life. *Length:* up to 1500 words. *Illustrations:* b&w photos, line, cartoons. *Payment:* by arrangement.

The Catholic Herald, Cristina Odone, Herald House, Lambs Passage, Bunhill Row, London EC1Y 8TQ *tel* 0171-588 3101 *fax* 0171-256 9728.
45p. W. Independent newspaper covering national and international affairs from a Catholic/Christian viewpoint as well as church news. *Length:* articles 600-1100 words. *Illustrations:* photos of Catholic and Christian interest, cartoons. *Payment:* by arrangement.

Catholic Pictorial (1961), David Mahon, Media House, Mann Island, Pier Head, Liverpool L3 1DQ *tel* 0151-236 2191 *fax* 0151-236 2216.
50p. W. News and photo features (maximum 800 words plus illustration) of Merseyside, regional and national Catholic interest only; also cartoons. Has a strongly social editorial and is a trenchant tabloid. *Payment:* by arrangement.

Catholic Times (relaunched 1993), Norman Cresswell, 1st Floor, St James's Buildings, Oxford Street, Manchester M1 6FP *tel* 0161-236 8856 *fax* 0161-237 5590.
40p. W. News (400 words) and news features (800 words) of Catholic interest. *Illustrations:* b&w photos. *Payment:* £30-£80; photos £50.

Cencrastus: Scottish & International Literature, Arts and Affairs (1979), Raymond Ross and Ruth Bradley, Unit One, Abbeymount Techbase, 2 Easter Road, Edinburgh EH8 8EJ *tel* 0131-661 5687.
£2.25 (back copies £2.50). Q. Articles, short stories, poetry, reviews. *Payment:* by arrangement. *Illustrations:* line, half-tone.

Certified Accountant, Brian O'Kane, Cork Publishing Ltd, 19 Rutland Street, Cork, Republic of Ireland *tel* (21) 313855 *fax* (21) 313496.
£2.50. M. Journal of the Chartered Association of Certified Accountants. Articles of accounting and financial interest. *Illustrations:* colour, cartoons. *Payment:* from £125 per 1000 words; by arrangement for illustrations.

Chapman (1969), Joy Hendry, 4 Broughton Place, Edinburgh EH1 3RX *tel* 0131-557 2207 *fax* 0131-556 9565.
£3.50. Q. (£14.00 p.a.) 'Scotland's Quality Literary Magazine.' Poetry, short stories, reviews, criticism, articles on Scottish culture. *Illustrations:* line, half-tone, cartoons. *Payment:* £8.00 per page; illustrations by negotiation.

Chat (1986), Terry Tavner, IPC Magazines Ltd, King's Reach Tower, Stamford Street, London SE1 9LS *tel* 0171-261 6565 *fax* 0171-261 6534.
55p. W. Tabloid weekly for women; fiction. *Length:* up to 1000 words. *Illustrations:* half-tone, colour. *Payment:* by arrangement.

Cheshire Life (1934), Patrick O'Neill, Town & County Magazines, Oyston Mill, Strand Road, Preston PR1 8UR *tel* (01772) 722022 *fax* (01772) 736496.
£1.90. M. Articles of county interest. *Length:* 800-1000 words. *Illustrations:* line and half-tone, 4-colour positives. Photos of definite Cheshire interest. *Payment:* by arrangement.

Chic (1995), Richard Barber, Northern & Shell plc, Northern & Shell Tower, City Harbour, London E14 9GL   *tel* 0171-987 5090   *fax* 0171-712 0069.
£1.70. M. In depth human interest articles aimed at women aged over 35. Show business interviews, 'at home' with personalities and stories about ordinary women. Submit written synopsis. *Length:* 2000-3000 words. *Illustrations:* all commissioned. *Payment:* by arrangement.

Child Education (1924), Gill Moore, Scholastic Publications Ltd, Villiers House, Clarendon Avenue, Leamington Spa, War. CV32 5PR   *tel* (01926) 887799   *fax* (01926) 883331.
£2.40. M. For teachers, pre-school staff, nursery nurses and parents concerned with children aged 3-8. Articles by specialists on practical teaching ideas and methods, child development, education news. *Length:* 800-1600 words. *Payment:* by arrangement. Profusely illustrated with photos, line drawings and cartoons; also large pictures in full colour.

The China Quarterly, Dr David Shambaugh, School of Oriental and African Studies, Thornhaugh Street, Russell Square, London WC1H 0XG   *tel* 0171-323 6129   *fax* 0171-580 6836.
£29/$56 p.a. Q. (£36/$70 institutions, £15/$28 students) Articles on contemporary China. *Length:* 8000 words approx.

Choice (1974), Editor-in-Chief: Sue Dobson, Apex House, Oundle Road, Peterborough PE2 9NP   *tel* (01733) 555123   *fax* (01733) 898487.
£1.90. M. Pre- and retirement magazine for 50+ readership. Positive attitude to life – experiences, hobbies, holidays, finance, relationships. About half the magazine *commissioned*. Unsolicited material accompanied by an sae will be read. If suggesting feature material, include selection of cuttings of previously published work. *Payment:* by agreement, on publication.

Chronicle & Echo, Northampton (1931), Mark Edwards, EMAP Newspapers Ltd, Upper Mounts, Northampton NN1 3HR   *tel* (01604) 231122   *fax* (01604) 233000.
27p. D. Articles, features and news – mostly commissioned – of interest to the Northampton area. *Length/illustrations:* varies. *Payment:* by negotiation.

Church of England Newspaper (1828), 10 Little College Street, London SW1P 3SH   *tel* 0171-976 7760   *fax* 0171-976 0783.
45p. W. Anglican news and articles relating the Christian faith to everyday life. Evangelical basis; almost exclusively commissioned articles. Study of paper desirable. *Length:* up to 1000 words. *Illustrations:* photos, line drawings, cartoons. *Payment:* c. £40 per 1000 words; photos £22, line by arrangement.

Church Times (1863), Paul Handley, 33 Upper Street, London N1 0PN   *tel* 0171-359 4570   *fax* 0171-226 3073.
45p. W. Articles on religious topics are considered. No verse or fiction. *Length:* up to 1000 words. *Illustrations:* news photos. *Payment:* £100 per 1000 words; Periodical Publishers' Association negotiated rates for illustrations.

Classic & Sportscar (1982), Ian Bond, Haymarket Magazines Ltd, 38-42 Hampton Road, Teddington, Middlesex TW11 0JE   *tel* 0181-943 5000   *telex* 8952440 HAYMRT G   *fax* 0181-943 5844.
£2.75. M. Features on classic cars and sportscars; shows, news and reviews, features and stories. *Length:* varies. *Illustrations:* half-tone, colour. *Payment:* £150 per 1000 words; varies for illustrations.

Classic Boat (1987), Robin Gates, Boating Publications Ltd, Link House, Dingwall Avenue, Croydon CR9 2TA   *tel* 0181-686 2599   *fax* 0181-781 6535.

£3.10. M. Cruising and technical features, restorations, events, new boat reviews, practical, maritime history; news. *Study of magazine essential:* read 3-4 back issues and send for contributors' guidelines. *Length:* 500-2000 words. *Illustrations:* colour and b&w photos; line drawings of hulls. *Payment:* £75-£100 per published page.

Classic Cars, Robert Coucher, IPC Magazines Ltd, King's Reach Tower, Stamford Street, London SE1 9LS *tel* 0171-261 5858 *fax* 0171-261 6731.
£2.75. M. Specialist articles on older cars. *Length:* from 500-4000 words (subject to prior contract). *Illustrations:* half-tone, colour, cartoons. *Payment:* by negotiation.

Classic CD (1990), Neil Evans, Future Publishing, 30 Monmouth Street, Beauford Court, Bath BA1 2BW *tel* (01225) 442244 *fax* (01225) 312228.
£3.95. M. Covers classical music on CD. Aims to inform, educate and entertain, with features on composers and performers, reviews and news. *Commissioned* material only. *Length:* up to 2000 words. *Illustrations:* colour and b&w photos, b&w line, including collage and cartoons. *Payment:* £125 per 1000 words; colour up to £300, b&w £35 ⅛ page.

Classic Stitches (1994), Mrs Bea Neilson, D.C. Thomson & Co. Ltd, 80 Kingsway East, Dundee DD4 8SL *tel* (01382) 462276 *telex* 76380 *fax* (01382) 452491.
£2.80. Bi-M. Creative needlework ideas and projects; needlework-based features on designers, collections, work-in-progress and exhibitions. *Length:* 1000-2000 words. *Illustrations:* colour photos, preferably not 35 mm. *Payment:* negotiable.

Classical Music (1976), Keith Clarke, Rhinegold Publishing Ltd, 241 Shaftesbury Avenue, London WC2H 8EH *tel* 0171-333 1742 *fax* 0171-333 1769 *e-mail* 100546.1127@compuserve.com
£2.45. F. News, opinion, features on classical music. All material commissioned. *Illustrations:* b&w photos and line; colour covers. *Payment:* minimum £85 per 1000 words; from £40 for illustrations.

Climber (1962), Tom Prentice, 7th Floor, The Plaza Tower, The Plaza, East Kilbride, Glasgow G74 1LW *tel* (01355) 246444 *fax* (01355) 263013.
£2.10. M. Articles on all aspects of mountaineering and hill walking in Great Britain and abroad, and on related subjects. *Study of magazine* essential. *Length:* 1500-2000 words, illustrated. *Illustrations:* colour transparencies/prints. *Payment:* according to merit.

Clocks (1978), John Hunter, Nexus Special Interests Ltd. Editorial address: 28 Gillespie Crescent, Edinburgh EH10 4HU *tel* 0131-229 5550.
£2.40. M. Well-researched articles on antique clocks and their makers, clock repair and restoration, and in general anything of interest to knowledgeable horologists. Sundials, barometers and associated scientific instruments are minority interests of Clocks readers. *Length:* 1500-3000 words. *Illustrations:* line, half-tone, colour; no cartoons. *Payment:* approx. £30 per 1000 words, £5 per b&w photo, £8 per colour print/transparency.

Clothes Show Magazine (1990), Jaynie Senior, BBC Worldwide Publishing, Woodlands, 80 Wood Lane, London W12 0TT *tel* 0181-576 2436 *fax* 0181-576 2424.
£1.60. M. Articles relating to fashion and beauty in a practical, accessible way. Submit ideas first, in writing, to the editor. *Length:* 1500-word, 4-page main feature; 600-word, 1-page. *Illustrations:* commissioned as necessary. *Payment:* up to £500 for main feature, £150 for 1-page; illustrations £150.

Club Mirror (1969), Dominic Roskrow, Quantum Publishing Ltd, 29-31 Lower Coombe Street, Croydon, Surrey CR9 1LX	*tel* 0181-681 2099	*fax* 0181-680 8828/2839.
£36.00 p.a. M. Features, news, drink news, catering news, legal and financial advice as a guide to the successful management of clubs. *Payment:* by arrangement. *Illustrations:* line, colour.

Coin News (1964), John W. Mussell, Token Publishing Ltd, PO Box 14, Honiton, Devon EX14 9YP	*tel* (01404) 831 878	*fax* (01404) 831 895.
£1.85. M. Articles of high standard on coins, tokens, paper money. *Length:* up to 2000 words. *Payment:* by arrangement.

Combat & Militaria (1983), Stephen Webb, Maze Media Ltd, Castle House, 97 High Street, Colchester, Essex CO1 1TH	*tel* (01206) 540621	*fax* (01206) 564214.
£1.95. M. Topical features on military subjects, preferably illustrated. *Length:* 1000-2500 words. *Illustrations:* colour prints and transparencies. *Payment:* by arrangement.

Commando, D.C. Thomson & Co. Ltd, Albert Square, Dundee DD1 9QJ	*tel* (01382) 223131	*fax* (01382) 322214; and 185 Fleet Street, London EC4A 2HS	*tel* 0171-242 5086	*fax* 0171-404 5694.
50p. 8 p.m. Fictional war stories told in pictures. Scripts should be of about 135 pictures. Synopsis required as an opener. New writers encouraged; send for details. *Payment:* on acceptance.

Commercial Motor (1905), Brian Weatherley, Reed Business Publishing, Quadrant House, The Quadrant, Sutton, Surrey SM2 5AS	*tel* 0181-652 3302/3303	*fax* 0181-652 8969.
£1.25. W. Technical and road transport articles only. *Length:* up to 1500 words. *Payment:* varies. *Illustrations:* drawings and photos.

Communicate (1980), Eddie Hold, The Economist Group, 15 Regent Street, London SW1Y 4LR	*tel* 0171-830 7000	*fax* 0171-839 1475.
Controlled circulation. M. Covers all aspects of telecommunications management: analysis pieces (200-700 words), features (800-1800 words), case studies (1800 words). *All material commissioned. Illustrations:* colour and b&w photos, line, diagrams. *Payment:* £180 per 1000 words; illustrations by negotiation.

Community Care (1974), Terry Philpot, Quadrant House, Reed Business Publishing, The Quadrant, Sutton, Surrey SM2 5AS	*tel* 0181-652 4861	*fax* 0181-652 4739.
£1.35. W. Articles of professional interest to local authority and voluntary body social workers, managers, teachers and students. *Preliminary letter* advisable. *Length:* 800-1400 words. *Payment:* at current rates. *Illustrations:* line, halftone.

Company (1978), Fiona McIntosh, National Magazine House, 72 Broadwick Street, London W1V 2BP	*tel* 0171-439 5000.
£1.80. M. Articles on a wide variety of subjects, relevant to young, independent women. Most articles are commissioned. *Payment:* usual magazine rate. *Illustrated.*

Computer Weekly (1966), Editor: Helena Sturridge, News Editor: Karl Schneider, Features Editor: David Evans, Reed Business Publishing Group, Quadrant House, The Quadrant, Sutton, Surrey SM2 5AS	*tel* 0181-652 3122	*telex* 892084 REEDBP G	*fax* 0181-652 3038.
£1.70. W. Feature articles on computer-related topics for business/industry

users. *Length:* 1200 words. *Illustrations:* b&w photos, line, cartoons. *Payment:* £150 per feature; negotiable for illustrations.

Computing (1973), Jerry Sanders, 32-34 Broadwick Street, London W1A 2HG *tel* 0171-316 9139 *fax* 0171-316 9160.
£100.00 p.a. W. Features and news items on corporate procurement and deployment of IT infrastructure, and on applications and implications of computers and telecommunications. Particular sections address the IT professional career development, and the desktop computing environment. *Length:* 1600-2200 words. *Payment:* by negotiation. *Illustrations:* colour photos, line drawings, cartoons.

Construction Europe, Paul Marsden, Southfields, Southview Road, Wadhurst, East Sussex TN5 6TP *tel* (01892) 784088 *fax* (01892) 784086.
Controlled circulation. M. Aimed at contractors, consultants and government/ international authorities. *Payment:* by negotiation.

Contemporary Art (1992), Lynne Green, 197 Knightsbridge, 8th Floor North, London SW7 1RB *tel* 0171-823 8373 *fax* 0171-823 7969.
£4.95. Q. Articles and reviews on all aspects of contemporary art; book reviews. *Length:* articles 1000-2000 words, reviews 750-1000 words. *Illustrations:* colour and b&w photos. *Payment:* from £120 per 1000 words; none for photos.

Contemporary Review (incorporating the **Fortnightly**) (1866), Dr Richard Mullen, Contemporary Review Co. Ltd, Cheam Business Centre, 14 Upper Mulgrave Road, Cheam, Surrey SM2 7AZ *tel* 0181-643 4846 *fax* 0181-241 7507.
£2.95. M. Independent review dealing with questions of the day, chiefly politics, international affairs, theology, literature, the arts. Mostly commissioned, but with limited scope for freelance authors with authoritative knowledge. Articles must be typewritten and double-spaced; 2000-3000 words. TS returned *only if sae enclosed.* Intending contributors should *study journal* before submitting (sample copy: £3.00 from the above address). *Payment:* £5 per page (500 words), 2 complimentary copies.

Control & Instrumentation (1958), Brian J. Tinham BSc, CEng, MInstMC, 30 Calderwood Street, Woolwich, London SE18 6QH *tel* 0181-855 7777 *fax* 0181-316 3422.
£60.00 p.a. M. Authoritative main feature articles on measurement, automation, control systems, instrumentation and data processing; also export, business and engineering news. *Length of articles:* 750 words for highly technical pieces, 1000-2500 words main features. *Payment:* according to value. *Illustrations:* photos and drawings of equipment using automatic techniques, control engineering personalities, cartoons.

Cosmetic World News (1949), M.A. Murray-Pearce, Caroline Marcuse, Norman Clare, 130 Wigmore Street, London W1H 0AT *tel* 0171-486 6757/8 *fax* 0171-487 5436.
£90.00 p.a. Bi-M. International news magazine of perfumery, cosmetics and toiletries industry. Worldwide reports, photo-news stories, articles (500-1000 words) on essential oils and new cosmetic raw materials, and exclusive information on industry's companies and personalities welcomed. *Payment:* by arrangement, minimum 10p per word. *Illustrations:* b&w and colour photos or colour separations.

Cosmopolitan (1972), Mandi Norwood, National Magazine House, 72 Broadwick Street, London W1V 2BP *tel* 0171-439 5000 *fax* 0171-439 5016.
£2.10. M. Short stories, articles. Commissioned material only. *Payment:* by arrangement. *Illustrated.*

Country (1901), Anthony Bush, The Country Gentlemen's Association, Hill Crest Mews, London Road, Baldock, Herts. SG7 6ND   *tel* (01462) 490206. £1.70. M. The Magazine of the Country Gentlemen's Association. Authoritative articles on wildlife, countryside and general interest. Gardening, cookery, travel. Send synopsis first. *Length:* 500-1000 words. *Payment:* by arrangement.

Country Garden & Smallholding (1975; as **Home Farm**), Helen Sears, Broad Leys Publishing Company, Buriton House, Station Road, Newport, Saffron Walden, Essex CB11 3PL   *tel* (01799) 540922   *fax* (01799) 541367. £1.85. M. The magazine for small-scale farmers. Practical, how-to articles, and seasonal features, on organic gardening, small-scale poultry and livestock keeping, country crafts, cookery and smallholdings. Approach editor in writing with ideas. *Length:* up to 2000 words. *Illustrations:* colour and b&w photos, line for instructive articles. *Payment:* £25 per 1000 words; photos £10 colour, £5 b&w, £35 cover.

Country Homes & Interiors (1986), Julia Watson, IPC Magazines Ltd, King's Reach Tower, Stamford Street, London SE1 9LS   *tel* 0171-261 6451   *fax* 0171-261 6895. £2.20. M. Articles on property, country homes, interior designs. *Illustrations:* colour. *Payment:* from £250 per 1000 words.

Country Life (1897), Clive Aslet, IPC Magazines Ltd, King's Reach Tower, Stamford Street, London SE1 9LS   *tel* 0171-261 7058   *fax* 0171-261 5139. £1.80. W. Illustrated journal chiefly concerned with British country life, social history, architecture and the fine arts, natural history, agriculture, gardening and sport. *Length of articles:* about 700, 1000 or 1300 words. *Illustrations:* mainly colour photos, cartoons. *Payment:* according to merit.

Country Living (1985), Susy Smith, National Magazine House, 72 Broadwick Street, London W1V 2BP   *tel* 0171-439 5000   *fax* 0171-439 5093. £2.20. M. Up-market magazine for country dwellers and townies who have the country at heart. *No* unsolicited material and *do not* send valuable transparencies; magazine cannot accept responsibility for loss of unsolicited material. *Illustrations:* line, half-tone, colour. *Payment:* by arrangement.

Country Quest, Brian Barratt, Cambrian Printers, Llanbadarn Road, Aberystwyth, Dyfed SY23 3TN   *tel* (01691) 627111   *fax* (01691) 615497. £1.50. M. Illustrated articles on matters relating to countryside, history and personalities of Wales and border counties. No fiction. Illustrated work preferred. *Length:* 500-1500 words. *Illustrations:* line, half-tone. *Payment:* by arrangement.

The Countryman (1927), Christopher Hall, Sheep Street, Burford, Oxon OX18 4LH   *tel* (01993) 822258. £2.00. Bi-M. Every department of rural life and progress except field sports. Party politics and sentimentalising about the country barred. Copy must be trustworthy, well-written, brisk, cogent and light in hand. Articles up to 1500 words. Good paragraphs and notes, first-class poetry and skilful sketches of life and character from personal knowledge and experience. Dependable natural history based on writer's own observation. Really good matter from old unpublished letters and MSS. *Illustrations:* b&w photos and drawings, but all must be exclusive and out of the ordinary, and bear close scrutiny. Humour welcomed if genuine. *Payment:* £40 per 1000 words minimum. Payment is usually very much in excess of these figures, according to merit.

Country-Side (1905), Dr David Applin, PO Box 87, Cambridge CB1 3UP   *tel/ fax* (01933) 314672.

£12.00 p.a. Q. Official organ of the British Naturalists' Association (BNA), the national body for naturalists. Original observations on wildlife and its protection, and on natural history generally, but not on killing for sport. *Preliminary letter* or study of magazine advisable. *Payment:* 1200 words plus pictures £50, shorter articles pro-rata. *Illustrations:* photos, drawings, cartoons.

County (1992), Howard M. Reynolds, Enterprise Magazines Ltd, Post & Mail House, 28 Colmore Circus, Birmingham B4 6AX   *tel* 0121-212 4141   *fax* 0121-212 2468.
£1.00. M. Articles of topical relevance or historical interest relating to Heart of England region of Birmingham and Warwickshire only. Prefer illustrated material. *Length:* 1200 words. *Illustrations:* line, half-tone, colour. *Payment:* £50 per 1200 words; according to quality for illustrations.

The Courier and Advertiser (1816 and 1801), D.C. Thomson & Co. Ltd, 80 Kingsway East, Dundee DD4 8SL   *tel* (01382) 223131   *telex* DCTHOM G 76380   *fax* (01382) 454590; and 185 Fleet Street, London EC4A 2HS   *tel* 0171-242 5086.
30p. D. Ind.

Coventry Evening Telegraph, Dan Mason, Corporation Street, Coventry CV1 1FP   *tel* (01203) 633633   *fax* (01203) 550869.
26p. D. Topical, illustrated articles, those with a Warwickshire interest particularly acceptable. *Length:* up to 600 words. *Payment:* by arrangement.

Creative Camera (1968), David Brittain, CC Publishing, 5 Hoxton Square, London N1 6NU   *tel* 0171-729 6993.
£3.95. Bi-M. Illustrated articles and pictures dealing with serious photography, sociology of, history of and criticism of photos; book and exhibition reviews. Arts Council supported. *Payment:* by arrangement. *Illustrations:* b&w, colour.

The Cricketer International (1921), Peter Perchard, Third Street, Langton Green, Tunbridge Wells, Kent TN3 0EN   *tel* (01892) 862551   *fax* (01892) 863755.
£2.45. M. Articles on cricket at any level. *Illustrations:* line, half-tone, colour, cartoons. *Payment:* £50 per 1000 words; illustrations minimum £17.50.

The Criminologist (1966), R.W. Stone, East Row, Little London, Chichester, West Sussex PO19 1PG   *tel* (01243) 775552   *fax* (01243) 779278.
£35.50 p.a. plus p&p. Q. Specialised material designed for an expert and professional readership on national and international criminology, the police, forensic science, the law, penology, sociology and law enforcement. Articles welcomed, up to 4000 words, from those familiar with the journal's style and requirements. *A preliminary letter* with a brief résumé is requested. *Payment:* according to merit. *Illustrations:* line and b&w photos.

Critical Quarterly (1959), Colin MacCabe. Address for contributions: Kate Mellor, The London Consortium, The British Film Institute, 21 Stephen Street, London W1P 2LN.
£27.50 p.a. Q. (£49.00 p.a. institutions) Fiction, poems, literary criticism. *Length:* 2000-5000 words. Interested contributors should *study magazine* before submitting MSS. *Payment:* by arrangement.

Critical Wave: The European Science Fiction & Fantasy Review (1987), Steve Green, Martin Tudor, 33 Scott Road, Olton, Solihull B92 7LQ   *tel* 0121-706 0108.
£2.45. 5 p.a. (£11.50 p.a.) Interviews with leading figures in the sf/fantasy/horror field; features on the genres; book, magazine, film, theatre and comic reviews; market reports; art portfolios (by arrangement); extensive convention and marts listing. *No* fiction or poetry. *Length:* by arrangement. *Illustrations:*

b&w photos and line – send photocopy samples of portfolios (single illustrations rarely used). *Payment:* none, but receive one complimentary copy of magazine.

CTN (Confectioner, Tobacconist, Newsagent), Anne Bingham, Maclaren House, 19 Scarbrook Road, Croydon CR9 1QH   *tel* 0181-277 5202   *fax* 0181-277 5216.
95p. W. (£48.00 p.a.) Trade news and brief articles illustrated when possible with photos or line drawings; also cartoons. Must be of current interest to retail confectioner-tobacconists and newsagents. *Length:* articles 600-800 words. *Payment:* by negotiation.

Cumbria (1951), Terry Fletcher, Dalesman Publishing Company Ltd, Stable Courtyard, Broughton Hall, Skipton, North Yorkshire BD23 3AE   *tel* (01756) 701381   *fax* (01756) 701326.
90p. M. Articles of genuine rural interest concerning Lakeland and Cumbria. Short *length* preferred. *Illustrations:* line drawings and first-class photos. *Payment:* according to merit.

Custom Car (1970), Tim Baggaley, Kelsey Publishing Ltd, Kelsey House, 77 High Street, Beckenham, Kent BR3 1AN   *tel* 0181-658 3531   *fax* 0181-650 8035.
£2.20. M. Customising, drag racing and hot rods. *Length:* by arrangement. *Payment:* by arrangement.

CWU Voice (formerly **UCW Journal**; 1920), Julia Simpson and Linda Quinn, CWU House, Crescent Lane, Clapham, London SW4 9RN   *tel* 0171-622 9977   *telex* 913585   *fax* 0171-720 2184.
Free to members. M. Main journal of CWU members. Articles on postal and telecommunications workers in the UK and abroad and on other questions of interest to a trade union readership. *Payment:* NUJ rates. *Illustrations:* line and colour.

Cycling Today (1993; as **New Cyclist**), Roger St Pierre, Stonehart Leisure Magazines Ltd, 67 Goswell Road, London EC1V 7EN   *tel* 0171-410 9410   *fax* 0171-410 9411.
£2.20. M. *Material mostly commissioned.* Accepts unsolicited travel/expedition features (UK and abroad), written to style (emphasis on anecdotes and on characters met, rather than bland travelogue) with professional-quality colour transparencies, including cycle action shots; and general cycling news. Interested to hear from health and fitness writers with some knowledge of cycling. *Length:* features 1500-2000 words, news 150-200 words. *Payment:* £150 per feature inc. pix; news £20 per item.

Cycling Weekly (1891), Andrew Sutcliffe, IPC Magazines Ltd, King's Reach Tower, Stamford Street, London SE1 9LS   *tel* 0171-261 5588   *fax* 0171-261 5758.
£1.25. W. Racing and technical articles; topical photos with a cycling interest also considered; cartoons. *Length:* not exceeding 1500 words. *Payment:* by arrangement.

Daily Express, Richard Addis, Ludgate House, 245 Blackfriars Road, London SE1 9UX   *tel* 0171-928 8000   *cables* Lon Express   *telex* 21841/21842   *fax* 0171-633 0244; Great Ancoats Street, Manchester M60 4HB   *tel* 0161-236 2112.
35p. D. Exclusive news: striking photos. Leader page articles, 600 words; facts preferred to opinions. *Payment:* according to value.

Daily Mail (1896), Paul Dacre, Northcliffe House, 2 Derry Street, London W8 5TT   *tel* 0171-938 6000   *fax* 0171-937 3251.

35p. D. Highest *payment* for good, exclusive news. Ideas welcomed for leader page articles, 500-800 words average. Exclusive news photos always wanted.

Daily Mirror (1903), Piers Morgan, 1 Canada Square, Canary Wharf, London E14 5AP *tel* 0171-293 3000 *fax* 0171-293 3758.
28p. D. Top *payment* for exclusive news and news pictures. Articles from freelances used, and ideas bought: send synopsis only. 'Unusual' pictures and those giving a new angle on the news are welcomed; also cartoons.

Daily Post (1855), Alastair Machray, PO Box 48, Old Hall Street, Liverpool L69 3EB *tel* 0151-227 2000 *fax* 0151-236 4682.
30p. D. Ind. Articles of general interest and topical features of special interest to North West England and North Wales. No verse or fiction. *Payment:* according to value. News and feature illustrations.

Daily Record, T. Quinn, Anderston Quay, Glasgow G3 8DA *tel* 0141-248 7000 *fax* 0141-204 0770. *London office:* 1 Canada Square, Canary Wharf, London E14 5AP *tel* 0171-293 3000.
27p. D. Topical articles, from 300-700 words; exclusive stories of Scottish interest and exclusive colour photos.

Daily Sport (1988), Jeff McGowan, 19 Great Ancoats Street, Manchester M60 4BT *tel* 0161-236 4466 *fax* 0161-236 4535 *Mercury Link* 19045750.
32p. Mon.-Fri. Factual stories and series. *Length:* up to 1000 words. *Illustrations:* b&w and colour photos, cartoons. *Payment:* £30-£5000.

Daily Star (1978), Phil Walker, Ludgate House, 245 Blackfriars Road, London SE1 9UX *tel* 0171-928 8000 *cables* Lon Express *telex* 21841/21842 *fax* 0171-620 1641.
25p. D. Hard news exclusives, commanding substantial payment. Major interviews with big-star personalities; short features; series based on people rather than things; picture features. *Payment:* short features £75-£100; full page £250-£300; double page £400-£600, otherwise by negotiation. *Illustrations:* line, halftone.

The Daily Telegraph (1855), Charles Moore, 1 Canada Square, Canary Wharf, London E14 5DT *tel* 0171-538 5000 *telex* 22874/5/6 *fax* 0171-538 6242.
40p. D. 70p. Sat. Ind. Articles on a wide range of subjects of topical interest considered. *Preliminary letter* and synopsis required. *Length:* 700-1000 words. *Payment:* by arrangement.
Telegraph Magazine (1964), Emma Soames. Free with Sat. paper. Short profiles (about 1600 words), articles of topical interest. *Preliminary study* of the magazine essential. *Illustrations:* all types. *Payment:* by arrangement.
Electronic Telegraph (1994), Ben Rooney. Available daily on Internet (World Wide Web) at http://www.telegraph.co.uk/. Free to Internet subscribers. Based on *The Daily Telegraph*, contains news, sport, City, features, Internet News, Hyperlinks to Archive.

Dairy Farmer and Dairy Beef Producer, Graeme Kirk, Wharfedale Road, Ipswich IP1 4LG *tel* (01473) 241122 *fax* (01473) 240501.
Controlled circulation. M. Authoritative articles dealing in practical, lively style with dairy farming. Topical controversial articles invited. Well-written, illustrated accounts of new ideas being tried on dairy farms are especially wanted. *Length:* normally 800-1400 words with colour photos. *Payment:* by arrangement.

Dairy Industries International (1936), Rebecca Wright, Wilmington House, Church Hill, Wilmington, Dartford, Kent DA2 7EF *tel* (01322) 277788 *fax* (01322) 276474.

£54.00 post free (UK). M. Covers the entire field of milk processing, the manufacture of products from liquid milk, and ice cream. Articles relating to dairy plant, butter and cheese making, ice cream making, new product developments and marketing, etc. *Payment:* by arrangement. *Illustrations:* colour transparencies/prints and Indian ink diagrams.

The Dalesman (1939), Terry Fletcher, Dalesman Publishing Company Ltd, Stable Courtyard, Broughton Hall, Skipton, North Yorkshire BD23 3AE *tel* (01756) 701381 *fax* (01756) 701326.
£1.00. M. Articles and stories of genuine rural interest concerning Yorkshire. Short *length* preferred. *Payment:* according to merit. *Illustrations:* line drawings and first-class photos preferably featuring people.

Dance & Dancers (1950), John Percival, 214 Panther House, 38 Mount Pleasant, London WC1X 0AP *tel/fax* 0171-837 2711.
£1.75. M. Specialist features, reviews on modern/classical dance, dancers. *Length:* by prior arrangement. *Payment:* by arrangement. *Illustrations:* line, half-tone; colour covers.

Dancing Times (1910), Editor: Mary Clarke, Editorial Adviser: Ivor Guest, The Dancing Times Ltd, Clerkenwell House, 45-47 Clerkenwell Green, London EC1R 0EB *tel* 0171-250 3006 *fax* 0171-253 6679.
£1.70. M. Ballet, contemporary dance and all forms of stage dancing, both from general, historical, critical and technical angles. Well-informed freelance articles are occasionally used, but only after preliminary arrangements. *Payment:* by arrangement. *Illustrations:* occasional line, action photos always preferred; colour invited.

The Dandy, D.C. Thomson & Co. Ltd, Albert Square, Dundee DD1 9QJ *tel* (01382) 223131 *fax* (01382) 322214; and 185 Fleet Street, London EC4A 2HS *tel* 0171-242 5086 *fax* 0171-404 5694.
40p. W. Comic strips for children. 10-12 pictures per single page story, 18-20 pictures per 2-page story. Promising artists are encouraged. *Payment:* on acceptance.

Dandy Comic Library, D.C. Thomson & Co. Ltd, Albert Square, Dundee DD1 9QJ *tel* (01382) 223131 *fax* (01382) 322214; and 185 Fleet Street, London EC4A 2HS *tel* 0171-242 5086 *fax* 0171-404 5694.
50p. 2 p.m. Extra-long comic adventure stories featuring the well-known characters from the weekly Dandy publication.

Darts World (1972), Tony Wood, World Magazines Limited, 9 Kelsey Park Road, Beckenham, Kent BR3 6LH *tel* 0181-650 6580 *fax* 0181-650 2534.
£1.50. M. Articles and stories with darts theme. *Illustrations:* half-tone, cartoons. *Payment:* £40-£50 per 1000 words; illustrations by arrangement.

Day by Day (1963), Patrick Richards, Woolacombe House, 141 Woolacombe Road, Blackheath, London SE3 8QP *tel* 0181-856 6249.
75p. M. Articles and news on non-violence and social justice. Reviews of art, books, films, plays, musicals and opera. Cricket reports. Occasional poems and very occasional short stories in keeping with editorial viewpoint. *Payment:* £2 per 1000 words. No *illustrations* required.

Dental Update (1973), Susan Joyce, George Warman Publications (UK) Ltd, 20 Leas Road, Guildford, Surrey GU1 4QT *tel* (01483) 304944 *fax* (01483) 303191.
£45.00 p.a. 10 p.a. (£20.00 p.a. students) Clinical articles, clinical quizzes. *Illustrations:* line, colour. *Payment:* £50-£100 per 1000 words; £50 cover photos only.

Derby Evening Telegraph, Mike Lowe, Northcliffe House, Meadow Road, Derby DE1 2DW   *tel* (01332) 291111   *fax* (01322) 253027.
28p. Mon.-Sat. Articles and news of local interest. *Payment:* by negotiation.

Derbyshire Life and Countryside (1931), Heritage House, Lodge Lane, Derby DE1 3HE   *tel* (01332) 347087/8/9   *fax* (01332) 290688.
£1.20. M. Articles, preferably illustrated, about Derbyshire life, people and history. *Length:* up to 800 words. Some short stories set in Derbyshire accepted, but verse not used. *Payment:* according to nature and quality of contribution. *Illustrations:* photos of Derbyshire subjects.

The Dickensian, Dickens House, 48 Doughty Street, London WC1N 2LF.
£9.50 p.a. 3 p.a. (£12.00 p.a. institutions; overseas rates on application) Published by The Dickens Fellowship. Welcomes articles on all aspects of Dickens' life, works and character. *Payment:* none. Contributions (enclose sae if return required) and editorial correspondence to the editor: Dr Malcolm Andrews, School of English, Rutherford College, University of Kent, Canterbury, Kent CT2 7NX   *fax* (01227) 827001.

Director (1947), Stuart Rock, Mountbarrow House, 12-20 Elizabeth Street, London SW1W 9RB   *tel* 0171-730 8320   *fax* 0171-235 5627.
£3.00. M. Authoritative business-related articles. Send synopsis of proposed article and examples of printed work. *Length:* 500-3000 words. *Payment:* by arrangement. *Illustrated* mainly in colour.

Dirt Bike Rider (1981), Roddy Brooks, Key Publishing Ltd, PO Box 100, Stamford, Lincs. PE9 1XQ   *tel* (01780) 55131   *fax* (01780) 57261.
£2.25. M. Features, track tests, coverage on all aspects of off-road motorcycling. *Length:* up to 1000 words. *Payment:* £80 per 1000 words. *Illustrations:* half-tone, colour, cartoons.

Disability Now (1957), Mary Wilkinson, Scope, 12 Park Crescent, London W1N 4EQ   *tel* 0171-636 5020   *fax* 0171-436 4582.
£14.00 p.a. M. (£27.00 organisations, £37.00 overseas) Topical, authoritative articles of interest to people with a wide range of disabilities, carers and professionals; also arts and book reviews. Contributions from people with disabilities particularly welcome. *Preliminary letter desirable. Length:* up to 1000 words. *Illustrations:* colour and b&w news photos, cartoons. *Payment:* from £85 per 1000 words; by arrangement for illustrations.

Diver (1953), Bernard Eaton, 55 High Street, Teddington, Middlesex TW11 8HA   *tel* 0181-943 4288   *fax* 0181-943 4312.
£2.50. M. Articles on sub aqua diving and underwater developments. *Length:* 1500-2500 words. *Illustrations:* line, half-tone and colour. *Payment:* by arrangement.

Doctor (1971), Helena Sturridge, Reed Healthcare, Quadrant House, The Quadrant, Sutton, Surrey SM2 5AS   *tel* 0181-652 8740   *telex* 892084 REEDBP G   *fax* 0181-652 8701.
£2.00. W. Commissioned articles and features of interest to GPs. *Length:* various. *Illustrations:* colour photos – news, features, clinical; some line. *Payment:* NUJ rates.

Dogs Today (1990), Beverley Cuddy, Pet Subjects Ltd, Pankhurst Farm, Bagshot Road, West End, Nr Woking, Surrey GU24 9QR   *tel* (01276) 858880   *fax* (01276) 858860.
£2.50. M. *Study of magazine essential* before submitting ideas. Interested in human interest dog stories, celebrity interviews, holiday features and anything

unusual – all must be entertaining and informative *and accompanied* by illustrations. *Length:* 800-1200 words. *Illustrations:* colour, preferably transparencies, colour cartoons. *Payment:* negotiable.

Dorset Evening Echo (1921), Mike Woods, Southern Newspapers plc, 57 St Thomas Street, Weymouth, Dorset DT4 8EU   *tel* (01305) 784804   *fax* (01305) 760387.
28p. D. News and occasional features (1000-2000 words). *Illustrations:* b&w photos. *Payment:* by negotiation.

Dorset Life – The Dorset Magazine (1967), John Newth, 95 North Street, Wareham, Dorset BH20 4AE   *tel* (01929) 551264.
£1.50. M. Articles (500-1200 words), photos (colour or b&w) and line drawings with a *specifically* Dorset theme. *Payment:* by arrangement.

The Downside Review, Dom Daniel Rees, Downside Abbey, Stratton-on-the-Fosse, Nr Bath, Somerset BA3 4RH   *tel* Stratton-on-the-Fosse (01761) 232 295.
£6.00. Q. (£22.00 p.a.) Articles and book reviews on theology, metaphysics, mysticism and modernism, and monastic and church history. *Payment:* not usual.

Drapers Record (formerly **DR The Fashion Business**) (1887), Sophie Hewitt-Jones, EMAP Maclaren, 67 Clerkenwell Road, London EC1R 5BH   *tel* 0171-417 2830   *fax* 0171-417 2832.
£1.65. W. Editorial aimed at fashion retailers, large and small. No unsolicited material. *Payment:* by negotiation. *Illustrations:* colour and b&w: photos, drawings and cartoons.

Dundee Evening Telegraph and Post, D.C. Thomson & Co. Ltd, 80 Kingsway East, Dundee DD4 8SL   *tel* (01382) 223131   *telex* DCTHOM 76380   *fax* (01382) 454590; and 185 Fleet Street, London EC4A 2HS   *tel* 0171-242 5086   *fax* 0171-404 5694.
25p. D.

Early Music (1973), Tess Knighton, Oxford University Press, 3 Park Road, London NW1 6XN   *tel* 0171-724 1707   *fax* 0171-723 5033   *e-mail* jnl.early -music@oup.co.uk
£9.50. Q. (£36.00 p.a., institutions £49.00 p.a.) Lively, informative and scholarly articles on aspects of medieval, renaissance, baroque and classical music. *Payment:* £20 per 1000 words. *Illustrations:* line, half-tone, colour.

East Anglian Daily Times (1874), Malcolm Pheby, 30 Lower Brook Street, Ipswich, Suffolk IP4 1AN   *tel* (01473) 230023   *fax* (01473) 211391.
33p. D. Features of East Anglian interest, preferably with pictures. *Length:* 500 words. *Illustrations:* colour, b&w. *Payment:* £50 per feature; illustrations NUJ rates.

East Lothian Life (1989), Pauline Jaffray, 2 Beveridge Row, Belhaven, Dunbar, East Lothian EH42 1TP   *tel/fax* (01368) 863593.
£2.00. Q. Articles and features with an East Lothian slant. *Length:* up to 1000 words. *Illustrations:* b&w photos, line, cartoons. *Payment:* negotiable.

Eastern Art Report (1989), Sajid Rizvi, Eastern Art Publishing/NEAR, Acre House, 69-76 Long Acre, London WC2E 9JH   *tel* 0171-379 3939/0181-392 1122   *fax* 0181-392 1422.
£6.00. Bi-M. (individual £25.00 p.a., institutions £40.00 p.a.) Original, well-researched articles on all aspects of the visual arts – Islamic, Indian, Chinese and Japanese; reviews. *Length* of articles: min. 1500 words. *Illustrations:* colour transparencies, b&w photos; no responsibility accepted for unsolicited material. *Payment:* by arrangement.

Eastern Daily Press (1870), Peter Franzen, Prospect House, Rouen Road, Norwich NR1 1RE *tel* (01603) 628311 *telex* 975276 ECNNCH G *fax* (01603) 612930; *London office:* House of Commons Press Gallery, House of Commons, SW1A 0AA *tel* 0171-219 3384 *fax* 0171-820 0304/5.
35p. D. Ind. Limited market for articles of East Anglian interest not exceeding 900 words.

Eastern Eye (1989), Sarwar Ahmed, Eastern Eye Publications Ltd, 138-148 Cambridge Heath Road, London E1 5QJ *tel* 0171-702 8012 *fax* 0171-702 7937.
49p. W. Articles, features and news of interest to Asians aged 16-36. *Length:* features, 1800 words. *Illustrations:* colour and b&w photos. *Payment:* £80 per 1000 words; photos £10.

The Echo (1875), A.G. Hughes, Echo House, Pennywell, Sunderland, Tyne & Wear SR4 9ER *tel* 0191-534 3011 *fax* 0191-534 5975 *ad-doc* DX60743.
27p. Mon.-Sat. Local news, features and articles. *Length:* 500 words. *Illustrations:* colour and b&w photos, line, cartoons. *Payment:* negotiable.

The Ecologist, Nicholas Hildyard and Sarah Sexton, Agriculture House, Bath Road, Sturminster Newton, Dorset DT10 1DU *tel* (01258) 473476 *fax* (01258) 473748.
£4.00. 6 p.a. Fully-referenced articles on economic, social and environmental affairs from an ecological standpoint. *Study* magazine first for level and approach. *Length:* 1000-5000 words. *Illustrations:* line, half-tone. *Payment:* by arrangement.

Economica (1921. New Series, 1934), Editors: Prof F.A. Cowell, Prof D.C. Webb, STICERD, London School of Economics, Houghton Street, London WC2A 2AE *tel* 0171-955 7855 *fax* 0171-242 2357.
£20.00. Q. (subscription rates on application) Learned journal covering the fields of economics, economic history and statistics. *Payment:* none.

The Economist (1843), Bill Emmott, 25 St James's Street, London SW1A 1HG *tel* 0171-830 7000.
£2.00. W. Articles staff-written.

Edinburgh Evening News, John McGurk, 20 North Bridge, Edinburgh EH1 1YT *tel* 0131-225 2468 *fax* 0131-225 7302.
24p. D. Ind. Features on current affairs, preferably in relation to our circulation area. Women's talking points, local historical articles; subjects of general interest.

Edinburgh Review (1969), Gavin Wallace and Robert Alan Jamieson, 22 George Square, Edinburgh EH8 9LF *tel* 0131-650 4689 *fax* 0131-662 4218.
£6.95. Bi-A. (£12.00 p.a.) Fiction, poetry, clearly written articles on Scottish and international cultural and philosophical ideas. *Payment:* by arrangement.

Education (1903), George Low, 5 Bentinck Street, London W1M 5RN *tel* 0171-935 0121 *fax* 0171-831 2855.
£1.75. W. Specialist articles on educational administration, all branches of education; technical education; universities; school building; playing fields; environmental studies; physical education; school equipment; school meals and health; teaching aids. *Length:* 1000 words. *Illustrations:* photos, cartoons. *Payment:* by arrangement.

Electrical Review (1872), T. Tunbridge, Reed Business Publishing, Quadrant House, The Quadrant, Sutton, Surrey SM2 5AS *tel* 0181-652 3113 *telex* 892084 REEDBP G *fax* 0181-652 8951.

£2.50. F. Technical and business articles on electrical and control engineering; outside contributions considered. Electrical news welcomed. *Illustrations:* photos and drawings, cartoons. *Payment:* according to merit.

Electrical Times (1891), Steve Hobson, Reed Business Publishing, Quadrant House, The Quadrant, Sutton, Surrey SM2 5AS   *tel* 0181-652 3115   *telex* 892084 REEDBP G   *fax* 0181-652 8972.
£2.25. M. Business and technical articles of interest to contractors and installers in the electrical industries, with illustrations as necessary. *Length:* 750 words. *Payment:* £150 per article. *Illustrations:* line, half-tone, colour, cartoons.

Elle (UK) (1985), Marie O'Riordan, EMAP Women's Group, 20 Orange Street, London WC2H 7ED   *tel* 0171-957 8383.
£2.20. M. Commissioned material only. *Payment:* by arrangement. *Illustrations:* colour.

Empire (1989), Mark Salisbury, Mappin House, 4 Winsley Street, London W1N 7AR   *tel* 0171-436 1515/1601   *fax* 0171-312 8249.
£2.25. M. Monthly guide to film and video: articles, features, news. *Length:* various. *Illustrations:* colour and b&w photos. *Payment:* approx. £125 per 1000 words; varies for illustrations.

The Engineer (1856), Adèle Kimber, 30 Calderwood Street, London SE18 6QH *tel* 0181-855 7777   *telex* 896238 MORGAN G   *fax* 0181-316 3040.
Controlled circulation. 34 p.a. (£90.00 p.a.) Articles, features and news on the business and technology of the engineering industry, including profiles, analysis and new products. *Length:* news up to 200 words, features average 1000 words. *Illustrations:* colour transparencies or prints, line diagrams, graphs. *Payment:* £150 per page; £50 per illustration.

English Historical Review (1886), Dr J.R. Maddicott, Dr J. Stevenson, Addison Wesley Longman Higher Education, Edinburgh Gate, Harlow, Essex CM20 2JE   *tel* (01279) 623623.
£83.00 p.a. Q. High-class scholarly articles, documents, and reviews or short notices of books. Contributions are not accepted unless they supply original information and should be sent direct to Dr J.R. Maddicott, Editor, E.H.R., Exeter College, Oxford OX1 3DP. Books for review should be sent to Dr J. Stevenson, Editor, E.H.R., Worcester College, Oxford OX1 2HB. *Payment:* none.

Envoi (1957), Roger Elkin, 44 Rudyard Road, Biddulph Moor, Stoke-on-Trent, Staffs. ST8 7JN   *tel* (01782) 517892.
£12.00 p.a. 3 p.a. New poetry, including sequences, collaborative works and translations, reviews, articles on modern poets and poetic style; poetry competitions; editorial criticism of subscribers' poems (with sae) at no charge. Sample copy: £3.00. *Payment:* 2 complimentary copies.

Esquire (1991), Rosie Boycott, National Magazine House, 72 Broadwick Street, London W1V 2BP   *tel* 0171-439 5000   *telegraphic address* Shanmag, London W1   *telex* 263879 NATMAG G   *fax* 0171-439 5067.
£2.40. M. Quality men's general interest magazine – articles, features. *No* unsolicited material or short stories. *Length:* various. *Illustrations:* colour and b&w photos, line. *Payment:* by arrangement.

Essentials (1988), IPC Magazines Ltd, King's Reach Tower, Stamford Street, London SE1 9LS   *tel* 0171-261 5540.
£1.40. M. Features, plus fashion, health and beauty, cookery. *Illustrations:* colour. *Payment:* by negotiation.

Essex Countryside (1952), Andy Tilbrook, Griggs Farm, West Street, Coggeshall, Essex CO6 1NT   *tel* (01376) 562578   *fax* (01376) 562581.

£1.50. M. Mostly articles of county interest. *Length:* approximately 1000 words. *Illustrations:* line, half-tone, colour.

Estates Gazette (1858), Helen Pearce, 151 Wardour Street, London W1V 4BN   *tel* 0171-437 0141   *fax* 0171-437 0294.
£1.85. W. Property, legislation, planning, architecture – articles, features and business news. *Length:* 1500-2000 words. *Illustrations:* colour, b&w photos, line, cartoons. *Payment:* none.

Euromoney (1969), Garry Evans, Nestor House, Playhouse Yard, London EC4V 5EX   *tel* 0171-779 8888   *telex* 928726/7 (editorial/research), 914553/4/5 (adv./survey/prod.)   *fax* 0171-779 8641.
£180.00 p.a. M. Articles of general interest on finance, banking and capital markets. *Length:* up to 6000 words. *Illustrations:* colour photos, cartoons. *Payment:* £250 per 1000 words; illustrations £50.

The European, Charles Garside, 200 Gray's Inn Road, London WC1X 8NE   *tel* 0171-418 7777   *fax* 0171-713 1840.
75p. Thu. News reports, analytical articles and features on subjects of interest and importance to Europe as a whole, including business affairs, sport, arts, literature, leisure, fashion. *Illustrations:* line, half-tone, colour transparencies, cartoons. *Payment:* by arrangement.
The European MagAZine: the A-Z of Europe, Andrew Harvey. Free with paper. Guide to current events in Europe including arts, fashion, travel, motoring, technology, health; also Élan, comprehensive events listing service. *Length:* features up to 1000 words. *Illustrations:* colour transparencies and artwork. *Payment:* by arrangement.

European Bookseller (1990), Marc Beishon, 15 Micawber Street, London N1 7TB   *tel* 0171-336 6650   *fax* 0171-336 6640.
£66.00 p.a. Bi-M. Articles, features, news, statistics for the European book trade. Database of Europe-wide, recently published titles (approx. 1000), subject classified. European Record Database – listing rights offers on all subjects. Free entry of unlimited number of titles open to subscribing publishers. *Length:* 200-2000 words. *Illustrations:* b&w photos. *Payment:* £100 per 1000 words; photos by agreement.

European Chemical News, John Baker, Reed Business Publishing, Quadrant House, The Quadrant, Sutton, Surrey SM2 5AS   *tel* 0181-652 3187   *fax* 0181-652 3375.
£5.00. W. Articles and features concerning business, markets and investments in the chemical industry. *Length:* 1000-2000 words; news items up to 400 words. *Payment:* £120-£150 per 1000 words.

European Drinks Buyer (1991), Heather Buckle, Crier Publications, Arctic House, Rye Lane, Dunton Green, Sevenoaks, Kent TN14 5HB   *tel* (01732) 451515   *fax* (01732) 451383.
Controlled free circulation. Bi-M. Articles of European interest on business, marketing, branding, catering, retail, duty free, EU legislation, packaging, labelling, product surveys, consumption trends. *No* unsolicited material but enquiries for editorial guidelines welcome (enclose sae/samples of published work). Overseas correspondents wanted. *Length:* features, profiles, interviews, opinion pieces 1000-2000 words, news 150-500 words. *Illustrations:* half-tone, colour. *Payment:* from £80 per 1000 words; none for illustrations.

European Frozen Food Buyer (1989), Alwyn Brice, Crier Publications, Arctic House, Rye Lane, Dunton Green, Sevenoaks, Kent TN14 5HB   *tel* (01732) 451515   *fax* (01732) 451383.

Controlled free circulation. Bi-M. Articles of European interest on business, marketing, branding, catering, retail, EU legislation, packaging, labelling, product surveys, food hygiene, consumption trends. *No* unsolicited material but enquiries for editorial guidelines welcome (enclose sae/samples of published work). Overseas correspondents wanted. *Length:* features, profiles, interviews 1000-2000 words, news 150-500 words. *Illustrations:* half-tone, colour. *Payment:* £80 per 1000 words; none for illustrations.

European Plastics News (1929), Andrew Beevers, EMAP Maclaren, Maclaren House, 19 Scarbrook Road, Croydon, Surrey CR9 1QH *tel* 0181-277 5000 *fax* 0181-277 5530.
£13.00. M. (£120.00 p.a.) Technical articles dealing with plastics and allied subjects. *Length:* depending on subject. *Illustrations:* b&w or colour photos/diagrams. *Payment:* by arrangement; none for illustrations.

Evening Chronicle, Neil Benson, Newcastle Chronicle and Journal Ltd, Thomson House, Groat Market, Newcastle upon Tyne NE1 1ED *tel* 0191-232 7500 *fax* 0191-232 2256.
25p. D. News, photos and features covering almost every subject of interest to readers in Tyne and Wear, Northumberland and Durham. *Payment:* according to value.

Evening Courier (1892), Edward Riley, PO Box 19, King Cross Street, Halifax HX1 2SF *tel* (01422) 365711 *fax* (01422) 330021.
28p. 2 per day. Mon.-Sat. Articles of local interest and background to news events. *Length:* up to 500 words. *Illustrations:* b&w photos. *Payment:* £25-£40 per article; photos per quality/size used.

Evening Echo (1969), Bob Dimond, Newspaper House, Chester Hall Lane, Basildon, Essex SS9 1RE *tel* (01268) 522792 *fax* (01268) 282884.
30p. Mon-Fri. Mostly staff-written; interested in Christmas features – submit ideas end November. *Length/illustrations:* by arrangement. *Payment:* by arrangement.

Evening Echo (1900), Gareth Weekes, Richmond Hill, Bournemouth, Dorset BH2 6HH *tel* (01202) 554601 *fax* (01202) 292115.
27p. Mon.-Sat. Local news and features. *Length:* up to 500 words. *Illustrations:* line, half-tone, colour, cartoons. *Payment:* by arrangement.

Evening Gazette (Teesside) (1869), Ranald Allan, North Eastern Evening Gazette Ltd, Borough Road, Middlesbrough TS1 3AZ *tel* (01642) 245401 *fax* (01642) 232014.
24p. Mon.-Sat. News, and topical and lifestyle features. *Length:* 600-800 words. *Illustrations:* line, half-tone, colour, graphics, cartoons. *Payment:* £50 per 1000 words; scale rate or by agreement for illustrations.

Evening News (1882), Bob Crawley, Prospect House, Rouen Road, Norwich NR1 1RE *tel* (01603) 628311 *fax* (01603) 612930.
27p. D. Ind. Interested in local news-based features. *Length:* up to 500 words. *Payment:* NUJ or agreed rates.

Evening Standard (1827), Max Hastings, Northcliffe House, 2 Derry Street, London W8 5EE *tel* 0171-938 6000.
30p. D. Ind. Articles of general interest considered, 1500 words or shorter; also news, pictures and ideas.
ES Magazine, Adam Edwards. Free with paper. W. Feature ideas, *exclusively* about London. *Payment:* by negotiation. *Illustrations:* all types.

Eventing (1984), Kate Green, IPC Magazines Ltd, Room 2105, King's Reach Tower, Stamford Street, London SE1 9LS *tel* 0171-261 5388 *fax* 0171-261 5429.

£2.50. M. News, articles, features, event reports and opinion pieces – all with bias towards the sport of horse trials. *Material mostly commissioned*, but all ideas welcome. *Length:* up to 1500 words. *Illustrations:* colour and b&w, mostly commissioned. *Payment:* by arrangement; illustrations £30-£45.

Everyday Practical Electronics (1971), Mike Kenward, Wimborne Publishing Ltd, Allen House, East Borough, Wimborne, Dorset BH21 1PF   *tel* (01202) 881749   *fax* (01202) 841692.
£2.45. M. Constructional and theoretical articles aimed at the student and hobbyist. *Length:* 1000-5500 words. *Payment:* £55-£90 per 1000 words depending on type of article. *Illustrations:* line, half-tone, cartoons.

Everywoman (1985), Lorna Russell, 9 St Albans Place, London N1 0NX   *tel* 0171-359 5496.
£2.20. M. Features, including news features, women's campaigns. *Study* of this feminist magazine essential. *No* short stories. Includes annual directory of women's businesses and organisations. *Illustrations:* line, half-tone, cartoons. *Payment:* for commissions, £50 per 1000 words.

Exchange & Mart (1868), Link House, West Street, Poole, Dorset BH15 1LL   *tel* (01202) 445180   *fax* (01202) 445189.
£1.20. W. Some reader interest editorial (consumer advice).

Executive PA (1991), Jean Postle, Hobsons Publishing plc, Bateman Street, Cambridge CB2 1LZ   *tel* (01223) 354551   *fax* (01223) 322850.
Complimentary. Q. Business to business for working senior secretaries. *Length:* 700-1400 words. *Illustrations:* colour. *Payment:* £110 per 1000 words; colour by negotiation.

Executive Woman (1987), Angela Giveon, Saleworld Ltd, 2 Chantry Place, Harrow, Middlesex HA3 6NY   *tel* 0181-420 1210   *fax* 0181-420 1691/3.
£2.25. Bi-M. News and features with a holistic approach to the world of successful working women. Strong business features; articles on management, personnel, networking and mentoring. *Length:* 500-1000 words. *Illustrations:* colour and b&w, line drawings. *Payment:* £150 per 1000 words; £50-£100.

Express & Echo (1904), Rachael Campey, Heron Road, Sowton, Exeter, Devon EX2 7NF   *tel* (01392) 442211   *fax* (01392) 442294/442287.
27p. Mon-Sat. Features and news of local interest. *Length:* features 500-800 words, news up to 400 words. *Illustrations:* colour. *Payment:* lineage rates; illustrations negotiable.

Express and Star (1874), Warren Wilson, Queen Street, Wolverhampton WV1 3BU   *tel* (01902) 313131   *fax* (01902) 319721; *London office:* Room 110, Temple Chambers, Temple Avenue, EC4Y 0DT.
27p. D.

The Face (1980), Richard Benson, Exmouth House, Pine Street, London EC1R 0JL   *tel* 0171-837 7270   *fax* 0171-837 3906.
£2.00. M. Articles on music, fashion, films, popular youth culture. Contributors must be familiar with the magazine, its audience and culture. *Illustrations:* half-tone, colour. *Payment:* £150 per 1000 words; illustrations approx. £120 per page.

Family Circle, IPC Magazines Ltd, King's Reach Tower, Stamford Street, London SE1 9LS   *tel* 0171-261 5000   *fax* 0171-261 5929.
£1.00. 13 p.a. Practical, medical human interest material – *mostly commissioned*. *Payment:* NUJ rates.

Family Law (1971), Elizabeth Walsh, Miles McColl, 21 St Thomas Street, Bristol BS1 6JS   *tel* (0117) 923 0600   *telex* 449119   *fax* (0117) 925 0486   *DX* 78161 Bristol.
£80.00 p.a. M. Articles dealing with all aspects of the law as it affects the family, written from a legal or socio-legal point of view. *Length:* from 1000 words. *Payment:* £15 per 1000 words, or by arrangement. No *illustrations.*

Family Tree Magazine (1984), Michael Armstrong, 61 Great Whyte, Ramsey, Huntingdon, Cambs. PE17 1HL   *tel* (01487) 814050.
£1.85. M. (£21.20 p.a.) Articles on any genealogically related topics. *Illustrations:* half-tone, line, cartoons. *Payment:* £20 per 1000 words; by arrangement for illustrations.

Farmers Weekly (incorporating **Power Farming**) (1934), Stephen Howe, Reed Business Publishing, Quadrant House, The Quadrant, Sutton, Surrey SM2 5AS   *tel* 0181-652 4911   *fax* 0181-652 4005.
£1.25. W. Articles on agriculture from freelance contributors will be accepted subject to negotiation.

Farming News (1983), Donald Taylor, 30 Calderwood Street, London SE18 6QH   *tel* 0181-855 7777   *telex* 896238   *fax* 0181-854 6795.
£1.20. W. (£60.00 p.a.) News, business, technical features and articles. *Payment:* by arrangement.

Fashion Forecast International (1946), Managing Editor: Stephen Higginson, 23 Bloomsbury Square, London WC1A 2JP   *tel* 0171-637 2211   *telex* 8954884 *fax* 0171-637 2248.
£30.00 p.a. UK/Europe, £40.00 p.a. outside Europe. 2 p.a. (Feb, Aug) **Hosiery Forecast** and **Lingerie Forecast** are included in each issue. Factual articles on fashions and accessories with forecast trends. *Length:* 800-1000 words. *Illustrations:* line, half-tone. *Payment:* by arrangement.

Fashion Weekly (1959), William Drew, EMAP Fashion, 67 Clerkenwell Road, London EC1R 5BH   *tel* 0171-417 2810   *fax* 0171-417 2812.
£1.50. 8 p.a. Fashion business magazine primarily for retailers. *Payment:* by arrangement. *Illustrations:* line, half-tone, colour.

FHM (For Him Magazine) (1987), Mike Soutar, EMAP Metro, Mappin House, 4 Winsley Street, London W1N 7AR   *tel* 0171-436 1515   *fax* 0171-312 8191.
£2.50. M. Features, fashion, grooming, travel (adventure) and men's interests. *Length:* 2000-3000 words. *Illustrations:* colour and b&w photos, line and colour artwork. *Payment:* by negotiation.

The Field (1853), IPC Magazines Ltd, King's Reach Tower, Stamford Street, London SE1 9LS   *tel* 0171-261 5198   *fax* 0171-261 5358.
£2.70. M. Specific, topical and informed features on the British countryside and country pursuits, including natural history, field sports, gardening and farming. Overseas subjects considered but opportunities for such articles are limited. No fiction or children's material. Articles, *length* 800-2000 words, by outside contributors considered; also topical 'shorts' of 200-300 words on all countryside matters. *Illustrations:* colour photos of a high standard. *Payment:* on merit.

Financial Accountant (1920), Garry Carter, Chartergate Publishing, 1 Northumberland Avenue, Trafalgar Square, London WC2N 5BW   *tel* 0171-872 5522   *fax* 0171-872 5611. Journal of The Institute of Financial Accountants, Burford House, 44 London Road, Sevenoaks, Kent TN13 1AS   *tel* (01732) 458080.
£12.00 p.a. Bi-M. Articles on accounting, management, company law, data processing, information technology, pensions, factoring, investment,

insurance, fraud prevention and general business administration. *Length:* 1000-2000 words. *Illustrations:* offset litho (mono or colour). *Payment:* by arrangement.

Financial Adviser (1987), David Turner, FT Business Information Ltd, Maple House, 149 Tottenham Court Road, London W1P 9LL   *tel* 0171-896 2525   *fax* 0171-896 2591.
Free to financial intermediaries working in financial services. W. (£50.00 p.a.) Topical personal finance news and features. *Length:* variable. *Payment:* by arrangement.

Financial Director (1984), Richard Shackleton, VNU Business Publications, VNU House, 32-34 Broadwick Street, London W1A 2HG   *tel* 0171-316 9000   *fax* 0171-316 9250.
£45.00 p.a. (free to finance directors). M. Features on financial and strategic management issues. *Length:* 1500-2000 words. *Illustrations:* colour and b&w photos, line drawings. *Payment:* £150 per 1000 words; photos, variable; line, £250-£300.

Financial Times (1888), Richard Lambert, Southwark Bridge, London SE1 9HL *tel* 0171-873 3000.
65p. D. Articles of financial, commercial, industrial and economic interest. *Length:* 800-1000 words. *Payment:* by arrangement.

Fire (1908), Simon Hoffman, Queensway House, 2 Queensway, Redhill, Surrey RH1 1QS   *tel* (01737) 768611   *telex* 948669 TOPJNL G   *fax* (01737) 761685.
£4.95. M. (£49.90 p.a.) Articles on firefighting and fire prevention from acknowledged experts only. *Length:* 1000 words. *Illustrations:* dramatic fire-fighting or fire brigade rescue colour photos sometimes bought. *Payment:* by arrangement.

First Steps (1994), Irene K. Duncan, D.C. Thomson & Co. Ltd, 80 Kingsway East, Dundee DD4 8SL   *tel* (01382) 223131   *fax* (01382) 452491.
£1.45. M. Cares about the mother and her needs as well as the baby. Interested in articles on pregnancy, birth and childcare, and fillers. *Illustrations:* colour transparencies and colour artwork. *Length/payment:* negotiable.

Fishkeeping Answers (1992), Managing Editor: Steve Windsor, EMAP Pursuit Publishing Ltd, Bretton Court, Bretton, Peterborough PE3 8DZ   *tel* (01733) 264666   *fax* (01733) 465353.
£2.00. M. Instructional articles on any aspect of fishkeeping. *Length:* up to 1500 words. *Illustrations:* colour transparencies or prints. *Payment:* by negotiation.

Flight International (1909), A. Winn, Reed Business Publishing, Quadrant House, The Quadrant, Sutton, Surrey SM2 5AS   *tel* 0181-652 3882   *telex* 892084 REEDBP G   *fax* 0181-652 3840.
£2.00. W. Deals with all branches of aerospace: operational and technical articles, illustrated by photos, engineering cutaway drawings; also news, para-graphs, reports of lectures, etc. News press days: Thu, Fri. *Illustrations:* tone, line, 2- and 4-colour. *Payment:* by agreement.

Fly-Fishing & Fly-Tying (1990), Mark Bowler, Rolling River Publications, Aber-feldy Road, Kenmore, Perthshire PH15 2HF   *tel/fax* (01887) 830526.
£2.00. 9 p.a. Fly-fishing and fly-tying articles, fishery features, limited short stories, some fishing travel. *Length:* 800-1500 words. *Illustrations:* colour photos. *Payment:* by arrangement.

FlyPast (1981), Ken Delve, Key Publishing Ltd, PO Box 100, Stamford, Lincs. PE9 1XQ   *tel* (01780) 55131   *fax* (01780) 57261.

£2.60. M. Articles and features on historic aviation. Particularly interested in personal recollections of flying or visits to interesting aeroplane collections anywhere in the world. *Length:* up to 3000 words. *Illustrations:* colour and b&w photos. *Payment:* £50 per 1000 words; £25 colour; £10 b&w.

Football Picture Story Library, D.C. Thomson & Co. Ltd, Albert Square, Dundee DD1 9QJ *tel* (01382) 223131 *fax* (01382) 322214; and 185 Fleet Street, London EC4A 2HS *tel* 0171-242 5086 *fax* 0171-404 5694. 50p. 2 p.m. Football stories for boys told in pictures.

For Women (1991), Ruth Corbett, Portland Publishing Ltd, 4 Selsdon Way, London E14 9GL *tel* 0171-538 8969 *fax* 0171-538 3690. £2.95. M. Women's general interest magazine with erotic emphasis. Features on sex, health and beauty; celebrity interviews; erotic fiction and photos. Submit written synopsis for features; erotic fiction welcomed on spec. *Length:* 1500-2000 words. *Illustrations:* colour and b/w photos, cartoons. *Payment:* £150 per 1000 words; £150 per illustration.

Fore! (1993), Paul Hamblin, EMAP Pursuit Publishing Ltd, Bretton Court, Bretton, Peterborough PE3 8DZ *tel* (01733) 264666 *fax* (01733) 267198. £2.25. M. Interested in off-beat features on golf – thought provoking, fun and occasionally irreverent. *Length:* up to 1000 words. *Illustrations:* colour, line, cartoons. *Payment:* £100 per 1000 words; illustrations per quality/size used.

Fortean Times (1973), Bob Rickard and Paul Sieveking, Box 2409, London NW5 4NP *tel/fax* 0171-485 5002. £2.20. M. The journal of strange phenomena, experiences, related subjects and philosophies. Articles, features, news, reviews. *Length:* 500-3000 words; longer by arrangement. *Illustrations:* colour photos, line and tone art, cartoons. *Payment:* by negotiation.

Fourth World Review (1984), John Papworth, Fourth World Educational Research Association Trust, 24 Abercorn Place, London NW8 9XP *tel* 0171-286 4366 *fax* 0171-286 2186. £ – at reader's discretion. Bi-M. For small nations, small communities and the human spirit. Original material on all aspects of society from the perspective of the human scale. Politics, but *not* party political, and economics. *Length:* 3000-5000 words. *Illustrations:* b&w cartoons. *Payment:* £10 per page; cartoons £25.

FRANCE Magazine (1989), Philip Faiers, FRANCE Magazine Ltd, FRANCE House, The Square, Stow-on-the-Wold, Glos. GL54 1BN *tel* (01451) 831398 *fax* (01451) 830869. £3.75. Q. An armchair journey to the real France – features and articles ranging from cuisine to customs to architecture to exploring the hidden France. Informed speculative submissions welcome. *Length:* 800-2500 words. *Illustrations:* colour transparencies. *Payment:* £100 per 1000 words; £50 per page/ pro rata for illustrations.

Freelance Market News (1963), Angela Cox, Sevendale House, 7 Dale Street, Manchester M29 7WL *tel* 0161-228 2362 *fax* 0161-228 3533. £25.00 p.a. 11 p.a. News items on editorial requirements of interest to writers, plus short articles on 'where to sell'. *Length:* articles up to 700 words. *Payment:* from £25 per 1000 words.

Freelance Writing & Photography (1965), Paul King, Weavers Press Publishing Ltd, Clarendon Court, Over Wallop, Stockbridge, Hants SO20 8HU *tel/fax* (01264) 782298.

£17.70 p.a. Bi-M. Articles, features, reviews, interviews, market news, competitions, tips and hints for the freelance writer and photographer. *No work will be considered* unless accompanied by an sae. Letter of enquiry or outline preferred in first instance. *Length:* 400-1800 words. *Illustrations:* line, half-tone, cartoons. *Payment:* £20 per 1000 words on acceptance; £5 per photo/illustration, £10 for cover picture.

Fresh Produce Journal (1895), David Hope-Mason, Lockwood Press Ltd, 430-438 Market Towers, New Covent Garden, 1 Nine Elms Lane, London SW8 5NN   *tel* 0171-622 6677   *fax* 0171-720 2047.
£1.60. W. Articles dealing with fruit trades on the marketing aspects of production but particularly importing, distribution and post-harvest handling; articles should average 500-700 words. *Payment:* by arrangement. *Illustrations:* half-tone.

The Friend (1843), Deborah Padfield, Drayton House, 30 Gordon Street, London WC1H 0BQ   *tel* 0171-387 7549.
75p. W. Quaker weekly paper. Material of interest to the Religious Society of Friends and like-minded people; political, social, economic or devotional, considered from outside contributors. *Length:* up to 1000 words. *Illustrations:* b&w or colour prints, b&w line drawings. *Payment:* none.

The Garden (1866), Ian Hodgson, Apex House, Oundle Road, Peterborough PE2 9NP   *tel* (01733) 898100   *fax* (01733) 890657.
£2.50. M. Journal of The Royal Horticultural Society. Features of horticultural or botanical interest on a wide range of subjects. *Commissioned material only. Length:* 1200-2500 words. *Illustrations:* 35mm or medium format colour transparencies, occasional b&w prints, botanical line drawings. *Payment:* £120 per 1000 words; varies for illustrations.

Garden Answers (1982), Adrienne Wild, EMAP Apex Publications Ltd, Apex House, Oundle Road, Peterborough PE2 9NP   *tel* (01733) 898100   *fax* (01733) 898433.
£2.00. M. Commissioned features and articles on all aspects of gardening. *Study of magazine* essential. Approach by letter with examples of published work. *Length:* 750 words. *Illustrations:* colour transparencies and artwork. *Payment:* by negotiation.

Garden News (1958), Jim Ward, EMAP Apex Publications Ltd, Apex House, Oundle Road, Peterborough PE2 9NP   *tel* (01733) 898100   *fax* (01733) 898433.
75p. W. Gardening news and features on gardeners and their methods of success. *Illustrations:* line, half-tone, colour, cartoons. *Payment:* by negotiation.

Gardens Illustrated (1993), Rosie Atkins, John Brown Publishing, The Boathouse, Crabtree Lane, Fulham, London SW6 6LU   *tel* 0171-381 6007   *fax* 0171-381 3930.
£3.30. Bi-M. Upmarket, inspirational glossy for those interested in garden history, plants and gardening merchandise. *Material mostly commissioned*; send synopsis, samples of past work and sae to the editor. *Length:* 1000 words. *Illustrations:* colour – usually commissioned. *Payment:* by negotiation.

Gas World International (1884), Neil Campbell, Petroleum Economist Ltd, Baird House, 15-17 St Cross Street, London EC1N 8VN   *tel* 0171-831 5588   *fax* 0171-831 4567.
£12.00. M. (£95.00 p.a., £120/$195 p.a. USA/Europe) Full news coverage and technical articles on all aspects of engineering and management in the gas

industry. *Length:* up to 2500 words. Pictures and news items of topical interest accepted. *Payment:* by arrangement.

Gay Times (1982), David Smith, Ground Floor, Worldwide House, 116-134 Bayham Street, London NW1 0BA   *tel* 0171-482 2576   *fax* 0171-284 0329. £2.50. M. Feature articles, full news and review coverage of all aspects of gay and lesbian life. *Length:* up to 2000 words. *Illustrations:* colour, line and half-tone, cartoons. *Payment:* by arrangement.

Geographical Journal (1893), Prof V. Gardiner, Royal Geographical Society (with the Institute of British Geographers), Kensington Gore, London SW7 2AR   *tel* 0171-589 5466   *fax* 0171-584 4447.
£20.00 (post free). 3 p.a. (£55.00 p.a.) Papers on all aspects of geography, including some read before the Royal Geographical Society. *Length:* up to 4500 words. *Payment:* for reviews. *Illustrations:* photos, maps and diagrams.

Geographical Magazine (1935), Lisa Sykes, Campion Interactive Publishing Ltd, under licence from the Royal Geographical Society, Carriage Row, 203 Eversholt Street, London NW1 1BW   *tel* 0171-391 8833   *fax* 0171-391 8835.
£2.30. M. Topical geography in a broad sense. *Length:* 1500 words. *Illustrations:* colour slides, b&w prints or vintage material; maps and graphs always needed; cartoons. *Payment:* £150 per 1000 words; illustrations by negotiation.

Geological Magazine (1864), Dr C.P. Hughes, Prof I.N. McCave, Dr N.H. Woodcock, Dr M.J. Bickle, Cambridge University Press, The Edinburgh Building, Shaftesbury Road, Cambridge CB2 2RU   *tel* (01223) 312393.
Bi-M. (£166.00 p.a. institutions, £38.00 p.a. students, US$282 USA/Canada/Mexico) Original articles on all earth science topics containing the results of independent research by experts. Also reviews and notices of current geological literature, correspondence on geological subjects – illustrated. *Length:* variable. *Payment:* none.

Gibbons Stamp Monthly, Hugh Jefferies, Stanley Gibbons Ltd, 5 Parkside, Ringwood, Hants BH24 3SH   *tel* (01425) 472363   *fax* (01425) 470247.
£1.85. M. (£22.20 p.a.) Articles on philatelic topics. Previous reference to the editor advisable. *Length:* 500-2500 words. *Payment:* by arrangement, £25 or more per 1000 words. *Illustrations:* photos.

Gifts International, Freda Parker, Timothy Benn Publishing, 244-249 Temple Chambers, Temple Avenue, London EC4Y 0BA   *tel* 0171-583 3030   *fax* 0171-583 4068.
£36.00 p.a. M. (£46-52 p.a. overseas) News of gift industry – products, trends, shops; articles on retailing, exporting, importing, manufacturing, crafts (UK and abroad). *Illustrations:* products, news, personal photos.

Girl About Town Magazine (1973), 7-9 Rathbone Street, London W1P 1AF   *tel* 0171-636 6651   *fax* 0171-255 2352.
Free. W. Articles of general interest to women. *Length:* about 1100-1500 words. *Payment:* negotiable.

Glasgow Evening Times (1876), John Scott, 195 Albion Street, Glasgow G1 1QP   *tel* 0141-552 6255   *fax* 0141-553 1355; *London office:* 127 Clerkenwell Road, EC1R 5DB   *tel* 0171-405 2121   *fax* 0171-405 1888.
28p. D.

Glaucus (1990), Andy Horton, Glaucus House, 14 Corbyn Crescent, Shoreham-by-Sea, West Sussex BN43 6PQ   *tel* (01273) 465433   *fax* (01273) 465433.
£20.00 p.a. Q. Official journal of the British Marine Life Study Society, aimed at the popular market. Observations and scientific research on the natural history, and related subjects, of the marine environment surrounding the

British Isles. Send sae for Guide to Submissions. *Length:* up to 2500 words. *Illustrations:* b&w line, occasional b&w photos. *Payment:* expenses only.

Gloucestershire Echo (1873), Anita Syvret, Cheltenham Newspaper Co. Ltd, 1 Clarence Parade, Cheltenham, Glos. GL50 3NZ *tel* (01242) 526261 *fax* (01242) 578395.
29p. D. Specialist articles with Gloucestershire connections; no fiction. *Material mostly commissioned. Length:* 350 words. *Payment:* £30 per article, negotiable.

Goldlife for 50-Forward (1989), Miss N. Parmer, 1st Floor, 5 Charterhouse Buildings, Goswell Road, London EC1M 7AN *tel* 0171-251 5489 *fax* 0171-251 5490.
£14.95 p.a. Bi-M. Celebrity profiles and articles, features and news of interest to the over 50s age group. *Length:* approx. 700 words. *Illustrated. Payment:* £150 per 1000 words; £20 per illustration.

Golf Monthly (1911), Colin Callander, IPC Magazines Ltd, King's Reach Tower, Stamford Street, London SE1 9LS *tel* 0171-261 7237 *fax* 0171-261 7240.
£2.40. M. Original articles on golf considered (not reports), golf clinics, handy hints. *Illustrations:* half-tone, colour, cartoons. *Payment:* by arrangement.

Golf Weekly, Bob Warters, EMAP Pursuit Publishing Ltd, Bretton Court, Bretton, Peterborough PE3 8DZ *tel* (01733) 465223 *fax* (01733) 267198.
£1.70. W. News, tournament reports and articles on golf of interest to golfers. *Payment:* 15p per word published. *Illustrations:* photos of golf news and new courses.

Golf World (1962), David Clarke, Advance House, 37 Millharbour, Isle of Dogs, London E14 9TX *tel* 0171-538 1031 *fax* 0171-538 4106.
£2.70. M. Expert golf instructional articles, 500-3000 words; general interest articles, personality features 500-3000 words. Little fiction. *Payment:* by negotiation. *Illustrations:* line, half-tone, colour, cartoons.

Good Housekeeping (1922), Pat Roberts Cairns, National Magazine House, 72 Broadwick Street, London W1V 2BP *tel* 0171-439 5000 *fax* 0171-439 5591.
£1.95. M. Articles of 1000-2500 words on topics of interest to intelligent women. No unsolicited features or stories accepted; approach by letter only. Domestic subjects covered by staff writers. Personal experiences and humorous articles occasionally used. *Payment:* magazine standards. *Illustrations:* mainly commissioned.

The Good Society Review (1993), Masry MacGregor, Holman's Press, Elm Lodge, Anstruther, Fife KY10 3HQ *tel* (01333) 310313.
£4.95. 2 p.a. (£10.00 p.a. inc. p&p) Documentary and creative writing on the arts, environment and society, to encourage the circulation of ideas relevant today and in ten years' time. *Length:* creative writing 300-1000 words, articles 300-2500 words, short poetry. *Illustrations:* one guest artist per issue. *Payment:* £17 per 1000 words, plus free copy.

GQ (1988), Angus MacKinnon, Vogue House, Hanover Square, London W1R 0AD *tel* 0171-499 9080 *telex* 27338 VOLON G *fax* 0171-495 1679.
£2.50. M. Style, fashion and general interest magazine for men. *Illustrations:* b&w and colour photos, line drawings, cartoons. *Payment:* by arrangement.

Gramophone, James Jolly, 177-179 Kenton Road, Harrow, Middlesex HA3 0HA *tel* 0181-907 4476 *fax* 0181-909 1599.
£3.10. M. Outside contributions are rarely used. Features on recording artists, technical articles, and articles about gramophone needs. *Length:* 500-1000 words preferred. *Payment:* by arrangement. *Illustrations:* line, half-tone.

Granta (1889; new series 1979), Ian Jack, 2/3 Hanover Yard, Noel Road, London N1 8BE   *tel* 0171-704 9776   *fax* 0171-704 0474.
£7.99. Q. Original fiction, non-fiction and journalism. *Length:* determined by content. *Illustrations:* photos. *Payment:* by arrangement.

Greetings Magazine (1992), Publisher: Malcolm Naish, Editor: Deborah Putsman, Lema Publishing, Unit No. 1, Queen Mary's Avenue, Watford, Herts. WD1 7JR   *tel* (01923) 250909   *fax* (01923) 250995.
£30.00 p.a. 10 p.a. (other rates on application) Official journal of the Greeting Card Association. Articles, features and news related to the greetings card and giftwrap industry. Mainly written in-house; some material taken from outside. *Length:* varies. *Illustrations:* line, colour and b&w photos. *Payment:* by arrangement.

Grimsby Evening Telegraph (1897), Peter Moore, 80 Cleethorpe Road, Grimsby, South Humberside DN31 3EH   *tel* (01472) 359232   *fax* (01472) 358859.
27p. D. Considers general interest articles. *Illustrations:* line, half-tone, colour, cartoons. *Payment:* by arrangement.

The Grocer (1861), A. de Angeli, William Reed, Broadfield Park, Crawley, West Sussex RH11 9RT   *tel* (01293) 613400   *fax* (01293) 610333.
45p. W. Trade journal: articles or news or illustrations of general interest to the grocery and provision trades. *Payment:* by arrangement.

The Grower (1923), Peter Rogers, Nexus Media Ltd, Nexus House, Azalea Drive, Swanley, Kent BR8 8HY   *tel* (01322) 660070   *fax* (01322) 667633.
£1.20. W. News and practical articles on commercial horticulture, preferably illustrated. *Illustrations:* photos, line drawings. *Payment:* by arrangement.

The Guardian (1821), Alan Rusbridger, 119 Farringdon Road, London EC1R 3ER   *tel* 0171-278 2332   *fax* 0171-239 9935; 164 Deansgate, Manchester M60 2RR   *tel* 0161-832 7200   *fax* 0161-832 5351.
Mon.-Fri. 45p. Sat. 60p. D. Ind. The paper takes few articles from outside contributors except on its specialist pages. Articles should not normally exceed 1200 words in *length. Illustrations:* news and features photos. *Payment:* from £170.83 per 1000 words; from £50.94 for illustrations.
The Guardian Weekend, Deborah Orr (free with Sat. paper). Features on world affairs, major profiles, food and drink, home life, the arts, travel, leisure, etc. Also good reportage on social and political subjects. *Illustrations:* b&w photos and line, cartoons. *Payment:* apply for rates.

Guernsey Evening Press and Star (1897), Graham Ingrouille, Braye Road, Vale, Guernsey, Channel Islands GY1 3BW   *tel* (01481) 45866   *fax* (01481) 48972.
30p. Mon.-Sat. News and feature articles. *Length:* 500-700 words. *Illustrations:* colour and b&w photos. *Payment:* by negotiation.

Guiding, Nora Warner, 17-19 Buckingham Palace Road, London SW1W 0PT   *tel* 0171-834 6242   *fax* 0171-828 8317.
£1.15. M. Official magazine of The Guide Association. Articles of interest to women of all ages, with special emphasis on youth work and the Guide Movement. Articles on simple crafts, games and the outdoors also welcome. *Length:* 500-1200 words. *Illustrations:* line, half-tone, colour, cartoons. *Payment:* £70 per 1000 words; £100 full colour page, £60 b&w – negotiable.

The Haiku Quarterly (1990), Kevin Bailey, 39 Exmouth Street, Kingshill, Swindon, Wilts. SN1 3PU   *tel* (01793) 523927.
£2.50. Q. (£9.00 p.a; £12.00 p.a. non-UK.) Haiku, Tanka and related forms; also longer traditional and experimental poetry. Book and magazine reviews. *Payment:* small. Commissioned *illustrations*.

Hairflair (1985), Hellena Barnes, Hair and Beauty Ltd, 4th Floor, 27 Maddox Street, London W1R 9LE   *tel* 0171-493 1081   *fax* 0171-499 6686.
£1.80. M. Hair, beauty, fashion – and related features – for the 16-35 age group. *Preliminary letter* essential. *Length:* 800-1000 words. *Illustrations:* colour and b&w photos, occasional line drawings. *Payment:* £100-£120 per 1000 words.

Hampshire—The County Magazine, 74 Bedford Place, Southampton SO15 2DF   *tel* (01703) 223591/333457.
£1.50. M. Factual articles concerning all aspects of Hampshire and Hampshire life, past and present. *Length:* 500-1500 words. *Payment:* £10 per 1000 words. *Illustrations:* photos and line drawings.

Harpers & Queen (1929), Fiona Macpherson, National Magazine House, 72 Broadwick Street, London W1V 2BP   *tel* 0171-439 5000   *fax* 0171-439 5506.
£2.70. M. Features, fashion, beauty, art, theatre, films, travel, interior decoration, mainly commissioned. *Illustrations:* line, wash, full colour and two- and three-colour, and photos.

Hartlepool Mail (1877), Christopher Cox, Northeast Press Ltd, Clarence Road, Hartlepool, Cleveland TS24 8BU   *tel* (01429) 274441   *fax* (01429) 869024.
27p. D. Features of local interest. *Length:* 500 words. *Illustrations:* colour, b&w photos, line, cartoons. *Payment:* by negotiation.

Health & Efficiency International (1900), Helen Ludbrook, 64 Great Eastern Street, London EC2A 3QR   *tel* 0171-739 5052   *fax* 0171-729 8053.
£2.00. M. (also publishes separate Q. and Bi-A. editions) Articles on naturist and human relationship matters. Naturist travel features; some health and humour. Wide scope for new writers; guidelines on request. *Length:* 750-1500 words. *Illustrations:* line, half-tone, colour transparencies, colour prints, cartoons. *Payment:* by negotiation.

Health & Fitness (1984), Sharon Walker, Nexus Media Communications, 50 Doughty Street, London WC1N 2NG   *tel* 0171-405 2055   *fax* 0171-405 6528.
£2.20. M. Articles on all aspects of health and fitness. *Illustrations:* line, half-tone, colour. *Payment:* by arrangement.

Healthy Eating (1990), Jane Last, Spendlove Centre, Charlbury, Oxfordshire OX7 3PQ   *tel* (01608) 811266   *fax* (01608) 811380.
£2.50. Bi-M. Articles on health and nutrition, how food affects the body, celebrity food and health stories. *Length:* 1000-1200 words. *Illustrations:* colour food photography and illustrations. *Payment:* £150-£250 per article; £30-£50 for illustrations; £25-£80 for transparencies.

Hello! (1988), Maggie Koumi, Wellington House, 69/71 Upper Ground, London SE1 9PQ   *tel* 0171-334 7404   *fax* 0171-334 7412.
£1.25. W. Personality-based features – showbusiness, celebrity, royalty; exclusive interviews. *Payment:* by arrangement. *Illustrated.*

The Herald (1783), George McKechnie, Caledonian Newspapers Ltd, 195 Albion Street, Glasgow G1 1QP   *tel* 0141-552 6255   *fax* 0141-552 2288; *London office:* Gray's Inn House, 127 Clerkenwell Road, EC1R 5DB   *tel* 0171-405 2121.
45p. D. Ind. Articles up to 1000 words.

Here's Health, Erika Harvey, EMAP Élan, 20 Orange Street, London WC2H 7ED   *tel* 0171-957 8383   *fax* 0171-930 4000.
£2.10. M. Articles on nutrition, alternative medicine, environment and health, natural treatment success stories. *Preliminary letter and clippings* essential. *Length:* 750-1800 words. *Payment:* on publication. *Illustrated,* including cartoons.

Heritage (1984), Siân Ellis, Bulldog Magazines Ltd, 4 The Courtyard, Denmark Street, Wokingham, Berks. RG40 2AZ *tel* (01734) 771677 *fax* (01734) 772903.
£2.95. Bi-M. Features on British topics only: towns and villages to visit, tours/off the beaten track, customs, craftsmen, people, all historic/heritage subjects. *Length:* 1200 words. *Illustrations:* colour transparencies. *Payment:* £100 per 1000 words; illustrations by negotiation.

Hertfordshire Countryside (1946), Sandra Small, Beaumonde Publications Ltd, 4 Mill Bridge, Hertford, Herts. SG14 1PY *tel* (01992) 553571 *fax* (01992) 587713.
£1.25. M. Articles of county interest. *Length:* 1000 words. *Payment:* £25 per 1000 words. *Illustrations:* line, half-tone, cartoons.

Hi-Fi News & Record Review (1956), Steve Harris, Link House, Dingwall Avenue, Croydon CR9 2TA *tel* 0181-686 2599 *fax* 0181-781 6046.
£2.75. M. Articles on all aspects of high quality sound recording and reproduction; also extensive record review section and supporting musical feature articles. Audio matter is essentially technical, but should be presented in a manner suitable for music lovers interested in the nature of sound. *Length:* 2000-3000 words. *Illustrations:* line, half-tone. *Payment:* by arrangement.

History (1916), H.T. Dickinson BA. DipEd. MA. PhD. DLitt. Editorial: History Department, University of Edinburgh, Edinburgh EH8 9JY *tel* 0131-650 3785. Published by Blackwell (Oxford) for the Historical Association, 59A Kennington Park Road, London SE11 4JH *tel* 0171-735 3901.
Q. (£16.00 p.a. for Historical Association members; £38.00 p.a. non-members) Historical articles and reviews by experts. *Length:* usually up to 8000 words. *Illustrations:* only exceptionally. *Payment:* none.

History Today (1951), Gordon Marsden, 20 Old Compton Street, London W1V 5PE *tel* 0171-439 8315.
£2.95. M. History in the widest sense – political, economic, social, biography, relating past to present; world history as well as British. *Length:* articles 3500 words; shorter news/views pieces 600-1200 words. *Illustrations:* from prints and original photos. Please do not send original material until publication is agreed. *Payment:* by arrangement.

Home and Country (1919), Amber Tokeley, 104 New King's Road, London SW6 4LY *tel* 0171-731 5777 *fax* 0171-736 4061.
£1.40. M. Official Journal of the National Federation of Women's Institutes for England and Wales. Publishes material related to the Federation's and members' activities; also considers articles of general interest to women, particularly country women, e.g. craft, environment, humour, health, rural life stories, of 800-1200 words. *Illustrations:* colour and b&w photos and drawings, cartoons. *Payment:* by arrangement.

Home and Family (1954), Margaret Duggan, The Mothers' Union, The Mary Sumner House, 24 Tufton Street, London SW1P 3RB *tel* 0171-222 5533 *fax* 0171-222 1591.
80p. Q. Short articles related to Christian family life. *Payment:* approx. £50 per 1000 words. *Illustrations:* line, half-tone, colour, usually commissioned.

Home Words (1870), Publisher: G.A. Knights, Chansitor Publications Ltd, St Mary's Works, St Mary's Plain, Norwich, Norfolk NR3 3BH *tel* (01603) 615995 *fax* (01603) 624483.
M. Illustrated C of E magazine insert. Articles of popular Christian interest with an Anglican slant (400-800 words) with relevant photos; also cartoons. *Payment:* by arrangement.

HomeFlair Magazine (1990), Dawn Leahey, Hamerville Magazines Ltd, Regal House, Regal Way, Watford, Herts. WD2 4YJ *tel* (01923) 237799 *fax* (01923) 246901.
£1.30. M. Homes' conversions, inspirational looks, what's new in products and design. Approach in writing, with samples of previously published work. *Length:* up to 1500 words. *Payment:* £120 per 1000 words. *Illustrated.*

Homes and Gardens (1919), Amanda Evans, IPC Magazines Ltd, King's Reach Tower, Stamford Street, London SE1 9LS *tel* 0171-261 5000 *fax* 0171-261 6247.
£2.10. M. Articles on home interest or design. *Length:* articles, 900-1000 words. *Illustrations:* all types. *Payment:* generous, but exceptional work required; varies.

Homes & Ideas (1993), Debbie Djordjević, IPC Magazines Ltd, King's Reach Tower, Stamford Street, London SE1 9LS *tel* 0171-261 7325 *fax* 0171-261 7495.
£1.50. M. Features on any aspect of style for the home. *Send* cuttings to the editor. *Length:* by arrangement. *Illustrations:* colour photos and drawings. *Payment:* NUJ rates plus; illustrations by arrangement.

Homestyle (1992), Lesley Hannaford-Hill, RAP Publishing, Vigilant House, 120 Wilton Road, London SW1V 1JZ *tel* 0171-233 9989 *fax* 0171-873 8557.
£1.20. M. Ideas and practical features on home and garden improvements. Merchandise reviews. *Length:* 2 or 4-page spreads. *Illustrations:* colour transparencies. *Payment:* by negotiation.

Horse and Hound, Arnold Garvey, IPC Magazines Ltd, King's Reach Tower, Stamford Street, London SE1 9LS *tel* 0171-261 6315 *fax* 0171-261 5429.
£1.30. W. Special articles, news items, photos, on all matters appertaining to horses, hunting; cartoons. *Payment:* by negotiation.

Horse & Pony (1980), Andrea Oakes, EMAP Pursuit Publishing Ltd, Bretton Court, Bretton, Peterborough PE3 8DZ *tel* (01733) 264666 *fax* (01733) 261984.
£1.00. F. All material relevant to young people with equestrian interests. *Payment:* on value to publication rather than length. *Illustrations:* colour, with a strong story line, cartoons.

Horse and Rider (1959), Managing Editor: Kate Austin, Editor: Alison Bridge, Haslemere House, Lower Street, Haslemere, Surrey GU27 2PE *tel* (01428) 651551 *fax* (01428) 653888.
£2.00. M. Sophisticated magazine covering all forms of equestrian activity at home and abroad. Good writing and technical accuracy essential. *Length:* 1500-2000 words. *Illustrations:* photos and drawings, the latter usually commissioned. *Payment:* by arrangement.

Horticulture Week, Vicky Browning, Haymarket Magazines Ltd, 60 Waldegrave Road, Teddington, Middlesex TW11 8LG *tel* 0181-943 5719.
£1.30. W. (£59.50 p.a.) News, technical and business journal for the nursery and garden centre trade, landscape industry and public parks and sports ground staff. Outside contributions considered and, if accepted, paid for. No fiction. *Length:* 500-1500 words. *Illustrations:* line, half-tone, colour. *Payment:* by arrangement.

Hortus (1987), David Wheeler, Bryan's Ground, Stapleton, Nr Presteigne, Herefordshire LD8 2LP *tel* (01544) 260001 *fax* (01544) 260015.
£30.00 p.a. Q. Articles on decorative horticulture: plants, gardens, history, design, literature, people; book reviews. *Length:* 1500-5000 words, longer by

arrangement. *Illustrations:* line, half-tone and wood-engravings. *Payment:* by arrangement.

Hospital Doctor (c.1980), Jane King, Reed Healthcare Publishing, Quadrant House, The Quadrant, Sutton, Surrey SM2 5AS   *tel* 0181-652 8763   *telex* 892048 REEDBP G   *fax* 0181-652 8701.
Free to 45,000 doctors. W. (£70.00 p.a.) *Commissioned* features of interest to all grades and specialities of hospital doctors; demand for news tip-offs. *Length:* features 800-1000 words. *Illustrations:* colour photos and transparencies. *Payment:* £120 per 1000 words features, £10 per 1000 words news; colour £100.

Hospitality (1980), Consultant Editor: Alan Sutton, 1st Floor, 67 West Street, Dunstable, Beds. LU6 1ST   *tel* (01582) 472266   *fax* (01582) 660872.
£4.20. Bi-M. Official magazine of the Hotel Catering & Institutional Management Association. Articles for a management readership on food, accommodation services and related topics in hotels, restaurants, tourism, educational establishments, the health service, industrial situations, educational and other institutions. *Illustrations:* photos, line, cartoons. *Payment:* by arrangement.

Hot Air (1984), Alex Finer, The Boathouse, Crabtree Lane, London SW6 6LU   *tel* 0171-381 6007   *fax* 0171-381 3930.
Free. Q. Inflight magazine for Virgin Atlantic Airways. Sport, trends/lifestyle, celebrities. *Length:* 1500-3000 words. *Illustrations:* high quality colour transparencies. *Payment:* by negotiation.

House & Garden, Susan Crewe, Vogue House, Hanover Square, London W1R 0AD   *tel* 0171-499 9080   *telex* 27338 VOLON G   *fax* 0171-629 2907.
£2.20. M. Articles (always commissioned), on subjects relating to domestic architecture, interior decorating, furnishing, gardening, household equipment, food and wine.

House Beautiful (1989), Caroline Atkins, National Magazine House, 72 Broadwick Street, London W1V 2BP   *tel* 0171-439 5500   *fax* 0171-439 5595.
£1.30. M. Specialist 'home' features for the homes of today. *Preliminary study* of magazine advisable. *Payment:* according to merit. *Illustrated.*

HouseBuilder, Ben Roskrow, 82 New Cavendish Street, London W1M 8AD   *tel* 0171-580 5588   *fax* 0171-323 0890.
£6.00. 11 p.a. Official Journal of the House-Builders Federation and National House-Building Council. Technical articles on design, construction and equipment of dwellings, estate planning and development, and technical aspects of house-building, aimed at those engaged in house and flat construction and the development of housing estates. *Preliminary letter* advisable. *Length:* articles from 500 words, preferably with illustrations. *Payment:* by arrangement. *Illustrations:* photos, plans, construction details, cartoons.

i-D Magazine (1980), Avril Mair, Universal House, 251-255 Tottenham Court Road, London W1P 0AB   *tel* 0171-813 6170   *fax* 0171-813 6179.
£2.20. M. Youth and general interest magazine: i-Deas, fashion, clubs, music, people. Will consider unsolicited material. *Illustrations:* colour and b&w photos. *Payment:* £100 per 1000 words; photos £50 per page.

Ideal Home (1920), Sally O'Sullivan, IPC Magazines Ltd, King's Reach Tower, Stamford Street, London SE1 9LS   *tel* 0171-261 5000.
£1.70. M. Lifestyle magazine, articles usually commissioned. Contributors advised to *study editorial content* before submitting material. *Payment:* according to material. *Illustrations:* usually commissioned.

The Illustrated London News (1842), Alison Booth, 20 Upper Ground, London SE1 9PF   *tel* 0171-805 5555   *fax* 0171-805 5911.

£2.50. 2-3 p.a. Magazine dealing chiefly with London and the UK, travel, adventure, environment and the quality of life. Interesting articles accepted and short stories for the annual Christmas Number; but most material commissioned. *Illustrations:* photos, drawings, cartoons – *all mostly commissioned. Payment:* usual rates; special rates for exclusive illustrations.

In Britain (1930), Andrea Spain, Premier Magazines, Haymarket House, 1 Oxendon Street, London SW1Y 4EE *tel* 0171-925 2544 *fax* 0171-976 1088. £2.00. M. (£19.95 p.a.) Upmarket features magazine about places and people in Britain. Some freelance material is accepted. *Illustrated. Payment:* by arrangement.

Independent (1986), Andrew Marr, One Canada Square, Canary Wharf, London E14 5DL *tel* 0171-293 2000 *fax* 0171-293 2435.
40p. D. 50p. Sat. Occasional freelance contributions; *preliminary letter* advisable. *Payment:* by arrangement.
Independent Magazine (1988), Michael Watts. Free with Sat. newspaper. Profiles and illustrated articles of topical interest; *all material commissioned. Preliminary study* of the magazine essential. *Length:* 500-3000 words. *Illustrations:* cartoons; commissioned colour and b&w photos. *Payment:* by arrangement.

Independent on Sunday (1990), Peter Wilby, One Canada Square, Canary Wharf, London E14 5DL *tel* 0171-293 2000 *fax* 0171-293 2043.
£1.00. W. News, features and articles. *Illustrated,* including cartoons. *Payment:* by negotiation.
The Sunday Review, Richard Askwith *tel* 0171-293 2000 *fax* 0171-293 2027. Free with paper. Original features of general interest with potential for photographic illustration. *Material mostly commissioned. Length:* 1000-5000 words. *Illustrations:* colour transparencies. *Payment:* £150 per 1000 words.

Index on Censorship (1972), Ursula Owen, Lancaster House, 33 Islington High Street, London N1 9LH *tel* 0171-278 2313 *fax* 0171-278 1878.
£7.99. Bi-M. (£36.00 p.a.) Articles up to 3000 words dealing with all aspects of free speech and political censorship. *Illustrations:* b&w, cartoons. *Payment:* £60 per 1000 words; £20 per illustration.

The Indexer (1958), Janet Shuter, The Old Chapel, Kings Road, Bembridge, Isle of Wight PO35 5NB *tel* (01983) 874514 *fax* (01983) 874656.
Free to members. 2 p.a. (subscription £25.00 p.a. from Journal Subscriptions Officer, Huntersquay, 33 Marlow Bottom, Marlow, Bucks. SL7 3LZ). Journal of the Society of Indexers, American Society of Indexers, Australian Society of Indexers, and Indexing & Abstracting Society of Canada. Articles of interest to professional indexers and providers and users of information in any form. *Payment:* none.

Infant Projects (1978), Jane Morgan, Scholastic Publications Ltd, Villiers House, Clarendon Avenue, Leamington Spa, Warwickshire CV32 5PR *tel* (01926) 887799 *fax* (01926) 883331.
£2.30. Bi-M. Practical articles suggesting project activities for teachers of children aged 4-8; *material mostly commissioned. Length:* 500-1000 words. *Illustrations:* b&w photos and line illustrations, colour posters. *Payment:* by arrangement.

Information and Software Technology (1959). *UK contact:* Prof Martin Shepperd, Department of Applied Computing & Electronics, Bournemouth University, Poole House, Talbot Campus, Fern Barrow, Poole, Dorset BH12 5BB *tel* (01202) 595078 *fax* (01202) 595314.
$395 US/£265 rest of world. M. Papers on software design and development

and the application of information processing in large organisations, especially multinationals. *Length:* 5000 words. *Illustrations:* line, half-tone.

The Inquirer (1842), Keith Gilley, 1-6 Essex Street, London WC2R 2HY   *tel* 0171-240 2384.
35p. F. Journal of news and comment for Unitarians and religious liberals. Articles, liberal and progressive in tone, of general religious, social, cultural and international interest. *Length:* up to 750 words. *Payment:* none.

Inside Edge (1990), Charles Frewin, Two Heads Publishing, 9 Whitehall Park, London N19 3TS   *tel* 0171-561 1606   *fax* 0171-501 1607.
£1.95. M. Cricket gossip and unusual stories; satirical humour and serious issues. Read the magazine for style. *Length:* (features) 1000 words. *Illustrations:* Unusual cricket photos. *Payment:* NUJ rates; £20.

Inspirations (1993), Deborah Barker, GE Publishing Ltd, 133 Long Acre, London WC2E 9AD   *tel* 0171-836 0519   *fax* 0171-836 0280.
£1.95. M. Practical features on all aspects of home interest – home design, cookery, crafts, gadgets. *Length:* 800-2000 words. *Payment:* by arrangement. *Illustrated.*

Insurance Age (1979), John Jackson, EMAP Business Communications, 33-39 Bowling Green Lane, London EC1R 0DA   *tel* 0171-505 8181.
M. News and features on general insurance, personal, commercial, private medical, health and Lloyd's of London. *Length:* 650 words. *Illustrations:* transparencies, colour and b&w photos. *Payment:* by negotiation.

Insurance Brokers' Monthly (1950), Brian Susman, 7 Stourbridge Road, Lye, Stourbridge, West Midlands DY9 7DG   *tel* Lye (01384) 895228.
£2.50. M. Articles of technical and non-technical interest to insurance brokers and others engaged in the insurance industry. Occasional articles of general interest to the City, on finance, etc. *Length:* 1000-1500 words. *Payment:* from £25 per 1000 words on last day of month following publication. Authoritative material written under true name and qualification receives highest payment. *Illustrations:* line and half-tone, 100-120 screen.

InterMedia (1970), Rex Winsbury, International Institute of Communications, Tavistock House South, Tavistock Square, London WC1H 9LF   *tel* 0171-388 0671   *fax* 0171-380 0623.
£70.00 p.a. Bi-M. International journal concerned with policies, events, trends and research in the field of communications, broadcasting, telecommunications and associated issues, particularly cultural and social. *Preliminary letter* essential. *Illustrations:* b&w line. *Payment:* by arrangement.

International Affairs (1922), Royal Institute of International Affairs, Chatham House, 10 St James's Square, London SW1Y 4LE   *tel* 0171-957 5700   *fax* 0171-957 5710.
£15.00. Q. (£39.00 p.a., institutions £56.00 p.a.) Serious long-term articles on international affairs; more than 100 books reviewed each quarter. *Preliminary letter* advisable. *Article length:* average 7000 words. *Illustrations:* none. *Payment:* by arrangement.

International Construction, A.J. Peterson, Ground Floor, Montrose House, 412-6 Eastern Avenue, Gants Hill, Ilford, Essex IG2 6NQ   *tel* 0181-518 2525   *fax* 0181-518 1020.
Controlled circulation. M. Articles dealing with new techniques of construction, applications of construction equipment and use of construction materials in any part of the world. *Length:* maximum 1500 words plus illustrations. *Illustrations:* line, half-tone, colour; some two-colour line illustrations used, cartoons. *Payment:* from £130 per 1000 words, plus illustrations.

Internet (1994), Neil Ellul, EMAP Computing, Greater London House, Hampstead Road, London NW1 7QZ   *tel* 0171-388 2430   *fax* 0171-383 5578.
£2.95. M. Magazine for consumer users, people who use the net at work and business users. Articles, news and features and guide to web sites on the Internet. *Length:* 800-1000 words. *Illustrations:* colour photos, cartoons. *Payment:* £150 per 1000 words.

Interzone (1982), David Pringle, 217 Preston Drove, Brighton, East Sussex BN1 6FL   *tel* (01273) 504710.
£2.75. M. (£30.00 p.a.) Science fiction and fantasy short stories, articles, interviews and reviews. *Please read magazine* before submitting. *Length:* 2000-6000 words. *Illustrations:* line, half-tone, colour. *Payment:* by arrangement.

Inverness Courier (1817), John Macdonald, PO Box 13, 9-11 Bank Lane, Inverness IV1 1QW   *tel* (01463) 233059   *fax* (01463) 243439.
35p. Tue.; 38p. Fri. Articles of Highland interest only. Unsolicited material accepted. *Illustrations:* colour and b&w photos. *Payment:* by arrangement.

Investors Chronicle, Ceri Jones, Greystoke Place, Fetter Lane, London EC4A 1ND   *tel* 0171-405 6969   *fax* 0171-405 5276.
£1.70. W. Journal covering investment and personal finance. Occasional outside contributions for surveys are accepted. *Payment:* by negotiation.

Involvement (1884), Anthony Barry, 42 Colebrooke Row, London N1 8AF   *tel* 0171-354 8040.
£32.00 p.a. UK, £45.00 p.a. overseas, post free. Q. Journal of the Involvement & Participation Association. Articles, mostly commissioned, on participation and involvement in industry, employee shareholding, joint consultation, the sharing of information, labour-management relations, workers participation, and kindred industrial subjects from the operational angle, with emphasis on the practice of particular enterprises, usually written by a member of the team involved, whether manager or workers, and with a strong factual background. *Length:* up to 2500 words. *Payment:* by negotiation.

Iron (1973), Peter Mortimer, 5 Marden Terrace, Cullercoats, North Shields, Northumberland NE30 4PD   *tel* (0191) 2531901.
£3.50 inc. postage. 3 p.a. Poems; short stories up to 6000 words in total. *Illustrations:* line, half-tone. *Payment:* £10 per page; £5 for illustrations.

Jane's Defence Weekly (1984), Carol Reed, Sentinel House, 163 Brighton Road, Coulsdon, Surrey CR5 2NH   *tel* 0181-700 3700   *telex* 916907 JANES G   *fax* 0181-763 1007.
£140.00 p.a. W. International defence news; military equipment; budget analysis, industry, military technology, business, political, defence market intelligence. *Payment:* minimum £125 per 1000 words used. *Illustrations:* line, half-tone, colour.

Jazz Journal International (1948), Publisher and Editor-in-Chief: Eddie Cook, Jazz Journal Ltd, 1/5 Clerkenwell Road, London EC1M 5PA   *tel* 0171-608 1348/1362   *fax* 0171-608 1292.
£2.80. M. Articles on jazz, record reviews. Prospective contributors should telephone or write before submitting material. *Payment:* by arrangement. *Illustrations:* photos.

Jewish Chronicle (1841), Edward J. Temko, 25 Furnival Street, London EC4A 1JT   *tel* 0171-405 9252.
40p. W. Authentic and exclusive news stories and articles of Jewish interest from 500-1500 words are considered. There is a lively arts and leisure section, as well as regular travel pages. *Payment:* by arrangement. *Illustrations:* of Jewish interest, either topical or feature.

Jewish Quarterly (1953), Elena Lappin, PO Box 2078, London W1A 1JR   *tel* 0171-629 5004   *fax* 0171-629 5110.
£3.95. Q. (£15.00 p.a., £17.50 p.a. Europe, £25.00 p.a. overseas) Articles of Jewish interest, literature, history, music, politics, poetry, book reviews, fiction. *Length:* 2000-3000 words. *Illustrations:* half-tone.

Jewish Telegraph (1950), Paul Harris, Telegraph House, 11 Park Hill, Bury Old Road, Prestwich, Manchester M25 0HH   *tel* 0161-740 9321   *fax* 0161-740 9325; 4A Roman View, Leeds LS8 2LW   *tel* (0113) 295 6000   *fax* (0113) 295 6006; Harold House, Dunbabin Road, Liverpool L15 6XL   *tel* 0151-475 6666/ 2222   *fax* 0151-475 2222; 43 Queen Square, Glasgow G41 2BD   *tel* 0141-423 9200/1/2   *fax* 0141-423 9200.
30p (Man.), 20p (Leeds), 25p (Liv.), 40p (Glas.). W. Non-fiction articles of Jewish interest, especially humour. Exclusive Jewish news stories and pictures, international, national and local. *Length:* 1000-1500 words. *Payment:* by arrangement. *Illustrations:* line, half-tone, cartoons.

The Journal (1912), David Worsfold, CII Journal, 58 Fleet Street, London EC4Y 1JU   *tel* 0171-353 1121   *fax* 0171-583 6069.
Free to members. 8 p.a. (£3.00) Journal of The Chartered Insurance Institute. Technical articles on all aspects of insurance. *Material mostly commissioned. Length:* 1200 words. *Payment:* £140 per 1000 words.

The Journal, Bill Bradshaw, Thomson House, Groat Market, Newcastle upon Tyne NE1 1ED   *tel* 0191-232 7500   *fax* 0191-261 8869.
28p. D. Ind.

Journal of Alternative and Complementary Medicine (1983), Graeme Miller, 9 Rickett Street, Fulham, London SW6 1RU   *tel* 0171-385 0012   *fax* 0171-385 4566.
£2.50. M. (£29.50 p.a.) Feature articles (*length:* up to 2000 words) and news stories (*length:* up to 250 words). Unsolicited material welcome but not eligible for payment unless commissioned. *Illustrations:* line, half-tone, colour. *Payment:* by negotiation.

Journalist, Tim Gopsill, NUJ, Acorn House, 314 Gray's Inn Road, London WC1X 8DP   *tel* 0171-278 7916   *fax* 0171-837 8143   *e-mail* the.journalist @mcr1.poptel.org.uk
50p. Bi-M. (£9.50 p.a., £13.00 p.a. overseas) Magazine of the National Union of Journalists (mailed to all members). Accepts material relating to journalism, trade unionism and general conditions in the newspaper industry. Mainly contributed by members, and outside written contributions not paid.

Junior Education (1977), Mrs Terry Saunders, Scholastic Publications Ltd, Villiers House, Clarendon Avenue, Leamington Spa, War. CV32 5PR   *tel* (01926) 887799   *fax* (01926) 883331.
£2.40. M. For teachers, educationalists and students concerned with children aged 7-12. Articles by specialists on practical teaching ideas and methods, plus in-depth coverage and debate on news issues in education. *Length:* 800-1200 words. *Payment:* by arrangement. *Illustrated* with b&w photos and line drawings; includes colour poster.

Junior Focus (1982), Kate Element, Scholastic Publications Ltd, Villiers House, Clarendon Avenue, Leamington Spa, War. CV32 5PR   *tel* (01926) 887799   *fax* (01926) 883331.
£2.30. M. Aimed at teachers of 7-12 year olds, each issue is based on a theme, closely linked with the National Curriculum. Includes A1 and A3 full-colour posters, 8 pages of photocopiable material and 12 pages of project notes. *All material commissioned. Length:* 1-4 pages. *Illustrations:* commissioned b&w

line; welcomes samples of work from new illustrators. *Payment:* £100 per double-page spread; varies for illustrations.

Just Seventeen (1983), EMAP Élan, 20 Orange Street, London WC2H 7ED *tel* 0171-957 8383 *fax* 0171-930 5728.

85p. W. Articles of interest to girls aged between 12 and 18: fashion, beauty, pop, and various features; real life and short stories up to 1500 words; quizzes. *Payment:* £150 per 1000 words. *Illustrations:* line, half-tone, colour, cartoons.

Justice of the Peace and Local Government Law (1837), F.W. Davies and Mark Watson-Gandy, Little London, Chichester, West Sussex PO19 1PG *tel* (01243) 775552.

£130.60 p.a. inc. postage. W. Professional journal. Articles on magisterial and local government law and associated subjects including family law, criminology, medico-legal matters, penology, police, probation (length preferred, under 1400 words). *Preliminary letter* welcomed although not essential. *Payment:* articles minimum £10 per column except when otherwise commissioned.

Kent Messenger, 6 and 7 Middle Row, Maidstone, Kent ME14 1TG *tel* (01622) 695666 *fax* (01622) 757227.

40p. Fri. Articles of special interest to Kent, particularly Maidstone, the Weald and Mid-Kent areas. *Payment:* state price. *Illustrations:* any format.

Kent Today, 395 High Street, Chatham, Kent ME4 4PG *tel* (01634) 830999 *fax* (01634) 829479 or 892484.

25p. Mon.-Fri. Paper with emphasis on news and sport, plus regular feature pages. National news; with editions covering the Medway Towns, Gravesend and Dartford, Swale, Maidstone. *Illustrations:* line, half-tone.

Kerrang! (1981), Phil Alexander, EMAP Metro Ltd, 52-55 Carnaby Street, London W1V 1PF *tel* 0171-437 8050 *fax* 0171-734 2287.

£1.50. W. News, views and reviews; the noise of the new generation. *All material commissioned. Illustrations:* colour. *Payment:* by arrangement.

Keyboard Review (1985), Sam Molineaux, Music Maker Publications, Alexander House, Forehill, Ely, Cambs. CB7 4AF *tel* (01353) 665577 *fax* (01353) 662489 *e-mail* kr@musicians-net.co.uk

£2.20. M. Interviews with keyboard/piano players; reviews of new keyboard-related equipment. *Length:* 900-2500 words. *Illustrations:* colour transparencies and photos. *Payment:* £70 per 1000 words.

Kids Alive! (The Young Soldier) (1881), Ken Nesbitt, 101 Queen Victoria Street, London EC4P 4EP *tel* 0171-236 5222 ext 2345 *fax* 0171-236 3491.

20p. W. (£25.54 p.a.) The Salvation Army's children's weekly. Stories, pictures, cartoon strips, puzzles etc., Christian-based with emphasis on education *re* addictive substances. *Payment:* by arrangement. *Illustrations:* half-tone, line and three-colour line, cartoons.

The Lady (1885), Arline Usden, 39-40 Bedford Street, Strand, London WC2E 9ER *tel* 0171-379 4717 *fax* 0171-497 2137.

65p. W. British and foreign travel, countryside, human-interest, celebrity interviews, animals, cookery, art and antiques, historic-interest and commemorative articles (*preliminary letter* advisable for articles dealing with anniversaries). *Length:* 900-1200 words; Viewpoint: 600 words. Annual Short Story Competition with prize of £1000 plus. Winning entries printed in magazine. *Illustrations:* colour transparencies, b&w photos and drawings. *Payment:* from £60 per 1000 words; varies for illustrations.

Lancashire Evening Post, Neil Hodgkinson, Oliver's Place, Fulwood, Preston PR2 9ZA *tel* (01772) 254841 *fax* (01772) 880173.

26p. D. Topical articles on all subjects. Area of interest Wigan to Lake District, Lancs, and coast. *Length:* 600-900 words. *Illustrations:* colour and b&w photos, cartoons. *Payment:* by arrangement.

Lancashire Evening Telegraph (1886), Peter Butterfield, Newspaper House, High Street, Blackburn, Lancs. BB1 1HT *tel* (01254) 678678.
26p. D. Will consider general interest articles, such as holidays, property, motoring, finance, etc. *Payment:* by arrangement.

Lancashire Life, Tony Skinner, Town & County Magazines, Oyston Mill, Strand Road, Preston PR1 8UR *tel* (01772) 722022 *fax* (01772) 736496.
£1.90. M. Quality features and photographic material of regional interest. *Payment:* by negotiation.

Lancashire Magazine (1977), Winston Halstead, 33 Beverley Road, Driffield, Yorkshire YO25 7SD *tel/fax* (01377) 253232.
£1.00. Bi-M. Articles about people, life and character of all parts of Lancashire. *Length:* 1500 words. *Payment:* £30-£35 approx. per published page. *Illustrations:* line, half-tone, colour.

Lancet (1823), Dr Richard Horton, 42 Bedford Square, London WC1B 3SL *tel* 0171-436 4981 *fax* 0171-323 6441.
£3.25. W. Research papers, review articles, editorials, correspondence and commentaries on the international medicosocial scene. Regular contributors are paid by arrangement; others should consult the editor before submitting.

Land & Liberty (1894), Fred Harrison, 177 Vauxhall Bridge Road, London SW1V 1EU *tel* 0171-834 4266.
£3.00. Q. (£12.00 p.a.) Articles on land economics, land taxation, land prices, land speculation as they relate to housing, the economy, production, politics. *Study of journal* essential. *Length:* up to 3000 words. *Payment:* by arrangement. *Illustrations:* half-tone.

The Lawyer (1987), Mary Heaney, Centaur Communications Group, 50 Poland Street, London W1V 4AX *tel* 0171-287 9800 *fax* 0171-734 0534.
£1.50. W. (£60.00 p.a.) News, articles, features and views of relevance to the legal profession. *Length:* 600-900 words. *Illustrations:* as agreed. *Payment:* £125 per 1000 words; by arrangement for illustrations.

Learned Publishing (1988) (successor to **ALPSP Bulletin**), Hazel K. Bell, 139 The Ryde, Hatfield, Herts. AL9 5DP *tel* (01707) 265201 *fax* (01707) 273601.
Free to members. Q. (£75.00 p.a.) Journal of the Association of Learned and Professional Society Publishers. Articles, reports and book reviews on publishing and learned societies: editorial, production, marketing and distribution, copyright. *Length:* 1000-4000 words. *Illustrations:* line, half-tone. *Payment:* none.

The Leicester Mercury (1874), Nick Carter, St George Street, Leicester LE1 9FQ *tel* (0116) 251 2512 *fax* (0116) 253 0645.
27p. Mon.-Sat. Occasional articles, features and news; submit ideas to editor first. *Length/payment:* by negotiation.

The Leisure Manager (1985), Jonathan Ives, The Institute of Leisure and Amenity Management, ILAM House, Lower Basildon, Reading, Berks. RG8 9NE *tel* (01491) 874222 *fax* (01491) 874059.
£25.00 p.a. Bi-M. Official Journal of The Institute of Leisure and Amenity Management. Articles on amenity, children's play, tourism, leisure, parks, entertainment, recreation and sports management. *Payment:* by arrangement. *Illustrations:* line, half-tone.

Leisure Painter (1966), Irene Briers, 63-65 High Street, Tenterden, Kent TN30 6BD *tel* (01580) 763315 *fax* (01580) 765411.
£2.05. M. Instructional articles on painting and fine arts. *Payment:* £60 per 1000 words. *Illustrations:* line, half-tone, colour, original artwork.

Leisureweek (1989), Michael Nutley, Centaur Publishing Ltd, St Giles House, 50 Poland Street, London W1V 4AX *tel* 0171-494 0300 *fax* 0171-734 2741.
£1.00. W. News and features relating to the leisure industry. *All material commissioned. Length:* features from 800 words, news from 200 words. *Illustrations:* line, half-tone. *Payment:* by agreement.

The Library (1889), M.C. Davies, Incunabula, Humanities & Social Sciences, The British Library, Great Russell Street, London WC1B 3DG *tel* 0171-412 7579 *fax* 0171-412 7736. Oxford University Press for the Bibliographical Society.
£60.00 p.a. Q. (£32.00 p.a. to members) Articles up to 15,000 words as well as shorter Notes, embodying original research on subjects connected with bibliography; reviews. *Illustrations:* line, half-tone. *Payment:* none.

Life and Work: Record of the Church of Scotland, 121 George Street, Edinburgh EH2 4YN *tel* 0131-225 5722 *fax* 0131-220 3113.
70p. M. Articles not exceeding 1000 words and news; poems and occasional stories. Study the magazine first. *Payment:* up to £45 per 1000 words, or by arrangement. *Illustrations:* photos and line, cartoons.

Lincolnshire Life (1961), Jez Ashberry, PO Box 81, Lincoln LN1 1HD *tel* (01522) 527127 *fax* (01522) 560035.
£1.30. M. Articles and news of county interest. *Length:* up to 1200 words. *Illustrations:* b&w and colour photos and line drawings. *Payment:* varies.

Lines Review (1952), Tessa Ransford, Edgefield Road, Loanhead, Edinburgh, Midlothian EH20 9SY *tel* 0131-440 0246 *fax* 0131-440 0315.
£2.00. Q. (£10.00 p.a.) Poetry, essays, criticism, reviews. *Illustrations:* line/half-tone for frontispiece only. *Payment:* £20 per 1000 words; £10 for illustrations.

The Linguist, Acting Editor: S.C. Eden, The Institute of Linguists, 24A Highbury Grove, London N5 2DQ *tel* 0171-359 7445 *fax* 0171-354 0202.
£5.00. Bi-M. (£25.00 p.a.) Articles of interest to professional linguists in translating, interpreting and teaching fields. Articles usually contributed, but *payment* by arrangement. All contributors have special knowledge of the subjects with which they deal. *Length:* 2000-3000 words. *Illustrations:* line, half-tone.

The Literary Review (1979), Auberon Waugh, 51 Beak Street, London W1R 3LF *tel* 0171-437 9392 *fax* 0171-734 1844.
£2.00. M. (£22.00 p.a.) Reviews, articles of cultural interest, interviews, profiles, monthly poetry competitions. Material mostly commissioned. *Length:* articles and reviews 800-1500 words. *Illustrations:* line and b&w photos. *Payment:* £25 per article; none for illustrations.

Live & Kicking Magazine (1993), Jeremy Mark, BBC Worldwide Publishing, Woodlands, Wood Lane, London W12 0TT *tel* 0181-576 3254 *fax* 0181-576 3267.
£1.30. M. Features and news stories on current pop, TV, film and sports stars with teenage appeal. *Length:* features 1000-1500 words. *Illustrations:* occasionally commission cartoons and caricatures. *Payment:* varies.

Liverpool Echo, John Griffith, PO Box 48, Old Hall Street, Liverpool L69 3EB *tel* 0151-227 2000.

28p. D. Ind. Articles of up to 600-800 words of local or topical interest; also cartoons. *Payment:* according to merit; special rates for exceptional material. This newspaper is connected with, but independent of, the Liverpool **Daily Post.** Articles not interchangeable.

Llais Llyfrau/Books in Wales (1964), R. Gerallt Jones, Katie Gramich, Lorna Herbert, Welsh Books Council, Castell Brychan, Aberystwyth, Dyfed SY23 2JB *tel* (01970) 624151 *fax* (01970) 625385.
£5.00 p.a. Q. Articles in Welsh and English on authors and their books, Welsh publishing; reviews and book lists. Mainly commissioned. *Payment:* by arrangement.

Local Government Chronicle (1855), David Pead, EMAP Business Publishing, 33-39 Bowling Green Lane, London EC1R 0DA *tel* 0171-837 1212 *fax* 0171-837 2725.
£2.45. W. Articles relating to financial, political, legal and administrative work of the local government manager. *Payment:* by arrangement. *Illustrations:* half-tone, cartoons.

The Local Historian (formerly **The Amateur Historian**) (1952), Dr Margaret Bonney, 7 Carisbrooke Park, Knighton, Leicester LE2 3PQ *tel* (0116) 270 5028. British Association for Local History, 25 Lower Street, Harnham, Salisbury, Wilts. SP2 8EY *tel* (01722) 320115 *fax* (01722) 413242.
£5.00. Q. Articles, popular in style but based on knowledge of research, covering methods of research, sources and background material helpful to regional, local and family historians – histories of particular places, people or incidents *not* wanted. *Length:* maximum 7000 words. *Illustrations:* line and photos. *Payment:* none.

LOGOS (1990), Gordon Graham, 5 Beechwood Drive, Marlow, Bucks. SL7 2DH *tel/fax* (01628) 477577.
£40.00 p.a. Q. (£62.00 p.a. institutions) In-depth articles on publishing, librarianship and bookselling with international or interdisciplinary appeal. *Length:* 3500-7000 words. *Payment:* 25 offprints/copy of issue.

London Magazine: A Review of the Arts (1954), Editor: Alan Ross, Deputy Editor: Jane Rye, 30 Thurloe Place, London SW7 2HQ *tel* 0171-589 0618.
£5.99. Bi-M. (£28.50 p.a.) Poems, stories (2000-5000 words), literary memoirs, critical articles, features on art, photography, sport, theatre, cinema, music, architecture, events, reports from abroad, drawings. Sae necessary. *Payment:* by arrangement.

London Review of Books (1979), Mary-Kay Wilmers, 28-30 Little Russell Street, London WC1A 2HN *tel* 0171-404 3336 *fax* 0171-404 3337.
£2.15. Bi-M. Features, essays, poems. *Payment:* by arrangement.

Looks Magazine, Annabel Goldstaub, EMAP Élan, 20 Orange Street, London WC2H 7ED *tel* 0171-957 8383 *fax* 0171-930 4191.
£1.50. M. Fashion, beauty and hair for 15-22 age range; features, especially with a celebrity bias. *No* unsolicited material, but ideas welcome. *Length:* up to 2000 words. *Illustrations:* colour, b&w. *Payment:* by arrangement.

Love Story (1987), Nexus Special Interests, Nexus House, Boundary Way, Hemel Hempstead, Herts. HP2 7ST *tel* (01442) 66551.
£1.75. Q. Contemporary romantic stories, 4500-7000 words. *No unsolicited MSS considered at present.*

Mail on Sunday (1982), Jonathan Holborow, Northcliffe House, 2 Derry Street, London W8 5TS *tel* 0171-938 6000 *telex* 28301 LDM G *fax* 0171-937 6721.
75p. W. Articles. *Payment:* by arrangement. *Illustrations:* line, half-tone; cartoons.

You, Dee Nolan (free with paper). Women's interest features. *Length:* 500-2500 words. *Payment:* by arrangement. *Illustrations:* full colour and b&w drawings commissioned; also colour photography.

Night & Day (1993) (free with paper). Jocelyn Targett   *tel* 0171-938 7051 *fax* 0171-937 7488.

Investigative journalism, profiles, personal columns and book reviews – *mostly commissioned. Length:* 3000 words for main feature; 1000 words for personal column. *Illustrations:* Colour photos.

Making Music (1986), Paul Quinn, Nexus Media Ltd, Nexus House, Swanley, Kent BR8 8HY   *tel* (01322) 660070   *fax* (01322) 615636.

£15.00 p.a. M. Technical, musicianly and instrumental features on rock, pop, blues, dance, world, jazz, soul; little classical. *Length:* 500-2500 words. *Payment:* £90 per 1000 words. *Illustrations:* colour, including cartoons and photos.

Management Today (1966), Charles Skinner, 176 Hammersmith Road, London W6 7JB   *tel* 0171-413 4566   *fax* 0171-413 4138.

£40.00 p.a. M. Company profiles and analysis – columns from 1000 words, features up to 3000 words. *Payment:* £250 per 1000 words. *Illustrations:* colour transparencies, usually commissioned.

Manchester Evening News, Michael Unger, 164 Deansgate, Manchester M60 2RD   *tel* 0161-832 7200   *editorial fax* 0161-834 3814   *features fax* 0161-839 0968.

30p. D. Feature articles of up to 1000 words, topical or general interest and illustrated where appropriate, should be addressed to the Features Editor. *Payment:* on acceptance.

Mandy/Judy, D.C. Thomson & Co. Ltd, Albert Square, Dundee DD1 9QJ   *tel* (01382) 223131   *fax* (01382) 322214; and 185 Fleet Street, London EC4A 2HS   *tel* 0171-242 5086   *fax* 0171-404 5694.

55p. W. Picture-story paper for schoolgirls. Serials and series in line drawings: 2 and 3 page instalments, 8-9 frames per page. Editorial co-operation offered to promising scriptwriters. *Payment:* on acceptance.

Mandy Library, D.C. Thomson & Co. Ltd, Albert Square, Dundee DD1 9QJ   *tel* (01382) 223131   *fax* (01382) 322214; and 185 Fleet Street, London EC4A 2HS   *tel* 0171-242 5086   *fax* 0171-404 5694.

50p. F. 64-page (about 140 line drawings) picture-stories for schoolgirls: adventure, animal, mystery, school, sport. Scripts considered; promising scriptwriters and artists encouraged. *Payment:* on acceptance.

Manx Life (1971), Ian Faulds, Trafalgar Press Ltd, 14 Douglas Street, Peel, Isle of Man IM5 1BA   *tel* (01624) 843881   *fax* (01624) 842353.

£17.70 p.a. Q. (other rates on application) Factual articles on historical or topical aspects of the social, commercial, agricultural or cultural activities and interests of the Isle of Man. *Payment:* by arrangement. *Illustrations:* line, half-tone, colour.

Marie Claire (1988), Juliet Warkentin, European Magazines Ltd, 2 Hatfields, London SE1 9PG   *tel* 0171-261 5240   *fax* 0171-261 5277.

£2.20. M. Feature articles of interest to today's woman; plus fashion, beauty, health, food, drink and travel. *Commissioned material* only. *Payment:* by negotiation. *Illustrated* in colour.

Market Newsletter (1965), John Tracy, Focus House, 497 Green Lanes, London N13 4BP   *tel* 0181-882 3315/6   *fax* 0181-886 5174.

Private circulation. M. Published by the Bureau of Freelance Photographers. Current information on markets and editorial requirements of interest to writers and photographers.

Marketing Week (1978), Stuart Smith, St Giles House, 50 Poland Street, London W1V 4AX   *tel* 0171-439 4222   *fax* 0171-439 9669.
£1.80. W. Aimed at marketing management. Accepts occasional features and analysis. *Length:* 1000-2000 words. *Payment:* £150 per 1000 words.

Mayfair (1966), Stephen Bleach, 2 Archer Street, London W1V 8JJ   *tel* 0171-734 5030   *fax* 0171-734 5030.
£2.25. M. Short humorous articles, sport, music, motoring. *Payment:* by arrangement. *Illustrations:* colour transparencies to illustrate highly visual feature ideas.

Medal News (1989), Diana Birch, Token Publishing Ltd, PO Box 14, Honiton, Devon EX14 9YP   *tel* (01404) 831878   *fax* (01404) 831895.
£2.20. 10 p.a. Well-researched articles on military history with a bias towards medals. *Length:* up to 2000 words. *Illustrations:* b&w preferred. *Payment:* £20 per 1000 words; none for illustrations.

Media Week (1985), Susannah Richmond, EMAP Media, 33-39 Bowling Green Lane, London EC1R 0DA   *tel* 0171-505 8341   *fax* 0171-505 8363.
£1.80. W. News and analysis of UK advertising media industry. *Illustrations:* full colour and b&w.

Melody Maker, Allan Jones, IPC Magazines Ltd, King's Reach Tower, Stamford Street, London SE1 9LS   *tel* 0171-261 6229   *fax* 0171-261 6706.
75p. W. Technical, entertaining and informative articles on rock and pop music. *Payment:* by arrangement. *Illustrations:* line, half-tone, colour.

Men Only (published by Paul Raymond: 1971), Nevile Player, 2 Archer Street, London W1V 8JJ   *tel* 0171-292 8000   *fax* 0171-734 5030.
£2.25. M. True life erotic stories – *no* erotic fiction; humour; short humorous columns (max. 600 words) on areas of male interest; glamour photography. *Payment:* by arrangement.

Methodist Recorder (1861), Michael Taylor, 122 Golden Lane, London EC1Y 0TL   *tel* 0171-251 8414.
45p. W. Methodist and Free Church newspaper; ecumenically involved. Limited opportunities for freelance contributors. *Preliminary letter* advised.

Middle East International (1971), Steve Sherman, 21 Collingham Road, London SW5 0NU   *tel* 0171-373 5228   *fax* 0171-370 5956.
£60.00 p.a. F. (other rates on application) Articles (1200-1600 words) and news stories on Middle East and Arab world-related topics. *Payment:* £80 per 1000 words.

Military Modelling, Ken Jones, Nexus Special Interests, Nexus House, Boundary Way, Hemel Hempstead, Herts. HP2 7ST   *tel* (01442) 66551   *fax* (01442) 66998.
£2.20. M. Articles on military modelling. *Length:* up to 2000 words. *Payment:* by arrangement. *Illustrations:* line, half-tone, colour.

Mind (1876), Prof Mark Sainsbury, Oxford University Press, Walton Street, Oxford OX2 6DP   *tel* (01865) 56767   *fax* (01865) 267773.
£7.00. Q. (£23.00 p.a. UK/Europe, $43.00 p.a. rest of world; institution rates on application) Review of philosophy intended for those who have studied and thought on this subject. Articles from about 5000 words; shorter discussion notes; critical notices and reviews. *Payment:* none.

Mizz (1985), Jeanette Baker, IPC Magazines Ltd, King's Reach Tower, Stamford Street, London SE1 9LS *tel* 0171-261 6319 *fax* 0171-261 6032.
80p. F. Articles on any subject of interest to 15-19-year-old girls. *Approach* in writing. *Payment:* by arrangement. *Illustrated.*

Mobile and Cellular Magazine (1989), Paul O'Rourke, Nexus Media, Nexus House, Azalea Drive, Swanley, Kent BR8 8HY *tel* (01322) 660070 *fax* (01322) 661257.
£38.00 p.a. M. Aimed at radio communications professionals – technical features, company profiles and news analysis; cartoons. *Length:* features up to 1500 words, analysis up to 800 words. *Payment:* £150 per 1000 words.

Model Boats (1964), John L. Cundell, Nexus Special Interests, Nexus House, Boundary Way, Hemel Hempstead, Herts. HP2 7ST *tel* (01442) 66551 *fax* (01442) 66998.
£2.20. M. Articles, drawings, plans, sketches of model boats. *Payment:* £25 per page; plans £100. *Illustrations:* line, half-tone.

Model Engineer (1898), Ted Jolliffe, Nexus Special Interests, Nexus House, Boundary Way, Hemel Hempstead, Herts. HP2 7ST *tel* (01442) 66551 *fax* (01442) 66998.
£1.75. 2 p.m. Detailed description of the construction of models, small workshop equipment, machine tools and small electrical and mechanical devices; articles on small power engineering, mechanics, electricity, workshop methods, clocks and experiments. *Payment:* up to £35 per page. *Illustrations:* line, half-tone, colour.

Modern Believing (formerly **Modern Churchman**; 1911), Dr George Pattison, The Modern Churchpeople's Union, King's College, Cambridge CB2 1ST *tel* (01223) 331100.
£4.00. Q. Covers contemporary and pastoral theology, ethics, politics, current affairs. *Length:* up to 3500 words. Intending contributors advised to write to the editor for a copy of instructions to authors.

Modern Language Review (1905), Modern Humanities Research Association, King's College, Strand, London WC2R 2LS.
£67.00 p.a. Q. (£80.00 overseas, $160.00 USA) Articles and reviews of a scholarly or specialist character on English, Romance, Germanic and Slavonic languages and literatures. *Payment:* none, but offprints are given.

Modern Painters (1986), Karen Wright, Fine Art Journals Ltd, Universal House, 251-255 Tottenham Court Road, London W1P 9AD *tel* 0171-636 6305 *fax* 0171-580 5615.
£4.95. Q. Journal of modern fine arts and architecture – *commissioned* articles and features; also interviews. *Length:* 1000-2500 words. *Payment:* £120 per 1000 words. *Illustrated.*

Modus, Geoffrey Thompson, Hamilton House, Mabledon Place, London WC1H 9BJ *tel* 0171-387 1441 *fax* 0171-383 7230.
£3.25. 8 p.a. (£26.00 p.a.) Official Journal of the National Association of Teachers of Home Economics and Technology: aimed at teachers and educationists. Articles on the teaching of home economics and technology, including textiles, nutrition, and social and technical background information for teachers. *Length:* up to 1500 words. *Payment:* by arrangement. *Illustrations:* line, half-tone, cartoons.

Mojo (1993), Mat Snow, EMAP Metro, Mappin House, 4 Winsley Street, London W1N 7AR *tel* 0171-436 1515 *fax* 0171-637 4925.

£2.50. M. Serious rock music magazine: interviews, news and reviews of books, live shows and albums. *Length:* up to 10,000 words. *Illustrations:* colour and b&w photos, colour caricatures. *Payment:* £150 per 1000 words; £250.

MoneyMarketing (1985), Patrick Collinson, Centaur Communications Ltd, St Giles House, 50 Poland Street, London W1V 4AX *tel* 0171-287 5678 *fax* 0171-734 9379.
£1.50. W. News, features, surveys and viewpoints; cartoons. *Length:* features from 900 words. *Illustrations:* b&w photos, colour and b&w line. *Payment:* £150 per 1000 words; colour line £200, b&w line £150.

Moneywise (1990), Matthew Vincent, Berkeley Magazines Ltd, 10 Old Bailey, London EC4M 7NB *tel* 0171-409 5273 *fax* 0171-409 5261.
£2.40. M. Financial and consumer interest features, articles and news stories. *Length:* 1500-2000 words. *Illustrations:* willing to see designers, illustrators and photographers for fresh new ideas. *Payment:* by arrangement.

The Month (1864), Tim Noble sj, 114 Mount Street, London W1Y 6AH *tel* 0171-491 7596 *fax* 0171-629 6936.
£1.30. M. Review of Christian thought, and world affairs, with arts and literary sections, edited by the Jesuit Fathers. *Preliminary letter* desirable. *Length:* up to 2500 words. *Payment:* by arrangement. *Illustrations:* b&w photos.

More! (1988), Tony Cross, EMAP Women's Group, 20 Orange Street, London WC2H 7ED *tel* 0171-957 8383 *fax* 0171-930 4637.
£1.10. F. News, features, 'how to' articles aimed at young, working women. *No* fiction. *Study of magazine* essential. *Length:* 1800 words. *Payment:* £150 per 1000 words. *Illustrated.*

Morning Star (formerly **Daily Worker,** 1930), John Haylett, The Morning Star Co-operative Society Ltd, 1-3 Ardleigh Road, London N1 4HS *tel* 0171-254 0033 *fax* 0171-254 5950 *e-mail* morsta@geo2.poptel.org.uk
40p. Daily newspaper for the Labour movement. Articles of general interest. *Illustrations:* photos, cartoons and drawings.

Mortgage Finance Gazette (1869), Neil Madden, Franey & Co. Ltd, South Quay Plaza, 183 Marsh Wall, London E14 9FS *tel* 0171-538 5386 *fax* 0171-538 8624.
£44.20 p.a. M. Articles on all aspects of building society management, mortgage finance, retail financial services. *Length:* up to 2000 words. *Payment:* by arrangement. *Illustrations:* line, half-tone.

Mother & Baby (1956), Sharon Parsons, EMAP Élan, Victory House, Leicester Place, Leicester Square, London WC2H 7BP *tel* 0171-437 9011 *telex* 266400 *fax* 0171-434 0656.
£1.50. M. Features and practical articles. *Length:* 1200-2400 words. *Payment:* by negotiation. *Illustrated.*

Motor Boat and Yachting (1904), Alan Harper, IPC Magazines Ltd, King's Reach Tower, Stamford Street, London SE1 9LS *tel* 0171-261 5333.
£2.50. M. General interest as well as specialist motor boating material welcomed. Features up to 2000 words considered on all aspects, sea-going and on inland waterways. *Payment:* varies. *Illustrations:* photos (mostly colour and transparencies preferred) and line, cartoons.

Motor Boats Monthly (1987), Kim Hollamby, Boating Publications Ltd, Link House, Dingwall Avenue, Croydon CR9 2TA *tel* 0181-686 2599 *fax* 0181-781 6065.
£2.50. M. News on motorboating in the UK and Europe, cruising features and anecdotal stories concerned with motorboating. *Mostly commissioned* – send

synopsis to editor. *Length:* news up to 200 words, features up to 4000 words. *Illustrations:* colour transparencies. *Payment:* by arrangement.

Motor Caravan Magazine (1985), Paul Carter, Link House Magazines Ltd, Link House, Dingwall Avenue, Croydon CR9 2TA   *tel* 0181-686 2599   *fax* 0181-781 6044.
£2.10. M. Practical features, touring features (home and abroad). *Length:* up to 1500 words. *Payment:* £35-£40 per page. *Illustrations:* line, half-tone, colour, cartoons.

Motor Cycle News (1955), Sean Warwick, EMAP National Publications Ltd, 20-22 Station Road, Kettering NN15 7HH   *tel* (01536) 411111   *fax* (01536) 411750.
95p. W. Features (up to 1000 words), photos and news stories of interest to motorcyclists.

Motorcaravan and Motorhome Monthly (MMM) (1966 as Motor Caravan and Camping), Penny Smith, 14 Eastfield Close, Andover, Hants SP10 2QP   *fax* (01264) 324794.
£2.40. M. Articles including motorcaravan travel, owner reports and DIY. *Length:* up to 2500 words. *Payment:* by arrangement. *Illustrations:* line, half-tone, colour prints and transparencies.

Motorcycle International (1985), Frank Westworth, PO Box 10, Whitchurch, Shropshire SY13 1ZZ   *tel* 0161-948 3480   *fax* 0161-941 6897.
£1.95. M. Motorcycle-related features, news and travel articles. *Length:* from 1000 words. *Illustrations:* colour transparencies. *Payment:* £100 per 1000 words or by negotiation; by negotiation for illustrations.

Ms London (1968), Cathy Howes, The Commuter Publishing Partnership, 7-9 Rathbone Street, London W1P 1AF   *tel* 0171-636 6651.
Free. W. Features and lifestyle pieces of interest to young professional working women. *All material commissioned*; contributors *must* live in the capital. *Length:* 1000-2000 words. *Illustrations:* no unsolicited illustrations; enquire first. *Payment:* by negotiation.

Museums Journal (1901), The Museums Association, 42 Clerkenwell Close, London EC1R 0PA   *tel* 0171-250 1834   *fax* 0171-250 1929.
£5.00. M. (free to members; £48.00 p.a. individuals; £72.00 p.a. institutions) Articles and news items on museum and art gallery policy, administration, architecture and display, notes on technical developments, book reviews. *Length:* 100-2500 words. *Illustrations:* line, half-tone, colour, cartoons. *Payment:* by agreement.

Music and Letters (1920). Editorial: Dr Nigel Fortune, Prof Tim Carter, Dr Katherine Ellis, Music Department, Royal Holloway, University of London, Egham, Surrey TW20 0EX   *tel* (01784) 443532. Other matters: Oxford University Press (Journals Production), 60 Walton Street, Oxford OX2 6DP.
£15.00. Q. Scholarly articles, up to 10,000 words, on musical subjects, neither merely topical nor purely descriptive. Technical, historical and research matter preferred. *Illustrations:* music quotations and plates. *Payment:* none.

The Music Review (1940), A.F. Leighton Thomas, Glyneithin, Burry Port, Dyfed SA16 0TA. Other matters: Black Bear Press, King's Hedges Road, Cambridge CB4 2PQ.
£15.00. Q. (£50.00 p.a.) Articles from 1500-8000 words dealing with any aspect of standard or classical music (no jazz). *Payment:* small, by arrangement.

Music Teacher (1908), Rhinegold Publishing Ltd, 241 Shaftesbury Avenue, London WC2H 8EH   *tel* 0171-333 1747   *fax* 0171-333 1769.

£2.75. M. Provides information and articles for both school and private music teachers. Articles and illustrations must both have a teacher, as well as a musical, interest. *Length:* articles 1000-3000 words. *Payment:* by arrangement.

Music Week (1959), Steve Redmond, Eighth Floor, Ludgate House, 245 Blackfriars Road, London SE1 9UL   *tel* 0171-620 3636   *fax* 0171-401 8035.
£2.80. W. (£103.00 p.a.) News and features on all aspects of producing, manufacturing, marketing and retailing music. *Payment:* by negotiation.

Musical Opinion (1877), Denby Richards, 2 Princes Road, St Leonards-on-Sea, East Sussex TN37 6EL   *tel* (01424) 715167   *fax* (01424) 712214.
£3.50. Q (plus supplements). Suggestions for contributions of musical interest, scholastic, educational, anniversaries, ethnic, and relating to the organ world. Record, video, CD-ROM, opera, festival, book, music reviews. All editorial matter must be commissioned. *Payment:* on publication. *Illustrations:* b&w photos, cartoons.

Musical Times (1844), Antony Bye, 79 Macaulay Square, London SW4 0RU   *tel* 0171-627 3202   *fax* 0171-482 5697.
£2.50. M. Musical articles, reviews, 200-4000 words. *All material commissioned.* *Illustrations:* music.

My Weekly (1910), D.C. Thomson & Co. Ltd, 80 Kingsway East, Dundee DD4 8SL   *tel* (01382) 223131   *fax* (01382) 452491; and 185 Fleet Street, London EC4A 2HS   *tel* 0171-242 5086   *fax* 0171-404 5694.
45p. W. Serials, from 30,000-80,000 words, suitable for family reading. Short complete stories of 1500-5000 words with humorous, romantic or strong emotional theme. Articles on television stars and on all subjects of women's interest. All contributions should appeal to women everywhere. *No preliminary letter* required. *Payment:* on acceptance. *Illustrations:* colour and b&w.

My Weekly Puzzle Time (1993), D.C. Thomson & Co. Ltd, Albert Square, Dundee DD1 9QJ   *tel* (01382) 223131   *fax* (01382) 322214.
£1.30. M. Broad range of puzzles appealing mainly to women. Entertainment value more important than intellectual. *Payment:* by arrangement. No *illustrations*.

My Weekly Story Library, D.C. Thomson & Co. Ltd, Albert Square, Dundee DD1 9QJ   *tel* (01382) 223131   *fax* (01382) 322214; and 185 Fleet Street, London EC4A 2HS   *tel* 0171-242 5086   *fax* 0171-404 5694.
50p. 4 p.m. 35,000-37,500-word romantic stories aimed at the post-teenage market. *Payment:* by arrangement; competitive for the market. No *illustrations*.

Natural World (1981), Linda Bennett, 20 Upper Ground, London SE1 9PF   *tel* 0171-805 5555   *fax* 0171-805 5911.
Free to members. 3 p.a. National magazine of The Wildlife Trusts. Short articles on UK nature conservation, particularly the work of The Wildlife Trusts; contributors normally have special knowledge of subjects on which they write. *Length:* up to 1200 words. *Payment:* by arrangement. *Illustrations:* line, colour.

Naturalist (1875), Prof M.R.D. Seaward MSc, PhD, DSc, The University, Bradford BD7 1DP   *tel* (01274) 384212   *telex* 51309   UNIBFD G   *fax* (01274) 384231   *e-mail* m.r.d.seaward@bradford.ac.uk
£20.00 p.a. Q. Original papers on all kinds of British natural history subjects, including various aspects of geology, archaeology and environmental science. *Length:* immaterial. *Illustrations:* photos and line drawings. *Payment:* none.

Nature (1869), Philip Campbell, Macmillan Magazines Ltd, Porters South, 4-6 Crinan Street, London N1 9XW   *tel* 0171-833 4000   *fax* 0171-843 4596. £4.00. W. Devoted to scientific matters and to their bearing upon public affairs. All contributors of articles have specialised knowledge of the subjects with which they deal. *Illustrations:* line, half-tone.

Nautical Magazine (1832), L. Ingram-Brown MIMgt, MBIM, MRIN, Brown, Son & Ferguson, Ltd, 4-10 Darnley Street, Glasgow G41 2SD   *tel* 0141-429 1234   *telegraphic address* Skipper, Glasgow   *fax* 0141-420 1694. £27.60 p.a. inc. postage (£31.80 p.a. overseas); 3 years £81.00 (£94.00 overseas). M. Articles relating to nautical and shipping profession, from 1500-2000 words; also translations. *Payment:* by arrangement. No *illustrations.*

Needlecraft (1991), Rebecca Bradshaw, Future Publishing Ltd, 30 Monmouth Street, Bath, Avon BA1 2BW   *tel* (01225) 442244   *fax* (01225) 484896   *e-mail* needlecraft@futurenet.co.uk £2.75. 4-weekly. Mainly project-based stitching designs with step-by-step instructions. Features with tight stitching focus (e.g. technique, personality). *Length:* 1000 words. *Illustrated. Payment:* £150-£200.

.net The Internet Magazine (1994), Richard Longhurst, Future Publishing Ltd, 30 Monmouth Street, Bath, Avon BA1 2BW   *tel* (01225) 442244   *fax* (01225) 423212   *e-mail* netmag@futurenet.co.uk £3.00. M. Articles, features and news on the Internet. *Length:* 1000-3000 words. *Payment:* £110 per 1000 words. *Illustrations:* colour.

New Beacon (1930; as **Beacon** 1917), Ann Lee, RNIB, 224 Great Portland Street, London W1N 6AA   *tel* 0171-388 1266. £1.50. M. Articles on all aspects of visual impairment. *Length:* from 500 words. *Payment:* £30 per 1000 words: *Illustrations:* half-tone. Also braille edition.

New Blackfriars (1920), Rev. Fergus Kerr OP, Blackfriars, 25 George Square, Edinburgh EH8 9LD   *tel* 0131-668 1776. £1.70. M. (£15.50 p.a.) Critical review, surveying the field of theology, philosophy, sociology and the arts, from the standpoint of Christian principles and their application to the problems of the modern world. Incorporates *Life of the Spirit. Length:* 2500-6000 words. *Payment:* by arrangement.

New Christian Herald, Herald House Ltd, 96 Dominion Road, Worthing, West Sussex BN14 8JP   *tel* (01903) 821082   *fax* (01903) 821081. 50p. W. Evangelical Christian paper with strong emphasis on news and current affairs. Features up to 700 words – profiles, the changing church, Christians, and contemporary culture (e.g. media, TV, music); cartoons. *No* short stories. *Payment:* £20-£50, depending on length/pictures used.

New Humanist (1885), Jim Herrick, Rationalist Press Association, Bradlaugh House, 47 Theobald's Road, London WC1X 8SP   *tel* 0171-430 1371   *fax* 0171-430 1271. £2.50. Q. Articles on current affairs, philosophy, science, literature and humanism. *Length:* 1000-3000 words. *Illustrations:* b&w photos. *Payment:* nominal; none for photos.

New Impact (1993), Managing Editor: Elaine Sihera, Anser House, PO Box 1448, Marlow, Bucks. SL7 3HD   *tel/fax* (01628) 481581. £26.00 p.a. (business). Bi-M. (£20.00 p.a. individual) 'Promoting enterprise, training and diversity.' Articles, features and news on any aspect of training, business and women's issues to suit a multicultural audience; also profiles of personalities, short stories. *Length:* 900-1000 words. *Illustrations:* b&w photos if related to profiles. *Payment:* £40 (depending on merit); none for photos.

New Internationalist (1973), Vanessa Baird, Chris Brazier, David Ransom, Nikki van der Gaag, 55 Rectory Road, Oxford OX4 1BW   *tel* (01865) 728181   *fax* (01865) 793152   *e-mail* newint@gn.apc.org
£2.20. M. (£24.85 p.a.) World issues, ranging from food to feminism to peace – examines one subject each month. *Length:* up to 2000 words. *Illustrations:* line, half-tone, colour, cartoons. *Payment:* £110 per 1000 words.

New Law Journal (1975), James Morton, Butterworth & Co. (Publishers) Ltd, Halsbury House, 35 Chancery Lane, London WC2A 1EL   *tel* 0171-400 2500   *fax* 0171-400 2583.
£3.00. 48 p.a. Articles and news on all aspects of the legal profession. *Length:* up to 1800 words. *Payment:* by arrangement.

New Library World (1898), MCB University Press, 60/62 Toller Lane, Bradford, West Yorkshire BD8 9BY   *tel* (01274) 777700   *fax* (01274) 785200.
£359.95 p.a. 7 p.a. Professional and bibliographical articles. Includes **Librarians' World** (6 p.a.), 16pp newsletter 'for librarians by librarians'. *Payment:* none.

New Musical Express, Steve Sutherland, IPC Magazines Ltd, 25th Floor, King's Reach Tower, Stamford Street, London SE1 9LS   *tel* 0171-261 5000   *fax* 0171-261 5185.
85p. W. Authoritative articles and news stories on the world's rock and movie personalities. *Length:* by arrangement. *Preliminary letter or phone call* desirable. *Payment:* by arrangement. *Illustrations:* action photos with strong news angle of recording personalities, cartoons.

New Scientist, Alun Anderson, IPC Magazines Ltd, King's Reach Tower, Stamford Street, London SE1 9LS   *tel* 0171-261 7301   *fax* 0171-261 6464   *e-mail* edit@mail.newsci.ipc.co.uk
£1.70. W. Authoritative articles of topical importance on all aspects of science and technology (*length:* 1000-3000 words); preliminary letter or telephone call desirable. Short items from specialists also considered for *Science, This Week, Forum* and *Technology.* Intending contributors should study recent copies of the magazine. *Payment:* varies but average £200 per 1000 words. *Illustrations:* line, half-tone, colour, cartoons.

New Statesman & Society (1988), Ian Hargreaves, Foundation House, Perseverance Works, 38 Kingsland Road, London E2 8DQ   *tel* 0171-739 3211   *fax* 0171-739 9307.
£1.65. W. Interested in news, reportage and analysis of current political and social issues at home and overseas, plus book reviews, poetry, general articles and coverage of the arts, environment and science seen from the perspective of the British Left but written in a stylish, witty and unpredictable way. *Length:* strictly according to the value of the piece. *Illustrations:* commissioned for specific articles, though artists' samples considered for future reference; occasional cartoons. *Payment:* by agreement.

New Theatre Quarterly (1985; as **Theatre Quarterly** 1971), Clive Barker, Simon Trussler, Great Robhurst, Woodchurch, Ashford, Kent TN26 3TB.
£13.00. Q. (£25.00 p.a.) Articles, interviews, documentation, reference material covering all aspects of live theatre. An informed, factual and serious approach essential. Preliminary discussion and synopsis desirable. *Payment:* by arrangement. *Illustrations:* line, half-tone.

The New Welsh Review (1988), Robin Reeves, Chapter Arts Centre, Market Road, Cardiff CF5 1QE   *tel/fax* (01222) 665529/515014.
£3.60. Q. (£15.00 p.a.) Articles, short stories, poems, book reviews, interviews and profiles. Especially, but not exclusively, concerned with Welsh writing

in English. Theatre in Wales section. *Length:* (articles) up to 4000 words. *Illustrations:* line, half-tone, cartoons; colour cover. *Payment:* £7-£15 per page prose; £8-£20 per poem; £10-£20 per review; £10-£20 per illustration.

New Woman (1988), Eleni Kyriacou, EMAP Élan, 20 Orange Street, London WC2H 7ED *tel* 0171-957 8383 *fax* 0171-930 7246.
£1.90. M. Features up to 2000 words. Occasionally accepts unsolicited articles; enclose sae for return. *Payment:* at or above NUJ rates. *Illustrated.*

New World, United Nations Association, 3 Whitehall Court, London SW1A 2EL *tel* 0171-930 2931 *fax* 0171-930 5893.
£1.00. 4 p.a. Review of UN activities, of UNA campaigns and of different viewpoints on major international issues confronting the United Nations. Occasionally takes cartoons. No *payment.*

The News, Portsmouth (1877), Geoffrey Elliott, The News Centre, Hilsea, Portsmouth PO2 9SX *tel* (01705) 664488 *fax* (01705) 673363.
25p. D. Articles of relevance to south-east Hampshire and West Sussex. *Length:* 600 words. *Illustrations:* photos, preferably in colour, cartoons. *Payment:* £50.

News of the World (1843), Phil Hall, 1 Virginia Street, London E1 9XR *tel* 0171-782 1000 *fax* 0171-583 9504.
55p. W. Takes freelance material. *Payment:* by negotiation.
Sunday Magazine (1981), Judy McGuire, Phase 2, 5th Floor, 1 Virginia Street, Wapping, London E1 9BD *tel* 0171-782 7900 *fax* 0171-782 7474. Free. W. Ideas and material from freelance writers always welcome. *Payment:* by arrangement.

19 (1968), April Joyce, IPC Magazines Ltd, King's Reach Tower, Stamford Street, London SE1 9LS *tel* 0171-261 6410.
£1.60. M. Glossy fashion and general interest magazine for young women aged 17 to 22 including beauty, music and social features of strong contemporary interest. All *illustrations* commissioned. *Payment:* by arrangement.

90 Minutes (1990), Eleanor Levy, IPC Magazines Ltd, King's Reach Tower, Stamford Street, London SE1 9LS *tel* 0171-261 7617 *fax* 0171-261 7474.
80p. W. Football features, news stories, interviews. *Length:* 50-1500 words. *Illustrations:* colour photos. *Payment:* £30-£100.

The Northern Echo (1870), David Flintham, Priestgate, Darlington, Co. Durham DL1 1NF *tel* (01325) 381313 *fax* (01325) 380539.
30p. D. Articles of interest to North-East and North Yorkshire; *all material commissioned. Preliminary study* of newspaper advisable. *Length:* 800-1000 words. *Illustrations:* line, half-tone, colour – mostly commissioned. *Payment:* by negotiation.

North-West Evening Mail (1898), Donald Martin, Newspaper House, Abbey Road, Barrow-in-Furness, Cumbria LA14 5QS *tel* (01229) 821835 *fax* (01229) 840164/832141.
27p. Mon.-Sat. 'The Voice of Furness and West Cumbria.' Articles, features and news. *Length:* 500 words. *Illustrations:* b&w photos and occasional artwork. *Payment:* £30; £10 for illustrations.

Nottingham Evening Post (1878), Forman Street, Nottingham NG1 4AB *tel* (0115) 948 2000 *fax* (0115) 964 4027.
27p. D. Will consider material on local issues.

Numismatic Chronicle (1839), Dr Mark Blackburn, Department of Coins and Medals, Fitzwilliam Museum, Cambridge CB2 1RB *tel* (01223) 332917 *fax* (01223) 332923.

£24.00 per annual volume. Journal of the Royal Numismatic Society. Articles on coins and medals. Articles relating to coins and medals are unpaid, and contributions should reach a high academic standard.

Nursery World, Ruth Beattie, Lector Court, 151-153 Farringdon Road, London EC1R 3AD   *tel* 0171-278 7441   *fax* 0171-278 3896.
90p. W. For all grades of primary school, nursery and child care staff, nannies, foster parents and all concerned with the care of expectant mothers, babies and young children. Authoritative and informative articles, 800 or 1600 words, and photos, on all aspects of child welfare and early education, from 0-8 years, in the UK. Practical ideas and leisure crafts. *No* short stories. *Payment:* by arrangement. *Illustrations:* line, half-tone, colour.

Nursing Times and Nursing Mirror (1905), Jane Salvage, Macmillan Magazines Ltd, Porters South, 4-6 Crinan Street, London N1 9XW   *tel* 0171-833 4600   *fax* 0171-843 4633.
95p. W. Articles of clinical interest, nursing education and nursing policy. *Illustrated* articles not longer than 2000 words. Contributions from other than health professionals sometimes accepted. Press day, Monday. *Illustrations:* photos, line, cartoons. *Payment:* NUJ rates; by arrangement for illustrations.

The Observer (1791), Will Hutton, 119 Farringdon Road, London EC1R 3ER *tel* 0171-278 2332.
£1.00. Sun. Ind. Some articles and illustrations commissioned. *Payment:* by arrangement.
The Observer Life Magazine, Michael Pilgrim   *tel* 0171-713 4175   *fax* 0171-713 4217. Free with paper. *Commissioned* features. *Length:* 2000-3000 words. *Illustrations:* first-class colour and b&w photos. *Payment:* NUJ rates; £150 per illustration.

Off Licence News (1970), William Reed Publishing Ltd, Broadfield Park, Crawley, West Sussex RH11 9RT   *tel* (01293) 613400   *fax* (01293) 610320.
£55 p.a. W. News and features for the off licence trade. *Length:* 1000-2000 words (features); news: flexible. *Payment:* £130 per 1000 words (features).

Office Secretary (1986), Danusia Hutson, Trade Media Ltd, Brookmead House, Thorney Leys Business Park, Witney, Oxon OX8 7GE *tel* (01993) 775545   *fax* (01993) 778884.
£9.50 p.a. Q. Serious features on anything of interest to senior secretaries/working women. *No* unsolicited MSS; ideas only. *Illustrations:* colour transparencies, cartoons. *Payment:* by negotiation.

OK! Weekly (1993), Richard Barber, Northern & Shell plc, Northern & Shell Tower, City Harbour, London E14 9GL   *tel* 0171-987 6262   *fax* 0171-515 6650.
£1.20. W. Celebrity interviews with exclusive photographs. Submit ideas in writing. *Length:* 2000 words. *Illustrations:* colour. *Payment:* £250-£500 per feature.

Oldham Evening Chronicle (1854), Philip Hirst, PO Box 47, Union Street, Oldham, Lancs. OL1 1EQ   *tel* 0161-633 2121   *fax* 0161-627 0905.
30p. Mon.-Fri. News and features on current topics and local history. *Length:* 1000 words. *Illustrations:* colour and b&w photos and line. *Payment:* £20-£25 per 1000 words; £16.32-£21.90 for illustrations.

The Oldie (1992), Richard Ingrams, 45-46 Poland Street, London W1V 4AU   *tel* 0171-734 2225   *fax* 0171-734 2226.
£1.80. F. General interest magazine reflecting attitudes of older people but aimed at a wider audience. Welcomes features (500-700 words) and ideas on all subjects. No interviews but profiles (900 words) for *Still With Us* section.

Will return MSS if sae enclosed. *Illustrations:* welcomes b&w and colour cartoons. *Payment:* approx. £80-£100 per 1000 words; minimum £30 for cartoons.

Opera, Rodney Milnes, 1A Mountgrove Road, London N5 2LU   *tel* 0171-359 1037   *fax* 0171-354 2700. Seymour Press Ltd, Windsor House, 1270 London Road, London SW16 4DH.
£2.50. 13 p.a. Articles on general subjects appertaining to opera; reviews; criticisms. *Length:* up to 2000 words. *Payment:* by arrangement. *Illustrations:* photos.

Opera Now (1989), Graeme Kay, 241 Shaftesbury Avenue, London WC2H 8EH   *tel* 0171-333 1740   *fax* 0171-333 1769.
£4.95. Bi-M. Articles, news, reviews on opera. All material commissioned only. *Length:* 150-1500 words. *Illustrations:* colour and b&w photos, line, cartoons. *Payment:* £120 per 1000 words.

Options (1982), Maureen Rice, IPC Magazines Ltd, King's Reach Tower, Stamford Street, London SE1 9LS   *tel* 0171-261 5000   *fax* 0171-261 7344.
£1.80. M. Aimed at women aged 25-35. Careers, emotional and sexual matters, health and well-being, women's issues, first-class celebrity interviews and profiles. *Mostly commissioned. Length:* 1000-3000 words. *Payment:* by arrangement.

Orbis (1968), Mike Shields, 199 The Long Shoot, Nuneaton, Warks. CV11 6JQ   *tel/fax/modem* (01203) 327440.
£15.00 p.a. Q. Poetry, prose pieces (up to 1000 words), reviews, letters. Annual competition for rhymed poetry. *Payment:* by arrangement. *Illustrations:* line.

The Organ (1921), Dr Brian Hick, 5 Aldborough Road, St Leonards-on-Sea, East Sussex TN37 6SE   *tel* (01424) 422225   *fax* (01424) 712214.
£16.00 p.a. Q. (£22.00 p.a. overseas) Articles, 1000-5000 words, relating to any type of organ: historical, technical and artistic; reviews of music, records. *Payment:* small. *Illustrations:* line, half-tone, colour.

Organic Gardening (1988), Basil Caplan, Wardnest Ltd, PO Box 4, Wiveliscombe, Taunton, Somerset TA4 2QY   *tel* (01984) 623998   *fax* (01984) 623998.
£2.00. M. Articles and features on all aspects of organic gardening. *All material commissioned. Length:* 600-2000 words. *Illustrations:* colour and b&w photos, line drawings, cartoons. *Payment:* by arrangement.

Our Baby (1994), Editor-in-Chief: Jayne Marsden, IPC Magazines Ltd, King's Reach Tower, Stamford Street, London SE1 9LS   *tel* 0171-261 7986   *fax* 0171-261 6542.
£1.35. M. Aimed at first-time mothers, including product information as well as health news and features on pregnancy and baby care; also readers' birth stories (£25 for 500 words). *Material mostly commissioned. Length:* varies. *Illustrations:* brilliant, colour photos of mums-and-dads-to-be and newborn babies. *Payment:* negotiable.

Our Dogs (1895), William Moores, Oxford Road Station Approach, Manchester M60 1SX   *tel* 0161-236 2660   *fax* 0161-236 5534/0892.
£1.25. W. Articles and news on the breeding and showing of pedigree dogs. *Illustrations:* b&w photos. *Payment:* NUJ rates; £7.50 per photo.

Outdoors Illustrated (1991), Fabian Russell-Cobb, Discovery Publications Ltd, Studio 2, 114-116 Walcot Street, Bath BA1 5BG   *tel* (01225) 443194   *fax* (01225) 443195.

£2.75. Bi-M. Features on adventure sports, active travel and outdoor life. *Material mostly commissioned. Length:* 1000-2000 words. *Illustrations:* colour transparencies. *Payment:* £90 per 1000 words; illustrations by negotiation.

Outposts Poetry Quarterly (1943), Roland John, 22 Whitewell Road, Frome, Somerset BA11 4EL   *tel/fax* (01373) 466653. *Founder:* Howard Sergeant MBE. £4.00. Q. (£12.00 p.a.) Poems, essays and critical articles on poets and their work; poetry competitions. *Payment:* by arrangement.

Oxford Poetry (1983), Sinéad Garrigan, Sam Leith, Magdalen College, Oxford OX1 4AU.
£2.40. 3 p.a. (£7.50 p.a.) Previously unpublished poems, both unsolicited and commissioned. *Payment:* none.

Parents (1976), Julia Goodwin, EMAP Élan, Victory House, Leicester Place, London WC2H 7BP   *tel* 0171-437 9011   *fax* 0171-434 0656.
£1.75. M. The magazine with smart solutions for today's mums. Articles on pregnancy, childbirth, general family health, food, fashion, child upbringing, development and early education up to age four, and marital relations. MSS with sae only. *Illustrations:* b&w or colour. *Payment:* in accordance with national magazine standards; by arrangement for illustrations.

Park Home & Holiday Caravan (formerly **Mobile & Holiday Homes**, 1960), Anne Webb, Link House, Dingwall Avenue, Croydon CR9 2TA   *tel* 0181-686 2599   *fax* 0181-781 6044.
£1.95. M. Informative articles on residential mobile homes (park homes) and holiday static caravans – personal experience articles, site features, news items. No preliminary letter. *Payment:* by arrangement. *Illustrations:* line, half-tone, colour transparencies, cartoons.

PC Direct (1991), Karen Packham, Ziff-Davis UK Ltd, Cottons Centre, Hay's Lane, London SE1 2QT   *tel* 0171-378 6800   *fax* 0171-378 1192.
£2.50. M. News, features, reviews and technical information for the direct computer buyer. *All material commissioned. Length:* 500-6000 words. *Illustrations:* colour photos and illustrations, including computer generated. *Payment:* £180 per 1000 words; varies for illustrations according to subject/ media.

PC Review, James Binns, Future Publishing, 30 Monmouth Street, Bath BA1 2BW   *tel* (01225) 442244   *fax* (01225) 446019.
£4.99. M. Features, previews, reviews of PC entertainment – commissioned only, by arrangement with the editor. *Illustrations:* colour transparencies; ideas for line art, diagrams, charts, etc. *Payment:* by negotiation.

Peace News for nonviolent revolution (1936), 5 Caledonian Road, London N1 9DX   *tel* 0171-278 3344   *fax* 0171-278 0444.
80p. M. Political articles based on nonviolence in every aspect of human life. *Illustrations:* line, half-tone. *Payment:* none.

Pensions World (1972), Stephanie Hawthorne, Tolley Publishing Co. Ltd, Tolley House, 2 Addiscombe Road, Croydon, Surrey CR9 5AF   *tel* 0181-686 9141   *fax* 0181-760 0588.
£55.00 p.a. M. Specialist articles on pensions, investment and law. *No* unsolicited articles; all material is *commissioned. Length:* 1500 words. *Payment:* by negotiation.

Penthouse Magazine, The International Magazine for Men (1965), Deric Botham, Northern & Shell Tower, PO Box 381, City Harbour, London E14 9GL   *tel* 0171-987 5090   *fax* 0171-987 2160.
£2.95. M. Serious and light-hearted factual articles on sex, relationships, motoring, adventure, general interest. *No* fiction. *Length:* 2000-3000 words.

Payment: by arrangement. *Illustrations:* cartoon strips, colour photo sets on 35 mm slide, and photos.

The People, Bridget Rowe, 1 Canada Square, Canary Wharf, London E14 5AP   *tel* 0171-293 3000   *fax* 0171-293 3517.
55p. Sun. Investigative features, single articles and series considered; pictures should be supplied with contributions if possible. Features should be of deep human interest, whether the subject is serious or light-hearted. Very strong sports following. Exclusive news and news-feature stories also considered. *Payment:* rates high, even for tips that lead to published news stories.
Yes! Free with paper. Feature articles. *Illustrations:* colour. *Payment:* by arrangement.

People Management, Rob MacLachlan, Personnel Publications Ltd, 17 Britton Street, London EC1M 5NQ   *tel* 0171-880 6200   *fax* 0171-336 7635.
£5.00. M. (£62.00 p.a.) Journal of the Institute of Personnel and Development. Features and news items on recruitment and selection, training and development; wage and salary administration; industrial psychology; employee relations; labour law; welfare schemes, working practices and new practical ideas in personnel management in industry and commerce. *Length:* up to 2500 words. *Payment:* by arrangement. *Illustrations:* photographers and illustrators should contact art editor.

People's Friend (1869), D.C. Thomson & Co. Ltd, 80 Kingsway East, Dundee DD4 8SL   *tel* (01382) 223131   *telex* 76380 DCTHOM G   *fax* (01382) 452491; and 185 Fleet Street, London EC4A 2HS   *tel* 0171-242 5086   *fax* 0171-404 5694.
45p. W. Illustrated weekly appealing to women of all ages and devoted to their personal and home interests, especially knitting, fashion and cookery. Serials (60,000-70,000 words) and complete stories (1500-3000 words) of strong romantic and emotional appeal. Stories for children are considered. *No preliminary letter* required. *Illustrations:* colour and b&w. *Payment:* on acceptance.

People's Friend Library, D.C. Thomson & Co. Ltd, 80 Kingsway East, Dundee DD4 8SL   *tel* (01382) 223131   *telex* 76380 DCTHOM G   *fax* (01382) 322214; and 185 Fleet Street, London EC4A 2HS   *tel* 0171-242 5086   *fax* 0171-404 5694.
80p. 2 p.m. 50,000-55,000-word family and romantic stories aimed at 30+ age group. *Payment:* by arrangement. No *illustrations*.

Perfect Home (1992), Julia Smith, DMG Home Interest Magazines Ltd, Times House, Station Approach, Ruislip, Middlesex HA4 8NB   *tel* (01895) 677677   *fax* (01895) 676027.
£1.60. M. Home-related features: readers' homes, craft, cookery, finance, DIY, show houses, product testing/reviews, gardening. *Length:* 800-1000 words. *Payment:* by merit. *Illustrated.*

Performance Car (1983), Brett Fraser, EMAP National Publications Ltd, Bushfield House, Orton Centre, Peterborough PE2 5UW   *tel* (01733) 237111   *fax* (01733) 231137.
£2.75. M. Articles, 2000-3000 words, on all aspects of cars. *Payment:* by arrangement. *Illustrations:* half-tone, colour, cartoons.

Period Living & Traditional Homes (1990), Clare Weatherall, EMAP Élan, Victory House, 14 Leicester Place, London WC2H 7BP   *tel* 0171-208 3245   *fax* 0171-434 0656.

£2.40. M. Articles and features on decoration, furnishings, renovation of period homes; traditional cookery; gardens, crafts, decorating in a period style. *Illustrated. Payment:* varies, according to work required.

Personal Computer World (1977), Ben Tisdall, VNU House, 32-34 Broadwick Street, London W1A 2HG   *tel* 0171-396 9000   *fax* 0171-396 9301   *e-mail* ben@compulink.co.uk
£2.95. M. Articles about computers; reviews. *Length:* 800-5000 words. *Payment:* from £130 per 1000 words. *Illustrations:* line, half-tone, colour.

Personal Finance (1994), Sarah Burnett, Charterhouse Communications Ltd, 4 Tabernacle Street, London EC2A 4LU   *tel* 0171-638 1916   *fax* 0171-638 3128.
£2.25. M. Articles and features on savings and investment, general family finance, of interest both to new investors and financially aware readers. *All material commissioned:* submit ideas in writing to the editor. *Length:* 1500-3000 words. *Illustrations:* colour and b&w photos, colour line drawings. *Payment:* £150-£200 per 1000 words; £50-£150 for illustrations.

The Pharmaceutical Journal (1841), D. Simpson FRPharmS, 1 Lambeth High Street, London SE1 7JN   *tel* 0171-735 9141   *telegraphic address/cables* Pharmakon, London SE1   *fax* 0171-735 7629.
£1.75. W. Official Journal of the Royal Pharmaceutical Society of Great Britain. Articles on any aspect of pharmacy may be submitted. *Payment:* by arrangement. *Illustrations:* half-tone, colour.

Photo Answers, Roger Payne, EMAP Apex Publications, Apex House, Oundle Road, Peterborough PE2 9NP   *tel* (01733) 898100   *fax* (01733) 894472.
£1.95. M. Magazine appealing to everyone interested in photography. Little opportunity for freelance writers, but always interested in seeing quality photos. *Payment:* upwards of £25 per published page, colour or mono. *Illustrations:* print, slide, line, half-tone.

photo pro (1989), David Kilpatrick, Icon Publications Ltd, Maxwell Place, Maxwell Lane, Kelso, Roxburghshire TD5 7BB   *tel* (01573) 226032   *fax* (01573) 226000.
£1.95. M. Illustrated features on professional and craft photography. *All material commissioned. Length:* 750-2500 words. *Illustrations:* b&w and colour photos. *Payment:* £50-£300 per feature, including photos. Rights to include one month's recompilation in PHOTON, Icon's World Wide Web Internet photo magazine.

Photo Technique (1993), Liz Walker (Associate Editor), IPC Magazines, Kings Reach Tower, Stamford Street, London SE1 9LS   *tel* 0171-261 5100   *fax* 0171-261 5404.
£2.35. Bi-M. News and practical topics of interest to amateur photographers, particularly accessible to beginners. Talkback and features accepted on spec. *Length:* 700-900 words (Talkback). *Illustrations:* maximum submisssion 20 prints or transparencies; no prints over 10 x 8 in. *Payment:* £100 per 1000 words; £90 per full page.

Pig Farming, Bryan Kelly, Wharfedale Road, Ipswich IP1 4LG   *tel* (01473) 241122   *fax* (01473) 240501.
£25.00 p.a. M. Practical, well-illustrated articles on all aspects of pigmeat production required, particularly those dealing with new ideas in pig management, feeding, housing, health and hygiene, product innovation and marketing. *Length:* 800-1200 words. *Payment:* by arrangement. *Illustrations:* line, half-tone, colour, cartoons.

Pilot (1968), James Gilbert, The Clock House, 28 Old Town, Clapham, London SW4 0LB   *tel* 0171-498 2506   *fax* 0171-498 6920   *e-mail* compuserve @100126,563
£2.40. M. Feature articles on general aviation, private and business flying. *Illustrations:* line, half-tone, colour, cartoons. *Payment:* £100-£800 per article on acceptance; £25 for each photo used.

The Pink Paper (1988), Andrew Saxton, 72 Holloway Road, London N7 8NZ   *tel*   0171-296   6000   *fax*   0171-296   0026   *e-mail*   positivetimes @posnet.co.uk
Free. W. The national newspaper for lesbians and gay men. Features (500-1500 words) and news (100-500 words) plus lifestyle section (features 700 words) on any gay-related subject. *Illustrations:* b&w photos and line plus colour 'scene' photos. *Payment:* £40-£100 for words; £45-£75 for illustrations.

Planet (1970-9; relaunched 1985), John Barnie, PO Box 44, Aberystwyth, Dyfed SY23 5BS   *tel* (01970) 611255   *fax* (01970) 623311.
£2.50. 6 p.a. (£12.00 p.a.) Short stories, poems, topical articles on Welsh current affairs, politics and society; articles on minority cultures throughout the world. New literature in English. *Length* of articles: 1000-3500 words. *Payment:* £40 per 1000 words for prose; £25 minimum per poem. *Illustrations:* line, half-tone, cartoons.

Plays & Players, Sandra Rennie, Northway House, 1379 High Road, London N20 9LP   *tel* 0181-343 8515   *fax* 0181-446 1410.
£2.50. M. Articles, reviews and photos on world theatre. *Payment:* by arrangement. *Illustrations:* line, photos.

PN Review, formerly **Poetry Nation** (1973), Michael Schmidt, 402 Corn Exchange Buildings, Manchester M4 3BY   *tel* 0161-834 8730   *fax* 0161-832 0084.
£4.00. Q. (£24.50 p.a.) Poems, essays, reviews, translations. *Payment:* by arrangement.

Poetry London Newsletter (1988), Tamar Yoseloff, Pascale Petit, Katherine Gallagher, Peter Daniels, 26 Clacton Road, London E17 8AR   *tel* 0181-520 6693   *fax* 0171-404 3598   *e-mail* pdaniels@easynet.co.uk   *WWW page* http://www.rmplc.co.uk/eduweb/sites/poetry/index.html
£12.00 p.a. 3 p.a. Poems of the highest standard, articles/reviews on any aspect of modern poetry; listings. Contributors must be very knowledgeable about contemporary poetry. *Payment:* £20 or four copies of the magazine.

Poetry Nottingham International (1941), Martin Holroyd, 39 Cavendish Road, Long Eaton, Nottingham NG10 4HY.
£2.00. Q. Poems. *Length:* not more than 30 lines. *Payment:* none, but complimentary copy.

Poetry Review, Peter Forbes, 22 Betterton Street, London WC2H 9BU   *tel* 0171-240 4810   *fax* 0171-240 4818.
£23.00 p.a. Q. (£26.00 p.a. institutions, schools and libraries) Poems, features and reviews; also cartoons. Send no more than six poems with sae. *Preliminary study* of magazine essential. *Payment:* £25-£30 per poem.

Poetry Wales (1965), First Floor, 2 Wyndham Street, Bridgend, Mid Glam. CF31 1EF. Books for review to: Amy Wack, 20 Denton Road, Canton, Cardiff CF5 1TE.
£2.50. Q. (£10.00 p.a. inc. postage) Poems mainly in English and mainly by Welsh people or resident: other contributors (and Welsh language poetry) also published. Articles on Welsh literature in English and in Welsh, as well as on poetry from other countries. Special features; reviews on poetry and wider matters. *Payment:* by arrangement.

Police Journal (1928), R.W. Stone QPM, Little London, Chichester, West Sussex
PO19 1PG   *tel* (01243) 787841   *fax* (01243) 779278.
£51.00 p.a. Q. Articles of technical or professional interest to the Police Service
throughout the world. *Payment:* by negotiation. *Illustrations:* half-tone.

Police Review (1893), Gary Mason, South Quay Plaza II, 183 Marsh Wall,
London E14 9FZ   *tel* 0171-537 2575   *fax* 0171-537 2560.
£1.25. W. News and features of interest to the police and legal professions.
Length: 200-2000 words. *Illustrations:* colour and b&w photos, line, cartoons.
Payment: NUJ rates.

The Political Quarterly (1930), Basil Blackwell Ltd, 108 Cowley Road, Oxford
OX4 1JF   *tel* (01865) 791100. Editor: Tony Wright MP, House of Commons,
Westminster, London SW1A 1AA. Books for review to be sent to the Literary
Editor, Bernard Crick, 8A Bellevue Terrace, Edinburgh EH7 4DT.
£53.50 p.a. 5 p.a. Journal devoted to topical aspects of national and international politics and public administration; takes a progressive, but not a party,
point of view. *Length:* average 5000 words. *Payment:* c. £60 per article.

Pony (1949), Janet Rising, Haslemere House, Lower Street, Haslemere, Surrey
GU27 2PE   *tel* (01428) 651551   *fax* (01428) 653888.
£1.15. M. Lively articles and short stories with a horsy theme aimed at young
readers, 8 to 14 years old. Technical accuracy and young, fresh writing essential.
Length: up to 800 words. *Payment:* by arrangement. *Illustrations:* drawings
(commissioned) and interesting photos, cartoons.

Popular Crafts, Charlotte Collis, Nexus Special Interests, Nexus House, Boundary Way, Hemel Hempstead, Herts. HP2 7ST   *tel* (01442) 66551.
£1.90. M. Covers all kinds of crafts. Projects with full instructions, profiles and
successes of craftspeople, news on craft group activities, readers' homes,
celebrity interviews, general craft-related articles. Welcomes written outlines
of ideas. *Payment:* by arrangement. *Illustrated*.

Post Magazine (1840), Stephen Womack, Timothy Benn Publishing Ltd, 58 Fleet
Street, London EC4Y 1JU   *tel* 0171-353 1107   *fax* 0171-583 6069.
£2.00. W. (£99.00 p.a.) *Commissioned* specialist articles on topics of interest
to insurance professionals; news, especially from overseas stringers. *Length:*
1700-2000 words. *Illustrations:* colour photos, colour and b&w cartoons and
line drawings. *Payment:* £150-£200 per 1000 words; photos £30-£60, cartoons/
line by negotiation.

Poultry World, John Farrant, Quadrant House, The Quadrant, Sutton, Surrey
SM2 5AS   *tel* 0181-652 4021   *fax* 0181-652 4748.
£1.80. M. Articles on poultry breeding, production, marketing and packaging.
News of international poultry interest. *Payment:* by arrangement. *Illustrations:*
photos, line.

PR Week (1984), Stephen Farish, Haymarket Marketing Publications, 174 Hammersmith Road, London W6 7JP   *tel* 0171-413 4520   *fax* 0171-413 4509.
Controlled circulation. W. (£60.00 p.a.) News and features on public relations.
Length: approx. 800-3000 words. *Payment:* £170 per 1000 words. *Illustrations:*
colour and b&w.

Practical Boat Owner (1967), Rodger Witt, Westover House, West Quay Road,
Poole, Dorset BH15 1JG   *tel* (01202) 680593.
£2.50. M. Articles of up to 2000 words in *length*, about practical matters
concerning the boating enthusiast. *Payment:* by negotiation. *Illustrations:*
photos or drawings.

Practical Fishkeeping (1966), Steve Windsor, EMAP Pursuit Publishing Ltd,
Bretton Court, Bretton, Peterborough PE3 8DZ   *tel* (01733) 264666.

£2.10. M. Instructional articles on fishkeeping with heavy emphasis on easily-absorbed information. *Payment:* by arrangement. *Illustrations:* line, half-tone, high quality colour transparencies of tropical fish, cartoons.

Practical Gardening (1960), Andrew Blackford, EMAP Garden Publications, Apex House, Oundle Road, Peterborough PE2 9NP   *tel* (01733) 898100   *fax* (01733) 898433.
£2.20. M. 500-1000 words on inspirational gardening subjects, particularly if oriented towards ideas for garden design, and well illustrated. *Payment:* from £120 per 1000 words. *Illustrations:* line, half-tone, colour.

Practical Householder (1955), John McGowan, Nexus Media Ltd, Warwick House, Azalea Drive, Swanley, Kent BR8 8HY   *tel* (01322) 660070   *fax* (01322) 667633.
£1.95. M. Articles about 1500 words in *length*, about practical matters concerning home improvement. *Payment:* according to subject. *Illustrations:* line, half-tone, cartoons.

Practical Motorist (1934), Ewan Scott, Arrowsmith Court, Station Approach, Broadstone, Dorset BH18 8PW   *tel* (01202) 657480   *fax* (01202) 659950.
£1.95. M. Practical articles on upkeep, servicing and repair and customising and performance improvements of all makes of cars; also practical hints and tips. *Payment:* according to merit. *Illustrations:* b&w, colour prints or transparencies, line drawings, cartoons.

Practical Parenting (1987), Editor-in-Chief: Jayne Marsden, IPC Magazines Ltd, King's Reach Tower, Stamford Street, London SE1 9LS   *tel* 0171-261 5058   *fax* 0171-261 5366.
£1.40. M. Articles on parenting, baby and childcare, health, psychology, education, children's activities, personal birth/parenting experiences. *Send synopsis*, with sae. *Illustrations: commissioned only*; colour: photos, line, cartoons. *Payment:* £100-£150 per 1000 words; illustrations by agreement.

Practical Photography (1959), Martyn Moore, Apex House, Oundle Road, Peterborough PE2 9NP   *tel* (01733) 898100   *fax* (01733) 894472.
£2.10. M. Features on any aspect of photography with practical bias. Mostly written by staff journalists, but freelance ideas welcome. Send brief synopsis *only* in first instance. *Illustrations:* line, half-tone, colour, cartoons. *Payment:* from £50 per 1000 words; from £10 b&w or colour.

Practical Wireless (1932), Rob Mannion, G3XFD, PW Publishing Ltd, Arrowsmith Court, Station Approach, Broadstone, Dorset BH18 8PW   *tel* (01202) 659910   *fax* (01202) 659950.
72p. M. Articles on the practical and theoretical aspects of amateur radio and communications. Constructional projects. *Illustrations:* in b&w and colour; photos, line drawings and wash half-tone for offset litho. *Payment:* by arrangement.

Practical Woodworking, Alan Mitchell, IPC Magazines Ltd, King's Reach Tower, Stamford Street, London SE1 9LS   *tel* 0171-261 6602.
£2.15. M. Articles of a practical nature covering any aspect of woodworking, including woodworking projects, tools, joints or timber technology. *Payment:* £65 per published page. *Illustrated.*

The Practitioner (1868), Howard Griffiths, 30 Calderwood Street, London SE18 6QH   *tel* 0181-855 7777   *fax* 0181-855 2406.
£6.50. M. (£52.00 p.a., $120.00 p.a. overseas) Articles of interest to GPs and vocational trainees, and others in the medical profession. *Payment:* approx. £150 per 1000 words.

Prediction (1936), Jo Logan, Link House, Dingwall Avenue, Croydon CR9 2TA *tel* 0181-686 2599 *fax* 0181-781 1164.
£1.80. M. Articles on astrology and all occult subjects. *Length:* up to 2000 words. *Payment:* by arrangement. *Illustrations:* for cover use only: large colour transparencies (i.e. not 35 mm).

Prep School, David Tytler, Stone Delf, Mottingham Lane, London SE9 4RW *tel* 0181-851 2706 *fax* 0181-851 4914.
£7.00 p.a. (on subscription) 3 p.a. Journal of the Preparatory School world: the magazine of IAPS and SATIPS. Articles of educational interest covering ages 4-13. *Length:* about 1000 words. *Illustrations:* line, half-tone. *Payment:* by arrangement.

The Press and Journal (1748), Derek Tucker, Lang Stracht, Aberdeen AB9 8AF *tel* (01224) 690222.
35p. D. Contributions of Scottish interest. *Payment:* by arrangement. *Illustrations:* half-tone.

Pride (1993), Deidre Forbes, 370 Coldharbour Lane, London SW9 8PL *tel* 0171-737 7377 *fax* 0171-274 8994.
£1.95. Bi-M. Celebrity interviews and lifestyle features of interest to young black women; also food, health and fitness, fashion and beauty. (Relaunched in 1994.) *Length:* 1000-3000 words. *Illustrations:* colour photos and drawings. *Payment:* £100 per 1000 words; £75 per illustration.

Priests & People, Rev. D.C. Sanders OP, Blackfriars, Buckingham Road, Cambridge CB3 0DD *tel* (01223) 359376.
£2.00. M. Journal of pastoral theology especially for parish ministry and for Christians of English-speaking countries. *Illustrations:* occasional b&w photos, cartoons. *Length* and *payment* by arrangement.

Prima (1986), Lindsay Nicholson, Portland House, Stag Place, London SW1E 5AU *tel* 0171-245 8700.
£1.40. M. Articles on fashion, crafts, health and beauty, cookery; features. *Illustrations:* half-tone, colour.

Printing World (1878), Gareth Ward, Miller Freeman Publishers Ltd, Miller Freeman House, Sovereign Way, Tonbridge, Kent TN9 1RW *tel* (01732) 364422 *fax* (01732) 377552.
£2.50. W. (£78.00 p.a., overseas £112.00 p.a.) Commercial, technical, financial and labour news covering all aspects of the printing industry in the UK and abroad. Outside contributions. *Payment:* by arrangement. *Illustrations:* line, half-tone, colour, cartoons.

Private Eye (1962), Ian Hislop, 6 Carlisle Street, London W1V 5RG *tel* 0171-437 4017 *fax* 0171-437 0705.
£1.00. F. Satire. *Payment:* by arrangement. *Illustrations:* b&w, line, cartoons.

Professional Nurse (1985), Andrew Heenan, Macmillan Magazines Ltd, Porters South, 4-6 Crinan Street, London N1 9SQ *tel* 0171-833 4000 *fax* 0171-843 4699.
£33.50 p.a. M. Articles of interest to the professional nurse. *Length:* articles: 2000-2500 words; letters: 250-500 words. *Payment:* by arrangement. *Illustrations:* line, half-tone, colour.

Professional Photographer (1961), Steve Hynes, MLP Ltd, Market Link House, Tye Green, Elsenham, Bishop's Stortford CM22 6DY *tel* (01279) 647555 *fax* (01279) 815300.
£2.00. M. Articles on professional photography, including technical articles, photographer profiles and coverage of issues affecting the industry. *Length:* 1000-2000 words. *Illustrations:* colour and b&w prints and transparencies,

diagrams if appropriate. *Payment:* £75 per page for articles and pro rata for illustrations.

Property Week (1982), Penny Guest, The Builder Group, 1 Millharbour, London E14 9RA *tel* 0171-560 4000 *fax* 0171-560-4012.
£2.00. W. News and features on commercial property, occupational management and financial issues. *Length:* by negotiation. *Illustrations:* contact art director, Peter Smith. *Payment:* £170 per 1000 words; up to £150-£200.

Publishing News (1979), Fred Newman, 43 Museum Street, London WC1A 1LY *tel* 0171-404 0304.
£1.50. W. Articles and news items on books and publishers. *Payment:* £80-£100 per 1000 words. *Illustrations:* half-tone, cartoons.

Pulse, Howard Griffiths, Miller Freeman Professional Ltd, 30 Calderwood Street, Woolwich, London SE18 6QH *tel* 0181-855 7777 *fax* 0181-855 2406.
£150.00 p.a. W. Articles and photos of direct interest to GPs. Purely clinical material can only be accepted from medically qualified authors. *Length:* up to 750 words. *Payment:* £150 average. *Illustrations:* b&w and colour photos.

Q Magazine (1986), Andrew Collins, EMAP Metro, Mappin House, 4 Winsley Street, London W1N 7AR *tel* 0171-436 1515 *fax* 0171-323 0680.
£2.20. M. Glossy modern guide to more than just rock music. *All material commissioned. Length:* 1200-2500 words. *Illustrations:* colour and b&w photos. *Payment:* £180 per 1000 words; illustrations by arrangement.

Quaker Monthly (1921), Elizabeth Cave, Quaker Home Service, Friends House, Euston Road, London NW1 2BJ *tel* 0171-387 3601 *fax* 0171-388 1977.
75p. M. (£11.70 p.a.) Articles, poems, reviews, expanding the Quaker approach to the spiritual life. Writers should be members or attenders of a Quaker meeting. *Illustrations:* line, half-tone. *Payment:* none.

RA Magazine (1983), Nick Tite, Royal Academy of Arts, Burlington House, Piccadilly, London W1V 0DS *tel* 0171-494 5657 *fax* 0171-287 9023.
£4.00. Q. Topical articles relating to the Royal Academy, its history and its exhibitions. *Length:* 500-1500 words. *Illustrations:* consult editor. *Payment:* £100 per 1000 words; illustrations by negotiation.

Radio Control Models and Electronics (1960), Kevin Crozier, Nexus Special Interests, Nexus House, Boundary Way, Hemel Hempstead, Herts. HP2 7ST *tel* (01442) 66551 *fax* (01442) 66998.
£1.70. M. Well-illustrated articles on topics related to radio control. *Payment:* £35 per published page. *Illustrations:* line, half-tone.

Radio Times, Nicholas Brett, BBC Worldwide Publishing, Woodlands, 80 Wood Lane, London W12 0TT *tel* 0181-576 3999 *fax* 0181-576 3160.
72p. W. Articles that preview the week's programmes on British television and radio. All articles are specially commissioned – ideas and synopses are welcomed but not unsolicited MSS. *Length:* 600-2500 words. *Payment:* by arrangement. *Illustrations:* in colour and b&w; photos, graphic designs or drawings.

Railway Gazette International, Murray Hughes, Reed Business Publishing, Quadrant House, The Quadrant, Sutton, Surrey SM2 5AS *tel* 0181-652 3739 *telex* 892084 REEDBP G *fax* 0181-652 3738.
£42.00 p.a. M. Deals with management, engineering, operation and finance of railways worldwide. Articles of practical interest on these subjects are considered and paid for if accepted. Illustrated articles, of 1000-3000 words, are preferred. A *preliminary letter* is required.

Railway Magazine (1897), Nick Pigott, IPC Magazines Ltd, King's Reach Tower, Stamford Street, London SE1 9LS   *tel* 0171-261 5821   *fax* 0171-261 5269.
£2.20. M. Illustrated magazine dealing with all railway subjects; no fiction or verse. Articles from 1500-2000 words accompanied by photos. *Preliminary letter* desirable. *Payment:* by arrangement. *Illustrations:* colour transparencies, half-tone and line.

Rambling Today (1935), Annabelle Birchall, 1-5 Wandsworth Road, London SW8 2XX   *tel* 0171-582 6878   *fax* 0171-587 3799.
Free to members. Q. Official magazine of The Ramblers' Association. Articles on walking, access to countryside and related issues. *Material mostly commissioned. Length:* about 1000 words. *Illustrations:* colour and b&w photos. *Payment:* by agreement.

Reader's Digest, Russell Twisk, The Reader's Digest Association Ltd, Berkeley Square House, Berkeley Square, London W1X 6AB   *tel* 0171-629 8144   *e-mail* excerpts@readersdigest.co.uk
£1.90. M. Original anecdotes – £150 for up to 150 words – are required for humorous features. Booklet 'Writing for Reader's Digest' available £2.50 post free.

Reading Evening Post (1965), Kim Chapman, 8 Tessa Road, Reading, Berks. RG1 8NS   *tel* (01734) 575833   *fax* (01734) 599363.
22p. D. Topical articles based on current news. *Length:* 800-1200 words. *Payment:* based on lineage rates. *Illustrations:* half-tone.

Red Pepper (1994), Hilary Wainwright, Socialist Newspaper (Publications) Ltd, 3 Gunthorpe Street, London E1 7RP   *tel* 0171-247 1702   *fax* 0171-247 1695   *e-mail* redpepper@online.rednet.co.uk
£1.95. M. Independent radical magazine: news and features on politics, culture and everyday life of interest to the left and greens. *Material mostly commissioned. Length:* news/news features 200-800 words, other features 800-2000 words. *Illustrations:* b&w photos, cartoons, graphics. *Payment:* by arrangement.

Red Tape (1911), Amanda Campbell, Civil and Public Services Association, 160 Falcon Road, Clapham Junction, London SW11 2LN   *tel* 0171-924 2727   *fax* 0171-924 1847.
Free to members. 10 p.a. (80p per issue non-members) Well-written articles on Civil Service, trade union and general subjects considered. *Length:* 750-1400 words. Also photos and humorous drawings of interest to Civil Servants. *Illustrations:* line, half-tone. *Payment:* NUJ rates.

Reform (1972), David Lawrence, 86 Tavistock Place, London WC1H 9RT   *tel* 0171-916 2020   *fax* 0171-916 2021 (mark: for 'Reform').
85p. M. Published by United Reformed Church. Articles of religious or social comment. *Length:* 600-1000 words. *Illustrations:* line, half-tone, colour, cartoons. *Payment:* by arrangement.

Report, 7 Northumberland Street, London WC2N 5DA   *tel* 0171-930 6441   *fax* 0171-930 1359.
£8.00 p.a. 8 p.a. (£12.00 p.a. overseas) Journal of the Association of Teachers and Lecturers (formerly Assistant Masters and Mistresses Association). Features, articles, comment, news about primary, secondary and further education. *Payment:* minimum £60 per 1000 words.

Retail Week (1988), Ian McGarrigle, EMAP Business Communications, Maclaren House, 19 Scarbrook Road, Croydon, Surrey CR9 1QH   *tel* 0181-277 5331   *fax* 0181-277 5344.

Controlled circulation. W. (£80.00 p.a.) Features and news stories on all aspects of retail management. *Length:* up to 1000 words. *Illustrations:* colour and b&w photos. *Payment:* £120 per 1000 words; photos at market rates.

The Rialto (1984), John and Rhiannon Wakeman, 32 Grosvenor Road, Norwich, Norfolk NR2 2PZ *tel* (01603) 666455.
£3.90. 3 p.a. (£10.00 p.a., £8.00 p.a. low income) Poetry and criticism. Sae essential. *Illustrations:* line. *Payment:* by arrangement.

Right Start (1989), Anita Bevan, Needmarsh Publishing Ltd, 71 Newcomen Street, London SE1 1YT *tel* 0171-403 0840 *fax* 0171-378 6883.
£1.50. Bi-M. Features on all aspects of pre-school and infant education, child health and behaviour. *No* unsolicited MSS. *Length:* 1200-1500 words. *Illustrations:* colour photos, line. *Payment:* varies.

Rugby World (1960), Alison Kervin, IPC Magazines Ltd, Kings Reach Tower, Stamford Street, London SE1 9LS *tel* 0171-261 6830 *fax* 0171-261 5419.
£2.25. M. Features and exclusive news stories on rugby. *Length:* approx. 1200 words. *Illustrations:* colour photos, cartoons. *Payment:* £120.

Runner's World (1979), Steven Seaton, Rodale Press Ltd, 7-10 Chandos Street, London W1M 0AD *tel* 0171-291 6000 *fax* 0171-291 6080.
£2.20. M. Articles on jogging, running and fitness. *Payment:* by arrangement. *Illustrations:* line, half-tone, colour, cartoons.

RUSI Journal, Editorial Manager: Alexandra Citron, Whitehall, London SW1A 2ET *tel* 0171-930 5854 *fax* 0171-321 0943.
£6.00. Bi-M. Journal of the Royal United Services Institute for Defence Studies. Articles on international security, the military sciences, defence technology and procurement, and military history; also book reviews and correspondence. *Length:* 3000-4000 words. *Illustrations:* b&w photos, maps and diagrams. *Payment:* £12.50 per printed page upon publication.

Safety Education (1966; founded 1937 as **Child Safety**; 1940 became **Safety Training**), Carole Wale, Royal Society for the Prevention of Accidents, Cannon House, The Priory Queensway, Birmingham B4 6BS *tel* 0121-200 2461 *telex* 336546 *fax* 0121-200 1254.
£6.85 p.a. for members of Safety Education Department. 3 p.a. (£13.60 p.a. non-members) Articles on every aspect of good practice in safety education including safety of teachers and pupils in school, and the teaching of road, home, water, leisure and personal safety by means of established subjects on the school curriculum. All ages. *Commissioned material only. Illustrations:* line, half-tone, colour. *Payment:* by negotiation.

Saga Magazine (1984), Paul Bach, The Saga Building, Middelburg Square, Folkestone, Kent CT20 1AZ *tel* (01303) 711523 *fax* (01303) 712699.
£12.95 p.a. 10 p.a. Articles relevant to interests of 50+ age group, and profiles of celebrities in same age group. *Length:* 1200-1800 words. *Illustrations:* colour transparencies, commissioned colour artwork. *Payment:* competitive rate.

Sainsbury's: The Magazine (1993), Michael Wynn Jones, New Crane Publishing, 20 Upper Ground, London SE1 9PD *tel* 0171-633 0266 *fax* 0171-401 9423.
95p. M. Features: general, food and drink, health, travel and humour; *all material commissioned. Length:* from 1500 words. *Illustrations:* colour and b&w photos and line illustrations. *Payment:* varies; £400 per full page for illustrations.

Satellite Times (1988), Nik Moore, 23 Mitcham Lane, Streatham, London SW16 6LQ *tel* 0181-677 7822 *fax* 0181-677 8223.
£2.00. M. Television and film personality articles and interviews, sports articles, music, competitions. *Payment:* by negotiation.

Scale Models International, Kelvin Barber, Nexus Special Interests, Nexus House, Boundary Way, Hemel Hempstead, Herts. HP2 7ST   *tel* (01442) 66551   *fax* (01442) 66998.
£1.95. M. Articles on scale models. *Length:* up to 2500 words. *Payment:* £25-£30 per page. *Illustrations:* line, half-tone, colour.

School Librarian (1937), Editor: Raymond Astbury; Review Editor: Keith Barker, The School Library Association, Liden Library, Barrington Close, Liden, Swindon, Wilts. SN3 6HF   *tel* (01793) 617838.
Free to members. Q. (£45.00 p.a. post free) The official Journal of the School Library Association. Reviews of books from pre-school to young adult age range with articles on authors and illustrators; also articles on school library organisation, use and skills. *Length:* up to 3000 words. *Payment:* by arrangement.

Science Progress, Prof David Phillips, Prof Robin Rowbury, Science Reviews, 41/43 Green Lane, Northwood, Middlesex HA6 3AE   *tel* (01923) 823586   *fax* (01923) 825066   *e-mail* scitech.demon.co.uk
£86.50 p.a. Q. (£95.00 p.a. overseas) Articles of 6000 words on new scientific developments, written so as to be intelligible to workers in other disciplines. Imperative to submit synopsis before full-length article. *Payment:* by arrangement. *Illustrations:* line, half-tone.

Scientific Computing World (1994), Dennis Moralee, IOP Publishing Ltd, Techno House, Redcliffe Way, Bristol BS1 6NX   *tel* (0117) 929 7481   *fax* (0117) 925 1942.
Free to qualifying subscribers. 10 p.a. Features on hardware and software developments for the scientific community, plus news articles and reviews. *Length:* 800-2000 words. *Illustrations:* colour transparencies, photos, electronic graphics. *Payment:* by negotiation.

Scootering (1985), Stuart Lanning, PO Box 46, Weston-super-Mare, Avon BS23 1AF   *tel* (01934) 414785.
£2.50. M. Custom, racing and vintage scooter features, plus technical information. Music features and related lifestyle pieces. *Payment:* by arrangement. *Illustrations:* half-tone, colour, cartoons.

Scotland on Sunday (1988), Brian Groom, North Bridge, Edinburgh EH1 1YT   *tel* 0131-225 2468   *telex* 72255   *fax* 0131-220 2443; Glasgow office   *tel* 0141-332 6163.
65p. W. Features on all subjects, not necessarily Scottish. *Payment:* £88 per 1000 words.

The Scots Magazine (1739), D.C. Thomson & Co. Ltd, 2 Albert Square, Dundee DD1 9QJ   *tel* (01382) 223131   *fax* (01382) 322214.
£1.10. M. Articles on all subjects of Scottish interest. Short stories, poetry, but must be Scottish. *Illustrations:* colour and b&w photos, drawings, cartoons. *Payment:* £22 per 1000 words; from £12.

The Scotsman (1817), James Seaton, 20 North Bridge, Edinburgh EH1 1YT   *tel* 0131-225 2468   *fax* 0131-226 7420.
42p. D. Ind. Considers articles, 800-1000 words, on political, economic and general themes, which add substantially to current information. Prepared to commission topical and controversial series from proved authorities. *Illustrations:* outstanding news pictures, cartoons. *Payment:* by arrangement.
The Scotsman Weekend. Free with Sat. paper. Features, reviews. *Illustrated.*

Scottish Book Collector (1987), Jennie Renton, c/o 36 Lauriston Place, Edinburgh EH3 9EZ   *tel* 0131-228 4837.
£1.50. Bi-M. Articles on collecting Scottish books; literary/bibliographical

articles on books published in Scotland or by Scottish writers. *Length:* 1500-2500 words. *Payment:* £25 per article.

Scottish Educational Journal, Simon Macaulay, Educational Institute of Scotland, 46 Moray Place, Edinburgh EH3 6BH *tel* 0131-225 6244 *fax* 0131-220 3151.
£8.10 p.a. 5 p.a., plus Specials.

The Scottish Farmer (1893), Alasdair Fletcher, The Plaza Tower, East Kilbride, Glasgow G74 1LW *tel* (013552) 46444 *fax* (013552) 63013.
£1.05. W. Articles on agricultural subjects. *Length:* 1000-1500 words. *Payment:* £80 per 1000 words. *Illustrations:* line, half-tone, cartoons (colour or b&w).

Scottish Field (1903), Archie Mackenzie, Special Publications, Royston House, Caroline Park, Edinburgh EH5 1QJ *tel* 0131-551 2942 *fax* 0131-551 2938.
£2.25. M. Will consider all material with a Scottish link and good photos. *Payment:* by negotiation.

Scottish Home and Country (1924), Stella Roberts, 42A Heriot Row, Edinburgh EH3 6ES *tel* 0131-225 1934 *fax* 0131-225 8129.
70p. M. Articles on crafts, cookery, travel, personal experience, village histories, country customs, DIY, antiques, farming; humorous rural stories; fashion, health, books. *Length:* up to 1000 words, preferably illustrated. *Illustrations:* colour prints/transparencies, b&w, cartoons. *Payment:* by arrangement.

Scouting, David Easton, The Scout Association, Baden-Powell House, Queens Gate, London SW7 5JS *tel* 0171-584 7030 *fax* 0171-590 5103.
£1.25. M. National Magazine of The Scout Association. Ideas, news, views, features and programme resources for Leaders and Supporters. Training material, accounts of Scouting events and articles of general interest with Scouting connections. *Illustrations:* photos – action shots preferred rather than static posed shots for use with articles or as fillers or cover potential, cartoons. *Payment:* on publication by arrangement.

Screen International, Boyd Farrow, EMAP Business Publishing, 33-39 Bowling Green Lane, London EC1R 0DA *tel* 0171-505 8080 *fax* 0171-505 8117.
£1.90. W. International news and features on every aspect of films, television and associated media. *Length:* variable. *Payment:* by arrangement.

Sea Angler (1973), Mel Russ, EMAP Pursuit Publishing Ltd, Bretton Court, Bretton, Peterborough PE3 8DZ *tel* (01733) 264666 *fax* (01733) 263294.
£1.95. M. Topical articles on all aspects of sea-fishing around the British Isles. *Payment:* by arrangement. *Illustrations:* colour.

Sea Breezes (1919), A.C. Douglas, Units 28-30, Spring Valley Industrial Estate, Braddan, Isle of Man IM2 2QS *tel* (01624) 626018 *fax* (01624) 661655.
£1.95. M. Factual articles on ships and the sea past and present, preferably illustrated. *Length:* up to 4000 words. *Illustrations:* line, half-tone, colour. *Payment:* by arrangement.

Select Magazine (1990), Andrew Harrison, EMAP Metro, Mappin House, 4 Winsley Street, London W1N 5AR *tel* 0171-436 1515 *fax* 0171-637 0456.
£1.85. M. Off-the-wall youth/music feature ideas for hip 18-25-year-olds. *Length:* decided on commissioning. *Illustrations:* colour and b&w rock/pop photography with an arty/provocative bent. *Payment:* £120 per 1000 words; illustrations £110 per page.

She (1955), Alison Pylkkanen, National Magazine House, 72 Broadwick Street, London W1V 2BP *tel* 0171-439 5000 *fax* 0171-439 5350.
£1.90. M. No unsolicited manuscripts. Ideas with synopses welcome on subjects ranging from health and relationships to child care and careers. *Payment:* NUJ freelance rates. *Illustrations:* photos, cartoons.

Ship & Boat International, Richard White, Royal Institution of Naval Architects, 10 Upper Belgrave Street, London SW1X 8BQ   *tel* 0171-235 4622   *telex* 265844 SINAI G   *fax* 0171-245 6959.
£50.00 p.a. M. Technical articles on the design, construction and operation of all types of specialised small ships and workboats. *Length:* 500-1500 words. *Payment:* by arrangement. *Illustrations:* line and half-tone, photos and diagrams.

Ships Monthly (1966), Robert Shopland, Waterway Productions Ltd, Kottingham House, Dale Street, Burton-on-Trent DE14 3TD   *tel* (01283) 564290   *fax* (01283) 561077.
£1.95. M. Illustrated articles of shipping interest – both mercantile and naval, preferably of 20th century ships. Well-researched, factual material only. No short stories or poetry. 'Notes for Contributors' available. Mainly commissioned material; preliminary letter essential, with sae. *Payment:* by arrangement. *Illustrations:* half-tone and line, colour transparencies and prints.

Shooting Times and Country Magazine (1882), John Gregson, IPC Magazines Ltd, King's Reach Tower, Stamford Street, London SE1 9LS   *tel* 0171-261 6180   *fax* 0171-261 7179.
£1.40. W. Articles on fieldsports, especially shooting, and on related natural history and countryside topics. *Length:* up to 2000 words. *Payment:* by arrangement. *Illustrations:* photos, drawings, colour transparencies.

The Short Wave Magazine (1937), Dick Ganderton, G8VFH, Arrowsmith Court, Station Approach, Broadstone, Dorset BH18 8PW   *tel* (01202) 659910   *fax* (01202) 659950.
£2.25. M. (£25.00 p.a.) Technical and semi-technical articles, 500-5000 words, dealing with design, construction and operation of radio receiving equipment. Radio-related photo features welcome. *Payment:* £55 per page. *Illustrations:* line, half-tone, cartoons.

Shout (1993), D.C. Thomson & Co. Ltd, Albert Square, Dundee DD1 9QJ   *tel* (01382) 223131   *fax* (01382) 200880; and 185 Fleet Street, London EC4A 2HS   *tel* 0171-242 5086   *fax* 0171-404 5694.
90p. F. 56-page colour gravure magazine for 12-16-year-old girls. Pop, film and 'soap' features and pin-ups; general features of teen interest; emotional features, fashion and beauty advice. *Illustrations:* colour transparencies. *Payment:* on acceptance.

The Shropshire Magazine (1950), Pam Green, The Leopard Press Ltd, 77 Wyle Cop, Shrewsbury, Shropshire SY1 1UT   *tel* (01743) 362175.
£1.00. M. Articles on topics related to Shropshire, including countryside, history, characters, legends, education, food; also home and garden features. *Length:* up to 1500 words. *Illustrations:* b&w photos, line drawings. *Payment:* £15-£20; illustrations by arrangement.

Shropshire Star (1964), Andy Wright, Ketley, Telford TF1 4HU   *tel* (01952) 242424   *fax* (01952) 254605.
26p. D. Evening paper – news and features. *No* unsolicited material; write to features editor with outline of ideas. *Payment:* by arrangement.

Sight and Sound (1932), Philip Dodd, 21 Stephen Street, London W1P 1PL   *tel* 0171-255 1444   *telex* 27624 BFILDN G   *fax* 0171-436 2327. Published by the British Film Institute.
£2.70. M. Topical and critical articles on the cinema of any country; book reviews; reviews of every film theatrically released in London; reviews of every video released; regular columns from the USA and Europe. *Length:* 1000-5000 words. *Payment:* by arrangement. *Illustrations:* relevant photos, cartoons.

The Sign (1905), Publisher: G.A. Knights, Chansitor Publications Ltd, St Mary's Works, St Mary's Plain, Norwich, Norfolk NR3 3BH   *tel* (01603) 615995   *fax* (01603) 624483.
5p. M. Leading national insert for C of E parish magazines. Articles of interest to parishes. Items should bear the author's name and address; return postage essential. *Length:* up to 400 words. *Illustrations:* unusual b&w photos, drawings considered. *Payment:* by arrangement.

Signal, Approaches to Children's Books (1970), Nancy Chambers, Lockwood, Station Road, South Woodchester, Stroud, Glos. GL5 5EQ   *tel* (01453 87) 3716/2208   *fax* (01453 87) 8599.
£3.95. 3 p.a. (£11.85 p.a.) Articles on any aspect of children's books or the children's book world. *Length:* no limit but average 2500-3000 words. *Payment:* £3 per printed page. *Illustrations:* line occasionally.

Simply Crafts (1994), Sue Marks, Nexus Special Interests Ltd, Nexus House, Boundary Way, Hemel Hempstead, Herts. HP2 7ST   *tel* (01442) 66551   *fax* (01442) 66998.
£2.25. M. Step-by-step craft projects and features on new techniques. *Length:* 1000-2000 words. *Illustrations:* colour photos and line illustrations, diagrams. *Payment:* by negotiation.

The Skier and The Snowboarder (1984), Frank Baldwin, 48 London Road, Sevenoaks, Kent TN13 1AS   *tel* (01732) 743644   *fax* (01732) 743647.
£2.50. 5 p.a. (Sept-May) Ski features, based around a good story. *Length:* 800-1000 words. *Illustrations:* colour action ski photos. *Payment:* by negotiation.

Sky Magazine, Mark Frith, Hachette Emap, Mappin House, 4 Winsley Street, London W1N 7AR   *tel* 0171-436 1515   *fax* 0171-637 0948.
£2.20. M. People, movies, music and style. *Length:* varies. *Illustrations:* colour and b&w photos. *Payment:* by arrangement.

Slimmer Magazine (1972), Claire Crowther, Turret Group plc, 177 Hagden Lane, Watford, Herts WD1 8LN   *tel* (01923) 228577   *fax* (01923) 221346.
£1.75. Bi-M. Features on health, nutrition, slimming. Personal weight loss stories. Sae essential. *Length:* 500 or 1500 words. *Payment:* £10 per 100 words.

Slimming Magazine (1969), Christine Michael, Victory House, 14 Leicester Place, London WC2H 7BP   *tel* 0171-437 9011   *telex* 266400   *fax* 0171-434 0656.
£1.75. 10 p.a. Articles on psychology, lifestyle and health related to diet and nutrition. *Approach* editor in writing with ideas. *Length:* 1000-1500 words. *Payment:* by negotiation.

Smallholder (1985), Liz Wright, Hook House, Hook Road, Wimblington, March, Cambs. PE15 0QL   *tel* (01354) 741182/(01366) 501035   *fax* (01354) 741182.
£1.90. M. Articles of relevance to small farmers about livestock and crops; items relating to the countryside considered. *Payment:* £20 per 1000 words or by arrangement. *Illustrations:* line, half-tone, cartoons.

Smash Hits, Kate Thornton, 2nd Floor, Mappin House, 4 Winsley Street, London W1N 7AR   *tel* 0171-436 1515   *fax* 0171-636 5792.
90p. F. News interviews and posters of pop, TV and film stars. *Illustrations:* colour photos. *Payment:* £100 per page and per photo.

Snooker Scene (1971), Clive Everton, Cavalier House, 202 Hagley Road, Edgbaston, Birmingham B16 9PQ   *tel* 0121-454 2931   *fax* 0121-452 1822.
£1.30. M. News and articles about snooker. *Payment:* by arrangement. *Illustrations:* photos.

Solicitors Journal (1856), 21-27 Lamb's Conduit Street, London WC1N 3NJ   *tel* 0171-242 2548   *fax* 0171-430 1729.
£1.65. W. Articles, by practising lawyers or specialist journalists, on subjects of practical interest to solicitors. Articles sent on spec should be on computer disk. *Length:* up to 1800 words. *Payment:* by negotiation.

Somerset Magazine (1977 as Somerset & West), Roy Smart, Smart Print Publications Ltd, 23 Market Street, Crewkerne, Somerset TA18 7JU   *tel* (01460) 78000   *fax* (01460) 76718.
£1.50. M. Articles, features with particular reference to county locations, facilities and other interests. *Length:* 1000-1500 words. *Illustrations:* line, halftone, colour (transparencies or prints). *Payment:* by arrangement.

Songwriting and Composing (1986), General Secretary: Carole Jones, Sovereign House, 12 Trewartha Road, Praa Sands, Penzance, Cornwall TR20 9ST   *tel* (01736) 762826   *fax* (01736) 763328.
Free to members. Q. Magazine of the Guild of International Songwriters and Composers. Short stories, articles, letters relating to songwriting, publishing, recording and the music industry. *Payment:* negotiable upon content £25-£60. *Illustrations:* line, half-tone.

South Wales Echo (1884), Keith Perch, Thomson House, Havelock Street, Cardiff CF1 1XR   *tel* (01222) 583583/223333   *fax* (01222) 583624.
26p. D. Evening paper – features, showbiz, news features, personality interviews. *Length:* up to 700 words. *Illustrations:* photos, cartoons. *Payment:* by negotiation.

The Southern Daily Echo (1888), Patrick Fleming, Newspaper House, Test Lane, Redbridge, Southampton SO16 9JX   *tel* (01703) 424777   *fax* (01703) 424770.
26p. D. News, articles, features, sport. *Length:* varies. *Illustrations:* line, halftone, colour. *Payment:* NUJ rates.

The Spectator (1828), Frank Johnson, 56 Doughty Street, London WC1N 2LL   *tel* 0171-405 1706   *fax* 0171-242-0603.
£1.90. W. Articles on current affairs, politics and the arts; book reviews; poetry. *Illustrations:* b&w, cartoons. *Payment:* on merit.

Speech and Drama (1951), Dr Paul Ranger, 4 Fane Road, Old Marston, Oxford OX3 0SA   *tel* (01865) 728304.
£6.50 p.a. 2 p.a. Covers theatre, drama and all levels of education relating to speech and drama; specialist articles only; preliminary abstract of 300 words; photos welcome. *Length:* 1500-2000 words. *Payment:* none, complimentary copy.

Spoken English (1968), Malcolm Dale, English Speaking Board (International), 26A Princes Street, Southport, Merseyside PR8 1EQ   *tel* (01704) 501730   *fax* (01704) 539637.
£20.00 p.a. (ESB membership inc. 2 issues of journal) Serious articles (1000+ words) on spoken English, communication ventures and training, poetry, drama, and English-teaching from primary to university levels, in Britain and overseas. *Payment:* by arrangement.

Sport (1994; formerly **Sport and Leisure**, 1949), Louise Fyfe, The Sports Council, 16 Upper Woburn Place, London WC1H 0QP   *tel* 0171-388 1277   *fax* 0171-383 5740.
£20.00 p.a. Bi-M. (£35.00 p.a. overseas) Articles on various sport development, physical education, sports politics, sponsorship, facilities and outdoor activities. *Length:* 500-1000 words. *Illustrations:* sports photographers encouraged; b&w photos. *Payment:* £120 per 1000 words; photos £50 per ½ page.

The Sporting Life, Tom Clarke, Mirror Group Newspapers Ltd, One Canada Square, Canary Wharf, London E14 5AP   *tel* 0171-293 3000   *fax* 0171-293 3758.
80p. D. National racing daily, with wide news and feature coverage, including bloodstock and betting; plus daily Sports Betting feature on general sports and betting. Also **Greyhound Life,** a daily pull-out, covering every angle of greyhound racing and betting. Interested in relevant news stories; features, photos and graphics are commissioned. *Payment:* by negotiation.

The Squash Player (1971), Ian McKenzie, 460 Bath Road, Longford, Middlesex UB7 0EB   *tel* (01753) 775511   *fax* (01753) 775512.
£39.95 p.a. 12 p.a. Covers all aspects of playing squash. All features are commissioned – discuss ideas with editor. *Length:* 1000-1500 words. *Illustrations:* unusual photos (e.g. celebrities), cartoons. *Payment:* £75 per 1000 words; £25-£40 for illustrations.

The Stage (incorporating **Television Today**; 1880), Brian Attwood, Stage House, 47 Bermondsey Street, London SE1 3XT   *tel* 0171-403 1818   *fax* 0171-357 9287.
80p. W. Original and interesting articles on professional stage and broadcasting topics may be sent for the editor's consideration. *Length:* 500-800 words. *Payment:* £100 per 1000 words.

Stamp Lover (1908), Michael Furnell, National Philatelic Society, British Philatelic Centre, 107 Charterhouse Street, London EC1M 6PT   *tel* 0171-490 4253.
£1.50. 6 p.a. Original articles on stamps and postal history. *Illustrations:* line, half-tone. *Payment:* by arrangement.

Stamp Magazine (1934), Richard West, Link House Publications, Link House, Dingwall Avenue, Croydon CR9 2TA   *tel* 0181-686 2599   *fax* 0181-781 6044.
£1.95. M. Informative articles and exclusive news items on stamp collecting and postal history. *No preliminary letter. Payment:* by arrangement. *Illustrations:* line, half-tone, colour.

Stand Magazine (1952), Jon Silkin, Lorna Tracy, Rodney Pybus, Peter Bennet, 179 Wingrove Road, Newcastle upon Tyne NE4 9DA   *tel/fax* 0191-273 3280.
£3.15 (inc. p&p). Q. (£10.95 p.a.) Poetry, short stories, translations, literary criticism. Send sae for return. Biennial Short Story Competition for unpublished original short story in English (see page 667) and alternates with biennial Poetry Competition. *Payment:* £25 per 1000 words of prose; £25 per poem.

Staple (1982), Bob Windsor, Donald Measham, Gilderoy East, Upperwood Road, Matlock Bath, Derbyshire DE4 3PD   *tel* (01629) 583867/582764.
£10.00 p.a. 4 p.a. (£15.00 outside Europe) Mainstream poems and short stories. *Payment:* £5-£10.

The Star (1887), Peter Charlton, York Street, Sheffield S1 1PU   *tel* (0114) 276 7676   *fax* (0114) 272 5978.
27p. D. Well-written articles of local character. *Length:* about 500 words. *Payment:* by negotiation. *Illustrations:* topical photos, line drawings, graphics, cartoons.

Steam Classic (1990), Peter Herring, Ebony, Trevithick House, Moorswater, Liskeard, Cornwall PL14 4LH   *tel* (01579) 340100/(01932) 225330   *fax* (01579) 340200/(01932) 254639.
£2.10. M. Features on the history, design and performance of British-built and overseas steam locomotives; news stories and features on present-day steam locomotive preservation. *Length:* 2000-3000 words. *Illustrations:* archive and contemporary colour transparencies and b&w photos; apply for list of specific

required material (topical material always welcome). *Payment:* approx. £50 per 1000 words; £20 colour, £10 b&w.

Street Machine (1979), Matthew Howell, EMAP National Publications Ltd, Bushfield House, Orton Centre, Peterborough PE2 5UW *tel* (01780) 51872 *fax* (01780) 66333.
£2.50. M. Articles on all modified cars and bodywork. *Length:* 800-1500 words. *Payment:* by arrangement. *Illustrations:* line, half-tone, colour.

Studio Sound (1959), Tim Goodyer, Miller Freeman Entertainment Ltd, Ludgate House, 245 Blackfriars Road, London SE1 9UR *tel* 0171-620 3636 *fax* 0171-401 8036.
£2.00. M. Articles on all aspects of professional sound recording. Technical and operational features on the functional aspects of studio equipment; general features on studio affairs. *Length:* widely variable. *Payment:* by arrangement. *Illustrations:* line, half-tone, colour.

The Sun (1969), Stuart Higgins, News Group Newspapers Ltd, Virginia Street, London E1 9XP *tel* 0171-782 7000 *telex* 262135 SUNEWS G *fax* 0171-488 3253.
25p. D. Takes freelance material, including cartoons. *Payment:* by negotiation.

The Sun (1985), Bob Bird, News International Newspapers, Scotland, 124 Portman Street, Kinning Park, Glasgow G41 1EJ *tel* (0141) 420 5200 *fax* (0141) 420 5248.
25p. D. Scottish edition of *The Sun*. *Illustrations:* transparencies, colour and b&w prints, colour cartoons. *Payment:* by arrangement.

Sunday Express (1918), Sue Douglas, Ludgate House, 245 Blackfriars Road, London SE1 9UX *tel* 0171-928 8000 *cables* Lon Express *telex* 21841/21842 *fax* 0171-620 1656.
65p. W. Exclusive news stories, photos, personality profiles and features of controversial or lively interest. *Length:* 800-1000 words. *Payment:* top rates.
Sunday Express Magazine, Jean Carr *fax* 0171-928 7262. Free. W. Homes, gardens, cookery, general interest features. *Length:* 1000 words. *Payment:* from £250 per 1000 words. *Illustrations:* colour, half-tone, artwork.

Sunday Mail, Jim Cassidy, Anderston Quay, Glasgow G3 8DA *tel* 0141-242 3403 *fax* 0141-242 3587; *London office:* 33 Holborn Circus, EC1P 1DQ.
55p. W. Exclusive stories and pictures (in colour if possible) of national and Scottish interest; also cartoons. *Payment:* above average.

Sunday Mercury, Peter Whitehouse, Colmore Circus, Birmingham B4 6AZ *tel* 0121-236 3366 *fax* 0121-233 0271.
50p. W. News specials or features of Midland interest. *Illustrations:* colour, b&w, cartoons. Special rates for special matter.

Sunday Mirror (1963), Tessa Hilton, 1 Canada Square, Canary Wharf, London E14 5AP *tel* 0171-293 3000 *fax* 0171-293 3073.
55p. W. Concentrates on human interest news features, social documentaries, dramatic news and feature photos. Ideas, as well as articles, bought. *Payment:* high, especially for exclusives.
Sunday Mirror Magazine (1988), Katy Bowen-Bravery *tel* 0171-293 3826 *fax* 0171-293 3835. Free. W. Human interest, celebrity articles, and original amusing ideas. *Length:* 1000 words. *Illustrations:* colour photos. *Payment:* articles and photographs high, especially for exclusives.

Sunday Post, D.C. Thomson & Co. Ltd, 144 Port Dundas Road, Glasgow G4 0HZ *tel* 0141-332 9933 *fax* 0141-331 1595; Albert Square, Dundee DD1 9QJ *tel* (01382) 223131 *fax* (01382) 201064; 185 Fleet Street, London EC4A 2HS *tel* 0171-404 0199 *fax* 0171-404 5694.

55p. W. Human interest, topical, domestic and humorous articles, and exclusive news; and short stories up to 2000 words. *Illustrations:* humorous drawings. *Payment:* on acceptance.
The Sunday Post Magazine (1988), Maggie Dun   *tel* (01382) 223131 ext 4147   *fax* (01382) 201064. Free. M. General interest articles. *Length:* 1000-2000 words. *Illustrations:* colour transparencies. *Payment:* varies.

Sunday Sport (1986), Tony Livesey, 19 Great Ancoats Street, Manchester M60 4BT   *tel* 0161-236 4466   *fax* 0161-236 2427.
55p. W.

The Sunday Sun (1919), Chris Rushton, Thomson House, Groat Market, Newcastle upon Tyne NE1 1ED   *tel* 0191-201 6330   *fax* 0191-230 0238.
55p. W. Immediate topicality and human sidelights on current problems are the keynote of the *Sunday Sun*'s requirements. Particularly welcomed are special features of family appeal and news stories of special interest to the North-East of England. Photos used to illustrate articles. *Length:* 200-800 words. *Payment:* normal lineage rates, or by arrangement. *Illustrations:* photos and line, cartoons.

Sunday Telegraph, Dominic Lawson, 1 Canada Square, Canary Wharf, London E14 5AR   *tel* 0171-538 5000   *fax* 0171-513 2504.
70p. W. Occasional freelance material accepted.
Sunday Telegraph Magazine (1995), Rebecca Tyrrel   *tel* 0171-538 7590   *fax* 0171-538 7074   *e-mail* sunmag@telegraph.co.uk Free with paper. *All material is commissioned.*

The Sunday Times (1822), John Witherow, 1 Pennington Street, London E1 9XW   *tel* 0171-782 5000.
£1.00. W. Special articles by authoritative writers on politics, literature, art, drama, music, finance and science, and topical matters. *Payment:* top rate for exclusive features. *Illustrations:* first-class photos of topical interest and pictorial merit very welcome; also topical drawings and cartoons.
Sunday Times Magazine   *tel* 0171-782 7000. Free with paper. W. Articles and pictures. *Illustrations:* colour and b&w photos. *Payment:* by negotiation.
The Sunday Times Scotland (1988), Will Peakin, Times Newspapers Ltd, 124 Portman Street, Kinning Park, Glasgow G41 1EJ   *tel* (0141) 420 5100   *fax* (0141) 420 5262.
Free with *The Sunday Times*. W. News, features and sport. *Illustrations:* colour photos, cartoons and graphics. *Payment:* £100 per feature; £50 for illustrations.

Superbike, Grant Leonard, Link House Magazines Ltd, Link House, Dingwall Avenue, Croydon CR9 2TA   *tel* 0181-686 2599   *fax* 0181-781 6042.
£2.20. M. Sports and high performance motorcycling, tests, reviews of related products, tuning and motorcycle sport. *Payment:* by arrangement. *Illustrations:* colour.

The Tablet (1840), John Wilkins, 1 King Street Cloisters, Clifton Walk, London W6 0QZ   *tel* 0181-748 8484   *fax* 0181-748 1550.
£1.25. W. The senior Catholic weekly. Religion, philosophy, politics, society, the arts. International coverage. Freelance work welcomed. *Length:* 1500 words. *Illustrations:* cartoons. *Payment:* by arrangement.

Take a Break (1990), John Dale, 25-27 Camden Road, London NW1 9LL   *tel* 0171-284 0909   *fax* 0171-284 3778.
46p. W. Lively, tabloid women's weekly. True life features, celebrities, health and beauty, family, travel; short stories (up to 1500 words); lots of puzzles. *Payment:* by arrangement. *Illustrated.*

tate: The Art Magazine (1993), Tim Marlow, Blueprint Media Ltd, Christ Church, Cosway Street, London NW1 5NJ *tel* 0171-262 2622 *fax* 0171-706 4811.
£2.95. 3 p.a. Independent visual arts magazine: features, news, interviews, reviews, previews and opinion pieces. *Length:* up to 5000 words. *Illustrations:* colour and b&w photos, but usually commissioned. *Payment:* negotiable.

The Tatler (1709), Jane Procter, Vogue House, Hanover Square, London W1R 0AD *tel* 0171-499 9080 *fax* 0171-409 0451.
£2.50. M. Smart society magazine favouring sharp articles, profiles, fashion and the arts. *Illustrations:* colour, b&w, but all commissioned.

The Teacher (1872), Mitch Howard, National Union of Teachers, Hamilton House, Mabledon Place, London WC1H 9BD *tel* 0171-380 4708 *fax* 0171-387 8458.
Free to NUT members. 8 p.a. Articles, features and news of interest to all those involved in the teaching profession. *Length:* 750 words. *Payment:* NUJ rates to NUJ members.

Telegraph & Argus (1868), Perry Austin-Clarke, Hall Ings, Bradford, West Yorkshire BD1 1JR *tel* (01274) 729511 *fax* (01274) 723634.
28p. D. Evening paper – news, articles and features relevant to or about the people of West Yorkshire. *Length:* up to 1000 words. *Illustrations:* line, half-tone, colour. *Payment:* features from £15; line from £5, b&w photos from £14.40, colour photos from £19.50.

Television (1950), Reed Business Publishing Ltd, Quadrant House, The Quadrant, Sutton, Surrey SM2 5AS *tel* 0181-652 8120 *fax* 0181-652 8956.
£2.35. M. Articles on the technical aspects of domestic TV and video equipment, especially servicing, long-distance television, constructional projects, satellite TV, video recording, teletext and viewdata, test equipment, monitors. *Payment:* by arrangement. *Illustrations:* photos and line drawings for litho.

Tempo, Calum MacDonald, Boosey & Hawkes, Music Publishers, Ltd, 295 Regent Street, London W1R 8JH *tel* 0171-580 2060 *fax* 0171-436 5675.
£2.50. Q. (£13.00 p.a.) Authoritative articles about 2000-4000 words on contemporary music. *Payment:* by arrangement. *Illustrations:* music type, occasional photographic or musical supplements.

Tennis World, Alastair McIver, Presswatch Ltd, The Spendlove Centre, Enstone Road, Charlbury, Oxford OX7 3PQ *tel* (01608) 811446.
£2.00. M. Tournament reports, topical features, personality profiles, instructional articles. *Length:* 600-1500 words. *Payment:* by arrangement. *Illustrations:* line, half-tone, colour.

TGO (The Great Outdoors) Magazine (1978), Cameron McNeish, Caledonian Magazines Ltd, 7th Floor, The Plaza Tower, East Kilbride, Glasgow G74 1LW *tel* (01355) 246444 · *fax* (01355) 263013.
£2.25. M. (£26.00 p.a.) Articles on walking or lightweight camping in specific areas, preferably illustrated. *Length:* 1200-1800 words. *Payment:* by arrangement. *Illustrations:* colour, cartoons.

that's life! (1995), Janice Turner, H. Bauer Publishing, 7th Floor, St Martin's House, 140 Tottenham Court Road, London W1 9LN *tel* 0171-388 6268; *Mercury* 19059412 *fax* 0171-388 6112.
45p. W. Dramatic true life stories about women. *Length:* average 1000 words. *Illustrations:* colour photos and cartoons. *Payment:* £650.

The Mag! (1995), Karen Ellison, Specialist Publications (UK) Ltd, Clifton Heights, Triangle West, Clifton, Bristol BS8 1EJ *tel* (0117) 9251696 *fax* (0117) 9251808.

39p. Bi-M. Short features on health, beauty, gardening, home improvements; celebrity interviews and human interest stories; short fiction. *Length:* approx. 800 words. *Illustrations:* colour transparencies, artwork and cartoons. *Payment:* £200 per feature; £200 for illustrations.

Theology (1920), Ann Loades, Theology Department, Abbey House, Palace Green, Durham DH1 3RS   *tel* 0191-374 2052.
£2.50. Bi-M. Articles and reviews on theology, ethics, Church and Society. *Length:* up to 3500 words. *Payment:* none.

Therapy Weekly (1974 as **Therapy**), Carol Harris, Macmillan Magazines Ltd, Porters South, 4-6 Crinan Street, London N1 9SQ   *tel* 0171-833 4000   *fax* 0171-843 4744.
Free to NHS and local authority therapists. W. (£42.50 p.a.) Articles of interest to chartered physiotherapists, occupational therapists and speech and language therapists. Guidelines to contributors available. *Send proposals only* initially. *Length:* up to 1000 words. *Illustrations:* colour and b&w photos, line, cartoons. *Payment:* by arrangement.

Third Way (1977), St Peters, Sumner Road, Harrow, Middlesex HA2 4BX   *tel* 0181-423 8494   *fax* 0181-423 5367.
£2.90. 10 p.a. Aims to present biblical perspectives on a wide range of current issues, e.g. sociology, politics, education, economics, industry and the arts. *Payment:* for articles: on publication.

This Caring Business (1985), Michael J. Monk, 1 St Thomas' Road, Hastings, East Sussex TN34 3LG   *tel* (01424) 718406   *fax* (01424) 718460.
£50.00 p.a. M. Specialist contributions relating to the commercial aspects of nursing and residential care, including hospitals. *Payment:* £75 per 1000 words. *Illustrations:* line, half-tone.

This England (1968), Roy Faiers, PO Box 52, Cheltenham, Glos. GL50 1YQ   *tel* (01242) 577775.
£3.20. Q. Articles on towns, villages, traditions, customs, legends, crafts of England; stories of people. *Length:* 250-2000 words. *Payment:* £20 per page and pro rata. *Illustrations:* line, half-tone, colour.

The Times (1785), Peter Stothard, 1 Pennington Street, London E1 9XN   *tel* 0171-782 5000   *telex* 262141   *fax* 0171-782 5436.
30p. D. 40p. Sat. Ind. Outside contributions considered from (1) experts in subjects of current interest; (2) writers who can make first-hand experience or reflection come readably alive. *No preliminary letter* is required, but telephone call to appropriate section editor is recommended. *Length:* up to 1200 words. **The Times Magazine,** Nicholas Wapshott. Free with Sat. paper. Features. *Illustrated.*

The Times Educational Supplement, Patricia Rowan, Admiral House, 66-68 East Smithfield, London E1 9XY   *tel* 0171-782 3000   *fax* 0171-782 3200.
90p. W. Articles on education written with special knowledge or experience; news items; books, arts and equipment reviews. Advisable to check with features, news or picture editor before submitting. *Illustrations:* suitable photos and drawings of educational interest, cartoons. *Payment:* standard rates, or by arrangement.

Times Educational Supplement Scotland (1965), Willis Pickard, 37 George Street, Edinburgh EH2 2HN   *tel* 0131-220 1100   *fax* 0131-220 1616.
90p. W. Articles on education, preferably 1100 words, written with special knowledge or experience. News items about Scottish educational affairs. *Illustrations:* line, half-tone. *Payment:* by arrangement.

Times Higher Education Supplement (1971), Auriol Stevens, Admiral House, 66-68 East Smithfield, London E1 9XY   *tel* 0171-782 3000   *fax* 0171-782 3300.

£1.00. W. Articles on higher education written with special knowledge or experience, or articles dealing with academic topics. Also news items. *Illustrations:* suitable photos and drawings of educational interest. *Payment:* by arrangement.

The Times Literary Supplement, Ferdinand Mount, Admiral House, 66-68 East Smithfield, London E1 9XY   *tel* 0171-782 3000   *dx* 98956 WAPPING   *fax* 0171-782 3100.

£1.90. W. Will consider poems for publication, literary discoveries and articles, particularly of an opinionated kind, on literary and cultural affairs. *Payment:* by arrangement.

Titbits (1881), Leonard Holdsworth, Caversham Communications, 2 Caversham Street, London SW3 4AH   *tel/fax* 0171-351 4995.

£1.20. M. Human interest articles; also show business, pop stars and medical, especially men's interest. No fiction. *Illustrations:* colour transparencies and photos, cartoons. *No* b&w. *Payment:* details on application.

Today's Golfer (1988), Neil Pope, EMAP Pursuit Publishing Ltd, Bretton Court, Bretton, Peterborough PE3 8DZ   *tel* (01733) 264666   *fax* (01733) 267198.

£2.60. M. Features and articles on golf. *Payment:* £150 per 1000 words. *Illustrations:* line, half-tone, colour.

Today's Horse (1990), Toni Cadden, Peenhill Ltd, 64 Great Eastern Street, London EC2A 3QR   *tel* 0171-739 5052   *fax* 0171-739 5053.

£1.75. M. 'For riding enthusiasts and horse lovers everywhere.' Articles, features and photo guides on all aspects of riding and horse care. *Length:* up to 1500 words. *Illustrations:* colour and b&w photos, line drawings. *Payment:* £60 per 1000 words; £5-£50 for illustrations.

Today's Runner (1985), Victoria Tebbs, EMAP Pursuit Publishing, Bretton Court, Bretton, Peterborough PE3 8DZ   *tel* (01733) 264666   *fax* (01733) 267198.

£2.20. M. Practical articles on all aspects of running lifestyle, especially road running training and events, and advice on health, fitness and injury. *Illustrations:* colour photos, cartoons. *Payment:* by negotiation.

Together with Children (1956), Mrs Pam Macnaughton, The National Society, Church House, Great Smith Street, London SW1P 3NZ   *tel* 0171-222 1672   *fax* 0171-233 2592.

£1.50. M. (£13.50 p.a.) Short, practical or topical articles and resources dealing with all forms of children's Christian education and all-age learning and worship. *Length:* up to 1200 words. *Illustrations:* line, half-tone. *Payment:* by arrangement.

Top of the Pops Magazine (1995), Peter Loraine, BBC Worldwide, 80 Wood Lane, London W12 0TT   *tel* 0181-576 3254   *fax* 0181-576 3267.

£1.25. M. Fun, lively and humorous articles on pop music aimed at fans of the television show aged 12-17 – *mostly commissioned*. *Length:* 700-1000 words (features). *Payment:* £200 per 1000 words.

Top Santé Health & Beauty (1993), Presse Publishing Ltd, 17 Radley Mews, Kensington, London W8 6JP   *tel* 0171-938 3033   *fax* 0171-938 5464.

£1.80. M. Articles, features and news on all aspects of health and beauty. Ideas welcome. *Length:* one-two pages. *Illustrations:* colour photos and drawings. *Payment:* £200 per 1000 words; illustrations by arrangement.

Toy Trader (1908), David Coombs, Turret Group plc, Turret House, 171 High Street, Rickmansworth, Herts WD3 1SN   *tel* (01923) 777000   *fax* (01923) 771297.
£52.00 p.a. M. Trade journal specialising in anything to do with games and toys, circulated to manufacturers and retailers. *Length:* by negotiation. *Illustrations:* cartoons. *Payment:* by negotiation.

Traveller (1970), Wexas Ltd, 45 Brompton Road, London SW3 1DE   *tel* 0171-581 4130   *telegraphic address* Wexas, London SW3   *telex* 297155 WEXAS G   *fax* 0171-581 1357.
£39.58 p.a. Q. Features usually based on long-haul and offbeat destinations, with a particular emphasis on cultural or anthropological angles. Recent features include: Mask-making in Mali; The Skeleton Coast of Namibia; New Year in Laos. *Length:* 1000-2000 words. *Illustrations:* first-class transparencies. *Payment:* £125 per 1000 words; colour £25 (£50 cover).

The Trefoil, Gillian Ellis, C.H.Q., The Guide Association, 17-19 Buckingham Palace Road, London SW1W 0PT   *tel* 0171-834 6242   *fax* 0171-828 8317.
Q. Official Journal of The Trefoil Guild. Articles on the activities of the Guild in the UK and overseas and on the work of voluntary organisations. *Length:* not more than 500 words. No fiction. *Illustrations:* photos. No *payment*.

Tribune, Editor: Mark Seddon; Reviews Editor: Caroline Rees, 308 Gray's Inn Road, London WC1X 8DY   *tel* 0171-278 0911.
£1.00. W. Political, literary, with Socialist outlook. Informative articles (about 700 words), news stories (250-300 words). No unsolicited reviews or fiction. *Payment:* by arrangement. *Illustrations:* cartoons and photos.

Trout and Salmon (1955), Sandy Leventon, EMAP Pursuit Publishing Ltd, Bretton Court, Bretton Centre, Peterborough PE3 8DZ   *tel* (01733) 264666   *fax* (01733) 263294.
£2.10. M. Articles of good quality with strong trout or salmon angling interest. *Length:* 400-2000 words, accompanied if possible by colour transparencies or good-quality colour prints. *Payment:* by arrangement. *Illustrations:* line, colour transparencies and prints, cartoons.

Trucking International (1983), Richard Simpson, A & S Publishing, Messenger House, 35 St Michael's Square, Gloucester GL1 1HX   *tel* (01452) 307181   *fax* (01452) 307170.
£1.80. M. For truck drivers, owner-drivers and small fleet operators: news, articles, features and technical advice. *Length:* 750-2500 words. *Illustrations:* mostly 35 mm colour transparencies. *Payment:* by negotiation.

TV Times, Liz Murphy, IPC Magazines Ltd, 10th Floor, King's Reach Tower, Stamford Street, London SE1 9LS   *tel* 0171-261 7000   *fax* 0171-261 7777.
60p. W. Features with an affinity to ITV, BBC1, BBC2, Channel 4, satellite and radio personalities and television generally. *Length:* by arrangement. *Photographs:* commissioned only. *Payment:* by arrangement.

Twinkle, D.C. Thomson & Co. Ltd, Albert Square, Dundee DD1 9QJ   *tel* (01382) 223131   *fax* (01382) 322214; and 185 Fleet Street, London EC4A 2HS   *tel* 0171-242 5086   *fax* 0171-404 5694.
50p. W. Picture stories, features and comic strips. Drawings in colour for gravure. Special encouragement to promising writers and artists. *Payment:* on acceptance.

The Unesco Courier (1948), Bahgat Elnadi, Adel Rifaat, Unesco, 1 rue Miollis, 75732 Paris Cedex 15, France   *tel* (1) 45 68 47 15   *telegraphic address* Unesco, Paris   *fax* (1) 45 66 92 70.
£17.00 p.a. Monthly in 30 language editions plus braille editions in French,

English, Spanish and Korean. Illustrated feature articles in the fields of science, culture, education and communication; promotion of international understanding; human rights. *Length:* 2000 words. *Illustrations:* colour and b&w photos, drawings, graphs, maps.

The Universe (1860), Joe Kelly, 1st Floor, St James's Buildings, Oxford Street, Manchester M1 6FP   *tel* 0161-236 8856   *fax* 0161-236 8530.
50p. W. Newspaper and review for Catholics. News stories, features and photos on all aspects of Catholic life required; also cartoons. MSS should not be submitted without sae. *Payment:* by arrangement.

Vanity Fair, The Condé Nast Publications Ltd, Vogue House, Hanover Square, London W1R 0AD   *tel* 0171-499 9080   *fax* 0171-499 4415. London Editor: Henry Porter   *tel* 0171-221 6228   *fax* 0171-221 6269.
£2.00. M. Style, media and politics for grown-up readers. *No* unsolicited MSS or illustrations. *Payment:* by arrangement. *Illustrated.*

The Vegan (1944), Richard Farhall, The Vegan Society, Donald Watson House, 7 Battle Road, St Leonards-on-Sea, East Sussex TN37 7AA   *tel* (01424) 427393   *fax* (01424) 717064.
£1.75. Q. Articles on animal rights, nutrition, cookery, agriculture, Third World, health. *Length:* approx. 1500 words. *Payment:* by arrangement. *Illustrations:* photos, cartoons, line drawings – foods, animals, livestock systems, crops, people, events; colour for cover.

Video Camera (1989), Philip Lattimore, W.V. Publications & Exhibitions Ltd, 57-59 Rochester Place, London NW1 9JU   *tel* 0171-485 0011   *fax* 0171-482 6249.
£2.40. M. Technique articles on how to use camcorders, especially for specific tricks or events. Material *mostly commissioned. Length:* 800-1000 words. *Illustrations:* colour photos, cartoons, diagrams. *Payment:* £90 per 1000 words; £90 per page for illustrations.

Viz (1979), Chris Donald, House of Viz, PO Box 1PT, Newcastle upon Tyne NE99 1PT.
£1.40. 6 p.a. Cartoons, cartoon scripts, articles. *Illustrations:* half-tone, line, cartoons. *Payment:* £300 per page (cartoons).

Vogue, Alexandra Shulman, Vogue House, Hanover Square, London W1R 0AD   *tel* 0171-499 9080   *telex* 27338 VOLON G   *fax* 0171-408 0559.
£2.80. M. Fashion, beauty, health, decorating, art, theatre, films, literature, music, travel, food and wine. *Length:* articles from 1000 words. *Illustrated.*

The Voice (1982), Annie Stewart, 370 Coldharbour Lane, London SW9 8PL   *tel* 0171-737 7377   *fax* 0171-274 8994.
65p. W. News stories, general and arts features of interest to black readers. *Illustrations:* colour and b&w photos, cartoons. *Payment:* £100 per 1000 words; £20-£35 for illustrations.

Voice Intelligence Report (1972), Ann Morris, 15A Lowndes Street, London SW1X 9EY   *tel* 0171-235 5966   *fax* 0171-259 6694.
£18.00. Q. (£48.00 p.a.) Background intelligence reports on the Press, media, Parliament, European Parliament, banking, diplomats, Saudi Arabia and the Arab Gulf countries, with specific reference to Middle East. All material commissioned. *Write* for specimen copy. *Illustrations:* none.

Vox (1990), Alan Lewis, IPC Magazines Ltd, 25th Floor, King's Reach Tower, Stamford Street, London SE1 9LS   *tel* 0171-261 6312   *fax* 0171-261 5627.
£2.20. M. Music and movies, aimed at 18-35 market – interviews, non-interview features, reviews. *Illustrations:* colour and b&w photos; commissioned illustrations and cartoons. *Payment:* by negotiation.

Wales on Sunday (1989), Thomson House, Havelock Street, Cardiff CF1 1XR *tel* (01222) 583583 *fax* (01222) 583725.
55p. W. Ind. General interest articles preferably with a Welsh connection, suitable for use in the national Sunday newspaper of Wales which offers comprehensive news, features and entertainments coverage at the weekend, with a particular focus on events in Wales.

Wanderlust (1993), Lyn Hughes, PO Box 1832, Windsor SL4 5YG *tel* (01753) 620426.
£2.50. Bi-M. Features on independent and special-interest travel. Send sae for 'Guidelines for contributors'. *Length:* up to 2500 words. *Illustrations:* colour (send stocklist first). *Payment:* by arrangement.

War Cry (1879), Captain Charles King, 101 Queen Victoria Street, London EC4P 4EP *tel* 0171-236 5222 *fax* 0171-236 3491.
20p. W. (£25.54 p.a. UK) Voluntary contributions; puzzles. *Illustrations:* line and photos, cartoons. Published by The Salvation Army.

Wasafiri (1984), Susheila Nasta, Queen Mary & Westfield College, English Department, Mile End Road, London E1 4NS *tel* 0171-775 3120.
£12.00 p.a. Bi-A. (£16.00 p.a. institutions) Published at University of London. Short stories, poetry, reviews, essays on literature and film. Submit MSS in duplicate, with an sae. *Illustrations:* b&w photos. *Payment:* none.

Waterways World (1972), Hugh Potter, Waterway Productions Ltd, Kottingham House, Dale Street, Burton-on-Trent, Staffs. DE14 3TD *tel* (01283) 564290.
£1.95. M. Feature articles on all aspects of inland waterways in Britain and abroad, including historical material; factual and technical articles preferred. No short stories or poetry. Send sae for 'Notes for WW Contributors'. *Payment:* £37 per 1000 words. *Illustrations:* colour transparencies or prints, line.

Wedding and Home (1985), IPC Magazines Ltd, King's Reach Tower, Stamford Street, London SE1 9LS *tel* 0171-261 7471 *fax* 0171-261 7459.
£3.10. Bi-M. Financial, travel, home and style, fashion and beauty, emotional, humour. Approach in writing. *Length:* 500-1500 words. *Illustrations:* colour and b&w photos. *Payment:* by negotiation.

The Weekly Journal (1992), Barbara Campbell, Positive Time & Space Ltd, 71A Wentworth Street, London E1 7TD *tel* 0171-247 5577 *fax* 0171-247 1727.
70p. W. Features, news, interviews, arts, society, business from an African Caribbean, multicultural perspective. *Length:* 300-3000 words. *Illustrations:* half-tone, cartoons. *Payment:* negotiable.

The Weekly News, D.C. Thomson & Co. Ltd, Albert Square, Dundee DD1 9QJ *tel* (01382) 223131; 137 Chapel Street, Manchester M3 6AA *tel* 0161-834 5122; 144 Port Dundas Road, Glasgow G4 0HZ *tel* 0141-332 9933; and 185 Fleet Street, London EC4A 2HS *tel* 0171-242 5086.
40p. W. Real-life dramas of around 2000 words told in the first person. Non-fiction series with lively themes or about interesting people. Keynote throughout is strong human interest. Joke sketches. *Illustrations:* cartoons. *Payment:* on acceptance.

Weight Watchers Magazine, Bloomsbury House Ltd, The Old School House, East Lodge Lane, Enfield, Middlesex EN2 8AS *tel/fax* 0181-366 9501.
£1.50. 8 p.a. Features page – health, beauty, news, astrology; food-orientated articles; success stories. *All material commissioned. Length:* ½-3 pages. *Illustrations:* colour photos and cartoons. *Payment:* by arrangement.

West Lancashire Evening Gazette (1929), Managing Editor: Philip Welsh, Blackpool Gazette & Herald Ltd, PO Box 20, Preston New Road, Blackpool FY4 4AU *tel* (01253) 839999 *fax* (01253) 694152.

27p. Mon.-Sat. Local news and articles of general interest, with photos if appropriate. *Length:* varies. *Payment:* on merit.

West Africa, Managing Editor: Kaye Whiteman, 43-45 Coldharbour Lane, London SE5 9NR　*tel* 0171-737 2946　*fax* 0171-978 8334.
£1.70. W. Weekly summary of West African news, with articles on political, economic and commercial matters, and on all matters of general interest affecting West Africa; also book reviews. Covers Ghana, Nigeria, Sierra Leone, The Gambia, French-speaking African States, former Portuguese West Africa, Liberia, South Africa, Namibia and Zaire. *Length:* articles about 1200 words. *Payment:* as arranged. *Illustrations:* half-tone.

Western Daily Press (1858), Ian Beales, Bristol United Press Ltd, Temple Way, Bristol BS99 7HD　*tel* (0117) 926 0080　*fax* (0117) 929 0971.
30p. D. National, international or West Country topics for features or news items, from established journalists, with or without *illustrations. Payment:* by negotiation.

The Western Mail (1869), Neil Fowler, Thomson House, Cardiff CF1 1XR　*tel* (01222) 223333　*fax* (01222) 583652.
32p. D. Ind. Articles of political, industrial, literary or general and Welsh interest are considered. *Illustrations:* topical general news and feature pictures, cartoons. *Payment:* according to value; special fees for exclusive news.

The Western Morning News (1860), Barrie Williams, Brest Road, Derriford, Plymouth PL6 5AA　*tel* (01752) 765500　*fax* (01752) 765535.
32p. D. Articles of 600-800 words, plus illustrations, considered on West Country subjects.

What Car? (1973), Mark Payton, Haymarket Motoring Magazines Ltd, 38-42 Hampton Road, Teddington, Middlesex TW11 0JE　*tel* 0181-943 5044　*fax* 0181-943 5959.
£2.85. M. Road tests, buying guide, consumer stories and used car features. *No* unsolicited material. *Illustrations:* colour and b&w photos, line drawings. *Payment:* by negotiation.

What's on TV (1991), Mike Hollingsworth, IPC Magazines Ltd, 10th Floor, King's Reach Tower, Stamford Street, London SE1 9LS　*tel* 0171-261 7769　*fax* 0171-261 7739.
45p. W. Features on TV programmes and personalities. *All material commissioned. Length:* up to 500 words. *Illustrations:* colour and b&w photos, cartoons. *Payment:* by agreement.

When Saturday Comes (1986), Andy Lyons, When Saturday Comes Ltd, 4th Floor, 2 Pear Tree Court, London EC1R 0DS　*tel* 0171-251 8595　*fax* 0171-490 1598.
£1.40. M. Features on football from the fans' perspective. Read the magazine for style first. *Length:* 500-2000 words. *Illustrations:* colour and b&w photos, occasional illustrations. *Payment:* £50-£100 for words; £50-£75 for illustrations.

Wisden Cricket Monthly (1979), David Frith, 6 Beech Lane, Guildford, Surrey GU2 5ES　*tel* (01483) 32573　*fax* (01483) 33153.
£2.50. M. Cricket articles of general interest. *Length:* up to 1000 words. *Payment:* by arrangement. *Illustrations:* half-tone, colour.

Woman (1937), Carole Russell, IPC Magazines Ltd, King's Reach Tower, Stamford Street, London SE1 9LS　*tel* 0171-261 5000　*fax* 0171-261 5997.
55p. W. Practical articles of varying length on all subjects of interest to women. No unsolicited fiction. *Payment:* by arrangement. *Illustrations:* colour transparencies, photos, sketches, cartoons.

Woman Alive (formerly **Christian Woman**) (1991), Elizabeth Proctor, Herald House Ltd, 96 Dominion Road, Worthing, West Sussex BN14 8JP *tel* (01903) 821082 *fax* (01903) 821081.
£1.60. M. Aimed at women aged 25-45. Celebrity interviews, topical features, Christian issues, 'Day in the life of' profiles of women in interesting occupations, Christian testimonies, fashion, beauty, health, crafts. Unsolicited material should include colour slides or b&w photos. *Length:* fillers 200-300 words, 'Day in the life of'/testimonies 750 words, interviews/features 1200 words. *Illustrations:* humorous photos, cartoons. *Payment:* by negotiation.

Woman and Home (incorporating **Living**) (1926), Orlando Murrin, IPC Magazines Ltd, King's Reach Tower, Stamford Street, London SE1 9LS *tel* 0171-261 5000 (and ask for relevant department) *fax* 0171-261 7346.
£1.50. M. Centres on the personal and home interests of the lively-minded woman with or without career and family. Articles dealing with fashion, beauty, leisure pursuits, gardening; things to buy and make for the home; features on people and places. Fiction: complete stories from 1000-5000 words in *length*. *Illustrations:* commissioned colour photos and sketches. *Please note:* non-commissioned work is rarely accepted and regrettably cannot be returned.

The Woman Journalist (1894), Barbara Haynes, 59 Grace Avenue, Maidstone, Kent ME16 0BS.
Free to members. 3 p.a. Periodical of the Society of Women Writers and Journalists. Short articles of interest to professional writers. *Payment:* none.

Woman's Journal (1927), Deirdre Vine, IPC Magazines Ltd, King's Reach Tower, Stamford Street, London SE1 9LS *tel* 0171-261 6622 *fax* 0171-261 7061.
£2.00. M. Magazine devoted to the looks and lives of intelligent women aged 30 plus: interviews and articles (1000-2000 words) dealing with topical subjects and personalities; fashion, beauty and health, food and houses. *Illustrations:* full colour, line and wash, first-rate photos. *Payment:* by arrangement.

Woman's Own, Keith McNeill, IPC Magazines Ltd, King's Reach Tower, Stamford Street, London SE1 9LS *tel* 0171-261 5474.
55p. W. Modern women's magazine aimed at the 20-35 age group. No unsolicited features; no unsolicited fiction accepted except for annual short story competition. *Illustrations:* colour and b&w: interior decorating and furnishing, fashion. Address work to relevant department editor. *Payment:* by arrangement.

Woman's Realm (1958), IPC Magazines Ltd, King's Reach Tower, Stamford Street, London SE1 9LS *tel* 0171-261 5000.
55p. W. Lively general interest weekly magazine. Articles on celebrities, topical subjects, cookery, fashion, beauty, home. Human interest real-life features; dramatic emotional stories, hard-hitting news stories, strong adventure and chilling ghost/supernatural stories. (Regretfully, no unsolicited features or fiction accepted.) *Payment:* by arrangement. *Illustrated.*

Woman's Story, Nexus Special Interests, Nexus House, Boundary Way, Hemel Hempstead, Herts. HP2 7ST *tel* (01442) 66551.
£1.75. Q. Contemporary stories, women's experiences, 4500-7000 words. *No unsolicited MSS considered at present.*

Woman's Weekly (1911), Olwen Rice, IPC Magazines Ltd, King's Reach Tower, Stamford Street, London SE1 9LS *tel* 0171-261 5000 *fax* 0171-261 6322.
50p. W. Lively, family-interest magazine. One serial, averaging 4000 words, each instalment of strong romantic interest, and several short stories of 1000-

2500 words of general emotional interest. Celebrity and strong human interest features; also inspirational and entertaining personal stories. *Payment:* by arrangement. *Illustrations:* full colour fiction illustrations, small sketches and photos.

Women's Art Magazine Heidi Reitniaier, Women's Art Library, Fulham Palace, Bishops Avenue, London SW6 6EA   *tel* 0171-731 7618   *fax* 0171-384 1110. £2.75. Bi-M. Interviews, book reviews and exhibition reviews on the work of contemporary and historical women artists. *Material mostly commissioned. Length:* up to 3000 words. *Illustrations:* b&w photos, line drawings. *Payment:* £30 per 1000 words; none for illustrations.

The Woodworker, Paul Richardson, Nexus Special Interests Ltd, Nexus House, Boundary Way, Hemel Hempstead, Herts. HP2 7ST   *tel* (01442) 66551   *fax* (01442) 66998.
£2.25. M. For the craft and professional woodworker. Practical illustrated articles on cabinet work, carpentry, wood polishing, wood turning, wood carving, rural crafts, craft history, antique and period furniture; also wooden toys and models, musical instruments; timber procurement, conditioning, seasoning; tool, machinery and equipment reviews. *Payment:* by arrangement. *Illustrations:* line drawings and photos.

Work Study, John Heap, Leeds Metropolitan University Learning Support Services, Calverley Street, Leeds LS1 3HE   *tel* (0113) 283 2600   *fax* (0113) 283 3123.
£349.00. 7 p.a. Authoritative articles on all aspects of work study including work measurement, method study, O&M, industrial engineering, payment systems. *Length:* 2000-4000 words. *Payment:* by arrangement. *Illustrations:* line, half-tone.

Workbox (1984), Linda Fancourt, Ebony, Trevithick House, Moorswater, Liskeard, Cornwall PL14 4LH   *tel* (01579) 340100   *fax* (01579) 340200.
£1.60. Bi-M. Features, of any length, on all aspects of needlecrafts. *No* 'how-to' articles. Send sae with enquiries and submissions. *Illustrations:* good b&w photos and colour transparencies; also line drawings. *Payment:* by agreement.

World Fishing (1952), Martin Gill, Oban Times Ltd, Royston House, Caroline Park, Edinburgh EH5 1QT   *tel* 0131-551 2942   *fax* 0131-551 2938.
£35.00 p.a. M. International journal of commercial fishing. Technical and management emphasis on catching, processing, farming and marketing of fish and related products; fishery operations and vessels covered worldwide. *Length:* 1000-2000 words. *Payment:* by arrangement. *Illustrations:* photos and diagrams for litho reproduction.

World Bowls, Keith Hale, 44 Oak Street, Southport, Lanc. PR8 6DD   *tel* (01704) 549054   *fax* (01704) 548900.
The official magazine of The English Bowling Association, The English Indoor Bowling Association, The English Women's Bowling Association and The English Women's Indoor Bowling Association. £1.95. M. Bowls related stories and features relating to indoor and outdoor bowls. *Illustrations:* colour transparencies and photos. *Payment:* by negotiation.

The World of Embroidery, The Embroiderers' Guild, PO Box 42B. East Molesey, Surrey KT8 9BB   *tel* 0181-943 1229.
£3.75. 6 p.a. (£22.50 p.a.) Articles on historical and contemporary embroidery by curators, artists and craftsmen; exhibition and book reviews; saleroom report; diary of events. *Illustrations:* line, half-tone, colour. *Payment:* by arrangement.

The World of Interiors (1981), Min Hogg, The Condé Nast Publications Ltd, Vogue House, Hanover Square, London W1R 0AD   *tel* 0171-499 9080   *fax* 0171-493 4013.
£2.90. M. All material commissioned: send synopsis/visual reference for article ideas. *Length:* 1000-1500 words. *Illustrations:* colour photos. *Payment:* £400 per 1000 words; photos from £100.

World Soccer (1960), Keir Radnedge, IPC Magazines Ltd, King's Reach Tower, Stamford Street, London SE1 9LS   *tel* 0171-261 5737   *fax* 0171-261 7474.
£2.00. M. Articles, features, news concerning football, its personalities and worldwide development. *Length:* 600-2000 words. *Illustrations:* colour and b&w photos, cartoons. *Payment:* by arrangement.

The World Today (1945), Graham Walker, The Royal Institute of International Affairs, Chatham House, 10 St James's Square, London SW1Y 4LE   *tel* 0171-957 5700   *fax* 0171-957 5710.
£2.50. M. Objective and factual articles on current questions of international affairs. *Length:* about 3000 words. *Payment:* £50 each article.

World's Children (1920), Lotte Hughes, Save the Children, 17 Grove Lane, London SE5 8RD   *tel* 0171-703 5400   *fax* 0171-708 2508.
Sent free to regular donors. Q. The magazine of Save the Children. Articles on child welfare and rights, related to Save the Children's work overseas and in the UK. *No* unsolicited features. *Length:* 500 words. *Payment:* by arrangement. *Illustrations:* colour and b&w photos.

Writers' Forum (1993), John Benton, 9/10 Roberts Close, Moxley, Wednesbury, West Midlands WS10 8SS   *tel* (01902) 497514.
£14.50 p.a. Q. Welcomes fillers and articles on any aspect of the craft and business of writing; *no* fiction or poetry (except for winners of the annual Open Writing Competition). *Length:* 300-1000 words. *Payment:* £6-£8 per 1000 words, pro rata more for fillers.

Writers' Monthly (1984), Alan L. Williams, 29 Turnpike Lane, London N8 0EP   *tel* 0181-342 8879   *fax* 0181-347 8847.
£37.50 p.a. M. Articles and features of interest to the freelance writer, author and playwright. Regular competitions and close links with literary agents. *Payment:* by negotiation. *Illustrations:* b&w.

Writers News (1989), Richard Bell, PO Box 4, Nairn IV12 4HU   *tel* (01667) 454441   *fax* (01667) 454401.
£41.60 p.a. (£36.60 p.a. CC/DD). M. News, competitions and articles on all aspects of writing. *Length:* 800-1500 words. *Illustrations:* line, half-tone. *Payment:* by arrangement.

Writing Magazine (1992), Richard Bell, PO Box 4, Nairn IV12 4HU   *tel* (01667) 454441   *fax* (01667) 454401.
£2.25. Bi-M. (free to subscribers of *Writers News*) Articles on all aspects of writing. *Length:* 800-1500 words. *Illustrations:* line, half-tone. *Payment:* by arrangement.

Writing Women (1981), Linda Anderson, Cynthia Fuller, Andrea Badenoch, Debbie Taylor, Unit 14, Hawthorn House, Forth Banks, Newcastle upon Tyne NE1 3SG.
£3.00. Poems, short stories. *Payment:* £25 per poem or per 1000 words.

Xenos (1990), S.V. Copestake, 29 Prebend Street, Bedford MK40 1QN   *tel* (01234) 349067.
£3.45. Bi-M. (£16.50 p.a.) Stories: sci-fi, fantasy, horror, occult, humour, detective, suspense, ripping yarns. *No gore, romance, domestic, or*

pornographic/experimental material. Annual short story competition with cash prizes: closing date 31 May. MSS must be well presented, accompanied by an sae or IRC and submitted one at a time. *Length:* 2000-10,000 words. Occasional *payment.*

Yachting Monthly (1906), Geoff Pack, IPC Magazines Ltd, King's Reach Tower, Stamford Street, London SE1 9LS   *tel* 0171-261 6040   *fax* 0171-261 7555.
£2.50. M. Technical articles, up to 2250 words, on all aspects of seamanship, navigation, the handling of sailing craft, and their design, construction and equipment. Well-written narrative accounts, up to 2500 words, of cruises in yachts. *Payment:* quoted on acceptance. *Illustrations:* b&w, colour transparencies, line or wash drawings, cartoons.

Yachting World (1894), Andrew Bray, IPC Magazines Ltd, King's Reach Tower, Stamford Street, London SE1 9LS   *tel* 0171-261 6800   *fax* 0171-261 6818.
£2.60. M. Practical articles of an original nature, dealing with sailing and boats. *Length:* 1500-2000 words. *Payment:* varies. *Illustrations:* colour transparencies, drawings, cartoons.

Yachts and Yachting (1947), Frazer Clark, 196 Eastern Esplanade, Southend-on-Sea, Essex SS1 3AB   *tel* (01702) 582245   *fax* (01702) 588434.
£2.10. F. Short articles which should be technically correct. *Payment:* by arrangement. *Illustrations:* line, half-tone, colour.

Yorkshire Evening Post (1890), C.H. Bye, PO Box 168, Wellington Street, Leeds LS1 1RF   *tel* (0113) 243 2701   *telex* 55425 YPOST G   *fax* (0113) 244 3430.
27p. Mon.-Sat. News stories and feature articles. *Illustrations:* colour and b&w, cartoons. *Payment:* by negotiation.

Yorkshire Evening Press (1882), Elizabeth Page, York and County Press, PO Box 29, 76-86 Walmgate, York YO1 1YN   *tel* (01904) 653051   *fax* (01904) 612853.
30p. D. Articles of North and East Yorkshire interest, humour, personal experience of current affairs. *Length:* 500-1000 words. *Payment:* by arrangement. *Illustrations:* line, half-tone, cartoons.

Yorkshire Gazette & Herald Series, Bob McMillan, PO Box 29, 76-86 Walmgate, York YO1 1YN   *tel* (01904) 653051   *fax* (01904) 611488.
30p. W. Stories, features and pictures of local interest. *Payment:* varies. *Illustrations:* line, half-tone, colour.

Yorkshire Life (1947), Tony Skinner, Town & County Magazines, Oyston Mill, Strand Road, Preston PR1 8UR   *tel* (01772) 722022   *fax* (01772) 736496.
£1.50. M. Topics of Yorkshire interest, with or without photos. *Length:* 200-500 words and 800-1500 words. *Payment:* varies. *Illustrations:* line, half-tone, colour.

Yorkshire Post (1754), Tony Watson, Wellington Street, Leeds LS1 1RF   *tel* (0113) 243 2701   *telex* 55245   *fax* (0113) 238 8537; *London office:* Ludgate House, 245 Blackfriars Road, SE1 9UY   *tel* 0171-921 5000.
32p. D. Authoritative and well-written articles on new topics or on topical subjects of general, literary or industrial interests. *Length:* 1200-1500 words. Contributions to *People*, a column about personalities in the news, are welcomed. *Illustrations:* photos and frequent pocket cartoons (single column width), topical wherever possible. *Payment:* by arrangement.

Yorkshire Ridings Magazine (1964), Winston Halstead, 33 Beverley Road, Driffield, Yorkshire YO25 7SD   *tel/fax* (01377) 253232.
£1.00. Bi-M. Articles exclusively about people, life and character of the three Ridings of Yorkshire. *Length:* up to 1500 words. *Payment:* approx. £30-£35 per published page. *Illustrations:* line, half-tone, colour.

You—see **Mail on Sunday.**

Young People Now (1989), Mary Durkin, National Youth Agency, 17-23 Albion Street, Leicester LE1 6GD   *tel* (0116) 247 1200   *fax* (0116) 247 1043. £2.00. M. (£22.80 p.a.) Informative articles, highlighting issues of concern to all those who work with young people – including youth workers, probation and social services, teachers and volunteers. Guidelines for contributors available on request.

Young Telegraph (1990), Damian Kelleher, Young Telegraph Ltd, 346 Old Street, London EC1V 9NQ   *tel* 0171-613 3376   *fax* 0171-613 3372. Free with Sat. *Daily Telegraph.* Short articles of interest to children aged 8-12 years. *Length:* 100-250 words. *Illustrations:* colour and b&w photos, cartoons. *Payment:* varies.

Your Dog (1994), Sarah Wright, EMAP Pursuit Publishing Ltd, Bretton Court, Bretton, Peterborough PE3 8DZ   *tel* (01733) 264666   *fax* (01733) 261984. £2.00. Bi-M. Articles and information of interest to dog lovers; features on all aspects of pet dogs. *Length:* approx. 1200 words. *Illustrations:* colour transparencies, prints and line drawings. *Payment:* £60 per 1000 words.

Your Garden (1993), Michael Pilcher, IPC Magazines Ltd, Westover House, West Quay Road, Poole, Dorset BH15 1JG   *tel* (01202) 680603 *fax* (01202) 674335. £1.80. M. Anything on gardening for the enthusiastic beginner. *Commissioned material only*; send brief synopsis of ideas. *Length:* 800-2000 words. *Illustrations:* colour photos and line. *Payment:* £100 per published 1000 words.

Yours (1973), Neil Patrick, Apex House, Oundle Road, Peterborough PE2 9NP   *tel* (01733) 555123   *fax* (01733) 898487. 70p. M. Features and news about/of interest to over-60s including nostalgia; short stories. *Study of magazine* essential; approach in writing. *Length:* articles up to 1000 words, short stories up to 1800 words. *Illustrations:* preferably colour transparencies/prints; will consider good b&w prints/line drawings, cartoons. *Payment:* at editor's discretion or by agreement.

YX (Youth Express) (1992), Gifty Tawiah, PO Box 405, Swindon, Wilts. SN1 1UZ   *tel* (01793) 514596   *fax* (01793) 514654. Free to secondary schools. 3 p.a. (termly) 'Hard'/environmental issues, music and sport, aimed at and mostly written by young people. *Length:* 300-400 words. *Illustrations:* cartoons. *Payment:* varies.

Zest (1994), Eve Cameron, National Magazine House, 72 Broadwick Street, London W1V 2BP   *tel* 0171-439 5000   *fax* 0171-439 5632. £1.95. Q. Lifestyle magazine with health and beauty at its core. *Commissioned material only:* health, fitness and beauty, features, news and shorts. *Length:* 50-2000 words. *Illustrations:* colour and b&w photos and line. *Payment:* £250 per 1000 words.

AUSTRALIA

Newspapers are listed under the towns in which they are published.

(Adelaide) Advertiser (1858), Rex Jory (acting editor), 121 King William Street, Adelaide, SA 5000   *tel* (08) 206 2220   *fax* (08) 206 3669; London: PO Box 481, 1 Virginia Street, E1 9BD   *tel* 0171-702 1355   *fax* 0171-702 1384. 70c Mon.-Fri., $1.00 Sat. Descriptive and news background material, 400-800 words, preferably with pictures; also cartoons.

(Adelaide) Sunday Mail (1912), K. Sullivan, 121 King William Street, Adelaide, SA 5000　*postal address* GPO Box 339, Adelaide, SA 5001　*tel* (08) 206 2796　*fax* (08) 206 3646.
$1.20. W.

Australasian Sporting Shooter, Ray Galea, Yaffa Publishing Group, 17-21 Bellevue Street, Surry Hills, NSW 2010　*tel* (02) 281 2333　*fax* (02) 281 2750.
$3.70. M. All aspects of game shooting, collecting, antiques, archery (associated with hunting), pistol shooting, clay target shooting, reloading, ballistics and articles of a technical nature. *Payment:* by arrangement.

Australian Angler's Fishing World, Jim Harnwell, Yaffa Publishing Group, 17-21 Bellevue Street, Surry Hills, NSW 2010　*tel* (02) 281 2333　*telex* AA 121887　*fax* (02) 281 2750.
$4.95. M. Rock, surf, stream, deep sea and game fishing, with comprehensive sections on gear, equipment and boats. *Payment:* by arrangement.

Australian Bookseller & Publisher (1921), Kim Hutchins, D.W. Thorpe, 18 Salmon Street, Port Melbourne, Victoria 3207　*tel* (03) 245 7370　*fax* (03) 245 7395.
$55.00 p.a. M. ($82.00 p.a. NZ/Asia; $93.00 p.a. USA/Canada; $99.00 p.a. UK/Europe).

The Australian Financial Review, Gregory Hywood, IBM Building, Level 25, 201 Sussex Street, Sydney 2001　*tel* (02) 282 2512　*fax* (02) 282 3137; London: 95 Fetter Lane, EC4A 1HE　*tel* 0171-242 0044　*fax* 0171-242 0066; New York: Suite 1002, 1500 Broadway, NY 10036　*tel* 212-398-9494.
$1.00. Mon.-Fri. Investment business and economic news and reviews; government and politics, production, banking, commercial, and Stock Exchange statistics; company analysis. General features in Friday *Weekend Review* supplement.

Australian Flying, James Ostinga, Yaffa Publishing Group, 17-21 Bellevue Street, Surry Hills, NSW 2010　*tel* (02) 281 2333　*fax* (02) 281 2750; London: Robert Logan, 64 The Mall, Ealing, W5 5LS　*tel* 0181-579 4836.
$5.25. 6 p.a. Appeals to pilots and owners of light and medium aircraft, as well as those associated with the aircraft industry. *Payment:* by arrangement.

Australian Geographic (1986), Howard Whelan, PO Box 321, Terrey Hills, NSW 2084　*tel* (02) 450 2344　*fax* (02) 450 2990.
$39.60 p.a. Q. (2-yr $79.20) Short articles and features about Australia, particularly life, technology and natural history in remote parts of the country. Material *mostly commissioned. Length:* articles, 300-800 words, features, 2000-3000 words. *Illustrations:* all commissioned. *Payment:* $500 per 1000 words; illustrations by negotiation.

Australian Home Beautiful (1913), W. Buttner, 32 Walsh Street, West Melbourne, Victoria 3003　*tel* (03) 320 7000　*fax* (03) 320 7410.
$4.20. M. Deals with home building, interior decoration, furnishing, gardening, cookery, etc. Short articles with accompanying photos with Australian slant accepted. *Preliminary letter* advisable. *Payment:* Australian average.

Australian House and Garden (1948), Stephanie King, 54 Park Street, Sydney, NSW 2000　*tel* (02) 282 8456　*fax* (02) 267 4912.
$4.50. M. Factual articles dealing with interior decorating, home design, gardening, wine, food. *Preliminary letter* essential. *Payment:* by arrangement. *Illustrations:* line, half-tone, colour.

Australian Journal of International Affairs, Dr Stephanie Lawson, Department of International Relations, RSPAS, Australian National University, Canberra, ACT 0200　*tel* (06) 249 2169　*fax* (06) 279 8010.

$34.00 p.a. Aus./NZ. 2 p.a. ($40.00 p.a. institutions Aus./NZ; other rates on application) Scholarly articles on international affairs. *Length:* 4000-7000 words. *Payment:* none.

The Australian Journal of Politics and History, Geoff Stokes and Ross Johnston, Department of History, University of Queensland, St Lucia, Queensland 4067 *tel* (07) 3365 3163 *fax* (07) 3365 1388.
$60.00. 3 p.a. (US $58.00, UK £33.00, inc. postage) Australian, Commonwealth, Asian, SW Pacific and international articles. Special feature: regular surveys of Australian Foreign Policy and State and Commonwealth politics. *Length:* 8000 words max. *Illustrations:* line, only when necessary. *Payment:* none.

Australian Photography (1950), Steve Packer, Yaffa Publishing Group, 17-21 Bellevue Street, Surry Hills, NSW 2010 *tel* (02) 281 2333 *fax* (02) 281 2750.
$3.95. M. Illustrated articles – picture-taking techniques, technical. *Length/illustrations:* 2000 words/colour and b&w prints or slides. *Payment:* $80 per page.

The Australian Quarterly (1929), Damian Grace, Ian Marsh, Australian Institute of Political Science, PO Box 145, Balmain, NSW 2041 *tel* (02) 810 5642 *fax* (02) 810 2406.
$55.00 p.a. individuals, $95.00 p.a. institutions. Q. ($65/$105 overseas) Peer-reviewed articles for the informed non-specialist on politics, law, economics, social issues, etc. *Length:* 3500 words preferred. *Payment:* none.

The Australian Way (1986), Brian Courtis, David Syme & Co. Ltd, 250 Spencer Street, Melbourne, Victoria 3000 *postal address* GPO Box 257c, Melbourne, Victoria 3001 *tel* (03) 601 2917 *fax* (03) 642 0852.
Free. M. Inflight magazine for Qantas Airways. Articles of international interest; profiles, third-person stories that use locations as a backdrop, pictorial essays and features on prominent Australians. *Length:* 800-1500 words. *Illustrations:* colour transparencies. *Payment:* by negotiation.

The Australian Women's Weekly, Nene King, Australian Consolidated Press Ltd, 54 Park Street, Sydney, NSW 2000 *tel* (02) 282 8000 *fax* (02) 267 4459.
$3.30. M. Fiction and features. *Length:* fiction 1000-10,000 words; features 750-2500 words plus colour or b&w photos. *Payment:* according to length and merit. *Fiction illustrations:* sketches by own artists and freelances.

(Brisbane) The Courier-Mail, C. Mitchell, Queensland Newspapers Pty Ltd, Campbell Street, Bowen Hills, Brisbane, Queensland 4006 *tel* (07) 3252 6011 *fax* (07) 3252 6696.
70c. D. Occasional topical special articles required. *Length:* 1000 words.

(Brisbane) Sunday Mail, Bob Gordon, Queensland Newspapers Pty Ltd, PO Box 130, Campbell Street, Bowen Hills, Brisbane, Queensland 4006 *tel* (07) 252 6011.
90c. W. Anything of general interest. *Length:* up to 1500 words. *Illustrations:* line, photos, b&w and colour, cartoons. *Payment:* by arrangement. Rejected MSS returned if postage enclosed.

The Bulletin with Newsweek, Lyndall Crisp, 54 Park Street, Sydney, NSW 2000 *tel* (02) 282 8200 *fax* (02) 267 4359.
$3.30. W. General interest articles, features; humour. *Length:* 750 words per page, max. 2100 words. *Illustrations:* colour photos and cartoons. *Payment:* $450 per 1000 words published; $100 colour cartoons and photos, according to size used.

Cleo (1972), Wendy Squires, Level 4, 54 Park Street, Sydney, NSW 2000 *tel* (02) 282 8617 *fax* (02) 267 4368.
$4.60. M. Articles (relationship, emotional, self-help) up to 3000 words, short quizzes. *Payment:* by negotiation.

Countryman, John Dare, 219 St Georges Terrace, Perth, Western Australia 6000 *tel* (09) 482 3322 *fax* (09) 482 3324.
70c. W. Agriculture, farming or country interest features and service columns. *Payment:* standard rates. *Illustrations:* line, half-tone, colour, cartoons.

Current Affairs Bulletin (1942), Managing Editor: Sue Phillips, CAB, 72 Bathurst Street, Sydney, NSW 2000 *tel* (02) 264 5726 *fax* (02) 267 7900.
$6.50. 6 p.a. ($40.00 p.a., $57.00 p.a. overseas) Authoritative well-documented articles on all national and international affairs: politics, economics, science, the arts, business and social questions. *Length:* 3000-5000 words. *Illustrations:* line, half-tone. *Payment:* none.

Dance Australia (1980), Karen van Ulzen, Yaffa Publishing Group, Box 606, GPO Sydney, NSW 2001 *tel* (02) 281 2333 *fax* (02) 281 2750.
$5.25. Bi-M. Articles and features on all aspects of dance in Australia. Material *mostly commissioned*, but will consider unsolicited contributions. *Length:* as appropriate. *Illustrations:* b&w photos, line drawings, cartoons. *Payment:* $150 per 1000 words; illustrations by negotiation.

Dolly (1970), Susie Pitts, 54 Park Street, Sydney, NSW 2000 *tel* (02) 282 8000 *fax* (02) 267 4911.
$3.50. M. Features on fashion, health and beauty, personalities, music, social issues and how to cope with growing up, etc. *Length:* not less than 1000 words. *Illustrations:* colour, b&w, line, cartoons. *Payment:* by arrangement.

Electronics Australia with ETI, Jamieson Rowe, PO Box 199, Alexandria, NSW 2015 *tel* (02) 9353 0620 *fax* (02) 9353 0613.
$5.50. M. Articles on technical television and radio, hi-fi, popular electronics, microcomputers and avionics. *Length:* up to 2000 words. *Payment:* by arrangement. *Illustrations:* line, half-tone, cartoons.

Elle (Australia) (1990), Deborah Thomas, 54 Park Street, Sydney, 2000 *tel* 61 2 282 8790 *fax* 61 2 267 4375.
$4.95. M. Profiles, news reports, cultural essays, fashion stories. *Length:* 300-3000 words. *Payment:* varies.

Geo Australasia (1978), Michael Hohensee, Geo Productions Pty Ltd, PO Box 1390, Chatswood, NSW 2057 *tel* (02) 411 1766 *fax* (02) 413 2689.
$7.95. Bi-M. ($55.00 p.a. surface mail; $85.00 p.a. airmail) Non-fiction articles on wildlife, adventure, culture and lifestyles, natural history and the environment in Australia, New Zealand, the Pacific and SE Asia. *Length:* 1500-3000 words. *Payment:* $600-$1500 by arrangement. *Illustrations:* photos, colour transparencies.

Guns Australia, Ray Galea, Yaffa Publishing Group Pty Ltd, 17-21 Bellevue Street, Surry Hills, NSW 2010 *tel* (02) 281 2333 *fax* (02) 281 2750.
$3.90. Bi-M. Articles, features, technical pieces, news. *All material commissioned. Length:* 2000 words. *Illustrations:* colour slides, b&w photos. *Payment:* $50 per page.

Herald of the South (1925), GPO Box 283, Canberra, ACT 2601 *tel/fax* (02) 970 6710.
$28.00 p.a. Q. Baha'i magazine with particular emphasis on religious approach to unity. Features, fiction and non-fiction. *Length:* up to 3500 words. *Illustrations:* colour and b&w photos. *Payment:* by negotiation.

HQ Magazine (1989), Shona Martyn, 54 Park Street, Sydney, NSW 2000   *tel*
(02) 282 8260   *telex* 120514 AA   *fax* (02) 267 3616.
$5.95. Q. General interest features and profiles for a literate readership.
Length: 1500-5000 words. *Illustrations:* colour and b&w photos. *Payment:* by
negotiation.

(Launceston) Examiner, Rod Scott, Box 99A, PO Launceston, Tasmania
7250   *tel* (003) 315 111   *telegraphic address* Examiner, Launceston   *fax* (003)
347 328.
65c. D. Accepts freelance material. *Payment:* by arrangement.

(Melbourne) Age, Bruce Guthrie, David Syme & Co. Ltd, 250 Spencer Street,
Melbourne, Victoria 3000   *tel* (03) 600 4211   *telex* 30331/30376/30449   *fax*
(03) 670 7514; London: 95 Fetter Lane, EC4A 1HE.
80c Mon.-Fri., $1.20 Sat. Independent liberal morning daily; room occasionally
for outside matter. An illustrated weekend magazine and literary review is
published on Saturday; accepts occasional freelance material.

(Melbourne) Australasian Post, News Editor: Denis Williams, Southdown Press,
32 Walsh Street, PO Box 1292K GPO, West Melbourne, Victoria 3003   *tel*
(03) 320 7000.
$2.20. W. Opening for casual contributions of topical factual illustrated articles
of Australian interest. General appeal. *Payment:* by arrangement.

(Melbourne) Herald Sun, Alan Oakley, HWT Tower, 40 City Road, Southbank,
Victoria 3006   *tel* (03) 9292 1999   *fax* (03) 9292 2105.
70c Mon.-Fri., 90c Sat., $1.20 Sun. Accepts freelance articles, preferably with
illustrations. *Length:* up to 750 words. *Illustrations:* half-tone, line, cartoons.
Payment: on merit.

(Melbourne) The Sunday Age (1989), Jill Baker, 250 Spencer Street, Melbourne,
Victoria 3000   *tel* (03) 600 4211   *fax* (03) 602 1856; London: 95 Fetter Lane,
EC4A 1HE   *tel* 0171-242 0044   *fax* 0171-242 0066.
70c. W. Features. *Length:* 500-2000 words. *Payment:* by arrangement.

(Melbourne) Sunday Herald Sun, Alan Howe, HWT Tower, 40 City Road,
Southbank, Victoria 3006   *tel* (03) 9292 2000   *telex* 30104/30124   *fax* (03)
9292 2080.
90c. W. Accepts freelance articles, preferably with illustrations. *Length:* up to
2000 words. *Illustrations:* colour. *Payment:* on merit.

Mode Australia (1973), Karin Upton Baker, ACP Publishing Pty Ltd, 54 Park
Street, Sydney, NSW 2001   *tel* (02) 282 8703   *fax* (02) 267 4456.
$5.50. Bi-M. Fashion, health and beauty, celebrity news. *Length:* 3000 words.
Illustrations: colour and b&w photos. *Payment:* $500 per 1000 words; $150.

Modern Boating (1965), Mark Rothfield, 180 Bourke Road, Alexandria, NSW
2015   *tel* (02) 693 6666   *fax* (02) 317 4615.
$5.95. M. Articles on all types of boats and boating. *Payment:* $130-$200 per
1000 words. *Illustrations:* half-tone, colour.

New Idea (1902), F. Wingett, 32 Walsh Street, PO Box 1292K GPO, Melbourne,
Victoria 3001   *tel* (03) 320 7000   *fax* (03) 320 7439.
$2.50. W. General interest women's magazine; news stories, features, fashion,
services, short stories of general interest to women of all ages. *Length:* stories,
500-4000 words: articles, 500-2000 words. *Payment:* on acceptance.

New Weekly (1993), Juliet Ashworth, 54 Park Street, Sydney, NSW 2000   *tel*
(02) 282 8285   *fax* (02) 264 6005.
$2.40. W. News and features on celebrities, food, health, fashion and sport.
Length: varies. *Illustrated. Payment:* by negotiation.

New Woman (1989), Josephine Brouard, 213 Miller Street, North Sydney, NSW 2059 *tel* (02) 9956 1000 *fax* (02) 9956 1088.
$4.50. M. Self-development for the thirty-something woman: articles, features, fashion, beauty, health, reviews and book excerpts. *Material mostly commissioned. Length:* average 1200 words. *Payment:* 50c a word. *Illustrated.*

Overland, John McLaren, PO Box 14146, Melbourne, Victoria 8001 *tel* (03) 9380 1152 *fax* (03) 9380 2586.
$8.00. Q. Literary and general. Australian material preferred. *Payment:* by arrangement. *Illustrations:* line, half-tone, cartoons.

People Magazine (national weekly news-pictorial), D. Naylor, 54 Park Street, Sydney, NSW 2000 *tel* (02) 282 8743 *fax* (02) 267 4365.
$2.70. W. Mainly people stories. Photos depicting exciting happenings, glamour, show business, unusual occupations, rites, customs. *Payment:* $300 per page, text and photos.

(Perth) Sunday Times (1897), Don Smith, 34 Stirling Street, Perth, Western Australia 6000 *tel* (09) 326 8326 *fax* (09) 221 1121.
$1.10. W. Topical articles to 800 words. *Payment:* on acceptance.

(Perth) The West Australian (1833), Paul Murray, 219 St Georges Terrace, Perth, Western Australia 6000 *tel* (09) 482 3111 *telegraphic address* Westralian, Perth *fax* (09) 324 1416.
70c Mon.-Fri., $1.20. Sat. Articles and sketches about people and events in Australia and abroad. *Length:* 300-700 words. *Payment:* Award rates or better. *Illustrations:* line, half-tone.

Poetry Australia (1964), John Millett, South Head Press, The Market Place, Berrima, NSW 2577 *tel* (048) 771 421.
$40 p.a. Q. Previously unpublished new poetry, and criticism. *Payment:* copy of magazine.

Quadrant, Robert Manne, 46 George Street, Fitzroy, Victoria 3065 *postal address* PO Box 1495, Collingwood, Victoria 3066 *tel* (03) 9417 6855 *fax* (03) 9416 2980.
$5.00. M. Articles, short stories, verse, etc. *Prose length:* 2000-5000 words. *Illustrations:* cartoons. *Payment:* minimum $90 articles/stories, $60 reviews, $40 poems; illustrations by arrangement.

Reader's Digest (Australian and New Zealand editions), Bruce Heilbuth, 26-32 Waterloo Street, Surry Hills, NSW 2010 *tel* (02) 690 6111 *fax* (02) 699 8165.
$3.95. M. Articles on Australian/New Zealand subjects by commission only. No unsolicited MSS accepted. *Length:* 2500-5000 words. *Payment:* up to $5000 per article; brief filler paragraphs, $50-$250. *Illustrations:* half-tone, colour.

Redoubt (1988), Managing Editor: Sally Clarke, Faculty of Communication, University of Canberra, PO Box 1, Belconnen, ACT 2616 *tel* (06) 201 2332 *fax* (06) 201 5300.
$8.50. Bi-A. Literary magazine: mainly poetry, short stories, reviews, articles. *Length:* short poetry; stories/articles, up to 3000 words; reviews up to 1000 words. *Illustrations:* b&w line and photos. *Payment:* by arrangement.

The Sun-Herald, Andrew Clark, GPO Box 506, Sydney, NSW 2001 *tel* (02) 282 2822 *fax* (02) 282 2151; London: John Fairfax (UK) Ltd, 95 Fetter Lane, EC4A 1HE *tel* 0171-242 0044.
$1.00. W. Topical articles to 1000 words; sections on politics, social issues, show business, finance and fashion. *Payment:* by arrangement.

(Sydney) The Daily Telegraph, Editor-in-Chief: John Hartigan, News Limited, 2 Holt Street, Surry Hills, NSW 2010   *tel* (02) 288 3000   *fax* (02) 288 3481.
70c D., 90c Sat. Modern feature articles and series of Australian or world interest. *Length:* 1000-2000 words. *Payment:* according to merit/length.

The Sydney Morning Herald (1831), Editor-in-Chief: John Alexander, PO Box 506, Sydney, NSW 2001   *tel* (02) 282 2858; London: 95 Fetter Lane, EC4A 1HE   *tel* 0171-242 0044   *fax* 0171-242 0066.
90c. D. Saturday edition has pages of literary criticism and also magazine articles, plus glossy colour magazine. Topical articles 600-4000 words. *Payment:* varies, but minimum $100 per 1000 words. *Illustrations:* all types.

Woman's Day, Bob Cameron, 54-58 Park Street, Sydney, NSW 2000   *tel* (02) 282 8000   *fax* (02) 267 2150.
$2.50. W. National women's magazine; news, show business, fiction, fashion, general articles, cookery, home economy.

CANADA

Newspapers are listed under the towns in which they are published.

ArtsAtlantic (1977), Joseph Sherman, Confederation Centre of the Arts, 145 Richmond Street, Charlottetown, Prince Edward Island C1A 1J1   *tel* 902-628-6138   *fax* 902-566-4648.
$29.95 for 4 issues. 3 p.a. ($45.95 for 8 issues) Features and reviews on the art history of Atlantic Canada, the work of contemporary artists and the ideas and issues affecting Canadian culture. *No* fiction or poetry. *All material commissioned*; send enquiries (plus CV and samples of published work). *Length:* reviews, 300-900 words, features, 1000-3000 words. *Illustrations:* colour and b&w. *Payment:* $75 per review, features 15c per word to $250 maximum; illustrations by negotiation.

The Beaver: Exploring Canada's History, Christopher Dafoe, Canadian National History Society, Suite 478, 167 Lombard Avenue, Winnipeg, Manitoba R3B 0T6   *tel* 204-988-9300   *fax* 204-988-9309.
$27.50 p.a. Bi-M. ($34.50 p.a. elsewhere) Articles, historical and modern, on Canadian history. *Length:* 1500-5000 words, with illustrations. *Payment:* on acceptance, approx. 10c per word. *Illustrations:* b&w and colour photos or drawings.

Books in Canada (1971), Norman Doidge, 427 Mount Pleasant Road, Toronto, Ontario M4S 2L8   *tel* 416-489-4755   *fax* 416-489-6045.
$3.95. 9 p.a. Commissioned reviews, informed criticism and articles on Canadian literary scene. *Query first* – do not send unsolicited material. *Payment:* 12c per word.

C Magazine (1972), Joyce Mason, PO Box 5, Station B, Toronto, Ontario M5T 2T2   *tel* 416-539-9495   *fax* 416-539-9903.
US$8.25. Q. Arts and artists' projects, features, reviews. Accept submissions. *Length:* features, varies; reviews, 500 words. *Illustrations:* b&w photos. *Payment:* $250-$500 features, $100 reviews.

Canadian Author, Welwyn Wilton Katz, PO Box 419, Campbellford, Ontario K0L 1L0   *tel* 705-653-0323   *fax* 705-653-0593.

$18.00 p.a. individual, $30.00 p.a. corporate. Q. (add $40.00 p.a. outside Canada) Published by Canadian Authors Association. Interested in an international view on writing techniques, profiles, interviews, freelance opportunities for Canadian writers. *Query only. Payment:* $30 per printed page.

The Canadian Forum, Duncan Cameron, 251 Laurier Avenue W, Suite 804, Ottawa, Ontario K1P 5J6 *tel* 613-230-3078 *fax* 613-233-1458.
$3.00. 10 p.a. ($23.54 p.a.) Articles on public affairs and the arts; book reviews. *Length:* up to 2500 words. *Payment:* varies. *Illustrations:* line and photos.

Canadian Interiors, Sheri Craig, Crailer Communications, 360 Dupont Street, Toronto, Ontario M5R 1V9 *tel* 416-966-9944 *fax* 416-966-9946.
$34.24 p.a. 8 p.a. (US$75.00 p.a. elsewhere) Articles on all aspects of the interior design industry. *Illustrations:* half-tone, colour.

Canadian Literature (1959), E.M. Kröller, 1855 West Mall, University of British Columbia, Vancouver, BC V6T 1Z2 *tel* 604-882-2780 *fax* 604-822-9452.
$15.00 plus postage. Q. Articles on Canadian writers and writing in English and French. *Length:* up to 5000 words. *Payment:* $5 per printed page.

Canadian Yachting (1974), Graham Jones, Kerrwil Publications Ltd, 395 Matheson Boulevard East, Mississauga, Ontario L4Z 2H2 *tel* 905-890-1846 *fax* 905-890-5769.
$2.95. 7 p.a. Features, news and views. *Query letters preferred. Length:* regulars, 1000-2000 words; features, 1800-2700 words. *Illustrations:* line, halftone, colour, cartoons. *Payment:* up to $350 regulars, up to $500 features; $50-$250 line, $30-$100 photos, $200 cover shots.

Chatelaine, Mildred Istona, 777 Bay Street, Toronto, Ontario M5W 1A7 *tel* 416-596-5425.
$2.00. M. Women's interest articles; Canadian angle preferred. *Payment:* on acceptance; from $1000.

The Dalhousie Review, Dr Alan Andrews, Dalhousie University Press Ltd, Sir James Dunn Building, Suite 314, Halifax, NS B3H 3J5 *tel* 902-494-2541.
$8.50 (plus postage). Q. ($30.00 p.a., $80.00 for 3 years; $40.00/$100.00 outside Canada) Articles on literary, political, historical, philosophical and social topics; fiction; verse; book reviews. *Length:* prose, normally not more than 5000 words; verse, preferably less than 40 words. *Payment:* $1 per printed page for fiction; $3 for 1st poem, $2 for each subsequent poem (per issue). Contributors receive two copies of issue and 15 offprints of their work. Usually not more than two stories and about 10 or 12 poems in any one issue.

Equinox (1982), Jim Cormier, 100-25 Sheppard Avenue West, North York, Ontario M2N 6S7 *tel* 416-733-7600 *fax* 416-218-3633.
$3.95. Bi-M. ($22.95 p.a. Canada; $29.00 p.a. USA; $35.00 elsewhere) Magazine of discovery in science, human cultures, technology and geography. Accepts articles on hard science topics (*length:* 100-500 words); welcomes queries (2-3-page outline) for specific assignments. *No* phone queries please. *Illustrations:* colour transparencies. *Payment:* by arrangement.

The Fiddlehead (1945), Don Mckay, Campus House, University of New Brunswick, PO Box 4400, Fredericton, NB E3B 5A3 *tel* 506-453-3501.
$9.00. Q. Reviews, poetry, short stories. *Payment:* approx. $10-$12 per printed page.

(Hamilton) The Spectator (1846), Publisher, Patrick J. Collins, 44 Frid Street, Hamilton, Ontario L8N 3G3 *tel* 905-526-3333.
75c Mon.-Fri., $1.50 Sat. Articles of general interest, political analysis and background; interviews, stories of Canadians abroad. *Length:* 800 words maximum. *Payment:* rate varies.

Inuit Art Quarterly (1986), Marybelle Mitchell, 2081 Merivale Road, Nepean, Ontario K2G 1G9 *tel* 613-224-8189 *fax* 613-224-2907.
$6.25. Q. Features, news and reviews on the Inuit art world. Freelance contributors are expected to have a thorough knowledge of the arts. *Length:* varies. *Illustrations:* colour and b&w photos and line. *Payment:* by arrangement; illustrations $50.

Journal of Canadian Studies, Michèle Lacombe, James Conley, Kerry Cannon, Trent University, Peterborough, Ontario K9J 7B8 *tel* 705-748-1279 *fax* 705-748-1655 *e-mail* jcb_rec@trentu.ca
$28.00 p.a. Q. ($45.00 p.a. institutions) Major academic review of Canadian studies. Articles of general as well as scholarly interest on history, politics, literature, society, arts. *Length:* 7000-10,000 words.

The Malahat Review (1967), Derk Wynand, University of Victoria, PO Box 1700, Victoria, BC V8W 2Y2 *tel* 604-721-8524.
$25.00 p.a. Q. ($35.00 p.a. overseas) Short stories, poetry, short plays, reviews, some graphics. *Payment:* $25 per magazine page. *Illustrations:* half-tone.

Performing Arts & Entertainment in Canada (PA&E) (1961), Karen Bell, 104 Glenrose Avenue, Toronto, Ontario M4T 1K8 *tel* 416-484-4534 *fax* 416-484-6214.
$8.00 p.a. Q. ($14.00 p.a. elsewhere) Feature articles on Canadian theatre, music, dance and film artists and organisations; technical articles on scenery, lighting, make-up, costumes, etc. *Length:* 800-1500 words. *Payment:* $150-$250, one month after publication. *Illustrations:* b&w photos, colour slides.

Photo Life (1976), Jacques Thibault, Toronto-Dominion Centre, Suite 2550, Box 77, Toronto, Ontario M5K 1E7 *tel* 800-905-7468 *fax* 800-664-2739.
$3.95. 8 p.a. Covers all aspects of photography of interest to amateur and professional Canadian photographers. *Length:* 1500-2500 words. *Illustrations:* colour and b&w photos. *Payment:* by arrangement.

Quebec Chronicle Telegraph (1764), Karen Macdonald, Quebec Chronicle-Telegraph Inc., 3484 chemin Ste-Foy, Quebec City, Quebec G1X 1S8 *tel* 418-650-1764.
40c. W. Covers local events within English community in Quebec City. Some feature articles.

Quill & Quire (1935), Scott Anderson, 70 The Esplanade, Suite 210, Toronto, Ontario M5E 1R2 *tel* 416-360-0044 *fax* 416-955-0794.
$45.00 p.a. (outside Canada 1-yr $75, 2-yr $134.72). 12 p.a. Articles of interest about the Canadian book trade. *Payment:* from $100. *Illustrations:* line, half-tone. Subscription includes *Canadian Publishers Directory*, 2 p.a.

Reader's Digest, Alexander Farrell, 215 Redfern Avenue, Montreal, Quebec H3Z 2V9 *tel* 514-934-0751.
$2.49. M. Original articles on all subjects of broad general appeal, thoroughly researched and professionally written. Outline or query *only*. *Length:* 3000 words approx. *Payment:* from $2700. Also previously published material. *Illustrations:* line, half-tone, colour.

(Toronto) The Globe and Mail (1844), Publisher: Roger Parkinson, Editor-in-Chief: William Thorsell, 444 Front Street West, Toronto, Ontario M5V 2S9.
50c. D. Unsolicited material considered. *Payment:* by arrangement.

Toronto Life (1967), John Macfarlane, 59 Front Street East, Toronto, Ontario M5E 1B3 *tel* 416-364-3333 *fax* 416-861-1169.
$2.50. M. Articles, profiles on Toronto and Torontonians. *Illustrations:* line, half-tone, colour.

Toronto Star (1892), One Yonge Street, Toronto, Ontario M5E 1E6   *tel* 416-367-2000; London: Level 4A, PO Box 495, Virginia Street, E1 9XY   *tel* 0171-833 0791.
30c Mon.-Fri., $1.00 Sat., 75c Sun. Features, life, world/national politics. *Payment:* by arrangement.

(Vancouver) Province (1898), Editor-in-Chief: Michael Cooke, 2250 Granville Street, Vancouver, BC V6H 3G2   *tel* 604-732-2007   *fax* 604-732-2378.
60c Mon.-Fri., $1.00. Sun.

Vancouver Sun, Editor-in-Chief: John Cruickshank, 2250 Granville Street, Vancouver, BC V6H 3G2   *tel* 604-732-2318   *fax* 604-732-2323; London: Southam News, 4th Floor, 8 Bouverie Street, EC4Y 8AX   *tel* 0171-583 7322.
60c Mon.-Thu., $1.00 Fri., Sat. Saturday Review, arts magazine, accepts contributions. Travel, Op-Ed pieces considered. *Payment:* by arrangement.

Wascana Review of Contemporary Poetry & Short Fiction (1966), Kathleen Wall, c/o English Department, University of Regina, Regina, Sask. S4S 0A2   *tel* 306-585-4311   *fax* 306-585-4827.
$7.00 p.a. Bi-A. ($8.00 p.a. outside Canada) Criticism, short stories, poetry, reviews. Manuscripts from freelance writers welcome. *Length:* prose, not more than 6000 words; verse, up to 100 lines. *Payment:* $3 per page for prose; $10 per printed page for verse; $3 per page for reviews. Contributors also receive two free copies of the issue.

Windspeaker (1983), Debora Lockyer, 15001-112 Ave NW, Edmonton, Alberta, T5M 2V6   *tel* 403-455-2700   *fax* 403-455-7639.
M. ($36.00 p.a.) National newspaper by and about Aboriginal people: articles, features, news, guest editorials. Write for 'Freelancer's guidelines'. *Length:* 300-800 words. *Illustrations:* prefer colour prints. *Payment:* $3.00 per published column inch; $15-$50 per photo.

Winnipeg Free Press (1872), John Dafoe, PO Box 9500, Winnipeg, Manitoba R2X 3A2   *tel* 204-694-2022.
25c Mon.-Fri., $1.25 Sat., 35c Sun. Some freelance articles. *Payment:* $100.

THE REPUBLIC OF IRELAND AND NORTHERN IRELAND

Africa: St Patrick's Missions, Rev. Gary Howley, St Patrick's, Kiltegan, Co. Wicklow   *tel* (0508) 73233   *fax* (0508) 73281.
£5.00 p.a. 9 p.a. Articles of missionary and topical religious interest. *Length:* up to 1000 words. *Illustrations:* line, half-tone, colour

Belfast Telegraph (1870), 124-144 Royal Avenue, Belfast BT1 1EB   *tel* (01232) 321242   *fax* (01232) 554506/554540 (editorial only).
26p. D. Any material relating to Northern Ireland. *Payment:* by negotiation.

The Big Issues (1994), Niall Skelly, 110 Amien Street, Dublin 3   *tel* (01) 8553969.
£1.00. F. Articles, features and news on the homeless, unemployed and social issues, plus general articles and celebrity interviews. *Length:* 800-3000 words. *Payment:* negotiable.

Books Ireland (1976), Editor: Jeremy Addis, Features Editor: Shirley Kelly, 11 Newgrove Avenue, Dublin 4   *tel/fax* (01) 2692185.
£1.50. M. (exc Jan, Jul, Aug; £15.00 p.a.) Reviews of Irish-interest and Irish-author books, articles of interest to librarians, booksellers and readers. *Length:* 800-1400 words. *Payment:* £35 per 1000 words.

Church of Ireland Gazette (1885, New Series 1963), Rev. Canon C.W.M. Cooper, 36 Bachelor's Walk, Lisburn, Co. Antrim BT28 1XN *tel* (01846) 675743 *fax* (01846) 675743.
30p. W. Church news, articles of religious and general interest. *Length:* 600-1000 words. *Payment:* according to length and interest.

The Cork Examiner (1841), Brian Looney, 1-6 Academy Street, Cork *tel* (021) 272722 *telex* 76014 *fax* (021) 275477.
80p. D. Features. Material *mostly commissioned. Length:* 1000 words. *Payment:* by arrangement.

Cyphers (1975), Leland Bardwell, Pearse Hutchinson, Eiléan Ní Chuilleanáin, Macdara Woods, 3 Selskar Terrace, Dublin 6 *fax* (01) 4978866.
£6.00 for 3 issues. Poems, fiction, articles on literary subjects, translations. *Payment:* £10 per page.

Evening Herald, Paul Drury, 90 Middle Abbey Street, Dublin 1 *tel* (01) 8731333.
55p. D. Articles. *Payment:* by arrangement. *Illustrations:* line, half-tone, cartoons.

Fortnight. An Independent Review of Politics and the Arts (1970), John O'Farrell, Martin Crawford, 7 Lower Crescent, Belfast BT7 1NR *tel* (01232) 232353/311337/324141 *fax* (01232) 232650.
£1.80. M. Current affairs analysis, reportage, opinion pieces, cultural criticism, book reviews, poems. *Illustrations:* line, half-tone, cartoons. *Payment:* by arrangement.

The Furrow (1950), Rev. Ronan Drury, St Patrick's College, Maynooth, Co. Kildare *tel* (01) 6286215 *fax* (01) 7083908.
£1.50. M. Religious, pastoral, theological, social articles. *Length:* 3000 words. *Payment:* average £15 per page (450 words). *Illustrations:* line, half-tone.

Hot Press (1977), Niall Stokes, 13 Trinity Street, Dublin 2 *tel* (01) 6795077/ 67955091 *fax* (01) 6795097.
£1.25. F. High-quality, investigative stories, or punchily written offbeat pieces, of interest to 16-39-year-olds, including politics, music, sport, sex, religion – whatever's happening on the street. *Length:* varies. *Illustrations:* b&w photos, colour sometimes used. *Payment:* by negotiation.

Hotel and Catering Review, Frank Corr, Jemma Publications Ltd, Marino House, 52 Glasthule Road, Sandycove, Co. Dublin *tel* (01) 2800000 *fax* (01) 2801818.
£22.00 p.a. M. Short news and trade news pieces. *Length:* approx. 200 words. Features. *Payment:* £80 per 1000 words. *Illustrations:* half-tone, cartoons.

HU (The Honest Ulsterman) (1968), Tom Clyde, 49 Main Street, Greyabbey, County Down BT22 2NF.
£2.00. 3 p.a. Poetry, short stories, reviews, critical articles, poetry pamphlets. *Payment:* by arrangement.

IMAGE (1974), Jane McDonnell, 22 Crofton Road, Dún Laoghaire, Co. Dublin *tel* (01) 2808415 *fax* (01) 2808309.
£1.50. M. Short stories of a high literary standard and of interest to women. *Length:* up to 3000 words. Interviews with actors, writers, etc.; human interest stories. *Payment:* by arrangement.

In Dublin (1976), Siobhán Cronin, 6-7 Camden Place, Dublin 2 *tel* (01) 4784322 *fax* (01) 4781055.
£1.50. F. Dublin-related news features, oddball items, humour and interviews. *Length:* 500-2000 words. *Payment:* £80 per 1000 words. *Illustrated.*

Ireland of the Welcomes, Letitia Pollard, Irish Tourist Board, Baggot Street Bridge, Dublin 2   *tel* (01) 6024000   *fax* (01) 6615775.
£2.00. Bi-M. Irish items with cultural, sporting or topographical background designed to arouse interest in Irish holidays. Mostly commissioned – *preliminary letter* preferred. *Length:* 1200-1800 words. *Payment:* by arrangement. *Illustrations:* scenic and topical, cartoons.

Ireland's Eye (1979), Lynn Industrial Estate, Mullingar, Co. Westmeath   *tel* (044) 48868.
70p. M. Articles, features, short stories with an Irish flavour; cartoons. *Length:* 1200-2000 words. *Payment:* £10-£15; £4 for cartoons.

Ireland's Own (1902), Austin Channing and Margaret Galvin, North Main Street, Wexford   *tel* (053) 22155   *fax* (053) 23801.
50p. W. Short stories: non-experimental, traditional with an Irish orientation (2000-2500 words); articles of interest to Irish readers at home and abroad (750-1000 words); general and literary articles (750-1000 words). Monthly special bumper editions, each devoted to a particular seasonal topic. Jokes and funny stories always welcome; suggestions for new features considered. *Payment:* varies according to quality and length. *Illustrations:* photos, cartoons.

Irish Farmers Journal (1948), Matthew Dempsey, Irish Farm Centre, Bluebell, Dublin 12   *tel* (01) 4501166   *fax* (01) 4520876.
£1.00. W. Readable, technical articles on any aspect of farming. *Length:* 700-1000 words. *Payment:* £100-£150 per article. *Illustrated.*

Irish Independent, Vincent Doyle, Independent House, 90 Middle Abbey Street, Dublin 1   *tel* (01) 8731666   *fax* (01) 8720304/8731787.
85p. D. Special articles on topical or general subjects. *Length:* 700-1000 words. *Payment:* editor's estimate of value.

Irish Journal of Medical Science (1st series 1832, 6th series January 1926, Volume 164, 1996), Royal Academy of Medicine, 6 Kildare Street, Dublin 2   *tel* (01) 6767650   *fax* (01) 6611684.
£15.00. M. (EU £60.00 post free; other rates on application) Official Organ of the Royal Academy of Medicine in Ireland. Original contributions in medicine, surgery, midwifery, public health, etc.; reviews of professional books, reports of medical societies, etc. *Illustrations:* line, half-tone, colour.

Irish Medical Times, Dr John O'Connell, 15 Harcourt Street, Dublin 2   *tel* (01) 4757461   *fax* (01) 4757467.
£1.90. W. (£96.90 p.a.) Medical articles, also humorous articles with medical slant. *Length:* 850-1000 words. *Payment:* £60 per 1000 words. *Illustrations:* line, half-tone, colour, cartoons.

The Irish News and Belfast Morning News (1855), Tom Collins, 113-117 Donegall Street, Belfast BT1 2GE   *tel* (01232) 322226   *fax* (01232) 337505.
28p. D. Articles of historical and topical interest. *Payment:* by arrangement.

Irish Printer (1974), Frank Corr, Jemma Publications Ltd, 52 Glasthule Road, Sandycove, Co. Dublin   *tel* (01) 2800000   *fax* (01) 2801818.
£22.00 p.a. M. Technical articles and news of interest to the printing industry. *Length:* 800-1000 words. *Illustrations:* colour and b&w photos. *Payment:* £80 per 1000 words; photos £30.

Irish Times, Conor Brady, 11-15 D'Olier Street, Dublin 2   *tel* (01) 6792022   *telex* 93639   *fax* (01) 6719407.
75p. D. Mainly staff-written. Specialist contributions (800-2000 words) by commission on basis of ideas submitted. *Payment:* at editor's valuation. *Illustrations:* photos and line drawings.

IT (Irish Tatler), Sarah Foot, 126 Lower Baggot Street, Dublin 2 *tel* (01) 6623158 *fax* (01) 6619757.
£1.95. M. General interest women's magazine: beauty, interiors, fashion, cookery, current affairs, fiction, reportage and celebrity interviews. *Length:* 2000-4000 words. *Payment:* by arrangement.

Krino (1986), Editor: Gerald Dawe; associate editors: Aodan MacPoilin, Eve Patten, Jonathan Williams, PO Box 65, Dún Laoghaire, Co. Dublin.
£5.00. 2 p.a. Poetry; fiction; work-in-progress; critical prose mostly on commissioned basis. *Illustrations:* line, half-tone. *Payment:* none, but complimentary copies of the magazine.

Modern Woman (1984), Margot Davis, Meath Chronicle Ltd, Market Square, Navan, Co. Meath, Republic of Ireland *tel* (046) 21442 *fax* (046) 23565.
50p. M. Articles and features on a wide range of subjects of interest to women over the age of 18 (e.g. politics, religion, health and sex). *Length:* 200-1000 words. *Illustrations:* colour and b&w photos, line drawings and cartoons. *Payment:* NUJ rates.

The Nationalist and Munster Advertiser (1890), Tom Corr, Queen Street, Clonmel, Co. Tipperary *tel* (052) 22211.
85p. W. Requirements by arrangement. *Payment:* £22 per 1000 words. *Illustrations:* artwork.

News Letter (1737), Geoff Martin, 46-56 Boucher Crescent, Boucher Road, Belfast BT12 6QY *tel* (01232) 680000 *fax* (01232) 664412.
32p. D. Pro-Union.

Poetry Ireland/Éigse Éireann (1981), Liam O'Muirthile, Bermingham Tower, Upper Yard, Dublin Castle, Dublin 2 *tel* (01) 6714632 *fax* (01) 6714634.
£5.00. Q. Poetry, short lyric and sections from long poems, articles and reviews. *Payment:* by arrangement.

Portadown Times & Craigavon News (1859), David Armstrong, 14 Church Street, Portadown BT62 1HY *tel* (01762) 336111.
56p. W. Articles. *Payment:* NUJ rates.

Reality (1936), Rev. Gerry Moloney CSSR, Redemptorist Publications, Orwell Road, Rathgar, Dublin 6 *tel* (01) 4922488 *fax* (01) 4922654.
80p. M. Illustrated magazine for Christian living. Articles on all aspects of modern life, including family, youth, religion, leisure. Illustrated articles, b&w photos only. Short stories. *Length:* 1000-1500 words. *Payment:* by arrangement; average £25 per 1000 words.

The Songwriter (1967), James D. Liddane, International Songwriters Association, PO Box 46, Limerick City *tel* (061) 228837.
Available to members only as part of membership fee. M. Articles on songwriting and interviews with music publishers and recording company executives. *Length:* 400-5000 words. *Payment:* from £75 per page and by arrangement. *Illustrations:* photos.

The Star (1989), Gerard O'Regan, Independent Star Ltd, Star House, 62a Terenure Road North, Dublin 6w *tel* (01) 4901228 *fax* (01) 4902193/4902188.
55p. D (Mon-Sat). General articles relating to news and sport, and features. *Length:* 1000 words. *Illustrations:* colour photos. *Payment:* by negotiation.

Studies, An Irish quarterly review (1912), Rev. Noel Barber SJ, 35 Lower Leeson Street, Dublin 2 *tel* (01) 6766785 *fax* (01) 6762984.

£3.50. Q. General review of social comment, literature, history, the arts. Articles written by specialists for the general reader. Critical book reviews. *Preliminary letter. Length:* 3500 words.

The Sunday Business Post (1989), Damien Kiberd, Merchants House, 27-30 Merchants Quay, Dublin 8   *tel* (01) 6799777   *fax* (01) 6796496/6796498.
85p. W. Features on financial, economic and political topics; also lifestyle, media and science articles. *Illustrations:* colour and b&w photos, graphics, cartoons. *Payment:* by negotiation.

Sunday Independent, Aengus Fanning, Independent House, 90 Middle Abbey Street, Dublin 1   *tel* (01) 8731333   *fax* (01) 8721914.
£1.00. W. Special articles. *Length:* according to subject. *Illustrations:* topical or general interest, cartoons. *Payment:* at editor's valuation.

Sunday Life (1988), Martin Lindsay, 124 Royal Avenue, Belfast BT1 1EB   *tel* (01232) 264300   *fax* (01232) 554507.
45p. W. Items of interest to Northern Ireland Sunday tabloid readers. *Payment:* by arrangement. *Illustrations:* colour and b&w, cartoons.

The Sunday Tribune (1980), Peter Murtagh, Tribune Publications plc, 15 Lower Baggot Street, Dublin 2   *tel* (01) 6615555   *fax* (01) 6615302.
£1.00. W. Newspaper containing news (inc. foreign), articles, features and photo features. *Length:* 600-2800 words. *Illustrations:* colour and b&w photos and cartoons. *Payment:* £100 per 1000 words; £100 for illustrations.

Technology Ireland (1969), Mary Mulvihill and Tom Kennedy, Forbairt (Irish Science and Technology Agency), Glasnevin, Dublin 9   *tel* (01) 8082345   *fax* (01) 8367122.
£25.00 p.a. M. Articles, features, reviews and news on current science and technology. *Length:* 1500-2000 words. *Illustrations:* line, half-tone, colour. *Payment:* varies.

U magazine (1978), Maura O'Kiely, Smurfit Publications Ltd, 126 Lower Baggot Street, Dublin 2   *tel* (01) 6608264   *fax* (01) 6619757.
£1.50. M. Ireland's review for women today. Special reports, interviews, analysis, fashion, humour, travel, health, arts. Material *mostly commissioned. Length:* 1000 words. *Illustrations:* line, half-tone, colour. *Payment:* varies.

Ulster Grocer (1972), Brian McCalden, Greer Publications, 151 University Street, Belfast BT7 1HR   *tel* (01232) 231634   *fax* (01232) 325736.
£1.50. M. Topical features (500-1000 words) on agribusiness – retail and manufacturing – and exhibitions; news (200 words) with a Northern Ireland bias. All features commissioned; no speculative articles accepted. *Illustrations:* colour and b&w photos. *Payment:* features £75, news £30; photos £40.

Waterford News & Star, Peter Doyle, 25 Michael Street, Waterford   *tel* (051) 75566   *fax* (051) 55281.
80p. W. News articles. *Payment:* by arrangement. *Illustrations:* line, half-tone.

Woman's Way (1963), Celine Naughton, Smurfit Publications Ltd, 126 Lower Baggot Street, Dublin 2   *tel* (01) 6623158   *fax* (01) 6619757.
75p. W. Short stories, personality interviews, general features. *Length:* 1000-1500 words. *Payment:* £25-£100 approx. *Illustrations:* line, half-tone, colour.

The Word (1936), Fr Tom Cahill svd, Divine Word Missionaries, Maynooth, Co. Kildare   *tel* (01) 6289564/6286391   *fax* (01) 6289184.
50p. M. Catholic illustrated for the family. Illustrated articles of general interest up to 2000 words and good picture features. *Payment:* by arrangement. *Illustrations:* photos and large colour transparencies, cartoons.

NEW ZEALAND

Newspapers are listed under the towns in which they are published.

(Auckland) New Zealand Herald (1863), P.J. Scherer, PO Box 32, Auckland *tel* (09) 379-5050 *fax* (09) 366-1568.
60c. D. Topical and informative articles 800-1100 words. *Payment:* minimum $50-$150. *Illustrations:* colour negatives or prints.

(Auckland) Sunday News (1963), Suzanne Chetwin, 155 New North Road, Auckland *tel* (09) 302-1300 *fax* (09) 358-3003.
$1.20. W. Will consider anything. *Length:* varies. *Illustrations:* colour and b&w photos and line. *Payment:* depends on quality.

(Auckland) Sunday Star-Times, Michael Prain, News Media Auckland Ltd, PO Box 1409, Auckland *tel* (09) 379-7626.
$1.20. Sun.

(Christchurch) The Press, D.W.C. Wilson, Private Bag 4722, Christchurch *tel* (03) 379-0940 *fax* (03) 364-8238.
40c. D. Articles of general interest not more than 1000 words. *Illustrations:* photos and line drawings, cartoons. *Payment:* by arrangement.

Christchurch Star (1868), Mike Fletcher, Tuam Street, Christchurch *tel* (03) 379-7100 *fax* (03) 366-0180.
Free. Bi-W. Will consider freelance material, excluding travel; also cartoons.

(Dunedin) Otago Daily Times (1861), G.T. Adams, PO Box 181, Dunedin *tel* (03) 477-4760 *fax* (03) 477-1313.
60c. D. Any articles of general interest up to 1000 words, but preference is given to NZ writers. Topical illustrations and personalities. *Payment:* current NZ rates.

The Gisborne Herald (1874), Iain Gillies, PO Box 1143, 64 Gladstone Road, Gisborne *tel* (06) 867-2099 *telegraphic address* Herald, Gisborne.
12c. D. Topical features of local interest. *Length:* 1000-1500 words. *Payment:* by arrangement. *Illustrations:* bromides.

Hawke's Bay Herald Tribune, J.E. Morgan, PO Box 180, Karamu Road North, Hastings *tel* (06) 878-5155 *fax* (06) 876-0655.
60c. D. Limited requirements. *Payment:* $30 upwards for articles, $10 upwards for photos. *Illustrations:* web offset.

(Invercargill) The Southland Times (1862), C.A. Lind, PO Box 805, Invercargill *tel* (03) 218-1909 *telegraphic address* Times, Invercargill *fax* (03) 214-9905.
60c. D. Articles of up to 800 words on topics of Southland interest. *Payment:* by arrangement. *Illustrations:* line, half-tone, colour, cartoons.

Management, Carroll du Chateau, Profile Publishing, PO Box 5544, Auckland *tel* (09) 358-5455 *fax* (09) 358-5462.
$5.95. M. Articles on the practice of management skills and techniques, individual and company profiles, coverage of business trends and topics. A NZ/Australian angle or application preferred. *Length:* 2000 words. *Payment:* by arrangement; minimum 23c per word. *Illustrations:* photos, line drawings.

(Napier) The Daily Telegraph (1871), K.R. Hawker, PO Box 343, Napier *tel* (06) 835-4488 *fax* (06) 835-1129.
60c. D. Limited market for features. *Illustrations:* line, half-tone, colour. *Payment:* $50 upwards per 1000 words; $20 a picture.

The Nelson Mail, David Mitchell, PO Box 244, 15 Bridge Street, Nelson *tel* (03) 548-7079   *fax* (03) 546-2802.
40c. D. Features, articles on NZ subjects. *Length:* 500-1000 words. *Payment:* up to $100 per 1000 words. *Illustrations:* half-tone, colour.

(New Plymouth) The Daily News (1857), Murray Goston, PO Box 444, Currie Street, New Plymouth   *tel* (06) 758-0559   *fax* (06) 758-6849.
50c. D. Articles preferably with a Taranaki connection. *Payment:* by negotiation. *Illustrations:* half-tone, cartoons.

New Truth and TV Extra, News Media Auckland Ltd, Hedley Mortlock, 155 New North Road, Auckland, PO Box 1074   *tel* (09) 302-1300   *fax* (09) 309-2279.
$1.50. W. Bold investigative reporting, exposés. *Length:* 500-1000 words, preferably accompanied by photos. *Payment:* about $150 per 500 words, extra for photos.

New Zealand Farmer, Hugh Stringleman, NZ Rural Press Ltd, PO Box 4233, 300 Great South Road, Greenlane, Auckland 5   *tel* (09) 520-9451   *fax* (09) 520-9459.
F. Authoritative, simply written articles on new developments in livestock husbandry, grassland farming, cropping, farm machinery, marketing. *Length:* 500 words. *Payment:* $200 per 1000 words.

New Zealand Listener (1939), Jenny Wheeler, PO Box 7, Auckland 1   *tel* (09) 623-1002   *fax* (09) 623-1011.
$2.60. W. Topical features of NZ and international interest; also features related to television and radio programmes. *Length:* up to 2000 words. *Illustrations:* colour and b&w, cartoons. *Payment:* by arrangement.

New Zealand Woman's Day (1989), Louise Wright, Private Bag 92512, Wellesley Street, Auckland   *tel* (09) 373-5408   *fax* (09) 357-0978.
$2.95. W. Celebrity interviews, exclusive news stories, short stories, gossip. *Length:* 1000 words. *Illustrations:* colour transparencies; payment according to use. *Payment:* £400.

New Zealand Woman's Weekly (1932), Sarah-Kate Lynch, NZ Magazines Ltd (Wilson & Horton), Private Bag, Dominion Road, Auckland 3   *tel* (09) 638-8105   *fax* (09) 630-9128.
$2.60. W. Pictorial features. Illustrated articles of general, family, celebrity interest, particularly with a NZ slant. *Length:* articles 600-1200 words. *Payment:* by arrangement. *Illustrations:* b&w, colour.

Straight Furrow (1933), Susan Grant, PO Box 715, Wellington   *tel* (04) 473-7269   *fax* (04) 473-1081.
$1.60. F. Factual news and features of interest to the farming/rural sector. *Length:* 500 words news, 1000 words features. *Illustrations:* colour and b&w photos. *Payment:* 25c per published word; $20 per published photo.

Takahe (1989), Takahe Collective Trust, PO Box 13335, Christchurch 8001   *tel* (03) 359-8133.
$32 p.a. international/$24 p.a. domestic. Q. Quality short fiction and poetry by both new and established writers. *Payment:* approx. $30 per item.

The Timaru Herald, B.R. Appleby, PO Box 46, Bank Street, Timaru   *tel* (03) 684-4129   *fax* (03) 688-1042.
50c. D. Topical articles. *Payment:* by arrangement. *Illustrations:* colour or b&w prints, cartoons.

(Wellington) The Evening Post (1865), S.L. Carty, PO Box 3740, 40 Boulcott Street, Wellington   *tel* (04) 474-0444   *fax* (04) 474-0237; *editor's fax* (04) 474-0536.
60c Mon.-Fri., 70c Sat. General topical articles, 600 words. *Payment:* NZ current rates or by arrangement. News *illustrations*, cartoons.

Your Home (1991), Sharon Newey, Australian Consolidated Press (New Zealand) Ltd, Private Bag 92512, Wellesley Street, Auckland   *tel* (09) 373-5408   *fax* (09) 377 6725.
$4.95. M. Advice, ideas and projects for homeowners – interiors and gardens. *Length:* 1000 words. *Illustrations:* good quality colour transparencies. *Payment:* 30c per word/$50 per transparency.

SOUTH AFRICA

Newspapers are listed under the towns in which they are published.

(Cape Town) Cape Times (1876), J.C. Viviers, Newspaper House, 122 St George's Street, Cape Town 8001   *tel* (021) 488-4911   *postal address* PO Box 11, Cape Town 8000; London: 1st Floor, 32-33 Hatton Garden, EC1N 8DL   *tel* 0171-405 3742.
R1.20. D. Contributions must be suitable for a daily newspaper and must not exceed 800 words. *Illustrations:* photos of outstanding South African interest.

Car (1957), John Wright, PO Box 180, Howard Place 7450   *tel* (021) 531-1391   *telegraphic address* Confrere   *telex* 526 933   *fax* (021) 531-3333.
R6.45. M. New car announcements with pictures and full colour features of motoring interest. *Payment:* by arrangement. *Illustrations:* colour, cartoons.

(Durban) The Mercury (1852), J.M. Patten, Natal Newspapers Ltd, 18 Osborne Street, Greyville 4001   *tel* (031) 308-2300   *fax* (031) 308-2333.
R2.00 Mon.-Fri. Serious background news and inside details of world events. *Length:* 700-900 words. *Illustrations:* photos of general interest.

Fair Lady, Roz Wrottesley, National Magazines, PO Box 1802, Cape Town 8000   *tel* (021) 406-2204; London: *tel* 0171-404 3216.
R4.54. F. Fashion, beauty, articles and stories for women including showbiz, travel, humour. *Length:* articles up to 2000 words, short stories approx. 3000 words; short novels and serialisation of book material. *Illustrations:* cartoons. *Payment:* on quality rather than length – by arrangement.

Femina Magazine, Jane Raphaely, Associated Magazines, Box 3647, Cape Town 8000   *tel* (021) 462-3070.
R6.95. M. For young married women and those who would like to be. Humour, good fiction, personalities, real-life drama, medical breakthroughs, popular science. *Payment:* by arrangement. *Illustrations:* line, half-tone, colour.

Independent Newspapers Holdings Ltd
Cape Town: **Argus,** D, R1.50, **Weekend Argus,** Sat., R3.50, **Cape Times,** R1.60; Durban: **Daily News,** R1.50, **The Saturday Paper,** R2.20, **Ilanga,** R1.20, **Post** (Natal), R2.00, **Natal Mercury,** R2.00, **Sunday Tribune,** R3.60; Johannesburg: **The Star,** R1.50, **Saturday Star,** R2.00, **Sunday Independent,** R5.00, **Sowetan,** R1.10; Pretoria: **Pretoria News,** R1.30. Accepts articles of general and South African interest; also cartoons. *Payment:* in accordance with an editor's assessment. Contributions should be addressed to PO Box 1014, Johannesburg 2000.

(Johannesburg) Sunday Times, K.F. Owen, PO Box 1090, Johannesburg 2000   *tel* (011) 497-2300   *fax* (011) 497-2623; London: South African Morning Newspapers Ltd, 32-33 Hatton Garden, EC1N 8DL   *tel* 0171-405 3742.
R3.00. Sun. Illustrated articles of political or human interest, from a South African angle if possible. Maximum 1000 words long and two or three photos. Shorter essays, stories and articles of a light nature from 500-750 words. *Payment:* average rate £100 a column. *Illustrations:* photos (colour or b&w) and line.

Natal Witness (1846), J.H. Conyngham, 244 Longmarket Street, Pietermaritzburg, KwaZulu-Natal 3201   *tel* (0331) 551-111   *fax* (0331) 551-122.
R1.30. D. Accepts topical articles. All material should be submitted direct to the editor in Pietermaritzburg. *Length:* 500-1000 words. *Payment:* average of R120 per 1000 words.

Republican Press, PO Box 32083, Mobeni 4060, Natal   *tel* (031) 422-041   *telegraphic address* Keur Durban; UK: Suite 15-17, The Outer Temple, 222-225 Strand, London WC2R 1BA   *tel* 0171-353 2580   *fax* 0171-353 2578.
Bona, R2.85. M. Articles on fashion, cookery, sport, music of interest to black people. *Length:* up to 3000 words. *Payment:* by arrangement. *Illustrations:* line, half-tone, colour, cartoons.
Farmer's Weekly (1911), C. Venter. R4.40. W. Articles, generally illustrated, up to 1000 words, on all aspects of practical farming and research with particular reference to conditions in Southern Africa. Includes women's section which accepts suitable, illustrated articles. *Illustrations:* line, half-tone, colour, cartoons. *Payment:* according to merit.
Garden and Home, Margaret Wasserfall. R6.56. M. Well-illustrated articles on gardening, suitable for southern hemisphere. Articles for home section on furnishings, flower arrangement, food. *Payment:* by arrangement. *Illustrations:* half-tone, colour, cartoons.
Living and Loving (1970), Fiona Wayman. R4.33. M. Romantic fiction, 1500-4000 words. Articles dealing with first-person experiences; baby, family and marriage, medical articles up to 3000 words. *Payment:* by merit. *Illustrations:* line, half-tone, colour, cartoons.
Personality, C. Backeberg. R3.42. W. Illustrated. Primarily an entertainment-oriented magazine but also a market for articles about people and places, preferably with South African angle. Strong news features and/or photo-journalism, 1000-4000 words, with b&w and colour photos. Short stories 1500-5000 words; also cartoons. *Payment:* by arrangement. *Illustrations:* usually commissioned.
Scope, D. Mullany. R5.30. F. Strong news features, well illustrated, about people and places in all parts of the world. *Length:* up to 4000 words. Short stories 1500-5000 words, serials from 20,000 words. *Illustrations:* half-tone, colour, cartoons.
Your Family, Angela Waller-Paton. R4.33. M. Cookery, knitting, crochet and homecrafts. Family drama, happy ending. *Payment:* by arrangement. *Illustrations:* continuous tone, colour and line, cartoons.

South African Yachting (1957), Neil Rusch, PO Box 3473, Cape Town 8000   *tel* (021) 461-7472   *fax* (021) 461-3758   *e-mail* 10077,260
R5.80. M. Articles on yachting, boating or allied subjects. *Payment:* R12 per 100 words. *Illustrations:* line, half-tone, cartoons; colour covers.

Southern Cross, PO Box 2372, Cape Town 8000   *tel* (021) 455-007   *telegraphic address* Catholic   *fax* (021) 453-850   *e-mail* SANGONET SNO194
R1.00. W. National English-language Catholic weekly. Catholic news reports, world and South African. 1000-word articles, cartoons of Catholic interest

acceptable from freelance contributors. *Payment:* 87.5c. per column cm for all copy used. *Illustrations:* photos, R6 per column width, cartoons.

World Airnews, Tom Chalmers, PO Box 35082, Northway, Durban 4065   *tel* (031) 84-1319   *fax* (031) 83-7115.
£30.00 p.a. M. Aviation news and features with an African angle. *Payment:* by negotiation.

UNITED STATES OF AMERICA

Because of the difficulties in providing an up-to-date list of US magazines and journals, the *Yearbook* does not contain a detailed list. For general reference purposes, readers are referred to the list of US publications in the Overseas volume of *Willings Press Guide* (Reed Information Services), available in most reference libraries.

Readers who are particularly interested in the US market are referred to the following (please note that any payments should be made in US funds). *Writer's Market*, an annual guidebook giving editorial requirements and other details of over 4000 US markets for freelance writing, published by **Writer's Digest Books**, 1507 Dana Avenue, Cincinnati, OH 45207 ($27.99, plus $4.00 postage and handling); *The Writer's Handbook*, a substantial volume published by **The Writer Inc.**, 120 Boylston Street, Boston, MA 02116 ($29.95 plus $17.34 for airmail, $3.97 for surface mail). It contains 110 chapters, each written by an authority, giving practical instruction on a wide variety of aspects of freelance writing and includes details of 3000 markets, payment rates and addresses.

The Writer Inc. also publish books on writing fiction, non-fiction, poetry, articles, plays, etc. and a monthly magazine *The Writer* ($35.00 p.a., must be in US funds) which contains articles of instruction on all writing fields, lists of markets for MSS and special features of interest to freelance writers everywhere.

Writer's Digest Books also publish the monthly magazine *Writer's Digest* ($27.00 + $10 surface post, $56.00 airmail per year) and the annual directories, *Novel and Short Story Writer's Market*, *Children's Writer's and Illustrator's Market*, *Poet's Market*, *Artist's & Graphic Designer's Market*, *Guide to Literary Agents* and many other books on creating and selling writing and illustrations.

For availability in the UK details may be obtained from: **Freelance Market News,** Sevendale House, 7 Dale Street, Manchester M29 7WL   *tel* 0161-228 2362   *fax* 0161-228 3533.

SUBMISSION OF MSS

When submitting material to US journals send your covering letter with the MS, together with International Reply Coupons. Make clear what rights are being offered for sale for some editors like to purchase MSS outright, thus securing world copyright, i.e. the traditional British market as well as the US market. MSS should be sent direct to the US office of the journal and not to any London office.

In many cases it is far better to send a preliminary letter giving a rough outline of your article or story. Enclose International Reply Coupons for a reply. Most magazines will send a leaflet giving guidance to authors.

Writing for Newspapers

JILL DICK

Imagine looking at a white space the size of a tennis court and knowing you have to fill it with words and pictures. This is the task newspaper editors face regularly and it's a wonder any can sleep at night for worrying about how they're going to do it. Not only must the space be filled, it must be temptingly – *irresistibly* – filled, if existing readers are to be kept happy and new ones attracted.

There have been great changes in the newspaper world in recent years and because staff have been reduced on many newspapers, more freelance work is being accepted than ever before. Quality writing counts above all else, as it always will. Competition is tough, with former staff members now among the competitors, but today's freelance writers have many advantages over their predecessors, such as being able to use modern technology.

Use of freelance copy on the Internet without the copyright-owners' permission is one of the less welcome changes to the working scene. More and more publishers now ask writers to sign over all rights in their copy before being paid; there has been much resistance and the ensuing battle rumbles on. Copyright is a valuable asset and writers should think very seriously before signing agreements robbing them of it.

A newspaper may be only ink on paper but it's alive, feeding on topicality, originality and the quality of the writing on its pages. Editors long to hear from contributors who identify with readers and understand what they want. Such contributors are never short of work and enjoy great personal satisfaction.

IDEAS

Newspapers' needs change from day to day or week to week, according to the frequency of publication and so to provide a list of topics to write about would not be helpful. Furthermore, mere lists of ideas can encourage stultified thinking – countless writers have stared at similar lists and tried to wrench inspiration from them; countless editors have seen (and rejected) the results. More is needed than an idea. A unique slant on one may be the pointer to a worthwhile venture but an idea is most likely to be successful when it arrives in your head jockeying for priority, albeit loosely at first, with a notion of how you're going to write it. Fishermen bait their hooks not with what they like, but with what fish like. Of the many hard lessons to learn about freelancing one of the toughest is that you have to write not just the stories that appeal to you, but the stories that will sell.

REPORTING

News writing can be dramatic but frequently it is writing about something quite prosaic: a report of a local council meeting, for instance, where an important decision is awaited affecting a keenly felt local issue. However, if someone were to accuse councillors of rigging the ballot you would not be just writing a report but filing a news story. If a newspaper is published the next morning you, as a freelance, could find yourself the only person able to write it.

Local reporters are hard-working folk at the very root of a paper's activities and a role where many leading journalists began learning their craft. They are likely to be out and about collecting information from tip-offs supplied by the

office, waiting to file the latest news on a 'running' story or they might be engaged
on any one of a dozen duties in the circulation area. Reporters carry considerable
responsibility in a challenging job that should not be undertaken without careful
consideration. Being committed to maintaining a flow of news from a small town
or village or district can be a chore when you want to go on holiday or if you are
ill, or if you suddenly don't feel like doing it. But the first rule of the job is to not
let your community down.

Doing the 'calls' will be a regular task. This means calling on the people or
organisations likely to tell you what's going on: the police and fire stations, local
hospitals, the town hall, the Citizens Advice Bureau, the morgue, the courts,
schools, health clinics, community centres – anywhere and everywhere in the
locality where a spokesperson is able and willing to give you news or the basis of
a news story to pass on to readers of the paper. Being a local reporter will almost
certainly bring you more rewards than cash. Your writing skills will benefit by
making quick decisions about your copy, learning how to present it clearly in
print and over the phone; you will develop an increasing perception of what is
and is not newsworthy and your confidence will grow.

MARKET STUDY

What we need to study is not newspapers but readers. Are they treated cheerfully,
with triviality, or as serious-minded thinkers? Are their main concerns domestic,
adventurous, romantic, or creative? Is the language used appropriate for imma-
ture youngsters or for folk with more experience of life? Above all, do *you* know
how to talk to them? Picture the very readers the paper is trying to reach and
think of someone you know who might be one.

There is no substitute for studying the papers you'd like to write for. Analyse
their content, their page layout and format and try to find out why they print
what they do. Even such attention to detail isn't infallible, for at best it can only
reveal what they were interested in when they went to press. As for what they'll
want tomorrow and next week . . .

Read newspaper advertisements carefully – after all, advertisers don't spend
large sums of money without precise reader-targeting. It can be very beneficial
for freelances to visualise readers through the eyes of the advertiser.

No matter where you live or work, whom you meet, how you spend your time
or what your hobbies and interests may be, there's a story. Feature, filler, news
item, article, review, regular series, specialist column, interview, diary item,
letter, anecdote, profile, preview; there is always something to be written. In
buying a paper readers instinctively ask themselves, 'What's in it for me?' You
are providing the answer.

There are several well-established market guides, the best being *Writers' &
Artists' Yearbook*, *Willings Press Guide* and *The Media Guide* (see page 126).

FEATURES

Written work submitted to editors or features editors may be referred to as a
feature, an article, a piece or just 'copy'. Call it what you wish, it needs to stop
them in their tracks ('We must buy this') or at least lure them enough to contact
you about development of a point here, getting a picture there and so on. A
feature is often tagged to a news event. For instance, it may give background
information on a running story about prison rioting when there's been trouble at
a nearby prison; reveal past histories of an unusual medical condition recently
occurring in the district; or reveal some awkward facts following the disappearance of charity funds. Whatever its theme, be careful your story is not out
of date, having been overtaken by more recent events.

Features may be based entirely on facts but it is their relevance to people that makes them viable. Make yourself the bringer of comfort, an inspiration, an instructor or a wallower in nostalgia. Give readers information about education, medical services, local transport, job opportunities – all these are important to people. This does not mean fill your piece with little more than your own opinion and personal experiences; unless you are famous or well known in the locality, such views are unlikely to be required.

It pays to look ahead, particularly in ways other writers may not. This is not always easy as you will have to do much of the work on an article before ever writing a word. A thinly researched piece lands on the reject pile if another author has taken more time and trouble to delve into the subject. Reference libraries offer extensive facilities for researching and the most comprehensive volume to help you is *Research for Writers* (see page 126).

As your pile of researched material grows so will your interest and enthusiasm. To write well you have to be interested in what you're writing, or at least make yourself interested. If you're not, why should anyone else be? Original freelance copy on an editor's desk is more welcome than a tea-break. A good feature writer can write about virtually anything. When you do so make it strong; make readers react in whatever way you choose – but make sure they do or feel *something*.

SPECIALIST SPOTS

Many freelances vow the best spot in a paper is a regular page/half-page/column all to themselves. It is not a commission won without effort, often over a number of years; editors need to know you will be able to sustain an unlimited time at the job, that your copy will constantly be fresh and innovative and, most importantly, that it will always arrive on time. But when satisfied about these criteria, many are only too glad to hand over responsibility for a portion of the paper. Making editors aware of your worth by previously selling them other copy is a good basis for asking for regular columns.

The golden rule that applies for *all* copy is that (short of real and rare emergencies) it must never be late. To be calm about accepting deadlines you need to plan ahead carefully and to know your own limits in terms of the research you may have to do for a particular item and the time it is likely to take you to write it. A good safety net is to have plenty of copy ready in your private store.

What types of regular columns are there? Their themes are boundless: nature, chess, horoscopes, crosswords, competitions, children's and women's pages, young mothers, pop music, pets, food – anything that interests people will make a good column. A few topics fall into a separate category, such as travel, sport, motoring, business and finance. These are nearly always covered by staff writers and freelance contributions to these sections have to be exceptional. A column will get you known and your work constantly read so you should be prepared for the feedback from readers. This can be one of the most rewarding aspects of column-running if you don't let it take up too much of your writing time. And at the end of every month you are guaranteed a pre-negotiated regular fee without having to invoice anyone.

REVIEWS

The distinctive task of reviewing books, drama, films, videos, radio and television programmes is seldom work for a newcomer to writing. Someone famous in another sphere might be invited to contribute – perhaps a politician or a top sportsperson – to attract readers with the name of the reviewer rather than the quality of the review but the established papers have their own trained and experienced staff reviewers. How, then, do you gain experience? For all categories of reviewing it is at the discretion of editors (or features editors) that you may be given a chance. And the only way to build up a solid reputation is to keep writing the copy they want when (or preferably just before) they want it.

LETTERS, FILLERS, ANECDOTES AND HUMOUR

Writers may complain that computerised page layout leaves fewer spaces for small items but, as in all marketing, it is a matter of finding your own openings. Distinguish between news and general fillers as a newspaper may confine itself to one variety. It is sometimes worthwhile amassing a good collection and filing them to the editor as a single package. To a freelance writer nothing observed or overheard is ever wasted and humour is nearly always welcome.

But the newspaper world is full of surprises: one writer persuaded the editor of her evening paper that a 'funny' corner would give readers at least one thing to laugh at every day. It is her column now and has been running for four years. It's easy to laugh at humour, not easy to write it and virtually impossible to teach someone how to do it. Lucky you if you know how.

BUSINESS

Never be deterred by the thought that a freelance writer must also be a seller – or be afraid to discuss what you will be paid for work accepted. *Bona fide* freelance writers generally pay tax once a year directly to their tax offices. This status allows you to claim many benefits, setting some of your expenses against tax and even working at a tax loss. To satisfy the Inland Revenue you must demonstrate that you are a professional writer, that you are trying to make a profit and that you are eligible to be taxed under Schedule D (see page 567). This means your taxable income from writing will be the amount you receive in fees less expenses wholly and exclusively incurred in the pursuit of your writing. If you hold another full-time job it may not be easy to substantiate your writing credentials, but being able to produce genuine records and receipts, and to demonstrate a proper businesslike approach to your writing work will help.

Write what they want – that's the simple recipe for success and if you write what the editor wants, space will always be found. Perhaps that last sentence sums up all we writers need to know.

Writing Magazine Articles

JOHN HINES

For the would-be writer there can be little doubt that magazine articles offer the easiest way to get into print. The magazine market is vast and is growing steadily. *Willings Press Guide 1996* recorded no less than 10,452 UK periodicals, excluding newspapers and annuals, and the majority of these rely on freelance contributions to fill their pages. New magazines appear almost daily and, although some founder, most of them survive. The subject material covered by these magazines is so varied that few writers would find their special interests not included.

The magazines range from the modest budget publications to the expensive glossies. Beginners can cut their teeth on the lower end of the market, knowing that, although the fees are modest, the competition is small. These publications provide an excellent start for building skills, self-confidence and credibility. The opportunity for steadily moving up-market is there for the taking, until the writer reaches the level which fulfils his or her ambitions.

The pathway to successful article writing is surprisingly simple: have a good idea for a subject; find a suitable market; produce an interesting and well-written article for that market; submit a professional-looking typescript; have a sound sales strategy throughout.

THE IDEA

Established article-writers usually have files bulging with ideas. They will include newspaper and magazine clippings, jottings from TV and radio programmes and personal observations. Almost anything which intrigues the writer or fires the imagination is worth a place in the ideas file.

There is an adage in the writing world that it pays to write about what you know. Certainly this is a good idea, for you write more comfortably and competently on a familiar subject, but the wise diversify as well.

In selecting subjects, it is most rewarding to pick those which interest you or, better still, fascinate you. They provide absorbing research and can result in articles rich in original thought with your enthusiasm showing through. As a freelance, you have the luxury of being able to pick and choose, so why not select those articles which are a pleasure to write?

MARKET STUDY

Successful writers know that effective market study is vital. Any editor will tell you that the vast majority of unsolicited material which lands on their desk is quite unsuitable. The material may be wrong in length, style or choice of subject. Yet studying a copy of the magazine could have helped to avoid these mistakes.

Try to read at least two recent copies of the magazine for which you are aiming to write. Analyse it carefully. Check the number of articles which are staff-written (the staff are usually listed in the front of the magazine). By studying several issues you may also discover that there are contributors with regular slots and so deduce the opportunities which exist for the freelance.

If the magazine looks promising, study the type of subject which the editor favours. Check the approximate length of the average article. Ask yourself if the magazine's style is one with which you would be comfortable or to which you could adapt.

Few writers seem to study the advertisements and this is a big mistake. Advertising agencies spend a great deal of money on painstaking expert research, aimed at identifying the typical reader. By studying the advertisements you can benefit from this valuable information which can be most helpful when slanting your article to the readers' interests.

Studying the *Writers' & Artists' Yearbook* can give you a good insight into the requirements of many magazines, even including the fees they pay.

Freelance Market News is the best market newsletter for the freelance (see page 126). However, the finest market information is that which freelances compile for themselves from personal experience. A card filing system is useful here but, like all market information, its value depends on its being kept up to date.

RESEARCH AND ACCURACY

Although some articles can be written from personal experience or knowledge, most articles require some sound current research. The public libraries can be very helpful, particularly if you enlist the help of the qualified librarian rather than the library assistant. The copyright libraries, of which the British Library is the best known, are superb. Would-be researchers must establish their bona-fides before being issued with a ticket.

All facts should be checked for accuracy, going back to the source wherever possible. The books of others are not infallible, even reference books. Errors can be embarrassing and inevitably attract unwelcome letters from readers. File researched material away for future use; an effective filing system is essential. The best book on the subject is *Research for Writers* by Ann Hoffmann (see page 126).

Research may entail interviewing people and this is a skill which the freelance should consider developing. For effective interviews, sound preparation is important. Research in advance as much as possible about the interviewee and their field of interest. Make a list of important questions in logical sequence. But be prepared to divert from your questions and follow any unexpected revelations. If you use a tape-recorder, test it beforehand and always carry spare batteries and tapes. It is essential to have a notebook as a back-up and to carry spare pens.

Sensitivity and courtesy should be the criteria for all interviewing for normal articles. Start with easy general questions. Guide the interview gently, but firmly. Wind up the interview as you began, on an easy note. The interviewee should be left with the feeling that it has been an enjoyable experience. Some inter-viewees ask if they can vet the finished article. You should always politely refuse, but do offer to allow them to withdraw anything they may regret saying.

(For more information on interviewing, see *Freelance Writing for Newspapers* and *The Way to Write Magazine Articles* in the further reading list on page 126.)

NON-LINEAR THINKING

A stumbling block for many inexperienced writers is beginning their article, particularly when faced with a daunting mass of notes, clippings and research references. Related research material must be associated and the various aspects considered in order of importance. However, when marshalling material, we often tend to arrange it in a linear fashion, rather like a shopping list. This tends to restrict our thinking on each point.

It has been found that non-linear thinking stimulates ideas and their logical development. I use this method as a framework for my articles, particularly those which are complex. Non-linear flow-of-thought patterns are easy to compile and to use. The subject is written in the centre of a large sheet of paper with the major aspects to be covered radiating from it. From these, further spurs are drawn, filling in other important material. Less significant points are added on minor spurs until all aspects are covered. Never discard these patterns; file them away for future use as a valuable concise reference to your research material.

(A detailed explanation of this method, together with illustrations of typical non-linear patterns, is given in *The Way to Write Magazine Articles*; more general coverage can be found in *Use Your Head*; see page 126.)

THE ARTICLE STRUCTURE

We all develop our own style, but it is important to learn to modify it to suit the requirements of our market. The majority of articles are relatively short and must put over their story crisply without wasting words. Often this can best be done with fairly short sentences and relatively short paragraphs. Never write long convoluted sentences which require reading more than once to understand.

The opening. The first paragraph of an article has special importance. It must grip the editor's attention immediately, its purpose being to force the editor to read on. You can often make your opening irresistible by selecting a point from your article which is intriguing, startling or even audacious.

The body. You will not sell an article on the strength of its opening. The body of the article must fulfil the promise of that good first paragraph. It is here that the main text or message of your article will be unfolded. Your thought patterns will help you to move logically from one aspect to the next in a smooth progression and ensure that nothing important is left out.

The end. The poor article appears to finish when the writer runs out of ideas. A good ending must aim to tie up any loose ends positively. The way it does this depends a great deal on the subject. It can be speculative – a look into the future, perhaps. It might go back to answer a question posed in the beginning.

Avoid a mere recap of the main text for this gives a weak ending. Try to set aside some 'meat' to include in the ending; this could leave the reader with a strong point to ponder over.

Dialogue. Dialogue can breathe life into an article and give it sparkle. It must be used judiciously, for over-use may unbalance the article. It is often effective when used appropriately as the first sentence of an article.

THE TYPESCRIPT

The conventional layout of the typescript is covered under **Preparation of Materials, Resources**. However, an article for the British magazine market needs the addition of a cover sheet with the writer's name and address in the top right-hand corner, the article's title centred halfway down the page followed by the writer's name. If you are using a pseudonym it goes here, not at the top.

About two-thirds down the page on the left you should type the number of words in the article. Two or three lines' space below, type in the rights which you are offering the editor. For normal practical purposes this would be First British Serial Rights, usually abbreviated to 'FBSR offered' – see below. The cover sheet is not used for USA markets.

For more details of typescript presentation, see *The Professional Typescript for Magazine Articles* in the further reading list on page 126.

ILLUSTRATIONS

Good illustrations enhance an article, making it more saleable. The writer/ illustrator also receives an extra fee. It is self-evident that all article writers should try to produce that editors' delight – the words and pictures package. If you are a reasonable photographer, you are halfway there. If you are not, there is little excuse for not trying with the modern fully automatic cameras.

Study magazines to see, not only whether they use black and white or colour, but also the way they use illustrations. Do they tend to be small and plentiful to assist in the understanding of the text? Does the editor favour large dramatic pictures, sometimes covering as much as a whole page or even two? Finally, can your pictures match those in the magazine?

Your pictures must be pin-sharp and properly exposed. They must avoid all the basic mistakes of composition which are outlined in any photographic primer. For black and white you should submit glossy, borderless prints, 254 × 203 mm (10 × 8 in). Transparencies are demanded by most quality magazines for their colour illustrations, although a small but growing number of periodicals will consider colour prints. You must always confirm that a magazine uses colour prints before submitting them. For covers, most magazines use 35 mm transparencies, but many prefer a larger format. (Illustrations are covered in depth in *The Way to Write Magazine Articles*; see page 126.)

Writers who turn to supplementing their writing with photography rarely look back. They report better sales and increased earnings.

RIGHTS

In offering First British Serial Rights you are inviting the magazine to publish your article once and for the first time in Britain. You are retaining the right to sell it elsewhere in the world. Some editors will try to wring all rights from you. Do not give way as it leaves the magazine free to sell your article worldwide and pocket the proceeds.

Second British Serial Rights are rarely sold, but a magazine may ask to buy them if they see your article in print and wish to reproduce it themselves. You would normally accept, but as Second Rights earn lower fees than First Rights, you should not make any particular effort to sell them. It pays to rewrite the original article, reslanting it to suit the new market and possibly introducing some new material. This effectively makes it a new article for which the First Rights may be legitimately offered.

THE SALES STRATEGY

Probably the most common reason for good articles failing to get published is lack of a sound sales strategy. A surprisingly large number of writers complete a good article and then peddle it hopefully around the markets. This is quite the wrong way. Your article must always be written specifically for the market you have in mind.

Your sales strategy should begin the moment you look at your material and can say: 'Yes, there is enough here for a good article.' You then use your market study to find a number of likely magazines which might publish such an article.

Query letters. The sound query letter is essential for sustained success in the article-writing field. Examine your list of possible magazines and arrange them in order of your preference. Select the top one and write your query letter to its editor. It should be brief and should state your idea for the article, mentioning any special slant you have in mind. If you are qualified in any way to write such an article or if you have a 'track-record' of writing in that field, you should say so. Also mention if you have suitable illustrations.

Ask the editor how many words he or she would like to see. It is particularly important to ask for the magazine's rates for contributors. Always enclose an sae. The query letter is your initial shop-window and its quality should be the best of which you are capable. If the editor turns down the idea, write immediately to the next magazine on your list and so on.

If the editor likes your idea, you may get a commission, but if you are unknown it is more likely that you will be asked to submit the article on spec. Some editors try to side-step divulging their rates in advance, but you must be professional and insist on knowing them.

An acceptance is the usual outcome from an editor's expression of interest. As you become better at matching subject to magazine, writing shrewd query letters and producing sound articles, your rejections should drop to virtually nil.

On acceptance, the professional freelance looks around for another outlet. Writing is easy, it is the research which takes the time. Make sure you get the maximum from your research (see above).

Payment. Some magazines pay on acceptance, but the majority pay on publication. Avoid those magazines which hold your material on spec with no guarantee of ultimate publication. They are not worthy of consideration. Never be afraid to question offers of low rates, for many editors will negotiate. If low rates are not improved upon, be professional and withdraw the offer of your article.

FRESH FIELDS

When you have written articles extensively on a subject, it may be worth considering whether the subject is suitable for a non-fiction book. If so, your articles could be valuable as evidence of your writing skills, your knowledge of the subject and the wide interest the subject can generate. Many writers have used their published articles as a means of gaining an advance contract for a non-fiction book. (This is covered in *The Way to Write Non-fiction*; see page 126.)

Writing for the European Union

BARBARA WOOD-KACZMAR

On 1 January 1995 the European Union passed another historic milestone when it grew from 12 member states to 15. Austria, Finland and Sweden joined to make a blonder, wealthier trading area of nearly 400 million. And although Norway rejected full membership, British writers and publishers will have unrestricted access to its markets as Norway and Iceland have signed up as economic partners. The British writers' home market, until recently confined to the UK, is now Europe, the world's largest trader.

The addition of the Nordic countries means for the first time British books are sold freely from the Arctic to the Mediterranean. And journalists benefit too. Sports writers gain the ski slopes of Austria, Norway and Sweden, energy specialists acquire Iceland's geothermal electricity and music writers now have Finland's Sibelius. Financial journalists will eventually net the bankers of Liechtenstein whenever that state unravels its customs arrangements with Switzerland – the Swiss voted to remain aloof from this European re-birth.

The birth pangs of creating a European single market have already brought turbulence to British magazine publishing. Familiar titles folded and new ones were launched to fight off the European invaders, but writers now benefit from a larger UK market. German newcomers *Take a Break* and *Bella* regularly head the women's bestseller list while Dutch publisher VNU has expanded the business and computer sectors.

And there is the greater challenge of writing for magazines in the EU. EMAP's aggressive policy of launching and acquiring European consumer titles provides new writing opportunities on the Continent – EMAP bought 38 French magazines including *L'Auto Journal*. But mergers may not always be good news. When Reed International combined with the Dutch publisher Elsevier to create one of the world's largest media empires, British journalists lost their union rights while Dutch writers kept theirs.

Right now, British writers are in a unique position to exploit the European market as the main EU business language is English. Advertisements in *The Guardian*'s media supplement reflect an upsurge in EU demand for English-speaking writers and presenters, especially for new pan-European radio and TV stations. Actively recruiting TV companies include London-based European Business News, Reuters' GMTV in Brussels, and the multilingual news channel

Euronews in France. And since the NUJ ran the first UK course to help TV comedy script writers get a foothold in Europe, training for print journalists has quickly followed. Cardiff University offers a midcareer MA in European Journalism while the European Media School specialises in multimedia applications. Journalists fluent in a second European language, especially German, are sought by computer, business, health and media titles both here and on the Continent. German will become increasingly dominant now Austria is a full EU member – and other EU writers are multilingual.

All speciality writers will find a magazine somewhere in the EU which publishes their topic. The language situation must be checked out first and various pitfalls avoided (see below). Otherwise the usual rules of good writing apply: an article must be tailored to the magazine style and written with respect for the sensitivities of its readers. Successful British writers will be happily surprised at the higher European fees.

1995 saw another bombshell with the introduction of a single European copyright – now extended to 70 years after an author's death. The good news for today's UK writers is their children and grandchildren will benefit – for an additional 20 years. The bad news for UK publishers is that out-of-copyright authors are back in, so cheap editions of Thomas Hardy will be dearer and composers from Elgar to Glen Miller can no longer be performed free.

HOW TO SUBMIT MSS TO EU MAGAZINES

Syndication (see page 141)

This is the easiest method for original MSS and also for articles previously published in the UK, if the UK rights only have been sold. A few syndicates report an increase in British writers selling to Europe but many have noticed little change.

Commission fees are usually around 50%, reflecting higher payments but both translation facilities and fees may vary. BIPS has no translation fee while Europress Features charges per page. Some syndicates may translate only one language, e.g. Features International translates only German. Illustrated material is preferred and the most popular subjects remain Royalty, international celebrities and science with a strong human interest. Recently, romantic fiction, real life crime and women's interests have become more sellable and travel features on TV locations and 'heritage' areas are more in demand. Unusual events in Britain have a shelf life of six weeks on the Continent but news items and political features are not required. Similarly, humour will not sell.

Pan-European magazines

Pan-European magazines are publications sold throughout the EU and aimed at an all-European readership, e.g. *Euromoney*, *Construction Europe* and *European Chemical News*. These English-language magazines and newspapers, e.g. *The European* and *Europa Times*, welcome freelance material tailored to their style. EMAP Images' *PC Review* is aimed at people who use computers for entertainment or non-business applications.

Other pan-Europeans change their language according to the country (e.g. *Prima*) and also their title (*Essentials* is called *Avantage* in France and *Pratica* in Italy). These women's publications are less easy to penetrate: each national title is geared to that market alone and there may be no connection between their different editions.

However, some magazine publishers will forward MSS from their London offices to their mainland counterparts. Others hire writers with linguistic skills as editorial consultants for continental editions (e.g. BBC's *Wildlife Magazine*'s German edition) or swap editorial with their continental partners (e.g. Reed

Business Publishing's *Motor Transport* and *Commercial Motor*). See *Willings Press Guide* for pan-European publishers' London offices.

Subjects in demand include science, medicine, consumer marketing, pollution and law.

Do it yourself

The go-it-alone approach is not difficult. Choose a country you have some knowledge of and an affinity for: then read the appropriate Department of Trade and Industry country profile for an idea of its business scene and publishing sector. These excellent profiles are in reference libraries or available from the DTI (see below).

Select your magazine from *Willings Press Guide*, the one essential tool. EU periodicals are in volume 2, listed according to country. Each entry includes subject, readership, editor's name, publisher and UK representative. An expanded classified list is helpful to speciality writers. English-language magazines are described as such but the few examples may be academic journals, not commercial concerns.

Send a preliminary letter to the editor along with a synopsis, photocopies of previous work and an International Reply Coupon. Never send MSS or photos unless commissioned and stipulate the material is for use only in the country of publication. Otherwise the publisher can claim copyright and peddle the rights worldwide. Similarly, make it clear your work should not be fed into a database or retrieval system without prior consent. Rates of pay should be agreed in advance.

The magazine's UK representative may provide back copies for commissioned writers: s/he may also know if the editor speaks English. Translation costs are sometimes deducted from your fee but double taxation exemption forms are no longer necessary.

Subjects in demand are environmental matters and interviews with famous people – it may be cheaper for an EU magazine editor to commission interviews from British writers on the spot. Hobbies, e.g. sailing, photography, camping and computers are also popular. And high quality photos need no translation – articles with photos are usually easy to sell.

SOLVING THE LANGUAGE PROBLEM

In descending order of English usage the EU countries are: Ireland, Holland, Germany, Belgium, Denmark, Sweden, Finland, Austria and Luxembourg; Portugal, Spain, France, Italy and Greece. Generally speaking, editors in countries in the second half expect correspondence as well as articles to be in their own language. But as areas popular with British tourists and expatriates, they may have small English-language publishing sectors worth investigating. And English is commercially acceptable in all Nordic countries.

Don't be tempted to translate your MSS yourself. The Institute of Translation and Interpreting (377 City Road, London EC1V 1NA *tel* 0171-713 7600; see page 631) maintains a national register of professional translators. Members of the Society of Authors may contact the Translators' Association, a specialised unit within their organisation. Fees for French, German, Italian and Spanish start from £35 per 1000 words but Greek and Scandinavian languages cost more. Highly technical texts can cost from £60 per 1000 words. Local colleges may offer private translation facilities but few provide a 24-hour service.

CHANGES IN BOOK PUBLISHING

With the retail value of the total Union book market estimated at over £15 billion, competition is fierce. EU book publishers have already moved into the

UK for access to the enormous English-language markets worldwide – see Cassell's *Directory of Publishing, Continental Europe* 1997. For the best deal on translation rights, a British agent is advisable.

Book sales should continue to hold up while VAT on British books is permitted to remain at zero. And authors should benefit from increased royalties: UK publishers may offer single, exclusive licences for the entire Union based on the UK price.

SOURCES OF INFORMATION

1. *Willings Press Guide*, volume 2 *Overseas*, 123rd edn, 1997; Reed Information Services, Windsor Court, East Grinstead House, East Grinstead, West Sussex RH19 1XA   *tel* (01342) 326972.
2. Cassell's *Directory of Publishing, Continental Europe* 1997; Cassell plc, Stanley House, 3 Fleet's Lane, Poole, Dorset BH15 3AJ   *tel* (01202) 670581   *fax* (01202) 666219.
3. DTI: Department of Trade and Industry (see page 513). For a country profile or publications catalogue contact DTI Export Publications, PO Box 55, Stratford-upon-Avon, Warks. CV37 9GE   *tel* (01789) 296212   *fax* (01789) 299096. The address for general queries is Exports to Europe Branch, Kingsgate House, 66-74 Victoria Street, London SW1E 6SW   *tel* 0171-215 5336. DTI library facilities are available at London and Regional offices.
4. Embassies (see pages 511-520). Most will supply lists of magazines and newspapers in their countries, publishers' and representatives' addresses (useful as changes are frequent) as well as circulation figures and names of editors. Some lists are more comprehensive than others! Embassies usually know the UK addresses of their countries' major publishers.
5. Chambers of Commerce are comprehensive information centres. Visitors may study reference books on publishing or photocopies may be supplied on request. Some Cultural Institutes are located outside London.
6. The European Commission discusses its proposals with professionals before legislation. Phone the London office (0171-973 1992) for information or to air your views.
7. The European Parliament is the only directly elected body in the EU. Your MEP or the London office (*tel* 0171-222 0411) should know of changes in the legislative pipeline affecting writers or their specialities.

HELPFUL ASSOCIATIONS

1. The National Union of Journalists can raise grievances, such as non-payment or breach of copyright, with European publishers either on its own or through its affiliated European unions. The NUJ maintains lists of EU unions of journalists (see page 619).
2. The Society of Authors (see page 598) normally advises on problems arising in the UK but it will refer a member having problems with a European publisher to the foreign authors' society, as all these belong to the Congress of European Writers' Organisations. However if disputes arise over payments the cost of going to law may be prohibitive. Writers who regularly or solely write for an EU country should join the relevant authors' society.
3. The Writers' Guild (see page 635) works out common European policies on Public Lending Rights and minimum terms publishing agreements through the biennial European Writers' Congress.

FURTHER READING

Buzan, Tony, *Use Your Head*, BBC, revised edn, 1995.

Dick, Jill, *Freelance Writing for Newspapers*, A. & C. Black, 1991.

Dick, Jill, *Writing for Magazines*, A. & C. Black, 2nd edn, Oct 1996.

Freelance Market News, Freelance Press Services, Lissadel Street, Salford M6 6GG (on subscription).

Hines, John, *The Professional Typescript for Magazine Articles*, Tanglewood, 1995.

Hines, John, *The Way to Write Magazine Articles*, Hamish Hamilton, repr. 1995.

Hines, John, *The Way to Write Non-fiction*, Hamish Hamilton, 1990. O.P.

Hoffmann, Ann, *Research for Writers*, A. & C. Black, 5th edn, 1996.

Howard, Godfrey, *The Good English Guide*, Pan Macmillan, 1994.

Legat, Michael, *The Nuts and Bolts of Writing*, Robert Hale, repr. 1993.

Peak, Steve (ed.), *The Media Guide*, Fourth Estate, annual.

The Oxford Writers' Dictionary, Oxford Reference, 1990.

Willings Press Guide, Reed Information Services, annual.

Recent UK Magazine Changes

The following changes have taken place since the last edition of the *Yearbook*.

Changes of Name and Mergers

Christian Herald *now* New Christian Herald
Country Garden *now* Country Garden & Smallholding
Embroidery *now* The World of Embroidery
The Great Outdoors *now* TGO (The Great Outdoors) Magazine
Involvement & Participation *now* Involvement
OK! Magazine *now* OK! Weekly
Poetry Nottingham *now* Poetry Nottingham International
Squash Player *now* The Squash Player
Together *now* Together with Children
Ulster News Letter *now* News Letter
Western Mail *now* The Western Mail
Woman and Home *now* Woman and Home (incorporating Living)
Woodworker *now* The Woodworker
The Young Soldier *now* Kids Alive! (The Young Soldier)

Newspapers and Magazines Ceased Publication

Daily Awaz International	Living
DAM	Panurge
Greenscene	PIC
HIM magazine	Today
i-to-i	Values

Classified Index of Newspapers and Magazines

Commonwealth and Irish Journals

This index can be only a broad classification. It should be regarded as a pointer to possible markets, and should be used with discrimination. Addresses for newspapers and magazines start on page 5.

Fiction (*See also* Literary)

All the following take short stories, unless otherwise stated. 'Long' refers to long complete stories, from 35,000 words upwards.

Active Life
Ambit
*The Australian Women's
  Weekly
Bad Attitude
Bella
Best
Bike
Catch
Chat
Cosmopolitan
*Fair Lady (SA) (also serials)
*Femina (SA)
*The Fiddlehead (Can.)
Fly-Fishing & Fly-Tying
Granta
*HU (The Honest Ulsterman)
  (Ire.)
The Illustrated London News
*IMAGE (Ire.)
Interzone

*Ireland's Eye
*Ireland's Own
  Iron
*IT (Ire.)
*(Johannesburg) Sunday Times
  (SA)
Just Seventeen
*Living and Loving (SA)
London Magazine
Love Story
*The Malahat Review (Can.)
My Weekly (also serials)
My Weekly Story Library
  (long only)
*New Idea (Aus.)
New Impact
People's Friend (also serials)
People's Friend Library (long
  only)
*Personality (SA)
*Quadrant (Aus.)

*Redoubt (Aus.)
*Reality (Ire.)
*Scope (SA)
Scots Magazine
Songwriting and Composing
Stand
Staple
Sunday Post
*Takahe (NZ)
Take a Break
The Mag!
*Wascana Review (Can.)
Woman and Home (also
  serials)
*Woman's Day (Aus.)
Woman's Own
Woman's Story
*Woman's Way (Ire.)
Woman's Weekly (also serials)
Xenos
Yours

Letters to the Editor

Art & Craft
*The Australian Woman's
  Weekly
BBC Gardeners' World
  Magazine
Bella
Best
The Big Issue
Buster
Catch
Chat
Child Education
Choice
Control & Instrumentation
Daily Express
Daily Star
*Dolly (Aus.)
Electrical Times
*Fair Lady (SA)
Family Circle
*Femina (SA)
First Steps
Freelance Market News

Freelance Writing &
  Photography
*The Furrow (Ire.)
Garden News
Goldlife for 50-Forward
Ideal Home
Junior Education
Mandy/Judy
Mobile & Holiday Homes
Modern Painters
Moneywise
Mother & Baby
Motor Caravan Magazine
My Weekly
News of the World
Our Baby
Penthouse
Police Journal
Practical Householder
Practical Parenting
Practical Photography
Practical Woodworking
Prima

Right Start
Saga Magazine
She
Shout
Slimming Magazine
Street Machine
Sunday Mail
Sunday Mirror
Take a Break
Television
that's life!
True Story
The Weekly News
What's on TV
Woman
*Woman's Day (Aus.)
Woman's Own
Woman's Realm
*Woman's Way (Ire.)
Woman's Weekly
Writers' Forum
Yours

Gossip Paragraphs

Aberdeen Evening Express
Aeroplane Monthly
African Business
Amateur Gardening
The Architects' Journal
Art Business Today
Art Monthly
Auto Express
BBC Music Magazine
Big!
The Big Issue
Bike
Blueprint
Boards
The Boatman
Bowls International
Bristol Evening Post
Broadcast
Building Design
Cage and Aviary Birds
Cambridge Evening News
Campaign
*Canadian Yachting
*(Cape Town) Cape Times
    (SA)
Car
Caravan Magazine
Carers World
Cat World
Catholic Pictorial
Cheshire Life
*(Christchurch) The Press (NZ)
Classic Boat
Classic Cars
Classical Music
Climber
Country Life
Cycling Weekly
Daily Mail
Daily Mirror
Daily Star
The Daily Telegraph
Derby Evening Telegraph
Dirt Bike Rider
Drapers Record
Edinburgh Evening News
Electrical Times
Euromoney
*Evening Herald (Ire.)
Eventing
Farming News

Fashion Weekly
Financial Weekly
First Steps
Freelance Market News
Fresh Produce Journal
Garden News
Geographical Magazine
Gibbons Stamp Monthly
Gifts International
Glasgow Evening Times
Goldlife for 50-Forward
Golf World
The Herald
Horse and Hound
*Hotel and Catering Review
    (Ire.)
Independent
Independent on Sunday
*Inuit Art Quarterly (Can.)
Inverness Courier
*Irish Farmers Journal
*Irish Medical Times
*Irish Printer
Jewish Chronicle
*(Johannesburg) Sunday Times
    (SA)
The Journal
Journalist
Justice of the Peace and Local
    Government Law
The Lawyer
Liverpool Echo
Mail on Sunday
Marketing Week
*(Melbourne) Australasian Post
Men Only
The Mirror
*Mode Australia
Mojo
Music Week
*(New Plymouth) The Daily
    News (NZ)
New Statesman & Society
The New Welsh Review
*New Zealand Listener
News of the World
The News, Portsmouth
Nursing Times and Nursing
    Mirror
The Oldie
Opera Now

Organic Gardening
PC Review
*Photo Life (Can.)
Pilot
The Pink Paper
Police Review
Practical Fishkeeping
The Press and Journal
Private Eye
Radio Times
Reading Evening Post
Red Pepper
Rugby World
Runner's World
The Scotsman
The Scottish Farmer
Sea Breezes
Shout
*South African Yachting
South Wales Echo
The Squash Player
The Stage
The Sun
*The Sun-Herald (Aus.)
*The Sunday Age (Aus.)
Sunday Express
*Sunday Independent (Ire.)
Sunday Mail
*Sunday News (NZ)
*The Sunday Press (Ire.)
Sunday Telegraph
The Tablet
tate: The Art Magazine
that's life!
Therapy Weekly
The Times
Titbits
Today's Runner
Wales on Sunday
Western Daily Press
The Western Mail
Woman
Woman's Realm
*Woman's Way (Ire.)
World Soccer
Writers' Forum
Yachts and Yachting
Yorkshire Evening Post
Yorkshire Evening Press
Yorkshire Life
Yorkshire Post

Brief Filler Paragraphs

Accountancy Age
Active Life
Aeroplane Monthly
Africa Confidential
African Business
Air Pictorial International

Amateur Gardening
Angler's Mail
The Architects' Journal
Art Monthly
Athletics Weekly
Auto Express

The Bath Chronicle
BBC Music Magazine
Bella
Big!
The Big Issue
Bike

Woman's Realm
The Woodworker
*World Airnews (SA)
World Fishing

World Soccer
Writers' Forum
Writers' Monthly
Yachts and Yachting

Yorkshire Evening Post
Yorkshire Evening Press
Yours

Puzzles and Quizzes

The newspapers and magazines listed below all take puzzles and/or quizzes, on an occasional or, in some cases, regular basis. Ideas must be tailored to suit each magazine or newspaper; approach in writing in the first instance.

Aberdeen Evening Express
*Adelaide Advertiser (Aus.)
*(Adelaide) Sunday Mail (Aus.)
*Argus South African Newspapers
Art Business Today
Athletics Weekly
*(Auckland) Sunday Star-Times (NZ)
Baptist Times
The Bath Chronicle
Bike
Bird Watching
Birmingham Evening Mail
Bolton Evening News
*Bona (SA)
Bowls International
*(Brisbane) Sunday Mail (Aus.)
Brownie
Cage and Aviary Birds
Cambridge Evening News
*Canadian Yachting
Carers World
Cat World
Catholic Gazette
The Catholic Herald
Catholic Pictorial
Choice
*(Christchurch) The Press (NZ)
*Christchurch Star (NZ)
Church of England Newspaper
*Cleo (Aus.)
Country Life
Country-Side
The Cricketer International
Daily Mail
Daily Mirror
Daily Star
*Daily Times (NZ)
The Dandy
Darts World
Dirt Bike Rider
Disability Now
*Dolly (Aus.)
*(Dunedin) Otago Daily Times (NZ)
East Lothian Life
The Echo
Electrical Times
Essentials

The European
Evening Courier
Evening Echo (Basildon)
Evening Echo (Bournemouth)
Evening Gazette (Teesside)
*Evening Herald (Ire.)
Evening News
Everyday with Practical Electronics
*Fair Lady (SA)
*Farmers Weekly (SA)
Financial Adviser
Football Picture Story Library
Fore!
*Garden and Home (SA)
Garden News
Gifts International
Glasgow Evening Times
Golf Monthly
Golf World
Grimsby Evening Telegraph
Guiding
Health & Efficiency International
The Herald
Here's Health
Hertfordshire Countryside
Horse and Hound
Horse & Pony
Hospital Doctor
*Hotel and Catering Review (Ire.)
HouseBuilder
The Illustrated London News
Independent Magazine
Independent on Sunday
*(Invercargill) The Southland Times (NZ)
Inverness Courier
*Ireland's Eye
*Ireland's Own
*Irish Medical Times
The Journal
Journalist
Just Seventeen
Kids Alive!
The Lady
Lancashire Evening Post
*(Launceston) Examiner (Aus.)
Liverpool Echo
*Living and Loving (SA)

Mail on Sunday
Mandy/Judy
*(Melbourne) Australasian Post
Men Only
Methodist Recorder
My Weekly Puzzle Time
New Christian Herald
*New Idea (Aus.)
New Impact
*(New Plymouth) The Daily News (NZ)
New Scientist
The New Welsh Review
*New Woman (Aus.)
New World
*New Zealand Listener
*New Zealand Woman's Weekly
The News, Portsmouth
19
North-West Evening Mail
Nottingham Evening Post
Nursing Times and Nursing Mirror
Opera
Opera Now
Park Home & Holiday Caravan
*Personality (SA)
*(Perth) The West Australian
Pilot
Pony
Practical Motorist
Practical Photography
The Practitioner
Publishing News
*Reality (Ire.)
Red Pepper
Red Tape
Runner's World
*Scope (SA)
The Scotsman
The Scottish Farmer
Scottish Homes and Country
She
The Short Wave Magazine
Shout
Shropshire Star
*South African Yachting
South Wales Echo
*Southern Cross (SA)

The Spectator
The Stage
Stamp Lover
The Star
The Sun
*The Sun-Herald (Aus.)
*Sunday Life (Ire.)
Sunday Mail
Sunday Mirror Magazine
*The Sunday Press (Ire.)
The Sunday Sun
The Sunday Times
*(Sydney) The Daily Telegraph
Mirror (Aus.)
The Tablet
Take a Break
Telegraph Magazine
TGO (The Great Outdoors)
Magazine

The Mag!
Therapy Weekly
The Times
The Times Educational
Supplement
Titbits
Today's Horse
Today's Runner
Trout and Salmon
Twinkle
The Universe
*(Vancouver) Province (Can.)
Vox
Wales on Sunday
War Cry
Waterways World
Weekend Guardian
The Weekly Journal
Weight Watchers Magazine

*(Wellington) The Evening
Post (NZ)
West Lancashire Evening
Gazette
Western Daily Press
The Western Mail
The Western Morning News
Woman
The Woodworker
*The Word (Ire.)
World Soccer
Young Telegraph
Yorkshire Evening Post
Yorkshire Evening Press
*Your Family (SA)
Yours

Newspapers

UK National Daily/Sunday Newspapers (*excluding* Northern Ireland)

Daily Express
Daily Mail
Daily Mirror
Daily Sport
Daily Star
The Daily Telegraph
Financial Times
The Guardian

Independent
Independent on Sunday
Mail on Sunday
News of the World
The Observer
The People
Scotland on Sunday
The Scotsman

The Sun
Sunday Express
Sunday Mirror
Sunday Sport
Sunday Telegraph
The Sunday Times
The Times
Wales on Sunday

UK National Weekly Newspapers (*excluding* Northern Ireland)

Asian Times
Caribbean Times

Eastern Eye
The European

The Voice
The Weekly Journal

UK Regional Newspapers (*excluding* Northern Ireland)

Aberdeen Evening Express
The Asian Age
The Bath Chronicle
Birmingham Evening Mail
The Birmingham Post
Bolton Evening News
Bristol Evening Post
Burton Mail
Cambridge Evening News
Chronicle and Echo
(Northampton)
The Courier and Advertiser
(Dundee)
Coventry Evening Telegraph
Daily Post (Liverpool)
Daily Record (Glasgow)
Derby Evening Telegraph
Dorset Evening Echo
Dundee Evening Telegraph &
Post

East Anglian Daily Times
Eastern Daily Press (Norwich)
The Echo (Sunderland)
Edinburgh Evening News
Evening Chronicle
(Newcastle)
Evening Courier (Halifax)
Evening Echo (Basildon)
Evening Echo (Bournemouth)
Evening Gazette (Teesside)
Evening News (Norwich)
Evening Standard (London)
Express & Echo (Exeter)
Express and Star
(Wolverhampton)
Glasgow Evening Times
Gloucestershire Echo
Grimsby Evening Telegraph
Guernsey Evening Press and
Star

Hartlepool Mail
The Herald (Glasgow)
Inverness Courier
The Journal (Newcastle)
Kent Messenger
Kent Today
Lancashire Evening Post
Lancashire Evening Telegraph
Leicester Mercury
Liverpool Echo
Manchester Evening News
The News, Portsmouth
The Northern Echo (Durham)
North-West Evening Mail
Nottingham Evening Post
Oldham Evening Chronicle
The Press and Journal
(Aberdeen)
Reading Evening Post
Shropshire Star

South Wales Echo
The Southern Daily Echo
  (Southampton)
The Star (Sheffield)
The Sun (Scotland)
Sunday Mail (Glasgow)
Sunday Mercury
  (Birmingham)

Sunday Post (Dundee/
  Glasgow)
The Sunday Sun (Newcastle)
The Sunday Tribune (Ire.)
Telegraph & Argus (Bradford)
The Weekly News (Scotland)
West Lancashire Evening
  Gazette

Western Daily Press (Bristol)
The Western Mail (Cardiff)
The Western Morning News
  (Plymouth)
Yorkshire Evening Post
Yorkshire Evening Press
Yorkshire Gazette & Herald
  Series
Yorkshire Post

UK National Colour Magazines (*excluding* Northern Ireland)

The European MagAZine
The Guardian Weekend
Independent Magazine
Night & Day (Mail on
  Sunday)
The Observer Life Magazine
The Scotsman Weekend

Sunday Express Magazine
Sunday Magazine (News of
  the World)
Sunday Mirror Magazine
The Sunday Post Magazine
The Sunday Telegraph
  Magazine

Sunday Times Magazine
Telegraph Magazine (Daily
  Telegraph)
The Times Magazine
Yes (The People)
You (Mail on Sunday)

Women's Interest Magazines
(*See also* Health and Home)

*The Australian Women's
  Weekly
Bad Attitude
Bella
Best
Black Beauty & Hair
*Bona (SA)
Catch
Chat
*Chatelaine (Can.)
Chic
Clothes Show Magazine
Company
Cosmopolitan
Country Living
*Elle (Australia)
Elle (UK)
Essentials
Everywoman
Executive PA
Executive Woman
*Fair Lady (SA)
Family Circle
*Femina (SA)
For Women
Girl About Town
Good Housekeeping
Hairflair

Harpers & Queen
Hello!
Home and Country
Home Words
*HQ (Aus.)
*IMAGE (Ire.)
*IT (Ire.)
Just Seventeen
Lady
*Living and Loving (SA)
Looks Magazine
Marie Claire
*Mode Australia
*Modern Woman (Ire.)
More!
Mother & Baby
Ms London
My Weekly
My Weekly Puzzle Time
*New Idea (Aus.)
New Woman
*New Woman (Aus.)
*New Zealand Woman's Day
*New Zealand Woman's
  Weekly
19
Nursery World
Office Secretary

OK! Magazine
Options
People's Friend
The Pink Paper
Pride
Prima
Right Start
She
Sunday Post
Take a Break
The Tatler
that's life!
The Mag!
*U magazine (Ire.)
Vanity Fair
Vogue
Wedding and Home
Woman
Woman Alive
Woman and Home
*Woman's Day (Aus.)
Woman's Journal
Woman's Own
Woman's Realm
*Woman's Way (Ire.)
Woman's Weekly
World's Children
*Your Family (SA)

Men's Interest Magazines

Arena
Attitude
Country
Esquire

FHM (For Him Magazine)
Gay Times
GQ
Masonic Square

Mayfair
Men Only
Penthouse
The Pink Paper

Children's and Young Adult Magazines

The Beano
Beano Comic Library
Big!
Brownie
Bunty
Bunty Library
Buster
Commando
The Dandy
Dandy Comic Library
*Dolly (Aus.)

Football Picture Story Library
Horse & Pony
*Hot Press (Ire.)
i-D Magazine
Just Seventeen
Live & Kicking Magazine
Looks Magazine
Mandy/Judy
Mandy Library
Mizz

Pony
Scouting
Shout
Sky Magazine
Smash Hits
Top of the Pops Magazine
Twinkle
Vox
Young Telegraph
YX

Subject Articles

Advertising, Design, Printing and Publishing (*See also* Literary)

Arena
*Australian Bookseller &
   Publisher
Blueprint
The Bookseller
British Journalism Review
British Printer
Building Design
Campaign

*Canadian Interiors
Exchange & Mart
The Face
Freelance Market News
Greetings Magazine
Indexer
InterMedia
*Irish Printer

Journalist
Learned Publishing
Market Newsletter
Media Week
PR Week
Printing World
Publishing News
The World of Interiors

Agriculture, Farming and Horticulture

Country Garden &
   Smallholding
Country Life
The Countryman
*Countryman (Aus.)
Country-Side
Dairy Farmer
Farmer's Weekly

*Farmer's Weekly (SA)
Farming News
The Field
Fresh Produce Journal
The Grower
Horticulture Week
*Irish Farmers Journal

*New Zealand Farmer
Pig Farming
Poultry World
Scottish Farmer
Smallholder
*Straight Furrow (NZ)
Town and Country Planning

Architecture and Building

The Architects' Journal
Architectural Design
Architectural Review
Architecture Today
Blueprint
Building
Building Design
Built Environment

Burlington Magazine
Construction Europe
Contemporary Review
Country Homes & Interiors
Country Life
Education
Estates Gazette
Homes and Gardens

House & Garden
HouseBuilder
Ideal Home
International Construction
Local Historian
Mortgage Finance Gazette
Museums Journal
Property Week

Art and Collecting

The Antique Collector
The Antique Dealer &
   Collectors Guide
Apollo
Art & Design
Art Business Today
Art Monthly
The Art Newspaper

Art Review
The Artist
Artists and Illustrators
Artists Newsletter
*ArtsAtlantic (Can.)
BBC Homes & Antiques
Burlington Magazine
*C Magazine (Can.)

Clocks
Coin News
Contemporary Art
Contemporary Review
Country Life
Creative Camera
Eastern Art Report
Gibbons Stamp Monthly

The Illustrated London News
*Inuit Art Quarterly (Can.)
Leisure Painter
Medal News
Modern Painters

Museums Journal
Numismatic Chronicle
RA Magazine
Stamp Lover
Stamp Magazine

tate: The Art Magazine
Women's Art Magazine
The World of Embroidery
The World of Interiors

Aviation

Aeromodeller
Aeroplane Monthly
Air International
Air Pictorial International

*Australian Flying
Flight International
FlyPast

Pilot
Transport
*World Airnews (SA)

Blind and Partially Sighted

Published by the Royal National Institute for the Blind (see under **United Kingdom Book Publishers**)

Access IT
After Hours
Aphra
Braille Chess Magazine
Braille Journal of
  Physiotherapy
Braille at Bedtime
Braille Music Magazine
Braille Radio Times
Braille Rainbow
Braille TV Times
British Journal of Visual
  Impairment
Busy Solicitor's Journal
Channels of Blessing
Come Gardening
ComputeIT

Contention
Conundrum
Daily Bread
Diane (Moon)
Eye Contact
Gleanings
Good Vibrations
High Browse (in braille and
  print)
In Touch (Moon)
Light of the Moon (Moon)
London Calling
The Magazine (Moon)
Moon Rainbow (Moon and
  braille)
New Beacon (in braille and
  print)

Physiotherapists' Quarterly
Piano Tuners' Quarterly
Progress
Rhetoric
Roundabout
Scientific Enquiry
Shaping Up
Shop Window
Soundings
Spotlight
Theological Times
Upbeat
The Weekender (Moon and
  braille)
You & Your Child

Business, Industry and Management

Achievement
Administrator
Brewing & Distilling
  International
Business Life
Business Scotland
BusinessAge
BusinessMatters
Communicate
Contemporary Review
Cosmetic World News
CWU Voice
Dairy Industries International
Director

Euromoney
European Chemical News
European Drinks Buyer
European Frozen Food Buyer
European Plastic News
Executive PA
Executive Woman
Fashion Forecast International
Fashion Weekly
Financial Director
Fire
Information and Software
  Technology
Involvement

Land & Liberty
Leisureweek
*Management (NZ)
Management Today
Mobile and Cellular Magazine
New Impact
Office Secretary
People Management
The Political Quarterly
*The Sunday Business Post
  (Ire.)
The Woodworker
Work Study

Cinema and Films

Campaign
Empire
New Statesman & Society

Screen International
Sight and Sound

Stand
Studio Sound

Computers

Computer Weekly
Computing
Internet

.net The Internet Magazine
PC Direct
PC Review

Personal Computer World
Scientific Computing World

Economics, Accountancy and Finance

Accountancy
Accountancy Age
Active Life
Africa Confidential
African Business
*The Australian Financial
  Review
The Banker
Business Scotland
Certified Accountant
Choice
Contemporary Review
Dairy Industries International

Economica
The Economist
Euromoney
Financial Accountant
Financial Adviser
Financial Director
Financial Times
Fourth World Review
The Grower
Insurance Age
Insurance Brokers' Monthly
Investors Chronicle
The Journal

Land & Liberty
Local Government Chronicle
MoneyMarketing
Moneywise
Mortgage Finance Gazette
New Statesman & Society
Pensions World
Personal Finance
Post Magazine
*Studies (Ire.)
Tribune
West Africa

Education

Amateur Stage
Art & Craft
British Journal of Special
  Education
Child Education
Education
Guiding
Infant Projects
Junior Education
Junior Focus
Linguist
Local Historian
Modern Language Review
Modus
Month

Museums Journal
Music Teacher
New Blackfriars
New Impact
New Statesman & Society
Nursery World
Parents
Practical Parenting
Prep School
*Reality (Ire.)
Report
Right Start
Safety Education
School Librarian
Scottish Educational Journal

Spoken English
The Teacher
Theology
The Times Educational
  Supplement
Times Educational
  Supplement Scotland
Times Higher Education
  Supplement
Together With Children
Tribune
The Unesco Courier
World's Children
Young People Now

Engineering and Mechanics (*See also* Architecture, Aviation, Business, Motor Transport, Nautical, Radio, Sciences)

Buses
Car Mechanics
Control & Instrumentation
Electrical Review
Electrical Times
*Electronics Australia
The Engineer

European Chemical News
Everyday with Practical
  Electronics
Fire
Gas World International
International Construction

Mobile and Cellular Magazine
Model Engineer
Practical Woodworking
Railway Gazette International
Railway Magazine
Transport

Gardening

Amateur Gardening
BBC Gardeners' World
  Magazine
Country
Country Garden &
  Smallholding
Country Life

The Field
The Garden
*Garden and Home (SA)
Garden Answers
Garden News
Gardens Illustrated

Homestyle
Hortus
House and Garden
Organic Gardening
Practical Gardening
Your Garden

Health and Home (*See also* Women's Interest Magazines)

Active Life
Aromatherapy
The Asda Magazine
*Australian Home Beautiful
*Australian House and Garden

BBC GoodFood
BBC Homes & Antiques
BBC Vegetarian GoodFood
*Canadian Interiors
Choice

Classic Stitches
Country Homes & Interiors
Cycling Today
First Steps
*Garden and Home (SA)

Goldlife for 50-Forward
Health & Efficiency
  International
Health & Fitness
Healthy Eating
Here's Health
Home and Family
Homes and Gardens
Homes and Ideas
HomeFlair Magazine
Homestyle
Hospitality
House & Garden
House Beautiful

Ideal Home
Inspirations
Jewish Telegraph
Modus
Our Baby
Parents
Perfect Home
Period Living & Traditional
  Homes
Practical Householder
Practical Parenting
Running Magazine
Safety Education
Saga

Sainsbury's: The Magazine
Scottish Home and Country
Slimmer Magazine
Slimming Magazine
The Mag!
Today's Runner
Vegan
Weight Watchers Magazine
The World of Embroidery
The World of Interiors
*Your Family (SA)
*Your Home (NZ)
Yours
Zest

History and Archaeology

Bedfordshire Magazine
Coin News
Contemporary Review
Country Quest
English Historical Review

Geographical Magazine
History
History Today
Illustrated London News
In Britain

Lancashire Life
Local Historian
Museums Journal
New Blackfriars
*Studies (Ire.)

Hotel, Catering and Leisure

Caterer & Hotelkeeper
Club Mirror
European Drinks Buyer
European Frozen Food Buyer

Hospitality
*Hotel and Catering Review
  (Ire.)

The Leisure Manager
Leisureweek

Humour and Satire

Private Eye

Viz

Inflight Magazines

*The Australian Way

Business Life

Hot Air

Legal and Police

The Criminologist
Family Law
Justice of the Peace and Local
  Government Law

The Lawyer
New Law Journal
Police Journal

Police Review
Solicitors Journal

Leisure Interests, Pets (*See also* Nautical, Sports)

Aeromodeller
Astronomy Now
Bird Keeper
Bird Watching
Birdwatch
Boards
British Birds
Camping Magazine
Caravan Magazine
Classic Stitches
Climber
Dogs Today
Family Tree Magazine
The Field
Fishkeeping Answers

Gibbons Stamp Monthly
Guiding
In Britain
Military Modelling
Model Boats
Model Engineer
Motor Caravan Magazine
Motorcaravan and Motorhome
  Monthly
Needlecraft
Our Dogs
Outdoors Illustrated
Park Home & Holiday
  Caravan
Popular Crafts

Radio Control Models
Rambling Today
Scale Models International
Scottish Field
Scouting
Simply Crafts
Stamp Lover
Stamp Magazine
Steam Classic
Today's Horse
The Woodworker
Workbox
Your Dog

Literary (See also Poetry)

*Australian Bookseller &
  Publisher
Author
The Book Collector
*Books in Canada
*Books Ireland
Books Magazine
The Bookseller
British Journalism Review
*Canadian Author
*The Canadian Forum
*Canadian Literature
Cencrastus
Chapman
Contemporary Review
Critical Quarterly
Critical Wave
*The Dalhousie Review (Can.)
The Dickensian
Edinburgh Review
European Bookseller
*Fiddlehead (Can.)
Freelance Market News
Freelance Writing &
  Photography

The Good Society Review
Granta
The Illustrated London News
Index on Censorship
The Indexer
*Journal of Canadian Studies
Journalist
Learned Publishing
The Library
Lines Review
The Literary Review
Llais Llyfrau
LOGOS
London Magazine
London Review of Books
*The Malahat Review (Can.)
Modern Languages
New Library World
New Statesman & Society
The New Welsh Review
The Oldie
Orbis
Outposts Poetry Quarterly
*Overland (Aus.)
Planet

Publishing News
*Quadrant (Aus.)
*Quill & Quire (Can.)
*Reality (Ire.)
*Redoubt (Aus.)
Scottish Book Collector
Signal
The Spectator
Stand
*Studies (Ire.)
*Takahe (NZ)
TGO (The Great Outdoors)
  Magazine
The Times Literary
  Supplement
Tribune
Wasafiri
*Wascana Review (Can.)
Woman Journalist
Writers' Forum
Writers' Monthly
Writers News
Writing Magazine
Writing Women
Xenos

Local Government and Civil Service

Justice of the Peace and Local
  Government Law
Local Government Chronicle

Public Service & Local
  Government

Red Tape

Marketing and Retailing

CTN
Drapers Record
Fashion Weekly
Gifts International

Greetings Magazine
The Grocer
Marketing Week
Off Licence News

Retail Week
Toy Trader
*Ulster Grocer

Medicine and Nursing

Balance
The British Deaf News
British Journal of General
  Practice
British Medical Journal
Carers World
Community Care
Dental Update
Disability Now

Doctor
Hospital Doctor
*Irish Journal of Medical
  Science
*Irish Medical Times
Journal of Alternative and
  Complementary Medicine
Lancet
Nursery World

Nursing Times
The Pharmaceutical Journal
The Practitioner
Professional Nurse
Pulse
Therapy Weekly
This Caring Business
Young People Now

Military

Army Quarterly & Defence
  Journal

Combat & Militaria
*Guns Australia

Jane's Defence Weekly
RUSI Journal

Motor Transport and Cycling

Auto Express
Autocar
Back Street Heroes

BBC Top Gear Magazine
Bike
Buses

Car
*Car (SA)
Car Mechanics

Classic & Sportscar
Classic Cars
Commercial Motor
Custom Car
Cycling Today
Cycling Weekly

Dirt Bike Rider
Motor Cycle News
Motorcycle International
Performance Car
Practical Motorist

Scootering
Street Machine
Superbike
Trucking International
What Car?

Music and Recording

Arena
BBC Music Magazine
Classic CD
Classical Music
Early Music
The Face
Gramophone
Hi-Fi News
i-D Magazine
Jazz Journal International
Kerrang!
Keyboard Review

Making Music
Melody Maker
Mojo
Music and Letters
The Music Review
Music Teacher
Music Week
Musical Opinion
Musical Times
New Musical Express
Opera
Opera Now

The Organ
Q Magazine
Select Magazine
Sky Magazine
Smash Hits
*Songwriter (Ire.)
Songwriting and Composing
Studio Sound
Tempo
Top of the Pops Magazine
Vox

Natural History (*See also* **Agriculture, Rural Life**)

The Aquarist and
  Pondkeeper
BBC Wildlife Magazine
Bird Keeper
Bird Watching
Birdwatch
British Birds
Budgerigar World
Cage and Aviary Birds

Cat World
The Dalesman
Dogs Today
The Ecologist
*Equinox (Can.)
*Geo Australasia
Geographical Magazine
Glaucus

Guiding
Horse & Pony
Natural World
Naturalist
Nature
Our Dogs
Pony
Practical Fishkeeping

Nautical and Marine

The Boatman
*Canadian Yachting
Classic Boat
Diver
*Modern Boating (Aus.)
Motor Boat and Yachting

Motor Boats Monthly
Nautical Magazine
Practical Boat Owner
Sea Breezes
Ship & Boat International
Ships Monthly

*South African Yachting
Transport
Yachting Monthly
Yachting World
Yachts and Yachting

Photography

Amateur Photographer
*Australian Photography
The British Journal of
  Photography
Camcorder User

Creative Camera
Freelance Writing &
  Photography
Photo Answers
*Photo Life (Can.)

photo pro
Photo Technique
Practical Photography
Professional Photographer
Video Camera

Poetry

Those magazines marked with a † only take the occasional poem. Check with the editor before submitting.

Acumen
Agenda
Ambit
Cencrastus
Chapman
†The Countryman

Critical Quarterly
*Cyphers (Ire.)
*The Dalhousie Review (Can.)
†Day by Day
Edinburgh Review
Envoi

*The Fiddlehead (Can.)
*Fortnight (Ire.)
The Good Society Review
The Haiku Quarterly
*HU (The Honest Ulsterman)
  (Ire.)

Iron
‡Jewish Quarterly
*Krino (Ire.)
‡Life and Work
Lines Review
The Literary Review
London Magazine
London Review of Books
*The Malahat Review (Can.)
New Statesman & Society
The New Welsh Review
Orbis
Outposts Poetry Quarterly

Oxford Poetry
Planet
PN Review
*Poetry Australia
*Poetry Ireland/Éigse Éireann
Poetry London Newsletter
Poetry Nottingham
International
Poetry Review
Poetry Wales
*Quadrant (Aus.)
‡Quaker Monthly
*Redoubt (Aus.)

The Rialto
‡The Scots Magazine
The Spectator
Stand Magazine
Staple
*Takahe (NZ)
‡The Times Literary
Supplement
‡Tribune
Wasafiri
*Wascana Review (Can.)
Writing Women

Politics

Africa Confidential
*Australian Journal of
International Affairs
*The Australian Journal of
Politics and History
*The Australian Quarterly
The China Quarterly
*The Big Issues (Ire.)
Contemporary Review
*Current Affairs Bulletin
(Aus.)

*Fortnight (Ire.)
Fourth World Review
The Illustrated London News
International Affairs
Justice of the Peace
Local Government Chronicle
Middle East International
New Blackfriars
New Christian Herald
New Internationalist
New Statesman & Society

Peace News
The Political Quarterly
Red Pepper
*Studies (Ire.)
Tribune
The Unesco Courier
Voice Intelligence Report
West Africa
The World Today

Radio, Television and Video

Broadcast
Campaign
*Electronics Australia
Empire
Gramophone
Hi-Fi News
InterMedia

New Statesman & Society
*New Zealand Listener
Opera Now
Practical Wireless
Radio Times
Satellite Times
Short-Wave Magazine

The Stage
Studio Sound
Television
Tribune
TV Times
What's on TV

Religion, Philosophy and New Age

Baptist Times
Catholic Gazette
The Catholic Herald
Catholic Pictorial
Catholic Times
Church of England Newspaper
*Church of Ireland Gazette
Church Times
Contemporary Review
Day by Day
The Downside Review
Fortean Times
Friend
*The Furrow (Ire.)
*Herald of the South (Aus.)
Home and Family

Home Words
Inquirer
Jewish Chronicle
Jewish Quarterly
Jewish Telegraph
Kids Alive!
Life and Work
Methodist Recorder
Mind
Modern Believing
Month
New Blackfriars
New Christian Herald
New Humanist
Priests & People

Quaker Monthly
*Reality (Ire.)
Reform
Sign
*Southern Cross (SA)
*Studies (Ire.)
Tablet
Theology
Third Way
Together with Children
Universe
War Cry
West Africa
Woman Alive
*Word (Ire.)

Rural Life and Country (See also Natural History)

Bedfordshire Magazine
Cheshire Life
Country

Country Life
Country Quest
The Countryman

Country-Side
County
Coventry Evening Telegraph

Cumbria
Dalesman
Derbyshire Life and
  Countryside
Dorset Life – The Dorset
  Magazine
East Lothian Life
Eastern Daily Press
Essex Countryside
The Field
Hampshire
Heritage

Hertfordshire Countryside
In Britain
Inverness Courier
*Ireland's Eye
The Lady
Lancashire Evening Post
Lancashire Life
Lancashire Magazine
Lincolnshire Life
The Local Historian
Manx Life
Rambling Today

The Scots Magazine
Scottish Field
Scottish Home and Country
Shooting Times and Country
  Magazine
The Shropshire Magazine
Somerset Magazine
This England
Waterways World
Yorkshire Life
Yorkshire Ridings Magazine

Sciences

The Criminologist
*Equinox (Can.)
Geological Magazine

Mind
Nature
New Scientist

Science Progress
Scientific Computing World
*Technology Ireland

Sports and Games (*See also* **Leisure Interests, Motoring, Nautical**)

Anglers' Mail
Angling Times
Athletics Weekly
*Australasian Sporting Shooter
*Australian Angler's Fishing
  World
Bowls International
Bridge International
British Chess Magazine
The Cricketer International
Darts World
Eventing
The Field
Fly-Fishing & Fly-Tying
Fore!
Golf Monthly

Golf Weekly
Golf World
*Guns Australia
Horse and Hound
Horse and Rider
Inside Edge
90 Minutes
Our Dogs
Outdoors Illustrated
Rugby World
Runner's World
Scottish Field
Sea Angler
Shooting Times
The Skier and
  The Snowboarder

Snooker Scene
Sport
The Sporting Life
The Squash Player
Tennis World
Today's Golfer
Today's Horse
Today's Runner
Trout and Salmon
When Saturday Comes
Wisden Cricket Monthly
*Word (Ire.)
World Bowls
World Fishing
World Soccer

Theatre, Drama and Dancing (*See also* **Cinema, Music**)

Amateur Stage
Ballroom Dancing Times
*Canadian Forum
Contemporary Review
Dance & Dancers
*Dance Australia
Dancing Times

The Illustrated London News
In Britain
New Statesman & Society
New Theatre Quarterly
*Performing Arts &
  Entertainment in Canada
Plays & Players

Radio Times
*Reality (Ire.)
Speech and Drama
The Stage
Tribune
TV Times

Travel and Geography

*Australian Geographic
*Australian Skiing
Caravan Magazine
Contemporary Review
*Equinox (Can.)
FRANCE Magazine
*Geo Australasia

Geographical Journal
Geographical Magazine
Heritage
The Illustrated London News
In Britain
*In Dublin (Ire.)

*Ireland of the Welcomes
The Local Historian
*Natal Witness (SA)
Outdoors Illustrated
Traveller
Wanderlust

Syndicates, News and Press Agencies

In their own interests writers and others are strongly advised to make preliminary enquiries before submitting MSS, and to ascertain terms of work. Commission varies. Strictly speaking, syndication is the selling and reselling of previously published work and the details given for agencies in the following list should be noted carefully. Some news and press agencies may handle original material.

Academic File (1985), The Centre for Near East, Afro-Asia Research (NEAR), Acre House, 69-76 Long Acre, London WC2E 9JH *tel* 0181-392 1122 *fax* 0181-392 1422. *Managing editor:* Sajid Rizvi; *executive editor:* Shirley Rizvi. Feature and photo syndication with special reference to the developing world and immigrant communities in the West.

Advance Features, Clarendon House, Judges Terrace, East Grinstead, West Sussex RH19 3AD *tel* (01342) 328562. *Managing editor:* Peter Norman. Supplies text and visual services to the national and regional press in Britain and newspapers overseas. Instructional graphic panels on a variety of subjects. Text services (weekly); 'agony' columns (teenagers), stars, nature, daily, weekly and theme crosswords. Daily and weekly cartoons for the regional press (not single cartoons).

A.L.I. Press Agency Ltd (1948), Boulevard Anspach 111-115, Bte 9, B9-1000 Brussels, Belgium *tel* 02 512 73 94 *fax* 02 512 03 30. *Director:* George Lans. All types of feature services except information and news: cartoons, puzzles, strips, comics, illustrations, picture stories, transparencies, articles of general interest, etc. for magazines, newspapers and books, especially illustrated books for children and adults. Syndication in all major countries. Commissions 35%, syndication 50%.

ANPS (Australasian News & Press Services) (D.J. Varney & Associates 1964), Box T 1834, GPO, Perth, W Australia 6001 *tel* (09) 293 1455 *fax* (09) 257 1558. Australian correspondents and representatives for the international media. Services provided: features and news for colour photo magazines; articles for consumer, trade, technical and professional journals; trade news summaries and newsletters. Full range of professional public relations and market research services available including film, television and stage writing, production and talent services.

The Associated Press Ltd (News Department), The Associated Press House, 12 Norwich Street, London EC4A 1BP *tel* 0171-353 1515 *telegraphic address* Associated Londonpsy *fax* 0171-353 8118.

Australian Associated Press (1935), 12 Norwich Street, London EC4A 1EJ *tel* 0171-353 0153 *fax* 0171-583 3563. News service to the Australian, New Zealand and Pacific Island press, radio and television.

BIPS—Bernsen's International Press Service Ltd, 9 Paradise Close, Eastbourne, East Sussex BN20 8BT *tel* (01323) 728760. *Editor:* Harry Gresty. Specialise in photo-features, both b&w and colour. Seek human interest, oddity, glamour, pin-ups, scientific, medical, etc., material suitable for marketing through own branches in London, San Francisco, Paris, Hamburg, Milan, Stockholm, Amsterdam (for Benelux), Helsinki.

Neil Bradley Puzzles (1981), Linden House, 34 Hardy Barn, Shipley, Derbyshire DE75 7JA *tel/fax* (01773) 768960. *Director:* Neil Bradley. Supplies visual puzzles to national and regional press; emphasis placed on variety and topicality with work based on current media listings. Work supplied on disk or prints to Mac or PC. Daily single frame and strip cartoons. Contact for free booklet and disk demo.

Bulls Presstjänst AB, Tulegatan 39, Box 6519, S-11383 Stockholm, Sweden *tel* (08) 23 40 20 *cables* Pressbull *fax* (08) 15 80 10; **Bulls Pressedienst GmbH,** Eysseneckstrasse 50, D-60322 Frankfurt am Main, Germany *tel* (069) 959 270 *cables* Pressbull *fax* (069) 959 27111; **Bulls Pressetjeneste A/S,** Ebbells Gate 3, N-0183 Oslo, Norway *tel* 22 20 56 01 *cables* Bullspress *fax* 22 20 49 78; **Bulls Pressetjeneste,** Östbanegade 9, 1th, DK-2100 Copenhagen, Denmark *tel* 31 38 90 99 *cables* Pressbull *fax* 31 38 25 16; **Bulls Finska Försäljnings AB,** Isonniitynkatu 7, Box 180, FIN-00521, Helsinki, Finland *tel* (90) 757 13 11 *fax* (90) 757 06 34; **Bulls Press,** ul. Chocimska 28, Pokoj 509, 00-791 Warsawa, Poland *tel/fax* (22) 49 80 18; **Bulls Press,** Pikk 29 A, EE 0001 Tallinn, Estonia *tel* (2) 501 84 85 *fax* (2) 631 41 65. *Market:* newspapers, magazines, weeklies and advertising agencies in Sweden, Denmark, Norway, Finland, Iceland, Poland, The Baltic States, Germany, Austria and German-speaking Switzerland. *Syndicates:* human interest picture stories; topical and well-illustrated background articles and series; photographic features dealing with science, people, personalities, glamour; genre pictures for advertising; condensations and serialisations of best-selling fiction and non-fiction; cartoons, comic strips, film and TV rights, merchandising and newspaper graphics on-line via modem or ISDN.

The Canadian Press (1919), Chief Correspondent: Helen Branswell. Associated Press House, 12 Norwich Street, London EC4A 1EJ *tel* 0171-353 6355 *fax* 0171-583 4238. London Bureau of the national news agency of Canada.

Capital Press Service, 2 Long Cottage, Church Street, Leatherhead, Surrey KT22 8EJ *tel* (01372) 377451. *Directors:* M. Stone, E.W. Stone; *news editor:* Mark Stone. Stories of trade, commerce and industry for trade papers in this country and abroad. Interested in air-cargo affairs and business travel (including hotels, luggage, guides, new routes via air, sea, road and train) for UK and US journals.

Central Press Features, 20 Spectrum House, 32/34 Gordon House Road, London NW5 1LP *tel* 0171-284 1433 *fax* 0171-284 4494. Supplies every type of feature to newspapers and other publications in 50 countries. Included in over 100 daily and weekly services are columns on international affairs, politics, sports, medicine, law, finance, computers, video, motoring, science, gardening, fashion, house and home, health and beauty, women's and children's features, strips, crosswords, cartoons and regular 6-12 article illustrated series of international human interest; also editorial material for advertising features.

J.W. Crabtree and Son (1919), 36 Sunbridge Road, Bradford BD1 2AA *tel* (01274) 732937 (office)/(01535) 655288 (home). News, general, trade and sport; information and research for features undertaken.

Daily & Sunday Telegraph Syndication, Ewan MacNaughton Associates, Alexandra Chambers, 6 Alexandra Road, Tonbridge, Kent TN9 2AA *tel* (01732) 771116 *fax* (01732) 771160. News, features, photography; worldwide distribution and representation.

Europa-Press, Saltmätargatan 8, 1st Floor, Box 6410, S-113 82, Stockholm, Sweden *tel* 8-34 94 35 *fax* 8-34 80 79. *Managing director:* Sven Berlin. *Market:* newspapers, magazines and weeklies in Sweden, Denmark, Norway and Finland. *Syndicates:* high quality features of international appeal such as topical articles, photo-features – b&w and colour, women's features, short stories, serial novels, non-fiction stories and serials with strong human interest, crime articles, popular science, cartoons, comic strips.

Europress Features (UK), 18 St Chads Road, Didsbury, near Manchester M20 9WH *tel* 0161-445 2945. Representation of newspapers and magazines in Europe, Australia, United States. Syndication of top-flight features with exclusive illustrations – human interest stories – showbusiness personalities. 30-35% commission on sales of material successfully accepted; 40% on exclusive illustrations.

Express Enterprises, division of Express Newspapers plc, Ludgate House, 245 Blackfriars Road, London SE1 9UX *tel* 0171-922 7902 *cable* Lon Express *telex* 21841 *fax* 0171-922 7871. Text and pictures from all Express titles. Archive from 1900. Numerous strips and political cartoons. Material handled worldwide for freelance journalists.

Features International, Tolland, Lydeard St Lawrence, Taunton TA4 3PS *tel* (01984) 623014 *fax* (01984) 623901. *Editorial director:* Anthony Sharrock. Syndicates features to magazines and newspapers throughout the world. The agency produces a wide range of material – mainly from freelance sources – including topical articles, women's features and weekly columns. Distributes directly to all English-language countries. Agents throughout the Common Market countries, Japan, the Americas and Eastern Europe. Buys copy outright and welcomes story ideas. *Sae essential.*

Gemini News Service, 9 White Lion Street, London N1 9PD *tel* 0171-833 4141 *fax* 0171-837 5118 *e-mail* Gemini@gn.apc.org *Editor:* Daniel Nelson; *managing director:* Bethel Njoku. Network of freelance contributors and specialist writers all over the world. Specialists in news-features of international, topical and development interest. Preferred length 800-1200 words.

Global Syndication & Literary Agency, Limited, 120 Westmont, Hemet, CA 92543, USA. *President:* A.D. Fowler. Interested in previously published books for possible syndication and placement of subsidiary rights. Our book reviewers always looking for non-fiction titles. US postage or International Reply Coupons required for return of material.

Graphic Syndication (1981), 4 Reyntiens View, Odiham, Hants RG29 1AF *tel* (01256) 703004. *Manager:* M. Flanagan. Cartoon strips and single frames supplied to newspapers and magazines in Britain and overseas. *Terms:* 50%.

India-International News Service, *Head office:* Jute House, 12 India Exchange Place, Calcutta 700001, India *tel* 2209563, 4791009 *telegraphic address* Zeitgeist. *Proprietor:* Ing H. Kothari BSc, DWP(Lond), FIMechE, FIE, FVI, FInstD. 'Calcutta Letters' and Air Mail news service from Calcutta. Specialists in industrial and technical news.

INS (International News Service)/Irish International News Service, 7 King's Avenue, Minnis Bay, Birchington-on-Sea, East Kent CT7 9QL *tel* (01843) 845022. *Editor and managing director:* Barry J. Hardy PC; *photo editor:* Jan Vanek. News, sport, book reviews, TV, radio, photographic department; also equipment for TV films, etc.

International Fashion Press Agency, Mumford House, Mottram Road, Alderley Edge, Cheshire SK9 7JF *tel* (01625) 583537 *fax* (01625) 584344. *Directors:* P. Bentham (managing), P. Dyson, L.C. Bentham, S. Fagette, J. Fox. Monitors and photographs international fashion collections and developments in textile and fashion industry. Specialist writers on health, fitness, beauty and personalities. Undertakes individual commissioned features. Supplies syndicated columns/pages to press, radio and TV (NUJ staff writers and photographers).

International Feature Service, 104 rue de Laeken, 1000 Brussels, Belgium *tel* 217-03-42 *fax* 217-03-42. *Managing director:* Max S. Kleiter. Feature articles, serial rights, tests, cartoons, comic strips and illustrations. Handles English TV-features and books; also production of articles for merchandising.

International Press Agency (Pty) Ltd (1934), PO Box 67, Howard Place 7450, South Africa *tel* (021) 531 1926 *fax* (021) 531 8789. *Manager:* Mrs T. Temple; *UK Office:* Mrs U.A. Barnett PhD (*managing editor*), 19 Avenue South, Surbiton, Surrey KT5 8PJ *tel/fax* 0181-390 4414. South African agents for many leading British, American and continental press firms for the syndication of comic strips, cartoons, jokes, feature articles, short stories, serials, press photos for the South African market.

ITAR-Tass Agency, Suite 12-20, Morley House, 314-320 Regent Street, London W1R 5AB *tel* 0171-580 5543 *fax* 0171-580 5547. General, economic and commercial news service to Russia and the CIS.

Joker Feature Service (JFS), PO Box 253, 6040 AG, Roermond, The Netherlands *tel* (0475) 337338 *fax* (0475) 315663. *Managing director:* Ruud Kerstens. Feature articles, serial rights, tests, cartoons, comic strips and illustrations, puzzles. Handles TV-features and books; also production for merchandising.

Knight Features (1985), 20 Crescent Grove, London SW4 7AH *tel* 0171-622 1467 *fax* 0171-622 1522. *Director:* Peter Knight; *associates:* Ann King-Hall, Gaby Martin, Andrew Knight, Giovanna Farrell-Vinay. Worldwide selling of strip cartoons and major features and serialisations. Exclusive agent in UK and Republic of Ireland for United Feature Syndicate and Newspaper Enterprise Association of New York.

London News Service, 68 Exmouth Market, London EC1R 4RA *tel* 0171-278 5661 *fax* 0171-278 8480 *telex* 94018004 FSNA G. *Editor:* John Rodgers. Worldwide syndication of features and photos.

Maharaja Features Pvt. Ltd, 5/226 Sion Road East, Bombay 400022, India *tel* 22-4097951 *fax* 22-4097801. *Editor:* K.R.N. Swamy; *managing editor:* K.R. Padmanabhan. Syndicates feature and pictorial material, of interest to Asian readers, to newspapers and magazines in India, UK and abroad. Specialists in well-researched articles on India by eminent authorities for publication in prestige journals throughout the world. Also topical features 1000-1500 words. *Illustrations:* b&w prints and colour transparencies.

Mirror Syndication International, Unique House, 21-31 Woodfield Road, London W9 2BA *tel* 0171-266 1133 *fax* 0171-266 2563. Supplies publishing material and international rights for news text and pictures from Mirror Group Newspapers and other large publishing houses. Extensive picture library of all subjects.

New Zealand Press Association, 12 Norwich Street, London EC4A 1EJ *tel* 0171-353 7040 *fax* 0171-583 3563.

News Blitz International, Via Guido Banti 34, 00191 Rome, Italy *tel* 333 26 41, 333 02 52 *fax* 333 26 51. *President:* Vinicio Congiu; *sales manager:* Gianni Piccione; *graphic, literary and television depts:* Giovanni Congiu. Syndicates cartoons, comic strips, humorous books with drawings, feature and pictorial material, environment, travels, throughout the world. Average rates of commission 60-40%, monthly report of sales, payment 60 days after the date of monthly report.

PA News Ltd (1868), 292 Vauxhall Bridge Road, London SW1V 1AE *tel* 0171-963 7000. *Chief executive:* Robert Simpson; *editor:* Paul Potts; *sales director:*

Clive Marshall. PA News: national news agency for the UK and Republic of Ireland. Comprehensive news, photo and information services, as well as extensive news cuttings and photo libraries. PA Sport: full coverage of national sport plus fast results service. PA Data Design: page-ready information – formatted sports results, TV listings, stocklists, racecards and weather reports.

Chandra S. Perera, Cinetra, 437 Pethiyagoda, Kelaniya-0490, Sri Lanka *tel* 94-1-521885 *cables* 94-1-521885 Colombo *telex* 94-1-21193/21213 OTS ATTN CHANDRA PERERA *fax* 94-1-323910/541414 ATTN CHANDRA PERERA. Press and TV news, news films on Sri Lanka and Maldives, colour and b&w photo news and features, photographic and film coverages, screenplays and scripts for TV and films, press clippings. Broadcasting, television and newspapers; journalistic features, news, broadcasting and TV interviews.

Pixfeatures, P.G. Wickman, 5 Latimer Road, Barnet, Herts. EN5 5NU *tel* 0181-449 9946 *fax* 0181-441 6246. Specialises in sale of picture features and news to British and European press.

Christopher Rann & Associates Pty Ltd (1977), 7th Floor, NZI House, 117 King William Street, Adelaide, SA 5000 *postal address* GPO Box 958, Adelaide, SA 5001 *tel* (08) 211 7771 *fax* (08) 212 2272. *Proprietors:* C.F. Rann, J.M. Jose. Full range of professional PR, press releases, special newsletters, commercial intelligence, media monitoring. Welcomes approaches from organisations requiring PR representation or press release distribution.

Republican Press (London), Suite 15-17, The Outer Temple, 222-225 Strand, London WC2R 1BA *tel* 0171-353 2580 *fax* 0171-353 2578. Acquire material for publication in South Africa.

Reuters Limited, 85 Fleet Street, London EC4P 4AJ *tel* 0171-250 1122 *telex* 28355/265952.

Singer Media Corporation, Seaview Business Park, 1030 Calle Cordillera, Unit 106, San Clemente, CA 92673 *tel* 714-498-7227. *Vice-President:* Helen J. Lee; *acquisitions:* Kristy Lee. Features (celebrity interviews and profiles, business, health, fitness, beauty, diet, self-help, how-to, etc.), cartoons, puzzles and quizzes of international appeal for international and domestic syndication. Represented in most countries abroad. No local or national material; no comic strips. Query first.

Solo Syndication Ltd (1978), 49-53 Kensington High Street, London W8 5ED *tel* 0171-376 2166 *fax* 0171-938 3165. *Chairman:* Don Short. Worldwide syndication of newspaper features, photos, cartoons, strips and book serialisations. Professional journalists only. *Commission:* 50/50. Agency represents the international syndication of Associated Newspapers (*Daily Mail, Mail on Sunday, Evening Standard*), IPC Magazines (*Woman, Woman's Own, Woman's Realm, Woman's Weekly*), *The European, The Guinness Book of Records, Guiness Publishing, News Ltd of Australia, New Idea* and *TV Week*, Australia, the *Johannesburg Star* and Argus South African Newspapers.

Southern Media Services (division of Maximedia Pty Ltd), PO Box 268, Springwood, NSW 2777, Australia *tel* (047) 514 967 *fax* (047) 515 545. *Directors:* Nic van Oudtshoorn, Daphne van Oudtshoorn. Illustrated features (colour and b&w) to newspapers and magazines in Australasia and many parts of the world. Also stock colour library. Assignments (news and feature stories, photos) accepted at moderate rates. Syndicates freelance features and photo features in Australia and abroad, but query before submitting. Commission 50% or by arrangement.

Swedish Features, Görwellsgatan 28B, 112 88 Stockholm, Sweden *tel* 8-738 32 74 *fax* 8-618 28 72. *Managing director:* Herborg Ericson. *Market:* newspapers, magazines and weeklies in Sweden, Norway, Denmark and Finland. *Syndicates:* high quality features of international appeal such as topical articles, photo-features – b&w and colour, women's features, short stories, serial novels, non-fiction stories and serials with strong human interest, popular science, cartoons, comic strips and TV features and TV personalities.

Syndicated International Network (S.I.N.) (1984), Second Floor, 208-209 Upper Street, Islington, London N1 1RL   *tel* 0171-359 0200   *fax* 0171-359 2228. *Managing director:* Marianne Lassen. Worldwide syndication of interview texts and photos, primarily of music and cinema artists. Unsolicited material always considered. *Commission:* 50%.

Peter Tauber Press Agency (1950), 94 East End Road, London N3 2SX   *tel* 0181-346 4165. UK and worldwide syndication of exclusive big name celebrity interviews, especially interviews with their associates or ex-associates. Also unique human interest features. *Commission:* 25%.

TEXT Syndication (1993), 26 Ingelow Road, London SW8 3QA   *tel* 0171-978 2116   *fax* 0171-627 0746. *Contact:* Amanda McKee. Specialises in syndicating previously published material worldwide for freelance journalists. Require high quality features of international appeal (including human interest, health, beauty, relationships, celebrity interviews, general features). Please enquire *before* submitting MSS. *Commission:* 50%.

TransAtlantic News Service, 7100 Hillside Avenue, Suite 304, Hollywood, CA 90046, USA   *tel* 213-874-1284. News and photo agency serving the British and foreign press, TANS supplies entertainment news, features and columns from Hollywood, and topical news in general from California. Covers all Hollywood events and undertakes commissions and assignments in all fields. Candid photos of stars at major Hollywood events a speciality.

United Press International, 408 Strand, London WC2R 0NG   *tel* 0171-333 0999 (news), 0171-468 1600 (admin), 0171-333 1666 (sports)   *fax* 0171-333 1670.

Universal Pictorial Press & Agency Ltd (1929), 29-31 Saffron Hill, London EC1N 8FH   *tel* 0171-421 6000   *fax* 0171-421 6006. *Managing director:* T.R. Smith. Syndication of daily press and library photo service to the national and provincial press, periodicals and television companies in the British Isles and overseas.

Visual Humour (1984), 5 Greymouth Close, Stockton-on-Tees, Cleveland TS18 5LF   *tel* (01642) 581847/0121-429 5861   *fax* (01642) 581847. *Contact:* Peter Dodsworth. Daily and weekly humorous cartoon strips; also single panel cartoon features (not single cartoons) for possible syndication in the UK and abroad. Picture puzzles also considered. Submit photocopy samples only initially, with sae.

Yaffa Newspaper Service of New Zealand, 29 Queens Avenue, Balmoral, Auckland 4, New Zealand   *tel* (09) 631 5225   *fax* (09) 631 0040.

Books

Book Publishers

SUBMITTING MATERIAL

The following essentials should be borne in mind when submitting material. First – choose the right publisher. It is a waste of time and money to send the MS of a novel to a publisher who publishes no fiction, or poetry to one who publishes no verse, though all too often this is done. By studying the entries in the *Yearbook*, examining publishers' lists of publications, or by looking for the names of suitable publishers in the relevant sections in libraries and bookshops, you will find the names of several publishers who might be interested in seeing your material.

Secondly – the approach. Many publishers will not accept unsolicited material – you must enquire first as to whether they would be willing to read the whole MS. A few publishers are prepared to speak on the telephone, allowing you to describe, briefly, the work on offer. Most prefer a preliminary letter (see below); and many publishers, particularly of fiction, will only see material submitted through a literary agent. It has to be said that some publishing houses, the larger ones in particular, may well employ all three methods!

When you send your preliminary letter, enclose with this a synopsis of the work, and two or three sample chapters, plus return postage (International Reply Coupons if writing from outside the UK). Writers have been known to send out such letters in duplicated form, an approach unlikely to stimulate a publishers' interest. Remember, also, that whilst every reasonable care will be taken of material in the publishers' possession, responsibility cannot be accepted if material is lost or damaged.

Fiction and poetry. To assist the writer of fiction, in particular, a classified list of publishers, by fiction genre, will be found on page 214. Those publishers willing to consider poetry are listed on page 217 (for adults) and page 247 (for children).

Children's books. Submission of material – both text and illustrations – for children's books requires particular consideration. Attention is therefore drawn to the article on page 241 on advice for this market. A classified list of publishers and packagers of children's books follows on page 244.

For more on the submission of manuscripts, see *Preparing and submitting a manuscript* on page 460.

SMALL PRESSES

It is beyond the scope of the *Yearbook* to list all the many smaller publishers which have either a limited output, or who specialise in poetry, avant-garde or other fringe publishing. Details are given of some of the better-known small poetry houses, but for a comprehensive listing, the reader is referred to *Small Presses & Little Magazines in the UK and Ireland*, available from HMSO Oriel Bookshop, The HMSO Oriel Bookshop, The Friary, Cardiff CF1 4AA   *tel* (01222) 395548.

SELF-PUBLISHING

Authors are strongly advised not to pay for the publication of their work. If a MS is worth publishing, a reputable firm of publishers will undertake publication at its own expense, except possibly for works of an academic nature. In this connection attention is drawn to the articles on *Self-publishing* and *Vanity Publishing*, at the end of this section, and to Michael Legat's article on *Publishing Agreements* on page 521.

UNITED KINGDOM

(For Northern Ireland publishers, see under Irish listings on page 223.)

* Member of the Publishers Association or Scottish Publishers Association

*AA Publishing (1979), Automobile Association, Fanum House, Basingstoke, Hants RG21 2EA   *tel* (01256) 20123   *telex* 858538 AABAS G   *fax* (01256) 22575. *Managing director:* John Howard, *marketing and international sales director:* S.J. Mesquita; *editorial manager:* Michael Buttler.
  Travel, atlases, maps, leisure interests, including Baedeker, Essential, Thomas Cook and Explorer Travel Guides.

*Abacus (1971)—see **Little, Brown and Company (UK).**

ABC, All Books for Children (1990), 33 Museum Street, London WC1A 1LD   *tel* 0171-436 6300   *telex* 21134 ABCDEF G   *fax* 0171-240 6923. *Managing director and publisher:* Susan Tarsky; *chairman:* Timothy Chadwick; *financial director:* Michael Raine. Division of The All Children's Co. Ltd.
  Children's picture books up to age seven; non-fiction for 7-11. Submit MSS with sae to Carol Mackenzie.

Absolute Press (1979), Scarborough House, 29 James Street West, Bath, Avon BA1 2BT   *tel* (01225) 316013   *fax* (01225) 445836. *Publisher:* Jon Croft. *Directors:* Amanda Hawkins (sales), Bronwen Douglas (marketing).
  Cookery, wine, travel, monographs in the Out Lines series.
  Absolute Classics (imprint). Classic European drama in translation, theatre books.

Abson Books Bristol (1970), 17 Fosseway Court, The Fosseway, Clifton, Bristol BS8 4EH   *tel* (0117) 973 4486. *Partners:* Anthea Bickerton, Pat McCormack. English speaking glossaries, guides, West Region. No fiction. No unsolicited MSS.

*Academic Press—see **Harcourt Brace & Co. Ltd.**

*Academy Editions (1967), 42 Leinster Gardens, London W2 3AN   *tel* 0171-402 2141   *fax* 0171-723 9540. *Director:* J.V. Stoddart. Imprint of Academy Group Ltd.
  Art, architecture, crafts, design, photography, urbanism, philosophy. *Series include Architectural Design* Profiles, Architectural Monographs, *Art and Design* Profiles, Art Monographs, and *UIA Journal, Journal of Philosophy and the Visual Arts, What Is . . .?.*

*Access Press—see **HarperCollins Publishers.**

Ace Books (1973), Age Concern England, 1268 London Road, London SW16 4ER *tel* 0181-679 8000 *fax* 0181-679 6069. *Manager:* Richard Holloway; *marketing:* Michael Addison.
Health and care, advice, leisure, finance, gerontology.

***Acorn Editions**—see **James Clarke & Co. Ltd.**

Actinic Press—see **Cressrelles Publishing Co. Ltd.**

***Addison Wesley Longman Ltd** (1995), Edinburgh Gate, Harlow, Essex CM20 2JE *tel* (01279) 623623 *fax* (01279) 431059 *e-mail* enq.order@awl.co.uk *Directors:* J. Larry Jones (USA), R.M. Woodward (USA), T.C. Davy, J.E. Robinson.
Addison Wesley Longman was established in 1995 with the merger of Longman and Addison-Wesley, both Pearson companies. It publishes materials for pupils and students from nursery-school to post-graduate level in virtually every country.

***Adlard Coles Nautical**—see **A. & C. Black (Publishers) Ltd.**

***Adlib**—see **Scholastic Children's Books.**

Airlife Publishing Ltd (1976), 101 Longden Road, Shrewsbury, Shropshire SY3 9EB *tel* (01743) 235651 *fax* (01743) 232944. *Directors:* Alastair Simpson (chairman and managing), Robert Pooley, Andrew Johnston (sales), John Gibbs, Peter Holmes (finance).
Aviation, technical and general, military.
Swan Hill Press (imprint). *Managing editor:* P. Coles. Natural history, wildlife, arts, travel, equestrian, fishing, country sports and pursuits.
Waterline Books (imprint). *Managing editor:* P. Coles. Sailing.

Alkin Books Ltd (1992), 28 Phillimore Walk, Kensington, London W8 7SA *tel/ fax* 0171-937 2351. *Managing director:* Mrs Amber G. Moore.
General non-fiction.

Ian Allan Ltd, Coombelands House, Coombelands Lane, Addlestone, Surrey KT15 1HY *tel* (01932) 855909 *fax* (01932) 854750. *Publishing manager:* Peter Waller.
Transport: railways, aircraft, shipping, road; naval and military history; reference books and magazines; sport and walking guides; no fiction.

***George Allen & Unwin Publishers Ltd**—acquired by **HarperCollins Publishers.**

J.A. Allen & Co. Ltd (1926), 1 Lower Grosvenor Place, Buckingham Palace Road, London SW1W 0EL *tel* 0171-834 0090/5606 *telegraphic address* Allenbooks, London *fax* 0171-976 5836. *Chairman and managing director:* Joseph A. Allen; *publishing manager:* Caroline Burt.
Specialist publishers of books on the horse and equestrianism including bloodstock breeding, racing, polo, dressage, horse care, carriage driving, breeds, veterinary and farriery. Technical books usually commissioned but willing to consider any serious, specialist MSS on the horse and related subjects. No fiction or autobiography.

W.H. Allen—acquired by **Virgin Publishing Ltd.**

***Allen Lane The Penguin Press**—see **Penguin Books Ltd.**

***Allison & Busby,** 179 Kings Cross Road, London WC1X 9BZ *tel* 0171-833 1042 *fax* 0171-833 1044. *Managing director and editor:* Peter Day; *rights:* Sarah Fulford.
Biography and memoirs, general, new, crime and international fiction, translations, writers' guides. Unsolicited MSS welcome (synopsis and two sample chapters initially) but sae essential.

AN Publications (1980), PO Box 23, Sunderland SR4 6DG *tel* 0191-567 3589 *fax* 0191-564 1600 *e-mail* anpubs@gn.apc.org *Commissioning editor:* Hannah Firth; *publisher:* Richard Padwick.
Information for the visual arts, including critical reviews, issues and news and practical advice.

Anaya—see **Collins & Brown.**

Andersen Press Ltd (1976), 20 Vauxhall Bridge Road, London SW1V 2SA *tel* 0171-973 9720 *telegraphic address* Literarius, London *telex* 261212 LITLDN G *fax* 0171-233 6263 *e-mail* 101370.533@compuserve.com *Managing director/publisher:* Klaus Flugge; *directors:* Philip Durrance, Denise Johnstone-Burt (editorial), Joëlle Flugge (company secretary).
Children's picture books and fiction (send synopsis and full MS with sae); *no* short stories. International co-productions.

Anness Publishing (1989), 88-89 Blackfriars Road, London SE1 8HP *tel* 0171-401 2077 *fax* 0171-633 9499. *Managing director:* Paul Anness; *publisher:* Joanna Lorenz.
Practical illustrated books on crafts, cookery and gardening, and children's non-fiction.
Lorenz Books (imprint). Lifestyle, cookery, crafts, gardening, and all practical illustrated subjects.
Ultimate Editions (imprint). Illustrated promotional and bargain books on practical subjects.

Antique Collectors' Club (1966), 5 Church Street, Woodbridge, Suffolk IP12 1DS *tel* (01394) 385501 *fax* (01394) 384434. *Managing director:* Diana Steel.
Fine art, antiques, gardening and garden history, architecture.

Anvil Press Poetry (1968), 69 King George Street, London SE10 8PX *tel/fax* 0181-858 2946. *Director:* Peter Jay.
Poetry. Submissions only with sae.

Apple Press (1984), The Old Brewery, 6 Blundell Street, London N7 9BH *tel* 0171-700 6700 *fax* 0171-700 4191. *Publisher:* Stephen Paul; *sales director:* David Rivers. Imprint of **Quarto Publishing plc**, book packagers.
Leisure, domestic and craft pursuits; cookery, gardening, sport, transport, militaria, fine and decorative art.

Arc Publications, Nanholme Mill, Shaw Wood Road, Todmorden, Lancs. OL14 6DA *tel* (01706) 812338 *fax* (01706) 818948. *Partners:* Rosemary Jones, Tony Ward (general editor), Angela Jarman; *associate editors:* Michael Hulse (international), David Morley (UK).
Poetry. Manuscripts with sae only.

Arena—see **Ashgate Publishing Ltd.**

*****Arkana**—see **Penguin Books Ltd.**

Arms & Armour Press—see **Cassell plc.**

*****E.J. Arnold Publishing Division**—acquired by **Thomas Nelson & Sons Ltd.**

Edward Arnold (1890)—see **Hodder Headline plc.**

*****Arrow Books Ltd**—see **Random House UK Ltd.**

Art Trade Press Ltd, 9 Brockhampton Road, Havant, Hants PO9 1NU *tel* (01705) 484943. *Editorial director:* J.M. Curley.
Publishers of *Who's Who in Art.*

Ashgate Publishing Ltd (1987), Gower House, Croft Road, Aldershot, Hants GU11 3HR *tel* (01252) 331551 *fax* (01252) 344405. *Chairman:* Nigel Farrow.
Arena (imprint). *Editor:* Jo Gooderham. Social work and public policy issues.
Avebury (imprint). *Editor:* Sarah Markham. Social sciences research publications, including economics, business, organisational and development studies, regional science, social work and policy, ethnic studies, criminology; joint imprint with **Cranfield University Press** includes aviation and aeronautics, business studies, and agricultural and food sciences.
Scolar Press (imprint). *Editors:* Nigel Farrow (art), Alec MacAulay (history), Rachel Lynch (music). Art, art history, print making, music studies, history of the book, history and literary studies.
Variorum (imprint). *Editor:* John Smedley. Early and medieval history.

Ashmolean Museum Publications (1972), Beaumont Street, Oxford OX1 2PH *tel* (01865) 278009/278010 *fax* (01865) 278018. *Publications officer:* Ian Charlton.
Fine and applied art, archaeology, history, numismatics.

Aslib (The Association for Information Management) (1924), 20-24 Old Street, London EC1V 9AP *tel* 0171-253 4488 *fax* 0171-430 01514. *Head of publications:* Sarah Blair.
Information management, librarianship, information science.

Associated University Presses—see **Golden Cockerel Press.**

The Athlone Press Ltd (1949), 1 Park Drive, London NW11 7SG *tel* 0181-458 0888 *fax* 0181-201 8115. *Directors:* Brian Southam (editorial), Doris Southam, Clive Bingley.
Anthropology, archaeology, architecture, art, economics, film studies, history, Japan, language, law, literature, medical, music, oriental, philosophy, politics, psychology, religion, science, sociology, cultural studies.

Atlantic Europe Publishing Co. Ltd (1989), Greys Court Farm, Greys Court, Henley on Thames, Oxon RG4 4PG *tel* (01491) 628188 *fax* (01491) 628189. *Directors:* Dr B.J. Knapp, D.L.R. McCrae.
Children's colour information books: science, geography, history, design and technology. Associate company: Earthscape Editions (*see* Book Packagers).

Aurum Press Ltd (1977), 25 Bedford Avenue, London WC1B 3AT *tel* 0171-637 3225 *fax* 0171-580 2469. *Directors:* André Deutsch (chairman), Bill McCreadie (managing), Piers Burnett (editorial), Sheila Murphy (marketing and rights), Ken Banerji.
General, illustrated and non-illustrated adult non-fiction: biography and memoirs, visual arts, film, home interest, travel.

Avebury—see **Ashgate Publishing Ltd.**

Award Publications Ltd (1954), 1st Floor, 27 Longford Street, London NW1 3DZ *tel* 0171-388 7800 *fax* 0171-388 7887. *Managing director:* Ron Wilkinson. Children's books: full colour picture story books; early learning, information and activity books.

Bernard Babani (Publishing) Ltd, The Grampians, Shepherds Bush Road, London W6 7NF *tel* 0171-603 2581/7296 *fax* 0171-603 8203. *Directors:* S. Babani, M.H. Babani BSc(Eng).
Practical handbooks on radio, electronics and computing.

*Baillière Tindall Ltd (1826)—see **Harcourt Brace & Co. Ltd.**

Duncan Baird Publishers (1994), Sixth Floor, Castle House, 75-76 Wells Street, London W1P 3RE *tel* 0171-323 2229 *fax* 0171-580 5692. *Directors:* Duncan

Baird (managing), Bob Saxton (editorial), Roger Walton (art), Alex Mitchell (international sales). Non-fiction, illustrated reference.

The Bankers' Almanac—see **Reed Information Services.**

*Bantam—see **Transworld Publishers Ltd.**

Barefoot Books Ltd (1993), PO Box 95, Kingswood, Bristol BS15 5BH *tel* (0117) 932 8885 *fax* (0117) 932 8881. *Publisher:* Tessa Strickland. Children's picture books: myth, legend, fairytale.

*Barrie & Jenkins—see **Random House UK Ltd.**

*Bartholomew—see **HarperCollins Publishers.**

Batsford Books (1843), 4 Fitzhardinge Street, London W1H 0AH *tel* 0171-486 8484 *fax* 0171-487 4296. *President:* Gerald Mizrahi; *chief executive:* Jules Perel; *directors:* Jim Gallacher (finance and company secretary), R.E. Huggins (Managing Director of Batsford Distribution); Penny Daniels (sales and marketing). Part of the Labyrinth Group.
Archaeology, architecture, bridge, building, art techniques, cinema, chess, fashion, costume, equestrian, country sports, craft, pottery, needlecraft, lace, embroidery, horticulture, junior reference, technical/professional, graphic design, woodworking. **Seaby** (imprint). Numismatics.

*BBC Worldwide Publishing, Woodlands, 80 Wood Lane, London W12 0TT *tel* 0181-576 2000.
BBC Books (division) *fax* 0181-576 2858. *Editorial manager:* Tracey Smith. Books tied in to BBC television and radio programmes of all subjects.
BBC Radio Collection (division) *tel* 0181-576 2567 *fax* 0181-576 3851. *Senior commissioning editor:* Mary Kalemkerian. Audio cassettes and CDs of BBC Radio and Television comedy, readings and dramatised serials for adults and children.
Network Books (imprint of BBC Books). Range of non-fiction titles tied in to non-BBC television programmes.
BBC Children's Books (imprint of BBC Books). *Head of children's books:* Rona Selby. Range of fiction and non-fiction titles tied in to BBC television programmes.

Bedford Square Press—see **NCVO Publications.**

Belitha Press Ltd (1980), London House, Great Eastern Wharf, Parkgate Road, London SW11 4NQ *tel* 0171-978 6330 *fax* 0171-223 4936. *Directors:* Cameron Brown (chairman), Peter Osborn (managing), Mary-Jane Wilkins (editorial), Mark Collins. Acquired by **Collins & Brown.**
Illustrated children's non-fiction for international co-editions: art, atlases, geography, history, natural history, reference, science.

*Bell & Hyman Ltd—acquired by **HarperCollins Publishers.**

Bellew Publishing Co. Ltd (1983), The Nightingale Centre, 8 Balham Hill, London SW12 9EA *tel* 0181-673 5611 *fax* 0181-675 2142. *Chairman:* Ian McCorquodale; *managing director:* Ib Bellew.
Sociology of religion, art and art criticism, some fiction, poetry.

David Bennett Books Ltd (1989), 23 Albion Road, St Albans, Herts. AL1 5EB *tel* (01727) 855878 *fax* (01727) 864085. *Managing director:* David Bennett. Highly illustrated children's fiction and non-fiction; baby books, play books and gift books for the young.

Berg Publishers (1983), 150 Cowley Road, Oxford OX4 1JJ *tel* (01865) 245104 *fax* (01865) 791165. *Managing director:* Peter Cowell.
Social anthropology, European studies, politics and economics, literature.

Berkswell Publishing Co. Ltd, PO Box 420, Warminster, Wilts. BA12 9XB *tel/fax* (01985) 840189. *Directors:* J.N.G. Stidolph, S.A. Abbott.
Books of local interest in Wessex, field sports, royalty. Ideas and MSS welcome. Also provide editorial, design, research, picture research, exhibition organisation and design.

Berlitz Publishing Co. Ltd (1960), Berlitz House, Peterley Road, Oxford OX4 2TX *tel* (01865) 747033 *fax* (01865) 779700. *Managing director:* Roger Kirkpatrick; *publisher:* Julian Parish.
Travel, language and related multimedia.

Bible Society, Stonehill Green, Westlea, Swindon, Wilts. SN5 7DG *tel* (01793) 418000 *telex* 44283 BIBLES G *fax* (01793) 418118.
Bibles, testaments, portions and selections in English and over 200 other languages; also books and audio-visual material on use of Bible for personal, education, church situations.

*Clive Bingley Ltd (1965)—see **Library Association Publishing Ltd.**

*Birnbaum—see **HarperCollins Publishers.**

*A. & C. Black plc (1807), 35 Bedford Row, London WC1R 4JH *tel* 0171-242 0946 *fax* 0171-831 8478. *Chairman and joint managing director:* Charles Black; *deputy chairman:* David Gadsby; *joint managing director:* Jill Coleman; *directors:* Paul Langridge, Terry Rouelett, Professor Leonard Marsh OBE; *company secretary:* Jenny Aspinall. Proprietors of A. & C. Black (Publishers) Ltd, Nautical Publishing Co. Ltd, Christopher Helm (Publishers) Ltd, Adlard Coles Ltd, The Herbert Press Ltd.

*A. & C. Black (Publishers) Ltd (1978), 35 Bedford Row, London WC1R 4JH *tel* 0171-242 0946 *fax* 0171-831 8478. *Chairman and joint managing director:* Charles Black; *joint managing director:* Jill Coleman; *directors:* Paul Langridge (rights), Janet Murphy (Adlard Coles Nautical), Terry Rouelett (distribution), Oscar Heini (production), Robert Kirk (Christopher Helm, ornithology). Subsidiary of **A. & C. Black plc.**
Children's and educational books (including music) for 3-15 years (preliminary enquiry appreciated – fiction guidelines available on request); ceramics, calligraphy, drama (*New Mermaid* series), fishing, reference (*Who's Who*), sport, theatre, travel (*Blue Guides*), books for writers.
Adlard Coles Nautical (imprint). *Editorial director:* Janet Murphy. Nautical.
Christopher Helm (imprint). *Editorial director:* Robert Kirk. Ornithology.
The Herbert Press (imprint). *Managing director:* David Herbert.

*Black Ace Books (1992), Ellemford Farmhouse, Duns, Berwickshire TD11 3SG *tel* (01361) 890370 *fax* (01361) 890287. *Publisher:* Hunter Steele; *art, publicity and sales:* Boo Wood.
New fiction, Scottish and general; new editions of outstanding recent fiction; some non-fiction, including history and philosophy. *No* unsolicited typescripts; preliminary letter essential. Send A4 sae for full details of imprint and current requirements.

Black Lace—see **Virgin Publishing Ltd.**

*Black Swan—see **Transworld Publishers Ltd.**

*Blackie Academic and Professional—see **Chapman & Hall Ltd.**

*Blackie Children's Books—see **Penguin Books Ltd.**

Blackstaff Press Ltd—see under Irish Book Publishers.

*****Blackwell Publishers** (Basil Blackwell Ltd) (1922), 108 Cowley Road, Oxford OX4 1JF   *tel* (01865) 791100   *telex* 837022   *fax* (01865) 791347. *Directors:* Nigel Blackwell (chairman), René Olivieri (managing), Philip Carpenter, Sue Corbett, Mark Houlton, John Davey, Stephan Chambers, Carolyn Dougherty.

Economics, education (academic), geography, history, industrial relations, linguistics, literature and criticism, politics, psychology, social anthropology, social policy and administration, sociology, theology, business studies, professional, law, reference, feminism, information technology, philosophy.

InfoSource International (division), InfoSource House, 54 Marston Street, Oxford OX4 1JU   *tel* (01865) 244068   *fax* (01865) 791347. *Directors:* René Olivieri, Mark Houlton. Computer-based training, skills assessment and instructor manuals. Specialist areas include: PC applications (e.g. Microsoft Excel, WordPerfect, Lotus 1-2-3), networks and Internet.

NCC Blackwell (imprint)   *fax* (01865) 798210. *Director:* Stephan Chambers. Professional and student books in computing/information technology. Specialist areas include: systems analysis and design, SSADM, PRINCE, security, open systems, communications and networking.

Shakespeare Head Press (imprint). Finely printed books; scholarly works.

*****Blackwell Science Ltd** (1939), Osney Mead, Oxford OX2 0EL   *tel* (01865) 206206   *fax* (01865) 721205   *WWW* http://www.blacksci.co.uk *Chairman:* Nigel Blackwell; *managing director:* Robert Campbell; *directors:* Jonathan Conibear, Peter Saugman (editorial), Martin Wilkinson (finance), John Strange (production), Bill Gibson (Boston).

Medicine, nursing, dentistry, veterinary medicine, life sciences, earth sciences, chemistry, professional including construction, allied health.

Blake Publishing (1991), 3 Bramber Court, 2 Bramber Road, London W14 9PB   *tel* 0171-381 0666   *fax* 0171-381 6868. *Chairman:* David Blake; *managing director:* John Blake; *assistant publisher:* Rosie Ries; *production editor:* Sadie Mayne.

Popular fiction and non-fiction, including biographies and true crime. *No* unsolicited fiction.

Blandford Press—see **Cassell plc.**

Bloodaxe Books Ltd (1978), PO Box 1SN, Newcastle upon Tyne NE99 1SN   *tel* 0191-232 5988   *fax* 0191-222 0020. *Directors:* Neil Astley, Simon Thirsk. Poetry, literary criticism, literary biography.

*****Bloomsbury Publishing plc** (1986), 2 Soho Square, London W1V 6HB   *tel* 0171-494 2111   *fax* 0171-434 0151   *e-mail* alan@bloombry.sonnet.co.uk *Chairman and managing director:* Nigel Newton; *directors:* David Reynolds (deputy managing and publishing), Liz Calder (publishing), Alan Wherry (publishing), Kathy Rooney (editorial), Sarah Beal (sales), Florence Whyte (publicity), Ruth Logan (rights), Penny Edwards (production), Emma Kirby (export/club), Colin Adams (finance), Matthew Hamilton (paperbacks).

Fiction, biography, illustrated, reference, travel in hardcover; trade paperback and mass market paperback.

Bloomsbury Children's Books (division). *Director:* Barry Cunningham. Picture books, fiction, novelty books.

*****Bodley Head**—see **Random House UK Ltd.**

*****Bodley Head Children's**—see **Random House UK Ltd.**

Bowker-Saur, Maypole House, Maypole Road, East Grinstead, West Sussex RH19 1HU *tel* (01342) 330100 *fax* (01342) 330191. *Directors:* Ira Siegal (chairman), Charles Halpin (managing).
Bibliographies, trade and reference directories, library and information science, electronic publishing, abstracts and indexes.
Hans Zell Publishers (imprint), PO Box 56, Oxford OX1 2SJ *tel* (01865) 511428 *fax* (01865) 311534/793298. Bibliographies, directories and other reference works; African studies, African literature (criticism only); development studies; studies on publishing and book development.

Boxtree Ltd (1986), Broadwall House, 21 Broadwall, London SE1 9PL *tel* 0171-928 9696 *fax* 0171-928 5632. *Directors:* S. Mahaffy (managing), D. Inman, A. Sington, M. Alcock, P. Roche (non-executive chairman), Susanna Wadeson (editorial), Humphrey Price (editorial), Christine Corton (production).
TV and film tie-ins (adult and children's non-fiction); illustrated and general non-fiction; mass market paperbacks linked to TV, film, rock and sporting events; humour.
Sapling (imprint). Children's media-related titles.
Newleaf (imprint). New Age titles.

*****Marion Boyars Publishers Ltd,** 24 Lacy Road, London SW15 1NL *tel* 0181-788 9522 *fax* 0181-789 8122. *Directors:* Marion Boyars, Arthur Boyars.
Belles-lettres and criticism, fiction, sociology, psychology, Briefings series, feminism, history of ideas, ideas in progress series, music, travel, drama, cinema, dance, biography.

Boydell & Brewer Ltd (1969), PO Box 9, Woodbridge, Suffolk IP12 3DF.
Medieval studies, history, literature, archaeology, art history, travel, country and sporting books. *No* unsolicited MSS.

BPP (Letts Educational) Ltd, trading as **Letts Educational** (1979), Aldine House, Aldine Place, London W12 8AW *tel* 0181-743 7514 *fax* 0181-743 8451. *Managing director:* Jonathan Harris; *publishing directors:* Richard Carr, Catherine Tilley.
Revision and exam preparation, and course books for the school, college and home study markets.

Brassey's (UK) Ltd (1886), 33 John Street, London WC1N 2AT *tel* 0171-753 7777 *fax* 0171-753 7795. *Directors:* Jenny Shaw BSc(Econ), MA, Major General A.J. Trythall CB, MA.
Defence and national security, international relations, weapons technology, military affairs, military biography, military history, Soviet studies, reference. Publisher to the Centre for Defence Studies.
Conway Maritime Press (imprint). Maritime and naval history, ship modelling.
Putnam Aeronautical Books (imprint). Technical and aviation reference.

*****Nicholas Brealey Publishing Ltd** (1992), 21 Bloomsbury Way, London WC1A 2TH *tel* 0171-430 0224 *fax* 0171-404 8311. *Managing director:* Nicholas Brealey.
Business, management, training, employment law, international affairs.

Breedon Books Publishing Co. Ltd (1981), 44 Friar Gate, Derby DE1 1DA *tel* (01332) 384235 *fax* (01332) 292755. *Directors:* Anton Rippon (chairman and editorial), Patricia Rippon, Graham Hales.
Sports, heritage, local history. *No* unsolicited MSS; preliminary letter essential.

Brimax Books—see Reed Books.

British Academic Press—see I.B. Tauris & Co. Ltd.

*The British Library (Publications) (1973), Marketing & Publishing Office, Public Services, 41 Russell Square, London WC1B 3DG   *tel* 0171-412 7704   *telex* 21462   *fax* 0171-412 7768. *Head of marketing and publishing:* Jane Carr; *managers:* David Way (publishing), Anne Young (product development), Karen Fermor (bookshop), Jenny McKinley (marketing).
Bibliography, book arts, music, maps, oriental, manuscript studies, history, literature, facsimiles, audio-visual, and multimedia CD-ROM.

*British Museum Press (1973), 46 Bloomsbury Street, London WC1B 3QQ   *tel* 0171-323 1234   *fax* 0171-436 7315. *Managing director:* Patrick Wright; *head of publishing:* Emma Way.
Art history, archaeology, numismatics, history, oriental art and archaeology, horology.

Brockhampton Press—see Hodder Headline plc.

James Brodie (1926), 15 Springfield Place, Lansdown, Bath BA1 5RA   *tel* (01225) 317706. *Directors:* Corinne Wimpress (secretary), Jeremy Wimpress. Literal classical translations.

*Brown, Son & Ferguson Ltd (1860), 4-10 Darnley Street, Glasgow G41 2SD   *tel* 0141-429 1234 (24 hours)   *telegraphic address* Skipper, Glasgow   *fax* 0141-420 1694. *Editorial director:* L. Ingram-Brown.
Nautical books; Scottish poetry and plays; Scout, Cub Scout, Brownie Guide and Guide story books.

Brown Wells & Jacobs Ltd (1970), Foresters Hall, 25/27 Westow Street, London SE19 3RY   *tel* 0181-771 5115   *fax* 0181-771 9994. *Managing director:* Graham Brown; *sales director:* Ailsa Brown.
Children's non-fiction novelty and pop-ups.

Burns & Oates Ltd (1847), Publishers to the Holy See, Wellwood, North Farm Road, Tunbridge Wells, Kent TN2 3DR   *tel* (01892) 510850   *fax* (01892) 515903. *Directors:* Charlotte de la Bedoyere, Hans Küpfer.
Theology, philosophy, spirituality, church history, books of Catholic interest and craft books with religious themes.

Burrows Publishing Ltd (1900), Publicity House, 106a Stafford Road, Wallington, Surrey SM6 9TD   *tel* 0181-773 9944   *fax* 0181-773 8888. *Managing director:* Paul Dipre.
Guidebooks, street plans and maps, industrial and economic development handbooks, business and industrial directories.

Butterworth & Co. (Publishers) Ltd, Halsbury House, 35 Chancery Lane, London WC2A 1EL   *tel* 0171-400 2500   *telex* 95678   *fax* 0171-400 2842. *Chairman and chief executive:* Neville Cusworth. Division of **Reed Elsevier (UK) Ltd.**
Law, tax and accountancy publishing.
British and Irish Legal Division. Legal books, journals and loose leaf services; tax and accountancy books, journals and loose leaf services.

Butterworth Architecture, Butterworth Heinemann UK—see Reed Educational and Professional Publishing.

Cadogan Books plc, London House, Parkgate Road, London SW11 4NQ   *tel* 0171-738 1961   *fax* 0171-924 5491. *Chairman:* Alewyn Birch; *managing director:* William Colegrave; *publisher:* David Campbell; *finance director:* Mark Bicknell; *managing director* (Cadogan Guides and Chess): Vicki Ingle; *publisher* (Cadogan Guides and Chess): Rachel Fielding; *sales director* (Cadogan Guides and Chess): Robert Beard. Travel (Cadogan Travel Guides); Cadogan Chess; now incorporating **Everyman's Library.**

*Calder Publications Ltd, 179 Kings Cross Road, London WC1X 9BZ *tel* 0171-833 1300. *Director:* John Calder.
European, international and British fiction and plays, art, literary, music and social criticism, biography and autobiography, essays, humanities and social sciences, European classics. *No unsolicited typescripts. Letters of inquiry must include an sae.* Series include: English National Opera Guides, New Paris Editions, Scottish Library, New Writing and Writers, Platform Books, Opera Library, Historical Perspectives.

*Cambridge University Press (1534), The Edinburgh Building, Shaftesbury Road, Cambridge CB2 2RU *tel* (01223) 312393 *telex* 817256 CUPCAM G *fax* (01223) 315052. *e-mail* information@cup.cam.ac.uk *WWW* http://www.cup.cam.ac.uk *Chief executive of the Press and University printer:* Anthony K. Wilson MA; *deputy chief executive and managing director (publishing division):* Jeremy Mynott MA, PhD.
Anthropology and archaeology, art and architecture, classical studies, computer science, educational (primary, secondary, tertiary), educational software, English language teaching, history, journals (humanities, social sciences and sciences), language and literature, law, mathematics, medicine, music, oriental, philosophy, politics, psychology, reference, science (physical and biological), social sciences, theology, religion. The Bible and Prayer Book.

*Canongate Books Ltd (1973), 14 High Street, Edinburgh EH1 1TE *tel* 0131-557 5111 *fax* 0131-557 5211. *Directors:* Jamie Byng, Hugh Andrew, Ronnie Shanks; *publishing director:* Stephanie Wolfe Murray.
Adult general non-fiction and fiction: Canongate Classics, Kelpie Paperbacks (children's fiction), Canongate Audio (audio books), art books, travel.
Payback Press (imprint). *Publishing director:* Jamie Byng. Afro-American and Jamaican culture: non-fiction, fiction, music, poetry and biography.

The Canterbury Press Norwich, St Mary's Works, St Mary's Plain, Norwich, Norfolk NR3 3BH *tel* (01603) 616563/612914 *fax* (01603) 624483. *Publisher:* G.A. Knights. Book publishing imprint of **Hymns Ancient and Modern Ltd,** music publishers.
C of E doctrine, theology, history and associated topics, music and liturgy.

*Jonathan Cape—see **Random House UK Ltd.**

*Jonathan Cape Children's Books—see **Random House UK Ltd.**

Carcanet Press Ltd (1969), 402 Corn Exchange Buildings, Manchester M4 3BQ *tel* 0161-834 8730 *fax* 0161-832 0084. *Director:* Michael Schmidt.
Poetry, memoirs (literary), Fyfield Series, translations, biography.

Carlton Books (1992), 20 St Anne's Court, Wardour Street, London W1V 3AW *tel* 0171-734 7338 *fax* 0171-434 1196. *Directors:* Jonathan Goodman (managing), John Maynard (operations), Piers Murray Hill (editorial), Russell Porter (design), Adrian Whitton (finance).
Popular music, sport, games, film, video, popular science, lifestyle, New Age, TV tie-ins, criminology.

Cartermill International Ltd—see **Pearson Professional Ltd.**

Frank Cass & Co. Ltd (1958), Newbury House, 890-900 Eastern Avenue, Newbury Park, Ilford, Essex IG2 7HH *tel* 0181-599 8866 *fax* 0181-599 0984. *Directors:* Frank Cass (managing), A.E. Cass, M.P. Zaidner.
History, African studies, Middle East studies, economic and social history, military and strategic studies, international affairs, development studies, academic journals.
Vallentine Mitchell (imprint). Jewish interest.
Woburn Press (imprint). Educational.

Cassell plc (1848), Wellington House, 125 Strand, London WC2R 0BB *tel* 0171-420 5555 *fax* 0171-240 7261. *Chairman and chief executive:* Philip Sturrock.
Arms & Armour Press (imprint). *Director:* Rod Dymott. Military history (land, sea, air, weaponry), military reference, military adventure non-fiction, modern defence/intelligence.
Blandford Press (imprint). *Director:* Rod Dymott. Aviculture, history, hobbies, music, natural history, practical handbooks, sport, New Age/mind, body, spirit.
Cassell (general imprint). *Editorial director:* Alison Goff. Cookery, poetry, lifestyle, gardening, word reference, art and craft, popular science, current affairs.
Cassell (general reference list). *Commissioning editor:* Nigel Wilcockson. General interest reference.
Cassell (academic reference list). *Director:* Janet Joyce. Foreign language, humanities, social science reference.
Cassell (professional lists). *Director:* Naomi Roth. Education, hotel and catering management, psychology and counselling, business and professional reference.
Cassell (contemporary studies lists). *Director:* Steve Cook. Gender studies, global issues, film studies.
Geoffrey Chapman (imprint). *Director:* Ruth McCurry. Religion and theology, particularly Roman Catholic.
Victor Gollancz Ltd (imprint). *Directors:* Chris Kloet (children's), Liz Knights (publishing and general non-fiction, science fiction and fantasy). Biography and autobiography, children's books, current affairs, fiction, crime fiction, science fiction, fantasy and macabre, history, music, humour, sociology, travel. In association with Peter Crawley: Master Bridge Series, historical architecture, cookery, general. Synopsis, sample chapters and sae requested before submitting MSS. No unsolicited MSS except for children's books.
Gollancz Witherby Ltd (imprint). *Editor:* Liz Knights. Sport.
Indigo (imprint). *Editor:* Mike Petty. Literary fiction and general non-fiction.
Leicester University Press (imprint). *Director:* Janet Joyce. Academic books, especially medieval history, museum studies, political theory.
Mansell Publishing (imprint). *Director:* Janet Joyce. Bibliographies in all academic subject areas and monographs in urban and regional planning, Islamic studies, librarianship, history.
Mowbray (imprint). *Director:* Ruth McCurry. Religion and theology, both Anglican and non-denominational.
New Orchard Editions (imprint). *Director:* Alan Smith. Antiques and collecting, children's, cookery, wines and spirits, gardening, history and antiquarian, illustrated and fine editions, military and war, natural history, reference and dictionaries, transport, travel and topography.
Pinter (imprint). *Director:* Janet Joyce. Academic and professional publishers specialising in social sciences including international relations, politics, economics, new technology, linguistics, communications and religious studies.
Studio Vista (imprint). *Commissioning editor:* Barry Holmes. Art, antiques and collecting, architecture and design, decorative arts, film books, practical art.
Vista (imprint). *Editor:* Jane Blackstock. Popular fiction and general non-fiction.
Ward Lock (imprint). *Director:* Alison Goff. Cookery, gardening, equestrian and outdoor pursuits, popular reference books, DIY, health.
Wisley Handbooks (imprint). *Trade publisher:* Barry Holmes. Gardening.

Castle House Publications Ltd (1973), 28-30 Church Road, Tunbridge Wells, Kent TN1 1JP *tel* (01892) 539606 *fax* (01892) 517773. *Director:* D. Reinders. Medical.

Kyle Cathie Ltd (1990), 20 Vauxhall Bridge Road, London SW1V 2SA *tel* 0171-973 9710 *fax* 0171-821 9258. *Publisher and managing director:* Kyle Cathie; *sales director:* Emma Bittleston.
History, natural history, health, biography, food and drink; craft; gardening; reference.

Catholic Truth Society (1868), 192 Vauxhall Bridge Road, London SW1V 1PD *tel* 0171-834 4392 *fax* 0171-630 1124. *Chairman:* Rt Rev. Peter Smith DCL, LLB; *general secretary:* Fergal Martin LLB, LLM.
General books of Roman Catholic and Christian interest, bibles, prayer books and pamphlets of doctrinal, historical, devotional or social interest. MSS of between 4000 and 5000 words or 2500 and 3000 words with up to six illustrations considered for publication as pamphlets, as well as larger MSS of up to 100,000 words.

Causeway Press Ltd (1982), PO Box 13, 129 New Court Way, Ormskirk, Lancs. L39 5HP *tel* (01695) 576048/577360 *fax* (01695) 570714. *Directors:* Mike Haralambos (chairman and editorial), Pauline Haralambos, Dave Gray (company secretary), David Alcorn.
School textbooks: mathematics, history, economics, business studies, sociology, politics, geography, technology.

*Cavendish Publishing Ltd (1990), The Glass House, Wharton Street, London WC1X 9PX *tel* 0171-278 8000 *fax* 0171-278 8080. *Publishing director:* Sonny Leong; *managing editor:* Jo Reddy.
A wide range of legal and medico-legal books and journals.

CBD Research Ltd (1961), 15 Wickham Road, Beckenham, Kent BR3 2JS *tel* 0181-650 7745 *fax* 0181-650 0768 *e-mail* 100702.32@compuserv.com *Directors:* G.P. Henderson, S.P.A. Henderson, C.A.P. Henderson, A.J.W. Henderson.
Directories, reference books, bibliographies, guides to business and statistical information.
Chancery House Press (imprint). Unusual non-fiction/reference works. Preliminary letter and synopsis with return postage essential.

Centaur Press (1954), Fontwell, Arundel, West Sussex BN18 0TA *tel* Eastergate (01243) 543302. *Directors:* Jon Wynne-Tyson, Jennifer M. Wynne-Tyson.
Philosophy, environment, humane education, biography. Principal series: The Kinship Library. A preliminary letter should be sent before submitting MS, enclosing an sae.

*Century—see **Random House UK Ltd.**

*Chadwyck-Healey Ltd (1971), The Quorum, Barnwell Road, Cambridge CB5 8SW *tel* (01223) 215512 *fax* (01223) 215514 *e-mail* marketing @chadwyck.co.uk *Chairman:* Sir Charles Chadwyck-Healey; *directors:* Steven Hall (managing), Michael Healy (editorial), Alison Moss (publishing).
CD-ROMs: News and business information, bibliographies and reference works, literature, arts, statistics, cartography and climate.

*Chambers—see **Larousse plc.**

Chancery House Press—see **CBD Research Ltd.**

Chansitor Publications Ltd, St Mary's Works, St Mary's Plain, Norwich, Norfolk NR3 3BH *tel* (01603) 615995 *fax* (01603) 624483. *Publisher:* G.A. Knights. Church Pulpit Year Book.
Religious and Moral Education Press (RMEP) (imprint). Books for teachers, primary and secondary schools on religious, moral, personal and social education.

Chapman (1989)—now incorporated into **The Orion Publishing Group Ltd.**

*****Chapman & Hall Ltd,** 2-6 Boundary Row, London SE1 8HN *tel* 0171-865 0066 *fax* 0171-522 9623. *Chief executive officer:* G. Burn. *Directors:* A. Davis (finance), M. Dunn (editorial, physical sciences and engineering), N. Dunton (editorial, biomedical), J. Lavender (electronic), G. McDonald (production), P. Read (editorial, Spon), B. ter Haar (sales and communications).
Scientific, technical, medical and professional publishers.
Blackie Academic and Professional (imprint). *Publisher:* J. Walmsley. Academic and professional, books for chemistry and food science.
E. & F.N. Spon Ltd (imprint). *Editorial director:* P. Read. Architecture, building, surveying, civil engineering, landscape architecture, construction, planning, sports sciences, leisure and recreation management.
Chapman & Hall is an International Thomson Publishing company.

Geoffrey Chapman—see **Cassell plc.**

Paul Chapman Publishing Ltd (1987), 144 Liverpool Road, London N1 1LA *tel* 0171-609 5315/6 *fax* 0171-700 1057. *Directors:* P.R. Chapman (managing), Marianne Lagrange (editorial).
Business, management, accounting, finance, economics, geography, environment, planning, education.

Chart Books Ltd (1995), Chart Warren, Seal, Sevenoaks, Kent TW15 OEJ *tel* (01732) 465515 *fax* (01732) 465595. *Executive directors:* Christine Pedersen (editorial/rights), Stephen Kirby (financial), Jenny Wilmot-Smith (editorial/publicity).
Children's picture books; novelty books; children's fiction.

*****Chatto & Windus**—see **Random House UK Ltd.**

Child's Play (International) Ltd (1972), Ashworth Road, Bridgemead, Swindon, Wilts. SN5 7YD *tel* (01793) 616286 *fax* (01793) 512795. *Chairman and publishing director:* Michael Twinn.
Children's educational books: board, activity and play books, fiction and non-fiction.

*****Church of Scotland Board of Communication**—see **The Saint Andrew Press.**

*****Churchill Communications Europe**—see **Pearson Professional Ltd.**

*****Churchill Livingstone**—see **Pearson Professional Ltd.**

Cicerone Press (1969), 2 Police Square, Milnthorpe, Cumbria LA7 7PY *tel* (015395) 62069 *fax* (015395) 63417. *Managing and sales director:* Dorothy Unsworth; *editorial director:* Walt Unsworth; *production director:* R.B. Evans.
Guidebooks to the great outdoors – walking, climbing, etc. – Britain, Europe, and world-wide; general books about the North of England. *No* fiction or poetry.

*****Clarendon Press**—see **Oxford University Press.**

Robin Clark Ltd (1976), 27 Goodge Street, London W1P 2LD *tel* 0171-636 3992 *fax* 0171-637 1866. *Director:* N.I. Attallah (chairman); *managing editor:* G. de Chamberet. Member of the Namara Group.
Fiction, biography, social history in paperback.

T. & T. Clark (1821), 59 George Street, Edinburgh EH2 2LQ   *tel* 0131-225 4703   *fax* 0131-220 4260. *Managing director:* Geoffrey F. Green MA, PhD. Theology, philosophy, law.

*****James Clarke & Co. Ltd** (1859), PO Box 60, Cambridge CB1 2NT   *tel* (01223) 350865   *fax* (01223) 366951   *e-mail* lutterworth.pr@dial.pipex.com *Managing director:* Adrian Brink.
Theology, academic, reference books.
Acorn Editions (imprint). Sponsored books.
Patrick Hardy Books (imprint of Lutterworth Press). Children's fiction.
Lutterworth Press (subsidiary). The arts, biography, children's books (fiction, non-fiction, picture, rewards), educational, environmental, general, history, leisure, philosophy, science, sociology, theology and religion.

Richard Cohen Books (1995), Basement Offices, 7 Manchester Square, London W1M 5RE   *tel* 0171-935 2099   *fax* 0171-935 2199. *Directors:* Richard Cohen (managing), H. Stuart Hughes (company secretary); *managing editor:* Patricia Chetwyn.
Fiction, biography, current affairs, travel, history, politics, the arts, sport.

*****Collins**—see **HarperCollins Publishers.**

Collins & Brown (1989), London House, Great Eastern Wharf, Parkgate Road, London SW11 4NQ   *tel* 0171-924 2575   *fax* 0171-924 7725. *Publisher:* Mark Collins; *chairman:* Cameron Brown; *directors:* Roger Bristow (art), Lucinda Richards (editorial).
Literature, history, practical photography, natural history, gardening, cookery, travel, DIY, crafts, music, biography, letters, art.
Anaya (imprint). Lifestyle, interiors, arts and crafts.

*****Condé Nast Books**—see **Random House UK Ltd.**

Conran Octopus—see **Reed Books.**

Conservative Political Centre (1945), 32 Smith Square, London SW1P 3HH   *tel* 0171-222 9000   *fax* 0171-233 2065. *Director:* Alistair B. Cooke OBE.
Politics, current affairs.

*****Constable & Co. Ltd** (1890), 3 The Lanchesters, 162 Fulham Palace Road, London W6 9ER   *tel* 0181-741 3663   *fax* 0181-748 7562. *Chairman and managing director:* Benjamin Glazebrook; *directors:* Richard Dodman, Miles Huddleston, Richard Tomkins, Jeremy Potter, Yvette Evans-Foster, Carol O'Brien.
Fiction: general, crime and suspense; general non-fiction: literature, biography, memoirs, history, politics, current affairs, food, travel and guidebooks, social sciences, psychology and psychiatry, counselling, social work, sociology, mass media.

*****Consumers' Association** (1957), 2 Marylebone Road, London NW1 4DF   *tel* 0171-830 6000   *fax* 0171-830 7660   *e-mail* editor@which.co.uk *Chief executive:* Sheila McKechnie; *assistant director:* Kim Lavely; *head of publishing:* Gill Rowley.
Travel, restaurant, hotel and wine guides, medicine, law and personal finance for the layman, gardening, education, DIY – all *Which?* branded titles.

Conway Maritime Press (1972)—see **Brassey's (UK) Ltd.**

Leo Cooper—see **Pen & Sword Books Ltd.**

*****Corgi, Corgi Children's Books**—see **Transworld Publishers Ltd.**

Cornwall Books—see **Golden Cockerel Press.**

Coronet—see **Hodder Headline plc.**

Council for British Archaeology (1944), Bowes Morrell House, 111 Walmgate, York YO1 2UA   *tel* (01904) 671417   *fax* (01904) 671384   *e-mail* 100271.456 @compuserve.com *Director:* Richard Morris; *managing editor:* Christine Pietrowski.
British archaeology – academic; practical handbooks; no general books.

Countryside Books (1976), 2 Highfield Avenue, Newbury, Berks. RG14 5DS   *tel* (01635) 43816   *fax* (01635) 551004. *Partners:* Nicholas Battle, Suzanne Battle.
Books of local or regional interest, usually on a county basis, walking, outdoor activity, local history; genealogy.

Cranfield University Press—see **Ashgate Publishing Ltd.**

*Creation Books (1990), 83 Clerkenwell Road, London EC1R 5AR   *tel* 0171-430 9878   *fax* 0171-242 5527. *Directors:* James Williamson, Peter Colebrook.
Films, media, art, horror, science fiction, pulp, graphic, counter culture, erotic, surreal, decadent, cult.
Velvet (imprint). Erotic fiction.

*Creed—see **Penguin Books Ltd.**

Cressrelles Publishing Co. Ltd (1973), 10 Station Road Industrial Estate, Colwall, Malvern, Worcs. WR13 6RN   *tel* (01684) 540154   *fax* (01684) 540154. *Directors:* Leslie Smith, Audrey Smith.
General publishing.
Actinic Press (imprint). Chiropody.

The Crowood Press (1982), The Stable Block, Ramsbury, Marlborough, Wilts. SN8 2HR   *tel* (01672) 520320   *fax* (01672) 520280. *Directors:* John Dennis (chairman), Ken Hathaway (managing).
Sport, motoring, climbing and walking, fishing, country sports, farming, natural history, gardening, DIY, crafts, dogs, equestrian, games.
Helmsman (imprint). Nautical.

Current Science Group, 34-42 Cleveland Street, London W1P 6LB   *tel* 0171-323 0323   *fax* 0171-580 1938. *Chairman:* Vitek Tracz; *chief executive:* Richard Charkin; *group managing director:* Anne Greenwood.
Biological sciences, medicine, chemistry, pharmaceutical science, general science, electronic publishing.

James Currey Ltd (1985), 54ʙ Thornhill Square, London N1 1BE   *tel* 0171-609 9026   *fax* 0171-609 9605. *Directors:* James Currey (editorial), Clare Currey, Keith Sambrook.
Academic studies of Africa, Caribbean, Third World: history, archaeology, economics, agriculture, politics, literary criticism, sociology.

Cygnus Arts—see **Golden Cockerel Press.**

Dalesman Publishing Co. Ltd (1939), Stable Courtyard, Broughton Hall, Skipton, North Yorks. BD23 3AE   *tel* (01756) 701381   *fax* (01756) 701326. *Chairman:* T.J. Benn; *managing director:* C.G. Benn; *publishing director:* T. Bennett; *general manager:* R. Flanagan.
Countryside books and magazines, walking, caving, humour, folklore, guides.

Terence Dalton Ltd (1966), Water Street, Lavenham, Sudbury, Suffolk CO10 9RN   *tel* (01787) 247572   *fax* (01787) 248267. *Directors:* T.A.J. Dalton, E.H. Whitehair (managing).
Maritime and aeronautical history, East Anglian interest and history.

The C.W. Daniel Company Ltd (1902), 1 Church Path, Saffron Walden, Essex CB10 1JP   *tel* (01799) 521909   *fax* (01799) 513462. *Directors:* Ian Miller, Jane Miller.

Natural healing, homoeopathy, aromatherapy, mysticism.
Health Science Press (imprint). *Directors:* Ian Miller, Jane Miller.
Homeopathy.
Neville Spearman Publishers (imprint). *Editorial director:* Sebastian Hobnut.
Mysticism.

Dartmouth Publishing Co. Ltd (1989), Gower House, Croft Road, Aldershot,
Hants GU11 3HR *tel* (01252) 331551 *fax* (01252) 344405 *e-mail*
gower@cityscape.co.uk *Managing director:* John Irwin.
International relations, law, management, politics.

*****Darton, Longman & Todd Ltd** (1959), 1 Spencer Court, 140-142 Wandsworth
High Street, London SW18 4JJ *tel* 0181-875 0155 *fax* 0181-875 0133. *Editorial director:* Morag Reeve.
Religious books and bibles, including the following themes: bible study, spirituality, prayer and meditation, anthologies, daily readings, healing, counselling
and pastoral care, bereavement, personal growth, mission, political, environmental and social issues, biography/autobiography, theological and historical
studies.

Darwen Finlayson Ltd—see **Phillimore & Co. Ltd.**

*****David & Charles plc** (1960), Brunel House, Newton Abbot, Devon TQ12
4PU *tel* (01626) 61121 *telex* 42904 BOOKS G *fax* (01626) 331367. *Directors:*
Neil A. Page (managing), Piers Spence (publishing), John Allgrove (sales and
marketing).
High quality illustrated non-fiction specialising in crafts, hobbies, art
techniques, cookery, gardening, natural history, equestrian, nautical, DIY.

Christopher Davies Publishers Ltd (1949), PO Box 403, Swansea SA1 4YF *tel*
(01792) 648825 *fax* (01792) 648825. *Directors:* Christopher Talfan Davies
(editorial), K.E.T. Colayera, D.M. Davies.
History, leisure books, sport and general of Welsh interest, Welsh dictionaries,
Triskele Books.

De Agostini Editions (1993), Interpark House, 7 Down Street, London W1Y
7DS *tel* 0171-318 8000 *fax* 0171-629 6230. *Chairman, publisher and managing director:* Simon McMurtrie; *directors:* Frances Gertler (publishing), Tim
Foster (art), Joanna Everard (rights), Isobel Robertson (sales), Lee Matthews
(production).
Adult illustrated reference: art, music, history, culture, health, science;
children's illustrated non-fiction (ages 0-8).

Dedalus Ltd (1983), 24 St Judith's Lane, Sawtry, Cambs. PE17 5XE *tel/fax*
(01487) 832382. *Chairman:* Juri Gabriel; *directors:* Eric Lane (managing),
Robert Irwin (editorial), Lindsay Thomas (marketing).
Original fiction in English and in translation; Empire of the Senses, Dedalus
European Classics, Surrealism and Literary Fantasy Anthologies.

Delta—see **Hodder Headline plc.**

J.M. Dent (1888)—now incorporated into **The Orion Publishing Group Ltd.**

*****André Deutsch Ltd** (1950), 106 Great Russell Street, London WC1B 3LJ *tel*
0171-580 2746 *fax* 0171-631-3253. *Chairman and chief executive:* T.G. Rosen-
thal; *directors:* Tim Forrester (managing), Steve Ayres, Ivan Dunleavy.
Art, belles-lettres, biography and memoirs, fiction, general, history, humour,
politics, travel, photography, cricket.

*****André Deutsch Children's Books**—see **Scholastic Children's Books.**

Dial—see **Reed Information Services.**

diehard (1993), 3 Spittal Street, Edinburgh EH3 9DY *tel* (0131) 229 7252. *Managing director:* Ian William King; *Marketing director:* Sally Evans King. Contemporary drama; literature and historic reprints.

Discovery Walking Guides Ltd (1994), 10 Tennyson Close, Dallington, Northampton NN5 7HJ *tel/fax* (01604) 752576. *Chairman:* Rosamund C. Brawn. Walking guides/plant and flower guides to popular European holiday destinations.

Eric Dobby Publishing Ltd (1992), 12 Warnford Road, Orpington, Kent BR6 6LW *tel/fax* (01622) 718962 *fax* (01622) 717089. *Managing director:* E.R. Dobby.
Biography, true crime, antiques (especially wristwatches), sport, dictionaries.

Doctor Who—see **Virgin Publishing Ltd.**

John Donald Publishers Ltd (1973), 138 St Stephen Street, Edinburgh EH3 5AA *tel* 0131-225 1146 *fax* 0131-220 0567. *Directors:* Gordon Angus, D.L. Morrison, J. Elder.
British history, archaeology, ethnology, local history, vernacular architecture, general non-fiction.

Dorling Kindersley Ltd (1974), 9 Henrietta Street, Covent Garden, London WC2E 8PS *tel* 0171-836 5411 *telex* 8954527 DEEKAY G *fax* 0171-836 7570 *WWW:* www.dk.com *Chairman:* Peter Kindersley; *deputy chairman and publisher:* Christopher Davis; *group directors:* Rod Hare (managing), John Sargent (ceo-US publishing), Peter Gill (finance), Anita Fulton (legal), Lyn Blackman (new business development); *subsidiary directors:* Stuart Jackman (group design), Martyn Longly (group production), David Holmes (managing, UK publishing), Daphne Razazan (adult editorial), Anne-Marie Bulat (adult art), Ruth Sandys (managing, children's), Linda Davis and Ingrid Selberg (children's fiction), Linda Cole (children's art), Sue Unstead (children's editorial), Jonathan Reed (managing, DK Direct), Katharine Thompson (managing, Vision), Alan Buckingham (managing, Multimedia), Peter Cartwright (managing, DKFL-Int.), Barbara Sharples (managing, DKFL-UK).
High quality illustrated books on non-fiction subjects, including health, atlases, travel, cookery, gardening, crafts and reference; also children's non-fiction, picture books and fiction. Specialists in international co-editions, CD-ROM and television/video creation.

*Doubleday (UK) (1989)—see **Transworld Publishers Ltd.**

*Doubleday Children's Books—see **Transworld Publishers Ltd.**

Dragon's World Ltd, Paper Tiger Books (1975), 7/9 St George's Square, London SW1V 2HX *tel* 0171-630 9955 *fax* 0171-630 9921. *Directors:* H.A. Schaafsma, C.M.A. Schaafsma, Pippa Rubinstein (editorial), Leslie Cramphorn (sales and marketing).
High quality illustrated books on fable and fantasy illustration and mythology, natural history, DIY and general interest subjects; children's illustrated classics, natural history and general non-fiction.

*Dryden Press—see **Harcourt Brace & Co. Ltd.**

Gerald Duckworth & Co. Ltd (1898), 48 Hoxton Square, London N1 6PB *tel* 0171-729 5986 *fax* 0171-729 0015. *Directors:* Stephen Hill (chairman), Robin

Baird-Smith (publisher and managing), Anna Haycraft (fiction), John Betts (editorial).
Mainly academic; also general and fiction.

Martin Dunitz Ltd (1978), The Livery House, 7-9 Pratt Street, London NW1 0AE *tel* 0171-482 2202 *fax* 0171-267 0159 *e-mail* 100626.3270 @compuserve.com *Directors:* Martin Dunitz, Ruth Dunitz, John Slaytor, Rosemary Allen.
Radiology, orthopaedics, metabolic bone disease, dermatology, dentistry, haematology, oncology, cardiology, rheumatology, pathology, plastic surgery, otolaryngology, sports medicine, allied health and nursing.

*Dutton Children's Books—see **Penguin Books Ltd.**

*Earthscan Publications Ltd (1987)—see **Kogan Page Ltd.**

*East-West Publications (UK) Ltd (1977), 8 Caledonia Street, London N1 9DZ *tel* 0171-837 5061 *fax* 0171-278 4429. *Chairman:* L.W. Carp; *editor:* B. Thompson.
General non-fiction, travel, Eastern studies, sufism.
Gallery Children's Books (imprint). Quality children's books.

*Ebury Press—see **Random House UK Ltd.**

*Edinburgh University Press, 22 George Square, Edinburgh EH8 9LF *tel* 0131-650 4218 *fax* 0131-662 0053. *Managing director:* Ms Vivian Bone; *editorial director:* Ms Jackie Jones.
Academic and general publishers. Archaeology, botany, cultural studies, Islamic studies, history, linguistics, literature (criticism), philosophy, politics, Scottish studies, theology, women's studies.
Polygon (imprint) *tel* 0131-650 4689. New international fiction, including translations, oral history, general, Scottish, social and political (Determinations series).

Educational Explorers (1962), 11 Crown Street, Reading, Berks. RG1 2TQ *tel* (01734) 873101 *fax* (01734) 873103. *Directors:* M.J. Hollyfield, D.M. Gattegno.
Educational, mathematics: *Numbers in colour with Cuisenaire Rods*, languages: *The Silent Way*, literacy, reading: *Words in Colour*; educational films.

Eel Pie—see **Plexus Publishing Ltd.**

Element Books (1978), The Old School House, The Courtyard, Bell Street, Shaftesbury, Dorset SP7 8BP *tel* (01747) 851448 *fax* (01747) 855721. *Directors:* Michael Mann (chairman and publisher), Annie Wilson (rights), David Alexander (managing), John Salkeld FCA, Julia McCutchen (editorial), Roger Lane (production), Theresa Franklin (international sales and marketing).
Health, personal development, popular psychology, astrology, philosophy, religion, colour illustrated books, and mass market non-fiction.

Edward Elgar Publishing Ltd (1986), 8 Lansdown Place, Cheltenham, Glos. GL50 2HU *tel* (01242) 226934 *fax* (01242) 262111 *e-mail* publicity @e-elgar.co.uk *Managing director:* Edward Elgar.
Economics and other social sciences.

Elliot Right Way Books (1946), Kingswood Buildings, Brighton Road, Lower Kingswood, Tadworth, Surrey KT20 6TD *tel* (01737) 832202 *fax* (01737) 830311. *Managing directors:* Clive Elliot, Malcolm Elliot.

Independent publishers of practical non-fiction 'how to' paperbacks. The low-price *Paperfronts* series includes games, pastimes, horses, pets, motoring, sport, health, business, public speaking and jokes, financial and legal, cookery, home and garden, popular education, family subjects and etiquette. Titles of a more specialist nature are covered in the larger-format *Right Way* series. Welcomes new ideas; editorial help provided.

ELM Publications (1977), Seaton House, Kings Ripton, Huntingdon, Cambs. PE17 2NJ *tel* (01487) 773238 *fax* (01487) 773359. *Managing director:* Sheila Ritchie.
Educational books and resources; books and training aids (tutor's packs and software) for business and management; software simulations; library and information studies. Telephone in the first instance, rather than send MSS. Please note: we publish mainly to curricula and course syllabi.

*Elm Tree Books—see **Penguin Books Ltd/Hamish Hamilton Ltd.**

Elsevier Science Ltd, The Boulevard, Langford Lane, Kidlington, Oxford OX5 1GB *tel* (01865) 843000 *fax* (01865) 843010. *Managing director:* M. Boswood; *publishing director (primary and reference):* P. Shepherd; *publishing director (magazines and newsletters):* D. Bousfield.
Journal, magazine and book publishers in science, technology and medicine. Imprints: **Pergamon, Elsevier Applied Science, Elsevier Trends Journals, Butterworth Heinemann Journals.**

Encyclopaedia Britannica International Ltd, Carew House, Station Approach, Wallington, Surrey SM6 0DA *tel* 0181-669 4355 *telex* 23866 ENBRI G *fax* 0181-773 3631. *Managing director:* Joe D. Adams.

Enitharmon Press (1969), 36 St George's Avenue, London N7 0HD *tel* 0171-607 7194 *fax* 0171-607 8694. *Director:* Stephen Stuart-Smith.
Poetry, literary criticism, translations, artists' books. No unsolicited MSS.

Epworth Press, c/o Methodist Publishing House, 20 Ivatt Way, Peterborough PE3 7PG *tel* (01733) 332202 *fax* (01733) 331201. *Editorial committee:* Dr Valerie Edden, Dr Dorothy Graham, Rev. Dr Ivor H. Jones, Rev. Dr John Newton, Rev. Gerald Burt (hon. sec.), Rev. Graham Slater (chairman), Rev. Michael J. Townsend.
Religion, theology, church history.

Eros Plus—see **Titan Books Ltd.**

Eurobook Ltd—see **Peter Lowe (Eurobook Ltd).**

Euromonitor plc (1972), 60-61 Britton Street, London EC1M 5NA *tel* 0171-251 8024 *telex* 262433 *fax* 0171-608 3149. *Directors:* T.J. Fenwick (managing), R.N. Senior (chairman).
Business and commercial reference, marketing information, European and International Surveys, directories.

Europa Publications Ltd, 18 Bedford Square, London WC1B 3JN *tel* 0171-580 8236 *fax* 0171-636 1664. *Directors:* C.H. Martin (chairman), P.A. McGinley (managing), J.P. Desmond, R.M. Hughes, P.G.C. Jackson, M.R. Milton, A.G. Oliver (editorial), J. Quinney.
Directories, international relations, reference, year books.

Evangelical Press of Wales (1955), Bryntirion, Bridgend, Mid Glamorgan CF31 4DX *tel* (01656) 655886 *fax* (01656) 656095. *Chief executive:* G. Wyn Davies. Theology and religion (in English and Welsh).

*Evans Brothers Ltd (1905), 2A Portman Mansions, Chiltern Street, London W1M 1LE *tel* 0171-935 7160 *telegraphic address* Byronitic, London W1 *telex* 8811713 EVBOOK G *fax* 0171-487 5034. *Directors:* S.T. Pawley (managing),

B.O. Bolodeoku (Nigeria), Brian D. Jones (international publishing), A.O. Ojora (Nigeria), M. Jackson, J.D. Solly; *editorial manager:* Su Swallow.
Educational books, particularly pre-school, school library and teachers' books for the UK, including the Rainbows series of graded information books for 5-8-year-olds; primary and secondary for Africa, the Caribbean and Hong Kong.

Everyman—see The Orion Publishing Group Ltd.

Everyman's Library, 79 Berwick Street, London W1V 3PF *tel* 0171-287 0035 *fax* 0171-287 0038. *Publisher:* David Campbell; *finance director:* Mark Bicknell. Now merged with **Cadogan Books plc.**
Clothbound reprints of the classics; Everyman's Children's Classics; Everyman's Travel Guides.

Exley Publications Ltd (1976), 16 Chalk Hill, Watford, Herts. WD1 4BN *tel* (01923) 250505 *fax* (01923) 818733/800440. *Directors:* Dalton Exley, Helen Exley (editorial), Lincoln Exley, Richard Exley.
Popular colour gift books for an international market. 50 new titles a year. No unsolicited MSS. Creative gift book series editors needed.

*Faber & Faber Ltd, 3 Queen Square, London WC1N 3AU *tel* 0171-465 0045 *fax* 0171-465 0034. *Chairman and managing director:* Matthew Evans; *directors:* John Bodley, Dennis Crutcher, Patrick Curran, Giles de la Mare, Valerie Eliot, T.E. Faber, Tom Kelleher, Joanna Mackle, Peter Simpson (company secretary).
High quality general fiction and non-fiction; all forms of creative writing, including plays. For current lists, write to the above address. Address all submissions (with sae or return postage) to the Editorial Department. In the case of MSS, preliminary letter required. For information on submission procedure ring 0171-465 0189.

Fabian Society (1884), 11 Dartmouth Street, London SW1H 9BN *tel* 0171-222 8877 *fax* 0171-976 7153 *e-mail* fabian-society@geo2.poptel.org.uk (also controls **NCLC Publishing Society Ltd**). *Research and publications officer:* Stephen Pollard.
Current affairs, economics, educational, environment, political economy, social policy.

Facts on File, c/o Roundhouse Publishing, PO Box 140, Oxford OX2 7FF *tel* (01865) 512682 *fax* (01865) 59594 *e-mail* 100637.3571@compuserve.com *Contact:* Alan Goodworth.
Non-fiction reference and information books in a broad range of disciplines.

J.B. Fairfax Press Ltd—see Merehurst Ltd/J.B. Fairfax Press Ltd.

Farming Press Books (1951), 2 Wharfedale Road, Ipswich, Suffolk IP1 4LG *tel* (01473) 241122 *fax* (01473) 240501. *Manager:* Roger Smith.
Agriculture, humour, veterinary; videos; audio.

Fernhurst Books (1979), Duke's Path, High Street, Arundel, West Sussex BN18 9AJ *tel* (01903) 882277 *fax* (01903) 882715. *Publisher:* Tim Davison.
Sailing, watersports.

*First and Best in Education Ltd (1992; incorporating **Hamilton House Publishing**), 32 Nene Valley Business Park, Oundle, Peterborough PE8 4HJ *tel* (01832) 274716 *fax* (01832) 275281 *e-mail* editors@rmplc.co.uk *Directors:* Tony Attwood, Philippa Attwood, Keith Buckby.
All education and business-related books. Currently actively recruiting new writers for schools and business; ideas welcome (*contact:* Vivienne Hill/Kirsty Meadows, editors). Sae must accompany submissions.

Fishing News Books Ltd (1953), Osney Mead, Oxford OX2 0EL *tel* (01865) 206206 *fax* (01865) 206096. *Manager:* Philip Saugman.
Commercial fisheries, aquaculture and allied subjects.

Fitzroy Dearborn Publishers (1994), 11 Rathbone Place, London W1P 1DE *tel* 0171-636 6627 *fax* 0171-636 6982 *e-mail* Fitzroy Dearborn 100420.3277@compuserve.com *Managing director:* Daniel Kirkpatrick; *senior commissioning editor:* Lesley Henderson; *marketing manager:* Kate Berney.
Reference books: history, design, art, literature, gender, business, science.

*Flamingo—see HarperCollins Publishers.

Flicks Books (1986), 29 Bradford Road, Trowbridge, Wilts. BA14 9AN *tel* (01225) 767728 *fax* (01225) 760418. *Partners:* Matthew Stevens (publisher), Aletta Stevens.
Cinema, television, related media.

*Flint River—see Philip Wilson Publishers Ltd.

*Floris Books (1978), 15 Harrison Gardens, Edinburgh EH11 1SH *tel* 0131-337 2372 *fax* 0131-346 7516. *Editor:* Christopher Moore.
Religion, science, Celtic studies, craft; children's books: picture and board books, fiction, activity books.

Focal Press—see Reed Educational and Professional Publishing Ltd.

*Fodor Guides—see Random House UK Ltd.

Folens Ltd (1987), Albert House, Apex Business Centre, Boscombe Road, Dunstable LU5 4RL *tel* (01582) 472788 *fax* (01582) 472575. *Managing director:* Malcolm Watson.
Primary and secondary educational books, learn at home books.

*Fontana—now HarperCollins Paperbacks.

*Fontana Press—see HarperCollins Publishers.

Forest Books (1984), 20 Forest View, Chingford, London E4 7AY *tel* 0181-529 8470 *telex* 891182 GECOMS G *fax* 0181-524 7890. *Managing director:* Brenda Walker.
Only international literature in English translation; poetry, plays, novels and short stories, especially East European literature. No unsolicited material please.

G.T. Foulis & Co.—see Haynes Publishing.

W. Foulsham & Co. Ltd (1819), The Publishing House, Bennetts Close, Cippenham, Berks. SL1 5AP *tel* (01753) 526769 *fax* (01753) 535003. *Managing director:* B.A.R. Belasco; *editorial director:* W. Hobson.
General know-how, cookery, health and alternative therapies, hobbies and games, gardening, sport, travel guides, DIY, collectibles, popular new age.
Quantum (imprint). *Editor:* Ian Fenton. Popular philosophy and practical psychology.
Raphael's (imprint). *Editor:* Ian Fenton. Astrology.

The Foundational Book Company, for The John W. Doorly Trust, PO Box 659, London SW3 6SJ *tel* 0171-584 1053. *Trustee for publications:* Mrs Peggy M. Brook.
Spiritual Science.

Foundery Press—see Methodist Publishing House.

*Fount—see HarperCollins Publishers.

Fourmat Publishing—see Tolley Publishing Co. Ltd.

Fourth Estate Ltd (1984), 6 Salem Road, London W2 4BU *tel* 0171-727 8993 *fax* 0171-792 3176. *Directors:* Victoria Barnsley (managing), Patric Duffy (financial), Christopher Potter (publishing), Joanna Prior (publicity and marketing), Stephen Page (sales).
Current affairs, literature, popular culture, fiction, humour, business, politics, science, popular reference, TV tie-ins. No unsolicited MSS.
Fourth Estate Paperbacks (imprint). Publishes paperback editions of Fourth Estate hardback titles.
Guardian Books (imprint). Books stemming from the *Guardian* newspaper.

*Framework Press Educational Publishers Ltd (1983), Parkfield, Greaves Road, Lancaster, Lancs. LA1 4TZ *tel* (01524) 39602 *fax* (01524) 841520. *Directors:* Brenda V. Abercrombie (editorial), Nicholas Abercrombie, David R. Green.
School and college management, staff development, vocational, English.

Free Association Books (1984), 57 Warren Street, London W1P 5PA *tel* 0171-388 3182 *fax* 0171-388 3187 *e-mail* fab@melmoth.demon.co.uk *Chairman and financial director:* T.E. Brown; *managing and editorial director:* Gill Davies.
Psychoanalysis, psychotherapy, counselling, cultural studies, social sciences.

W.H. Freeman, Macmillan Press Ltd, Houndmills, Basingstoke, Hants RG21 6XS *tel* (01256) 29242 *fax* (01256) 479476. *Sales director:* E. Warner.
Science, technical, medicine, economics, psychology, archaeology.

*Freeway—see Transworld Publishers Ltd.

*Samuel French Ltd (1830), 52 Fitzroy Street, London W1P 6JR *tel* 0171-387 9373 *fax* 0171-387 2161. *Directors:* Charles Van Nostrand (chairman), John Bedding (managing), Amanda Smith, Paul Taylor.
Publishers of plays and agents for the collection of royalties.

*FT Law & Tax—see Pearson Professional Ltd.

*David Fulton Publishers Ltd (1987), 2 Barbon Close, Great Ormond Street, London WC1N 3JX *tel* 0171-405 5606 *fax* 0171-831 4840. *Managing director:* David Fulton; *editorial director:* John Owens.
Initial and continuing teacher education (special needs, primary and secondary), educational management and psychology, geography (for undergraduates). Unsolicited MSS not returned.

Gaia Books Ltd, 66 Charlotte Street, London W1P 1LR *tel* 0171-323 4010 *fax* 0171-323 0435; and 20 High Street, Stroud, Glos. GL5 1AS *tel* (01453) 752985 *fax* (01453) 752987. *Managing director:* Joss Pearson; *directors:* David Pearson, Lars Kjeldsen, Tor Svensson.
Illustrated reference books on ecology, natural living, health, mind. Submissions (outline and sample chapter) to managing director.

Gairm Publications, incorporating Alex MacLaren & Sons (1875), 29 Waterloo Street, Glasgow G2 6BZ *tel/fax* 0141-221 1971. *Editorial director:* Derick Thomson.
(Gaelic and Gaelic-related only) dictionaries, language books, novels, poetry, music, children's books, quarterly magazine.

*Gallery Children's Books—see East-West Publications (UK) Ltd.

Garnet Publishing Ltd (1991), 8 Southern Court, South Street, Reading RG1 4QS *tel* (01734) 597847 *fax* (01734) 597356. *Managing director:* Kenneth Banerji.
Art, architecture, photography and general, mainly on Middle and Far East, and Islam.

Ithaca Press (imprint). Post-graduate academic works, especially on the Middle East.

Gateway Books (1982), The Hollies, Wellow, Nr Bath, Avon BA2 8QJ *tel* (01225) 835127 *fax* (01225) 840012. *Publisher:* Alick Bartholomew.
Popular psychology, spirituality, health and healing, earth mysteries, ecology, self help, metaphysics and alternative science. Please do not send unsolicited MSS – outline and sample welcome.

The Gay Men's Press—see **GMP Publishers Ltd.**

*****Geddes & Grosset Ltd** (1988), David Dale House, New Lanark ML11 9DJ *tel* (01555) 665000 *fax* (01555) 665694. *Directors:* Ron Grosset, Mike Miller, David Geddes.
Popular reference including cookery; children's picture books, non-fiction and activity books.

Gee & Son (Denbigh) Ltd (1808), Chapel Street, Denbigh, Clwyd LL16 3SW *tel* (01745) 812020 *fax* (01745) 812825. *Directors:* E. Evans, E.M. Evans.
Oldest Welsh publishers. Books of interest to Wales, in Welsh and English.

*****Geographia**—now **Bartholomew**; see **HarperCollins Publishers.**

*****GeoInformation International**—see **Pearson Professional Ltd.**

*****Stanley Gibbons Publications** (1856), Parkside, Christchurch Road, Ringwood, Hants BH24 3SH *tel* (01425) 472363 *fax* (01425) 470247. *Chairman:* P.I. Fraser.
Philatelic handbooks, stamp catalogues and albums, *Gibbons Stamp Monthly*.

Robert Gibson & Sons Glasgow Ltd (1885), 17 Fitzroy Place, Glasgow G3 7SF *tel* 0141-248 5674 *fax* 0141-221 8219. *Directors:* R.G.C. Gibson, M. Pinkerton, H.C. Crawford, N.J. Crawford (editorial).
Bibliography and library science; educational and textbooks.

Ginn & Co.—see **Reed Educational and Professional Publishing Ltd.**

*****Mary Glasgow Publications**—merged with **Stanley Thornes (Publishers) Ltd.**

GMP Publishers Ltd (1979), PO Box 247, Swaffham, Norfolk PE37 8PA *tel* (01366) 328101 *fax* (01366) 328102. *Publishers:* Aubrey Walter, David Fernbach.
The Gay Men's Press (imprint). Modern, popular, historical/literary fiction, including translations from European languages, biography and memoir, history, drama, health, social and political questions, literary criticism; *Gay Modern Classics:* reprints of gay fiction/non-fiction from the past 100 years; *Éditions Aubrey Walter:* male photography both art and glamour, fine-art editions of gay artists.
Heretic Books (imprint). Ecology, animal liberation, green politics, Third World.

Godfrey Cave—see **Penguin Books Ltd.**

Golden Cockerel Press, 16 Barter Street, London WC1A 2AH *tel* 0171-405 7979 *fax* 0171-404 3598 *e-mail* lindesa@ibm.net *Contact:* Tamar Lindesay.
Academic.
Associated University Presses (imprint). Literary criticism, art, music, history, film, theology, philosophy, Jewish studies, politics, sociology.
Cornwall Books (imprint). Antiques, history, film.
Cygnus Arts (imprint). The arts.

Victor Gollancz Ltd (1927)—see **Cassell plc.**

Gollancz Witherby Ltd—see **Cassell plc.**

Gomer Press (1892), Llandysul, Dyfed SA44 4BQ *tel* (01559) 362371 *fax* (01559) 363758. *Directors:* Jonathan Lewis, John H. Lewis, Dyfed Elis-Gruffydd; *editor:* Mairwen Prys Jones.
Books in Welsh; biography, local history. Fiction with Welsh background for schoolchildren.

Gower Publishing Ltd (1967), Gower House, Croft Road, Aldershot, Hants GU11 3HR *tel* (01252) 331551 *fax* (01252) 344405. *Managing director:* Christopher Simpson.
Practical management and business reference.

*Grafton—now HarperCollins Paperbacks.

Graham & Whiteside Ltd (1995), Tuition House, 5-6 Francis Grove, London SW19 4DT *tel* 0181-947 1011 *fax* 0181-947 1163. *Directors:* A.M.W. Graham, H.C.H. Whiteside, R.M. Whiteside, P.L. Murphy.
Directories for international business and professional markets.

Granta Publications Ltd (1982), 2/3 Hanover Yard, Noel Road, London N1 8BE *tel* 0171-704 9776 *fax* 0171-704 0474. *Book publisher:* Frances Coady; *magazine editor:* Ian Jack.
Fiction, autobiography, political non-fiction.

Green Books (1987), Foxhole, Dartington, Totnes, Devon TQ9 6EB *tel/fax* (01803) 863843. *Managing director:* John Elford.
Environment (practical and philosophical). *No* fiction or children's books. *No* MSS; synopsis and covering letter please.

Green Print—see Merlin Press Ltd.

Greenhill Books/Lionel Leventhal Ltd (1984), Park House, 1 Russell Gardens, London NW11 9NN *tel* 0181-458 6314 *fax* 0181-905 5245. *Managing director:* Lionel Leventhal.
Military history.

Gresham Books Ltd, The Gresham Press, PO Box 61, Henley-on-Thames, Oxon RG9 3LQ *tel/fax* (01734) 403789. *Chief executive:* Mrs M.V. Green.
Hymn books, prayer books, wood engraving.

Grub Street (1989), The Basement, 10 Chivalry Road, London SW11 1HT *tel* 0171-924 3966/738 1008 *fax* 0171-738 1009. *Directors:* John B. Davies, Anne Dolamore.
Adult non-fiction: aviation history, cookery, health and reference.

Guardian Books—see Fourth Estate Ltd.

Guild of Master Craftsman Publications Ltd (1979), Castle Place, 166 High Street, Lewes, East Sussex BN7 1XU *tel* (01273) 477374/478449 *fax* (01273) 486300. *Managing director:* Alan Phillips.
Practical, illustrated woodworking and crafts.

*Guinness Publishing Ltd (1954), 33 London Road, Enfield, Middlesex EN2 6DJ *tel* 0181-367 4567 *cables* Mostest, Enfield *fax* 0181-367 5912. *Joint publishing directors:* Michael Feldman, Ian Castello-Cortes.
The Guinness Book of Records and general and recreational reference books.

Gwasg Gee—see Gee & Son (Denbigh) Ltd.

Peter Halban Publishers Ltd (1986), 42 South Molton Street, London W1Y 1HB *tel* 0171-491 1582 *fax* 0171-629 5381. *Directors:* Martine Halban, Peter Halban.
General non-fiction; history and biography; Jewish subjects and Middle East. No unsolicited MSS considered; preliminary letter essential.

Robert Hale Ltd (1936), Clerkenwell House, 45-47 Clerkenwell Green, London EC1R 0HT *tel* 0171-251 2661 *fax* 0171-490 4958. *Directors:* John Hale (managing and editorial), Robert J. Hale (production), Robert Kynaston (financial), Martin Kendall (marketing), Betty Weston (rights).
Adult general non-fiction and fiction.

*Hamish Hamilton Ltd (1931)—see **Penguin Books Ltd.**

*Hamish Hamilton Children's Books—see **Penguin Books Ltd.**

*Hamilton House Publishing—see **First and Best in Education Ltd.**

Hamlyn—see **Reed Books.**

Hamlyn Children's Non-fiction—see **Reed Books.**

*Harcourt Brace & Co. Ltd, 24-28 Oval Road, London NW1 7DX *tel* 0171-267 4466 *fax* 0171-482 2293/485 4752. *Managing director:* Bill M. Barnett.
Scientific and medical.
Academic Press (division). *Managing director:* Jan Velterop. Academic and reference.
Baillière Tindall Ltd (division). *Editorial director:* Sean Duggan. Medical, veterinary, nursing, pharmaceutical books and journals.
Dryden Press (division). *Managing director:* Bill M. Barnett. Educational books (college, university), economics, business.
W.B. Saunders Co. Ltd (division). *Editorial director:* Sean Duggan. Medical and scientific.

*Patrick Hardy Books—see **James Clarke & Co. Ltd.**

*Harlequin Mills & Boon Ltd (1908), Eton House, 18-24 Paradise Road, Richmond, Surrey TW9 1SR *tel* 0181-948 0444 *fax* 0181-288 2899. *Chairman:* J.T. Boon CBE; *managing director:* A. Flynn; *directors:* A.W. Boon, S. Cummings (financial), M.N. Saraceno (production), R. Hedley (hardback and export sales), K. Stoecker (editorial), R. Guzner (direct marketing), G. Howe (paperback sales), H. O'Neil (retail marketing and exports), J. Oldham (human resources).
Mills & Boon (imprint). *Senior editors:* T. Shapcott, S. Hodgson. Contemporary romance fiction in paperback and hardback.
Mira Books (imprint). *Senior editor:* L. Fildew. Women's fiction.
Medical & Historical (series). *Senior editor:* E. Johnson. Romance fiction.
Silhouette (imprint). *Senior editor:* L. Stonehouse. Popular romantic women's fiction.

*HarperCollins Publishers (1819), 77-85 Fulham Palace Road, Hammersmith, London W6 8JB *tel* 0181-741 7070 *telex* 25611 COLINS G *fax* 0181-307 4440.
Executive chairman and publisher: Eddie Bell; *divisional managing directors:* Adrian Bourne (Trade), Eileen Campbell (Thorsons/Religious), Jeremy Westwood (Cartographic), Robin Wood (Reference/Dictionaries), Kate Harris (Education/College); *publishers:* Stuart Proffitt (Trade), Ian Craig (Children's).
All fiction and trade non-fiction must be submitted through an agent. Unsolicited submissions should be made in the form of a typewritten synopsis.
Access Press (imprint). Travel guides.
Bartholomew (imprint). Maps, atlases, electronic products.
Birnbaum (imprint). Travel guides.
Collins (imprints). Collins Crime, Collins Classics, Collins Educational, Collins bibles, Collins Liturgical Books, Collins Dictionaries, Collins Cobuild, Collins Gems, Collins New Naturalist Library, Collins Willow, Collins Longman.

HarperCollins Publishers—*continued*

Collins (children's imprint). *Publishing director:* Gail Penston. Includes Jets, Yellow Storybooks, Red Storybooks, fiction for older children and toddler books.

Collins Children's Audio (imprint). *Publishing director:* Gail Penston.

Collins Children's Non-fiction (imprint). *Publishing director:* David Howgrave-Graham.

Collins Children's Books (imprint). *Publishing director:* Gail Penston.

Collins Picture Lions (imprint). *Publishing director:* Gail Penston. Children's picture paperbacks.

Collins Tracks (imprint). *Publishing director:* Gail Penston. Young adult books.

Flamingo (imprint). *Editorial director:* Philip Gwyn Jones. Literary fiction both hardback and paperback.

Fontana Press (imprint). *Editorial director:* Philip Gwyn Jones. Paperback intellectual non-fiction.

Fount (imprint). *Managing director:* Eileen Campbell. Religious.

HarperCollins (imprints). Audiobooks, hardbacks (fiction and non-fiction), paperbacks (fiction and non-fiction), religious.

HarperCollins Broadcasting Consultancy. *Contact:* Cresta Norris. Exploits TV and film rights across the company.

HarperCollins Electronic Products. *Managing director:* Kate Harris. CD-ROM, floppy disk and on-line. Specialises in special interest, children's, reference and interactive fiction.

HarperCollins World. *Marketing director:* Henrietta Silver. General trade titles imported into the UK market.

Lions (imprint). *Publishing director:* Gail Penston. Children's books.

Marshall Pickering (imprint). *Managing director:* Eileen Campbell. Theology, music, popular religion, illustrated children's, wide range of Christian books.

Nicholson (imprint). *Managing director:* Jeremy Westwood. London maps, atlases and guidebooks. Waterways maps and guidebooks.

Pandora Press (imprint). *Managing director:* Eileen Campbell. Feminist press publishing. General non-fiction: biography, arts, media, health, current affairs, reference and sexual politics.

Thorsons (imprint). *Managing director:* Eileen Campbell. Complementary medicine, health and nutrition, business and management, self-help and positive thinking, popular psychology, parenting and childcare, astrology, tarot and divination, mythology and psychic awareness.

Times Books (imprint). *Managing director:* Jeremy Westwood. World atlases and maps, thematic atlases, reference, guides and crosswords.

Tolkien (imprint). *Projects director:* David Brawn; *editorial director:* Jane Johnson.

Voyager (imprint). *Editorial director:* Jane Johnson. Science fiction, fantasy fiction and media tie-ins.

Harrap, 43-45 Annandale Street, Edinburgh EH7 4AZ *tel* 0131-557 4571 *fax* 0131-557 2936. *Chairman:* John Clement; *sales director:* Robert Snuggs; *publishing manager:* Katharine Coates. Subsidiary of **Larousse plc.**
Bilingual dictionaries.

Harvard University Press—see under United States Book Publishers; all material originates in North America.

*Harvester Wheatsheaf—see **Prentice Hall Europe.**

The Harvill Press (1946), 84 Thornhill Road, London N1 1RD　*tel* 0171-609 1119　*fax* 0171-609 2019　*e-mail* harvill@leopards.demon.co.uk　*Publisher and chairman:* Christopher MacLehose; *directors:* John Mitchinson (managing), Guido Waldman (editorial), Rachael Kerr (marketing); *managing editor:* Sarah Westcott; *rights manager:* Katharina Bielenberg.
English-language and world literature in translation (mainly literary fiction, but including non-fiction and some first-class narrative thrillers); monographs in the fields of ethnography, art, ballet, horticulture and natural history; Africana.

Hawk Books (1986), Suite 309, Canalot Studios, 222 Kensal Road, London W10 5BN　*tel* 0181-969 8091　*fax* 0181-968 9012. *Director:* Patrick Hawkey.
Comics, nostalgia, juveniles, art.

Haynes Publishing, Sparkford, Yeovil, Somerset BA22 7JJ　*tel* North Cadbury (01963) 440635　*telex* 46212 HAYNES G　*fax* (01963) 440023. *Directors:* J.H. Haynes (chairman), A.C. Haynes, I.P. Mauger, S.L. Reed, D.J. Reach (editorial), A.J. Sperring, K.C. Fullman (managing), C. Davies, D.J. Hermelin, N. Barnard.
Car and motorcycle owners workshop manuals, car handbooks/servicing guides, do-it-yourself books, aircraft, trains, nautical.
G.T. Foulis & Co. (imprint). *Editor:* Darryl Reach. Motoring/motorcycling, marque and model history, practical maintenance and renovation, related biographies, motor/motorcycle sport, aircraft, nautical, aviation.
Haynes (imprint). Home and Leisure Division. *Editor:* Nicholas Barnard. Home DIY and leisure activities (e.g. cycling).
Oxford Illustrated Press (imprint). *Editor:* Darryl Reach. Well-illustrated non-fiction books, sport, leisure and travel guides, car books, art books, general.
Oxford Publishing Company (OPC Railbooks) (imprint). *Editor:* Peter Nicholson. Railway transport.
Patrick Stephens Ltd (imprint). *Editorial director:* Darryl Reach. Aviation, biography, maritime, military and wargaming, model making, motorcycling, motoring and motor racing, railways and railway modelling.

Hazar Publishing Ltd (1992), 147 Chiswick High Road, London W4 2DT　*tel* 0181-742 8578　*fax* 0181-994 1407. *Managing director:* Greg Hill; *children's editor:* Rio Brown; *adult non-fiction editor:* Marie Clayton.
Children's picture and novelty books; adult non-fiction: architecture and design.

Headland Publications (1970). *Editorial office:* Tŷ Coch, Galltegfa, Llanfwrog, Ruthin, Clwyd LL15 2AR, and 38 York Avenue, West Kirby, Wirral, Merseyside L48 3JF. *Director and editor:* Gladys Mary Coles.
Poetry, anthologies of poetry and prose. *No* unsolicited MSS.

Headline Book Publishing Ltd—see **Hodder Headline plc.**

Headstart—see **Hodder Headline plc.**

Health Science Press—see **The C.W. Daniel Company Ltd.**

William Heinemann—see **Reed Books.**

Heinemann Educational—see **Reed Educational and Professional Publishing Ltd.**

Heinemann English Language Teaching—see **Reed Educational and Professional Publishing Ltd.**

Heinemann Young Books—see **Reed Books.**

Helicon Publishing Ltd (1992), 42 Hythe Bridge Street, Oxford OX1 2EP　*tel* (01865) 204204　*fax* (01865) 204205　*e-mail* 7477.3250@compuserve.com *Directors:* David Attwooll (managing), Michael Upshall (publishing); *editorial*

director (subject reference): Anne-Lucie Norton; *associate editorial director* (general reference): Hilary McGlynn, Tony Ballsdon (production), Brigid Macleod (sales and marketing).
General trade reference, hardback and paperback; electronic reference.

*Christopher Helm—see **A. & C. Black (Publishers) Ltd.**

Helmsman—see **The Crowood Press.**

Henderson Publishing plc (1990), Tide Mill Way, Woodbridge, Suffolk IP12 1BY *tel* (01394) 380622 *fax* (01394) 380618. *Managing director:* Barrie Henderson; *managing editor:* Lucy Bater.
Children's books: picture books, activity, novelty, non-fiction.

*The Herbert Press Ltd (1972), 35 Bedford Row, London WC1R 4JH *tel* 0171-404 5621 *fax* 0171-404 7706. *Chairman:* Charles Black; *directors:* David Herbert (managing), Jill Coleman. Subsidiary of **A. & C. Black plc.**
Art, architecture, design, crafts, art nostalgia, fashion and costume, natural history, archaeology, illustrated non-fiction.

Heretic Books (1982)—see **GMP Publishers Ltd.**

Nick Hern Books Ltd (1988), 14 Larden Road, London W3 7ST *tel* 0181-740 9539 *fax* 0181-746 2006. *Publisher:* Nick Hern.
Theatre, professionally produced plays. Initial letter required.

Hilmarton Manor Press (1964), Calne, Wilts. SN11 8SB *tel* Hilmarton (01249) 760208 *fax* (01249) 760379. *Editorial director:* Charles Baile de Laperriere.
Fine art, photography, antiques, visual arts.

*Hippo (1980)—see **Scholastic Children's Books.**

Hippopotamus Press (1974), 22 Whitewell Road, Frome, Somerset BA11 4EL *tel/fax* (01373) 466653. *Editors:* Roland John, Anna Martin.
Poetry, essays, criticism. Publishes *Outposts Poetry Quarterly*. Poetry submissions from new writers welcome.

*HMSO Books. *Head Office:* St Crispins, Duke Street, Norwich NR3 1PD *tel* (01603) 695532 *telex* 97301 *fax* (01603) 695317; *distribution and order point:* HMSO Books Publication Centre, PO Box 276, London SW8 5DT *tel* 0171-873 0011 *telex* 297138; *HMSO bookshops* (retail): 49 High Holborn, London WC1V 6HB *tel* 0171-873 0011 *fax* 0171-831 1326; 9-21 Princess Street, Albert Square, Manchester M60 8AS *tel* 0161-834 7201 *fax* 0161-833 0634; 71 Lothian Road, Edinburgh EH3 9AZ *tel* 0131-228 4181 *fax* 0131-229 2734; 68/69 Bull Street, Birmingham B4 6AD *tel* 0121-236 9696 *fax* 0121-236 9699; 33 Wine Street, Bristol BS1 2BQ *tel* (0117) 926 4306 *fax* (0117) 929 4515; 16 Arthur Street, Belfast BT1 4GD *tel* (01232) 238451 *fax* (01232) 235401; HMSO Oriel Bookshop, The Friary, Cardiff CF1 4AA *tel* (01222) 395548 *fax* (01222) 384347; plus HMSO agents (see Yellow Pages).
Archaeology, architecture, art, current affairs, directories and guidebooks, educational (primary, secondary, technical, university), general, history, naval and military, practical handbooks, reference, science, sociology, year books. As the Government Publisher, **HMSO** publishes only material sponsored by Parliament, Government Departments and other official bodies. Consequently it cannot consider unsolicited work submitted by private citizens.

Hobsons Publishing plc (1974), Bateman Street, Cambridge CB2 1LZ *tel* (01223) 460366 *fax* (01223) 323154. *Directors:* Charles Sinclair (chairman), Martin Morgan (managing), Robert Baker (deputy managing), Roger Dalzell, David Hepburn, Andrew Round, Chris Letcher; *company secretary:* Stuart Mott.

Careers guidance, PSE, science, business studies, leisure, *Johansens Guides*. Publishers under licence to CRAC – Careers Research & Advisory Centre.

Hodder Children's Books—see **Hodder Headline plc.**

Hodder Headline plc (1993), 338 Euston Road, London NW1 3BH   *tel* 0171-873 6000   *fax* 0171-873 6024. *Chairman:* The Earl of Donoughmore (non-executive); *group chief executive:* Tim Hely Hutchinson; *deputy chief executive:* Mark Opzoomer CA Canada, MBA; *directors:* Martin Neild (managing, Hodder & Stoughton General), Sue Fletcher (deputy managing, Hodder & Stoughton General), John Lloyd (non-executive), Mary Tapissier (managing, children's, chairman, religious), Eric Major (managing, religious), Amanda Ridout (managing, Headline), Malcolm Edwards (managing, Australia and New Zealand), Brian Steven (managing, Educational), Richard Stileman (managing, Edward Arnold), Mandy Warnford-Davis (non-executive), Christopher Weston (non-executive).

Edward Arnold (division). *Managing director:* Richard Stileman; *humanities:* Chris Wheeler; *medical, science and engineering:* Nicki Dennis. Academic and professional books and journals.

Brockhampton Press (division). *Managing director:* John Maxwell; *sales director:* Jack Cooper. Promotional books.

Headline Book Publishing Ltd (division). *Managing director:* Amanda Ridout; *non-fiction:* Alan Brooke; *fiction:* Jane Morpeth. Publishes under **Headline**, **Headline Feature**, **Headline Review**. Commercial fiction (hardback and paperback); popular non-fiction including: biography, cinema, design and film, food and wine, countryside, TV tie-ins and sports yearbooks.

Headline Delta (imprint of Headline Book Publishing). *Associate publisher:* Mike Bailey. General erotica.

Headline Liaison (imprint of Headline Book Publishing). *Associate publisher:* Mike Bailey. Erotica for both sexes, to be read separately, or with a partner.

Hodder Children's Books (division). *Managing director:* Mary Tapissier; *publishing director:* Fiona Kenshole. Publishes under **Hodder & Stoughton**, **Knight**, **Picture Knight**, **Hodder Dargaud**, **Headstart**, **Test Your Child**, **Signature**. Picture books, fiction and non-fiction.

Hodder & Stoughton Educational (division). *Managing director:* Brian Steven; *humanities, science and mathematics:* David Lea; *languages, business and psychology:* Tim Gregson-Williams. Publishes under **Hodder & Stoughton Educational**, **Teach Yourself**, **Headway**. Textbooks for the primary, secondary, tertiary and further education sectors and for self-improvement.

Hodder & Stoughton General (division). *Managing director:* Martin Nield; *deputy managing director:* Sue Fletcher; *non-fiction:* Roland Philipps; *horror:* Nick Austin; *Sceptre:* Carole Welch; *fiction:* Carolyn Mays, Carolyn Caughey; *audio:* Rupert Lancaster. Publishes under **Hodder & Stoughton**, **Coronet**, **New English Library**, **Sceptre**. Commercial and literary fiction; biography, autobiography, history, self-help, humour, travel and other general interest non-fiction; audio.

Hodder & Stoughton Religious (division). *Managing director:* Charles Nettleton; *editorial directors:* Emma Sealey (bibles and liturgical), Judith Longman (religious trade). Publishes under **New International Version of the Bible**, **Hodder Christian** paperbacks. Bibles, commentaries, liturgical works (both printed and software), wide range of Christian paperbacks.

Hodder & Stoughton (1868)—see **Hodder Headline plc.**

Hodder Dargaud—see **Hodder Headline plc.**

*Hogarth Press—see **Random House UK Ltd.**

*Ellis Horwood Ltd (1973)—see **Prentice Hall Europe.**

How To Books Ltd (1991), Plymbridge House, Estover Road, Plymouth, Devon PL6 7PZ *tel* (01752) 202369. *Managing director:* R.E. Ferneyhough; *secretary:* M.W. Beevers FCA.
How To series of personal achievement paperbacks covering student life, careers, employment and expatriate topics, practical business skills, creative/media skills, education, family reference and personal development.

Hugo's Language Books Ltd (1864), Old Station Yard, Marlesford, Woodbridge, Suffolk IP13 0AG *tel* (01728) 746546 *fax* (01728) 746236. *Editorial director:* Robin Batchelor-Smith.
Hugo's language books and courses.

Hunt & Thorpe (1989), Laurel House, Station Approach, New Alresford, Hants SO24 9JH *tel* (01962) 735633 *fax* (01962) 735320. *Partners:* John Hunt, Debbie Thorpe.
Children's and adult religious, full colour books for the international market. Manuscripts welcome; send sae.

*C. Hurst & Co. (Publishers) Ltd (1967), 38 King Street, London WC2E 8JZ *tel* 0171-240 2666, (night) 0181-852 9021 *fax* 0171-240 2667. *Directors:* Christopher Hurst, Michael Dwyer.
Scholarly 'area studies' covering contemporary history, politics, social studies and the religions of Asia and Africa.

*Hutchinson—see **Random House UK Ltd.**

*Hutchinson Children's—see **Random House UK Ltd.**

ICSA Publishing (1981), Campus 400, Maylands Avenue, Hemel Hempstead, Herts. HP2 7EZ *tel* (01442) 881900 *fax* (01442) 252544. *Managing director:* Clare Grist.
Professional business books for the private, public and voluntary sectors. Publish titles for The Institute of Chartered Secretaries and Administrators.

Impact Books Ltd (1985), Axe and Bottle Court, 70 Newcomen Street, London SE1 1YT *tel* 0171-403 3541 *fax* 0171-407 6437. *Chairman:* Jean-Luc Barbanneau (publisher); *directors:* David Skinner, David Collins, Roy Greenslade.
Travel writing, illustrated country books, practical guides and reference. No unsolicited MSS. Send synopsis and sample first.

In Print Publishing Ltd (1990), 9 Beaufort Terrace, Brighton, East Sussex BN2 2SU *tel* (01273) 682836 *fax* (01273) 620958 *e-mail* iprintad @pavilion.co.uk *Directors:* Alastair Dingwall, John Edmondson.
Special interest travel (including literary guides), Japan, South-east Asia, guides to teaching English.

*InfoSource International—see **Blackwell Publishers.**

Institute of Personnel and Development, IPD House, 35 Camp Road, Wimbledon, London SW19 4UX *tel* 0181-971 9000 *fax* 0181-263 3333. *Head of publishing:* Judith Tabern.
Personnel management, training and development.

Institute of Physics Publishing, Techno House, Redcliffe Way, Bristol BS1 6NX *tel* (0117) 929 7481 *fax* (0117) 929 4318 *e-mail* revill @ioppublishing.co.uk *Books publisher:* Jim Revill.
Monographs, graduate texts, conference proceedings, in physics and physics-related science and technology, and popular science titles.

*Inter-Varsity Press, 38 De Montfort Street, Leicester LE1 7GP   *tel* (0116) 255 1754   *fax* (0116) 254 2044. *Managing editor:* Mrs S.J. Heald.
Theology and religion.

*Irwin—see Times Mirror International Publishers Ltd.

Ithaca Press—see Garnet Publishing Ltd.

Arthur James Ltd (1935), 4 Broadway Road, Evesham, Worcs. WR11 6BH   *tel* (01386) 446566   *fax* (01386) 446717. *Editorial director:* John Hunt; *managing director:* Ian Carlile.
Religion, sociology, psychology.

Jane's Information Group, 163 Brighton Road, Coulsdon, Surrey CR5 2NH   *tel* 0181-763 1030   *telex* 916907   *fax* 0181-763 1005. *Managing director:* Alfred Rolington.
Military, aviation, naval, defence, non-fiction, reference.

Jarrold Publishing (1770), Whitefriars, Norwich NR3 1TR   *tel* (01603) 763300   *fax* (01603) 662748. *Managing director:* Antony Jarrold; *publishing director:* Caroline Jarrold. Division of Jarrold & Sons Ltd.
UK travel guidebooks, pictorial books and calendars. About 30 titles a year. Unsolicited MSS, synopses and ideas welcome but approach in writing before submitting to Donald Greig, Senior Editor.

Jewish Chronicle Publications, C/o Vallentine Mitchell, Newbury House, 900 Eastern Avenue, Ilford, Essex IG2 7HH   *tel* 0181-599 8866   *fax* 0171-405 9040. *Executive director:* M. Weinberg.
Theology and religion, reference; *Jewish Year Book*, *Jewish Travel Guide*.

Johnson Publications Ltd (1946), 130 Wigmore Street, London W1H 0AT   *tel* 0171-486 6757   *fax* 0171-487 5436. *Directors:* M.A. Murray-Pearce, Z.M. Pauncefort.
Perfume, cosmetics, beauty culture, aromatherapy and essential oils, including dictionaries, *objets d'art*, advertising, marketing, biography and memoirs. Return postage should be sent with unsolicited MSS.

Jordan Publishing Ltd, 21 St Thomas Street, Bristol BS1 6JS   *tel* (0117) 923 0600   *fax* (0117) 925 0486   *DX* 78161 Bristol. *Managing director:* Richard Hudson.
Law, particularly company and family (including the *Family Law Journal*), company administration, business, finance, looseleaf services.

*Michael Joseph Ltd (1935)—see **Penguin Books Ltd.**

The Journeyman Press—see Pluto Publishing Ltd.

Karnak House (1979), 300 Westbourne Park Road, London W11 1EH   *tel/fax* 0171-221 6490. *Directors:* Dimela Yekwai (chairman), Amon Saba Saakana (editorial), Gloria Flaxman (administration), Seheri Sujai (art).
Specialists in African/Caribbean studies worldwide: anthropology, education, Egyptology, fiction, history, language, linguistics, literary criticism, music, parapsychology, philosophy, prehistory.

Kelly's—see Reed Information Services.

The Kenilworth Press Ltd (1989; incorporates **Threshold Books**, 1970), Addington, Buckingham MK18 2JR   *tel* (0129 671) 5101   *fax* (0129 671) 5148. *Directors:* David Blunt, Deirdre Blunt.
Equestrian, including official publications for the British Horse Society.

Kenyon-Deane, 10 Station Road Industrial Estate, Colwall, Malvern, Worcs. WR13 6RN *tel* (01684) 540154 *fax* (01684) 540154. *Directors:* Leslie Smith, Audrey Smith.
Plays and drama textbooks, especially for amateur dramatic societies. Specialists in plays for women.

*****Laurence King Publishing** (1991), 71 Great Russell Street, London WC1B 3BN *tel* 0171-831 6351 *fax* 0171-831 8356. *Directors:* Robin Hyman (chairman), Laurence King (managing), Lesley Ripley Greenfield (editorial: college and fine arts), Judith Rasmussen (production). Imprint of **Calmann and King Ltd**, book packagers.
Art, design, decorative art.

*****Kingfisher**—see **Larousse plc.**

*****Jessica Kingsley Publishers** (1986), 116 Pentonville Road, London N1 9JB *tel* 0171-833 2307 *fax* 0171-837 2917. *Director:* Jessica Kingsley.
Psychology, psychotherapy, therapy, social work, higher education policy, regional studies, education.
Penton Press (imprint). Materials science, engineering.

*****Kingsway Communications Ltd,** Lottbridge Drove, Eastbourne, East Sussex BN23 6NT *tel* (01323) 410930 *fax* (01323) 411970. *Joint managing directors:* John Paculabo, Brian Davies; *director of publishing:* Richard Herkes.
Christian theology for laymen. No poetry. *All submissions must have Evangelical Christian content.* Please send synopsis/2 sample chapters only to the Editorial Department with return postage.

Kluwer Publishing (1972), Croner House, London Road, Kingston-upon-Thames, Surrey KT2 6SR *tel* 0181-547 3333 *fax* 0181-547 2637. *Directors:* Hans Staal (managing), Chris Hilton-Childs (finance). Subsidiary of Croner Publications Ltd.
Law, taxation, finance, insurance, looseleaf information services.

Knight—see **Hodder Headline plc.**

Charles Knight Publishing—see **Tolley Publishing Co. Ltd.**

Knockabout Comics (1975), 10 Acklam Road, London W10 5QZ *tel* 0181-969 2945 *fax* 0181-968 7614. *Editors:* Tony Bennett, Carol Bennett.
Humorous and satirical comic strips for an adult readership.

*****Kogan Page Ltd** (1967), 120 Pentonville Road, London N1 9JN *tel* 0171-278 0433 *telex* 263088 KOGAN G *fax* 0171-837 6348. *Managing director:* Philip Kogan; *directors:* Pauline Goodwin (editorial), Peter Chadwick (production and editorial), Gordon Watts (financial), Philip Mudd (editorial), Jonathan Sinclair-Wilson (Earthscan, editorial), Mike Baggallay (sales and marketing).
Education, training, educational and training technology, journals, business and management, human resource management, transport and distribution, marketing, sales, advertising and PR, finance and accounting, directories, small business, careers and vocational, personal finance, environment.
Earthscan Publications Ltd (subsidiary). *Directors:* Philip Kogan, Jonathan Sinclair-Wilson (editorial). Third world and environmental issues including politics, sociology, environment, economics, current events, geography, health.

Kompass—see **Reed Information Services.**

*****Ladybird Books Ltd** (1924), Beeches Road, Loughborough, Leics. LE11 2NQ *tel* (01509) 268021 *fax* (01509) 234672. *Chairman:* Peter Mayer. Division of **Penguin Books Ltd.**

Children's books for 0-10 year-olds—babies, toddlers, preschoolers, general and home educational (infants, primary, junior and secondary).

Lampada Press—see **The University of Hull Press.**

*Larousse plc. London office: Elsley House, 24-30 Great Titchfield Street, London W1P 7AD   *tel* 0171-631 0878   *fax* 0171-323 4694; Edinburgh office: 43-45 Annandale Street, Edinburgh EH7 4AZ   *tel* 0131-557 4571   *fax* 0131-557 2936. *Chairman:* John Clement; *directors:* Marc Zagar (finance), Robert Snuggs (sales and marketing), Gerry Kelly (special sales). See also **Harrap.**
Chambers (imprint). *Publishing director:* Robert Allen. Dictionaries, reference and local interest.
Kingfisher (imprint). *Publishing directors:* Chester Fisher (non-fiction), Ann-Janine Murtagh (fiction). Children's books.
Larousse (imprint). *Publishing directors:* Robert Allen, Jim Miles. Reference books and bilingual dictionaries.

Lawrence & Wishart Ltd, 99A Wallis Road, London E9 5LN   *tel* 0181-533 2506   *fax* 0181-533 7369. *Directors:* S. Davison (editorial), J. Rodrigues, B. Kirsch, M. Seaton, M. Perryman, A. Greenaway.
Cultural studies, current affairs, history, socialism and Marxism, political philosophy, politics, popular culture.

*Legend—see **Random House UK Ltd.**

Leicester University Press (1951)—see **Cassell plc.**

Lennard Publishing, Windmill Cottage, Mackerye End, Harpenden, Herts. AL5 5DR   *tel* (01582) 715866   *fax* (01582) 715121. *Directors:* K.A.A. Stephenson, R.H. Stephenson. Division of **Lennard Associates Ltd.**
General adult non-fiction. No unsolicited MSS.

Letts Educational—see **BPP (Letts Educational) Ltd.**

Levinson Books Ltd (1994), Greenland Place, 115-123 Bayham Street, London NW1 0AG   *tel* 0171-424 0488   *fax* 0171-424 0499. *Executive officers:* Joanna Levinson (managing director), Kate Burns (senior editor), Louise Millar (art director).
Children's books for the pre-school market, including: picture flats, activity and novelty books; also fiction and non-fiction for the 5-7 and 7-9 age groups.

Lewis Masonic (1870), Coombelands House, Coombelands Lane, Addlestone, Surrey KT15 1HY   *tel* (01932) 820560   *fax* (01932) 821258.
Masonic books; *Masonic Square Magazine.*

Liaison—see **Hodder Headline plc.**

John Libbey & Co. Ltd (1979), 13 Smiths Yard, Summerley Street, London SW18 4HR   *tel* 0181-947 2777   *telex* 94013503 JOHN G   *fax* 0181-947 2664   *e-mail* libbey@earlsfield.win.uk.net *Directors:* John Libbey, G. Cahn.
Medical: nutrition, obesity, epilepsy, neurology, diabetes. Film/cinema.

*Library Association Publishing, 7 Ridgmount Street, London WC1E 7AE   *tel* 0171-636 7543   *fax* 0171-636 3627. *Managing director:* Janet Liebster.
Library and information science, information technology, reference works, directories, bibliographies.
Clive Bingley Ltd (imprint). Library and information science, reference works.

Frances Lincoln Ltd (1977), 4 Torriano Mews, Torriano Avenue, London NW5 2RZ   *tel* 0171-284 4009   *fax* 0171-485 0490. *Directors:* Frances Lincoln (managing), Erica Hunningher (editorial, adult books), Janetta Otter-Barry (editorial, children's books).

Illustrated, international co-editions: gardening, interiors, health, crafts, cookery, children's books.

*Lion Publishing plc (1971), Peter's Way, Sandy Lane West, Oxford OX4 5HG *tel* (01865) 747550 *fax* (01865) 747568. *Directors:* David Alexander, Pat Alexander, Tony Wales, Mark Beedell, Robin Keeley, Denis Cole, Rebecca Winter (editorial), Dy Leyland, Peter Young.
Reference, paperbacks, illustrated children's books, educational, gift books, religion and theology; all reflecting a Christian position.

*Lions—see **HarperCollins Publishers.**

*Little, Brown and Company (UK) (1988), Brettenham House, Lancaster Place, London WC2E 7EN *tel* 0171-911 8000 *fax* 0171-911 8100. *Chief executive and publisher:* Philippa Harrison; *directors:* David Young (managing), B. Boote (editorial), A. Samson (editorial), David Kent (home sales), Nigel Batt (financial), Charles Viney (export sales), Terry Jackson (marketing).
Hardback and paperback fiction, general non-fiction and illustrated books. *No unsolicited MSS.*
Abacus (division). *Editorial director:* Richard Beswick. Trade paperbacks.
Illustrated (division). *Editorial director:* Vivien Bowler. Hardback photographic and art books.
Orbit (imprint). *Editor:* Colin Murray. Science fiction and fantasy paperbacks.
Virago (division). *Editor:* Lennie Goodings. Fiction, including Modern Classics Series, biography, autobiography and general non-fiction which highlight all aspects of women's lives.
Warner (division). *Editorial directors:* Barbara Boote, Alan Samson, Hilary Hale, Imogen Taylor. Paperbacks: original fiction and non-fiction; reprints.
X Libris (imprint). *Editor:* Helen Goodwin. Erotic fiction for women.

*Liverpool University Press (1901), Senate House, Liverpool L69 3BX *tel* 0151-794 2232/7 *fax* 0151-708 6502. *Publisher:* Robin Bloxsidge.
Academic and scholarly books in a range of disciplines. Special interests: art history, education, European and American literature, social, political, economic and ancient history, archaeology, veterinary science, urban and regional planning. Major new science fiction criticism series established 1995.

Y Lolfa Cyf. (1967), Talybont, Ceredigion SY24 5HE *tel* (01970) 832304 *fax* (01970) 832782 *e-mail* ylolfa@netwales.co.uk *WWW* http://www. ylolfa.wales.com *Directors:* Robat Gruffudd, Enid Gruffudd; *editor:* Eiry Jones.
Welsh-language popular fiction and non-fiction, music, children's books; Welsh-language tutors; English-language political books and a range of Welshinterest books for the tourist market.

Lonely Planet Publications (1973), The Barley Mow Centre, 10 Barley Mow Passage, Chiswick, London W4 4PH *tel* 0181-742 3161 *fax* 0181-742 2772 *e-mail* 100413.3551@compuserve.com *WWW* lonelyplanet.com *Directors:* Tony Wheeler, Jim Hart, Maureen Wheeler; *general manager UK:* Charlotte Hindle.
Travel guidebooks, atlases, phrasebooks, language-learning audio packs, travel literature.

*Longman Group—see **Addison Wesley Longman Ltd.**

*Longman Training—now **Training Direct**—see **Pearson Professional Ltd.**

Lorenz Books (1994)—see **Anness Publishing.**

Peter Lowe (Eurobook Ltd) (1968), PO Box 52, Wallingford, Oxon OX10 0XU *tel* (01865) 749033 *fax* (01865) 749044. *Directors:* P.S. Lowe, R. Lowe.
Publishers of natural history, popular science and related subjects as illustrated non-fiction. Age 12+ but no general fiction or teen fiction.

Lund Humphries Publishers Ltd, Park House, 1 Russell Gardens, London NW11 9NN *tel* 0181-458 6314 *fax* 0181-905 5245. *Managing director:* Lionel Leventhal.
Art, architecture, graphic art and design, Arabic language.

*****Lutterworth Press** (1799)—see **James Clarke & Co. Ltd.**

Macdonald Young Books (1994), 61 Western Road, Hove, East Sussex BN3 1JD *tel* (01273) 722561 *fax* (01273) 329314. *Publishing director:* Roberta Bailey.
Fiction, non-fiction, picture books and story books for children from pre-school to teenage.

*****McGraw-Hill Book Company Europe,** McGraw-Hill House, Shoppenhangers Road, Maidenhead, Berks. SL6 2QL *tel* (01628) 23432 *fax* (01628) 770224. *Group vice president, UK:* Fred J. Perkins; *directors:* Andrew Phillips (editorial), Peter Kitley (financial).
Technical, scientific, professional reference.

*****Macmillan Interactive Publishing**—see **Macmillan Publishers Ltd.**

*****Macmillan Press Ltd**—see **Macmillan Publishers Ltd.**

*****Macmillan Publishers Ltd,** 25 Eccleston Place, London SW1W 9NF *tel* 0171-881 8000. *Chairman:* N.G. Byam Shaw; *directors:* R. Barker, M. Barnard, C.J. Paterson, A. Soar, A.J. Sutherland, G.R.U. Todd.

Macmillan Children's Books Ltd (division). *Publisher:* Kate Wilson; *editorial director (picture books and properties):* Alison Green; *editorial director (fiction):* Marion Lloyd; *editorial director (non-fiction and poetry):* Susie Gibbs. Publishes under **Macmillan, Pan.** Picture books, fiction, poetry, non-fiction, early learning, pop-up, novelty. *No* unsolicited material.

Macmillan Education (division), Houndmills, Basingstoke, Hants RG21 6XS *tel* (01256) 29242 *fax* (01256) 479985. *Managing director:* Christopher Harrison; *publishing director:* Alison Hubert; *sales director:* John G. Watson. School and College books in all subjects for all ages, including English Language Teaching.

Macmillan General Books (division). *Managing director:* Ian S. Chapman; *editor-in-chief:* Peter Straus. Publishes under **Macmillan, Pan, Papermac, Sidgwick & Jackson**.
Macmillan (1865). *Publisher:* Maria Rejt; *executive editorial director (fiction):* Suzanne Baboneau. Novels, detective fiction, sci-fi, fantasy and horror. *Editorial directors (non-fiction):* Georgina Morley, Catherine Hurley, Judith Hannam. Autobiography, biography, business and industry, crafts and hobbies, economics, gift books, health and beauty, history, humour, natural history, travel, philosophy, politics and world affairs, psychology, theatre and drama, gardening and cookery, encyclopaedias.
Pan (1947). *Publisher:* Peter Lavery. Fiction: novels, detective fiction, sci-fi, fantasy and horror. Non-fiction: sports and games, theatre and drama, travel, gardening and cookery, encyclopaedias.
Papermac (1965). *Publisher:* Jon Riley; *editor:* Tanya Stobbs. Series non-fiction: history, biography, science, political economy, cultural criticism and art history.

Macmillan Publishers Ltd—*continued*

Picador (1972). *Publisher:* Jon Riley; *editorial director:* Ursula Doyle. Literary international fiction and non-fiction.

Sidgwick & Jackson (1908). *Editorial director:* Georgina Morley. Military and war, music, pop and rock.

MSS, synopses and ideas welcome. Send to submissions editor, with return postage.

Macmillan Interactive Publishing (division). *New media development director:* Fionnuala Duggan.
CD-ROM and on-line.

Macmillan Press Ltd (division), Houndmills, Brunel Road, Basingstoke, Hants RG21 6XS *tel* (01256) 29242 *fax* (01256) 479476. *Managing director:* D. Knight; *publishing directors:* H. Holt (journals), T.M. Farmiloe (scholarly), S. O'Neill (academic and professional reference), S. Kennedy (higher education), J. Winkler (further education). Textbooks, monographs and works of reference in academic, professional and vocational subjects; medical and scientific journals; directories.

*****Julia MacRae Books** (1979)—see **Random House UK Ltd.**

Magi Publications (1987), 22 Manchester Street, London W1M 5PG *tel* 0171-486 0925 *fax* 0171-486 0926. *Publisher:* Monty Bhatia; *editor:* Linda Jennings. Quality children's picture books. New material will be considered from authors and illustrators, but please enquire first.

*****Mainstream Publishing Co. (Edinburgh) Ltd** (1978), 7 Albany Street, Edinburgh EH1 3UG *tel* 0131-557 2959 *fax* 0131-556 8720. *Directors:* Bill Campbell, Peter MacKenzie.
Biography, autobiography, art, photography, sport, health, guidebooks, humour, literature, fiction, current affairs, history, politics.

Mammoth—see **Reed Books.**

Management Books 2000 Ltd (incorporating **Mercury Books**), 125A The Broadway, Didcot, Oxon OX11 8AW *tel* (01235) 815544 *fax* (01235) 817188. *Directors:* N. Dale-Harris, A. Finn, R.C. Postema (editorial).
Business books.

*****Manchester University Press** (1912), Oxford Road, Manchester M13 9NR *tel* 0161-273 5539 *fax* 0161-274 3346 *e-mail* mup@man.ac.uk *Editorial director:* Vanessa Graham.
Works of academic scholarship: literary criticism, art, architecture, urban studies, cultural studies, history, politics, economics; general books on North of England; specialises in international law, Spanish, Italian, German and French texts; sociology, special education; sixth form/student texts.

Mandarin—see **Reed Books.**

Mandrake of Oxford (1986), PO Box 250, Oxford OX1 1AP *tel* (01865) 243671 *fax* (01865) 243671 *e-mail* krm@mandrake.compulink.co.uk *WWW* http://www.compulink.co.uk/mandrake/welcome.htm *Directors:* Kris Morgan, Shantidevi Nath.
Occult and bizarre.

Mansell Publishing—see **Cassell plc.**

*****Manson Publishing Ltd** (1992), 73 Corringham Road, London NW11 7DL *tel* 0181-905 5150 *fax* 0181-201 9233. *Managing director:* Michael Manson.
Medical, scientific, veterinary.

Mantra Publishing Ltd (1984), 5 Alexandra Grove, London N12 8NU *tel* 0181-445 5123 *fax* 0181-446 7745. *Managing director:* M. Chatterji.
Multicultural children's books/cassettes; dual language books/cassettes; South Asian literature – teenage fiction, translations.

*Marshall Pickering—see **HarperCollins Publishers.**

Martin Books, Grafton House, 64 Maids Causeway, Cambridge CB5 8DD *tel* (01223) 366733 *fax* (01223) 461428. *Editorial director:* Janet Copleston.
Imprint of Simon & Schuster Consumer Group.
Cookery, gardening, illustrated non-fiction and sponsored publishing.

*Kenneth Mason Publications Ltd (1958), Dudley House, 12 North Street, Emsworth, Hants PO10 7DQ *tel* (01243) 377977 *fax* (01243) 379136. *Directors:* Kenneth Mason (chairman), Piers Mason (managing), Michael Mason, Anthea Mason.
Nautical, slimming, health, fitness; technical journals.

Meadowfield Press Ltd (1976), I.S.A. Building, Hackworth Industrial Park, Shildon, Co. Durham DL4 1LH *tel* Bishop Auckland (01388) 773065 *telex* 587188 *fax* (01388) 774888. *Directors:* Dr J.G. Cook (editorial), M. Cook, J.A. Verdon, A.M. Creasey.
Microbiology, zoology, archaeology, botany, biology.

*Medical & Historical—see **Harlequin Mills & Boon Ltd.**

Medici Society Ltd, 34-42 Pentonville Road, London N1 9HG *tel* 0171-837 7099 *fax* 0171-837 9152.
Publishers of Medici Prints, greetings cards and other colour reproductions. Art and children's books. Preliminary letter with brief details of the work requested; mark for the attention of The Art Department.

Melrose Press Ltd (1969), 3 Regal Lane, Soham, Ely, Cambs. CB7 5BA *tel* (01353) 721091 *fax* (01353) 721839. *Directors:* R.A. Kay, J.M. Kay, B.J. Wilson, N.S. Law (editorial), C. Emmett FCA, V.A. Kay, J.E. Pearson.
International biographical reference works, including *International Authors & Writers Who's Who*, *International Who's Who in Poetry* and *Poets' Encyclopedia*.

*The Mercat Press (1970), James Thin Ltd, 53-59 South Bridge, Edinburgh EH1 1YS *tel* 0131-556 6743 *fax* 0131-557 8149 *e-mail* james.thin.ltd @almac.co.uk *Chairman:* D. Ainslie Thin; *editorial managers:* Tom Johnstone, Seán Costello.
Scottish books of general and academic interest. *No* fiction.

Merehurst Ltd/J.B. Fairfax Press Ltd, Ferry House, 51/57 Lacy Road, London SW15 1PR *tel* 0181-780 1177 *fax* 0181-780 1714. *Directors:* Debbie Kent (sales and marketing), Shirley Patton (publishing), Kirsten Schlesinger (rights), Roger Potter (finance).
Crafts and hobbies, cake decorating, cookery, homes and interiors, children's non-fiction, gardening.

Merlin Press Ltd, 2 Rendlesham Mews, Rendlesham, Nr Woodbridge, Suffolk IP2 2SZ *tel* (01394) 461313 *fax* (01394) 461314. *Directors:* M.W. Eve, P.M. Eve.
Radical history and social studies. Letters/synopsis only please.
Green Print (imprint). Green politics and the environment. Letter/synopses to Julie Millard (commissioning editor).
Seafarer Books (imprint). Books on traditional sailing, mainly narrative; also travel literature. Letter/synopses to Martin Eve (commissioning editor).

Merrow Publishing Co. Ltd (1951), I.S.A. Building, Hackworth Industrial Park, Shildon, Co. Durham DL4 1LH *tel* Bishop Auckland (01388) 773065 *telex*

587188   *fax* (01388) 774888. *Directors:* Dr J.G. Cook (editorial), M. Cook, J.A. Verdon, A.M. Creasey.
Textiles, plastics, popular science, scientific.

Methodist Church, Division of Education and Youth, 2 Chester House, Pages Lane, Muswell Hill, London N10 1PR   *tel* 0181-444 9845   *fax* 0181-365 2471.
Theology and religion.

Methodist Publishing House (1773), 20 Ivatt Way, Peterborough PE3 7PG   *tel* (01733) 332202   *fax* (01733) 331201.
Hymn and service books, general religious titles, church supplies.
Foundery Press (imprint). Ecumenical titles.

Methuen—see **Reed Books.**

Methuen Academic—incorporated in **Routledge.**

Methuen Children's Books—see **Reed Books.**

Michelin Tyre plc (1989), Tourism Department, The Edward Hyde Building, 38 Clarendon Road, Watford, Herts. WD1 1SX   *tel* (01923) 415000   *telex* 919071   *fax* (01923) 415052. *Head of tourism department:* D.C. Brown.
Tourist guides, maps and atlases, hotel and restaurant guides; children's activity books.

Milestone Publications (1967), Forestside House, Forestside, Rowlands Castle, Hants PO9 6EE   *tel* (01705) 631468   *fax* (01705) 631322   *e-mail* scope @mail.britnet.co.uk   *WWW*   http://www.britnet.co.uk/scope   *Managing director:* Nicholas J. Pine.
Heraldic china, antique porcelain, business, economics.

Millennium—see **The Orion Publishing Group Ltd.**

J. Garnet Miller Ltd (1951), 10 Station Road Industrial Estate, Colwall, Malvern, Worcs. WR13 6RN   *tel* (01684) 540154   *fax* (01684) 540154. *Directors:* Leslie Smith, Audrey Smith.
Drama, theatre, plays.

Harvey Miller Publishers, 197 Knightsbridge, London SW7 1RB   *tel* 0171-584 7676   *fax* 0171-823 7969. *Editor-in-chief:* Elly Miller. Imprint of G+B Arts International.
Art history.

Miller Freeman Information Services, Riverbank House, Angel Lane, Tonbridge, Kent TN9 1SE   *tel* (01732) 362666   *telex* 95132 BENTON G   *fax* (01732) 367301.
Over 35 directories for business and industry.

Mills & Boon (Publishers) Ltd—now **Harlequin Mills & Boon Ltd.**

Minerva—see **Reed Books.**

Mira Books—see **Harlequin Mills & Boon Ltd.**

The MIT Press—see under United States Book Publishers; all material originates in North America.

Mitchell Beazley—see **Reed Books.**

Monarch Publications, Broadway House, The Broadway, Crowborough, East Sussex TN6 1HQ   *tel* (01892) 652364   *fax* (01892) 663329. *Publisher:* Tony Collins, Jane Collins.
Christian books: (Monarch) issues of faith and society; (MARC) leadership, mission, evangelism; (Mitre) Christian drama and humour. Submit synopsis/ 2 sample chapters *only* with return postage please.

Mondo—see **Titan Books Ltd.**

Moorland Publishing Co. Ltd (1972), Moor Farm Road, Ashbourne, Derbyshire DE6 1HD *tel* (01335) 344486 *fax* (01335) 346397. *Managing director:* C.L.M. Porter.
Travel, gardening.

*****Mosby, Mosby Wolfe, Mosby Wolfe Medical Communications**—see **Times Mirror International Publishers Ltd.**

The Mothers' Union (1876), 24 Tufton Street, London SW1P 3RB *tel* 0171-222 5533 *fax* 0171-222 1591.
Religious, educational and social subjects connected with marriage and the family; religious books for adults and children; quarterly magazine *Home and Family*.

Mowbray—see **Cassell plc.**

Multimedia Books Ltd—see **Prion Books.**

*****John Murray (Publishers) Ltd** (1768) 50 Albemarle Street, London W1X 4BD *tel* 0171-493 4361 *telegraphic address* Guidebook, London W1 *fax* 0171-499 1792. *Chairman:* John R. Murray (general books marketing); *managing director:* Nicholas Perren; *directors:* Grant McIntyre (general editorial), Judith Reinhold (educational marketing); *company secretary:* Philip Carter.
General: art and architecture, biography and autobiography, letters and diaries, travel, exploration and guidebooks, Middle East, Asia, India and sub-continent, general history, health education, aviation, craft and practical. *No* unsolicited MSS please.
Educational: biology, chemistry, physics, business studies, economics, management and law, English, geography and environmental studies, history and social studies, mathematics, modern languages, special educational needs, technical subjects. Also self teaching in all subjects in *Success Studybook* series.

*****National Christian Education Council** (incorporating **Hillside Publishing** and **International Bible Reading Association**), 1020 Bristol Road, Selly Oak, Birmingham B26 6LB *tel* 0121-472 4242 *fax* 0121-472 7575.
Books on all aspects of Christian education. Material for children's work in the Church, also RE material for day schools. Activity, visual and resource material, religious drama and religious music.

National Poetry Foundation (1981), 27 Mill Road, Fareham, Hants PO16 0TH *tel* (01329) 822218. *Founder/trustee:* Johnathon Clifford.
Poetry.

The National Trust (1895), 36 Queen Anne's Gate, London SW1H 9AS *tel* 0171-222 9251 *fax* 0171-222 5097. *Publisher:* Margaret Willes.
History, cookery, architecture, guidebooks, children's non-fiction. *No* unsolicited MSS.

The Natural History Museum Publications (1881), Cromwell Road, London SW7 5BD *tel* 0171-938 8761 *fax* 0171-938 8709 *e-mail* t.brannan@nhm.ac.uk *Editorial manager:* Trudy Brannan.
Natural sciences; entomology, botany, geology, palaeontology, zoology.

*****Nautical Books**—now **Adlard Coles Nautical**; see **A. & C. Black (Publishers) Ltd.**

*****NCC Blackwell**—see **Blackwell Publishers.**

NCVO Publications (incorporating **Bedford Square Press**), Regent's Wharf, 8 All Saints Street, London N1 9RL *tel* 0171-713 6161 *fax* 0171-713 6300. Imprint of the National Council for Voluntary Organisations.
Practical guides, reference books, directories and policy studies on voluntary sector concerns including management and trustee development, legal, finance and fundraising, self-help and Europe.

*Thomas Nelson & Sons Ltd (1798), Nelson House, Mayfield Road, Walton-on-Thames, Surrey KT12 5PL *tel* (01932) 252211 *telegraphic address* Thonelson, Walton-on-Thames *fax* (01932) 246109 *e-mail* nelinfo@nelson.co.uk *Directors:* Rod E. Gauvin (managing), John Tuttle, Nick White.
Educational (infant, primary, secondary), college and multimedia, educational books for Caribbean and SE Asia.

*Network Books—see **BBC Worldwide Publishing.**

New Beacon Books (1966), 76 Stroud Green Road, London N4 3EN *tel* 0171-272 4889. *Directors:* John La Rose, Sarah White, Michael La Rose, Janice Durham.
Small specialist publishers: general non-fiction, fiction, poetry, critical writings, mainly concerning the Caribbean, Africa, Afro-America, Black Europe. No unsolicited MSS.

New Cavendish Books (1973), 3 Denbigh Road, London W11 2SJ *tel* 0171-229 6765/792 9984 *fax* 0171-792 01027.
Specialist books for the collector; art reference books and Thai guidebooks. **White Mouse Editions Ltd** (imprint). *Contact:* Chris Shelley. Transport.

New English Library (1957)—see **Hodder Headline plc.**

*New Holland (Publishers) Ltd, Chapel House, 24 Nutford Place, London W1H 6DQ *tel* 0171-724 7773 *fax* 0171-258 1293. *Managing director:* John Beaufoy; *publishing directors:* Charlotte Parry-Crooke, Yvonne McFarlane (home interest).
Illustrated books on natural history and travel, cookery, cake decoration, needlecrafts and handicrafts, interior design, DIY, gardening.

New Orchard Editions—see **Cassell plc.**

New Playwrights' Network, Flat 4, Brocklehurst Manor, 25 Brocklehurst Avenue, Macclesfield, Cheshire SK10 2RX *tel/fax* (01625) 425312. *Publishing director:* J.C.F. Gray.
General plays for the amateur, one-act and full length.

Newleaf—see **Boxtree Ltd.**

Nexus (1988)—see **Virgin Publishing Ltd.**

Nexus Special Interests Ltd, Nexus House, Boundary Way, Hemel Hempstead, Herts. HP2 7ST *tel* (01442) 66551 *fax* (01442) 66998. *Manager:* B. Laughlin.
Modelling, model engineering, woodworking, aviation, railways, military, crafts, electronics, home brewing and winemaking.

*NFER-NELSON Publishing Co. Ltd (1981), Darville House, 2 Oxford Road East, Windsor, Berks. SL4 1DF *tel* (01753) 858961 *fax* (01753) 856830. *Business development director:* Ian Florance.
Testing, assessment and management publications and services for education, business and health care.

*Nicholson (1967)—see **HarperCollins Publishers.**

James Nisbet & Co. Ltd (1810), 78 Tilehouse Street, Hitchin, Herts. SG5 2DY *tel* (01462) 438331 *fax* (01462) 431528. *Directors:* Miss E.M. Mackenzie-Wood, Mrs A.A.C. Bierrum.
Dictionaries, educational (infants, primary, secondary), business management.

Northcote House Publishers Ltd (1985), Plymbridge House, Estover Road, Plymouth, Devon PL6 7PZ *tel* (01752) 735251 *fax* (01752) 695699. *Directors:* B.R.W. Hulme, A.V. Hulme; *secretary:* M.W. Beevers FCA.
Careers, education and education management, educational dance and drama, English literature (*Writers and their Work*).

W.W. Norton & Company (1980), 10 Coptic Street, London WC1A 1PU *tel* 0171-323 1579 *fax* 0171-436 4553 *telegraphic address* Gavia, London WC1. *Managing director:* Alan Cameron.
History, biography, current affairs, sailing, English and American literature, economics, music, psychology, science.

Notting Hill Electronic Publishers (1995), 31 Brunswick Gardens, London W8 4AW *tel* 0171-229 0591 *fax* 0171-727 6641 *e-mail* 100444.232 @compuserve.com *Chairman:* Andreas Whittam Smith; *directors:* Ben Whittam Smith, Rachael Broughton (sales and marketing), Timothy Warren (art).
Electronic publishing on-line and off-line on CD-ROM platform: food and wine, sport, popular science, music, art and biography.

The Octagon Press Ltd (1972), PO Box 227, London N6 4EW *tel* 0181-348 9392 *fax* 0181-341 5971 *e-mail* octagon@schredds.demon.co.uk *Managing director:* George R. Schrager.
Psychology, philosophy, Eastern religion. Unsolicited MSS not accepted.

The Oleander Press (1960), 17 Stansgate Avenue, Cambridge CB2 2QZ *tel* (01223) 244688 *telegraphic address* Oleander. *Managing director:* P. Ward.
Language, literature, Libya, Arabia and Middle East, Indonesia and Far East, Cambridgeshire, travel, medical history, reference. Preliminary letter required before submitting MSS; please send sae for reply.

*Oliver & Boyd—see **Addison Wesley Longman Ltd.**

Michael O'Mara Books Ltd (1985), 9 Lion Yard, Tremadoc Road, London SW4 7NQ *tel* 0171-720 8643 *fax* 0171-627 8953. *Chairman:* Michael O'Mara; *managing director:* Lesley O'Mara; *editorial director:* David Roberts.
General non-fiction: Royal books, history, ancient history, humour, anthologies and biography.

*Omnibus Press/Music Sales Ltd** (1976), 8/9 Frith Street, London W1V 5TZ *tel* 0171-434 0066 *fax* 0171-439 2848. *Sales and marketing manager:* Hilary Dunlon.
Rock music biographies, books about music.

Oneworld Publications (1984), 185 Banbury Road, Oxford, Oxon OX2 7AR *tel* (01865) 310597 *fax* (01865) 310598 *e-mail* oneworld@cix.compulink.co.uk *Directors:* Juliet Mabey (editorial), Novin Doostdar (marketing).
Social issues, psychology, self-help, religion, inter-religious dialogue, philosophy.

Onlywomen Press Ltd (1974), 40 St Lawrence Terrace, London W10 5ST *tel* 0181-960 7122 *fax* 0181-960 2817 *e-mail* 100756.1242@compuserve.com *Managing director:* Lilian Mohin.
Lesbian feminist theory, fiction, poetry and cultural criticism.

Open Books Publishing Ltd (1974), Beaumont House, New Street, Wells, Somerset BA5 2LD   *tel* (01749) 677276   *fax* (01749) 670760. *Directors:* P. Taylor (managing), C. Taylor.
Books on gardening.

Open Eye Publishing—see **Special Event Books.**

*****Open University Press** (1977), Celtic Court, 22 Ballmoor, Buckingham MK18 1XW   *tel* (01280) 823388   *fax* (01280) 823233. *Directors:* John Skelton (managing), Jacinta Evans (editorial), Sue Hadden (production), Barry Clarke (financial).
Education, management, psychology, sociology, criminology, counselling, health and social welfare, women's studies.

Orbit (1989)—see **Little, Brown and Company (UK).**

*****Orchard Books** (1985)—see **The Watts Publishing Group.**

Orion (1992)—see **The Orion Publishing Group Ltd.**

Orion Children's Books (1993)—see **The Orion Publishing Group Ltd.**

The Orion Publishing Group Ltd (1992), Orion House, 5 Upper St Martin's Lane, London WC2H 9EA   *tel* 0171-240 3444   *fax* 0171-240 4822. *Directors:* Lord Cuckney (chairman), Anthony Cheetham (chief executive), Peter Roche (managing).
No unsolicited MSS; approach in writing in the first instance.
Illustrated (division). *Contact:* Michael Dover. Illustrated non-fiction: design, cookery, wine, gardening, art and architecture, natural history and personality based books.
Mass Market (division). *Contact:* Susan Lamb. Mass market fiction and non-fiction under **Everyman, Orion** and **Phoenix** imprints.
Millennium (imprint of Orion). *Contact:* Caroline Oakley. Science fiction and fantasy.
Orion (division). *Directors:* Rosemary Cheetham, Jane Wood. Hardcover fiction and non-fiction.
Orion Children's Books (division)   *fax* 0171-240 4823. *Managing director and publisher:* Judith Elliott. Children's fiction and non-fiction.
Phoenix House (imprint of Weidenfeld & Nicolson). *Director:* Maggie McKernan. Literary fiction.
Weidenfeld & Nicolson (division). *Publisher:* Ion Trewin. General non-fiction, biography, autobiography, history and travel.

Osprey—see **Reed Books.**

*****Peter Owen Ltd,** 73 Kenway Road, London SW5 0RE   *tel* 0171-373 5628/370 6093   *fax* 0171-373 6760. *Directors:* Peter L. Owen (managing).
Art, belles-lettres, biography and memoirs, fiction, general, theatre.

Owl Press (1990), PO Box 315, Downton, Salisbury, Wilts. SP5 3YE   *tel/fax* (01243) 572988. *Managing editors:* Anne Musgrove, Marjorie Hewitt.
Adult humour and gift books.

Oxford Illustrated Press—see **Haynes Publishing.**

Oxford Publishing Company (OPC Railbooks)—see **Haynes Publishing.**

*****Oxford University Press** (1478), Walton Street, Oxford OX2 6DP   *tel* (01865) 56767   *cables* Clarendon Press, Oxford   *telex* 837330 CLARPRESS G   *fax* (01865) 56646. *Chief executive and secretary to the delegates:* James Arnold-Baker; *finance director:* Roger Boning; Arts and Reference Division: *managing director:* Ivon Asquith; Science, Medical and Journals Division:

managing director: John Manger; Educational Division: *managing director:* Peter Mothersole; ELT Division: *managing director:* Bill Andrewes.

Anthropology, archaeology, architecture, art, belles-lettres, oibles, bibliography, children's books (fiction, non-fiction, picture), commerce, current affairs, dictionaries, drama, economics, educational (infants, primary, secondary, technical, university), English language teaching, electronic publishing, essays, general history, hymn and service books, journals, law, maps and atlases, medical, music, oriental, philosophy, poetry, political economy, prayer books, reference, science, sociology, theology and religion, educational software. Academic books published under the imprint **Clarendon Press.** Trade paperbacks published under the imprint of **Oxford Paperbacks.**

*Paladin—now merged with **Flamingo;** see **HarperCollins Publishers.**

*Pan (1947)—see **Macmillan Publishers Ltd.**

*Pan Macmillan Ltd—now **Macmillan General Books.**

*Pan Macmillan Children's Books Ltd—now **Macmillan Children's Books Ltd.**

*Pandora Press—see **HarperCollins Publishers.**

*Papermac—see **Macmillan Publishers Ltd.**

*Partridge Press (1987)—see **Transworld Publishers Ltd.**

*The Paternoster Press, PO Box 300, Carlisle, Cumbria CA3 0QS *tel* (01228) 512512 *fax* (01228) 514949 *e-mail* 100526.3434@compuserve.com *Director of publishing services:* Pieter Kwant.

Biblical studies, Christian theology, ethics, history, mission.

*Stanley Paul—see **Random House UK Ltd.**

Pavilion Books (1980), 26 Upper Ground, London SE1 9PD *tel* 0171-620 1666 *fax* 0171-620 1314. *Chairman:* Richard Humphreys; *directors:* Sir Tim Rice, Michael Parkinson, Colin Webb (managing), Pamela Webb, Tim James, Trevor Dolby, Vivien James, Desmond Higgins, Neil Palfreyman, Terry Shaugnessy, Fiona Brownlee.

Cookery, gardening, travel, humour, sport, art, children's.

*Payback Press (1995)—see **Canongate Books Ltd.**

*Pearson Professional Ltd, Maple House, 149 Tottenham Court Road, London W1P 9LL *tel* 0171-896 2000 *fax* 0171-896 2099. *Chief executive:* Peter Warwick.

Cartermill International Ltd, Technology Centre, St Andrews, Fife KY16 9EA *tel* (01334) 477660 *fax* (01334) 477180. *Managing director:* M. Campbell. Print and electronic research and information management products and services on science, technology and industry; health and social care reference; business intelligence and current affairs.

Churchill Communications Europe (division), Maple House, 149 Tottenham Court Road, London W1P 9LL *tel* 0171-896 2111 *fax* 0171-896 2112. *Managing director:* P. Mitchell; *directors:* A. Dryburgh, D. Riding.

Full-service medical communications for pharmaceutical companies—i.e. sponsored publishing, drug registration, patient education, etc.

Churchill Livingstone (division), Robert Stevenson House, 1-3 Baxter's Place, Leith Walk, Edinburgh EH1 3AF *tel* 0131-556 2424 *telex* 262433 MONREF G *fax* 0131-558 1278. *Divisional directors:* Andrew Stevenson, Peter Shepherd (nursing and allied health), Peter Richardson (healthcare information and management), John Richardson (publishing services), Mary Law (nursing and allied health), Timothy Wright (sales). Medical books and journals for students, trainees and practitioners; books and journals in nursing, midwifery,

Pearson Professional Ltd—*continued*

physiotherapy, complementary medicine, and other allied health disciplines. Note: preliminary letter recommended before submitting MSS.

FT Law & Tax (division), formerly **Longman Law Tax and Finance**, 21-27 Lamb's Conduit Street, London WC1N 3NJ *tel* 0171-242 2548 *fax* 0171-831 8119. *Managing director:* C. Stibbs. *Divisional directors:* A.R. Wells, M. Staunton. Books and professional journals on law, business, taxation, pensions, insurance, government contracting, finance and accountancy.

GeoInformation International (division), 307 Cambridge Science Park, Milton Road, Cambridge CB4 4ZD *tel* (01223) 423020 *fax* (01223) 425787. *Managing director:* Seppe Cassettari. Digital geographical information. Publishes *GIS Europe, Mapping Awareness* magazines.

Pitman Publishing (division), 128 Long Acre, London WC2E 9AN *tel* 0171-379 7383 *telegraphic address* Ipandsons, London WC2 *telex* 261367 PITMAN G *fax* 0171-240 5771. *Managing director:* Rod Bristow; *publishing directors:* Simon Lake (educational), Mark Allin (professional). Business education, management, professional studies, M & E Handbooks.

Training Direct (imprint), formerly **Longman Training**, Edinburgh Gate, Harlow, Essex CM20 2JE *tel* (01279) 623850 *fax* (01279) 623795. *Managing director:* Mike Smith. Video and technology-based multimedia interactive training resources for use in business and industry.

*Pelham Books (1959)—see **Penguin Books Ltd.**

Pen & Sword Books Ltd, 47 Church Street, Barnsley, South Yorkshire S70 2AS *tel* (01226) 734222 *fax* (01226) 734438. *Chairman:* Sir Nicholas Hewitt, Bt; *managing director:* Leo Cooper; *director and company secretary:* T.G. Hewitt.
Military history.
Leo Cooper (imprint), 190 Shaftesbury Avenue, London WC2H 8JL *tel* 0171-836 3141 *fax* 0171-240 9247. Specialist military publisher.
Pen & Sword Paperbacks (imprint).

*Penguin Books Ltd, Bath Road, Harmondsworth, Middlesex UB7 0DA *tel* 0181-899 4000 *telex* 933349 *fax* 0181-899 4099. *London office* 27 Wrights Lane, W8 5TZ *tel* 0171-416 3000 *telex* 917181/2 *fax* 0171-416 3099. *Founder:* Sir Allen Lane; *chief executive:* Peter Mayer; *directors:* Peter Carson, Roger Clarke, Stephen Hall, Tony Lacey, John Rolfe, Nigel Williams, Jonathan Yglesias, Sally Floyer, Susan Watt, Clare Alexander, Cecily Engle, Andrew Welham, Pat McCarthy, Philippa Milnes-Smith, Fran Supple, Anthony Forbes Watson (managing).
Allen Lane The Penguin Press (imprint) *fax* 0171-416 3274. *Editorial director:* Alistair Rolfe. Hardback non-fiction titles of academic and intellectual interest, principally but not exclusively the humanities. Unsolicited MSS and poetry discouraged.
Arkana (imprint). *Contact:* Janice Brent. 'Mind, body and spirit' list. Please do not submit unsolicited proposals.
Blackie Children's Books (imprint) *fax* 0171-416 3086. Publishers of *Topsy and Tim.* No unsolicited MSS.
Dutton Children's Books (imprint) *fax* 0171-416 3086. *Editorial director:* Rosemary Stones. Children's fiction, poetry, picture books, novelties and gift books. Unsolicited MSS to be sent to the Children's Reader, enclosing an sae.
Elm Tree Books (imprint of **Hamish Hamilton Ltd**). 'How-to' books on the media.
Godfrey Cave (imprint), 42 Bloomsbury Street, London WC1B 3QJ *tel* 0171-636 9177 *fax* 0171-636 9091. General non-fiction, reprints, remainders.

Penguin Books Ltd—*continued*

Hamish Hamilton Ltd (subsidiary)　*tel* 0171-416 3000　*fax* 0171-416 3274. *Editorial director:* Kate Jones. Fiction, belles-lettres, biography and memoirs, current affairs, general, history, literature, politics, travel. Synopses and non-fiction ideas welcome; unsolicited fiction MSS discouraged.

Hamish Hamilton Children's Books (imprint). *Editorial director:* Jane Nissen. Children's fiction and picture books. Unsolicited MSS, synopses and ideas welcome.

Michael Joseph Ltd (subsidiary)　*tel* 0171-416 3000　*fax* 0171-416 3293. *Publishing director:* Susan Watt. Biography and memoirs, current affairs, fiction, history, humour, travel, crafts, sports, handbooks, general leisure, illustrated books. Unsolicited MSS discouraged; synopses and ideas welcome.

Pelham Books (imprint of Michael Joseph Ltd)　*tel* 0171-416 3000　*fax* 0171-416 3293. *Contact:* Susan Watt. *Pears Cyclopaedia*, *Junior Pears Encyclopaedia*. Autobiographies of men and women in sport, sports handbooks, hobbies, crafts and pastimes, practical handbooks on dogs and other pets, country pursuits.

Penguin (imprint)　*fax* 0171-416 3193. *Publishing director:* Tony Lacey. Adult paperback books – wide range of fiction, non-fiction, classics, TV and film tie-ins. No unsolicited fiction or poetry.

Penguin Audiobooks. *Contact:* Jan Paterson.

Penguin Electronic Publishing (imprint)　*fax* 0171-416 3198. *Contact:* Guy Gadney.

Puffin (imprint)　*fax* 0171-416 3086. *Editorial director:* Philippa Milnes-Smith. Children's paperback books – mainly reprints: fiction, poetry, picture books, limited non-fiction, film and TV tie-ins.

RoC and **Creed** (imprints)　*fax* 0171-416 3293. *Contact:* Luigi Bonomi. Science fiction, fantasy and dark fantasy. Unsolicited MSS discouraged; synopses and ideas welcome.

Signet (imprint)　*fax* 0171-416 3293. *Contact:* Luigi Bonomi. Mass market fiction and non-fiction paperbacks. Unsolicited MSS discouraged; synopses and ideas welcome.

Ventura Publishing Ltd (subsidiary)　*fax* 0171-416 3199. *Publisher:* Sally Floyer. Eric Hill's *Spot*.

Viking (imprint)　*fax* 0171-416 3274. *Publishing director:* Clare Alexander. Fiction, general non-fiction; literature, biography, autobiography, current affairs, popular science, travel, popular culture and reference. Please do not submit unsolicited MSS for fiction; approach in writing only.

Viking Children's Books (imprint)　*fax* 0171-416 3086. *Editorial director:* Rosemary Stones. Fiction, poetry, picture books. Unsolicited MSS discouraged; synopses and ideas welcome.

Frederick Warne & Co. Ltd (subsidiary)　*fax* 0171-416 3199. *Publisher:* Sally Floyer. Beatrix Potter, Flower Fairies, Orlando.

***Penton Press**—see **Jessica Kingsley Publishers.**

Pergamon—see **Elsevier Science Ltd.**

Peterloo Poets (1976), 2 Kelly Gardens, Calstock, Cornwall PL18 9SA　*tel* (01822) 833473. *Publishing director:* Harry Chambers; *trustees:* Rosemarie Bailey, Linda Squire, David Selzer. *Honorary president:* Charles Cansley CBE. Poetry.

Phaidon Press Ltd, Regent's Wharf, All Saints Street, London N1 9PA　*tel* 0171-843 1000　*fax* 0171-843 1010. *Chairman:* Richard Schlagman; *directors:* Paula Kahn (managing), Andrew Price (financial), Frances Johnson (production),

David Jenkins (editorial), David Graham (sales), Amanda Renshaw (international editions).
Fine art, architecture, design, decorative arts, photography, music.

George Philip—now **Philips**—see **Reed Books.**

Phillimore & Co. Ltd (1870) (incorporating **Darwen Finlayson Ltd**), Shopwyke Manor Barn, Chichester, West Sussex PO20 6BG   *tel* (01243) 787636   *fax* (01243) 787639. *Directors:* Philip Harris JP (chairman), Noel Osborne MA, FSA (managing), Ian Macfarlane FCA (financial), Hilary Clifford Brown (marketing).
Local and family history; architectural history, archaeology, genealogy and heraldry; also Darwen County History series and History from the Sources series.

Phoenix House—see **The Orion Publishing Group Ltd.**

Piatkus Books (1979), 5 Windmill Street, London W1P 1HF   *tel* 0171-631 0710   *fax* 0171-436 7137   *e-mail* piatkus.books@dial.pipex.com *Managing director:* Judy Piatkus; *directors:* Philip Cotterell (marketing), Gill Cormode (editorial).
Self-help, health, mind, body and spirit, business, careers, women's interest, fiction, how-to and practical, popular psychology, cookery, parenting and childcare, biography and paranormal.

*Picador—see **Macmillan Publishers Ltd.**

Piccadilly Press (1983), 5 Castle Road, London NW1 8PR   *tel* 0171-267 4492   *fax* 0171-267 4493. *Directors:* Brenda Gardner (chairman and managing), Philip Durrance (secretary).
Children's hardback books and parents' interest trade paperbacks; trade paperback teenage information, humour and sports books.

Picture Knight—see **Hodder Headline plc.**

*Pimlico (1991)—see **Random House UK Ltd.**

Pinter (1973)—see **Cassell plc.**

Pitkin Guides—see **Reed Books.**

*Pitman Publishing (1845)—see **Pearson Professional Ltd.**

The Playwrights Publishing Company (1990), 70 Nottingham Road, Burton Joyce, Notts. NG14 5AL   *tel* (0115) 931 3356. *Proprietor:* Liz Breeze; *consultant:* Tony Breeze.
One-act and full-length drama: serious work and comedies, for mixed cast, all women or schools. Reading fee and sae required.

Plexus Publishing Ltd (1973), 55A Clapham Common Southside, London SW4 9BX   *tel* 0171-622 2440   *fax* 0171-622 2441. *Directors:* Terence Porter (managing), Sandra Wake (editorial).
Film, music, biography, popular culture, fashion.
Eel Pie (imprint). Film, music, biography, popular culture, fashion.

Pluto Publishing Ltd (1968), 345 Archway Road, London N6 5AA   *tel* 0181-348 2724   *fax* 0181-348 9133. *Directors:* Roger van Zwanenberg (managing), Anne Beech (editorial).
Community studies, sociology, social and political science including economics, history; cultural, international, women's studies, legal studies, anthropology, media studies.
The Journeyman Press (trade imprint). Feminist, biography, social history, media handbooks.

Pocket Books—see **Simon & Schuster.**

*Point—see **Scholastic Children's Books.**

The Policy Press (1996) (incorporating **SAUS Publications**), University of Bristol, Rodney Lodge, Grange Road, Bristol BS8 4EA *tel* (0117) 9738797 *fax* (0117) 9737308 *e-mail* tpp@bris.ac.uk *Publishing manager:* Alison Shaw; *book editor:* Dawn Louise Pudney; *marketing and sales manager:* Julia Mortimer; *journals manager/book editor:* Liz McCarty.
Community care; public policy, social policy; family policy and child welfare; health, housing, employment and urban studies; governance.

*Polygon—see **Edinburgh University Press.**

Prentice Hall Europe, Campus 400, Maylands Avenue, Hemel Hempstead, Herts. HP2 7EZ *tel* (01442) 881900 *telex* 82445 *fax* (01442) 882099. *President:* Joseph J. Marcelle.
Business and economics, computer science, engineering, physics, mathematics, politics, sociology and social policy, psychology, health studies, literature, trade computing.
Also incorporates the following imprints: **Prentice Hall/Harvester Wheatsheaf, Ellis Horwood, Woodhead-Faulkner.**

Prion Books (formerly **Multimedia Books Ltd**) (1986), Unit L, 32-34 Gordon House Road, London NW5 1LP *tel* 0171-482 4248 *fax* 0171-482 4203 *e-mail* books@prion.co.uk *Managing director:* Barry Winkleman.
Psychology and health, food, environment, cars, cookery, wine and spirits, film, popular culture.

Prism Press (1974), The Thatched Cottage, Partway Lane, Hazelbury Bryan, Sturminster Newton, Dorset DT10 2DP *tel* (01258) 817164 *fax* (01258) 817635. *Director:* Julian King.
Non-fiction, including health, food, psychology, politics, ecology. Synopses and ideas welcome, but *no* complete MSS.

P.S.I. Policy Studies Institute, 100 Park Village East, London NW1 3SR *tel* 0171-468 0468 *fax* 0171-388 0914. *Director:* Pamela Meadows.
Economic, industrial and social policy, political institutions, social sciences, arts and cultural industries.

*Puffin—see **Penguin Books Ltd.**

Putnam Aeronautical Books—see **Brassey's (UK) Ltd.**

Quadrille Publishing (1994), 3rd Floor, 9 Irving Street, London WC2H 7AT *tel* 0171-839 7117 *fax* 0171-839 7118. *Directors:* Alison Cathie (managing), Anne Furniss (publishing), Jane O'Shea (editorial), Mary Evans (art), Marlis Ironmonger (commercial).
Illustrated non-fiction: cookery, craft, health and medical, gardening and interiors.

Quantum—see **W. Foulsham & Co. Ltd.**

Quartet Books Ltd (1972), 27 Goodge Street, London W1P 2LD *tel* 0171-636 3992 *telex* 919034 NAMARA G *fax* 0171-637 1866. *Chairman:* N.I. Attallah; *managing director:* Jeremy Beale. Member of the Namara Group.
General fiction and non-fiction, foreign literature in translation, classical music, jazz, contemporary music, biography.

Queen Anne Press, Windmill Cottage, Mackerye End, Harpenden, Herts. AL5 5DR *tel* (01582) 715866 *fax* (01582) 715121. *Directors:* K.A.A. Stephenson, R.H. Stephenson. Division of **Lennard Associates Ltd.**
Sport and leisure activities. No unsolicited MSS.

Quiller Press Ltd, 46 Lillie Road, London SW6 1TN   *tel* 0171-499 6529   *fax* 0171-381 8941. *Directors:* J.J. Greenwood, A.E. Carlile.
Publishers of sponsored books: guidebooks, history, industry, humour, architecture, cookery, collectables, country sports.

Radcliffe Medical Press Ltd (1987), 18 Marcham Road, Abingdon, Oxon OX14 1AA   *tel* (01235) 528820   *fax* (01235) 528830   *e-mail* medical@radpress .win.uk.net *Directors:* Andrew Bax (managing), Gill Nineham (editorial), Margaret McKeown (financial); *head of marketing:* Gregory Moxon.
Medicine: management in primary care; management in secondary care; health service development; minimally invasive therapies; clinical management. Dentistry: practice management. Pharmacy.

****Random House UK Ltd,** 20 Vauxhall Bridge Road, London SW1V 2SA   *tel* 0171-973 9670   *telex* 299080 RANDOM G   *fax* 0171-233 6058. *Chairman and chief executive:* Gail Rebuck; *directors:* Simon Master (deputy chairman), Simon King (publishing), Piet Snyman (chairman, children's division), Amelia Thorpe (managing, Ebury Press), Mike Broderick (UK sales), Anthony McConnell (finance), David Pemberton (operations), Susan Sandon (publicity and marketing), Juliet Annan (rights), Stephen Esson (production), Joanna Page (personnel).
Arrow Books Ltd (imprint)   *tel* 0171-973 9700   *fax* 0171-233 6127. *Directors:* Simon King (managing), Andy McKillop (publishing), Kate Farquhar-Thomson (publicity). Fiction, non-fiction, science fiction, fantasy, crime, humour, film tie-ins.
Barrie & Jenkins (imprint of Ebury Press)   *tel* 0171-973 9710/9670   *fax* 0171-233 6057. *Managing director:* Julian Shuckburgh. Art, antiques and collecting, architecture, decorative and applied arts.
Jonathan Cape (imprint)   *tel* 0171-973 9730   *fax* 0171-233 6117. *Directors:* Dan Franklin, Robin Robertson, Tom Maschler, Tony Colwell, Rachel Cugnoni (publicity). Archaeology, biography and memoirs, current affairs, drama, economics, fiction, history, philosophy, poetry, sociology, travel. Imprint: **Bodley Head.**
Century (imprint)   *tel* 0171-973 9680   *fax* 0171-233 6127. *Directors:* Simon King (managing), Kate Parkin (publishing), Mark Booth, Oliver Johnson, Nicky Eaton (publicity). Fiction, classics, romance, biography, autobiography, general non-fiction, film tie-ins; **Century Business Books.**
Chatto & Windus (imprint)   *tel* 0171-973 9740   *fax* 0171-233 6123. *Directors:* Jonathan Burnham (publishing), Rosemary Davidson (publicity). Art, belles-lettres, biography and memoirs, cookery, crime/thrillers, current affairs, drama, essays, fiction, history, illustrated books, poetry, politics, psychoanalysis, translations, travel, hardbacks and paperbacks. Imprint: **Hogarth Press.** No unsolicited MSS.
Condé Nast Books (imprint of Ebury Press). *Editorial director:* Julian Shuckburgh. Highly illustrated home interest books, fashion and beauty, food.
Ebury Press Special Books (division)   *tel* 0171-973 9690   *fax* 0171-233 6057. *Directors:* Amelia Thorpe (managing), Caroline Buckland (special sales), Nicola Cowen (publicity), Fiona MacIntyre (publishing), Julian Shuckburgh (associate publisher), Denise Bates (editorial); Rae Shirvington (rights manager). Cookery, health, beauty, photography, crafts, biography, antiques, hobbies, gardening, natural history, DIY, diaries, stationery. Publishes books from *Good Housekeeping, Cosmopolitan, Harpers & Queen, She, Esquire, Country Living, House Beautiful* magazines.
Fodor Guides (imprint of Ebury Press). World-wide annual travel guides.
Hutchinson (imprint)   *tel* 0171-973 9680   *fax* 0171-233 6129. *Directors:* Simon King (managing), Sue Freestone (publishing), Anthony Whittome, Paul Sidey

Random House UK Ltd—*continued*

(editorial), Alex Hippisley-Cox (publicity). Belles-lettres, biography, memoirs, thrillers, crime, current affairs, general fiction, history, politics, translations, travel, film tie-ins.

Legend (imprint of Arrow Books Ltd). *Directors:* John Jarrold (editorial), Kate Farquhar-Thomson (publicity). Science fiction and fantasy.

Optima—see **Vermilion.**

Stanley Paul (imprint of Ebury Press) *tel* 0171-973 9690 *fax* 0171-233 6057. *Publishing director:* Julian Shuckburgh. Sport, games, hobbies and handicrafts, sporting biographies, practical books on breeding, care, training and general management of dogs.

Pimlico (imprint) *tel* 0171-973 9730 *fax* 0171-828 7213. *Publishing director:* Will Sulkin. History, biography, literature.

Random House Audio Books *tel* 0171-973 9700.

Random House Children's Books (division) *tel* 0171-973 9750. *Directors:* Piet Snyman (chairman), Martina Challis (managing), Caroline Roberts (publishing), Margaret Conroy (publishing), Julia Macrae (publishing), Tom Maschler (publishing), Linda Summers (rights). Publishes under **Bodley Head Children's, Jonathan Cape Children's Books, Hutchinson Children's, Julia MacRae Books, Red Fox, Tellastory.** Picture books, fiction, poetry, music, non-fiction, audio cassettes.

Rider (imprint of Ebury Press). *Publishing director:* Fiona MacIntyre; *editorial consultant:* Judith Kendra. Buddhism, religion and philosophy, psychology, ecology, health and healing, mysticism, meditation and yoga.

Random House New Media *fax* 0171-233 6129. *Directors:* Anthony Askew, Mike Brunt (sales). Interactive multimedia, education and entertainment.

Studio Editions Ltd (imprint of Ebury Press). *Directors:* K.T. Forster (rights), David Nash (Studio Designs), Ken Fox (sales and marketing). Art and design, history, cartography, Victoriana and nostalgia, music, mythology, military and aviation, children's non-fiction and novelty; social stationery.

Vermilion (imprint of Ebury Press). *Editorial director:* Fiona MacIntyre; *senior editor:* Sarah Sutton. Paperback practical self-help, health, fitness, guidebooks, practical parenting.

Vintage (imprint). *Publisher:* Caroline Michel; *associate publishing director:* Will Sulkin. Quality fiction and non-fiction.

Raphael's—see **W. Foulsham & Co. Ltd.**

*****The Reader's Digest Association Ltd,** Berkeley Square House, Berkeley Square, London W1X 6AB *tel* 0171-629 8144 *telegraphic address* Readigest, London W1 *telex* 264631 *fax* 0171-499 9751. *Managing director:* S.N. McRae; *editorial directors:* R.G. Twisk (magazine editor), R.S. Hosie (general books editor).

Monthly magazine, condensed and series books; also DIY, car maintenance, gardening, medical, handicrafts, law, touring guides, encyclopaedias, dictionaries, nature, folklore, atlases, cookery.

Reaktion Books (1988), 11 Rathbone Place, London W1P 1DE *tel* 0171-580 9928 *fax* 0171-580 9935. *General editor:* Michael R. Leaman.

Art history, cultural studies, architecture, museum studies, travel literature and history.

*****Red Fox**—see **Random House UK Ltd.**

William Reed Directories, Merchant House, 4A Reading Road, Pangbourne, Berks RG8 7LL *tel* (01734) 844111 *fax* (01734) 841579. *Managing director:* Maria Atkin; *editorial manager:* Helen Turner.

Publishers of leading business to business directories and reports, including The Grocer Marketing Directory and The Grocer Food & Drink Directory.

Reed Information Services (1983), Windsor Court, East Grinstead House, East Grinstead, West Sussex RH19 1XA   *tel* (01342) 326972   *telegraphic address* Infoservices, East Grinstead   *telex* 95127 INFSER G   *fax* (01342) 335612   *e-mail* ris@dial.pipex.com   *WWW* www.reedinfo.co.uk   *Chief executive:* R.J.E. Dangerfield; *managing director:* K. Burton.
Worldwide provider of business information and services. The range includes some of the most respected and valued imprints in business publishing, such as **Kompass, Kelly's, Dial** and **The Bankers' Almanac**.

Reed Books, Michelin House, 81 Fulham Road, London SW3 6RB   *tel* 0171-581 9393   *fax* 0171-225 9424   *e-mail* cd49@dial.pipex.com   *WWW* www @reedbooks.co.uk   *Chief executive:* Sandy Grant; *executive directors:* Chris Hunt, Derek Freeman, Peter Murphy. Consumer book publishing subsidiary of Reed Elsevier (UK) Ltd.
Brimax Books (imprint), Units 4/5, Studland Park Industrial Estate, Exning Road, Newmarket, Suffolk CB8 7AU   *tel* (01638) 664611   *fax* (01638) 665220. *Managing director:* Patricia Gillette. Mass market picture books for children.
Conran Octopus (imprint), 37 Shelton Street, London WC2H 9HN   *tel* 0171-240 6961   *fax* 0171-836 9951. *Publishing director:* John Wallace. Quality illustrated books, particularly lifestyle, cookery, gardening.
Hamlyn (imprint)   *fax* 0171-225 9458. *Publishing director:* Laura Bamford. Popular illustrated non-fiction, particularly cookery, gardening, craft, sport, film tie-ins, rock'n'roll.
Hamlyn Children's Non-Fiction (imprint)   *fax* 0171-225 9731. Illustrated non-fiction and reference books for children.
William Heinemann (imprint)   *fax* 0171-225 9095. *Publisher:* Tom Weldon. Fiction and general non-fiction. No unsolicited MSS and synopses considered.
Heinemann Young Books (imprint)   *fax* 0171-225 9731. *Managing director:* Jane Winterbotham. Books for children including quality picture books, novels, anthologies.
Mammoth (imprint)   *fax* 0171-225 9731. *Managing director:* Jane Winterbotham. Children's paperbacks, licensed characters and tie-ins.
Mandarin (imprint)   *fax* 0171-225 9095. *Publisher:* Tom Weldon. Paperback fiction and general non-fiction. No unsolicited MSS and synopses considered.
Methuen (imprint)   *fax* 0171-225 9095. *Publisher:* Michael Earley. Drama, humour, fiction, music, arts, plays. No unsolicited MSS or synopses considered.
Methuen Children's Books (imprint)   *fax* 0171-225 9731. *Managing director:* Jane Winterbotham. Books for children including picture books and fiction for babies to early teens.
Minerva (imprint)   *fax* 0171-225 9095. *Editorial director:* Geoff Mulligan. Paperback literary fiction and non-fiction.
Mitchell Beazley (imprint)   *fax* 0171-225 9458. *Publishing director:* Jane Aspden. Quality illustrated books, particularly antiques, gardening, craft and interiors, wine.
Osprey (imprint)   *fax* 0171-225 9458. *Managing director:* Jonathan Parker. Militaria, aviation, automotive.
Philips (imprint)   *fax* 0171-225 9458. *Publishing director:* John Gaisford. Atlases, maps, astronomy, encyclopaedias, globes.
Pitkin Guides (imprint), Healey House, Dene Road, Andover, Hants SP10 2AA   *tel* (01264) 334303   *fax* (01264) 334110. *Managing director:* Ian Corsie. Illustrated souvenir guides.

Reed Books—*continued*

Secker and Warburg (imprint) *fax* 0171-225 9095. *Publisher:* Max Eilenberg. Literary fiction, general non-fiction. *No* unsolicited MSS/synopses.

Sinclair-Stevenson (imprint) *fax* 0171-225 9095. *Senior editorial director:* Penelope Hoare. Fiction and general non-fiction. No unsolicited MSS or synopses considered.

Reed Educational and Professional Publishing Ltd, Halley Court, Jordan Hill, Oxford OX2 8EJ *tel* (01865) 311366 *fax* (01865) 314641. *Chief executive:* William Shepherd.

Butterworth Architecture (imprint). *Editorial director:* Peter Dixon; *publisher:* Neil Warnock-Smith. Architecture, the environment, planning, townscape, building technology; general.

Butterworth Heinemann UK, Linacre House, Jordan Hill, Oxford OX2 8EJ *tel* (01865) 311366 *fax* (01865) 310898. *Managing director:* Philip Shaw. Books and electronic products across business, technical, medical and open learning fields for students and professionals.

Focal Press (imprint) *fax* (01865) 314572. *Publishing director:* Peter Dixon; *senior commissioning editor:* Margaret Riley. Professional, technical and academic books on photography, broadcasting, film, television, radio, audiovisual and communication media.

Ginn & Co. (imprint), Prebendal House, Parson's Fee, Aylesbury, Bucks. HP20 2QZ *tel* (01296) 394442 *fax* (01296) 393433. *Managing director:* Nigel Hall. Textbook/other educational resources for primary and secondary schools.

Heinemann Educational (imprint) *fax* (01865) 314140. *Managing director:* Bob Osborne. Textbooks/literature/other educational resources for all levels.

Heinemann English Language Teaching (imprint) *fax* (01865) 414193. *Managing director:* Mike Esplen. English language teaching books and materials.

See also **Butterworth & Co. (Publishers) Ltd.**

Religious and Moral Education Press (RMEP)—see **Chansitor Publications Ltd.**

***Rider**—see **Random House UK Ltd.**

Rivelin Grapheme Press (1984), Merlin House, Church Street, Hungerford, Berks. RG17 0JG *tel* (01488) 684645 *fax* (01488) 683018. *Director:* Snowdon Barnett.
Poetry. Please do not send unsolicited MSS.

Rivers Oram Press (1991), 144 Hemingford Road, London N1 1DE *tel* 0171-607 0823 *fax* 0171-609 2776. *Directors:* Elizabeth Rivers Fidlon (managing), Anthony Harris.
Non-ficton: social and political science, current affairs, social history, gender studies, sexual politics, cultural studies and photography.

Robinson Publishing Ltd (1983), 7 Kensington Church Court, London W8 4SP *tel* 0171-938 3830 *fax* 0171-938 4214 *e-mail* 100560.3511 @compuserve.com *Publisher:* Nicholas Robinson; *editorial director:* Mark Crean.
Fiction: anthologies, horror, fantasy, women's romantic; general non-fiction includes health, self-help, true crime, puzzles, military history. Children's: anthologies, fiction, humour, games. Do not send MSS; letters/synopses only, please.

*Robson Books (1973), Bolsover House, 5-6 Clipstone Street, London W1P 8LE *tel* 0171-323 1223/637 5937 *telegraphic address* Robsobook, London W1 *fax* 0171-636 0798. *Managing director:* Jeremy Robson.
General, biography, music, humour.

*RoC—see **Penguin Books Ltd.**

George Ronald (1939), 46 High Street, Kidlington, Oxon OX5 2DN *tel* (01865) 841515 *fax* (01865) 841230. *Managers:* W. Momen, E. Leith.
Religion, specialising in the Baha'i Faith.

Barry Rose Law Publishers Ltd (1972), Little London, Chichester, West Sussex PO19 1PG *tel* (01243) 775552/779174 *fax* (01243) 779278.
Law, local government, police, legal history.

Rosendale Press Ltd (1987), Suite 515, Premier House, 10 Greycoat Place, London SW1P 1SB *tel* 0171-222 8866 *fax* 0171-799 1416. *Chairman:* Timothy S. Green; *editorial director:* Maureen P. Green.
Food and drink, gourmet guides/travel, business and investment, health and lifestyle.

Roundhouse Publishing Ltd (1991), PO Box 140, Oxford OX2 7FF *tel* (01865) 512682 *fax* (01865) 59594 *e-mail* 100637.3571@compuserve.com *Publisher:* Alan T. Goodworth.
Film, cinema, and performing arts; reference books.

*Routledge, 11 New Fetter Lane, London EC4P 4EE *tel* 0171-583 9855 *cables* Elegiacs, London EC4 *telex* 263398 ROUT G *fax* 0171-842 2298. *Managing director:* Janice Price; *publishing director:* Peter Sowden; *finance director:* David Tebbutt; *marketing director:* Tim Westbrook.
Addiction, anthropology, archaeology, Asian studies, classical studies, counselling, criminology, development and environment, dictionaries, economics, education, geography, health, history, Japanese studies, library science, language, linguistics, literary criticism, media and culture, performance studies, philosophy, politics, psychiatry, psychology, reference, social administration, social studies/sociology, women's studies. **Routledge** is an International Thomson Publishing company.

Royal National Institute for the Blind (1868), PO Box 173, Peterborough, Cambs. PE2 6WS *tel* (0345) 023153 (for price of a local call) *fax* (01733) 371555.
Magazines and books for blind people, in braille and Moon embossed types. Also tape-recorded books (*Talking Books* and cassette library). For complete list of magazines see page 134.

*Sage Publications Ltd (1971), 6 Bonhill Street, London EC2A 4PU *tel* 0171-374 0645 *fax* 0171-374 8741. *Directors:* David Hill (managing), Lynn Adams, Ian Eastment, Stephen Barr, Mike Birch, Matt Jackson, David F. McCune (USA), Sara Miller McCune (USA).
Social sciences, behavioural sciences, humanities, software.

*The Saint Andrew Press, 121 George Street, Edinburgh EH2 4YN *tel* 0131-225 5722 *fax* 0131-220 3113. *Publishing manager:* Lesley A. Taylor. Section of **Church of Scotland Board of Communication.**
Theology and religion, church and local history.

St Pauls (1948), St Pauls House, Middlegreen, Slough, Berks. SL3 6BT *tel* (01753) 520621 *fax* (01753) 574240.
Theology, ethics, spirituality, biography, education, general books of Roman Catholic and Christian interest.

St Paul's Bibliographies (1974), West End House, 1 Step Terrace, Winchester, Hants SO22 5BW *tel* (01962) 860524 *fax* (01962) 842409 *e-mail* stpaul-b@winterb.demon.co.uk *Managing director:* Robert S. Cross.
Bibliography and scholarly works on the history of the Book and the book trade.

Salamander Books Ltd (1973), 129-137 York Way, London N7 9LG *tel* 0171-267 4447 *cables* Salamander, London N7 *fax* 0171-267 5112. *Directors:* Jan Jacobs (chairman), Ray Bonds (managing), David Spence.
Cookery, crafts, children's, military, natural history, music, gardening, hobbies, pets, transport, sports.

Salvationist Publishing and Supplies Ltd, 117-121 Judd Street, London WC1H 9NN *tel* 0171-387 1656 *fax* 0171-383 3420. *Editorial director:* Lieut-Colonel Ray Caddy.
Devotional books, theology, biography, worldwide Christian and social service, children's books, music.

Sapling—see **Boxtree Ltd.**

***W.B. Saunders Co. Ltd**—see **Harcourt Brace & Co. Ltd.**

K.G. Saur—see **Bowker-Saur.**

SAUS Publications—see **The Policy Press.**

S.B. Publications (1987), c/o 19 Grove Road, Seaford, East Sussex BN25 1TP *tel* (01323) 893498. *Proprietor:* Stephen Benz.
Local history (illustrated by postcards/old photographs), local themes (e.g. walking books, guides), maritime history, transport, specific themes.

Scala—see **Philip Wilson Publishers Ltd.**

Scarlet Press (1990), 5 Montague Road, London E8 2HN *tel* 0171-241 3702 *fax* 0171-275 0031. *Editorial director:* Avis Lewallen.
Women's studies, lesbian, cultural studies, history, politics, health.

Sceptre—see **Hodder Headline plc.**

Schofield & Sims Ltd (1901), Dogley Mill, Fenay Bridge, Huddersfield HD8 0NQ *tel* (01484) 607080 *fax* (01484) 606815 *e-mail* 100641.252 @compuserve.com *Directors:* John S. Nesbitt (chairman), J. Stephen Platts (managing), J. Brierley (sales).
Educational: infants, primary, secondary, children's books.

***Scholastic Children's Books,** Communications House, 1-19 New Oxford Street, London WC1A 1NU *tel* 0171-421 9000 *fax* 0171-421 9001. *Director:* David Fickling. *Character and preschool publisher:* Penny Morris. Imprint of **Scholastic Ltd.**
Adlib (imprint). *Editorial director:* David Fickling. Quality teenage fiction.
André Deutsch Children's Books (imprint). *Editorial director:* David Fickling. Children's fiction and non-fiction.
Hippo (imprint). *Managing editor:* Anne Finnis. Children's paperbacks – fiction and non-fiction. *No* unsolicited MSS.
Point (imprint). *Editor:* Julia Moffatt. Fiction for 11+: horror, crime, romance, fantasy, science fiction.

***Scholastic Ltd** (1964), Villiers House, Clarendon Avenue, Leamington Spa, Warks. CV32 5PR *tel* (01926) 887799 *fax* (01926) 883331. *London office:* Communications House, 1-19 New Oxford Street, London WC1A 1NU *tel* 0171-421 9000 *fax* 0171-421 9001. *Directors:* D.M.R. Kewley (managing), M.R. Robinson (USA), R.M. Spaulding (USA), D.J. Walsh (USA).
Children's division—see **Scholastic Children's Books.**

Direct marketing. Children's book clubs and school book fairs.
Educational division. *Publishing director:* Anne Peel. Publishers of books for teachers (Bright Ideas and other series), primary classroom resources and magazines for teachers (*Child Education, Junior Education* and others).

Science Museum Publications, Science Museum, Exhibition Road, London SW7 2DD   *tel* 0171-938 8211   *telex* 21200 SCMLIB G   *fax* 0171-938 8213   *e-mail* a.hodson@nmsi.ac.uk *Publications manager:* Anna Hodson.
History of science and technology, public understanding of science, including books for children.

*****SCM Press Ltd** (1929), 9-17 St Albans Place, London N1 0NX   *tel* 0171-359 8033   *fax* 0171-359 0049. *Managing director and editor:* John Bowden; *directors:* Margaret Lydamore (associate editor and company secretary), Linda Foster, Roger Pygram (finance).
Theological books with special emphasis on biblical, philosophical and modern theology; books on sociology of religion and religious aspects of current issues.

Scolar Press—see Ashgate Publishing Ltd.

Scottish Academic Press (1969), 56 Hanover Street, Edinburgh EH2 2DX   *tel* 0131-225 7483   *fax* 0131-225 7662. *Editor:* Dr Douglas Grant.
All types of academic books and books of Scottish interest.

*****Scottish Cultural Press** (1992), PO Box 106, Aberdeen AB9 8ZE   *tel* (01224) 583777   *fax*   (01224)   575337   *WWW*   http://www.johnsmith.co.uk/ publishsctcltin.htm *Director:* Jill Dick.
Literature, poetry, history, archaeology, biography and environmental history. **Scottish Children's Press** Scottish fiction, Scottish non-fiction and Scots language.

The Scout Association, Baden-Powell House, Queen's Gate, London SW7 5JS   *tel* 0171-584 7030   *fax* 0171-590 5103. *General editor:* David Easton.
Technical books dealing with all subjects relevant to Scouting and monthly journal *Scouting.*

*****Scripture Union** (1867), 207-209 Queensway, Bletchley, Milton Keynes, Bucks. MK2 2EB   *tel* (01908) 856000   *fax* (01908) 856111.
Christian books and Bible reading materials for people of all ages; educational and worship resources for churches; children's fiction and non-fiction; adult non-fiction.

Seaby (1926)—see **Batsford Books.**

Seafarer Books—see Merlin Press Ltd.

Search Press Ltd (1962), Wellwood, North Farm Road, Tunbridge Wells, Kent TN2 3DR   *tel* (01892) 510850   *fax* (01892) 515903. *Directors:* Charlotte de la Bedoyère (editorial), The Hon. G.E. Noel, Ruth B. Saunders.
Arts, crafts, leisure, organic gardening.

Secker and Warburg—see Reed Books.

*****Serif** (1993), 47 Strahan Road, London E3 5DA   *tel/fax* 0181-981 3990. *Editorial director:* Stephen Hayward.
International fiction, politics, history, Irish studies, cookery. *No* unsolicited MSS.

Seren Books (1981), First Floor, 2 Wyndham Street, Bridgend CF31 1EF   *tel/ fax* (01656) 767834. *Director:* Mick Felton.
Poetry, fiction, drama, history, film, literary criticism, biography, art – mostly with relevance to Wales.

Serpent's Tail (1986), 4 Blackstock Mews, London N4 2BT　*tel* 0171-354 1949　*fax* 0171-704 6467. *Director:* Peter Ayrton.
Modern fiction in paperback: literary and experimental work, first novels and work in translation. Approach with query letter please; do *not* send complete MSS. Sae essential as is familiarity with list.

Settle Press (1983), 10 Boyne Terrace Mews, London W11 3LR　*tel* 0171-243 0695. *Directors:* D. Settle (managing), M. Carter (editorial).
Travel guidebooks and general.

Severn House Publishers, 9-15 High Street, Sutton, Surrey SM1 1DF　*tel* 0181-770 3930　*fax* 0181-770 3850. *Chairman:* Edwin Buckhalter; *managing editor:* Deborah Smith.
Adult fiction: romances, thrillers, detective, adventure, war, science fiction; film and TV tie-ins. Accepts unsolicited MSS only through a literary agent.

*****Shakespeare Head Press** (1904)—see **Blackwell Publishers.**

Sheed & Ward Ltd (1926), 14 Coopers Row, London EC3N 2BH　*tel* 0171-702 9799　*fax* 0171-702 3583. *Directors:* M.T. Redfern, K.G. Darke, A.M. Redfern.
Publishers of books, mostly by Catholics. History, philosophy, theology, catechetics, scripture and religion.

*****Sheldon Press**—see **Society for Promoting Christian Knowledge.**

Sheldrake Press (1979), 188 Cavendish Road, London SW12 0DA　*tel* 0181-675 1767　*fax* 0181-675 7736. *Publisher:* J.S. Rigge.
History, travel, architecture, cookery, music; stationery.

Shepheard-Walwyn (Publishers) Ltd (1971), Suite 34, 26 Charing Cross Road, London WC2H 0DH　*tel* 0171-240 5992　*fax* 0171-379 5770. *Directors:* A.R.A. Werner, M.M. Werner.
History, political economy, philosophy; illustrated gift books, some originated in calligraphy; Scottish interest.

John Sherratt & Son Ltd, Hotspur House, 2 Gloucester Street, Manchester M1 5QR　*tel* 0161-236 9963　*fax* 0161-236 2026. *Managing director:* P.A. Westaway.
Educational (primary, secondary, technical, university), medical, practical handbooks, collectors' books.

Shire Publications Ltd (1966), Cromwell House, Church Street, Princes Risborough, Bucks. HP27 9AA　*tel* (01844) 344301　*fax* (01844) 347080. *Directors:* J.P. Rotheroe, J.W. Rotheroe.
Discovering paperbacks, Shire Albums, Shire Archaeology, Shire Natural History, Shire Ethnography, Shire Egyptology, Shire Garden History.

*****Sidgwick & Jackson** (1908)—see **Macmillan Publishers Ltd.**

Sigma Press (1979), 1 South Oak Lane, Wilmslow, Cheshire SK9 6AR　*tel* (01625) 531035　*fax* (01625) 536800　*e-mail* sigma.press@zetnet.co.uk *WWW* http://www.zetnet.co.uk/coms/sigma.press *Partners:* Graham Beech, Diana Beech.
Leisure (country walking, cycling, regional heritage, football, cookery, folklore); popular science; computing.

Signature—see **Hodder Headline plc.**

*****Signet**—see **Penguin Books Ltd.**

*****Silhouette**—see **Harlequin Mills & Boon Ltd.**

Simon & Schuster (1986), West Garden Place, Kendal Street, London W2 2AQ *tel* 0171-316 1900 *fax* 0171-402 0639. *Directors:* Nick Webb (managing), Jo Frank (editorial, fiction), Martin Fletcher (editorial, mass-market fiction and Touchstone), Mary Pachnos (rights), Helen Gummer (editorial, non-fiction), Bob Kelly (international sales and marketing).
Fiction; non-fiction: reference, music, travel, mass-market paperbacks.
Pocket Books (imprint). Mass-market fiction and non-fiction paperbacks.
Touchstone (imprint). Quality upmarket fiction and non-fiction paperbacks.

Simon & Schuster International—now **Prentice Hall Europe.**

Sinclair-Stevenson—see **Reed Books.**

Skoob Books Ltd (1979), 25 Lowman Road, London N7 6DD *tel/fax* 0171-609 0699. *Director:* I.K. Ong; *editorial:* M. Lovell.
Literary guides, cultural studies, esoterica/occult, oriental literature. Unsolicited summaries and samples with sae only; no MSS.

Slow Dancer Press (1977), Flat 2, 59 Parliament Hill, London NW3 2TB. *Director:* John Harvey.
Poetry. Send letter before submitting material.

Smith Gryphon Ltd (1990), Swallow House, 11-21 Northdown Street, London N1 9BN *tel* 0171-278 2444 *fax* 0171-833 5680. *Chairman and managing director:* Robert Smith.
Biography, autobiography, rock music, cinema, true crime, topical issues, finance and business, wine, food and cookery, illustrated, and personality-led fiction.

***Colin Smythe Ltd** (1966), PO Box 6, Gerrards Cross, Bucks. SL9 8XA *tel* (01753) 886000 *fax* (01753) 886469. *Directors:* Colin Smythe (managing and editorial), Peter Bander van Duren, A. Norman Jeffares, Ann Saddlemyer, Leslie Hayward.
Biography, literary criticism, folklore, Irish interest and Anglo-Irish literature.

***Society for Promoting Christian Knowledge** (1698), Holy Trinity Church, Marylebone Road, London NW1 4DU *tel* 0171-387 5282 *fax* 0171-388 2352. *Director of publishing:* Simon Kingston.
Sheldon Press (imprint). *Publisher:* Joanna Moriarty. Popular medicine, health, self-help, psychology, business.
SPCK (imprint). *Senior editor:* Alex Wright (theology and academic); *senior editor:* Rachel Boulding (liturgy, prayer, spirituality); *editor:* Lucy Gasson (biblical studies, educational resources, mission); *editor:* Naomi Starkey (gospel and culture, worldwide); *publisher:* Joanna Moriarty (pastoral care).
Triangle (imprint). *Editor:* Naomi Starkey. Popular Christian paperbacks.

Sotheby's Publications—see **Philip Wilson Publishers Ltd.**

Souvenir Press Ltd, 43 Great Russell Street, London WC1B 3PA *tel* 0171-580 9307-8 and 637 5711/2/3 *telegraphic address* Publisher, London *fax* 0171-580 5064. *Managing director:* Ernest Hecht BSc(Econ), BCom; *executive director:* Jeanne Manchee.
Archaeology, biography and memoirs, educational (secondary, technical), fiction, general, humour, practical handbooks, psychiatry, psychology, sociology, sports, games and hobbies, travel, supernatural, parapsychology, illustrated books.

***SPCK**—see **Society for Promoting Christian Knowledge.**

Neville Spearman Publishers—see **The C.W. Daniel Company Ltd.**

Special Event Books (1995), Unit 18, City Business Centre, Brighton Road, Horsham, West Sussex RH13 5BA *tel* (01403) 274598 *fax* (01403) 274599. *Publisher:* Barry O'Dwyer.
Books for corporate profiles, business anniversary publications and special events.
Open Eye Publishing (imprint). Books for the visual communications industry: advertising, design, illustration, graphics.

Specialist Crafts Ltd (formerly **Dryad**), PO Box 247, Leicester LE1 9QS *tel* (0116) 251 0405 *fax* (0116) 251 5015. *Joint managing director:* P.A. Crick.
'How to' booklets on various art and craft skills. *Specialist Crafts 500 series* full colour craft booklets and patterns. Suppliers of over 7000 art and craft items.

*Spellmount Ltd** (1984), The Old Rectory, Staplehurst, Kent TN12 0AZ *tel* (01580) 893730 *fax* (01580) 893731. *Proprietor:* Jamie A.G. Wilson.
Ancient, 15th-20th century history/military history.

*Spindlewood** (1980), 70 Lynhurst Avenue, Barnstaple, Devon EX31 2HY *tel* (01271) 71612 *fax* (01271) 25906. *Directors:* Michael Holloway, Anne Holloway.
Children's picture books; young adult and children's fiction.

*E. & F.N. Spon Ltd** (1834)—see **Chapman & Hall Ltd.**

Springboard—see **Yorkshire Art Circus.**

*Springer-Verlag London Ltd** (1972), Sweetapple House, Catteshall Road, Godalming, Surrey GU7 3DJ *tel* (01483) 418800 *fax* (01483) 415151 *e-mail* postmaster@svl.co.uk *Managing director:* John Watson; *executive directors:* C. Michaletz, D. Goetz.
Medicine, computing, engineering, astronomy, mathematics.

Stacey International (1974), 128 Kensington Church Street, London W8 4BH *tel* 0171-221 7166 *fax* 0171-792 9288. *Directors:* Tom Stacey (managing), C.S. Stacey; *publishing executive:* Kitty Carruthers.
Illustrated non-fiction, encyclopaedic books on regions and countries, Islamic and Arab subjects, world affairs, art, travel, belles-lettres.

Stainer & Bell Ltd (1906), PO Box 110, Victoria House, 23 Gruneisen Road, London N3 1DZ *tel* 0181-343 3303 *fax* 0181-343 3024. *Directors:* Bernard Braley ACIS (chairman), Keith Wakefield (joint managing), Carol Wakefield (joint managing and secretary), Joan Braley, John Hosier CBE, Antony Kearns.
Books on music, religious communication.

*Harold Starke Publishers Ltd,** Pixey Green, Stradbroke, Eye, Suffolk IP21 5NG *tel* (01379) 388334 *fax* (01379) 388335; and 203 Bunyan Court, Barbican, London EC2Y 8DH *tel* 0171-588 5195. *Directors:* Harold K. Starke, Naomi Galinski (editorial).
Specialist, scientific, medical, reference.

Patrick Stephens Ltd (1967)—see **Haynes Publishing.**

Sterling Publishing Group plc (1978), PO Box 839, 86-88 Edgware Road, London W2 2YW *tel* 0171-258 0066 *telex* 8953130 ESPEPE G *fax* 0171-723 5766. *Chairman:* R. Harrison; *managing director:* R.M. Summers; *directors:* D.M. Coughlan, R. Panton Corbett, R.G.B. Heller, C.E. Whitley.
Reference, management and technology directories, leisure, commemorative publishing, exhibition organising.

*Stevens and Sons Ltd** (founded 1799; incorporated 1889)—see **Sweet & Maxwell Ltd.**

Stride Publications (1980), 11 Sylvan Road, Exeter, Devon EX4 6EW *e-mail* rml@madbear.demon.co.uk *Managing editor:* Rupert M. Loydell.
Poetry, short story collections, literary experimental novels, contemporary music and visual arts, theology of arts. Submissions in writing only.

*Studio Editions Ltd—see **Random House UK Ltd.**

Studio Vista—see **Cassell plc.**

Summersdale Publishers (1990), 46 West Street, Chichester, West Sussex PO19 1RP *tel* (01243) 771107 *fax* (01243) 786300. *Editors:* Alastair Williams, Stewart Ferris.
Cookery, biography, sport, humour, popular psychology, business and travel.

Sunflower Books, 12 Kendrick Mews, London SW7 3HG *tel* 0171-589 1862 *telex* 269388 LONHAN G *fax* 0171-589 1862. *Directors:* P.A. Underwood (editorial), J.G. Underwood, S.J. Seccombe.
Travel guidebooks.

Sussex Academic Press (1994), 18 Chichester Place, Brighton BN2 1FF *tel* (01273) 699533 *fax* (01273) 621262 *e-mail* 100101.377@compuserve.com *Editorial director:* Anthony Grahame.
British history and Middle East studies. Also **The Alpha Press**. Religion and sport.

Sutton Publishing Ltd (1978), Phoenix Mill, Far Thrupp, Stroud, Glos. GL5 2BU *tel* (01453) 731114 *fax* (01453) 731117. *Directors:* David Prigent, Peter Clifford (publishing), Richard Bryant, Christopher Sackett, Nicholas Mills, Alan Plank, David Hogg.
General and academic publishers of high quality fully illustrated books, including history, travel, military, countryside, topography, regional interest, local history, railways, literature, biography, archaeology.

Swan Hill Press—see **Airlife Publishing Ltd.**

Swedenborg Society, 20-21 Bloomsbury Way, London WC1A 2TH *tel* 0171-405 7986.
The Writings of Swedenborg.

*Sweet & Maxwell Ltd (founded 1799; incorporated 1889), South Quay Plaza, 183 Marsh Wall, London E14 9FT *tel* 0171-538 8686 *fax* 0171-538 8625. *Directors:* A. Kinahan, C. Tullo, P. Riddle, B. Grandage, S. Leach, C. Blake, S. Grenier.
Law.
Stevens and Sons Ltd (imprint). Law.

Take That Ltd (1986), PO Box 200, Harrogate, N. Yorks HG1 4XB *tel* (01423) 507545 *fax* (01423) 507545 *e-mail* 100563.3643@compuserve.com *Managing director:* Chris Brown.
Internet/computing, business, gambling, illustrated humour. Send sae with synopsis/samples.

Tamarind Ltd (1987), PO Box 296, Camberley, Surrey GU15 1QW *tel* (01276) 683979 *fax* (01276) 685365. *Managing director:* Verna Wilkins.
Multicultural children's picture books and educational material. Publications give a high positive profile to black children. Unsolicited material welcome with return postage.

Tango Books—children's fiction and non-fiction imprint of **Sadie Fields Productions Ltd**, book packagers.

Tate Gallery Publishing Ltd (1996), Millbank, London SW1P 4RG *tel* 0171-887 8869/70 *fax* 0171-887 8878. *Managing director:* Celia Clear; *senior manager:*

Brian McGahon; *retail manager:* Rosemary Bennett; *marketing manager:* Mark Eastment; *production manager:* Tim Holton.
Publishers for the Tate Gallery in London, Liverpool and St Ives. Exhibition catalogues, general and educational books, diaries, calendars, posters and stationery in the field of British and modern art.

I.B. Tauris & Co. Ltd (1983), Victoria House, Bloomsbury Square, London WC1B 4DZ   *tel* 0171-916 1069   *fax* 0171-916 1068. *Director:* I. Bagherzade (chairman and managing); *executive officers:* Anna Enayat (editorial director), Jonathan McDonnell (sales and marketing director).
Modern history, politics, international relations, economics, current affairs, Middle East, cultural studies.
British Academic Press (imprint). Academic monographs and research dissertations in history, political science and social sciences.
Tauris Academic Studies (imprint). Academic monographs on history, politics, international relations, economics, international law.
Tauris Parke Books (imprint). Illustrated books on architecture, design, cultural history and travel.

Tauris Parke Books—see **I.B. Tauris & Co. Ltd.**

*Taylor & Francis Group Ltd, 1 Gunpowder Square, London EC4A 3DE   *tel* 0171-503 0490. *Group publishing director (editorial):* Stephen Neal.
Educational (university), science: physics, mathematics, chemistry, electronics, natural history, pharmacology and drug metabolism, toxicology, technology, history of science, ergonomics, production engineering, remote sensing, geographic information systems, psychology.

Telegraph Books (1920), The Daily Telegraph, 1 Canada Square, Canary Wharf, London E14 5DT   *tel* 0171-538 6829   *fax* 0171-538 6064. *Manager:* Vicky Unwin.
Business, personal finance, crosswords, sport, travel and guides, cookery and wine, general, gardening, history – all by *Telegraph* journalists and contributors, and co-published with major publishing houses.

*Tellastory—see **Random House UK Ltd.**

The Templar Company plc (1980), Pippbrook Mill, London Road, Dorking, Surrey RH4 1JE   *tel* (01306) 876361   *fax* (01306) 889097. *Directors:* Amanda Wood (publishing), Ruth Huddleston (sales and marketing), Graeme East (financial), Richard Carlisle (communications).
Children's novelty and gift books; picture books; illustrated educational, particularly natural history; marketing and communications literature.

Test Your Child—see **Hodder Headline plc.**

*Thames and Hudson Ltd, 30-34 Bloomsbury Street, London WC1B 3QP   *tel* 0171-636 5488   *fax* 0171-636 4799   *e-mail* mail@thbooks.demon.co.uk
Chairman: E.U. Neurath; *managing director:* T.M. Neurath; *directors:* E. Bates (company secretary), J.R. Camplin (editorial), T.L. Evans (sales and marketing), C.A. Ferguson (production), W. Guttmann, S. Huntley, C.M. Kaine (design), I.H.B. Middleton (rights), N. Stangos (editorial), T.J. Flood (finance), P. Hughes CBE.
Illustrated non-fiction for an international audience, especially art, architecture, graphic design, garden and landscape design, archaeology, cultural history, historical reference, fashion, photography, ethnic arts, mythology and religion.

Thames Publishing (1970), 14 Barlby Road, London W10 6AR   *tel* 0181-969 3579   *fax* 0181-969 1465. *Publishing manager:* John Bishop.
Books about music (not pop), particularly British composers and musicians. Preliminary letter essential.

D.C. Thomson & Co. Ltd – Publications, Dundee DD1 9QJ   *tel* (01382) 223131   *telegraphic address* Courier, Dundee   *telex* 76380   *fax* (01382) 322214. *London office:*   185 Fleet Street, EC4A 2HS   *tel* 0171-242 5086   *telegraphic address* Courier, London, EC4   *fax* 0171-404 5694. Publishers of newspapers and periodicals.
Children's books (annuals), based on weekly magazine characters; fiction.

*****Stanley Thornes (Publishers) Ltd** (incorporating **Mary Glasgow Publications**), Ellenborough House, Wellington Street, Cheltenham, Glos. GL50 1YW   *tel* (01242) 228888   *fax* (01242) 221914   *e-mail* mktng:sthornes@rmplc.co.uk   *Managing director:* David Smith; *directors:* Brian Carvell, Kevin Waterman, Paul Vinson, Oliver Gadsby.
Educational: primary, secondary, further education books, higher education, professional.

*****Thorsons—see HarperCollins Publishers.**

*****Times Books—see HarperCollins Publishers.**

*****Times Mirror International Publishers Ltd (TMIP Ltd),** 5th Floor, Lynton House, 7-12 Tavistock Square, London WC1H 9LB   *tel* 0171-388 7676   *fax* 0171-391 6555. *President:* Tim Hailstone; *vice presidents:* Fiona Foley (publishing), Jim Donohue (sales and marketing), Melanie Laing (human resources).
Irwin (imprint). *Publisher:* Cathy Peck. Business and economic textbooks for the European and South African markets, often adapted from products of Richard D. Irwin, USA.
Mosby (imprint). *Publisher:* Cathy Peck. International student textbooks and postgraduate works of reference in full colour in medicine, nursing and bio-medical sciences.
Mosby Wolfe (imprint). *Publisher:* Fiona Foley. International colour atlases in medicine, biomedical science, dentistry and veterinary medical.
Mosby Wolfe Medical Communications (division). *Managing director:* Derrick Holman. Supplies the global pharmaceutical industry with medically relevant educational and promotional programmes in support of ethical drugs. Produces books, ideas, slides and multimedia programmes for the clinical and consumer health markets. Also runs the co-editions and translation rights businesses.

Titan Books Ltd (1981), 42-44 Dolben Street, London SE1 0UP   *tel* 0171-620 0200   *fax* 0171-620 0032. *Publisher and managing director:* Nick Landau; *editorial director:* Katy Wild.
Graphic novels, including Aliens and Batman, featuring comic strip material; film and TV tie-ins, fiction and fact books, including Star Wars and Star Trek; crime fiction; humour. True crime under the **Mondo** imprint. Erotic fiction under the **Eros Plus** imprint. *No* fiction or children's proposals and no unsol-icited material without preliminary letter please; send large sae for current author guidelines.

*****Tolkien—see HarperCollins Publishers.**

Tolley Publishing Co. Ltd (1916), Tolley House, 2 Addiscombe Road, Croydon, Surrey CR9 5AF   *tel* 0181-686 9141   *fax* 0181-681 7986. *Directors:* Graham Wilson (chairman), Harry King (managing), Robert McKay (divisional chief executive), Kelvin Ladbrook (divisional chief executive), Robin Webb (elec-tronic products), Nicholas Parmée (editorial), Peter Diggles (finance and administration).

Law, taxation, accountancy, business.

Fourmat Publishing (division). *Publisher:* Carol Doyle-Linden; *commissioning editor:* Irene Kaplan. Books and legal forms for lawyers, business and the professions.

Charles Knight Publishing (division). *Publisher:* Carol Doyle-Linden; *managing editor:* S.C. Cotter. Looseleaf legal works and periodicals on local government law, construction law and technical subjects.

Touchstone—see **Simon & Schuster.**

*****Training Direct**—see **Pearson Professional Ltd.**

*****Transworld Publishers Ltd,** 61-63 Uxbridge Road, London W5 5SA   *tel* 0181-579 2652   *fax* 0181-579 5479. *Chairman:* Stephen Rubin; *managing director:* Mark Barty-King; *deputy managing director:* Barry Hempstead (operations); *publishers:* Patrick Janson-Smith (adult trade books), Ursula Mackenzie (hardbacks), Tony Mott (paperbacks). Subsidiary of Bertelsmann AG.

Bantam (imprint). *Publishing director:* Francesca Liversidge. Paperback general fiction and non-fiction.

Bantam Press (imprint). *Publishing director:* Sally Gaminara. Fiction, general, cookery, business, crime, health and diet, history, humour, military, music, paranormal, self-help, science, travel and adventure, biography and autobiography.

Bantam Children's Books (division). *Publisher:* Philippa Dickinson. Paperback young adult books and series.

Black Swan (imprint). *Editorial director:* Bill Scott-Kerr. Paperback quality fiction.

Corgi (imprint). *Editorial director:* Bill Scott-Kerr. Paperback general fiction and non-fiction.

Corgi Children's Books (division). *Publisher:* Philippa Dickinson. Children's paperback picture books, fiction and poetry.

Doubleday (UK) (imprint). *Publisher:* Marianne Velmans. General fiction and non-fiction.

Doubleday Children's Books (imprint). *Publisher:* Philippa Dickinson. Hardback picture books, fiction and poetry for children.

Freeway (imprint). *Editorial director:* Philippa Dickinson. Paperback young adult books.

Partridge Press (imprint). *Publishing manager:* Debbie Beckerman. Sport and leisure.

Also: **IDG Computer Books** and **Expert Gardening Books.**

*****Trentham Books Ltd** (1968), Westview House, 734 London Road, Oakhill, Stoke-on-Trent, Staffs. ST4 5NP   *tel* (01782) 745567/844699   *fax* (01782) 745553   *e-mail* tb@trentham.books.co.uk   *WWW* http://www.ftech.net/ -trentham *Directors:* Professor S.J. Eggleston (managing), Gillian Klein (editorial), Barbara Wiggins (executive). *Editorial office:* 28 Hillside Gardens, London N6 5ST   *tel* 0181-348 2174.

Education (including specialist fields – multicultural issues, equal opportunities, bullying, design and technology, early years), social policy, sociology of education, European education. Does not publish books for use by children or fiction, biography and poetry.

*****Triangle**—see **Society for Promoting Christian Knowledge.**

Trotman & Company Ltd (1970), 12 Hill Rise, Richmond, Surrey TW10 6UA   *tel* 0181-940 5668   *fax* 0181-948 9267. *Chairman:* A.F. Trotman; *publishing director:* Morfydd Jones.

Higher education guidance, careers, classroom resources.

Two Heads Publishing (1992), 9 Whitehall Park, London N19 3TS *tel* 0171-561 1606 *fax* 0171-561 1607 *e-mail* twoheads.demon.co.uk *Publisher:* Charles Frewin.
London-based guides, sport, cycling books.

*Two-Can Publishing (1987), 346 Old Street, London EC1V 9NQ *tel* 0171-613 3376 *fax* 0171-613 3371 *e-mail* server@twocan.demon.co.uk *Directors:* Andrew Jarvis (chairman), Ian Grant (marketing), Sara Lynn (creative).
Children's: reference and non-fiction books, magazines, video and multimedia products.

UCL Press Ltd (1991), University College London, Gower Street, London WC1E 6BT *tel* 0171-380 7707 *fax* 0171-413 8392. *Publisher and chief executive:* R.F.J. Jones; *marketing director:* N.J.R. Esson.
Art, architecture, archaeology, history, language, literature and literary theory, philosophy, computing, physics, psychology, cultural studies, planning and geography, social research methods, sociology.

Ultimate Editions—see Anness Publishing.

Unicorn Books, 16 Laxton Gardens, Paddock Wood, Kent TN12 6BB *tel* (01892) 833648 *fax* (01892) 833577. *Director:* R. Green.
Militaria, music, transport.

*University of Exeter Press (1958), Reed Hall, Streatham Drive, Exeter, Devon EX4 4QR *tel* (01392) 263066 *fax* (01392) 263064 *e-mail* uep @exeter.ac.uk *Publisher:* Simon Baker.
Academic and scholarly books on history, local history (Exeter and the South West), archaeology, classical studies, English literature, medieval English, linguistics, modern languages, European studies, maritime studies, mining history, politics, Arabic studies, American studies.

The University of Hull Press & Lampada Press (1983/1991), Cottingham Road, Hull, North Humberside HU6 7RX *tel* (01482) 465322 *telex* 592592 KHMAIL G. FAO HULIB 375 *fax* (01482) 465936. *Assistant registrar:* Miss J.M. Smith.
General interest: economic and social history, history, local history, modern languages, English, geography, law, music.

University of Wales Press (1922), 6 Gwennyth Street, Cathays, Cardiff CF2 4YD *tel* (01222) 231919 *fax* (01222) 230908 *e-mail* press@wales.ac.uk *Editorial director:* Ned Thomas.
Academic and educational (Welsh and English). Publishers of *Welsh History Review, Studia Celtica, Llên Cymru, Delta, Y Gwyddonydd, Efrydiau Athronyddol, Contemporary Wales, Welsh Journal of Education, Journal of Celtic Linguistics, ALT-J (Association for Learning Technology Journal)*.

Merlin Unwin Books (1990), 58 Broad Street, Ludlow, Shropshire SY8 1GQ *tel* (01584) 877456 *fax* (01584) 877457. *Proprietor:* Merlin Unwin.
Fishing.

*Unwin Hyman Ltd—acquired by HarperCollins Publishers.

*Unwin Hyman Academic—incorporated in Routledge.

*Usborne Publishing (1973), Usborne House, 83-85 Saffron Hill, London EC1N 8RT *tel* 0171-430 2800 *telex* 8953598 *fax* 0171-430 1562. *Directors:* T.P. Usborne, Jenny Tyler (editorial), Robert Jones, David Lowe, Keith Ball, D. Harte, L. Hunt.
Children's books: reference, practical, craft, natural history, science, languages, history, geography, fiction.

Vallentine Mitchell (1950)—see **Frank Cass & Co. Ltd.**

Variorum—see **Ashgate Publishing Ltd.**

*Velvet—see **Creation Books.**

*Ventura Publishing Ltd—see **Penguin Books Ltd.**

*Vermilion—see **Random House UK Ltd.**

Verso Ltd (1970), 6 Meard Street, London W1V 3HR *tel* 0171-437 3546 *fax* 0171-734 0059 *e-mail* 100434.1414@compuserve.com *Directors:* Colin Robinson (managing and editorial), Robin Blackburn, Tariq Ali, Perry Anderson; *executive chairman:* Lucy Heller.
Politics, sociology, economics, history, philosophy, cultural studies.

*Viking—see **Penguin Books Ltd.**

*Viking Children's Books—see **Penguin Books Ltd.**

*Vintage—see **Random House UK Ltd.**

*Virago—see **Little, Brown and Company (UK).**

Virgin Books—see **Virgin Publishing Ltd.**

Virgin Publishing Ltd, 332 Ladbroke Grove, London W10 5AH *tel* 0181-968 7554 *fax* 0181-968 0929. *Chairman:* Robert Devereux; *directors:* Robert Shreeve (managing), Richard Branson; *management:* Peter Darvill-Evans (publisher, fiction), Philip Dodd (publisher, illustrated), Ana Panoho (rights), John Bond (marketing), Nicky Stonehill (publicity), Ray Mudie (sales), Michael Cohen (financial); Mal Peachey (senior editor, general).
Black Lace (imprint). *Editor:* Kerri Sharp. Erotic fiction by women for women.
Doctor Who (imprint). *Editor:* Rebecca Levene. Novelisations and large format fan books based on the series under licence from the BBC.
Nexus (imprint). *Publisher:* Peter Darvill-Evans. Erotic fiction.
Virgin Books (imprint). *Editorial:* Mal Peachey (general), Philip Dodd (illustrated), Rod Green (film and TV tie-ins and humour), Peter Darvill-Evans (fiction). Popular culture: entertainment, showbiz, arts, film and TV, music, humour, biography and autobiography, popular reference, true crime, children's books, mainly juvenile fiction.

Virtue Books Ltd, Edward House, Tenter Street, Rotherham S60 1LB *tel* (01709) 365005 *fax* (01709) 829982. *Directors:* Peter E. Russum, Margaret H. Russum, Michael G. Virtue (editorial).
Books for the professional chef, catering and drink.

*Voyager—see **HarperCollins Publishers.**

Walker Books Ltd (1979), 87 Vauxhall Walk, London SE11 5HJ *tel* 0171-793 0909 *fax* 0171-587 1123. *Directors:* David Ford, David Heatherwick, Wendy Boase, David Lloyd, Amelia Edwards, Judy Burdsall, Harold G. Gould OBE, Henryk Wesolowski, Rick Richter, Sarah Foster.
Children's – mainly picture books; junior and teenage fiction.

Warburg Institute, University of London, Woburn Square, London WC1H 0AB *tel* 0171-580 9663 *fax* 0171-436 2852.
Cultural and intellectual history, with special reference to the history of the classical tradition.

Ward Lock—see **Cassell plc.**

Ward Lock Educational Co. Ltd (1952), BIC Ling Kee House, 1 Christopher Road, East Grinstead, West Sussex RH19 3BT *tel* (01342) 318980 *fax* (01342) 410980. *Directors:* Au Bak Ling (chairman, Hong Kong), Au King Kwok (Hong Kong), Au Wai Kwok (Hong Kong), Albert Kw Au (Hong

Kong), Au Chun Kwok (Hong Kong); *general manager:* Penny Kitchenham.
Primary and secondary pupil materials, Kent Mathematics Project: KMP
BASC for primary and KMP Main for secondary, Reading Workshops, Take
Part Series and Take Part Starters, teachers' books, music books, Target Series
for the National Curriculum: Target Science and Target Geography, religious
education, environmental studies.

*Frederick Warne & Co. Ltd—see **Penguin Books Ltd.**

Warner Chappell Plays Ltd, 129 Park Street, London W1Y 3FA   *tel* 0171-514
5236   *fax* 0171-514 5201. *Editorial director:* Michael Callahan.
Stage plays only, in both acting and trade editions. Preliminary letter essential.

Warner—see **Little, Brown and Company (UK).**

Waterline Books (1991)—see **Airlife Publishing Ltd.**

*Franklin Watts (1969)—see **The Watts Publishing Group.**

*The Watts Publishing Group, 96 Leonard Street, London EC2A 4RH   *tel* 0171-
739 2929   *fax* 0171-739 2318. *Directors:* Francesca Dow (editorial: Orchard),
Philippa Stewart (editorial: Franklin Watts), Marlene Johnson (managing),
Rita Ireland (production), George Spicer (sales), Sarah Odedina (rights).
Division of Grolier Ltd.
Orchard Books (division). *Editorial director:* Francesca Dow. Children's pic-
ture books, fiction, poetry, novelty books, board books.
Franklin Watts (division). *Publishing director:* Philippa Stewart. Children's
illustrated non-fiction, reference, education.

*Wayland Publishers Ltd (1969), 61-61A Western Road, Hove, East Sussex BN3
1JD   *tel* (01273) 722561   *fax* (01273) 329314. *Managing director:* D.J. Smith;
directors: R. Bailey (general manager), S. White-Thompson (product development), F.M. Jane (finance), B. Nevin (sales).
Children's information books for ages 4-18.

Websters International Publishers Ltd (1983), 2nd Floor, Axe & Bottle Court,
70 Newcomen Street, London SE1 1YT   *tel* 0171-407 2846   *fax* 0171-407
6437. *Chairman and publisher:* Adrian Webster; *managing director:* Jean-Luc
Barbanneau; *publishing director:* Susannah Webster.
Wine, food, travel and health.

Weidenfeld & Nicolson (1948)—see **The Orion Publishing Group Ltd.**

*Which? Books—see **Consumers' Association.**

*J. Whitaker & Sons Ltd, 12 Dyott Street, London WC1A 1DF   *tel* 0171-420
6000   *fax* 0171-836 2909. *Directors:* Peter Allsop, Robin Baum, John Lycett,
Jonathan Nowell, Chris Ostrom, Paul Pounsford, Tom Sweetman, David
Whitaker (chairman), Sally Whitaker (managing), Martin Whitaker.
Reference including *Whitaker's Almanack* (1869), *The Bookseller* (1858),
Whitaker's Books in Print (1874), and other book trade directories.

White Mouse Editions Ltd (1979)—see **New Cavendish Books.**

Whittet Books Ltd (1976), 18 Anley Road, London W14 0BY   *tel* 0171-603
1139   *fax* 0171-603 8154. *Directors:* Annabel Whittet, John Whittet.
Natural history, countryside, transport, pets, horses.

*Whurr Publishers Ltd (1987), 19B Compton Terrace, London N1 2UN   *tel* 0171-
359 5979   *fax* 0171-226 5290. *Managing director:* Colin Whurr.
Disorders of human communication, medicine, psychology, psychiatry, occupational therapy, physiotherapy, business.

***John Wiley & Sons Ltd** (incorporating **Interscience Publishers**), Baffins Lane, Chichester, West Sussex PO19 1UD *tel* (01243) 779777 *fax* (01243) 775878 *e-mail* europe@wiley.co.uk *Chairman:* The Duke of Richmond; *managing director:* J.H. Jarvis; *publishing director, STM division:* M. Dixon; *publishing director, professional division:* S. Mair.
Physics, chemistry, mathematics, statistics, engineering, computer science, biology, medicine, earth science, psychology, business, economics, finance, law.

***Neil Wilson Publishing Ltd** (1992), 303A The Pentagon Centre, 36 Washington Street, Glasgow G3 8AZ *tel* 0141-221 1117 *fax* 0141-221 5363 *e-mail* nwp@cqm.co.uk *WWW* http://www.colloquium.co.uk/nwp *Managing director:* Neil Wilson.
Scottish interest, biography, history, food and drink, hill walking, travel, humour, true crime, Irish interest.

***Philip Wilson Publishers Ltd** (1975), 143-149 Great Portland Street, London W1N 5FB *tel* 0171-436 4490 *fax* 0171-436 4403. *Chairman:* P. Wilson; *managing director:* A. White; *publishing director:* A. Jackson.
Fine and applied art, architecture, museums.
Flint River (imprint). Countries.
Scala (imprint). Museums.
Sotheby's Publications (imprint). Art, art history, architecture, collectables.

The Windrush Press (1987), Little Window, High Street, Moreton-in-Marsh, Glos. GL56 0LL *tel* (01608) 652012/652025 *fax* (01608) 652125. *Managing director:* Geoffrey Smith; *publishing director:* Victoria Huxley.
History, military history, travel, biography, humour, local interest.

Wisley Handbooks—see Cassell plc.

Woburn Press (1968)—see **Frank Cass & Co. Ltd.**

The Women's Press (1978), 34 Great Sutton Street, London EC1V 0DX *tel* 0171-251 3007 *fax* 0171-608 1938. *Directors:* Kathy Gale (publishing), Mary Hemming (sales).
Books by women in the areas of literary fiction, crime novels, biography and autobiography, health, politics, handbooks, literary criticism, psychology and self-help, the arts.
Livewire (imprint). Books for teenagers.

Woodhead Publishing Ltd (1989), Abington Hall, Abington, Cambridge CB1 6AH *tel* (01223) 891358 *fax* (01223) 893694 *e-mail* woodhead @dial.pipex.com *Managing director:* Martin Woodhead; *finance director:* Duncan Leeper.
Materials engineering, welding, textiles, finance, investment, banking, business, food science and technology.

***Woodhead-Faulkner** (1972)—see **Prentice Hall Europe.**

World International Ltd, Deanway Technology Centre, Wilmslow Road, Handforth, Cheshire SK9 3ET *tel* (01625) 650011 *fax* (01625) 650040. *Directors:* Ian Findlay (managing), David Sheldrake (production), Michael Herridge (editorial), Peter Hey, Andrew Maddock.
Books for children of all ages; early learning, activity, annuals; character publishing including *Mr Men.*

***X Libris—see Little, Brown and Company (UK).**

***Yale University Press London** (1961), 23 Pond Street, London NW3 2PN *tel* 0171-431 4422 *fax* 0171-431 3755. *Managing director:* John Nicoll.

Art, architecture, history, economics, political science, literary criticism, Asian and African studies, religion, philosophy, psychology, history of science.

Yorkshire Art Circus (1986), School Lane, Glass Houghton, Castleford, West Yorkshire WF10 4QH *tel* (01977) 550401 *fax* (01977) 512819 *e-mail* ian.daley@poptel.org.uk *Books co-ordinator:* Reini Schühle.
Specialises in new writing by first-time authors. Publishes autobiography, community books, fiction and local interest (Yorkshire/Humberside). No local history, children's, reference or nostalgia. Unsolicited MSS discouraged; authors should send for fact sheet first.
Springboard (1993) (imprint). Fiction.

Young Library (Assetpulse Ltd) (1982), PO Box 2231, Reading RG4 9YP *tel* (01734) 722805 *fax* (01734) 722544. *Director:* Roger Bonnett.
Highly illustrated non-fiction for children's libraries, including geography, history, natural history, social and urban studies, science and technology, and reference.

*Zed Books Ltd (1976), 7 Cynthia Street, London N1 9JF *tel* 0171-837 4014 (general)/0171-837 0384 (editorial) *fax* 0171-833 3960 *e-mail* zed @zedbooks.demon.co.uk *Editors:* Robert Molteno, Louise Murray.
Social sciences on international issues; women's studies, cultural studies, development and environmental studies; area studies (Africa, Asia, Caribbean, Latin America, Middle East and the Pacific).

Hans Zell Publishers—see **Bowker-Saur.**

Zoë Books Ltd (1990), 15 Worthy Lane, Winchester, Hants SO23 7AB *tel* (01962) 851318 *fax* (01962) 843015. *Directors:* I.Z. Dawson (managing publishing), A.R. Davidson. Publishers of children's information books for the school and library markets in the UK; specialists in co-editions for world markets. Opportunities for freelances with relevant experience.

The plot

You have expanded your idea, you have created your characters around it, and now you have to work these into a detailed credible plot. At the outset, though, you have to have a 'feel' for everything that you have done so far; if you don't really like your characters or you are not really inspired by the idea, then what follows from hereon will not make much impact. If you become bored with the book, then that will be passed on to the editor who reads it. You have to convince yourself that this is a book which people will read avidly; without that motivation you may as well go back to the beginning and start looking for another idea and creating new characters. Don't delude yourself. If you are not sure it is right, begin again. It is frustrating but it is preferable to get it right at the beginning.

from *Writing Horror Fiction* by Guy N. Smith (A & C Black, £8.99).
See order form on page 690.

Classified Index of UK Publishers of Fiction

Addresses for UK publishers start on page 148.

Gerald Duckworth & Co.
Faber & Faber
Fourth Estate
Gairm Publications
Victor Gollancz
Granta Publications
Robert Hale
Hamish Hamilton
HarperCollins Publishers
Headline Book Publishing
William Heinemann
Hodder & Stoughton
Hutchinson Books
Michael Joseph
Karnak House

Little, Brown
Y Lolfa Cyf. (Welsh language)
Macmillan
Mainstream Publishing Co.
Methuen
New English Library
Orion
Peter Owen
Pan Books
Penguin Books
Piatkus Books
Pimlico
Pocket Books
Quartet Books
Random House UK

Sceptre
Secker and Warburg
Serpent's Tail
Signet
Simon & Schuster
Sinclair-Stevenson
Souvenir Press
Touchstone
Viking
Vintage
Virago Press
Warner
Worldwide Books
Yorkshire Art Circus

Historical

Bantam
Bantam Press
Bellew
Black Ace Books
Marion Boyars Publishers
Canongate Books
Jonathan Cape
Robin Clark
Richard Cohen Books
Constable & Co.
André Deutsch
diehard
Doubleday (UK)

Fourth Estate
Victor Gollancz
Robert Hale
HarperCollins Publishers
Headline Book Publishing
William Heinemann
Hodder & Stoughton
Hutchinson Books
Michael Joseph
Karnak House
Little, Brown
Mainstream Publishing Co.
Orion

Peter Owen
Pan
Penguin Books
Piatkus Books
Pimlico
Random House UK
Sceptre
Simon & Schuster
Sinclair-Stevenson
Souvenir Press
Vintage
Virago Press
Warner

Literary

Abacus
Bantam
Bantam Press
Black Ace Books
Black Swan
Bloomsbury Publishing
Marion Boyars Publishers
Calder Publications
Canongate Books
Jonathan Cape
Chatto & Windus
Robin Clark
Richard Cohen Books
Constable & Co.
Corgi
Dedalus
André Deutsch
diehard
Doubleday (UK)
Faber & Faber

Flamingo
Forest Books
Fourth Estate
Gairm Publications
Victor Gollancz
Granta Publications
Robert Hale
Hamish Hamilton
HarperCollins Publishers
Harvill
William Heinemann
Hodder & Stoughton
Hutchinson Books
Karnak House
Little, Brown
Macmillan
Mainstream Publishing Co.
Methuen
Orion
Peter Owen

Pan
Penguin Books
Phoenix
Picador
Pimlico
Polygon
Random House UK
Sceptre
Scottish Cultural Press
Secker and Warburg
Serif
Serpent's Tail
Sinclair-Stevenson
Skoob Books
Souvenir Press
Stride Publications
Viking
Vintage
Virago Press
The Women's Press

Romantic

Bantam
Bantam Press

Black Swan
Blake Publishing

Corgi
Coronet

Doubleday (UK)
Robert Hale
Harlequin Mills & Boon
Headline Book Publishing
William Heinemann
Hodder & Stoughton

Little, Brown
Macmillan
Monarch Publications
Orion
Pan
Piatkus Books

Random House UK
Robinson Publishing
Silhouette
Souvenir Press
Warner

Science Fiction/Fantasy

Arrow Books
Bantam
Bantam Press
Black Swan
Blake Publishing
Corgi
Coronet
Victor Gollancz
HarperCollins Publishers

Headline Book Publishing
Hodder & Stoughton
Legend
Little, Brown
Millennium
New English Library
Orbit
Orion
Pan

Penguin Books
Random House UK
Robinson Publishing
RoC
Severn House Publishers
Titan Books
The Women's Press

Short Stories

Bellew
Bloomsbury Publishing
Marion Boyars Publishers
Jonathan Cape
Chatto & Windus
Constable & Co.
Creation Books
Faber & Faber
Forest Books
Fourth Estate

Gairm Publications
Granta Publications
Hamish Hamilton
William Heinemann
Hodder & Stoughton
Karnak House
Little, Brown
Mainstream Publishing Co.
Peter Owen
Pan

Penguin Books
Polygon
Random House UK
Robinson Publishing
Secker and Warburg
Serpent's Tail
Severn House Publishers
Sinclair-Stevenson
Stride Publications
Yorkshire Art Circus

Other

Erotic

Black Lace
Creation Books
Delta
Eros Plus
Liaison
Nexus
Velvet

Graphic

Creation Books
Titan Books

Horror

Chapman
Creation Books
Robinson Publishing
Warner

Humour

Black Swan
Corgi
Victor Gollancz
Warner

International

Allison & Busby
Serif

New/Experimental

Serpent's Tail
Stride Publications

Translations

Marion Boyars Publishers
Dedalus
The Harvill Press
Quartet Books
Serpent's Tail

War

Severn House Publishers

Westerns

Robert Hale
Severn House Publishers

Classified Index of UK Publishers of Poetry

Addresses for UK publishers start on page 148; see classified index on page 247 for publishers of poetry for children.

Anvil Press Poetry
Arc Publications
Bellew Publishing
Bloodaxe Books
Jonathan Cape
Carcanet Press
Cassell plc
Chatto & Windus
Enitharmon Press

Faber & Faber
Forest Books
Gairm Publications
Headland Publications
Hippopotamus Press
National Poetry Foundation
New Beacon Books
Onlywomen Press
Oxford University Press

Payback Press
Penguin Books
Peterloo Poets
Random House UK
Rivelin Grapheme Press
Scottish Cultural Press
Seren Books
Slow Dancer Press
Stride Publications

Classified Index of UK Publishers of Multimedia

Addresses for UK publishers start on page 148.

Academic Press
Addison Wesley Longman
BBC Worldwide Publishing
Berlitz Publishing (language
  and travel related only)
Blackwell Publishers
  (InfoSource International)
The British Library
  (Publications)
Chadwyck-Healey
Current Science Group
Dorling Kindersley Multimedia
Dragon's World

HarperCollins Electronic
  Products
Helicon Publishing
Hodder Headline
McGraw Hill
Macmillan Interactive
  Publishing
Mosby Wolfe Medical
  Communications
Thomas Nelson
Notting Hill Electronic
  Publishers

Oxford University Press
Penguin Electronic Publishing
Random House New Media
Reed Educational Electronic
  Publishing
Thames & Hudson
Training Direct (Pearson
  Professional Ltd)
Two-Can Publishing
Usborne Publishing
The Watts Publishing Group
Wayland Publishers

AUSTRALIA

*Member of the Australian Publishers Association

Access Press (1979), 11 Palmerston Street, Northbridge, Western Australia 6003 *postal address* PO Box 132, Northbridge, Western Australia 6865 *tel* (09) 328 9188 *fax* (09) 328 4605. *Managing editor*: Helen Weller. Australiana, fiction, poetry, children's, history, general. Privately financed books published and distributed.

****Addison Wesley Longman Australia Pty Ltd,** 95 Coventry Street, South Melbourne, Victoria 3205 *tel* (03) 9697 0666 *fax* (03) 9699 2041. *Managing director:* Robert W. Fisher. Educational, academic and trade publishers.

****Allen & Unwin Pty Ltd,** 9 Atchison Street, PO Box 8500, St Leonards, NSW 2065 *tel* (02) 9901 4088 *fax* (02) 9906 2218. General trade, including fiction and children's books, academic, especially social science and history.

****The Australian Council for Educational Research Ltd,** 19 Prospect Hill Road, Private Bag 55, Camberwell, Victoria 3124 *tel* (03) 9277 5555 *fax* (03) 9277 5500. Range of books and kits: for teachers, trainee teachers, parents, psychologists, counsellors, students of education, researchers.

Blackwell Science, 54 University Street, Carlton, Victoria 3053 *tel* (03) 9347 0300 *telegraphic address* Blackwell, Melbourne *fax* (03) 9347 5001. *Editorial director:* Mark Robertson. Medical, healthcare, life, earth sciences, professional.

****Brooks Waterloo Publishers**—imprint of **Jacaranda Wiley Ltd.**

****Butterworths,** 271-273 Lane Cove Road, North Ryde, NSW 2113 *tel* (02) 335 4444 *fax* (02) 335 4655. *Managing director:* D.J. Jackson; *editorial and deputy managing director:* J. Broadfoot. Division of Reed International Books Australia Pty Ltd. Legal, tax and commercial

****Cambridge University Press Australian Branch,** 10 Stamford Road, Oakleigh, Melbourne, Victoria 3166 *tel* (03) 9568 0322 *fax* (03) 9563 1517. *Director:* Kim W. Harris. Academic, educational, reference, English as a second language.

Craftsman House (1981), 20 Barcoo Street, Roseville East, NSW 2069 *postal address* PO Box 480, Roseville, NSW 2069 *tel* (02) 417 1033 *fax* (02) 417 1501. *Directors:* Nevill Drury (publishing), Martin Gordon; Nichola Dyson Walker (marketing manager). Australian and European fine arts.

Dominie Pty Ltd, Drama Department, 8 Cross Street, Brookvale, NSW 2100 *tel* (02) 9905 0201 *fax* (02) 9905 5209. Australian representatives of publishers of plays and agents for the collection of royalties for Samuel French Ltd, incorporating Evans Plays and Samuel French Inc., The Society of Authors, ACTAC, and Bakers Plays of Boston.

Elephas Books (1989), 1/18 Mooney Street, Bayswater, WA 6053 *tel* (09) 370 1461 *fax* (09) 341 8952. *Principals:* Alan J. Falkson, Rune Karlson. How-to and informational subjects.

Samuel French Ltd—see **Dominie Pty Ltd.**

****HarperCollins Publishers Pty Limited,** 25-31 Ryde Road, Pymble, NSW 2073 *postal address* PO Box 321, Pymble, NSW 2073 *tel* (02) 9952 5000 *fax* (02) 9952 5555. *Managing director:* Barrie Hitchon. Australiana, literature, poetry, fiction, general non-fiction and reference, sport, children's books, gift and stationery.

*Hill of Content Publishing Co. Pty Ltd (1965), 86 Bourke Street, Melbourne, Victoria 3000 *tel* (03) 662 2282 *fax* (03) 662 2527. *Directors:* M. Slamen, M.G. Zifcak, Michelle Anderson. Health, general, lifestyle.

*Hodder Headline Australia Pty Ltd, 10-16 South Street, (Locked Bag 386), Rydalmere, NSW 2116 *tel* (02) 9638 5299 *fax* (02) 9684 4942. *Directors:* Malcolm Edwards (managing), Tim Hely Hutchinson, Lisa Highton, Mary Howell, Richard Bartlett, Michael Burge, David Cocking, Mark Opzoomer. General, illustrated non-fiction, children's, religious, educational books.

*Jacaranda Wiley Ltd, 33 Park Road, Milton, Queensland 4064 *tel* (07) 3859 9755 *fax* (07) 3859 9715; 184-186 Glenferrie Road, Malvern, Victoria 3144 *tel* (03) 9576 1011 *fax* (03) 9576 1132; Suite 4A, 113 Wicks Road, North Ryde, NSW 2113 *tel* (02) 805 1100 *fax* (02) 805 1597 *e-mail* headoffice @jacwiley.com.au *Managing director:* P. Donoughue. Educational, technical, atlases, professional, reference, trade.

*Kangaroo Press Pty Ltd (1980), 3 Whitehall Road, Kenthurst, NSW 2156 *postal address* PO Box 6125 Dural Delivery Centre, Dural, NSW 2158 *tel* (02) 654 1502 *fax* (02) 654 1338 *e-mail* 100231.230@compuserve.com *Directors:* David Rosenberg, Priscilla Rosenberg. Gardening, craft, Australian history and natural history, collecting, fitness, transport, children's non-fiction.

*The Law Book Company Ltd, 50 Waterloo Road, North Ryde, NSW 2113 *tel* (02) 936 6444 *fax* (02) 888 9706.

*Lonely Planet Publications (1973), PO Box 617, Hawthorn, Victoria 3122 *tel* (03) 9819 1877 *fax* (03) 9819 6459 *e-mail* talkaus@lonelyplanet.com.au *Publisher:* Tony Wheeler. Travel guidebooks, walking guides, travel atlases, phrasebooks, travel literature and audio packs.

*Thomas C. Lothian Pty Ltd, 11 Munro Street, Port Melbourne, Victoria 3207 *tel* (03) 9645 1544 *fax* (03) 9646 4882. *Chairman and managing director:* P. Lothian; *directors:* E. McDonald, G. Matthews, B. Hilliard. Juveniles, health, gardening, general literature, craft, educational, reference, Australian history, business.

*Macmillan Education Australia Pty Ltd, 107 Moray Street, South Melbourne, Victoria 3205 *tel* (03) 699 8922 *fax* (03) 690 6938; Suite 310, Henry Lawson Business Centre, Birkenhead Point (Cary Street), Drummoyne, NSW 2047 *tel* (02) 719 8944 *fax* (02) 719 8613. *Directors:* Brian Stonier (executive chairman), John Rolfe (managing), N. Byam Shaw (UK), Margaret Brownie, Peter Debus, Peter Huntley, Brian McCurdy, Rex Parry, George Smith; *company secretary/financial controller:* Terry White. Educational books.

*Melbourne University Press, 268 Drummond Street, Carlton, Victoria 3053 *postal address* PO Box 278, Carlton South, Victoria 3053 *tel* (03) 9347 3455 *fax* (03) 9349 2527. *Chairman:* Professor J.R.V. Prescott; *director:* Brian Wilder. Academic, scholastic and cultural; educational textbooks and books of reference.

*Mimosa Publications Pty Ltd—see **Weldon International Pty Ltd.**

*Thomas Nelson Australia, 102 Dodds Street, South Melbourne, Victoria 3205 *tel* (03) 9685 4111 *fax* (03) 9685 4199. Educational books.

*Oxford University Press, Australia, 253 Normanby Road, South Melbourne, Victoria 3205 *postal address* GPO Box 2784Y, Melbourne, Victoria 3001 *tel* (03) 9646 4200 *fax* (03) 9646 3251. *Managing director:* Marek Palka. Australian history, biography, literary criticism, general, but excluding fiction; school books in all subjects.

*Pan Macmillan Australia Pty Ltd, Level 18, 31 Market Street, Sydney, NSW 2000 *tel* (02) 9261 5611 *fax* (02) 9261 5047. *Directors:* Ross Gibb (managing), James Fraser (publishing), Roxarne Burns (publishing), Siv Toigo (finance), Peter Phillips (sales), Jeannine Fowler (publicity). Fiction, non-fiction, children's.

*Pearson Professional (Australia) Pty Ltd, Kings Gardens, 95 Coventry Street, South Melbourne, Victoria 3205 *tel* (03) 9699 5400 *fax* (03) 9696 5205. *Managing director:* Peter Hylands. Medical, legal and business and professional publishers.

*Penguin Books Australia Ltd (1946), (PO Box 257), 487 Maroondah Highway, Ringwood, Victoria 3134 *tel* (03) 871 2400 *telegraphic address* Penguinook, Melbourne *fax* (03) 870 9618. *Managing director:* P.J. Field; *publishing director:* R.P. Sessions. Fiction, general non-fiction, current affairs, sociology, economics, environmental, travel guides, anthropology, politics, children's, health, cookery, gardening, pictorial and general books relating to Australia under **Penguin Books** and **Viking** imprints.

*Random House Australia Pty Ltd, 20 Alfred Street, Milsons Point, NSW 2061 *tel* (02) 9954 9966 *fax* (02) 9954 4562. *Managing director:* E.F. Mason. General, non-fiction, fiction, children's.

*Reed Books Australia, 22 Salmon Street, Port Melbourne, Victoria 3207 *tel* (03) 245 7111 *fax* (03) 245 7333. *Managing director:* Adrian Collette. General fiction and non-fiction, children's books, reference.

Reeve Books (1987), 11 Palmerston Street, Northbridge, Western Australia 6003 *postal address* PO Box 132, Northbridge, Western Australia 6865 *tel* (09) 328 9188 *fax* (09) 328 4605. *Managing director and editor:* Helen Weller. Biography, local history, general non-fiction. Commissioned works only.

*Rigby Heinemann (1982), 22 Salmon Street, Port Melbourne, Victoria 3207 *tel* (03) 9245 7111 *fax* (03) 9245 7333. *Managing director:* Louise Rice. Division of Reed Books. Art, chemistry, chemical engineering, environmental studies, geography, geology, health, nutrition, history, mathematics, physics, languages. Primary and Secondary.

*Scholastic Australia Pty Ltd (1968), PO Box 579, Lindfield 2070 *tel* (02) 416400 *fax* (02) 4169877. *Managing director:* Ken Jolly. Children's fiction/non-fiction; educational materials for elementary schools, teacher reference.

*Transworld Publishers (Aust) Pty Limited (1981), Ground Floor, 40 Yeo Street, Neutral Bay, NSW 2089 *tel* (02) 9908 4366 *fax* (02) 9953 8563. *Managing director:* Geoffrey Rumpf. Bio, self-help, personal awareness, health, parenting and childcare, sports, current affairs, social history.

University of Queensland Press (1948), PO Box 42, St Lucia, Queensland 4067 *tel* (07) 365 2127 *telex* UNIVQLD AA 40315 PRESS *fax* (07) 3365 7579 *e-mail* uqpbris@peg.apc.org.au *General manager:* L.C. Muller. Scholarly works, tertiary texts, Australian fiction, young adult fiction, poetry, history, general interest.

*Viking—see **Penguin Books.**

*Weldon International Pty Ltd, 107 Union Street, North Sydney, NSW 2060 *tel* (02) 9955 0091 *fax* (02) 9955 9390. *Chairman:* Kevin Weldon.

Mimosa Publications Pty Ltd (division). Primary school education.

Weldon Owen (division). Cookery, natural science, aerial photography, encyclopedic reference works, young readers' non-fiction.

Weldon Russell (division). Illustrated non-fiction including natural history, cookery, gardening, ancient history, general reference books and gift books.

*Wild & Woolley P (1974), PO Box 41, Glebe, NSW 2037 *tel* (02) 692 0166 *fax*
(02) 552 4320 *WWW* http://www.fastbooks.com.au *Director:* Pat Woolley.
Offers short-run paperback printing for self-publishing writers.

CANADA

*Member of the Canadian Publishers' Council
†Member of the Association of Canadian Publishers

Butterworths, 75 Clegg Road, Markham, Ontario L6G 1A1 *tel* 905-479-
2665 *fax* 905-479-2826.

*Canada Publishing Corporation (1844), 164 Commander Boulevard, Scar-
borough, Ontario M1S 3C7 *tel* 416-293-8141 *fax* 416-293-9009. Publishers
of elementary and secondary school textbooks; general trade/consumer publications including cookbooks, business, sport and fiction; professional and
reference materials; annual publications, including *Canadian Global Almanac*
and *Who's Who in Canada*.

Canadian Stage and Arts Publications Ltd, 104 Glenrose Avenue, Toronto,
Ontario M4T 1K8 *tel* 416-484-4534 *fax* 416-484-6214. *President and
publisher:* George Hencz. Primarily interested in children's books of an educational nature, art books. Also publishes quarterly *Performing Arts & Entertainment in Canada* (*editor:* Karen Bell).

Carswell, Thomson Professional Publishing, Corporate Plaza, 2075 Kennedy
Road, Scarborough, Ontario M1T 3V4 *tel* 416-609-8000 *fax* 416-298-5094.
Chairman/ceo: Ross M. Inkpen. Law, tax, business reference.

The Charlton Press (1952), 2010 Yonge Street, Toronto, Ontario M4S 1Z9 *tel*
416-488-4653 *fax* 416-488-4656. *President:* W.K. Cross. Collectibles, numismatics, Sportscard price catalogues.

*Copp Clark Ltd, 2775 Matheson Boulevard East, Mississauga, Ontario L4W
4P7 *tel* 905-238-6074 *fax* 905-238-6075. *President:* Robert F. Gurnham.
Professional publishers. Preliminary letter required before submitting MSS.

†Douglas & McIntyre Ltd (1964), 1615 Venables Street, Vancouver, BC V5L
2H1 *tel* 604-254-7191 *fax* 604-254-9099. General list, including Greystone
Books imprint: Canadian biography, art and architecture, natural history,
history, native studies, Canadian fiction. Children's division (Groundwood
Books) specialises in fiction and illustrated flats. No unsolicited MSS.

†ECW Press (1979), 2120 Queen Street E, Toronto, Ontario M4E 1E2 *tel*
416-694-3348 *fax* 416-698-9906 *e-mail* ecw@sympatico.ca *President:* Jack
David; *secretary-treasurer:* Robert Lecker. Literary criticism, indexes,
bibliographies, biographies, guidebooks.

Fitzhenry & Whiteside Limited (1966), 195 Allstate Parkway, Markham, Ontario
L3R 4T8 *tel* 905-477-9700 *fax* 905-477-9179 *toll free* 1-800-387-9776.
Director: Sharon Fitzhenry. Trade, educational, college books.

*Gage Educational Publishing Company—see Canada Publishing Corporation.

*Gold Eagle Books—see Harlequin Enterprises Ltd.

Harcourt Brace & Company Canada, Ltd, 55 Horner Avenue, Toronto, Ontario
M8Z 4X6 *tel* 416-255-4491 *fax* 416-255-4046.

*Harlequin Enterprises Ltd (1949), 225 Duncan Mill Road, Don Mills, Ontario
M3B 3K9 *tel* 416-445-5860 *fax* 416-445-8655. *President and ceo:* Brian E.
Hickey. Romance, action adventure, mystery.

Gold Eagle Books (imprint). *Senior editor and editorial co-ordinator:* Feroze Mohammed. Series action adventure fiction.

Harlequin Books (imprint). *Editorial director:* Randall Toye. Contemporary and historical romance fiction in series.

Mira Books (imprint). *Senior editor and editorial co-ordinator:* Dianne Moggy. Women's fiction: contemporary and historical dramas, family sagas, romantic suspense and relationship novels.

Silhouette Books (imprint). *Editorial director:* Isabel Scrift. Contemporary romance fiction in series.

Worldwide Library (imprint). *Senior editor and editorial co-ordinator:* Feroze Mohammed. Contemporary mystery fiction. Reprints only.

HarperCollins Canada, 1995 Markham Road, Scarborough, Ontario M1B 5M8 *tel* 416-321-2241 *fax* 416-321-3033; **HarperCollins Publishers Ltd,** Suite 2900, Hazelton Lanes, 55 Avenue Road, Toronto, Ontario M5R 3L2 *tel* 416-975-9334 *fax* 416-975-9884. Publishers of general literature, trade and reference, religious, mass market paperbacks, children's books.

Irwin Publishing, division of General Publishing Co. Ltd, 1800 Steeles Avenue W, Concord, Ontario L4K 2P3 *tel* 905-660-0611 *fax* 905-660-0676 *e-mail* irwin@irwin-pub.com *President:* Brian O'Donnell; *chairman:* Jack Stoddart. Educational books at the elementary, high school and college levels.

†**Kids Can Press Ltd,** 29 Birch Avenue, Toronto, Ontario M4V 1E2 *tel* 416-925-5437 *fax* 416-960-5437. *Publisher:* Valerie Hussey. Juvenile/young adult books.

†**Lester Publishing Ltd** (1991), 56 The Esplanade, Suite 507A, Toronto, Ontario M5E 1A7 *tel* 416-362-1032 *fax* 416-362-1647. *President and publisher:* Malcolm Lester. Biography, history, fiction, children's.

Lone Pine Publishing (1980), 206, 10426-81 Avenue, Edmonton, Alberta T6E 1X5 *tel* 403-433-9333 *fax* 403-433-9646. *Publisher and president:* Grant Kennedy; *editor-in-chief:* Shane Kennedy. Natural history, recreation and wildlife guidebooks, gardening, popular history.

†**McClelland & Stewart Inc.** (1906), 481 University Avenue, Suite 900, Toronto, Ontario M5G 2E9 *tel* 416-598-1114 *fax* 416-598-7764. *Chairman, president and ceo:* Avie Bennett. General.

†**McGill-Queen's University Press** (1969), 3430 McTavish Street, Montreal, Quebec H3A 1X9 *tel* 514-398-3750 *fax* 514-398-4333 *e-mail* mqup @printing.lan.mcgill.ca and Queen's University, Kingston, Ontario K7L 3N6 *tel* 613-545-2155 *fax* 613-545-6822 *e-mail* mqup@qucdn.queensu.ca Academic.

*****McGraw-Hill Ryerson Ltd,** 300 Water Street, Whitby, Ontario L1N 9B6 *tel* 905-430-5000 *fax* 905-430-5020. Educational and trade books.

†**Macmillan Canada** (1905), division of **Canada Publishing Corporation,** 29 Birch Avenue, Toronto, Ontario M4V 1E2 *tel* 416-963-8830 *fax* 416-923-4821. Trade book publishers.

*****Maxwell Macmillan Canada**—acquired by **Prentice Hall Canada Inc.**

Mira Books (1994)—see **Harlequin Enterprises Ltd.**

*****Nelson Canada** (1914), 1120 Birchmount Road, Scarborough, Ontario M1K 5G4 *tel* 416-752-9100 *telex* 06-963813 *fax* 416-752-9646. *Directors:* Herb Hilderley (president), Martin Keast, Andrew Clowes, Dick Parkinson. Elementary, high school, college textbooks; measurement and guidance; children's library.

†**Oberon Press,** 400-350 Sparks Street, Ottawa, Ontario K1R 7S8   *tel/fax* 613-238-3275. General.

***Oxford University Press, Canada,** 70 Wynford Drive, Don Mills, Ontario M3C 1J9   *tel* 416-441-2941   *fax* 416-444-0427. *Managing director:* Susan Froud. General, educational and academic.

***Pippin Publishing Ltd,** Suite 800, 481 University Avenue, Toronto, Ontario M5G 2E9   *tel* 416-598-1866   *fax* 416-598-1565. *President and editorial director:* Jonathan Lovat Dickson. ESL/EFL, teacher reference, adult basic education, school texts (all subjects).

***Prentice Hall Canada Inc.** (1960), 1870 Birchmount Road, Scarborough, Ontario M1P 2J7   *tel* 416-293-3621   *telex* 065-25184   *fax* 416-299-2529. *President:* Brian Heers. Academic, technical, educational, children's and adult, trade.

†**Quarry Press** (1965), PO Box 1061, Kingston, Ontario K7L 4Y5   *tel* 613-548-8429   *fax* 613-548-1556. *Publisher:* Bob Hilderley. Fiction, poetry, children's, biography, historical non-fiction, travel, folk stories.

***Silhouette Books**—see **Harlequin Enterprises Ltd.**

***Stoddart Publishing Co. Ltd,** 34 Lesmill Road, Don Mills, Ontario M3B 2T6   *tel* 416-445-3333   *fax* 416-445-5967. Fiction and non-fiction.

Tundra Books Inc., 345 Victoria Avenue, Suite 604, Montreal, Quebec H3Z 2N2   *tel* 514-932-5434   *fax* 514-484-2152. High quality children's picture books; art books.

†**University of Toronto Press Inc.,** 10 St Mary Street, Suite 700, Toronto, Ontario M4Y 2W8   *tel* 416-978-5171 (editorial); 416-978-2239 (administration)   *fax* 416-978-4738 (editorial/administration). *President and publisher:* George L. Meadows.

***Worldwide Library**—see **Harlequin Enterprises Ltd.**

THE REPUBLIC OF IRELAND AND NORTHERN IRELAND

*Member of the Irish Book Publishers' Association

***Anvil Books/The Children's Press** (1964), 45 Palmerston Road, Dublin 6   *tel* (01) 4973628   *cables* Anvil, Dublin. *Directors:* Rena Dardis (managing), Margaret Dardis (editorial). Anvil: history, biography; Children's Press: adventure, humour, fantasy.

***Appletree Press Ltd** (1974), 19-21 Alfred Street, Belfast BT2 8DL   *tel* (01232) 243074   *telex* 9312100435   *fax* (01232) 246756. *Director:* John Murphy. Biography, cookery, guidebooks, history, Irish interest, literary criticism, music, photographic, social studies, sport, travel.

***Attic Press** (1984), 29 Upper Mount Street, Dublin 2   *tel* (01) 6616128   *fax* (01) 6616176   *e-mail* atticirl@iol.ie   *WWW* http://www.iol.ie//-atticirl/ *Directors:* Róisín Conroy, Maeve Kneafsey, Ann Harper, Gretchen Fitzgerald. Books by and about women in the areas of social and political comment, fiction, women's studies, humour, reference guides and handbooks.
Basement Press (imprint). Fiction and non-fiction by men and women.

***Blackstaff Press Ltd** (1971), 3 Galway Park, Dundonald BT16 0AN   *tel* (01232) 487161   *fax* (01232) 489552. *Managing director:* Anne Tannahill. Fiction, poetry, biography, history, art, academic, natural history, sport, politics, music, education, fine limited editions.

The Blackwater Press—imprint of **Folens Publishing Company.** General non-fiction, Irish interest.

****Brandon Book Publishers Ltd** (1982), Cooleen, Dingle, Co. Kerry *tel* (066) 51463 *fax* (066) 51234. *Directors:* Steve MacDonogh, Bernard Goggin. Biography, literature, politics, fiction, travel (Ireland), history, children's folklore.

****Catholic Communications Institute of Ireland, Inc.**—see **Veritas Publications.**

****Cló Iar-Chonnachta Teo.** (1985), Indreabhán, Conamara, Co. Galway *tel* (091) 593307 *fax* (091) 593362. *Director:* Micheál Ó Conghaile; *editor:* Nóirín Ní Ghrádaigh; *general manager:* Deirdre O'Toole. Mostly Irish-language publications – novels, short stories, plays, poetry, songs, history; cassettes (writers reading from their works in Irish and English).

****Cork University Press** (1925), University College, Cork *tel* (021) 902980 *fax* (021) 273553. *Publisher:* Sara Wilbourne. Irish literature, history, cultural studies, medieval studies, and English literature.

Dolmen Press Ltd—stock acquired by **Colin Smythe Ltd**; see UK list.

The Educational Company of Ireland, PO Box 43a, Ballymount Road, Walkinstown, Dublin 12 *tel* (01) 4500611 *fax* (01) 4500993. *Executive directors:* F.J. Maguire (chief executive), O. Mulcahy, R. McLoughlin. Trading unit of Smurfit Services Ltd. Educational MSS on all subjects in English or Gaelic.

C.J. Fallon (1927), Lucan Road, Palmerstown, Dublin 20 *tel* (01) 6265777 *fax* (01) 6268225. *Directors:* H.J. McNicholas (managing), P. Tolan (financial), N. White (editorial). Educational text books.

Folens Publishing Company, Unit 8, Broomhill Business Park, Broomhill Road, Tallaght, Dublin 24 *tel* (01) 4515311 *fax* (01) 4515306. *Chairman:* Dirk Folens; *directors:* John O'Connor (managing), Anna O'Donovan (secondary), Deirdre Whelan (primary). Educational (primary, secondary, comprehensive, technical, in English and Irish), educational children's magazines.

****Four Courts Press** (1969), Kill Lane, Blackrock, Co. Dublin *tel* (01) 2892922 *fax* (01) 2893072. *Managing director:* Michael Adams. Theology, church history, medieval and Celtic studies, 17th and 18th century studies, art, film studies.

The Gallery Press (1970), Loughcrew, Oldcastle, Co. Meath *tel/fax* (049) 41779. *Editor and publisher:* Peter Fallon. *Allied company:* Deerfield Publications Inc., Massachusetts. Poetry, drama, occasionally fiction, by Irish authors. Also, hand-printed limited editions poetry.

****Gill & Macmillan Ltd** (1968), Goldenbridge, Inchicore, Dublin 8 *tel* (01) 4531005 *fax* (01) 4541688. Biography or memoirs, educational (secondary, university), history, sociology, theology and religion, popular psychology, literature, cookery, current affairs, guidebooks, professional (law, accountancy, tax).

The Goldsmith Press (1972), Newbridge, Co. Kildare *tel* (045) 433613 *fax* (045) 434648. *Directors:* D. Egan, V. Abbott; *secretary:* Bernadette Smyth. Literature, art, Irish interest, poetry.

****Government Supplies Agency,** Publications Division, 4-5 Harcourt Road, Dublin 2 *tel* (01) 6613111 *fax* (01) 4752760. Parliamentary publications.

****Institute of Public Administration** (1957), Vergemount Hall, Clonskeagh, Dublin 6 *tel* (01) 2697011 *fax* (01) 2698644. *Assistant director general and publisher for the Institute:* Jim O'Donnell. Government, economics, politics, law, social policy and administrative history.

*Irish Academic Press Ltd (1974), Kill Lane, Blackrock, Co. Dublin *tel* (01) 2892922 *fax* (01) 2893072. *Directors:* Stewart Cass, Frank Cass, Michael Philip Zaidner. Publishes under the imprints **Irish University Press** and **Irish Academic Press**. Scholarly books especially in 19th and 20th century history and literature.

The Kavanagh Press Ltd (1989), Newbridge, Co. Kildare *tel* (045) 433613 *fax* (045) 434648. *Directors:* Desmond Egan, Vivienne Abbott. Poetry, Irish interest, literary criticism, Irish history, art; cassettes.

*The Lilliput Press Ltd (1984), 4 Rosemount Terrace, Arbour Hill, Dublin 7 *tel/ fax* (01) 6711647. *Managing director:* Antony T. Farrell. General and Irish literature: essays, biography/autobiography, fiction, criticism; Irish history; Irish art; contemporary culture; nature and environment.

Marino Books (1994)—see **The Mercier Press.**

*The Mercier Press (1944), PO Box 5, 5 French Church Street, Cork *tel* (021) 275040 *fax* (021) 274969. *Directors:* G. Eaton (chairman), J.F. Spillane (managing), M.P. Feehan, D.J. Keily, M.L. McNamara, J. O'Donoghue. Irish literature, folklore, history, politics, humour, ballads, education, theology, law.
Marino Books (imprint), 16 Hume Street, Dublin 2 *tel* (01) 6615299 *fax* (01) 6618583. *Publisher:* Jo O'Donoghue. Fiction, children's fiction, current affairs, health, mind and spirit, general non-fiction.

*Oak Tree Press (1991), Merrion Building, Lower Merrion Street, Dublin 2 *tel* (01) 6761600 *fax* (01) 6761644. *Directors:* Brian O'Kane, Rita O'Kane; *general manager:* David Givens. Law, accountancy, business management.

O'Brien Educational (1976), 20 Victoria Road, Rathgar, Dublin 6 *tel* (01) 4923333 *fax* (01) 4922777. *Directors:* Michael O'Brien, Bride Rosney. Humanities, science, environmental studies, history, geography, English, Irish, art, commerce, music, careers, media studies.

*The O'Brien Press Ltd (1974), 20 Victoria Road, Rathgar, Dublin 6 *tel* (01) 4923333 *fax* (01) 4922777. *Directors:* Michael O'Brien, Ide Ni Laoghaire, Ivan O'Brien. Folklore, nature, fiction, architecture, topography, history, general, illustrated books, sport, true crime, anthropology, children's (fiction and non-fiction), biography; tapes for children. Series include *Lucky Tree Books*, *Junior Biography Library*, *Urban Heritage*, *Other World Series* (science fiction/fantasy/horror for juveniles).

On Stream Publications Ltd (1986), Currabaha, Cloghroe, Blarney, Co. Cork *tel/fax* (021) 385798. *Owner:* Rosalind Crowley. Cookery, wine, travel, human interest non-fiction, local history and practical books.

*Poolbeg Press Ltd (1976), 123 Baldoyle Industrial Estate, Baldoyle, Dublin 13 *tel* (01) 8321477 *fax* (01) 8321430. *Directors:* Philip MacDermott (managing), Ivan Kerr, Kieran Devlin. Fiction, public interest, women's interest, history, politics, current affairs, Business Poolbeg, Children's Poolbeg, Beachwood.

Round Hall Sweet & Maxwell, Brehon House, 4 Upper Ormond Quay, Dublin 7 *tel* (01) 8730101 *fax* (01) 8720078. *Managing director:* Bart D. Daly. Law.

Stationery Office—see **Government Supplies Agency.**

*Town House and Country House (1981), Trinity House, Charleston Road, Ranelagh, Dublin 6 *tel* (01) 4972399 *fax* (01) 4970927. *Directors:* Treasa Coady, Jim Coady. General illustrated non-fiction, popular fiction, art, archaeology and biography.

****Veritas Publications,** division of the **Catholic Communications Institute of Ireland, Inc.,** Veritas House, 7/8 Lower Abbey Street, Dublin 1   *tel* (01) 8788177   *fax* (01) 8786507. *UK:* Veritas Book & Video Distribution Ltd, Lower Avenue, Leamington Spa, Warks. CV31 3NP   *tel* (0926) 451 730   *fax* (0926) 451 733. Religion, including social and educational works, and material relating to the media of communication.

****Wolfhound Press** (1974), 68 Mountjoy Square, Dublin 1   *tel* (01) 8740354   *fax* 8720207. *Publisher:* Seamus Cashman; *editor:* Susan Houlden. Literary studies and criticism, fiction, art, biography, history, young readers, children's and teenage fiction, law, gift titles, cookery, general non-fiction.

NEW ZEALAND

*Member of the New Zealand Book Publishers' Association

****Addison Wesley Longman,** Private Bag 102908, North Shore Mail Centre, Glenfield, Auckland 10   *tel* (09) 444-4968   *fax* (09) 444-4957. NZ educational books.

Ashton Scholastic Ltd—see **Scholastic New Zealand Ltd.**

****Auckland University Press** (1966), University of Auckland, Private Bag 92019, Auckland   *tel* (09) 373-7528   *fax* (09) 373-7465. *Director:* Elizabeth Caffin. NZ history, NZ poetry, Maori and Pacific studies, politics, sociology, literary criticism, art history, biography, media studies, women's studies.

****David Bateman Ltd** (1979), Tarndale Grove, Albany Business Park, Bush Road, Albany, Auckland   *postal address* PO Box 100242 North Shore Mail Centre, Auckland 10   *tel* (09) 415-7664   *fax* (09) 415-8892. *Chairman and publisher:* David L. Bateman; *directors:* Janet Bateman, Paul Bateman (joint managing), Paul Parkinson (joint managing). Natural history, gardening, encyclopedias, sport, art, cookery, historical, juvenile, travel, motoring, maritime history, business.

Bush Press Communications Ltd (1979), 4 Bayview Road, Hauraki Corner, Takapuna, Auckland 1309   *postal address* PO Box 33-029, Takapuna, Auckland 1309   *tel/fax* (09) 486-2667. *Governing director and publisher:* Gordon Ell. NZ non-fiction, particularly outdoor, nature, travel, architecture, crafts, Maori, popular history; children's non-fiction.

****Butterworths of New Zealand Ltd,** 203-207 Victoria Street, Wellington   *tel* (04) 385-1479   *fax* (04) 385-1598. *Publishing director:* James Clarke. Law, accountancy.

****The Caxton Press,** 113 Victoria Street, Christchurch, PO Box 25-088   *tel* (03) 366-8516   *fax* (03) 365-7840. *Director:* E.B. Bascand. Fine printers and publishers since 1935 of NZ books of many kinds, including biography, history, natural history, travel, gardening.

****Dunmore Press Ltd** (1970), PO Box 5115, Palmerston North   *tel* (06) 358-7169   *fax* (06) 357-9242. *Directors:* Murray R. Gatenby, Valerie K. Gatenby. Education, history, sociology, business studies.

****Godwit Publishing Ltd** (1994), PO Box 34-683, Birkenhead, Auckland   *tel* (09) 480-5410   *fax* (09) 480-5930. *Publisher:* Jane Connor; *executive director:* Brian Phillips. Art, lifestyle, literature and natural history.

Grantham House Publishing (1984), PO Box 17-256, Wellington 6033   *tel* (04) 476-4625   *fax* (04) 476-3048. *Publisher and chief executive:* Graham C. Stewart; *editorial:* Anna Rogers, Lorraine Olphert. Antiques and collecting, architecture and design, aviation, gardening, history and antiquarian, illustrated and fine editions, military and war, nautical, transport, railways, tramways.

*HarperCollins Publishers (New Zealand) Ltd, PO Box 1, Auckland   *tel* (09) 443-9400   *fax* (09) 443-9403. Publishers of general literature, teen fiction, non-fiction, reference books, trade paperbacks.

*Hodder Moa Beckett Publishers Ltd, PO Box 100-749, North Shore Mail Centre, Auckland 1330   *tel* (09) 478-1000   *fax* (09) 478-1010. *Managing director:* Neil Aston; *publishing director:* John Blackwell. Sport, gardening, cooking, travel, atlases, general, fiction, children's.

Mallinson Rendel Publishers Ltd (1980), 7 Grass Street, PO Box 9409, Wellington   *tel* (04) 385-7340   *fax* (04) 385-4235. *Directors:* Ann Mallinson, David Rendel. Children's, general NZ books, aviation.

*Nelson Price Milburn Ltd, PO Box 38-945, Wellington Mail Centre, Wellington   *located at* 1 Te Puni Street, Petone   *tel* (04) 568-7179   *fax* (04) 568-2115. Children's fiction, primary school texts, especially school readers and maths, secondary educational.

New Zealand Council for Educational Research (1933), Box 3237, Education House, 178-182 Willis Street, Wellington 1   *tel* (04) 384-7939   *fax* (04) 384-7933. *Director:* Anne Meade; *publisher:* Peter Ridder. Education, including educational policy and institutions, vocational education and adult learning, early childhood education, higher education, educational achievement tests, Maori language and education, curriculum and assessment, etc.

*Oxford University Press, PO Box 11-149, Ellerslie, Auckland 5   *tel* (09) 525-8020   *fax* (09) 525-1072. *NZ academic and trade publisher:* Linda Cassells.

*Random House New Zealand Ltd (1977), Private Bag 102950, North Shore Mail Centre, Auckland 10   *tel* (09) 444-7197   *fax* (09) 444-7524. *Managing director:* J. Rogers. Fiction, general non-fiction, gardening, business, health.

*Reed Publishing (New Zealand) Ltd, incorporating Reed Consumer Books and Heinemann Education, 39 Rawene Road, Private Bag 34901, Birkenhead, Auckland 10   *tel* (09) 480-4950   *fax* (09) 480-4999. *Chairman:* Sandy Grant; *managing director:* Alan Smith. NZ literature, specialist and general titles, primary, secondary and tertiary textbooks. *Imprints:* George Philip, Conran Octopus, Mitchell Beazley, Reed Publishing Group Australia Pty Ltd, Heinemann Young Books, Secker & Warburg, Hamlyn, Bounty, Dean, Buzz, Minerva, Mandarin, Cedar, Methuen Drama, Brimax, Budget Books, Octopus Publishing Group, Ginn & Company, Heinemann Education Books, Rigby Heinemann (Australia), Rigby (USA), Heinemann Education Books Inc. (USA).

*Scholastic New Zealand Ltd (1962), 21 Lady Ruby Drive, East Tamaki, Auckland   *postal address* Private Bag 94407, Greenmount, Auckland   *tel* (09) 274-8112   *fax* (09) 274-8114. *Managing director and publisher:* Graham Beattie; *finance director and operations manager:* David Peagram. Children's books.

*Shortland Publications Ltd (1984), 360 Dominion Road, Auckland   *tel* (09) 638-7128   *fax* (09) 638-6422. *Managing director:* Avelyn Davidson. Children's books: reading material (ages 5-12), science/non-fiction (ages 5-14).

*University of Otago Press (1958), University of Otago, PO Box 56, Dunedin   *tel/fax* (03) 479-8807   *fax* (03) 479-8385. *Managing editor:* Wendy Harrex. Student texts and scholarly works in all disciplines and general books, including

Maori and women's studies, natural history and environmental studies, health and fiction.

*Victoria University Press** (1974), Victoria University of Wellington, PO Box 600, Wellington *tel* (04) 496-6580 *fax* (04) 496-6581. *Editor:* Fergus Barrowman. Academic, scholarly books on NZ history, sociology, political history, architecture, economics, law, zoology, biology; also fiction, plays, poetry.

Viking Sevenseas Ltd, 23b Ihakara Street, Paraparaumu *tel* (04) 297-1990 *telegraphic address* Vikseven *fax* (04) 297-1990. *Managing director:* M.B. Riley. Factual books on New Zealand only.

SOUTH AFRICA

*Member of the South African Publishers' Association

Ashanti Publishing (Pty) Ltd (1987)—acquired by **William Waterman Publications.**

*Jonathan Ball Publishers (Pty) Ltd,** 10-14 Watkins Street, Denver Ext. 4, Johannesburg *postal address* PO Box 33977, Jeppestown 2043 *tel* (011) 622 2900 *fax* (011) 622 3553.
Ad Donker (division). Africana, literature, history, academic.
Jonathan Ball/HarperCollins (division). General publications, reference books, business, history, politics.
Delta Books (division). General non-fiction.

Cambridge University Press, 1 The Moorings, Portswood Ridge, Victoria & Alfred Waterfront, Cape Town 8001 *tel* (021) 419-8414. *Director:* Tony Seddon.

Ad Donker (Pty) Ltd (1973)—see **Jonathan Ball Publishers (Pty) Ltd.**

HarperCollins Publishers (SA) (Pty) Ltd—see **Jonathan Ball Publishers (Pty) Ltd.**

*Juta & Company Ltd** (1853), PO Box 14373, Kenwyn 7790 *tel* (021) 797-5101 *fax* (021) 762-7424. Educational, academic, professional and legal publishers.

Lovedale Press, Private Bag X1346, PO Lovedale 5702, Alice Ciskei 5700 *tel* (0404) 31-135 *fax* (0404) 31-871. Educational, religious and general book publications for African market.

*Maskew Miller Longman (Pty) Ltd,** Howard Drive, Pinelands 7405 *postal address* PO Box 396, Cape Town 8000 *tel* (021) 531-7750 *telex* 526053 *fax* (021) 531-4049. Educational and general publishers.

*Oxford University Press (Southern African Branch),** 5th Floor, Harrington House, 37 Barrack Street, Cape Town 8001 *postal address* PO Box 1141, Cape Town 8000 *tel* (021) 457-266 *fax* (021) 457-265. *Managing director:* Kate McCallum.

*David Philip Publishers (Pty) Ltd** (1971), PO Box 23408, Claremont 7735, Western Cape *tel* (21) 644-136 *fax* (21) 643-358. *Managing directors:* David Philip, Marie Philip; *directors:* Russell Martin, Bridget Impey. Academic, history, social sciences, politics, theology, biography, belles-lettres, reference books, fiction, educational, children's books.

*Ravan Press (Pty) Ltd** (1972), 6th Floor, Randhill, 104 Bordeaux Drive, Randburg *postal address* PO Box 145, Randburg 2125 *tel* (011) 789-7636 *fax* (011) 789-7653. *Managing director:* Glenn Moss. South African studies: history, politics, social studies; fiction, literature, children's, educational.

*Shuter and Shooter (Pty) Ltd (1925), 230 Church Street and 199 Pietermaritz Street, Pietermaritzburg 3201, Natal   *postal address* PO Box 109, Pietermaritzburg 3200   *tel* (0331) 946-830/948-881   *telegraphic address* Shushoo   *fax* (0331) 943-096/427-419. *Publishing director:* D.F. Ryder. Primary and secondary educational, science, biology, history, maths, geography, English, Afrikaans, biblical studies, music, teacher training, agriculture, accounting, school readiness, dictionaries, African languages.

*Southern Book Publishers (Pty) Ltd, PO Box 3103, Halfway House, Gauteng 1685   *tel* (011) 315-3633/7   *fax* (011) 315-3810. Publishers of general non-fiction books, especially natural history, as well as those of South African interest.

*Struik Publishers (Pty) Ltd, PO Box 1144, Cape Town 8000. Division of The Struik Publishing Group (Pty) Ltd   *tel* (021) 462-4360   *fax* (021) 461-9378/462-4379. *Managing director:* Dick Wilkins. General illustrated non-fiction.

*Struik Winchester Publishers, PO Box 1144, Cape Town 8000. Division of Struik Publishers   *tel* (021) 455-573   *fax* (021) 462-4379/461-9378. *Managing director:* Dick Wilkins. Natural history, cultural history, Africana.

*J.L. Van Schaik Publishers (1914), PO Box 12681, Hatfield, Pretoria 0028   *tel* (012) 342-2765   *fax* (012) 433-563. Publishers of books in English, Afrikaans and African languages. Specialists in non-fiction, dictionaries, textbooks and fiction in eleven official languages.

*William Waterman Publications Pty Ltd (incorporating Ashanti Publishing, Justified Press, Justified Press for Juniors), PO Box 5091, Rivonia 2128   *tel* (011) 882-1408   *fax* (011) 882-1559. *Directors:* Murray J. Bolton, Nicholas W. Combrinck (managing). General non-fiction, military history, literature, poetry, children's educational.

*Witwatersrand University Press, PO Wits, 2050   *tel* (011) 484-5910   *fax* (011) 484-5971   *e-mail* wup@iafrica.com

UNITED STATES OF AMERICA

*Member of the Association of American Publishers, Inc.

Abbeville Press (1977), 488 Madison Avenue, 23rd Floor, New York, NY 10022   *tel* 212-888-1969   *fax* 212-644-5085. *Publisher and president:* Robert Abrams. Art and illustrated books.

Abingdon Press, PO Box 801, Nashville, TN 37202-0801   *tel* 615-749-6404   *fax* 615-749-6512. Editorial offices for academic books: 2495 Lawrenceville Highway, Decatur, GA 30033-3240   *tel* 404-636-6001   *fax* 404-636-5894. *Editorial director:* Neil M. Alexander. General interest, professional, academic and reference – primarily directed to the religious market.

Academy Chicago Publishers (1975), 363 West Erie Street, Chicago, IL 60610   *tel* 312-751-7300   *fax* 312-751-7306. *Directors:* Anita Miller, Jordan Miller. Fiction, mystery, biography, travel, books of interest to women; quality reprints.

And/Or Books (1974), PO Box 2246, Berkeley, CA 94702   *tel* 510-548-2124. Imprint of **Ronin Publishing, Inc.** Health and nutrition, life styles. No unsolicited work.

Andrews & McMeel, 4900 Main Street, Kansas City, MO 64112   *tel* 816-932-6700   *fax* 816-932-6706. *Vice-president and editorial director:* Donna Martin. General trade publishing, with emphasis on humour and consumer reference.

Arcade Publishing, 141 Fifth Avenue, New York, NY 10010 *tel* 212-475-2633 *fax* 212-353-8148. *President and publisher:* Richard Seaver; *associate publisher and marketing director:* Jeannette Seaver; *general manager:* Cal Barksdale. General, including adult hard cover and paperbacks.

Atlantic Monthly Press—see **Grove/Atlantic, Inc.**

*Avon Books (1941), The Hearst Corporation, 1350 Avenue of the Americas, New York, NY 10019 *tel* 212-261-6800 *fax* 212-261-6895. *Senior vp and publisher:* Lou Aronica. All subjects, fiction and non-fiction.

Walter H. Baker Company (1845), 100 Chauncy Street, Boston, MA 02111 *tel* 617-482-1280 *fax* 617-482-7613. *President:* Charles Van Nostrand; *editor:* John B. Welch. Plays and books on the theatre. Also agents for plays. *UK agents:* Samuel French Ltd, 52 Fitzroy Street, London W1P 6JR.

*Bantam Doubleday Dell Publishing Group Inc., 1540 Broadway, New York, NY 10036 *tel* 212-354-6500 *telex* 7608009 *fax* 212-782-9597. *Chairman, president and ceo:* Jack Hoeft. Fiction, classics, biography, health, business, general non-fiction, social sciences, religion, sports, science, audio tapes.

Barron's Educational Series, Inc. (1941), 250 Wireless Boulevard, Hauppage, NY 11788 *tel* 516-434-3311 *fax* 516-434-3723. *President:* Manuel H. Barron; *executive vice president:* Ellen Sibley. Test preparation, juvenile, cookbooks, crafts, business, pets, gardening.

*Beacon Press, 25 Beacon Street, Boston, MA 02108 *tel* 617-742-2110 *fax* 617-723-3097. *Director:* Helene Atwan. General non-fiction in fields of religion, ethics, philosophy, current affairs, gender studies, environmental concerns, African-American studies, anthropology and women's studies, nature.

Bergh Publishing, Inc. (1983), 20 East 53rd Street, Suite 7E, New York, NY 10022 *tel* 212-593-1040 *fax* 212-593-4638. *Chairman and ceo:* Sven-Erik Bergh MA(Oxon). Quality popular non-fiction, especially yearbooks, culinary and cook books. Query first with sase.

*R.R. Bowker, 121 Chanlon Road, New Providence, NJ 07974 *tel* 908-464-6800 *fax* 908-464-3553. *President:* Ira T. Siegel. A Reed Reference Publishing company. Bibliographies and reference tools for the book trade and literary and library worlds, available in hardcopy, on microfiche, on-line and CD-ROM. Reference books for music, art, business, computer industry, cable industry and information industry.

Boyds Mills Press (1990), 815 Church Street, Honesdale, PA 18431 *tel* 717-253-1080 *fax* 717-253-0179. *Publisher:* Kent Brown Jr; *president:* Clay Winters; *editorial director:* Larry Rosler; *art director:* Tim Gillner. Fiction and non-fiction trade books for children.

Brassey's, Inc. (1984), 1313 Dolley Madison Boulevard, Suite 401, McLean, VA 22101 *tel* 703-442-4535. *Publisher:* Franklin D. Margiotta PhD. Foreign policy, defence, national and international affairs, military history, intelligence, biography, sports.

George Braziller Inc. (1954), 60 Madison Avenue, New York, NY 10010 *tel* 212-889-0909 *fax* 212-689-5405. *Publisher:* George Braziller. Art, architecture, history, biography, fiction, poetry, science.

*Cambridge University Press (North American branch), 40 West 20th Street, New York, NY 10011 *tel* 212-924-3900 *fax* 212-691-3239. *Director:* Barbara Colson.

Candlewick Press (1991), 2067 Massachusetts Avenue, Cambridge, MA 02140 *tel* 617-661-3330 *fax* 617-661-0565. Children's books – 6 months to

14 years: picture books, novels, non-fiction, novelty books. We are currently unable to accept submissions.

Capra Press (1969), PO Box 2068, Santa Barbara, CA 93120 *tel* 805-966-4590 *fax* 805-965-8020. *Publisher:* Noel Young. Fiction, natural history, animals.

Carroll & Graf Publishers, Inc. (1983), 260 Fifth Avenue, New York, NY 10001 *tel* 212-889-8772. *President:* Herman Graf; *publisher:* Kent Carroll; *subrights:* Jennifer Prior. Mystery and science fiction, popular fiction, history, biography, literature, business, sports.

Chilton Book Company, Trade Division, 1 Chilton Way, Radnor, PA 19089-0230 *tel* 610-964-4100 *fax* 610-964-2926. *General manager:* Christopher J. Kuppig; *executive editor:* Jeff Day; *acquisitions editor:* Mary Green. Antiques and collectibles, sewing and crafts, consumer automotive, professional and technical.

Chronicle Books, 275 Fifth Street, San Francisco, CA 94103; from 1 Dec 97: 85 Second Street, San Francisco, CA 94105 *tel* 415-777-7240 *fax* 415-777-2289 *WWW* www.chronbooks.com *Publisher:* Jack Jensen; *associates:* Christine Carswell, Caroline Herter, Nion McEvoy, Victoria Rock. Cooking, art, fiction, general, children's, gift, new media, gardening, regional, nature.

Coffee House Press (1984), 27 N 4th Street, Suite 400, Minneapolis, MN 55401 *tel* 612-338-0125 *fax* 612-338-4004. *Publisher:* Allan Kornblum. Literary fiction and poetry.

***Columbia University Press**, 562 West 113th Street, New York, NY 10025 *tel* 212-666-1000 *fax* 212-316-3100. *Editor-in-chief:* Kate Wittenberg; *UK:* 1 Oldlands Way, Bognor Regis, West Sussex PO22 9SA *tel* (0243) 842165 *fax* (0243) 842167. General reference works in print and electronic formats, translations and serious non-fiction of more general interest.

Concordia Publishing House (1869), 3558 S Jefferson Avenue, St Louis, MO 63118 *tel* 314-268-1000 *fax* 314-268-1329. *Executive vp, editorial:* Dr Earl Gaulke. Religious books, Lutheran perspective. Few freelance MSS accepted; query first.

Contemporary Books Inc., 180 North Stetson, Suite 1200, Chicago, IL 60601 *tel* 312-540-4500 *fax* 312-540-4657. *Vice president and editorial director:* Nancy Crossman; *publisher:* Christine Albritton. Non-fiction.

***The Continuum Publishing Company, Inc.** (1980), 370 Lexington Avenue, New York, NY 10017-6503 *tel* 212-953-5858 *fax* 212-953-5944. *Chairman and publisher:* Werner Mark Linz. General non-fiction, education, literature, psychology, politics, sociology, literary criticism, religious studies.

***Cornell University Press** (including **ILR Press** and **Comstock Publishing Associates**) (1869), Sage House, 512 East State Street, Ithaca, NY 14850 *tel* 607-277-2338 *fax* 607-277-2374. *Director:* John G. Ackerman. Scholarly books.

Council Oak Books (1984), 1350 East 15th Street, Tulsa, OK 74120-5801 *tel* 918-587-6454 *fax* 918-583-4995. *Publisher and president:* Michael Hightower; *publishers/vice presidents:* Sally Dennison PhD, Paulette Millichap. Non-fiction: native American, multicultural, life skills, life accounts, Earth awareness, meditation.

The Countryman Press, Inc. (1973), PO Box 175, Lincoln Corners, Rte 4W, Woodstock, VT 05091 *tel* 802-457-1049 *fax* 802-457-3250. *Publisher:* Carl Taylor; *editor-in-chief:* Helen Whybrow. Mysteries, outdoor recreation guides for anglers, hikers, cyclists, anglers, canoeists and skiers, US travel guides, New England non-fiction, how-to books, country living books, books on nature and the environment, classic reprints and general non-fiction. *No* unsolicited MSS.

Crown Publishing Group, 201 East 50th Street, New York, NY 10022 *tel* 212-572-2100 *fax* 212-940-7400. *President and publisher:* Michelle Sidrane. General fiction, non-fiction, illustrated books.

Devin-Adair Publishers, Inc. (1911), 6 North Water Street, Greenwich, CT 06830 *tel* 203-531-7755. Conservative politics, health and ecology, Irish topics, gardening and travel, homeopathy and holistic health books.

*****Doubleday**—see **Bantam Doubleday Dell Publishing Group Inc.**

Dover Publications, Inc. (1941), 31 E 2nd Street, Mineola, NY 11501 *tel* 516-294-7000 *fax* 516-742-6953. *Vp, editorial:* Stanley Appelbaum. Art, architecture, antiques, crafts, juvenile, food, history, folklore, literary classics, mystery, language, music, math and science, nature, design and ready-to-use art.

Dryden Press, City Center Tower II, 301 Commerce Street, Suite 3700, Fort Worth, TX 76102 *tel* 817-334-7500 *fax* 817-334-0878. *Publisher:* Elizabeth Widdicombe. College textbooks.

*****Dutton/Signet,** division of Penguin USA, 375 Hudson Street, New York, NY 10014 *tel* 212-366-2000 *fax* 212-366-2666. General publishers. General non-fiction, including biographies, adventure, history, travel; fiction, mysteries, juveniles, quality paperbacks.

*****Dutton Children's Books,** 375 Hudson Street, 3rd Floor, New York, NY 10014 *tel* 212-366-2600 *fax* 212-366-2011. *President and publisher:* Christopher Franceschelli; *editor in chief:* Lucia Monfried; *executive editor:* Donna Brooks; *director of operations:* Karen Lotz. Picture books, young adult novels, non-fiction photographic books.

Faber and Faber, Inc. (1976), 53 Shore Road, Winchester, MA 01890 *tel* 617-721-1427 *fax* 617-729-2783. *Publisher:* Tom Kelleher; *senior editors:* Valerie J. Cimino, Dan Weaver. Adult non-fiction: film, popular music, ethnic and cultural works, travelogues, anthologies, literary novels, popular science, women's issues, gay and lesbian fiction and non-fiction.

Facts On File Inc. (1940), 11 Penn Plaza, 15th Floor, New York, NY 10001-2006 *tel* 212-967 8800 *fax* 212-967 9196. *President:* Mark McDonnell; *executive vp and publisher:* Beverley Balaz. General reference books and services for colleges, libraries, schools and general public.

Farrar, Straus & Giroux Inc., 19 Union Square West, New York, NY 10003 *tel* 212-741-6900 *cables* Farrarcomp *fax* 212-633-9385. *Executive vp and editor-in-chief:* Jonathan Galassi. General publishers.

Firebrand Books (1986), 141 The Commons, Ithaca, NY 14850 *tel* 607-272-0000. *Editor and publisher:* Nancy K. Bereano. Feminist and lesbian fiction and non-fiction.

Four Walls Eight Windows (1987), 39 West 14th Street, Room 503, New York, NY 10011 *tel* 212-206-8965 *fax* 212-206-8799. *Publisher:* John Oakes. Fiction, graphic works, novels, memoirs, art, African-American studies, current affairs, biography, environment, health. *No* unsolicited submissions accepted.

Samuel French Inc., 45 West 25th Street, New York, NY 10010 *tel* 212-206-8990 *fax* 212-206-1429. Play publishers and authors' representatives (dramatic).

David R. Godine, Publisher Inc. (1970), PO Box 9103, Lincoln, MA 01773   *tel* 617-259-0700   *fax* 617-259-9198. *President:* David R. Godine; *editorial director:* Mark Polizzotti. Fiction, photography, poetry, art, biography, children's, essays, history, typography, architecture, nature and gardening, music, cooking, words and writing, mystery and ghost stories.

Greenwillow Books, division of **William Morrow & Co., Inc.,** 1350 Avenue of the Americas, New York, NY 10019   *tel* 212-261-6500   *fax* 212-261-6619. *Senior vice-president and editor-in-chief:* Susan Hirschman. Children's book.

Grosset & Dunlap, Inc., 200 Madison Avenue, New York, NY 10016   *tel* 212-951-8700. *Vp and publisher:* Jane O'Connor. Children's mass market: easy-to-reads, series books, activity books, board books.

Grove/Atlantic, Inc., 841 Broadway, New York, NY 10003-4793   *tel* 212-614-7850   *fax* 212-614-7886. *Publisher:* Morgan Entrekin. MSS of permanent interest, fiction, biography, autobiography, history, current affairs, social science, belles-lettres, natural history. *Imprints:* **Atlantic Monthly Press, Grove Press.**

Grove Press—see **Grove/Atlantic, Inc.**

*****Harcourt Brace & Company,** 525 B Street, Suite 1900, San Diego, CA 92101   *tel* 619-231-6616   *fax* 619-699-6320. *President:* Rubin Pfeffer; *managing editor:* Marianna Lee; 15 East 26th Street, New York, NY 10010. General publishers. Fiction, history, biography, etc.; college and school textbooks of all kinds; children's; technical; reference; religious; dictionaries.

*****HarperCollins Publishers** (1817), 10 East 53rd Street, New York, NY 10022   *tel* 212-207-7000   *cables* Harpsam, NY   *telex* 12-5741(dom.), 6-2501(intl). *President and chief executive officer:* Anthea Disney. HarperCollins San Francisco: 1160 Battery Street, San Francisco, CA 94111   *tel* 415-477-4400   *fax* 415-477-4444. *London:* HarperCollins Publishers, 77-85 Fulham Palace Road, Hammersmith, London W6 8JB. Fiction, history, biography, poetry, science, travel, juvenile, educational, business, technical and religious. *No* unsolicited material; all submissions must come through a literary agent.

*****Harvard University Press,** 79 Garden Street, Cambridge, MA 02138-1499   *tel* 617-495 2600   *fax* 617-495-5898. *Director:* William P. Sisler; *editor-in-chief and assistant director:* Aida D. Donald. History, philosophy, literary criticism, politics, economics, sociology, music, science, classics, social sciences.

Hastings House, 141 Halstead Avenue, Mamaroneck, NY 10543   *tel* 914-835-4005   *fax* 914-835-1037. *Publisher:* Hy Steirman; *director of operations:* Richard Cadier. Non-fiction, general, consumer, travel, cooking, controversy and how-to.

*****D.C. Heath and Co.,** Raytheon Co., 125 Spring Street, Lexington, MA 02173   *tel* 617-860-1357/1340   *fax* 617-860-1260/1508. *International sales director:* Vince Duggan. Elementary, secondary, college textbooks.

Hill & Wang (1956), division of **Farrar, Straus & Giroux Inc.,** 19 Union Square West, New York, NY 10003   *tel* 212-741-6900   *fax* 212-633-9385. *Publisher:* Elisabeth Sifton; *senior editor:* Arthur W. Wang. General non-fiction, history, drama.

Hippocrene Books, Inc. (1971), 171 Madison Avenue, New York, NY 10016   *tel* 212-685-4371   *fax* 212-779-9338. *President and editorial director:* George Blagowidow; *publisher and director of marketing:* Jacek Galazka. Foreign language books, foreign language dictionaries, travel, military history, Polonia, general trade.

Holiday House (1935), 425 Madison Avenue, New York, NY 10017 *tel* 212-688-0085 *fax* 212-421-6134. *President:* John Briggs; *vp and editor-in-chief:* Regina Griffin. General children's books.

Holmes & Meier Publishers Inc. (1969), 160 Broadway, New York, NY 10038 *tel* 212-374-0100 *fax* 212-374-1313. *Executive editor:* Katharine Turok. History, biography, political science, art, costume, Jewish studies, international affairs, Latin American studies, sociology, theatre (history), women's studies, fiction in translation, Africana publishing.

*****Henry Holt and Company, Inc.** (1866), 115 West 18th Street, New York, NY 10011 *tel* 212-886-9200 *fax* 212-633-0748. *Associate publisher, editor-in-chief adult books:* William Strachan; *associate publisher, editor-in-chief books for young readers:* Marjorie Cuyler; *associate publisher, editorial director reference books:* Ken Wright; *publisher, Twenty-First Century Books:* Jeanne Vestal; *editorial director MIS Press and M&T Books:* Paul Farrell; *associate publisher, editorial director Metropolitan Books:* Sara Bershtel; *associate publisher, editorial director Owl Books:* Gregory Hamlin. History, biography, nature, science, self-help, novels, mysteries; books for young readers; trade paperback line, computer books.

*****Houghton Mifflin Company** (1832), 222 Berkeley Street, Boston, MA 02116 *tel* 617-351-5000 *telex* 4430255 HMHQ UI. *Executive vp and publisher, trade and reference division:* Joseph A. Kanon. Fiction, biography, history, works of general interest of all kinds, both adult and juvenile; also school and college textbooks in all departments, and standardised tests. Best length: 75,000-180,000 words; juveniles, any reasonable length.

Indiana University Press (1950), 601 North Morton Street, Bloomington, IN 47404-3797 *tel* 812-855-4203 *fax* 812-855-7931. *Director:* John Gallman. African studies, Russian and East European studies, semiotics, literary criticism, music, history, women's studies, Jewish studies, African-American studies, film, folklore, philosophy, medical ethics, archaeology, anthropology.

*****The Johns Hopkins University Press** (1878), 2715 North Charles Street, Baltimore, MD 21218-4319 *tel* 410-516-6971 *fax* 410-516-6968. *Director:* Dr Willis Regier. History, literary criticism, classics, politics, economic development, environmental studies, biology, medical genetics, consumer health.

Keats Publishing Inc. (1971), 27 Pine Street, PO Box 876, New Canaan, CT 06840 *tel* 203-966-8721. *President and publisher:* Norman Goldfind. Natural health, nutrition and medical books.

Alfred A. Knopf Inc. (1915), subsidiary of **Random House, Inc.,** 201 East 50th Street, New York, NY 10022 *tel* 212-751-2600 *telegraphic address* Knopf, New York *fax* 212-572-2593 *WWW* http://www.randomhouse.com General literature, fiction, belles-lettres, sociology, politics, history, nature, science, etc.

Lippincott-Raven Publishers (1792), a Wolters Kluwer company, 227 East Washington Square, Philadelphia, PA 19106 *tel* 215-238-4200 *cables* Lippcot, Phila. *President and ceo:* Mary M. Rogers; *president:* J.W. Lippincott, III; *publishers:* Kathey Alexander (medical), Donna Hilton (nursing). Medical and nursing books and journals.

*****Little, Brown & Company,** 34 Beacon Street, Boston, MA 02108 *tel* 617-227-0730 *cables* Brownlit, Boston. General literature, especially fiction, non-fiction, biography, history, trade paperbacks, books for boys and girls, law, medical books. Art and photography books under the **Bulfinch Press/New York Graphic Society Books** imprint.

Lothrop, Lee & Shepard Books (1859), division of **William Morrow & Co., Inc.,** 1350 Avenue of the Americas, New York, NY 10019 *tel* 212-261-6641 *fax* 212-261-6648. *Vice-president/editor-in-chief:* Susan Pearson. Children's books only.

Lyons & Burford, Publishers, 31 West 21st Street, New York, NY 10010 *tel* 212-620-9580 *fax* 212-929-1836. *Publishers:* Nick Lyons, Peter Burford. Outdoor sport, natural history, general sports, art.

*McGraw-Hill Co., 1221 Avenue of the Americas, New York, NY 10020 *tel* 212-512-2000. *College books:* Sieb Adams; *professional and reference books:* Theodore Nardin. Professional and reference: engineering, scientific, business, architecture, encyclopedias; college textbooks; high school and vocational textbooks: business, secretarial, career; trade books; microcomputer software; training courses for industry.

*Macmillan Publishing USA—reference imprint of **Simon & Schuster.**

McPherson & Company (1974), PO Box 1126, 148 Smith Avenue, Kingston, NY 12401 *tel/fax* 914-331-5807. *Publisher:* Bruce R. McPherson. Literary fiction; non-fiction: art criticism, writings by artists, filmmaking, etc; occasional general titles (e.g. anthropology). No poetry. No unsolicited MSS; query first.

Mercury House (1985), 785 Market Street, Suite 1500, San Francisco, CA 94103 *tel* 415-974-0729 *fax* 415-974-0832. *Executive editor:* Thomas Christensen. Fiction; non-fiction: biography/memoirs, contemporary issues, translations, nature/environment, literary travel, women's issues, philosophy and personal growth. Material only accepted through agents.

Milkweed Editions (1979), 430 First Avenue North, Suite 400, Minneapolis, MN 55401 *tel* 612-332-3192 *fax* 612-332-6248. *Publisher and editor:* Emilie Buchwald. Fiction, poetry, essays, literature, children's novels and biographies (ages 8-14).

*The MIT Press (1961), 55 Hayward Street, Cambridge, MA 02142 *tel* 617-253-5646 *fax* 617-258-6779. *Director:* Frank Urbanowski; *editor-in-chief:* Laurence Cohen. Architecture, art and design, cognitive sciences, neuroscience, linguistics, computer science and artificial intelligence, economics, philosophy, environment and ecology, natural history.

Morehouse Publishing Co., PO Box 1321, Harrisburg, PA 17105 *tel* 717-541-8130 *fax* 717-541-8128. *President:* Kenneth Quigley; *Publisher:* E. Allen Kelley. Religious books, religious education, texts, seminary texts, children's books.

Morrow Jr. Books, division of **William Morrow & Co., Inc.,** 1350 Avenue of the Americas, New York, NY 10019 *tel* 212-261-6500 *fax* 212-261-6689. *Vp/editor-in-chief:* David Reuther. Children's books only. *No* unsolicited material accepted.

William Morrow & Co., Inc., 1350 Avenue of the Americas, New York, NY 10019 *tel* 212-261-6500 *fax* 212-261-6595. *Senior vice-president/editor-in-chief:* William Schwalbe. General literature, fiction and juveniles. *Imprints:* Greenwillow Books, Lothrop, Lee & Shepard, Morrow Jr Books, Tambourine Books, Mulberry/Beech Tree/Tupelo.

The Naiad Press, Inc. (1973), PO Box 10543, Tallahassee, FL 32302 *tel* 904-539-5965 *fax* 904-539-9731. *Ceo:* Barbara Grier. Lesbian fiction; non-fiction: bibliographies, biographies, essays.

*Thomas Nelson, Inc. (1978), Nelson Place at Elm Hill Pike, PO Box 141000, Nashville, TN 37214-1000 *tel* 615-889-9000 *fax* 615-391-5225. *President of* *publishing:* Byron Williamson. Bibles, religious, non-fiction and fiction general trade, stationery gift items.

W.W. Norton & Company, Inc., 500 Fifth Avenue, New York, NY 10110 *tel* 212-354-5500 *fax* 212-869-0856. General fiction and non-fiction, music, boating, psychiatry, economics, family therapy, social work, reprints, college texts, science.

Orchard Books (1987), 95 Madison Avenue, New York, NY 10016 *tel* 212-951-2600 *fax* 212-213-6435. *President and publisher:* Neal Porter. Books for children and young adults; picture books, fiction and photo essays.

Ottenheimer Publishers Inc. (1890), 10 Church Lane, Baltimore, MD 21208 *tel* 410-484-2100 *fax* 410-486-8301. *Directors:* Allan T. Hirsh, Jr, Allan T. Hirsh, III. Juvenile and adult non-fiction, reference.

*The Overlook Press, 149 Wooster Street, 4th Floor, New York, NY 10012 *tel* 212-477-7162 *fax* 212-477-7525. *Editorial director:* Tracy Carns. Non-fiction, fiction, children's books.

*Oxford University Press, Inc., 198 Madison Avenue, New York, NY 10016 *tel* 212-726-6000 *fax* 212-726-6455. Scholarly, professional, reference, bibles, college textbooks, religion, medicals, music.

*Pantheon Books, division of **Random House, Inc.,** 201 East 50th Street, New York, NY 10022 *tel* 212-572-2564 *fax* 212-572-6030. Fiction, mysteries, belles-lettres, translations, philosophy, history and art, sociology, psychology, juvenile.

*Pelican Publishing Company (1926), PO Box 3110, Gretna, LA 70054 *tel* 504-368-1175 *fax* 504-368-1195. *Publisher and president:* Milburn Calhoun. Art and architecture, cookbooks, travel, music, business, children's.

*Penguin USA, 375 Hudson Street, New York, NY 10014 *tel* 212-366-2000 *fax* 212-366-2666. General books, fiction, non-fiction, biography, sociology, poetry, art, travel, children's books.

*Penn State Press (1956), 820 North University Drive, University Park, PA 16802 *tel* 814-865-1327 *fax* 814-863-1408 *WWW* 56t3@psu.edu *Senior editor, humanities:* Philip Winsor; *editor, history and social science:* Peter Potter. Art history, literary criticism, religious studies, philosophy, political science, sociology, history, Russian and East European studies, Latin American studies and medieval studies.

The Permanent Press and Second Chance Press (1978), RD 2, Noyac Road, Sag Harbor, NY 11963 *tel* 516-725-1101. *Directors:* Martin Shepard, Judith Shepard. Quality fiction.

Praeger Publishers, Greenwood Publishing Group, Inc., 88 Post Road West, Westport, CT 06881 *tel* 203-226-3571 *fax* 203-222-1502. *Editor-in-chief:* James R. Dunton. Non-fiction on international relations, social sciences, economics, reference, contemporary issues, urban affairs, psychology, education.

*Prentice Hall—imprint of **Simon & Schuster.**

Price Stern Sloan (1963), 11835 Olympic Boulevard, Los Angeles, CA 90064 *tel* 310-477-6100 *fax* 310-445-3933. *Publisher:* Tanni Tytel. Children's books: pop-ups, novelty/lift-flaps, activity books, board books.

The Putnam Berkley Group Inc., 200 Madison Avenue, New York, NY 10016 *tel* 212-951-8400. All types of literature; history, economics, political science, natural science, and standard literature; fiction; children's books.

Rand McNally, PO Box 7600, Chicago, IL 60680 *tel* 708-392-8100. *Chairman and ceo:* Andrew McNally IV; *executive editor:* Jon M. Leverenz. Maps, guides, atlases, educational publications, globes and children's geographical titles and atlases.

*Random House, Inc., 201 East 50th Street, New York, NY 10022 *tel* 212-751-2600. General publishers.

Rawson Associates, 1230 Avenue of the Americas, New York, NY 10020 *tel* 212-632-4941 *fax* 212-632-4918. *Publisher:* Eleanor S. Rawson. Adult nonfiction of wide general interest.

Rizzoli International Publications, Inc. (1976), 300 Park Avenue South, New York, NY 10010 *tel* 212-387-3400 *fax* 212-387-3535/3636. *President and ceo:* Judith R. Joseph. Art, architecture, photography, fashion, gardening, design, gift books, cookbooks; children's books.

Rodale Press, Inc. (1930), 33 East Minor Street, Emmaus, PA 18098 *tel* 610-967-5171 *fax* 610-967-8961. *President, book division:* Pat Corpora; *editor-in-chief, book division:* Bill Gottlieb. Health, women's health, men's health, fitness, gardening, woodworking, do-it-yourself, quilting, crafts, healthy cooking, psychological self-help.

Ronin Publishing Inc., Box 1035, Berkeley, CA 94701 *tel* 510-540 6278 *fax* 510-548-7326 *e-mail* roninpub@aol.com New Age business, controlled substances, visionary, underground comix. Preliminary letter essential; no unsolicited MSS or artwork.

Routledge, Inc., 29 West 35th Street, New York, NY 10001 *tel* 212-244-3336 *telegraphic address* Algernon, New York *telex* 6801368 *fax* 212-563-2269. *Directors:* William P. Germano (editorial). Literary criticism, history, philosophy, psychology and psychiatry, politics, women's studies, education, anthropology, religion, lesbian and gay studies, classical studies.

Rutledge Hill Press (1982), 211 Seventh Avenue North, Nashville, TN 37219 *tel* 615-244-2700 *fax* 615-244-2978. *President:* Lawrence M. Stone; *editorial director:* Charla Honea. Regional books, cookbooks, books on quilts, gift books.

*St Martin's Press, Inc., 175 Fifth Avenue, New York, NY 10010 *tel* 212-674-5151 *telegraphic address* Saintmart, New York *fax* 212-420-9314. Trade, reference, college.

Saunders College, The Public Ledger Building, 150 South Independence Mall West, Suite 1250, Philadelphia, PA 19106 *tel* 215-238-5500 *fax* 215-238-5660. College textbooks.

*Scribner (1846)—imprint of **Simon & Schuster.**

*Simon & Schuster, 1230 Avenue of the Americas, New York, NY 10020 *tel* 212-698-7000. *President and ceo:* Jonathan Newcomb. General fiction, nonfiction, children's and young adult books, CD-ROM and multimedia products, travel guides, reference books; educational books, multimedia materials and integrated learning systems; English-as-a-Second Language and English Language Teaching materials; computer-use books, business and professional books, audio-visual products, health care journals, training programs and computer-based learning systems.

Soho Press Inc. (1986), 853 Broadway, New York, NY 10003 *tel* 212-260-1900 *fax* 212-260-1902. *Publisher:* Juris Jurjevics; *associate publisher:* Laura Hruska. Literary fiction, commercial fiction, mystery, thrillers, travel, memoir, general non-fiction.

*Stanford University Press, Stanford, CA 94305-2235   *tel* 415-723-9434   *fax* 415-725-3457. *Director:* Norris Pope. Scholarly non-fiction.

Strawberry Hill Press (1973), 3848 SE Division Street, Portland, OR 97202   *tel* 503-235-5989. *President:* Jean-Louis Brindamour PhD; *executive vice-president and art director:* Ku Fu-Sheng; *treasurer:* Edward E. Serres. Health, self-help, cookbooks, philosophy, religion, history, drama, science and technology, biography, mystery, Third World. No unsolicited MSS; preliminary letter and return postage essential.

Tambourine Books (1990), division of **William Morrow & Co., Inc.,** 1350 Avenue of the Americas, New York, NY 10019   *tel* 212-261-6661   *fax* 212-261-6668. *Vice-president and editor-in-chief:* Paulette C. Kaufmann; *senior editor:* Lenny Hort; *art director:* Golda Laurens. Juvenile and young adult books.

Taplinger Publishing Co., Inc. (1955), PO Box 1324, New York, NY 10185   *tel* 201-432-3257   *telegraphic address* Taplinpub. *Vice president:* Theodore Rosenfeld. Calligraphy, literature (including translated works into English), music, art and art criticism, non-fiction.

Theatre Arts Books, division of **Routledge, Inc.,** 29 West 35th Street, New York, NY 10001   *tel* 212-244-3336. *President:* John von Knorring; *editorial director:* William Germano. Successor to the book publishing department of Theatre Arts (1921-1948). Theatre, performance, dance and allied books – acting techniques, costume, tailoring, etc.; a few plays.

Tor Books (1980), 175 Fifth Avenue, 14th Floor, New York, NY 10010   *tel* 212-388-0100   *fax* 212-388-0191. *President and publisher:* Tom Doherty. Subsidiary of **St Martin's Press, Inc.** Fiction: general, historical, western, suspense, mystery, horror, science fiction, fantasy, humour, juvenile, classics (English language); non-fiction: adult and juvenile.

*Charles E. Tuttle Co., Inc. (1949), 153 Milk Street, Boston, MA 02109   *tel* 802-773-8930/802-773-8229   *cables* Tuttbooks   *fax* 802-773-6993. *President:* Peter Ackroyd; and Suido I-chome, 2-6 Bunkyo-ku, Tokyo 112, Japan   *tel* 811-7106-9   *cables* Tuttbooks, Tokyo   *telex* 0272-3170 TUTBKS J   *fax* 811-6953. *President:* Nicholas J. Ingleton. Oriental art, culture, Eastern philosophy, martial arts, health.

The University of Alabama Press (1945), Box 870380, Tuscaloosa, AL 35487   *tel* 205-348-5180   *fax* 205-348-9201. *Director:* Nicole Mitchell; *managing editor:* Elizabeth May. American and Southern history, rhetoric and speech communication, Judaic studies, linguistics, literary criticism, anthropology and archaeology, history of American science and technology.

The University of Arkansas Press (1980), The University of Arkansas, 201 Ozark Street, Fayetteville, AR 72701   *tel* 501-575-3246   *fax* 501-575-6044. *Director:* Miller Williams. History, literary criticism, biography, poetry, fiction.

University of California Press, 2120 Berkeley Way, Berkeley, CA 94720   *tel* 510-642-4247   *fax* 510-643-7127. *Director:* James H. Clark. Publishes scholarly books, books of general interest, series of scholarly monographs and scholarly journals. *UK:* University Presses of California, Columbia, and Princeton, 1 Oldlands Way, Bognor Regis, West Sussex PO22 9SA   *tel* (01243) 842165   *fax* (01243) 842167.

*University of Chicago Press, 5801 South Ellis Avenue, Chicago, IL 60637   *tel* 312-702-7700   *fax* 312-702-9756. *Director:* Morris Philipson. Scholarly books and monographs, religious and scientific books, general trade books, and 54 scholarly journals.

University of Illinois Press (1918), 1325 South Oak Street, Champaign, IL 61820 *tel* 217-333-0950 *fax* 217-244-8082. *Director:* Richard L. Wentworth. American studies (history, music, literature), poetry, working-class and ethnic studies, communications, regional studies, art and photography, architecture, philosophy and women's studies.

The University of Massachussetts Press (1964), PO Box 429, Amherst, MA 01004-0429 *tel* 413-545-2217 *cables* Masspress *fax* 413-545-1226. *Director:* Bruce G. Wilcox. Scholarly books and works of general interest: American studies and history, black and ethnic studies, women's studies, cultural criticism, architecture and environmental design, literary criticism, poetry, fiction, philosophy, political science, sociology, books of regional interest.

The University of Michigan Press (1930), 839 Greene Street, PO Box 1104, Ann Arbor, MI 48106 *tel* 313-764-4388 *fax* 313-936-0456. *Director:* Colin Day; *assistant director:* Mary Erwin; *executive editor:* LeAnn Fields; *managing editor:* Christina Milton. Scholarly works in literature, classics, history, theatre, women's studies, political science, law, anthropology, economics, archaeology; textbooks in English as a second language; regional trade titles, health policy and management.

University of Missouri Press (1958), 2910 LeMone Boulevard, Columbia, MO 65201 *tel* 573-882-7641 *fax* 573-884-4498. *Director and editor-in-chief:* Beverly Jarrett; *acquisitions editor:* Clair Willcox. American and European history, American, British and Latin American literary criticism, journalism, political philosophy, art history, regional studies; short fiction.

University of New Mexico Press (1929), 1720 Lomas Boulevard NE, Albuquerque, NM 87131-1591 *tel* 505-277-2346 *fax* 505-277-9270. *Director:* Elizabeth C. Hadas. Western history, anthropology and archaeology, Latin American studies, photography, multicultural literature.

***The University of North Carolina Press** (1922), PO Box 2288, 116 South Boundary Street, Chapel Hill, NC 27514 *tel* 919-966-3561 *fax* 919-966-3829. *Director:* Kate Douglas Torrey. American history, American studies, Southern studies, European history, women's studies, Latin American studies, political science, anthropology and folklore, classics, regional trade.

***University of Oklahoma Press** (1928), 1005 Asp Avenue, Norman, OK 73019-0445 *tel* 405-325-5111 *fax* 405-325-4000. *Director:* George Bauer. History of American West, American Indian studies, Mesoamerican studies, classical studies, women's studies, natural history, political science.

University of Pennsylvania Press (1869), Blockley Hall, 418 Service Drive, Philadelphia, PA 19104-6097 *tel* 215-898-6261 *telegraphic address* PNSYL PRESS *fax* 215-898-0404. *Director:* Eric Halpern. American and British history, anthropology, art, architecture, biological sciences, business, cultural studies, economics, folklore, history of science, technology and medicine, human rights, law, literature, medicine, Pennsylvania regional studies, women's studies.

University of Washington Press (1909), PO Box 50096, Seattle, WA 98145-5096 *tel* 206-543-4050 *telex* 4740096 UWUI *fax* 206-543-3932. *Director:* Patrick Soden; *associate director and editor-in-chief:* Naomi B. Pascal. Anthropology, Asian-American studies, Asian studies, art and art history, aviation history, environmental studies, forest history, Jewish studies, literary criticism, marine sciences, Middle East studies, music, regional studies, including history and culture of the Pacific Northwest and Alaska, Native American studies, resource management and public policy, Russian and East European studies, Scandinavian studies.

Van Nostrand Reinhold (1848), 115 Fifth Avenue, New York, NY 10003 *tel* 212-254-3232 *fax* 212-475-2548. *President:* Marianne J. Russell. A division of International Thomson Publishing. Professional and reference publisher of information products for culinary arts/hospitality, architecture/design, environmental sciences and business technology.

***Viking**—see **Penguin USA.**

Walker & Co. (1960), 435 Hudson Street, New York, NY 10014 *tel* 212-727-8300 *fax* 212-727-0984. *Publisher:* George Gibson; *mystery:* Michael Seidman; *juvenile:* Emily Easton. General publishers, biography, popular science, health, business, mystery/suspense, westerns, juveniles, early childhood education, parenting, self-help.

***Warner Books Inc.** (1973), 1271 Avenue of the Americas, 9th Floor, New York, NY 10020 *tel* 212-522-7200 *fax* 212-522-7991. *President:* Laurence J. Kirshbaum. Fiction and non-fiction, hardcovers, trade paperbacks, mass market paperbacks.

Franklin Watts, Sherman Turnpike, Danbury, CT 06813 *tel* 203-797-3500 *fax* 203-797-6986. *Vp and editorial director:* John W. Selfridge. School and library books for grades K-12.

Westminster John Knox Press, 100 Witherspoon Street, Louisville, KY 40202-1396 *tel* 502-569-5043 *fax* 502-569-5113. *Editorial manager:* Stephanie Egnotovich. Religious, academic, reference, general.

Whispering Coyote Press, Inc. (1989), 300 Crescent Court, Suite 850, Dallas, TX 75201 *tel* 214-871-5599 *fax* 214-871-5577. *President:* Lou Alpert. Children's picture books.

Workman Publishing Co. (1968), 708 Broadway, New York, NY 10003 *tel* 212-254-5900 *fax* 212-254-8098. *President:* Peter Workman. General non-fiction, calendars.

Writers and Readers Publishing Inc. (1974), PO Box 461, Village Station, New York, NY 10014 *tel* 212-982-3158 *fax* 212-777-4924. *Publisher:* Glenn Thompson. Imprints: Black Butterfly Children's Books and Harlem River Press; also For Beginners Series. Specialises in multicultural and African centric children's books. *Editors:* Ron David (For Beginners Series), Patricia Allen (Harlem River Press and Young For Beginners Series), Deborah Dyson (Black Butterfly Children's Books).

Writer's Digest Books, 1507 Dana Avenue, Cincinnati, OH 45207 *tel* 513-531-2222 *fax* 513-531-4744. Market Directories, books for writers, photographers and songwriters. **North Light Books:** fine art and graphic arts instruction books; **Betterway Books:** how-to in home building, remodelling, woodworking, sports, home organisation, theatre.

***Yale University Press,** 302 Temple Street, New Haven, CT 06511 *postal address* PO Box 209040, New Haven, CT 06520 *tel* 203-432-0960 *telex* 963531 *fax* 203-432-0948/2394. *Director:* John G. Ryden; *London:* 23 Pond Street, Hampstead, NW3 2PN *tel* 0171-431 4422 *fax* 0171-431 3755. Scholarly books and art books.

Writing and Illustrating Children's Books

CAROLINE SHELDON

Sammy the Squirrel, Cyril the Slug, Teddy the Traffic Light . . . mention such titles to a group of children's book editors and they all recognise yesterday's pile of rejected manuscripts. To a man (or in fact generally to a woman) they are looking for something with more originality and punch. The best way to get a feel of what children's publishers are publishing today is to read a large range of children's books published now and over the last thirty years. They cover an enormous spectrum in length and content – from simple, highly illustrated picture book stories to full length novels for teenagers, and most children's publishers' lists cover the whole range. The following is a brief *vade mecum* for the submission of children's manuscripts.

WRITING CHILDREN'S BOOKS

Observe all the rules of submission as for other work – a doubled-spaced, attractively presented manuscript; a covering letter giving information about yourself and your writing; return postage; no bulky ring binders that burst open in the post. Mention any experience of working with children.

Picture books. There is limited opportunity for authors to get involved in bath books or board books, and therefore picture books are generally the youngest end of the age range for writers. The high cost of printing in full colour necessitates a long print run of copies to keep the unit cost down. To achieve this, collaboration with an American, European or other foreign publisher is essential. Thus a publisher has to believe a book is really going to make its mark in the international market before taking it on. It is a very competitive field, but ask most publishers what they are short of and they will say good picture book texts – which just proves how difficult they are to write successfully. Almost all picture books are 32 pages long with 12-14 spreads (i.e. double-pages) of full colour illustration. The number of words varies from none (it has been done; the author provided the storyline to which the artist worked) to a maximum of about 2500. The book has to encompass a big enough idea to make it something of an event, yet not deal with issues too wide to resolve within the limits of the page size and design. A narrative with a strong beginning, middle and end is needed to encourage the reader to turn the pages. Even some successful authors in the area find their publisher or agent may reject five stories before one magically slips into place. So be warned, it's tough . . .

Picture book manuscripts should be typed as a series of numbered pages each with its own text. Detailed descriptions of the illustrations and instructions to the illustrator are almost always a mistake. However, if there is something that should be included in the picture, but this is not clear from the text, this should be pointed out.

Younger fiction. This area of publishing is designed for children who are reading their first whole novels. Texts tend to be anything from 2000 to 7500 words long; in many cases the books will be illustrated with much line illustration breaking up the words on the page. Generally, publishers don't want a use of restricted vocabulary, but writers should remember that, particularly at the bottom end of the age range, they are writing for children who have just learnt to read. Novels for this age range can be published as individual books but often publishers put them out under an umbrella series name. It is advantageous in getting your book placed to have investigated a series before approaching the publisher and checked that your book fits in to that series in terms of length and interest level. You can indicate in a covering letter that you have planned that it will be illustrated but don't give illustration notes in the manuscript.

The following are some currently published series with the approximate word length of the manuscript and the age group at which the books are aimed.

Publisher	Series name	Word length	Age group	Comments
Andersen Press	Tigers	3000-5000	6-9	B&w illustrations on every page
A. & C. Black	Jets	2500	6-8	B&w illustrations on every page
	Jumbo Jets	4000-5000	7-9	B&w illustrations on every page
	Chillers	4000-5000	7-9	B&w illustrations on every page
	Dingbats	4000-5000	10-13	B&w illustrations on every page
Hamish Hamilton	Cartwheels	1000	4-8	Full colour illustrations
	Gazelles	4000	5-8	B&w illustrations on every page
	Antelopes	7500	6-9	B&w illustrations on every page
	Surfers	10,000-12,000	9-12	B&w illustrations
HarperCollins	Colour Jets	2500	6-9	Colour illustrations on every page
	Yellow Storybooks	2000-3000	6-8	B&w illustrations on every page
	Red Storybooks	6000-8000	6-8	B&w illustrations
Heinemann	Blue Bananas	1000-1500	3-5	Full colour illustrations
	Yellow Bananas	3000	6-9	Full colour illustrations
Hodder	Read Alone	2000-4000	6-8	B&w illustrations on every page
	Story Book	8000-12,000	7-9	B&w illustrations
Kingfisher	Beginners	1000-1500	5-7	Full colour illustrations
Macdonald Young Books	Story Books	2000-3000	6-9	Colour and b&w illustrations
	Shivery Storybooks	2000-2500	6-9	Colour and b&w illustrations
Methuen	Read Aloud	8000	5-7	B&w line illustrations
Orchard	Beginners	1000	5-7	B&w illustrations on every page
	Read Alone	2000-4000	7-9	B&w illustrations on every page
Puffin	Ready, Steady, Read	1500	5-7	B&w illustrations on every page
Red Fox	Read Alone	3000 or 7000	6-9	B&w illustrations on every page
Transworld	Corgi Pups	2000-2500	5-8	B&w illustrations on every page
	Young Corgi	3000-7000	6-8	B&w illustrations

Publisher	Series name	Word length	Age group	Comments
Viking	Read Alone	2500	6-8	B&w illustrations on every page
	Kites	6000	7-9	B&w illustrations
Walker	Sprinters	3000-4000	6-8	B&w illustrations on every page

General fiction. Children's novels for the 9-plus age group are mainly published as individual books. Generally, they are shorter than children's books read by previous generations. Any books over 40,000 words will have to face the problems of a higher price than the publisher would like. Each book stands on its own merits and publishers are looking for authors whose work they like and whom they believe will go on to write a number of books for their list.

There are also a number of extremely successful fiction series for older children that have recently become established. Scholastic commission books for their Point series with genres including horror, romance, crime and science fiction, and Puffin commission books for their Gothic series Dark Enchantments. In each case, the publisher would be interested in a proposal for the series with sample chapters.

Non-fiction. Non-fiction is an area almost exclusively covered by specialists. Some publishers have much of their non-fiction written by their own staff. If you are interested in this area, nothing can replace a research trip to a good children's library or bookshop to establish who is publishing what, and how your work or field of interest could fit in.

ILLUSTRATING CHILDREN'S BOOKS

Illustrating children's books is a highly professional field but one in which there is always room for new talent. Most illustrators working in children's books have an art school background but there are also those who have come to it without formal training. The work available varies from illustrations for full colour picture books, to jackets and black-and-white line illustrations for novels, to non-fiction illustration.

Illustrators looking for work in this area should try to make appointments to show their portfolios to either the Art Director or Children's Book Editor at a publishing house and to show their work to suitable agents. A portfolio should show as wide a range of work as possible – it is well worth working up some line black-and-white illustrations for children's novels for the 6-10 age range since so much bread-and-butter work is commissioned in this area. Once you have achieved this, people are more likely to be interested in spending time with you developing your special picture book project. The main complaints of those who look at prospective illustrators' portfolios is that the work shown is too stylised and sophisticated, and there is not an obvious application to children's book illustration. If you find it difficult to get an appointment, send in a photocopied folder of samples of your work together with a letter outlining the type of work for which you are looking.

My advice would always be to send colour photocopies of work, never the original artwork; even if the photocopies don't do full justice to the colour, publishers are experienced at spotting the sort of quality that makes them want to see more.

WHICH COMES FIRST – THE WRITER OR THE ILLUSTRATOR?

Unless you are best buddies with a best selling illustrator or writer, it is best to present your work individually. It is an unwanted complication to have wonderful artwork tied in to an amateurish text, or a nice text illustrated by an artist whose work won't stand up in the very competitive picture book market. Publishers are experienced in matching the work of writers and artists and my advice is that the individual work should stand on its own. Having said that, at the younger end of children's publishing, life is much simpler if you are a writer/illustrator.

Classified Index of UK Children's Book Publishers and Book Packagers

See pages 148 and 258 for UK book publishers and book packagers.

Picture Books

Book publishers

ABC, All Books for Children
Andersen Press
Award Publications
Bantam
Barefoot Books
BBC Books
David Bennett Books
A. & C. Black
Blackie Children's Books
Bloomsbury Children's Books
Bodley Head Children's Books
Brimax Books
Jonathan Cape Children's
 Books
Chart Books
Child's Play International
J.M. Dent
André Deutsch Children's
 Books
Dorling Kindersley
Dragon's World
Floris Books
Gairm Publications (Gaelic)
Gallery Children's Books
Victor Gollancz

Hamish Hamilton Children's
 Books
HarperCollins Publishers
Hawk Books
Hazar Publishing
Heinemann Young Books
Henderson Publishing
Hippo Books
Hodder & Stoughton
Hunt & Thorpe
Hutchinson Children's Books
Kingfisher
Ladybird Books
Levinson Books
Frances Lincoln
Lion Publishing
Little, Brown and Company
 (UK)
Peter Lowe (Eurobook Ltd)
Lutterworth Press
Macdonald Young Books
Macmillan Children's Books
Julia MacRae Books
Magi Publications

Mammoth
Mantra Publishing
Medici Society
Methuen Children's Books
Michael O'Mara Books
Orchard Books
Orion Children's Books
Oxford University Press
Pavilion Books
Piccadilly Press
Puffin
Red Fox
Scripture Union
Spindlewood
Tamarind
Tango Books
The Templar Company
Transworld Publishers
Usborne Publishing
Ventura Publishing
Viking Children's Books
Walker Books
Frederick Warne
World International

Book packagers

Aladdin Books
Albion Press
Andromeda Oxford
Breslich & Foss
Geddes & Grosset
Graham-Cameron Publishing

Angus Hudson
Marshall Editions
Playne Books
Mathew Price
Sadie Fields Productions
The Templar Company

Tucker Slingsby
Ventura Publishing (*Spot* books
 by Eric Hill)
Victoria House Publishing
Zigzag Publishing

Fiction

Book publishers

Adlib
Andersen Press

Bantam
Barefoot Books

BBC Children's Books
David Bennett Books

A. & C. Black
Bloomsbury Children's Books
Bodley Head Children's Books
Brimax Books
Brown, Son & Ferguson (Scout/
    Guide)
Canongate Books
Jonathan Cape Children's
    Books
Chart Books
Child's Play (International)
J.M. Dent
André Deutsch Children's
    Books
Dorling Kindersley
Dutton's Children's Books
Faber & Faber
Floris Books
Gairm Publications (Gaelic)
Victor Gollancz
Gomer Press
Hamish Hamilton Children's
    Books

Patrick Hardy Books
HarperCollins Publishers
Hawk Books
Heinemann Young Books
Hippo
Hodder & Stoughton
Hutchinson Children's Books
Kingfisher
Ladybird Books
Frances Lincoln
Lion Publishing
Y Lolfa Cyf. (Welsh)
Peter Lowe (Eurobook Ltd)
Lutterworth Press
Macdonald Young Books
Macmillan Children's Books
Julia MacRae Books
Mammoth
Mantra Publishing
Methuen Children's Books
Michael O'Mara Books
Orchard Books
Orion Children's Books

Oxford University Press
Pavilion Books
Piccadilly Press
Point
Puffin
Red Fox
Robinson Publishing
Schofield & Sims
Scottish Children's Press
Scripture Union
Spindlewood
Tango Books
D.C. Thomson & Co Ltd –
    Publications
Titan Books (film/TV tie-ins)
Transworld Publishers
Usborne Publishing
Viking Children's Books
Virgin Books
Walker Books
The Women's Press
World International

Book packagers

Albion Press
Oyster Books

Mathew Price
Signpost Books

Touchstone Publishing
Victoria House Publishing

Non-Fiction

Book publishers

ABC, All Books for Children
Anness Publishing
Atlantic Europe Publishing Co
Bantam
BBC Children's Books
Belitha Press
David Bennett Books
A. & C. Black
Boxtree (film/TV tie-ins)
Brimax Books
Brown Wells & Jacobs
Child's Play International
J.M. Dent
André Deutsch Children's
    Books
Dorling Kindersley
Dragon's World
Evans Brothers
Exley Publications
Geddes & Grosset
Hamlyn Children's Non-Fiction
HarperCollins Publishers
Heinemann Young Books

Henderson Publishing
Hippo
Hodder & Stoughton
Kingfisher
Ladybird Books
Levinson Books
Frances Lincoln
Lion Publishing
Little, Brown and Company
    (UK)
Y Lolfa Cyf (Welsh)
Peter Lowe (Eurobook Ltd)
Lutterworth Press
Macdonald Young Books
Macmillan Children's Books
Julia MacRae Books
Mantra Publishing
Medici Society
Merehurst
Michelin Tyre
The National Trust
New Orchard Editions
Oxford University Press

Pavilion Books
Piccadilly Press
Puffin
Riverswift
Salamander Books
Sapling (film/TV tie-ins)
Science Museum Publications
Schofield & Sims
Scottish Children's Press
Scripture Union
Studio Editions
Tango Books
The Templar Company
Transworld Publishers
Two-Can Publishing
Usborne Publishing
Walker Books
Frederick Warne
Watts Books
Wayland
The Women's Press
World International
Young Library

Book packagers

Aladdin Books
Albion Press
Bender Richardson White

Breslich & Foss
Brown Wells & Jacobs
Philip Clark

Earthscape Editions
Geddes & Grosset
Graham-Cameron Publishing

Lionheart Books
Marshall Editions
Orpheus Books
Oyster Books

Mathew Price
Signpost Books
The Templar Company
Touchstone Publishing

Tucker Slingsby
Victoria House Publishing
Zigzag Publishing
Zoe Books

Other

Activity and novelty

Book publishers

Andersen Press
Atlantic Europe Publishing Co
Award Publications
BBC Books
Belitha Press
David Bennett Books
Bloomsbury Children's Books
Brimax Books
Brown Wells & Jacobs
Chart Books
Child's Play International
Dorling Kindersley
Dragon's World
Dutton's Children's Books
Exley Publications
Floris Books
Geddes & Grosset

Hamlyn Children's Non-Fiction
Hazar Publishing
Heinemann Young Books
Henderson Publishing
Hippo
Kingfisher
Ladybird Books
Levinson Books
Frances Lincoln
Lion Publishing
Macmillan Children's Books
Mammoth
Methuen Children's Books
Michelin Tyre
Michael O'Mara Books
Orchard Books

Orion Children's Books
Oxford University Press
Pavilion Books
Piccadilly Press
Puffin
Salamander Books
Scripture Union
Studio Editions
Tango Books
The Templar Company
Transworld Publishers
Two-Can Publishing
Usborne Publishing
Walker Books
Frederick Warne
World International

Book packagers

Aladdin Books
Andromeda Oxford
Bellew Publishing
Breslich & Foss
Brown Wells & Jacobs
Earthscape Editions

Geddes & Grosset
Graham-Cameron Publishing
Angus Hudson
Oyster Books
Mathew Price
Sadie Fields Productions

Signpost Books
The Templar Company
Tucker Slingsby
Victoria House Publishing
Zigzag Publishing
Zoe Books

Audiobooks

Book publishers

BBC Books
Canongate Books
HarperCollins Publishers
Henderson Publishing
Hodder Headline

Ladybird Books
Frances Lincoln
Mantra Publishing
Random House Audio Books

Tellastory
Transworld Audio Books
Usborne Publishing
Watts Books

Multimedia

Book publishers

BBC Books
Dorling Kindersley
Dragon's World
Ginn
HarperCollins
Heinemann Educational

Hodder Headline
Macmillan
Oxford University Press
Puffin
Random House
Thomas Nelson

Two-Can Publishing
Usborne Publishing
Frederick Warne
Watts Books
Wayland Publishers

Book packagers

Bender Richardson White

Earthscape Editions

Zigzag Publishing

Music

Book publishers

A. & C. Black
Canongate Books
Child's Play International

Exley Publications
Gallery Children's Books
Henderson Publishing

Mantra Publishing
Scripture Union
Usborne Publishing

Poetry

Book publishers

Andersen Press
Bantam
A. & C. Black
Bloomsbury Children's Books
Bodley Head Children's Books
Jonathan Cape Children's
 Books
André Deutsch Children's
 Books

Dutton's Children's Books
Faber & Faber
HarperCollins Publishers
Heinemann Young Books
Hutchinson Children's Books
Kingfisher
Lutterworth Press
Macmillan Children's Books
Mammoth

Methuen Children's Books
Orchard Books
Oxford University Press
Puffin
Red Fox
Transworld Publishers
Usborne Publishing
Viking Children's Books
Walker Books

Book packagers

Albion Press

Religion

Book publishers

Gallery Children's Books
Hamlyn Children's Non-Fiction
HarperCollins Publishers
Angus Hudson
Hunt & Thorpe

Lion Publishing
Lutterworth Press
Marshall Pickering
Medici Society
The Mothers' Union

Oxford University Press
Salvationist Publishing and
 Supplies
Scripture Union Publishing

Book packagers

Albion Press
Graham-Cameron Publishing

Angus Hudson
Marshall Editions

Oyster Books
Victoria House Publishing

LITERARY AGENTS FOR CHILDREN'S BOOKS

The following literary agents are prepared to consider work suitable for children's
books, from both authors and illustrators (see page 397); see also the art agents
listing on page 329.

The Agency (London) Ltd
Peter Bryant (Writers)
Curtis Brown
Anne Drexl
A.M. Heath & Co Ltd (Michael Thomas)
Juvenilia
Jennifer Luithlen Agency
Eunice McMullen Children's Literary Agent Ltd
M.C. Martinez Literary Agency

Maggie Noach Literary Agency
The Peters, Fraser & Dunlop Group Ltd
 (Rosemary Canter)
Murray Pollinger
Rogers, Coleridge & White Ltd
Elizabeth Roy Literary Agency
Rosemary Sandberg Ltd
Caroline Sheldon Literary Agency
Ed Victor Ltd (Sophie Hicks)

Pictures into Print

DAVID ASKHAM

Imagine completing a book-length manuscript, accompanied by a fine selection of your own photographs, only to discover that the publisher requires colour *transparencies*, whereas your illustrations are in the form of colour *prints*!

To an author such a set-back can be highly demoralising. Apart from the frustrations of lost time and opportunities, there is the daunting prospect of a major re-shoot of the photography, a costly conversion of negatives into transparencies, or facing up to hiring photographs from a picture library at a cost probably not included in the original budget.

Of course the street-wise photographer would probably not make such a fundamental mistake. Increasingly, however, more and more writers are undertaking the provision of their own photographs to illustrate their written work. And why not? Modern cameras are well-endowed with automatic features to simplify the task and are quite capable of yielding results perfectly acceptable for reproduction.

So this article is intended primarily for writers who wish to make a success of supplying their own photography. It will not transform them into multi-talented professional photographers. That would be wildly optimistic. Rather it will help them avoid basic mistakes, such as that mentioned earlier, and give some useful pointers to success.

It should be stressed, however, that an author should know and respect the upper limits of his or her photographic capabilities. A publisher will not thank you for second-rate results. If in doubt, consider engaging a talented colleague, though your agreement needs to take account of the ultimate division of labour. At all times be honest with your editor about the degree of confidence you have in providing acceptable photography.

On the positive side, many authors have acquired and developed photographic skills to the point where their work is highly accomplished in its own right. But first – back to basics.

BASIC REQUIREMENTS

Before embarking on any photography it is essential first to elicit a publisher's or editor's requirements. In the case of a book-length project the contract should set out, precisely, what the author accepts and is obliged to produce in terms of numbers of pictures and their breakdown, where appropriate, into colour or monochrome images. Check also whether colour pictures are required in the form of colour transparencies (slides – but not in glass mounts) or colour prints. With illustrated features, it is less usual to have a written contract prior to production. Nevertheless, a letter should spell out the salient facts concerning the provision of pictures.

The question of fees and reproduction rights should also be addressed, not only for text but also for the illustrations. Publishers have budgets for their editorial needs and prior agreement on fees is essential if the contributing author is not to finish the commitment unwittingly well out of pocket. While photographic film may appear a relatively inexpensive item, travel to distant locations can inflate overall costs. Thought, therefore, must be given to the question of expenses.

Where colour is concerned, transparencies (derived from colour reversal or slide film) provide the better source for high quality reproduction than do colour prints. Gradually this situation may change as reproduction techniques continue to develop. To be safe, however, always check with your publisher before deviating from industry standards. If in any doubt when, for example, you are producing pilot material to form the basis of a book proposal, do use colour slide film. Then, if the proposal is accepted, you have already made a valuable start with your photography.

Editors rarely influence the choice of pictorial content of images produced by authors, provided the pictures offered meet certain criteria and accepted standards. So, while the author would appear to enjoy unbridled freedom in deciding what pictures to take and supply to the publisher, the editor will only be satisfied if your pictures are truly relevant to the manuscript and the aim of your work, and are also of a satisfactory quality. Let us now look at these aspects in more detail.

PICTURE RELEVANCE

Images should complement and help to clarify the text. Additionally they can beautify and add interest. Picture subjects often suggest themselves. However there is a potential trap in sacrificing relevance when the most appropriate pictures are unavailable or difficult to acquire.

Take an example of a non-fiction book about London Midland and Scottish Railway locomotives which would clearly require illustrations of some, if not all, of the models described. It would be quite misleading to intermix pictures of the London and North Western Railway locomotives unless a specific point of comparison or contrast was being made. Without such justification, readers could become confused, misled and eventually lose interest in the book. The author's credibility would suffer. Fortunately such lack of relevance should be spotted at the editorial stage and the author be required to rectify the error.

A biographer seeking to illustrate the boyhood home environment of an historical figure would be lucky indeed to find the actual dwelling, let alone the atmosphere of the period, unless immortalised in a museum. In the absence of contemporary artwork, it becomes acceptable to show the current locale provided captions clearly account for the time-shift.

Occasionally a publisher will have preferences or fixed ideas on the need for certain illustrations. Provided these ideas are feasible and reasonable they should be respected and added to the author's list of picture requirements.

PICTURE QUALITY

Next to relevance comes picture quality which is vitally important. Photographs should be *sharp* and *clear*. Modern cameras are capable of yielding high definition results provided the lens is correctly focused on the principal subject and the camera is held steady at the time of exposure. The latter calls for practice and suggestions for success appear in instruction manuals and books.

Paradoxically, a photograph may appear to be sharp but at the same time suffer from lack of clarity. Why should this be?

Usually the cause of such obfuscation is conflict and confusion in the picture area, caused by lack of thought at the time of exposure. Remedies lie in isolating the main subject by using certain simple techniques such as careful framing, differential focus or employing contrasting tones or colour.

It should be realised that no amount of camera automation will substitute for skill on the part of the photographer. Only the photographer can compose the picture in such a way as to communicate his or her ideas clearly and unambiguously to the reader.

Quality results also depend on reliable equipment, films, processing and presentation. Avoid skimping in any of these areas. It is not necessary to invest a small fortune in photographic equipment. A modern 35mm camera of a reputable make will serve an author well. Choose wisely taking counsel from a learned colleague or trusted dealer. Use fresh films and have them processed by a professional laboratory rather than a cut-price corner shop.

While the emphasis has been on colour photography, most of the principles apply equally to monochrome pictures. Black and white photography will continue to be an important source of illustration in publishing.

It is becoming more difficult to find good processors of black and white films which is why many photographers set up a small darkroom to print their own 10″ × 8″ or whole plate enlargements. In extremis, however, publishers can derive impressive black and white illustrations from colour transparency originals, albeit at a cost.

ADMINISTRATION

Once you start producing your own pictures for publication, it is important to consider their administration.

Each picture should be presented in such a way that your name, address, telephone number, reference and caption is clearly related to the subject. Records should be kept of pictures stored in your library and of those held by publishers. Despite all reasonable care losses will occasionally occur. Depending on circumstances, compensation should be claimed.

Colour transparencies need to be mounted, handled, stored and transmitted with extreme care if damage is to be avoided. Never mount colour transparencies intended for publication in glass.

Depending on urgency, pictures can be dispatched by post or courier services. In all cases they should be carefully packed and insured, if so inclined, according to their value.

Questions of copyright are addressed in detail in a separate chapter of this book (see page 540). Normally an author retains copyright both of his or her literary and artistic works unless these are assigned to a publisher. It is customary to assign only limited rights – e.g. First British Serial Rights for an article, or Single Reproduction Rights (qualified by territory and time if appropriate) – for pictures unless special circumstances prevail.

Occasionally problems arise in the reproduction of historic photographs, such as those produced, for example, by Henry Fox Talbot and other pioneering practitioners. By any definition these old pictures would be out of copyright by virtue of the time elapsed since the photographer's death. However trustees or independent commercial libraries often levy hire charges if material in their possession is subsequently reproduced.

In summary, authors are well placed to produce their own photography to illustrate their literary works. With sensible understanding of publishers' requirements and thoughtful application with the camera, writers will derive extra pleasure and profit from seeing their pictures, as well as words, in print.

Top Hundred Chart of
1995 Paperback Fastsellers

ALEX HAMILTON

In the pages which follow this preamble readers will find a table of the 100 highest sales figures for paperbacks uttered during 1995 by British publishers. It is an annual survey, which I have compiled for *The Guardian* newspaper since 1979, but for readers encountering it for the first time it would perhaps be useful to describe its terms of reference and indicate certain limitations.

An important distinction has first to be made between 'bestsellers' and the term used here – 'fastsellers'. The former have the real commercial pedigree. Sometimes, but not always, they have made a very visible showing in the fastseller lane, but among bestselling authors there are hundreds whose books have made a slow start and only through the cumulative sales over many years vindicate the faith of the original publisher. Among many examples of those whose sales in their lifetimes were modest but the posthumous interest spectacular, two durable cases are D.H. Lawrence and George Orwell.

Again, while serious poets never repeat Lord Byron's success in becoming a bestseller and 'famous overnight', and the only two works with short lines in a decade of fastsellers were collections of comic verse, a poet such as T.S. Eliot, not to mention Shakespeare and Chaucer, will over the long haul rack up sales in millions. And an outside event, such as the award of the Nobel Prize to Seamus Heaney in 1995, produces an immediate selling bonanza.

The bread and butter of publishing has long been Bibles, classic authors, cookbooks, dictionaries and other reference books, and these are also the bridge for the trade into CD-ROM. Although the larger bulk of counter sales, and of library borrowings, consists of fiction, the topselling individual titles for this century, with figures over 20 million copies, include most of these categories. However, the gross figures worldwide, hardcover and paperback, with translations, of prolific authors such as Agatha Christie, Alistair MacLean, Mickey Spillane, Stephen King and Catherine Cookson are claimed to be between 50 million and 300 million copies.

The individual titles of such popular authors would generally show up in topical bestseller lists, but not always. Dennis Wheatley, for instance, had a very big following in Britain, but the 'British' quality he prided himself on did not travel, and overseas he was hardly read. Something like it happens also with Barbara Cartland who, with more than 500 titles, is so prolific as to compete with herself: her individual books are never bestsellers but all together they do loom large.

The fastselling list which follows consists of the outpourings of the parish pump, meaning that it is limited to paperbacks which have appeared for the first time in that year from British publishers (regardless of their hardcover provenance). It is tempting to include old titles revived to synchronise with film releases and television serials, because these tie-ins have a strong influence (a good example this year would be Michael Crichton's 1982 title *Congo*, which sold 135,000 more) but except when the figure is very large, I try to exclude them.

Since 1979 there were always, until the recession of the Nineties, between 102 and 125 titles which passed the 100,000 mark – a convenient round figure for those who like to make comparisons. (This year there were 110.) While publishers inevitably highlight the performances of their own authors, it was never my aim to make the list look like a competition. Nor should it be seen as a yardstick of

No	Title	Genre	Author	Imprint
1	The Chamber	Thriller	John Grisham (US)	Arrow
2	The Glass Lake	Novel	Maeve Binchy (Ire)	Orion
3	The Fist of God	Thriller	Frederick Forsyth (Br)	Corgi
4	Debt of Honour	Thriller	Tom Clancy (US)	HarperCollins
5	Tinker's Girl	Novel	Catherine Cookson (Br)	Corgi
6	The Body Farm	Crime	Patricia Cornwell (US)	Warner
7	Wild Horses	Thriller	Dick Francis (Br)	Pan
8	Nothing Lasts Forever	Novel	Sidney Sheldon (US)	HarperCollins
9	Insomnia	Horror	Stephen King (US)	NEL
10	Accident	Romance	Danielle Steel (US)	Corgi
11	Twelve Red Herrings	Stories	Jeffrey Archer (Br)	HarperCollins
12	Justice is a Woman	Saga	Catherine Cookson (Br)	Corgi
13	A Brief History of Time	Science	Stephen Hawking (Br)	Bantam
14	The Gift	Romance	Danielle Steel (US)	Corgi
15	Everything to Gain	Novel	Barbara T. Bradford (Br)	HarperCollins
16	Hollywood Kids	Romance	Jackie Collins (Br)	Pan
17	Day After Tomorrow	Thriller	Allan Folsom (US)	Warner
18	Simisola	Crime	Ruth Rendell (Br)	Arrow
19	Tom Clancy's Op Centre	Thriller	Clancy & Pieczenik (US)	HarperCollins
20	The Long Walk to Freedom	Autobiog	Nelson Mandela (SA)	Abacus
21	Another Woman	Novel	Penny Vincenzi (Br)	Orion
22	The Ghosts of Sleath	Horror	James Herbert (Br)	HarperCollins
23	Tiger Eyes	Romance	Shirley Conran (Br)	Pan
24	Soul Music	Fantasy	Terry Pratchett (Br)	Corgi
25	Interesting Times	Fantasy	Terry Pratchett (Br)	Corgi
26	Daughters of Cain	Crime	Colin Dexter (Br)	Pan
27	Inca Gold	Thriller	Clive Cussler (US)	HarperCollins
28	Tom Clancy's Mirror Image	Thriller	Clancy & Pieczenik (US)	HarperCollins
29	An Imaginative Experience	Novel	Mary Wesley (Br)	Black Swan
30	Dark Rivers of the Heart	Thriller	Dean Koontz (US)	Headline
31	A-Z of Behaving Badly	Humour	Nye & Dornan (Br)	Pavilion
32	Interview with a Vampire	Film tie-in	Anne Rice (US)	Warner
33	Lovers	Novel	Judith Krantz (US)	Bantam
34	Fury	Thriller	Colin Forbes (Br)	Pan
35	On Dangerous Ground	Thriller	Jack Higgins (Br)	Signet
36	The Hippopotomus	Novel	Stephen Fry (Br)	Arrow
37	The Power	Thriller	Colin Forbes (Br)	Pan
38	Sheba	Thriller	Jack Higgins (Br)	Signet
39	Botham	Autobiog	Ian Botham (Br)	HarperCollins
40	X Files: Goblins	TV tie-in	Charles L. Grant (US)	HarperCollins
41	Heart of Danger	Thriller	Gerald Seymour (Br)	HarperCollins
42	A Little Badness	Saga	Josephine Cox (Br)	Headline
43	Snow Falling on Cedars	Thriller	David Guterson (US)	Bloomsbury
44	X Files: Whirlwind	TV tie-in	Charles L. Grant (US)	HarperCollins
45	Last Human	Novel	Doug Naylor (Br)	Penguin
46	Men are from Mars, Women are from Venus	Psychology	John Gray (US)	Thorsons
47	Icebound	Thriller	Dean Koontz (US)	Headline
48	The Scold's Bridle	Crime	Minette Walters (Br)	Pan
49	Where's Wally in Hollywood	Juvenile	Martin Handford (Br)	Walker
50	Writing Home	Autobiog	Alan Bennett (Br)	Faber

Price £	Month	Home	Export	Total	Gross £	No
5.99	Apr	760,495	370,038	1,130,533	6,771,893	1
5.99	June	683,270	296,135	979,405	5,866,636	2
5.99	Feb	424,372	343,027	767,399	4,596,720	3
5.99	Aug	423,012	263,633	686,645	4,113,004	4
4.99	Oct	513,297	127,111	640,408	3,195,636	5
5.99	July	418,608	157,908	576,516	3,453,331	6
5.99	Nov	397,198	168,205	565,403	3,386,764	7
4.99	Apr	260,850	288,878	549,728	2,743,143	8
5.99	July	388,564	160,734	549,298	3,290,295	9
4.99	Aug	412,001	133,230	545,231	2,720,703	10
4.99	July	310,259	220,845	531,104	2,650,209	11
4.99	Mar	369,909	143,650	513,559	2,562,659	12
6.99	Apr	164,872	335,859	500,731	3,500,110	13
4.99	Nov	388,651	99,037	487,688	2,433,563	14
4.99	Aug	352,586	132,828	485,414	2,422,216	15
5.99	July	273,168	155,954	429,122	2,570,441	16
5.99	May	257,418	102,391	359,809	2,155,256	17
5.99	Oct	284,070	72,444	356,514	2,135,519	18
4.99	Apr	164,782	171,582	336,364	1,678,456	19
8.99	Oct	119,470	215,312	334,782	3,009,690	20
5.99	July	208,516	124,912	333,428	1,997,234	21
4.99	June	277,525	45,958	323,483	1,614,180	22
5.99	June	241,090	75,146	316,236	1,894,254	23
4.99	May	261,663	51,919	313,582	1,564,774	24
4.99	Nov	256,414	52,433	308,847	1,541,147	25
4.99	Oct	252,017	53,481	305,498	1,524,435	26
5.99	Mar	165,386	135,907	301,293	1,804,745	27
5.99	Nov	130,989	160,405	291,394	1,745,450	28
5.99	Jan	247,665	33,308	280,973	1,683,028	29
5.99	Nov	172,522	107,691	280,213	1,678,476	30
7.99	Oct	241,419	27,000	268,419	2,144,668	31
5.99	Jan	134,442	128,260	262,702	1,573,585	32
5.99	Apr	162,997	95,787	258,784	1,550,116	33
5.99	Dec	150,629	98,170	248,799	1,490,306	34
4.99	June	176,696	71,624	248,320	1,239,117	35
5.99	Mar	188,137	53,678	241,815	1,448,472	36
4.99	Jan	134,047	104,796	238,843	1,191,827	37
4.99	Oct	168,201	69,470	237,671	1,185,978	38
5.99	Sep	217,751	17,234	234,985	1,407,560	39
4.99	April	177,494	55,507	233,001	1,162,675	40
5.99	Dec	191,864	37,369	229,233	1,373,106	41
5.99	Sep	204,193	22,696	226,889	1,359,065	42
5.99	May	201,111	25,439	226,550	1,357,035	43
4.99	June	157,335	64,985	222,320	1,109,377	44
5.99	Nov	165,458	39,208	204,666	1,225,949	45
7.99	Jan	53,590	150,793	204,383	1,633,020	46
4.99	Aug	129,331	68,800	198,131	988,674	47
4.99	May	142,602	54,539	197,141	983,734	48
4.99	July	96,629	99,355	195,984	977,960	49
7.99	Oct	185,503	8,806	194,309	1,552,529	50

No	Title	Genre	Author	Imprint
51	Cold Shoulder	Thriller	Lynda La Plante (Br)	Pan
52	Playing for the Ashes	Novel	Elizabeth George (US)	Bantam
53	Far Side Gallery 5	Humour	Gary Larson (US)	Warner
54	Gump & Co	Humour	Winston Groom (US)	Black Swan
55	The Container Garden Expert	Gardening	D.G. Hessayon (Br)	Expert
56	The Seventh Scroll	Adventure	Wilbur Smith (SA)	Macmillan
57	The Hot Zone	Science	Richard Preston (US)	Corgi
58	Calvin & Hobbes 10th Anniv.	Humour	Bill Watterson (US)	Warner
59	More than Riches	Saga	Josephine Cox (Br)	Headline
60	Sophie's World	Novel	Jostein Gaader (Nor)	Phoenix
61	Faith	Thriller	Len Deighton (Br)	HarperCollins
62	The Hidden City	Fantasy	David Eddings (US)	HarperCollins
63	A Parliamentary Affair	Novel	Edwina Currie (Br)	Coronet
64	Nest of Vipers	Thriller	Linda Davies (Br)	Orion
65	Ruby	Romance	"Virginia Andrews" (US)	Pocket Books
66	Circle of Friends	Film tie-in	Maeve Binchy (Ire)	Coronet
67	First Offence	Thriller	Nancy T. Rosenberg (US)	Orion
68	Taltos	Novel	Anne Rice (US)	Arrow
69	Kolymsky Heights	Thriller	Lionel Davidson (Br)	Mandarin
70	Apollo 13	Film tie-in	Jim Lovell (US)	Coronet
71	Darkest Hour	Romance	"Virginia Andrews" (US)	Pocket Books
72	Trainspotting	Novel	Irvine Welsh (Br)	Minerva
73	Original Sin	Crime	P.D. James (Br)	Faber
74	The Bulb Expert	Gardening	D.J. Hessayon (Br)	Expert
75	The Raiders	Novel	Harold Robbins (US)	Pocket Books
76	Superplonk	Drink	Malcolm Gluck (Br)	Coronet
77	Pot of Gold	Novel	Judith Michael (US)	Warner
78	Midnight in the Garden	Crime	John Berendt (US)	Vintage
79	Downing Street Years	Autobiog	Margaret Thatcher (Br)	HarperCollins
80	Green River Rising	Thriller	Tim Willocks (Br)	Arrow
81	Silence of Strangers	Saga	Audrey Howard (Br)	Coronet
82	Self Defence	Thriller	Jonathan Kellerman (US)	Warner
83	A Son of the Circus	Novel	John Irving (US)	Black Swan
84	Made in Africa	Travel	Bill Bryson (US)	Minerva
85	Parson Harding's Daughter	Novel	Caroline Harvey (Br)	Corgi
86	Eyes of a Child	Thriller	Richard N. Patterson (US)	Arrow
87	The Tick Tock Man	Novel	Terence Strong (Br)	Mandarin
88	Borrowed Time	Novel	Robert Goddard (Br)	Corgi
89	Guilt by Association	Novel	Susan R. Sloan (US)	Warner
90	Making of Pride and Prejudice	TV tie-in	Birtwhistle & Conklin (Br)	Penguin
91	Looking for Trouble	Autobiog	Peter de la Billiere (Br)	HarperCollins
92	Brother Cadfael's Penance	Crime	Ellis Peters (Br)	Warner
93	Daughters of Arabia	Biography	Jean Sasson (US)	Bantam
94	Everville	Fantasy	Clive Barker (US)	HarperCollins
95	Remember Me	Suspense	Mary Higgins Clark (US)	Pocket Books
96	Summer Madness	Novel	Susan Lewis (Br)	Mandarin
97	Echoes of Yesterday	Saga	Mary Jane Staples (Br)	Corgi
98	Final Cut	Novel	Michael Dobbs (Br)	HarperCollins
99	Jigsaw	Thriller	Campbell Armstrong (Br)	Corgi
100	Closing Time	Novel	Joseph Heller (US)	Pocket Books

Price £	Month	Home	Export	Total	Gross £	No
4.99	Aug	112,111	78,597	190,708	**951,633**	51
4.99	Feb	111,266	77,214	188,480	**940,515**	52
8.99	Nov	117,313	67,804	185,117	**1,664,202**	53
5.99	Oct	126,054	51,679	177,733	**1,064,621**	54
4.99	Apr	149,823	26,410	176,233	**879,403**	55
9.99	Nov	171,116	2,593	173,709	**1,735,353**	56
4.99	Aug	107,074	65,002	172,076	**858,659**	57
8.99	Oct	120,002	48,981	168,983	**1,519,157**	58
5.99	Mar	133,860	27,626	161,486	**967,301**	59
6.99	Feb	0	161,080	161,080	**1,125,949**	60
4.99	Sep	98,539	59,259	157,798	**787,412**	61
5.99	July	77,365	78,032	155,397	**930,828**	62
5.99	Mar	117,587	35,893	153,480	**919,345**	63
4.99	Apr	64,940	84,348	149,288	**744,947**	64
4.99	Aug	100,042	48,215	148,257	**739,802**	65
5.99	Mar	63,877	84,309	148,186	**887,634**	66
4.99	Sep	105,043	42,586	147,629	**736,669**	67
5.99	Sep	75,490	71,337	146,827	**879,494**	68
5.99	Mar	137,335	7,471	144,806	**867,388**	69
5.99	Aug	95,678	46,391	142,069	**850,993**	70
4.99	Jan	93,334	47,900	141,234	**704,758**	71
5.99	July	130,113	4,110	134,223	**803,996**	72
8.99	Apr	106,258	27,775	134,033	**1,204,957**	73
4.99	Aug	107,673	18,271	125,944	**628,461**	74
4.99	Aug	70,081	55,624	125,705	**627,268**	75
4.99	Nov	125,511	0	125,511	**626,300**	76
5.99	Feb	78,744	45,686	124,430	**745,336**	77
5.99	June	47,696	74,347	122,043	**731,038**	78
9.99	Mar	86,608	35,331	121,939	**1,218,171**	79
4.99	May	87,633	33,475	121,108	**604,329**	80
5.99	Nov	97,667	22,925	120,592	**722,346**	81
5.99	June	66,164	53,973	120,137	**719,621**	82
7.99	Sep	61,679	57,320	118,999	**950,802**	83
6.99	July	116,985	1,691	118,676	**829,545**	84
4.99	Mar	91,759	26,460	118,219	**589,913**	85
5.99	Oct	70,278	46,697	116,975	**700,680**	86
4.99	May	110,197	6,473	116,670	**582,183**	87
5.99	Dec	84,170	31,539	115,709	**693,097**	88
5.99	Nov	76,510	36,782	113,292	**678,619**	89
9.99	Sep	108,393	4,796	113,189	**1,130,758**	90
6.99	Aug	107,023	6,048	113,071	**790,366**	91
4.99	Oct	88,373	23,699	112,072	**559,239**	92
4.99	Feb	39,380	71,880	111,260	**555,187**	93
5.99	Apr	62,917	48,115	111,032	**665,082**	94
4.99	July	56,015	54,017	110,032	**549,060**	95
5.99	June	81,483	26,847	108,330	**648,897**	96
4.99	Oct	107,054	506	107,560	**536,724**	97
4.99	Oct	93,068	14,323	107,391	**535,881**	98
4.99	Sep	56,213	50,559	106,772	**532,792**	99
5.99	May	69,520	36,337	105,857	**634,083**	100

publishing efficiency, or solvency. The high-profile books which achieve six-figure sales are a vital part of the trade, but the list has little significance in the assessment of quality, policy and financial acumen in any one publishing house. It is possible to go broke with a runaway fastseller – on more than one occasion the success of a single book has led to an unrealistic expansion; on the other hand there are many attractive and profitable imprints which never come within hailing distance of having a title in this list. The best way to look at it is as a reflection of popular taste accentuated by increasingly sophisticated marketing.

Though one naturally suspects a distortion for titles published at the end of the period, one finds (checking some months later) that it has rarely made much difference. The significant sale of new paperbacks, particularly by authors with a regular following, takes place within a very few weeks of their appearance on the racks. However, a few do enter the magic circle of bestsellers: during the Eighties the highest cumulative sales were for books by Sue Townsend and Jeffrey Archer, each passing five million, which had sold 400,000 and a million respectively in their first year.

Surveyed over a period, these lists indicate a rather conservative attitude on the part of buyers. It is not very common for a book to appear in the top 20 (which earn between them much the same as the rest of the list put together) which has not appeared before somewhere on the list. Once properly established on it, an author only has to turn in a regular supply of similar works to stay on it. So, being comfortable with a formula is a psychological asset for those wanting to compete in this market but, like actors who are typecast, they may find too late that the market will then not allow them to escape. One among several stories of authors corralled in their own fantasies relates that thriller writer Peter Cheyney gave his publisher a book unlike the rest of his oeuvre and was told to bury it, lest its publication confuse his loyal following.

The dominant figures of the Eighties were Wilbur Smith (now with more than 20 novels past the million), Barbara Taylor Bradford, Dick Francis, Len Deighton, Stephen King, Catherine Cookson, Jeffrey Archer, Danielle Steel and Victoria Holt, with Jilly Cooper coming through at the end, particularly in the UK market. The 1990s have not yet seen any very significant shift, save the introduction as frontrunners of John Grisham and Maeve Binchy. It is the author's name that matters most, as shown by the fact that of a thousand titles only four have been volumes of short stories, two with sales over 750,000 copies, because they were by Frederick Forsyth and Jeffrey Archer, and two with 500,000 (Archer again, and Rosamund Pilcher).

Some 80% of the bulk is usually fiction. The regular elements of the non-fiction remainder are diet books, the horoscope division of astrology, joke books, showbiz lives and exploitations based on big movies (anything by Spielberg, for instance). Of the fiction, genres take up most of the slots, particularly adventure yarns, thrillers, horror stories, family sagas and a mixed bag of romances, from historical to 'Gothic' to the now faded bodice-rippers and 'shopping romances' (likewise dropping), and career conflict stories under the vague umbrella of 'women's fiction'. There seems to be no overt category of 'men's fiction' that might once have included authors like Mickey Spillane and Harold Robbins, or today would correspond to the focus and tone of laddish magazines. Perhaps there is an inkling in the popularity of heroics by SAS men, war commanders and pilots who have been shot down, but it is not yet a developed genre.

It is curious, since more than half the buyers have always been women, that for most of the Eighties hardly more than a quarter of the authors were women, but in the last six years the mould has been broken. They have had a steadily increasing presence, from 25% rising to level at between 35% and 40%.

Science fantasy is more likely to show than science fiction of a harder, more experimental kind. Westerns never figured at all, despite the sometime fame on the range of authors like Zane Grey, Louis L'Amour and J.T. Edson.

There are rarely more than ten or a dozen titles in any list that could count on reviews from serious book pages, and most of these appear some way down, though in recent years, broadly since the television focus on it, the Booker Prize has taken winners into the fastseller list. (But not always: this year for the first time in a decade it failed, doubtless because the winning book was too difficult and specialised to have the booksellers' support.) When it does work this award seems to establish the book rather than the author, and the only winner to keep a place with subsequent books is Anita Brookner. No other literary award has yet resulted in a 100,000 paperback sale for the author.

The highest selling title for the Eighties happens to have been a juvenile, *The Secret Diary of Adrian Mole Aged 13¾*, whose author Sue Townsend is said to have been embarrassed when she heard that the publishers had a print run of 70,000 in hand, and begged them to reduce it because she could not bear to think of them risking so much on her behalf. With this and a sequel she very nearly equals the total sale for 11 titles of the best-known author in children's fiction, the late Roald Dahl. The latter's death left the role of natural market leader vacant, a position apparently now being filled by Terry Pratchett.

Horror books that can be racked at children's eye level, such as Scholastic's Point Horror series, are examples of a perennially popular genre. But on the whole, 1995 was a poor year for children's books. There was nothing to match the previous year's Mighty Morphin Power Rangers.

The trade as a whole had a peculiar year, with a brilliant summer that emptied the shops, a lottery frenzy that knocked £60 million a week out of people's disposable income, a horrendous rise of 30% in paper costs, and some alarming wobbles among the major bookshop chains. All this was capped by the collapse of the Net Book Agreement, the 'sheet-anchor' of fair trading since 1899. The prospect of discounting, however, seemed to concern hard-cover books rather than paperbacks.

Amidst this painful scenario the fastsellers list is one feature that remains almost eerily stable, as if these books had an independent orbit. The two most popular price points, £4.99 and £5.99, have precisely the same representation as last year, 41 and 44 respectively. The average price has risen from £5.75 to £5.87. Export has held up well (32%), and the aggregate, home and abroad, has risen to 26 million books for a turnover of £151 million.

Casting about for evidence of those genres which have been spoken of optimistically in recent times, it seems few fulfil their promise. Those that do are new subdivisions in the major categories of thriller, horror and romance. The Western has disappeared into the sunset; the modest flutter in travel writing subsided; fantasy now does better than hardcore SF; and 'green books', after looking as if they would be as uplifting commercially as sermons in the late 19th century, have not much expanded their original niche market. The current vogue for courtroom drama stems from the success of American lawyer John Grisham, and X-Files novelisations are having a run of sorts. Looking at incipient genres, and the way that some are being fuelled with many varieties of religious speculation, it is to be feared that enough millennial books will appear to form a road block.

A charming phenomenon of the year came about through Penguin's promotion of its 60th anniversary with mini-format paperbacks priced at 60p. Excerpts from its classics and modern backlists peppered the bestseller lists from July onward. Even with tiny profit margins, a gross sale of 19 million from a list of 130 titles was a nice result, and during 1996 other publishers began working up similar Lilliputian ventures.

Book Packagers

Many modern illustrated books are created by book packagers, whose special skills are in the areas of book design and graphic content. Children's interests and informational how-to are the usual subject areas; such books match up the expertise of specialist writers, artists and photographers, usually freelances, with the craftsmanship of in-house desk editors and art editors.

Packaged books are often expensive to produce, beyond the cost parameters set by traditional publishers for their own markets; the packager recoups the expense by pre-selling titles to publishers in various countries. Thus packaged books are usually international in content and approach, avoiding local interests such as cricket or Cornish cream teas.

The working style in most packagers' offices is more akin to magazine publishing than to traditional book publishing, with creative groups concentrating on the complexities of integrating words and pictures for individual titles rather than merely manuscript editing for a broad publishing list.

The many opportunities for freelance writers, specialist contributors and consultants, photographers and illustrators will usually be short-term and high pressure; packagers rarely spend more than a year on any title. As packaged books are frequently the work of more than one 'author' and because of the complications of the overseas rights deals that will be made and the formulae for a packager's earnings, which are obviously only a proportion of a book's retail price, flat fees are often suggested rather than royalty agreements. Where royalties are appropriate, they will be based on the packager's receipts, but the expectation is that there will be more foreign language editions than a traditional publisher can achieve.

The Book Packagers Association (*Secretary:* Rosemary Pettit, 93a Blenheim Crescent, London W11 2EQ) is the forum for the exchange of creative and commercial experience in this branch of the publishing industry. The BPA has devised standard contracts to cover members' relationships with contributors and customers.

* Member of the Book Packagers Association

Aladdin Books Ltd (1980), 28 Percy Street, London W1P 0LD *tel* 0171-323 3319 *telex* 21115 ALADIN G *fax* 0171-323 4829. *Directors:* Charles Nicholas, Lynn Lockett. Full design and book packaging facility.

Albion Press Ltd (1984), Spring Hill, Idbury, Oxon OX7 6RU *tel* (01993) 831094 *fax* (01993) 831982. *Directors:* Emma Bradford, Neil Philip. Quality integrated illustrated titles specialising in literature, social history, fine and graphic arts, cookery, children's books. Supply finished books. Publishers' commissions undertaken.

Alphabet & Image Ltd (1972), Marston House, Marston Magna, Yeovil, Somerset BA22 8DH *tel/fax* (01935) 851331. *Directors:* Anthony Birks-Hay, Leslie Birks-Hay. Complete editorial, picture research, photographic, design and production service for illustrated books on ceramics, fine art, horticulture, architecture, history, etc.

Andromeda Oxford Ltd (1986), 11-15 The Vineyard, Abingdon, Oxon OX14 3PX *tel* (01235) 550296 *fax* (01235) 550330. *Directors:* M. Ritchie (managing), M. Desebrock, J. Taylor, M. Smith, J.G. Bateman, C. Sparling, D. Hall.

Illustrated reference titles for the international market for children and adults. Its subsidiary Andromeda Interactive Ltd publishes CD-ROMs.

*BCS Publishing Ltd (1993), 1 Bignell Park Barns, Kirtlington Road, Chesterton, Bicester, Oxon OX6 8TD   *tel* (01869) 324423   *fax* (01869) 324385. *Directors:* Steve McCurdy (managing and art), Candida Hunt (publishing), Deena Daher. Creation, editorial and design of highly illustrated general interest books for the co-edition market. Opportunities for freelances.

Bellew Publishing Co. Ltd (1983), The Nightingale Centre, 8 Balham Hill, London SW12 9EA   *tel* 0181-673 5611   *fax* 0181-675 2142. *Chairman:* Ian McCorquodale; *managing director:* Ib Bellew. Adult and children's illustrated titles from origination of idea through concept and design to production. Opportunities for freelances.

Bender Richardson White (1990), PO Box 266, Uxbridge, Middlesex UB9 5NX   *tel* (01895) 832444   *fax* (01895) 835213. *Partners:* Lionel Bender, Kim Richardson, Ben White. Book and multi-media packaging, specialising in children's natural history, science and family information. Opportunities for freelances.

Bison Books Ltd (1974), Kimbolton House, 117A Fulham Road, London SW3 6RL   *tel* 0171-823 9222   *fax* 0171-244 7139. *Managing director:* S.L. Mayer. Non-fiction illustrated titles principally history, military history, weaponry, natural history, transport, travel, sport, art, entertainment.

BLA Publishing Ltd (1981), BIC Ling Kee House, 1 Christopher Road, East Grinstead, West Sussex RH19 3BT   *tel* (01342) 318980   *fax* (01342) 410980. *Directors:* Au Bak Ling (chairman, Hong Kong), Au King Kwok (Hong Kong), Au Chun Kwok (Hong Kong), Albert Kw Au (Hong Kong), Au Wai Kwok (Hong Kong). *General manager:* Penny Kitchenham. High quality illustrated reference books, particularly science dictionaries and encyclopedias, for the international market.

*Book Packaging and Marketing (1990), 3 Murswell Lane, Silverstone, Towcester, Northants. NN12 8UT   *tel/fax* (01327) 858380. *Proprietor:* Martin F. Marix Evans. Illustrated general and informational non-fiction and reference for adults, especially travel, military history, countryside, health and fitness. Product development and project management; editorial and marketing consultancy. Opportunities for freelances.

*Breslich & Foss (1978), 20 Wells Mews, London W1P 3FJ   *tel* 0171-580 8774   *fax* 0171-580 8784. *Directors:* Paula G. Breslich, K.B. Dunning. Books produced from MS to bound copy stage from in-house ideas. Specialising in the arts, crafts, gardening, gift and novelty, children's.

*Brown Packaging Ltd (1989), 255-257 Liverpool Road, London N1 1LX   *tel* 0171-607 9039   *fax* 0171-700 5673. *Managing director:* Ashley Brown; *marketing director:* Stasz Gnych; *rights director:* Sara Ballard. Book, partwork and continuity set packaging services for trade, promotional and international publishers. Subject areas include military, aviation, gardening, music, sport and craft. Opportunities for freelances.

Brown Wells & Jacobs Ltd (1981), Foresters Hall, 25-27 Westow Street, London SE19 3RY   *tel* 0181-771 5115   *fax* 0181-771 9994. *Director:* Graham Brown. Design, editorial, illustration and production of high quality non-fiction illustrated children's books. Specialities include pop-ups and novelties. Opportunities for freelances.

Calmann and King Ltd (1976), 71 Great Russell Street, London WC1B 3BN   *tel* 0171-831 6351   *fax* 0171-831 8356. *Directors:* Robin Hyman, Laurence King,

Judy Rasmussen, Lesley Ripley Greenfield. Illustrated books on design, art, history, nature, architecture for international co-editions.

Cameron Books (1976), PO Box 1, Moffat, Dumfriesshire DG10 9SU *tel* (01683) 220808 *fax* (01683) 220012. *Directors:* Ian A. Cameron, Jill Hollis. Illustrated non-fiction including architecture, design, fine arts (including environmental and land art), the decorative arts and crafts, antiques, collecting, natural history, environmental studies, social history, film, food. **Edition** (1975). Design, editing, typesetting, production work from concept to finished book for other publishers.

Carroll & Brown Ltd (1989), 5 Lonsdale Road, London NW6 6RA *tel* 0171-372 0900 *fax* 0171-372 0460. *Directors:* Amy Carroll (managing), Denise Brown (creative). Editorial and design through to final film of cookery, health, crafts and life style titles. Opportunities for freelances.

*****Philip Clark Ltd** (1981), 53 Calton Avenue, Dulwich Village, London SE21 7DF *tel* 0181-693 5605 *fax* 0181-299 4647. *Director:* Philip Clark. Illustrated non-fiction for the international co-edition market. Titles include the Travellers Wine Guides series; consultancy service.

Diagram Visual Information Ltd (1967), 195 Kentish Town Road, London NW5 8SY *tel* 0171-482 3633 *fax* 0171-482 4932. *Director:* Bruce Robertson. Research, writing, design and illustration of reference books, supplied as film, computer disks or manufactured copies. Opportunities for freelances.

Earthscape Editions (1987), Greys Court Farm, Greys Court, Henley on Thames, Oxon RG9 4PG *tel* (01491) 628188 *fax* (01491) 628189. *Partners:* B.J. Knapp, D.L.R. McCrae. High quality, full colour, illustrated children's books, including co-editions, for education and library market. Also multimedia productions. Sae with MSS essential. Opportunities for freelances. Associate company: Atlantic Europe Publishing (see UK Book Publishers).

*****Eddison Sadd Editions Ltd** (1982), St Chad's House, 148 King's Cross Road, London WC1X 9DH *tel* 0171-837 1968 *fax* 0171-837 2025. *Directors:* Nick Eddison, Ian Jackson, Maria White, David Owen, Elaine Partington, Charles James. Illustrated non-fiction books for the international co-edition market.

Equinox (Oxford) Ltd—acquired by **Andromeda Oxford Ltd.**

Gardenhouse Editions (1980), 15 Grafton Square, London SW4 0DQ *tel* 0171-622 1720 *fax* 0171-720 9114. *Managing director:* Lorraine Johnson. Practical and art-related books on gardening, cookery, interior design, fashion, architecture.

Geddes & Grosset Ltd (1988), David Dale House, New Lanark ML11 9DJ *tel* (01555) 665000 *fax* (01555) 665694. *Directors:* R. Michael Miller, Ron Grosset, David Geddes. Complete packaging service to bound books, production, editorial project and joint venture management, premium deals. Opportunities for freelances.

Graham-Cameron Publishing (1984), The Studio, 23 Holt Road, Sheringham, Norfolk NR26 8NB *tel* (01263) 821333 *fax* (01263) 821334. *Directors:* Mike Graham-Cameron, Helen Graham-Cameron. Educational and children's books; sponsored publications. Illustration agency, editorial and production services. *No* unsolicited MSS please.

Angus Hudson Ltd (1971), Concorde House, Grenville Place, Mill Hill, London NW7 3SA *tel* 0181-959 3668 *fax* 0181-959 3678. *Directors:* Angus Hudson (chairman), Nicholas Jones (managing), Stephen Price (production), Geoffrey Benge, William Brooks. Children's and religious international co-editions, from concept to finished copies. Publishing imprints: Candle Books and Concorde House Books.

Lennard Books, Windmill Cottage, Mackerye End, Harpenden, Herts. AL5 5DR *tel* (01582) 715866 *fax* (01582) 715121. *Directors:* K.A.A. Stephenson, R.H. Stephenson. Division of **Lennard Associates Ltd.** Sport, personalities, TV tie-ins, humour.

Lexus Ltd (1980), 205 Bath Street, Glasgow G2 4HZ *tel* 0141-221 5266 *fax* 0141-226 3139. *Director:* P.M. Terrell. Reference book publishing (especially bilingual dictionaries) as contractor, packager, consultant; translation.

Lionheart Books (1985), 10 Chelmsford Square, London NW10 3AR *tel* 0181-459 0453 *fax* 0181-451 3681. *Partners:* Lionel Bender (editorial), Madeleine Bender (editorial), Ben White (design). Handle all aspects of editorial and design packaging of, mostly, children's illustrated science, natural history and history projects.

*****Market House Books Ltd** (1981), 2 Market House, Market Square, Aylesbury, Bucks. HP20 1TN *tel* (01296) 84911 *fax* (01296) 437073. *Directors:* Dr Alan Isaacs, Dr John Daintith, P.C. Sapsed. Compilation of dictionaries, encyclopedias, and reference books.

*****Marshall Cavendish Books** (1969), 119 Wardour Street, London W1V 3TD *tel* 0171-734 6710 *telex* 23880 MARCAV G *fax* 0171-439 1423. *Head of books:* Ellen Dupont. Cookery, crafts, gardening, do-it-yourself, general illustrated non-fiction.

*****Marshall Editions Ltd** (1977), 170 Piccadilly, London W1V 9DD *tel* 0171-629 0079 *fax* 0171-834 0785. *Directors:* Richard Harman, Bruce Marshall, Barbara Anderson, Barry Baker, Ed Day. Highly illustrated non-fiction, for the adult and children's co-edition markets, including science and natural history, fitness and well-being, lifestyle and leisure interests.

National Cartoon Company of Ireland Ltd (1992), St Josephs, Portland Row, Dublin 1, Republic of Ireland *tel* (01) 8551290 *fax* (01) 8551291. *Directors:* Vincent Poklewski-Koziell, Grainne O'Rourke, Dudley Stewart. High quality illustrated books for adults and children.

Orpheus Books Ltd (1992), 4 Church Green, Witney, Oxfordshire OX8 6AW *tel* (01993) 774949 *fax* (01993) 700330. *Executive directors:* Nicholas Harris (editorial, design and marketing), Joanna Turner (production and administration). Children's illustrated non-fiction/reference. Opportunities for freelance artists.

Oyster Books (1985), Unit 4, Kirklea Farm, Badgworth, Axbridge, Somerset BS26 2QH *tel* (01934) 732251 *fax* (01934) 732514. *Directors:* Jenny Wood, Tim Wood, Ali Brooks. Specialises in high-quality children's books and book/toy gift items.

Playne Books (1987), Trefin, Haverfordwest, Pembrokeshire SA62 5AU *tel* (01348) 837073 *fax* (01348) 837063. *Director:* David Playne; *editor:* Gill Davies. Specialises in highly illustrated adult non-fiction and books for very young children. All stages of production undertaken from initial concept (editorial, design and manufacture) to delivery of completed books.

*****Mathew Price Ltd** (1983), The Old Glove Factory, Bristol Road, Sherborne, Dorset DT9 4HP *tel* (01935) 816010 *fax* (01935) 816310. *Chairman:* Mathew Price. Illustrated fiction and non-fiction children's books for all ages for the international market.

Quarto Children's Books Ltd, 3rd Floor, The Fitzpatrick Building, 188/194 York Way, London N7 9QP   *tel* 0171-607 3322   *fax* 0171-700 2951 *Creative director:* Louise Jervis. Highly illustrated non-fiction children's books.

Quarto Publishing plc (1976), **Quintet Publishing Ltd** (1984), The Old Brewery, 6 Blundell Street, London N7 9BH   *tel* 0171-700 6700   *fax* 0171-700 4191. *Directors:* L.F. Orbach, R.J. Morley, M.J. Mousley. International co-editions.

Sadie Fields Productions Ltd (1983), 3D West Point, 36/37 Warple Way, London W3 0RG   *tel* 0181-746 1171   *fax* 0181-746 1170. *Directors:* Sheri Safran, David Fielder. Creates and produces international co-productions of pop-up, novelty and picture and board books for children.

***Savitri Books Ltd** (1983), 115 J Cleveland Street, London W1P 5PN   *tel* 0171-436 9932   *fax* 0171-580 6330. *Director:* Mrinalini S. Srivastava. Packaging, design, production.

Signpost Books Ltd (1988), 25 Eden Drive, Headington, Oxford OX3 0AB   *tel* (01865) 60444   *fax* (01865) 751399. *Directors:* Dorothy Wood, Sally Wood. Project development, editorial, design and production through to finished books, film or CRC. Specialises in children's fiction, non-fiction and novelty. Opportunities for freelances.

Sports Book Specialists, Grove Meadow, Jordans Way, Jordans, Bucks. HP9 2SP   *tel/fax* (01494) 873137. *Managing editor:* C. Plumridge. Division of **Lennard Associates Ltd.** Sports projects.

The Templar Company plc, Pippbrook Mill, London Road, Dorking, Surrey RH4 1JE   *tel* (01306) 876361   *fax* (01306) 889097. *Directors:* Richard Carlisle (creative), Amanda Wood (managing), Ruth Huddleston (sales and marketing), Graeme East (financial). Children's gift, novelty, picture and illustrated information books; most titles aimed at international co-edition market. Established links with major co-publishers in USA, Australia and throughout Europe.

Thames Head, BIC Ling Kee House, 1 Christopher Road, East Grinstead, West Sussex RH19 3BT   *tel* (01342) 318980   *fax* (01342) 410980. Division of **BLA Publishing Ltd.** Illustrated international co-editions: general non-fiction, militaria, history, travel guides and practical crafts.

***Toucan Books Ltd** (1985), Fourth Floor, 32-38 Saffron Hill, London EC1M 8BS   *tel* 0171-404 8181   *fax* 0171-404 8282. *Directors:* Robert Sackville West, Adam Nicolson, Jane MacAndrew. International co-editions; editorial, design and production services.

Touchstone Publishing Ltd (1989), Gissing's Farm, Fressingfield, Eye, Suffolk IP21 5SH   *tel* (01379) 588044   *fax* (01379) 588055. *Directors:* Roger Goddard-Coote (managing), Edwina Conner (publishing). High quality, illustrated children's fiction and non-fiction for trade and institutional markets worldwide. Supply CRC, film or finished books. Publishers' commissions undertaken.

Tucker Slingsby (1993), 3G London House, 66-68 Upper Richmond Road, Putney, London SW15 2RP   *tel* 0181-874 3400   *fax* 0181-874 3004. *Directors:* Janet Slingsby, Del Tucker. Creation, editorial and design to disk or film, of children's books, magazines and general interest adult books. Commissioned work undertaken. Opportunities for freelances.

Ventura Publishing Ltd, 27 Wrights Lane, London W8 5TZ   *tel* 0171-416 3000   *telex* 917181 PENGRP G   *fax* 0171-416 3070. *Publisher:* Sally Floyer. Specialises in production of the *Spot* books by Eric Hill.

Victoria House Publishing Ltd (1980), 4 North Parade, Bath BA1 1LF *tel* (01225) 463401 *fax* (01225) 460942. *Director:* Michael J. Morris. Fully owned subsidiary of Reader's Digest Association Inc. Packagers of mass market and novelty children's books under Reader's Digest Children's Books imprint.

Webb & Bower (Publishers) Ltd (1975), 9 Duke Street, Dartmouth, Devon TQ6 9PY *tel* (01803) 835525 *fax* (01803) 835552. *Director:* Richard Webb. Specialises in licensing illustrated non-fiction books.

*Wordwright (1987), 25 Oakford Road, London NW5 1AJ *tel* 0171-284 0056 *fax* 0171-284 0041. *Directors:* Charles Perkins, Veronica Davis. Full packaging/production service – from original concept to delivery of film or finished copies. Produces illustrated non-fiction. Also assesses and prepares MSS for the US market.

*Zigzag Publishing (1989), The Barn, Randolph's Farm, Brighton Road, Hurstpierpoint, West Sussex BN6 9EL *tel* (01273) 832777 *fax* (01273) 835511. *Directors:* Dr T.C. Potter, B. Austin, G. Sutton. Children's books and multimedia. Opportunities for freelances.

Doing It On Your Own – Self-publishing

PETER FINCH

Why bother?
You've tried all the usual channels and been turned down; your work is uncommercial, specialised, technical, out of fashion; you are concerned with art while everyone else is obsessed with cash; you need a book out quickly; you want to take up small publishing as a hobby; you've heard that publishers make a lot of money out of their authors and you'd like a slice – all reason enough. But be sure you understand what you are doing before you begin.

But isn't this cheating? It can't be real publishing – where is the critical judgement? Publishing is a respectable activity carried out by firms of specialists. Writers of any ability never get involved

But they do. Start self-publishing and you'll be in good historical company: Horace Walpole, Balzac, Walt Whitman, Virginia Woolf, Gertrude Stein, John Galsworthy, Rudyard Kipling, Beatrix Potter, Lord Byron, Thomas Paine, Mark Twain, Upton Sinclair, W.H. Davies, Zane Grey, Ezra Pound, D.H. Lawrence, William Carlos Williams, Alexander Pope, Robbie Burns, James Joyce, Anaïs Nin and Lawrence Stern. All these at some time in their careers dabbled in doing it themselves. William Blake did nothing else. He even made his own ink, handprinted his pages and got Mrs Blake to sew on the covers.

But today it's different?
Not necessarily. This is not vanity publishing we're talking about although if all you want to do is produce a pamphlet of poems to give away to friends then self-publishing will be the cheapest way. Doing it yourself today can be a valid form of business enterprise. Being twice shortlisted for the Booker Prize sharpened Timothy Mo's acumen. Turning his back on the mass-market paperbacks, he published *Brownout on Breadfruit Boulevard*, his latest prizewinner, himself. Michael Tod's badger trilogy, *The Silver Tide*, has been paperbacked by Orion, and as an example to us all Jill Paton Walsh's self-published *Knowledge of Angels* was shortlisted for the Booker Prize.

Can anyone do it?

Certainly. If you are a writer then a fair number of the required qualities will already be in hand. If, in addition, you can put up a shelf then the manufacture of the book to go on it will not be beyond you. The more able and practical you are then the cheaper the process will be. The utterly inept will need to pay others to help them, but it will still be self-publishing in the end.

Where do I start?

With research. Read up on the subject. Make sure you know what the parts of a book are. Terms like *verso*, *recto*, *prelims*, *dummy*, *typeface* and *point size* all have to lose their mystery. You will not need to become an expert but you will need a certain familiarity. Don't rush. Learn.

What about ISBN numbers?

International Standard Book Numbers – a standard bibliographic code, individual to each book published, are used by booksellers and librarians alike. They are issued free of charge by the Standard Book Numbering Agency, 12 Dyott Street, London WC1A 1DF. Write giving the basic details of your proposed book and, if appropriate, you will receive an ISBN by return.

Next?

Put your book together – be it the typed pages of your novel, your selected poems or your story of how it was in the war – and see how large a volume it will make. Follow the details on preparation of typescript given elsewhere in this yearbook. No real idea of what your book should look like? Anything will not do. Go to your local bookshop and hunt out a few contemporary examples of volumes produced in a style you would like to emulate. Ask the manager for advice. Take your typescript and your examples round to a number of local printers (find these through *Yellow Pages*) and ask for a quote. This costs nothing and will give you an idea of what the enterprise is likely to involve. Anthony Rowe Ltd (Bumper's Way, Bristol Road, Chippenham SN14 6LM) are specialists in low runs from camera ready copy, and will quote you a price. Book-in-Hand Ltd (20 Shepherds Hill, London N6 5AH) and Evergreen Graphics (Meadow Lane, West Wittering, Chichester, West Sussex PO20 8LR) are also both worth consulting. A number of others advertise their services in the writers' magazines. Many are worth a look but tread with care. Don't rush.

How much?

It depends. How long is a piece of string? You will not get a pamphlet of poems out for less than a few hundred pounds while a hardbacked work of prose will come in well above £4000. Unit cost is important. The larger the number of copies you have printed the less each will cost. Print too many and the total bill will be enormous. Books are no longer cheap; perhaps they never were.

Can I make it cost less?

Yes. Do some of the work yourself. If it's poems and you are prepared to manage with text set by home word processor then that can make a considerable saving. Could you accept home production, run the pages off on an office photocopier, then staple the sheets? Such productions can be very presentable. Access to equipment running a desktop publishing program will give even better results. Home binding, if your abilities lie in that direction, can save a fair bit. What it all comes down to is the standard of production you want and indeed at whom your book is aimed. Books for the commercial market place need to look like their fellows; specialist publications can afford to be more eccentric.

Who decides how it looks?

You do. No one should ever ask a printer simply to produce a book. You should plan the design of your publication with as much care as you would a house extension. Books which sell are those which stand out in the bookshop. Spend as much time and money as you can on the cover. It is the part of the book your buyer will see first. Look at the volumes in bookshop displays, especially those in the window. Imitate British paperback design – it's the best in the world.

How many copies should I produce?

Small press poetry pamphlets sell about 300 copies, new novels sometimes manage 1000, literary paperbacks 10,000, mass-market blockbusters over a million. But that is generally where there is a sales team and whole distribution organisation behind the book. You are an individual. You must do everything yourself. Do not, on the one hand, end up with a prohibitively high unit cost by ordering too few copies. One hundred of anything is usually a waste of time. On the other hand can you really sell 3000? Will shops buy in dozens? They will probably only want twos and threes. Take care. Research your market first.

How do I sell it?

With all your might. This is perhaps the hardest part of publishing. It is certainly as time consuming as both the writing of the work and the printing of it put together. To succeed here you need a certain flair and you should definitely not be of a retiring nature. If you intend selling through the trade (and even if you don't you are bound to come into contact with bookshop orders at some stage) your costing must be correct and *worked out in advance*. Shops will want at least 33% of the selling price as discount. You'll need about the same again to cover your distribution, promotion and other overheads, leaving the final third to cover production costs and any profit you may wish to make. Multiply your unit production cost by at least 4. Commerical publishers often multiply by as much as 9.

Do not expect the trade to pay your carriage costs. Your terms should be 33% post free on everything bar single copy orders. Penalise these by reducing your discount to 25%. Some shops will suggest that you sell copies to them on *sale or return*. This means that they only pay you for what they sell and then only after they've sold it. This is a common practice with certain categories of publications and often the only way to get independent books into certain shops; but from the self-publisher's point of view it should be avoided if at all possible. Cash in hand is best but expect to have your invoices paid by cheque at a later date. Buy a duplicate pad in order to keep track of what's going on. Phone the shops you have decided should take your book or turn up in person and ask to see the buyer. Letters and sample copies sent by post will get ignored. Get a freelance distributor to handle all of this for you if you can. Check the trade section of Cassell's *Directory of Publishing* or advertise for one in *The Bookseller*. If you can contract one they will want another 12% or so commission on top of the shops' discount – but expect to have to go it alone.

What about promotion?

A vital aspect often overlooked by beginners. Send out as many review copies as you can, all accompanied by slips quoting selling price and name and address of the publisher. Never admit to being that person yourself. Invent a name, it will give your operation a professional feel. Ring up newspapers and local radio stations ostensibly to check that your copy has arrived but really to see if they are prepared to give your book space. Try to think of an angle for them, anything around which they can write a story. Buying advertising space rarely pays for itself but good local promotion with 100% effort will generate dividends.

What about depositing copies at the British Library?

Under the Copyright Acts the British Library, the Bodleian Library, Oxford, The University Library, Cambridge, The National Library of Scotland, the Library of Trinity College Dublin and the National Library of Wales are all entitled to a free copy of your book which must be sent to them within one month of publication. One copy should go direct to the Legal Deposit Office at The British Library, Boston Spa, Wetherby, West Yorkshire LS23 7BY. The other libraries use an agent, Mr A.T. Smail, at 100 Euston Street, London NW1 2HQ *tel* 0171-388 5061. Contact him directly to find out how many copies he requires. Many self-publishers object to sending books out for nothing but there are advantages. Data on your title will be used by the libraries as part of their bibliographic services and the book itself will eventually form part of a comprehensive national printed archive and be made available to the public.

What if I can't manage all this myself?

You can employ others to do it for you. If you are a novelist and you opt for a package covering everything, it could set you back more than £10,000. A number of publishers and associations advertise such services in writers' journals and in the Sunday classifieds. *Authors. Publish with us.* is a typical ploy. They will do a competent job for you, certainly, but you will still end up having to do the bulk of the selling yourself. It is a costly route, fraught with difficulty. Do the job on your own if you possibly can.

And what if it goes wrong?

Put all the unsolds under the bed or give them away. It has happened to lots of us. Even the big companies who are experienced at these things have their regular flops. It was an adventure and you did get your book published. On the other hand you may be so successful that you'll be at the London Book Fair selling the film rights and wondering if you've reprinted enough. Whichever way it goes – good luck.

Where to learn more

Finch, Peter, *How To Publish Yourself*, Allison & Busby, 1991

Foster, Charles, *Editing, Design and Book Production*, Journeyman, 1993

Godber, Bill, Webb, Robert, and Smith, Keith, *Marketing For Small Publishers*, Journeyman, 1992

Kritzinger, Ann, *Brief Guide to Self-Publishing*, Scriptmate Editions, 1991.

Spicer, Robert, *How To Publish A Book*, How To Books, 1993

Zeitlyn, Jonathan, *Print: How You Can Do It Yourself!*, Journeyman, 1992

Organisations which can help

Association of Little Presses, 89A Petherton Road, London N5 2OT *tel* 0171-226 2657. Membership £12.50. Offers advice, publishes a catalogue of small independent publications, produces a newsletter, organises book fairs. Write for their booklet *Self-Publishing: Not So Difficult After All.*

Password (Books) Ltd, 23 New Mount Street, Manchester M4 4DE *tel* 0161-953 4009. Runs publishing training courses for small and self-publishers; grants available.

Author-Publisher Enterprise, 7 Kingsland Road, West Mersea, Essex CO5 8RB *tel* (01206) 382558. Membership £25. A self-publishers' self-help organisation. Runs courses, lectures; publishes *Write to Publish*, an essential self-publisher's newsletter; compiles a catalogue of members' publications; and a directory of services. Self-publishers should certainly join the A-PE.

Vanity Publishing

Reputable publishers very rarely ask authors to pay for the production of their work, to contribute to its cost, or to undertake purchase of copies. Exceptions may be a book of an extremely specialised nature with a very limited market, or perhaps the first book of poems by a talented new writer. In such cases, especially if the book makes a significant contribution to its subject, an established and reliable publisher may be prepared to accept a subvention from the author to make publication possible, and such financial grants often come from scientific or other academic foundations or funds. This is a very different procedure from that of the *vanity publisher* who claims to perform, for a fee to be paid by the author, all the many functions involved in publishing a book.

In their effort to secure business vanity publishers will usually give exaggerated praise to an author's work and arouse equally unrealistic hopes of its commercial success. However, when authors pay vanity publishers they are paying simply for the manufacture of copies. If all they want is a book which they can show with pride to their family and friends – then no harm may come of it. But 'manufacture' should not be confused with 'publication'. True publishers invest *their own* money in the whole publishing process: editorial, design, manufacturing, selling, distribution. The vanity publisher invests *the author's* money in but one part of this process: manufacture.

The distressing reports we have received from embittered victims of vanity publishers underline the importance of reading extremely carefully the contracts offered by such publishers. Often these will provide for the printing of, say, 2000 copies of the book, usually at a quite exorbitant cost to the author, but will leave the 'publisher' under no obligation to bind more than a very limited number. Frequently, too, the author will be expected to pay the cost of any effective advertising, while the 'publisher' makes little or no effort to promote the distribution and sale of the book. Again, the names and imprints of vanity publishers are well known to literary editors, and their productions therefore are rarely, if ever, reviewed or even noticed in any important periodical. Similarly, such books are hardly ever stocked by booksellers.

To reiterate: except in rare instances, never pay for 'publication', whether for a book, an article, a lyric, or a piece of music. If a work is worth publishing, sooner or later a publisher will be prepared to publish it at his or her own expense. However, writers who cannot resist the temptation of seeing their work in print, in book form, should consider the possibility of self-publishing (see page 263). If, after all, a writer decides to approach a vanity publisher, even though he or she has to pay a substantial sum, it should first be established just how much or how little the publisher will provide and do in return for the payment demanded.

FURTHER READING

Clifford, Johnathon, *Vanity Press & the Proper Poetry Publishers* (1994), £6.00, and *Vanity Publishers: Marketing – the Facts and the Fiction – A Report* (1995), £15.00; both published by Johnathan Clifford. Available from 27 Mill Road, Fareham, Hants PO16 0TH   *tel/fax* (01329) 822218.

Poetry

Poetry into Print

JOHN WHITWORTH

I have never edited a poetry magazine nor worked in a publishing house. But I *have* submitted hundreds of poems and I have had dealings, most of them happy, with a number of publishers of poetry. My advice will therefore be from the handle end of the long spoon that poets use to sup with those they would persuade or bamboozle into printing, even paying for, their work.

There are two things to say at the outset. Do not expect to make more than pin money *directly* from publication of your work. You may, in the fullness of time, make quite a tidy sum *indirectly* – I mean you get work because you are a published poet: readings, workshops, reviewing and so forth, if you like any of that sort of thing. But if you get £50 for a poem from a national magazine you may feel very satisfied, and as for your published slim volumes – they will not sell in four figures, nor do the publishers, except in a very few instances, expect them to. In a sense nearly all poetry publishing is vanity publishing. Nobody is in it for the money.

And, secondly, as one poet put it to me, do not have too much respect for the taste of individual literary editors. She is right. An editor is not God (whatever he or she thinks). Remember that, though it can be hard if you are diffident and most poets are). But this person is just like you; the fact that he or she (nearly always he) is warming an editorial chair may mean many things. It certainly does not mean papal infallibility. If Snooks of the *Review* sends back your work, despatch it immediately to Snurd of the *Supplement*. And if Snurd concurs with Snooks, they may both be wrong, indeed neither may actually have read through (or at all) what you sent. Grit your teeth and send to Snarl and then to Snivel. Do not be discouraged by rejection. If your poems are as good as you can make them and have been submitted in as professional a way as you can manage, then just keep on sending them out. I started writing poems in 1968, wrote my first good one in 1972, and was paid my first proper money (£40 from the Arts Council) in 1976. The first book was published in 1980. So patience and a thick skin are big advantages.

It does help, of course, to have read the magazine you are making submissions to. This will prevent you sending your bawdy ballad to *PN Review* or concrete poetry to *The Spectator*. And I am assuming that you actually are interested in the *craft* of poetry and the names of, say, Milton, Tennyson and Eliot mean something to you. You will also be interested to know what Heaney, Hughes,

Harrison, Carol Ann Duffy and Fiona Pitt-Kethley actually do. You don't have
to like it, but you ought to want to know about it. If no one is writing anything
remotely like your work, perhaps you should ask yourself why that might be. On
the other hand, remember the words of Charlie Coburn, the old music-hall
singer: 'I sang my song to them, and they didn't like it. So I sang it again, and
they still didn't like it. So I sang it a third time and one of them thought he might
just get to like it if I changed the tune and altered the words. So I sang it again,
just exactly the same way, and after a bit they all liked it.'

SUBMITTING YOUR WORK TO MAGAZINES

I asked a number of poets about this. Some of them surprised me by saying they
never submitted to magazines at all, because they disliked being rejected. I must
say I think that a rather craven attitude, but you *can*, if you are talented enough,
carve out a poetic reputation through workshops and readings. You must be
good at putting yourself about in public and have the time and energy to expend
on it.

All who did submit work regularly agreed on a number of basics:

1. Submit your poem on an A4 sheet (or the computer-paper rough equivalent),
typed or printed out from a word processor. One poet, David Phillips, reckoned
his percentage of successful submissions had gone up appreciably since he bought
his word processor, and he assumed it was because his work now looked much
more professional. It might be, of course, that it has just got better. Do not type
it in italic, capitals or mock cursive. Keep it simple.
2. Put your name and address at the bottom of each poem. Editors, reasonably,
do not keep your letters, only the poems that interest them. You might consider
one of those rubber stamps. I know a number of poets who have them, though
I don't myself.
3. Fold the poem once and put it into the sort of envelope designed to take A4
folded once. I don't know why poets like to scrunch their verses into tiny
envelopes, but don't do it. Don't go to the other extreme either and send it
decorated with admonitions not to bend, etcetera. Include a stamped, self-
addressed envelope of the same size. This really is important. Shakespeare
himself would be consigned to the wpb without an appropriate sae.
4. Do not send just one poem. Do not send 20 poems. Send enough to give a
reasonable flavour of your work – say about four or five. Long poems are less
likely to be accepted than short poems, for very obvious reasons. If you write
different *kinds* of things, then make sure your selection covers a fair few of these
kinds. Send what you think of as your best work, but do not be surprised if what
is finally accepted is the one you put in at the last minute, 'to make the others
look better' as Larkin lugubriously puts it. And if an editor says he or she likes
your work and would like to see more, then *send* more as soon as possible. The
editor wasn't just being polite. Editors aren't. It was said because it was meant.
5. At this point there is generally some po-faced stuff about *never* sending the
same poem to more than one editor simultaneously. As it happens, I don't do
this, but it appears that some well-known poets do. And indeed, if Snurd of the
Supplement sits on your poems for six months, what are you supposed to do,
since the polite follow-up letter recommended will, almost certainly, have no
effect at all, except to waste your time and your stamps? The real reason for not
making multiple submissions is the embarrassment of having to make grovelling
noises when the same poem is accepted by two editors at once. I once, inad-
vertently, won two microscopic prizes in poetry competitions for the same poem.
What did I do? I kept my mouth shut and cashed the cheques, that's what I did.

6. You wouldn't have been daft enough to send off your *only* copies of poems
to Snurd, would you? *Of course* he lost them and it's all your own silly fault. No
you can't sue him through the civil courts, but you'll know better next time. Send
photocopies and keep your originals. No, editors don't mind photocopies. Why
should they? They look a lot better than the original all covered in Tippex
anyway.

7. Keep your covering letter short, but if you have been published in reputable
places then it will do no harm to say so. This advice comes from Duncan Forbes.
Selling poems is very like selling anything else, so blow your own trumpet, but
don't blow for too long. Don't ask the editor for help in the advancement of your
poetic career. Editors don't care, and anyway, what do they know? Being rude
won't help either. I know artists are supposed to be rude and a lot of them are,
too, but it hasn't actually helped them to anything except an ulcer or a punch on
the nose.

WHICH MAGAZINES?

You *could* start with *The Times Literary Supplement* but I wouldn't advise it.
One editor (not from the *TLS*) said honestly that he tended to reject, more or
less unread, poems from anyone he had never heard of. Before you play with
the big boys perhaps you ought to have some sort of a record in the little
magazines. Some of these pay and some do not. The size of the cheque seems
to depend on the size of the Arts Council grant rather than the quality of the
magazine, though I suppose the two ought to have some sort of relationship.
What matters is not the cash but whether you feel proud or ashamed to be seen
in the thing. The Poetry Library at the South Bank Centre (Royal Festival Hall,
London SE1 8XX) publishes a list of poetry magazines, and if you can get along
there (very convenient for Waterloo Station and open 11-8 for seven days a
week), you can nose around among the back numbers and see what is appealing
to you. If you can't do that, then a letter with an sae will get you the list. The
one I am looking at has well over a hundred titles, from photocopied and stapled
compilations all the way up to *Poetry Review*, the magazine of the Poetry Society,
to which I suggest you subscribe (for your own benefit, and not the Poetry
Society's). Judge where you think you will fit in, and buy yourself a big sheet of
second-class stamps. Send off your work and be prepared to be reasonably
patient. Most editors reply in the end. Little magazines have a high mortality
rate, so be prepared for a particularly crushing form of disappointment – having
your work accepted by a magazine which promptly ceases publication. It happens
to us all; it goes on happening to me. The Poetry Library also sends out for an
sae of about 70p a satisfying wodge of bumph about poetry publishing in general.
Worth the money.

Some inexperienced poets seem very worried that editors will filch their 'ideas'
and pay them nothing, but poems are not made up of ideas; they are made up
of words, and if anyone prints your poem without permission they are infringing
your copyright and you can threaten them with all sorts of horrible things. But,
honestly, this is a buyer's market, and even the editor of that badly photocopied
rag has more material than he can use. I ought to mention the *Poetry Now*
anthologies, widely advertised, always trawling for contributions. This looks like
vanity publishing (see page 267) but it isn't. You don't have to pay, you sometimes
even get royalties and your poem doesn't have to be very good.

There seems to be a new kind of organisation that solicits poems. Often with
names like Global or International, they don't ask for money up front, so are
not exactly vanity presses. But they encourage you in marketers' prose to buy
super-duper anthologies for £40 or so. Harmless, I suppose, but I'd rather appear
in something less pretentious along with some poets I had actually heard of.

I have already recommended *Poetry Review*. *Poetry Wales* and *The New Welsh Review* are both beautifully produced, though they lack *PR*'s bite and attack, and there is a certain amount of relentless celticity. *HU* (*The Honest Ulsterman*) is unpretentious to look at, but consistently interesting and intelligent – you don't have to be at all Irish to contribute either. *Ambit* is lively with good artwork; the editors take ages to look at submissions. *Iron* is run by a relic of the 60s (Peter Mortimer who has a little boy called Dylan). The quality of the work has steadily improved along with the quality of the production. Mortimer is a most conscientious editor too, and replies promptly and individually. *Stand* has a wide distribution – a rather *Guardian*-y feel to the poems and opinions. *London Magazine* is as good as ever – Alan Ross scribbles cryptic encouragement on poems that don't quite make it. *PN Review* is a Leavisite dinosaur with very rude reviewers, an offshoot of the publisher Carcanet (or the other way round) and prints a wide range of poems. *Edinburgh Review* also has rude reviewers. This is a personal list – magazines I read from time to time. (See the classified list on page 138 for the poetry magazines listed in this *Yearbook*.

The two literary heavyweights are *The Times Literary Supplement* and *The London Review of Books*, and both publish poetry. The *TLS* does not publish Fiona Pitt-Kethley's ruderies. P.J. Kavanagh at *The Spectator* publishes poems every week. There are poems in *The Independent* and *The Guardian*. I have in front of me a list from *Poetry Now* running to four pages of local newspapers that publish poetry if you can believe it. If all else fails you can get yourself a modem and publish your poems on the Internet. Then readers can tell you what they think by e-mail!

BOOK PUBLICATION

Every poet wants to get a book out. How do you do it? One pretty sure way is to win a big prize in a competition, the National or the biennial Arvon or Harry Chambers' Peterloo, though a high proportion of the winners have published books already, which seems unfair of them. Otherwise, you wait until you have reached the stage of having had two or three dozen poems published in reputable places; then you type out enough poems for a collection, traditionally 64pp but collections seem to be getting longer, and send them out, keeping your own copy and including return postage. I suppose you do. I first got published by talking to Anthony Thwaite in a pub; everybody needs a slice of luck. I know some excellent poets who are still trying to place their first book and, contrariwise, there are books from big publishers that are complete disasters in every way. Poetry, like most things, goes in fashions. But don't be in a hurry. Wait until you have some sort of a reputation in the magazines and small presses. Neil Astley at Bloodaxe reckons more than 90 per cent of what comes through his letterbox he sends back, and he has usually had an eye on the successful ones before they got around to submitting.

Who do you send out to? Faber are still out in front (though they did turn down Larkin's *The Less Deceived*, the most influential book of English poems in the last 50 years). It is not that their 1990s poets are all better, but Faber promote them heavily and care about them. And being a Faber poet puts you in the company of Eliot and Larkin. Penguin are reviving their excellent Modern Poets series, so they may join Faber on the railway bookstalls. Most other big publishers do poetry – fortunes wax and wane with the person, often a poet, nearly always a man, in the editorial chair.

But being published by a household name does not mean selling thousands – hundreds are more common. Publishers like to have poetry on their list as a badge of virtue, but often they don't want to know much about it, they don't promote it and they don't persist with it. The book sinks or swims, and usually it sinks.

Specialist poetry presses (some, though not all of which, publish nothing but poetry) produce books that look every bit as good and, in most cases, sell every bit as well (or badly). Bloodaxe, Peterloo and Carcanet, none of them London-based, are leaders in the field.

Bloodaxe sounds fearsomely dismissive, but the name is from a Viking who conquered Northumberland. They have more titles and possibly better poets than Faber but they still fail the railway bookstall test. 'From traditional formalists to post-modernists', says Neil Astley. Bloodaxe poets tend to be young and come from north of Watford. Carcanet publish both Elizabeth Jennings and John Ashberry, which indicates Michael Schmidt's catholicity and willingness to go outside this country. He sees them as extending the Wordsworthian tradition of the common voice and welcomes manuscripts, though he wishes people would read some of the books on his list first. This is good advice; every publisher has a style, just as every magazine has. His latest find is Sophie Hannah, the infant phenomenon. If infancy is long past, then Harry Chambers at Peterloo is worth a try. He published a first book by Kirkpatrick Dobie in the poet's eighty-fourth year. Dana Gioia, the American 'new formalist' and Ursula Fanthorpe are his biggest guns.

Anvil are London-based and do a lot of poetry in translation. Enitharmon have Duncan Forbes, the most underrated poet now writing, Seren is Welsh, Peepal Tree is ethnic and The Women's Press is women.

There are a lot more excellent small presses and information on them is available from the following:

The Association of Little Presses (ALP), 89a Petherton Road, London N5 2QT. They (they appear to be Bob Cobbing, the grand old man of concrete poetry) put out a newsletter and a catalogue for £2.40 + 60p p&p.

The Oriel Bookshop (Welsh Arts Council Bookshop, The Friary, Cardiff CF1 4AA) publishes *Small Presses and Little Magazines of the UK and Ireland*.

Small Press Listings is available quarterly from The National Small Press Centre, Middlesex University, White Hart Lane, London N17 8HR *tel* 0181-362 6058.

Light's List is just that, a list of over 600 small press magazines. It costs £1.00 plus A5 sae from Photon Press, The Light House, 29 Longfield Road, Tring, Herts. HP23 4DG.

The Poetry Library (address earlier) has a Current Awareness List for Asian and Afro-Caribbean Poetry. Mine is 38pp of bookshops, competitions, libraries, magazines, organisations, UK publishers and workshops.

COMPETITIONS

Some poets are very snooty about these, though I can't think why. Of course they are popular because they make money for the organisers. Think of the numbers: a biggish competition may attract 10,000 entries paying £3 a time. That gives an income of £30,000, enough to pay for some good prizes, a fair bit of promotion, fees for the judges and running costs, and still leave a nice bit in the kitty. But, from the poet's end, it is a good deal too. Though unknowns (everybody starts as an unknown, don't they?) only occasionally win the big prizes, they do pick up the smaller ones quite often, and that can be a great encouragement when you need it. The competitions (I have judged two big ones and a number of little ones) are organised fairly (I organise one too), and everyone does have an equal chance. So why *not* have a go? If you are just starting out, then enter the competitions with first prizes of hundreds rather than thousands of pounds. The big guns probably won't enter these. You can find details of current competitions on page 275.

VANITY PUBLISHING/SUBSIDY PUBLISHING

Never give a publisher money. That is what they give to you. If you want your work in print and nobody will do it for you without a cheque, then do it yourself. Self-publishers have made money before now, though not usually (I think) with poetry. You could probably buy yourself an Amstrad with the money you save by *not* answering that advertisement!

A LAST WORD

Invest some time, invest some money. Buy yourself, if not a word processor, at least a decent typewriter and some nice paper. Buy some books of poetry and try to see how your favourites do it. If you're a joiner, join a local group. Your local Regional Arts Board will know who they are. The Muse chooses her favourites, but be a bit welcoming.

Poetry Organisations

MARY ENRIGHT
The Poetry Library

SOCIETIES

The Poetry Society, 22 Betterton Street, London WC2H 9BU *tel* 0171-240 4810 *fax* 0171-240 4818. The Poetry Society has been operating for over 80 years and exists to help poets and poetry thrive in Britain today. Its principal activities include the publication of *Poetry Review* and *Poetry News*; involvement in promotions such as National Poetry Day; running an information and training service; administration of the W.H. Smith-sponsored Poets-in-Schools scheme and the annual National Poetry Competition; provision of 'The Script' critical service.

Its new centre – 'The Poetry Place' – includes a café, reading room, meeting space and access to the Internet. Open to members and friends of the Society, which is open to all. You can also visit the Place via the Society's Internet website; 'The Poetry Map' is at http://www.bbcnc.org.uk/online/poetry *e-mail* poetrysoc@dial.pipex.com

Poetry Ireland, Bermingham Tower, Upper Yard, Dublin Castle, Dublin 2, Republic of Ireland *tel* (01) 6714632 *fax* (01) 6714634. Poetry Ireland acts as the Irish Poetry Society and also runs the Austin Clarke Library, a reference library of over 10,000 titles. It publishes *Poetry Ireland Review*, a quarterly magazine, organises readings in Dublin and nationally, and runs the Writers in Schools scheme.

European Association for the Promotion of Poetry, European Poetry Centre, 'The Seven Sleepers', J.P. Minckelersstraat 168, B-3000 Louvain, Belgium *tel* (16) 235351.

Regional Arts Boards. The officers responsible for literature in the Regional Arts Boards can provide information on local poetry groups, workshops and societies. Many Boards give grant aid to local publishers and magazines and help fund festivals and readings, etc.; some run critical services. A list of the relevant officers is available on receipt of an sae from the Information Service, The Arts Council of England, 14 Great Peter Street, London SW1P 3NQ.

LIBRARIES

The Poetry Library, Royal Festival Hall, South Bank Centre, London SE1 8XX *tel* 0171-921 0943/0664 *fax* 0171-921 0939. The Poetry Library was founded in 1953 by the Arts Council of Great Britain (now the Arts Council of England). It is now part of the Literature section of the South Bank Centre and can be found on Level 5 of the Royal Festival Hall. Its two principal roles are to collect and preserve all poetry published in the UK in this century, and to act as a public lending library. Two copies of all titles are purchased, allowing one to be available for consultation and the other to go out on loan. Books may be borrowed by those outside London through the national Inter-Library Lending network. The collection of about 30,000 titles is all in the English language, although it includes translations from all over the world. There is a large children's section, as well as poetry on cassette, record and video.

As well as the normal functions of all libraries, the Poetry Library also runs an active information service on all poetry-related activities, and offers advice to the new poet. Current awareness lists are produced and are available by post on receipt of a large sae. They include lists of magazines, competitions, bookshops, groups and workshops, evening classes, festivals, etc. and are updated regularly. The Library also stocks the full range of British poetry magazines as well as a large selection from abroad.

Membership of the Library is free, and is open to all on production of proof of identity and current address.

The Scottish Poetry Library, Tweeddale Court, 14 High Street, Edinburgh EH1 1TE *tel* 0131-557 2876. Founded in 1984, the Scottish Poetry Library is run along similar lines to the Poetry Library in London, specialising in twentieth-century poetry written in Scotland, in Scots, Gaelic and English. It also collects some pre-twentieth century poetry and contemporary poetry from all over the world. Information and advice on all poets is given and visits by individuals, groups and schools are welcome. Borrowing is free of charge and there is a membership scheme at £10.00 p.a., which includes use of members' reading room and regular newsletter. It has branches in libraries and arts centres throughout Scotland and also runs a mobile library service. Readings and exhibitions are regularly organised, particularly during the Edinburgh Festival.

Northern Poetry Library, County Library, The Willows, Morpeth, Northumberland NE61 1TA *tel* (01670) 512385. Founded in 1968, the Northern Arts Poetry Library serves the area covered by the Northern Arts Regional Board, i.e. Tyne and Wear, Durham, Northumberland, Cumbria and Cleveland. Its collection contains over 6000 titles of mostly British material. It is run by Northumberland Public Library as one of its special services.

The British Haiku Society Library, 27 Park Street, Westcliff-on-Sea, Essex SS0 7PA. The BHS Library is a collection of books, magazines and cassettes in haiku and related forms. It is a mail-order, members only lending library. Details on membership from the above address.

Public libraries. Public libraries can be an invaluable source of information on writing activities in the area in addition to having collections of modern poetry for loan. Some also have literature field workers or writers-in-residence, who can be very helpful to beginners.

COMPETITIONS AND AWARDS

There are literally hundreds of poetry competitions going on throughout the year, varying widely in quality and quantity of entries and prizes. The two most important are the National Poetry Competition run by the Poetry Society and the biennial Arvon Foundation International Poetry Competition. Details of these and other competitions can be found under **Literary prizes and awards**. The Poetry Library produces a free list, updated monthly, of these and other competitions, and is available on receipt of a large sae.

There are several prestigious awards for poetry, most awarded annually to published poets, and therefore non-competitive. A complete list of prizes is included in the *Guide to Literary Prizes 1995*, published by Book Trust (45 East Hill, London SW18 2QZ), 8th edn, 1995. Also available from the same address is a free leaflet on grants and awards.

BOOKSHOPS

Not all general bookshops have a strong modern poetry section but there are some which specialise in poetry. The principal ones are the following:

The Poetry Bookshop/Alan Halsey
22 Broad Street
Hay-on-Wye
Herefordshire HR3 5DB

HMSO Oriel Bookshop
The Friary
Cardiff CF1 4AA

Peter Riley
27 Sturton Street
Cambridge CB1 2QG

These and other good bookshops stocking a range of poetry are listed by the Poetry Library; this list is divided into London and outside London areas and can be obtained by sending a large sae.

FESTIVALS

Literature festivals have become increasingly popular and prestigious in the past few years and are now held in almost every part of the country. Again information on what is happening in your area should be readily available from your local library and Regional Arts Board. A selection of literature festivals is listed on page 672 and the British Council keeps a list of forthcoming literature festivals. Send an A4 or A5 size sae to the Information Officer, Literature Department, British Council, 11 Portland Place, London W1N 4EJ.

PERFORMANCE VENUES

In London the best way to keep up to date with readings and poetry events is through the weekly listing magazines, *Time Out* and *What's On in London*. The main London venues are the Voice Box in the South Bank Centre, Apples and Snakes Performance Poetry at Battersea Arts Centre, the Blue Nose Café and Terrible Beauty at the Troubadour Coffee House.

Outside London, local listings magazines should be helpful and Regional Arts Boards and public libraries will have details of all literature events happening in their area.

POETRY GROUPS AND WORKSHOPS

Joining a poetry group can be an excellent way to get useful help and advice on writing and publishing. Groups vary enormously; if possible, try a few in your area to find the one most congenial to your style. They tend to wax and wane, but your Regional Arts Board and local library should have up-to-date information on those currently active. You could also consult *Poetry Groups Register*, published by Blaxland Family Press, 12 Matthews Road, Taunton, Somerset TA1 4NH *tel* (01823) 257634.

The Poetry Library compiles a list of groups and workshops for the Greater London area; this is updated regularly and available on receipt of a large sae.

WRITING COURSES

There is currently much more available than ever before in the area of short-term creative writing courses, as writers-in-residence are appointed by Regional Arts Boards, and by libraries, colleges, prisons, etc. There is also a choice of residential writing courses of which the long established ones are run by the Arvon Foundation and the Tŷ Newydd. All areas of writing are covered, as well as poetry.

Arvon Foundation

The Arvon Foundation runs three centres, in Yorkshire, Devon and Inverness-shire, and has wide experience of residential writing courses. Most last for about five days and offer tuition by working writers. Full details of annual courses may be obtained from: The Arvon Foundation at Lumb Bank, Hebden Bridge, West Yorkshire HX7 6DF; The Arvon Foundation at Totleigh Barton, Sheepwash, Beaworthy, Devon EX21 5NS; The Arvon Foundation at Moniack Mhor, Teavarran, Kiltarlity, Beauly, Inverness-shire IV4 7HT.

Tŷ Newydd

Courses here are run along similar lines to the Arvon Houses with a wide variety of courses offered. Some of the tutors used are Welsh writers though there is a good mix. Full details can be obtained from Taliesin, Tŷ Newydd, Llanystumdwy, Criccieth, Gwynedd LL52 0LW.

Other courses

East Midlands Arts runs a number of residential writing courses from June 1996 to April 1997 located at Leicester University. Again, a variety of types of writing is covered and details for future courses are available from East Midlands Arts, Mountfields House, Epinal Way, Loughborough, Leics. LE11 0QE.

The Poets' House in Northern Ireland runs courses in poetry only. Three two-week courses are offered over the summer months; an MA in creative writing is also available. Details from The Poets' House, 79 Portmuck Road, Islandmagee, Co. Antrim BT40 3TP.

Information on other such courses can be obtained from the Regional Arts Boards, local libraries or the Poetry Library.

POETRY FOR CHILDREN AND YOUNG ADULTS

Poetry Society Education

Poetry Society Education promotes poetry throughout the formal education sector and beyond. It offers a wide range of services and facilities to teachers, young people and students, running activities such as the W.H. Smith Poets-in-Schools scheme and Poets in Hospitals. In addition to publishing a range of materials including the *Teachers' Poetry Resources File*, poetry posters and the *Young Poetry Pack*, Poetry Society Education also produces teaching resources for Education members of the Poetry Society. Other services include training courses and events for students, teachers, readers and writers. These occur both on-site at The Poetry Place and at selected venues around the country. INSET is also available – along with an Advice and Information Service which puts schools in touch with poets and works to keep young writers informed about competitions, magazines and ways to develop their creative writing. Publications may be obtained via the Publications Officer. Further information about educational services can be obtained from the Education Development Officer, The Poetry Society, 22 Betterton Street, London WC2H 9BU   *tel* 0171-240 4810.

The Poetry Library

The Poetry Library has a large children's section of about 4000 books incorporating the SIGNAL Collection of Children's Poetry. It runs an Education service for teachers and schools, which includes class visits and poet-led workshops. A Teachers' Information Pack covering all aspects of poetry in education is available, as are selected reading lists for different age groups.There is a special collection of books and materials for teachers and poets involved in education; the teachers' membership scheme offers special loan facilities to use books in the classroom. Details from the Children's Section, The Poetry Library, Royal Festival Hall, London SE1 8XX.

Young Book Trust

Young Book Trust is the children's division of Book Trust. Its aims are to promote reading and offer advice and information on all aspects of children's reading and books. It runs a library of all children's books published over the last two years. It organises Children's Book Week, held usually in October, co-ordinating national activities throughout the week. It also offers an information service, including information on authors (Authorbank), and publishes a newsletter. A subscription service is available for schools, libraries, colleges, bookshops and publishers. Details from Young Book Trust, Book House, 45 East Hill, London SW18 2QZ.

National Association of Writers in Education

NAWE is a national organisation which aims to widen the scope of writing in education, and co-ordinate activities between writers, teachers and funding bodies. It publishes a magazine, *Writing in Education*, and a national directory of writers who work in schools, colleges and the community. Membership details and further information from NAWE, PO Box 1, Sheriff Hutton, York YO6 7YU   *tel* (01653) 618429.

Competitions

The number of good poetry competitions for children are limited; below is a list of the main annual ones.

W.H. Smith Young Writers Competition This is an annual open competition for original writing – poems, stories, plays or articles – by children aged 16 and under. Information is available from W.H. Smith Young Writers Competition, Strand House, 7 Holbein Place, Sloane Square, London SW1W 8NR.

Welsh Academy Young Writers Competition This is a national competition in which poetry and prose are acceptable in three categories, the upper limit being 18. The closing date is usually July. Information from Young Writers Competition, PO Box 328, Cardiff CF2 4XL.

BBC Radio 4 Young Poetry Competition First launched in 1994, there are three age categories between 8-21 years for poems written for Radio. Details from BBC Radio 4 Young Poetry Competition, BBC Broadcasting House, Whiteladies Road, Bristol BS8 2LR.

The Roald Dahl Foundation Poetry Competition Annual competition divided into four age groups, between 7 and 17 years. Details from The Roald Dahl Foundation Poetry Competition, PO Box 1375, 20 Vauxhall Bridge Road, London SW1V 2SA.

FURTHER READING FOR POETS

ALP, *Catalogue of Little Press Books in Print*, Association of Little Presses

Baldwin, Michael, *The Way to Write Poetry*, Hamish Hamilton, 1982

Bolton, Marjorie, *The Anatomy of Poetry*, Routledge, 1990

Chevalier, Tracy (ed.), *Contemporary Poets*, 5th edn, St James Press, 1991

Chisholm, Alison, *The Craft of Writing Poetry*, Allison & Busby, 1992

Chisholm, Alison, *A Practical Poetry Course*, Allison & Busby, 1994

Clifford, Johnathon, *Metric Feet and Other Gang Members*, Johnathon Clifford, 1993

Clifford, Johnathon, *Vanity Press & The Proper Poetry Publishers*, Johnathon Clifford, 1994

Corti, Doris, *Writing Poetry*, Thomas & Lochar, 1994

Fairfax, John and Moat, John, *The Way to Write*, Elm Tree Books, 1981

Fergusson, Rosalind, *The Penguin Rhyming Dictionary*, Penguin Books, 1992

Finch, Peter, *How to Publish Your Poetry*, Allison & Busby, 1985

Finch, Peter, *The Poetry Business*, Seren Books, 1994

Finch, Peter, *Small Presses and Little Magazines of the UK and Ireland: an address list*, Oriel

Fulton, Len, *Directory of Poetry Publishers*, 9th edn, Dustbooks, USA

Fulton, Len, *The International Directory of Little Magazines and Small Presses*, 29th edn, Dustbooks, USA

Gortschacher, Wolfgang, *Little Magazines Profiles*, University of Salzburg, 1993

Hamilton, Ian, *The Oxford Companion to Twentieth-Century Poetry in English*, Oxford University Press, 1994

Hyland, Paul, *Getting into Poetry*, Bloodaxe, 1992

Jerome, Judson, *1996 Poet's Market: Where and How to Publish Your Poetry*, Writer's Digest Books, USA

Lendennie, Jessie, *The Salmon Guide to Poetry Publishing in Ireland*, Salmon Publishing, 1989

Livingstone, Dinah, *Poetry Handbook for Readers & Writers*, Macmillan, 1992

Myers, Jack & Simms, Michael, *Longman Dictionary and Handbook of Poetry*, Longman, 1989

PALPI Poetry and Little Press Information, Association of Little Presses

Preminger, Alex, *New Princeton Encyclopedia of Poetry and Poetics*, 3rd rev. edn, Princeton University Press, USA, 1993

Roberts, Philip Davies, *How Poetry Works: the Elements of English Poetry*, Penguin Books, 1991

Sansom, Peter, *Writing Poems*, Bloodaxe, 1994

Scannell, Vernon, *How to Enjoy Poetry*, Piatkus, 1987

Scripts for theatre, tv, radio and film

Marketing a Play

JULIA JONES

As soon as a play is written, it is protected under the copyright laws of this country. No formalities are necessary here to secure copyright protection but it is a good plan to deposit a copy with the bank and take a dated receipt for it, so as to be able to prove the date of its completion, if this should be necessary at some time either, for example, to enforce a claim for infringement of copyright or to rebut such a claim. The copyright belongs to the author unless and until it is parted with; and this should never be done, since the copyright is in effect the sum total of all the author's rights in the work. An author should, so far as possible, deal separately with the component rights which go to make up the copyright and grant limited licences for the principal rights with, where customary or necessary, limited interests in the ancillary rights. A West End production agreement (see below) illustrates this principle.

The author can try to market the play personally, but once a play is accepted, it is wise to have professional assistance. All aspects of a contract are open for negotiation and the contractual complications are best handled by a reputable literary agent.

Although most ambitious young playwrights visualise a West End opening for their plays, the first step, except for the established dramatist, is usually to try to place the play with a company known to be interested in presenting new plays. It is wise to write to the company first, giving salient details, such as type of play, size of cast, number of sets, etc., and ask if the management would be willing to read it. This saves the frustration and expense of copies of the play being kept for long periods by managements who have no interest in it. Do not send your only copy of the play away – this seems obvious, but many authors have suffered the torment of having to rewrite from memory when the only copy has been lost. (See also the list of literary agents specialising in plays on page 324.) It is also possible to get a first production by entering the play for the various competitions which appear from time to time, but in this case great care should be taken to study the rules and ensure that the organisers of the competition do not acquire unreasonably wide rights and interests in the entries.

Many repertory companies will give a new play a try-out production in the hope that it will be seen by London managements and transfer to the West End. For the run at the repertory company's own theatre the company will receive a licence for a given period from a fixed date and pay the author a royalty of about

5 per cent calculated on the gross box office receipts. In return for the risk involved in presenting a new play, the repertory company will expect a share in the author's earnings from subsequent professional stage productions of the play during a limited period (usually two years). Sometimes on transfer the West End management will agree to take over responsibility for part or all of this payment.

The contract, for repertory or West End production, or for the use of any other rights in the play, should specify precisely the rights to which it refers, the territory covered, the period of time covered, the payments involved and make it clear that all other rights remain the property of the author.

For a first-class production in the West End of London, usually preceded by a short provincial tour, the author's contract will include clauses dealing with the following main heads of agreement. The substance, as well as the phrasing of these clauses will vary considerably, but those given below probably represent the average, as do the figures in brackets, which must not be assumed to be standard:

1. UK option

In consideration of a specified minimum sum (between £500 and £1000) as a non-returnable advance against royalties, the Manager shall have the exclusive option for a specified period (almost always twelve months) to produce the play in a first-class theatre in the West End of London (preceded possibly by a tour of a specified number of weeks) with an extension for a further period upon payment of a further similar sum.

2. UK licence

When the Manager exercises his or her option he or she shall have the UK licence for a specified period (three or five years) from the date of the first performance under the licence, such licence to terminate before the expiry of the specified period if:
(a) the play is not produced before a specified date;
(b) (i) less than a specified number (between 50 and 75) of consecutive professional performances are given and paid for in any year; or
(ii) the Manager has not paid at the beginning of any year a non-returnable advance against royalties. This variant on clause (b) (i) prevents the rights being tied up for a year while waiting to check if the qualifying performances have been given and is thus desirable from the author's point of view.

3. US option

If the Manager gives a specified number (usually 24) of consecutive performances in the West End he or she shall have an option exercisable within a specified period of the first West End performance (six weeks) to produce the play on Broadway on payment of a specified non-returnable advance on royalties (between £500 and £1000).

4. US licence

When the Manager exercises his or her option the Broadway licence shall be for a specified period (three years) on terms not less favourable than those specified in the Approved Production Contract of the Dramatists' Guild of America.

5. Other rights

Provided the play has run for the qualifying period (usually 24 performances) the Manager acquires interests in some of the other rights as follows:
(i) *Repertory.* The author should reserve these rights, paying the Manager a share (one-third) of his or her royalties for a specified period (two years after the end of the West End run or the expiry of the West End licence, whichever is the shorter). The author agrees not to release these rights until after the end of the

West End run without the Manager's consent, this consent not to be unreasonably withheld. It is recommended that a play should be released to theatres on the A list immediately after the end of the West End run, and to theatres on the B list within three months from the end of the West End run, if an option for a tour has not been taken up by then, otherwise at the end of the tour. The theatres on these lists are those recommended by the Theatres' National Committee for immediate and early release of plays to repertory.

(ii) *Amateur.* The author should reserve these rights and pay the Manager no share in his or her royalties, but should undertake not to release these rights for an agreed period, to allow the repertory theatres to have maximum clear run.

(iii) *Radio, television and video.* The author should reserve these rights but it may well be in his or her interest not to release them until some time after the end of the West End run. During the run of the play in the West End, however, the Manager may arrange for an extract from the play to be broadcast or televised for publicity purposes, the author's fee for such broadcast or television performances being paid to him or her in full without any part of it going to the Manager.

(iv) *Film.* If the Manager has produced the play for the qualifying period it is expected that the author will pay the Manager a percentage (often 20 per cent) of the author's net receipts from the disposal of the film rights, if these rights are disposed of within a specified period (one year) from the last West End performance. If the Manager has also produced the play on Broadway for the qualifying period the author is expected to allow him or her a further percentage (20 per cent) of the author's net receipts from the disposal of the film rights if the rights are disposed of within a specified time (one year) of the last Broadway performance. This is a field where the established dramatist can, not unnaturally, strike a much better bargain than the beginner. In no case, however, should the total percentage payable to the Manager exceed 40 per cent.

(v) *Foreign language.* These rights should be reserved to the author, the Manager receiving no share of the proceeds.

(vi) *Cassette.* These rights should be specifically reserved to the author.

Other clauses which should appear include:

(a) A royalty clause setting out the royalties which the author shall receive from West End and touring performances of the play – usually a scale rising from 5 per cent through $7\frac{1}{2}$ per cent to 10 per cent. If the author is registered for VAT, provision for VAT should be included here.

(b) Cast approval, etc. The author should be consulted about the casting and the director of the play, and in some cases may be able to insist on approval of the casting of a particular part.

(c) Rehearsals, scripts, etc. The author should be entitled to attend all rehearsals of the play and no alteration in the title or script should be made without the author's consent. All approved alterations in or suggestions for the script should become the author's property. In this clause also should appear details about supply of tickets for the author for opening performances and any arrangements for tickets throughout the West End run.

(d) Credits. Details of billing of the author's name on posters, programmes and advertising matter should be included.

(e) Lord Chamberlain's licence. The Theatres Act 1968 abolishes the power of the Lord Chamberlain to censor stage plays and play licences are no longer required. However, it is obligatory for managers to deposit a copy of the script on which the public performance of any new play is based with the Keeper of Manuscripts, British Library, Great Russell Street, London WC1B 3DG, within one month of the performance.

(f) The author will normally warrant that the play contains nothing that is obscene or defamatory or that infringes copyright.

There must also be:
(g) An accounting clause giving details of payment and requiring a certified statement of box office receipts.
(h) A clause giving the conditions under which the agreement may be assigned or sub-leased.
(i) A termination clause, stating the conditions under which the agreement shall terminate.

ARRANGEMENTS FOR OTHER RIGHTS AFTER THE FIRST-CLASS RUN OF THE PLAY

Provincial or repertory
The author or the author's representative will license provincial or repertory performances for a fixed royalty on the gross box office receipts – usually 10 per cent for a new play immediately after its West End run, dropping perhaps to 7½ per cent in later years.

Amateur
The author or the author's representative will license amateur performances of the play for a flat fee (normally between £20 and £30).

Publication
A firm specialising in acting editions of plays may offer to publish the play, in which case it will expect to license amateur performances and collect the fees on a commission basis (20 per cent to 50 per cent). The publication contract will also usually provide for the author to receive a royalty of 10 per cent of the published price of every copy sold.

Radio and television
Careful negotiation is required and care should be taken that repeat fees for repeat performances are included in the contract in addition to the initial fee for the first broadcast.

Film rights
Professional advice is absolutely necessary when dealing with a film contract as there are many complications. The rights may be sold outright or licensed for a number of years – usually not less than 7 or 10 or more than 15. The film company normally acquires the right of distribution throughout the world in all languages and expects a completely free hand in making the adaptation of the play into a film.

Foreign rights
It is usual to grant exclusive foreign language rights for the professional stage to an agent or translator who will arrange for a translation to be prepared and produced – it is wise to ask for evidence of the quality of the translator's work unless the translator is very well known. The financial arrangement is usually an advance against royalties for a given period to enable a translation to be prepared and then a licence to exploit the translation for a further period after production (usually 5 years).

Markets for Stage Plays

It is not easy for a new or comparatively unknown writer to find a management willing to present his or her play. The English Stage Company at the Royal Court Theatre and some other similarly enterprising organisations present a number of plays by new authors. However, new and inexperienced writers may find it easier to persuade amateur drama groups or provincial repertory theatres to present their work. Other markets may be found in the smaller fringe theatres.

The Stage reports productions of most new plays first produced by repertory theatres; study of this journal may reveal other potential markets for plays.

The Arts Council of England publishes a brochure, *Schemes for Writers & Theatre Companies*, which gives details of various forms of assistance available to playwrights and to theatres wishing to commission new plays. The help given by the Arts Council includes Bursaries (including the John Whiting Award) and help to writers who are being commissioned or encouraged by a theatre company. There is a number of Resident Dramatists' Attachment Awards available. Copies of the brochure and further information may be obtained from The Drama Director, The Arts Council of England, 14 Great Peter Street, London SW1P 3NQ.

It is probable that competitions for full-length and one-act plays and other special opportunities for new plays will be announced after the *Yearbook* has gone to press, and writers with plays on the stocks would do well to watch carefully for announcements in the Press, especially *The Observer*, *The Author*, *Amateur Stage* and *The Stage*.

Sketches for revues and broadcasting and plays for youth organisations are in demand. Sketches are usually bought outright, but in any case authors should know what rights they will be disposing of before accepting any offer.

In every case it is advisable to send a preliminary letter before submitting a manuscript. Suggestions for the preparation of manuscripts will be found in the article **Preparing and submitting a manuscript**.

Writers of plays are also referred to **Marketing a Play** and to the sections on **Radio** and **Television**. See page 140 for a list of **magazines** dealing with the theatre.

LONDON

Bush Theatre, Shepherd's Bush Green, London W12 8QD   *tel* 0171-602 3703   *fax* 0171-602 7614. *Literary manager:* Joanne Reardon. Welcomes unsolicited full-length scripts (accompanied by 1 small and 1 large sae); commissions writers at an early stage in their career; produces six premieres a year.

Michael Codron Ltd, Aldwych Theatre Offices, Aldwych, London WC2B 4DF   *tel* 0171-240 8291   *fax* 0171-240 8467.

Ray Cooney Presentations Ltd, Hollowfield Cottage, Littleton, Surrey GU3 1HN   *tel* (01483) 440 443   *fax* (01483) 32068. *Contact:* H.S. Udwin.

English Stage Company Ltd, Royal Court Theatre, Sloane Square, London SW1W 8AS   *tel* 0171-730 5174   *fax* 0171-730 4705. *Literary manager:* Graham Whybrow. New plays.

Greenwich Theatre Ltd, Greenwich Theatre, Crooms Hill, London SE10 8ES   *tel* 0181-858 4447. *Contact:* artistic director.

Hampstead Theatre, Swiss Cottage Centre, Avenue Road, London NW3 3EX   *tel* 0171-722 9224   *fax* 0171-722 3860. *Contact:* Ben Jancovich. New plays and the occasional modern classic. After initial assessment, promising scripts are then read by the literary manager and/or artistic director. It can therefore take 2-3 months to reach a decision.

Bill Kenwright Ltd, 59 Shaftesbury Avenue, London W1V 8JA   *tel* 0171-439 4466   *fax* 0171-437 8370. *General manager:* Max Finbow.

King's Head Theatre, 115 Upper Street, London N1 1QN   *tel* 0171-226 8561   *fax* 0171-226 8507. *Contact:* general manager.

Brian Kirk Associates, 3 Wigton Place, London SE11 4AN   *tel* 0171-820 0077   *fax* 0171-820 1237.

Knightsbridge Theatrical Productions Ltd, 21 New Fetter Lane, London EC4A 1JJ   *tel* 0171-583 8687   *fax* 0171-583 1040. *Contact:* Mrs Sheila H. Gray.

Lyric Theatre Hammersmith, King Street, London W6 0QL   *tel* 0181-741 0824   *fax* 0181-741 7694. *Chief executive:* Sue Storr; *artistic director:* Neil Bartlett. A producing theatre as well as a receiving venue for work by new writers, translators, performers and composers.

Man in the Moon Theatre, 392 King's Road, Chelsea, London SW3 5UZ   *tel* 0171-351 5701   *fax* 0171-351 1873. *Associate director:* Jacqui Somerville. Theatre and studio space; medium-scale company. Broad range of plays produced in-house (24-40 a year), including new writing; scripts from new writers considered.

Orange Tree Theatre, 1 Clarence Street, Richmond, Surrey TW9 2SA   *tel* 0181-940 0141   *fax* 0181-332 0369.

Questors Theatre, Mattock Lane, Ealing, London W5 5BQ   *tel* 0181-567 0011   *fax* 0181-567 8736. *Theatre manager:* Elaine Orchard; *marketing manager:* Colin Jervis. Annual Playwriting Competition with £1000 prize.

Royal National Theatre, South Bank, London SE1 9PX   *tel* 0171-928 2033   *fax* 0171-620 1197. Little opportunity for the production of unsolicited material, but submissions welcomed. Send to Jack Bradley, Literary Manager, together with an sae.

Royal Shakespeare Company, Barbican Theatre, Barbican, London EC2Y 8BQ   *tel* 0171-628 3351   *fax* 0171-374 0818. *Literary manager:* Colin Chambers.

Soho Theatre Company, 24 Mortimer Street, London W1N 7RD   *tel* 0171-436 8833   *fax* 0171-436 8844. *Artistic director:* Abigail Morris; *literary manager:* Paul Sirett. Always on the look out for new plays and playwrights and welcome unsolicited scripts. These are read by a professional panel who write a detailed critical report. Also offer various levels of workshop facilities, including rehearsed reading and platform performances, for promising playwrights, and in-depth script development with the Artistic Director and Literary Manager. See also the Verity Bargate Award on page 646.

Tabard Theatre, 2 Bath Road, Turnham Green, Chiswick, London W4 1LW   *tel* 0181-995 6035   *fax* 0181-747 8256. *Contact:* artistic director. Produces a number of shows each year, ranging from classic to contemporary world theatre.

Theatre Royal, Stratford East, Gerry Raffles Square, Newham, London E15 1BN   *tel* 0181-534 7374 ext 225   *fax* 0181-534 8381. *Assistant to the directors:* Paul Everitt.

The Tricycle Theatre Company, Tricycle Theatre, 269 Kilburn High Road, London NW6 7JR   *tel* 0171-372 6611   *fax* 0171-328 0795. *Contact:* Nicolas Kent.

Triumph Proscenium Productions Ltd, Suite 4, Waldorf Chambers, 11 Aldwych, London WC2B 4DA   *tel* 0171-836 0186   *fax* 0171-240 7511.

Turnstyle, Duke of York's Theatre, St Martin's Lane, London WC2N 4BG   *tel* 0171-240 9891   *fax* 0171-379 5748. *General manager:* Meryl Faiers.

Unicorn Theatre for Children, Arts Theatre, 6-7 Great Newport Street, London WC2H 7JB   *tel* 0171-379 3280   *fax* 0171-836 5366. *Administrative director:* Christopher Moxon; *artistic director:* Richard Williams. Six productions a year, in repertoire, for children aged 4-12 – new writing and adaptations.

Warehouse Theatre, Dingwall Road, Croydon CR0 2NF   *tel* 0181-681 1257. *Artistic director:* Ted Craig. New playwriting theatre producing up to six in-house productions each year. New scripts usually accepted via the International Playwriting Festival held annually in November (see page 656).

Michael White Productions Ltd, 48 Dean Street, London W1V 5HL   *tel* 0171-734 7707   *fax* 0171-734 7727. No unsolicited scripts.

PROVINCIAL

Abbey Theatre, Lower Abbey Street, Dublin 1, Republic of Ireland   *tel* (01) 8748741   *fax* (01) 8729177. *Artistic director:* Patrick Mason; *general manager:* Martin Fahy. Mainly produces plays written by Irish authors or on Irish subjects. Foreign plays are however regularly produced.

Yvonne Arnaud Theatre Management Ltd, Yvonne Arnaud Theatre, Millbrook, Guildford, Surrey GU1 3UX   *tel* (01483) 440077   *fax* (01483) 564071. Receives and produces Number One touring and pre-West End product.

Belgrade Theatre, Belgrade Square, Coventry CV1 1GS   *tel* (01203) 256431   *fax* (01203) 550680. Produces new plays both in the main house and studio. Scripts for consideration should be addressed to the Joint Artistic Directors. Please enclose sae.

Birmingham Repertory Theatre Ltd, Broad Street, Birmingham B1 2EP   *tel* 0121-236 6771   *fax* 0121-236 7883. *Artistic director:* Bill Alexander; *literary manager:* Ben Payne. Aims to provide a platform for the best work from new writers from both within and beyond the West Midlands region. The development, commissioning and production of new writing takes place across the full range of the theatre's programme including: the Main House (capacity 900); the Studio, a space dedicated to new work; and its biannual Community tours. Unsolicited submissions are welcome largely from the point of view of beginning a relationship with a writer. Priority in such development work is given to writers from the region.

Bristol Old Vic Company, Theatre Royal, King Street, Bristol BS1 4ED   *tel* (0117) 949 3993   *fax* (0117) 949 3996. *Director's office:* Sheila Pearce; *artistic director:* Andy Hay. Programme includes classical and new plays. New writing encouraged. New scripts read by experienced reader for a fee, currently £10.

The Byre Theatre of St Andrews Ltd, Abbey Street, St Andrews KY16 9LA   *tel* (01334) 476288   *fax* (01334) 475370. *Artistic director:* Ken Alexander. Open all year, operating as a summer rep., and as a touring venue for the rest of the year. Producing five plays between June and October; also, touring with TIE productions. Has a commitment to new writing, hosting the Byre Writers' Group, Scotland's leading training ground for new playwrights.

Chester Gateway Theatre Trust Ltd, Chester Gateway Theatre, Hamilton Place, Chester CH1 2BH   *tel* (01244) 344238   *fax* (01244) 317277. *Artistic director:* Jeremy Raison.

Chichester Festival Theatre Productions Company Ltd, Chichester Festival Theatre, Oaklands Park, Chichester, West Sussex PO19 4AP *tel* (01243) 784437 *fax* (01243) 787288. *Director:* Duncan C. Weldon; *general manager:* Paul Rogerson. Festival season Apr-Oct in Festival Theatre and Minerva Theatre; rest of year seasons of touring plays, opera, ballet, dance, jazz, orchestral concerts and Minerva Movies.

Churchill Theatre, High Street, Bromley, Kent BR1 1HA *tel* 0181-464 7131 *fax* 0181-290 6968. *Contact:* theatre director. Full-length plays; comedies, thrillers, dramas, new plays considered.

Theatr Clwyd, Mold, Clwyd CH7 1YA *tel* (01352) 756331 *fax* (01352) 758323.

Colchester Mercury Theatre Ltd, Balkerne Gate, Colchester, Essex CO1 1PT *tel* (01206) 577006 *fax* (01206) 769607. *Artistic director and chief executive:* Pat Trueman.

The Coliseum Theatre, Fairbottom Street, Oldham OL1 3SW *tel* 0161-624 1731 *fax* 0161-624 5318. *Artistic director:* Warren Hooper. Special interest in musicals and comedies. Contact by letter initially.

Contact Theatre Company, Oxford Road, Manchester M15 6JA *tel* 0161-274 3434 *fax* 0161-273 6286. *Artistic director:* Benjamin Twist. Interested in exciting, theatrical plays for a younger (under 25) audience.

Crucible Theatre, 55 Norfolk Street, Sheffield S1 1DA *tel* (0114) 276 0621 *fax* (0114) 270 1532. *Artistic director:* Deborah Paige. Large-scale producing house with smallish studio.

Derby Playhouse Ltd, Theatre Walk, Eagle Centre, Derby DE1 2NF *tel* (01332) 363271 *fax* (01332) 294412.

Druid Theatre Company, Druid Lane Theatre, Chapel Lane, Galway, Republic of Ireland *tel* (091) 568617/568660 *fax* (091) 563109 *e-mail* druid@iol.ie. *General manager:* Jane Daly; *artistic director:* Garry Hynes.

The Duke's Playhouse, Moor Lane, Lancaster LA1 1QE *tel* (01524) 67461 *fax* (01524) 846817. *Artistic director:* to be appointed; *general manager:* Penny McPhillips.

Dundee Repertory Theatre, Tay Square, Dundee DD1 1PB *tel* (01382) 227684. *Artistic director:* Hamish Glen.

Everyman Theatre, 5-9 Hope Street, Liverpool L1 9BH *tel* 0151-708 0338 *fax* 0151-709 0398. *Artistic director:* Peter Rowe.

Everyman Theatre, Regent Street, Cheltenham, Glos. GL50 1HQ *tel* (01242) 512515 *fax* (01242) 224305. *Chief executive:* Philip Bernays.

Grand Theatre, Singleton Street, Swansea SA1 3QJ *tel* (01792) 475242 *fax* (01792) 475379. *General manager:* Gary Iles.

Haymarket Theatre Company, The Haymarket Theatre, Wote Street, Basingstoke, Hants RG21 1NW *tel* (01256) 55844 *fax* (01256) 57130. *Theatre director:* Adrian Reynolds. Mounts seasons of plays, many of which are designed for co-production with London managements.

Leicester Haymarket Theatre, Belgrave Gate, Leicester LE1 3YQ *tel* (0116) 253 0021 *fax* (0116) 251 3310.

Library Theatre Company, St Peter's Square, Manchester M2 5PD *tel* (0161) 234 1913 *fax* (0161) 228 6481. *Contact:* artistic director. Contemporary drama, classics, plays for children. Aims to produce drama which illuminates the contemporary world; scripts from new writers considered.

Liverpool Repertory Theatre Ltd, Liverpool Playhouse, Williamson Square, Liverpool L1 1EL *tel* 0151-709 8478 *fax* 0151-709 7113. *Theatre manager:* Caroline Parry.

New Victoria Theatre, Etruria Road, Newcastle under Lyme ST5 0JG *tel* (01782) 717954 *fax* (01782) 712885. *Theatre director:* Peter Cheeseman. Europe's first purpose built theatre in the round, presenting major classics, adaptations, contemporary plays, documentaries. New plays limited.

New Victoria Theatre, Peacocks Arts & Entertainment Centre, Woking, Surrey GU21 1GQ *tel* (01483) 747422 *fax* (01483) 740477. *Contact:* Robert Cogo-Fawcett, c/o Theatre Royal, Sawclose, Bath BA1 1ET *tel* (01225) 448815. Large-scale touring house. Interested to co-produce or produce.

Northampton Repertory Players Ltd, The Royal Theatre, Guildhall Road, Northampton NN1 1EA *tel* (01604) 38343 *fax* (01604) 602408. Presents plays for main house, studio, theatre-in-education, community touring and youth theatre. Please send scripts, indicating which area of work they are for, to Michael Napier Brown, Artistic Director.

Northcott Theatre, Stocker Road, Exeter, Devon EX4 4QB *tel* (01392) 56182. *Artistic director:* John Durnin.

Northern Stage Company, Newcastle Playhouse, Barras Bridge, Newcastle upon Tyne NE1 1RH *tel* 0191-232 3366 *fax* 0191-261 8093. *Artistic director:* Alan Lyddiard.

Nottingham Playhouse, Nottingham Theatre Trust Ltd, Wellington Circus, Nottingham NG1 5AF *tel* (0115) 947 4361 *fax* (0115) 947 5759. *Artistic director:* Martin Duncan. Works closely with communities of Nottingham and Nottinghamshire; presents best of innovative and world theatre. Takes six months to read unsolicited MSS.

Nuffield Theatre, University Road, Southampton SO17 1TR *tel* (01703) 315500 *fax* (01703) 315511. *Script executive:* Penny Gold.

Octagon Theatre, Howell Croft South, Bolton BL1 1SB *tel* (01204) 529407 *fax* (01204) 380110. *Administrative director:* Amanda Belcham; *artistic director:* Lawrence Till. Repertory season Sept-June, including new plays and contemporary theatre.

The Oxford Stage Company, 15-19 George Street, Oxford OX1 2AU *tel* (01865) 723238 *fax* (01865) 790625. *Contact:* marketing manager.

Palace Theatre, Clarendon Road, Watford, Herts. WD1 1JZ *tel* (01923) 235455 *fax* (01923) 819664. *Contact:* Giles Croft.

Palace Theatre Trust Ltd, London Road, Westcliff-on-Sea, Essex SS0 9LA *tel* (01702) 347816 *fax* (01702) 435031. *Theatre secretary:* Iris Stewart. Subsidised repertory theatre producing a programme of predominantly modern British drama with some foreign writers, particularly American. Most new work is done in small, 100-seater studio.

The Park Community Theatre Company (1985), South Hill Park Arts Centre, Bracknell, Berks. RG12 7PA *tel* (01344) 427272 *fax* (01344) 411427. *Community Theatre officer:* Jonathan Holloway. Main house and experimental studio. Welcomes new writers.

Peacock Theatre, The Abbey Theatre, Lower Abbey Street, Dublin 1, Republic of Ireland *tel* (01) 8748741 *fax* (01) 8729177. *Artistic director:* Patrick Mason; *general manager:* Martin Fahy. Experimental theatre associated with the Abbey Theatre; presents mostly new writing as well as exploring the entire canon of world drama.

Perth Theatre Ltd, 185 High Street, Perth PH1 5UW   *tel* (01738) 638123   *fax* (01738) 624576. *Artistic director:* Michael Winter; *general manager:* Paul McLennan. Three-weekly repertory programme Aug-May of plays, musicals, revivals and new writing; also studio and theatre-in-education work.

Plymouth Theatre Royal, Theatre Royal, Royal Parade, Plymouth, Devon PL1 2TR   *tel* (01752) 668282   *telex* 45115 TROYAL G   *fax* (01752) 671179. *Chief executive:* Adrian Vinken; *producer:* Grahame Morris.

Queen's Theatre Hornchurch (Havering Theatre Trust Ltd), Billet Lane, Hornchurch, Essex RM11 1QT   *tel* (01708) 456118   *fax* (01708) 452348. *Contact:* Tony Hill. Medium scale regional repertory company producing popular comedy, drama and musicals. Scripts from new writers welcome especially as co-productions with commercial producer or additional funding.

Royal Exchange Theatre Company Ltd, St Ann's Square, Manchester M2 7DH   *tel* 0161-833 9333   *fax* 0161-832 0881. *General manager:* Patricia Weller. Provides a varied programme of major classics, new plays, musicals, contemporary British and European drama; also explores the creative work of diverse cultures.

Royal Lyceum Theatre Company Ltd, Royal Lyceum Theatre, Grindlay Street, Edinburgh EH3 9AX   *tel* 0131-229 7404   *fax* 0131-228 3955. *Artistic director:* Kenny Ireland; *associate literary director:* Tom McGrath.

Salisbury Playhouse, Malthouse Lane, Salisbury, Wilts. SP2 7RA   *tel* (01722) 320117   *fax* (01722) 421991. *Artistic director:* Jonathan Church. Regional repertory theatre producing a broad programme of classical and modern plays.

Scarborough Theatre Trust Ltd, Stephen Joseph Theatre, Westborough, Scarborough, North Yorkshire YO11 1JW   *tel* (01723) 370540   *fax* (01723) 360506. *Literary manager:* Connal Orton.

Sherman Theatre (1974), Senghennydd Road, Cardiff CF2 4YE   *tel* (01222) 396844   *fax* (01222) 665581. *General manager:* Margaret Jones. Plays mainly for 15-25 age range.

Swan Theatre, The Moors, Worcester WR1 3EF   *tel* (01905) 726969   *fax* (01905) 723738. *Artistic director:* Jenny Stephens.

Thorndike Theatre, Church Street, Leatherhead, Surrey KT22 8DF   *tel* (01372) 376211   *fax* (01372) 362595. *Contact:* theatre manager.

Traverse Theatre, 10 Cambridge Street, Edinburgh EH1 2ED   *tel* 0131-228 3223   *fax* 0131-229 8443. *Dramaturge:* Ella Wildridge.

Watermill Theatre Ltd, Bagnor, Newbury, Berks. RG20 8AE   *tel* (01635) 45834. *Contact:* Jill Fraser. Small professional theatre. Interested in all types of new work, including drama and musicals, suitable for small stage and auditorium.

The West Yorkshire Playhouse, Playhouse Square, Quarry Hill, Leeds LS2 7UP   *tel* (0113) 244 2141   *fax* (0113) 244 8252. *Artistic director:* Jude Kelly; *literary co-ordinator:* Claire Malcolm. Twin auditoria complex – with a policy of encouraging new writing; community theatre; Young People's Theatre programme.

Windsor Theatre Company (Capoco Ltd), Theatre Royal, Windsor, Berks. SL4 1PS   *tel* (01753) 863444   *fax* (01753) 831673. *Artistic director:* Mark Piper. Interested mainly in comedies and thrillers.

The Wolsey Theatre, Civic Drive, Ipswich, Suffolk IP1 2AS   *tel* (01473) 218911   *fax* (01473) 212946. *Administrative director:* Lorna Anderson; *artistic director:* Antony Tuckey.

York Citizens' Theatre Trust Ltd, Theatre Royal, St Leonard's Place, York YO1 2HD *tel* (01904) 658162 *fax* (01904) 611534. *Executive director:* Elizabeth Jones; *artistic director:* John Doyle. Repertory productions, tours.

TOURING COMPANIES

Black Theatre Co-Operative Ltd, 8 Bradbury Street, London N16 8JN *tel* 0171-249 9150 *fax* 0171-275 9440. *Artistic director:* Felix Cross; *marketing officer:* Gillian Christie. Interested in Black plays, especially those that relate to the experiences of Black people both in Britain and outside Britain.

Bristol Express Theatre Company, 16 Frederick Street, Totterdown, Bristol BS4 3AZ *tel* (0117) 9717279. *Artistic director:* Andy Jordan. Most productions are new plays; scripts from new writers considered.

Compass Theatre Company, Carver Street Institute, 24 Rockingham Lane, Sheffield S1 4FW *tel* (0114) 275 5328 *fax* (0114) 278 6931. *General manager:* William Jones.

Gay Sweatshop, The Holborn Centre, Three Cups Yard, Sandland Street, London WC1R 4PZ *tel* 0171-242 1168 *fax* 0171-242 3143. *Joint artistic directors:* James Neal-Kennerley, Lois Weaver. Interested in developing (often commissioning) scripts into full production of new plays by lesbian and gay writers.

The Hiss & Boo Company, 24 West Grove, Walton-on-Thames, Surrey KT12 5NX *tel* (01932) 248931 *fax* (01932) 248946 *e-mail* 100547.1656 @compuserve.com Not much scope for new plays, but will consider comedy thrillers/chillers and plays/musicals for children. Send synopsis first. Plays/synopses will be returned only if accompanied by an sae.

Hull Truck Theatre Co. Ltd, Hull Truck Theatre, Spring Street, Hull HU2 8RW *tel* (01482) 224800 *fax* (01482) 581182. *General manager:* Simon Stallworthy.

Live Theatre, 8 Trinity Chare, Quayside, Newcastle upon Tyne NE1 3DF *tel* 0191-261 2694 *fax* 0191-232 2224. *Artistic director:* Max Roberts. Interested in new plays which relate to the present and/or history, culture and concerns of the region and which are accessible to a wide audience.

The London Bubble (Bubble Theatre Company), 3/5 Elephant Lane, London SE16 4JD *tel* 0171-237 4434 *fax* 0171-231 2366.

M6 Theatre Company, Hamer C.P. School, Albert Royds Street, Rochdale, Lancs. OL16 2SU *tel* (01706) 355898 *fax* (01706) 711700. *Contact:* Aileen Lebrocguy-Cox. Theatre-in-education company providing high quality, educational, innovative and relevant live theatre for children and for audiences who may not normally have access to theatre.

Made in Wales, Aberdare House, Mount Stuart Square, Cardiff CF1 6DJ *tel* (01222) 484017 *fax* (01222) 484016. *Artistic director:* Jeff Teare. Three productions per year of new plays relevant to Wales; scripts from new writers considered.

Major Road Theatre Company, 29 Queens Road, Bradford, West Yorkshire BD8 7BS *tel* (01274) 480251 *fax* (01274) 548528. *Artistic director:* Graham Devlin.

New Perspectives Company, The Old Library, Leeming Street, Mansfield, Notts. NG18 1NG *tel* (01623) 635225 *fax* (01623) 635240. *Artistic director:* Gavin Stride. Has a policy of employing writers for new work. Regret unsolicited scripts returned, unless writers are local to the East Midlands region.

NTC Touring Theatre Company (formerly Northumberland Theatre Company), The Playhouse, Bondgate Without, Alnwick, Northumberland NE66 1PQ *tel* (01665) 602586. *Artistic director:* Gillian Hambleton. Performs a wide cross-section of work: new plays, extant scripts, classics and theatre for young people. Particularly interested in non-naturalism, physical theatre and plays with direct relevance to rural audiences.

Orchard Theatre Company, 108 Newport Road, Barnstaple, North Devon EX32 9BA *tel* (01271) 71475 *fax* (01271) 71825. *Administrator:* Frederica Notley.

Paines Plough, 4th Floor, 43 Aldwych, London WC2B 4DA *tel* 0171-240 4533 *fax* 0171-240 4534. *Artistic director:* Penny Ciniewicz; *literary development manager:* Mark Ravenhill. Tours new plays nationally. Works with writers to develop their skills and voices through courses, workshops, free script reading service and surgeries. Encourages writers to bridge the gap between arthouse and commercial plays with entertaining and provocative work for audiences beyond the London fringe and West End. Welcomes new scripts from writers. For script reading service send 2 saes for response and return of script.

Proteus Theatre Company (1981), Fairfields Arts Centre, Council Road, Basingstoke, Hants RG21 3DH *tel* (01256) 54541. *Administrative director:* Katherine Ives; *artistic director:* Chris Baldwin; *community and education officer:* Alison Jones. Small-scale touring company. Presents three plays per year, at least one a new play; also 2-3 projects which may include commissioned written pieces of drama.

Quicksilver Theatre for Children (formerly Theatre of Thelema), 4 Enfield Road, London N1 5AZ *tel* 0171-241 2942 *fax* 0171-254 3119. *Artistic director:* Guy Holland. Tours schools and theatres London and nationwide. Produces three plays a year for specific age ranges: 3-5-year-olds, 7-11-year-olds and 6+ years and family audiencies. Particularly interested in visual, physical and music theatre.

Red Ladder Theatre Co., Cobden Avenue, Lower Wortley, Leeds LS12 5PB *tel* (0113) 279 2228 *fax* (0113) 231 0660. *Artistic director:* Kully Thiarai. Theatre performances for young people (14-25) in youth clubs and small-scale theatre venues. Commissions at least two new plays each year. Training/residentials for youth workers/young people.

Red Shift Theatre Company, 9 The Leathermarket, Weston Street, London SE1 3ER *tel* 0171-378 9787 *fax* 0171-378 9789.

Solent Peoples Theatre, The Heathfield Centre, Valentine Avenue, Sholing, Southampton SO19 0EQ *tel* (01703) 443943 *fax* (01703) 440752. *Administrative director:* Caroline Routh.

The Sphinx Theatre Co. Ltd, 25 Short Street, London SE1 8LJ *tel* 0171-401 9993/4 *fax* 0171-401 9995. *Artistic director:* Sue Parrish. Women writers only.

Stage One Theatre Company, 34 Jasmine Grove, London SE20 8JW *tel* 0181-778 5213 *fax* 0181-778 1756. Scripts from new writers considered; send to Buddy Dalton, c/o 11 Cannon Place, Hampstead, London NW3 1EH.

Talawa Theatre Company, 3rd Floor, 23/25 Great Sutton Street, London EC1V 0DN *tel* 0171-251 6644 *fax* 0171-251 5969. *Contact:* A.W. Nyachae. Scripts from new writers considered.

Theatre Centre, Hanover School, Noel Road, Islington, London N1 8BD *tel* 0171-354 0110 voice/minicom *fax* 0171-359 7562. *Contact:* Jackie Alexis. National touring theatre for young people – schools, art centres, venues.

Theatre Workshop Company, 34 Hamilton Place, Edinburgh EH3 5AX *tel*
(0131) 225 7942 *fax* (0131) 220 0112. *Contact:* Robert Rae. Plays include new
writing/community/children's. Scripts from new writers considered.

UK PUBLISHERS SPECIALISING IN THE PUBLICATION OF PLAYS

Playwrights are reminded that it is unusual for a publisher of trade editions of
plays to publish plays which have not had at least reasonably successful, usually
professional, productions *on stage* first. See listing beginning on page 148 for
addresses.

Faber & Faber Ltd   J. Garnet Miller Ltd
Samuel French Ltd   New Playwrights' Network
Nick Hern Books Ltd   The Playwrights Publishing Company
Kenyon-Deane   Warner Chappell Plays Ltd
Methuen, Reed Books

Writing for Broadcasting

JOCELYN HAY
Chairman, Voice of the Listener and Viewer

The pace of change in broadcasting is increasing at an alarming rate but while
this complicates the scene for writers it also brings new opportunities for those
prepared to adapt to the new environment.

In the next few years we shall see an explosion of new television and radio
channels but only one – Channel 5 Television, due to come on air in January
1997 – will be available to the majority of UK households on the same 'free to
air' terms as BBC, ITV and Channel 4. The rest will be satellite, cable or digital
terrestrial channels for which viewers will almost certainly have to pay a monthly
subscription and, on occasions, an additional surcharge for particular programmes or premium events. The first such 'pay per view' programme broadcast
in the UK was the Bruno/Tyson fight in March 1996 for which BskyB subscribers
had to pay an additional fee of nearly £15. More than half a million chose to do
so and such economics are playing havoc with the market for broadcast sporting
rights.

The terrestrial channels BBC, ITV, Channel 4 – and Channel 5 when it is
launched – are all required to broadcast a wide diversity of high quality
programmes, more than 50 per cent of which must be of European origin.
Satellite and cable channels do not bear any of the same positive requirements
on range and quality. Many also rely heavily on imported – mostly American –
programming, although in a welcome move BskyB recently commissioned its
first costume drama and a 26-part 'soap' from UK producers.

Competition from the new channels is inevitably taking audiences and revenue
from the existing channels but it is also forcing the BBC and ITV to rethink their
programme strategies. The result is a greater focus on high quality British drama
and programming. Good news for writers.

There is also a significant move to commission more programmes with a
regional flavour. ITV has always broadcast programmes that reflect its regional
company structure and the tradition continues with the series *Wycliffe* from
Westcountry Television and *World in Action* from Granada. The BBC has made
a conscious decision to switch more production out of London by creating

'Centres of Excellence' in different regional cities. This is already being reflected in popular drama series such as *Ballykissangel, Hamish McBeth, Our Friends from the North*, and in more programmes being produced under a new 'Bi-media' Head of Radio and TV Drama in Wales.

Writers should take advantage of this trend and use their specialist knowledge not only to vary the settings of their stories but to look for opportunities in other genres and departments. For example, the historical documentary series *Strange Landscape*, broadcast in 1995, was commissioned by the BBC's religious department in Manchester. Youth programmes are also commissioned from Manchester, the BBC's specialist Natural History Unit is based in Bristol and Birmingham is a centre for radio drama.

BBC Radio still offers the best and largest market for writers wanting to break into broadcasting. Radio costs are lower than those of television, the range of programmes is greater and radio provides a marvellous testing ground for new ideas and new writers, especially in soaps and comedy. Many have learnt their craft by contributing items to Radio 4's *Week Ending* and Radio 2's *The News Huddlines*, and many successful television comedy series had their first airing on BBC Radio. Even the market for radio drama is changing, however, and writers must study the schedules and listen regularly to the output if they are to succeed.

Writers should also keep an eye on the politics. The BBC has a new Royal Charter and Agreement, a new Chairman, a new Managing Director of Radio and in 1997 it could have a new Director General. The new Charter gives the BBC a stable constitution for the next 10 years but the new Agreement guarantees the licence fee only for the next five. After that, the BBC may be funded by advertising, sponsorship, subscription or any other means the Government deems fit. Losing the licence fee may sound attractive to some, but how will BBC Radio be funded if the BBC is forced to move to subscription television, as was recommended by the 1988 Government White Paper on Broadcasting? BBC Radio currently gets nearly a quarter of the licence fee income but will it be able to continue its patronage of writers and musicians if this is cut? And will radio drama be so well funded if all drama goes bi-media?

One area that seems to be growing and that certainly should not be scorned is that of competitions. They cover every genre, from poetry to drama, but are especially valuable for radio and television playwrights. Most competitions have clear objectives, often to encourage young writers or to develop an understanding of the problems of disability or ethnic minorities. Most are designed to encourage new writers. However, the Sacred Earth Drama Trust, which is looking for plays that explore the relationship between young people and the natural world, and the PAWS Fund (Public Awareness of Science and Engineering), which is seeking ideas for television plays and series set in a contemporary science or engineering context, both give grants to accomplished scriptwriters. Prizes and grants are often generous but publication or the broadcast of a winning work is often the greatest benefit, bringing recognition to an unknown writer plus valuable experience of the production process. Regional Arts Councils and reference libraries should have details of most major competitions and a copy of the Book Trust's annual *Guide to Literary Prizes* (Book Trust, Book House, 45 East Hill, Wandsworth, London SW18 2QZ   *tel* 0181-870 9055). The Society of Authors (see page 637) and the New Playwrights Trust (see page 623) are other good sources of information and help.

The essential message for writers is to be flexible and willing to learn, not least about the new multimedia genres which the convergence of television and computer technologies makes possible. These include interactive games, drama and educational packages on CD-ROM. A visit to a computer shop will soon show how varied and exciting the possibilities are.

So the market may be changing but it is certainly not all gloom. Budgets will be lower than in the past, and writers need to be prepared to take advantage of new markets, perhaps accommodating the needs of sponsors and other financial partners. But the good news is that more channels means that more programmes will be needed to fill them. Viewers soon tire of repeats and with more choice they will shun cheap, shoddy programming and that should benefit writers. Provided they keep abreast of developments and up to date with skills, the rewards of the writer will be high.

Writing for Television

BILL CRAIG
Past-President of The Writers' Guild of Great Britain

'Television drama' is a generic term which covers several varied and specialist areas of writing for the domestic screen. Since each differs from the others in terms of requirements and rewards and since each is definable in copyright terms, let's start by identifying them.

The television play is a one-off creation of a single mind and talent and absolutely the property of its author. As a form it is the vehicle for the talents of newest and least-experienced writers in the medium and also for those who are held in the highest regard. It is (for practical reasons) the traditional point of entry for the tyro. There has been some reduction in the number of plays produced annually but the BBC and certain ITV companies are still in the market for 30, 60 and 90 minute slot-length works. If the bad news is that they get several thousand unsolicited manuscripts every year, the good news is that they are all read. No script-unit will risk missing out on an undiscovered genius.

The same observations (with some modification) would apply to the original series or serial: that is, a multi-part work of sole authorship and of finite length. They tend to be written by established television writers who have a proven ability to go the necessary distance, but a new writer with an attractive idea can come in through this door.

What's the procedure? Invest some time and talent and write the play. A commission on a synopsis is unlikely without some evidence that you can write interesting action, dialogue and characters. With the finite series/serial – write the first episode and synopsise the rest.

The situation-comedy is the most highly paid area of television writing – and understandably so. It calls for a quirky and idiosyncratic mind, and its overriding imperative – to make the viewer laugh – subordinates all of the other dramatic tools to this end. If it's difficult to play Beethoven's *Ninth* on a one-stringed fiddle, then it's Hell to do it for a run of six episodes. The sit-com is unique in screen drama in so far as most of them are played before live studio audiences. Once upon a time, they were constructed around individual comedians. Some still are, but for several years now the practice has been to cast according to the script with actors who can play comedy. And that's not a bad thing, is it?

Again, this form is an original in copyright terms, though dual authorships are not uncommon. A synopsis is pretty useless (ever tried to explain a joke?), so write the pilot-script and briefly indicate where you can go with other episodes.

We now come to a significant point of departure and go into those areas where the copyright is split with another party.

First, the drama-series: *Bramwell*, *The Bill*, *Casualty*, et al. These are definable as a series of original and self-contained scripts using the same characters and backgrounds throughout. The format – that is, the characters and general ambience – will be owned or leased by the production organisation. They represent a substantial part of television drama, but it is rare for a writer without previous screen experience to be commissioned to write for them. It is quite pointless to submit a speculative script or synopsis: the series you are seeing now was recorded months ago.

Serials, such as *Coronation Street, Brookside, Take the High Road* and *Emmerdale*, will occasionally try out new writers, but the production pressures on reliability and deadline delivery dates don't allow for too many risks to be taken outside what is usually an established and pretty permanent writing team.

Dramatisation and Adaptation are terms which are interchanged in an ignorantly casual manner; they are not the same thing. A dramatisation is the conversion of a prose-work to a screenplay. An adaptation is a similar conversion of a dramatic work. The difference is considerable, and the screen credit should reflect this fact.

There has been a great increase in the number of dramatisations made from novels. Again, these are usually written by writers with a track record in television, but occasionally the author of the book to be dramatised will be approached to write the screenplay. If you don't come under either of those headings, then you probably wouldn't get very far by simply suggesting that you'd like to dramatise this or that novel. Adaptations are usually 'in-house' works.

All of this leaves uncovered an odd and often lucrative area – the format. It is possible to sell an idea for a series without ever having written a script. But make sure that your submission is as detailed as it possibly can be in terms of background, main characters and development. Doing it the simple way in this instance can mean finding out that fifty other people have had the same simple idea. And selling an idea carries no guarantee that you'll be asked to write the scripts.

Script layout and presentation. Use A4. Type it or have it typed. Blank margin about 10 cm on the left hand side. Directions and character names in capitals, dialogue in capitals and lower case, double spaced. Don't go mad with directions; keep them functional and indicative. Don't be intimidated by camera directions; use them only when they make a dramatic point you want to get across.

Number and head the scenes thus: 1. INT. JOE'S ROOM. DAY Avoid nonsense action directions such as 'Her inner resilience manifests itself in a way reminiscent of the wind howling across her native moors'. If you mean she's from Yorkshire, just say it.

There are several books on the subject of layout and technique. Two which come to mind are *Writing for Television* by Gerald Kelsey (Black) and *The Way to Write for Television* by Eric Paice (Elm Tree Books). Another on scriptwriting is *Writing Comedy* by Ronald Wolfe (Hale).

Given success to your efforts, you will be contracted under the terms of the relevant agreement between the British Broadcasting Corporation or the ITV Network Centre and the Writers' Guild of Great Britain, 430 Edgware Road, London W2 1EH. The Guild has sole bargaining rights in the television drama rates, its agreements are complex and comprehensive and several of the rights and benefits contained in them are available to Guild members only.

Payments are made in stages: BBC – half on commission, half on acceptance; ITV Network Centre – half on commission, a quarter on delivery, a quarter on acceptance. A new system of part-networking has come into being. The initial fee is lower than that paid for a full network transmission, but increments are payable for each franchise area that transmits the programme.

The foregoing comments apply mainly to programmes produced by the British Broadcasting Corporation or the ITV companies. The increasingly important independent production sector should not, however, be ignored, since many of their productions are primarily intended for television screening.

These programmes are made by either entirely independent production organisations or subsidiaries of the ITV companies (e.g. *Wexford*, Meridian).

Generally speaking, the scripts are laid out in film format (see **Screenplays for Films** on page 323) although some, since they produce on tape, might prefer the television format. The procedures described above for submitting unsolicited work should be observed.

Contracts should conform to the terms laid down by the agreement between the Writers' Guild of Great Britain and the Producers Alliance for Cinema and Television (PACT). Again, the agreement is comprehensive and covers all forms and aspects of screen drama. Payment is made in four stages: treatment, first draft, second draft and principal photography. Further exploitation is also covered.

Further useful information and addresses may be found in a booklet called *Contacts*. The 1996-97 edition is available from November from *The Spotlight*, 7 Leicester Place, London WC2H 7BP *tel* 0171-437 7631.

Dating letters

Letters all too frequently present the researcher with unforeseen problems. Far too many people had (and still have) the habit of dating their correspondence 'Thursday', 'Sunday, 12th' or 'Amsterdam, Monday', or – which is worse from the researcher's point of view – of not dating them at all. You should also be aware that some individuals are prone to stuff free hotel or club stationery into their briefcases and to use it weeks or even months later, so that although such correspondence may be dated, you cannot be absolutely certain that the writer was actually resident at the hotel or club at the time: if there is any doubt at all in your mind on this score, try to verify the date and/or place in another source.

If, on first reading, a letter does not appear to offer any clue of this kind, do not despair. Re-examine it closely for mention of any family, national or world event – perhaps the death of a well-known person, an exhibition or play seen, a new novel read, and so on, the dates of which can then be checked out in the national press, *Whitaker's Almanack* and other sources. Letters that you cannot even guess at dating should be kept apart from the rest; sooner or later, as work progresses, you are more than likely to stumble on some information (nearly always when you are not looking for it) that will enable you to slot such letters into their right sequence.

from *Research for Writers* by Ann Hoffmann (A & C Black, £11.99).
See order form on page 690.

British Broadcasting Corporation

Potential contributors to the BBC should be aware that the needs of television and radio are quite different. Writers should study in detail the possible outlets by watching and listening to programmes, and tailor their work to fit them. Because of the length of time taken by the various BBC departments to consider the many hundreds of unsolicited scripts received each year, writers may like to consider submitting their work through an agent who, having contacts with producers or script editors, will know current requirements.

TELEVISION

Drama

Original dramas for film (50, 75 and 90 minutes) are sought. Plays and screenplays using few locations and small casts are advantageous. No standardised layout or technical instructions are required in any scripts. However, well-spaced presentation with dialogue and stage directions clearly distinguished is essential. New writers should always present sample scripts with any submission of ideas being presented to Series, Serials or Single Drama.

New Writing Initiatives for Single Drama include: *Black Screen* (c/o Frances-Anne Solomon) looking for 75-90 minute screenplays from black and Asian writers; *MIDA* co-development fund looking for any length of screenplay from writers based in the northwest (c/o Roger Shannon at *MIDA*, Liverpool); *Screen on the Tube* (a BBC/BFI co-development scheme) looking for feature screenplays (c/o Frances-Anne Solomon); and *Brief Encounters* (c/o Jenny Killick) looking for 11-minute screenplays for new writers and directors.

Since the BBC has opened its doors to national and international independent drama markets, competition is very fierce indeed and all unsolicited scripts will therefore be rigorously sifted.

Scripts should be submitted to the appropriate Development Executive in Series, Serials and Single Drama at BBC Drama Group, Centre House, 56 Wood Lane, London W12 7SB.

Entertainment Group

The Comedy Dept Script Development Unit welcomes new 30-minute comedy series. Only original formats, preferably mainly studio based, are required. We prefer to see a completed half-hour script rather than an idea or outline, novel or treatment, etc. We do not read sketch material. The Comedy Unit reads and responds to all comedy script submissions, but it is a highly competitive market.

We issue brief sitcom writing guidelines. If you wish to receive them please send an A4 stamped addressed envelope to the following address: Room 4127, BBC Television Centre, Wood Lane, London W12 7RJ.

Scripts should be submitted to: The Script Editors, Room 4127, BBC Television Centre, Wood Lane, London W12 7RJ.

RADIO

Short stories

Short stories specially written for broadcasting will be considered for the 'short story' slot on Radio 4. A story written for a 15-minute broadcasting space should be between 2000 and 2300 words in length. Unsolicited material is considered but it has to compete with regularly commissioned work. Submissions should be addressed to the Producer, Short Story.

Drama Department

The Department broadcasts 400 hours of new plays and adaptations every year, in addition to readings. There is therefore a very large market regularly available to the freelance writer. A free leaflet, *Writing Plays for Radio*, giving basic guidance on the technique of radio writing and also on the market is available from the Chief Producer, Plays (Radio Drama), BBC, Broadcasting House, Portland Place, London W1A 1AA. Submissions should be addressed to the Chief Producer, Plays or Series and Serials. Allow up to two months for a reply.

Music

At the heart of the BBC's music policy is a commitment to high-quality, live music-making in all its forms and across the full range of styles and periods. Audition sessions for professional soloists and ensembles are held every other week, except in July and August, with an outside professional assessor on the listening panel. The BBC also regularly commissions new works from a wide range of composers both nationally and internationally for all its house orchestras and the BBC Singers as well as for other groups and special occasions. These too have broadened their range in recent years to include jazz, electronic and radiophonic media.

The BBC makes best endeavours to consider all unsolicited scores and tapes for broadcast. This is carried out chiefly by the Music Department's New Music unit, and where further opinions are sought, they are put before the Readers on the New Music Panel, who provide objective advice to the production teams without bias or prejudice.

Light Entertainment

Light Entertainment Radio is interested in receiving scripts or ideas for series of half-hour sitcoms or panel games, principally for Radio 4. Before submitting material, please read the writers' guidelines – explaining such matters as length, layout, structure and so on – available (enclosing an A4 sae) from the Senior Producer, Scripts (Light Entertainment Radio), BBC, Room 1013, Broadcasting House, Portland Place, London W1A 1AA, where the material should ultimately be sent.

Two programmes, *Week Ending* and *The News Huddlines*, are interested in using unsolicited topical sketches during the course of their run. *Week Ending* holds a weekly writers' meeting at which anyone is welcome, at the above address. Details (and times of deadlines) can be obtained by ringing 0171-580 4468 and asking for the production office of the programme concerned. All fees are a matter for negotiation with the Corporation's Copyright Department.

BROADCASTING RIGHTS AND TERMS

Contributors are advised to check latest details of fees with the BBC.

Specially written material for television

From 1 April 1996 the rates for one performance of a 60-minute original television play were a minimum of £4728 for a play written by a beginner and a 'going rate' of £7450 for an established writer, or *pro rata* for shorter or longer timings. Fees for submitted material are paid on acceptance, and for commissioned material half on commissioning and half on acceptance as being suitable for television.

Fees for a 50-minute episode in a series during the same period were a minimum of £3900 for a beginner and a 'going rate' of £5634 for an established writer.

Fees for a 50-minute dramatisation were a minimum of £2721 for a beginner and a £4010 'going rate' for an established writer.

Fees for a 50-minute adaptation of an existing stage play or other dramatic work were a minimum of £1640 for a beginner and a £2403 'going rate' for an established writer.

All fees were subject to negotiation above the minima.

Specially written light entertainment sketch material for television

The rates for sketch material range from £31.31 per minute for beginners with a 'going rate' of £62.62 for established writers.

The fee for a quickie or news item is half the amount of the writer's per minute rate.

Fees for submitted material are payable on acceptance and for commissioned material half on signature and half on acceptance.

Published prose and poems for television (from 23 January 1995)

Prose works, £17.21 per minute.
Poems £19.97 per *half* minute.

Stage plays and source material for television

Fees for stage plays and source novels are negotiable.

Specially written material for radio

Fees are assessed on the basis of the type of material, its length, the author's status and experience in writing for radio. From 1 July 1995 rates for specially written radio dramas in English (other than educational programmes) are £37.82 a minute for beginners and a 'going rate' of £57.58 a minute for established writers, which rate covers two broadcasts.

Fees for submitted material are paid on acceptance, and for commissioned material half on commissioning and half on acceptance as being suitable for broadcasting.

Short stories specially written for radio from 1 May 1995

Fees range from £117.00 for 15 minutes.

Published material for radio (from 1 July 1995)

Domestic radio:
Dramatic works: £11.36 per minute.
Prose works: £11.36 per minute.
Prose works required for dramatisation: £8.86 per minute.
Poems: £11.36 per *half* minute.
World Service Radio (English):
Dramatic works: £5.69 per minute for broadcasts within a 7-day period.
Prose works: £5.69 per minute for broadcasts within a 7-day period.
Prose works required for dramatisation: £4.43 per minute for broadcasts within a 7-day period.
Poems: £5.69 per *half* minute for broadcasts within a 7-day period.
For Foreign Language Services approximately one-fifth of the rate for English Language Services.

Repeats in BBC programmes

Further proportionate fees are payable for repeats.

Use abroad of recordings of BBC programmes

If the BBC sends abroad recordings of its programmes for use by overseas broadcasting organisations on their own networks or stations, further payments accrue to the author, usually in the form of additional percentages of the basic fee paid for the initial performance or a royalty based on the percentage of the distributors' receipts. This can apply to both sound and television programmes.

Value Added Tax

A self-billing system for VAT was introduced in January 1978 for programmes made in London. This now covers radio, external services and television.

TALKS FOR TELEVISION

Contributors to talks will be offered the standard Television talks contract which provides the BBC certain rights to broadcast the material in a complete, abridged and/or translated manner, and which provides for the payment of further fees for additional usage of the material whether by television, domestic radio or external broadcasting. The contract also covers the assignment of material and limited publication rights. Alternatively a contract taking all standard rights may be negotiated. Fees are arranged by the contract authorities in London and the Regions.

TALKS FOR RADIO

Contributors to talks for domestic Radio and World Service broadcasting may be offered either: the standard talks contract which takes rights and provides for residual payments, as does the Television standard contract above; or be offered an STC (Short Talks Contract) which takes all rights except print publication rights where the airtime of the contribution does not exceed five minutes and which has set fees or disturbance money payable; or an NFC (No Fee Contract) where no payment is made which provides an acknowledgement that a contribution may be used by the BBC.

ADDRESSES

Letters addressed to speakers c/o the BBC will be forwarded, but may be opened before being forwarded. Letters marked 'Personal' are forwarded unopened.

LONDON

BBC Corporate Headquarters and BBC Network Radio: Broadcasting House, London W1A 1AA   *tel* 0171-580 4468   *fax* 0171-637 1630.

BBC Network Television: Television Centre, Wood Lane, London W12 7RJ   *tel* 0181-743 8000.

BBC Worldwide Television and BBC Worldwide Publishing: Woodlands, 80 Wood Lane, London W12 0TT   *tel* 0181-743 5588.

BBC World Service: Bush House, PO Box 76, London WC2B 4PH   *tel* 0171-240 3456.

BBC White City: 201 Wood Lane, London W12 7TS   *tel* 0181-752 5252.

BBC Written Archives: Caversham Park, Reading, Berks. RG4 8TZ   *tel* (01734) 472742.

MIDLANDS AND EAST REGION

Birmingham: Broadcasting Centre, Pebble Mill, Birmingham B5 7QQ   *tel* 0121-414 8888.

Nottingham: York House, Mansfield Road, Nottingham NG1 3JB   *tel* (0115) 955 0500.

Norwich: St Catherine's Close, All Saint's Green, Norwich, Norfolk NR1 3ND *tel* (01603) 619331.

NORTH REGION

Manchester: New Broadcasting House, PO Box 27, Oxford Road, Manchester M60 1SJ   *tel* 0161-200 2020.

Leeds: Broadcasting Centre, Woodhouse Lane, Leeds LS2 9PN   *tel* (0113) 244 1188.

Newcastle: Broadcasting Centre, Barrack Road, Newcastle upon Tyne NE99 2NE   *tel* 0191-232 1313.

SOUTH REGION

Bristol: Broadcasting House, Whiteladies Road, Bristol BS8 2LR   *tel* (0117) 973 2211.

Elstree: Clarendon Road, Borehamwood, Herts. WD6 1JF   *tel* 0181-953 6100.

Southampton: Broadcasting House, Havelock Road, Southampton SO14 7PU   *tel* (01703) 226201.

Plymouth: Broadcasting House, Seymour Road, Mannamead, Plymouth PL3 5BD   *tel* (01752) 229201.

NORTHERN IRELAND

Belfast: Broadcasting House, Ormeau Avenue, Belfast BT2 8HQ   *tel* (01232) 338000.

BBC Radio Foyle: 8 Northland Road, Londonderry BT48 7NE   *tel* (01504) 262244.

SCOTLAND

Glasgow: Broadcasting House, Queen Margaret Drive, Glasgow G12 8DG   *tel* 0141-339 8844.

Edinburgh: Broadcasting House, 5 Queen Street, Edinburgh EH2 1JF   *tel* 0131-225 3131.

Aberdeen: Broadcasting House, Beechgrove Terrace, Aberdeen AB9 2ZT   *tel* (01224) 625233.

Inverness (Radio Nan Gaidheal): 7 Culduthel Road, Inverness IV2 4AD   *tel* (01463) 221711.

Orkney: Castle Street, Kirkwall, Orkney KW15 1DF   *tel* (01856) 873939.

Selkirk: Municipal Buildings, High Street, Selkirk TD7 4BU   *tel* (01750) 21884.

Shetland: Brentham House, Lerwick, Shetland ZE1 0LR   *tel* (01595) 4747.

Solway: 'Elmbank', Lovers' Walk, Dumfries DG1 1NZ   *tel* (01387) 68008.

Stornoway (Radio Nan Gaidheal): Rosebank, Church Street, Stornoway, Isle of Lewis PA87 2LS   *tel* (01851) 705000.

WALES

Cardiff: Broadcasting House, Llantrisant Road, Llandaff, Cardiff CF5 2YQ   *tel* (01222) 572888.

Bangor: Broadcasting House, Meirion Road, Bangor, Gwynedd LL57 2BY   *tel* (01248) 370880.

Swansea: Broadcasting House, 32 Alexandra Road, Swansea SA1 5DT   *tel* (01792) 654986.

BBC LOCAL RADIO STATIONS

Local Radio also affords opportunities for writers to submit short stories and plays. A number of stations hold play-writing or short story competitions where the winners have their work broadcast. Others consider original work from local writers. Material should be submitted to the Assistant Editor.

Bedfordshire: BBC Three Counties Radio, PO Box 3CR, Luton, Beds. LU1 5XL   *tel* (01582) 411000.

Birmingham: BBC Radio WM, Pebble Mill Road, Birmingham B5 7SD   *tel* 0121-414 8484.

Bristol: BBC Radio Bristol, PO Box 194, Bristol BS99 7QT   *tel* (0117) 974 1111.

Cambridgeshire: BBC Radio Cambridgeshire, Broadcasting House, 104 Hills Road, Cambridge CB2 1LD   *tel* (01223) 259696.

Cleveland: BBC Radio Cleveland, PO Box 95FM, Newport Road, Middlesbrough, Cleveland TS1 5DG   *tel* (01642) 225211.

Cornwall: BBC Radio Cornwall, Phoenix Wharf, Truro, Cornwall TR1 1UA   *tel* (01872) 75421.

Coventry: BBC CWR, 25 Warwick Road, Coventry CV1 2WR   *tel* (01203) 559911.

Cumbria: BBC Radio Cumbria, Annetwell Street, Carlisle, Cumbria CA3 8BB   *tel* (01228) 592444.

Derby: BBC Radio Derby, PO Box 269, Derby DE1 3HI   *tel* (01332) 361111.

Devon: BBC Radio Devon, PO Box 5, Broadcasting House, Seymour Road, Mannamead, Plymouth, Devon PL1 1XT   *tel* (01752) 260323.

Dorset: Dorset FM, Portfolio House, Princes Street, Dorchester DT1 1TP   *tel* (01305) 269654.

Essex: BBC Essex, 198 New London Road, Chelmsford, Essex CM2 9AB   *tel* (01245) 262393.

Gloucestershire: BBC Radio Gloucestershire, London Road, Gloucester GL1 1SW   *tel* (01452) 308585.

Guernsey: BBC Radio Guernsey, Commerce House, Les Banques, St Peter Port, Guernsey, CI   *tel* (01481) 728977.

Hereford and Worcester: BBC Hereford and Worcester, Hylton Road, Worcester WR2 5WW   *tel* (01905) 748485.

Humberside: BBC Radio Humberside, 9 Chapel Street, Hull HU1 3NU   *tel* (01482) 323232.

Jersey: BBC Radio Jersey, 18 Parade Road, St Helier, Jersey, CI *tel* (01534) 870000.

Kent: BBC Radio Kent, Sun Pier, Chatham, Kent ME4 4EZ *tel* (01634) 830505.

Lancashire: BBC Radio Lancashire, 26 Darwen Street, Blackburn, Lancs. BB2 2EA *tel* (01254) 262411.

Leeds: BBC Radio Leeds, Broadcasting House, Woodhouse Lane, Leeds LS2 9PN *tel* (0113) 244 2131.

Leicester: BBC Radio Leicester, Epic House, Charles Street, Leicester LE1 3SH *tel* (0116) 262 6688.

Lincolnshire: BBC Radio Lincolnshire, PO Box 219, Newport, Lincoln LN1 3XY *tel* (01522) 511411.

London: BBC GLR, 35c Marylebone High Street, London W1A 4LG *tel* 0171-224 2424.

Manchester: BBC GMR, PO Box 951, Oxford Road, Manchester M60 1SD *tel* 0161-200 2000.

Merseyside: BBC Radio Merseyside, 55 Paradise Street, Liverpool L1 3BP *tel* 0151-708 5500.

Newcastle: BBC Radio Newcastle, Broadcasting Centre, Barrack Road, Newcastle upon Tyne NE99 1RN *tel* 0191-232 4141.

Norfolk: BBC Radio Norfolk, Norfolk Tower, Surrey Street, Norwich, Norfolk NR1 3PA *tel* (01603) 617411.

Northampton: BBC Radio Northampton, Broadcasting House, Abington Street, Northampton NN1 2BE *tel* (01604) 239100.

Nottingham: BBC Radio Nottingham, York House, Mansfield Road, Nottingham NG1 3JB *tel* (0115) 955 0500.

Sheffield: BBC Radio Sheffield, Ashdell Grove, 60 Westbourne Road, Sheffield S10 2QU *tel* (0114) 268 6785.

Shropshire: BBC Radio Shropshire, 2-4 Boscobel Drive, Shrewsbury, Shropshire SY1 3TT *tel* (01743) 248484.

Solent: BBC Radio Solent, Broadcasting House, Havelock Road, Southampton SO14 7PW *tel* (01703) 631311.

Somerset: BBC Somerset Sound, 14-15 Paul Street, Taunton, Somerset TA1 3PF *tel* (01823) 252437.

Stoke-on-Trent: BBC Radio Stoke, Cheapside, Hanley, Stoke-on-Trent, Staffs. ST1 1JJ *tel* (01782) 208080.

Suffolk: BBC Radio Suffolk, Broadcasting House, St Matthews Street, Ipswich IP1 3EP *tel* (01473) 250000.

Surrey: BBC Southern Counties Radio, Broadcasting Centre, Guildford, Surrey GU2 5AP *tel* (01483) 306306.

Swindon: BBC Wiltshire Sound, Broadcasting House, Prospect Place, Swindon, Wilts. SN1 3RW *tel* (01793) 513626.

Thames Valley: BBC Radio Thames Valley FM, 269 Banbury Road, Oxford OX2 7DW *tel* (01865) 311444.

York: BBC Radio York, 20 Bootham Row, York YO3 7BR *tel* (01904) 641351.

Independent Broadcasting

NATIONAL AND SATELLITE TELEVISION

Channel 5 Broadcasting Ltd, 22 Long Acre, London WC2E 9LY *tel* 0171-497 5225 *fax* 0171-497 5222. The fifth and last national 'free to air' terrestrial 24-hour television channel, due to come on air in January 1997, commissioning a wide range of programmes to suit all tastes.

Channel Four Television Corporation, 124 Horseferry Road, London SW1P 2TX *tel* 0171-396 4444 *fax* 0171-306 8347. Commissions and purchases programmes (does not make them) for broadcast during the whole week throughout the United Kingdom (except Wales).

GMTV, London Television Centre, Upper Ground, London SE1 9TT *tel* 0171-827 7000 *fax* 0171-827 7001. ITV's national breakfast television service, 6.00-9.25 a.m., seven days a week.

ITN, 200 Gray's Inn Road, London WC1X 8XZ *tel* 0171-833 3000. Provides the national and international news programmes for all ITV areas.

Teletext Ltd, 101 Farm Lane, London SW6 1QJ *tel* 0171-386 5000 *fax* 0171-386 5002.

BSkyB, 6 Centaurs Business Park, Grant Way, Isleworth, Middlesex TW7 5QD *tel* 0171-705 3000 *fax* 0171-705 3030/3113.

ITV Network Centre, 200 Gray's Inn Road, London WC1X 8HF *tel* 0171-843 8000 *fax* 0171-843 8158.

Independent Television Commission (ITC), 33 Foley Street, London W1P 7LB *tel* 0171-255 3000 *fax* 0171-306 7800. Licenses and regulates all commercially funded UK television services, including cable and satellite services as well as terrestrial services.

REGIONAL TELEVISION

It is advisable to check before submitting any ideas/material – in all cases, scripts are preferred to synopses. Programmes should be planned with natural breaks for the insertion of advertisements. These companies also provide some programmes for Channel 4.

Anglia Television Ltd, Anglia House, Norwich NR1 3JG *tel* (01603) 615151 *fax* (01603) 631032; 48 Leicester Square, London WC2H 7FB *tel* 0171-389 8555 *fax* 0171-930 8499. Provides programmes for the East of England, daytime discussion programmes, drama and Survival natural history programmes for the ITV Network. Drama submissions only through an accredited agency or similar source.

Border Television plc, The Television Centre, Carlisle CA1 3NT *tel* (01228) 25101. Provides programmes for The Borders and the Isle of Man, during the whole week. Ideas for programmes, but not drama programmes, are considered from outside sources. Suggestions should be sent to Neil Robinson, Controller of Programmes.

Carlton Broadcasting, 101 St Martin's Lane, London WC2N 4AZ *tel* 0171-240 4000 *fax* 0171-240 4171. Provides ITV programmes for London and the South East from Monday to Friday.

Central Broadcasting, Central House, Broad Street, Birmingham B1 2JP *tel* 0121-643 9898 *fax* 0121-643 4897; The Television House, Lenton Lane, Nottingham NG7 2NA *tel* (0115) 986 3322 *fax* (0115) 964 5552; Unit 9, Windrush Court, Abingdon Business Park, Abingdon, Oxon OX1 1SA *tel* (01235) 554123 *fax* (01235) 524024. Provides ITV programmes for the East, West and South Midlands seven days a week.

Channel Television, The Television Centre, St Helier, Jersey JE2 3ZD *tel* (01534) 816816 *fax* (01534) 816817. Provides programmes for the Channel Islands during the whole week relating mainly to Channel Islands news and current affairs.

Grampian Television plc, Queens Cross, Aberdeen AB9 2XJ *tel* (01224) 846846 *fax* (01224) 846800; Albany House, 68 Albany Road, West Ferry, Dundee DD5 1NW *tel* (01382) 739363; 23-25 Huntly Street, Inverness IV3 5PR *tel* (01463) 242624; Seaforth House, 54 Seaforth Road, Stornoway PH87 2SH *tel* (01851) 704433 *fax* (01851) 706406. Provides programmes for North Scotland during the whole week.

Granada Television Ltd, Granada Television Centre, Manchester M60 9EA *tel* 0161-832 7211; 36 Golden Square, London W1R 4AH *tel* 0171-734 8080. The ITV franchise holder for the North West of England. Produces programmes across a broad range for both its region and the ITV Network. It is advisable for writers to make their approach through agents who would have some knowledge of Granada's current requirements.

HTV Ltd, HTV Wales, The Television Centre, Culverhouse Cross, Cardiff CF5 6XJ *tel* (01222) 590590; HTV West, The Television Centre, Bristol BS4 3HG *tel* (0117) 977 8366. Provides programmes for Wales and West of England during the whole week. Produces programmes for home and international sales.

LWT, The London Television Centre, London SE1 9LT *tel* 0171-620 1620. Provides programmes for Greater London and much of the Home Counties area from Friday 5.15 p.m. to Monday 6.00 a.m. (excluding 6.00-9.25 a.m. on Sat/Sun).

Meridian Broadcasting, Television Centre, Southampton, Hants SO14 0PZ *tel* (01703) 222555 *fax* (01703) 335050. The ITV franchise holder for the South and South East. Meridian is a publisher contractor and commissions independent production companies.

Scottish Television Enterprises, Cowcaddens, Glasgow G2 3PR *tel* 0141-300 3000 *telex* 77388 *fax* 0141-300 3030. Wholly owned subsidiary of Scottish Television, making drama and other programmes for the ITV network. Material: ideas and formats for long-form series with or without a Scottish flavour. Approach in the first instance to the Controller of Drama, Robert Love.

Tyne Tees Television Ltd, The Television Centre, City Road, Newcastle upon Tyne NE1 2AL *tel* 0191-261 0181 *fax* 0191-261 2302; 15 Bloomsbury Square, London WC1A 2LJ *tel* 0171-312 3700. Serving the North of England seven days a week, 24 hours a day.

Ulster Television plc, Havelock House, Ormeau Road, Belfast, Northern Ireland BT7 1EB *tel* (01232) 328122 *fax* (01232) 246695. Provides programmes for Northern Ireland during the whole week.

Westcountry Television Ltd, Langage Science Park, Plymouth PL7 5BG *tel* (01752) 333333 *fax* (01752) 333444. Provides programmes for South West England throughout the week. In-house production mainly news, regional current affairs and topical features; other regional features commissioned from independent producers. Conduit to the Network for independent production packages.

Yorkshire Television Ltd, The Television Centre, Leeds LS3 1JS *tel* (0113) 243 8283 *fax* (0113) 244 5107; Television House, 15 Bloomsbury Square, London WC1A 2LJ *tel* 0171-312 3700. Yorkshire Television is a Network Company which produces many programmes for the ITV Network and the Yorkshire area seven days a week. Material preferred submitted through agents.

INDEPENDENT NATIONAL RADIO

Virgin Radio, 1 Golden Square, London W1R 4DJ *tel* 0171-434 1215 *fax* 0171-434 1197.

Classic FM, Academic House, 24-28 Oval Road, London NW1 7DQ *tel* 0171-284 3000 *fax* 0171-713 2630.

Talk Radio UK, 3rd Floor, 76 Oxford Street, London W1N 0TR *tel* 0171-636 1089 *fax* 0171-636 1053.

IRN (Independent Radio News), 1 Euston Centre, Euston Road, London NW1 3JG *tel* 0171-388 4558 *fax* 0171-388 4449. National news provider to all UK commercial radio stations, including live news bulletins, sport and financial news, and coverage of the House of Commons.

The Radio Authority, Holbrook House, 14 Great Queen Street, London WC2B 5DG *tel* 0171-430 2724 *fax* 0171-405 7062. Licenses and regulates Independent Radio. Plans frequencies, awards licences, regulates programming and radio advertising, and plays an active role in the discussion and formulation of policies which affect the Independent Radio industry and its listeners.

Association of Independent Radio Companies (AIRC), Radio House, 46 Westbourne Grove, London W2 5SH *tel* 0171-727 2646 *fax* 0171-229 0352. AIRC is the trade association of the commercial radio companies in the UK; non-broadcast companies may also join as associate members.

INDEPENDENT LOCAL RADIO

Aberdeen: NorthSound One FM and NorthSound Two, 45 King's Gate, Aberdeen AB2 6BL *tel* (01224) 632234.

Alton: Wey Valley Radio, Prospect Place, Mill Lane, Alton, Hants GU34 2SY *tel* (01420) 544444 *fax* (01420) 544044.

Aylesbury: Mix 96, Friars Square Studios, 11 Bourbon Street, Aylesbury, Bucks. HP20 2PZ *tel* (01296) 399396 *fax* (01296) 398988.

Ayr: West Sound, Radio House, 54A Holmston Road, Ayr KA7 3BE *tel* (01292) 283662 *fax* (01292) 283665.

Bedford: Chilton Radio East and Chilton Radio SuperGold East, Broadcast Centre, Goldington Road, Bedford, Beds MK40 3LS *tel* (01234) 272400 *fax* (01234) 218580.

Belfast: 96.7 BCR, Russell Court, Claremont Street, Lisburn Road, Belfast, Northern Ireland BT9 6JX *tel* (01232) 438500 *fax* (01232) 230505.

Belfast: Downtown Radio/Cool FM, Kiltonga Industrial Estate, Newtownards, Co. Down, Northern Ireland BT23 4ES *tel* (01247) 815555 *fax* (01247) 818913.

Birmingham: 96.4FM BRMB/XTRA-AM, Radio House, Aston Road North, Birmingham B6 4BX *tel* 0121-359 4481 *fax* 0121-359 1117.

Birmingham: Choice FM, 95 Broad Street, Birmingham B15 1AU *tel* 0121-616 1000 *fax* 0121-616 1011.

Birmingham: Radio XL 1296 AM, KMS House, Bradford Street, Birmingham B12 0JD *tel* 0121-753 5353 *fax* 0121-753 3111.

Blackpool: Radio Wave, 965 Mowbray Drive, Blackpool, Lancs. FY3 7JR *tel* (01253) 304965 *fax* (01253) 301965.

Borders: Radio Borders, Tweedside Park, Galashiels TD1 3TD *tel* (01896) 759444 *fax* (01896) 759494.

Bournemouth: Two Counties Radio, 5 Southcote Road, Bournemouth, Hants BH1 3LR *tel* (01202) 294881 *fax* (01202) 299314.

Bradford: Sunrise FM, 30 Chapel Street, Little Germany, Bradford BD1 5DN *tel* (01274) 735043 *fax* (01274) 728534.

Bradford/Huddersfield & Halifax: The Pulse, Forster Square, Bradford BD1 5NE *tel* (01274) 731521 *fax* (01274) 392031.

Brighton: Festival Radio, 6B Steine Gardens, Brighton, East Sussex BN2 1WB *tel* (01273) 777373 *fax* (01273) 205585.

Brighton: South Coast Radio, Radio House, PO Box 2000, Brighton, East Sussex BN14 2SS *tel* (01273) 430111 *fax* (01273) 430098.

Brighton: Southern FM, Radio House, PO Box 2000, Brighton, East Sussex BN41 2SS *tel* (01273) 430111 *fax* (01273) 430098.

Bristol: GWR Radio, PO Box 2000, Bristol BS99 7SN *tel* (0117) 984 3200 *fax* (0117) 984 3202.

Bury St Edmunds: SGR-FM, PO Box 250, Bury St Edmunds, Suffolk IP33 1AD *tel* (01473) 461000 *fax* (01473) 741200.

Cambridge & Newmarket: Q 103 FM, PO Box 103, The Vision Park, Chivers Way, Histon, Cambridge CB4 4WW *tel* (01223) 235255 *fax* (01223) 235161.

Cardiff & Newport: Red Dragon FM, West Canal Wharf, Cardiff CF1 5XJ *tel* (01222) 384041 *fax* (01222) 384014.

Cardiff & Newport: Touch AM, PO Box 99, Cardiff CF1 5YJ *tel* (01222) 273878 *fax* (01222) 84014.

Carlisle: CFM, PO Box 964, Carlisle, Cumbria CA1 3NG *tel* (01228) 818964.

Central Scotland: SCOT FM, Central Radio Scotland Ltd, Number 1, Albert Quay, Leith, Edinburgh EH6 7DN *tel* 0131-554 2266 *fax* 0131-554 2266.

Ceredigion: Radio Ceredigion, Yr Hen Ysgol Cymraeg, Ffordd Alexandra, Aberystwyth, Dyfed SY23 1LF *tel* (01970) 627999.

Channel Tunnel: Channel Travel Radio, Eurotunnel, UK Terminal, PO Box 2000, Folkestone, Kent CT18 8XY *tel* (01303) 283873 *fax* (01303) 283874.

Cheltenham: Cheltenham Radio, Radio House, PO Box 99, Cheltenham, Glos. GL53 7YX *tel* (01242) 261555.

Chichester, Bognor Regis & Littlehampton: Spirit FM, 9-10 Dukes Court, Bognor Road, Chichester, West Sussex PO19 2FX *tel* (01243) 773600 *fax* (01243) 786464.

Colchester: SGR Colchester, Abbeygate Two, 9 Whitewell Road, Colchester, Essex CO2 7DE *tel* (01206) 575859 *fax* (01206) 561199.

Cornwall/Plymouth/West Devon: Pirate FM102, Carn Brea Studios, Wilson Way, Redruth, Cornwall TR15 3XX *tel* (01209) 314400 *fax* (01209) 314345.

Coventry: Mercia FM and Mercia Classic Gold 1359, Hertford Place, Coventry CV1 3TT *tel* (01203) 868200 *fax* (01203) 868202.

Coventry: KIX 96, Ringway House, Hill Street, Coventry CV1 4AN *tel* (01203) 525656 *fax* (01203) 551744.

Darlington & Newport Aycliffe: A1 FM, Radio House, 11 Woodland Road, Darlington, Co. Durham DL3 7BJ *tel* (01325) 381032 *fax* (01325) 461235.

Derby: Ram FM, The Market Place, Derby DE1 3AA *tel* (01332) 292945 *fax* (01332) 292229.

Dumfries: South West Sound, Campbell House, Bankend Road, Dumfries DG1 4TH *tel* (01387) 50999 *fax* (01387) 65629.

Dumfries: West Sound, Campbell House, Bankend Road, Dumfries DG1 4TH *tel* (01387) 250999 *fax* (01387) 265629.

Dundee/Perth: Radio Tay AM (PO Box 123), Tay FM (PO Box 1028), 6 North Isla Street, Dundee DD1 9UF *tel* (01382) 200800 *fax* (01382) 593252.

Eastbourne/Hastings: Southern FM, PO Box 2000, Brighton, East Sussex BN41 2SS *tel* (01273) 430111 *fax* (01273) 430098.

Edinburgh: Forth FM, Forth House, Forth Street, Edinburgh EH1 3LF *tel* 0131-556 9255.

Edinburgh: Max AM, Forth House, Forth Street, Edinburgh EH1 3LF *tel* 0131-556 9255 *fax* 0131-558 3277.

Exeter/Torbay: Gemini Radio, Hawthorn House, Exeter Business Park, Exeter, Devon EX1 3QS *tel* (01392) 444444 *fax* (01392) 444433.

Fort William: Nevis Radio, Inverlochy, Fort William, Inverness-shire PH33 6LU *tel* (01397) 700007 *fax* (01397) 701007.

Glasgow: Clyde 1 FM and Clyde 2, Clydebank Business Park, Clydebank, Glasgow G81 2RX *tel* 0141-306 2200 *fax* 0141-306 2265.

Gloucester & Cheltenham: Severn Sound, Broadcast Centre, Southgate Street, Gloucester GL1 2DQ *tel* (01452) 423791 *fax* (01452) 529446.

Guernsey: Island FM, 12 Westerbrook, St Sampson, Guernsey GY2 4QQ, Channel Islands *tel* (01481) 42000 *fax* (01481) 49676.

Guildford & Haslemere: Radio Mercury FM West, The Friary, PO Box 964, Guildford, Surrey *tel* (01483) 451964 *fax* (01483) 31612.

Guildford, Haslemere, Reigate & Crawley: Mercury Extra AM, Broadfield House, Brighton Road, Crawley, West Sussex RH11 9TT *tel* (01293) 519161 *fax* (01293) 560927. Broadcasting to Surrey, Sussex and Hampshire.

Harlow: Ten 17, Latton Bush Centre, Southern Way, Harlow, Essex CM18 7BU *tel* (01279) 432415 *fax* (01279) 445289.

Harrogate: Stray FM, Stray Studios, PO Box 972, Station Parade, Harrogate HG1 5YF *tel* (01423) 522972 *fax* (01423) 522922.

Hereford/Worcester: Radio Wyvern, Barbourne Terrace, Worcester WR1 3JZ *tel* (01905) 612212.

High Wycombe: elevenSEVENTY, PO Box 1170, High Wycombe, Bucks HP13 6YT *tel* (01494) 446611 *fax* (01494) 445400 *news fax* (01494) 447272.

Humberside: Viking FM, Commercial Road, Hull HU1 2SG   *tel* (01482) 325141   *fax* (01482) 587067.

Inverness, Moray Firth Radio, PO Box 271, Inverness IV3 6SF   *tel* (01463) 224433   *fax* (01463) 243224.

Inverurie: North East Community Radio, Town House, Inverurie, Aberdeenshire AB51 0US   *tel* (01467) 632878   *fax* (01467) 632969.

Ipswich: SGR·FM, Radio House, Alpha Business Park, Whitehouse Road, Ipswich IP1 5LT   *tel* (01473) 461000   *fax* (01473) 741200.

Isle of Wight: Isle of Wight Radio, Dodnor Park, Newport, Isle of Wight PO30 5XE   *tel* (01983) 822557   *news tel* (01933) 821777   *fax* (01983) 821690.

Jersey: Channel 103, 6 Tunnell Street, St Helier, Jersey JE2 4LU, Channel Islands   *tel* (01534) 888103.

Kettering: KCBC Radio, PO Box 1584, Kettering, Northants. NN16 8PU   *tel* (01536) 412413   *fax* (01536) 517390.

King's Lynn: KL·FM96·7, PO Box 77, 18 Blackfriars Street, King's Lynn, Norfolk PE30 1NN   *tel* (01553) 772777   *fax* (01553) 767200.

Leeds/Wakefield/West Yorkshire: Radio Aire FM/Magic 828, PO Box 2000, 51 Burley Road, Leeds LS3 1LR   *tel* (0113) 245 2299   *fax* (0113) 242 1380   *news fax* (0113) 242 3985.

Leicester: Leicester Sound FM, Granville House, Granville Road, Leicester LE1 7RW   *tel* (0116) 256 1300   *fax* (0116) 256 1303.

Leicester: Sabras Sound, Radio House, 63 Melton Road, Leicester LE4 6PN   *tel* (0116) 261 0666   *fax* (0116) 266 7776.

Lincoln: Lincs FM, Witham Park, Waterside South, Lincoln LN5 7JN   *tel* (01522) 549900   *fax* (01522) 549911.

Liverpool: Radio City, 8 Stanley Street, Liverpool L1 6AF   *tel* 0151-227 5100   *newsdesk tel* 0151-471 0216   *fax* 0151-471 0333.

London (General and Entertainment Service): Capital Radio, Euston Tower, London NW1 3DR   *tel* 0171-608 6080   *fax* 0171-387 2345.

London (Brixton): Choice FM, 16-18 Trinity Gardens, London SW9 8DP   *tel* 0171-738 7969.

London (Haringey): London Greek Radio, Florentia Village, Vale Road, London N4 1TD   *tel* 0181-800 8001   *fax* 0181-800 8005.

London, Greater: Country 1035, PO Box 1035, London SW6 3QQ   *tel* 0171-384 1175   *fax* 0171-384 1177.

London, Greater: Festival Radio, Universal House, 251 Tottenham Court Road, London W1P 9AD   *tel* 0171-580 5668   *fax* 0171-580 5669.

London, Greater: 106·2 Heart FM, The Chrysalis Building, Bramley Road, London W10 6SP   *tel* 0171-221 2213.

London, Greater: J FM, 26/27 Castlereagh Street, London W1H 6DJ   *tel* 0171-706 4100   *fax* 0171-723 9742.

London, Greater: Kiss 100 FM, Kiss House, 80 Holloway Road, London N7 8JG   *tel* 0171-700 6100   *fax* 0171-700 3979.

London, Greater: London News 97·3FM and London News Talk 1152AM, 72 Hammersmith Road, London W14 8YE   *tel* 0171-973 1152   *fax* 0171-973 8833.

London, Greater: Melody FM, 180 Brompton Road, London SW3 1HF *tel* 0171-581 1054 *fax* 0171-581 7000.

London, Greater: Premier Radio, Glen House, Stag Place, London SW1E 5AG *tel* 0171-233 6705 *fax* 0171-233 6706.

London, Greater: Spectrum Radio, 80 Silverthorne Road, Battersea, London SW8 3XA *tel* 0171-627 4433 *fax* 0171-627 3409.

London, Greater: Sunrise Radio 1458AM, Sunrise House, Sunrise Road, Southall, Middlesex UB2 4AU *tel* 0181-574 6666 *fax* 0181-813 9800.

London, Greater: Virgin Radio London, 1 Golden Square, London W1R 4DJ *tel* 0171-434 1215 *fax* 0171-434 1197.

London, Greater: Viva! 963 AM, Golden Rose House, 26-27 Castlereagh Street, London W1H 6DJ *tel* 0171-706 9963 *fax* 0171-723 9742.

Londonderry: Q102·9 FM, The Old Waterside, Railway Station, Duke Street, Waterside, Londonderry, Northern Ireland BT47 1DH *tel* (01504) 44449.

Ludlow: Sunshine 855, Sunshine House, Waterside, Ludlow, Shropshire SY8 1GS *tel* (01584) 873795 *fax* (01584) 875900.

Luton/Bedford: Chiltern Radio, Chiltern Road, Dunstable, Beds. LU6 1HQ *tel* (01582) 666001.

Maidstone & Medway/East Kent: Invicta FM and Invicta SuperGold, Radio House, John Wilson Business Park, Whitstable, Kent CT5 3QX *tel* (01227) 772004 *fax* (01227) 771558.

Manchester: Fortune 1458, PO Box 1458, Quay West, Trafford Park, Manchester M17 1FL *tel* 0161-872 1458 *fax* 0161-872 0206.

Manchester: Kiss 102, Kiss House, PO Box 102, Manchester M60 1GJ *tel* 0161-228 0102 *fax* 0161-228 1020.

Manchester: Piccadilly Radio, 127-131 The Piazza, Piccadilly Plaza, Manchester M1 4AW *tel* 0161-236 9913 *fax* 0161-228 1503.

Mid Ulster: Townland Radio 828 AM, PO Box 828 Cookstown, Co. Tyrone BT80 9LQ *tel* (016487) 64828 *fax* (016487) 63828.

Milton Keynes: FM 103 Horizon, Broadcast Centre, Crownhill, Milton Keynes MK8 0AB *tel* (01908) 269111 *fax* (01908) 564893.

Montgomeryshire: Radio Maldwyn (The Magic 756), The Park, Newtown, Powys SY16 2NZ *tel* (01686) 623555 *phone-in tel* (01686) 624756 *fax* (01686) 623666.

North Devon: Lantern FM, The Light House, 17 Market Place, Bideford, Devon EX39 2DR *tel* (01237) 424444 *fax* (01237) 423333.

North East: Century Radio, PO Box 100, Gateshead NE8 2YY *tel* 0191-477 6666 *fax* 0191-477 5660.

North Lancashire/South Cumbria: The Bay 96·9 FM, PO Box 969, St George's Quay, Lancaster LA1 3LD *tel* (01524) 848747 *fax* (01524) 848787.

North Wales Coast: Marcher Coast FM, 41 Conway Road, Colwyn Bay, Clwyd LL28 5AB *tel* (01492) 534555 *fax* (01492) 535248.

North West: Jazz FM, The World Trade Centre, Exchange Quay, Manchester M5 3EJ *tel* 0161-877 1004 *fax* 0161-877 1005.

Northampton: Northants Radio, Broadcast Centre, The Enterprise Park, Boughton Green Road, Northampton NN2 7AH *tel* (01604) 792411 *fax* (01604) 721934.

Norwich & Great Yarmouth: Amber Radio, PO Box 4000, Norwich NR3 1DB *tel* (01603) 630621 *fax* (01603) 666353.

Norwich & Great Yarmouth: Broadland 102·4 FM, St George's Plain, 47-49 Colegate, Norwich NR3 1DB *tel* (01603) 630621 *fax* (01603) 666252.

Nottingham: TRENT FM, 29-31 Castle Gate, Nottingham NG1 7AP *tel* (0115) 952 7000.

Nottingham & Derby: GEM AM, 29-31 Castle Gate, Nottingham NG1 7AP *tel* (0115) 952 7000 *fax* (0115) 958 8614.

Oxford/Banbury: Fox FM, Brush House, Pony Road, Oxford OX4 2XR *tel* (01865) 748787 *fax* (01865) 748721.

Paisley: Q96, 26 Lady Lane, Paisley PA1 2LG *tel* 0141-887 9630 *fax* 0141-887 0963.

Peterborough: Classic Gold 1332 AM, PO Box 225, Queensgate Centre, Peterborough PE1 1XJ *tel* (01733) 346225 *fax* (01733) 896400.

Peterborough: 102·7 Hereward FM, PO Box 225, Queensgate Centre, Peterborough, Cambs. PE1 1XJ *tel* (01733) 460600 *fax* (01733) 281445.

Pitlochry & Aberfeldy: Heartland FM, Atholl Curling Rink, Lower Oakfield, Pitlochry, Perthshire PH16 5DS *tel* (01796) 474040 *fax* (01796) 474007.

Plymouth: Plymouth Sound, Earl's Acre, Plymouth PL3 4HX *tel* (01752) 227272 *fax* (01752) 670730.

Portsmouth & Southampton: South Coast Radio, Radio House, Fareham, Hants PO15 5SH *tel* (01489) 589911 *fax* (01489) 589453.

Portsmouth/Southampton/Winchester: Ocean FM, Radio House, Fareham, Hants PO15 5TA *tel* (01489) 589911 *fax* (01489) 589453.

Portsmouth, Southampton & Winchester: Power FM, Radio House, Whittle Avenue, Segensworth West, Fareham, Hants PO15 5SH *tel* (01489) 589911 *fax* (01489) 589453.

Preston & Blackpool: Red Rose Radio, PO Box 301, St Paul's Square, Preston, Lancs. PR1 1YE *tel* (01772) 556301 *fax* (01772) 201917.

Reading/Basingstoke: 210 Classic Gold, PO Box 2020, Reading, Berks. RG31 7RZ *tel* (01734) 254400 *fax* (01734) 254456.

Reading/Basingstoke & Andover: 2-TEN FM, PO Box 210, Reading, Berks. RG31 7RZ *tel* (01734) 254400 *fax* (01734) 254456.

Reigate & Crawley: Radio Mercury FM East, Broadfield House, Brighton Road, Crawley, West Sussex RH11 9TT *tel* (01293) 519161 *fax* (01293) 565663.

St Albans/Watford: Oasis Radio, Broadcast Centre, 7 Hatfield Road, St Albans, Herts. AL1 3RS *tel* (01727) 831966.

Salisbury: Spire FM, City Hall Studios, Malthouse Lane, Salisbury, Wilts. SP2 7QQ *tel* (01722) 416644 *fax* (01722) 415102.

Scarborough: Yorkshire Coast Radio, 62 Falsgrave Road, Scarborough, North Yorkshire YO12 5AX *tel* (01723) 500962 *fax* (01723) 501050.

Severn Estuary: Galaxy Radio, Broadcast Centre, Portland Square, Bristol BS2 8RZ *tel* (0117) 924 0111 *fax* (0117) 924 5589.

Shaftesbury: Gold Radio, Longmead, Shaftesbury, Dorset SP7 8QQ *tel* (01747) 855711 *fax* (01747) 855722.

Sheffield & Rotherham/Barnsley/Doncaster: Hallam FM and Great Yorkshire Gold, Radio House, 900 Herries Road, Hillsborough, Sheffield S6 1RH *tel* (0114) 285 3333/852121 *fax* (0114) 285 3159.

Shetland Islands: SIBC, Market Street, Lerwick, Shetland ZE1 0JN *tel* (01595) 695299 *fax* (01595) 695696.

Southend/Chelmsford/Harlow: Essex FM, Breeze and Ten 17, Radio House, Clifftown Road, Southend-on-Sea, Essex SS1 1SX *tel* (01702) 333711 *fax* (01702) 345224.

Staffordshire & Cheshire: Signal Radio, Stoke Road, Stoke-on-Trent, Staffs. ST4 2SR *tel* (01782) 747047 *fax* (01782) 744110.

Stirling: Central 103·1 FM, John Player Building, Stirling Enterprise Park, Stirling FK7 7YJ *tel* (01786) 451188 *fax* (01786) 461883.

Stockport: Signal Radio Cheshire, Regent House, Heaton Lane, Stockport, Cheshire SK4 1BX *tel* 0161-480 5445 *fax* 0161-429 7680.

Sunderland: Sun City 103·4, PO Box 1034, Sunderland, Tyne and Wear SR1 3YZ *tel* 0191-567 3333 *fax* 0191-567 0888.

Swansea: Sound Wave 96·4 FM, Victoria Road, Gowerton, Swansea, West Glamorgan SA4 3AB *tel* (01792) 893751 *fax* (01792) 898841.

Swansea: Swansea Sound 1170 MW, Victoria Road, Gowerton, Swansea, West Glamorgan SA4 3AB *tel* (01792) 893751 *fax* (01792) 898841.

Swindon/West Wiltshire: GWR Radio, PO Box 2000, Swindon, Wilts. SN4 1WQ *tel* (01793) 440300 *fax* (01793) 440302.

Taunton & Yeovil: Orchard FM, Haygrove House, Shoreditch, Taunton, Somerset TA3 7BT *tel* (01823) 338448.

Teesside: TFM Radio, Yale Crescent, Stockton-on-Tees, Cleveland TS17 6AA *tel* (01642) 615111 *fax* (01642) 674402.

Tendring: Mellow 1557, The Media Centre, 2 St John's Wynd, Culver Square, Colchester, Essex CO1 1WQ *tel* (01206) 764466 *fax* (01206) 764672.

Thamesmead: RTM (Independent Radio Thamesmead), Thamesmead Town Offices, Harrow Manorway, London SE2 9UG *tel* 0181-311 3112 *fax* 0181-312 1930.

Tonbridge, Tunbridge Wells & Sevenoaks: KFM, 1 East Street, Tonbridge, Kent TN9 1AR *tel* (01732) 369200 *fax* (01732) 369201.

Tyne and Wear: Metro FM, Long Rigg, Swalwell, Newcastle upon Tyne NE99 1BB *tel* 0191-420 0971 *fax* 0191-488 9222.

West Cumbria: CFM, PO Box 964, Carlisle CA1 3NG *tel* (01228) 818964 *fax* (01228) 819444.

West Midlands: 100·7 Heart FM, PO Box 1007, 1 The Square, 111 Broad Street, Edgbaston, Birmingham B15 1AS *tel* 0121-626 1007.

Weymouth & Dorchester: Wessex FM, Trinity Street, Dorchester, Dorset DT1 1DJ *tel* (01305) 250333 *fax* (01305) 250052.

Whitstable: Invicta Radio, PO Box 100, Whitstable, Kent CT5 3YR *tel* (01227) 772004 *fax* (01227) 771558.

Windsor, Slough & Maidenhead: Star FM, The Observatory Shopping Centre, Slough, Berks. SL1 1LH *tel* (01753) 551016 *fax* (01753) 512277.

Wolverhampton & the Black Country/Shrewsbury & Telford: Beacon Radio, 267 Tettenhall Road, Wolverhampton WV6 0DQ *tel* (01902) 838383; 28 Castle Street, Shrewsbury SY1 2BQ *tel* (01743) 232271.

Wolverhampton & the Black Country/Shrewsbury & Telford: WABC, 267 Tettenhall Road, Wolverhampton WV6 0DQ   *tel* (01902) 838383   *fax* (01902) 755163 or 838266.

Wrexham, Chester & Deeside, Wirral and North Wales: Marcher Sound/Sain-Y-Gororau, The Studios, Mold Road, Wrexham, Clwyd LL11 4AF   *tel* (01978) 752202   *fax* (01978) 759701.

York: Minster FM, PO Box 123, Dunnington, York YO1 5ZX   *tel* (01904) 488888   *fax* (01904) 488878.

Yorkshire/Lincolnshire: Great Yorkshire Gold, Radio House, 900 Herries Road, Sheffield S6 1RH   *tel* (0114) 285 2121   *fax* (0114) 285 3159; Forster Square, Bradford BD1 5NE   *tel* (01274) 731521   *fax* (01274) 392031; Commercial Road, Hull HU1 2SG   *tel* (01482) 325141   *fax* (01482) 587067.

Overseas Radio and Television Companies

AUSTRALIA

Australian Broadcasting Corporation, Box 9994, GPO, Sydney, NSW 2001. Manager for Europe: Australian Broadcasting Corporation, 54 Portland Place, London W1N 4DY. Provides television and radio programmes in the national broadcasting service; operates Radio Australia; operates the international television service, Australia Television; and co-ordinates a network of six symphony orchestras and stages concerts throughout Australia.

ABC television restricts its production resources to work closely related to the Australian environment. ABC radio also looks principally to Australian writers for the basis of its drama output. However, ABC radio is interested in reading or auditioning new creative material of a high quality from overseas sources and this may be submitted in script or taped form. No journalistic material is required. Talks on international affairs are commissioned.

ATN Channel 7, Australian Television Network, Amalgamated Television Services Pty Ltd, Television Centre, Epping, NSW 2121   *tel* (02) 877 7777   *telegraphic address* Telecentre, Sydney   *telex* AA 20250   *fax* (02) 877 7886. Unsolicited material not accepted.

BTQ Channel 7, Brisbane TV Limited, Sir Samuel Griffith Drive, Mt Coot-tha, GPO Box 604, Brisbane 4001   *tel* (07) 3369 7777   *fax* (07) 3368 2970. *Network director, children's programs:* Dina Browne. Children's educational-type series, children's entertainment programmes. Writers should have a thorough understanding of Australian culture.

HSV Channel 7 Melbourne, HSV Channel 7 Pty Ltd, 119 Wells Street, South Melbourne, Victoria 3205   *tel* (03) 697 7777. No unsolicited material accepted.

National Nine Network (TCN-9 Sydney, GTV-9 Melbourne, QTQ-9 Brisbane, NWS-9 Adelaide, STW-9 Perth), c/o 24 Artarmon Road, Willoughby, NSW 2068   *tel* (02) 9906 9999   *fax* (02) 9958 2279. *Network program director:* John Stephens; *network director of drama:* Kris Noble; *network director program development:* David Lyle. Interested in receiving material from freelance writers strictly on the basis of payment for material or ideas used. No necessity for writers to be Australian-based, but membership of the Australian Writers' Guild helpful.

CANADA

Canadian Broadcasting Corporation, PO Box 8478, Ottawa, Ontario K1G 3J5 *tel* 613-724-1200.

REPUBLIC OF IRELAND

Radio Telefis Eireann, Donnybrook, Dublin 4 *tel* (01) 2083111 *telex* 93700 *fax* (01) 2083080. The Irish national broadcasting service operating radio and television.

Television: Ongoing production of both a rural and an urban drama serial. Treatments and character profiles accepted for one-off drama productions, drama series and situation comedies, preferably set in Ireland or of strong Irish interest, with preferred durations of commercial half hour or hour length. Forwarding of fully dialogued submissions not encouraged. Before submitting material to Current Affairs, Drama, Features or Young People's programmes, authors are advised to write to the department in question.

Radio: short stories (length 13-14 minutes) in Irish or English suitable for broadcasting; plays (running 30, 60 or 90 minutes) are welcomed and paid for according to merit. Guidelines on writing for radio drama are available from the RTE Radio Drama Department, Radio Centre, Donnybrook, Dublin 4.

Independent Radio and Television Commission, Marine House, Clanwilliam Place, Dublin 2 *tel* (01) 6760966 *fax* (01) 6760948. Statutory body with responsibility for independent broadcasting. At present there are 21 local radio stations operating in Ireland, in addition to one special interest/community station and one Irish language station. During 1995, 11 community and community of interest radio stations came on-air as part of an 18-month pilot community radio project. It is hoped that a new national independent radio station will be in operation towards the end of 1996. The IRTC is currently in the process of negotiations regarding the establishment of a national independent television service.

NEW ZEALAND

Radio New Zealand Ltd, PO Box 2092, Wellington, C1 *tel* (04) 474-1555 *telex* NZ31031 *fax* (04) 474-1340. *Chief executive:* Joan Withers. A 24-hour state-owned radio enterprise, with editorial and programming independence, controlling a NZ-wide group of over 40 commercial/community stations, two commercial networks and two public service non-commercial networks, and a shortwave service directed primarily to the Pacific area.

Television New Zealand Ltd, PO Box 3819, Auckland *tel* (09) 377-0630 *fax* (09) 375-0918. *Chairman:* Norman Geary; *group chief executive:* Chris Anderson. TVNZ is a state-owned enterprise with production facilities in all four main centres. It owns and operates TV ONE, TV2 and subsidiary companies, South Pacific Pictures Ltd, Avalon Studios Ltd, Broadcast Communications Ltd and Horizon Pacific Television, which operates five regional television stations.

SOUTH AFRICA

South African Broadcasting Corporation, Private Bag XI, Auckland Park 2006 *tel* (011) 714-9111 *fax* (011) 714-3106. Operates five national radio networks, eight regional radio services and three television services.

Markets for Radio Programmes

Almondell Productions (1993), 144 Mansefield, East Calder, West Lothian EH53 0JQ   *tel/fax* (01506) 881483. *Contact:* David Calder. Scripts for docs and speech-based programmes; no plays.

Boom Media Ltd (1993), 25 Market Place, Halesworth, Suffolk IP19 8DA   *tel* (01986) 875000   *fax* (01986) 875050. *Director:* Nick Patrick. Features and docs with an East Anglian bias, sports' features, popular culture, East Anglian drama.

Business Sound Ltd (1989), Unit 9, Bramley Business Centre, Station Road, Bramley, Surrey GU5 0AZ   *tel* (01483) 898868   *fax* (01483) 894056. *Managing director:* Michael Bartlett. Ideas and synopses for packages for the corporate training market; docs. No unsolicited material; initial approach by phone, please.

Fast Forward Radio Productions (1994), A132, Riverside Business Centre, Bendon Valley, London SW18 4LZ   *tel* 0181-875 9999   *fax* 0181-875 0344. *Producer:* Adrian Quine. Travel, music, current affairs.

Festival Radio productions (Level Broadcast Ltd) (1989), 6ʙ Steine Gardens, Brighton, East Sussex BN2 1WB   *tel* (01273) 777373   *fax* (01273) 205585. *Director:* Daniel Nathan. Plays, docs and features.

The Fiction Factory (1993), 201 Greenwich High Road, London SE10 8NB   *tel* 0181-853 5100   *fax* 0181-293 3001   *e-mail* drama@mill.cityscape.co.uk *Creative director:* John Taylor. Plays, dramatisations, readings, documentaries, arts features and children's drama mainly for BBC radio (R4, R2, World Service etc). Ideas for all radio genres considered.

The Flying Dutchman Company (1988), 5-7 Hughes Mews, 143 Chatham Road, London SW11 6HJ   *tel* 0171-223 9067   *fax* 0171-585 0459. *Partner:* Michael Cameron. Plays, docs and other programmes on all topics.

GRF Christian Radio (1948), 342 Argyle Street, Glasgow G2 8LY   *tel* 0141-221 9447   *fax* 0141-332 9187   *e-mail* grf.radio@scet.org.uk *Programme controller:* Brian W. Muir. Docs on ethical/moral/religious issues; mini-dramas (up to four minutes) on religious themes; one-minute scripts; children's programmes (religious/educational).

Heavy Entertainment Ltd (1992), 208-209 Canalot Studios, 222 Kensal Road, London W10 5BN   *tel* 0181-960 9001/2   *fax* 0181-960 9003. *Company directors:* David Roper, Nick St George. Full-length plays, docs and comedy programmes.

Hispania (1993), 17 Montrose Court, Edgware Road, London NW9 5BS   *tel* 0181-905 5000. *Head of Hispanic service:* Bruno Giorgi. Short plays and docs suitable for broadcasting in Spanish, so material translated into Spanish an advantage. Scripts for international and national radio competitions.

Mike Hopwood Productions Ltd (1991), Conway House, Cheapside, Hanley, Stoke-on-Trent, Staffs. ST1 1JJ   *tel* (01782) 201319   *fax* (01782) 289115. *Editor:* Mike Hopwood. Plays, docs, comedy, soaps, light entertainment.

Independent Productions Ltd (1990), 46ᴀ Willowtree Road, Hale, Altrincham, Cheshire WA14 2EG   *tel* 0161-928 6105   *fax* 0161-928 6105. *Director:* Tony Hawkins. Scripts and ideas for commercials and promotions for independent radio.

IRDP, PO Box 518, Manningtree, Essex CO11 1XD *tel* (01206) 299088. New writing schemes for radio and theatre, and professional independent productions.

Mediatracks (1987), 93 Columbia Way, Blackburn, Lancs. BB2 7EA *tel/fax* (01254) 691197. *Contact:* Steve Johnson. Pop-music and general interest docs for BBC local radio network.

Partners in Sound Ltd, 63 Spencer Rise, London NW5 1AR *tel* 0171-485 0873 *mobile* (01973) 221479 *fax* 0171-428 0541/482 2218 *e-mail* @compuserve 74077,2265 *Director:* Ian Willox. Scripts for plays, docs and other programmes.

Planet 24 (1991), Norex Court, Thames Quay, 195 Marsh Wall, London E14 9SG *tel* 0171-345 2424 *fax* 0171-345 9400. *Development executive:* Tracey Macleod. Scripts, synopses and ideas for plays, docs and other programmes.

Rewind Productions Ltd (1989), The Media Centre, 131-151 Great Titchfield Street, London W1P 8AE *tel* 0171-577 7770 *fax* 0171-577 7771. *Managing director:* Chris Parry-Davies. Plays, docs, popular and classical music, comedy and game shows.

Saffron Productions Ltd (1985), Craigs End, Stambourne, Halstead, Essex CO9 4NQ *tel* (01440) 785200 *fax* (01440) 785775. *Managing director/executive producer:* Victor Pemberton; *director programmes:* David Spenser. Ideas for one-hour plays, and drama series, serials, docs and other programmes.

ScreenPlay Ltd (1987), 25 Cleveland Road, Brighton, East Sussex BN1 6FF *tel* (01273) 708610 *fax* (01273) 708611 *e-mail* bobshep@pavilion.co.uk *Managing director:* Robert J. Shepherd. Scripts for drama and comedy, particularly series and serials. Unsolicited material occasionally considered. Send synopsis and sample dialogue in first instance; sae essential for return of material.

SH Radio (1988), Robert Symes, Green Dene Cottage, Honeysuckle Bottom, East Horsley, Surrey KT24 5TD *tel/fax* (01483) 283223; Mary-Jean Hasler, 22 Carew Road, Ealing, London W13 9QL *tel* 0181-567 2100. Music series, documentary features and broadcast/non-broadcast commercial material, voice over for films.

Smooth Operations (1992), PO Box 286, Cambridge CB1 4TW *tel* (01223) 880835 *fax* (01223) 881647. *Executive producers:* Nick Barraclough, John Leonard. Scripts and ideas for docs and series with popular music theme.

Soundbite Productions Ltd (1991), 55 Tasman Road, Stockwell, London SW9 9LZ *tel/fax* 0171-274 1349. *Managing director:* Lizzie Jackson. Well-thought-out ideas and research for series and programmes for BBC Radio and World Service. Material only accepted from those with a proven track record in radio or TV.

Splash Sound Productions (1982), 1 Mossley Hill Drive, Liverpool L17 1AJ *tel/fax* 0151-724 5813. Ideas for plays, serials, musical drama and comedy.

Testbed Productions (1992), 10 Margaret Street, London W1N 7LF *tel* 0171-436 0555 *fax* 0171-436 2800. *Directors:* Viv Black, Nick Baker. Docs and other programmes; ideas for interviews, feature series, magazine, plays and panel/quiz games.

Markets for Screenplays

JEAN McCONNELL

The recommended approach for placing material is through a recognised literary agent, but most film companies have a story department to whom material can be sent for consideration. But it is a good idea to check with the company first to make sure it is worth your while.

It is a fact that many of the feature films these days are based on already best-selling books, but there are some companies, particularly those with a television outlet, which will sometimes accept unsolicited material if it seems to be exceptionally original. It is obviously sensible to try to sell your work to a company which is currently in active production, such as those listed below. *But again remember the best way to achieve success is through the knowledge and efforts of a literary agent.*

When a writer submits material direct to a company, some of the larger ones, usually those American based, may request that a Release Form be signed before they are prepared to read it. This document is ostensibly designed to absolve the company from any charge of plagiarism if they should be working on a similar idea; also to limit their liability in the event of any legal action. Writers must make up their own minds whether they wish to sign this but, in principle, it is not highly recommended.

Markets for Screenplays and Television Programmes

Aardman Animations (1972), Gas Ferry Road, Bristol BS1 6UN   *tel* (0117) 984 8485   *fax* (0117) 984 8486. *Producer, broadcast/features:* Michael Rose. Specialists in model animation, looking for screenplays for adults and families for cinema and TV.

Agran Barton Television Ltd (1993), The Yacht Club, Chelsea Harbour, London SW10 0XA   *tel* 0171-351 7070   *fax* 0171-352 3528. *Contacts:* Linda Agran and Nick Barton. Screenplays for cinema; drama and factual TV programmes.

Anglia Television Entertainment (1988), 48 Leicester Square, London WC2H 7FB   *tel* 0171-321 0101   *fax* 0171-930 8499. *Managing director:* Sarah Lawson. Synopses for television drama or mini-series, non-factual programme ideas.

British Lion Screen Entertainment (1927), Pinewood Studios, Iver, Bucks. SL0 0NH   *tel* (01753) 651700   *fax* (01753) 656391. *Contact:* Peter Snell. Screenplays and treatments for cinema; TV drama and sitcoms. No unsolicited material.

Brook Associates Ltd, 21-24 Bruges Place, Randolph Street, London NW1 0TF   *tel* 0171-482 6111   *fax* 0171-284 0626. *Development executives:* Anne Lapping, Phillip Whitehead, Udi Eichler. Screenplays for TV; TV documentaries, current affairs and drama.

Catalyst Television Ltd (1991), Brook Green Studios, 186 Shepherds Bush Road, London W6 7LL   *tel* 0171-603 7030   *fax* 0171-603 9519. *Contact:* Head of Drama Development. Screenplays/novels for adaptation for TV. Will only consider material submitted through an agent.

Celador Productions Ltd (1983), 39 Long Acre, London WC2E 9JT   *tel* 0171-240 8101   *fax* 0171-836 1117. *Contacts:* Paul Smith (game shows), Nic Phillips (sitcoms). Popular entertainment TV programmes: comedy, entertainment, game show productions, 'people show' ideas, light documentary.

Chatsworth Television Ltd (1980), 97-99 Dean Street, London W1V 5RA   *tel* 0171-734 4302   *fax* 0171-437 3301. *Head of drama development:* Stephen Jeffery-Poulter – film and TV drama scripts; *head of entertainment:* Justin Scroggie – infotainment, entertainment and game show formats. *No* sitcoms.

Children's Film and Television Foundation Ltd, Elstree Studios, Borehamwood, Herts. WD6 1JG   *tel* 0181-953 0844   *fax* 0181-207 0860. Not a production company; finances script development, especially for feature films (principally television) aimed at children between 5 and 12 years old.

Childsplay Productions Ltd (1984), 8 Lonsdale Road, London NW6 6RD   *tel* 0171-328 1429   *fax* 0171-328 1416. *Contact:* Kim Burke. Children's (not pre-school) and family TV programming. Chiefly drama; some unsolicited work accepted but telephone first to discuss.

The Comic Strip Ltd (1980), 8-10 Great Titchfield Street, London W1P 7AA   *tel* 0171-462 6006   *fax* 0171-436 0632. *Contact:* Rebecca Jeffrey, Peter Richardson. Screenplays for cinema and TV; ½-hour comedy and drama series.

Compass Film Productions Ltd (1974), 175 Wardour Street, London W1V 3FB   *tel* 0171-734 8115   *fax* 0171-439 6456. *Contact:* Simon Heaven. Screenplays for TV; cultural, educational and sponsored TV programmes.

The Walt Disney Company Ltd, Avon House, Kensington Village, Avonmore, London W14 8TS   *tel* 0171-605 2400   *fax* 0171-605 2593. Screenplays not accepted by London office. *Must be submitted by an agent* to The Walt Disney Studios in Burbank, California.

Diverse Production Ltd (1982), Gorleston Street, London W14 8XS   *tel* 0171-603 4567   *fax* 0171-603 2148. *Drama producer:* Laurence Bowen. Film and TV drama.

Fairwater Films Ltd (1982), 68 Vista Rise, Llandaff, Cardiff CF5 2SD   *tel/fax* (01222)   578488   *e-mail* tonybarnes@bbcnc.org.uk   and   100756,3440 @compuserve.com *Managing director:* Tony Barnes. Animation for cinema and TV; live action entertainment. All material should be submitted through an agent.

The First Film Company Ltd (1984), 38 Great Windmill Street, London W1V 7PA   *tel* 0171-439 1640   *fax* 0171-437 2062. *Producers:* Roger Randall-Cutler, Sophie Bankes, Simon Flind. Screenplays for cinema. All material should be submitted through an agent.

Focus Films (1982), The Rotunda Studios, rear of 116-118 Finchley Road, London NW3 5HT   *tel* 0171-435 9004   *fax* 0171-431 3562. *Contact:* head of development. Screenplays for cinema. Will only consider material submitted through an agent.

Mark Forstater Productions Ltd, Unit 66, Pall Mall Deposit, 124-126 Barlby Road, London W10 6BL   *tel* 0181-964 1888   *fax* 0181-960 9819. *Contact:* Rosie Homan. Film and TV production. No unsolicited scripts, please.

Front Page Films (1985), 23 West Smithfield, London EC1A 9HY   *tel* 0171-329 6866   *fax* 0171-329 6844. *Contact:* script editor. Screenplays for cinema. Material only accepted through agents.

Noel Gay Television (1987), 6th Floor, 76 Oxford Street, London W1N 0AT   *tel* 0171-412 0400   *fax* 0171-412 0300. *Contact:* head of development. Screenplays for cinema and TV; entertainment and drama.

Granada Film (1989), 36 Golden Square, London W1R 4AH   *tel* 0171-494 6388   *fax* 0171-494 6360. *Head of film:* Pippa Cross. Screenplays for cinema and TV: major commercial feature films, smaller UK-based films, internationally financeable TV movies. No unsolicited material.

Hammer Film Production Ltd, Millennium Studios, Elstree Way, Borehamwood, Herts. WD6 1SF   *tel* 0181-207 4011   *fax* 0181-905 1127. *Contact:* Graham Skeggs. Completed screenplays and published books for cinema and TV development: drama/mystery/horror/ghost. *No* unsolicited material.

Hartswood Films (1981), Shepperton Studios, Studios Road, Shepperton, Middlesex TW17 0QD   *tel* (01932) 572294   *fax* (01932) 572299. *Producer:* Beryl Vertue; *development:* Elaine Cameron. Screenplays for cinema and TV; comedy and drama. No unsolicited material.

Hat Trick Productions Ltd (1986), 10 Livonia Street, London W1V 3PH   *tel* 0171-434 2451   *fax* 0171-287 9791. *Contact:* Denise O'Donoghue. Situation and drama comedy series and light entertainment shows.

Jim Henson Productions Ltd (1979), 30 Oval Road, London NW1 7DE   *tel* 0171-428 4000   *fax* 0171-428 4001. *Contact:* director of development. Screenplays for cinema and TV; fantasy, family and children's programmes – usually involving puppetry or animatronics. All material should be submitted through an agent.

Hightimes Productions (1981), 5 Anglers Lane, Kentish Town, London NW5 3DG   *tel* 0171-482 5202   *fax* 0171-485 4254. *Production executive:* Tony Humphreys. Screenplays for TV; light entertainment, comedy and drama.

Illuminations (1982), 19-20 Rheidol Mews, Rheidol Terrace, London N1 8NU   *tel* 0171-226 0266   *fax* 0171-359 1151. *Contact:* Linda Zuck. Screenplays for TV; cultural documentaries, arts and entertainment for broadcast TV. All material should be submitted through an agent.

Initial Film & Television Ltd (1985), 74 Black Lion Lane, London W6 9BE   *tel* 0181-741 4500   *fax* 0181-741 9416. *Head of development, drama department:* Leonora Martin. Screenplays for cinema and TV; music; drama series, serials and one-offs. All material should be submitted through an agent.

Kensington Films and Television Ltd (1993), 60 Charlotte Street, London W1P 2AX   *tel* 0171-927 8458   *fax* 0171-927 8444. Screenplays for cinema and TV drama. Send material to Margot Gavan Duffy or Lucy Guard.

Brian Lapping Associates (1988), 21 Bruges Place, Randolph Street, London NW1 0TF   *tel* 0171-482 5855   *fax* 0171-284 01626. *Contact:* Brian Lapping. Screenplays for TV; documentary series, studio programmes.

Little Bird Company Ltd (1982), 91 Regent Street, London W1R 7TA   *tel* 0171-434 1131   *fax* 0171-434 1803. *Development executives:* J. Cavendish, M. Pope. Screenplays for cinema and TV.

Little Dancer Ltd (1992), Avonway, 3 Naseby Road, Crystal Palace, London SE19 3JJ   *tel* 0181-653 9343. *Producer:* Robert Smith. Screenplays for cinema and TV; drama.

London Film Productions Ltd, 35 Davies Street, London W1Y 1FN   *tel* 0171-499 7800   *fax* 0171-499 7994. *Chairman:* J. Eliasch. No unsolicited material considered.

Malone Gill Productions Ltd (1978), Canaletto House, 39 Beak Street, London W1R 3LD *tel* 0171-287 3970 *fax* 0171-287 8146. *Contact:* Georgina Denison. TV programmes.

Maya Vision Ltd (1982/3), 43 New Oxford Street, London WC1A 1BH *tel* 0171-836 1113 *fax* 0171-838 5169. *Producer/director:* Rebecca Dobbs. Features, TV dramas and documentaries. No unsolicited scripts.

New Blitz TV, Via Guido Banti 34, 00191 Rome, Italy *tel* 333 26 41 *fax* 333 26 51. *Television department:* Giovanni A. Congiu. Importation and dubbing TV series, documentaries, educational films and video for schools. Material from freelance sources required.

Oxford Scientific Films Ltd (1968), Lower Road, Long Hanborough, Oxon OX8 8LL *tel* (01993) 881881 *fax* (01993) 882808. *Managing director:* Karen Goldie-Morrison. Natural history and science-based programmes for broadcast, multimedia, educational and advertising markets. See also entry in picture agencies and libraries section.

Penumbra Productions Ltd (1981), 21A Brondesbury Villas, London NW6 6AH *tel* 0171-328 4550 *fax* 0171-328 3844. *Contact:* H.O. Nazareth. Drama for feature films and TV; documentaries for TV; non-broadcast videos to commissions.

Picture Palace Films Ltd (1971), 53a Brewer Street, Soho, London W1R 3FD *tel* 0171-734 6630 *fax* 0171-734 8574. *Contact:* Malcolm Craddock. Screenplays for cinema and TV; low budget films; TV drama series. Material only considered if submitted through an agent.

Planet 24 (1992), The Planet Building, 195 Marsh Wall, Thames Quay, London E14 9SG *tel* 0171-345 2424 *fax* 0171-345 9400. *Contact:* Development Department. Screenplays for cinema and TV; drama and comedy for TV and radio.

Portman Productions Ltd (1970), 105 Ladbroke Grove, London W11 1TG *tel* 0171-468 3400 *fax* 0171-468 3499. *Head of development:* Katherine Butler. Cinema and TV.

Portobello Pictures Ltd (1987), 42 Tavistock Road, London W11 1AW *tel* 0171-379 5566 *fax* 0171-379 5599. *Contact:* Eric Abraham. Screenplays for cinema and TV; drama.

Primetime Television (1968), Seymour Mews House, Seymour Mews, Wigmore Street, London W1H 9PE *tel* 0171-935 9000 *telex* 22872 TVFILM G *fax* 0171-935 1992 or 0171-487 3975. *Contacts:* Victoria Hull, Judy Craymer. Screenplays for TV and TV programmes of international interest, especially drama and documentary series. One-page synopsis *must* accompany any unsolicited script.

Red Rooster Film & Television Entertainment Ltd (1982), 29 Floral Street, London WC2E 9DP *tel* 0171-379 7727 *fax* 0171-379 5756. *Contacts:* Julia Ouston, Tim Vaughan and Jill Green (drama), Sue Birbeck (comedy). Screenplays for cinema and TV; long-running series: drama, children and entertainment. All material should be submitted through an agent.

Regent Productions Ltd (1982), The Mews, 6 Putney Common, London SW15 1HL *tel* 0181-789 5350 *fax* 0181-789 5332. *Contact:* William G. Stewart. Screenplays for TV; drama, situation comedies.

RM Associates Ltd (1982), 46 Great Marlborough Street, London W1V 1DB *tel* 0171-439 2637 *telex* 24549 RMALTD G *fax* 0171-439 2316. *Contact:* Meckie Offermanns. Music and arts programmes: opera, dance, music, arts features and documentary series.

Saffron Productions Ltd (1985), Craigs End, Stambourne, Halstead, Essex CO9 4NQ   *tel* (01440) 785200   *fax* (01440) 785775. *Contacts:* Victor Pemberton, David Spenser. Drama and factual TV programmes; non-broadcast videos. Ideas/synopses only.

Specific Films, 25 Rathbone Street, London W1P 1AG   *tel* 0171-580 7476   *fax* 0171-494 2676. *Contact:* Melanie Claus. Comedy screenplays for cinema.

Spitting Image Productions Ltd and Lawless Films (1983), Cairo Studios, 4 Nile Street, London N1 7ZZ   *tel* 0171-251 2626   *fax* 0171-251 2066. *Head of development:* Jenny Landreth. Screenplays for film and TV; TV programmes, including 'live action' areas of comedy.

Talisman Films Ltd (1991), 5 Addison Place, London W11 4RJ   *tel* 0171-603 7474   *fax* 0171-602 7422. *Contact*: Alan Shallcross. Screenplays for cinema and TV. Material *only considered* if submitted through an agent.

TalkBack Productions (1989), 36 Percy Street, London W1P 0LN   *tel* 0171-323 9777   *fax* 0171-637 5105. TV situation comedies and comedy dramas. Send unsolicited material to PA to Managing Director; material through an agent to Peter Fincham or Sioned William.

Tiger Aspect Productions Ltd (1993), 5 Soho Square, London W1V 5DE   *tel* 0171-434 0672   *fax* 0171-287 1448. *Contact:* Colette Blair. TV comedy drama and sitcoms. All material should be submitted through an agent.

Triple Vision Ltd (1983), Folly Lodge, Folly Lane, North Wooton, Somerset BA4 4ER   *tel/fax* (01749) 890610. *Contact:* Terry Flaxton. Screenplays for cinema and TV; arts/drama and documentaries, plays. Material only accepted through agents.

Twentieth Century Fox Productions Ltd, Twentieth Century House, 31-32 Soho Square, London W1V 6AP   *tel* 0171-437 7766   *fax* 0171-434 2170. Will not consider unsolicited material.

Twenty Twenty Television (1982), 20 Kentish Town Road, London NW1 9NX   *tel* 0171-284 2020   *telex* 914951 ZOZOTV G   *fax* 0171-284 1810. *Executive producer:* Claudia Milne. Current affairs, documentaries, travel films, science and educational programmes, drama documentaries.

UBA Ltd (1983), 6 Cambria Street, London SW6 2EE   *tel* 0171-371 0160   *fax* 0171-384 3181. *Contact:* Peter Shaw. Screenplays for cinema and TV of international interest; TV drama and mini series. All material should be submitted through an agent.

Warner Bros. Productions Ltd, 135 Wardour Street, London W1V 4AP   *tel* 0171-437 5600. Screenplays for cinema. Will only consider material submitted through an agent.

Warner Sisters Film & TV Ltd (1984), Canalot Studios, 222 Kensal Road, London W10 5BN   *tel* 0181-960 3550   *fax* 0181-960 3880. Screenplays for cinema and TV; TV programmes. All material should be submitted through an agent.

Michael White Productions Ltd (1963), 48 Dean Street, London W1V 5HL   *tel* 0171-734 7707   *fax* 0171-734 7727. Screenplays for cinema and TV. No unsolicited scripts.

Working Title Films (1984), 76 Oxford Street, London W1N 9FD   *tel* 0171-307 3000   *fax* 0171-307 3001/2/3. *Head of development (films):* Debra Hayward; *TV:* Simon Wright. Screenplays for film and TV – drama and comedy.

World Productions Ltd, 17 Golden Square, London W1R 4BB   *tel* 0171-734 3536   *fax* 0171-734 3585. *Head of development:* Serena Cullen. Screenplays for TV; TV drama series and serials.

Zenith Productions Ltd, 43-45 Dorset Street, London W1H 4AB   *tel* 0171-224 2440   *fax* 0171-224 3194. Screenplays for cinema; TV drama. No unsolicited scripts.

Screenplays for Films

JEAN McCONNELL

Despite the old saying that the plot of the best movie can be written on a postcard, film companies do not actually welcome a plot on a postcard. Nor is it enough simply to send a story in narrative form. You should be prepared to write your idea into a full screenplay. In consequence, it is advisable to check as far as possible in case a company is already working on a similar idea and your efforts are likely to be wasted.

LAYOUT

1. Use A4 size typing paper.
2. It is not necessary to put in elaborate camera directions. A shooting script will be made later. Your job is to write the master scenes, clearly broken down into each incident and location.
3. Your screenplay will tell your story in terms of visual action and dialogue spoken by your characters. If you intend it to be a full-length feature film, running about 1½ hours, your script will be about 100-130 pages long.
4. The general layout of a page of screenplay can be seen from the specimen on page 323. The following points should be noted.
(a) Each scene should be numbered on the left and given a title which indicates whether the scene is an interior or an exterior, where it takes place, and the lighting conditions, i.e. Day or Night. The situation of each scene should be standardised; don't call your 'sitting room' a 'lounge' the next time you come to it, or people will think you mean a different place.
(b) Note that the dialogue is spaced out, with the qualifying directions such as '(frowning)' on a separate line, slightly inset from the dialogue. Double space each speech from the previous one.
(c) Always put the names of the characters in CAPITALS, except when they occur in the actual dialogue. Double space the stage directions from the dialogue, but single space the lines of the stage directions themselves.
(d) Leave at least a 4 cm margin on the left hand and a reasonably wide right-hand margin. It is false economy to cram the page. Type on one side of the sheet only.
(e) If you have to make a correction, cross it out neatly and type the whole section out again. But don't irritate your reader with too many corrections. Better to re-type the page.
(f) Only give the camera directions when you feel it to be essential. For instance, if you want to show something from a particular character's point of view, or if you think you need it to make a point, i.e. 'HARRY approaches the cliff edge and looks down. LONG SHOT – HARRY'S POINT OF VIEW. ALICE fully-clad is walking into the sea. CUT TO: CLOSE UP OF HARRY'S HORRIFIED

FACE.' Note the camera directions are put in capital letters on a separate line, as in the specimen page.

PREPARATION OF MANUSCRIPT

1. Make at least two copies, and never send your very last copy out to anyone. It will invariably be lost.
2. The length of your manuscript will depend on whether you are submitting a feature film, a short film for children, say, or a documentary. But it is better to present a version which is too short rather than too long.
3. Prepare the title page in the same way as for a story or article to an editor, except that it is not necessary to state the number of words.
4. If you give a list of characters, do not suggest the actor or actress you would like to play it. This is a decision to be made elsewhere and relies on many factors about which you cannot know. Don't attach character sketches, as these should appear in the body of the screenplay.
5. Bind your screenplay, giving it a front and back cover, and securing the pages firmly.

SUBMISSION

Attach a stamped, addressed envelope to your manuscript whether sending it through an agent or direct. Remember that if film companies state that they will only consider material sent through an agent, they definitely mean it.

Most companies have Story Departments to which you should address your material. As Story Editors are very busy people, you can make their life easier by complying with the following rules.
1. If you have based your screenplay on someone else's published work you should make the fact clear in a covering letter, stating *(a)* that the material is no longer in copyright, or *(b)* that you yourself own the copyright, or at least an option on it, or *(c)* that you have not obtained the copyright but have reason to believe that there would be no difficulty in doing so.
2. Apart from a note of any relevant credits you may already possess, do not regale the Editor with your personal details, unless they bear a direct relation to the material submitted. For instance, if your story concerns a brain surgeon, then it would be relevant for the Editor to know that you actually are one. Otherwise, trust your work to stand on its own merit.
3. There is no need to mention if your work has been turned down by other companies, however regretfully. The comments of others will not influence a Story Editor one way or the other.
4. Don't pester the company if you don't get a reply, or even an acknowledgement, for some weeks. Most companies will formally acknowledge receipt and then leave you in limbo for at least six weeks. However, after a passage of three months or more, a brief letter asking politely what has happened is in order. A telephone call is unlikely to be helpful. It is possible the company may have liked your work enough to have sent it to America, or to be getting further readers' opinions on it. This all takes time. If they don't like it, you will certainly get it back in due course.
5. Accept that this is really a tough market; for this there are at least three reasons. One, films cost so much to make these days that the decision to go ahead is only taken after a great many important factors have been satisfied and an even greater number of important people are happy about it. Two, the number of films made is small in relation to, say, books published or TV plays produced.

13   (continued)

She moves across the barn to the door, where she turns.

ELIZABETH
I still think the police ought to know.

She goes out. ALAN stands immobile until her
footsteps retreat, and then he sighs with relief.
He darts quickly to the large wine vat, climbs
up and begins heaving at the lid.

CUT TO:

14   EXT. FARMYARD DAY

DONALD intercepts ELIZABETH as she crosses yard.

DONALD
What does he say?

ELIZABETH
Nothing.

DONALD
(frowning)

Right! Now it's my turn.

He starts for the barn. ELIZABETH watches him
anxiously.

CUT TO:

15   INT. BARN DAY

DONALD's shadow falls across the threshold.
He hesitates while his eyes get used to the gloom.

DONALD
Alan?

ALAN lets the lid of the vat fall and jumps down.
He stands quite still as DONALD crosses the barn
and stands staring at him. The two men are silent
a moment.

DONALD
(then, with realisation)
You knew it was there, didn't you?

CLOSE SHOT — DONALD'S POINT OF VIEW
ALAN'S face is haggard.

ALAN
I hoped to God it wouldn't be.
Nobody will ever understand.

Three, writing a screenplay calls for knowledge and appreciation of the technicalities of film-making, as well as the ability to combine dialogue, action and pictures, visualising the story throughout in the language of the cinema.

6. Try to get an agent. A good agent will give you a fair opinion of your work and, if your work is worthwhile, then the agent is the one who will know the particular film company to whom it can be sold.

Literary Agents Specialising in Plays, Films, Television and Radio

Full particulars about these and other agents will be found in the section beginning on page 397. US literary agents are marked with an asterisk.

A & B Personal Management Ltd
*American Play Company Inc.
Artellus Ltd
Yvonne Baker Associates
*Berman, Boals & Flynn, Inc.
Blake Friedman Literary,
  TV & Film Agency Ltd
Rosemary Bromley Literary
  Agency
Peter Bryant (Writers)
Casarotto Ramsay Ltd
Jonathan Clowes
Elspeth Cochrane Agency
Rosica Colin Ltd
Jane Conway-Gordon
Cruickshank Cazenove Ltd
Curtis Brown
*Curtis Brown Ltd
Judy Daish Associates Ltd
Felix De Wolfe
*Ann Elmo Agency
Fact & Fiction Agency Ltd
Film Rights Ltd
*Frieda Fishbein Ltd
Laurence Fitch Ltd
Jill Foster Ltd
*Robert A. Freedman Dramatic
  Agency, Inc.
French's
Vernon Futerman Associates
Jüri Gabriel
Kerry Gardner Management
Eric Glass
*Gregory & Radice Authors' Agents
David Higham Associates Ltd
Valerie Hoskins
ICM Ltd
Michael Imison Playwrights Ltd
International Copyright Bureau Ltd
Harry Joyce Ltd
Juvenilia
*Ben F. Kamsler Ltd
*The Lazear Agency Inc.

Lemon Unna & Durbridge Ltd
*Ellen Levine Literary Agency, Inc.
Barbara Levy Literary Agency
Christopher Little Literary Agent
Andrew Mann Ltd
*The Evan Marshall Agency
Judy Martin
*Elisabeth Marton Agency
Blanche Marvin
MBA Literary Agents
*Scott Meredith Literary Agency
  Inc.
*Helen Merrill Ltd
Richard Milne
*William Morris Agency Inc.
William Morris Agency (UK)
  Ltd
*Fifi Oscard Associates, Inc.
The Peters Fraser & Dunlop
  Group Ltd
*PMA Literary and Film Management,
  Inc.
PVA Management Ltd
Radala & Associates
*Renaissance-Swanson Film Agency, Inc.
Tessa Sayle Agency
*Susan F. Schulman Literary &
  Dramatic Agents Inc.
The Sharland Organisation Ltd
Sheil Land Associates Ltd
Caroline Sheldon Literary Agency
*The Shukat Company Ltd
*Singer Media Corporation
Micheline Steinberg Playwrights' Agent
*Sterling Lord Literistic, Inc.
*Gloria Stern Agency
Jon Thurley
*Austin Wahl Agency, Inc.
*Wallace Literary Agency, Inc.
Warner Chappell Plays Ltd
A.P. Watt Ltd
*Sandra Watt and Associates

Illustration and design

Freelancing for Beginners – an Illustrators' Guide

FIG TAYLOR

WHY FREELANCE?

It is a harsh fact that full-time posts for illustrators are not only highly specialised but sadly very rare. Because the needs of those who commission illustration tend to change on a regular basis, most artists have little choice but to offer their skills to a variety of clients in order to make a living. Thus you will be entering a hugely competitive arena and a professional attitude towards targeting, presenting, promoting and delivering your work will be vital to your success. Equally crucial is a realistic understanding of how the illustration industry works and of your place within the scheme of things. Without adequate research into your chosen field of interest it is all too easy to approach inappropriate clients – a frustrating and disheartening experience for both parties, to say nothing of its being both expensive and time-consuming.

SO WHO COMMISSIONS ILLUSTRATION?

Magazines and newspapers. Whatever your eventual career goals, your first stop, for research, should be your largest local newsagent. Most illustrators receive their first commissions from editorial clients who, whilst offering comparatively modest fees, are actively keen to try out fresh talent. Briefs are by and large fairly loose, though deadlines can be short, particularly in the case of daily and weekly publications. However, fast turnover also ensures a swift appearance in print – proof positive of your professional status to clients in other, more lucrative, spheres. Given then that it is possible to use the editorial field as a springboard, it is essential to appreciate its breadth when seeking to identify your own individual market. Between them, magazines and newspapers accommodate an infinite variety of illustrative styles and techniques. Do not limit your horizons by approaching only the most obvious titles and/or those you would read yourself. Consider also trade and professional journals, free publications and those available on subscription from membership organisations or charities. Remember, the more potential clients you uncover, the brighter your future will be.

Greetings cards. Many decorative, humorous and fine-art biased illustrators are interested in providing designs for greetings cards and giftwrap, where there is a definite market for their skills. As with editorial, fees are unlikely to be high but many small card companies are keen to use new or lesser known artists. You

325

may be expected to produce samples of artwork on a speculative basis prior to receiving a definite commission – therefore it makes sense to target those companies who are likely to be most responsive.

In addition to card shops and the gift departments of larger stores (many of whom employ commissioning buyers for their own ranges), you may find trade fairs such as London's bi-annual Top Drawer and Birmingham's International Spring and Autumn Shows yield the best results for your research. Geared primarily towards buyers, trade fairs offer you the opportunity to check out the forthcoming ranges of numerous card, stationery and giftware manufacturers as well as enabling you to make contacts.

Be warned, however, that most exhibitors will be far too busy selling to go through your work there and then. It is best to make a separate appointment to do this after the fair has ended. For further details, contact Top Drawer organisers, P&O Events Ltd, Earls Court Exhibition Centre, Warwick Road, London SW5 9TA *tel* 0171-370 8185 or Trade Promotion Services Ltd, who organise the International Shows, at Exhibition House, 6 Warren Lane, London SE18 6BW *tel* 0181-855 9201.

Book publishing. With the exception of adult illustrated non-fiction, where the emphasis is on decorative, specialist and technical illustration, the majority of publishers are interested in full-colour figurative work for use on paperback and hardback bookcovers. Strong, realistic work which shows the figure in a narrative context is invaluable to those who commission massmarket fiction, which includes such genres as historical and contemporary romance, thrillers, family sagas, horror, science fiction and fantasy. On the whole publishing deadlines are civilised and massmarket covers well paid. Those whose work is more stylised or experimental would be better advised to approach those smaller imprints and independent publishing houses who deal with more literary, upmarket fiction. Although fees are significantly lower and commissions less frequent, briefs are less restrictive and a wider range of styles can be accommodated.

Children's publishers use a diversity of styles, covering the gamut from baby books, activity and early-learning through to full-colour picture books, older children's novels with black and white spot-illustrations and teenage fiction and non-fiction. Author/illustrators are particularly welcomed by picture book publishers – though, whatever your style, you must be able to draw children well and to sustain a character throughout a narrative.

Design. It is unnecessary for you to have design training in order to approach a design group for illustration work. However, it is advisable that you be in print. Both designers and their clients – who are largely uncreative and will ultimately be footing the bill – will be impressed and reassured by relevant, published work. Although fees are higher than those in editorial and publishing, this third-party involvement generally means a more restrictive brief. Deadlines may vary while styles favoured range from conceptual through to realistic, decorative, humorous and technical.

For research purposes you may find it useful to peruse *Design Week* or the monthly *Creative Review* (both published by Centaur Communications, 49-50 Poland Street, London W1V 4AX *tel* 0171-439 4222), or the monthly *Graphics International* (published by Creative Magazines Ltd, 35 Britannia Row, London N1 8QH *tel* 0171-226 1739). Design groups have different biases and specialities – some, for instance, might concentrate on packaging while others may deal exclusively with corporate and financial literature.

The Creative Handbook (published by the Media Division of Reed Information Services, Windsor Court, East Grinstead House, East Grinstead, West Sussex RH19 1XA *tel* 01342 326 972), available from some reference libraries, carries many listings. Individual contact names are also available at a price from File

FX, who specialise in providing creative suppliers with up-to-date information on commissioning clients in all spheres. Contact them at Unit 14, 83-93 Shepperton Road, London N1 3DF   *tel* 0171-226 6646.

Advertising. As with design, you should ideally be quite well established before seeking commissions in advertising. Fees can be high, deadlines short and clients extremely demanding. Advertising agencies currently use significantly less illustration than clients in other areas and have a tendency to 'play safe' stylistically. What little illustration they do commission might be incorporated into direct mail or press advertising, hoardings or, very occasionally, animated for television – fees will vary depending on whether a campaign is locally or nationally based.

Most agencies employ an art buyer to look at portfolios. A good one will know what each creative team is working on at any given time and may refer you to specific art directors. Agency listings and client details may be found in the BRAD Agencies & Advertisers (published by Emap Media, Emap Business Communications, 33-39 Bowling Green Lane, London EC1R 0DA   *tel* (subscriptions department) 0171-505 8293), and ALF (Account List File, published by DMS Group Limited, Ramillies House, 1-2 Ramillies Street, London W1V 1DF   *tel* 0171-287 0030), available in reference libraries. The Campaign Portfolio (published by Haymarket Business Publications, 174 Hammersmith Road, London W6 7JP   *tel* 0171-413 4306), is a yearly showcase for agencies' work while File FX (see Design section), can supply individual contact names. Magazines such as *Creative Review* and Haymarket's weekly, *Campaign*, also carry agency news.

PORTFOLIO PRESENTATION

Obviously, the more outlets you can find for your talents the better. However, do not be tempted to develop a myriad of styles in an attempt to please every client you see. Firstly it's unlikely that you will and secondly, in the UK market, you'll stand a better chance of being remembered for one strong, consistent style. You'll also get far more commissions that way. Thus, when assembling your professional portfolio, try to exclude samples which are, in your own eyes, weak, irrelevant, uncharacteristic or simply unenjoyable to do – it is worth noting that even published work counts for little if the content is substandard. For maximum impact, aim to focus solely on your strengths. Should you be one of those rare, multi-talented individuals who find it hard to limit themselves stylistically, try splitting conflicting media or subject matter into separate portfolios geared towards different types of clients.

Having no formal illustrative training need not be a handicap providing your portfolio accurately reflects the needs of potential clients. With this is mind, some find it useful to assemble 'mock-ups' using existing magazine layouts. By responding to the copy, working in proportion to original images and replacing them with your own illustrations, both you and the client will be able to see how your work will look in context. Eventually, as you become more established, you'll be able to augment these with published pieces.

Ideally, your folder should be of the zip-up, ringbound variety and never any bigger than A2 as clients usually have very little desk-space. Complexity of style and diversity of subject matter will be key elements in deciding how many pieces to include but all should be neatly, consistently mounted on lightweight paper or card and placed inside protective plastic leaves. Professional photographs of originals are acceptable to clients, as are good quality lasercopies or bubblejet prints. However, tacky, out-of-focus snapshots are not. Avoid also including too many sketchbooks and academic studies – particularly life drawings, which are anathema to clients. It will be taken for granted that you know how to draw from observation.

INTERVIEWS AND BEYOND

Making appointments can be hard work but clients take a dim view of spontaneous visits from passing illustrators. Having identified the most relevant person to see (either from a written source or by asking the company directly), clients are best approached by letter or telephone call. Most magazines and publishing houses are happy to see freelances though portfolio 'drop-offs' are becoming increasingly common within the industry. Some clients will automatically take photostats of your work for their files, however it is always advisable to have some form of self-promotional material to leave behind – a full-colour A6 postcard, for instance, would be ideal for this purpose. In the case of larger companies, it is also worth asking your contact if others might be interested in your work. Word-of-mouth has a distinct advantage over cold-calling.

Cleanliness, punctuality and enthusiasm are more important to clients than the kind of clothes you wear – as is a professional attitude towards taking and fulfilling a brief. A thorough understanding of what a job entails is paramount from the outset. You will need to know all your client's requirements regarding roughs; format, size and flexibility of artwork; preferred medium and whether the image is to be executed in colour or black and white. You will also need to know when the deadline is. Never, under any circumstances, agree to undertake a commission unless you are certain you can deliver on time and always work within your limitations. Talent is nothing without reliability.

BE ORGANISED!

Once your career is off the ground it is imperative to keep organised records of all your commissions. Contracts can be verbal as well as written though details – financial and otherwise – should always be confirmed in writing and duplicated for your files. Likewise, file away corresponding client faxes, letters and order-forms. *Survive – the Illustrators Guide to a Professional Career* and *Rights – the Illustrators Guide to Professional Practice*, published by the Association of Illustrators, offer artists a wealth of practical, legal and ethical information. Subjects covered include contracts, licences, royalties, copyright and ownership of artwork. Contact them at 1st Floor, 32-38 Saffron Hill, London EC1N 8FH or telephone 0171-831 7377 for details.

MONEY

Try not to undertake a commission before agreeing on a fee, although this may not always prove practicable in the case of rush-jobs. Most publishing and editorial fees are fixed and, unfortunately, there are no hard and fast rules for negotiation where design and advertising are concerned. As a pointer, however, take into consideration the type of client involved and the distribution of the final printed product – obviously a national 48 sheet poster advertising a well-known supermarket chain is likely to pay better than a local press advertisement for a poodle parlour! Some illustrators find it helpful to work out a daily rate incorporating various overheads such as rent, heating, materials, travel and telephone charges – while others prefer to negotiate on a flat fee basis. Some clients will actually tell you if they've a specific figure in mind, though you may have to put them on the spot. Certainly, as you become more established, you'll be able to use comparable jobs as benchmarks when negotiating a fee.

Basic book-keeping – making a simple, legible record of all your financial transactions, both incoming and outgoing – will be vital to your sanity once the taxman starts to loom. It will also make your accountant's job easier, thereby saving you money. If your annual turnover is less than £15,000, it is unnecessary to provide the Inland Revenue with detailed accounts of your earnings. Information regarding your turnover, allowable expenses and net profit may simply be entered on your tax return. Although an accountant is not integral to this process, many find it advantageous to employ one. The tax system is complicated and dealing with the Inland Revenue can be stressful, intimidating and time-consuming – not least since the introduction of changes regarding 'self-assessment', which will apply from the 1996-1997 tax year onwards (see page 567). Accountants offer invaluable advice on tax allowances, National Insurance and tax assessments as well as dealing expertly with the Revenue on your behalf – thereby enabling you to attend to the business of illustrating.

Art Agents and Commercial Art Studios

In their own interests, artists are advised to make preliminary enquiries before submitting work, and to ascertain terms of work. Commission varies but averages 25-30 per cent. **The Association of Illustrators** (full details on page 613) provides a valuable service for illustrators, agents and clients.

*Member of The Society of Artists Agents

A.L.I. Press Agency Ltd, Boulevard Anspach 111-115, B9–1000 Brussels, Belgium *tel* 012 512 73 94 *fax* 012 512 013 30. *Director:* G. Lans. Cartoons, comics, strips, puzzles, entertainment features, illustrations for covers. All feature material for newspapers and magazines. Large choice of picture stories for children and adults. Market for transparencies: paintings, portraits, nudes, landscapes, handicrafts. Interest in video productions.

Allied Artists Ltd, 31 Harcourt Street, London W1H 1DT *tel* 0171-724 8809 *fax* 0171-262 8526. *Director:* Gary Mills. Represent over 40 artists specialising in highly finished realistic figure illustration for magazines, books, video, plates, prints and advertising. Also offers extensive library of second rights illustrations for syndication.

Arena (1970), 144 Royal College Street, London NW1 0TA *tel* 0171-267 9661 *fax* 0171-284 0486. *Contacts:* Tamlyn Hennessey, Valerie Paine, Alison Eldred and Charlotte Phillips. Representing 45 artists working mostly for book covers, children's books and design groups. *Average commission:* 30%.

Art Solutions (1992), 4 Granville Road, Sevenoaks, Kent TN13 1ER *tel/fax* (01732) 458917. *Directors:* Michael Wells (managing), Anne Buky (sales). Unusually varied and versatile artwork suitable for reproduction on greetings cards, giftwrap, stationery, ceramics and gifts of all kinds; children's and adult's publishing. *Commission:* 30%.

Aspect Art (1994), Courtyard Unit E5, The Old Imperial Laundry, 71-73 Warriner Gardens, London SW11 4XW *tel/fax* 0171-720 5439. *Partners:* Lady Vanessa Brown and M.T.G. O'Donovan. Architectural art in any medium to sell, commission or exhibit; also publish original prints. *Commission:* 30%.

Associated Freelance Artists Ltd, 124 Elm Park Mansions, Park Walk, Chelsea, London SW10 0AR *tel* 0171-352 6890 *fax* 0171-352 8125. *Directors:* Eva

Morris, Doug FitzMaurice. Freelance illustrators mainly in children's and educational fields; and lots of greetings cards.

Bardon Art, S.L. (1957), Gran Via de los Corts Catalanes 806, Barcelona E-08013, Spain *tel* (3) 245 56 84 *fax* (3) 246 30 19. *Directors:* Jordi Macabich, Barry Coker, Mercè Biadiu, Montserrat Serra. Picture strips for newspapers and comic magazines, cartoons, illustrations for juvenile books.

Sarah Brown Agency (1977), 10 The Avenue, Ealing, London W13 8PH *tel* 0181-998 0390 *fax* 0181-843 1175. *Contact:* Brian Fennelly. Illustrations for publishing and advertising. Sae essential for unsolicited material. *Commission:* 25% UK, 33⅓% USA.

*****Beint & Beint** (1976), 3 Richborne Terrace, London SW8 1AR *tel* 0171-793 7000 *fax* 0171-735 2565. Illustrations in a variety of styles for advertising, design groups and publishing.

Central Illustration Agency (1983), 36 Wellington Street, London WC2E 7BD *tel* 0171-240 8925/836 1106 *fax* 0171-836 1177. *Director:* Brian Grimwood. Illustrations for design, publishing and advertising. *Commission:* 30%.

Barry Everitt Associates, 23 Mill Road, Stock, Essex CM4 9LJ *tel* (01277) 840639 *fax* (01277) 841223. *Director:* Barry M. Everitt. UK/international representation for artists, illustrators and designers seeking high quality markets for their work. Greetings cards, fine art prints, calendars, collectors' ceramics, giftware, books, etc. Sae required for return of work. *Commission:* negotiable.

Jacqui Figgis (1995), The Glasshouse, 11 Lettice Street, London SW6 4EH *tel* 0171-610 9933 *fax* 0171-610 9944. *Director:* Jacqui Figgis. Illustrations for advertising, design, publishing and editorial. *Commission:* 30%.

*****Folio Illustrators' & Designers' Agents** (1976), 10 Gate Street, Lincoln's Inn Fields, London WC2A 3HP *tel* 0171-242 9562 *fax* 0171-242 1816. All areas of illustration.

*****Garden Studio** (1929), 23 Ganton Street, Soho, London W1V 1LA *tel* 0171-287 9191 *fax* 0171-287 9131 *e-mail* 100763.21@compuserve.com *WWW* http://www.elfande.co.uk/gardenstudio.html *Agents:* John Havergal, Harry Lyon-Smith. Worldwide all-round coverage. *Commission:* 33⅓% (publishing 25%).

Simon Girling & Associates (1985), 61B High Street, Hadleigh, Suffolk IP7 5DY *tel* (01473) 824083 *fax* (01473) 827846. Representing over 50 illustrators, accepting commissions for book publishing (children's and adult), encyclopaedias, magazines, dust jackets, as well as a portfolio of licensed characters. *Commission:* 30%.

Graham-Cameron Illustration (1988), The Studio, 23 Holt Road, Sheringham, Norfolk NR26 8NB *tel* (01263) 821333 *fax* (01263) 821334. *Partners:* Mike Graham-Cameron, Helen Graham-Cameron. All forms of illustration for publishing, communications and advertising. Specialises in children's books and educational materials.

The Guild of Aviation Artists (1971), Bondway Business Centre, 71 Bondway, London SW8 1SQ *tel/fax* 0171-735 0634. *President:* Michael Turner PGAvA; *secretary:* Hugo Trotter DFC. Professional body of 350 artists specialising in aviation art in all mediums. The Guild sells, commissions and exhibits members' work. *Commission:* 25%.

Hambleside Ltd (1990), Winton Road, Petersfield, Hants GU32 3HA *tel* (01730) 231010 *fax* (01730) 231117. *Directors:* D.R. Yellop, R.A. Jeffery,

M.G.W. Goodman, W.J.Cumper, R.B. Gamble (USA). Design studio specialising in all forms of promotional graphics, advertising and marketing. Enquiries from technical illustrators and special effect photographers welcome.

*John Hodgson Agency (1965), 38 Westminster Palace Gardens, Artillery Row, London SW1P 1RR *tel* 0171-580 3773 *fax* 0171-222 4468. Illustrations for publishing, advertising, design. Sae with samples please. *Commission:* 25%.

Image by Design (1987), Lydford Farm, Highbury Street, Coleford, Bath BA3 5NS *tel/fax* (01373) 812393. *Partners:* John R. Brown, Burniece M. Brown. Artwork for prints, greetings cards, calendars, posters, stationery, book publishing, jigsaw puzzles, tableware, ceramics. *Commission:* negotiable.

*Kathy Jakeman Illustration, 20 Trefoil Road, Wandsworth, London SW18 2EQ *tel* 0181-875 9525 *fax* 0181-874 4874. Illustration for publishing – especially children's; also design, editorial and advertising. Please send sae with samples. *Commission:* 25%.

David Lewis Illustration Agency (1974), Worlds End Studios, 134 Lots Road, Chelsea, London SW10 0RJ *tel* 0171-351 3401 *fax* 0171-351 5044. *Contacts:* David Lewis, Andrew Newcombe. All types of illustration for a variety of applications but mostly suitable for book publishing purposes. Samples or letters sent without return postage will not be acknowledged/returned. *Average commission:* 30%.

Libba Jones Associates (1983), Hopton Manor, Hopton, Nr Wirksworth, Derbyshire DE4 4DF *tel* (01629) 540353 *fax* (01629) 540577. *Contacts:* Libba Jones, Ieuan Jones. High quality artwork and design for china, greetings cards and giftwrap, jigsaw puzzles, calendars, prints, posters, stationery, book illustration, fabric design. Submission of samples required for consideration.

*John Martin & Artists Ltd, 26 Danbury Street, Islington, London N1 8JU *tel* 0171-734 9000 *fax* 0171-226 6069. *Directors:* W. Bowen-Davies, C.M. Bowen-Davies, B.L. Bowen-Davies. Illustrations for children (educational and fictional), dust jackets, paperbacks, magazines, encyclopedias, advertising. Return postage for any artwork sent please.

Meiklejohn Illustration (1971), 28 Shelton Street, Covent Garden, London WC2H 9HP *tel* 0171-240 2077 *fax* 0171-836 0199. *Contacts:* Chris Meiklejohn, Paul Meiklejohn, Malcolm Sanders. All types of illustration.

N.E. Middleton, 20 Trefoil Road, Wandsworth, London SW18 2EQ *tel* 0181-875 9525 *fax* 0181-874 4874. Designs for greetings cards, stationery, prints, calendars and china. Sae with samples, please.

*Maggie Mundy Illustrators' Agency, Britannia House, 1-11 Glenthorne Road, London W6 0LF *tel* 0181-741 5862 *fax* 0181-748 5532. Represents 25 artists in varying styles of illustration for children's books.

*The Organisation (1986), The Basement, 69 Caledonian Road, London N1 9BT *tel* 0171-833 8268 *fax* 0171-833 8269. *Partners:* Jane Buxton and Lorraine Owen. All aspects of illustration from advertising campaigns, book covers, print, packaging, editorial work through to working directly with clients both in the UK and abroad. *Commission:* 30%.

Oxford Illustrators Ltd (1968), Aristotle Lane, Oxford OX2 6TR *tel* (01865) 512331 *fax* (01865) 512408 *e-mail* oxford_illust@compuserve.com Studio of 25 full-time illustrators working for publishers, business and industry. All types of artwork including science, technical, airbrush, graphic, medical, biological, botanical, natural history, figure, cartoon, maps, diagrams, and charts. Artwork supplied as PMT, bromide, film or on 3½in Mac or PC disk, Syquest or optical, with both b&w and colour proofs. *Not* an agency.

***Pennant Illustration** (1992), Yukon Court, 6 Yukon Road, London SW12 9PU   *tel* 0181-673 8008   *fax* 0181-673 4227. *Director:* Matthew Doyle. Illustrations for publishing, design and advertising. Samples *must* be accompanied by an sae. *Commission:* 25%.

Linda Rogers Associates (1975), PO Box 330, 1 Bloomsbury House, 9 Guilford Street, London WC1N 1PX   *tel* 0171-242 01975   *fax* 0171-405 0876. *Partners:* Linda Rogers, Peter Sims. Represent a group of artists and designers covering all fields of illustration, but specialising in educational and general children's books and magazines. Replies only with sae.

Specs Art, 93 London Road, Cheltenham, Glos. GL52 6HL   *tel* (01242) 515951   *fax* (01242) 518862. *Partners:* Roland Berry and Stephanie Prosser. High quality illustration work for advertisers, publishers and all other forms of visual communication.

Summer Lane Pictures Ltd (1993), Lower Tower Street, Birmingham B19 3NE   *tel* 0121-359 6269   *fax* 0121-333 5366. *Managing director:* Malcolm McGivan. Design-led licensing agency offering a wide variety of images, linking artists and illustrators with manufacturers in the gift and publishing industries; in-house reproduction facilities available. Sae with samples essential.

Temple Rogers Artists' Agency, 120 Crofton Road, Orpington, Kent BR6 8HZ   *tel* (01689) 826249   *fax* (01689) 896312. *Contact:* Patrick Kelleher. Illustrations for children's educational books, picture strips and magazine illustrations. *Commission:* by arrangement.

2D Illustration Agency (1986), 114 Ladbroke Grove, London W10 5NE   *tel* 0171-727 5243/8685   *fax* 0171-727 9680. *Proprietors:* Brian Whitehead, Mair Ellis. Stylised, contemporary illustrations for advertising, design and publishing, Europe-wide. Sae with samples please. *Commission:* 30% UK, 35% overseas.

Vicki Thomas Associates (1985), 19 Hickman Close, Fulmer Road, London E16 3TA   *tel* 0171-511 5767   *fax* 0171-473 5177. *Consultant:* Vicki Thomas. Considers the work of illustrators and designers working in greetings and gift industries, and promotes such work to gift, toy, publishing and related industries. Written application and b&w photocopies required. *Commission:* from 30%.

Wildlife Art Agency (1992), Studio 16 Muspole Workshops, 25-27 Muspole Street, Norwich, Norfolk NR3 1DJ   *tel* (01603) 617868   *fax* (01603) 219017. *Contact:* Sarah Whittley. Illustrations of all things natural, including gardening and food. Clients range from children's/adults' books, greetings cards, design and advertising agencies. Sae must be included with work submitted for consideration. *Commission:* 30%.

Michael Woodward Licensing (1980), Parlington Hall, Aberford, West Yorkshire LS25 3EG   *tel* (0113) 281 3913   *fax* (0113) 281 3911. *Proprietor:* Michael R. Woodward. International art agency with subsidiary offices overseas. Specialists in greetings cards, stationery, posters, prints, calendars and gift products. Character merchandising division. Freelance artists please send samples with sae. *Terms:* on application.

Markets for Drawings, Designs and Verses for Greetings Cards and Social Stationery

In their own interest, artists are advised to write giving details of the work which they have to offer, and asking for requirements before submitting the work.

*Member of the Greeting Card Association

*Abacus Cards Ltd (1991), Gazeley Road, Kentford, Newmarket, Suffolk CB8 7QB *tel* (01638) 552399 *fax* (01638) 552103. *Partners:* Jeff Fothergill and Brian Carey; *art director:* Bev Demant. Quality greetings cards and giftwrap. Most subjects considered; submit artwork or transparencies. Will consider copy/ideas/jokes for humour cards.

*The Andrew Brownsword Collection (1975), Kelston Park, Kelston, Bath BA1 9AE. *Sales director:* John Curtis. Contemporary and traditional imagery for greetings cards, giftwrap and social stationery. Submit transparencies of original artwork, or original artwork. Will consider verses.

*The Bucentaur Gallery Ltd (1977), Eastway, Fulwood, Preston PR2 9WS *tel* (01772) 662800 *fax* (01772) 662909. *Contact:* Head of Design. Fine art, traditional greetings cards: florals, animals, wildlife, cottages, etc., plus traditional Christmas subjects. All submissions to be accompanied by an sae; original artwork, or minimum 5 × 4 in transparencies, photographs or laser copies of originals. No verses please.

*Card Connection Ltd (1992), Park House, South Street, Farnham, Surrey GU9 7QQ *tel* (01252) 733177 *fax* (01252) 735644. *Managing director:* Simon Hulme; *product manager:* Gabriella Baldwin-Purry. Cute, humour, traditional, floral, contemporary, sport. Submit artwork, or 5 × 4 in transparencies of originals. No verses.

*Carlton Cards Ltd, Mill Street East, Dewsbury, West Yorkshire WF12 9AW *tel* (01924) 465200. *Marketing director:* Keith Auty. All types of artwork, any size; submit as colour roughs, colour copies or transparencies. *Creative director for alternative ranges:* Ged Backland (especially interested in humorous artwork and ideas).

C.C.A. Stationery Ltd, Eastway, Fulwood, Preston PR2 9WS *tel* (01772) 662800. Publishers of personalised wedding stationery and Christmas cards. Pleased to consider original artwork, preferably of relevant subject matter; Christmas verses considered.

The Classic Card Company Ltd—Classic/Valentines, James Street West, Bath BA1 2BS *tel* (01225) 444228 *fax* (01225) 444214. Greetings cards for all occasions; giftwrap, artwork in colour; sentimental and humorous editorial verses considered.

*Gallery Five Ltd (1960), 121 King Street, London W6 9JG *tel* 0181-741 8394 *fax* 0181-741 4444. *Contact:* D.J. Walser (art director). Send samples which give an idea of style; or phone for an appointment on the day (i.e. no forward appointments). No verses.

*Gibson Greetings International Ltd (1991), Gibson House, Hortonwood 30, Telford, Shropshire TF1 4ET *tel* (01952) 608333 *fax* (01952) 608363. *Product director:* Jan Duncan. Everyday, wedding and all seasonal illustrations:

cute, humorous, juvenile age, traditional landscapes and subjects; giftwrap and calendars. Greeting card traditional and humorous verse.

*Giesen & Wolff (UK) Ltd (1908), Kaygee House, Rothersthorpe Crescent, Northampton NN4 9JD *tel* (01604) 709499 *fax* (01604) 709399. *Contact:* Studio Manager. Illustrations: cute characters, wedding, sympathy, juvenile age subjects, traditional landscapes, humour – anything suitable for everyday and all seasonal occasions. Will consider verses.

The Gift Business (1986), Lower Tower Street, Birmingham B19 3NE *tel* 0121-359 7088 *fax* 0121-333 5366. *Managing director:* Trevor Jones; *sales and marketing director:* Sue Hammond. Commercial decorative art with broad appeal – especially classic and contemporary floral imagery, William Morris designs, fine art – for greetings cards and gift stationery.

Graphic Humour (1984), 4 Britannia Centre, Point Pleasant, Wallsend, Tyne and Wear NE28 6HQ *tel* 0191-295 4200 *fax* 0191-295 3916. Risqué and everyday artwork ideas for greetings cards; short, humorous copy. Also unusual and Victorian photos/illustrations for use as humorous greetings cards.

*Greetings Cards By Noel Tatt Ltd (1954/1988), Appledown House, Barton Business Park, Appledown Way, New Dover Road, Canterbury, Kent CT1 3AA *tel* (01227) 455540 *fax* (01227) 458976. *Directors:* Noel Tatt, Vencke Tatt, Jarle Tatt, Diane Tatt, Richard Parsons. Greetings cards and giftwrap.

*Hallmark Cards Ltd, Hallmark House, Station Road, Henley-on-Thames, Oxon RG9 1LQ *tel* (01491) 578383 *fax* (01491) 578817. *Chairman and chief executive:* A. Brownsword; *managing director UK:* Trish Davis; *product director:* B. Arganbright. Humorous editorial ideas considered, including short jokes and punchlines. Submit all ideas to the Editorial Department. *No* traditional verse.

Hambledon Studios Ltd, Hambledon House, Marlborough Road, Accrington, Lancs. BB5 6BX *tel* (01254) 872255/872266 *fax* (01254) 872079. *Art managers:* D. Jaundrell, J. Ashton, D. Fuller, N. Harrison, K. Ellis; *creative director:* M. Smith. Designs suitable for reproduction as greetings cards. *Brands:* Arnold Barton, Donny Mac, Reflections, New Image.

*Hammond Gower Publications (1985), 14 Tideway Yard, Mortlake High Street, London SW14 8SN *tel* 0181-878 5210 *fax* 0181-876 1487. *Directors:* Nicci Hammond, Mike Gower, Alan Daly. Greetings cards and giftwrap: children's, contemporary, occasions, blank cards. All types of artwork considered: paintings, silk, line drawing, embroidery, etc.

Hanson White (1958), 9th Floor, Wettern House, 56 Dingwall Road, Croydon, Surrey CR0 0XH *tel* 0181-680 1885 *fax* 0181-760 0093. *Product development manager:* Sarah Garratt. Artwork for greetings cards, giftwrap and related stationery items: cute, humorous, contemporary, fine art. Humorous copy lines, including rude jokes, poems and punchlines; occasionally accept non-humorous verses.

*Images & Editions (1984), Bourne Road, Essendine, Nr Stamford, Lincs. PE9 4UW *tel* (01780) 57118 *fax* (01780) 54629. *Directors:* Lesley Forrow, Maurice Miller. Greetings card artwork: cute, floral, animals.

Jodds (1988), PO Box 353, Kidlington, Oxon OX5 2UU *tel* (01865) 331437 *fax* (01865) 331007. *Partners:* M. Payne and J.S. Payne. Bright contemporary art style greetings cards which include humour; must give out a warm feel. Submit colour photocopies with sae. No verses.

*Jooles Ltd (1988), Unit 5, St Margaret's Business Centre, Drummond Place, Moor Mead Road, Twickenham, Middlesex TW1 1JN *tel* 0181-744 1333 *fax*

0181-891 4295. *Contact:* Maggie Waller, Art Co-ordinator. Write with sae for submission of artwork. Artwork for greetings cards: humorous, traditional, cute.

Thomas Leach Ltd, 54 Ock Street, Abingdon, Oxon OX14 5DE *tel* (01235) 520444 *fax* (01235) 554270. *Contact:* David Leach. Line drawings of religious subjects suitable for reproduction as Christmas or Easter cards.

Leeds Postcards (1979), PO Box 84, Leeds LS1 1HU *tel* (0113) 246 8649 *fax* (0113) 243 6730. Workers co-operative. Publishers and producers of campaign postcards (and greetings cards) for left wing political campaigns, the women's movement, environmental and campaigns for international justice. Joint publishers of Women Artists Cards. No verses.

*Henry Ling & Son (London) Ltd, Chiddingstone Causeway, Nr Tonbridge, Kent TN11 8JP *tel* (01892) 870333 *fax* (01892) 870466. *Contact:* Product manager – greetings cards. Artwork for greetings cards; no verses.

M.G. Management (1995), 22 Maze Street, Darcy Lever, Bolton, Lancs. BL3 1SB *tel* (01204) 384768. *Partners:* Marcia J. Galley and Andrew J. Galley. Consultant for writers of verse; cute, inspirational, seasonal, occasions; prose and punchlines. Also consultant for artists/photographers to complement same areas both in UK and overseas. All samples must bear name and address.

Medici Society Ltd, 34-42 Pentonville Road, London N1 9HG *tel* 0171-837 7099 *fax* 0171-837 9152. Requirements: full colour paintings suitable for reproduction as greetings cards. Preliminary letter with brief details of work requested; mark for the attention of The Art Department.

*The Paper House Group plc, Shepherd Road, Gloucester, Glos. GL2 6EL *tel* (01452) 423451 *fax* (01452) 410312. *Product director:* Neil Holliday. Publishers of greetings cards, humorous and fine art. *Brands:* Elgin Court, Parnassus Gallery, Aries Design and The Humour Factory. Submit original artwork, or transparencies or photographs of originals.

*Paperlink Ltd (1986), 346-348 Kennington Road, London SE11 4LD *tel* 0171-582 8244 *fax* 0171-587 5212. *Directors:* Louise Tighe, Jo Townsend, Tim Porte, Tim Purcell. Publishers of ranges of humorous and contemporary art greetings cards, giftwrap, calendars, notelets, mugs, T-shirts, prints. Produce products under licence for charities.

Pomegranate Europe Ltd (1993), Fullbridge House, Fullbridge, Maldon, Essex CM9 4LE *tel* (01621) 851646 *fax* (01621) 852426. *Sales director:* Dave Harris. Contemporary art for cards, calendars and gift stationery. Will consider original artwork or transparencies of originals.

*Nigel Quiney Publications Ltd, Cloudesley House, Shire Hill, Saffron Walden, Essex CB11 3FB *tel* (01799) 520200 *fax* (01799) 520100. *Director:* Stewart F.E. Stott. Everyday and seasonal greetings cards (sizes: 7×5, 9×6 and 12×9 in) and giftwrap. Submit original artwork or 5×4 in transparencies of originals.

*Rainbow Cards Ltd (1977), Albrighton Business Park, Newport Road, Albrighton, Wolverhampton, West Midlands WV7 3ET *tel* (01902) 374347. *Directors:* M. Whitehouse, R. Fellows, J. Whitehouse, I. Mackintosh. Artwork for greetings cards. No verses.

*The Really Good Card Company Ltd (1987), Unit 1, 26 Grove Street, Summertown, Oxford OX2 7JT *tel* (01865) 512315 *fax* (01865) 510256. *Director:* David Hicks. Do not send original artwork; send photocopies or snapshots with sae. No verses.

Felix Rosenstiel's Widow & Son Ltd, Fine Art Publishers, 33-35 Markham Street, London SW3 3NR *tel* 0171-352 3551. Invite offers of original oil paintings and strong watercolours of a professional standard for reproduction as picture prints for the picture framing trade. Any type of subject considered.

*****Royle Publications Ltd,** Royle House, Wenlock Road, London N1 7ST *tel* 0171-253 7654. *Creative director:* Richard D'Arcy. Greetings cards, calendars, fine art reproductions and social stationery.

*****Scandecor Ltd** (1967), 3 The Ermine Centre, Hurricane Close, Huntingdon, Cambs. PE18 6XX *tel* (01480) 456395 *fax* (01480) 456269. *Director:* G. Huldtgren. Drawings all sizes.

*****Second Nature Ltd** (1981), 10 Malton Road, London W10 5UP *tel* 0181-960 0212 *fax* 0181-960 8700. *Marketing/publishing director:* Rod Schragger. Contemporary artwork for greetings cards; jokes for humorous range; short modern sentiment.

W.N. Sharpe Ltd—now **The Classic Card Company Ltd.**

Solomon & Whitehead Ltd, Lynn Lane, Shenstone, Staffs. WS14 0DX *tel* (01543) 480696 *fax* (01543) 481619. Fine art prints and limited editions, framed and unframed.

Noel Tatt Ltd (1954), Coombe House, Coombe Valley Road, Dover, Kent CT17 0EU *tel* (01304) 211644 *fax* (01304) 240470. *Directors:* Noel Tatt, Vencke Tatt, Derek Bates, Anthony Sharpe, Paul Tatt, Robert Dixon. Greetings cards, prints, postcards.

United Greeting Card Co. (UK) Ltd (1969), River Park, Billet Lane, Berkhamsted, Herts. HP4 1EL *tel* (01442) 871381. *Directors:* R.H. Seddon, M. Howard. Ideas and artwork for humorous, cute and general greetings cards.

Valentines—see **The Classic Card Company Ltd.**

*****Waverley 1770 Ltd** (1770), Godalming Business Centre, Woolsack Way, Godalming, Surrey GU7 1XW *tel* (01483) 426277 *fax* (01483) 426947. *Publishing director:* Rosemary French; *design manager:* Hayley Bebb. Gift stationery (calendars, notecards, giftwrap). Colour illustrations; cute/traditional/floral. Submit original artwork or 5 × 4 in transparencies; all enquiries to Hayley Bebb. No verses.

Webb Ivory (Burton) Ltd, Queen Street, Burton-on-Trent, Staffs. DE14 3LP *tel* (01283) 566311. High quality Christmas cards and paper products.

See also **Newspapers and magazines, Book publishers** and **Book packagers**; and **Literary agents** (particularly for children's books).

It is recommended that artists read the article on copyright in the **Copyright and libel** section; the **Publishing practice** section for information about formal agreements.

A Serious Look at Marketing Cartoons

JOHN BYRNE

Although in the business of being funny, cartoonists can be quite a morose bunch, bemoaning the passing of the original *Punch* and complaining that the market for general cartoons is growing smaller. Yet many of the most lucrative merchandising properties in recent years, from *Garfield* to *Judge Dredd*, started life as cartoons. Freelance cartooning has its share of ups and downs, but there are still many opportunities for comic artists and for illustrators and writers, too. Many cartoonists are certainly accomplished artists, but today funny ideas and sharp captions are just as important as the visuals. Writers with comic flair may consider collaborating with an artist or even trying their own simple drawings.

RESEARCH AND PRESENTATION

See page 339 for UK newspapers and magazines which currently take cartoons.

Study the publication you are planning to submit to. What cartoon subjects feature most frequently, especially for joke or 'gag' cartoons (see Markets): Married couples? Children? Animals? Are all the cartoons domestic or office based, or is there a mixture? Are the characters drawn in semi-realistic or more distorted styles? Are the jokes mainly in the captions or is the humour visual?

Be aware of changing fashions in humour. Thanks to Gary Larson's *The Far Side* the pun, formerly derided as a low form of wit, is currently very much in vogue. Consider technical details: Are the cartoons colour or black and white? What shape are they? It is pointless sending portrait-shaped cartoons to publications that only use landscape ones.

While most magazines still typeset cartoon captions, some now accept handdrawn captions or balloons. Avoid spelling mistakes for which cartoonists are notorious and which often result in rejection of otherwise saleable drawings. This can also happen if a clever cartoon becomes illegible when reduced to printed size. Editors often squeeze cartoons into very small spaces – be sure your drawings are simple and bold enough to survive reduction.

See also copyright (page 540) and libel (page 559).

SUBMISSION

A preliminary letter saves wasted effort and can yield useful information. Busy editors find unsolicited phone calls very unamusing – but one call you will need to make is to check exactly *who* to address your letter to: full-time cartoon editors are rare and the person who chooses cartoons can be anyone from the art director to the person in charge of the puzzle page. Sending a number of cartoons together increases the chance of at least one being accepted, but quality is better than quantity. A few good jokes will get a better response when the editor doesn't have to extract them from a mountain of 'fillers'.

Rejections. While current fashions in cartoons encompass a wide range of styles, both visual and in terms of being funny, humour is still very subjective. Rejections are a fact of life for even the most successful cartoonists, but one editor's rejected cartoon may be snapped up by another publication.

One way to lessen the sting is to have several submissions on the go at once. A strong pre-paid envelope will ensure that work comes back in one piece, ready for its next expedition. (Put your name and address on the back of each cartoon in case it gets detached from the main bundle.) If you are sending lots of cartoons back and forth to different publications it is wise to create a filing system. Otherwise you'll inevitably receive the dreaded response 'You've sent this one before . . . and it wasn't funny the first time'.

MARKETS

General gag cartoons. The demise of *The Cartoonist*, *Squib* and other brave attempts to launch cartoon magazines in the wake of *Punch* may suggest that the traditional gag cartoon is an endangered species. However, magazines like *Private Eye* and *The Spectator* still publish joke or gag cartoons alongside more topical items and new cartoon magazines continue to appear. At the time of writing even *Punch* is being resurrected.

Topical cartoons. Topical cartoons are a good market for the quick-witted artist. Remember that the cartoon must still be topical *on the day it is published*. This is (relatively) easy if the cartoon is for a newspaper coming out the next day, but a topical cartoon can become very outdated in the time it takes a weekly or fortnightly magazine to publish. Faxing roughs to the editor can save time. If accepted, you may need to produce finished artwork to very tight deadlines.

Do try to get your cartoons back after publication – people featured in topical cartoons sometimes ask to buy the original artwork.

Specialist and trade publications. This is an under-exploited market for cartoonists who are able to tailor jokes to particular subjects – but remember you are dealing with an expert audience. A stereotypical cartoon chef may suffice for general cartoons, but you'd better get the terminology and different uniforms right for *Bakery World* or *Catering*.

Try creating your own markets. Think about jobs you've had, past or present, or your particular sports, hobbies and interests. No matter how obscure, there may be a related publication just waiting to be brightened up by your combination of cartoon skills and specialist knowledge.

Strip cartoons, regular features and syndication. For regular comic strips or cartoon features, editors need to see that you can produce not only funny material but that you can maintain a consistent output. Submit a good supply of roughs along with examples of finished cartoons to show that you can sustain the idea. The same applies when approaching a syndicate with your strip and feature ideas (see page 141 for names and addresses of syndicates). Cartoons may be in syndication for a long time, and in different countries, so very topical humour and local references are best avoided. If cartoons are syndicated in other languages humour based on verbal puns may not translate very well.

Other. The lists of greetings cards publishers (page 333) and merchandising agents (page 433) should suggest other markets for cartoons, and cartoons are often used to illustrate books for both adults and children (see page 148 for list of UK publishers). Some of the art agents listed on page 329 represent cartoonists.

ORGANISATIONS

For specialist advice, and to meet other members of what can be a solitary profession, try The Cartoonists' Guild and The Cartoonists' Club of Great Britain (both at Strawberry Vale, Twickenham TW1 4SE) or the Comics Creators Guild (171 Oldfield Grove, Surrey Quays, London SE16 2NE).

The life of a full-time funny person can be precarious, but properly researching and tailoring work to specific markets and adopting an organised approach to submissions should greatly reduce your rejection collection.

FURTHER READING

Byrne, John, *Learn to Draw Cartoons*, HarperCollins, 1995.
Hall, Robin, *The Cartoonist's Workbook*, A. & C. Black, 1995.
Hewson, Bill and Thompson, Ross, *How to Draw and Sell Cartoons*, North Light, 1985.
Whitaker, Steve, *The Encyclopaedia of Cartooning Techniques*, Headline, 1994.

Classified Index of UK Markets for Cartoons in Newspapers and Magazines

Listed below are newspapers and magazines which take cartoons – either occasionally, or on a regular basis. Approach *in writing* in first instance (see listing starting on page 5 for addresses) to ascertain the editor's requirements.

Newspapers and Colour Supplements

Aberdeen Evening Express
Birmingham Evening Mail
Daily Mail
Daily Mirror
Daily Sport
The Echo
The European
Evening Echo
Evening Gazette (Teesside)
Glasgow Evening Times
Grimsby Evening Telegraph
The Guardian Weekend
Hartlepool Mail
The Herald

The Independent Magazine
The Independent on Sunday
The Journal
Lancashire Evening Post
Liverpool Echo
Mail on Sunday
The News, Portsmouth
Nottingham Evening Post
The Scotsman
South Wales Echo
The Star
The Sun
Sunday Mail

Sunday Mercury
The Sunday Sun
The Sunday Times
Telegraph Magazine
The Times
The Weekly Journal
The Weekly News
Western Daily Press
The Western Mail
Yorkshire Evening Post
Yorkshire Evening Press
Yorkshire Post
Young Telegraph

Consumer and Special Interest Magazines

Aeroplane Monthly
Air International
Amateur Photographer
The Aquarist and Pondkeeper
Athletics Weekly
The Author
Back Street Heroes
Bad Attitude
Baptist Times
BBC Vegetarian GoodFood
Bella
Best
Big!
Bike
Bird Watching
Boards
Bowls International

British Chess Magazine
Bunty
Buster
Cage and Aviary Birds
Cat World
Catch
Catholic Gazette
The Catholic Herald
Catholic Pictorial
Chapman
Church of England Newspaper
Classic Cars
Classic CD
Computer Weekly
Computing
Country Life
The Countryman

Country-Side
The Cricketer International
Cycling Weekly
The Dandy
Darts World
Dirt Bike Rider
Disability Now
Dogs Today
East Lothian Life
The Economist
Euromoney
Everyday with Practical
  Electronics
Everywoman
Financial Adviser
Football Picture Story Library
Fore!

Fortean Times
Fourth World Review
Freelance Writing &
  Photography
Garden News
Gay Times
Geographical Magazine
Golf Monthly
Golf World
Guiding
Health & Efficiency
  International
Here's Health
Hertfordshire Countryside
Home and Country
Home Words
Horse and Hound
Horse & Pony
Index on Censorship
Jewish Telegraph
Just Seventeen
Kids Alive!
Life and Work
Live & Kicking Magazine
Mandy/Judy
Men Only
Modus
Money Week
Motor Boat and Yachting
Motor Caravan Magazine
Musical Opinion
My Weekly Puzzle Time

New Christian Herald
New Internationalist
New Musical Express
New Scientist
New Statesman & Society
The New Welsh Review
New World
Office Secretary
The Oldie
Opera Now
Organic Gardening
Park Home & Holiday
  Caravan
Penthouse
Performance Car
Pilot
Planet
Poetry Review
Pony
Practical Fishkeeping
Practical Householder
Practical Motorist
Practical Photography
Priests & People
Private Eye
Red Pepper
Reform
Runner's World
Scootering
The Scots Magazine
Scottish Homes and Country
Scouting

She
The Short Wave Magazine
Sight and Sound
Smallholder
The Spectator
The Squash Player
The Tablet
Take a Break
TGO (The Great Outdoors)
  Magazine
The Times Educational
  Supplement
Titbits
Today's Runner
Tribune
Trout and Salmon
Twinkle
The Universe
The Vegan
Viz
The Voice
Vox
War Cry
The Weekly Journal
Weight Watchers Magazine
What's on TV
Woman
Woman Alive
World Soccer
Yachting Monthly
Yachting World
Yours
YX

Business and Professional Magazines

Accountancy
Art Business Today
British Printer
Broadcast
Building Design
Carers World
Certified Accountant
Child Education
Control and Instrumentation
CTN
Drapers Record
Education
Electrical Review

Electrical Times
Hospitality
House Builder
International Construction
Journalist
Local Government Chronicle
Marketing Week
Mobile and Cellular Magazine
Museums Journal
Music Teacher
Nursing Times and Nursing
  Mirror

Pig Farming
Police Review
Post Magazine
Printing World
Publishing News
Red Tape
The Scottish Farmer
Solicitors Journal
Therapy Weekly
Toy Trader
Waterways World

Photography

The Freelance Photographer and the Agent

BRUCE COLEMAN

Photographic agencies and libraries have a dual role in the service they provide. They meet the needs and demands of picture editors, picture researchers and art buyers and, at the same time, provide a service to the freelance photographer. The enterprising photographer, wishing to penetrate the publishing market, would do well to consider employing the services of an agent whose knowledge of current trends and client contact will gear the photographer's output to the requirements of the markets. The complexities of reproduction rights are best left to an agent – that's if you wish to protect the copyright of your work!

Selecting the right agent very much depends on your type of work and you should, therefore, take a look at several agencies before choosing the one you think will be of advantage to you. Some agents, for example, work in the syndication area, selling news and topical pictures to the world's press; others are in the stock business maintaining a library of photographers' work orientated to the editorial market. Agents normally do not sell pictures outright but lease them for a specific use and fee from which they deduct a commission. A good photograph in the hands of a good agent can be published several times over and bring in royalties for many years.

Before submitting your work to an agent, a preliminary letter is recommended enquiring whether the agent is accepting new photographers and asking for details of their specific needs.

The agent will wish to see an initial presentation of at least two hundred photographs and photographers should indicate the number of photographs they plan to submit in the course of a year. Agents are keen to encourage the active photographer who can supply a regular stream of good quality work. Serious attention should be given to the caption of every picture as this can often mean the difference between a sale or a rejection. A caption should be brief and legible and an example of a good nature caption would be:

> Spotted Hyena (*C. crocuta*)
> Serengeti
> Aggressive behaviour

or, a geographical caption:

> Canada: Northwest Territories
> Inuit fur trappers and dogsled

Some time spent on the presentation of your work, editing for composition, content, sharpness and, in the case of transparencies, colour saturation, will

341

create a favourable impression. When submitting original colour transparencies, to ensure they are protected from damage and also to facilitate easy examination, place them in clear plastic sleeves, never between glass. Do not submit transparencies which you may require for personal use as it is impossible for an agent to recall pictures at short notice from his client.

One final point, never supply similar photographs to more than one agent as the problems created by almost identical pictures appearing, say, on a calendar or a greetings card can be embarrassing and costly to rectify. Indeed, for this reason, many agents insist on an exclusive arrangement between themselves and their photographers.

How to run your own Picture Library

JOHN FELTWELL

Photographers seeking to have someone else place their work should consider the possibilities of engaging a photographic agency (*see* Bruce Coleman's piece above). Photographers wishing to market their work themselves, either as specialist libraries listed below, or those wishing to establish a library, might find useful the following guidelines and tips.

It is important to draw up strict terms of business to cover items such as search fee, holding fee, and particularly loss or damage to original transparencies (£500 or more per transparency. See also *Picture Research* article.) Remember that the loss/damage fee is subject to tax as earnings. A month is a reasonable time for transparencies to be reviewed, thereafter a weekly holding fee per transparency is recommended, unless stated otherwise. Search fees may or may not be waived if transparencies are accepted. Reproduction rights should be calculated according to territorial limitations, whether one-time non-exclusive UK only, English speaking countries, world rights, etc., as well as size (small 'editorial' size to front cover). Sliding scales are required and bulk discounts. Agree fees, including future fees, before publication; restrict all electronic rights.

Beware of and budget for use of transparencies by editors, and especially design studios, for preparation of 'dummies'; pictures used may not be accounted for in-house by the resident picture researcher if acquired by editors, sub-editors, etc. Forbid any slide projection of transparencies. Be wary of the use of transparencies from which artists can derive ideas, unless arranged, and of publicity/advertising companies who generate computer models and logos, and bill accordingly. Beware of supplying private individuals who are naive to procedures. Some libraries ask for an official letter of request from the publisher.

The photographer's transparencies are treasured possessions. Unfortunately *some* publishers and magazines do not see it like that and treat them as dispensable and with some irreverence. You can be sure that picture researchers who are members of SPREd (full details at end of *Picture Research* article) know all about looking after transparencies and they are safe in their hands.

Make sure that dispatched transparencies (all sleeved) are well packed by whatever means and sent (by messenger/courier or by Registered Plus post with Consequential Loss Insurance) and are properly insured – and that the recipient knows when his or her liability starts and finishes. This includes transit to printers away from publishers' premises. Once accepted, transparencies may lie up for several months waiting to be used. This can run on to a year, unless strictly controlled. Arrange for payment three months after acceptance or on publication, whichever happens first, otherwise it might be on publication, some time off, or never. Specify that transparencies are returned from printers in a clean condition without any printers' solvents, but with original mounts.

The British Association of Picture Libraries and Agencies (BAPLA) (18 Vine Hill, London EC1R 5DX *tel* 0171-713 1780 *fax* 0171-713 1211) mostly represents commercial and institutional libraries. Smaller libraries, who are perhaps more vulnerable to disputes, can only be assisted (the right is reserved) by BAPLA after first year membership (currently (1996) £375 + VAT).

Picture Agencies and Libraries

For a **classified index** of picture agencies and libraries, see page 369.

Before submitting examples of work, photographers are advised to write a preliminary letter to ascertain terms and conditions. Usually, colour transparencies are required: medium and large format (minimum of 56 mm sq) are preferred to 35 mm. Only top quality transparencies should be submitted; inferior work is never accepted. *Postage for return material should be enclosed.*

Photographers are also referred to the markets for greetings cards and calendars on page 376, and to the children's book publishers and packagers classified index on page 244; also to the main Newspapers and Magazines (page 5), and Book Publishers (page 147), listings.

*Member of the British Association of Picture Libraries and Agencies

*A.A. & A. Ancient Art & Architecture Collection, 6 Kenton Road, Harrow-on-the-Hill, Middlesex HA1 2BL *tel* 0181-422 1214 *fax* 0181-426 9479. Specialises in the history of civilisations of the Middle East, Mediterranean countries, Europe, Asia, Americas, from ancient times to recent past, their arts, architecture, beliefs and peoples.

*A-Z Botanical Collection Ltd, Bedwell Lodge, Cucumber Lane, Essendon, Hatfield, Herts. AL9 6JB *tel* (01707) 649091 *fax* (01707) 649091. Colour transparencies of plant life worldwide, 6 × 6, 35 mm.

*Abode Interiors Photographic Library (1993), Albion Court, 1 Pierce Street, Macclesfield, Cheshire SK11 6ER *tel* (01625) 500070 *fax* (01625) 500910. *Contact:* Mary Jarvis or Judi Goodwin. Colour photo library specialising in English and Scottish house interiors of all styles, types and periods. High quality material only; terms by agreement.

Academic File News Photos (1985), The Centre for Near East, Afro-Asia Research (NEAR), Acre House, 69-76 Long Acre, London WC2E 9JH *tel* 0181-392 1122 *fax* 0181-392 1422. *Director:* Sajid Rizvi. Daily news coverage in UK and general library of arts, cultures, people and places, with special reference to the Middle East, North Africa and Asia. New photographers welcomed to cover UK and abroad.

*Ace Photo Agency (1980), Satellite House, 2 Salisbury Road, Wimbledon, London SW19 4EZ *tel* 0181-944 9944 *fax* 0181-944 9940. General library: people, industry, business, travel, commerce, skies, sport, music and natural history. Worldwide syndication. Sae for enquiries. Very selective editing policy. *Terms:* 50%.

*Action Plus (1986), 54-58 Tanner Street, London SE1 3LL *tel* 0171-403 1558 *fax* 0171-403 1526. Comprehensive and creative coverage of action, venues and personalities in over 120 sports and leisure activities, worldwide. Extensive colour and b&w library of high quality work from staff and contributing photographers. *Terms:* 50%.

Lesley and Roy Adkins Picture Library (1989), Longstone Lodge, Aller, Langport, Somerset TA10 0QT *tel* (01458) 250075 *fax* (01458) 250858. Colour library covering archaeology and heritage; prehistoric, Roman and medieval sites and monuments; landscape, countryside, architecture, towns, villages and religious monuments. Catalogue available.

Aerofilms (1919), Hunting Aerofilms Ltd, Gate Studios, Station Road, Borehamwood, Herts. WD6 1EJ *tel* 0181-207 0666 *fax* 0181-207 5433. Comprehensive library – over 1½ million photos going back to 1919 – of vertical and oblique aerial photographs of UK; large areas with complete cover.

Air Photo Supply (1963), 42 Sunningvale Avenue, Biggin Hill, Kent TN16 3BX *tel* (01959) 574872. Aircraft and associated subjects, South-East England, colour and monochrome. No other photographers' material required.

*Bryan and Cherry Alexander Photography (1973), Higher Cottage, Manston, Sturminster Newton, Dorset DT10 1EZ *tel* (01258) 473006 *fax* (01258) 473333. Polar regions with emphasis on Eskimos, Lapps and the modern Arctic, Antarctica.

Rev. J. Catling Allen, St Giles House, Little Torrington, Devon EX38 8PS *tel* (01805) 622497. Library of colour transparencies (35 mm) and b&w photos of Bible Lands, including archaeological sites and the religions of Christianity, Islam and Judaism. Medieval abbeys and priories, cathedrals and churches in Britain. Also historic, rural and scenic Britain. (Not an agent or buyer.)

Allied Artists Ltd (1983), 31 Harcourt Street, London W1H 1DT *tel* 0171-724 8809 *fax* 0171-262 8526. *Contact*: Gary Mills. Agency for illustrators, with colour library of realistic figurative illustrations available for syndication.

*Allsport Photographic Ltd (1972), 3 Greenlea Park, Prince George's Road, London SW19 2JD *tel* 0181-685 1010 *fax* 0181-648 5240. International sport and leisure.

American History Picture Library, 3 Barton Buildings, Bath BA1 2JR *tel* (01225) 334213. Photographs, engravings, colour transparencies covering the exploration, social, political and military history of North America from 15th to 20th century. Conquistadores, Civil War, gangsters, Moon landings, etc.

*Andes Press Agency (1983), 26 Padbury Court, London E2 7EH *tel* 0171-613 5417 *fax* 0171-739 3159. *Director:* Carlos Reyes. Social, political and economic aspects of Latin America, Africa, Asia, Middle East, Europe and Britain; specialises in Latin America and contemporary world religions.

*Heather Angel, Highways, 6 Vicarage Hill, Farnham, Surrey GU9 8HJ *tel* (01252) 716700 *fax* (01252) 727464. Colour transparencies (35 mm and 2¼ in square) with worldwide coverage of natural history and biological subjects including animals, plants, natural habitats (deserts, polar regions, rainforests, wetlands, etc.), landscapes, gardens, close-ups and underwater images; also man's impact on the environment – pollution, acid rain, urban wildlife, etc. Large China file. Detailed catalogues on request by *bona fide* picture researchers.

*Animal Photography (1955), 4 Marylebone Mews, New Cavendish Street, London W1M 7LF *tel* 0171-935 0503 *fax* 0171-487 3038. Horses, dogs, cats, small pets, East Africa, Galapagos.

*Aquarius Picture Library, PO Box 5, Hastings, East Sussex TN34 1HR *tel* (01424) 721196 *fax* (01424) 717704. *Contact:* David Corkill. Showbusiness specialist library with over one million colour and b&w images: film stills, classic portraiture, candids, archive material to present. New material added every week. Archival situation stills for advertising and magazine illustration use. Also television, vintage pop, opera, ballet and stage. Worldwide representation and direct sales. Collections considered, either outright purchase or 50%-50% marketing.

*Aquila Photographics, Haydon House, Alcester Road, Studley, Warks. B80 7AN *tel* (01527) 852357 *fax* (01527) 857507 *e-mail* interbirdnet @dial.pipex.com Specialists in ornithological subjects, but covering all aspects of natural history, also pets and landscapes, in both colour and b&w.

*Arcaid Architectural Photography and Picture Library, The Factory, 2 Acre Road, Kingston, Surrey KT2 6EF *tel* 0181-546 4352 *fax* 0181-541 5230. 'The built environment'– international collection: architecture, interior design, gardens, travel, museums, historic and contemporary. *Terms:* 50%.

*Archivio Veneziano (formerly **Venice Picture Library**) (1990), c/o Unesco, Piazza San Marco 63, 30124 Venice, Italy *tel/fax* (041) 520 2119. *Curator:* Sarah Quill. Specialises in Venice, covering most aspects of the city, islands and lagoon, especially their architecture, conservation and the environment. Commissions undertaken; visitors are welcome by appointment.

Arctic Camera, Derek Fordham (1978), 66 Ashburnham Grove, Greenwich, London SE10 8UJ *tel/fax* 0181-692 7651. Colour transparencies of all aspects of Arctic life and environment.

*Ardea London Ltd, 35 Brodrick Road, London SW17 7DX *tel* 0181-672 2067 *fax* 0181-672 8787. Su Gooders. Specialist worldwide natural history photographic library of animals, birds, plants, fish, insects, reptiles, worldwide scenics.

*Aspect Picture Library Ltd (1971), 40 Rostrevor Road, London SW6 5AD *tel* 0171-736 1998/731 7362 *fax* 0171-731 7362. General library including wildlife, tribes, cities, industry, science, Space.

The Associated Press Ltd, News Photo Department, The Associated Press House, 12 Norwich Street, London EC4A 1BP *tel* 0171-353 1390 (colour and b&w request), 0171-353 1515 ext 4264 (library manager) *fax* 0171-353 0836. News, features, sports.

Attard Photolibrary (1992), 5 Brewer Street, London W1R 3FN *tel* 0171-434 4444 *fax* 0171-287 3977. *Director:* Nigel Attard. Specialises in people: lifestyle, romance, contemporary themes. *Terms:* 50%.

Australia Pictures (1988), 28 Sheen Common Drive, Richmond, London TW10 5BN *tel* 0181-876 3637 *fax* 0181-876 3637 *tel/fax* 0181-898 0150. *Contact:* John Miles. Comprehensive library covering Australia, Aboriginals and their art, indigenous peoples, underwater, Tibet, Peru, Bolivia, Iran, Irian Jaya, Pakistan, Yemen.

Aviation Photographs International (1970), 15 Downs View Road, Swindon, Wilts. SN3 1NS *tel* (01793) 497179 *fax* (01793) 434030. All types of aviation and military subjects. Assignments undertaken.

*Aviation Picture Library (Austin J. Brown) (1970), 35 Kingsley Avenue, West Ealing, London W13 0EQ *tel* 0181-566 7712 *fax* 0181-566 7714 *cellphone* (01860) 670073. Worldwide aviation photographic library, including dynamic views of aircraft. Aerial and travel library including Europe, Caribbean, USA, and East and West Africa. Material taken since 1960. Specialising in air-to-air and air-to-ground commissions.

B. & B. Photographs (1974), Prospect House, Clifford Chambers, Stratford upon Avon, Warks. CV37 8HX   *tel* (01789) 298106   *fax* (01789) 292450. 35 mm / medium format colour library of horticulture (especially pests and diseases) and biogeography (worldwide), natural history (especially Britain) and biological education. Other photographers' work not represented.

Bandphoto Agency (division of **UPPA Ltd**), 29-31 Saffron Hill, London EC1N 8FH   *tel* 0171-421 6000   *fax* 0171-421 6006. International news and feature picture service for British and overseas publishers.

*Barnaby's Picture Library, 19 Rathbone Street, London W1P 1AF   *tel* 0171-636 6128/9   *fax* 0171-637 4317. General library of 4 million photos, colour and b&w, illustrating yesterday, today and tomorrow. Requires photographs for advertising and editorial publication. Photographs not purchased, sender retains copyright.

*Barnardo's Photographic Archive (1874), Tanners Lane, Barkingside, Ilford, Essex IG6 1QG   *tel* 0181-550 8822   *fax* 0181-550 0429. Extensive collection of b&w and colour images dating from 1874 to the present day covering social history with the emphasis on children and child care. Also 300 films dating from 1905.

*BBC Hulton Picture Library—see **Hulton Getty Picture Collection.**

Dr Alan Beaumont, 52 Squires Walk, Lowestoft, Suffolk NR32 4LA   *tel* (01502) 560126. Worldwide collection of monochrome prints and colour transparencies (35 mm and 6 × 7 cm) of natural history, countryside, windmills and aircraft. Subject lists available. No other photographers required.

Bee Photographs—see **Heritage & Natural History Photography.**

Stephen Benson Slide Bureau, 45 Sugden Road, London SW11 5EB   *tel* 0171-223 8635. World: agriculture, archaeology, architecture, commerce, everyday life, culture, environment, geography, science, tourism. Speciality: South America, the Caribbean, Australasia, Nepal, Turkey, Israel and Egypt. Assignments undertaken.

BIPS-Bernsen's International Press Service Ltd, 9 Paradise Close, Eastbourne, East Sussex BN20 8BT   *tel* (01323) 728760. (For full details see page 141.)

Bird Images (1989), 28 Carousel Walk, Sherburn in Elmet, North Yorkshire LS25 6LP   *tel/fax* (01977) 684666. *Principal:* P. Doherty. Specialist in the birds of Britain and Europe. Expert captioning service available.

*John Birdsall Photography (1980), 75 Raleigh Street, Nottingham NG7 4DL   *tel* (0115) 978 2645   *fax* (0115) 978 5546   *e-mail* j.birdsall@mcrl.poptel.org.uk *Contact:* Clare Marsh. Contemporary social documentary library covering children, youth, old age, health, disability, education, housing, work; also Nottingham and surrounding area; Spain – commissions and stock pictures.

*The Anthony Blake Photo Library, 54 Hill Rise, Richmond, Surrey TW10 6UB   *tel* 0181-940 7583   *fax* 0181-948 1224. Food and wine images from around the world, including raw ingredients, finished dishes, shops, restaurants, markets, agriculture and viticulture. Commissions undertaken. Contributors welcome. Brochure available on request.

John Blake Picture Library (1975), 74 South Ealing Road, London W5 4QB   *tel* 0181-840 4141   *fax* 0181-566 2568. *Manager:* Alan Denny. General topography of England, Europe and the rest of the world. Landscapes, architecture, churches, gardens, countryside, towns and villages. Horse trials covered including Badminton and Gatcombe Park. *Terms:* 50%.

Blitz International News & Photo Agency (1988), Stubcroft Studios, Stubcroft Farm, Stubcroft Lane, East Wittering, Nr Chichester, West Sussex PO20 8PJ *tel* (01243) 671469. *Contact:* Simon Green. Comprehensive library of colour transparencies and monochrome prints (35 mm, medium and large formats). Action and sports photography (especially yachting and motorsport, including Le Mans 24hr race), travel, natural history, landscapes and aerial, agriculture, reportage, personalities, news, advertising shots, general. Commissions undertaken and photographers accepted. Catalogue on request. *Terms:* 50%.

Bodleian Library, Oxford OX1 3BG *tel* (01865) 277153/277214 *fax* (01865) 277182. Photographic library of 32,000 35 mm colour transparencies, of subjects mostly from medieval manuscripts with iconographical index to illuminations; 35 mm filmstrips available for immediate sale (not hire); other formats to order.

Bookart Architecture Picture Library (1991), 1 Woodcock Lodge, Epping Green, Hertford SG13 8ND *tel* (01707) 875253 *fax* (01707) 875286. Modern and historic buildings, landscapes, works of named architects in Great Britain, Europe, Scandinavia, North America, India, South-East Asia, Japan, North and East Africa; modern sculpture. Listed under style, place and personality.

Boxing Picture Library, 3 Barton Buildings, Bath BA1 2JR *tel* (01225) 334213. Prints, engravings and photos of famous boxers, boxing personalities and famous fights from 18th century to recent years.

*****Bridgeman Art Library** (1971), 17-19 Garway Road, London W2 4PH *tel* 0171-727 4065 *fax* 0171-792 8509 *e-mail* info@bridgeman.co.uk Comprehensive source of fine art images for publication. Acts as agent for over 600 museums, galleries and private collections around the world. Large format colour transparencies. Currently holds more than 75,000 different images and is growing by 300 every week. Fully computerised, the image database runs on a custom-written free text keyword search system. CD-ROM catalogues.

Britain on View Photographic Library, official photographic library for British Tourist Authority and English Tourist Board. Colour library operated on their behalf by **Mirror Syndication International.** Encompasses all aspects of Britain: coast, countryside, villages, towns, pageantry, landmarks, historic houses and the British people. For details of b&w, contact Manager, Design, BTA, Thames Tower, Black's Road, London W6 9EL *tel* 0181-846 9000 *fax* 0181-563 0302.

David Broadbent/Peak District Pictures (1989), 66 Norfolk Street, Glossop, Derbyshire SK13 9RA *tel/fax* (01457) 862997. The Peak District fully covered, landscape, natural history, birds a speciality; sports. Commissions undertaken. New material welcome. *Terms:* 50%.

*****Brooklands Museum Picture Library** (1987), Brooklands Museum, Brooklands Road, Weybridge, Surrey KT13 0QN *tel* (01932) 857381 *fax* (01932) 855465. *Contact:* John Pulford, Curator of Collections or Julian Temple, Curator of Aviation. About 40,000 b&w and colour prints and slides. Subjects include Brooklands motor racing 1907-39; British aviation and aerospace 1908 to present day – particularly BAC, Hawker, Sopwith and Vickers aircraft built at Brooklands. Visits by appointment.

Hamish Brown, Scottish Photographic, 26 Kirkcaldy Road, Burntisland, Fife KY3 9HQ *tel* (01592) 873546. Photographs and 35 mm transparencies of Scottish sites and topographical, Morocco, mountain ranges of Europe, Africa, India and South America. Commissions undertaken. No pictures purchased.

Butterflies (1990), 27 Lucastes Lane, Haywards Heath, West Sussex RH16 1LE *tel* (01444) 454254. *Proprietors:* Dr J. Tampion, Mrs M.D. Tampion. Worldwide: butterflies, silkmoths, hawkmoths, adults, larvae, pupae, their foodplants, poisonous plants, wild, garden and greenhouse plants, botanical and gardening science, ecology, environment. Articles and line illustrations also available; commissions undertaken. *Terms:* 50%.

*Camera Press Ltd (1947), 21 Queen Elizabeth Street, London SE1 2PD *tel* 0171-378 1300 *fax* 0171-278 5126. B&w prints and colour transparencies covering British Royalty, portraits of world statesmen, politicians, entertainers, reportage, humour, nature, pop, features. *Terms:* 50%.

Camerapix—see C.P.L. (Camerapix Picture Library).

*J. Allan Cash Photolibrary (J. Allan Cash Ltd), 74 South Ealing Road, London W5 4QB *tel* 0181-840 4141 *fax* 0181-566 2568. *Manager:* Alan Denny. Worldwide photographic library: travel, landscape, natural history, sport, industry, agriculture. Details available for photographers interested in contributing.

*The Central Press Photos Ltd—see Hulton Getty Picture Collection.

*Cephas Picture Library, Hurst House, 157 Walton Road, East Molesey, Surrey KT8 2DX *tel* 0181-979 8647 *fax* 0181-224 8095. People, places, agriculture, industry, religion, architecture, travel, food and wine, crafts; wine industry and vineyards. *Terms:* 50%.

*City Syndication Ltd—see Monitor Syndication.

*Michael Cole Camerawork (1945), The Coach House, 27 The Avenue, Beckenham, Kent BR3 2DP *tel/fax* 0181-658 6120. Probably the world's largest tennis library. Archives include 50 years of Wimbledon. All current major events covered – worldwide media and sports companies supplied.

Bruce Coleman Inc., 117 East 24th Street, New York, NY 10010-2919, USA *tel* 212-979-6252 *fax* 212-979-5468 *e-mail* 72757,1343@compuserve.com *President:* Norman Owen Tomalin. Specialising exclusively in colour transparencies. All formats from 35 mm acceptable. All subjects required.

Bruce Coleman Ltd, 16 Chiltern Business Village, Arundel Road, Uxbridge, Middlesex UB8 2SN *tel* (01895) 257094 *fax* (01895) 272357. Colour transparencies on natural history, ecology, environment, geography, archaeology, anthropology, agriculture, science, scenics and travel.

*Collections (1990), 13 Woodberry Crescent, London N10 1PJ *tel* 0181-883 0083 *fax* 0181-883 9215. The British Isles only; places, people, buildings, industry, leisure; specialist collections on customs, castles, bridges, London, emergency services; also family life from pregnancy through birth, childhood, education to being grown up.

*Colorific Photo Library, The Innovation Centre, 225 Marsh Wall, London E14 9FX *tel* 0171-515 3000 *fax* 0171-538 3555. Handles the work of top international photographers, most subjects currently on file, upwards of 250,000 images. Represents the following agencies: Black Star (New York), Contact Press Images (New York/Paris), Visages (Los Angeles/New York), Icone (Paris), Regards (Paris), ANA Press (Paris). Also represents *Sports Illustrated*.

*Sylvia Cordaiy Photo Library (1990), 72 East Ham Road, Littlehampton, West Sussex BN17 7BQ *tel/fax* (01903) 715297. Worldwide travel and architecture, global environmental topics, wildlife and domestic animals, veterinary, comprehensive UK files, ocean racing. *Terms:* 50%.

C.P.L. (Camerapix Picture Library), 8 Ruston Mews, London W11 1RB *tel* 0171-221 0077 *fax* 0171-792 8105; and PO Box 45048 Nairobi, Kenya *tel* 223511/334398 *telex* 22576 *fax* 217244. Kenya, Tanzania, Pakistan, Jordan, Namibia, Nepal, Maldives, Mauritius, Seychelles, Zimbabwe; portraits, agriculture, industry, tribal cultures, landscapes; wildlife including rare species; extensive collection on Aldabra Island; Islamic portfolio: Mecca, Medina, Muslim pilgrimage. News material available and special assignments arranged. Further material available from collection held in Nairobi.

Crafts Council Picture Library (1973), 44A Pentonville Road, Islington, London N1 9BY *tel* 0171-806 2503 or 0171-278 7700 ext. 300 *fax* 0171-837 7700. Large, medium and small format transparencies. Coverage includes ceramics, jewellery, textiles, metal and silver, furniture, wood, glass, knitting, weaving, bookbinding, fashion accessories, toys and musical instruments supplied by selected makers and from *Crafts* magazine.

Peter Cumberlidge Photo Library (1982), 9 St Mary's Close, Llanfair Kilgeddin, Abergavenny, Gwent NP7 9YE *tel* (01873) 880610/880757 *fax* (01873) 858717. *Contact:* Jane Cumberlidge. Nautical, travel and coastal colour transparencies 35 mm and 6 × 6 cm; specialities: boats, harbours, marinas, inland waterways. Travel and holiday subjects Northern Europe and Mediterranean. No other photographers' material required.

Cumbria Picture Library (1990), PO Box 33, Kendal, Cumbria LA9 4SU *tel* (015394) 48894 *fax* (015394) 48294. *Contact:* Eric Whitehead. Specialist picture library with over 40,000 images covering every aspect of Cumbria and The Lake District. Subjects include: places, people, events, customs, outdoor pursuits and landscapes; snooker photos by Eric Whitehead. The library holds work from many photographers and commissions are accepted.

*Lupe Cunha (1987), Photo-Arte Gallery, 19 Ashfield Parade, London N14 5EH *tel* 0181-882 6441 *fax* 0181-882 6303. Specialist library on all aspects of childhood from pregnancy to school age, also women's interest and health/ medical with focus on the patient and nursing care. Commissioned photography undertaken. Also represents collection on Brazil for Brazil Photo Agency. *Terms:* 50%.

*Sue Cunningham Photographic, 56 Chatham Road, Kingston upon Thames, Surrey KT1 3AA *tel* 0181-541 3024 *fax* 0181-541 5388. Growing collection of international subjects (not only travel); South America, Africa, Central and Western Europe. Also UK, especially London, Cornwall.

The Dance Library (1983), 12 Southwick Mews, London W2 1JG *tel* 0171-262 6300 *fax* 0171-262 6400. Contemporary and historical dance: classical ballet, jazz, tap, disco, popping, ice dancing, musicals, variety, folk, tribal rites and rituals.

Das Photo (1975), Chalet le Pin, Domaine de Bellevue 181, 6940 Septon, Belgium *tel* (086) 32 24 26; c/o Old School House, Llanfilo, Brecon, Powys LD3 0RH *tel* (01874) 711953. Arab countries, Americas, Europe, SE Asia, Amazon, world festivals, archaeology, people, biblical, motor bikes, education, schools, modern languages.

Barry Davies (1983), Dyffryn, Bolahaul Road, Cwmffrwd, Carmarthen, Dyfed SA31 2LP *tel/fax* (01267) 233625. Natural history, landscape (especially waterfalls), Egypt, children, outdoor activities and general subjects. Formats 35 mm, 6 × 6 cm, 6 × 7 cm, 5 × 4 in. Other photographers' work not accepted.

Dennis Davis Photography (1984), 9 Great Burrow Rise, Northam, Bideford, Devon EX39 1TB *tel* (01237) 475165. Gardens, wild and garden flowers, domestic livestock including rare breeds and poultry, agricultural landscapes, architecture – interiors and exteriors, landscape, coastal, rural life. Commissions welcomed. No other photographers required.

*James Davis Travel Photography, 65 Brighton Road, Shoreham, West Sussex BN43 6RE *tel* (01273) 452252 *fax* (01273) 440116. *Proprietor:* Paul Seheult. Stock transparency library specialising in worldwide travel photos. Suppliers to publishers, advertising agents, etc.

*Peter Dazeley, The Studios, 5 Heathmans Road, Parsons Green, London SW6 4TJ *tel* 0171-736 3171 *fax* 0171-371 8876. Extensive golf library dating from 1970. Colour and b&w coverage of major tournaments. Constantly updated, with over 250,000 images of players (male and female), courses worldwide, action shots, portraits, trophies, including miscellaneous images: clubs, balls and teaching shots.

George A. Dey (1986), 'Drumcairn', Aberdeen Road, Laurencekirk, Kincardineshire AB30 1AJ *tel* (01561 37) 8845. Scottish Highland landscapes, Highland Games, forestry, seabirds, castles of NE Scotland, gardens, spring, autumn, winter scenes, veteran cars, North Holland, New Zealand (North Island).

Douglas Dickins Photo Library (1946), 2 Wessex Gardens, Golders Green, London NW11 9RT *tel* 0181-455 6221. Worldwide collection of colour transparencies (mostly 6 × 6 cm, some 35 mm) and b&w prints (10 × 8 in originals), specialising in Asia, particularly India and Indonesia; also, USA, Canada, France, Austria and Switzerland, Japan, China, Burma.

Gordon Dickson (1975) Flagstones, 72 Catisfield Lane, Fareham, Hants PO15 5NS *tel* (01329) 842131. Colour transparencies of fungi, in natural habitat; also wildflowers, butterflies, moths, beetles. No other photographers required.

*C.M. Dixon, The Orchard, Marley Lane, Kingston, Canterbury, Kent CT4 6JH *tel* (01227) 830075 *fax* (01227) 831135. Europe and Ethiopia, Iceland, Sri Lanka, Tunisia, Turkey, former USSR. Main subjects include agriculture, ancient art, archaeology, architecture, clouds, geography, geology, history, horses, industry, meteorology, mosaics, mountains, mythology, occupations, people.

Earth Images Picture Library (1989), PO Box 43, Keynsham, Bristol BS18 2TH *tel/fax* (0117) 986 1144/(01275) 839643. *Director:* Richard Arthur. Earth from Space (satellite remote sensing); earth science and art-in-science imagery – from cosmic to sub-atomic.

*Ecoscene (1987), Sally Morgan, The Oasts, Headley Lane, Passfield, Liphook, Hants GU30 7RX *tel* (01428) 751056 *fax* (01428) 751057. Natural history, specialising in the environment and ecology. Subjects include animal and plant species, habitats, conservation, energy, industry, all forms of pollution; worldwide coverage. *Terms:* 55% to photographer.

*English Heritage Photographic Library (1984), 23 Savile Row, London W1X 1AB *tel* 0171-973 3338/3339 *fax* 0171-973 3330. Wide range of high quality, large format colour transparencies, ranging from ancient monuments to artefacts, legendary castles to stone circles, elegant interiors to industrial architecture and post-war listed buildings.

Environmental Investigation Agency (1985), 15 Bowling Green Lane, London EC1R 0BD *tel* 0171-490 7040 *fax* 0171-490 0436. *Photograph co-ordinator:* Tamara Gray. Specialist library covering animal abuse, trade in endangered species, abuse of the environment; also animals in their natural environment.

Greg Evans International Photo Library (1979), 91 Charlotte Street, London W1P 1LB *tel* 0171-636 8238 *fax* 0171-637 1439. Comprehensive, general colour library with over 300,000 transparencies. Subjects include: abstract, aircraft, arts, animals, beaches, business, children, computers, couples, families, food/restaurant, women, industry, skies, sports (action and leisure), UK scenics, worldwide travel. Visitors welcome; combined commissions undertaken; first search fee. Photographers' submissions welcome. Please phone for free brochure.

*****Mary Evans Picture Library,** 59 Tranquil Vale, Blackheath, London SE3 0BS *tel* 0181-318 0034 *fax* 0181-852 7211. Millions of historical illustrations in colour and b&w covering all aspects of the past, emphasis on social conditions and cultural activities. Portraits, topography, science and many specialist subjects, notably women's rights, psychical research, psychology (Freud). Many special collections including individual photographers 1930s to 1960s.

Eyeline Photography (1979), 259 London Road, Cheltenham, Glos. GL52 6YG *tel/fax* (01242) 513567. Watersports, particularly sailing and powerboating, worldwide; equestrian events; windvanes; scenics.

*****Famous** (1990), Studio 4, Limehouse Cut, 46 Morris Road, London E14 6NQ *tel* 0171-537 7055 *fax* 0171-537 7056 *e-mail* 100741.1754@compuserve.com Colour pictures and features library covering music, film and TV personalities. *Commission:* 50%.

*****Feature-Pix Colour Library—see World Pictures.**

*****Financial Times Pictures,** Number One, Southwark Bridge, London SE1 9HL *tel* 0171-873 3671 *fax* 0171-873 4606. Colour and b&w library serving *The Financial Times*. Specialises in world business, industry and commerce; world politicians and statespeople; cities and countries; plus many other subjects. Library updated daily.

*****Fogden Natural History Photographs** (1980), Mid Cambushinnie Cottage, Kinbuck, Dunblane, Perthshire FK15 9JU *tel/fax* (01786) 822069. *Library manager:* Susan Fogden. Wide natural history coverage, including camouflage, warning coloration, mimicry, breeding strategies, feeding, animal/plant relationships, environmental studies, especially in rain forests and deserts.

Ron and Christine Foord, 155b City Way, Rochester, Kent ME1 2BE *tel/fax* (01634) 847348. Colour picture library of 1000 species of wild flowers; British insects, garden flowers, pests and diseases, indoor plants, cacti, countryside views.

*****Footprints Colour Picture Library** (1991), Goldfin Cottage, Maidlands Farm, Broad Oak, Rye, East Sussex TN31 6BJ *tel/fax* (01424) 883078. *Proprietor:* Paula Leaver. Specialises in underwater and above water coverage of holiday destinations in the tropics; also food and flowers by Debbie Patterson.

*****Forest Life Picture Library** (1983), Forestry Commission, 231 Corstorphine Road, Edinburgh EH12 7AT *tel* 0131-334 0303 *fax* 0131-334 4473. *Manager:* Douglas Green. Tree species, forest and woodland management, employment, landscapes, wildlife, flora and fauna, conservation, sport and leisure.

*****Werner Forman Archive** (1975), 36 Camden Square, London NW1 9XA *tel* 0171-267 1034 *fax* 0171-267 6026. Art, architecture, archaeology, history and peoples of ancient, oriental and primitive cultures.

*****Fortean Picture Library,** Henblas, Mwrog Street, Ruthin, Clwyd LL15 1LG *tel* (01824) 707278 *fax* (01824) 705324. Library of colour and b&w pictures covering all strange phenomena: UFOs, Loch Ness Monster, ghosts, Bigfoot, witchcraft, etc.; also antiquities (especially in Britain – prehistoric and Roman sites, castles, churches).

Fotoccompli–The Picture Library (1989), 11 Ampton Road, Edgbaston, Birmingham B15 2UH   *tel* 0121-454 3305   *fax* 0121-454 9257. Comprehensive library, ranging from abstracts to zoology, serving all of Britain, especially the Birmingham and West Midlands areas. *Terms:* 50%; minimum retention period – three years.

Fotomas Index, 12 Pickhurst Rise, West Wickham, Kent BR4 0AL   *tel/fax* 0181-776 2772. Specialises in supplying pre-20th century (mostly pre-Victorian) illustrative material to publishing and academic worlds, and for television and advertising. Complete production back-up for interior décor, exhibitions and locations.

*Fox Photos—see Hulton Getty Picture Collection.

Freelance Focus (1988), 7 King Edward Terrace, Brough, North Humberside HU15 1EE   *tel/fax* (01482) 666036. *Contact:* Gary Hicks. UK/international network of photographers. Over two million stock pictures available, covering all subjects, worldwide, at competitive rates. Assignments undertaken for all types of clients. Further details/subject list available on request. Also publishes directory of photographers and photo libraries/agencies.

Frontline Photo Press Agency (1988), 18 Wall Street, Norwood, Australia 5067   *postal address* PO Box 162, Kent Town, Australia 5071   *tel* (08) 8333 2691   *fax* (08) 8364 0604   *e-mail* fppa@tne.net.au *Director:* Carlo Irlitti. Stock photo agency, picture library and photographic press agency with 300 images. Covers sport, people, personalities, travel, scenics, environmental, agricultural, industrial, natural history, concepts, science, medicine, social documentary and press images. Seeking worldwide contributors. Assignments undertaken. Write or fax for submission guidelines, photo requirements and other details. *Terms:* 60% to photographer (stock); assignment rates negotiable.

Frost Historical Newspaper Collection, 8 Monks Avenue, New Barnet, Herts. EN5 1DB   *tel/fax* 0181-440 3159. Headline stories from 60,000 British and overseas newspapers reporting major events since 1850.

Brian Gadsby Picture Library, Route des Pyrénées, Labatut-Riviere 65700, Hautes Pyrénées, France   *tel* 62 96 38 44. Colour (2¼ in sq, 6 × 4.5 cm, 35 mm) and b&w prints. Wide range of subjects but emphasis on travel, natural history, children. Catalogue on request by picture researchers. No other photographers' material required.

*Galaxy Picture Library (1992), 1 Milverton Drive, Ickenham, Uxbridge, Middlesex UB10 8PP   *tel* (01895) 637463   *fax* (01895) 623277   *e-mail* galaxypix@compuserve.com *Contact:* Robin Scagell. Astronomy: specialities include the night sky, amateur astronomy, astronomers and observatories.

*Garden Matters Photographic Library (1993), Dr John Feltwell, Marlham, Henley's Down, Battle, East Sussex TN33 9BN   *tel* (01424) 830566   *fax* (01424) 830224   *e-mail* 100572.115@compuserve.com **Plants 5000:** over 5000 scientifically named species of garden flowers, wild plants, trees (over 700 species), grasses, crops, herbs, spices, houseplants, carnivorous plants, climbers and roses. **General gardening** and how-to, gardening techniques, garden design and embellishments, cottage gardens, USA designer-gardens, 200 garden portfolios from 16 states in the USA, 100 portfolios from 12 European countries. Several photographers now represented.

Leslie Garland Picture Library (1985), 69 Fern Avenue, Jesmond, Newcastle upon Tyne NE2 2QU *tel* 0191-281 3442 *fax* 0191-281 3442. Colour library of all subjects in the geographic areas of Northumberland, Durham, Tyne and Wear, Cleveland, Cumbria, Lancashire, North Yorkshire and Norway. Details available for photographers interested in contributing – please send sae. *Terms:* 50%.

*Colin Garratt—see **Railways – Milepost 92½.**

*Genesis Space Photo Library (1990), Greenbanks, Robins Hill, Raleigh, Bideford, Devon EX39 3PA *tel* (01237) 471960 *fax* (01237) 472060. *Contact:* Tim Furniss. Specialises in rockets, spacecraft, spacemen, Earth, Moon, planets.

*Geo Aerial Photography (1992), 4 Christian Fields, London SW16 3JZ *tel/fax* 0181-764 6292, (0115) 981 5474 or (0115) 981 9418. *Director:* J.F.J. Douglas. Air-to-air and air-to-ground colour library: natural and cultural/man-made landscapes and individual features. Commissions undertaken. *Terms:* 50%.

*GeoScience Features, 6 Orchard Drive, Wye, Kent TN25 5AU *tel* (01233) 812707 *fax* (01233) 812707. *Director:* Dr Basil Booth. Colour library (35 mm to 5 × 4 in). Animals, biology, birds, botany, chemistry, earth science, ecology, environment, geology, geography, habitats, landscapes, macro/micro, peoples, plants, travel, sky, weather, wildlife and zoology; Americas, Africa, Australasia, Europe, India, South-East Asia. Incorporates K.S.F. and R.I.D.A. photolibraries.

*Geoslides (1968), 4 Christian Fields, London SW16 3JZ *tel/fax* 0181-764 6292 or (0115) 981 9418. *Library director:* John Douglas. Broadly based and substantial collections from Africa, Asia, Antarctic, Arctic and sub-Arctic areas, Australia (Blackwood Collection). Worldwide commissions undertaken. Photographs for all types of publications, television, advertising. *Terms:* 50% on UK sales.

Mark Gerson Photography, 3 Regal Lane, Regents Park Road, London NW1 7TH *tel* 0171-286 5894 *fax* 0171-267 9246. Portrait photographs of personalities, mainly literary, in colour and b&w from 1950 to the present. No other photographers' material required.

Global Syndications (1990), Chartwood Towers, Punchbowl Lane, Dorking, Surrey RH5 4ED *tel* (01306) 741213 *fax* (01306) 875347. *Managing editor:* Sam Hall. Colour transparencies of all aspects of Arctic life and environment, particularly Eskimo (Inuit) and Lapps (Sami); Scandinavia and UK (landscapes, people, etc.). Assignments undertaken. No other photographers required.

John Glover Photography (1979), Fairfield, Hale House Lane, Churt, Farnham, Surrey GU10 2NQ *tel* (01428) 717196 *fax* (01428) 717129. Gardens and gardening, from overall views of gardens to plant portraits with Latin names; UK landscapes including ancient sites, Stonehenge, etc.

*Martin and Dorothy Grace (1984), 40 Clipstone Avenue, Mapperley, Nottingham NG3 5JZ *tel* (0115) 920 8248 *fax* (0115) 962 6802. General British natural history, specialising in native trees, shrubs, flowers, habitats and ecology.

Tim Graham (1970), 31 Ferncroft Avenue, London NW3 7PG *tel* 0171-435 7693 *fax* 0171-431 4312. Royal Family in this country and on tours; background pictures on royal homes, staff, hobbies, sports, cars, etc.; English and foreign country scenes; international heads of state and VIPs.

Greater London Record Office, 40 Northampton Road, London EC1R 0HB *tel* 0171-332 3820 *fax* 0171-833 9136. Over 350,000 photographic prints and 1,500,000 negatives of London and the London area from c.1860 to 1986.

Especially strong on local authority projects, including schools, public housing and open spaces.

Robert Haas Photo Library (1978), 11 Cormont Road, Camberwell, London SE5 9RA　*tel* 0171-326 1510. Holland, Greek Islands, Morocco, Scottish oil industry, Notting Hill Carnival, skies. *Specialities:* people; New York City, Lloyd's of London, Docklands.

*****Robert Harding Picture Library,** 58-59 Great Marlborough Street, London W1V 1DD　*tel* 0171-287 5414　*fax* 0171-631 1070. Photographic library. Require photographs of outstanding quality for advertising and editorial use, all subjects considered particularly lifestyle.

Harper Horticultural Slide Library, 219 Robanna Shores, Seaford, VA 23696, USA　*tel* 804-898-6453　*fax* 804-890-9378. 160,000 35 mm slides of plants, gardens and native habitats.

Heritage & Natural History Photography, Dr John B. Free, 37 Plainwood Close, Summersdale, Chichester, West Sussex PO19 4YB　*tel* (01243) 533822. Archaeology, history, agriculture: Arabia, China, India, Iran, Japan, Kenya, Mediterranean countries, Mexico, Nepal, North America, Oman, Russia, Thailand, UK. Bees and bee keeping, insects and small invertebrates, tropical crops and flowers.

Historical Picture Service, 3 Barton Buildings, Bath BA1 2JR　*tel* (01225) 334213. Engravings, prints and photos on all aspects of history from ancient times to 1920. Special collection Old London: buildings, inns, theatres, many of which no longer exist.

Pat Hodgson Library & Picture Research Agency, Jasmine Cottage, Spring Grove Road, Richmond, Surrey TW10 6EH　*tel* 0181-940 5986. Small collection of b&w historical engravings, book illustrations, ephemera, etc.; some colour and modern photos. Subjects include history, Victoriana, ancient civilisations, occult, travel. Text written and research undertaken on any subject. Of special interest to educational publishers, film makers and exhibition designers.

*****Holt Studios International (Agriculture, Horticulture, Environment)** (1981), The Courtyard, 24 High Street, Hungerford, Berks. RG17 0NF　*tel* (01488) 683523　*fax* (01488) 683511. Worldwide agriculture, horticulture, crops and associated pests (and their predators), diseases and deficiencies, farming people and practices, livestock, machinery, landscapes, diverse environments, natural flora and fauna.

Horizon International Creative Images (1978). Photographer enquiries: Horizon International, Horizon House, Route de Picaterre, Alderney, Channel Islands　*fax* (01481) 823880; picture research and UK sales enquiries: Images Colour Library Ltd, 12-14 Argyll Street, London W1V 1AB　*tel* 0171-734 7344　*fax* 0171-287 3933. General stock library covering travel, people, sport, business, industry, etc.

*****David Hosking** FRPS, Pages Green House, Wetheringsett, Stowmarket, Suffolk IP14 5QA　*tel* (01728) 861113　*fax* (01728) 860222. Natural history subjects, especially birds covering whole world. Also Dr D.P. Wilson's unique collection of marine photos.

*****Houses & Interiors Photographic Features Agency** (1985), 18 Church Street, Ticehurst, Wadhurst, East Sussex TN5 7AH　*tel/fax* (01580) 200905. *Contact:* Richard Wiles. Stylish house interiors and exteriors, home dossiers, renovations, architectural details, interior design, gardens and houseplants. Also step-by-step photographic sequences of DIY subjects, fresh and dried flower arrangements and gardening techniques. Colour only. Commissions undertaken. *Commission:* Library 50%, Agency negotiable.

*Hulton Getty Picture Collection, Unique House, 21-31 Woodfield Road, London W9 2BA *tel* 0171-266 2662 *fax* 0171-289 6392 *e-mail* 100530,101 @compuserve.com *WWW* http://www.u-net.com/hulton One of the largest picture resources in Europe, with over 15 million b&w and colour images. Specialises in social history, Royalty, transport, war, fashion, sport, entertainment, people, places and early photography. Collections include *Picture Post, Express, Evening Standard,* Keystone, Fox and Topical Press. Manages Syndication International; only London agents for the Reuter News Picture Service; publisher of CD-ROMs for creative image access.

*The Hutchison Library (1976), 118b Holland Park Avenue, London W11 4UA *tel* 0171-229 2743 *fax* 0171-792 0259. General colour library; worldwide subjects: agriculture, environments, festivals, human relationships, industry, landscape, peoples, religion, towns, travel.

*The Illustrated London News Picture Library, 20 Upper Ground, London SE1 9PF *tel* 0171-805 5585 *fax* 0171-805 5905. Engravings, photos, illustrations in b&w and colour from 1842 to present day, especially 19th and 20th century social history, wars, portraits, Royalty. Travel archive including The Thomas Cook collection.

*The Image Bank (1979), 17 Conway Street, Fitzrovia, London W1P 6EE *tel* 0171-312 0300 *fax* 0171-391 9111; **Image Bank Scotland,** 14 Alva Street, Edinburgh EH2 4QG *tel* 0131-225 1770 *fax* 0131-225 1660; **Image Bank Manchester,** 4 Jordan Street, Manchester M15 4PY *tel* 0161-236 9226 *fax* 0161-236 8723. General library of still and moving imagery from the world's top artists. Digital search facilities and CD catalogues.

Image Diggers (1980), 618B Finchley Road, London NW11 7RR *tel/fax* 0181-455 4564. *Contact:* Neil Hornick. Stills archive covering performing arts, popular culture, human interest, natural history, architecture, nautical, children and people, strange phenomena, religions and other. Also audio and video for research purposes and ephemera including magazines, books, comic books, sheet music, postcards.

*Images Colour Library Ltd (1983), 15/17 High Court Lane, The Calls, Leeds LS2 7EU *tel* (0113) 243 3389 *fax* (0113) 242 5605. *Leeds office manager:* Jess Diebel; and 12-14 Argyll Street, London W1V 1AB *tel* 0171-734 7344 *fax* 0171-287 3933. *London office manager:* Cara Botting. General, contemporary stock library including people, business, UK and world travel, industry and sport. *Terms:* 50%.

*Images of Africa Photobank (1983), 11 The Windings, Lichfield, Staffs. WS13 7EX *tel* (01543) 262898 *fax* (01543) 417154. *Contact:* David Keith Jones. Colour and b&w covering wildlife, traditional and modern people, land, resources, beauty, tourist attractions, hotels and lodges, National Parks and Reserves. *Terms:* 50%.

*Imperial War Museum (1917), Photograph Archive, Lambeth Road, London SE1 6HZ *tel* 0171-416 5000 *fax* 0171-416 5379. National archive of over five million photos, dealing with war in the 20th century involving the armed forces of Britain and the Commonwealth countries. Visitors' Room (IWM All Saints Annexe, Austral Street, SE11 – five minutes walk from main building) open by appointment Mon-Fri. Enquiries should be as specific as possible; prints made to order.

International Press Agency (Pty) Ltd (1934), PO Box 67, Howard Place 7450, South Africa   *tel* (021) 531 1926   *fax* (021) 531 8789. Press photos for South African market.

Isle of Wight Pictures (1985), 60 York Street, Cowes, Isle of Wight PO31 7BS   *tel* (01983) 290366   *fax* (01983) 297282. *Proprietor:* Patrick Eden. Covers all aspects of the Isle of Wight, including Cowes Week, sailing events, nautical aspects. Any picture not on file can be shot on request.

Japan Archive (1993), 9 Victoria Drive, Horsforth, Leeds, West Yorkshire LS18 4PN   *tel* (0113) 258 3244. *Contact:* S.R. Turnbull. Japan: modern, daily life, architecture, religion, history, personalities, gardens, natural world.

Jazz Index (1979), 26 Fosse Way, London W13 0BZ   *tel/fax* 0181-998 1232. Photo library of jazz, blues and contemporary musicians. Also photos of instruments, clubs, crowds at concerts. Photos sold on behalf of photographers. *Terms:* 50%.

Joe Filmbase (1991), 208A Belgravia Workshop, 159 Marlborough Road, London N19 4NF   *tel* 0171-561 0909   *fax* 0171-561 0966. General library specialising in Africa and Europe. *Terms:* 3-year contract.

JS Library International (1979) 101A Brondesbury Park, London NW2 5JL   *tel* 0181-451 2668   *fax* 0181-459 0223. The Royal Family, worldwide travel pictures, particularly the African continent, stage and screen celebrities, authors, worldwide general material. New material on any subject, in any quantity, always urgently required; features also required. Assignments undertaken.

Just Europe (1989), 50 Basingfield Road, Thames Ditton, Surrey KT7 0PD   *tel/fax* 0181-398 2468. Specialises in Europe – major cities, towns, people and customs. Assignments undertaken; background information available; advice and research service.

*Keystone Collection—see **Hulton Getty Picture Collection.**

Lakeland Life Picture Library (1979), Langsett, Lyndene Drive, Grange-over-Sands, Cumbria LA11 6QP   *tel* (015395) 33565 (answer phone). English Lake District: industries, crafts, sports, shows, customs, architecture, people. Also provides colour and b&w, illustrated articles. Not an agency. Catalogue available on request.

*Landscape Only (1986), c/o Images Colour Library Ltd, 12-14 Argyll Street, London W1V 1AB   *tel* 0171-734 7344   *fax* 0171-287 3933. Outdoor landscapes of villages and countryside worldwide by some of the leading landscape photographers. *Terms:* 50%.

*Frank Lane Picture Agency Ltd, Pages Green House, Wetheringsett, Stowmarket, Suffolk IP14 5QA   *tel* (01728) 860789   *fax* (01728) 860222. Natural history and meteorology.

Michael Leach, Brookside, Kinnerley, Oswestry, Shropshire SY10 8DB   *tel/fax* (01691) 682639. General worldwide wildlife and natural history subjects, with particular emphasis on mammals and urban wildlife. Comprehensive collection of owls from all over the world. No other photographers required.

*Link Picture Library (1983), 33 Greyhound Road, London W6 8NH   *tel* 0171-381 2261/2433   *fax* 0171-385 6244   *e-mail* lib@linkpics.demon.co.uk *Proprietor:* Orde Eliason. Specialist archives on South Africa, India and music; also general stock library; electronic images on Photo CD Disc. Commissions accepted. *Terms:* 50%.

The Billie Love Historical Collection (1969), Reflections, 3 Winton Street, Ryde, Isle of Wight PO33 2BX   *tel* (01983) 812572   *fax* (01983) 564331. *Proprietor:* Billie Love. Photos (late 19th century-1930s), engravings, coloured lithographs, covering subjects from earliest times, people, places and events up to the Second World War; also more recent material.

*Ludvigsen Library Ltd (1984), 73 Collier Street, London N1 9BE   *tel* 0171-837 1700   *fax* 0171-837 1776. *Photographic resources:* Neil King. Vintage, antique and classic cars; cars of all countries; historical motor sports events (Formula 1, Le Mans, US racing, motor shows).

*The MacQuitty International Collection, 7 Elm Lodge, River Gardens, Stevenage Road, London SW6 6NZ   *tel* 0171-385 6031   *tel/fax* 0171-384 1781. 300,000 photos covering aspects of life in 70 countries: archaeology, art, buildings, flora and fauna, gardens, museums, people and occupations, scenery, religions, methods of transport, surgery, acupuncture, funeral customs, fishing, farming, dancing, music, crafts, sports, weddings, carnivals, food, drink, jewellery and oriental subjects. Period: 1920 to present day.

*Mander & Mitchenson Theatre Collection, The Mansion, Beckenham Place Park, Beckenham, Kent BR3 2BP   *tel* 0181-658 7725   *fax* 0181-663 0313. Prints, drawings, photos, programmes, etc., theatre, opera, ballet, music hall, and other allied subjects including composers, playwrights, etc. All periods. Available for books, magazines, TV.

Mansell Collection Ltd, 42 Linden Gardens, London W2 4ER   *tel* 0171-229 5475   *fax* 0171-792 0469. General historical material up to the 1920s, 1930s.

John Massey Stewart, 20 Hillway, Highgate, London N6 6QA   *tel* 0181-341 3544   *fax* 0181-341 5292. Large collection Russia, including topography, people, culture, Siberia, plus Russian and Soviet history, 3000 pre-revolutionary PCs, etc. Also Britain, Europe, Asia (including Mongolia and South Korea), Alaska, USA, Israel, Sinai desert, etc.

*S. & O. Mathews, The Old Rectory, Calbourne, Isle of Wight PO30 4JE   *tel* (01983) 531247   *fax* (01983) 531253. Gardens, flowers and landscapes.

Chris Mattison, 138 Dalewood Road, Beauchief, Sheffield S8 0EF   *tel* (0114) 236 4433. Colour library specialising in reptiles and amphibians; other natural history subjects; habitats and landscapes in Africa, SE Asia, South America, USA, Mexico, Mediterranean. Captions or detailed copy supplied if required. No other photographers' material required.

Merseyside Photo Library (1989), Suite 1, Egerton House, Tower Road, Birkenhead, Wirral L41 1FN   *tel* 0151-650 6975   *fax* 0151-650 6976 (operated by Ron Jones Associates). Library specialising in images of Liverpool and Merseyside but includes other destinations.

Microscopix (1986), Middle Travelly, Beguildy, Nr Knighton, Powys LD7 1UW   *tel/fax* (01547) 510242. Scientific photo library specialising in scanning electron micrographs and photomicrographs for technical and aesthetic purposes. Commissioned work, both biological and non-biological, undertaken offering a wide variety of applicable microscopical techniques.

Military History Picture Library, 3 Barton Buildings, Bath BA1 2JR   *tel* (01225) 334213. Prints, engravings, photos, colour transparencies covering all aspects of warfare and uniforms from ancient times to present.

*Mirror Syndication International, Unique House, 21-31 Woodfield Road, London W9 2BA   *tel* 0171-266 1133   *fax* 0171-266 2563. Photo library specialising in current affairs, personalities, royalty, sport, cinema and travel. Agents for

Mirror Group Newspapers, The British Tourist Authority and other leading magazine publishers.

Monitor Syndication (1960), 17 Old Street, London EC1V 9HL   *tel* 0171-253 7071   *fax* 0171-250 0966. *Contact:* Ian Hendry. Specialists in portrait photos of leading national and international personalities from politics, trade unions, entertainment, sport, Royalty and well-known buildings in London. Incorporates the **City Syndication** library.

Motorcycles Unlimited (1993), 106 Wilberforce Road, Finsbury Park, London N4 2SU   *tel* 0171-354 1229   *fax* 0171-704 0646. *Owner:* Roland Brown. Bikes of all kinds, from latest roadsters to classics, racers to tourers. Detailed information available on all machines pictured.

Mountain Dynamics (1990), Heathcourt, Morven Way, Monaltrie, Ballater AB35 5SF   *tel* (013397) 55081   *fax* (013397) 55526. *Proprietor:* Graham P. Adams. Scottish and European mountains – from ground to summits – in panoramic (6×17 cm), 5×4 in and medium format. Commissions undertaken. *Terms:* 50%.

Mountain Visions (1984), Graham and Roslyn Elson, 25 The Mallards, Langstone, Havant, Hants PO9 1SS   *tel* (01705) 478441. Colour transparencies of mountaineering, skiing, and associated travel, in Europe, Africa, Himalayas, Arctic, Far East and Australia. Do not act as agents for other photographers.

*****David Muscroft Photography** and **David Muscroft Picture Library** (1977), 16 Broadfield Road, Heeley, Sheffield S8 0XJ   *tel* (0114) 258 9299   *fax* (0114) 255 0113. Large, varied and expanding library on babyhood, family, pregnancy, supplying all the UK's baby magazines.

The Mustograph Agency, 19 Rathbone Street, London W1P 1AF   *tel* 0171-636 6128/9   *fax* 0171-637 4317. Britain only: b&w general subjects of countryside life, work, history and scenery.

*****National Maritime Museum Picture Library,** National Maritime Museum, Park Row, Greenwich, London SE10 9NF   *tel* 0181-312 6631   *fax* 0181-312 6722. *Picture library manager:* Christopher Gray. Maritime, transport, time and space and historic photographs.

*****National Motor Museum, Beaulieu,** Motoring Picture Library, Beaulieu, Hants SO42 7ZN   *tel* (01590) 612345   *fax* (01590) 612655. All aspects of motoring, cars, commercial vehicles, motor cycles, personalities, etc. Illustrations of period scenes and motor sport. Also large library of 5×4 in and smaller colour transparencies of veteran, vintage and modern cars, commercial vehicles and motor cycles. Over 700,000 images in total.

*****Natural History Photographic Agency**—see **NHPA.**

Natural Image, Dr Bob Gibbons (1982), 31 Shaftesbury Road, Poole, Dorset BH15 2LT   *tel/fax* (01202) 675916. Colour library covering natural history, habitats, countryside and gardening (UK and worldwide); special emphasis on conservation. Commissions undertaken. *Terms:* 50%.

News Blitz International, Via Guido Banti 34, 00191 Rome, Italy   *tel* 333 26 41/ 333 02 52   *fax* 333 26 51. *Contact:* Giovanni A. Congiu. News and general library.

Newsfocus Press Photograph Agency (1989), 49 Westmere Drive, Mill Hill, London NW7 3HG   *tel* (0956) 693158. *Contact:* David Fowler. Specialises in colour and b&w portrait photos of leading British and international personalities, especially politics, entertainment, Royalty, trade unions, media. No search/service fees to clients. *Terms:* 50%; occasional outright purchase.

*NHPA (Natural History Photographic Agency), 57 High Street, Ardingly, West Sussex RH17 6TB   *tel* (01444) 892514   *fax* (01444) 892168. Represents more than 100 of the world's leading natural history photographers covering a wide range of wildlife, marine life, domestic animals and pets, plants, landscapes and environmental subjects. Specialisations include the unique high-speed photography of Stephen Dalton, comprehensive coverage on North America and Africa, and the ANT collection of Australasian material (for which NHPA is UK agent). Recent additions to the files include strong coverage from Chile, Papua New Guinea, Scandinavia, Antarctica, the Caribbean and Madagasca. Pictures are generally supplied to companies and institutions only, and are sent to freelance writers and artists by agreement with their publisher or commissioning company.

*The Northern Picture Library, Greenheys Business Centre, 10 Pencroft Way, Manchester M15 6JJ   *tel* 0161-226 2007   *fax* 0161-226 2022. *Proprietor:* Roy Conchie. General library covering Britain, the world, industry, sport, leisure, etc. Submissions considered from photographers.

*Operation Raleigh—see Raleigh International.

Orion Press, 1-13 Kanda Jimbocho, Chiyoda-ku, Tokyo 101, Japan   *tel* (03) 3295-1400   *fax* (03) 3295-0227. All subjects in all formats.

*Christine Osborne Pictures/MEP (1984), 53A Crimsworth Road, Vauxhall, London SW8 4RJ   *tel/fax* 0171-720 6951. Colour and b&w. Africa, Middle East/Gulf, SE Asia/Pacific and Australasia, Indo-Pak sub-continent. Special stock on: travel and tourism, religion, people and way-of-life, ethnic cultures, foods, crafts. *Terms:* 50%.

*Oxford Scientific Films Ltd, Photo Library, Long Hanborough, Oxon OX8 8LL   *tel* (01993) 881881   *fax* (01993) 882808. World renowned, first class collection of colour transparencies of wildlife and natural science images and special effects supplied by over 300 photographers worldwide. UK agents for *Animals Animals* and Photo Researchers, New York, *Okapia*, Frankfurt and *PLA*, Australia. Now also incorporating the **Survival Anglia Photo Library.** Please phone or fax your details for free catalogue.

*PA News Photo Library (1902), 292 Vauxhall Bridge Road, London SW1V 1AE   *tel* 0171-963 7032/34/35   *fax* 0171-963 7066. Over five million photos dating from the turn of the century, covering news, sport, royalty and showbiz. Library updated daily. Searches undertaken, or customers are welcome to browse.

*Panos Pictures (1986), 9 White Lion Street, London N1 9PD   *tel* 0171-837 7505   *fax* 0171-278 0345   *e-mail* panospics@corporate.nethead.co.uk Third World and Eastern European documentary photos focusing on social, political and economic issues with a special emphasis on environment and development. Files on agriculture, conflict, education, energy, environment, family life, festivals, food, health, industry, landscape, people, politics, pollution, refugees, religions, rural life, transport, urban life, water, weather. *Terms:* 50%.

*Papilio Natural History & Travel Library (1988), 44 Palestine Grove, Merton, London SW19 2QN   *tel/fax* 0181-687 2202. *Contacts:* Robert Pickett, Justine Bowler. Worldwide coverage of natural history and environmental subjects including travel section; commissions undertaken.

*Ann & Bury Peerless, 22 King's Avenue, Minnis Bay, Birchington-on-Sea, Kent CT7 9QL   *tel* (01843) 841428   *fax* (01843) 848321. Art, craft (including textiles), archaeology, architecture, dance, iconography, miniature paintings, manuscripts, museum artefacts, social, cultural, agricultural, industrial, historical, political, educational, geographical subjects and travel in India, Pakistan, Bangladesh, Afghanistan, Burma, China, Egypt, Iran, Israel, Kenya, Libya, Malta, Malaysia, Morocco, Nepal, Russia (Moscow, St Petersburg, Samarkand and Bukhara, Uzbekistan), Sri Lanka, Spain, Sudan, Taiwan, Tunisia, Uganda, Zambia and Zimbabwe. Specialist material on historical and world religions: Hinduism, Buddhism, Jainism, Judaism, Christianity, Confucianism, Islam, Sikhism, Taoism, Zoroastrianism (Parsees of India).

Chandra S. Perera Cinetra (1958), 437 Pethiyagoda, Kelaniya-0490, Sri Lanka *tel* (1) 521885 *telex* 21193/21213 *fax* (1) 541414/323910. B&w and colour library including news, wildlife, religious, social, political, sports, adventure, environmental, forestry, nature and tourism. Photographic and journalistic features on any subject.

*****Photo Flora** (1982), 46 Jacoby Place, Priory Road, Birmingham B5 7UN *tel* 0121-471 3300. Comprehensive collection of British wild plants; Mediterranean wild plants and travel; Egypt, India, Tibet, China, Nepal, Thailand, Mexico.

Photo Library International, PO Box 75, Leeds LS7 3NZ *tel* (0113) 262 3005 *fax* (0113) 262 5366. Colour transparencies only. Most subjects. New material always welcome.

Photo Link (1990), 126 Quarry Lane, Northfield, Birmingham B31 2QD *tel/ fax* 0121-475 8712. *Contact:* Mike Vines. Colour and b&w aviation library, covering subjects from 1909 to the present day. Specialises in air-to-air photography. Assignments undertaken.

*****Photo Resources,** The Orchard, Marley Lane, Kingston, Canterbury, Kent CT4 6JH *tel* (01227) 830075 *fax* (01227) 831135. Ancient civilisations, art, archaeology, world religions, myth, and museum objects covering the period from 30,000 BC to AD 1900. European birds, butterflies, trees.

*****Photofusion,** 17A Electric Lane, Brixton, London SW9 8LA *tel* 0171-738 5774 *fax* 0171-738 5509. Collection of 50,000 b&w photos and 15,000 colour transparencies on contemporary social issues, including disability, education, family, health, homelessness and work.

*****The Photographers' Library** (1978), 81A Endell Street, Covent Garden, London WC2H 9AJ *tel* 0171-836 5591 *fax* 0171-379 4650. Requires transparency material on worldwide travel, industry, agriculture, commerce, sport, people, leisure, girls, scenic. Colour only. *Terms:* 50%.

*****Pictor International Ltd,** Lymehouse Studios, 30-31 Lyme Street, London NW1 0EE *tel* 0171-482 0478 *fax* 0171-267 1396. Offices in 18 countries. All subjects. *Rates:* 50%.

*****Picturepoint Ltd**—see **Topham Picturepoint.**

Sylvia Pitcher (1968), 75 Bristol Road, Forest Gate, London E7 8HG *tel/fax* 0181-552 8308. Specialist in blues, jazz, old-time country and bluegrass, cajun and zydeco musicians; also towns, rural scenes, details, record labels, and still life etc. relevant to the music.

Pixfeatures (Mr P.G. Wickman), 5 Latimer Road, Barnet, Herts. EN5 5NU *tel* 0181-449 9946 *fax* 0181-441 6246. Picture-features, preferably topical. Especially for sale to British, German and Spanish magazines. *Terms:* 35% of all sales, unless otherwise arranged.

*****Planet Earth Pictures** (1969), The Innovation Centre, 225 Marsh Wall, London E14 9FX *tel* 0171-293 2999 *fax* 0171-293 2998. All aspects of natural history and the natural environment, farming, fishing, pollution and conservation.

*Popperfoto (Paul Popper Ltd), The Old Mill, Overstone Farm, Overstone, Northampton NN6 0AB   *tel* (01604) 670670   *fax* (01604) 670635. Offer documentary and feature photos (b&w and colour) from all countries of the world. Collection includes Exclusive News Agency, Odhams Periodicals Photo Library, Conway Picture Library, Reuters, United Press International (UPI) Library, Planet, Agence-France Presse, European Pressphoto Agency and Bob Thomas Sports Photography.

Power Pix International Picture Library—see **S. & I. Williams, Power Pix International Picture Library**.

*Premaphotos Wildlife, Amberstone, 1 Kirland Road, Bodmin, Cornwall PL30 5JQ   *tel* (01208) 78258   *fax* (01208) 72302. Library of 35 mm transparencies; wide range of natural history subjects from around the world. Invertebrate behaviour a speciality.

*Press Association Photos (news picture service of The Press Association)—see **PA News Photo Library**.

Pro-file Photo Library (1982), 2B Winner Commercial Building, 401-403 Lockhart Road, Hong Kong   *tel* (852) 2574 7788   *fax* (852) 2574 8884; 62A Smith Street, Chinatown, Singapore 058964   *tel* (65) 324-3747   *fax* (65) 324-3748. *Director:* Neil Farrin. General photo library. *Terms:* 50%.

*Punch Cartoon Library (1841), 100 Brompton Road, Knightsbridge, London SW3 1ER   *tel* 0171-225 6711/6710   *fax* 0171-225 6712. Comprehensive collection of cartoons and illustrations, indexed under subject categories: humour, historical events, politics, fashion, sport, personalities, etc.

*Railways – Milepost 92½ (1969), Milepost 92½, Newton Harcourt, Leics. LE8 9FH   *tel* (0116) 259 2068   *fax* (0116) 259 3001. Comprehensive collection of railway photos, including British Rail's library of railway and scenic pictures of the UK and abroad, Colin Garratt's collection of world steam trains and thousands of other professional railway photos.

*Raleigh International Picture Library (1978), Raleigh House, 27 Parson's Green Lane, London SW6 4HS   *tel* 0171-371 8585   *fax* 0171-371 5116. *Contact:* May Morton. Source of stock colour images from locations around the world: the 100,000+ images are updated eight times a year. Open to researchers by appointment, 9.30-5.30 weekdays.

*Retna Pictures Ltd (1984), 1 Fitzroy Mews, Cleveland Street, London W1P 5DQ   *tel* 0171-209 0200   *fax* 0171-383 7151. Library of colour transparencies and b&w prints of rock and pop performers, show business personalities, celebrities, actors and actresses. Also extensive lifestyle and stock library.

*Retrograph Nostalgia Archive Ltd (1984), 164 Kensington Park Road, London W11 2ER   *tel* 0171-727 9378   *answerphone* (outside office hours) 0171-727 9426   *fax* 0171-229 3395. Worldwide advertising, packaging, posters, decorative and fine art illustrations from 1880-1970. Special collections include Victoriana illustrations and scraps (1860-1901), fashion and beauty (1880-1980), RetroTravel Archive: travel and tourism, RetroGourmet Archive: food and drink (1890-1950). Research service and Image Consultancy services; RetroMontages: Victorian montage design service. Free colour leaflets on request.

Rich Research (1978), 1 Bradby House, Carlton Hill, St John's Wood, London NW8 9XE   *tel/fax* 0171-624 7755. *Director:* Diane Rich. Speedy and innovative picture research service. Visuals found for all sectors of publishing and the media. Stock images, commissioned photography and artwork. Negotiations of rights and fees.

*Ann Ronan at Image Select, Kebbell House, Delta Gain, Carpenters Park, Watford, Herts. WD1 5BE   *tel* 0181-421 3131   *fax* 0181-421 3896. Woodcuts, engravings, etc., social and political history plus history of science and technology, including military and space.

Roundhouse Ornithology Collection (1991), c/o John Stewart-Smith, 24 Carneton Close, Crantock, Newquay, Cornwall TR8 5RY   *tel/fax* (01637) 830546. Colour library specialising in birds of UK, Europe, Middle East (especially), North Africa, Far East and South America.

*Royal Geographical Society Picture Library (1830), 1 Kensington Gore, London SW7 2AR   *tel/fax* 0171-584 4381 (direct line)   *tel* 0171-589 5466 ext 152   *fax* 0171-584 4447. *Contact:* picture library manager. Worldwide coverage of geography, travel, exploration, expeditions and cultural environment from 1870s to the present.

*The Royal Photographic Society (1853), The Octagon, Milsom Street, Bath BA1 1DN   *tel* (01225) 462841   *fax* (01225) 448688. Exhibitions; library of books, photos and photographic equipment.

Royal Society for Asian Affairs, 2 Belgrave Square, London SW1X 8PJ   *tel* 0171-235 5122. Archive library of original 19th and 20th century b&w photos, glass slides, etc., of Asia. Publishes *Asian Affairs* 3 p.a.

*Royal Society of Chemistry Library and Information Centre, Burlington House, Piccadilly, London W1V 0BN   *tel* 0171-437 8656   *fax* 0171-287 9798. Science photographs and prints.

Dawn Runnals Photographic Library (1985), 5 St Marys Terrace, Kenwyn Road, Truro, Cornwall TR1 3SW   *tel* (01872) 79353. General library: land and seascapes, flora and fauna, sport, animals, people, buildings, boats, harbours, miscellaneous section and some specialised subjects – details on application. Other photographers' work not accepted. Sae appreciated with enquiries.

*The Russia and Republics Photo Library (1988), Conifers House, Cheapside Lane, Denham, Uxbridge, Middlesex UB9 5AE   *tel* (01895) 834814   *fax* (01895) 834028. *Library manager:* Mark Wadlow. Colour photo library specialising in cities, towns, famous landmarks and people. Do not accept other photographers' work.

*Peter Sanders Photography (1987), 9 Meades Lane, Chesham, Bucks. HP5 1ND   *tel/fax* (01494) 773674. Specialises in Islamic world, but now expanding into other world religions, beliefs and cultures.

Steffi Schubert, Wildlife Conservation Collection Photographic Library (1990), Avondale Farm, Southwold Road, Holton, nr Halesworth, Suffolk IP19 8PW   *tel/fax* (01986) 872777. All aspects of British wildlife and fauna.

*Science Photo Library (1979), 112 Westbourne Grove, London W2 5RU   *tel* 0171-727 4712   *fax* 0171-727 6041. Scientific photography of all kinds – medicine, technology, Space, nature. 100,000 different images.

*Science & Society Picture Library (1993), Science Museum, Exhibition Road, London SW7 2DD   *tel* 0171-938 9750   *fax* 0171-938 9751. Subjects include: science and technology, medicine, industry, transport, social documentary and the media. Extensive collection; images drawn from the Science Museum in London, the National Railway Museum in York and the National Museum of Photography, Film and Television in Bradford. Free brochure available on request.

Scotland in Focus Picture Library (1988), 22 Fleming Place, Fountainhall, Galashiels, Selkirkshire TD1 2TA   *tel/fax* (01578 760) 256. Library specialising in all aspects of Scotland, including British wildlife and natural history subjects.

All Scottish material required on 35 mm and upwards, medium format preferred. Photographers must enclose return postage. *Commission:* 50%.

SCR Photo Library (1943), Society for Co-operation in Russian and Soviet Studies, 320 Brixton Road, London SW9 6AB   *tel* 0171-274 2282   *fax* 0171-274 3230. Russian and Soviet life and history. Comprehensive coverage of cultural subjects: art, theatre, folk art, costume, music; agriculture and industry, architecture, armed forces, education, history, places, politics, science, sport. Also posters and theatre props, artistic reference and advice. Research by appointment only.

*Seaco Picture Library (1995), Sea Containers House, 20 Upper Ground, London SE1 9PF   *tel* 0171-805 5831/5834   *fax* 0171-805 5926. Stills and video footage of: container shipping; fast ferries and ports; produce and fruit farming – India and Africa; hotels and resorts in Botswana, South Africa, Portugal, the United States, Brazil, Italy and Australia; the Venice Simplon-Orient-Express and Oriental Express luxury tourist train services and the recently launched Road to Mandalay cruiseship.

*Sealand Aerial Photography Ltd (1976), Goodwood Airfield, Goodwood, Chichester, West Sussex PO18 0PH   *tel* (01243) 781025   *fax* (01243) 531422. Aerial photo coverage of any subject that can be photographed from the air in the UK. Most stock on 2¼ in format colour negative/transparency. Subjects constantly updated from new flying.

*S & G Press Agency Ltd, 68 Exmouth Market, London EC1R 4RA   *tel* 0171-278 1223   *fax* 0171-278 8480. Press photos and vast photo library. Send photos, but negatives preferred.

Mick Sharp (1981), Eithinog, Waun, Penisarwaun, Caernarfon, Gwynedd LL55 3PW   *tel/fax* Llanberis (01286) 872425. Archaeology, ancient monuments, architecture, churches, countryside, environment, history, landscape, travel and tourism. Emphasis on British Isles, but material from many other countries including France, Iraq, Morocco and USA. Access to other similar photo collections. B&w prints from 5 × 4 in negatives, and 35 mm and 6 × 4.5 cm colour transparencies.

*Shout Picture Library (1994), 10 Sutton Close, Aston-le-Walls, Northants NN11 6UJ   *tel* (mobile) (0973) 226793   *fax* (01295) 660518. *Contact:* John Callan. Specialises in the emergency services: fires, road traffic accidents, surgery, various police and hospital units. Commissions accepted; terms as recommended by BAPLA.

*Brian and Sal Shuel—see **Collections.**

Sites, Sights and Cities (1990), PO Box 92, Penzance, Cornwall TR18 2XL   *tel/fax* (01736) 65790. *Director:* Paul Devereux. Ancient monuments, mainly in Britain, Egypt, Greece and USA; city features in UK, Europe and USA; general nature shots.

*Skishoot – Offshoot (1986), 28 Dalebury Road, London SW17 7HH   *tel* 0181-767 0059   *fax* 0181-767 6680. *Librarian:* Caroline Ellerby. Library specialising in all aspects of skiing. Also travel (especially France). Assignments undertaken. *Terms:* 50%.

*Skyscan Photolibrary (1984), Oak House, Toddington, Cheltenham, Glos. GL54 5BY   *tel* (01242) 621357   *fax* (01242) 621343. Based on a unique collection of aerial images of British landscapes, cities, heritage sites, patterns, etc., taken from a tethered balloon which produces unusual viewpoints and very high definition photos. Now expanding to include other aerial collections i.e. air-to-ground, air-to-air, balloons, etc. *Terms:* 50%.

*The Slide File (1978), 79 Merrion Square South, Dublin 2, Republic of Ireland *tel* (01) 6766850 *fax* (01) 6624476. Specialises in Eire and Northern Ireland: landscapes, Irish natural history, agriculture and industry, Irish people and their traditions, Celtic heritage.

Patrick Smith Associates (1964), Gloucester House, High Street, Borth, Dyfed SY24 5HZ *tel/fax* (01970) 871296. South London 1950-1977, mid-Wales, aviation; also The Patrick Smith Collection of London photos, now in The Museum of London.

*Society for Anglo-Chinese Understanding (1965), Sally & Richard Greenhill Photo Library, 357a Liverpool Road, London N1 1NL *tel* 0171-607 8549 *fax* 0171-607 7151. Colour and b&w prints of China, late 1960s-1989.

Society for Co-operation in Russian and Soviet Studies—see SCR Photo Library.

Source Photographic Archives (1974), 66 Claremont Road, Sandymount, Dublin 4, Republic of Ireland *tel* (01) 6607090. *Director:* Thomas Kennedy. Mostly recent photos by living photographers on many different subjects.

*Spectrum Colour Library, 41-42 Berners Street, London W1P 3AA *tel* 0171-637 1587 *fax* 0171-637 3681. Extensive general library of high-quality transparencies, for worldwide marketing, including electronically. Photographer's information pack available. Purchases photos and collections of photos.

*Sporting Pictures (UK) Ltd, 7A Lambs Conduit Passage, Holborn, London WC1R 4RG *tel* 0171-405 4500 *fax* 0171-831 7991. *Director:* Crispin J. Thruston; *librarian:* Justin Downing. Specialises in sports, sporting events, sportsmen.

Peter Stiles Picture Library, 4 Rockingham Close, Durrington, Worthing, West Sussex BN13 2NU *tel/fax* (01903) 503147. Specialises in horticulture, plus natural history, pictorial views. Sequences and illustrated features. Own pictures only. Commissions undertaken.

*The Still Moving Picture Company (1991), 67A Logie Green Road, Edinburgh EH7 4HF *tel* 0131-557 9697 *fax* 0131-557 9699. 250,000 pictures of Scotland and all things Scottish; sport (Allsport agent for Scotland).

*Still Pictures Whole Earth Photo Library (1970), 199 Shooters Hill Road, Blackheath, London SE3 8UL *tel* 0181-858 8307 *fax* 0181-858 2049. *Proprietor:* Mark Edwards. Specialises in environment and Third World issues and nature; includes industry, agriculture, indigenous peoples and cultures and endangered species. *Commission:* 50%.

*Tony Stone Images, Worldwide House, 116 Bayham Street, London NW1 0BA *tel* 0171-267 8988 *fax* 0171-722 9305. International photo library. Subjects required: travel, people, natural history, commerce, industry, technology, sport, etc. Check first with Creative Department. *Terms:* 50%.

*Survival Anglia Photo Library (1960)—see **Oxford Scientific Films Ltd.**

Sutcliffe Gallery, 1 Flowergate, Whitby, North Yorkshire YO21 3BA *tel* (01947) 602239 *fax* (01947) 820287. Collection of 19th century photography, all by Frank M. Sutcliffe Hon. FRPS (1853-1941), especially inshore fishing boats and fishing community; also farming interests. Period covered 1872 to 1910.

Charles Tait Photo Library (1978), Kelton, St Ola, Orkney KW15 1TR *tel* (01856) 873738/875003 *fax* (01856) 875313 *e-mail* charles @velvia.demon.co.uk Colour photo library specialising in islands: coverage includes Orkney, Shetland and Western Isles (including North Rona, Sula Sgeir), as well as many parts of Scotland and France; also Venice. Subjects include archaeology, landscapes, transport, industry, seascapes, events, people and wildlife, especially seabirds and seals. Panoramic landscapes using Alpa Rotocam a speciality. Publisher of postcards, calendars and guidebooks. All transparencies with detailed computer captions and bar coded.

The Tank Museum Photo Library & Archive (c.1946), The Tank Museum, Bovington, Dorset BH20 6JG *tel* (01929) 403463 *fax* (01929) 405360. International collection, from 1900 to present, of armoured fighting vehicles and military transport, including tanks, armoured cars, personnel carriers, self-propelled artillery carriers, missile launchers, cars, lorries and tractors.

***Telegraph Colour Library,** The Innovation Centre, 225 Marsh Wall, London E14 9FX *tel* 0171-987 1212 *fax* 0171-538 3309. Stock photography agency covering a wide subject range: business, sport, people, industry, animals, medical, nature, space, travel and graphics. Sameday service for all UK clients. Free catalogues available upon request.

Theatre Museum, National Museum of the Performing Arts, 1E Tavistock Street, Covent Garden, London WC2E 7PA *tel* 0171-836 7891 *fax* 0171-836 5148. In addition to extensive public displays on live entertainment, the Museum has an unrivalled collection of programmes, playbills, prints, photos, plays, books and press cuttings relating to performers and productions from the 17th century onwards. Available by appointment, free of charge through the Study Room, open Tues-Fri, 1030-1630. Reprographic services available.

***Three Lions**—see **Hulton Getty Picture Collection.**

***Topham Picturepoint,** PO Box 33, Edenbridge, Kent TN8 5PB *tel* (01342) 850313 *fax* (01342) 850244. Historic library: personalities, warfare, Royalty, topography, France, natural history and world travel. World news file from original sources: UPI, INP, Press Association, Central News, Planet News, Alfieri, Pictorial Press, Syndicated Features Ltd, etc. New photographers – sample submission of 50 transparencies; 5-year contract, 50% commission.

***B.M. Totterdell Photography** (1989), Constable Cottage, Burlings Lane, Knockholt, Kent TN14 7PE *tel* (01959) 532001. Specialist volleyball library, covering all aspects of the sport.

Transworld/Scope, 26 St Cross Street, London EC1N 8UH *tel* 0171-831 0013 *fax* 0171-831 4549. *Contact:* Valerie Dobson. Colour: situations/beauty pictures.

***Travel Images** (1990), The White House, 25 Jubilee Lane, Farnham, Surrey GU10 4TA *tel* (01252) 794994 *fax* (01252) 794094. *Sales and marketing manager:* Frances Allen. Comprehensive travel library, covering over 80 countries.

***Travel Ink Photo & Feature Library** (1988), The Old Coach House, 14 High Street, Goring-on-Thames, Nr Reading, Berks RG8 9AT *tel* (01491) 873011 *fax* (01491) 875558 *e-mail* abbie@travink.demon.co.uk Travel, tourism and lifestyles covering around 150 countries – including the UK. Specialist sections include Hong Kong (including construction of the Tsing Ma Bridge), North Wales and Greece.

Travel Photo International, 8 Delph Common Road, Aughton, Ormskirk, Lancs. L39 5DW *tel/fax* (01695) 423720. Touristic interest including scenery, towns, monuments, historic buildings, archaeological sites, local people. Specialises in travel brochures and books. *Terms:* 50%.

***Tropix Photographic Library** (1973), 156 Meols Parade, Meols, Wirral, Merseyside L47 6AN *tel/fax* 0151-632 1698. All human and environmental aspects of tropics, sub-tropics and non-tropical developing countries. Environmental issues are accepted from locations worldwide. New collections welcome but preliminary enquiry in writing essential; send four first class stamps for details. *Terms:* 50%.

Ulster Photographic Agency (1985), 22 Casaeldona Park, Belfast, Northern Ireland BT6 9RB *tel* (01232) 795738. Motoring and motorsport. *Terms:* 50% or outright purchase.

Universal Pictorial Press & Agency Ltd (UPPA) (1929), 29-31 Saffron Hill, London EC1N 8FH *tel* 0171-421 6000 *fax* 0171-421 6006. Notable Royal, political, company, academic, legal, diplomatic, church, military, pop, arts, entertainment and sports personalities and well-known views and buildings. Commercial, industrial, corporate and public relations photo assignments undertaken.

John Vickers Theatre Collection, 27 Shorrolds Road, London SW6 7TR *tel* 0171-385 5774. Archives of British theatre and portraits of actors, writers and musicians by John Vickers from 1938-1974.

Vidocq Photo Library (1983), 162 Burwell Meadow, Witney, Oxon OX8 7GD *tel/fax* (01993) 778518. Extensive coverage of wide range of subjects. Register of Photographers includes many specialists who market their work exclusively through the library. New photographers welcome. Please submit list of categories covered – do not send photographs. *Terms:* 50%.

Viewfinder Colour Photo Library (1984), 3 Northload Street, Glastonbury, Somerset BA6 9JJ *tel* (01458) 832600 *fax* (01458) 832850. Colour library covering industry, agriculture, transport, people, worldwide travel and the British Isles in detail; also world religions. *Terms:* 50%.

The Charles Walker Collection (1983), c/o Images Colour Library Ltd, 12-14 Argyll Street, London W1V 1AB *tel* 0171-734 7344 *fax* 0171-287 3933. *London office manager:* Cara Botting. World's largest archive of colour pictures relating to the occult, magical, esoteric, mystical and mythological traditions.

Simon Warner, Whitestone Farm, Stanbury, Keighley, West Yorkshire BD22 0JW *tel/fax* (01535) 644644. Landscape photographer with own stock pictures of northern England, North Wales and NW Scotland.

Waterways Photo Library (1976), 39 Manor Court Road, London W7 3EJ *tel* 0181-840 1659 *fax* 0181-567 0605. *Contact:* Derek Pratt. British inland waterways; canals and rivers; bridges, aqueducts, locks and all waterside architectural features; watersports; waterway holidays, boats, fishing; town and countryside scenes. No other photographers' work required.

Weimar Archive (1983), 8-9 The Incline, Coalport, Telford, Shropshire TF8 7HR *tel* (01952) 680050 *fax* (01952) 587184. Germany, specialising in World War I, Weimar Republic and Third Reich; but all aspects of social, political and cultural life in central Europe from Middle Ages until 1945; plus a comprehensive collection of German painting and sculpture, Soviet posters and cartoons 1917-1945, and German Democratic Republic.

Welfare History Picture Library (1975), Heatherbank Museum of Social Work, Caledonian University, Park Campus, 1 Park Drive, Glasgow G3 6LP *tel* 0141-337 4402 *fax* 0141-337 4500. Social history and social work, especially child welfare, poorhouses, prisons, hospitals, slum clearance, women's movement, social reformers and their work. Catalogue on request.

Westcountry Pictures (1989), 23 Southernhay West, Exeter, Devon EX1 1PR *tel* (01392) 426640 *fax* (01392) 51745. *Contact:* Peter Cooper. All aspects of Devon and Cornwall.

Western Americana Picture Library, 3 Barton Buildings, Bath BA1 2JR *tel* (01225) 334213. Prints, engravings, photos and colour transparencies on the American West, cowboys, gunfighters, Indians, including pictures by Frederic Remington and Charles Russell, etc. Interested in buying pictures on American West.

Roy J. Westlake ARPS, West Country Photo Library, 31 Redwood Drive, Plympton, Plymouth PL7 3FS *tel/fax* (01752) 336444. Landscapes, seascapes, architecture, leisure activities, etc., for tourist brochures, advertising, books, magazines, calendars, etc. Also camping, caravanning and inland waterways subjects in Britain, including rivers and canals. Some world travel. Other photographers' work not accepted.

*Eric Whitehead Picture Agency and Library—see Cumbria Picture Library.

Derek G. Widdicombe, Worldwide Photographic Library, 'Oldfield', High Street, Clayton West, Huddersfield HD8 9NS *tel/fax* (01484) 862638 *pager* (0839) 764024. Landscapes, seascapes, architecture, human interest of Britain and abroad. Moods and seasons, buildings and natural features. Holds copyright of Noel Habgood FRPS Collection.

*Wilderness Photographic Library, Mill Barn, Broad Raine, Sedbergh, Cumbria LA10 5ED *tel* (015396) 20196 *fax* (015396) 21293. *Director:* John Noble FRGS. Specialist library in mountain and wilderness regions, especially polar. Associated aspects of people, places, natural history, geographical features, exploration and mountaineering, adventure sports, travel.

*Wildlife Matters Photographic Library (1980), Dr John Feltwell, Marlham, Henley's Down, Battle, East Sussex TN33 9BN *tel* (01424) 830566 *fax* (01424) 830224 *e-mail* 100572.115@compuserve.com Ecology, conservation and environment; habitats and pollution; agriculture and horticulture; general natural history, entomology; Mediterranean wildlife; rainforests (Central America and Indonesia); aerial pics of countryside UK, Europe, USA.

*David Williams Picture Library (1989), 50 Burlington Avenue, Glasgow G12 0LH *tel* 0141-339 7823 *fax* 0141-337 3031. Specialises in colour transparencies of Scotland and Iceland (2¼ in and 35 mm). Subjects include landscapes, towns, villages, buildings, antiquities, geology and physical geography. Catalogue available. Commissions undertaken.

S. & I. Williams, Power Pix International Picture Library (1968), Castle Lodge, Wenvoe, Cardiff CF5 6AD *tel* (01222) 595163 *fax* (01222) 593905. Worldwide travel, people and views, girl and 'mood-pix', sub-aqua, aircraft, flora, fauna, agriculture, children. Agents worldwide.

*Windrush Photos (1991), 99 Noah's Ark, Kemsing, Sevenoaks, Kent TN15 6PD *tel* (01732) 763486 *fax* (01732) 763285. *Owner:* David Tipling. Wildlife, especially birds; any aspect of the environment from pollution to country crafts; Far East and Middle East travel. Photographic and features commissions undertaken. *Terms:* 60% to the photographer.

Timothy Woodcock (1983), 45 Lyewater, Crewkerne, Somerset TA18 8BB *tel* (01460) 74488 *fax* (01460) 74988. British and Eire landscape, seascape, architecture and heritage; children, parenthood, adults and education; gardens and containers; mountain biking. Location commissions undertaken. *Terms:* 50%.

*Woodmansterne Publications Ltd, 1 The Boulevard, Blackmoor Lane, Watford, Herts. WD1 8YW *tel* (01923) 228236 *fax* (01923) 245788. Britain, Europe, Holy Land; architecture, cathedral and stately home interiors; general art subjects; museum collections; natural history, butterflies, geography, volcanoes, transport, Space; opera and ballet; major state occasions; British heritage.

*World Pictures (formerly **Feature-Pix Colour Library**), 85a Great Portland Street, London W1N 5RA   *tel* 0171-437 2121/436 0440   *fax* 0171-439 1307. *Directors:* Gerry Brenes, Joan Brenes, David Brenes. Over 600,000 medium and large format colour transparencies aimed at travel and travel-related markets. Extensive coverage of cities, countries and specific resort areas, together with material of an emotive nature, i.e. children, couples and families on holiday, all types of winter and summer sporting activities, motoring abroad, etc. *Terms:* 50%; major contributing photographers 60%.

Murray Wren Picture Library, 3 Hallgate, London SE3 9SG   *tel* 0181-852 7556. Outdoor nudes; nudist holiday resorts and activities in Europe and elsewhere; historic and erotic art of the nude through the ages. Media enquiries only; no new photographers required.

The Allan Wright Photo Library t/a Cauldron Press Ltd (1986), The Stables, Parton, Castle Douglas, Kirkcudbrightshire, Scotland DG7 3NB   *tel* (016444) 70260   *fax* (016444) 70202. North Sea oil, offshore life 'on the rigs', Dumfries and Galloway, Argyll and Scottish highlands, scenic and environmental.

*York Archaeological Trust Picture Library (1987), Piccadilly House, 55 Piccadilly, York YO1 1PL   *tel* (01904) 663044/663000   *fax* (01904) 640029. *Picture librarian:* C. Daniell. York archaeology covering Romans, Dark Ages, Vikings and Middle Ages; traditional crafts; scenes of York and Yorkshire.

Yorkshire in Focus, 75A Selby Road, Garforth, Leeds LS25 1LR   *tel* (0113) 286 3016. Transparencies, 35 mm/6 × 9 cm. Landscapes, rivers, buildings, tourist attractions in Yorkshire and the north. Camping and caravanning subjects: sites, caravans, motor caravans, tents and all equipment. Large collection of touristy stock subjects. Assignments undertaken.

*Zoological Society of London (1826), Regent's Park, London NW1 4RY   *tel* 0171-449 6293   *fax* 0171-586 5743. *Librarian:* Ann Sylph. Archive collection of photographs, paintings and prints, from the 16th century onwards, covering almost all vertebrate animals, many now extinct or rare, plus invertebrates.

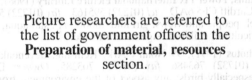

Picture researchers are referred to the list of government offices in the **Preparation of material, resources** section.

Classified Index of Picture Agencies and Libraries

This index gives the major subject area(s) only of each entry in the main listing which begins on page 343, and should be used with discrimination.

Aerial Photography

Aerofilms Ltd
Aviation Picture Library

Geo Aerial Photography
Sealand Aerial Photography

Skyscan Photolibrary

Africa

Academic File News Agency
Animal Photography
Hamish Brown, Scottish
    Photographic
Sue Cunningham
    Photographic

David Hosking (animals)
Images of Africa Photobank
Joe Filmbase

Link Picture Library
    (South Africa)
Panos Pictures
Tropix Photographic Library

Agriculture and Farming

The Anthony Blake Photo
    Library
Blitz International News &
    Photo Agency
Dennis Davis Photography

Frontline Photo Press Agency
Heritage & Natural History
    Photography
Frank Lane Picture Agency
    Ltd

Holt Studios International
Planet Earth Pictures
Seaco Picture Library
Sutcliffe Gallery

Aircraft and Aviation

Air Photo Supply
Aviation Photographs
    International
Aviation Picture Library

Dr Alan Beaumont
Brooklands Museum Picture
    Library

Photo Link
Patrick Smith Associates

Archaeology, Antiquities, Ancient Monuments and Heritage

A.A. and A. Ancient Art &
    Architecture Collection
Lesley and Roy Adkins
    Picture Library
Rev. J. Catling Allen
C.M. Dixon
English Heritage Photo
    Library

Werner Forman Archive
Fortean Picture Library
Heritage & Natural History
    Photography
Pat Hodgson Library
Chandra S. Perera Cinetra
Mick Sharp

Sites, Sights and Cities
Skyscan Balloon Photography
Woodmansterne Publications
    Ltd
York Archaeological Trust
    Picture Library

Architecture, Houses and Interiors

A.A. & A. Ancient Art and
    Architecture Collection
Abode Interiors
ARCAID Architectural
    Photography and Picture
    Library

Archivio Veneziano
Bookart Architecture Picture
    Library
Dennis Davis Photography
English Heritage Photo
    Library

Houses & Interiors
    Photographic Features
    Agency
Woodmansterne Publications
    Ltd

Art, Sculpture and Crafts

A.A. & A. Ancient Art and
    Architecture Collection
Abode Interiors Photographic
    Library
Academic File News Agency

Archivio Veneziano
Bodleian Library
Bookart Architecture Picture
    Library
Bridgeman Art Library

Crafts Council Picture Library
Werner Forman Archive
Photo Resources
Retrograph Nostalgia Archive
    Ltd

Asia

Academic File News Agency
Douglas Dickins Photo
  Library
Japan Archive
Link Picture Library (India)

Ann & Bury Peerless
Photo Flora
Royal Society for Asian
  Affairs

Society for Anglo-Chinese
  Understanding
Travel Ink Photo & Feature
  Library (Hong Kong)

Australia and New Zealand

Australia Pictures

George A. Dey

Britain (See also Ireland, Scotland)

Rev. J. Catling Allen
John Blake Picture Library
Britain on View Photographic
  Library
David Broadbent/Peak
  District Pictures
Collections
Cumbria Picture Library
English Heritage Photo
  Library
Fotoccompli—The Picture
  Library
Leslie Garland Picture Library
  (North England)

Global Syndications
Isle of Wight Pictures
Just Europe
Lakeland Life Picture Library
  (Lake District)
Landscape Only
Merseyside Photo Library
The Mustograph Agency
Patrick Smith Associates
  (Wales)
Spectrum Colour Library
Travel Ink Photo & Feature
  Library (Wales)
Vidocq Photo Library

Viewfinder Colour Photo
  Library
Simon Warner (North
  England)
Westcountry Pictures (Devon,
  Cornwall)
Roy J. Westlake
Derek G. Widdicombe
Timothy Woodcock
Woodmansterne Publications
  Ltd
York Archaeological Trust
  Picture Library
Yorkshire in Focus

Business, Industry and Commerce

Financial Times Pictures

Camping and Caravanning

Roy J. Westlake

Yorkshire in Focus

Children and People (See also Social Issues)

Attard Photolibrary
Barnardo's Photographic
  Archive
Collections
Lupe Cunha

Brian Gadsby Picture Library
Robert Haas Photo Library
The Hutchinson Library
David Muscroft Picture
  Library

Photofusion
Telegraph Colour Library
Timothy Woodcock

Cities and Towns (See also London)

Lesley and Roy Adkins
  Picture Library
Financial Times Pictures

Robert Haas Photo Library
Sites, Sights and Cities

Skyscan Photolibrary
Waterways Photo Library

Civilisations, Cultures and Way of Life

Bryan and Cherry Alexander
  Photography
Werner Forman Archive

Christine Osborne Pictures/
  MEP
Photo Resources

Still Pictures Whole Earth
  Photo Library

Countryside and Rural Life (See also Landscapes)

Dr Alan Beaumont
Ron and Christine Foord
Forest Life Picture Library
Tim Graham

Isle of Wight Pictures
Lakeland Life Picture Library
Sutcliffe Gallery

Waterways Photo Library
Wildlife Matters Photographic
  Library

Developing Countries

Geoslides
Christine Osborne Pictures/
    MEP

Panos Pictures
Still Pictures Whole Earth
    Photo Library

Tropix Photographic Library

Environment, Conservation, Ecology and Habitats

Heather Angel
Aquila Photographics
Ardea London Ltd
Dr Alan Beaumont
Butterflies
Bruce Coleman Ltd
George A. Dey (forestry,
    natural history)
Ecoscene
Environmental Investigation
    Agency

Fogden Natural History
    Photographs
Forest Life Picture Library
Martin and Dorothy Grace
Harper Horticultural Slide
    Library
Holt Studios International
Frank Lane Picture Agency
    Ltd
Chris Mattison
Natural Image

NHPA
Papilio Natural History &
    Travel Library
Planet Earth Pictures
Premaphotos Wildlife
Still Pictures Whole Earth
    Photo Library
Tropix Photographic Library
Wildlife Matters Photographic
    Library
Windrush Photos

Europe and Eastern Europe (*excluding* UK/Ireland)

Archivio Veneziano (Venice)
Das Photo
James Davis Travel
    Photography
Douglas Dickins Photo
    Library
C.M. Dixon

Lesley Garland Picture
    Library (Norway)
Global Syndications
    (Scandinavia)
Joe Filmbase
Just Europe
Panos Pictures (Eastern
    Europe)

Russia & Republics
    Photolibrary
Vidocq Photo Library
Weimar Archive (Germany)
David Williams Picture
    Library (Iceland)

Food

The Anthony Blake Photo
    Library
Cephas Picture Library

Footprints Colour Picture
    Library

Retrograph Nostalgia Archive

Gardens, Gardening and Horticulture (*See also* Plant Life)

A-Z Botanical Collection
Ardea London Ltd
B. & B. Photographs
Butterflies
Collections
Dennis Davis Photography
Forest Life Picture Library

Garden Matters Photographic
    Library
John Glover Photography
Harper Horticultural Slide
    Library
Holt Studios
    International

Houses & Interiors
    Photographic Features
    Agency
S. & O. Mathews
Natural Image
Peter Stiles Picture Library
Timothy Woodcock

General and Stock Libraries

Ace Photo Agency
Aspect Picture Library Ltd
Bandphoto Agency
Barnaby's Picture Library
Stephen Benson Slide Bureau
Blitz International News &
    Photo Agency
J. Allan Cash Photolibrary
Cephas Picture Library
Bruce Coleman Inc.
Bruce Coleman Ltd
Colorific Photo Library
Sylvia Cordaiy Photo Library

C.P.L. (Camerapix Picture
    Library)
Barry Davies
C.M. Dixon
Greg Evans International
    Photo Library
Fotoccompli—The Picture
    Library
Freelance Focus
Frontline Photo Press Agency
Geo Aerial Photography
GeoScience Features
Geoslides

Robert Harding Picture
    Library
Horizon International
    Creative Images
Hulton Deutsch Collection
The Hutchison Library
The Image Bank
Images Colour Library
Joe Filmbase
Lears Magical Lanterns
    Museum
The MacQuitty International
    Collection

News Blitz International
The Northern Picture Library
Orion Press
Photo Library International
Photofusion
The Photographers' Library
Pictor International Ltd
Popperfoto (Paul Popper Ltd)
Pro-file Photo Library
Raleigh International Picture
  Library
Retna Pictures Ltd

Rich Research
Royal Geographical Society
  Picture Library
The Royal Photographic
  Society
Dawn Runnals Photographic
  Library
S & G Press Agency Ltd
Source Photographic Archives
Spectrum Colour Library
Tony Stone Images

Telegraph Colour Library
Universal Pictorial Press &
  Agency Ltd (UPPA)
Vidocq Photo Library
Viewfinder Colour Photo
  Library
Derek G. Widdicombe
S. & I. Williams, Power Pix
  International Picture
  Library
Yorkshire in Focus

Geography, Biogeography and Topography

Arctic Camera
B. & B. Photographs

John Blake Picture Library

Geoslides

Glamour, Moods and Nudes

Attard Photolibrary
The Photographers' Library
Transworld/Scope

S. & I. Williams, Power Pix
  International Picture
  Library

Murray Wren Picture Library

Health and Medicine

Lupe Cunha
Royal Society of Chemistry
  Library

Science & Society Picture
  Library

Shout Picture Library

High-Tech, High-Speed, Macro/Micro, Special Effects and Step-by-Step

Earth Images Picture Library
  (high-tech)
Houses & Interiors
  Photographic Features
  Agency (step-by-step)

The Image Bank (high-tech,
  special effects)
Microscopix
NHPA (high-speed)

Oxford Scientific Films Ltd,
  Photo Library (special
  effects)

History

Barnardo's Photographic
  Archive
Bodleian Library
Mary Evans Picture Library
Frost Historical Newspaper
  Collection
Historical Picture Service

Pat Hodgson Library
The Billie Love Historical
  Collection
Mansell Collection Ltd
Pixfeatures
The Royal Photographic
  Society

Royal Society of Chemistry
  Library
Science & Society Picture
  Library
Topham Picturepoint
Weimar Archive (Europe)

Illustrations, Prints, Engravings, Lithographs and Cartoons

Allied Artists Ltd
Bodleian Library
Mary Evans Picture Library

The Illustrated London News
  Picture Library
The Billie Love Historical
  Collection

Punch Cartoon Library
Royal Society of Chemistry
  Library
Zoological Society of London

Ireland

Picturepoint

The Slide File

Source Photographic Archives

Landscapes and Scenics

Bookart Architecture Picture
  Library

Cumbria Picture Library
Barry Davies

James Davis Travel
Photography

George A. Dey (Scottish)
Eyeline Photography
Geo Aerial Photography
John Glover Photography
Isle of Wight Pictures
Landscape Only
S. & O. Mathews
Chris Mattison

Scotland in Focus Picture
  Library
Mick Sharp
Skyscan Photolibrary
Peter Stiles Picture Library
The Still Moving Picture
  Company

Charles Tait Photo Library
Simon Warner
Roy J. Westlake
Derek G. Widdicombe
The Allan Wright Photo
  Library

Latin America

Andes Press Agency
Das Photo

Fogden Natural History
  Photographs

London

ARCAID Architectural
  Photographic and Picture
  Library
Greater London Record
  Office

Historical Picture Service
The Illustrated London News
  Picture Library

Monitor Syndication
Skyscan Photolibrary
Patrick Smith Associates

Middle East

Academic File News Agency
Stephen Benson Slide Bureau
Das Photo

Christine Osborne Pictures/
  MEP

Ann & Bury Peerless

Military and Armed Forces

Air Photo Supply
Aviation Photographs
  International

Imperial War Museum
Military History Picture
  Library

The Tank Museum Photo
  Library & Archive

Mountains

Hamish Brown, Scottish
  Photographic
Mountain Dynamics

Mountain Visions
Royal Geographical Society
  Picture Library

Wilderness Photographic
  Library

Natural History (*See also* Environment, Plant life)

A-Z Botanical Collection
Heather Angel
Animal Photography
Aquila Photographics
Ardea London Ltd
B. & B. Photographs
Dr Alan Beaumont
Bird Images
David Broadbent/Peak
  District Pictures (birds)
Butterflies
Bruce Coleman Ltd
Sylvia Cordaiy Photo Library
Barry Davies
Gordon Dickson (fungi,
  insects)
Ecoscene
Environmental Investigation
  Agency

Fogden Natural History
  Photographs
Ron and Christine Foord
  (insects)
Footprints Colour Picture
  Library
Brian Gadsby Picture Library
Geoscience Features
Martin and Dorothy Grace
Heritage & Natural History
  Photography (insects,
  especially bees)
David Hosking (birds)
Image Diggers
Michael Leach (owls)
Chris Mattison (reptiles,
  amphibians)
Natural Image
NHPA

Oxford Scientific Films Ltd,
  Photo Library
Papilio Natural History &
  Travel Library
Planet Earth Pictures
Premaphotos Wildlife
Roundhouse Ornithology
  Collection
Steffi Schubert, Wildlife
  Conservation Collection
  Photographic Library
Scotland in Focus Picture
  Library
Peter Stiles Picture Library
Still Pictures Whole Earth
  Photo Library
Wildlife Matters Photographic
  Agency
Windrush Photos
Zoological Society of London

Nautical and Maritime

Peter Cumberlidge Photo
Library

National Maritime Museum
Picture Library

Seaco Picture Library

News, Features and Photo Features

Academic File News Photos
The Associated Press Ltd
Bandphoto Agency
BIPS
Blitz International News &
Photo Agency

Financial Times Pictures
Frost Historical Newspaper
Collection
International Press Agency
(Pty) Ltd
News Blitz International

PA News Photo Library
Chandra S. Perera Cinetra
Pixfeatures
S & G Press Agency Ltd
Topham Picturepoint

North America

American History Picture
Library

Douglas Dickins Photo
Library

Western Americana Picture
Library

Nostalgia, Ephemera and Advertising

Fotomas Index

Retrograph Nostalgia Archive
Ltd

Performing Arts (Theatre, Dance, Music)

Aquarius Picture Library
Camera Press Ltd
The Dance Library
Famous
Image Diggers

Jazz Index
Link Picture Library (music)
Mander & Mitchenson
Theatre Collection

Sylvia Pitcher
Theatre Museum
John Vickers Theatre
Collection

Personalities and Portraits (*See also* **Royalty**)

Aquarius Picture Library
Camera Press Ltd
Famous
Financial Times Pictures
Mark Gerson Photography
Tim Graham
Pat Hodgson Library
(historical)
JS Library International

Mander & Mitchenson
Theatre Collection
Monitor Syndication
Newsfocus Press Photograph
Agency
Punch Cartoon Library
Retna Pictures Ltd
The Royal Photographic
Society

Royal Society of Chemistry
Library
Syndication International Ltd
Topham Picturepoint
Universal Pictorial Press &
Agency Ltd (UPPA)
John Vickers Theatre
Collection

Plant Life (*See also* **Gardens**)

A-Z Botanical Collection Ltd
Heather Angel
Aquila Photographics
Ron and Christine Foord
Garden Matters Photographic
Library

John Glover Photography
Martin and Dorothy Grace
Harper Horticultural Slide
Library

Photo Flora
Premaphotos Wildlife
Source Photographic Archives

Polar and Arctic

Bryan and Cherry Alexander
Photography
Arctic Camera

Global Syndications
Royal Geographical Society
Picture Library

Wilderness Photographic
Library

Religions and Religious Monuments

Lesley and Roy Adkins
Picture Library
Rev. J. Catling Allen

Andes Press Agency
Ann & Bury Peerless

Photo Resources
Peter Sanders Photography

Royalty

Camera Press Ltd
Tim Graham
JS Library International

Monitor Syndication
Newsfocus Press Photograph
Agency

Syndication International Ltd

Russia

John Massey Stewart
The Russia and Republics
Photo Library

SCR Photo Library

Science, Technology and Meteorology

Ace Photo Agency
Earth Images Picture Library
Leslie Garland Picture Library
GeoScience Features

Frank Lane Picture Agency
Ltd
Microscopix
Ann Ronan at Image Select

Science Photo Library
Science & Society Picture
Library

Scotland

Hamish Brown, Scottish
Photographic
George A. Dey (castles,
Highland Games)
Scotland in Focus Picture
Library

The Still Moving Picture
Company
Charles Tait Photo Library
Simon Warner

David Williams Picture
Library
The Allan Wright Photo
Library

Social Issues and Social History

Andes Press Agency
Barnardo's Photographic
Archive
John Birdsall Photography
Mary Evans Picture
Library

Greater London Record
Office
Imperial War Museum
Photofusion

Ann Ronan at Image Select
Shout Picture Library
Welfare History Picture
Library

South America

Animal Photography
(Galapagos)
Australia Pictures

Stephen Benson Slide Bureau
Lupe Cunha (Brazil)

Sue Cunningham
Photographic (Brazil)
David Hosking (Falklands)

Space and Astronomy

Aspect Picture Library
Earth Images Picture Library
Galaxy Picture Library

Genesis Space Photo Library
National Maritime Museum
Picture Library

Science Photo Library

Sport and Leisure

Action Plus
Allsport Photographic Ltd
The Associated Press Ltd
John Blake Photo Library
(equestrian)
Boxing Picture Library
Michael Cole Camerawork
Cumbria Picture Library
(snooker)

Peter Dazeley (golf)
Eyeline Photography
(watersports, equestrian)
Frontline Photo Press Agency
Mountain Visions (skiing)
Skishoot – Offshoot
Sporting Pictures (UK) Ltd
The Still Moving Picture
Company

B M Totterdell Photography
(volleyball)
Ulster Photography Agency
(motorsport)
Universal Pictorial Press &
Agency Ltd (UPPA)
World Pictures

Strange Phenomena, Occult and Mystical

Fortean Picture Library
Image Diggers

Sites, Sights and Cities

The Charles Walker
Collection

Transport (Cars and Motoring, Railways)

Brooklands Museum Picture
Library
Ludvigsen Library
Motorcycles Unlimited

National Maritime Museum
Picture Library
National Motor Museum.
Beaulieu

Railways—Milepost 92½
Science & Society Picture
Library
Ulster Photographic Agency

Travel and Tourism

Ace Photo Agency
Air Photo Supply
ARCAID Architectural
Photography and Picture
Library
Aspect Picture Library
Aviation Picture Library
Bandphoto Agency
The Anthony Blake Photo
Library
Britain on View Photographic
Library
Cephas Picture Library
Sylvia Cordaiy Picture
Library
Peter Cumberlidge Photo
Library
Sue Cunningham
Photographic
James Davis Travel
Photography

Ecoscene
Greg Evans International
Photo Library
Footprints Colour Picture
Library
Fotoccompli—The Picture
Library
Brian Gadsby Picture Library
The Hutchinson Library
The Illustrated London News
Picture Library
JS Library International
Just Europe
Landscape Only
Mountain Visions
Papilio Natural History &
Travel Library
Photo Flora
The Photographers' Library

Raleigh International Picture
Library
Peter Sanders Photography
Seaco Picture Library
Mick Sharp
Skishoot – Offshoot
Spectrum Colour Library
Charles Tait Photo Library
Telegraph Colour Library
Travel Images
Travel Ink Photo & Feature
Library
Travel Photo International
Viewfinder Colour Photo
Library
Wilderness Photographic
Library
Windrush Photos
World Pictures

Waterways

Peter Cumberlidge Photo
Library

Waterways Photo Library

Roy J. Westlake

Markets for Transparencies and Photographs for Greetings Cards, Calendars and Viewcards

Before submitting examples of work, in their own interest, photographers are advised to write a preliminary letter to ascertain requirements, including terms and conditions. Only top quality material should be submitted; inferior work is never accepted. *Postage for return of material should be enclosed.*

*Member of the Greeting Card Association

*Abacus Cards Ltd (1991), Gazeley Road, Kentford, Newmarket, Suffolk CB8 7QB *tel* (01638) 552399 *fax* (01638) 552103. *Partners:* Jeff Fothergill and Brian Carey; *art director:* Bev Demant. Quality greetings cards. Florals, garden scenes, still lifes etc.; submit 35mm transparencies or larger formats.

*Chapter and Verse (1981), Granta House, 96 High Street, Linton, Cambs. CB1 6JT *tel* (01223) 891951 *fax* (01223) 894137. Buildings, animals, flowers, scenic, or domestic subjects in series, suitable for greetings cards and postcards. All sizes of transparency. No verses.

Dennis Print and Publishing, Printing House Square, Melrose Street, Scarborough, North Yorkshire YO12 7SJ *tel* (01723) 500555 *fax* (01723) 501488/500545. Interested in first-class transparencies for reproduction as local view postcards and calendars. 3¼ × 2¼ in or 35 mm transparencies ideal for postcard reproduction.

*Giesen & Wolff (UK) Ltd (1908), Kaygee House, Rothersthorpe Crescent, Northampton NN4 9JD *tel* (01604) 709499 *fax* (01604) 709399. *Contact:* Art Manager. Transparencies, 2¼ in sq minimum: floral studies, still life.

Hambledon Studios Ltd, Hambledon House, Marlborough Road, Accrington, Lancs. BB5 6BX *tel* (01254) 872255/872266 *fax* (01254) 872079. *Art managers:* D. Jaundrell, J. Ashton, D. Fuller, N. Harrison, K. Ellis; *creative director:* M. Smith. Photos for reproduction as greetings cards. *Brands:* Arnold Barton, Donny Mac, Reflections, New Image.

*Images & Editions (1984), Bourne Road, Essendine, Nr Stamford, Lincs. PE9 4UW *tel* (01780) 57118 *fax* (01780) 54629. *Directors:* Lesley Forrow, Maurice Miller. Greetings cards, giftwrap, gift products and social stationery: flowers, gardens and landscape, animals, especially cats and teddy bears. Any format accepted; transparencies preferred.

Jane's Information Group, Sentinel House, 163 Brighton Road, Coulsdon, Surrey CR5 2NH *tel* 0181-700 3700 *telex* 916907 JANES G *fax* 0181-700 1006. Considers defence, aerospace and transportation transparencies.

Jarrold Publishing (1770), Whitefriars, Norwich NR3 1TR *tel* (01603) 763300 *fax* (01603) 662748. *Managing director:* Antony Jarrold; *publishing director:* Caroline Jarrold. Transparencies (35 mm or larger) for calendars. Verses not required.

Pomegranate Europe Ltd (1993), Fullbridge House, Fullbridge, Maldon, Essex CM9 4LE *tel* (01621) 851646 *fax* (01621) 852426. *Sales director:* Dave Harris. Photographs or transparencies (any size) for cards, calendars, postcards and posters: art, architecture, the environment, Third World issues and art, history, politics and photography.

J. Salmon Ltd, 100 London Road, Sevenoaks, Kent TN13 1BB *tel* (01732) 452381 *fax* (01732) 450951. Picture postcards, calendars, local view booklets and greeting cards.

*Scandecor Ltd (1967), 3 The Ermine Centre, Hurricane Close, Huntingdon, Cambs. PE18 6XX *tel* (01480) 456395 *fax* (01480) 456269. *Director:* G. Huldtgren. Transparencies all sizes.

See also the **Articles, reports and short stories** and the **Books** sections for lists of magazines and publishers.

Picture research

Picture Research

JENNIE KARRACH

Picture research is the art of obtaining pictures – photos and illustrations – suitable for reproduction, which suit the project's brief, budget and deadline. It also includes the clearance of permissions, copyright, the negotiation of rights and fees, and the eventual return of pictures to their owners at the end of the project. Given the incidence of pictures in daily life it can be appreciated that picture researchers are responsible for supplying a vast range of clients, in the book and magazine industry, both publishers and packagers, advertising agencies, film, television and video companies, newspapers and exhibition organisers. Although the skills involved in picture research are relevant in all these contexts, the type of pictures required varies enormously. As a result researchers tend to specialise in the type of work they undertake, and they may well have a specialist knowledge of one particular area, such as science and technology.

Picture researchers are employed either as staff members or freelance by the hour, day, for the duration of the project, as appropriate. An employee working full time on a long-running project may have time to carry out extensive research, but freelance work is often constrained by the client's budget and schedule. It is here that experience counts. Knowing where to find material quickly to suit the brief saves time and therefore money. The researcher's fees are often included in the total budget, so that although the final deadline for delivery of pictures to the client may be a month away, the total allowed for picture research amounts to three days' work. It may be that this is unrealistic, and that the job will require five days. These details all need to be clarified at the outset and some sort of agreement listing the picture brief, deadlines, budget and invoicing particulars needs to be drawn up. It is important to put everything in writing so that in the event of dispute both parties can refer back to the agreement. Pictures themselves are often worth large amounts of money, and in the event of loss it will become difficult to agree who will pay compensation unless this has been pre-arranged. It can also prove difficult to collect payment for work completed, so it may be advisable to agree upon regular payments and an advance to cover expenses such as travel, postage and telephone, etc.

THE BRIEF

It is important to clarify the brief so that both parties, the picture researcher and the editor/design team, are agreed upon the image required. It may be that the picture requested needs no further description – a work of art, by a well-known artist, e.g. *The Mona Lisa* by Leonardo da Vinci, to be used in colour. Or it may be that the picture is to depict an historical event which occurred long before the advent of photography. What is required? A photo of a contemporary manuscript which describes the incident, or perhaps a contemporary illumination exists. Or does the client have in mind an illustration executed by a more recent artist, perhaps a nineteenth-century engraving? Or perhaps a photograph of the remains of an historic site? It may be that the client has no one image in mind, but rather needs to evoke a specific mood, or provoke a reaction. This is often the case in advertising campaigns. Pictures are highly subjective, and what is evocative to some will appear bleak to others. A good picture researcher is able to capture the image conjured up in a picture meeting, responding to the ideas of an art director or editor.

It may be that the picture required must be a specific shape – portrait (upright) or landscape (horizontal), or it may need to have an area lacking in detail, such as sky, into which text can fit. Or a dark area suitable for text reversal. If there are too many design constraints it may be cost effective to commission a photographer, rather than to search for a non-existent 'existing' photo.

THE BUDGET, RIGHTS AND DEADLINE

Once the brief has been agreed, the budget, rights and deadline must be confirmed. These are interdependent. Picture fees increase according to the size and use made of the image; for instance, a picture used at quarter-page size in a school textbook will cost less than one used quarter-page size in a glossy, adult non-fiction book. Fees vary according to the media: books, magazines, television, video, CD-ROM, etc. The print run/circulation of a book/magazine also affects the price charged for use. Fees are calculated also according to the rights requested. The larger the territory, the larger the fee, although the percentage increase between the various categories will vary from agency to agency. The territories sold are usually: UK only; UK and first foreign edition; English language, world rights, excluding US; English language, world rights, including US; world rights, all languages. It may well be that, as the European Union attempts to remove trade barriers, the rights available will change.

Other fees will need to be budgeted for. Many commercial picture agencies charge 'research' or 'service' fees. These may be linked to the amount of material they are loaning or there may be a fixed charge levied. In both cases the source should advise of this at the initial enquiry stage. Some will only charge if a personal visit is not possible and pictures are despatched by a member of their staff. The levying of these fees can erode the total picture budget quickly. It is not unusual to receive a service fee of £30, which may be acceptable if this is the only source used, and the pictures obtained are accepted by the client. However, on projects where a selection of pictures to cover a wider range of topics is required, many sources will have to be approached. It is worth discussing service fees at the outset. It is not unknown for agencies to waive or reduce them if it increases the likelihood of a sale. Some only charge the service fee if all pictures are returned and none selected for use. Other sources do not loan out material but instead sell copy transparencies or prints. This is usually the case with museums who can supply a transparency of a particular object or manuscript, but are unable to respond to a vague request for a selection of pictures for possible use. A transparency of reproduction quality may cost £20, or more, if a 'rush job' surcharge is added on.

Most commercial picture libraries or agencies operate on a loan system. Pictures are selected and loaned for an agreed period, usually a month. After this time material not required should be returned and some indication given as to the fate of the pictures still held. Is a subsequent picture selection to be made, or are those retained going to be used? If material is kept longer than the agreed loan period, then holding fees may be charged. These should only be levied if a reminder sent fails to elicit news of the pictures or return. (Freelance picture researchers need to make sure that such reminders are forwarded to them either by the source or sent on by the client.) Holding fees are charged per picture, per week over the deadline, and are usually waived if a reasonable extension to the free loan period is requested.

PICTURE SOURCES

Sources are many and various. They include government departments, institutions, companies, libraries, commercial picture libraries and agencies, individual collectors, and individual photographers. Some of these sources supply pictures without charge, but that is not to say that they are necessarily easy to obtain, or that no copyright pertains. Many sources are not primarily concerned with the supply of pictures and give it low priority. Access to the collection may be limited to research students and those who hold a reader's card. Enquiries may have to be made in writing, and the idea of urgency is an alien one. Or lack of resources may prevent an efficient service.

There is no one source book which lists all picture sources and if one existed it would run to many volumes and be in need of constant updating. Commercial libraries and agencies maintain a high profile, advertising by mail shots to prospective clients. The larger ones produce glossy catalogues, usually free, which include a selection of their images, enough to give a flavour of the type of stock held.

New technology is affecting picture storage and use. Some large agencies produce CD-ROMs which clients can purchase for future reference. These discs allow rapid viewing of thousands of images. On-line facilities at news agencies allow quick transmission of pictures to clients and use of the World Wide Web via the Internet enables subscribers to browse and download high resolution images for use. There are serious implications for copyright control resulting from electronic storage, e.g. unauthorised use or manipulation of photographs.

'General stock libraries' hold pictures which fall into the following broad categories: travel, architecture, food, business, science/medicine, people, sport, nature, animals, transport, etc. They would almost certainly hold pictures of famous foreign landmarks, e.g. the Eiffel Tower, photographed from the ground, the air, by night, by day, with lovers . . . It is much more difficult to find pictures of less glamorous sites. Street furniture, cars and pedestrians date quickly, and some agencies, keen to keep pictures saleable for as long as possible, will attempt to keep such features to a minimum. The result is strange; London, peopled only by bobbies and red buses, Venice reduced to St Mark's Square and gondoliers on the Grand Canal, Los Angeles depicted by traffic on freeways. This problem extends to the 'people' pictures, which tend to be stereotypes posed by models. It is not impossible to find pictures of 'real' people going about everyday activities, but it can be time-consuming. Directories cannot hope to express the nuances of photographic collections, and it is only over time, after visits to many sources, that an overview of the range available will emerge. Specialist picture libraries are usually one-subject libraries, and cover the whole range of picture needs. The level of captioning is usually higher in specialist sources as the photographer has expert knowledge. It can be the case that a good quality photograph badly captioned is rendered useless. A photo filed in the 'elderly people' category of a general stock agency showed a woman standing in a slight depression in the desert somewhere. The woman was actually a famous anthropologist, but her name meant nothing to the library so she had been miscaptioned and then wrongly filed. It may be that for certain purposes any train, boat, car, etc. will be acceptable, but if the picture required is of a specific model then it is frustrating to find insubstantial captions and undated pictures.

USE OF PHOTOS

Once pictures have been found which fit the brief, the next stage is clearance for use. Permission must be sought from the copyright holder for use of particular photos in set contexts. The supply of photos does not automatically guarantee permission to reproduce. It may be that the agency or picture source is not the copyright holder, and permission has to be sought elsewhere. This is often the case with photos of works of art still in copyright. The artist, or the artist's estate, may be represented by a copyright protection society such as DACS (Design and Artists Copyright Society – see page 607), which will approach the estate or artist on behalf of a picture researcher and, if permission is granted, often subject to conditions, issue a licence. Conditions could include the right to approve colour proofs. The production department or designer of the project would therefore need to be informed to allow time in the schedule. DACS have reciprocal representation agreements with similar copyright protection societies in some 26 countries. This simplifies a copyright enquiry considerably but sufficient time should be allowed for clearance. It may take a day or several weeks. If the copyright holder and the supplier of the photograph are not one and the same, then a fee may be due to both parties.

It may be that the context in which the photo is to appear is a sensitive one, perhaps an article about child abuse, divorce, AIDS, or that the caption is to make some derogatory statement about the subject. If this is the case it is important to be honest about the context with the supplier of the photo. If the article is educational and positive in its approach, then the photo will play a different role from one appearing in an exposé of shameful goings on. It is prudent to enquire whether the photographer has obtained 'model release' from the subject in the photo. In return for a sum of money the model grants the photographer the right to sell the photos taken. This is standard procedure at photo sessions, where a particular shot has been commissioned by a client, or a personality has granted a shoot. The release may have certain riders attached as to use, precisely to avoid certain contexts.

It may be that the agency grants permission to use the photo in a sensitive area, but insists on a declaration appearing with it or with the photo credits 'all photos posed by models'. Or it may be that the agency or photographer do not have model release for the photo. At present in the UK, if a person is photographed in public they cannot prevent that photo being published. Hence the breed of paparazzi photographers. There is as yet no law protecting against the invasion of privacy. (The situation is different in the USA.) As a result many British photo libraries hold photos of members of the public, taken 'in the public domain' for which they hold no model release. Most agencies reproduce the following or similar statement in their Terms & Conditions: 'although the agency takes all reasonable care, the agency shall not be liable for any loss or damage suffered by the client or by any third party arising from any defect in the picture or its caption, or in any way from its reproduction.' The onus is put onto the picture user. It is fair to say that if the context of the photo is an innocent one, most members of the public are pleased to be in the spotlight, and require no more than a complimentary copy of the book, magazine, or whatever.

CAPTIONS

It is important for picture researchers to make caption writers aware that litigation may result from derogatory or inappropriate captions. Staff researchers should attempt to prevent pictures which were obtained for one project, e.g. a book on health care, being transferred to another, such as a booklet on safe sex. Freelance researchers would be well advised to include a paragraph in the agreement mentioned above which would disclaim responsibility for use by the client of pictures supplied in any use other than that stated in the brief, and any subsequent copyright infringement by the client. It is not unknown for clients to withhold information or mislead picture researchers as to the length of the print run, or the production of foreign language editions.

Picture researchers do not generally write captions themselves but may be asked to provide information for captions. This can be very time-consuming if the pictures do not already have a reasonable amount of caption information attached, supplied by the source or photographer.

CREDITS AND COPYRIGHT

Once pictures have been selected, captioned, and sized for the project in hand, the credit or acknowledgement list will need to be drawn up. This usually includes a courtesy line thanking the various picture sources for permission to reproduce photographs. Sources are either listed alphabetically, with page numbers as to where their pictures appear, or the name of the source appears next to the picture.

Under the provisions of the Copyright, Designs and Patents Act 1988, photographers have 'moral rights' which include the right to be identified as the author of a photograph (see page 548). Newspapers, magazines, encyclopedias, and other works of reference, are exempt from crediting contributors, but most will include credits as a matter of course. Under the terms of the 1988 Act photography is copyright for the same duration and in the same way as other works of art. This was for 50 years after the death of the photographer until 1 January, 1996 when 'the Term Directive' was implemented (see page 540). The Term Directive harmonised copyright laws throughout the European Union and it extends the term of copyright in the UK to 70 years after the death of the photographer. Commissioned work, where previously the copyright belonged to the commissioner, is now the property of the photographer. This means that photos can only be kept for a limited period after a photo session, and rights must be agreed in the same way as for stock library images. All photos, used and unused, must be returned to the photographer. Staff photographers as employees do not own copyright on their photos.

A short booklet, *The ABC Guide to UK Photographic Copyright*, has been produced by the British Photographers Liaison Committee (BPLC) which summarises the changes in copyright relevant to photographers brought about by the 1988 Act. Details may be obtained from the Association of Photographers (address opposite).

LAST STAGES

The pictures are now ready to go off to the printer. A final check should be made to see that they have not been damaged by any of the people who have handled them – editors, designers, etc. If the printer returns photos damaged it will be easier to refute claims that pictures were already scratched if everything is checked as a matter of course. If prints or transparencies are damaged, a fee to compensate the agency or photographer is due. This will vary in amount according to whether the picture was an original or a duplicate. Some photographs are irreplaceable. The amount due for loss is stated in the Terms & Conditions listed on the reverse of most delivery notes. This may be in the region of £400 for an original. Sometimes pictures are not damaged irreparably but are returned by the printer with torn mounts, or still sticky from origination. It is best to return such pictures to the printer for cleaning, in case any damage occurs during a DIY cleaning session. Pictures should then be returned to their owners and one or two copies of the book or proofs supplied as evidence of use, as stated in the Terms & Conditions of the source.

GETTING INTO PICTURE RESEARCH

This can be difficult as employers are loath to employ people without experience, and some picture sources are nervous about loaning pictures. A job with a picture library would give an insight into that particular source and might lead into a job as a picture researcher. Jobs in picture libraries, and picture research work, are advertised in the Creative, Media and Sales section of *The Guardian* on Saturdays and Mondays. Sometimes such ads appear in *The Bookseller*, the weekly publishing journal, and *Campaign*, the weekly advertising magazine. These may all be available at the local library. Salaries tend to be low initially as one learns the skills involved. The idea of working freelance may appeal but it is difficult to obtain enough freelance work without the contacts amassed over a period of time. Many picture researchers build up experience working for an employer full time, and then go freelance. This is not without risks. Getting enough work; getting paid for work completed; sorting out tax; National Insurance; motivation; and loneliness are some of the problems which may arise.

USEFUL DIRECTORIES

Picture Sources UK, Rosemary Eakins, Macdonald, 1985. Now out of print but may be available through a library.

Picture Researcher's Handbook, Hilary & Mary Evans, 6th edition, Blueprint Routledge, £39.00 (£42.50 inc. p&p), available from bookshops and The Mary Evans Picture Library, 59 Tranquil Vale, London SE3 0BS   *tel* 0181-318 0034   *fax* 0181-852 7211.

BAPLA Directory, £10. This lists all the current members of the British Association of Picture Libraries and Agencies (BAPLA), at present totalling around 300. Copies available from Sarah Saunders, BAPLA, 18 Vine Hill, London EC1R 5DX   *tel* 0171-713 1780   *fax* 0171-713 1211.

1995 Directory of Photographers, £12.95 inc. p&p, GHP Publishing, Freepost (HU593), Brough HU15 1BR   *tel* (01482) 666036. Fully indexed source book, with over 430 entries of advertising, editorial and commercial photographers, picture libraries and agencies.

USEFUL ORGANISATIONS

BAPLA – see above.

DACS (Design and Artists Copyright Society), St Mary's Clergy House, 2 Whitechurch Lane, London E1 7QR   *tel* 0171-247 1650   *fax* 0171-377 5855.

Association of Photographers, 9-10 Domingo Street, London EC1Y 0lTA   *tel* 0171-608 1441   *fax* 0171-253 3007. Includes fashion and advertising photographers amongst its members.

SPREd (The Society of Picture Researchers and Editors) – see page 384.

Picture Research Course

The Book House Training Centre offers training in picture research in the form of a two-day course, twice yearly (June and December), designed for those working in book publishing. The objective of the course is to give a professional approach to the search for and use of suitable sources; to make picture researchers aware of all the implications of their task: suitability for reproduction, legal and financial aspects, efficient administration.

Details of the course, with the outline of the programme, may be obtained from Book House Training Centre, 45 East Hill, Wandsworth, London SW18 2QZ *tel* 0181-874 2718/4608 *fax* 0181-870 8985.

The London School of Publishing offers a 10-week course in picture research four times a year. Each course takes place between 6.30-8.30pm, one evening per week; a certificate is only awarded on successful completion of a project. A two-day intensive course is also offered twice a year. Further details can be obtained from the Course Director, John Dalton, at David Game House, 69 Notting Hill Gate, London W11 3JS *tel* 0171-221 3399.

SPREd (Society of Picture Researchers and Editors)

SPREd was formed in 1977 as a professional body for picture researchers and picture editors. It is not a trade union but a society for people who work in similar fields, and who wish to share problems and exchange information on all aspects of dealing with illustrations. Its main aims are:

1. To promote the recognition of picture research as a profession, requiring particular skills and knowledge.
2. To promote and maintain professional standards and ethics within the profession.
3. To bring together those involved in the research and publication of visual material and to provide a forum for the exchange of information.
4. To encourage the use of trained researchers throughout publishing and other media, and to ensure common professional standards in all areas of picture use.
5. To provide guidance and advice to its members.

All picture researchers need a wide circle of contacts and a good knowledge of sources. Picture researchers tend to encounter the same problems and have the same need for up-to-date information, but they tend to work in isolation from each other. SPREd sets out to be a clearing house for information. More importantly, it provides an opportunity for researchers to meet each other informally and to exchange ideas and discuss problems. It can be a great relief to discover that others have already met and overcome the very difficulties that are worrying you.

To this end SPREd runs meetings for members, and publishes an occasional magazine to which non-members may subscribe. Advertising space may be purchased in this magazine.

SPREd members sign a Code of Practice which sets out the professional standards expected from a SPREd member and states the responsibilities of a picture researcher.

For further details about SPREd write, enclosing an sae, to The Secretary, 455 Finchley Road, London NW3 6HN *tel* 0171-431 9886/7.

Music

Introduction to Music Publishing

PETER DADSWELL
The Music Publishers' Association Ltd

Although we live in an age in which music is everywhere and is taken for granted, aspiring composers and songwriters abound. Some desperately seek instant fame and fortune firmly convinced that they are gifted with creative talent; others harbour more modest ambitions and are content to see their work in print in the hope that it will eventually gain recognition and critical acclaim. It is the music publisher's lot to try and serve such individuals at a time when new music is competing on an unprecedented scale with other forms of leisure-time occupation and entertainment.

This brief introduction to a few aspects of music publishing will help those interested in making their compositions available to a wider audience, be it educational or the public at large, and tries to dispel a little of the mystique which unfortunately still surrounds music publishing activity.

The role of the music publisher is to find, nurture, promote and protect the original creative output of composers, authors and songwriters by administering their business interests so that they are properly rewarded for the use of their works. Creativity and the commercial acumen required to exploit fully the music produced are seldom to be found in the same person although some do possess the necessary entrepreneurial skills to do both! In most cases, however, it is not possible to be a prolific writer and take care of the fairly demanding degree of promotion or administration needed in professional, and dynamic, modern music publishing. It is only a music publisher who knows what to charge for the use of a copyright musical work in a given situation. Too often the Association receives enquiries from songwriters, composers, agents and even lawyers seeking advice on how much to ask for from users; this is where the expertise of a music publisher is so valuable.

SUBMISSIONS OF COMPOSITIONS TO MUSIC PUBLISHERS

The first hurdle to be overcome in the music publishing process is obtaining acceptance of a work by a music publisher. Thorough research is worthwhile as it is important to establish the kinds of works already in a particular publisher's catalogue, since it is patently foolish to submit a choral work to a brass or wind band specialist!

385

Popular music

Most publishers will listen to unsolicited material submitted on cassettes although there are now some who no longer do so because they will only deal with writers with a known track record. There have been a number of cases where music publishers, record companies and major artists have been frivolously accused of stealing musical works from unknown writers; some music publishers who have been involved in time-wasting litigation have therefore made it their policy not to deal with anyone who is not strongly recommended or referred by reputable colleagues in the industry. All tapes or discs (some creators now produce demonstration compact discs) in this field should be sent in clearly marked with the title, author's name and a short covering letter giving full details of the address and telephone number. A stamped addressed envelope must be enclosed. Only the best items should be submitted and a selection of the two or three most representative works from the songwriter's output will suffice for assessment. Bear in mind that publishers listen to vast quantities of material and the response will rarely be immediate; delays must not be unreasonable, however, and reputable publishers should give an initial indication fairly promptly but it is important to be patient with them. Beware of any company asking for a fee to listen to new music – such a practice is most unusual and ought to be treated with the utmost caution.

The Music Publishers' Association Ltd (MPA), 3rd Floor, Strandgate, 18-20 York Buildings, London WC2N 6JU *tel* 0171-839 7779 publishes a regularly updated members list.

Although artists who do not write music are looking for material to record it is not generally a good idea to send it to them direct; they are busy people and are usually recording or touring. It puts them in a difficult position if they are constantly receiving cassettes, which will probably be passed on to a manager, agent, record producer or record company, and adds to the possibility of the material going astray.

These days many writers regularly perform their own material in pubs, halls and clubs either as individual performers or as members of a band; like record companies many publishers use talent scouts hunting for new creative sounds and publishing projects are frequently begun as a result of seeing and hearing a live performance. In fact it is probably much more common for songwriters to become published through these encounters than as a consequence of a music publisher signing a writer from hearing a demonstration tape. There are a number of Songwriter Showcases and similar events in the London area, details of which can be obtained from the MPA. Most venues throughout the country putting on 'gigs' accept tapes and decide whether they will allow singer/songwriters or new bands to perform at the premises; such exposure also provides an opportunity to have creative effort heard by music publishing personnel. The Internet is starting to be used as a forum for new music but there are obvious risks in using this method of exposure.

It is not normally possible to market song lyrics on their own. Music publishers prefer listening to complete works – songs with words and music. It is therefore important for someone who is unable to compose music, or who recognises that their strength is in writing lyrics, to team up with a person who can produce music prior to approaching a music publisher. If a person who writes words only is unable to display sufficient initiative or enterprise in finding a collaborator, it is unlikely that a publisher will consider lyrics in isolation. Enthusiastic popular song lyricists can normally find partners through music contacts or through friends, or by advertising in the music or local press, and they may also find co-writers by joining the British Academy of Songwriters, Composers and Authors (BASCA; 34 Hanway Street, London W1P 9DE). If, however, a composer or lyricist has already managed to establish a music industry reputation as a specialist in either discipline, a music publisher will provide a matching service and encourage 'co-writes'.

Music primarily intended for print and performance by orchestras, bands and choirs

Other genres of music in a 'serious' or 'classical' style or for the educational market require a different approach. It is most unlikely that a work sent in by someone without reasonably advanced formal musical training or knowledge of compositional techniques will be of a sufficient standard to be accepted. Many talented composers attract the attention of publishers whilst they are still at music college, university or taking a specialist further education course although there are very well-known exceptions who did not follow the established routes. Principals, professors of music and tutors will often be familiar with publishing staff and refer their most talented protégés to them. Promotional staff are also constantly attending concerts to hear new works. The Society for the Promotion of New Music (West Heath Studios, 174 Mill Lane, London NW6 1TB) plays an important role in launching the careers of young composers and does much to encourage them in a variety of ways.

Anyone interested in publication of educational or classical music should submit their material in a similar fashion to that required for popular music for editorial scrutiny, except that the music publisher needs to assess the manuscript or, if it is an opera or musical, a synopsis of the work. Tutorial or instructional works should be submitted in full. Taped extracts of vocal, instrumental, orchestral or band works accompanying the manuscripts are also acceptable.

The composition of music for films, television and for advertising is also a popular and interesting specialist field. This too is an area where the MPA and the organisations listed in the next section can offer preliminary guidance.

COMPETITIONS AND CONTESTS AS A ROUTE FOR SUCCESS

Competitions and contests are events which are monitored by music publishers and the most prestigious of these in the popular music world is the Eurovision Song Contest and its UK preliminary 'Song for Europe'. In recent years the Vivian Ellis Prize sponsored by the Performing Right Society (PRS) has been recognised as a major national competition to encourage composers and librettists to write for the musical stage. Various bodies such as broadcasters, music colleges, commercial sponsors, professional orchestras, trusts and foundations offer prizes to young composers or run competitions for composition. Such events are useful for music publishers.

A publisher expressing positive interest in a musical work should be prepared to explain the basics of any proposed business relationship at the outset. The administrative aspects cannot be overlooked as, whilst creative matters are likely to be discussed in some detail, the aspiring composer or songwriter may not be aware of such matters as normal recommended usage values, accounting time scales and the role of the music industry collecting societies. It is desirable that a composer should be advised to obtain expert independent advice from either a lawyer with experience in the music business or one of the established composer organisations, such as the Association of Professional Composers (APC), BASCA (previously mentioned), Composers' Guild (all at 34 Hanway Street, London W1P 9DE), the Incorporated Society of Musicians (ISM; 10 Stratford Place, London W1N 9AE) or the Musicians' Union (MU; 60-62 Clapham Road, London SW9 0JJ), prior to signing any legally binding document.

DO IT YOURSELF?

As competition is so intense and music publishers are currently minimising their risks in what is essentially a very speculative operation anyway, with the advent of desktop music publishing and origination in the classical world and the use of sequencers or MIDI recorders in the pop sphere, some composers consider this to be the preferable route for them to take, particularly if their work has been rejected by established publishing houses. There are royalty and tax advantages in opting to self-publish, but there are also considerable drawbacks as much work is involved if the promotion and administration is to be really effective. Investment money to start up is required and sufficient capital must be available to print and distribute the works or make recordings for promotional purposes. Careful consideration is recommended for this option.

MUSIC PUBLISHING CONTRACTS

Quite simply the publishing contract will say that the publisher will promote the writer's music and look after their business interests in return for a share in the income it generates. The rights granted under copyright law in the musical works are transferred by the creator to the music publisher and a share of any resultant income is agreed; the more the music is used, the greater the income. The creator and music publisher have other clearly specified obligations to each other and the interests of each should be fairly balanced.

The publishing contract must be clear, unambiguous, comprehensive and should be honoured in both the letter and the spirit showing the obligations of creator and music publisher. Lawyers make a living by using complex language to express basic facts. Ideally agreements should be short, easy to understand and drawn up in plain English. Too many words and lengthy documents can cause problems and it is to be hoped the day will come when less money will be spent on legal costs because contracts are drawn up on a simple basis.

Matters which particularly need to be stated include:

- a title which identifies the musical work(s) and, where appropriate, the nature, agreed length and scope of the work(s).
- the nature of the rights conferred – the ownership of the copyright (an assignment or an exclusive licence), territories and duration. The term (period) of an exclusive agreement should not be excessive.
- the timescale for delivery of the work or manuscript (where appropriate) and for publication of the printed music.
- the payments, royalties and advances (if any) to be paid, what they are for and when they are due.
- the provisions for sub-publishing (licensing); these should not 'erode' income in the publisher's favour.
- the termination and reversion (where appropriate) provisions of the contract.

Even allowing for the wide diversity of musical genres and of music publishing, whether classical, educational, popular, media or background music, it is possible broadly to define the areas of exploitation and administration carried out by the music publisher. Generally speaking the exploitation or promotion of a musical work will involve one or more of the following activities: the release of a commercial sound recording; the issue of a synchronisation licence for an audio-visual use of the work (the incorporation of songs or music in a film soundtrack or television programme); the publication of the work in print for sale or hire; the public performance; the broadcast.

On commercial sound recordings a royalty of 8.5% of the dealer price of each sound carrier, exclusive of VAT, is shared between the music publisher and the composer(s)/authors(s), and, if appropriate, the other copyright musical works on the record. The composer and publisher divisions should always be specified in the publishing agreement. The percentages to be received by the composer and music publisher for public performances and broadcasts of the musical work will also be detailed. These rights are, for the majority of compositions, traditionally assigned to the Performing Right Society and the royalties arising from the exercise of these rights are paid directly to each party.

Royalties for the sales of printed music are generally expressed as a percentage of the retail selling price of the publication and the normal royalty is 10% of this amount. Composers will, if successful, earn royalties on virtually every conceivable use of their music and these days it plays an integral part in feature films, advertising campaigns, television productions and commercial videos, plus all kinds of miscellaneous use such as by service providers or Web sites on the Internet, off-line multimedia products such as CD-ROMs and enhanced CDs, in computer games, telephone lines, musical greetings cards and even underwear! These too must be properly licensed and paid for, but at a time when publishing is exploding into multimedia and many other startling new areas, the proper control of such usage is becoming increasingly difficult. Music publishing is rapidly becoming even more complex as the music is no longer bound to a particular medium as information and entertainment can be accessed with no regard for the media upon which it is delivered. Digital information transmission has effectively separated the content from the carrier.

Music publishers may offer contracts on a work by work basis or an exclusive contract to accept a number of works over a specified period. Exclusive agreements normally state that if a work is not exploited within a reasonable period of time, the composer/writer should have the option to call for the work to be returned.

The publishing contract, in dealing with administration, should undertake to protect the copyright in the work and preserve the moral rights of the composer. The music publisher should also register the works with appropriate collecting societies such as the Performing Right Society Ltd and the Mechanical-Copyright Protection Society Ltd (MCPS). Reasonable requests for additional information should receive favourable consideration.

The creator in return will need to guarantee that works created are original and do not contain substantial portions, copies or 'samples' of other material. Delivery times for all works must be adhered to.

Most music publishers will still ask for a full assignment of all rights for the life of copyright for all works to enable them to generate enough income to carry on the publishing process, and use the money to reinvest in the composer they wish to sign and the others on their books.

ARRANGING

Copyright in a musical work lasts for the life of the composer plus 70 years from the end of the year of that person's death. If it is a vocal work and the words have been written by someone else they too cannot be tampered with without the author's permission. Under copyright law the arrangement (such as alteration, adaptation, orchestration) of any copyright musical work in printed or manuscript form for commercial exploitation (making available for sale) requires the prior written permission of the original copyright owner of that work, who is usually the music publisher. Arrangers must contact the original publisher prior to undertaking any arrangement since it is that publisher's responsibility either to permit the arrangement to proceed or, for contractual or other reasons, to prohibit such an arrangement. Permissions to make arrangements of copyright works may be subject to a written licence requiring the payment of a fee or royalty to the original publisher or composer. Other terms and conditions may also be appropriate and these will be notified when the approach to the original publisher is made. It is dangerous to submit or offer an arrangement to a music publisher for publication without evidence from the original publisher that all necessary clearances have been made. Any difficulties in tracing the copyright owners of musical works should be referred to the PRS, MCPS or the MPA.

THE PHOTOCOPYING DILEMMA

Part of the role of the music publisher is to protect composers against copyright infringement by any means. Apart from the commercial piracy of sound recordings, videos, printed music and home taping, which have deprived composers of income, indiscriminate unauthorised photocopying over the last 25 years or so has seriously threatened the livelihood of many composers who have been published. Such infringement has narrowed the repertoire of works available. The use and availability of unsupervised, high-speed, photocopying machines has also harmed the 'consumers' of musical works whether amateur or professional. As printed music is the catalyst for many live, broadcast and recorded performances of copyright music, photocopying has stifled additional exploitation on behalf of creators by music publishers, depriving them both of further income. In the UK, an equitable solution to the problem has been found; the contents of the Code of Fair Practice have been agreed between publishers and users. It is available from the Music Publishers' Association and attempts to define 'fair dealing for printed music' enshrining two general principles as follows:

a) Copyright owners (composers and their publishers) recognise the need of musicians and students for reasonable access to copyright material so that their music may be widely performed and studied.
b) At the same time, composers and their publishers must be properly compensated for their work so that the economic incentive and means for the creation and publication of music continue to exist. It follows that copying to evade purchase or hire will always be wrong.

Voluntary blanket licensing schemes are felt by music publishers to be appropriate for some types of copyright works but not for printed music which is specifically excluded from these arrangements. Blanket licensing schemes administered by the Copyright Licensing Agency Ltd are dealt with on page 536. Such arrangements are considered by most music publishers in the UK unsuitable for music as it is virtually impossible to specify clear parameters to permit photocopying which would not conflict with the normal method of exploitation, publishing the music. There are also other important reasons why printed music has to be treated separately. Reading music is a specialist matter for initiates and it is published in very much smaller units than textbooks and other literary works so that in most cases the copying of entire works is quick and easy. With music, the infringer generally wishes to copy the whole work, whereas it is rare for a student or researcher to need to copy a complete novel or textbook.

The MPA is currently reviewing the subject in the light of present-day circumstances to consider whether any change in policy is needed.

THE COLLECTING SOCIETIES

Part of the administrative role of the music publisher is to know precisely how the activities, practices, rules and regulations of these organisations (PRS and MCPS) affect the operation of the business; see pages 622 and 617 for more details.

FURTHER READING

Bagehot, R., *Music Business Agreements*, Waterlow, 1989

British Music Education Yearbook, Rhinegold Publishing

British Music Yearbook, Rhinegold Publishing

Copying Music – A Code of Fair Practice agreed between composers, publishers and users, rev. edn, Music Publishers' Association. 1992

Copyright, Designs & Patents Act 1988, HMSO

The Creative Role of the Music Publisher, International Publishers Copyright Council for the IPA (available from MPA)

Dann, Allan and Underwood, John, *How to Succeed in the Music Business*, Wise Publications, 1948

de Freitas, Denis, *The British Copyright Council's Guide to Copyright and Rights in Performances in the United Kingdom*, British Copyright Council, 1990

Ehrlich, Cyril, *Harmonious Alliance – A History of the Performing Right Society*, Performing Right Society, 1989

Gunning, Annie, *The Composer's Guide to Music Publishing*, 2nd edn, The Association of Professional Composers, 1994.

Gibson, James, *Getting Noticed: A Musician's Guide to Publicity and Self-promotion*, 2nd rev. edn, Omnibus Press, 1990

Homewood, Susan and Matthews, Colin, *The Essentials of Music Copying – A Manual for Composers, Copyists and Processors*, Music Publishers' Association

Lester, David and Mitchell, Paul, *Joynson-Hicks on UK Copyright Law*, Sweet & Maxwell, 1989

Music Week Directory (annual published by *Music Week*)

Rachlin, Harvey, *The Songwriter's and Musician's Guide to Making Successful Demos*, 2nd rev. edn, Omnibus Press, 1989

Music Publishers

The publishers in the following list are all members of the Performing Right Society except those marked †. The list does not include all publisher-members of the Performing Right Society.

Lyrics without a musical setting are not accepted unless stated by individual firms

†**Baker Music** (1984), Postgate House, Lartington, Co Durham DL12 9DA *tel* (01833) 650040 *fax* (01833) 650006. *Managing director:* Bernard Baker. European music – all instruments; books on and about music. Welcomes submissions and ideas from new composers.

Banks Music Publications (Ramsay Silver), The Old Forge, Sand Hutton, York YO4 1LB *tel* (01904) 468472 *fax* (01904) 468679. Publishers of choral and instrumental music.

Bardic Edition, 6 Fairfax Crescent, Aylesbury, Bucks. HP20 2ES *tel/fax* (01296) 28609 *e-mail* 101464.2670@compuserve.com Piano, vocal, chamber, choral, educational, orchestral, Grainger Society Edition, Copperplate Music, Drumblade Music, William Grant Still Music.

†**Bärenreiter** (1925), Burnt Mill, Elizabeth Way, Harlow, Essex CM20 2HX *tel* (01279) 417134 ext 224/236 *fax* (01279) 429401 *Director:* Christopher

Jackson. Music for strings, wind, piano, organ, choral, solo voice, chamber, orchestral; collected editions, scores, books on music.

A. & C. Black (Publishers) Ltd (1978), 35 Bedford Row, London WC1R 4JH *tel* 0171-242 0946 *fax* 0171-831 8478. *Editor:* Sheena Roberts. Song books and instrumental books for children.

Boosey & Hawkes Music Publishers Ltd, 295 Regent Street, London W1R 8JH *tel* 0171-580 2060 *fax* 0171-291 7218. *Managing director:* Trevor Glover. General and educational.

Bosworth & Co. Ltd (1889), 14-18 Heddon Street, London W1R 8DP *tel* 0171-734 4961 *fax* 0171-734 0475 *e-mail* bosworthlon@cityscape.co.uk Orchestral, chamber, instrumental, operetta, church, educational, piano, string, recorder and recorder ensemble, and part-songs.

Bourne Music Ltd, Standbrook House, 2/5 Old Bond Street, London W1X 3TB *tel* 0171-493 6412 *fax* 0171-493 6583. Popular and educational music.

Brampton Music International Ltd (1970), 3rd Floor, 9 Carnaby Street, London W1V 1PG *tel* 0171-437 1958 *fax* 0171-437 3852. *Managing director:* Tony Hall. Pop, soul, dance.

Breitkopf & Härtel (1719), Castle House, Ivychurch, Romney Marsh, Kent TN29 0AL *tel/fax* (01797) 344011. *Contact:* Robin Winter. Baroque, classical, romantic and contemporary music.

Bugle Songs Ltd (1979), Bugle House, 21A Noel Street, London W1V 3PD *tel* 0171-439 2282 *fax* 0171-439 7649. *Director:* Miles Copeland III. Popular. Will consider tapes, demo discs, etc.

Cambridge University Press (1534), The Edinburgh Building, Shaftesbury Road, Cambridge CB2 2RU *tel* (01223) 312393 *telex* 817256 CUPCAM G *fax* (01223) 315052. *Music editor:* Penny Souster BA, ARCM. Books on music and history of music; music books and music for schools.

Cathedral Music Ltd (1977), Maudlin House, Westhampnett, Chichester, West Sussex PO18 0PB *tel* (01243) 776325 *fax* (01243) 539604. *Managing director:* Richard Barnes. All classical music, but weighted towards choral.

Chester Music (1860), 8-9 Frith Street, London W1V 5TZ *tel* 0171-434 01066 *fax* 0171-287 6329. Classical, contemporary and educational music.

†**Cló Iar-Chonnachta Teo.** (1985), Indreabhán, Conamara, Co Galway, Republic of Ireland *tel* (091) 593307 *fax* (091) 593362. *Director:* Micheál Ó Conghaile; *music editor:* Nóirín Ní Ghrádaigh; *general manager:* Deirdre O'Toole. Specialises in traditional (*sean-nós*) singing and traditional Irish music.

CMA Publications (1987), 10 Avenue Road, Kingston, Surrey KT1 2RB *tel* 0181-541 0857 *fax* 0181-974 8120. *Proprietor:* Geraldine Russell-Price. Contemporary music: instrumental, solo, ensemble, band, orchestral, Grade 4 – professional.

Complete Music Ltd, 3rd Floor, Bishops Park House, 25-29 Fulham High Street, London SW6 3JH *tel* 0171-731 8595 *fax* 0171-384 1854. *Chairman:* Iain McNay; *managing director:* Martin Costello. Modern/pop music of all kinds; vocal and instrumental.

Con Moto Publications UK (1984 as Mostyn Music), 17 Mostyn Street, Dukinfield, Cheshire SK16 5JS *tel/fax* 0161-343 2423. *Partners:* Maureen Cresswell, Tony Cresswell. Brass band, wind band, ensembles and solos, junior band (brass and wind), the John Golland and Thomas Pitfield collections.

†**Cramer Music** (1824), 23 Garrick Street, London WC2E 9AX   *tel* 0171-240 1612   *fax* 0171-240 2639. General and educational.

De Wolfe Ltd, 80-88 Wardour Street, London W1V 3LF   *tel* 0171-439 8481-6   *fax* 0171-437 2744. Symphonic recorded orchestral (English and foreign); comprehensive library of recorded music on CD and tape; extensive effects library; original film scores; recording studio.

†**East-West Publications (UK) Ltd** (1977), 8 Caledonia Street, London N1 9DZ   *tel* 0171-837 5061   *fax* 0171-278 4429. *Chairman:* L.W. Carp; *editor:* B. Thompson. Piano, guitar, recorder and vocal music.

Emerson Edition Ltd (1972), Windmill Farm, Ampleforth, North Yorkshire YO6 4HF   *tel* (01439) 788324   *fax* (01439) 788715. *Managing director:* June Emerson. Music for wind instruments, and music from Albania.

EMI Music Publishing Ltd, 127 Charing Cross Road, London WC2H 0EA   *tel* 0171-434 2131   *fax* 0171-434 3531. Popular and standard.
Comprising Dix Ltd, EMI Songs Ltd, EMI United Partnership Ltd, B. Feldman & Co. Ltd, Francis, Day & Hunter Ltd, KPM Music Group, The Peter Maurice Music Co. Ltd, Keith Prowse Ltd, Reynolds Music, Robbins Music Corp. Ltd, Screen Gems-EMI Music Ltd, Lawrence Wright Music Ltd, Virgin Music Publishers Ltd, ATV Music Ltd.

Faber Music Ltd (1966), 3 Queen Square, London WC1N 3AU   *tel* 0171-833 7906 or 0171-278 7436   *fax* 0171-278 3817. *Directors:* Robin Boyle (chairman), Thomas H. Pasteur (chief executive), Martin Kingsbury (vice-chairman & director of publishing), Sally Cavender, Piers Hembry, Richard King. A general list of the highest quality, comprising both old and new music, and music books.

Fentone Music Ltd, Fleming Road, Earlstrees, Corby, Northants. NN17 4SN   *tel* (01536) 260981   *fax* (01536) 401075. Educational and classical music.
Agents for Fenette Music, Earlham Press, Mimram Music, Edizioni Bèrben, Ancona, Italy, F & R. Walsh Publications, London, London Orchestral Series, Luck's Music Library, Detroit, Norsk Musikforlag, Oslo, XYZ International, Amsterdam, Real Musical, Madrid, E.F. Kalmus, USA.

First Time Music (Publishing) UK Ltd (1986), Sovereign House, 12 Trewartha Road, Praa Sands, Penzance, Cornwall TR20 9ST   *tel* (01736) 762826   *fax* (01736) 763328. *Managing director:* Roderick G. Jones. Popular, country, folk, gospel music; music for choirs – in all styles.

Forsyth Bros. Ltd (1857), 126 Deansgate, Manchester M3 2GR   *tel* 0161-834 3281   *fax* 0161-834 0630. Educational piano and instrumental music; modern teaching material; modern recorder music published. UK distributors of *Music Minus One* and *Pocket Songs*.

Friendly Music, PO Box 53, Cranbrook, Kent TN17 3ZX   *tel* (01580) 713281. *Proprietor:* Jonathan Rutland. Collections of solos and duets for woodwind instruments; also quartets and quintets.

Glocken Verlag Ltd (1946), 12-14 Mortimer Street, London W1N 7RD   *tel* 0171-580 2827   *fax* 0171-436 9616. *Directors:* R.M. Toeman, R.G. Holt. Musical works by Franz Lehar.

Cwmni Cyhoeddi Gwynn Cyf., Y Gerlan, Heol Y Dŵr, Penygroes, Gwynedd LL54 6LR   *tel* (01286) 881797. Publishers of Welsh educational and international choral music. Official music publishers to the Welsh Folk Song Society, The Welsh Folk Dance Society, The Court of the National Eisteddfod.

Hughes & Son, Publishers (1820), Parc Tŷ Glas, Llanishen, Cardiff CF4 5DU *tel* (01222) 741484 *telex* 94017032 SIAN G *fax* (01222) 741474. Welsh music, Welsh language, television related material, educational publications, novels.

Hymns Ancient and Modern Ltd, trading under the imprint of **The Canterbury Press Norwich,** St Mary's Works, St Mary's Plain, Norwich, Norfolk NR3 3BH *tel* (01603) 612914/616563 *fax* (01603) 624483. *Directors:* The Very Revd Professor Henry Chadwick KBE (chairman), Dr Allan Wicks, Dr Lionel Dakers, Sir Richard O'Brien, Mr Patrick Coldstream; *publisher:* Gordon Knights. The leading hymn book publisher in the UK for churches, schools and other institutions.

†**International Music Publications Ltd,** Woodford Trading Estate, Southend Road, Woodford Green, Essex IG8 8HN *tel* 0181-551 6131 *fax* 0181-551 3919. Standard and popular, educational, instrumental tutors, tutorial videos.

Alfred A. Kalmus Ltd, 48 Great Marlborough Street, London W1V 2BN *tel* 0171-437 5203 *fax* 0171-437 6115. Sole representatives of Universal Edition AG, Vienna, Universal Edition (London) Ltd; Theodore Presser Co, International Music Co, Boelke-Bomart Inc., European American Music Corp., Helicon Inc., Bourne Music, Belmont Music, Trio Associates, all USA; Doblinger Edition, Vienna, PWM Editions, Cracow (complete Chopin-Paderewski), Harmonia, Hilversum, Berandol, Canada, Boccaccini and Spada, Italy, Aldo Bruzzichelli, Italy, Musikwissenschaftlicher Verlag, Austria, Musica Rara, France, Fraser-Enoch, Kent; Olivan Press, London; Broekmans & Van Poppel, Amsterdam; Power Music, West Yorkshire, Virgo Music, West Midlands, Itchy Fingers Publications, London, Hug Musikverlag/Foetisch, Zürich.

Edward Kassner Music Co. Ltd (1939), Exmouth House, 11 Pine Street, London EC1R 0JH *tel* 0171-837 5020 *fax* 0171-837 4795. *Directors:* Edward Kassner (chairman), David Kassner (managing), Victoria Haslam (copyright manager). Pop music, including rock 'n' roll, country, jazz, ballads, rock and film music.

†**Alfred Lengnick & Co. Ltd** (1893), Pigeon House Meadow, 27 Grove Road, Beaconsfield, Bucks. HP9 1UR *tel* (01494) 681216 *fax* (01494) 670443. *General manager:* Sally Willison; *creative director:* David Willison. Division of **Complete Music Ltd.** Specialise in English contemporary music.

MCA Music Ltd, West 6, 77 Fulham Palace Road, London W6 8JA *tel* 0181-741 8686 *fax* 0181-741 8646. *Managing director:* Paul Connolly. General and popular vocal music. Includes ATV Music Ltd and Northern Songs.

Maecenas Europe, 5 Bushey Close, Old Barn Lane, Kenley, Surrey CR8 5AU *tel* 0181-660 4766/1349 *fax* 0181-668 5273. *Directors:* Malcolm Binney, Maggie Barton, Ray Lee. Classical, including educational, choral, keyboard and other instrumental; pop, guitar, textbooks, etc.

Momentum Music Ltd (1983), 17-19 Alma Road, Wandsworth, London SW18 1AA *tel* 0181-871 2121 *fax* 0181-871 2745. *Directors:* A. Heath, M. Mills. Indie. Welcomes tapes.

†**M.S.M. Music Publishers** (incorporating **Leonard, Gould & Bolttler**), Gilbert House, 406 Roding Lane South (off Woodford Avenue), Woodford Green, Essex IG8 8EY *tel* 0181-551 1282 *fax* 0181-550 8377. General and educational.

†**Music Exchange (Manchester) Ltd** (1965), Claverton Road, Manchester M23 9ZA *tel* 0161-946 1234 *fax* 0161-946 1195. *Directors:* S.W. Taylor (managing), J.F. Taylor, A. Osborn, G. Burns. Educational, all grades: instrumental, vocal, tutors.

Music Sales Ltd, 8-9 Frith Street, London W1V 5TZ *tel* 0171-434 0066 *fax* 0171-439 2848/734 2246/287 6329. General, popular, classical and educational. Handles copyright, sale and rental of sheet music and other print-related media for: Associated Music Publishers Inc., Chester Music Ltd, Campbell Connelly & Co. Ltd, Cinephonic Music Co. Ltd, Cross Music Ltd, Dash Music Ltd, Dorsey Brothers Music Ltd, Edwin Ashdown Limited, Emergency Music Ltd, Evergreen Music Ltd, Glad Music Ltd, Glendale Music Ltd, Golden Apple Productions, G. Schirmer Inc., Harrison Music Co. Ltd, High-Fye Music Ltd, Hournew Music Ltd, Ivy Music Ltd, J. Curwen & Sons Ltd, Montclare Music Co. Ltd, Noel Gay Music Publishing Ltd, Novello & Company Ltd, Shapiro Bernstein & Co. Ltd, Shawnee Press Inc., Skidmore Music Ltd, Twangy Music Ltd, Union Musical Ediciones, Veronica Music Ltd, Edition Wilhelm Hansen.

Novello & Co. Ltd (1811), 8/9 Frith Street, London W1V 5TZ *tel* 0171-434 0066 *fax* 0171-287 6329. Classical and modern orchestral, instrumental, vocal and choral music, church music, school and educational music books.

Octava Music Co. Ltd (1938), 12-14 Mortimer Street, London W1N 7RD *tel* 0171-580 2827 *fax* 0171-436 9616. *Contact:* R.M. Toeman. Theatrical and music publishers.

Orestes Music Publishing Ltd (1986), 112 Gunnersbury Avenue, Ealing, London W5 4HB *tel* 0181-993 7441 *fax* 0181-992 9993. *Directors:* Dee O'Reilly, Hazel Hemmings. Pop, New Age, dance, musicals.

Oxford University Press, Music Department, Walton Street, Oxford OX2 6DP *tel* (01865) 56767 *telex* 837330 *fax* (01865) 267749. Orchestral, instrumental, operatic, choral, vocal works, church and organ music by early and modern composers, educational music, classroom material, books on music.

Paterson's Publications Ltd—acquired by **Novello & Co. Ltd.**

Peters Edition Ltd (1938), 10-12 Baches Street, London N1 6DN *tel* 0171-253 1638. Copyright/Hire: *tel* 0171-251 5094; Promotion/Editorial: *tel* 0171-251 6732 *fax* 0171-490 4921. Classical and contemporary music (piano, organ, other instrumental, vocal, choral and brass). Peters Edition, Hinrichsen Edition, Litolff Edition, Belaieff Edition, Heinrichshofen, Henmar Press, Edition Kunzelmann and Lienau-Schlesinger.

G. Ricordi & Co. (London) Ltd (1808), The Bury, Church Street, Chesham, Bucks. HP5 1JG *tel* (01494) 783311 *telegraphic address* Ricordi, Chesham *fax* (01494) 784427. Publishers of Italian opera, music for piano, classical and contemporary, operatic arias, songs, choral large scale works and part songs for all voices, orchestral works, classical and contemporary, instrumental, string, woodwind, brass tutors, exercises, etc., guitar music of all types.

Roberton Publications, The Windmill, Wendover, Aylesbury, Bucks. HP22 6JJ *tel* (01296) 623107. *Partners:* Kenneth Roberton, Margaret Roberton. Choral and educational; also piano, chamber, orchestral, and music for all instruments. Represent Leslie Music Supply, Oakville, Ontario.

Schott & Co. Ltd (1835), 48 Great Marlborough Street, London W1V 2BN *tel* 0171-437 1246 *fax* 0171-437 0263. Classical/contemporary/educational music/books. Eulenburg Miniature Scores and Orchestral Parts, Schott London, Mainz, Madrid, New York, Paris, Tokyo, Toronto. Agents for Amadeus Verlag, Winterthur; Bardic Edition, Aylesbury; Carl Fischer, New York; G. Henle Verlag, Munich; Magnamusic, Sharon; MMB Music Inc., St Louis; Musisca, Topsham; Pro Musica, Leipzig; Schott Freres, Brussels; Studio 49 Percussion Instruments, Munich; Zen-On Recorders, Tokyo.

Sea Dream Music (1976), 236 Sebert Road, Forest Gate, London E7 0NP *tel* 0181-534 8500. *Senior partner:* S.A. Law. Christian-based rock, blues and folk.

R. Smith & Co. Ltd (1857), c/o Chester Music Ltd, 8-9 Frith Street, London W1V 5TZ. Wind/brass band, wind/brass ensemble, educational.

Spartan Press Ltd (1989), Old Brewery House, Redbrook, Monmouth NP5 4LU *tel* (01600) 712482 *fax* (01600) 712483. *Directors:* M.T.R. Goddard, P.D. Goddard. Educational music for teachers/students.

†**Sphemusations,** Gramercy House, 12 Northfield Road, Onehouse, Stowmarket, Suffolk IP14 3HF *tel* (01449) 613388. Serious music, brass band, choral, keyboard music, instrumental and educational; records of modern works; tapes.

Stainer & Bell Ltd, PO Box 110, Victoria House, 23 Gruneisen Road, London N3 1DZ *tel* 0181-343 3303 *fax* 0181-343 3024. Serious music of all kinds: instrumental, choral, songs, educational and religious; tutors.
Book and music publishers including the imprints of Augener, Belton Books, Galliard, Stainer & Bell, A. Weekes, Joseph Williams.

Sylvester Music Co. Ltd, 80-82 Wardour Street, London W1V 3LF *tel* 0171-437 4933/4 *fax* 0171-437 2744. Popular and orchestral music. Comprehensive library of recorded music on CD and tape; extensive effects library; specially composed scores; transfers to tape and film.

Thames Publishing (1970), 14 Barlby Road, London W10 6AR *tel* 0181-969 3579. Serious music of all types, particularly vocal, choral and instrumental. MSS welcome *but should always be preceded by a letter*.

United Music Publishers Ltd (1932), 42 Rivington Street, London EC2A 3BN *tel* 0171-729 4700 *fax* 0171-739 6549. Contemporary British works. Agents for the principal French music publishing houses and specialists in the distribution of French and other foreign music.

Universal Edition (London) Ltd, 48 Great Marlborough Street, London W1V 2BN *tel* 0171-437 5203 *fax* 0171-437 6115. Serious music of all types.

Vanderbeek & Imrie Ltd (1983), 15 Marvig, Lochs, Isle of Lewis HS2 9QP *tel/ fax* (01851) 880216. *Directors:* Martyn Imrie, M.E.H. Hunter OBE, J.M. Imrie. 20th century serious contemporary music; 15th and 16th century Latin church music.

Warner Chappell Music Ltd, 129 Park Street, London W1Y 3FA *tel* 0171-629 7600 *fax* 0171-499 9718. Popular, standard and show music.
Brussels, Munich, Johannesburg, Los Angeles, Madrid, Milan, Bussum, Nashville, New York, Paris, Stockholm, Sydney, Tokyo, Toronto, Buenos Aires, Vienna, Rio de Janeiro, Copenhagen, Hamburg, Athens, Hong Kong, Tel-Aviv, Kuala Lumpur, Mexico, Oslo, Lima, Lisbon, Singapore, Caracas.

†**Warren & Phillips** (1906), 126 Deansgate, Manchester M3 2GR *tel* 0161-834 3281 *fax* 0161-834 0630. Educational piano and instrumental music; modern teaching material.

Josef Weinberger Ltd (1885), 12-14 Mortimer Street, London W1N 7RD *tel* 0171-580 2827 (4 lines) *fax* 0171-436 9616. *Directors:* R.G. Holt, R.M. Toeman; *executive directors:* G. Barker, K. Dixon, G. Kingsley, J. Schofield. Musical theatre, contemporary classical, educational and religious music.

Workers' Music Association (1936), 240 Perry Rise, Forest Hill, London SE23 2QT *tel* 0181-699 2250. General music organisation with emphasis on the social aspects of music. Publications; Music courses.

Agents

Literary Agents

The primary task of a literary agent is to look after a writer's commercial interests and to exploit fully the rights in the material he or she handles. This can mean anything from placing work with a British publisher to the sale of US, translation, dramatic, film, TV, audio, electronic or other rights. Agents can also supply editorial guidance, advise on career strategy, and – in the increasingly fluid and unpredictable world of modern publishing – provide the author with a degree of continuity.

What agents cannot be expected to do is comment at length on unsuitable work or sell the unsaleable. Nor can they guarantee that the writer's life is without disappointments.

When approaching an agent, try to define your needs and choose an agent who seems most likely to meet them. Work from an up-to-date edition of this yearbook. Do bear in mind that it is not good practice to send work to more than one agent at the same time. Either ring or write a preliminary letter to the agent/s of your choice to ascertain whether the agent is taking on new clients. Describe as succinctly as possible the nature of your work, your future plans, and give any biographical information that might be germane to your writing. When submitting your work, make sure the manuscript is typed, double-spaced, with wide margins, on one side of the paper only, pages numbered, and put loose in a folder. Enclose return postage.

Enquire about the agent's terms. Some of this information will be given in the listing that follows, but make sure you understand how the agency operates. Does it use associates for the sale of subsidiary rights, and how does this affect commission? Does it have a letter of agreement for its clients which details its terms of business?

The Association of Authors' Agents (see page 598) is the trade association of British agents. Members, designated with an asterisk in the following list, meet regularly and are committed to a code of practice. They do not charge authors a reading fee. Agents that do charge a reading fee usually refund the fee (which covers a report on the MS) on acceptance of the material by a publisher. This fee is not to be confused with commission, which is the agreed percentage charged by the agent to the author and deducted by the agent from publishers' advances, royalties earned and any other monies paid to the author.

All agents listed below were circulated with a questionnaire designed to provide pertinent information. They are asked to keep this information up to date. The list does not purport to be exhaustive. If any who are not included would like to receive a copy of the questionnaire and to be considered for inclusion, application should be made to the publishers.

UNITED KINGDOM

*Full member of the Association of Authors' Agents

A & B Personal Management Ltd (1982), 5th Floor, Plaza Suite, 114 Jermyn Street, London SW1Y 6HJ   *tel* 0171-839 4433   *fax* 0171-930 5738. *Directors:* R.W. Ellis, R. Ellis.
Full-length MSS. Scripts for TV, theatre, cinema; also novels, fiction and non-fiction (home 12½%, overseas 15%), performance rights (12½%). Synopsis required initially from writers submitting work for first time. No reading fee for synopsis, plays or screenplays, but fee charged for full-length MSS. Return postage required.

*The Agency (London) Ltd (incorporating **Lemon Unna & Durbridge Ltd**) (1995), 24 Pottery Lane, London W11 4LZ *tel* 0171-727 1346   *fax* 0171-727 9037. *Directors:* Stephen Durbridge, Sheila Lemon, Leah Schmidt, Sebastian Born, Julia Kreitman, Girsha Reid, Bethan Evans, Wendy Gresser, Hilary Delamere.
Represents writers for theatre, film, television, radio and children's writers and illustrators. Adult novels represented only for existing clients. Commission 10% unless sub-agents employed overseas; works in conjunction with agents in USA and overseas. No unsolicited MSS. Preliminary letter including publishing/production history and sae essential.

*Aitken & Stone Ltd, incorporating **Hughes Massie Ltd,** 29 Fernshaw Road, London SW10 0TG   *tel* 0171-351 7561   *fax* 0171-376 3594. *Directors:* Gillon Aitken, Brian Stone, Sally Riley, Antony Harwood.
Full-length MSS (home 10%, USA 15%, translations 20%). Preliminary letter and return postage essential. *Authors* include Pat Barker, Agatha Christie Estate, Sebastian Faulks, Germaine Greer, Alan Hollinghurst, Susan Howatch, A.L. Kennedy, V.S. Naipaul, Caryl Phillips, Paul Theroux.

*Jacintha Alexander Associates (1981), 47 Emperor's Gate, London SW7 4HJ   *tel* 0171-373 9258   *fax* 0171-373 4374. *Managing director:* Julian Alexander.
Full length MSS. General fiction and non-fiction (home 10-15%, overseas 20%). No poetry, plays, textbooks or children's books. Film or TV scripts handled for established clients only. Works with agents worldwide. No reading fee but preliminary letter, synopsis and sae essential.

*Darley Anderson Literary, TV and Film Agency, Estelle House, 11 Eustace Road, London SW6 1JB   *tel* 0171-385 6652   *fax* 0171-386 5571. *Proprietor:* Darley Anderson; *associates:* Pippa Dyson (film/TV), Elizabeth Wright (crime/fantasy/erotica), Kerith Biggs (foreign rights).
Full-length MSS. Popular, commercial fiction and non-fiction. Special fiction interests: all types of thrillers and crime (cosy/hard boiled/historical); women's fiction including contemporary, 20th century romantic sagas, love stories, erotica and women in jeopardy; horror; fantasy; comedy; and Irish novels. Special non-fiction interests: celebrity autobiographies, biographies, true life women in jeopardy, diet, beauty, health, cookery, popular psychology, self-improvement, inspirational, popular religion and supernatural (home 15%, US/translation 20%, film/TV/radio 20%). No poetry, plays or academic books. Can arrange PR and author publicity and specialist financial advice; editorial guidance on selected MSS. Preliminary letter, synopsis and first three chapters. Return postage/sae essential. Overseas associates: Mitchell Rose Agency (New York), Renaissance-Swanson Film Agency (LA/Hollywood) and leading foreign agents worldwide. *Authors* include Jane Adams, Tessa Barclay, Lee Child, Martina Cole, Joseph Corvo, Debbie Frank, Martica

Heaner, Beryl Kingston, Frank Lean, Deborah McKinlay, Lesley Pearce, Allan Pease, Adrian Plass, Fred Secombe, Jane Walmsey.

Artellus Ltd (1986), 30 Dorset House, Gloucester Place, London NW1 5AD *tel* 0171-935 6972 *fax* 0171-487 5957. *Director:* Leslie Gardner; *chairman:* Gabriele Pantucci.
Full-length and short MSS; scripts for films (home 10%, overseas 12½-20%). Crime, science fiction, historical, contemporary and literary fiction; non-fiction: science, art history, current affairs, biography, general history. Works directly in USA and with agencies in Europe, Japan and Russia. Will suggest revision. No reading fee.

Associated Publicity Holdings Ltd (1987), 1-6 Clay Street, London W1H 3FS *tel* 0171-486 4889 *fax* 0171-486 4885. *Managing director:* Jonathan G. Harris.
Full-length and short MSS: non-fiction, particularly sport (home 10%, overseas 20%), performance rights (15%); will suggest revision. Works with foreign agencies. No reading fee.

Yvonne Baker Associates (1987), 8 Temple Fortune Lane, London NW11 7UD *tel* 0181-455 8687 *fax* 0181-458 3143.
Television, film (12½%), theatre, radio (10%). Particularly interested in contemporary drama and TV comedy drama series. No books, short stories, articles, poetry. No reading fee but preliminary letter essential with full information and sae.

*Blake Friedmann Literary, TV & Film Agency Ltd (1977), 37-41 Gower Street, London WC1E 6HH *tel* 0171-631 4331 *fax* 0171-323 1274. *Directors:* Carole Blake, Julian Friedmann, Barbara Jones, Conrad Williams.
Full-length MSS. Fiction: thrillers, women's novels and literary fiction; non-fiction: investigative books, biography, travel; no poetry or plays (home 15%, overseas 20%). Specialise in film and television rights; place journalism and short stories for existing clients only. Represented worldwide in 26 markets; in USA by Writers House Inc. Preliminary letter, synopsis and first two chapters preferred. No reading fee. *Authors* include Gilbert Adair, Ted Allbeury, Jane Asher, Teresa Crane, Barbara Erskine, Maeve Haran, John Harvey, Ken Hom, Glenn Meade, Lawrence Norfolk, Joseph O'Connor, Michael Ridpath, Robyn Sisman, Craig Thomas.

David Bolt Associates, 12 Heath Drive, Send, Surrey GU23 7EP *tel/fax* (01483) 721118.
Specialises in biography, fiction, theology. Full-length MSS (home 10%, overseas 19%; all other rights including film, video and television 10%). No unsolicited short stories or play scripts. Will sometimes suggest revision. Works in association with overseas agencies worldwide. Preliminary letter essential. Reading fee terms on application. *Authors* include Chinua Achebe, David Bret, Arthur Jacobs, James Purdy, Joseph Rhymer, Colin Wilson.

Rosemary Bromley Literary Agency. Avington, Winchester, Hants SO21 1DB *tel/fax* (01962) 779656.
Specialises in biography, travel, leisure, cookery, health (home 10%, overseas from 15%.) No poetry. No reading fee. *No* unsolicited MSS; enquiries unaccompanied by return postage will not be answered. For children's books see **Juvenilia.**

*Felicity Bryan, 2A North Parade, Banbury Road, Oxford OX2 6PE *tel* (01865) 513816 *fax* (01865) 310055.
Fiction and general non-fiction; no light romance, science fiction, short stories, plays or children's (home 10%, overseas 20%). Translation rights handled by

Andrew Nurnberg Associates; works in conjunction with US agents. Return postage essential.

Peter Bryant (Writers) (1980), 94 Adelaide Avenue, London SE4 1YR   *tel* 0181-691 9085   *fax* 0181-692 9107.
Special interests: animation, children's fiction and TV comedy; also handles drama scripts for theatre, radio and television (home/USA 10%). Overseas associate: Hartmann and Stauffacher, Germany. No reading fee for the above categories, but sae essential for all submissions. *Authors* include Isabelle Amyes, Roy Apps, Joe Boyle, Lucy Daniel, Jimmy Hibbert, Jan Page, Ruth Silvestre, Peter Symonds, George Tarry.

Diane Burston (1984), 46 Cromwell Avenue, Highgate, London N6 5HL   *tel* 0181-340 6130.
General fiction and non-fiction, full-length MSS (home 10%, overseas 20%, USA 15%), short stories (15%). No unsolicited MSS; preliminary enquiry and sae essential. Reading service available on request.

Bycornute Books, 76a Ashford Road, Eastbourne, East Sussex BN21 3TE   *tel* (01323) 726819   *fax* (01323) 649053. *Director:* Asia Haleem.
Specialises in illustrated books on sacred art, comparative religion, mythology, cosmology, astrology, iconography, symbolism, metaphysics, art history and popular archaeology/ancient history (*not* fiction, poetry, children's, psychic studies or psychology); associated cardboard novelties. Full-length and short MSS (10%). Will suggest revision. *Authors* include Gordon Strachan, Asia Shepsut, Peter Clough, Robertson of Strathloch, Anne Macaulay.

*Campbell Thomson & McLaughlin Ltd, 1 King's Mews, London WC1N 2JA   *tel* 0171-242 0958   *fax* 0171-242 2408. *Directors:* John McLaughlin, Charlotte Bruton, Hal Cheetham.
Full-length book MSS (home 10%, overseas up to 20% including commission to foreign agent). No poetry, plays or television scripts, short stories or children's books. USA agents represented: Raines & Raines, The Fox Chase Agency, Inc. Representatives in most European countries. Preliminary letter with sae first, please. No reading fee, but return postage required. Subsidiary company: **Peter Janson-Smith Ltd.**

*Carnell Literary Agency (1951), Danes Croft, Goose Lane, Little Hallingbury, Herts. CM22 7RG   *tel* (01279) 723626. *Proprietor:* Pamela Buckmaster.
All MSS except poetry. Specialises in science/fantasy fiction. Works in conjunction with many foreign agents (home 10%, overseas 10% or 19% through sub-agent). No new submissions at present – list closed.

Casarotto Ramsay Ltd (1992; formerly **Margaret Ramsay Ltd,** 1953), National House, 60-66 Wardour Street, London W1V 3HP   *tel* 0171-287 4450   *fax* 0171-287 9128. *Directors:* Tom Erhardt, Jenne Casarotto.
MSS – theatre, films, television, sound broadcasting only (10%). Works in conjunction with agents in USA and in all foreign countries. Preliminary letter essential. No reading fee. *Authors* include Alan Ayckbourn, Peter Barnes, Edward Bond, Caryl Churchill, Christopher Hampton, David Hare, Larry Kramer, Willy Russell, Martin Sherman, David Wood.

Mic Cheetham Literary Agency (1994), 138 Buckingham Palace Road, London SW1W 9SA   *tel* 0171-730 3027   *fax* 0171-730 3027/0037. *Director:* Mic Cheetham.
General and literary fiction, science fiction, general non-fiction (home 10%, overseas 20%); film, TV and radio rights (10-15%); will suggest revision. Works with The Marsh Agency for foreign rights. No unsolicited MSS.

*Judith Chilcote (1990), 8 Wentworth Mansions, Keats Grove, London NW3 2RL *tel* 0171-794 3717 *fax* 0171-794 7431.
Commercial fiction, non-fiction – sports, self-help, alternative medicine, cinema, current affairs, TV tie-ins (home 15%, overseas 20-25%). *No* short stories, science fiction, children's, poetry. Works in conjunction with overseas agents and New York affiliate. UK representative for Cader Books and Carol Publishing. No reading fee but preliminary letter with three chapters only, CV and sae essential. *Authors* include Jane Alexander, Jane Gordon, Philippa Kennedy, Douglas Thompson.

Teresa Chris Literary Agency (1988), 16 Castellain Mansions, Castellain Road, London W9 1HA *tel* 0171-289 0653. *Director:* Teresa Chris.
All fiction, especially crime, women's commercial, general and literary fiction; all non-fiction, especially health, cooking, business, arts and crafts. *No* science fiction, horror, fantasy, short stories, poetry, academic books (home 10%, USA 15%, rest 20%). Own US office: Thompson & Chris Literary Agency. No reading fee. No unsolicited MSS accepted without introductory letter describing work and enclosing sae.

Christy & Moore Ltd—see **Sheil Land Associates Ltd.**

*Serafina Clarke (1980), 98 Tunis Road, London W12 7EY *tel* 0181-749 6979 *fax* 0181-740 6862.
Full-length MSS (home 15%, overseas 20%). Works in conjunction with agents overseas. No reading fee, but preliminary letter, 2 sample chapters and return postage essential.

*Mary Clemmey (1992), 6 Dunollie Road, London NW5 2XP *tel/fax* 0171-267 1290.
High quality fiction and non-fiction with an international market (home 10%, overseas 20%), performance rights (15%). *No* children's books, science fiction or fantasy. Works in conjunction with US agent. No reading fee. Small exclusive agency, approach by letter (including sae) first.

*Jonathan Clowes Ltd (1960), 10 Iron Bridge House, Bridge Approach, London NW1 8BD *tel* 0171-722 7674 *fax* 0171-722 7677. *Directors:* Jonathan Clowes, Ann Evans, Brie Burkeman.
Full-length MSS fiction and non-fiction; no academic or text books (home/USA 15%, translation 19%). Television, film, theatre and radio. Works in association with agents in most foreign countries.

Elspeth Cochrane Agency (1960), 11-13 Orlando Road, London SW4 0LE *tel* 0171-622 0314 (actors); 0171-622 4279 (writers) *fax* 0171-622 5815. *Contacts:* Elspeth Cochrane, Angela Frewin (actors); Nicholas Turrell (writers).
Send synopsis with covering letter in first instance (home and overseas 12½%), performance rights (12½%). No reading fee. *Authors* include Anne Charleston, John Carson, David Giles, Richard Olivier, Robert Tanitch, David Pinner, Royce Ryton, Malcolm Needs.

Rosica Colin Ltd (1949), 1 Clareville Grove Mews, London SW7 5AH *tel* 0171-370 1080 *telegraphic address* Colrep, London SW7 *fax* 0171-244 6441. *Directors:* Sylvie Marston, Joanna Marston.
All full-length MSS (excluding sci-fi and poetry); also theatre, film and sound broadcasting (home 10%, overseas 10-20%). No reading fee, but may take 3-4 months to consider full MSS. Send synopsis only in first instance, with letter outlining writing credits and whether MS has been previously submitted, plus return postage. *Authors* include Richard Aldington, Simone de Beauvoir (in UK), Samuel Beckett (publication rights), Steven Berkoff, Alan Brownjohn, Donald Campbell, Nick Dear, J.T. Edson, Bernard Farrell, Rainer Werner

Fassbinder (in UK), Jean Genet, Franz Xaver Kroetz, Heiner Müller (in UK), Graham Reid, Botho Strauss (in UK), Wim Wenders (in UK).

*Jane Conway-Gordon (1982), in association with Andrew Mann Ltd, 1 Old Compton Street, London W1V 5PH *tel* 0171-494 0148 *fax* 0171-287 9264. Full length MSS, performance rights (home 10%, overseas 20%). Represented in all foreign countries. No reading fee but preliminary letter and return postage essential.

*Rupert Crew Ltd (founded by F. Rupert Crew, 1927), 1A King's Mews, London WC1N 2JA *tel* 0171-242 8586 *telegraphic address* Authorship, Holb., London *fax* 0171-831 7914. *Directors:* Kathleen A. Crew, Doreen Montgomery, Caroline Montgomery.
International representation, handling volume and subsidiary rights in fiction and non-fiction properties (home 10-15%, elsewhere 20%); *no* plays, poetry, journalism or short stories. No reading fee, but preliminary letter and sae essential. Also acts independently as publishers' consultants.

Cruickshank Cazenove Ltd (1983), 97 Old South Lambeth Road, London SW8 1XU *tel* 0171-735 2933 *fax* 0171-820 1081. *Director:* Harriet Cruickshank.
Film, television and theatre scripts (home 10%, overseas varies). Works with agents abroad. No reading fee but preliminary letter essential with sae. Also agent for directors and designers.

*Curtis Brown, Haymarket House, 28/29 Haymarket, London SW1Y 4SP *tel* 0171-396 6600 *fax* 0171-396 0110. *Chairman:* Paul Scherer. *Managing director:* Jonathan Lloyd; *directors:* Diana Baring, Tim Curnow (Australia), Sue Freathy, Giles Gordon, Diana Mackay, Anthea Morton-Saner, Peter Murphy, Peter Robinson, Vivienne Schuster, Michael Shaw, Elizabeth Stevens.
Agents for the negotiation in all markets of novels, general non-fiction, children's books and associated rights (home 10%, USA, Canada and foreign 20%). Preliminary letter required; no reading fee. MSS for films, theatre, television and radio. Also agents for directors and designers. Return postage essential.

Judy Daish Associates Ltd (1978), 2 St Charles Place, London W10 6EG *tel* 0181-964 8811 *fax* 0181-964 8966. *Agents:* Judy Daish, Sara Stroud, Deborah Harwood.
Theatre, film, television, radio (rates by negotiation). No unsolicited MSS.

The Caroline Davidson Literary Agency (1988), 5 Queen Anne's Gardens, London W4 1TU *tel* 0181-995 5768 *fax* 0181-994 2770.
Specialises in literary fiction and non-fiction of all kinds, including highly illustrated books, academic and reference works (12½%); will suggest revision. No reading fee, but preliminary letter with book proposal and/or sample text, CV and sae required. *Authors* include Robert Baldock, Maggie Black, Elizabeth Bradley, Lynda Brown, Andrew Dalby, Emma Donoghue, Willi Elsener, Anissa Helou, Paul Hillyard, Tom Jaine, Bernard Lavery, J.P. McEvoy, Huon Mallalieu, Rena Salaman, Roland Vernon.

Merric Davidson Literary Agency (1990), Oakwood, Ashley Park, Tunbridge Wells, Kent TN4 8UA *tel/fax* (01892) 514282.
Specialising in contemporary adult fiction (home 10%, overseas 20%). No unsolicited MSS. Preliminary letter with synopsis, author information and sae, though very few new clients taken on. No initial reading fee, may suggest revision, subsequent editorial advice by arrangement. *Authors* include Valerie Blumenthal, Louise Doughty, Alison Habens, Elizabeth Harris, Alison MacLeod, Mark Pepper.

Felix De Wolfe, Manfield House, 376-9 Strand, London WC2R 0LR *tel* 0171-379 5767 *fax* 0171-836 0337.
Theatre, films, television, sound broadcasting, fiction (home 10-12½%, overseas 20%). Works in conjunction with many foreign agencies.

Dorian Literary Agency (1986), Upper Thornehill, 27 Church Road, St Marychurch, Torquay, Devon TQ1 4QY *tel/fax* (01803) 312095. *Proprietor:* Mrs D. Lumley.
Full-length MSS. Specialises in women's fiction, SF, fantasy and horror, crime, thrillers and mainstream (home 10%, USA 15%, translations 20-25%), performance rights (10%). No poetry, children's or short stories. Works in conjunction with agencies in most countries; negotiates direct with USA. No reading fee; preliminary letter with sample material essential; return postage essential. *Authors* include Brian Lumley, Dee Williams, Amy Myers, Stephen Jones.

Anne Drexl (1988), 8 Roland Gardens, London SW7 3PH *tel* 0171-244 9645.
Special interest in women's fiction, glitzy, family sagas, crime fiction and non-fiction. Also illustrated books for young readers, activity titles, and juvenile fiction (home 12½%, overseas 20-25%). Works in conjunction with foreign agencies and negotiates direct with foreign publishers. No reading fee, but no unsolicited MSS; return postage and preliminary letter essential.

Toby Eady Associates Ltd (1968), 3rd Floor, 9 Orme Court, London W2 4RL *tel* 0171-792 0092 *fax* 0171-792 0879. *Directors:* Toby Eady, Alexandra Pringle.
Books on Africa, the Middle East, China, fiction, non-fiction (home 10%, overseas 20%), performance rights (10%). Works with overseas associates. No reading fee, but return postage essential. *Authors* include Jung Chang, Bernard Cornwell, Julia Blackburn, Barbara Trapido, Esther Freud, Tim Pears.

***Faith Evans Associates** (1987), Clerkenwell House, 45 Clerkenwell Green, London EC1R 0EB *tel* 0171-490 2535 *fax* 0171-490 4958.
Small select agency (home 15%, overseas 20%). Sub-agents in most countries. No phone calls, scripts or unsolicited MSS. *Authors* include Melissa Benn, Eleanor Bron, Helena Kennedy, Seumas Milne, Roger Mugford, Christine Purkis, Sheila Rowbotham, Lorna Sage, Marion Urch, Andrea Weiss, Elizabeth Wilson.

Fact & Fiction Agency Ltd, 16 Greenway Close, London NW9 5AZ *tel* 0181-205 5716. *Directors:* Roy Lomax, Vera Lomax.
Television and radio – comedy only (home 10%, overseas 15%). By introduction only.

***John Farquharson Ltd**—see **Curtis Brown.**

Film Rights Ltd (1932), 483 Southbank House, Black Prince Road, Albert Embankment, London SE1 7SJ *tel* 0171-735 8171. *Directors:* Maurice Lambert, Laurence Fitch, Brendan Davis, Joan Potts.
Theatre, films, television and sound broadcasting (10%). Represented in USA and abroad.

Laurence Fitch Ltd (1952) (incorporating The London Play Company; 1922), 483 Southbank House, Black Prince Road, Albert Embankment, London SE1 7SJ *tel* 0171-735 8171. *Directors:* F.H.L. Fitch, Joan Potts, Brendan Davis.
Theatre, films, television and sound broadcasting. Also works with several agencies in New York and in Europe. *Authors* include The Estate of the Late Dodie Smith, Ray Cooney, John Chapman, Carlo Ardito, John Graham, Edward Taylor, Judy Allen, Dawn Lowe-Watson, Peter Coke, Glyn Robbins.

Jill Foster Ltd (1978), 3 Lonsdale Road, London SW13 9ED *tel* 0181-741 9410 *fax* 0181-741 2916.
  Theatre, films, television, sound broadcasting (12½%). Particularly interested in film and television comedy and drama. No novels or short stories. No reading fee. Preliminary letter essential.

Fox & Howard Literary Agency (1992), 4 Bramerton Street, Chelsea, London SW3 5JX *tel* 0171-352 8691 *fax* 0171-352 8691. *Partners:* Chelsey Fox, Charlotte Howard.
  Full-length MSS. General non-fiction: biography, naval, military and popular history, current affairs, reference, business, self-help, health and mind, body and spirit (home 10%, overseas 20%); will suggest revision where appropriate. *No* poetry, plays, short stories, children's, science fiction, fantasy or horror. No reading fee, but preliminary letter and synopsis with sae essential. *Authors* include Sir Rhodes Boyson, Dr Graham Handley, Anthony Kemp, Betty Parsons.

*****Fraser & Dunlop Ltd, Fraser & Dunlop Scripts Ltd**—see **The Peters Fraser & Dunlop Group Ltd.**

French's, 9 Elgin Mews South, London W9 1JZ *tel* 0171-266 3321 *fax* 0171-286 6716. *Director:* John French.
  All MSS; specialises in novels and screenplays (home/overseas 10%); theatre, films, television, radio (10%). Reading service available, details on application. Sae must be enclosed with all MSS.

*****Vernon Futerman Associates** (1984), 159 Goldhurst Terrace, London NW6 3EU *tel* 0171-625 9601 *fax* 0171-625 9601. *Directors:* Vernon Futerman (managing), Guy Rose, Alexandra Groom.
  Specialises in academic (science, humanities), art, politics, current affairs, literary criticism, showbusiness, travel and plays for theatre, film and TV. Full-length MSS (home 12½-17½%, overseas 17½-22½%), performance rights (12½-17½%). Works in conjunction with overseas agents. Will suggest revision. No reading fee; preliminary letter with synopsis and sae essential. No unsolicited MSS. *Authors* include Éve Eckstein, Russell W. Howe, Hugo du Plessis, Prof Wu Ningkun, Ernie Wise, Valerie Grosvenor Myer, Desmond Harding, Judy Upton.

Jüri Gabriel, 35 Camberwell Grove, London SE5 8JA *tel/fax* 0171-703 6186.
  Quality fiction and non-fiction (current specialisations: medical, military, practical art, popular academic); radio, television and film. Full-length MSS (home 10%, overseas 20%), performance rights (10%); will suggest revision where appropriate. No short stories, articles, verse or books for children. No reading fee; return postage essential. Jüri Gabriel is the chairman of Dedalus (publishers) and was a writer/translator for 20 years. *Authors* include Nigel Cawthorne, Diana Constance, James Hawes, Robert Irwin, Sian James, 'Mark Lloyd', David Miller, Prof Cedric Mims, John Outram, Ewen Southby-Tailyour, Dr Terence White, Herbert Williams, John Wyatt, Dr Robert Youngson.

Kerry Gardner Management (1975), 15 Kensington High Street, London W8 5NP *tel* 0171-937 4478 *fax* 0171-376 2587.
  Specialises in performance rights – represents playwrights, and film, TV and radio scriptwriters (10%). Works in conjunction with overseas agents. No reading fee.

Eric Glass Ltd (1932), 28 Berkeley Square, London W1X 6HD *tel* 0171-629 7162 *fax* 0171-499 6780. *Director:* Janet Glass.

Full-length MSS only; also theatre, films, television, and sound broadcasting. No unsolicited MSS. No reading fee. Sole representatives of the French Society of Authors (Societé des Auteurs et Compositeurs Dramatiques).

*Christine Green Authors' Agent (1984), 40 Doughty Street, London WC1N 2LF   *tel* 0171-831 4956   *fax* 0171-405 3935.
Fiction and general non-fiction. Full-length MSS (home 10%, overseas 20%). Works in conjunction with agencies in Europe and Scandinavia. No reading fee, but preliminary letter and return postage essential.

*Greene & Heaton Ltd (1962), 37 Goldhawk Road, London W12 8QQ   *tel* 0181-749 0315   *fax* 0181-749 0318. *Directors:* Carol Heaton, Timothy Webb; *associate agent:* Judith Murray.
Full-length MSS, fiction and non-fiction (home 10%, overseas 20%, translation 20%). *No* plays, TV or film scripts, or children's books. Works in conjunction with agencies in most countries. No reading fee. Preliminary letter and return postage required.

*Gregory & Radice Authors' Agents (1987), 3 Barb Mews, London W6 7PA   *tel* 0171-610 4676   *fax* 0171-610 4686. *Partners:* Jane Gregory, Dr Lisanne Radice (editorial), Pippa Dyson (film and television rights).
Full-length MSS; fiction and non-fiction. Specialise in crime fiction, commercial and literary fiction, thrillers and politics. Particularly interested in books with potential for sales abroad and/or to film and television (home 15%, articles, USA and translation 20%, film/TV rights 15%). No short stories, plays, film scripts, science fiction, fantasy, poetry, academic or children's books. Represented in all foreign markets. No reading fee, editorial advice given to own authors. No unsolicited MSS: preliminary letter, synopsis and first three chapters essential plus return postage.

David Grossman Literary Agency Ltd (1976), 118b Holland Park Avenue, London W11 4UA   *tel* 0171-221 2770   *fax* 0171-221 1445.
Full-length MSS (home 10-15%, overseas 20% including foreign agent's commission), performance rights (15%). Works in conjunction with agents in New York, Europe, Japan. No reading fee, but preliminary letter required.

The Guidelines Partnership (1986), 18 Pretoria Road, Cambridge CB4 1HE   *tel* (01223) 314668   *fax* (01223) 364619. *Partners:* Geoff Black, Stuart Wall, Linda Black, Eleanor Wall.
Specialises in educational texts and exam-related study guides for most ages and most subject areas (home 15%, overseas 20%); will suggest revision where appropriate. Works with overseas educational publishers. No reading fee. Preliminary letter or fax essential.

*A.M. Heath & Co. Ltd (1919), 79 St Martin's Lane, London WC2N 4AA   *tel* 0171-836 4271   *cables* Script, London   *telegraphic address* Script, London WC2   *fax* 0171-497 2561. *Directors:* Michael Thomas, William Hamilton, Sara Fisher, Sarah Molloy.
Full-length MSS (home 10-15%, USA 20%, translation 20%), performance rights (15%). Agents in USA and all European countries and Japan. No reading fee.

*David Higham Associates Ltd (1935), 5-8 Lower John Street, Golden Square, London W1R 4HA   *tel* 0171-437 7888   *fax* 0171-437 1072. *Directors:* Bruce Hunter, Jacqueline Korn, Anthony Crouch, Elizabeth Cree, Anthony Goff, Ania Corless.
Agents for the negotiation of all rights in fiction, general non-fiction, plays, film and television scripts (home 10%, USA/translation 20%). USA associate

agency: Harold Ober Associates Inc. Represented in all foreign markets. Preliminary letter and return postage essential. No reading fee.

*Vanessa Holt Ltd (1989), 59 Crescent Road, Leigh-on-Sea, Essex SS9 2PF *tel* (01702) 73787 *fax* (01702) 471890.
General adult fiction and non-fiction (home 10%, overseas 20%). Works in conjunction with many foreign agencies. No reading fee, but preliminary letter essential.

Valerie Hoskins Associates, 20 Charlotte Street, London W1P 1HJ *tel* 0171-637 4490 *fax* 0171-637 4493. *Proprietor:* Valerie Hoskins.
Film, television and radio only (12.5% home and maximum 20% overseas). No reading fee, but sae appreciated. Works in conjunction with overseas agents. *No* unsolicited MSS; preliminary letter essential.

Howard Seddon Associates (1988), BM Box 1129, London WC1N 3XX *tel* (01923) 229784 *fax* (01923) 229784. *Partners:* Dr Keith H. Seddon, Sarah J. Howard.
Full-length MSS. Fiction: fantasy, gothic, horror, literary; non-fiction: folklore, New Age, occult, philosophy, religion, social issues (home 15%, overseas 20%); will suggest revision where appropriate (will also undertake revision; fees variable). No unsolicited MSS; preliminary letter, CV and sae essential. Reading fee may be charged. Full reading and report service available.

*Tanja Howarth Literary Agency (1970), 19 New Row, London WC2N 4LA *tel* 0171-240 5553/836 4142 *fax* 0171-379 0969.
Full-length MSS. General fiction and non-fiction, thrillers, contemporary and historical women's novels and sagas (home 15%, USA/translation 20%). Represented in the USA by various agents. Please submit preliminary letter, synopsis and three sample chapters with return postage. No reading fee.

ICM Ltd, Oxford House, 76 Oxford Street, London W1R 1RB *tel* 0171-636 6565 *fax* 0171-323 0101. *Directors:* Duncan Heath, Susan Rodgers, Michael Foster, Ian Amos, Paul Lyon-Maris.
Specialises in scripts for film, theatre, TV, radio (home 10%, overseas 10%). Part of International Creative Management Inc., Los Angeles and New York. No reading fee.

Michael Imison Playwrights Ltd (formerly Dr Jan Van Loewen Ltd), 28 Almeida Street, London N1 1TD *tel* 0171-354 3174 *fax* 0171-359 6273. *Directors:* Michael Imison MA, Tamsyn Imison BSc.
Specialises in stage plays, also cover radio, TV, film (home 10%, overseas 15%), no fiction or general MSS. Represented in all major countries. No reading fee. No unsolicited scripts; recommendation from known theatre professional required.

*Intercontinental Literary Agency (1965), The Chambers, Chelsea Harbour, Lots Road, London SW10 0XF *tel* 0171-351 4763 *fax* 0171-351 4809. Anthony Guest Gornall and Nicki Kennedy.
Concerned only with translation rights for The Peters Fraser & Dunlop Group Ltd, London and Harold Matson Company, Inc., New York.

International Copyright Bureau Ltd (1905), 22A Aubrey House, Maida Avenue, London W2 1TQ *tel* 0171-724 8034 *fax* 0171-724 7662. *Directors:* Joy Westendarp, J.C.H. Hadfield.
Theatre, films, television, radio (home 10%, overseas 19%). Works in conjunction with agents in New York and most foreign countries. Preliminary letter essential.

International Management Group, Pier House, Strand on the Green, Chiswick, London W4 3NN *tel* 0181-233 5137 *fax* 0181-233 5001. *Chairman:* Mark H.

McCormack; *agents:* Jean Cooke (UK), Julian Bach, David Chalfant, Mark Reiter (US), Fumiko Matsuki (Japan).
Represents sports celebrities, classical musicians and broadcasting personalities (home/US 15%, elsewhere 25%). No reading fee.

International Scripts (1979), 1 Norland Square, Holland Park, London W11 4PX *tel* 0171-229 0736 *fax* 0171-792 3287. *Directors:* H.P. Tanner, J. Lawson.
Specialises in full-length contemporary and women's fiction, horror, general non-fiction (home 15%, overseas 20-25%), performance rights (15-20%); *no* poetry or short stories. Works with overseas agents worldwide. Preliminary letter required. Return postage required for MSS plus a £30.00 reading fee (for which a report will be provided). *Authors* include Richard Laymon, Anna Jacobs, Mary Ryan, Ed Gorman, Julie Harris, Peter Haining, Graham Masterton, John and Anne Spencer.

Mary Irvine (1974), 11 Upland Park Road, Oxford OX2 7RU *tel* (01865) 513570.
Specialises in women's fiction and family sagas. No plays, scripts, children's books, short stories or poetry (home 10%, USA 15%, translations 20%). Works with agents in USA, Europe, Japan. No unsolicited MSS. Preliminary letter essential and return postage required. No reading fee.

*****John Johnson (Authors' Agent) Ltd** (1956), Clerkenwell House, 45-47 Clerkenwell Green, London EC1R 0HT *tel* 0171-251 0125 *fax* 0171-251 2172.
Full-length MSS (home 10%, overseas direct 15%, with subagent maximum of 20%). Works in conjunction with agents in USA and many European countries. No unsolicited MSS.

*****Jane Judd Literary Agency** (1986), 18 Belitha Villas, London N1 1PD *tel* 0171-607 0273 *fax* 0171-607 0623.
Full-length MSS only (home 10%, overseas 20%). Works with agents in USA and most foreign countries. No reading fee, but preliminary letter with synopsis and sae essential.

Juvenilia (1973), Avington, Winchester, Hants SO21 1DB *tel/fax* (01962) 779656. *Proprietor:* Mrs Rosemary Bromley.
Full-length MSS for the children's market, fiction and non-fiction (home 10%, overseas from 15%), illustration (20%), performance rights (10%). Short stories only if specifically for picture books, radio or TV. No verse. No unsolicited MSS; preliminary letter with sae and full details essential. No reading fee. Postage for acknowledgement and return of material imperative.

*****Michelle Kass Associates** (1991), 36-38 Glasshouse Street, London W1R 5RH *tel* 0171-439 1624 *fax* 0171-734 3394. *Proprietor:* Michelle Kass.
Full-length MSS. Fiction and drama (screen and stage) (home 10%, overseas 15-20%), performance rights (10%); will suggest revision where appropriate. Works with agents overseas. No reading fee. Preliminary letter and return postage required.

*****Frances Kelly Agency** (1978), 111 Clifton Road, Kingston upon Thames, Surrey KT2 6PL *tel* 0181-549 7830 *fax* 0181-547 0051.
Full-length MSS. Non-fiction: general and academic, reference and professional books, all subjects (home 10%, overseas 20%), television, radio (10%). No reading fee, but no unsolicited MSS; preliminary letter with synopsis, CV and return postage essential.

Peter Knight Agency (1985), 20 Crescent Grove, London SW4 7AH *tel* 0171-622 1467 *fax* 0171-622 1522. *Director:* Peter Knight; *associates:* Ann King-Hall, Gaby Martin, Andrew Knight, Giovanna Farrell-Vinay.

Motor sports, cartoon books for both adults and children, and factual and biographical material (commission dependent upon authors and territories). No poetry, science fiction or cookery. Overseas associates: United Media (USA), Auspac Media (Australia). No unsolicited MSS. Send letter accompanied by CV and sae with synopsis of proposed work.

*Lemon Unna & Durbridge Ltd—see **The Agency (London) Ltd**

*Barbara Levy Literary Agency (1986), 64 Greenhill, Hampstead High Street, London NW3 5TZ *tel* 0171-435 9046 *fax* 0171-431 2063. *Director:* Barbara Levy; *associate:* John Selby (solicitor).
Full-length MSS only; also films, television and radio (home 10%, overseas by arrangement). No reading fee, but informative preliminary letter and return postage essential.

Limelight Management (1991), 54 Marshall Street, London WC1V 1LR *tel* 0171-734 1218 *fax* 0171-287 1998. *Directors:* Fiona Lindsay, Linda Shanks.
Full-length and short MSS. Food, wine, health, crafts, gardening (home 10%, overseas 20%), TV and radio rights (10-20%); will suggest revision where appropriate. No reading fee.

*The Christopher Little Literary Agency (1979), 48 Walham Grove, London SW6 1QR *tel* 0171-386 1800 *fax* 0171-381 2248 *e-mail* 100555.3137 @compuserve.com *Contacts:* Christopher Little, Patrick Walsh (fiction, non-fiction); *office manager:* Bryony Evens.
Commercial and literary full-length fiction and non-fiction and film/TV scripts. Special interests: crime, thrillers, autobiographies, popular science and narrative and investigative non-fiction. Also makes a particular speciality out of packaging celebrities for the book market and representing book projects for journalists. Rights representative in the UK for six US literary agencies (home 15%; US, translation, motion picture 20%). No reading fee. Send detailed letter ('giving a summary of present and future intentions together with track record, if any'), synopsis and/or first two chapters and sae in the first instance. *Authors* include Felice Arena, Linford Christie, Damon Hill, Anna Pasternak, Clare Latimer, Ginny Elliot, James Whitaker, Alistair MacNeill, Candace Robb, Harriet Castor, Sanjida O'Connell, Simon Gandolfi, Storm Constantine, Paula Hamilton, Frankie Dettori, Peter Rosenberg, Marcus Berkmann, Tom Holland, David Thomas, Vivienne Savory, Simon Beckett, Wilbur Wright, John Spurling, Samantha Phillips, Alvin Rakoff, Laura Thompson, Colin Cameron, Mike Dash, Brian Hall, A.J. Quinnell.

London Independent Books (1971), 26 Chalcot Crescent, London NW1 8YD *tel* 0171-706 0486 *fax* 0171-724 3122. *Proprietor:* Carolyn Whitaker.
Specialises in commercial and fantasy fiction, cinema, jazz, show business, travel. Full-length MSS (home 15%, overseas 20%), films, television and sound broadcasting (15%). Will suggest revision of promising MSS. No reading fee. *Authors* include Bruce Crowther, Nigel Frith, Keith Grey, Andre Launay, Glenn Mitchell, Connie Monk, Emma Sinclair.

Jennifer Luithlen Agency (1986), The Rowans, 88 Holmfield Road, Leicester LE2 1SB *tel* (0116) 273 8863 *fax* (0116) 273 5697. *Agent:* Jennifer Luithlen.
Children's books; adult fiction: crime, historical, saga (home 10%, overseas 20%), performance rights (15%); will suggest revision where appropriate. Handles translation sales direct. No reading fee. *Not actively looking for new clients. No unsolicited MSS* without prior telephone call.

*Lutyens & Rubinstein (1993), 231 Westbourne Park Road, London W11 1EB *tel* 0171-792 4855 *fax* 0171-792 4833. *Directors:* Sarah Lutyens, Felicity Rubinstein.

Fiction and non-fiction, commercial and literary (home 10%, overseas 20%). Send outline/2 sample chapters and sae. No reading fee.

Duncan McAra (1988), 30 Craighall Crescent, Edinburgh EH6 4RZ *tel/fax* 0131-552 1558. Thrillers and literary fiction; non-fiction: art, architecture, archaeology, biography, film, military, travel (home 10%, overseas by arrangement). Preliminary letter with sae essential. No reading fee.

Maclean Dubois (Writers & Agents) (1977), Hillend House, Hillend, Edinburgh EH10 7DX *tel* 0131-445 5885 *fax* 0131-445 5898. *Directors:* Charles Maclean, Ross Leckie, Geraldine Coates, James Hardie, Patrick Maguire. Full-length MSS and proposals. Scottish literature, history and topography; food and drink, especially Scotch whisky (home 10%, overseas 15%); will suggest revision, fee payable. Reading fee.

Eunice McMullen Children's Literary Agent Ltd (1992), 38 Clewer Hill Road, Windsor, Berks. SL4 4BW *tel* (01753) 830348 *fax* (01753) 833459. *Director:* Eunice McMullen.
All types of children's books, particularly picture books (home 10%, overseas 15%). No unsolicited scripts without prior letter. *Authors* include Wayne Anderson, Reg Cartwright, Richard Fowler, Charles Fuge, Simon James, Colin and Moira Maclean, Graham Oakley, Sue Porter, Jim Riordan, Carol Thompson, David Wood.

*Andrew Mann Ltd (1974), in association with Jane Conway-Gordon, 1 Old Compton Street, London W1V 5PH *tel* 0171-734 4751 *fax* 0171-287 9264. *Directors:* Anne Dewe, Tina Betts.
Full-length MSS. Scripts for television, cinema, radio and theatre (home 10%, USA 19%, Europe 19%). Associated with agents worldwide. No reading fee, but no unsolicited MSS without preliminary enquiry and sae.

Manuscript ReSearch (1988), PO Box 33, Bicester, Oxon OX6 7PP *tel* (01869) 323447 *fax* (01869) 324096. *Proprietor:* T.G. Jenkins.
Full-length MSS. Specialises in crime/thrillers, biographies (home 10%, overseas 20%), performance rights (15%); short MSS only from established clients. Professional line by line editing and laser printing £3.00 per A4 page. No reading fee, but sae for script return essential.

*The Marsh Agency (1994), 138 Buckingham Palace Road, London SW1W 9SA *tel* 0171-730 1124 *fax* 0171-730 0037 *e-mail* 100614.1702@compuserve.com *Partners:* Paul Marsh, Susanna Nicklin.
Specialisation: translation rights (10%).

Judy Martin (1990), 138 Buckingham Palace Road, London SW1W 9SA *tel* 0171-730 3779 *fax* 0171-730 3801.
Fiction, non-fiction, film and TV tie-ins, film and TV scripts; *no* plays, poetry or children's stories (home 15%, overseas 20%), performance rights (15%). Translation rights handled by The Marsh Agency. No reading fee, but sae required for all unsolicited MSS, together with details of publishing history.

M.C. Martinez Literary Agency (1988), 60 Oakwood Avenue, Southgate, London N14 6QL *tel* 0181-886 5829. *Proprietor:* Mary Caroline Martinez.
Fiction, children's books, arts and crafts, interior design, alternative health, cookery, DIY, travel, biographies, popular music, sport and business. Also scripts for television, radio and theatre. Specialises in fiction, children's and alternative health. No unsolicited typescripts. No reading fee but an admin fee may be charged where appropriate. DTP service available. Preliminary letter with synopsis and sae required (home 15%; US, overseas and translation 20%; performance rights 20%). Telephone first, possible change of address. *Authors*

include Faustin Charles, Carol Donockley, Alan Fisk, David Holbrook, Nina Milton, Dorothy Thompson, Carol Turner, Roger Stevens, Sylvia Wickham.

Blanche Marvin, 21A St John's Wood High Street, London NW8 7NG   *tel/fax* 0171-722 2313.
Full-length MSS (home 12½% + 12½% overseas), performance rights. No reading fee but return postage essential. *Authors* include Christopher Bond.

*MBA Literary Agents Ltd (1971), 45 Fitzroy Street, London W1P 5HR   *tel* 0171-387 2076/4785   *fax* 0171-387 2042. *Directors:* Diana Tyler, John Richard Parker, Meg Davis, Ruth Needham, Timothy Webb.
Full-length MSS; no poetry (home 10%, overseas 20%), theatre, television, radio (10%), films (10-15%). Works in conjunction with agents in most countries. No reading fee. No unsolicited material. *Authors* include Jeffrey Caine, Glenn Chandler, Campbell Armstrong, Maggie Furey, Valerie Georgson, Andrew Hodges, Roy Lancaster, Paul J. McAuley, Anne McCaffrey, Anne Perry, Iain Sinclair, Tom Vernon, Douglas Watkinson, Fred Warrington, Sir Roger Penrose, Patrick Wright, Valerie Windsor, Elspeth Sandys and the estate of B.S. Johnson.

Richard Milne Ltd (1956), 15 Summerlee Gardens, London N2 9QN   *tel* 0181-883 3987. *Directors:* R.M. Sharples, K.N. Sharples.
Specialises in scripts for films, television, sound broadcasting (10%). Unable to represent any additional authors at present.

*William Morris Agency (UK) Ltd (1965), 31/32 Soho Square, London W1V 6HH   *tel* 0171-434 2191   *fax* 0171-437 0238   *e-mail* adl@wma.com   *Contacts:* Stephen M. Kenis (films), Jane Annakin (television and theatre), Stephanie Cabot (books).
Worldwide theatrical and literary agency with offices in New York, Beverly Hills and Nashville, and associates in Munich and Sydney. Represents theatre, television, film and radio scripts; fiction and general non-fiction (television, theatre, film and UK book 10%, US book and translation 20%). No unsolicited material or MSS.

Judith Murdoch Literary Agency (1993), 19 Chalcot Square, London NW1 8YA   *tel* 0171-722 4197.
Full-length fiction only (home 15%, overseas 20%). No genre novels, science fiction/fantasy, poetry, short stories or children's. Must send first two chapters and synopsis with preliminary letter. Return postage/sae essential. Editorial advice given; no reading fee. Translation rights handled by The Marsh Agency.

Negotiate Ltd (1986), Gavin Kennedy, 22 Braid Avenue, Edinburgh EH10 6EE   *tel* 0131-452 8404   *fax* 0131-452 8388.
Specialises in the negotiation of author's contracts and subsidiary rights. Established authors only or new authors with draft contract from a publisher. Preliminary letter or fax please.

*Maggie Noach Literary Agency (1982), 21 Redan Street, London W14 0AB   *tel* 0171-602 2451   *fax* 0171-603 4712.
General fiction and non-fiction; non-illustrated children's books. Full-length MSS (home 15%, US/translation 20%). No scientific, academic or specialist non-fiction; no poetry, plays, short stories or books for the very young. Encourages promising young writers but *very* few new clients taken on as it is considered vital to give individual attention to each author's work. Unsolicited MSS not welcome. Approach by letter (*not by telephone*), giving a brief description of the book and enclosing a few sample pages. Return postage essential. No reading fee.

*Andrew Nurnberg Associates Ltd, Clerkenwell House, 45-47 Clerkenwell Green, London EC1R 0HT   *tel* 0171-417 8800   *fax* 0171-417 8812.
Specialises in the sale of translation rights of English and American authors into European languages.

Alexandra Nye, Writers & Agents (1991), Cauldhame Cottage, Sheriffmuir, Dunblane, Perthshire FK15 0LN   *tel* (01786) 825114. *Director:* Alexandra Nye.
Literary fiction, historical, biographies; no poetry or plays (home 10%, overseas 20%, translation 15%). Will suggest revision where appropriate. Send preliminary letter and synopsis in first instance; sae essential for return. No reading fee. Critical service available at a charge.

David O'Leary Literary Agency (1988), 10 Lansdowne Court, Lansdowne Rise, London W11 2NR   *tel* 0171-229 1623   *telex* 27636 AEZRA G   *fax* 0171-727 9624.
Popular general fiction and non-fiction: special interests Russia, Ireland, history, science (home 10%, overseas 20%), performance rights (15%). Will suggest revision; no reading fee. Write or call before submitting MSS. *Authors* include Alexander Cordell, Jim Lusby, Alex Keegan, James Kennedy, Edward Toman.

*Deborah Owen Ltd (1971), 78 Narrow Street, Limehouse, London E14 8BP   *tel* 0171-987 5119/5441   *fax* 0171-538 4004. Deborah Owen, Gemma Hirst.
Full-length MSS (home 10%, overseas 15%). All types of literary material except plays, scripts, children's books, short stories or poetry. No unsolicited MSS. No new authors at present. *Authors* include Ellis Peters, Amos Oz, Murray Smith, Delia Smith.

*Mark Paterson & Associates (1955), 10 Brook Street, Wivenhoe, Colchester, Essex CO7 9DS   *tel* (01206) 825433/4   *fax* (01206) 822990.
Book-length MSS; general but with special experience in psychoanalysis, psychotherapy, history, copyright and education (20% worldwide including sub-agents' commission). No articles or short stories except for existing clients. Preliminary letter with synopsis, sample material and sae essential. *Authors* include Sigmund Freud, Anna Freud, Hugh Brogan, Donald Winnicott, Peter Moss, Sir Arthur Evans, Dorothy Richardson, Hugh Schonfield, Georg Groddeck, Patrick Casement.

John Pawsey (1981), 60 High Street, Tarring, Worthing, West Sussex BN14 7NR   *tel* (01903) 205167   *fax* (01903) 205167.
Full-length popular fiction and non-fiction MSS (home 10-15%, overseas 19%). No unsolicited material, poetry, short stories, journalism or original film and stage scripts. Preliminary letter and return postage with all correspondence essential. Works in association with agencies in the USA, Europe and the Far East. Will suggest revision if MS sufficiently promising. No reading fee. *Authors* include Jonathan Agnew, Dr David Lewis, Peter Hobday, Jon Silverman.

*Maggie Pearlstine Associates Ltd (1989), 31 Ashley Gardens, Ambrosden Avenue, Westminster, London SW1P 1QE   *tel* 0171-828 4212   *fax* 0171-834 5546.
Full-length MSS, fiction and non-fiction. Special interests: commercial fiction, illustrated non-fiction, home and leisure, health, biography, history and politics (home 10-12½%, overseas 20%). No children's or poetry; only deals with scripts and short stories by authors already on its books. No unsolicited MSS. Preliminary letter required and sae. No reading fee. *Authors* include James Cox, John Drews, Mary Evans Young, Glorafilia, Prof Roger Gosden, Roy Hattersley, Prof Lisa Jardine, Charles Kennedy, Prof Nicholas Lowe, Sara

Morrison, Lesley Regan, Jack Straw, Dr Thomas Stuttaford, Brian Wilson, Prof the Lord Winston, Tony Wright.

*A.D. Peters & Co. Ltd—see **The Peters Fraser & Dunlop Group Ltd.**

*The Peters Fraser & Dunlop Group Ltd, 503/4 The Chambers, Chelsea Harbour, Lots Road, London SW10 0XF *tel* 0171-344 1000 *fax* 0171-352 7356/351 1756. *Directors:* Michael Sissons (joint chairman), Anthony Jones (joint chairman), Anthony Baring (managing director), Kenneth Ewing, Pat Kavanagh, Tim Corrie, Maureen Vincent, Norman North, Mark Lucas, Caroline Dawnay, Ginette Chalmers. *Incorporating* A.D. Peters & Co. Ltd, Fraser & Dunlop Scripts Ltd, Fraser & Dunlop Ltd, June Hall Literary Agency Ltd. *Associated agencies:* Intercontinental Literary Agency, Sterling Lord Literistic (New York), Chelsea West Inc. (New York).
Specialists in the negotiation of all rights in general fiction and non-fiction, film and television scripts, plays, and certain specialist and academic works. Children's MSS and illustrations to Peters Fraser & Dunlop Children's List, Rosemary Canter (home/overseas 10-20%). No unsolicited MSS accepted. We ask for an introductory letter from the author describing the work offered, with sae. No reading fee.

Laurence Pollinger Ltd, 18 Maddox Street, London W1R 0EU *tel* 0171-629 9761 *fax* 0171-629 9765. *Directors:* Gerald J. Pollinger, Margaret Pepper, Lesley Hadcroft, Juliet Burton; *secretary:* Denzil De Silva.
All material except original film stories, poetry and freelance journalistic articles. Dramatic associate, Micheline Steinberg. *Commission:* 15%, except for translation (20%), which may include the commission to the associate in the territory concerned. No reading fee. An editorial contribution may be requested.

*Murray Pollinger (1969), 5-8 Lower John Street, Golden Square, London W1R 4HA *tel* 0171-437 7888 *fax* 0171-437 1072. Now part of David Higham Associates Ltd.
Agents for the negotiation in all markets of adult fiction and non-fiction, children's fiction and picture books (home 10%, overseas 20%). Preliminary letter with synopsis required, together with return postage; also names of agents and publishers previously contacted. No reading fee.

*Shelley Power Literary Agency Ltd (1976), Le Montaud, 24220 Berbiguières, France *tel* 53 29 62 52 *fax* 53 29 62 54. Also based in the UK.
General fiction and non-fiction. Full-length MSS (home 10%, USA and translations 19%). No children's books, poetry or plays. Works in conjunction with agents abroad. No reading fee, but preliminary letter with sae for return from UK essential. *Authors* include Madge Swindells, William Gibson, Elizabeth Hand, Michael Swanwick, Richard Stern, Peter Lambley and Roger Wilkes.

PVA Management Ltd, Hallow Park, Worcester WR2 6PG *tel* (01905) 640663 *fax* (01905) 641842. *Managing director:* Paul Vaughan.
Full-length MSS (home 15%, overseas 20%), performance rights (15%). Please send synopsis and sample chapters together with return postage.

Radala & Associates (1970), 17 Avenue Mansions, Finchley Road, London NW3 7AX *tel* 0171-794 4495 *fax* 0171-431 7636. *Director:* Richard Gollner; *associates:* Neil Hornick, Anna Swan, Andy Marino.
Full-length MSS (home 10%, overseas 15%). Fiction and non-fiction. Books, television, sound broadcasting. Electronic publishing division, including video, audio tape, computer program packages for multi-media publishing production companies.

Margaret Ramsay Ltd—now **Casarotto Ramsay Ltd.**

Jim Reynolds Associates (1988), 7 Banbury Lane, Byfield, Daventry, Northants.
NN11 6UX *tel/fax* (01327) 261542. *Director:* Ann Reynolds.
Full-length MSS – biography, social, political and military history, current
affairs, investigative journalism, cricket (home 10%, overseas 19%); will
suggest revision where appropriate. Works in conjunction with foreign
agencies. No reading fee. Sae with preliminary enquiry, please.

*Rogers, Coleridge & White Ltd (1967), 20 Powis Mews, London W11 1JN *tel*
0171-221 3717 *telegraphic address* Debrogers, London W11 *fax* 0171-229
9084. *Directors:* Deborah Rogers, Gill Coleridge, Patricia White (USA);
consultant: Ann Warnford-Davis.
Full-length book MSS, including children's books (home 10%, USA 15%,
translations 20%). *USA associate:* International Creative Management, Inc.
No unsolicited MSS please, and no submissions by fax. No reading fee.

Elizabeth Roy Literary Agency (1990), White Cottage, Greatford, Nr Stamford,
Lincs. PE9 4PR *tel/fax* (01778) 560672.
Women's fiction, crime fiction, children's books – writers and illustrators (home
10-15%, overseas 20%). Will suggest revision. Preliminary letter, synopsis and
sample chapters essential with names of publishers and agents previously
contacted. Return postage essential. No reading fee.

Hilary Rubinstein Books (1992), 61 Clarendon Road, London W11 4JE *tel*
0171-792 4282 *fax* 0171-221 5291. *Director:* Hilary Rubinstein.
Full-length MSS. Fiction and non-fiction (home 10%, overseas 20%); will
suggest revision where appropriate. *No* plays, scripts, children's books or
poetry. No reading fee, but *no* unsolicited MSS without preliminary letter or
call. *Authors* include Eric Lomax, Donna Williams.

Uli Rushby-Smith and Shirley Stewart (1993), 72 Plimsoll Road, Islington, London N4 2EE *tel/fax* 0171-354 2718. *Directors:* Uli Rushby-Smith, Shirley
Stewart.
Full length MSS only. Fiction and non-fiction, commercial and literary (home
10%, USA/foreign 20%). Work in conjunction with foreign sub-agents in
some countries. UK representatives of Curtis Brown Ltd, New York and
Henry Holt & Co, Inc., New York. Send outline, sample chapters and sae;
no reading fee.

Rosemary Sandberg Ltd (1991), 6 Bayley Street, London WC1B 3HB *tel* 0171-
304 4110 *fax* 0171-304 4109. *Directors:* Rosemary Sandberg, Ed Victor,
Graham Greene CBE.
Children's – writers and illustrators, general fiction and non-fiction (home 10-
15%, overseas 20%). Absolutely no unsolicited MSS.

*Tessa Sayle Agency, 11 Jubilee Place, London SW3 3TE *tel* 0171-823 3883 (5
lines) *fax* 0171-823 3363. *Publishing:* Rachel Calder; *film, TV, theatre:* Jane
Villiers.
Full-length MSS (home 10%, overseas 20%), film, TV, theatre (home 10%,
overseas 15-20%). USA Associates: Darhansoff & Verrill, 1220 Park Avenue,
New York, NY 10128. Represented in all foreign countries. No reading fee,
but preliminary letter and return postage essential.

The Sharland Organisation Ltd (1988), 9 Marlborough Crescent, Bedford Park,
London W4 1HE *tel* 0181-742 1919 *fax* 0181-995 7688. *Directors:* Mike
Sharland, Alice Sharland.
Specialises in film, television, stage and radio rights throughout the world
(home 15%, overseas 20%); also negotiates multimedia, interactive TV deals
and computer game contracts. Works in conjunction with overseas agents. Sae
required.

*Sheil Land Associates Ltd (1962), incorporating Christy & Moore Ltd (1912) and Richard Scott Simon Ltd (1971), 43 Doughty Street, London WC1N 2LF *tel* 0171-405 9351 *fax* 0171-831 2127. *Agents:* Anthony Sheil, Sonia Land, Vivien Green, Robert Kirby, Simon Trewin, John Rush (film/drama/TV), Benita Edzard (foreign rights department).

Full-length general and literary fiction, biography, travel, cookery, humour (home 10%, USA/translations 20%); theatre, film, radio and TV scripts (home 10%, overseas 20%). Preliminary letter and return postage essential. *Authors* include Peter Ackroyd, Melvyn Bragg, John Banville, Catherine Cookson, Josephine Cox, John Fowles, Susan Hill, HRH The Prince of Wales, Michael Ignatieff, John Keegan, Tom Sharpe, Rose Tremain, John Wilsher. **Foreign Rights Department** (1985), 19 John Street, London WC1N 2DL *tel* 0171-405 7473 *fax* 0171-405 5239. Benita Edzard, Anthony Sheil, Sonia Land, Susy Behr. Translation rights only.

*Caroline Sheldon Literary Agency (1985), 71 Hillgate Place, London W8 7SS *tel* 0171-727 9102. *Proprietor:* Caroline Sheldon; *associate:* Pippa Dyson (film/TV).

Full-length MSS. General fiction, women's fiction, and children's books (home 10%, overseas 20%). No reading fee. Synopsis and first three chapters with large sae in case of return required initially.

Jeffrey Simmons, 10 Lowndes Square, London SW1X 9HA *tel* 0171-235 8852 *fax* 0171-235 9733.

Specialises in adult fiction, biography, autobiography, show business, law, crime, politics, world affairs. Full-length MSS (home from 10%, overseas from 15%). Will suggest revision. No reading fee, but preliminary letter essential. *Authors* include Michael Bentine, Billy Boy, Clive Collins, Margaret Crosland, Euphrosyne Doxiadis, Anne-Marie Edwards, Fred Lawrence Guiles, James Haskins, Keith Wright.

*Richard Scott Simon Ltd—see **Sheil Land Associates Ltd.**

Carol Smith (1976), 25 Hornton Court, Kensington High Street, London W8 7RT *tel* 0171-937 4874 *fax* 0171-938 5323 *CIS e-mail* 100067,1643

Full-length MSS, fiction and non-fiction; specialise in commercial contemporary novels and welcome beginners (home 10%, USA/translation 20%). No science fiction, short stories, children's books, poetry, plays or TV scripts. No reading fee but preliminary letter essential. Please enclose return postage. MSS submissions by invitation only – write, don't phone! *Authors* include Sarah Harrison, Ruth Hamilton, John Cornwell, Mike Wilks, Claire Macdonald.

Solo Literary Agency Ltd (1978), 49-53 Kensington High Street, London W8 5ED *tel* 0171-376 2166 *fax* 0171-938 3165. *Directors:* Don Short (managing), Wendy Short (secretary).

Specialises in celebrity and autobiographical books. Fiction from established authors only (home 15%, overseas 20%). No reading fee. *Authors* include Peter Essex, James Oram, Nicholas Davies, Barbra Paskin, Rick Sky.

*Abner Stein, 10 Roland Gardens, London SW7 3PH *tel* 0171-373 0456 *fax* 0171-370 6316.

Full-length and short MSS (home 10%, overseas 20%). No reading fee, but no unsolicited MSS; preliminary letter and return postage required.

Micheline Steinberg Playwrights' Agent (1987), 110 Frognal, London NW3 6XU *tel* 0171-433 3980 *fax* 0171-794 8355.

Full-length MSS – theatre, films, television, radio (home 10%, overseas 15%). Dramatic Associate for Laurence Pollinger Ltd; works in conjunction with agents in USA and other countries. No reading fee, but preliminary letter essential and return postage with MSS.

Rochelle Stevens & Co. (1984), 2 Terretts Place, Upper Street, London N1 1QZ *tel* 0171-359 3900 *fax* 0171-354 5729. *Proprietor:* Rochelle Stevens; *associate:* Frances Grannum.
Drama scripts for film, television, theatre and radio (10%); will suggest revision where appropriate. No reading fee, but preliminary letter and return postage essential.

Peter Tauber Press Agency (1950), 94 East End Road, London N3 2SX *tel* 0181-346 4165. *Directors:* Peter Tauber, Robert Tauber.
Non-fiction: hard-hitting top celebrity auto/biographies; innovative slimming books. Fiction: highest quality commercial women's fiction, thrillers and horror. No poetry, short stories, plays, children's or foreign books. *Commission:* 20%. Please send synopsis, author CV, first three chapters, copies of all previous rejections, an sae, and for fiction writers a non-returnable, no-obligation submission fee of £50. Replies only on these terms.

J.M. Thurley Management (1976), 213 Linen Hall, 162-168 Regent Street, London W1R 5TA *tel* 0171-437 9545/6 *fax* 0171-287 9208. *Associates:* Jon Thurley MA, Patricia Preece BA.
Literary and dramatic work for all media (home 10-15%, overseas 20%). American and European representation arranged geared to specific projects. No reading fee. Where substantial creative/editorial imput required, commission charged at 15%.

*****Lavinia Trevor** (1993), 6 The Glasshouse, 49A Goldhawk Road, London W12 8QP *tel* 0181-749 8481 *fax* 0181-749 7377.
Fiction and non-fiction for the general trade market. No reading fee.

*****Jane Turnbull** (1986), 13 Wendell Road, London W12 9RS *tel* 0181-743 9580 *fax* 0181-749 6079.
Fiction and non-fiction (home 10%, USA 15%, translation 20%), performance rights (15%). No science fiction, romantic fiction, children's or short stories. Works in conjunction with Aitken, Stone & Wylie for sale of translation rights. No reading fee but preliminary letter and sae essential.

*****Harvey Unna & Stephen Durbridge (1975) Ltd**—see **The Agency (London) Ltd.**

*****Ed Victor Ltd** (1976), 6 Bayley Street, Bedford Square, London WC1B 3HB *tel* 0171-304 4100 *telegraphic address* Victorious, London W1 *fax* 0171-304 4111. *Directors:* Ed Victor, Graham C. Greene CBE, Carol Ryan, Leon Morgan, Margaret Phillips, Sophie Hicks.
Full-length MSS, fiction and non-fiction, but no short stories, film/TV scripts, poetry or plays (home 15%, USA 15%, translation 20%), performance rights (15%). Represented in all foreign markets. No unsolicited MSS. Sophie Hicks (children's) – writers and illustrators. *Authors* include Douglas Adams, Joan Collins, Sir Ranulph Fiennes, Josephine Hart, Jack Higgins, Erica Jong, Kathy Lette, Iris Murdoch, Nigel Nicolson, Erich Segal, Will Self, and the estates of Irving Wallace, Raymond Chandler, Sir Stephen Spender.

S. Walker Literary Agency (1939), 96 Church Lane, Goldington, Bedford MK41 0AS *tel* (01234) 216229. *Partners:* Alan Oldfield, Cora-Louise Oldfield; *consultant:* E.K. Walker.
Full-length novels only (home 10%, overseas 20% including 10% to overseas agent). Do not handle short topical articles, poetry or fictional short stories. Works in conjunction with agencies in most European countries, and also negotiates directly with foreign publishers. No unsolicited synopses or MSS. No reading fee.

Warner Chappell Plays Ltd (formerly **English Theatre Guild Ltd**) (1938), part of **Warner Chappell Music Ltd,** 129 Park Street, London W1Y 3FA   *tel* 0171-514 5236   *fax* 0171-514 5201.
Specialises in stage plays. Works in conjunction with overseas agents. Preliminary letter essential.

***Watson, Little Ltd,** 12 Egbert Street, London NW1 8LJ   *tel* 0171-722 9514   *fax* 0171-586 7649. *Directors:* Sheila Watson, Amanda Little.
Full-length MSS. Special interests: business books, popular science, psychology, all leisure activities, fiction; no short stories or play scripts (home 10%, serial 15%, overseas 19%; electronic rights 20%; all other rights including film, video and television 10%). Works in association with US agencies and many foreign agencies. Preliminary letter please.

***A.P. Watt Ltd** (1875), 20 John Street, London WC1N 2DR   *tel* 0171-405 6774   *fax* 0171-831 2154 (books)/0171-430 1952 (drama). *Directors:* Caradoc King, Linda Shaughnessy, Rod Hall, Lisa Eveleigh, Nick Marston, Derek Johns.
Full-length MSS; dramatic works for all media (home 10%, US and foreign 20% including commission to US or foreign agent). No poetry. Works in conjunction with agents in USA and most European countries and Japan. No reading fee. No unsolicited MSS.

***Dinah Wiener Ltd,** 27 Arlington Road, London NW1 7ER   *tel* 0171-388 2577   *fax* 0171-388 7559.
Full-length MSS only, fiction and general non-fiction (home 15%, overseas 20%), film and television in association (15%). No plays, scripts, poetry, short stories or children's books. No reading fee, but preliminary letter and return postage essential.

Elisabeth Wilson (1979), 24 Thornhill Square, London N1 1BQ   *tel* 0171-609 1965   *fax* 0171-609 6045.
Rights agent and consultant on illustrated books (home/overseas 10%).

UNITED STATES OF AMERICA

*Member of the Association of Authors' Representatives

In all cases, and in their own interests, writers are advised to send a preliminary letter with a self-addressed, stamped envelope (or an International Reply Coupon if writing from outside the USA) and to ascertain terms before submitting MSS.

American Play Company Inc., 19 West 44th Street, Suite 1204, New York, NY 10036   *tel* 212-921-0545   *fax* 212-869-4032. *President:* Sheldon Abend.

***The Axelrod Agency** (1983), 54 Church Street, Lenox, MA 01240   *tel* 413-637-2000   *fax* 413-637-4725. *President:* Steven Axelrod.
Full-length MSS. Fiction and non-fiction, software (home 10%, overseas 20%), film and TV rights (10%); will suggest revision where appropriate. Works with overseas agents. No reading fee.

***The Balkin Agency Inc.,** PO Box 222, Amherst, MA 01004   *tel* 413-548-9835   *fax* 413-548-9836. *Director:* Richard Balkin.
Full-length MSS – adult non-fiction only (home 15%, overseas 20%). Query first. May suggest revision. *European and British representative:* Christopher Little Agency. No reading fee.

***Virginia Barber Literary Agency, Inc.** (1974), 101 Fifth Avenue, New York, NY 10003   *tel* 212-255-6515   *fax* 212-691-9418. *President:* Virginia Barber; *contacts:* Jennifer Rudolph Walsh, Alyson Becker, Jay Mandel, Nina Evtuhov.

General fiction and non-fiction (home 15%, overseas 20%), performance rights (15%); will suggest revision. Has co-agents in all major countries; Abner Stein handles UK rights. No reading fee.

*Berman, Boals & Flynn, Inc., 225 Lafayette Street, Suite 1207, New York, NY 10012 *tel* 212-966-0339 *fax* 212-966-0389. *Agents:* Lois Berman, Judy Boals, Jim Flynn.
Dramatic writing only (and only by recommendation).

*Georges Borchardt Inc. (1967), 136 East 57th Street, New York, NY 10022 *tel* 212-753-5785 *fax* 212-838-6518. *Directors:* Georges Borchardt, Anne Borchardt.
Full-length and short MSS (home/British 15%, translations 20%), performance rights (10%). Agents in most foreign countries. No unsolicited MSS. No reading fee.

*Brandt & Brandt Literary Agents Inc., 1501 Broadway, New York, NY 10036 *tel* 212-840-5760 *fax* 212-840-5776.
Full-length and short MSS (home 15%, overseas 20%), performance rights (10%). *British representative:* A.M. Heath & Co. Ltd. No reading fee.

*The Helen Brann Agency Inc., 94 Curtis Road, Bridgewater, CT 06752 *tel* 203-354-9580 *fax* 203-355-2572.

*Maria Carvainis Agency, Inc., 235 West End Avenue, New York, NY 10023 *tel* 212-580-1559 *fax* 212-877-3486. *President:* Maria Carvainis.
Fiction: all categories (except science fiction), especially general fiction/literary and mainstream; mystery, thrillers and suspense; fantasy; historical, Regency and category romance. Non-fiction: young adult and children's; political and film biographies; medicine and women's health; business, finance, psychology and popular science (home 15%, overseas 20%). Maria Carvainis views the author's editorial needs and career development as integral components of the literary agent's role, in addition to the negotiation of intricate contracts. Works in conjunction with foreign, TV and movie agents. No reading fee. Query first; no unsolicited MSS.

*Martha Casselman, Literary Agent (1978), PO Box 342, Calistoga, CA 94515 *tel* 707-942-4341 *fax* 707-942-4358.
Food and cookbook, other adult non-fiction (combined home/overseas 25%); will suggest revision where appropriate. *No* fiction, poetry or textbooks; no MSS; include return postage with query. Works with overseas agents. No reading fee.

Faith Childs Literary Agency, Inc. (1990), 275 West 96th Street, New York, NY 10025 *tel* 212-662-1232 *fax* 212-662-1456. *Director:* Faith Hampton Childs. *Associates:* Emily E. Bernard, Arlene T. Stoltz.
Literary fiction; non-fiction (home 15%, overseas 20%). Works in conjunction with overseas agents. Will suggest revision. No reading fee.

*Ruth Cohen, Inc. Literary Agency (1982), PO Box 7626, Menlo Park, CA 94025 *tel* 415-854-2054.
Requires quality writing: women's contemporary fiction, Regencies, historical romances; mysteries; juvenile – picture books to middle grade novels and young adult novels (home 15%, overseas 20%), film, TV rights (15%); will suggest revision. Works in conjunction with overseas agents. Send query letter and 25 opening pages plus sase. No reading fee.

*Frances Collin Literary Agent (successor to **Marie Rodell-Frances Collin Literary Agency,** 1948), PO Box 33, Wayne, PA 19087-0033 *tel* 610-254-0555.
Full-length MSS (specialisations of interest to UK writers: mysteries, women's fiction, history, biography, science fiction, fantasy) (home 15%, overseas

20%), performance rights (20%). No screenplays. Works in conjunction with agents worldwide. No reading fee. No unsolicited MSS please. Letter queries must include sufficient international postage response coupons.

*Don Congdon Associates, Inc. (1983), 156 Fifth Avenue, Suite 625, New York, NY 10010   *tel* 212-645-1229   *fax* 212-727-2688. *Agents:* Don Congdon, Michael Congdon, Susan Ramer.
Full-length and short MSS. General fiction and non-fiction (home 10%, overseas 19%), performance rights (10%); will sometimes suggest revision. Works with co-agents overseas. No reading fee, but *no* unsolicited MSS – query first.

*Richard Curtis Associates Inc. (1970), 171 East 74th Street, New York, NY 10021   *tel* 212-772-7363   *fax* 212-772-7393. *President:* Richard Curtis; *associates:* Amy Victoria Meo, Laura Tucker.
All types of commercial fiction; also non-fiction (home 15%, overseas 20%), multimedia, film, TV rights (15%). Works in conjunction with overseas agents. Will suggest revision. No reading fee.

*Curtis Brown Ltd, 10 Astor Place, New York, NY 10003   *tel* 212-473-5400. *Chairman:* Perry Knowlton; and 1750 Montgomery Street, San Francisco, CA 94111   *tel* 415-954-8566. *Contact:* Peter Ginsberg.
Fiction and non-fiction, juvenile, film and TV rights. No unsolicited MSS; query first with sase. No reading fee; handling fees.

*Joan Daves Agency (founded in 1952 by Joan Daves), 21 West 26th Street, New York, NY 10010   *tel* 212-685-2663   *fax* 212-685-1781. *Director:* Jennifer Lyons; *assistant:* Edward Lee. Subsidiary of **Writers House Inc.**
Full-length MSS or a detailed outline of n-f projects (home 15%, overseas 20%). No reading fee. No unpublished writers.

Elaine Davie Literary Agency (1986), 620 Park Avenue, Rochester, NY 14607   *tel* 716-442-0830. *President:* Elaine Davie.
Full-length MSS. Specialises in books by and for women, especially genre romance (home 15%, overseas 20%); will sometimes suggest revision. Works with overseas agents. No reading fee, but preliminary letter with sase essential.

*Sandra Dijkstra Literary Agency (1981), 1155 Camino del Mar, Suite 515, Del Mar, CA 92014   *tel* 619-755-3115. *President:* Sandra Dijkstra.
Adult fiction, especially literary/contemporary, mystery/suspense; non-fiction: current affairs, memoir/biography, science, health, history and psychology/self-help, business, how-to; selected children's projects (home 15%, overseas 20%). Works in conjunction with foreign agents. Will suggest revision. No reading fee. Send first 50 pages and sase for response/return. No faxed queries accepted. Response period 2-8 weeks; do not call to enquire.

*Donadio & Ashworth, Inc., 121 West 27th Street, Suite 704, New York, NY 10001   *tel* 212-691-8077   *fax* 212-633-2837.
Literary book agents, fiction and non-fiction.

Dorese Agency, 37965 Palo Verde Drive, Cathedral City, CA 92234   *tel* 619-321-1115   *fax* 619-321-1049. Alyss Barlow Dorese.
Specialises in true crime, non-fiction.

Peter Elek Associates (1979), PO Box 223, Canal Street Station, New York, NY 10013   *tel* 212-431-9368/9371   *fax* 212-966-5768   *e-mail* 73174.2515 @compuserve.com *Directors:* Peter Elek, Helene W. Elek.
Full-length and short MSS. Adult and illustrated adult non-fiction: style, culture, popular history, popular science, current affairs; juvenile picture books (home 15%, overseas 20%), performance rights (20%); will sometimes suggest

revision. Works with overseas agents. No reading fee. Experienced in licensing for multimedia, on-line and off-line.

*Ann Elmo Agency, Inc., 60 East 42nd Street, New York, NY 10165 *tel* 212-661-2880 *fax* 212-661-2883. *Director:* Lettie Lee.
Full-length fiction and non-fiction MSS (home 15%, overseas 20%), theatre, films, television (15%). Will suggest revision when MSS is promising. Works with foreign agencies. No reading fee.

Frieda Fishbein Ltd, 2556 Hubbard Street, Brooklyn, NY 11235 *tel* 212-247-4398. *Contacts:* Heidi Carlson, Douglas Michael.
TV, plays, books, screenplays, film and TV rights. No unsolicited MSS; query first. Reading fee for new writers, or published writers in a new genre.

Forthwrite Literary Agency (1988), 3579 E Foothill Boulevard, Suite 327, Pasadena, CA 91107 *tel* 818-798 0793. *Owner:* Wendy L. Zhörne.
How-to, self-help and general non-fiction. Subjects include: business books, animals, art, horticulture/gardening, archaeology, European history (especially English), biography, health (especially homeopathy and alternative medicines), parenting, coffee table (illustrated) books, crafts (bobbin lace, handicrafts, etc.), nature, psychology. Send IRC with query. Response in 8 weeks.

*The Fox Chase Agency Inc., The Public Ledger Building, Room 930, Independence Square, Philadelphia, PA 19106 *tel* 215-625-2450 *fax* 215-574-9190.

*Robert A. Freedman Dramatic Agency, Inc. (formerly **Harold Freedman Brandt & Brandt Dramatic Dept., Inc.**), 1501 Broadway, Suite 2310, New York, NY 10036 *tel* 212-840-5760.
Plays, motion picture and TV scripts. Send letter of enquiry first, with sase.

*Samuel French Inc., 45 West 25th Street, New York, NY 10010 *tel* 212-206-8990 *fax* 212-206-1429. *President:* Charles R. Van Nostrand.
Play publishers and authors' representatives.

*Jay Garon-Brooke Associates Inc., 101 West 55th Street, Suite 5K, New York, NY 10019 *tel* 212-581-8300 *fax* 212-581-8397.
Specialises in fiction. Writer must be referred by an editor or a client. Will not read unsolicited MSS. *London:* Abner Stein *tel* 0171-373 01456.

*Gelfman Schneider Literary Agents, Inc., 250 West 57th Street, Suite 2515, New York, NY 10107 *tel* 212-245-1993 *fax* 212-245-8678. *Directors:* Jane Gelfman, Deborah Schneider.
General adult fiction and non-fiction (home 15%, overseas 20%). Works in conjunction with Curtis Brown, London. Will suggest revision. No reading fee.

*Goodman Associates, Literary Agents (1976), 500 West End Avenue, New York, NY 10024 *tel* 212-873-4806 *fax* 212-580-3278. *Partners:* Arnold P. Goodman, Elise Simon Goodman.
Adult book length fiction and non-fiction (home 15%, overseas 20%). No reading fee.

*Sanford J. Greenburger Associates, Inc., 55 Fifth Avenue, New York, NY 10003 *tel* 212-206-5600 *fax* 212-463-8718. *Contacts:* Heide Lange, Faith Hamlin, Beth Vesel, Theresa Park, Elyse Cheney.
Fiction and non-fiction, film and TV rights. No unsolicited MSS; query first. No reading fee.

*John Hawkins & Associates, Inc. (formerly **Paul R. Reynolds, Inc.**) (1893), 71 West 23rd Street, Suite 1600, New York, NY 10010 *tel* 212-807-7040 *fax*

212-807-9555. *President:* John Hawkins; *vice-president:* William Reiss; *foreign rights:* Moses Cardona; *permissions:* Gladys Guadalupe; *other agents:* Elinor B. Sidel, J. Warren Frazier.
Fiction, non-fiction, juvenile.

*Heacock Literary Agency, Inc. (1978), 1523 6th Street, Suite 14, Santa Monica, CA 90401   *tel* 310-393-6277. *President:* Rosalie G. Heacock; *associate agent:* Robin Henning.
Adult non-fiction: self-help, health/medicine, science/technology, philosophy/psychology, art, women's studies, biography. Fiction including mystery/suspense, action/adventure, mainstream (home 15%, overseas 15%-25%). Will suggest revision; no reading fee but charges for expenses. Works in conjunction with overseas agents. No unsolicited MSS or facsimile submissions. Send synopsis, say why you wrote the book, include bio and 1-2 sample chapters plus sase.

*The Jeff Herman Agency (1986), 500 Greenwich Street, Suite 501c, New York, NY 10013   *tel* 212-940-0540   *fax* 212-941-0614.
Business, reference, popular psychology, computers, health and beauty, spirituality, general non-fiction (home/overseas 15%); will suggest revision where appropriate. Works with overseas agents. No reading fee.

Frederick Hill Associates (1979), 1842 Union Street, San Francisco, CA 94123   *tel* 415-921-2910   *fax* 415-921-2802; *branch office:* 8446½ Melrose Place, Los Angeles, CA 90069   *tel* 213-852-0830   *fax* 213-852-0426.
Full-length fiction and non-fiction (home 15%, overseas 20%). Will suggest revision. Works in conjunction with agents in Scandinavia, France, Germany, Holland, Japan, Spain. No reading fee.

*IMG Literary, 22 East 71st Street, New York, NY 10021   *tel* 212-772-8900   *fax* 212-772-2617.
Fiction (no science fiction) and non-fiction. Send query letter with sase for response.

InterLicense, Ltd (1982), 200 Gate Five Road, Suite 207, Sausalito, CA 94965   *tel* 415-331-7460   *fax* 415-331-6940. *Executive director:* Manfred Mroczkowski.
International administration of creative rights in non-fiction, self-help and esoterica, children's books (home/overseas 15%-33%). No reading fee.

*International Creative Management, Inc., 40 West 57th Street, New York, NY 10019   *tel* 212-556-5600   *telex* 125422/661562 ICMNYK   *fax* 212-556-5665.
No unsolicited MSS, please; send query letters.

*JCA Literary Agency Inc., Suite 1103, 27 West 20th Street, New York, NY 10011   *tel* 212-807-0888. *Contacts:* Jane Cushman, Jeff Gerecke, Tony Outhwaite.
Adult fiction and non-fiction. No unsolicited MSS; query first.

Ben F. Kamsler Ltd (1990), 5501 Noble Avenue, Van Nuys, CA 91411   *tel* 818-785-4167   *fax* 818-988-8304. *Directors:* Ben Kamsler, Irene Kamsler.
Full-length novel MSS, plays, TV specials, screenplays (home 10%, overseas 20%), performance rights (10%). Will suggest revision on promising MSS. No reading fee, but preliminary letter with sase essential.

*Barbara S. Kouts, Literary Agent (1980), PO Box 560, Bellport, NY 11713   *tel* 516-286-1278   *fax* 516-286-1538.
Full-length MSS. Fiction and non-fiction, children's and adult (home 10%, overseas 20%); will suggest revision. Works with overseas agents. No reading fee. Query first.

*The Robert Lantz-Joy Harris Literary Agency, 156 Fifth Avenue, Suite 617, New York, NY 10010   *tel* 212-924-6249   *fax* 212-924-6609. *President:* Joy Harris.

The Lazear Agency Inc. (1984), 430 First Avenue North, Suite 416, Minneapolis, MN 55401   *tel* 612-332-8640   *fax* 612-332-4648. *Directors:* Jonathon Lazear, Eric Vrooman, Dennis Cass, Susanne Moncur.
Full-length MSS. Adult/young adult fiction and non-fiction; juvenile; film and TV rights/software; syndication (home 15%, overseas 20%); will suggest revision. Works with overseas agents. No reading fee. No unsolicited MSS; query first with #10 sase.

*Lescher & Lescher Ltd (1966), 67 Irving Place, New York, NY 10003   *tel* 212-529-1790   *telegraphic address* Micawber   *fax* 212-529-2716. *Directors:* Robert Lescher, Susan Lescher.
Full-length and short MSS (home 15%, overseas 25%). No unsolicited MSS; query first with sase. No reading fee.

*Ellen Levine Literary Agency Inc. (1980), Suite 1801, 15 East 26th Street, New York, NY 10010   *tel* 212-899-0620   *fax* 212-725-4501. *Contacts:* Elizabeth Kaplan, Diana Finch, Louise Quayle.
Full-length MSS: biography, contemporary affairs, women's issues, history, science, literary and commercial fiction (home 15%, overseas 20%); in conjunction with co-agents, theatre, films, television (15%). Will suggest revision. Works in conjunction with agents in Europe, Japan, Israel, Brazil, Argentina, Australia, Far East. *UK representative:* A.M. Heath. No reading fee; preliminary letter and sase essential.

*Margret McBride Literary Agency (1981), 7744 Fay Avenue, Suite 201, La Jolla, CA 92037   *tel* 619-454-1550   *fax* 619-454-2156; and 11684 Ventura Blvd., Suite 956, Studio City, CA 91604   *tel* 818-508-0031   *fax* 818-508-0039. *President:* Margret McBride; *vp, associate agent:* Winifred Golden; *associate agent (L.A. office):* Kim Sauer.
Full-length and short MSS. Mainstream fiction and non-fiction; *no* poetry or children's books (home 15%, overseas 25%). No reading fee. Submit query letter with sase to Clare Horn.

*Gerard McCauley Agency, Inc., PO Box 844, Katonah, NY 10536   *tel* 914-232-5700.
Specialises in history, biography, science for general reader.

*Anita D. McClellan Associates, 50 Stearns Street, Cambridge, MA 02138   *tel* 617-576-6950. *Director:* Anita D. McClellan.
General fiction and non-fiction. Full-length MSS (home 15%, overseas 20%). Will suggest revision for agency clients. No unsolicited MSS. Send preliminary letter and sase bearing US postage or International Reply Coupon.

*McIntosh & Otis Inc. (1928), 310 Madison Avenue, New York, NY 10017   *tel* 212-687-7400   *fax* 212-687-6894. *Adult:* Julie Fallowfield; *juvenile:* Dorothy Markinko, Renée Cho; *film and TV:* Evva Joan Pryor.
Adult and juvenile literary fiction and non-fiction, film and TV rights. No unsolicited MSS; query first with outline, sample chapters and sase. No reading fee.

*Carol Mann Agency (1977), 55 Fifth Avenue, New York, NY 10003   *tel* 212-206-5635   *fax* 212-675-4809. *Associates:* Carol Mann, Gareth Esersky; *rights:* Gail Feinberg.
Psychology, popular history, biography, general non-fiction; fiction (home 15%, overseas 20%). Works in conjunction with foreign agents. No reading fee.

*Elaine Markson Literary Agency (1973), 44 Greenwich Avenue, New York, NY 10011   *tel* 212-243-8480   *fax* 212-691-9014. *Directors:* Elaine Markson, Geri Thoma, Sally Wofford-Girand.
Full-length MSS. Literary and mainstream commercial fiction (no genre); biography, sociology, history, popular culture, feminism (home 15%, overseas 20%), performance rights (10%); will suggest revision. Works with overseas agents. No reading fee.

*Mildred Marmur Associates Ltd (1987), 2005 Palmer Avenue, Suite 127, Larchmont, NY 10538-2469   *tel* 212-949-6055   *fax* 212-949-0329. *President:* Mildred Marmur; *associate agent:* Jennie Dunham.
Serious non-fiction, literary fiction, juveniles. Full-length and short MSS (home licences 15%, overseas licences 20%), performance rights (15%). Works with co-agents in all major countries. No reading fee. Queries must include sase or International Reply Coupons.

The Evan Marshall Agency (1987), 6 Tristam Place, Pine Brook, NJ 07058-9445   *tel* 201-882-1122   *fax* 201-882-3099. *President:* Evan Marshall.
General fiction and non-fiction (home 15%, overseas 20%); screenplays, teleplays (20%). Works in conjunction with overseas agents. Will suggest revision; no reading fee but $38 handling fee for unpublished writers.

*Elisabeth Marton Agency, 1 Union Square, Suite 612, New York, NY 10003   *tel* 212-255-1908   *fax* 212-691-9061. *Owner:* Tonda Marton.
Stage plays only.

*Harold Matson Company, Inc. (1937), 276 Fifth Avenue, New York, NY 10001   *tel* 212-679-4490   *cables* Halmatson   *fax* 212-545-1224.
Full-length MSS (home 10%, UK 19%, translation 19%). No unsolicited MSS. No reading fee.

Scott Meredith Literary Agency Inc. (1946), 845 Third Avenue, New York, NY 10022   *tel* 212-751-4545   *fax* 212-755-2972. *President:* Arthur Klebanoff; *vice-president:* Lisa J. Edwards; *foreign rights:* Lawrence P. Ganem.
Full-length and short MSS. General fiction and non-fiction, books and magazines, juveniles, plays, TV scripts, motion picture rights and properties (home 10%, overseas 20%), performance rights (10%). Will read unsolicited MSS, queries, outlines. Single fee charged for readings, criticism and assistance in revision. *London:* A.M. Heath & Co. Ltd.

*Helen Merrill Ltd, 435 West 23rd Street, Suite 1A, New York, NY 10011   *tel* 212-691-5326   *fax* 212-727-0545.

*William Morris Agency Inc., 1325 Avenue of the Americas, New York, NY 10019   *tel* 212-586-5100.

*Multimedia Product Development Inc. (1971), 410 South Michigan Avenue, Suite 724, Chicago, IL 60605   *tel* 312-922-3063   *fax* 312-922-1905. *Contact:* Jane Jordan Browne.
General fiction and non-fiction (home 15%, overseas 20%), performance rights (15%). Works in conjunction with foreign agents. Will suggest revision; no reading fee.

*Jean V. Naggar Literary Agency (1978), 216 East 75th Street, Suite 1E, New York, NY 10021   *tel* 212-794-1082. *President:* Jean V. Naggar; *agents:* Anne Engel, Frances Kuffel.
Mainstream commercial and literary fiction (no formula fiction); non-fiction: psychology, science, biography (home 15%, overseas 20%), performance rights (15%). Works in conjunction with foreign agents. No reading fee.

Ruth Nathan Agency (1981), 80 Fifth Avenue, Suite 706, New York, NY 10011 *tel/fax* 212-675-6063. *Director:* Ruth Nathan.
Fine art, decorative arts, show biz, biographies pertaining to those areas; fiction (Middle Ages only) and true crime (home 15%, overseas 10%-15%). No reading fee.

*New England Publishing Associates, Inc. (1982), PO Box 5, Chester, CT 06412 *tel* 203-345-READ *fax* 203-345-3660. *Directors:* Elizabeth Frost Knappman, Edward W. Knappman.
Serious non-fiction for the adult market (home 15%, overseas varies), performance rights (varies). Works in conjunction with foreign publishers. No reading fee; will suggest revision – if undertaken; 15% fee for placing MSS.

*Harold Ober Associates Inc. (1929), 425 Madison Avenue, New York, NY 10017 *tel* 212-759-8600 *fax* 212-759-9428. *Directors:* Phyllis Westberg, Henry Dunow, Wendy Schmalz, Anne Edelstein.
Full-length MSS (home 15%, British 20%, overseas 20%), performance rights (10%). Will suggest revision. *London representative:* David Higham Associates. No reading fee.

*Fifi Oscard Agency Inc., 24 West 40th Street, New York, NY 10018 *tel* 212-764-1100 *fax* 212-840 5019. *President:* Fifi Oscard; *agents:* Ivy Fischer Stone, Kevin McShane, Nancy Murray.
Full-length MSS (home 15%, overseas 20%), performance rights (10%). Will suggest revision. Works in conjunction with many foreign agencies. No reading fee, but no unsolicited submissions.

*James Peter Associates, Inc. (1981), 151 Sunset Lane, PO Box 772, Tenafly, NJ 07670 *tel* 201-568-0760 *fax* 201-568 2959. *Contact:* Bert Holtje.
Non-fiction, especially history, politics, popular culture, health, psychology, reference, biography (home 15%, overseas 20%). Foreign rights handled by: Bobbe Siegel, 41 West 83rd Street, New York, NY 10024. Will suggest revision. No reading fee.

The Pimlico Agency Inc., Box 20447, Cherokee Station, New York, NY 10021 *tel* 212-628-9729 *fax* 212-535-7861. *Contact:* Christopher Shepard; *directors:* Kay McCauley, Kirby McCauley.
Specialise in general non-fiction and science fiction, horror and fantasy.

PMA Literary and Film Management, Inc. (1976), 132 West 22nd Street – 12th Floor, New York, NY 10011 *tel* 212-929-1222 *fax* 212-206-0238 *e-mail* pmalitfilm@aol.com *President:* Peter Miller.
Full-length MSS, specialising in commercial fiction, true crime, biography, Hollywood history and all books with global publishing and film and television production potential (home 15%, overseas 25%), films, television (10-20%). Works in conjunction with agents worldwide. Preliminary enquiry with career goals, synopsis and resumé essential.

*Raines & Raines (1961), 71 Park Avenue, New York, NY 10016 *tel* 212-684-5160. *Directors:* Theron Raines, Joan Raines, Keith Korman.
Full-length MSS (home 15%, overseas 20%). Works in conjunction with overseas agents. No unsolicited MSS.

Renaissance–A Literary Talent Agency (1934), 8523 Sunset Boulevard, Los Angeles, CA 90069 *tel* 310-289-3636 *fax* 310-289-3637. *Partners:* Joel Gotler, Alan Nevins, Irv Schwarz; *agents:* Steve Fisher, Brian Lipson.
Full-length MSS. Fiction and non-fiction, plays (home 15%, overseas 20%), film and TV rights (home 10%, overseas 20%), performance rights. No unsolicited MSS; query first, submit outline. No reading fee.

*Helen Rees Literary Agency (1982), 308 Commonwealth Avenue, Boston, MA 02115 *tel* 617-262-2401 *fax* 617-236-0133.
Full-length MSS. Business books, self-help, biography, autobiography, political, literary fiction (home 15%); will suggest revision. Works with foreign agent. No reading fee. Submit query letter with sase.

Mitchell Rose Literary Agency (1987), 688 Avenue of the Americas, Suite 303, New York, NY 10010 *tel* 212-929-1401 *fax* 212-929-9819 *e-mail* 71324,1413@compuserve.com *President:* Mitchell Rose.
Popular culture, health, history, general-non-fiction, distinctive fiction, ethnic issues (home 15%, overseas 20%); will suggest revision. No reading fee.

*Rosenstone/Wender, 3 East 48th Street, 4th Floor, New York, NY 10017 *tel* 212-832-8330 *fax* 212-759-4524. *Contacts:* Phyllis Wender, Susan Perlman Cohen, Hannah Wallace.
Fiction, non-fiction, film and TV rights. No unsolicited MSS; query first. No reading fee.

Robin Rue, 310 Madison Avenue, New York, NY 10017 *tel* 212-687-1122 *fax* 212-972-1756.
Fiction, non-technical non-fiction.

*Russell & Volkening Inc., 50 West 29th Street, New York, NY 10001 *tel* 212-684-6050 *fax* 212-889-3206. *Contacts:* Jennie Dunham, Timothy Seldes, Joseph Regal.
General fiction and non-fiction, film and TV rights. No screenplays. No unsolicited MSS; query first with letter and sase. No reading fee.

*Susan F. Schulman Literary & Dramatic Agents Inc., 454 West 44th Street, New York, NY 10036 *tel* 212-713-1633 *fax* 212-581-8830.
Agents for negotiation in all markets (with co-agents) of fiction, general non-fiction, children's books, academic and professional works, and associated subsidiary rights including plays, film and television (home 15%, UK 7½%, overseas 20%). Return postage required.

*Charlotte Sheedy Literary Agency, Inc., 65 Bleecker Street, New York, NY 10012 *tel* 212-780-9800 *fax* 212-780-0308. *Contact:* Charlotte Sheedy.
Fiction and non-fiction, film and TV rights. No unsolicited MSS; query first with outline and sample chapters. No reading fee.

*The Shukat Company Ltd, 340 West 55th Street, Suite 1A, New York, NY 10019 *tel* 212-582-7614 *fax* 212-315-3752 *e-mail* shukat@interramp.com *President:* Scott Shukat; *contact:* Patricia McLaughlin.
Theatre, films, novels, television, radio (15%). No reading fee. No unsolicited material accepted.

Singer Media Corporation, Seaview Business Park, 1030 Calle Cordillera, Unit 106, San Clemente, CA 92673 *tel* 714-498-7227. *Directors:* Helen J. Lee (vice-president), Kristy Lee (acquisitions).
Interested in foreign language reprint rights and syndication rights of published non-fiction and fiction. Represented in most countries abroad (home 15%, overseas 20%). Published authors only. No unsolicited MSS; query first.

The Spieler Agency (1982), 154 West 57th Street, Room 135, New York, NY 10019 *tel* 212-757-4439 *fax* 212-333-2019. *Directors:* F. Joseph Spieler, Lisa M. Ross, John F. Thornton; West Coast Office, 1328 6th Avenue, Berkeley, CA 94710 *tel* 510-528-2616 *fax* 510-528-8117. *Principal agent:* Victoria Shoemaker.
Full- and short-length MSS. History, politics, ecology, business, consumer reference, some fiction (home 15%, overseas 20%). No reading fee.

*Philip G. Spitzer Literary Agency, 50 Talmage Farm Lane, East Hampton, NY 11937 *tel* 516-329-3650 *fax* 516-329-3651.
General fiction and non-fiction; specialises in mystery/suspense, sports, politics, biography, social issues.

*Stepping Stone Literary Agency (1974), 59 West 71st Street, Suite 9B, New York, NY 10023 *tel* 212-362-9277 *fax* 212-501-8240. *President:* Sarah Jane Freymann; *associate:* Katharine Sands.
Fiction and non-fiction, especially commercial and mainstream fiction (home/ overseas 15%). Works in conjunction with Abner Stein and Marsh & Sheil in London. No reading fee.

Sterling Lord Literistic, Inc., 65 Bleecker Street, New York, NY 10012 *tel* 212-780-6050 *cables* Literistic New York *fax* 212-780-6095. *Directors:* Peter Matson, Sterling Lord, Philippa Brophy, Jody Hotchkiss.
Full-length and short MSS (home 15%, overseas 19%), performance rights (10%). Will suggest revision. UK representative (non-exclusive): The Peters Fraser & Dunlop Group Ltd. No reading fee.

*Gloria Stern Agency (1984), 12535 Chandler Boulevard, Suite 3, North Holly-wood, CA 91607-1934 *tel* 818-508-6296 *fax* 818-508-6296. *Director:* Gloria Stern.
Fiction and films (home 10%, overseas 15%). Reading fee; consultation fee for revisions; some author expenses for placing MSS.

*Roslyn Targ Literary Agency, Inc., 105 West 13th Street, New York, NY 10011 *tel* 212-206-9390 *fax* 212-989-6233.
Full-length MSS. Affiliates in most foreign countries. No reading fee; pre-liminary letter with sase essential.

*Susan P. Urstadt, Inc., Agency (1975), PO Box 1676, New Canaan, CT 06840 *tel* 203-972-8226 *fax* 203-966-2249. *Director:* Susan P. Urstadt; *agent:* Joanne Fredericks.
All quality non-fiction, especially biography, decorative arts, gardening, food, health, history, natural history, medical, performing arts and popular reference (home 15%, overseas 20%). No reading fee. Query first, enclosing a sase.

*Ralph Vicinanza Ltd, 111 8th Avenue, Suite 1501, New York, NY 10011 *tel* 212-924-7090.
Popular fiction (especially science fiction, fantasy, mystery, thrillers), non-fiction (history, science). No unsolicited MSS (home 10%, overseas 20%).

Austin Wahl Agency, Ltd (1935), 1820 North 76th Court, Elmwood Park, IL 60635-3631 *tel* 708-456-2301. *President:* Thomas Wahl.
Full-length and short MSS (home 15%, overseas 20%), theatre, films, tele-vision (10%). No reading fee; professional writers only.

*Wallace Literary Agency, Inc. (1988), 177 East 70th Street, New York, NY 10021 *tel* 212-570-9090 *fax* 212-772-8979. *Directors:* Lois Wallace, Thomas C. Wallace.
Full-length MSS; no cookery, humour, how-to; film, television, theatre for agency clients. Will suggest revision. No unsolicited MSS; no faxed queries.

Watkins/Loomis Agency, Inc., 133 East 35th Street, New York, NY 10016 *tel* 212-532-0080 *cables* Anwat, Newyork *fax* 212-889-0506. *President:* Gloria Loomis; *associate:* Nicole Aragi; *contact:* Lily Oei.
Fiction and non-fiction, art, film and TV rights. No unsolicited MSS; query first with sase. No reading fee. *London:* Abner Stein (UK), The Marsh Agency (foreign).

Sandra Watt and Associates (1978), 8033 Sunset Boulevard, Suite 4053, Hollywood, CA 90046   *tel* 213-653-2339. *Owner:* Sandra Watt.

Lead women's fiction, suspense, mysteries, New Age, cyber-punk; psychological self-help, gardening, single-volume reference works; screenplays (home 15%, overseas 25%), films (10%). Works in conjunction with foreign agents. Will suggest revision; no reading fee; $100 marketing fee for unpublished authors.

Wecksler-Incomco (1971), 170 West End Avenue, New York, NY 10023   *tel* 212-787-2239   *fax* 212-496-7035. *President:* Sally Wecksler; *associate:* Joann Amparan.

Illustrated books, non-fiction, some literary fiction, children's books (home 12-15%, overseas 20%); will suggest revision where appropriate. No reading fee.

*****Rhoda Weyr Agency** (1983), 151 Bergen Street, Brooklyn, NY 11217   *tel* 718-522-0480   *fax* 718-522-0410.

General non-fiction and fiction with particular interest in science, history, biography. Full-length MSS for fiction; proposal for n-f (home 15%, overseas 20%), performance rights (15%). Co-agents in all foreign markets. Sase required.

*****Writers House Inc.** (1974), 21 West 26th Street, New York, NY 10010   *tel* 212-685-2400   *fax* 212-685-1781. *President:* Albert Zuckerman; *executive vice-president:* Amy Berkower.

Full-length MSS. Popular and literary fiction, novels for children and young adults, history, biography, popular science, how-to books in business, health, nutrition and popular psychology (home 15%, overseas 20%). No reading fee.

The Wylie Agency, Inc., 250 West 57th Street, Suite 2114, New York, NY 10107   *tel* 212-246-0069   *fax* 212-586-8953. *Directors:* Andrew Wylie (president), Sarah Chalfant, Bridget Love.

Literary fiction/non-fiction (home 10%, overseas 20%). No unsolicited MSS accepted. New London office: The Wylie Agency UK, Ltd.

*****Mary Yost Associates, Inc.** (1958), 59 East 54th Street, Suite 73, New York, NY 10022   *tel* 212-980-4988   *telegraphic address* Mybooks.

Full-length and short MSS (home and overseas 10%). Works with individual agents in all foreign countries. Will suggest revision. No reading fee.

*****Susan Zeckendorf Associates Inc.** (1978), 171 West 57th Street, New York, NY 10019   *tel* 212-245-2928. *President:* Susan Zeckendorf

Literary fiction, women's commercial fiction, mysteries, thrillers, science, music (home 15%, overseas 20%), film, TV rights (15%). Works in conjunction with overseas agents. Will suggest revision. No reading fee.

Other Literary Agents

Most of the agents whose names and addresses are given below work in association with an agent in London.

In all cases, and in their own interests, writers are advised to send a preliminary letter and to ascertain terms before submitting MSS or books.

ARGENTINA

International Editors Co., Avenida Cabildo 1156, 1426 Buenos Aires   *tel* 786-0888/788-2992   *fax* 541-786-0888/552-5832.

Lawrence Smith BA (1938), Avenida de los Incas 3110, 1426 Buenos Aires *tel* 552-5012 *cables* Litagent, Baires *fax* 54-1-8045508/54-1-5525012.

AUSTRALIA

Curtis Brown (Australia) Pty Ltd, 27 Union Street, Paddington, Sydney, NSW 2021 *tel* (02) 331 5301/361 6161 *fax* (02) 360 3935.

Literary Resources (1992), 6/88A Kurraba Road, Neutral Bay, NSW 2089 *fax* (02) 9909 3752. *Principal:* Doug Nancarrow. Full-length and short MSS, adult fiction and non-fiction (home 10%, overseas 20%), performance rights (10%); will suggest revision. Works with overseas agents. One-off reading fee for unpublished authors only.

BRAZIL

Agencia Literária Balcells Mello e Souza Riff, Rua Visconde de Pirajá, 414 s1 1108 Ipanema, 22410-002 Rio de Janeiro, RJ *tel* (55-21) 287-6299 *fax* (55-21) 267-6393. *Contact:* Lucia de Mello e Souza Riff.

Karin Schindler, Rights Representative (formerly **Dr J.E. Bloch Literary Agency**), Caixa Postal 19051, 04599-970 São Paulo, SP *tel* 241-9177 *fax* 241-9077.

CANADA

Acacia House Publishing Services Ltd (1985), 51 Acacia Road, Toronto, Ontario M4S 2K6 *tel/fax* 416-484-8356. *Managing director:* Mrs Frances A. Hanna. Literary fiction and non-fiction, quality commercial fiction, most non-fiction, except business books; selective quality children's list, mainly fiction (15% English language worldwide, 30% translation), performance rights (15-30%). *No* science fiction, horror or occult. Works with overseas agents. Reading fee on MS over 200pp, where an evaluation is also provided.

EASTERN EUROPE

Artisjus. Agency for Literature and Theatre of the Hungarian Bureau for the Protection of authors' rights, Mészáros u. 15-17, 1016 Budapest, Hungary *postal address* H-1538 Budapest, Pf. 593, Hungary *tel* 1-212-15-53 *fax* 1-212-15-52.

Aura-Pont, Theatrical and Literary Agency Ltd (1990), Radlická 99, Prague 5, Czech Republic *tel/fax* (0422) 53 99 09, 53 63 51. *Director:* Zuzana Ježková. Handles authors' rights in books, theatre, film, TV, radio software – both Czech and foreign, literary scouting for Czech publishers (home 10%, overseas 15%); will suggest revision.

Dilia Theatrical and Literary Agency, Krátkého 1, Prague 9, 190 03, Czech Republic *tel* (02) 82 68 41/8 *fax* (0422) 82 40 09.

Interlit Services Ltd (1993), PO Box 125, 130 00 Prague 3, Czech Republic *tel* (02) 78 19 324 *tel/fax* 78 10 327. *Directors:* Klaus Flugge, Otakar Bozejowski; *manager:* Alena Šmídová. Sells rights to Czech and Slovak publishers, including fiction, sci-fi, popular science and esoteric (home 10%).

Lex Copyright (1991), Szemere utca 21, 1054 Budapest, Hungary *tel* (1) 132 9340 *fax* (1) 131 6181. *Director:* Dr Gyorgy Tibor Szanto. Specialises in representing American and British authors in Hungary.

Lita Slovak Literary Agency, Partizánska 21, 815 30 Bratislava, Slovakia   *tel/ fax* 42 7 313645   *telegraphic address* Lita, Bratislava.

Andrew Nurnberg Associates Prague, s.r.o, Seifertova 81, Prague 3, Czech Republic   *tel/fax* (42) 2274895. *Contact:* Petra Tobiskova.

Prava i Prevodi (1983), Koste Jovanovica 18, 11000 Belgrade, Yugoslavia   *tel* (11) 460 290   *fax* (11) 472 146. *Director:* Predrag Milenkovic. Specialises in representing American and British authors in former Eastern Europe (15 languages).

FRANCE

Bureau Littéraire International Marguerite Scialtiel, 14 rue Chanoinesse, 75004 Paris   *tel* (1) 43 54 71 16. *Contact:* Geneviéve Ulmann.

Agence Hoffman, 77 boulevard Saint-Michel, 75005 Paris   *tel* (1) 43 26 56 94   *cables* Aghoff   *telex* 203605   *fax* (1) 43 26 34 07.

Mme Michelle Lapautre, 6 rue Jean Carriès, 75007 Paris   *tel* (1) 47 34 82 41   *fax* (1) 47 34 00 90.

La Nouvelle Agence, 7 rue Corneille, 75006 Paris   *tel* (1) 43 25 85 60   *fax* (1) 43 25 47 98. *Contact:* Mary Kling.

GERMANY (*See also* SWITZERLAND)

Brigitte Axster, Dreieichstr. 43, D-60594 Frankfurt/Main   *tel* 069-629856   *fax* 069-623526.

Geisenheyner & Crone, Gymnasiumstrasse 31B, 70174 Stuttgart   *tel* 0711-293738   *fax* 0711-2261748.

Agence Hoffman, Bechsteinstrasse 2, 80804 Munich   *tel* 089-308 48 07   *fax* 089-308 21 08.

Michael Meller Literary Agency (1988), PO Box 400 323, 80703 Munich   *tel* (089) 366371   *fax* (089) 366372. Full-length MSS. Fiction and non-fiction, screenplays for films and television (home 15%, overseas 20%). Own US office. No reading fee.

Thomas Schlück, Literary Agency, Hinter der Worth 12, 30827 Garbsen   *tel* 05131-93053   *fax* 05131-93045.

INDIA

Ajanta Books International (1975), 1 U.B. Jawahar Nagar, Bungalow Road, Delhi 110007   *tel* 2926182, 7258630   *telegraphic address* AJANTA BOOKS INT   *telex* 03179032 TCS IN   *fax* 91-11-7132908/7213076. *Proprietor:* S. Balwant. Full-length MSS in social sciences and humanities (commission varies according to market – Indian books in Indian and foreign languages, foreign books into Indian languages). Will suggest revision; charges made if agency undertakes revision; reading fee.

IRELAND

Jonathan Williams Literary Agency (1981), 2 Mews, 10 Sandycove Avenue West, Sandycove, Co. Dublin, Republic of Ireland   *tel/fax* (01) 2803482. *Director:* Jonathan Williams. General fiction and non-fiction, preferably by Irish authors (home 10%). Will suggest revision; usually no reading fee.

ISRAEL

I. Pikarski Ltd Literary Agency (1977), 200 Hayarkon Street, PO Box 4006, Tel Aviv 61040 *tel* 03-5270159/5231880 *fax* 03-5270160. *Director:* Ilana Pikarski. General trade publishing and merchandising rights.

ITALY

Eulama SRL (1962), Via Guido de Ruggiero 28, 00142 Rome *tel* (06) 540 73 09 *fax* (06) 540 87 72. *Directors:* Harald Kahnemann, Karin von Prellwitz, Norbert von Prellwitz, Maria G. Ocello von Prellwitz. Quality fiction and non-fiction, social sciences, politics, philosophy, religion, psychology, education, linguistics, architecture, urban studies (home 15%, overseas 20%); will suggest revision where appropriate. Works with overseas agents. No reading fee.

Grandi Associati SRL (1988), Via Caradosso 12, 20123 Milan *tel* (02) 469 55 41/481 89 62 *fax* (02) 481 951 018. *Directors:* Laura Grandi, Stefano Tettamanti. Provides publicity and foreign rights consultation for publishers and authors as well as sub-agent services; will suggest revision where appropriate. Reading fee.

ILA–International Literary Agency–USA (1969), I-18010 Terzorio-IM *tel* (0184) 48 40 48 *fax* (0184) 48 72 92. Publishers' and authors' agent, interested only in series of best-selling and mass market books by proven, published authors with a track record. Also interested in published books on antiques and collectibles.

Agenzia Letteraria Internazionale SRL, Via Fratelli Gabba 3, 20121 Milan *tel* (02) 86 54 45/86 46 34 18/86 15 72 *telex* 323574 Linali I *fax* (02) 87 62 22.

News Blitz International, Via Guido Banti 34, 00191 Rome *tel* (06) 33 32 641/ 33 30 252 *fax* (06) 33 32 651. *Literary department:* Giovanni A. Congiu.

JAPAN

The English Agency (Japan) Ltd (1979), Sakuragi Building 4ᴘ, 6-7-3 Minami Aoyama, Minato-ku, Tokyo 107 *tel* 03-3406 5385 *fax* 03-3406 5387. *Managing director:* William Miller. Handles work by English-language writers living in Japan; arranges Japanese translations for internationally established publishers, agents and authors; arranges Japanese localisations for CD-ROM. Standard commission: 10%. Own representatives in New York and London. No reading fee.

Orion Literary Agency, 1-58 Kanda-Jimbocho, Chiyoda-ku, Tokyo 101 *tel* 03-3295-1405 *fax* 03-3295-4366.

NETHERLANDS

Auteursbureau Greta Baars-Jelgersma (1951), Bovensteweg 46, NL-6585 KD Mook *tel* (024) 696 14 70 *fax* (024) 696 24 39. Literature; illustrated co-productions, including children's, art, handicraft, hobby and nature (home/ overseas 20%). Works with overseas agents. Occasionally charges a reading fee.

International Drama Agency, Ilperveldstraat 82, 1024 PJ Amsterdam *tel* (020) 636 77 54/634 08 04 *fax* (020) 636 73 55. *Contact:* Francis Lonnee.

Internationaal Literatuur Bureau B.V., Postbus 10014, 1201 DA, Hilversum *tel* (035) 621 35 00 *fax* (035) 621 57 71 *e-mail* mkohn@worldaccess.nl *Contact:* Menno Kohn.

NEW ZEALAND

Glenys Bean Literary Agency (1989), PO Box 47-098, Auckland 2 *tel/fax* (09) 378-6287. Adult and children's fiction, educational, non-fiction, film, TV, radio (home, UK 15%, foreign rights 20%). Represented by Sanford Greenburger (USA); translations – Sheil Land (UK). Preliminary letter, synopsis and sae required.

Richards Literary Agency (1977), 3-49 Aberdeen Road, Castor Bay, Auckland 9 *postal address* PO Box 31240, Milford, Auckland 9 *tel* (09) 410-5681 *fax* (09) 410-6389. *Partners:* Ray Richards, Barbara Richards. Full-length MSS, fiction, non-fiction, juvenile, educational, academic books; films, television, radio (home 10%, overseas 10-20%). Preliminary letter, synopsis with sae required. No reading fee.

NIGERIA

Joe–Tolalu & Associates (Nigeria) Ltd (1983), Plot 14, Block A, Surulere Industrial Road, Ogba, PO Box 7031, Ikeja, Lagos *tel* 01-4925078, 059-412041. *Directors:* Joseph Omosade Awolalu, Tosin Awolalu, Foluke Awolalu, Dimeji Popoola. Full-length MSS: fiction and non-fiction; Christian literature; short MSS: picture books only (home 10-15%, overseas 15-20%; translation 15%, performance/film/TV 10%); will suggest revision. Works with overseas agents. Preliminary letter essential; no reading fee.

PORTUGAL

Ilidio da Fonseca Matos, Avenida Gomes Pereira, 105-3°-B, 1500 Lisbon *tel* 716 29 88 *fax* 715 44 45.

RUSSIA

Prava i Prevodi (1993), 14-12 Sadovaya Triumfalnaya, 103006 Moscow, Russia *tel* (095) 209 2263 *fax* (095) 883 6050. *Director:* Konstantin Palchikov. Specialises in representing American and British authors in Russia, Latvia, Lithuania, Estonia and Ukraine.

SCANDINAVIA, including FINLAND and ICELAND

A/S Bookman, Nørregade 45, DK-1165 Copenhagen K, Denmark *tel* 33 14 57 20 *fax* 33 12 00 07. Handles rights in Denmark, Sweden, Norway, Finland and Iceland for foreign authors.

Gösta Dahl & Son, AB, Aladdinsvägan 14, S-161 38 Bromma, Sweden *tel* 08 25 62 35 *fax* 08 25 11 18.

Lennart Sane Agency AB (1969), Holländareplan 9, S-374 34 Karlshamm, Sweden *tel* 0454 123 56 *fax* 0454 149 20. *Directors:* Lennart Sane, Elisabeth Sane, Ulf Töregård. Fiction, non-fiction, children's books, film and TV scripts; will suggest revision where appropriate. No reading fee.

Leonhardt & Høier Literary Agency aps, Studiestraede 35, DK-1455 Copenhagen K, Denmark *tel* 33 13 25 23 *cables* Leolitag *fax* 33 13 49 92.

Gustaf von Sydow (1988), Lorensbergsvägen 76, S 136 69 Haninge, Sweden *tel/fax* 08 776 10 54. *Directors:* Gustaf von Sydow, Elizabeth von Sydow. Handles television, film, celebrity and news features in Sweden, Norway, Denmark and Finland. Literary agent working in Sweden, Norway, Denmark and Finland.

Sane Töregård Agency (1995), Holländareplan 9, S-374 34 Karlshamn, Sweden *tel* (46) 454 12356 *fax* (46) 454 14920. *Directors:* Lennart Sane, Elisabeth Sane, Ulf Töregård. Represents authors, agents and publishers in Scandinavia and Holland for rights in fiction, non-fiction and children's books.

SOUTH AFRICA

Frances Bond Literary Services (1985), 32B Stanley Teale Road, Westville North 3630, KwaZulu-Natal *postal address* PO Box 223, Westville 3630 *tel* (031) 824532 *fax* (031) 822620. *Managing editor:* Frances Bond; *chief editor:* Eileen Molver.

International Press Agency (Pty) Ltd, PO Box 67, Howard Place 7450 *tel* (021) 5311926 *fax* (021) 5318789. *Manager:* Terry Temple. *UK office:* Ursula A. Barnett, 19 Avenue South, Surbiton, Surrey KT5 8PJ *tel/fax* 0181-390 4414.

Literary Dynamics (formerly **Isabel Cooke Literary Agency**; 1985), PO Box 51037, Musgrave 4062 *tel/fax* (031) 222139/3092913. *Managing editor:* Isabel Cooke. Full-length MSS, fiction and non-fiction, screenplays; public speaking consultant, literary consultant to industry; reading fee for in-depth evaluation.

Sandton Literary Agency (1982), PO Box 785799, Sandton 2146 *tel* (011) 4428624. *Directors:* J. Victoria Canning, M. Sutherland. Full-length MSS and screenplays; lecture agents. Letter or telephone call first, please. Works in conjunction with Renaissance-Swan Film Agency, Inc., Los Angeles, USA.

SPAIN

A.C.E.R. Literary Agency (1959), Amor de Dios 1, 28014 Madrid *tel* 1-369-2061 *fax* 1-369-2052. *Directors:* Elizabeth Atkins, Laure Merle d'Aubigné. Represents UK, US, French and German publishers for Spanish and Portuguese translation rights; represents Spanish- and Portuguese-language authors (home/overseas 10%); will suggest revision where appropriate. £20 reading fee.

Miss Carmen Balcells, Agencia Literaria Carmen Balcells, Diagonal 580, Barcelona 08021 *tel* 200-89-33, 200-85-65 *cables* Copyright, Barcelona *telex* 50459 COPY E *fax* 200-70-41.

Mercedes Casanovas Literary Agency (1980), Teodora Lamadrid 29, 08022 Barcelona *tel* 212-47-91 *fax* 417-90-37. Literature, non-fiction, children's books (home 10%, overseas 20%). Works with overseas agents. No reading fee.

Raquel de la Concha, Plaza de las Salesas 9, 1°B-28004 Madrid *tel* 308-55-85 *fax* 308-56-00. *Director:* Raquel de la Concha. Representing foreign fiction, non-fiction, children's books and Spanish authors. No reading fee.

International Editors Co., S.A., Rambla Cataluña 63, 3°-1ª, 08007 Barcelona *tel* 215-88-12 *fax* 487-35-83.

Lennart Sane Agency AB (1965), Paseo de Mejico 65, Las Cumbres-Elviria, E-29600 Marbella (Malaga) *tel* (9) 52 83 41 80 *fax* (9) 52 83 31 96. Fiction, non-fiction, children's books, film and TV scripts; will suggest revision where appropriate. No reading fee.

Julio F. Yañez, Agencia Literaria, Via Augusta 139, 6°-2ª, 08021 Barcelona *tel* 200-71-07 *fax* 209-48-65.

SWITZERLAND

Paul & Peter Fritz AG Literary Agency, Jupiterstrasse 1, CH-8032 Zürich *postal address* Postfach, CH-8032 Zürich *tel* (01) 381 41 40 *fax* (01) 381 20 35. Represents authors, agents and publishers in German-language areas.

Liepman AG, Maienburgweg 23, CH-8044 Zürich *tel* (01) 261 76 60 *cables* Litagent *fax* (01) 261 01 24. Dr Ruth Liepman, Eva Koralnik, Ruth Weibel. Represents authors, agents and publishers from all over the world for German translation rights, and authors from MSS on for world rights.

Mohrbooks Literary Agency, Klosbachstrasse 110, CH-8032 Zürich *tel* (01) 251 16 10 *fax* (01) 262 52 13. Rainer Heumann, Sabine Ibach.

Niedieck Linder AG, Zollikerstrasse 87, Postbox 217, CH-8034 Zürich *tel* (01) 381 65 92 *fax* (01) 381 65 13. Represents German-language authors and Italian-language authors on the German market.

WEST INDIES

CMS Literary Agency (1994), PO Box 993, Road Town, Tortola, British Virgin Islands *tel/fax* 809-495-9202. *Directors:* Ginger Hodge, George Graham. Children's and adult fiction; Caribbean literature and poetry (10%). Will suggest revision; no reading fee. Willing to work with other agencies in publishing Caribbean writers.

Listen to speech

Listen to yourself on a tape recorder. The experience of hearing yourself recorded for the first time is usually unpleasant. Who is this stranger with the funny squeaky voice and the appalling vowels? Do you really sound like that? Your friends assure you it is exactly like you, just as they do when they show you an unflattering snapshot. It is a curious fact that the microphone seems to exaggerate individual vowel traits. You will never before have heard your voice as others hear it, because in the ordinary way it reverberates inside your head as well as coming to your ears across an air gap. But this stranger is the person your audience will meet. If you are to write successfully for yourself you must study your own style of speech, come to terms with your own vocal personality, and construct the sort of sentences that will sit easily on your tongue.

from *Writing for Radio* by Rosemary Horstmann (A & C Black, £6.99).
See order form on page 690.

Merchandising Agents

A number of agents specialise in the handling of rights connected with the promotion of characters from books, television programmes, etc., or with the books and programmes themselves. This is a selective listing, both of agents and of properties handled.

BBC Licensing, BBC Worldwide Ltd, Woodlands, 80 Wood Lane, London W12 0TT   *tel* 0181-576 2725   *fax* 0181-743 0393. Representing BBC TV and Radio and a selection of copyright owners.
Properties: *Animal Hospital, Animals of Farthing Wood, Antiques Roadshow, The Archers, BBC News & Current Affairs, BBC Sport, Big Break, Blue Peter, The Busy World of Richard Scarry, Clothes Show, Dad's Army, Doctor Who, EastEnders, Every Second Counts, Fireman Sam, Food & Drink, Gardeners' World, The Generation Game, Grandstand, Hairy Jeremy, Heartbreak High, Keeping Up Appearances, Live & Kicking, Mastermind, Match of the Day, Monty – the Dog Who Wears Glasses!, Morag the Cow, Mr Blobby, Noddy, Noel's House Party, Oakie Doke, One Foot in the Grave, One Man & his Dog, Only Fools & Horses, Otis the Aardvark, People's Century, Pingu, Plasmo, The Prince of Atlantis, A Question of Sport, Radio 1, Radio 2, Radio 3, Radio 4, Radio 5 Live, Reeves & Mortimer, The Silver Brumby, Songs of Praise, Spider, Teletubbies, Telly Addicts, Top Gear, Top of the Pops, Wallace & Gromit, William's Wish Wellingtons.*

Copyright Promotions Ltd (1974), 12th Floor, Metropolis House, 22 Percy Street, London W1P 0DN   *tel* 0171-580 7431   *fax* 0171-631 1147. *Joint managing director:* Angela Farrugia; *group communications manager:* Catherine Pauk.
Properties: *Star Wars, Indiana Jones, Young Indiana Jones, Spider-Man, Fantastic Four, Ironman, The Incredible Hulk, Mask Animation, Sky Dancers, Dragon Flyz, Test and County Cricket Club, Story Store, Judge Dredd, Judge Dredd the Movie, Mr Men* and *Little Miss, Pink Panther, Sonic the Hedgehog* (Sega); Kate Veal originals: *Oliver Otter & Friends, Cherished Teddies, Reboot, Wind in the Willows, Willows in Winter, Manga Video, Cosmopolitan* (Hearst Magazines), *Boyzone, Dennis the Menace, Desperate Dan, Minnie the Minx, Bash Street Kids;* The Hanna Barbera Portfolio Inc.: *Jonny Quest, The Flintstones, Scooby Doo, Yogi Bear, Top Cat, Wacky Races, Banana Splits, Tom & Jerry,* Turner Movies (over 3500 classic films), *Zig and Zag, X Files, Brockum Rock Groups, Dan Dare, Tank Girl, Teenage Mutant Hero Turtles, Mad Gadget, Mighty Morphin Power Rangers Movie.*

The Copyrights Company (UK) Ltd, Manor Barn, Milton, Nr Banbury, Oxon OX15 4HH   *tel* (01295) 721188   *fax* (01295) 720145; *London office:* 7 Square Rigger Row, Plantation Wharf, York Road, London SW11 3TZ   *tel* 0171-924 3292   *fax* 0171-924 3208. *Directors:* Nicholas Durbridge (managing), Linda Pooley, Mark Robinson, Julie Nellthorp, Karen Addison.
Properties include *Beatrix Potter, Paddington Bear, Brambly Hedge, Postman Pat, Flower Fairies,* and other book-related properties for merchandise licensing.

Hawk Books, 309 Canalot Studios, 222 Kensal Road, London W10 5BN   *tel* 0181-969 8091   *fax* 0181-968 9012. *Director:* Patrick Hawkey.
Properties: *Billy Bunter, Dopey Dinosaur.*

Link Licensing Ltd (1986), 7 Baron's Gate, 33-35 Rothschild Road, Chiswick, London W4 5HT *tel* 0181-996 4800 *fax* 0181-747 9452. *Directors:* Claire L. Derry, David A. Hamilton, Martin Weigold.

Properties: *Asterix, Barbie, Camberwick Green, Caribou Kitchen, Christopher Crocodile, Creature Comforts, The Forgotten Toys, Goosebumps, The Hedgehogs of Leafy Lane, Magic Roundabout, The Magic School Bus, Natural History Museum, Jane Hissey's Old Bear & Friends, Percy the Park Keeper, The Slow Norris, Very Hungry Caterpillar, Wind in the Willows, What-A-Mess.*

Marvel Entertainment Group, Arundel House, 13-15 Arundel Street, London WC2R 3DX *tel* 0171-208 4500 *fax* 0171-497 8844.

Properties include *The Marvel Super-Heroes, Spider-Man, X-Men, Iron Man, Fantastic Four.*

Patrick, Sinfield (PSL) (1980), 95 White Lion Street, London N1 9PF *tel* 0171-837 5440 *fax* 0171-837 5334. *Directors:* Christopher Patrick, John Sinfield.

Represent properties of: Space Productions Ltd (*Gerry Anderson's Space Precinct*), Vivid Imaginations Ltd (*Teeny Weeny Families*), Gaumont Media (*Highlander* – the animated series), Nikelodeon (*Aaahh!! Real Monsters, Clarissa Explains It All, Ren & Stimpy, Rocko's Modern Life, Rugrats*), MTV (*MTV logo, Beavis and Butt-Head*), UFS (*Dilbert, Snoopy, Fido Dido*), Paws Inc. (*Garfield*), Capcom (*Street Fighter II, Mega Man*), Titan Sports (*World Wrestling Federation*), Zorro Productions (*Zorro*), Binney & Smith (*Crayola*), Michelle Lovric (*Love Letters*).

Michael Woodward Creations (1979), Parlington Hall, Aberford, West Yorkshire LS25 3EG *tel* (0113) 281 3913 *fax* (0113) 281 3911. *Contacts:* Michael Woodward, Janet Woodward (licensing director), Rebecca Sheavyn (licensing manager).

International licensing company with own in-house studio. Artist management, licensing, design and character concepts for worldwide merchandising. Current properties include: *Teddy Tum Tum, Railway Children, Animal Magic, Oceana, Beaky & Bumpy & Friends, Ragamuffins, Melting Pot, Grow-Tesk, Awe' Kids, Oddbods.* New concepts considered. Sae with synopsis/illustrations; scripts only not accepted.

Shaping the play

Although the notion of the well-made play with its neatly arranged beginning, middle and end is now a thing of the past, structure remains one of the principal problems which bedevil playwrights. Because events unfold in the here and now before our eyes – not in a vague past where their exact chronology and exactly 'who knows what and when' can be fudged – their sequence can be crucial. Moving an event from one scene and placing it elsewhere, whether earlier or later, can have untold and peculiar consequences.

from *Writing a Play* by Steve Gooch (A & C Black, £8.99).
See order form on page 690.

PART TWO

General Information

Preparation of materials, resources

Books, Research and Reference Sources for Writers

MARGARET PAYNE ALA

Almost every writing project will involve the use of books or research at some stage. Some references are quickly found; others require accumulating numerous books or information files on a specific topic and visits to specialist libraries or other relevant places or people. Although research can be an interest or pleasure in itself, it can also be time-consuming, cutting into writing or earning time. Even checking a single fact can take hours or days if you ask the wrong question or check the wrong source first. No article or book can hope to solve all problems – sometimes there are no answers, or the lack of information is itself the answer – but a few guidelines as to routines and sources may save much time and money. The following is an introduction to printed sources. For a more detailed approach, including guides to original and unpublished material, it is recommended you consult Ann Hoffmann's *Research for Writers* (Black, 5th edn 1996, £11.99), a most useful book which covers methods, sources, specific organisations and specialist libraries.

Suggestions for a core collection of reference books to own are given below under 'A writer's reference bookshelf'. The final choice of title often depends on personal preference and interests, space, the frequency with which it needs to be consulted, its cost and the proximity of your nearest public reference library. Anyone living in or near a large city has an advantage over the country dweller. Those living within easy reach of London have the best advantage of all: a choice of major reference libraries; a variety of specialist sources such as headquarters of various societies, companies and organisations; academic and other specialist libraries and the government. Often a question can be answered much nearer home, but you may find the further back in time you go, or the more detailed your research, the further afield you need to travel.

CHECKING A FACT

What do you really want to know?

Clarifying your question in advance can save much work for you or your researcher. If you want to check someone's date of birth and know the person is alive or very recently dead and in *Who's Who*, then ask for that book, or phrase your telephone request so that the librarian goes straight to that source. Do not start with general questions such as 'Where are the biographies?' In a branch library you may be shown sections of individual lives; on the telephone you are adding to British Telecom's profits and your telephone bill, as well as wasting time. If the person is dead, did he or she die recently enough to have a newspaper obituary – it often mentions the date of birth – or long enough ago to be in a volume of *Who Was Who* or the *Dictionary of National Biography*? Never assume that information that you know is necessarily common knowledge; it needs to be specified.

Go straight to the index.

Most reference books are arranged in alphabetical order but, if not, they should have an index. Some indexes may seem inadequate, but have you used the right key word? A good index should refer you from the one not used. For example, some will use carpentry and ignore woodwork as an entry. Others will ignore both and go straight to the object to be made or repaired. If there is no index, turn first to the contents page, as in some books the index is at the front rather than the back.

Is it important to be up to date?

Most books have the date of publication on the back of the title page. Is the answer given one which may be surpassed or superseded? Despite some instant publishing, when dealing with statistics most books have a built in obsolescence. There is a cut-off date when the text goes to the printer and the updating must wait for the next edition. Some current events are too recent to be found in books at all, although well documented at the time in newspapers and magazines (see below).

If in doubt, re-check your answer.

If the answer is of importance, try not to depend on one source. Mistakes can occur in print or in transcribing. Sometimes it is necessary to check another source for verification or to obtain another point of view. In all cases you should . . .

Note your source.

Even if you think you will remember, always note where you find your information, preferably next to the answer, or in a card file or book where it can be easily found. Note the title, author, publisher and date of publication as well as the page number. Nothing is more annoying than having to undertake the same search twice.

RESEARCHING A SUBJECT

Reference has already been made to Ann Hoffmann's book for detail, but Kipling's six honest serving men can still be the basis for any subject: What? Why? When? How? Where? Who? cover aspects of most enquiries. The starting point depends on the writer's personal knowledge of the subject. Where it is unfamiliar always start from the general and go on to the particular. An article in an encyclopedia can fill in the background and often recommend bibliographies or other references. If an article in the *Encyclopaedia Britannica* is too detailed or too complex, try *The World Book*. The latter may be in the children's library, but because it has to appeal to a wider readership, the text and illustrations are clearer. Avoid a detailed book on the subject until you need it; it may tell you more than you want to know.

The following sources are suggestions as sources of information, but not all will be relevant to your subject.

Reference libraries. Use the largest one in your vicinity for encylopedias, specialised reference books, annuals and for back numbers of newspapers and periodicals. Ask for *Walford's Guide to Reference Material*. The three volumes list the standard reference works of subjects, most of which should be available for consultation.

Lending libraries. Find the class number of the books you want, and see what is available.

Special libraries. *The Aslib Directory of Information Sources in the United Kingdom* should be available in your reference library. It gives details of special libraries of industries, organisations and societies.

Catalogues, bibliographies and subject guides. Some libraries publish their catalogues, but this is becoming less frequent. There is a series of subject catalogues to the British Library (formerly the British Museum Library) up to 1975 and the *British National Bibliography* updates this (*see* 'Compiling a bibliography' below).

Newspapers and bibliographies. There is a monthly index to *The Times*, cumulated annually, which often provides the date of an event. The index also includes the *The Times Supplements*. For periodical articles, begin with the *British Humanities Index*, and, if necessary, check also the specialist indexes and abstracting journals such as *Current Technology Index*. Your public library can often locate runs of periodicals and magazines, and the interloan service can obtain specific periodical articles if you have the details. *Profile*, an on-line index to quality newspapers, is the most up to date available, but retrospective only to 1985 and few libraries have the facility as yet. *Clover* is a printed index to the same broadsheet press.

COMPILING A BIBLIOGRAPHY

Checking what books are already available may reveal both the range of titles already in print and the potential market for your work. If yours is to be the tenth book on the subject published in the last two years, saturation point may be near. On the other hand, if you know the books and believe you can do better, or have evolved a different approach, you can mention this in a covering letter to a potential publisher. A quick way to evaluate what is available is by checking the shelves of a public library or bookstore, but it should be remembered that in a library, many of the best books will be on loan. This practice also makes one aware of publishers' interests.

A more comprehensive and systematic list of recent books can be compiled by consulting the *British National Bibliography*, a cumulating list based on the copyright books in the British Library, with advance notice (up to three months) of new books through the Cataloguing in Publication scheme. The arrangement is by the Dewey Decimal Classification used in all public libraries. Other subject lists are less satisfactory to consult. The British Museum (now British Library) has a series of subject indexes up to 1975, and many British books are included in the American *Cumulative Book Index* (1928 on). *Whitaker's Books in Print* is predominantly an author-title list, but does index some books under the key word of a subtitle; as its name implies, out of print books are excluded.

Facilities now exist to obtain a bibliography on any subject by using one of the computer data banks based on the British Library, the Library of Congress or commercial firms. The difficulties are expense (£25.00 per hour) and finding local access points.

OBTAINING BOOKS

Books in print. In 1995 95,064 different books were published in the United Kingdom alone, joining the many thousands of other titles still in print from previous years. The number of books available means that the chances of finding a copy of what you want on your bookseller's shelf, when you want it, may be slim. But if it is in print it can be ordered for you, although delivery times vary with each publisher. Most large bookshops and libraries now have the monthly microfiche editions of *Whitaker's Books in Print* giving details of author, publisher, price, number of pages and international standard book number (ISBN). The latter is often useful for speeding the order.

Out of print books present more difficulty. Generally the older the book, the more difficult it may be to obtain. Such books are no longer available from the publishers, who retain only a file copy, all other stocks having been sold. Therefore unless you are lucky enough to find an unsold copy on a bookseller's shelves, it must be sought in the second-hand market or through a library loan. There are many specialist second-hand and antiquarian booksellers, and a number of directories listing them and their interests. The most well known are *Sheppard's Book Dealers in the British Isles*, now published by R. Joseph. Copies of these should be in your local reference library. Many advertise in *Book and Magazine Collector*, a monthly magazine, which has an extensive 'wants' column.

Public libraries should be able to obtain books for you, whether or not they are in print, either from their own stock, from other libraries in the system or through the interloan scheme. This operates through the British Lending Library, but all requests must go through your library as you cannot apply direct. Your local library tickets may sometimes be used in other libraries, but different issuing systems have discouraged this in recent years. Most library systems now have a databased catalogue of all branch stock.

A WRITER'S REFERENCE BOOKSHELF

However good and accessible a public library may be, there are some books required for constant or instant consultation, which should be within easy reach of your work area. The choice of title may vary, but the following list is offered as suggestions for a core collection.

1. **Dictionaries.** With the use of word processor packages, a dictionary is no longer quite so essential for spelling checks, although still needed to clarify definitions and meanings. A book is often easier to consult, and portable. The complete *Oxford English Dictionary* is not, and although the definitive work, neither the full nor the compact edition with its magnifying glass, nor the two volume *Shorter Oxford Dictionary* is easy to handle for quick reference, so a one volume dictionary is more practical. The number of new words and meanings coming into vogue suggests a replacement every five years or so, or supplementing your choice by a good paperback edition. If you use an old copy, you will be surprised by the improved format and readability of the new editions.

The most popular one volume dictionaries are the *Concise Oxford Dictionary* (8th edn 1991, £13.99 – 80,000 definitions), *Chambers' English Dictionary* (6th edn 1993, £19.99 – 150,000 entries, appealing to crossword addicts), *The Collins English Dictionary* (HarperCollins, 4th edn 1994, £22.99 – 110,000 entries). A recommended paperback dictionary is *Oxford Paperback Dictionary* (rev. edn 1994, £5.50 – 50,000 entries). If you write for the American market, it is advisable also to have an American dictionary to check variant spellings and meanings. The equivalent of the Oxford family of dictionaries is Webster's, the most popular one volume edition being *Webster's New World Dictionary* (Prentice-Hall, 4th edn 1994, £17.95).

2. **Roget's Thesaurus.** When the exact word or meaning eludes you, a thesaurus may help clear a mental block. There are many versions of Roget available, both in hardback and paperback, including a revision by E.M. Kirkpatrick (Longman, 1987, £15.99) and a paperback edition from Penguin (1984, £4.99). *The Bloomsbury Thesaurus* (Bloomsbury, 1993, £15.99) is a new compilation which includes 1000 knowledge categories and 1500 quotations.

3. **Grammar and English usage.** A wide choice is available but Fowler's *Modern English Usage* remains a standard work (2nd edn revised Sir Ernest Gowers, Oxford UP, £13.95 and £6.99 paperback). Many prefer Sir Ernest Gowers' *Complete Plain Words* (4th edn 1994 revised Sidney Greenbaum and Jane Whitcut, Penguin, £6.99). More recent works are *The Oxford Guide to English Usage* (Oxford UP, 2nd edn 1994, £4.99), and Michael Legat's *The Nuts and Bolts of Writing* (Hale, 1989, £9.95 and £5.99).

4. **Encyclopedias and annuals.** Multi-volume encyclopedias are both expensive and space consuming. They are best left for consultation at the nearest reference library, where the most up-to-date versions should be available, unless your need justifies ownership. Of the single volumes, *Pears Cyclopaedia* contains a surprising amount of general information and a new edition is issued annually (Pelham Books, 1995-6, £14.99). For those concerned with current affairs, the complete edition of *Whitaker's Almanack* has valuable statistics and information on government and countries, as well as many miscellaneous facts not found elsewhere. For annual replacement if constantly used.

5. **Atlases, gazetteers and road maps.** These also need replacing with updated editions from time to time. An old edition can be misleading with recent changes of placenames and metrication. The *The Times Atlas of the World* is the definitive work, but it is expensive and bulky for quick reference. The *The Times Concise Atlas of the World* (Times Books, 7th edn 1995, £45.00) has the most comprehensive gazetteer-index. It is a little more manageable but still requires special shelving.

With the building of the M25 and other motorways, many existing road atlases of Britain may be out of date and need replacing. There are many paperback editions at 3 miles to 1 inch (1:190,080) for less than £5.00, but most detailed is *A-Z Great Britain Road Atlas* (Geographers A-Z, 1994, £6.95; 1:250,000) with 31,000 place names and 56 town maps. Others are *A-Z Great Britain Road Atlas* (1995, £12.95; and £5.95 paperback; 1:152,064) and *Ordnance Survey Road Atlas of Great Britain* (Hamlyn, 1993, £16.99 and £10.99). The *Reader's Digest Driver's Atlas of the British Isles* (1992, £21.95) includes Ireland. For London and environs *Greater London Street Atlas* (Nicholson, rev. edn 1993, £25.99 and £14.99) is a detailed 3.17 miles to 1 inch, 1:20,000 street map for the whole M25 area.

6. **Literary companions and dictionaries.** There are many to choose from, and frequency of consultation will determine whether all or some of the following are desirable. *Brewer's Dictionary of Phrase and Fable* (Cassell, 15th edn 1994, £18.99) and its companion volume *Brewer's Twentieth Century Dictionary of Phrase and Fable* (Cassell, 1991, £16.95 and £10.99 paperback) avoid many distractions by settling queries, as does *The Oxford Companion to English Literature* (5th edn edited by Margaret Drabble, Oxford UP, 1985, £25.00). This new edition complements rather than replaces Sir Paul Harvey's earlier editions. Either can be used for checking an author's work, but the definitive and exhaustive lists are to be found in the *New Cambridge Bibliography of English Literature*. The four volumes and the index volume can be found in major reference libraries.

7. Books of quotations. Once divorced from their text and unattributed, quotations are not easy to trace. This should be a warning to any writer or researcher to note author, title and page number to any item copied. Tracing quotations often needs resort to more than one collection, but the most popular anthologies are *The Oxford Dictionary of Quotations* (4th edn, Oxford UP, 1992, £25.00) and the *Bloomsbury Dictionary of Quotations* (Bloomsbury, 2nd edn 1991, paperback, £12.99) and *The New Penguin Dictionary of Quotations* (Penguin, 1993, £6.99).

8. Biographical dictionaries. *Pears Cyclopaedia* contains a brief but useful section, but for a fuller working tool the standard works are *Chambers' Biographical Dictionary* (Chambers, 5th edn 1990, £35.00, paperback £19.99 – 15,000 entries) or the American-biased *Webster's New Biographical Dictionary* (Merriam-Webster Inc, 1990, £17.95 – 150,000 entries). Frequency of consultation will determine whether you need a personal copy of *Who's Who* or the *Concise Dictionary of National Biography*, which are available in most libraries.

9. Dates, anniversaries and names. A brief guide to anniversaries is included in the Journalists' Calendar section of this book (see page 444). *Everyman's Dictionary of Dates* (Dent, 7th rev. edn, 1987, o.p.) and *The Independent Book of Anniversaries* (Headline, 1993, £20.00 and £8.99) are useful. Leslie Dunkling's *Guinness Book of Names* (Guinness, 7th edn 1995, £11.99) is an encyclopedic source on its subject from first names to places and pubs, with a comprehensive index.

10. Working directories for writers. A current copy of *Writers' & Artists' Yearbook* is essential, as recent moves and mergers have made so many publishers' details out of date. It is useful for very much more information besides that found in the first section. Browse through, or use the index, in spare moments to familiarise yourself with its contents for future reference.

Frequency of consultation will determine whether you also need *Willings Press Guide* (annual, British Media Publications). *Benn's Media Directory* (Benn, 2 vols. annual) is expensive; both are very comprehensive in their coverage of British and overseas newspapers, magazines and other media information. *Cassell's Directory of Publishing* complements all the above, but gives more information about publishing personnel not found elsewhere.

SOME BOOKS ABOUT WRITING AND THE BOOK TRADE

Like the world in general, the book trade has changed and is changing so rapidly today that it is difficult to keep up to date with current events. More bookshops are to be found in the high streets, but not all are charter booksellers undertaking to supply any book in print; many cater only for 'remainder' sales of publishers' unsold stocks, as warehouse space is needed for new titles. In large publishing houses marketing and accounting departments may have as much authority as editors alone once had, and many publishers are diversifying from print to multimedia, from audiobooks to CD-ROM versions of established reference books. At the moment the latter may be more expensive and still experimental in format, but as the majority of people become computer literate, this media may well be a shape of things to come in the non-fiction field.

Computerisation has already affected a great many aspects of publishing and some editors now ask for material on compatible computer disk. Mergers and takeovers of companies and periodicals continue, although this does not reduce the number of titles published annually. For these reasons, much of the material in older books may be inapplicable, although some details remain important for historical reasons. The following is a selection from recent publications. It does not include any of the many books on writing specific types of novels or articles, which are best examined in a library or bookshop before purchase.

Bolt, David, *The Author's Handbook*, Piatkus Books, 1986, £9.95 and £5.95. Written to fill some of the gaps in the author's search for information.

Bonham-Carter, Victor, *Authors by Profession, volume 2: From the Copyright Act 1911 until the End of 1981*, Bodley Head, 1984, O.P. Volume 1 published by the Society of Authors covered the history of authorship up to 1911; the present volume brings it closer to date.

Clark, Giles N., *Inside Book Publishing: a career builder's guide*, Blueprint, 2nd edn 1994, £12.99. Intended to give an overview to young publishers, it describes the processes and business of modern publishing.

Legat, Michael, *An Author's Guide to Publishing*, Robert Hale, 2nd edn 1991, £6.99. Assumes no experience of publishing; a useful, clear introduction with a glossary.

Legat, Michael, *Writing for Pleasure and Profit*, Robert Hale, 2nd edn 1993, paperback £6.99. The best of the recent introductions to writing, covering novels, non-fiction and other topics briefly but clearly.

Mumby, F.A., *Publishing and Bookselling in the Twentieth Century*, Unwin Hyman, 6th edn, paperback 1984, O.P. Revised by Ian Norrie to include events up to 1970, this is the best historical survey.

Owen, Peter (ed.), *Publishing Now*, Peter Owen, 1993, £12.95. Collection of articles by leading figures on various aspects of the book trade today and tomorrow.

Waterhouse, Keith, *Waterhouse on Newspaper Style*, Penguin, 1993, £6.99. Based on the *Daily Mirror* house style, it contains much information on writing succinctly and clearly.

Don't tell, show

There is a sense in which it is meaningless to separate writing about people from any other kind of writing. Just as there is no special way to write about cats, or revolutions, or snow, there is no special way to write about people. Some text books frequently exhort you to USE VIVID WORDS as if this were the key to making people 'come alive'. The question to ask is 'come alive for what, and how?' It depends on what you want to 'do' with a character, and that depends on the kind of story you want to write, and the character's role within it. You will not want to describe in detail every waiter who serves your hero a cup of coffee – but if your hero is feeling threatened by the world then to describe the waiter's contemptuous manner may help to create the desired atmosphere of oppression. The description of the waiter is not done for its own sake, but because it makes him play a part in the story.

from *Word Power* by Julian Birkett (A & C Black, £9.99).
See order form on page 690.

Journalists' Calendar
1997

SELECTED ANNIVERSARIES

January

1 Travellers' cheques, called 'Circular Notes', first issued, 1772

The first British Medical Officer of Health appointed, 1847

Airline uniforms first worn, 1922

Lord Trenchard appointed as the first Marshal of the Royal Air Force, 1927

Ownership of British coal mines and Cable & Wireless Ltd transferred to the nation, 1947

Maurice Chevalier, singer and actor, died 1972

2 Nathaniel Bacon, American colonial leader, born 1642

The first motor van manufactured in Britain, a chain-driven 1½ ton steam van, delivered 1897

3 Beatrice d'Este, patron of the arts and diplomat, died 1497

Ray Milland, actor, born 1905

Jack Ruby, who shot President Kennedy's assassin Lee Oswald in 1963, died while awaiting retrial, 1967

4 Donald Campbell, English water speed record holder, died 1967

The first woman judge, Rose Heilbron, sat at the Old Bailey, 1972

5 Sir Ernest Shackleton, explorer, died 1922

6 Alexander Scriabin, composer, born 1872

The first slalom race took place in Murren, Switzerland, 1922

7 The first British intercontinental airline service (London-Cairo, Imperial Airways) departed, 1927

The first transatlantic telephone service, London-New York (£15/3min), started 1927

8 Denis Wheatley, novelist, born 1897

Shirley Bassey, singer, born 1937

David Bowie, singer and actor, born 1947

Chou En-lai, former premier of China, died 1976

The UK Government launched a major campaign to inform the British public about AIDS, 1987

9 Clive Dunn, actor, born 1922

Sir Anthony Eden resigned as Prime Minister, 1957

UK national coal strike began, 1972

10 Buffalo Bill (William F.) Cody, US showman, died 1917

Terrence Kilmartin, former literary editor of the *Observer*, born 1922

Harold Macmillan became Prime Minister, 1957

Nubar Sarkis Gulbenkian, industrialist, diplomat and philanthropist, died 1972

11 The first diabetic, Leonard Thompson, was treated with insulin, 1922

12 Sir Isaac Pitman, inventor of shorthand, died 1897

Production of civilian gas masks started in Britain, 1937

Dame Agatha Christie, author, died 1976

13 The first parachute jump by a British service flier (from 600ft), 1917

14 The first Municipal Lending Library in Britain opened by Canterbury Corporation, 1847

Rev. Wilson Carlile, founder of the Church Army, born 1847

The first public opinion poll was conducted in Britain according to Dr Gallup's sampling method, 1937

Covent Garden Opera Company's first production, Bizet's *Carmen*, performed 1947

Humphrey Bogart, actor, died 1957

Sir Anthony Eden, statesman, died 1977

15 Molière, dramatist, baptised 1622

Haberdasher John Hetherington wore the first top hat in London, 1797

The Irish Free State recognised, 1922

The first commentary of a team game in Britain and the first BBC sports commentary given at Twickenham, England *v* Wales Rugby International, 1927

16 The first Russian Tsar, Ivan the Terrible, crowned, 1547

Arturo Toscanini, conductor, died 1957

17 Keith Chegwin, TV and radio personality, born 1957

Jeremy Thorpe elected leader of the Liberal Party, 1967

18 Hungarian Writers' Union dissolved, 1957

The first plastic warship, 500-ton minehunter *HMS Wilton*, launched from Southampton, 1972

19 Nigel Nicolson, author and former Conservative MP, born 1917

The first play written specially for TV, *The Underground Murder Mystery*, shown 1937

21 The Earl of Surrey, poet and soldier, executed 1547

The letters of Junius last appeared, 1772

Franz Grillparzer, dramatist and poet, died 1872

Recognition of taxi-cabs in Britain, 1907

Aubrey Singer, producer and former deputy director-general of BBC, born 1927

The first supersonic airliner in passenger service, BA Concorde and AF Concorde, took off simultaneously at 11.40am, 1976

22 The first broadcast football commentary, 1927

Treaty of Accession to EEC signed in Brussels by UK, Denmark, Ireland and Norway, 1972

Ceasefire agreement in Lebanon, 1976

23 Pierre Bonnard, painter, died 1947

Princess Caroline of Monaco, born 1957

The first hover freight Ramsgate-Calais journey, 1967

Paul Robeson, actor, singer and leader in the Black civil rights movement, died 1976

25 Raymond Baxter, broadcaster and writer, born 1922

Al Capone, Chicago gangster, died 1947

26 The first Borough Engineer in Britain appointed 1847

Michael Bentine, humorist, born 1922

The first film by a camerawoman (Diane Tammes), *Women of Marrakesh*, transmitted 1977

27 John Ogdon, pianist, born 1937

UK, USA and USSR signed treaty banning nuclear weapons from outer space, 1967

28 Henry VII, King of England, born 1457

Henry VIII, King of England, died 1547

Ronnie Scott, jazz musician, born 1927

Reynaldo Hahn, composer, died 1947

29 Sir William Rothenstein, artist, born 1872

30 Charles I beheaded at Whitehall, 1649

Vanessa Redgrave, actress, born 1937

Boris Spassky, chess champion, born 1937

France abolished exchanged control system and freed the gold market, 1967

British troops shot 13 civilians during illegal march in Londonderry, 'Bloody Sunday', 1972

The first woman jockey (Muriel Naughton) competed under National Hunt Rules, 1976

31 The first VD clinic opened in London Lock Hospital, 1747

Franz Schubert, composer, born 1797

Trans-Iranian pipeline completed, 1957

February

1 Germany began unrestricted submarine warfare, 1917

Renata Tebaldi, soprano, born 1922

Don Everly, of the Everly Brothers, born 1937

The first turbo-prop airliner entered into scheduled service in Britain, 1957

2 The first petrol-driven motor van manufactured in Britain carried a pay-load for the first time, 1897

Ulysses by James Joyce published, 1922

4 More than 23,000 people killed in Guatemala earthquake, 1976

6 Limitation of Armaments Conference in Washington ended 1922

7 Peter Jay, writer and broadcaster, born 1937

Jenny Bazeley became the first woman to referee an all-male soccer match, 1976

The first woman jockey (Diana Thorne) won a race under National Hunt Rules, 1976

8 Sir Victor Gollancz, publisher, died 1967

9 Norman Adams, painter, born 1927

State of Emergency proclaimed in UK, 1972

10 USSR signed a peace treaty with Finland, 1947

11 Thomas Alva Edison, inventor, born 1847

E.W. Swanton, veteran cricket writer, born 1907

Mark Bonham-Carter, former Liberal MP and first chairman of the Race Relations Board, born 1922

12-13 The first Volunteer Regiment to win battle honour was Castlemartin Yeomanry for its defence of Fishguard against French invasion, 1797

14 Battle of Cape St Vincent, 1797

Lois Maxwell, actress (Miss Moneypenny in James Bond films), born 1927

15 The first session of Permanent Court of International Justice, 1922

16 Philip Melanchthon, Church reformer, born 1497

The first law journal, *Journal du Paris*, published 1672

Nylon was first developed and patented, 1937

18 Helen Gurley Brown, writer, born 1922

Dr Robert Oppenheimer, pioneer of the American atom bomb, died 1967

19 Sir Henry Savile, scholar and philanthropist, died 1622

The Peace of Tolentino, 1797

Charles Blondin, acrobat and tightrope walker, died 1897

The first Women's Institute founded in Stoney Creek, Ontario, 1897

The first prison concert performed at Pentonville, 1922

Britain's first continuous TV serial, *Emergency Ward 10*, began in 1957

20 Sidney Poitier, actor, born 1927

The first post buses in Britain ran in Monmouthshire, 1967

21 W.H. Auden, poet, born 1907

Jilly Cooper, novelist, born 1937

The first daytime TV soap opera in the US, *A woman to Remember*, began in 1947

22 The first purpose-built cinema in Britain at Central Hall, Colne, Lancs., opened 1907

London Gazette announced that the Queen had granted to the Duke of Edinburgh 'the style and dignity of a Prince of the United Kingdom' and that he would henceforth be known as 'Prince Philip, Duke of Edinburgh', 1957

Indonesian President Dr Sukarno surrendered all powers to Premier General Suharto, 1967

IRA bomb at Aldershot killed 7 people, 1972

Andy Warhol, artist, died 1987

23 Anton Mosimann, chef, born 1947

L.S. Lowry, painter, died 1976

24 Don John of Austria, soldier, born 1547

Thomas Coutts, banker, died 1822

The first feature film presented by command of the Sovereign: *Tom Brown's Schooldays*, 1917

Tony Miles became the first British International Grand Master chessplayer, 1976

25 Anthony Burgess, author, born 1917

Tom Courteney, actor, born 1937

26 The first £1 note issued by the Bank of England, 1797

Publication of the US Tower Commission report (appointed to investigate the activities of the National Security Council in the Iran arms deal scandal), 1987

27 Dame Ellen Terry, actress, born 1847

The first wedding at which the bridal couple left in a motor car took place in Paris, 1897

Mervyn Jones, author, born 1922

28 The British Protectorate over Egypt ended, 1922

Coal miners returned to work in UK, 1972

March

1 Designation of the first National Park, Yellowstone, Wyoming, 1872

2 Horace Walpole, Earl of Orford, politician and writer, died 1797

John Gardner, composer, born 1917

Margaret Barbieri, ballet dancer, born 1947

3 Alexander Graham Bell, inventor, born 1847

Danny Kaye, actor and entertainer, died 1987

4 Peter Skellern, singer, born 1947

The first North Sea gas piped ashore by BP, 1967

Cyril Grimes became the first person to receive £0.5 million as an individual football pool prize, 1972

The first Hovercraft fatality: 4 people died aboard the *Seaspeed SR-N6* at Southsea, 1972

President Reagan admitted mistakes and accepted full responsibility for Iran arms deal scandal, 1987

6 Valentina Nikolayeva-Tereshkova, first woman in space, born 1937

Ghana declared independence, 1957

Zoltán Kodály, composer, died 1967

Svetlana Alliluyeva, Stalin's daughter, requested asylum at US embassy in Delhi, 1967

Townsend Thoresen cross-Channel ferry *Herald of Free Enterprise* capsized off Zeebrugge, Belgium, 1987

7 The first jazz record, *The Dixie Jazz Band One Step*, released, 1917

8 Russian Revolution began at Petrograd, 1917

9 Mary Anning, palaeontologist, died 1847

11 Baghdad captured by the British, 1917

Anne Warburton became the first woman to serve as British ambassador (to Denmark), 1976

First radio external broadcasting service was inaugurated with a short-wave transmission from the Netherlands to the Dutch East Indies, 1927

12 Elizabeth Vaughan, soprano, born 1937

Googie Withers, actress, born 1917

13 Lesley Collier, ballet dancer, born 1947

14 The first filming of a US president was outgoing President Grover Cleveland at the inauguration of McKinley, 1897

Provisional government established in Russia, 1917

German retreat to the Hindenburg Line began, 1917

Pam Ayres, poet, born 1947

The first helicopter pilot's licence issued, 1947

15 The first women MPs were elected in Finland, 15-17 March 1907

Tsar of Russia abdicated, 1917

Ry Cooder, folk and blues guitarist, born 1947

16 Rosa Bonheur, painter, born 1822

The first football Cup Final was played in London, 1872

17 The first wide-screen film, a 15-minute production of the Corbett-Fitzsimmons championship, shown in 1897

Ferdinand von Zeppelin, inventor of the airship, died 1917

18 The first stamp auction in Britain was held at Sotheby's, 1872

Mr Attlee delivered the first Party Political Broadcast under new BBC scheme, 1947

Torrey Canyon oil tanker disaster, 1967

19 Sergei Diaghilev, ballet master, born 1872

20 Dame Vera Lynn, singer, born 1917

21 Flight trials of the first British guided missile took place at Upavon, 1917

22 Wilhelm I, Emperor of Germany, born 1797

Motor cabs in Britain first fitted with a taxi-meter, 1907

23 Cristóbal Balenciaga, courturier, died 1972

24 Benjamin Luxon, baritone, born 1937

Field Marshal Montgomery of Alamein died 1976

25 St Catherine of Siena, nun and mystic, born 1347

Elton John, singer and composer, born 1947

The European Community established: treaty signed at Rome, 1957

26 The first Battle of Gaza, 1917

27 Alfred, comte de Vigny, writer, born 1797

Henri Murger, writer, born 1822

Cyrus Vance, former US Secretary of State, born 1917

Mstislav Rostropovich, cellist and composer, born 1927

28 Women's Army Auxiliary Corps (WAAC), the first official servicewomen in Britain, founded 1917

Karol Szymanowski, composer, died 1937

Broadcast of the first breakfast-time television in Britain, Good Morning Television, 1977

29 Emmanuel Swedenborg, scientist and theologican, died 1772

Joyce Carey, novelist, died 1957

Lord Rank, J. Arthur Rank, film magnate, died 1972

The Queen opened the exhibition of the tomb of Tutankhamen treasures at British Museum, London, 1972

30 The Treaty of Fez made Morocco a French protectorate, 1912

Warren Beatty, actor, born 1937

Northern Ireland came under direct rule from London, 1972

31 Francis I, King of France, died 1547

April

1 King George II (of Greece), died 1947

Butler Act raised the compulsory school-leaving age to 15 years, 1947

Hounslow Borough Council was the first local authority in Britain to offer free contraceptives, 1972

Max Ernst, artist, died 1976

2 The first airline steward, Jack Anderson, served on Daimler Airways London-Paris flight, 1922

Oxford *v* Cambridge Boat Race first broadcast, 1927

Denis Tuohy, BBC TV presenter, born 1937

The first woman to ride in the Grand National was Charlotte Brew on *Barony Fort*, 1977

3 Edward Everett Hale, writer, born 1822

Johannes Brahms, composer, died 1897

5 Howard Hughes, millionaire recluse, died 1976

6 USA declared war on Germany, 1917

The first collision between airliners, Northern France, 1922

Gerry Mulligan, jazz musician, born 1927

The first TV performer (professional artiste): a short act of monologue and song by comedian A. Dolan during an experimental transmission, 1927

Henry Ford, motor engineer and manufacturer, died 1947

The Scarman Tribunal report on violence and civil disturbances in Northern Ireland in 1969 published, 1972

7 Opening of the first purpose-built prisoner of war camp in Britain, Norman Cross Depot, for the reception of French POWs, 1797

8 Sir Henry Hadow, musicologist, died 1937

9 The last man to be beheaded in Britain was Lord Lovat, Scottish Jacobite, 1747

The Canadians stormed Vimy Ridge, northern France, 1917

Valerie Singleton, broadcaster, born 1937

USSR and Iraq signed 15-year treaty of friendship, 1972

10 Joseph Pulitzer, newspaper proprietor and journalist, born 1847

Britain, USA and USSR with 46 other countries signed convention outlawing biological weapons, 1972

11 Manuel Quintana, writer, born 1772

Erskine Caldwell, author, died 1987

Primo Levi, writer, died 1987

13 John Braine, author, born 1922

Edward Fox, actor, born 1937

15-16 Naval mutiny at Spithead, 1797

Explosion at Texas City, near Galveston, USA caused over 600 deaths, 1947

Apollo 16 launched to moon, 1972

17 Henry Vaughan, poet, born 1622

Thornton Wilder, writer, born 1897

19 Sydney Harpley, sculptor, born 1927

North Vietnam aircraft attacked US Seventh Fleet in Gulf of Tonkin, 1972

20 Christian X, King of Denmark, died 1947

21 The first wedding in Britain at which the bridal couple left in a motor car, 1897

Greek military junta took power over the country, 1967

22 Laurier Lister, theatre director, born 1907

Sir Sidney Nolan, painter, born 1917

First operational fibre-optic telephone cable in service, 1977

23 Lord Anson, explorer, born 1697

Bernadette McAliskey, *née* Devlin, youngest MP in the House of Commons when elected at 21, born 1947

24 The first Rugby League championship, 1897

The first space fatality admitted by the Russians occurred (Col. Vladamir Mikhailovich Komarov), 1967

25 Thomas Faber, publisher, born 1927

26 Jack Douglas, actor-comedian, born 1927

Spanish town of Guernica destroyed by German aircraft, 1937

The first instant home movies demonstrated by Polaroid Corp, Mass: Polavision system enabled film to be viewed 95 seconds after filming, 1977

27 Sheila Scott, record-breaking aviator, born 1927

Dr Kwame Nkrumah, Ghanaian politician, died 1972

First commercially sponsored steeplechase: Whitbread Gold Cup at Sandown Park, 1957

28 Jack Nicholson, actor, born 1937

The *Kon-Tiki* expedition set sail from Peru, 1947

29 Fred Zinnemann, film director, born 1907

30 The first dial weighing machine patented by John Clais in London, 1772

The first iron steamship, *Aaron Manby*, completed, 1822

The first quadraphonic broadcasts in Britain, inaugurated by BBC on radios 1 and 3, 1977

May

1 Gary Bertini, conductor, born 1927

The first British airliner with cooked meals on board: London-Paris flights on Imperial Airways' luxury Silver Wing, 1927

The first TV sports series, *Sporting Magazine*, broadcast by BBC (monthly), 1937

J. Edgar Hoover, former director of FBI, died 1972

2 Bianca Jagger born 1947

The first mobile TV unit in Britain was delivered just in time to televise the Coronation procession 10 days later, the BBC's first major outside broadcast, 1937

Bertrand Russell International War Crimes Tribunal opened in Stockholm: USA found guilty of aggression in Vietnam, 1967

3 Marisa Robles, harpist, born 1937

John Sachs, disc jockey, born 1957

5 Holy Roman Emperor Leopold II born 1747

6 The *Hindenburg* airship disaster, 1937

The first ladies' race held in Britain under Jockey Club rules was the Goya Stakes, held at Kempton Park. The winner was Meriel Tufnell on outsider *Scorched Earth*, 1972

William Casey, former director of the CIA, died 1987

7 The first Isle of Man TT Races, 1907

The first open zoo, Hamburg Tierpark, opened 1907

Ruth Prawer Jhabvala, novelist and screenplay writer, born 1927

Elisabeth Söderström, soprano, born 1927

8 The first speedway racing in Britain took place at Camberley Heath, 1927

Harry Gordon Selfridge, department store pioneer, died 1947

10 The first Mother's Day was initiated by Miss Anna Jarvis in Philadelphia, 1907

The first woman to be called to the English Bar was Oxford lecturer Dr Ivy Williams, 1922

11 The first sportsman to be knighted for service to cricket was Sir Pelham Warner, 1937

The first British radio sports commentary broadcast: Arthur Burrows described the Ted Kid Lewis *v* Georges Carpentier fight at Olympia, 1922

12 Leslie Charteris, author, born 1907

Dr Miriam Stoppard, writer and broadcaster, born 1937

King George VI was first monarch to appear live on TV at the Coronation procession, 1937

John Masefield, poet, died 1967

Stansted chosen as site of London's third airport, 1967

13 Dame Daphne du Maurier, author, born 1907

Clive Barnes, theatre and dance critic, born 1927

The first regular schools TV service in Britain was inaugurated, 1957

14 The first steamship to circumnavigate the world, *HMS Driver*, arrived at Spithead, England, 1847

The first British cricket commentary (Essex *v* NZ), broadcast 1927

Rita Hayworth, US film star, died 1987

15 Daniel O'Connell, Irish Catholic political leader, died 1847

The first British hydrogen bomb dropped over Christmas Island region, 1957

17 Birgit Nilsson, soprano, born 1922

20 Treaty of Jedda signed 1927

The first non-stop solo transatlantic flight (New York-Paris) made by Charles Lindbergh, 20-21 May 1927

Earl of Iveagh, head of the Guinness clan, born 1937

22 Blackwall Tunnel opened 1897

Lord Olivier, actor, born 1907

Cecil Day-Lewis, poet, died 1972

23 Mutiny at the Nore, 1797

John D. Rockefeller, financier and philanthropist, died 1937

24   Battle of Pinchincha, 1822

25   The first 24-hour motor race, the Endurance Derby, was held at Point Breeze, Philadelphia, 1907

27   Sir John Cockcroft, nuclear physicist and Nobel Prize winner, born 1897

Christopher Lee, actor, born 1922

Sir Francis Chichester arrived in Plymouth after a solo circumnavigation of the world, 1967

28   Neville Chamberlain appointed Prime Minister, 1937

Alfred Adler, psychoanalyst, died 1937

Nigerian Government announced a decree to split the country into 12 states within the Federation, 1967

Duke of Windsor (Edward VIII) died 1972

29   West German pilot, Mathias Rust, landed his light aircraft in Red Square, Moscow, 1987

30   Eastern Region of Nigeria under Colonel Ojukwu announced secession and declared itself Republic of Biafra, 1967

31   Denholm Elliott, actor, born 1922

June

1   Sir Frank Whittle, aviator and inventor of the British jet engine, born 1907

The first broadcast horse race commentary in Britain was The Derby, 1927

The first premium bond winner (£1000) announced, 1957

2   Duke of Windsor married Mrs Wallis Warfield, 1937

Arthur Ransome, author, died 1967

The first woman rabbi (Sally Priesand) ordained at Isaac M. Wise Temple, Cincinnati, Ohio, 1972

Andrés Segovia, guitarist, died 1987

4   The first transatlantic aeroplane passenger flight, New York–Germany, 1927

The first London double-decker bus with pneumatic tyres came into service, 1927

Supermarket trolleys were first introduced, 1937

US black militant Angela Davis, charged with murder, kidnapping and conspiracy in August 1970, acquitted by an all-white jury in San José, 1972

5   Marshall Plan announced; speech at Harvard on financial aid to Europe, 1947

David Hare, playwright, born 1947

Outbreak of war between Arab states and Israel, 1967

6   The first British-built petrol van sold, 1897

Derek Jewell, music writer, born 1927

J. Paul Getty, oil billionaire and art collector, died 1976

7   Battle of Messines, 1917

Jean Harlow, actress, died 1937

Dorothy Parker, writer and wit, died 1967

8   Sir Michael Levey, art historian, born 1927

9   The first airliner night flight, France–England, 1922

Dame Sybil Thorndike, actress, died 1976

10   Judy Garland, actress and singer, born 1922

11   Dame Millicent Fawcett, women's rights campaigner, born 1847

Sir John Franklin, Arctic explorer, died 1847

Dame Beryl Grey, ballet dancer, born 1927

12   The first bullfighter killed in ring, Seville, 1747

Léon Goossens, oboist, born 1897

14   Jerome K. Jerome, writer, died 1927

16   Duke of Marlborough, soldier, died 1722

Erich Segal, author, born 1937

Burglars arrested in the Democratic Party headquarters, Watergate Building, 1972

17   Dean Martin, actor and singer, born 1917

China claimed to have exploded a hydrogen bomb, 1967

19   Sir James Barrie, writer, died 1937

Salman Rushdie, author, born 1947

20   Greyhound racing began at White City, London, 1927

Cassius Clay, world boxing champion, sentenced to 5 years' imprisonment for refusing to be drafted into US army, 1967

21   The first British military walkie-talkie demonstrated, 1937

Lawn tennis at Wimbledon first televised, 1937

22   Queen Victoria's Diamond Jubilee, 1897

Fred Astaire, dancer and singer, died 1987

23   The first women's international chess championship opened, 1897

Margaret Lane, novelist and biographer, born 1907

Prof James Meade, economist and Nobel Prize winner, born 1907

Most Rev. and Rt Hon. John Habgood, Archbishop of York, born 1927

24 John Cabot, discoverer of mainland North America, sighted land (probably Cape Breton Island, Nova Scotia, 1497

Mick Fleetwood, of Fleetwood Mac, born 1942

26 American Expeditionary Force reached France, 1917

The first colour photos transmitted by wire: San Francisco to New York for *New York World*, 1927

27 The first bank cash dispenser in Britain introduced by Barclays, 1967

28 The first British prime minister filmed: Lord Salisbury at Buckingham Palace garden party, 1897

Correlli Barnett, historian, born 1927

29 The first broadcast commentary of lawn tennis from Wimbledon, 1927

30 Buddy Rich, jazz drummer, born 1917

July

1 Louis Blériot, aviator, born 1872

The first Air Force unit, the Aeronautical Division of the Office of the Chief Signal Officer of the US Army, established 1907

The 999 telephone emergency service started, 1937

The first colour TV service in Britain launched, 1967

2 Aviator Amelia Earhart disappeared in South Pacific, 1937

3 Ken Russell, film director, born 1927

Tom Stoppard, playwright, born 1937

The first local TV station in Britain was inaugurated by Greenwich Cablevision, 1972

4 Neil Simon, playwright, born 1927

5 Ernst Hoffmann, writer and composer, died 1822

6 Sigismund II, King of Poland, died 1572

John Paul Jones, naval adventurer, born 1747

Lord Runciman, ship owner, born 1847

The first purpose-built motor-racing track opened at Brooklands, Weybridge, Surrey, 1907

Vladimir Ashkenazy, pianist and conductor, born 1937

Outbreak of civil war in Nigeria, 1967

7 Christopher Stone became the first disc jockey in Britain, 1927

Nigerian Government attacked Biafra, 1967

8 Edmund Burke, statesman and political writer, died 1797

Percy Bysshe Shelley, poet, drowned off Leghorn, Italy, 1822

The first of the Ziegfeld Follies opened in New York, 1907

9 Edmund Burke, writer, died 1797

David Hockney, painter, born 1937

Announcement of Princess Elizabeth's betrothal to Lieutenant Philip Mountbatten, 1947

Atomic Energy Authority announced discovery of a new element (Element 102) by team of Swedish, British and US scientists at Nobel Institute, 1957

10 Reg Smythe, creator of *Andy Capp*, born 1917

11 George Gershwin, composer, died 1937

The Aga Khan III died 1957

12 Frank Windsor, actor, born 1927

Race riots in Newark, New Jersey 1967

13 The first voting by ballot in Britain was introduced by Act, 1872

14 The first radio transmission at sea made by Guglielmo Marconi to a tug in Gulf of Snezia, 1897

16 Roald Amundsen, explorer, born 1872

The first polo match in Britain (Lancers *v* Life Guards), 1872

Barbara Stanwyck, actress, born 1907

17 George V renounced the German titles of the Royal Family; dynasty renamed the House of Windsor, 1917

18 Benito Juárez, Mexican statesman, died 1872

19 George Hamilton IV, singer, born 1937

20 Guglielmo Marconi, physicist and inventor, died 1937

21 The Tate Gallery, London, officially opened, 1897

22 Gregor Mendel, botanist, born 1822

Carl Sandburg, poet, died 1967

The Mormons first reached the site of Salt Lake City, 1847

23 Elspeth Huxley, author, born 1907

David Essex, singer and actor, born 1947

24 Wilfrid Josephs, composer of TV and film scores, born 1927

26 Independence of Liberia, first African colony to secure independence, 1847

27 Martin Ennals of Amnesty International, 1977 Nobel Peace Prize winner, born 1927

Sexual Offences Act 1967 came into force amending law on homosexuality, 1967

29 The first radio broadcast in Britain of a comedy programme: *Listening In*, 1922

30 Meredith Davies, conductor, born 1922

31 The third battle of Ypres began 1917

Peter Nichols, playwright, born 1927

August

2 TUC and CBI signed agreement to set up independent conciliation service, 1972

3 Henry V, King of England, died 1422

The first radio broadcast in Britain of a play: *The Wolf*, 1922

5 Alan Howard, actor, born 1937

The expulsion of Ugandan Asians announced by President Amin, 1972

6 Robert Mitchum, actor, born 1917

Sir Freddie Laker, entrepreneur, born 1922

Barbara Windsor, actress, born 1937

Dr David Owen resigned as leader of the Social Democratic Party following a vote in favour of merger negotiations with the Liberal Party, 1987

7 Camille Chamoun, former President of Lebanon, died 1987

8 Dustin Hoffman, actor, born 1937

10 Captain Odom's flight round the world completed in 73 hours, 5 minutes, 1947

11 Enid Blyton, author, born 1897

Raymond Leppard, conductor, born 1927

Anna Massey, actress, born 1937

12 Fulton Mackay, actor, born 1922

13 William Caxton, the first English printer, born 1422

Fidel Castro, Cuban revolutionary, born 1927

The first promenade concert was broadcast from Queen's Hall, 1927

14 Feliks Topolski, painter and illustrator, born 1907

Alfred Harmsworth (Lord Northcliffe), founder of the *Daily Mail*, died 1922

15 The first parliamentary election held under the provisions of the Act permitting voting by ballot, 1872

India became independent, 1947

René Magritte, surrealist painter, died 1967

16 Elvis Presley, singer, died 1977

The first licence to use a postage meter in Britain issued by GPO to Prudential Assurance Co, 1922

17 Rudolf Hess, Hitler's former deputy, committed suicide in Spandau prison, 1987

18 William Hudson, writer and naturalist, died 1922

Robert Redford, actor, born 1937

William Rushton, humorist, born 1937

The first ship reached North Pole: Soviet atomic icebreaker *Arktika*, 1977

19 The first taxis in Britain, run by The London Electric Cab Co., began operating electric cabs in the City and West End, 1897

Edward Rayne, Royal shoemaker, born 1922

Alastair Sim, actor, died 1976

Groucho Marx, film comedian, died 1977

14 people died when Michael Ryan ran amok in Hungerford, Berks, 1987

20 Jan de Witt, Dutch statesman, died 1672

21 Ettore Bugatti, car designer and manufacturer, died 1947

The first woman fire fighter (Mary Langdon) appointed, 1976

23 Sir Brian Young, former director-general of the IBA, born 1922

Albert Roussel, composer, died 1937

Roy Chadwick, aircraft designer responsible for Lancaster bomber, died 1947

Willy Russell, playwright, born 1947

Race riots in Detroit, 1967

24 Massacre of St Bartholomew, 1572

Sir Max Beerbohm, writer, born 1872

Charles Causley, poet, born 1917

René Lévesque, former premier of Quebec, born 1922

26 Sir Francis Chichester, yachtsman, died 1972

Lotte Lehmann, soprano, died 1976

28 The first radio commercial broadcast in New York, 1922

Duke of Argyll, born 1937

Prince William of Gloucester killed in air race crash, 1972

John Huston, film director, died 1987

30 Mary Shelley, writer, born 1797

31 Malaya became independent, 1957

September

1 Charles Douglas-Home, former editor of *The Times*, born 1937

Siegfried Sassoon, writer, died 1967

Iceland extended its fishing limits from 12 to 50 miles, 1972

2 Shakespeare first broadcast, 1922

Baron Pierre de Coubertin, who conceived the Modern Olympic Games, died 1937

3 James Hannington, first Bishop of Eastern Equatorial Africa, born 1847

4 Dame Margaret Drummond, WRNS, born 1917

Black September massacre at Munich Olympics, 1972

7 The first ship to circumnavigate the world, the *Victoria*, arrived in Spain after 3-year voyage, 1522

Brazil became independent, 1822

9 Mao Zedong (Mao Tse-tung), Chinese political leader and Marxist theoretician, died 1976

10 Battle of Pinkie (near Musselburgh, Lothian), 1547

Mary Wollstonecraft, women's rights campaigner, died 1797

The first motorist to be convicted of drunken driving, taxi driver George Smith, charged, 1897

Wilfred Scawen Blunt, poet and traveller, died 1922

12 The first prisoners' wages in Britain introduced, 1937

13 Leopold Stokowski, conductor and composer, died 1977

14 The first motor-racing fatality in Britain, 1907

Russia proclaimed a republic, 1917

Isadora Duncan, ballet dancer and choreographer, died 1927

Tomás Masaryk, founder-president of the Czechoslovakian Republic, died 1937

16 Sir Anthony Panizzi, chief librarian of the British Museum (1856-66), born 1797

Earl of Cardigan, commander of the Charge of the Light Brigade in the Crimean War, born 1797

The first building acquired for preservation in Britain: Shakespeare's birthplace sold to United Shakespeare Committee, 1847

17 The first programme of sound-on film productions to be presented in public was shown in Berlin before an invited audience of 1000, 1922

18 First Ugandan Asians arrived by aeroplane from Uganda, 1972

20 Treaty of Ryswick signed, 1697

The first animal clinic in Britain established in Liverpool by RSPCA, 1917

Jean Sibelius, composer, died 1957

Queen Elizabeth launched new Cunarder, *Queen Elizabeth II*, 1967

21 Latvia proclaimed independence, 1917

Haakon VII, King of Norway, died 1957

22 Earliest known marine insurance policy in Britain issued to John Broke for vessel *Santa Maria*, 1547

The first transatlantic automatic flight, 1947

23 The first motoring fatality on a public highway: a 9-year-old child was crushed by a London taxi, 1897

The first repertory theatre company's production, *David Ballard*, performed at Midland Hotel Theatre, 1907

24 Norway voted against membership of the EEC in referendum, 1972

25 The first petrol bus service was advertised in *Bradford Observer*, 1897

William Faulkner, novelist, born 1897

26 Pope Paul VI, born 1897

Edgar Degas, artist, died 1917 (some say 27th)

Hugh Lofting, children's novelist and creator of Dr Dolittle, died 1947

27 Lord (Bernard) Miles, actor, stage director and founder of the Mermaid Theatre, London, born 1907

The first 3D feature film, *The Power of Love*, premiered in Los Angeles, 1922

28 The Holy Roman Emperor Henry VI died 1197

Michael Somes, ballet dancer, born 1917

30 Rula Lenska, actress, born 1947

TWA inaugurated direct Los Angeles-London service over the Polar route, 1957

The first broadcast by woman BBC newscaster, Armine Sandford, 1957

Radio 1 first on air at 7am with disc jockey Tony Blackburn, 1967

October

1 The first recorded sale of pneumatic tyres, 1847

Sandy Gall, former TC newscaster, born 1927

2 Paul von Hindenburg, statesman and soldier, born 1847

Lord Todd, chemist and Nobel Prize winner, born 1907

3 Earl of Bradford, restauranteur, born 1947

Sir Malcolm Sargent, conductor, died 1967

Jean Anouilh, dramatist, died 1987

4 Sir Roger Keyes, naval officer, born 1872

Prof Max Planck, German physicist, died 1947

The first Soviet satellite, *Sputnik I*, launched, 1957

5 Robert Adams, sculptor and designer, born 1917

7 Marie Lloyd, music-hall singer, died 1922

The first Royal broadcast: HRH The Prince of Wales, addressed the Boy Scouts of Britain, 1922

The first cross-Channel swim by an Englishwoman: Mercedes Gleitze, 1927

Christopher Booker, author, born 1937

8 Sir Edward Eveleigh, appeal court judge, born 1917

Merle Park, ballet dancer, born 1937

Lord Romsey, film producer, born 1947

Che Guevara died 1967

The first statutory breathalyser test in Britain administered 1967

9 André Maurois, writer, died 1967

Lord Hailsham of St Marylebone, former Lord Chancellor, born 1907

Clare Luce, (*née* Boothe) politician, feminist and author, died 1987

10 UK Road Safety Act providing for breath tests came into force, 1967

11 Battle of Camperdown, 1797

Bobby Charlton, former footballer, born 1937

Jodrell Bank radio telescope went into operation, 1957

Atomic Energy Authority announced overheating of one of the two Windscale Reactors, 1957

13 The first British veteran car rally, from Grays Inn Road to Olympia, 1927

14 Roger Moore, actor, born 1927

The first level supersonic flight made by Captain Charles Yeager, California, 1947

Dame Edith Evans, actress, died 1976

15 Prof Arthur Schlessinger, special assistant to Presidents Kennedy and Johnson, born 1917

Mata Hari shot on charges of spying, 1917

Naval base of Trincomalee handed to Sri Lanka by Britain, 1957

16 The first gliding meet was held at Itford, Sussex, 16-21 Oct. 1922

Max Bygraves, singer and comedian, born 1922

Günter Grass, writer, born 1927

Hurricane-force winds swept southern Britain, 1987

17 John Wilkes, political agitator and libertine who subsequently became Lord Mayor of London, born 1727

Queen Elizabeth II visited Yugoslavia, the first British monarch to visit a communist country, 1972

18 Antonio Canaletto, artist, born 1697

George C. Scott, actor, born 1927

Rheims Cathedral reconsecrated, 1937

19 Lord Rutherford, scientist, died 1937

The first member of the Royal Family to be portrayed on stage during their lifetime was HRH Queen Elizabeth the Queen Mother: played as the Duchess of York by Amanda Reiss in *Crown Matrimonial* at Haymarket Theatre, 1972

On Wall Street, the Dow Jones Index fell by 508 points; stock markets around the world also plunged sharply, 1987

Jacqueline du Pré, cellist, died 1987

20 *The Sunday Times* first published, 1822

Benito Mussolini seized power in Italy, 1922

Ray Buckton, former General Secretary of ASLEF, born 1922

The first original radio script of any kind, *Cockney Fragment from Life*, broadcast 1922

21 Crusaders first arrived in front of Antioch, 1097

Demonstrations against Vietnam War took place in London, Washington and other capitals, 1967

22 The first parachute descent by an aeronaut made over the Parc Monceau, Paris: André-Jacques Garnerin released from a balloon at 2230ft, 1797

Joan Fontaine, actress, born 1917

23 Battle of Caporetto began, 1917

Lester Piggott, jockey, jailed for 3 years for tax offences, 1987

24 Francis Palgrave, poet and anthologist, died 1897

The first comic strip in a newspaper, 'Yellow Kid', appeared in the supplement of the *New York Journal*, 1897

Christian Dior, fashion designer, died 1957

25 Foot and mouth epidemic began in Shropshire, 1967

26 The Territorial Army inaugurated in Britain, 1907

Shah of Iran crowned, 1967

North Vietnam published text of agreement between it and the USA, 1972

The London City Airport opened, 1987

27 Abortion Act 1967 and Leasehold Reform Act passed

Dangerous Drugs Act 1967 came into force, 1967

The first sound newsreel issued by Fox Movietone News, 1927

28 Cleo Laine, singer, born 1927

André Masson, painter, died 1987

29 Joseph Goebbels, Nazi leader, born 1897

Ratification by the three Governments of the Customs Union known as 'Benelux', 1947

Green Paper on The Future of Northern Ireland published, 1972

November

1 Radio licences introduced in Britain, 1922

Ezra Pound, poet, died 1972

Naomi Mitchison, writer, born 1897

The first woman chartered surveyor, Irene Martin, appointed, 1922

2 Balfour Declaration about a national home for the Jews in Palestine, 1917

3 The first satellite to carry an animal launched, 1957

The first £100,000 Premium Bond prize won, 1976

4 Felix Mendelssohn-Bartholdy, composer, died 1847

Sir Anthony Lousada, solicitor and patron of the arts, born 1907

Tutankhamen's tomb discovered by Lord Carnarvon and Howard Carter, 1922

Second Soviet earth-satellite launched, 1957

5 The first automatic traffic lights in Britain began functioning at Princes Square, Wolverhampton, 1927

Rail crash at Hither Green killed 49 people, 1967

7 October Revolution began in Russia, 1917

The first Communist Government was formed in Russia under Lenin following the Bolshevik Revolution (25 Oct. by the Russian calendar), 1917

World water speed record of 239.07mph established by Donald Campbell in *Bluebird* on Coniston Water, 1957

President Nixon elected for second term, 1972

8 The first woman Minister of State, Alexandra Kollantai, appointed People's Commissar of Social Welfare in the revolutionary Bolshevik Government formed by Lenin, 1917

Bram Stoker, creator of Count Dracula, born 1847

The first charitable appeal broadcast in Britain by Frank Gill for London Hospitals, 1922

The first BBC local radio station on air, 1967

IRA bomb exploded at Remembrance Day service in Enniskillen, County Fermanagh, 1987

9 The first newspaper photograph transmitted by wire: portrait of King Edward sent Paris-London in 12 min (8 Nov.), published 1907

The first high definition tele-recording made (Remembrance Day Ceremony at the Cenotaph), 1947

10 William Hogarth, painter, born 1697

11 The first radio broadcasting external service in Britain, an experimental Empire service, inaugurated by the BBC from Chelmsford, 1927

13 The first helicopter achieved free flight: twin rotor machine designed by Paul Cornu test flown at Lisieux, 1907

14 Sir Charles Lyell, geologist, born 1797

BBC began its first daily broadcasting service, 1922

15 Sir Sacheverell Sitwell, poet and art critic, born 1897

Aneurin Bevan, Labour politician and architect of the National Health Service, born 1897

The first election results radio broadcast in Britain, 1922

Peter Phillips, son of Mark and Princess Anne, born 1977

17 Alain René Le Sage, novelist and playwright, died 1747

Auguste Rodin, sculptor, died 1917

The first communist MP in Britain, J.T. Walton Newbold, elected 1922

Peter Cook, comedian, born 1937

Jacques Anquetil, racing cyclist, died 1987

18 Marcel Proust, novelist, died 1922

Man Ray, artist, died 1976

Fire at Kings Cross underground station: 30 people died, 1987

19 Indira Gandhi, former Prime Minister of India, born 1917

20 Henry Francis Lyte, hymn writer, died 1847

Battle of Cambrai, 1917

Wedding of Princess Elizabeth (Queen Elizabeth II), 1947

22 Vasco da Gama sailed round the Cape of Good Hope, 1497

Prof Sir Andrew Huxley, Nobel Prize-winning physiologist and President of the Royal Society, born 1917

23 The first Royal Command Film Performance given at Windsor Castle by command of Queen Victoria, 1897

Central Criminal Court found Herbert Selby's *Last Exit to Brooklyn* obscene, 1967

André Malraux, author and statesman, died 1976

24 Lilian Baylis, theatrical manager, died 1937

25 Flight of jet-propelled Meteor, Edinburgh-London at 617.50mph, 1947

26 Charles Schulz, creator of *Peanuts*, born 1922

27 President de Gaulle in press conference ruled out early negotiations for UK entry into EEC, 1967

28 Alberto Moravia, Italian novelist, born 1907

29 Gaetano Donizetti, composer, born 1797

Horace Greeley, founder and editor of the New York *Tribune*, died 1872

The first motorcycle race in Britain held at Sheen House, Richmond, 1897

30 The first Football International played: England *v* Scotland, 1872

The first aircraft carrier to be designed and completed as such, made its first sea trials, 1922

Frank Ifield, singer, born 1937

Beniamino Gigli, opera singer, died 1957

Sir Compton Mackenzie, novelist, died 1972

James Baldwin, writer, died 1987

December

1 Gordon Crosse, composer, born 1937

The first railway milk tanker (glass-lined) in Britain used 1927

2 Hernán Cortés, conqueror of Mexico, died 1547

The rebuilt St Paul's Cathedral opened, 1697

Samuel Courtauld, chairman of Courtaulds Ltd and patron of art and culture, died 1947

Francis, Cardinal Spellman, Archbishop of New York, died 1967

3 Battle of Cambrai ended, 1917

The first heart transplant operation performed by Dr Christiaan Barnard, 1967

The first English Mass in Britain introduced in all RC churches, 1967

5 The first radio broadcast children's programme in Britain, *Children's Corner*, transmitted from BBC's Birmingham station, 1922

6 4 members of Angry Brigade found guilty of conspiracy to cause explosions, 1972

7 The first boxing referee officiated inside ring, 1907

Withdrawal of last British troops from Italy, 1947

8 Lord Diplock, law lord and last judge to serve beyond the age of 75, born 1907

Lucian Freud, painter, born 1922

The first esperanto broadcast: Miss Gladys Cosmetto sang *Until*, 1922

9 Jerusalem surrendered to the British, 1917

Donny Osmond, singer, born 1957

Cunarder *Queen Mary* arrived at Long Beach, California, ending its last voyage, 1967

10 The first postmark slogan in Britain used: 'Buy British War Bonds Now', 1917

11 Sheila Walker, former chief commissioner of the Girl Guides, born 1917

The first public appearance of Concorde, the Anglo-French supersonic airliner, at Toulouse, 1967

12 Royal Automobile Club founded as The Automobile Club of Great Britain, 1897

US Voodoo jet fighter-bomber set world speed record of 1207.60mph, 1957

13 Henrich Heine, poet, born 1797

Sellotape was first marketed, 1937

14 Research workers at Stanford University announced manufacture in test tube of DNA, 1967

16 Alphonse Daudet, novelist, died 1897

17 The first British radio transmission at sea, 1897

Simon Bates, disc jockey, born 1947

Dorothy L. Sayers, thriller writer, died 1957

18 The first motor gun-carrier used in warfare, 1907

The first woman barrister to appear as counsel in an English court, Helena Normanton, received first brief, 1922

The first woman solicitor in Britain, Carrie Morrison, admitted, 1922

19 Eamon Andrews, (*This is Your Life*), born 1922

London-Moscow air service inaugurated, 1957

20 Erich von Ludendorff, German general, died 1937

Diplock Commission on Legal Changes in Northern Ireland reported, 1972

21 Jane Fonda, actress, born 1937

The first feature-length colour cartoon talkie, Walt Disney's *Snow White and the Seven Dwarfs*, shown 1937

23 The first orchestral radio broadcast in Britain transmitted, 1922

The first daily news broadcasts in Britain started, 1922

24 Matthew Arnold, poet, born 1822

Ava Gardner, American actress, born 1922

The first play written for radio, *The Truth about Father Christmas*, broadcast, 1922

25 Vasco da Gama discovered Natal, 1497

The first religious programme broadcast in Britain, 1922

The first Royal Christmas TV broadcast by Queen Elizabeth II, 1957

Sir Charles Chaplin, film actor, died 1977

27 Louis Pasteur, founder of the science of bacteriology, born 1822

26 John Wilkes, political agitator, died 1797

28 St Francis de Sales, nobleman and ecclesiastic, died 1622

Maurice Ravel, composer, died 1937

Victor Emanuel III, former King of Italy, died 1947

30 Zululand annexed to Natal, 1897

King Michael of Romania abdicated, 1947

Alfred North Whitehead, philosopher and mathematician, died 1947

31 The first national rationing in Britain: 8oz sugar per week, 1917

Use of the lance in the British Army abandoned, except for ceremonial use, 1927

Anthony Hopkins, actor, born 1937

Compiled by the Information Bureau.

This list has been compiled from a variety of sources and is designed as a guideline only. As some anniversary dates are disputed in different sources, all dates should be checked further before embarking on any major project involving any of these dates.

Sexism, Racism, Ageism and other Isms

KAREN JUDD

In recent years more emphasis has been placed on protecting the feelings of women and minority groups: ethnic groups, the elderly, the disabled. Particularly in non-fiction writing, and specifically in textbooks, unintentional slurs were frequently made against minority groups.

It is not my intention to censor, nor can it be yours. In textbooks, however, censorship is common and often desirable; ethnic slurs of even the most innocent kind must be removed from the books our children learn values from. There is also movement towards eliminating sexual stereotyping and ageism from schoolbooks and this trend is good.

But you will still come across written materials that have references you don't like, because, after all, people should be able to write whatever they want. What should you do if you find a racist comment in something you're editing? Don't change it. Ask the publisher for her or his policy. Then perhaps point out the offending passage to the author. Perhaps it was an oversight, and the author would be embarrassed if it found its way into print. There is a difference, for example, in referring to 'Jack, a black from South Carolina' and 'Jack, a black man from South Carolina.' Intentional or not, the effect of the second example is a put-down. So *ask*. But you don't have the right to determine what some other person's morals should be and whether he or she should refrain from bigotry.

Ageism is a form of intolerance directed towards older people. It implies that just because of age, an older person is not able to function as well as a younger one. How true is that really? Older people may lack the speed and endurance of the young, but they may be just as active. A person's brains do not deteriorate just because the eyesight or hearing may fade at a certain age. Watch for ageist references, and point them out to the author or publisher.

Sexism, of course, is the area of most concern these days. Although we were always told to treat ethnic minorities with respect, we were also subjected, wherever we went, to references to *he* that included both men and women. Well, I'm here to tell you that *he* does *not* include women; *he* refers to men and *she* refers to women. Getting rid of sexism means changing not only our thought patterns but our language patterns as well. No longer is *salesman* an acceptable word for men and women who sell. No longer can we say *poetess* without implying that a woman poet is somehow inferior to a man poet.

Most publishers want to be non-sexist, but they don't want to put words in the author's mouth. They say that if the author has made no attempt to be non-sexist, the copy-editor should not overdo the changes. Authors are gradually learning to make their prose non-sexist, but it's not always easy for someone who has always thought of men as principals and women as teachers. And it's not just male authors who think this way. I once saw a manuscript authored by two women who referred throughout to authors as *he*! Copy-editors must be on the lookout for sexist references, and they should point them out to the publisher if they feel awkward telling the author. Sexist references fall into two main categories: sexist or non-inclusive language and sexual stereotyping.

SEXIST OR NON-INCLUSIVE LANGUAGE

It is not always possible to correct sexist language, but there are some things that can be done. Here are a few hints.

1. Recast sentences into the plural to avoid references to *his* or *her*.

Original Version	*Revised Version*
The student should do his homework each evening.	Students should do their homework each evening.

2. Alternate references to *his* or *her*. This method works well in certain subject areas, such as child development, where it would be awkward or impossible to always use plural or *he* or *she*. Thus one paragraph can describe a child as *she* and another as *he*.

3. Do not characterise professions by sex.

Original Version	*Revised Version*
the male nurse	the nurse
the authoress	the author
a Girl Friday	a personal assistant [or aide]

It may also be convenient to indicate sex by a pronoun: 'The writer sent her manuscript to the publisher.' And frequently it doesn't matter what the person's sex is anyway.

4. Avoid, wherever practical, words that use the suffix *-man* in the traditional sense of 'male'.

Original Version	*Revised Version*
salesman	salesperson
fireman	fire fighter
foreman	supervisor
policeman	police officer

However, this generalisation doesn't always work. Many people find *chairperson* absurd. Other words are simply too new to be appropriate at this time. A *midshipman* right now can be male or female; with luck, in a few years there will be another word. And what about *freshman*? Will it be replaced by *fresher*? Don't invent words just for the purpose of eliminating the *-man* suffix everywhere it appears. But do be sensitive to women's participation in all areas.

5. Never draw parallels using non-parallel words.

Original Version	*Revised Version*
man and wife	husband and wife
men's room, ladies' room	men's room, women's room
men and girls	men and women; boys and girls

6. Except in dialogue, query all put-downs of women, such as 'the little woman' (would you say 'the little man'?) 'My girl will get it', or 'my helpmeet'. *Wife*, *secretary*, *lover* and *friend* are perfectly acceptable words. Fortunately, the problem of put-downs comes up seldom in writing; unfortunately, it occurs far too often in speech.

STEREOTYPING

When you copyedit, think about the pictures being painted by the author. Are they complete, or have some groups been omitted? Are they stereotypical? Are women the nurses and men the doctors? Women can take any position they wish: telephone installers, judges, even homemakers. So can men; they can be nurses, teachers and, yes, even homemakers. Blacks and whites and everyone else can hold jobs in all areas. The old, the young and the disabled can be useful members of society.

Be alert when you copyedit. Do not allow any group to be left out by virtue of language or stereotyping. An entire segment of the population may feel that such-and-such a book or article or brochure is not intended for them. Elimination of sexism is so important in educational publishing, in fact, that the copy-editor may be asked to keep a running tally of references to boys and girls to make sure they are equal, and to include the disabled in a certain percentage of pictures. But make changes in sexist, ageist or ethnic stereotyping and language *cautiously*, and then only with the approval of the publisher.

Reprinted, by permission of Crisp Publications Inc. from *Copyediting, a practical guide* by Karen Judd (Robert Hale). 'Karen Judd's *Copyediting* is precisely what it claims to be, a *practical* guide to all aspects of the craft. Publishers' editors will surely admire its range and depth. Authors will find it invaluable as a reference work that comprehensively covers points of style and setting and, thanks to an excellent index, is easy to look up.' – Hugh Rae in *The Author* (journal of The Society of Authors).

Preparing and Submitting a Manuscript

PREPARATION

Many publishers refuse even to consider handwritten manuscripts. No publisher will accept them as final copy. If you cannot afford to have the whole script typed before acceptance, there are ways round the problem; see below under Preliminary Letter.

Note that the terms 'manuscript' and 'typescript' are interchangeable in present usage, and both are used below.

CONSISTENCY

Be as consistent as possible in your choice of variant spellings, use of sub-headings, etc. If you want to know more about the technicalities of preparing a manuscript for the printer, consult *Copy-editing* by Judith Butcher, Cambridge University Press, 3rd edn 1992, £24.95 or *Copyediting* by Karen Judd, Robert Hale, 1995, £17.99 (see also page 458). Much of this is outside the author's scope, but dipping into these books will make you aware of points of style and consistency.

TYPING

A neatly typed manuscript is essential, not only to make a good impression on a publisher and a publisher's reader (see below), but the publisher's copy editor also needs a 'clean' manuscript in order to mark it up for setting. Typesetters must be able to read your typescript quickly and accurately, plus interpret the code of marks made by the copy editor or designer.

Authors are increasingly using word processors for the advantages they have to offer over the traditional typewriter (see **Word Processing** article on page 475). For ordinary typescripts, use the black ribbon. For plays, use red for names of characters, stage directions, etc., and black for dialogue. If a two-colour ribbon is not available use capitals for character names and underline stage directions in red by hand. Keep a fairly new ribbon in the typewriter so that it is black but not splodgy. Remember that typewriter maintenance is a tax-deductible expense!

Use a standard A4 typewriter paper, one side only. It is helpful but not essential if manuscripts are typed to a width of sixty characters per line. This makes it easier for printers and publishers to calculate the extent of a work and so – using copyfitting tables – to work out the space occupied when it is printed.

Margins. Good margins are essential, to enable the copy editor to include instructions to the printer. Allow a left-hand margin of about 3 cm, and generous margins on the right-hand, top and bottom of the page.

Double spacing. This is necessary to allow space for any corrections to be made to the typescript, either by you or by the copy editor. Double spacing means a *full* line of space between two lines of copy – not half a line of space.

Numbering. Pages (or folios as publishers prefer to call them to distinguish them from the pages of the final book) should be numbered throughout. If you need to include an extra folio after, say, folio 27, call it 27a and write at the foot of folio 27: 'Folio 27a follows'. Then write at the foot of 27a: 'Folio 28 follows'. Don't do this too often or you will confuse and irritate your readers.

Front page. Your manuscript will need a front page (unnumbered). Type the title about halfway down the page, with your name (or pen name) immediately beneath. In the bottom left-hand corner, type your name and address, plus the word count (see below). It is worth including your name and address on the last page also, just in case the first folio becomes detached.

At all costs, **keep a duplicate of the manuscript**, with all the latest changes to the text included on it.

WORD COUNT

To estimate the length or *extent* of a manuscript, calculate the average number of words per page over, say, eight pages. Multiply the average by the number of pages in the manuscript, making allowances for half-pages at the end of chapters, etc. This will give you the approximate number of words, which should be shown on the front page of the manuscript. If you are using a word processor, the word count facility in your program will speed up this task.

CORRECTIONS TO TYPESCRIPT

Keep your corrections to the final typescript to a minimum. Often the publisher's editor will suggest a few additional changes, and once these are included, the typescript may have become very messy. If the publishers then feel it is not in a fit state for the typesetter they may well ask you to have it retyped.

PRESENTATION

Publishers prefer to handle each folio separately, so do not use a binder which will make this impossible; ring binders are acceptable. Alternatively you can use a cardboard envelope folder: in this case, clip the pages of each chapter together, but never staple them. The typescript can be protected by placing a piece of stiff card at front and back.

SUBMISSION

CHOOSING YOUR PUBLISHER

You can save time and postage if you check first that you are sending your typescript to a firm that will consider it. Publishers specialise. It is no use sending a work of romantic fiction to a firm that specialises in high-brow novels translated from obscure languages. It is still less use to send it to a firm which publishes no fiction at all. (For fiction publishers, see the classified index on page 214.)

Look in your library or bookshop for books which are in some way similar to yours, and find out who publishes them. Remember, though, that paperbacks are often editions of books published first in hardback editions.

PRELIMINARY LETTER

This will also save you time, money and probably frustration. Most publishers prefer to see a brief preliminary letter together with a synopsis of the book and the first couple of chapters. From this material the publisher can judge whether the book will fit the list, in which case you will be asked to send the complete manuscript. This is one way of avoiding paying a typing bill until it looks as though the investment in the manuscript may be worthwhile.

There is no point whatsoever in asking for an interview: the publisher will prefer to consider the manuscript on its own merits.

POSTAGE OF MANUSCRIPTS

Packing is important and padded bags are ideal. Manuscripts can, of course, be sent by ordinary first or second class mail; alternatively, you can use Recorded Delivery, which has to be signed for.

Always send postage to cover the return of your manuscript or, if you prefer, explain that you will arrange to pick it up from the publisher's office. (Again, if your manuscript has been rejected the publisher will not be willing to discuss the reasons in person.)

WHAT IS THE PUBLISHER DOING WITH YOUR MANUSCRIPT?

There is usually a considerable interval between submission and the publisher's decision. Most publishers acknowledge receipt of manuscripts; if you do not receive one it is advisable to check that your manuscript has arrived. Apart from that, it is not worth chasing the publisher for a quick decision: if pressed, the publisher will probably reject, purely because this is the safer decision.

You should hear from the publisher within about two months. During this time the manuscript will either have been read 'in-house' or it will have been sent to one or more advisers whose opinions the publisher respects. Favourable readers' reports may mean that the publisher will immediately accept the manuscript, particularly if it fits easily into the current publishing programme.

On the other hand, a reader's report may be glowing, but the publisher may still hesitate. Publishers want to be sure they will be able to sell a book profitably, so may obtain further opinions, and estimates from printers, to judge whether the book could be produced at a reasonable price.

If you have not had a decision after two months, write either a tactful letter saying 'I don't want to rush you, but . . .' or, alternatively, request an immediate decision and be prepared to start again with another publisher. If your book is topical you have a right to a speedy decision, but it is as well to establish this early on.

ILLUSTRATIONS

If illustrations form a large part of your proposed book and you expect to provide them yourself, then they should be included with the manuscript. If you are sending specimen pages you should include also some sample illustrations: this applies largely to children's picture books and to travel and technical books. Do not send the originals – send duplicate photographs, photocopies of line drawings and so on so that little harm is done if illustrations go astray.

In the case of a children's book, if you intend to illustrate it yourself, obviously one finished piece of artwork is essential, plus photocopies of roughs for the rest (the final artwork may have to be drawn to a particular size and the number of illustrations fixed according to the format chosen by the publisher). If you have written a children's story, or the text for a picture book, do *not* ask a friend to provide the illustrations; the publisher who likes your story may well not like your friend's artwork. Of course this does not apply when an artist and author work closely together to develop an idea, but in that case it is best to start by finding a publisher who likes the artist's work before submitting the story.

Travel manuscripts should be accompanied by a sketch map to show the area you are writing about, so the publisher has sufficient detail with which to follow your manuscript. Irreplaceable material should not be sent speculatively.

Many illustrated books these days have illustrations collected by the publishers. It is best to establish early on who is responsible for the illustration costs: an attractive royalty offer might be less attractive if you have to gather the pictures, obtain permission for use, and foot the bills.

QUOTATIONS

It is normally the author's responsibility to obtain (and pay for) permission to quote written material which is still in copyright. Permission should always be sought from the publisher of the quoted work, not from the author. Fees for quotation vary enormously: for fashionable modern writers permission may be costly, but in other cases only a nominal fee is charged. There is no standard scale of fees. It is permissible to quote up to about 200 words for the purpose of criticism or review, but this does not apply to use in anthologies, nor does it apply to poetry. And it is a concession, not a right. Even though this is your area of responsibility, your publisher will be able to give you some advice.

PROOF READING

As author you will see either one or two stages of proofs. Sometimes you will be shown the finalised copy of the typescript immediately before it goes to the typesetter. If so, this is really your last chance to make changes which will not tend to sour relations with your publisher! Take the opportunity to comb through the manuscript, and if there are changes which you suspect you will want to make in proof, make them now. There was a time when authors could virtually rewrite their books in galley proof, and revise them again at page, but those days are long gone! (See **Correcting Proofs** for the conventional proof-correcting marks.)

Although modern printing is highly mechanised, corrections are time-consuming and may involve extensive handwork, making them far more costly than the original setting. You will probably have signed a contract undertaking to pay the cost of corrections (other than printer's errors) over say 10 per cent or 15 per cent of the cost of composition. This does not mean that you can change ten or fifteen lines in every hundred.

Increasingly often only one stage of proofs is used in book production, and there is rarely any need for the author to see more than one stage. The proofs may be in several forms. It could be that you will be asked to check *computer printouts* which bear no resemblance to the finished book but which do contain everything that will appear in that book. *Galley proofs* hold columns of continuous text. *Page proofs* have been made up into pages, including page numbers, headlines, illustrations, and so on. It is prohibitively expensive to make corrections at this stage, except to the printer's own errors.

It is worth noting that in the production of highly illustrated books such as children's or 'coffee table' books, the fitting together of the pictures and text on each page is an important stage. The designer or editor may have to 'cut and paste' and make minor modifications to the text to make the final result come together happily.

Correcting Proofs

The following notes and table are extracted from BS 5261: Part 2: 1976 (1995) and are reproduced by permission of the British Standards Institution, 2 Park Street, London W1A 2BS, from whom copies of the complete Standard may be obtained.

NOTES ON COPY PREPARATION AND PROOF CORRECTION

The marks to be used for marking-up copy for composition and for the correction of printers' proofs shall be as shown in table 1.

The marks in table 1 are classified in three groups as follows.

(a) Group A: general.
(b) Group B: deletion, insertion and substitution.
(c) Group C: positioning and spacing.

Each item in table 1 is given a simple alpha-numeric serial number denoting the classification group to which it belongs and its position within the group.

The marks have been drawn keeping the shapes as simple as possible and using sizes which relate to normal practice. The shapes of the marks should be followed exactly by all who make use of them.

For each marking-up or proof correction instruction a distinct mark is to be made:

(a) in the text: to indicate the exact place to which the instruction refers;
(b) in the margin: to signify or amplify the meaning of the instruction.

It should be noted that some instructions have a combined textual and marginal mark.

Where a number of instructions occur in one line, the marginal marks are to be divided between the left and right margins where possible, the order being from left to right in both margins.

Specification details, comments and instructions may be written on the copy or proof to complement the textual and marginal marks. Such written matter is to be clearly distinguishable from the copy and from any corrections made to the proof. Normally this is done by encircling the matter and/or by the appropriate use of colour (see below).

Proof corrections shall be made in coloured ink thus:

(a) printer's literal errors marked by the printer for correction: green;
(b) printer's literal errors marked by the customer and his agents for correction: red;
(c) alterations and instructions made by the customer and his agents: black or dark blue.

Table 1. Classified list of marks

NOTE. The letters M and P in the notes column indicate marks for marking-up copy and for correcting proofs respectively.

Group A   General

Number	Instruction	Textual mark	Marginal mark	Notes
A1	Correction is concluded	None	/	P Make after each correction
A2	Leave unchanged	– – – – – – under characters to remain	⨀	M P
A3	Remove extraneous marks	Encircle marks to be removed	✕	P e.g. film or paper edges visible between lines on bromide or diazo proofs
A3.1	Push down risen spacing material	Encircle blemish	⊥	P
A4	Refer to appropriate authority anything of doubtful accuracy	Encircle word(s) affected	(?)	P

Group B   Deletion, insertion and substitution

Number	Instruction	Textual mark	Marginal mark	Notes
B1	Insert in text the matter indicated in the margin	⋏	New matter followed by ⋏	M P Indentical to B2
B2	Insert additional matter identified by a letter in a diamond	⋏	⋏ Followed by for example Ⓐ	M P The relevant section of the copy should be supplied with the corresponding letter marked on it in a diamond e.g. Ⓐ
B3	Delete	/ through character(s) or ⊢——⊣ through words to be deleted	∂	M P
B4	Delete and close up	⁀/ through character or ⊢)(—⊣ through characters e.g. charac⌢ter charac⌢ter	∂̃	M P

Table 1 *(continued)*

Number	Instruction	Textual mark	Marginal mark	Notes
B5	Substitute character or substitute part of one or more word(s)	/ through character or ├────────┤ through word(s)	New character or new word(s)	M P
B6	Wrong fount. Replace by character(s) of correct fount	Encircle character(s) to be changed	⊗	P
B6.1	Change damaged character(s)	Encircle character(s) to be changed	✕	P This mark is identical to A3
B7	Set in or change to italic	────── under character(s) to be set or changed	⊔	M P Where space does not permit textual marks encircle the affected area instead
B8	Set in or change to capital letters	═══════ under character(s) to be set or changed	≡	
B9	Set in or change to small capital letters	═══════ under character(s) to be set or changed	═	
B9.1	Set in or change to capital letters for initial letters and small capital letters for the rest of the words	═══════ under initial letters and ═══════ under rest of the word(s)	≡	
B10	Set in or change to bold type	∿∿∿∿∿ under character(s) to be set or changed	∿	
B11	Set in or change to bold italic type	∿∿∿∿∿ under character(s) to be set or changed	⊔̰	
B12	Change capital letters to lower case letters	Encircle character(s) to be changed	≢	P For use when B5 is inappropriate

Table 1 *(continued)*

Number	Instruction	Textual mark	Marginal mark	Notes
B12.1	Change small capital letters to lower case letters	Encircle character(s) to be changed	╪	P For use when B5 is inappropriate
B13	Change italic to upright type	Encircle character(s) to be changed	⊔	P
B14	Invert type	Encircle character to be inverted	↻	P
B15	Substitute or insert character in 'superior' position	/ through character or ∧ where required	⌐ under character e.g. ⌐2	P
B16	Substitute or insert character in 'inferior' position	/ through character or ∧ where required	L over character e.g. L2	P
B17	Substitute ligature e.g. ffi for separate letters	⊢———⊣ through characters affected	⌒ e.g. ffi	P
B17.1	Substitute separate letters for ligature	⊢———⊣	Write out separate letters	P
B18	Substitute or insert full stop or decimal point	/ through character or ∧ where required	⊙	M P
B18.1	Substitute or insert colon	/ through character or ∧ where required	⊙	M P
B18.2	Substitute or insert semi-colon	/ through character or ∧ where required	⁏	M P

Table 1 *(continued)*

Number	Instruction	Textual mark		Marginal mark	Notes
B18.3	Substitute or insert comma	/	through character	,⁄	M P
		∧	where required		
B18.4	Substitute or insert apostrophe	/	through character	⸰	M P
		∧	where required		
B18.5	Substitute or insert single quotation marks	/	through character	and/or	M P
		∧	where required		
B18.6	Substitute or insert double quotation marks	/	through character	and/or	M P
		∧	where required		
B19	Substitute or insert ellipsis	/	through character	• • •	M P
		∧	where required		
B20	Substitute or insert leader dots	/	through character	(• • •)	M P Give the measure of the leader when necessary
		∧	where required		
B21	Substitute or insert hyphen	/	through character	⊢–⊣	M P
		∧	where required		
B22	Substitute or insert rule	/	through character	⊢—⊣	M P Give the size of the rule in the marginal mark e.g. ⊢ 1 em ⊣ ⊢ 4 mm ⊣
		∧	where required		

Table 1 *(continued)*

Number	Instruction	Textual mark	Marginal mark	Notes
B23	Substitute or insert oblique	/ through character or ⋀ where required	(/)	M P

Group C Positioning and spacing

Number	Instruction	Textual mark	Marginal mark	Notes
C1	Start new paragraph			M P
C2	Run on (no new paragraph)			M P
C3	Transpose characters or words	between characters or words, numbered when necessary		M P
C4	Transpose a number of characters or words	3 2 1 | | |	1 2 3	M P To be used when the sequence cannot be clearly indicated by the use of C3. The vertical strokes are made through the characters or words to be transposed and numbered in the correct sequence
C5	Transpose lines			M P
C6	Transpose a number of lines		——— 3 ——— 2 ——— 1	P To be used when the sequence cannot be clearly indicated by C5. Rules extend from the margin into the text with each line to be transposed and numbered in the correct sequence
C7	Centre	[enclosing matter to be centred]	[ ]	M P
C8	Indent			P Give the amount of the indent in the marginal mark

Table 1 *(continued)*

Number	Instruction	Textual mark	Marginal mark	Notes
C9	Cancel indent	(textual mark)	(marginal mark)	P
C10	Set line justified to specified measure	⊢[and/or]⊣	↔	P Give the exact dimensions when necessary
C11	Set column justified to specified measure	↔	↔	M P Give the exact dimensions when necessary
C12	Move matter specified distance to the right	enclosing matter to be moved to the right	(marginal mark)	P Give the exact dimensions when necessary
C13	Move matter specified distance to the left	enclosing matter to be moved to the left	(marginal mark)	P Give the exact dimensions when necessary
C14	Take over character(s), word(s) or line to next line, column or page	(textual mark)		P The textual mark surrounds the matter to be taken over and extends into the margin
C15	Take back character(s), word(s), or line to previous line, column or page	(textual mark)		P The textual mark surrounds the matter to be taken back and extends into the margin
C16	Raise matter	over matter to be raised / under matter to be raised	(marginal mark)	P Give the exact dimensions when necessary. (Use C28 for insertion of space between lines or paragraphs in text)
C17	Lower matter	over matter to be lowered / under matter to be lowered	(marginal mark)	P Give the exact dimensions when necessary. (Use C29 for reduction of space between lines or paragraphs in text)
C18	Move matter to position indicated	Enclose matter to be moved and indicate new position		P Give the exact dimensions when necessary

Table 1 *(continued)*

Number	Instruction	Textual mark	Marginal mark	Notes
C19	Correct vertical alignment	‖ ‖	‖	P
C20	Correct horizontal alignment	Single line above and below misaligned matter e.g. mi$_s$aligne$_d$	⎯⎯ ⎯⎯	P The marginal mark is placed level with the head and foot of the relevant line
C21	Close up. Delete space between characters or words	linking ⌒ characters	⌒	M P
C22	Insert space between characters	between characters affected	Y	M P Give the size of the space to be inserted when necessary
C23	Insert space between words	between words affected	Y	M P Give the size of the space to be inserted when necessary
C24	Reduce space between characters	between characters affected	⋀	M P Give the amount by which the space is to be reduced when necessary
C25	Reduce space between words	between words affected	⋀	M P Give amount by which the space is to be reduced when necessary
C26	Make space appear equal between characters or words	between characters or words affected	Y	M P
C27	Close up to normal interline spacing	(each side of column linking lines)	⎞⎛	M P The textual marks extend into the margin

Marked galley proof of text

(B9.1) =/   At the sign of the red pale   ⅄/ (C22)

(B13) ⚏/   *The Life and Work of William Caxton,* by H W Larken

(C7) []/   [An Extract]   ⌒/ (B10)

(C9)   Few people, even in the field of printing, have any clear   =/ (B9)
conception of what William Caxton did or, indeed, of
what he was. Much of this lack of knowledge is due to the
absence of information that can be counted as factual
and the consequent tendency to vague information.   i.l/ (B1)

(B12) ≠/   Though it is well known that Caxton was born in the
county of Kent, there is no information as to the precise
place. In his prologue to the *History of Troy*, William Caxton   ⊘/ (A2)
(B18.5)   wrote 'for in France I was never and was born and   .../ (B19)
learned my English in Kent in the Weald where I doubt
not is spoken as broad and rude English as in any place   ⅄/ (C23)
(B18.5)   of England.' During the fifteenth century there were a
great number of Flemish cloth weavers in Kent; most   ⌐/ (C1)
(B6) Ⓚ/   of them had come to England at the instigation of
Edward III with the object of teaching their craft to the
English. So successful was this venture that the English   t/ (B5)
(B17) fl/   cloth trade flourished and the agents who sold the cloth
(the mercers) became very wealthy people. There have b   ∂/ (B3)
(C8)   There have been many speculations concerning the origin
of the Caxton family and much research has been carried
out. It is assumed often that Caxton's family must have   ⌐/ (C3)
(B14) Ω/   been connected with the wool trade in order to have
secured his apprenticeship to an influential merchant.
(A4) ?/   W. Blyth Crotch (*Prologues and Epilogues of William*   ⊔/ (B7)
(B7)   *Caxton*) suggests that the origin of the name Caxton (of
which there are several variations in spelling) may be
traced to Cambridgeshire but notes that many writers
have suggested that Caxton was connected with a family
(A3.1)   at Hadlow or alternatively a family in Canterbury.   ═/ (C20)
(B18.1) ⊙/   Of the Canterbury connection a William Caxton
became freeman of the City in 1431 and William Pratt,
a mercer who was the printer's friend, was born there.
(B15)   H.R. Plomer suggests that Pratt and Caxton might possibly
have been schoolboys together, perhaps at the school St.   Ⓐ/ (B2)
Alphege. In this parish there lived a John Caxton who
(C26)   used as his mark three cakes over a barrel (or tun) and
who is mentioned in an inscription on a monument in
the church of St. Alphege.   ✗/ (A3)
In 1941, Alan Keen (an authority on manuscripts)
secured some documents concerning Caxton; these are   ≠/ (B12.1)
(B8) =/   now in the BRITISH MUSEUM. Discovered in the library of
(B6) Ⓚ/   Earl Winterton at Shillinglee Park by Richard Holworthy,
the documents cover the period 1420 to 1467. One of
(C27)   Winterton's ancestors purchased the manor of West
Wratting from a family named Caxton, the property
being situated in the Weald of Kent.
There is also record of a property mentioning Philip   ⌐/ (C2)
Caxton and his wife Dennis who had two sons, Philip   ∂/ (B4)
(B18) ⊙/   (born in 1413) and William.
Particularly interesting in these documents is one
(C27)   recording that Philip Caxton junior sold the manor of
Little Wratting to John Christemasse of London in 1436,   1e Ⱶ/ (B22)
the deed having been witnessed by two aldermen, one of   (C14)
whom was Robert Large, the printer's employer.
(B18.3) ,/   Further, in 1439 the other son, William Caxton, con   Ⱶ/ (B21)
Wratting to John Christemasse, and an indenture of 145?   2
concerning this property mentions one William Caxton   3/ (C6)
veyed his rights in the manor Bluntes Hall at Little   1
alias Causton. It is an interesting coincidence to note that
the lord of the manor of Little Wratting was the father of
(C21) ⌒/   Margaret, Duchess of Burgundy.   ⅄/ (C25)
In 1420, a Thomas Caxton of Tenterden witnessed the   (+1pt (C28)
(C19) |||/   will of a fellow townsman; he owned property in Kent and
appears to have been a person of some importance.   ) −1pt (C29)

¹ See 'William Caxton'

Ⓐ *attached to Christchurch Monastery in the parish of*

Revised galley proof of text incorporating corrections

At the Sign of the Red Pale

The Life and Work of William Caxton, *by H W Larken*

An Extract

FEW PEOPLE, even in the field of printing, have any clear conception of what William Caxton did or, indeed, of what he was. Much of this lack of knowledge is due to the absence of information that can be counted as factual and the consequent tendency to vague generalisation.

Though it is well known that Caxton was born in the county of Kent, there is no information as to the precise place. In his prologue to the *History of Troy*, William Caxton wrote '. . . for in France I was never and was born and learned my English in Kent in the Weald where I doubt not is spoken as broad and rude English as in any place of England.'

During the fifteenth century there were a great number of Flemish cloth weavers in Kent; most of them had come to England at the instigation of Edward III with the object of teaching their craft to the English. So successful was this venture that the English cloth trade flourished and the agents who sold the cloth (the mercers) became very wealthy people.

There have been many speculations concerning the origin of the Caxton family and much research has been carried out. It is often assumed that Caxton's family must have been connected with the wool trade in order to have secured his apprenticeship to an influential merchant.

W. Blyth Crotch (*Prologues and Epilogues of William Caxton*) suggests that the origin of the name Caxton (of which there are several variations in spelling) may be traced to Cambridgeshire but notes that many writers have suggested that Caxton was connected with a family at Hadlow or alternatively a family in Canterbury.

Of the Canterbury connection: a William Caxton became freeman of the City in 1431 and William Pratt, a mercer who was the printer's friend, was born there. H. R. Plomer[1] suggests that Pratt and Caxton might possibly have been schoolboys together, perhaps at the school attached to Christchurch Monastery in the parish of St. Alphege. In this parish there lived a John Caxton who used as his mark three cakes over a barrel (or tun) and who is mentioned in an inscription on a monument in the church of St. Alphege.

In 1941, Alan Keen (an authority on manuscripts) secured some documents concerning Caxton; these are now in the British Museum. Discovered in the library of Earl Winterton at Shillinglee Park by Richard Holworthy, the documents cover the period 1420 to 1467. One of Winterton's ancestors purchased the manor of West Wratting from a family named Caxton, the property being situated in the Weald of Kent. There is also record of a property mentioning Philip Caxton and his wife Dennis who had two sons, Philip (born in 1413) and William.

Particularly interesting in these documents is one recording that Philip Caxton junior sold the manor of Little Wratting to John Christemasse of London in 1436—the deed having been witnessed by two aldermen, one of whom was Robert Large, the printer's employer. Further, in 1439, the other son, William Caxton, conveyed his rights in the manor Bluntes Hall at Little Wratting to John Christemasse, and an indenture of 1457 concerning this property mentions one William Caxton alias Causton. It is an interesting coincidence to note that the lord of the manor of Little Wratting was the father of Margaret, Duchess of Burgundy.

In 1420, a Thomas Caxton of Tenterden witnessed the will of a fellow townsman; he owned property in Kent and appears to have been a person of some importance.

[1] See 'William Caxton'

Table 1 *(continued)*

Number	Instruction	Textual mark	Marginal mark	Notes
C28	Insert space between lines or paragraphs			M P The marginal mark extends between the lines of text. Give the size of the space to be inserted when necessary
C29	Reduce space between lines or paragraphs			M P The marginal mark extends between the lines of text. Give the amount by which the space is to be reduced when necessary

Natural dialogue

What your play does not need is genuine authentic natural dialogue. If that surprises you, as it does some people, I suggest you try a little experiment. Set up a recorder and tape your friends or family talking without letting them know what you are doing. What you will hear will be genuine, authentic, natural dialogue and unless your friends are exceptionally brilliant conversationalists you will find it quite impossible to listen to them.

The experiment will demonstrate to you that what we take to be natural dialogue when we hear it coming from the mouths of television actors is nothing of the sort. It is very carefully edited and contrived.

from *Writing for Television* by Gerald Kelsey (A & C Black, £9.99).
See order form on page 690.

Word Processing

RANDALL McMULLAN

Word processing equipment now glistens on display in superstores and in High Street shops. There is little need to explain the basic ideas and advantages of moving words about on a screen before we print them, but we can consider how to write more effectively and more professionally while using our word processor. Your choice of computer hardware and software does affect these targets and a section at the end of this article suggests some guidelines for purchasing.

Methods of writing are very personal but they all involve a comfortable interaction between yourself and something mechanical, even if the equipment has to be a pad and pencil on your knee in front of the fire. But before you become set in the way you use the keyboard and screen of your word processor, do consider the information in the following sections. They contain techniques used by authors which may improve your efficiency, your income, your sanity – and even your writing.

CREATING

If your creative habit depends upon letting the words flow, like Enid Blyton in her hidey-hole, then the word processor is an ideal companion. You can be a 'sprinter' or a 'fingertip' writer and rapidly get your narrative or ideas onto the screen. There is no need to stop; the layout and the order doesn't matter, you can work on those later.

More reflective methods of creation involve the use of reference materials, notes, outlines, ordering and assembly of portions of text. Any word processor allows you to develop personalised routines for these actions but you can also try some of the software packages which support these operations.

For example, many word processors have an 'outliner' which helps you to order your thoughts by using hierarchies of headings or 'layers' of text. If such ordered working is too much of a straight-jacket then you may like the type of writing tool which searches your notes and offers links between sections containing similar words and ideas.

The well-known word processing programs include an indexing tool which may sound more useful than it may prove to be. You will still have to provide the thought, make the decisions, flag words or insert flagged phrases in the text. The indexer will then automatically sort and merge all your references with correct page numbers and update this index if you change the text.

A Thesaurus is a more successful companion to a word processor and can lead you through pleasant webs of cross-references. Other programs will analyse your writing and give a report on content and style. The grammatical comments are often debatable and a report on your sexism or pomposity may irritate you, but a correct analysis of the reading age of your text may surprise you.

A sample of other writers' tools on the market have names which give a clue to their purpose: Storyspace, Plot unlimited, Poetry Processor, WordPerfect Rhymer, Idea Fisher, IdeaList, Quotemaster, Lexica, StyleWriter, Readability Plus, Concise Oxford Dictionary, Oxford Concordance, Oxford Science Shelf.

Now that CD-ROMs are standard in modern computers, the size, speed and utility of these reference works have increased dramatically. Available, for example, is a single CD-ROM which contains complete texts of out-of-copyright classics from Aristotle through Shakespeare to Wilde. The texts can be quickly searched for key words, displayed in a window on screen, and pasted into your own work as desired.

INPUTTING TEXT

You should abandon two habits from typewriter days: correcting errors as you enter, and typing 'over' existing text. You can't truly 'process' the words until all the words are there on the screen. Correcting, polishing and rearranging text are more efficient when done later as separate editing operations.

Don't stop for a typing mistake, even when you know you have just made one. Errors can be fixed automatically by the spell checker at an editing stage. On some word processors, typos can be automatically corrected as you write. The software can be set by you to change 'hte', for example, into 'the' – as you type.

Save, save, save your work as you write. It costs nothing and secures everything. Your creation on screen is transient until it is magnetically saved onto the hard disk or onto a floppy disk. A save command is usually a simple keystroke which should be given at the end of every page, every ten minutes, when the phone rings, and when the cat approaches the keyboard.

The physical aspects of putting text into the word processor should also be considered. You can learn or improve your typing skills from the various cheap and popular programs which use your screen and keyboard to train the eyes and fingers. If you intend to remain a two-finger typist, then at least keep each hand on its correct side of the keyboard.

Take rests and avoid long uninterrupted periods at the keybord. This action will help to minimise the risk of repetitive strain injury (RSI) to the hands and arms. The pain and disability of RSI has always been a risk for non-stop keyboardists, quill pen clerks and other repetitive workers such as chicken pluckers. So locate the phone and the files *away* from the word processor; moving and stretching is good for you.

EDITING

Copy your work before making changes. Duplicate your work before and after making changes as you may be glad to go back to yesterday's version. Let the spell checker run through your entire text to correct the typos and the misspelt words. Remember that this tool can't correct for sense and that a correctly spelt word may still be the wrong word. Some of these wrong words can only be detected when your brain is in a different mode. The best editing is often done by making a paper copy which you read and mark up while away from your work area, preferably the next day.

As you make changes to text you need not 'overwrite' old text, as in typewriter days. Keep the word processor in normal 'insert' mode and let any text in front of your screen cursor be 'pushed along' in front of your new writing. The two versions can then be compared on the screen before deleting the unwanted text.

Become fluent in the commands of your word processor which allow you to mark 'blocks' of text and then copy or move them to new locations. A block of text can also be copied into a separate file document for use in future documents or for repeated insertion into your current document. Any stored text can be 'inserted' into the current text at the place where you have left the screen cursor. You can therefore open a new blank document and 'boilerplate' a new assembly of text out of existing saved text.

FORMATTING

The final layout and the style of print on the page should be thought of as a separate process carried out after the creation and the editing of text. A publishing house prefers to receive your work as totally unformatted plain text, as do desktop publishing programs described in the accompanying article on desktop publishing (see page 479).

Ideally your plain text should contain no indents, no padded word spaces, no alignments, no centring, no line spaces and no carriage returns except to start new paragraphs. The save command of your word processor should somewhere have an option of 'plain (or ASCII) text'. Seek the agreement of the final publisher before using underlining, emboldening, large font and other effects.

Plain text looks cramped and uninspiring so you may, for creative reasons, wish to work with a copy of your text laid out in a form which resembles the final page. After inputting your text unformatted you can keep a copy of the plain text version before doing your fancy version. To control some writing projects you may need to set up your page to a certain width of line and length. Word processors can save these personal formats as blank templates.

Modern word processors do have powerful desktop publishing features which allow you to do final page layout on the word processor screen if you desire. These activities, which require the skills and knowledge described in the desktop publishing article, are inspiring to some writers and of little interest to others.

HOUSEKEEPING

Authors can never be too rich, too thin, or have too many computer copies of their work. Each electronic document is stored as an electronic file or folder on the magnetic disk with a file or folder name chosen by yourself. Use a document or file 'copy' command to make a clone copy of your work but with a different filename.

If your work is being stored on the hard disk fitted inside your computer, then make a copy onto a portable floppy disk at daily intervals. Keep several floppy disk copies, some of them in a different room or building. If the computer fails, or is stolen, then you will be glad to go back to last week's version of your work.

Word processing files take up relatively little disk space compared to other computer files such as graphics. You can probably fit your entire year's writing onto one floppy disk but please don't do so as it may develop a fault and trap your masterpiece in a magnetic limbo. Floppy disks are so cheap that they are given away on magazine covers.

TRAINING

Please *read* about your word processor; other writers have written to you! If you don't have a manual or a book then display the screen help items, print them out, and read them in bed. You don't need to spend money on a training course as you can't damage your word processor by experimenting. But you can remain ignorant of a feature which is just what you have been wanting to know about.

All modern word processors offer high level features such as automated routines (macros), printing envelopes and labels, and mail shots. If you want to use these features you should learn about them and try them.

EQUIPMENT

The simple broad aim is to use the same hardware as those people with whom you work or from whom you can obtain support. It is a fact that around 90 per cent of the market for business PCs belongs to the IBM PC/Intel families of machines made by a wide variety of manufacturers, not usually IBM.

The ability to gain information, swap disks, share equipment is often more important than other considerations. For most people that choice will be an IBM-compatible PC. For some it will be an Apple. The Apple Macintosh range has always used a 'graphical interface' which executes commands by moving a pointer on screen and 'clicking' the mouse. Modern PC-compatibles are now supplied with Microsoft Windows which provides a graphical interface similar to the Macintosh.

The PC and the Apple 'platforms' are slowly converging and the leading word processing packages work on both types of machine with minimal differences. The word processor packages being bought for modern offices are mainly Microsoft Word for Windows, and WordPerfect in several forms.

There are several dozen other word processing packages which have been in use over the years and they all do everything that most writers require. Conversion software allows you to convert text in one major format to another major format, although fancy layouts may become mangled. Most word processors should also be able to exchange information via the plain text or ASCII format.

The purchase of computer goods often relates to how you personally buy an item like a washing machine or TV. You may purchase at a John Lewis department store and arrange for full delivery and installation, or you might bring the equipment home from a Comet warehouse in an unopened box and set it up yourself.

It is common to buy computer equipment by mail order and credit card from reputable discount warehouses, so buy a magazine like *MicroMart* or *Personal Computer World* to get an idea of prices. Otherwise choose a dealer in a convenient location and use your magazine prices to negotiate a suitable package of price and help.

Dark fantasy

You don't need a one-eyed, foul-breathed monster with a rusty knife, or an indescribable something (covered in slime), to conjure up terrors in the human heart. Some crumpled sheets, a crowded bus: these are the kinds of things you see out of the corner of your eye. It is their very ordinariness that makes them so sinister. These are the kinds of things that well up from the innermost recesses of the mind, the unconscious if you like, or that part of the imagination that is not sunny and creative, and take you by surprise. This is dark fantasy: the shadow side of the human soul.

from *Writing Fantasy Fiction* by Sarah Le Fanu (A & C Black, £8.99).
See order form on page 690.

Desktop Publishing

RICHARD WILLIAMS

ESSENTIAL EQUIPMENT

This article gives you some general guidance on buying desktop publishing equipment and software – because of the rapid pace of change you should read the specialist computer magazines for more detailed and up-to-date information. Look for a machine which more than meets your current needs, and preferably one that can be upgraded, because each release of a program is likely to require more power, machine memory and hard disk capacity than the last. IBM-compatible PCs probably have the greatest number of programs, but the Macintosh is favoured by the DTP and graphics professionals, so programs which they use tend to come out first on this machine (and some specialised ones never make it to the IBM machines). In either case, go for a reasonable sized monitor screen – these are normally classified by the screen diagonal and the smallest useful size is 15". For sustained work 17" is probably the minimum and professionals tend to use 20 or 21" screens.

A mouse is essential for DTP work. These have always been provided with Macs, and nowadays are almost always included with IBM-compatible machines. If not, resist the temptation to buy a cheap model.

Inkjet printers cost very little more that dot matrix machines, but give better quality results, and are much quieter. Laser printers are a bit more expensive than inkjets, and slightly noisier (though much quieter than dot matrix) but give the best quality, are faster, and cost less per page for consumables. If you will be using your own printer to proof work for commercial printing, a Postscript printer is worth considering. Although costing more than the standard type, this should give a much better match between proof and final output, because Postscript is almost universally used to produce the final bromide or film.

OPTIONAL EXTRAS

A CD-ROM drive gives you access to illustrations in electronic form, ready to drop into the page. These can be either your own photos transferred to Photo CDs, or commercial collections of stock photos and drawn 'clip art'. You can also use the huge range of fonts now available in this format. These drives are now relatively cheap, and are often included in machines. If not, one can be easily added. If you also want to use it for multimedia and games, make sure that it is at least a quadruple speed drive and buy a sound card as well (these often come bundled with drives).

A scanner is another useful extra, to convert existing paper illustrations into electronic form. The choice is between relatively cheap compact scanners which are best suited for occasional use and monochrome originals, and the more expensive flatbeds which can quickly scan an A4 page in colour. OCR (optical character reading) software, often bundled with these, can convert existing typed or printed text to electronic format, avoiding the need to re-type it.

SOFTWARE

Desktop publishing programs have tended to polarise between the inexpensive, but competent, and the expensive and fully professional. For anyone doing a significant amount of DTP work the extra cost of the high end programs will be worthwhile, just for their power and ease of use (though not necessarily ease of learning). If you are not sure, start with one of the low end programs which will give you a clearer idea of your requirements if, or when, you come to buy a more powerful program.

DESIGNING THE PUBLICATION

Planning is the most important first step in creating a document or publication. Before starting work you need to be clear what kind of document it is, and who it is aimed at. At the practical level you should decide, roughly at least, how many pages there will be, what size, and how they are to be printed and bound. Obviously these decisions are often interlinked – your choice of page size will be limited if it is to be produced by laser printer, photocopier or quick printer, but much wider if it is to be commercially printed. Before you set up the page layout, spend as much time as you can looking critically at other publications. See what works, and what doesn't, and don't be afraid to copy.

When you start, work on just a few pages at first, the minimum needed to show all the possibilities in the document as a whole. For something simple, like a novel, you only need a double page spread of ordinary text, another spread for chapter start and finish, and possibly a single page for the table of contents. Non-fiction is usually more complex, and may require extra pages to show the treatment of headings and illustrations plus an index if present. Work on until you are happy with the result, then try a sample chapter as a check before laying out the rest of the book. Problems can then be solved at an early stage, and changes made, with a minimum impact on the work already done.

Try to avoid over elaborate page designs. Use elements such as lines and boxes with a purpose, to clarify rather than ornament, and remember that white space has a vital role to play. Most programs allow you to set up a grid of guidelines, so use these to give pages a structure, particularly important in illustrated works.

USING TYPEFACES SENSIBLY

Because DTP programs allow access to lots of typefaces, beginners tend to use too many – the basic rule is to use no more than two individual typefaces on a page, and get the necessary variety with different sizes and weights. One popular scheme is to combine a sans-serif face for headings with a serif face for text. This gives both variety and readability (serif faces are generally reckoned to be more legible for large amounts of text, except at very small sizes).

Beginners also err by carrying over the conventions of the typewriter, with plentiful use of capitals and underlining. In print this is unnecessary – use upper case (capital letters) sparingly, and don't use underlines at all. Instead use either bold or italics for emphasis: bold for an isolated word or phrase, but italics for a longer passage, which would otherwise be over-emphatic.

Other common mistakes are using two spaces after a full stop, two hyphens for a dash, and the normal typewriter single and double quotation marks. For professional looking results, make sure there is only a single space, use proper dashes and opening and closing quotation marks, and avoid indents in the first paragraph after a heading.

THE RIGHT SPACING

The correct balance of spacing between letters, words and lines is crucial for legibility. Here the basic rule is that spacing between letters should be less than between words, and that between words less than between lines. Provided the relationship between these elements is correct, the actual amount of spacing is a matter of taste.

The ideal page should have an even texture, avoiding obvious variations in spacing from line to line. Letter spacing should normally be fixed, and word spacing should not be less than two thirds, or more than one and a half times the average setting. This may cause problems with shorter lines, but the solution here is intelligent use of hyphenation (avoiding more than two successive hyphens) and use of unjustified text for short lines. The ideal line length is generally reckoned to be about 60 to 70 characters – much less gives problems with spacing, whilst longer lines are more difficult to read.

Space should be used to differentiate headings from body text, with at least as much space below a heading as between paragraphs, and more above, so that it clearly relates to the following text.

To ensure that text in adjoining columns lines up across the page, the total space occupied by a heading (the type itself, plus space above and below) must always be a multiple of the point size of the body text. Resist the temptation to use too many different levels of heading – three should be enough for almost any purpose.

Even with these rules to guide you, experimentation will be necessary to get a satisfactory combination of typefaces, and the various types of spacing. Don't skimp this, but persevere until you are really happy with the result – if it doesn't look right, then it probably isn't. If you are not sure, put the sample page on one side for a day or more, so that you come back to it with a fresh eye.

ADDING TEXT AND ILLUSTRATIONS

Once you are happy with the layout and typography of your sample pages, you are ready to apply these to the whole text. You should be able to do this by creating 'styles' which format a paragraph in a single operation by 'tagging' it. The foolproof method is to prepare text in the word processor without any formatting at all, then use the appropriate style to format it in the DTP program. Text can also be tagged in a word processor, but this requires more expert knowledge.

Although simple graphics can be created in many DTP programs, it is better to use a separate program to create illustrations – a drawing program for diagrams and charts, a spreadsheet for graphs. Avoid the so-called paint programs if possible – these can give a jagged look to the finished result. If you must use one of these, make sure you create the illustration at least the size of the printed version and preferably larger.

Photographs can liven up a text page, but only if properly handled. Two common faults are to include too much detail for the size of the picture, and to print it too dark. Cropping can get rid of extraneous detail, and most DTP or graphics programs can do this.

Dot gain (the tendency of half-tone dots to be larger on paper than on the printing plate) causes photos to print darker than the original. This can be compensated for either in scanning or in the DTP program itself. Conventionally screened photos should take this into account, and pasting these into a bromide rather than scanning them may be the simplest solution.

FINAL STAGES

Make sure that you check the final proofs carefully – any mistakes not found then will be expensive to correct later. Spell checkers need to be used intelligently – they are great for catching obvious errors but are no substitute for careful manual proof reading.

One task that normally has to wait for this stage is the preparation of an index. Although DTP programs can help in this, the process still requires human intervention, and for anything more than a simple index a professional indexer will give a much better result.

FINAL OUTPUT

Conventional printing is expensive for short runs, so consider using either a high quality copier in a quick printer, or one of the new machines which are a hybrid of copier and printer. For longer runs it is better to use a commercial printer. The first time you do so, get some sample pages (the ones you produced for deciding on layout and typography) run off by the printer or service bureau. Any sensible firm will be happy to do this, knowing that snags found at this stage will avoid much worse problems later.

Although some service bureaux will accept files in the format of the DTP program, Postscript files are easier for them to handle and the final output is more likely to match your proofs. If you are using a Windows-based program, make sure that the bureau can handle output in this format and has the appropriate fonts (Mac fonts may not be compatible.)

When you send a job to a service bureau or printer, list the files that you want to be output, and enclose proofs with the disks so that they can see how the finished job should look. For anything more than a short document, break it up into separate files of a few pages each, which makes it easier to recover from any problems. Doing this and getting sample pages printed beforehand should cope with most potential problems, but make sure they have a telephone number to contact you if necessary.

FURTHER READING

Inevitably in a short article such as this it is only possible to give a brief introduction to the subject. There are too many books dealing with individual programs or topics to list individually, but the following books on general topics may be useful:

Jones, Robert, *DTP The Complete Guide to Corporate Desktop Publishing*, Cambridge University Press, 1988
Miles, John, *Design for Desktop Publishing*, John Taylor Book Ventures, 1992

Sensitive areas

Always bear in mind that novels with 'teens' logos are well known to be popular with the under-twelves, who are naturally eager to come to grips with the adult world. Many of them enjoy identifying with the much older teenage characters in books and are fascinated by tales of sexual encounters, but it seems only fair for you, as a writer, to make sure your readers are aware of the risks involved.

from *Writing for the Teenage Market* by Ann de Gale (A & C Black, £8.99).
See order form on page 690.

Writing Courses in Higher Education

DYMPHNA CALLERY

Why study writing? What's to be gained?

If you want to act or play the flute, you'll jump at the chance to train. And whether you've been writing for years or have just discovered an interest in it, you'll find that a course in writing offers a great deal, not least the impetus to write. Goals are set and you learn to produce to a deadline. A course promotes a disciplined approach to crafting for anyone who has been exploring writing on their own and the advice of experienced tutors and professionals can help to focus a direction in your writing that's hard to find on one's own. And it doesn't matter how old you are either, for courses in Higher Education these days welcome students of all ages and backgrounds. Studying writing, either as part of a degree or at postgraduate level, can enhance your writing skills and augment your chances in the publishing world or the workplace. But above all, it gives you the opportunity to improve and enrich your work.

What's available: BA degrees

At undergraduate level, several institutions have developed opportunities for Creative Writing to be taken as part of a degree in English, such as Sheffield Hallam University, one of the pioneers in this field. Others recognise that there is a place for writing courses within the broader context of the Creative Arts, Cultural Studies or Film Studies, and therefore writing courses are offered within those programmes. Some, such as Liverpool John Moores University, offer the opportunity to study Imaginative Writing as one half of a two subject degree. Currently, Bournemouth University is the only one offering a full programme – in Scriptwriting for Film and Television. But more and more institutions are developing courses in writing, so check with your local institution to see what's on offer.

What's available: MA degrees

Postgraduate courses are for those who already have a degree or the equivalent. Some focus on specific genres – such as the novel at East Anglia and Manchester, play-writing at Birmingham, or screen-writing at the Northern Film School – but most emphasise the process of discovery and re-discovery through writing practice. Students are usually assessed on a mixture of original creative work and critical writing. The study of critical theory is a component of all MA courses, but don't let that put you off, for although initially some of it can seem difficult or challenging, there are payoffs – you'll find yourself stretched intellectually as well as creatively. The basic assumption is that developing critical and analytical skills both enhances intellectual development and helps you to evaluate your own work. Through analysing narrative structure, for example, you can improve your storylining and plotting. You may even find yourself writing in genres or styles that you had never before considered.

Why have these courses developed?

Creative Writing has been a growth area in the Higher Education sector during the last ten years. This trend follows the American system where undergraduate options and Masters Degrees in Writing have been common for some time, producing a wealth of successful writers. The basis of this increasing trend in Britain is not that writing *ought* to be taught, but that it *can* be. If you haven't already got a degree, then now may be the time to consider developing your writing and gaining a qualification at the same time. If you already have a degree than why not consider following a full- or part-time writing course at postgraduate level?

How do these courses work? How can you 'study' writing? Surely it's better to 'do' it?

The main principle of these courses is that you learn by 'doing'. Just as an art student produces work in a studio, so writing students produce portfolio material. Most courses offer a framework of group workshops where material is generated and discussed. This is the principle of the 'writers' group'. However, the aim is not just to provide a supportive atmosphere in which writers can air their work, but to create a forum for critical debate. As someone who has experienced this workshop process (I recently completed the MA in Writing Studies at Edge Hill College) I can vouch for the success of this mode of study from the participating point of view. As someone who now teaches on the degree programme at Liverpool John Moores University, I find that this method of working nurtures talent and encourages experimentation.

In many instances, students are expected to read past and contemporary literature as well as critical theory. This not only invokes the old adage that the more you read the better you write, but that viewing these works from a critical standpoint facilitates the ability to read your own and others' work with more insight. By the end of such a course you will probably find yourself far better read than you were at the beginning, more aware of your own potential, and probably more critical too.

Who does the teaching? What qualifications do they have?

The majority of tutors on these programmes are themselves practising and published writers, some – e.g. Andrew Motion, David Edgar – more well known than others, e.g. Jenny Newman, Jeremy Hooker. Whilst committed to their own writing they are keen to share their ideas and encourage new writers. They recognise that writing can be a lonely pursuit and that there's a great deal to be gained in an environment where creative problems and ideas are openly discussed. Any course worth its salt will incorporate visits from professional writers which means that your work may be read and commented upon by someone with a proven track record in the 'business'. Don't expect the course to offer contacts with publishers, editors or agents unless they specifically mention this in their information. But, tutors may be able to suggest the kind of publisher who might be interested in your work and many universities have their own writing magazines for which students' work is welcomed.

Being a student

There are benefits to be gained from becoming a student, not least of which is access to libraries and, in some institutions, access to IT and DTP machines and training. Whether part-time or full-time, you automatically become a member of your university or college library, and postgraduate students may apply for membership of the British Library. University libraries have, like those in the public sector, been hit by reductions in funding yet they are still often repositories of considerable excellence. And they frequently take periodicals, including some poetry titles, which are not available elsewhere.

Believe it or not, there are perks associated with being a student. Whether part-time or full-time, under forty or over fifty, you are entitled to join the Student Union and thereby gain access to such benefits as cheap travel, reduced price cinema and theatre tickets, etc. Most universities these days have post-graduate societies and mature student organisations. Many have cheap catering and bar facilities, and some of the more enlightened ones have crèches for those with small children (although there are normally charges for this service).

Who is eligible?

Although most of the undergraduate courses which include Creative Writing will expect English Literature at A level (generally with two other subjects), the majority of universities now welcome applications from those who have undertaken a BTEC or an Access to Higher Education course. Admissions policies in many institutions are flexible when dealing with mature applicants (for these purposes mature means those over 21), particularly those candidates who have work/life experience.

MA courses in all aspects of Creative Writing will usually expect applicants to have a degree, but not necessarily in a related field such as English Literature. They positively welcome applications from mature students, who make up the majority of students on these courses. Some will accept work experience in a related field, such as teaching, television production, journalism or publishing, as an equivalent entry qualification. All will require the submission of a portfolio of writing on which they base their assessment of your potential for the programme they offer. Some institutions will accept candidates purely on the basis of this, while others prefer to interview selected candidates.

How and when should I apply?

First contact the institutions that interest you. Follow their instructions for application procedures for courses. Visit the campus (some colleges may even let you sit in on a class or lecture). However, lecturing staff are notoriously under pressure these days, so don't expect individual attention. At this stage you are a potential applicant, not a student.

Although these courses usually begin in September/October, applications are considered much earlier in the year, for example the closing date for the MA in Playwriting Studies at Birmingham is mid-January. Applications for BA degrees are normally processed during November–March for the subsequent year. Check with the institution first and make sure you apply early as places tend to be filled on a first-come first-served basis.

How much does it cost?

Providing you have not previously been in receipt of a grant, you should be eligible for a full maintenance grant, which includes tuition fees, for an undergraduate degree. Your local authority will give you information. Some institutions with modular programming allow students to register for certain courses on a part-time basis, paying as they go. Check with the institution to see what is offered in this respect.

Fees for MA degrees vary but are generally in the region of £1200-£2000 for a full-time MA (nearer £6000 for foreign students). Most will allow payment in termly instalments. Part-time courses are usually considerably cheaper and of course the cost is spread over two years. Their fees range from £200-£500 (approx.) per year. Few grants are awarded for postgraduate courses, especially in the Arts, unless the first degree is exceptional. However, if you are accepted for a full-time MA you are eligible to apply for funding to the British Academy. Further information is available from: The British Academy, Postgraduate Studentships Office, Block 1, Spur 15, Government Buildings, Honeypot Lane, Stanmore, Middlesex HA7 1AX.

Many students support themselves by part-time work, and since most courses require two to four attendances a week during term time, this is not too difficult. Beware of trying to marry a full-time job with a full-time course as this is virtually impossible given the amount of reading and *writing* you will be expected to do.

And afterwards?

The major benefit of a writing course in Higher Education comes in improving your writing, but you may also find it moves you further towards that goal of 'being a writer'. Remember that Ian McEwan was a graduate of UEA's course and, although you may not be the next Booker Prize winner, there is little doubt that graduates of these courses succeed in getting published in a variety of ways, from magazines to children's books. It is also worth noting that having a higher qualification may open up opportunities for you to make use of your skills in related work, such as teaching creative writing or undertaking residencies for writers.

BA courses with components in creative writing

BA Combined Arts
University College, Scarborough, North Riding College, Filey Road, Scarborough, North Yorks. YO11 3AZ   *tel* (01723) 362393.

BA Combined Studies
Manchester Metropolitan University, All Saints, Manchester M15 6BH   *tel* 0161-247 2000.

BA Creative Arts
Bath College of Higher Education, Newton Park, Bath BA2 9BN   *tel* (01225) 873701.

Crewe and Alsager Faculty, All Saints, Manchester M15 6BH   *tel* 0161-247 2000.

University of Glamorgan, Pontypridd, Mid Glamorgan CF37 1DL   *tel* (01443) 480480.

Lancaster University, Lancaster LA1 4YW   *tel* (01524) 65201.

BA Creative Arts Studies
University of Sunderland, Langham Tower, Ryhope Road, Sunderland SR2 7EE   *tel* 0191-515 2000.

BA Cultural Studies
Norfolk Institute of Art and Design, St George Street, Norwich, Norfolk NR3 1BB   *tel* (01603) 610561.

BA Drama
University of Hull, Drama Department, Hull HU6 7RX   *tel* (01482) 466210.
University of Exeter, Exeter, Devon EX4 4QW   *tel* (01392) 264580.

BA Drama and Theatre Studies
Roehampton Institute, Senate House, Roehampton Lane, London SW15 5PU   *tel* 0181-392 3000.

BA Drama, Theatre and Television Studies
King Alfred's College, Winchester, Hants. SO22 4NR   *tel* (01962) 841515.

BA English
Edge Hill College of Higher Education, St Helen's Road, Ormskirk, Lancs. L39 4QP   *tel* (01695) 575171.

University of Wolverhampton, Wulfruna Street, Wolverhampton WV1 1SB   *tel* (01902) 321000.

BA English Studies
Sheffield Hallam University, Pond Street, Sheffield S1 1WB   *tel* (0114) 272 0911.

BA English and Creative Studies
University of Portsmouth, University House, Winston Churchill Avenue, Portsmouth PO1 2UP   *tel* (01705) 843082.

BA English Literature with Creative Writing
University of East Anglia, Norwich NR4 7TJ   *tel* (01603) 56161.

BA Film and Drama
Reading University, PO Box 217, Reading RG6 2AH   *tel* (01734) 875123.

BA Imaginative Writing
Liverpool John Moores University, School of Media, Critical and Creative Arts, Dean Walters Building, St James Road, Liverpool L1 7BR   *tel* 0151-231 5007/5009.

BA Modular Scheme
University of Derby, Kedleston Road, Derby DE22 1GB   *tel* (01332) 62222.

BA Performance Writings
Dartington College of Arts, Totnes, Devon TQ9 6EJ   *tel* (01803) 863234.

BA Related Arts and English
West Sussex Institute of Higher Education, The Dome, Upper Bognor Road, Bognor Regis, West Sussex PO21 1HR   *tel* (01243) 865581.

BA Scriptwriting for Film and Television
Bournemouth University, Talbot Campus, Fern Barrow, Poole, Dorset BH12 5BB   *tel* (01202) 314144.

BA Theatre Degree: Writers' Course
Rose Bruford College of Speech and Drama, Lamorbey Park, Sidcup, Kent DA15 9DF   *tel* 0181-300 3024.

BA Theatre and Media Drama
University of Glamorgan, Pontypridd, Mid Glamorgan CF37 1DL   *tel* (01443) 482573.

BA Theatre Studies
Royal Holloway and Bedford New College, University of London, Egham Hill, Egham, Surrey TW20 0EX   *tel* (01784) 443922.

BA Writing and Publishing
Middlesex University, School of English, Cultural and Communication Studies, White Hart Lane, London N17 8HR   *tel* 0181-362 5000.

MA courses in creative writing

Many of these programmes also offer a Postgraduate Diploma in Writing – please check with individual institutions.

All courses begin in October and run through an academic year unless otherwise indicated. (FT = full-time; PT = part-time)

MA in Creative Writing (1yr FT   2yr PT)
A combination of taught courses and workshops led by tutors who are practising and published writers with intervention from professionals, e.g. Gillian Clark and Fay Weldon. *Contact:* Jeremy Hooker, Bath College of Higher Education, Newton Park, Newton St Loe, Bath BA2 9BN   *tel* (01225) 873701.

MA in Creative Writing: 1 Fiction, 2 Script and Screen (1yr FT)
Founded by Malcolm Bradbury and now with Andrew Motion in the driving seat, this is the premier course for aspiring novelists and is geared to 'those who are already writing seriously'. *Contact:* Professor Christopher Bigsby, School of English and American Studies, University of East Anglia, Norwich NR4 7TJ   *tel* (01603) 56161.

MA in Creative Writing (1yr FT   2yr PT)
Open to people already able to produce publishable work, students on this course write a book: a novel, collection of stories or poems, a film/play script. Visits from major authors. *Contact:* Professor David Craig, Bowland College, Lancaster University, Lancaster LA1 4YN   *tel* (01524) 65201 ext 4590.

MA in Creative Writing (1yr FT)
This course examines the crafting techniques of major writers of the novel, short story or poetry, and includes written three-hour examinations on these as well as original writing. *Contact:* Professor Douglas Dunn, School of English, University of St Andrews, Fife KY16 9AL   *tel* (01334) 62666.

MA in Film & Television Scriptwriting (Fiction) (1yr FT Jan.-Dec.)
Designed for those who have already achieved a body of writing, or those with appropriate professional experience. Focuses on original scriptwriting and contextual studies. *Contact:* Ian Macdonald, Head of Northern School of Film and Television, Leeds Metropolitan University, 2-8 Merrion Way, Leeds LS2 8BT *tel* (0113) 283 2600.

MA in Novel Writing (1yr FT plus 1yr writing)
This new course is unique in offering a twelve-month taught course, followed by the writing of a novel under tutor supervision during the following year. Taught by published writers. *Contact:* Dr Richard Francis, The Postgraduate Admissions Secretary, Department of American Studies, University of Manchester, Oxford Road, Manchester M13 9PL *tel* 0161-275 3054.

MA in Playwriting Studies (1yr FT)
This course is led by David Edgar and features input from several major playwrights, e.g. Alan Bennett, Charlotte Keatley, as well as theatre directors such as Max Stafford Clark. *Contact:* Dr Brian Crow, Department of Drama and Theatre Arts, The University of Birmingham, Edgbaston B15 2TT *tel* 0121-414 5993.

MA in Screenwriting (2yr PT) A hands-on practical course in writing for screen and the role of the writer in the film and television industry. The course operates via workshops/seminars and individual tuition. Jimmy McGovern is a regular tutor. *Contact:* Harry Pepp, Liverpool John Moores University, School of Media, Critical and Creative Arts, Dean Walters Building, St James Road, Liverpool L1 7BR *tel* 0151-231 5020.

MA in Screenwriting and Screen Research (2yr PT Jan.-Dec.)
The course prepares students to pursue careers as writers and researchers in film and television via a workshop and portfolio programme. Also useful for script editing. *Contact:* Phil Parker, School of Media, London College of Printing and Distributive Trades, Back Hill, Clerkenwell, London EC1R 5EN *tel* 0171-735 8484.

MA in Teaching & Practice of Creative Writing (1yr FT)
For writers with an interest in teaching Creative Writing as well as teachers interested in creative writing practice. The experienced group of tutors include Anne Cluysenaar. *Contact:* Norman Schwenk, School of English Studies, Journalism & Philosophy, University of Wales College of Cardiff, PO Box 94, Cardiff CF1 3XE *tel* (01222) 874241.

MA in Theatre Arts (1yr FT)
Play writing features as an optional area of study in this new degree which provides opportunities to study theatre disciplines in a professional context. *Contacts:* Professor Vera Gottlieb/Nesta Jones, Goldsmiths College, University of London, Lewisham Way, London SE14 6RW *tel* 0181-692 7171.

MA in Writing (2yr PT)
A unique flexible-learning scheme which offers students the opportunity to develop their book-length manuscript under the guidance of university tutors and prize-winning writers. *Contact:* Tony Curtis, School of Humanities and Social Sciences, University of Glamorgan, Treforest, Pontypridd, Mid Glamorgan CF37 1DL *tel* (01443) 482551.

MA in Writing (1yr FT)
After general workshops, students can specialise in fiction, scriptwriting, poetry or teaching in the classroom. Taught by working writers including Jane Rogers

and Barry Hines. *Contact:* Robert Miles, English Department, Sheffield Hallam University, 32 Collegiate Crescent, Sheffield S10 2BP   *tel* (0114) 272 0911.

MA in Writing Studies (2yr PT)

A course which combines advanced level writers' workshops with closely related courses in critical theory and contemporary writing. *Contact:* MA in Writing Studies Course Tutor, Edge Hill College of Higher Education, St Helens Road, Ormskirk, Lancs. L39 4QP   *tel* (01695) 575171.

Other higher education courses of interest

Creative Writing for Performance (1yr FT)

Diploma course offering training in writing for theatre, screen and radio. Tutors have included Alan Drury (radio) and Stephen Wyatt (film). *Contact:* Linda Roe, Central School of Speech and Drama, Embassy Theatre, Eton Avenue, London NW3 3HY   *tel* 0171-722 8183.

Scriptwriting for Television, Stage and Radio (1yr FT)

Aimed at those wanting to explore creative scriptwriting in a small group with personal supervision. *Contact:* Tony Dinner, Thames University, St Mary's Road, London W5 5RF   *tel* 0181-231 2271.

Interviews

Interviews form an important element in news reports. The reporter's task is to use skill with words to set a scene and bring it to life for the listener, and then to avoid the limelight by eliciting as much of the story as possible from the key people involved.

Interviewing is both a skill and an art. The interviewer must have a clear idea of the purpose of the recording and the length of time it will eventually be allowed to run.

Interviews in news bulletins usually have to be short and to the point. The reporter must evoke factual responses and avoid leading questions which allow simple 'yes' or 'no' replies. Thus, not:

Q. Mr Jones, I believe you were standing in the doorway when the thunderbolt fell?

A. Yes.

but:

Q. Mr Jones, where were you when the thunderbolt fell?

A. Standing in the doorway...

from *Writing for Radio* by Rosemary Horstmann (A & C Black, £6.99). See order form on page 690.

Editorial, Literary and Production Services

For a **classified list** of editorial, literary and production services, see page 505.

The following specialists offer a wide variety of services to writers (both new and established), to publishers, journalists and others. Services include advice on MSS, editing and book production, indexing, translation, research and writing.

'A Feature Factory' Editorial Services (incorporating **Academic Projects**), 4 St Andrews Court, 53 Yarmouth Road, Norwich NR7 0EW   *tel* (01603) 435229. *Editors:* Dr Dennis Chaplin, Leigh-Anne Perryman. Produces company magazines, brochures, company histories, press releases/features (including same-day turnaround), advertisement features, ghostwriting, dtp, research briefs for press/broadcasting, backgrounders, writing and research tuition.

Abbey Writing Services (1989), Portsmouth Cottage, St Mary Bourne, Andover, Hants SP11 6BP   *tel/fax* (01264) 738556. *Director:* John McIlwain. Comprehensive writing, project management and editorial service. Writing of most non-fiction types: areas of expertise include guidebooks, dictionaries and education.

Academic File (The Centre for Near East Afro-Asia Research) (NEAR) (1985), Acre House, 69-76 Long Acre, London WC2E 9JH   *tel* 0181-392 1122   *fax* 0181-392 1422. *Director:* Sajid Rizvi. Research, advisory and consultancy services related to politics, economics and societies of the Near and Middle East, Asia and North Africa and related issues in Europe. Risk analysis, editorial assessment, editing and publishing design and production.

Advice and Criticism Service, Hilary Johnson, 5 St Agnes Gate, Wendover, Bucks. HP22 6DP   *tel* (01296) 623260   *fax* (01296) 623601. Authors' consultant: detailed and constructive assessment of typescripts/practical advice regarding publication. Current organiser Romantic Novelists' Association's New Writers' Scheme. Publishers' reader. Specialities: crime/thrillers/popular women's fiction.

Alpha Word Power (1985), 3 Bluecoat Buildings, Claypath, Durham DH1 1RF   *tel* 0191-384 7219   *fax* 0191-384 3767   *e-mail* 100270.2023 @compuserve.com Publishing services: camera-ready copy, word processing, text from and/or to disk, desk editing, proof-reading, liaison with printers/binders/graphic design; full secretarial services; business services. Specialise in versatility and speed of turnaround.

Lucia Alvarez de Toledo (1979), 138B Melrose Avenue, London NW2 4JX   *tel* 0181-450 5344   *fax* 0181-452 9005. Research, interpreting, translation, subtitles, voice overs, proof-reading, editing, copy-writing, into/from English, Spanish, French, Italian.

Anvil Editorial Associates (1966), Lleifior, Malltraeth, Bodorgan, Anglesey, Gwynedd LL62 5AF   *tel/fax* Bodorgan (01407) 840688. *Director:* Dr H. Bernard-Smith. Comprehensive editorial service, including editing, copy-editing, and proof-reading. Planning, preparation, writing and editing of books, house journals, company histories, reports, brochures, promotional literature, pamphlets, and scripts. In-house photography. Full MS service.

Archaeological Consultants, Lesley and Roy Adkins, Longstone Lodge, Aller, Langport, Somerset TA10 0QT   *tel* (01458) 250075   *fax* (01458) 250858.

Work with an archaeological, historical and heritage theme undertaken, including all types of research, critical assessment of MSS, contract writing for publishers, project management, copy-editing, indexing, some illustration, and picture research.

Arioma Editorial Services, Gloucester House, High Street, Borth, Dyfed SY24 5HZ *tel/fax* (01970) 871 296. *Partners:* Moira Smith, Patrick Smith. Research, co-writing, ghost-writing, dtp, complete book production service. Specialities: military, naval, aviation history and autobiography.

Arkst Publishing Ltd (1995), 1 Lindsey House, Lloyd's Place, Blackheath, London SE3 0QF *tel* 0181-297 9997 *fax* 0181-297 1990. *Director:* James H. Willis FRCP (Edin). General editing of MSS; also rewriting. Independent appraisal of MSS – fiction and non-fiction.

Aspect (1984), PO Box 43, Thatcham, Berks. RG19 4WH *tel* (01635) 871802 *fax* (01635) 871803. *Proprietor:* Graham Jones. Writing, editing, copy-editing, production of newspapers, magazines and books.

Linda Auld Associates (1981), Brewer's Cottage, Brook Street, Yoxford, Suffolk IP17 3EZ *tel/fax* (01728) 668198. *Proprietor:* Linda Auld. Project management, managing editing, rewriting, copy-editing, proof-reading, indexing, on-screen editing. All subjects. Member of Society of Freelance Editors and Proofreaders.

Auteursbureau Greta Baars-Jelgersma (1951), Bovensteweg 46, NL-6585 KD Mook, The Netherlands *tel* (024) 696-1470 *fax* (024) 696-2439. Specialises in international co-printing of illustrated books; translations from German, English, French and Sworn interpreter and translator Scandinavian languages.

Authors' Advisory Service (1972), 21 Campden Grove, Kensington, London W8 4JG *tel* 0171-937 5583. All typescripts professionally evaluated in depth and edited by long-established publishers' reader specialising in constructive advice to new writers and with wide experience of current literary requirements. Critic and reader for literary awards. Lecture service on the craft and technique of writing for publication.

Authors Appraisal Service (1988), 12 Hadleigh Gardens, Boyatt Wood, Eastleigh, Hants SO5 4NP *tel* (01703) 368863. *Literary consultant:* J. Evans. Critical appraisal of all types of manuscript, specialising in romantic and historical fiction. Competitive rates. Preliminary letter first please.

Authors' Research Services (1966), Richard Wright, 32 Oak Village, London NW5 4QN *tel* 0171-284 4316. Offers comprehensive research service to writers, academics and business people worldwide, including fact checking, bibliographical references and document supply. Specialises in English history, social sciences, business.

Ayrshire Business Services (1989), 84 Main Street, Monkton, Ayrshire KA9 2QL *tel/fax* (01292) 477339. *Owner/manager:* Janet Spufford. Full manuscript service – word processing or desktop publishing; assists new authors with placement of book and liaises with agent/publisher on behalf of author.

Laraine Bamrah, 61 rue de Parmain, 95430 Butry sur Oise, Auvers sur Oise, France *tel* (1) 34 73 09 75 *fax* (1) 34 08 81 36. British freelance writer and researcher resident in France's 'Impressionist' valley. Editorial, commercial picture and script research, especially EFL, tourism. Production assistant and liaison for radio, TV and film. Translations from French.

Richard A. Beck (1991), 49 Curzon Avenue, Stanmore, Middlesex HA7 2AL *tel* 0181-427 0480. Editing, proof-reading, indexing, research, writing and rewriting. Reduced rates for new authors, senior citizens, the unemployed, etc.

Beswick Writing Services (1988), Francis Beswick, 19 Haig Road, Stretford M32 0DS   *tel* 0161-865 1259. Editing, research, information books. Special interests: religious, ecology, outdoor activities, philosophical and educational. Expertise in correspondence courses and Open Learning materials.

Black Ace Book Production (1990), Ellemford Farmhouse, Duns, Berwickshire TD11 3SG   *tel* (01361) 890370   *fax* (01361) 890287. *Directors:* Hunter Steele, Boo Wood. Book production and text processing, including text capture (or scanning), editing, proofing to camera-ready/film, printing and binding, jacket artwork and design. Delivery of finished books; can sometimes help with distribution.

Blair Services (1992), Blair Cottage, Aultgrishan, Melvaig, Gairloch, Wester Ross IV21 2DG   *tel/fax* (01445) 771228. *Director:* Ian Mertling-Blake MA. DPhil. Editing and revision: fiction and non-fiction (such as prospectus for schools and other educational purposes). Also specialist academic revision for books/articles on archaeology and associated subjects.

Book Production Consultants (1973), 25-27 High Street, Chesterton, Cambridge CB4 1ND   *tel* (01223) 352790   *fax* (01223) 460718   *e-mail* apl@bpccam .demon.co.uk *Directors:* A.P. Littlechild, C.S. Walsh. Complete publishing service: writing, editing, designing, illustrating, translating, indexing, artwork; production management of printing and binding; specialised sales and distribution; advertising sales. For books, journals, manuals, reports, magazines, catalogues, electronic media.

Books-in-Hand Ltd, 20 Shepherds Hill, London N6 5AH   *tel/fax* 0181-341 7650. Ann Kritzinger (managing), Kim Spanoghe (technical), Amanda Little (secretary). Fast high-tech production of cost-effective short-run books for self-publishers, from typescript (or disk) to bound copies (hardbacks or paperbacks, sewn or unsewn).

Bookwatch Ltd (1982), 15-up, East Street, Lewin's Yard, Chesham, Bucks. HP5 1HQ   *tel* (01494) 792269   *fax* (01494) 784850. *Directors:* Peter Harland, Jennifer Harland. Market research, bestseller lists, syndicated reviews, features. Publishers of *Books in the Media*, weekly for booksellers and librarians.

Brittan Design Partnership (1978), Clarence House, 35 Clarence Street, Market Harborough, Leics. LE16 7NE   *tel* (01858) 466950   *fax* (01858) 434632. *Partners:* Derek W. Brittan MCSD, Jean E. Brittan, Nick J. Brittan. Complete editorial, design and publishing service; in-house typesetting; high end computer graphics and pre-press; film production.

Brooke Projects, 21 Barnfield, Urmston, Manchester M41 9EW   *tel* 0161-746 8140   *fax* 0161-746 8132   *e-mail* urmston@brooke.u-net.com Research, editing and contract writing. Specialises in business, management, tourism, history, biography, social science.

Mrs D. Buckmaster (1966), 51 Chatsworth Road, Torquay, Devon TQ1 3BJ   *tel* (01803) 294663. General editing of MSS, specialising in traditional themes in religious, metaphysical and esoteric subjects; also success and inspirational books or articles.

John Button (1991), 14 Manor House Way, Brightlingsea, Colchester, Essex CO7 0QN   *tel/fax* (01206) 302769. Copy-editing and proof-reading, specialising in legal, financial, taxation, business education and corporate identity publications; Legal Reference Library series.

Calderbridge Associates (1995), 3 Lion Chambers, Huddersfield, West Yorkshire HD1 1ES *tel/fax* (01484) 512817. *Directors:* R. Sharp, B. Bedar. MSS criticism and advice; editing; proof-reading; word processing; multimedia/internet services.

Cambridge Language Services Ltd (1982), 64 Baldock Street, Ware, Herts SG12 9DT *tel* (01223) 325880/325945 *fax* (01223) 325594 *e-mail* s.allen-mills @cup.cam.ac.uk *Managing director:* Paul Procter BA. Suppliers to publishers, societies and other organisations of customised database management systems, with advanced retrieval mechanisms, and electronic publishing systems for the preparation of dictionaries, reference books, encyclopaedias, catalogues, journals, archives. PC (Windows) based.

Causeway Resources (1989), 8 The Causeway, Teddington, Middlesex TW11 0HE *tel/fax* 0181-977 8797. *Director:* Keith Skinner. Genealogical, biographical and historical research, specialising in police history and true crime research.

Central Office of Information, Hercules Road, London SE1 7DU *tel* 0171-928 2345. The Government executive agency which procures and provides publicity and information services to government departments, other executive agencies and public sector bodies.

Vanessa Charles (1975), 38 Ham Common, Richmond, Surrey TW10 7JG *tel/fax* 0181-940 9225. Design and book production services.

Karyn Claridge Book Production (1989), 244 Bromham Road, Biddenham, Bedford MK40 4AA *tel* (01234) 347909. Complete book production management service offered from MS to bound copies; graphic services available; sourcing service for interactive book projects.

Combrógos (1990), Mr Meic Stephens, 10 Heol Don, Whitchurch, Cardiff CF4 2AU *tel* (01222) 623359 *fax* (01222) 529202. Specialises in books (including fiction and poetry) about Wales or by Welsh authors, providing a full editorial service and undertaking arts and media research.

Copywriting One-to-One (1994), Cowieslinn, Eddleston, Peeblesshire EH45 8QZ *tel/fax* (01721) 730 350. *Director:* Patrick Quinn. Correspondence course in copywriting with telephone helpline.

Ingrid Cranfield (1972), 16 Myddelton Gardens, Winchmore Hill, London N21 2PA *tel* 0181-360 2433. Advisory and editorial services for authors and media, including critical assessment, rewriting, proof-reading, copy-editing, writing of marketing copy, indexing, research, interviews, transcripts. Special interests: geography, travel, exploration, adventure (own archives), language, education, youth training, Japanese art. Translations from German and French.

Creative Comics, Denis Gifford, 80 Silverdale, Sydenham, London SE26 4SJ *tel* 0181-244 9846. Specialises in strip cartoons and comics for both adults and children, custom-tailored to clients' requirements. Everything from jokes, puzzles and single strips, to serials and complete comics, books, supplements and giveaways.

David A. Cross, Philemon's, 9a Wildman Street, Kendal, Cumbria LA9 6EN *tel* (01539) 722465. Research and information service; editing texts, specialising in art history, English literature, biography and genealogy; creative writing tutorials; lectures on artists and writers of the Lake District.

Margaret Crush (1980), Moonfleet, Burney Road, West Humble, Dorking, Surrey RH5 6AU *tel* (01306) 884347. Editing, copy-editing, writing, rewriting and proof-reading for publishers, especially illustrated books.

D & N Publishing (1991), The Stable Block, Crowood Lane, Ramsbury, Marlborough, Wilts. SN8 2HR   *tel* (01672) 521211   *fax* (01672) 521322. *Partners:* David and Namrita Price-Goodfellow. Complete project management including commissioning, editing, picture research, illustration and design, page layout, indexing, printing and repro. All stages managed in-house and produced on Apple Macintoshes running QuarkXPress and Freehand.

Meg and Stephen Davies, 31 Egerton Road, Ashton, Preston, Lancs. PR2 1AJ   *tel* (01772) 725120   *fax* (01772) 723853. Indexing at general and postgraduate level in the arts and humanities. Can offer indexes on PC disk. Also proof-reading and copy-editing. Registered indexer with Society of Indexers since 1971; member of Society of Freelance Editors and Proofreaders.

DOLPHIN ECS (1987), 38 Gyles Park, Stanmore, Middlesex HA7 1AW   *tel* 0181-952 8329   *fax* 0181-952 5075. *Directors:* R. and Y. Dennis. Translation, editing and typesetting services to publishing, commerce, industry and government.

Rosemary Dooley (1973), Crag House, Witherslack, Grange-over-Sands, Cumbria LA11 6RW   *tel* (015395) 52286   *fax* (015395) 52013   *e-mail* musicbks@rdooley.demon.co.uk Editorial advice, editing, copy-editing, specialising in books about music.

Dr Andrew Duncan (1986), 19 Rainham Road, London NW10 5DL   *tel/fax* 0181-969 8332. Professional researcher working in historical and contemporary sources.

Editorial/Visual Research (1973), Angela Murphy, 21 Leamington Road Villas, London W11 1HS   *tel* 0171-727 4920. Comprehensive research service including historical, literary, film and picture research for writers, publishers, film and television companies. Services also include copy-writing, editing, and travel and feature writing.

Dr Martin Edwards (1985), 2 Highbury Hall, 22 Highbury Road, Weston-super-Mare, Avon BS23 2DN   *tel/fax* (01934) 621261. Specialist editorial and research service in the medico-scientific field: including copy-editing, co-editorial/-authorship, proof-reading, abstracting and conference productions. Special interest in the improvement of foreign texts.

Lewis Esson Publishing (1989), 45 Brewster Gardens, London W10 6AQ   *tel* 0181-969 0951   *fax* 0181-968 1623. Project management of illustrated books in areas of food, art and interior design; editing and writing of food books.

etr (Edward Twentyman Resources) (1992), 4 Little Green, Cheveley, Nr Newmarket, Suffolk CB8 9RG   *tel* (01638) 731332   *fax* (01638) 731152   *e-mail* etwentyman@cix.compulink.co.uk *Proprietor:* Edward Twentyman. Employment agency specialising solely in freelance people in publishing.

First Edition Translations Ltd (1981), 6 Wellington Court, Wellington Street, Cambridge CB1 1HZ   *tel* (01223) 356733   *fax* (01223) 321488. *Directors:* Judy Boothroyd, Sarah Walsh. Translation, interpreting, editing, proof-reading, indexing, dtp; books, manuals, reports, journals and promotional material.

FJN Associates (1990), Little Theobald, Sandy Cross, Heathfield, East Sussex TN21 8BT   *tel* (01435) 866653   *fax* (01435) 868998. *Partners:* Frederick J. Nixon, Brenda Mellen Nixon. Comprehensive DTP and editorial service including magazine and newsletter design and production; advice to authors, editing and preparation of manuscripts for submission to publishers/editors; proof-reading.

James Wilson Flegg (1970), via Paolini 11, 10138 Turin, Italy *tel/fax* (011) 4331192. Language consultant; writing, ghosting, copy-editing, translation, abstracting; projects and commissions undertaken.

Christine Foley Secretarial Services (1991), Glyndedwydd, Login, Whitland, Carmarthenshire SA34 0TN *tel/fax* (01994) 448414. *Partners:* Christine Foley, Michael Foley. Word processing service: preparation of MSS from handwritten/typed notes and audio-transcription. Complete secretarial support.

Brian J. Ford, Rothay House, 6 Mayfield Road, Eastrea, Cambs. PE7 2AY *tel/fax* (01733) 350888. Scientist and adviser on scientific matters; author, producer/director scientific films and programmes in addition to editor/contributor to many leading books and journals. Has hosted many leading BBC television and radio programmes, and overseas documentaries.

Freelance Editorial Services (1975), Bill Houston BSc. DipLib. MPhil. 45 Bridge Street, Musselburgh, Midlothian EH21 6AA *tel* 0131-665 7825. Editing, proof-reading, indexing, abstracting, translations, bibliographies; particularly scientific and medical.

Freelance Market News (1967), Sevendale House, 7 Dale Street, Manchester M29 7WL *tel* 0161-228 2362 *fax* 0161-228 3533. Market Research Department for freelance writers issues a monthly Market News service the *Freelance Market News*; £29 p.a. A good rate of pay made for news of editorial requirements. Agents for the UK for the American Writer Inc. and Writer's Digest Books, including *The Writer's Handbook*; also the American *Writer's Market*.

Shelagh Furness (1992), Hallgarth Farmhouse, The Hallgarth, Durham, Co. Durham DH1 3BJ *tel* 0191-384 3840. Research and information service, specialising in environmental, scientific and geographical topics, also North East England; word processing service.

Geo Group & Associates, 4 Christian Fields, London SW16 3JZ *tel/fax* 0181-764 6292. Visual aid production services: slide packs, packaging. Photo library. Commission photography (including aerial photography). Research and publishing consultancy.

C.N. Gilmore (1987), 6c St Michael's Road, Bedford MK40 2LT *tel* (01234) 346142. Sub-editing, copy-editing, slush-pile reading, reviewing. Will also collaborate. Undertakes work in all scholarly and academic fields as well as fiction and practical writing.

Global Syndications (1988), Chartwood Towers, Punchbowl Lane, Dorking, Surrey RH5 4ED *tel* (01306) 741213 *fax* (01306) 875347. *Managing director:* Sam Hall. Research, editing, design, layout, proof-reading and print liaison; picture research and photo library – also preparation of artwork; will compile magazines, books, etc. from start to finish; brochures, newsletters and annual reports a speciality.

Graham-Cameron Publishing (1984), The Studio, 23 Holt Road, Sheringham, Norfolk NR26 8NB *tel* (01263) 821333 *fax* (01263) 821334. *Partners:* Helen Graham-Cameron, Mike Graham-Cameron. Complete editorial, including writing, illustration and production services.

Grahame & Grahame Editorial (1989), 18 Chichester Place, Brighton, East Sussex BN2 1FF *tel* (01273) 699533 *fax* (01273) 621262. *Directors:* Tony and Anita Grahame. Copy-editing; complete book production service; consultancy on all aspects of non-fiction publishing.

Guildford Reading Services (1978), 17 Burwood Gardens, Ash Vale, Aldershot, Hants GU12 5HN   *tel* (01483) 504325/(01252) 317950. *Director:* B.V. Varney. Proof-reading, press revision, copy preparation, sub-editing.

Bernard Hawton, 6 Merdon Court, Merdon Avenue, Chandler's Ford, Hants SO53 1FP   *tel* (01703) 267400. Proof-reading, copy-editing.

Heath Associates (1988), Garden Flat, 15 South Hill Park Gardens, London NW3 2TD   *tel/fax* 0171-435 4059. *Proprietor:* Richard Williams. Consultancy on desktop publishing, word processing and graphics programs for IBM PC; design and illustration specialising in academic and technical works; writing and editing for computing and related topics.

Antony Hemans (1981), Maranatha, 1 Nettles Terrace, Guildford, Surrey GU1 4PA   *tel* (01483) 574511. Biographical and historical research, specialising in industrial archaeology – railways, canals and shipping, air, military and naval operations, genealogy.

Robert Holland-Ford Associates, 103 Lydyett Lane, Barnton, Northwich, Cheshire CW8 4JT   *tel* (01606) 76960. *Director:* Robert Holland-Ford. Impresarios, concert/lecture agents.

Rosemary Horstmann, 1 Kinmond Court, Kenilworth Street, Leamington Spa CV32 4QU   *tel* (01926) 883689. Broadcasting scripts evaluated; general consultancy on editorial and marketing matters; lectures, writing workshops. Send sae for brochure.

E.J. Hunter, 6 Dorset Road, London N22 4SL   *tel* 0181-889 0370. Editing, copy-editing, proof-reading; appraisal of MSS. Special interests: novels, short stories, drama, children's stories; primary education, alternative medicine, New Age.

Hurst Village Publishing (1989), Henry and Elizabeth Farrar, High Chimneys, Davis Street, Hurst, Reading RG10 0TH   *tel* (01734) 345211   *fax* (01734) 320348. Offers design, photography, typesetting, printing and binding services, using the latest desktop publishing programs, photographic equipment and high resolution colour and laser printers.

Society of Indexers, 38 Rochester Road, London NW1 9JJ   *tel* 0171-916 7809 (see pages 508 and 614 for further details).

Indexing Specialists (1965), 202 Church Road, Hove, East Sussex BN3 2DJ   *tel* (01273) 738299   *fax* (01273) 323309   *e-mail* indspec@pavilion.co.uk *Director:* Richard Raper BSc. DTA. Indexes for all types of books, journals and reference publications on professional, scientific and general subjects; copy-editing, proof-reading services; consultancy on indexing and training projects.

The Information Bureau (formerly **Daily Telegraph Information Bureau**), 51 The Business Centre, 103 Lavender Hill, London SW11 5QL   *tel* 0171-924 4414   *fax* 0171-924 4456. *Contact:* Jane Hall. Offers an on-demand research service on a variety of subjects including current affairs, business, marketing, history, the arts, media and politics. Resources include range of cuttings amassed by the bureau since 1948.

Ken Jackson (1985), 30 The Boundary, Langton Green, Tunbridge Wells, Kent TN3 0YB   *tel* (01892) 545198. Copy-editing, proof-reading, indexing, particularly of technical, historical or religious MSS.

JG Editorial (1988), 54 Mount Street, Lincoln LN1 3JG   *tel* (01522) 549180   *fax* (01522) 575883. *Directors:* Janet Goss, Jenni Goss, John Goss. Independent critique service for fiction, general non-fiction (no poetry), and academic/business/professional books; rewriting/ghosting; word processing/presentation/keying (MSS or audio); project management; editorial reports; copy and disk editing (IBM and AppleMac); proof-reading. Design/indexing/PR by arrangement.

Hugh Lamb (1983), 10 The Crescent, Westmead Road, Sutton, Surrey SM1 4HU *tel* 0181-661 1936. Experienced journalist, proof-reader and anthologist offers proof-reading for publishers and typesetters; experienced in book, magazine and institution work.

Leeds Postcards (Northern Trading Co-operative Ltd) (1979), PO Box 84, Leeds, West Yorkshire LS1 4HT *tel* (0113) 246 8649 *fax* (0113) 243 6730. *Directors:* Richard Honey, Christine Hankinson, Alison Sheldon. Publishing, printing and distribution service for artists, campaigns and unions, specialising in postcards and greeting cards.

Library Research Agency (1974), Burberry, Devon Road, Salcombe, Devon TQ8 8HJ *tel* (01548 84) 2769. *Directors:* D.J. Langford MA, B. Langford. Research and information service for writers, journalists, artists, businessmen from libraries, archives, museums, record offices and newspapers in UK, USA and Europe. Sources may be in English, French, German, Russian, Serbo-Croat, Bulgarian, and translations made if required.

Miles Litvinoff (1984), 104 Doyle Gardens, London NW10 3SR *tel/fax* 0181-965 3427. Writer and editor on environment, human rights, development and history. Writing, editing, commissioning, co-authorship, rewriting, project management, editorial advice; especially environment, Third World, human rights, history and biography, social science, current affairs, popular science and natural history, education, young people's non-fiction.

Dr Kenneth Lysons MA. MEd. DPA. DMS. FCIS. FInstPS. FBIM (1986), Lathom, Scotchbarn Lane, Whiston, Nr Prescot, Merseyside L35 7JB *tel* 0151-426 5513. Company and institutional histories, support material for organisational management and supervisory training, house journals, research and reports service. Full secretarial support.

Duncan McAra (1988), 30 Craighall Crescent, Edinburgh EH6 4RZ *tel/fax* 0131-552 1558. Consultancy on all aspects of general trade publishing; editing; proof correction. Main subjects include art, architecture, archaeology, biography, film, military and travel.

McText (1986), Denmill, Tough, By Alford, Aberdeenshire AB33 8EP *tel/fax* (019755) 62582. *Partners:* K. and Duncan McArdle. Editing, copy-editing, proof-reading. Specialist interests: archaeology, equestrian.

Manuscript Appraisals (1984), 95 Bramble Road, Eastwood, Leigh-on-Sea, Essex SS9 5HA *tel* (01437) 563822. *Proprietor:* Raymond J. Price; *consultants:* N.L. Price MBIM, Mary Hunt. Independent appraisal of authors' MSS (fiction and non-fiction, but no poetry) with full editorial guidance and advice. In-house editing, copy-editing, rewriting and proof-reading if required. Interested in the work of new writers.

Marlinoak (1984), 22 Eve's Croft, Birmingham B32 3QL *tel/fax* 0121-475 6139. *Proprietors:* Alan L. Billing MIM, Hazel J. Billing JP. BA. DipEd. Preparation of scripts, plays, books, MSS service, ghostwriting, proof reading, research; also audio-transcription, word processing and full secretarial facilities.

M.C. Martinez (1988), 60 Oakwood Avenue, Southgate, London N14 6QL *tel* 0181-886 5829. *Partners:* Mary Martinez, Françoise Budd. Advice and evaluation of MSS; critical assessment of MSS specialising in fiction and children's books; full desktop publishing service; translation in French and Spanish. Possible change of address; please telephone first.

James Moore Associates (1975), 51 Firs Chase, West Mersea, Essex CO5 8NN *tel/fax* (01206) 382073. *Partners:* James Moore BCom, Inge Moore. Advisory/consultancy services, editing of MSS, proof-reading, translation from/into German, from French, Dutch, Spanish. Special subjects: educational (especially language courses), music, travel, sailing, ships and the sea.

Susan Moore Editorial Services (1994), 65 Albion Road, London N16 9PP *tel/fax* 0171-923 2480. Troubleshooting service for publishers, packagers and agents: co-authorship with specialists, ghostwriting, re-writing, translation fine tuning, re-drafting.

Morley Adams (1917), 20 Spectrum House, 32/34 Gordon House Road, London NW5 1LP *tel* 0171-284 1433   *fax* 0171-284 4494. *Editor:* Mike Hutchinson. Specialists in the production of crosswords and other puzzles, quizzes, etc.

Murder Files (1994), Marienau, Brimley Road, Bovey Tracey, Devon TQ13 9DH *tel* (01626) 833487   *fax* (01626) 835797. *Director:* Paul Williams. Crime writer and researcher specialising in UK murders. Holds information on thousands of well-known and not so well-known murders dating from 1400 and press cuttings on murder cases from 1920 to date.

Elizabeth Murray (1975), 3 Gower Mews Mansions, Gower Mews, London WC1E 6HR   *tel/fax* 0171-636 3761. Literary, biographical, historical, crime, military, cinema, genealogy research for authors, journalists, radio and television from UK, European and USA sources.

My Word! (1994), 19 King Edward Road, Rugby, Warwickshire CV21 2TA   *tel* (01788) 571294   *fax* (01788) 550957   *e-mail* 101457.1402@compuserve.com *Partners:* Roddie Grant, Janet Grant. Complete DTP service; word processing service either to hard copy or disk; editing, copy-editing and proof-reading. Work done includes books, magazines, theses and CVs.

Paul Nash (1979), Munday House, Aberdalgie, Perth PH2 0QB   *tel/fax* (01738) 621584. Indexer specialising in sciences, technology and environment, management and computer science. Winner of Library Association Wheatley Medal 1992/93.

Paul H. Niekirk (1976), 40 Rectory Avenue, High Wycombe, Bucks. HP13 6HW   *tel* (01494) 527200. Text editing for works of reference and professional and management publications, particularly texts on law; freelance writing; editorial consultancy and training; marketing consultancy and research.

Northern Writers Advisory Services (1986), 77 Marford Crescent, Sale, Cheshire M33 4DN   *tel* 0161-969 1573. *Proprietor:* Jill Groves. Offers word processing, copy-editing, proof-reading and desktop publishing to small publishers, societies and authors.

Northgate Training (1978), Scarborough House, 29 James Street West, Bath BA1 2BT   *tel* (01225) 339733   *fax* (01225) 429151. *Directors:* M.R. Lynch, J.M. Bayley. Writing and design of management games and training exercises. Specialists in distance and open learning training packages.

Oriental Languages Bureau, Lakshmi Building, Sir P. Mehta Road, Fort, Bombay 400001, India   *tel* 2661258/2665640   *telegraphic address* Orientclip   *fax* 2664598. *Proprietor:* Rajan K. Shah. Undertakes translations and printing in all Indian languages and a few foreign languages.

Ormrod Research Services (1982), Weeping Birch, Burwash, East Sussex TN19 7HG   *tel* (01435) 882541. Comprehensive research service; literary, historical, academic, biographical, commercial. Critical reading with report, editing, indexing, proof-reading, ghosting.

Oxprint Design (1974), Aristotle House, Aristotle Lane, Oxford OX2 6TR *tel* (01865) 512331 *fax* (01865) 512408. *Directors:* Per Saugman, John Webb (managing), Peter Lawrence BA(Hons), Andrew King (company secretary). Design, typesetting, editorial, illustrating scientific, educational and general books. Specialists in project management. Macintosh desktop and bureau facilities, computer aided design and illustration.

Pageant Publishing (1978), 1 Weir Gardens, Bridge Street, Pershore, Worcs. WR10 1AJ *tel* (01386) 561125 *fax* (01386) 561119. *Director:* Gillian Page. Consultancy on all aspects of academic publishing: publication of academic journals.

Pages Editorial & Publishing Services (1995), Ballencrieff Cottage, Ballencrieff Toll, Bathgate, West Lothian EH48 4LD *tel/fax* (01506) 632728. *Director:* Susan Coon. Editorial and production service of magazines/newspapers for companies or for commercial distribution; promotional literature; publishing service for authors wishing to self-publish.

Geoffrey D. Palmer (1987), 47 Burton Fields Road, Stamford Bridge, York YO4 1JJ *tel/fax* (01759) 372874. Editorial and production services, including STM and general copy-editing, artwork editing, proof-reading and indexing. Pre-press project management.

Roger Palmer Ltd (1993), 18 Maddox Street, London W1R 9PL *tel* 0171-499 8875 *fax* 0171-499 9580. *Director:* Roger Palmer; *senior consultant:* Stephen Aucutt. Drafts, advises on and negotiates all media contracts for publishers, agents, packagers, authors and others; undertakes contractual audits and devises contracts systems; provides advice on copyright and related issues; provides training and seminars. Special terms for members of the Society of Authors.

Penman Literary Service, Mark Sorrell, 185 Daws Heath Road, Benfleet, Essex SS7 2TF *tel* (01702) 557431. Advisory, editorial and typing service for authors. Rewriting, re-drafting, ghostwriting, proof-reading; critical assessment of MSS.

Phoenix 2 (1994), Lantern House, Lodge Drove, Woodfalls, Salisbury, Wilts SP5 2NH *tel* (01725) 512200 *fax* (01725) 511122. *Partners:* Bryan Walker, Amanda Walker. Writing, editing, sub-editing, typesetting and design of magazines, newsletters, journals, brochures and promotional literature. Specialist areas are business, tourism, social affairs and education.

Christopher Pick, 41 Chestnut Road, London SE27 9EZ *tel* 0181-761 2585 *fax* 0181-761 6388. Publications consultancy advice, project management, writing and editing for companies and private, public-sector and voluntary-sector organisations: e.g. training manuals, strategy documents, research reports, brochures, company histories. Author and editor of non-fiction books for all popular markets. Special interests: modern social and political history, travel, heritage and current affairs.

Picture Research Agency, Pat Hodgson, Jasmine Cottage, Spring Grove Road, Richmond, Surrey TW10 6EH *tel* 0181-940 5986. Illustrations found for books, films and television. Written research also undertaken particularly on historical subjects, including photographic and film history. Small picture library.

Reginald Piggott (1962), Decoy Lodge, Decoy Road, Potter Heigham, Norfolk NR29 5LX *tel* (01692) 670384. Cartographer to the University Presses and academic publishers in Britain and overseas. Maps and diagrams for academic and educational books.

PJ Typecraft (1990), 21 Kingsbury Road, St John's, Worcester WR2 4JH   *tel* (01905) 426393. *Partners:* P.M. Jones, J.L. Jones. Proof-reading and copy-editing, all subjects but specialising in science and mathematics; complete word processing and typesetting service, including design and page layout.

Keith Povey Editorial Services (1980), North Burrow, Bratton Clovelly, Oke-hampton, Devon EX20 4JJ   *tel* (01837) 871296   *fax* (01837) 871369. Copy-editing, indexing, proof-reading, publisher/author liaison. Partnership with T & A Typesetting Services, Suite 2, Tramway Offices, Mellor Street, Rochdale, Lancs. OL12 6AA   *tel* (01706) 861662   *fax* (01706) 861673. Specialist book-typesetting to CRC and negs, graphic design.

Victoria Ramsay (1981), Abbots Rest, Chilbolton, Stockbridge, Hants SO20 6BE   *tel* (01264) 860251   *fax* (01264) 860026. Freelance editing, copy-editing and proof-reading; non-fiction research and writing of promotional literature and pamphlets. Any non-scientific subject undertaken. Special interests: education, cookery, travel, Africa and Caribbean and works in translation.

Reading and Righting (Robert Lambolle Services) (1987), 618B Finchley Road, London NW11 7RR   *tel/fax* 0181-455 4564. MSS/script analysis and evaluation service: fiction, non-fiction, stage plays and screenplays; editorial services; one-to-one tutorials, creative writing courses, lectures and research.

S. Ribeiro Literary Services (1986), 42 West Heath Court, North End Road, London NW11 7RG   *tel* 0181-458 9082. Experienced editor and writing tutor. MSS appraisal, including notes, analysis, rewriting and editing. New writers welcome. Editing on disk, all systems. Guidance in submission to publishers. Specialities: fiction, autobiography, travel, poetry, rewriting. Also, creative writing tuition, by post or in person.

Rich Research (1978), 1 Bradby House, Carlton Hill, St John's Wood, London NW8 9XE   *tel/fax* 0171-624 7755. *Director:* Diane Rich. Speedy and innovative picture research service. Visuals found for all sectors of publishing and the media. Stock images, commissioned photography and artwork. Negotiation of rights and fees.

Anton Rippon Press Services, 20 Chain Lane, Mickleover, Derby DE3 5AJ   *tel* (01332) 512379/384235   *fax* (01332) 292755. Writer and researcher on historical, sociological and sporting topics. Features, programmes, brochures produced; ghost writing. Radio and film documentary scripts. Complete book production service available.

Vernon Robinson Editorial Services (1973), 114 Blinco Grove, Cambridge CB1 4TT   *tel* (01223) 244414. Copy-editing and proof-reading of all educational books, specialising in science, maths, engineering, economics, computer science, biology, etc. Also English correction of technical MSS translated into English for European publishers.

Roger Smithells Ltd, Editorial Services, Garth Cottage, 26 High Street, Buriton, Petersfield, Hants GU31 5RX   *tel* (01730) 262369   *fax* (01730) 260722. Journalistic specialists in everything relating to travel and holidays; newspaper and magazine articles; TV and radio scripts; compilers of travel books.

Sandhurst Editorial Consultants (1991), 36 Albion Road, Sandhurst, Camberley, Surrey GU17 8BP   *tel* (01252) 877645   *fax* (01252) 890508. *Partners:* Lionel Browne, Janet Browne. Specialists in technical, professional and reference work. Project management, editorial development, writing, ghosting, text processing, and general editorial consultancy.

Sandton Literary Agency (1982), PO Box 785799, Sandton 2146, South Africa   *tel* (011) 442-8624. *Directors:* J. Victoria Canning, M. Sutherland.

Evaluating, editing and/or indexing book MSS. Preparing reports, company histories, house journals, etc. Ghost writing and ghost painting. Critical but constructive advice to writers. Lecture agents. Please write or phone first.

Sarratt Information Services (1986), 68 St Andrews Road, Henley-on-Thames, Oxon RG9 1JE *tel* 0181-422 4384. *Directors:* D.M. Brandl MIInfSci, G.H. Kay BSc. CEng. MIChemE. MBCS. Research bibliographies compiled, references checked, indexes compiled. Specialists in bioengineering, bio materials and disability information research.

Science Unit, Rothay House, 6 Mayfield Road, Eastrea, Cambs. PE7 2AY *tel/fax* (01733) 350888. Independent scientific consultancy specialising in microscopical matters and new directions in science. Advises on programmes and publications in general scientific field. Activities are world-wide, with publications in many overseas and foreign-language editions.

SciText (1988), 18 Barton Close, Landrake, Saltash, Cornwall PL12 5BA *tel/fax* (01752) 851451. Dr Brian Gee. Proof-reading and editing in science, engineering and the history of science and technology; IBM compatible PC.

Scriptmate (1985), 20 Shepherd's Hill, London N6 5AH *tel/fax* 0181-341 7650. Ann Kritzinger. Reports and revision suggestions given on unpublished work in the fields of fiction, non-fiction and drama by freelance team of 46 specialist readers.

Mrs Ellen Seager, 3 Hereford Court, Hereford Road, Harrogate, North Yorkshire HG1 2PX *tel* (01423) 509770. Critical assessment of fiction and non-fiction work with helpful direction, tuition and advice; creative writing tutor; ghost writing; publishing and market information.

SeaStar Editorial Services, 10 Trinity Road, Rothwell, nr Kettering, Northants NN14 6HY *tel* (01536) 710129. *Proprietor:* Terry Scott. MSS revision and rewriting; compilation, keying-in for floppy disk, disk conversion; desktop publishing services; printer liaison.

Serpentine Editorial (1991), 50 Quaker's Hall Lane, Sevenoaks, Kent TN13 3TU *tel/fax* (01732) 457360. *Partners:* Molly Perham, Julian Rowe. Publishing service for children's books: editing, writing and re-writing, planning and management of complete projects to CRC; DTP on PC or Apple Mac. All subjects, but science a speciality.

SFEP – Society of Freelance Editors and Proofreaders; see page 611.

Joan Shannon – Freelance Services (1991), 41A Newal Road, Ballymoney, Co. Antrim, Northern Ireland BT53 6HB *tel* (012656) 62953 *fax* (012656) 65019. Writing, general, specialising in disability and geographical/historical in a Northern Ireland context. Full or part book production service, photography (mostly scenic/landscape), desktop design and word processing.

Christine Shuttleworth (1981), Flat 1, 25 St Stephen's Avenue, London W12 8JB *tel/fax* 0181-749 8797. Indexing (with MACREX program), copy-editing, proof-reading, non-technical translation from German. Registered Indexer and Council member, Society of Indexers; member, Society of Freelance Editors and Proofreaders, Translators' Association.

I.R. Sinclair (1984), Saltire, Livermere Road, Gt Barton, Bury St Edmunds, Suffolk IP31 2RZ *tel/fax* (01284) 788312 (please ring before faxing). Technical writing (electronics and computing). Typesetting to CRC, particularly mathematical setting.

Small Print (1986), The Old School House, 74 High Street, Swavesey, Cambridge CB4 5QU *tel* (01954) 231713 *fax* (01954) 232777 *e-mail* info @smallprt.demon.co.uk *Proprietor:* Naomi Laredo. Editorial, project management, and audio production services, specialising in ELT and foreign language courses for secondary schools and home study; also phrase books, travel guides, general humanities. Translation from/to and editing in many European and Asian languages.

Robert and Jane Songhurst (1976), 3 Yew Tree Cottages, Grange Lane, Sandling, Nr Maidstone, Kent ME14 3BY   *tel* Maidstone (01622) 757635. Literary consultants, authors' works advised upon (fees by agreement), literary and historical research, feature writing, reviewing, editing, proof-reading.

Mrs Gene M. Spencer (1970), 63 Castle Street, Melbourne, Derbyshire DE73 1DY   *tel* (01332) 862133. Editing, copy-editing and proof-reading; feature writing; theatrical profiles; book reviews; freelance writing.

SPREd – Society of Picture Researchers and Editors; see page 384.

Strand Editorial Services (1974), 16 Mitchley View, South Croydon, Surrey CR2 9HQ   *tel/fax* 0181-657 1247. *Joint principals:* Derek and Irene Bradley. Provides a comprehensive service to publishers, editorial departments, and public relations and advertising agencies. Proof-reading a speciality.

Streetwise Town Plans Ltd, 3 Rayleigh Road, Basingstoke, Hants. RG21 1TJ   *tel* (01256) 28186. *Contacts:* P.J. Corcoran, Rosemary Corcoran. Top quality computer-generated maps of almost every town in Europe, plus major towns and cities throughout the world. All maps personalised to order.

Hans Tasiemka Archives (1950), 80 Temple Fortune Lane, London NW11 7TU   *tel* 0181-455 2485   *fax* 0181-455 0231. *Proprietor:* Mrs Edda Tasiemka. Comprehensive newspaper cuttings library from 1850s to the present day on all subjects for writers, publishers, picture researchers, film and TV companies.

Lyn M. Taylor (UK), 1 Eglinton Crescent, Edinburgh EH12 5DH   *tel* 0131-225 6152   *fax* 0131-467 6260. National comprehensive editorial service for publishers and printers: copy-editing and proof-reading in all subjects. Specialises in complex scientific and medical. Hard copy or disk.

Teamwork (1973), Unit 5, Spurlings Yard, Spurlings Road, Fareham PO17 6AB   *tel* (01329) 829135   *fax* (01329) 829136. *Proprietors:* Mrs D. Emmerson, N. Emmerson. Typesetting, paste-up, camera-ready artwork, design and preparation of books to print stage, illustration, proof-reading, indexing, general editing and research services.

Tecmedia Ltd (1972), Unit 4, The Courtyard, Whitwick Business Park, Stenson Road, Coalville LE67 4JP   *tel* (01530) 815800   *fax* (01530) 813452. *Managing director:* J.D. Baxter. Specialists in the design, development and production of mixed media training and information packages, newsletters and brochures.

Teral Research Services (1980), Alan C. Wood, 111 The Avenue, Bournemouth, Dorset BH9 2UX   *tel* (01202) 519220 and Terry C. Treadwell, 45 Forest View Road, Bournemouth, Dorset BH9 3BH   *tel/fax* (01202) 516834. Research and consultancy on military aviation, army, navy, defence, space, weapons (new and antique), police, intelligence, medals, uniforms and armour.

3 & 5 Promotion (1985), Crag House, Witherslack, Grange-over-Sands, Cumbria LA11 6RW   *tel* (015395) 52286   *fax* (015395) 52013   *e-mail* musicbks @rdooley.demon.co.uk *Proprietor:* Rosemary Dooley. Collaborative publishers' exhibitions: music and health care; advertising: music and dance.

John Vickers, 27 Shorrolds Road, London SW6 7TR   *tel* 0171-385 5774. Archives of British Theatre photographs by John Vickers, from 1938-1974.

Gordon R. Wainwright, 22 Hawes Court, Sunderland SR6 8NU   *tel/fax* 0191-548 9342. Criticism, advice and revision for publishers. Articles on education and training matters supplied to newspapers, journals and magazines. Training in report writing, rapid reading, effective meetings, etc. Lecture service. Consultancy service in all aspects of communication. Travel writing assignments undertaken.

Caroline White (1985), 78 Howard Road, Walthamstow, London E17 4SQ *tel/fax* 0181-521 5791. Research and writing of features for newspapers, magazines and radio, specialising in health and social issues. Corporate literature and reports. Written and spoken Italian, Spanish and French. Project management of illustrated books.

David Winpenny (1991), 17 Newlands Drive, York YO2 5PQ *tel/fax* (01904) 784616 *e-mail* 101456.1270@compuserve.com Writer and editor, including research and writing of features, news stories, brochures, speeches, advertising copy. Special interest in architectural history, the arts, music, landscape, heritage, business and the North.

Rita Winter Editorial Services (1988), 'Kilrubie', Eddleston, Peeblesshire, Scotland EH45 8QS *tel* (01721) 730353. Copy-editing and proof-reading (English and Dutch). Subjects: current affairs, sociology, philosophy, art, literature, education, theology, history, classics, African and European studies, general non-fiction. Special interests: reference works, dictionaries and art.

The Word Service (1994), Bob Gallagher, 143 Sirdar Road, Wood Green, London N22 6QS *tel* 0181-888 6962. Radio drama script analysis, evaluation and polishing; copy-editing and proof-reading; research, specialising in Irish history, literary lives and the history of psychiatry.

Wordwise (1990), 37 Elmthorpe Road, Wolvercote, Oxford OX2 8PA *tel* (01865) 510098 *fax* (01865) 310556. *Director:* Valerie Mendes. Provides a range of publishing services, including creative writing (particularly for children); editing; educational, arts and humanities and English Language Teaching publishing; report analysis and full project management.

Working Press (1987), 54 Sharsted Street, London SE17 3TN *tel* 0171-735 6221 *fax* 0171-582 7021. *Directors:* Stefan Szczelkun, Sarah Richardson, Howard Slater. Agency for self-publication by and support for working-class artists and cultural activists.

Richard M. Wright (1977), 32 Oak Village, London NW5 4QN *tel* 0171-284 4316. Indexing, copy-editing, specialising in politics, history, business, social sciences.

Write Line Critical Service (1988), 130 Morton Way, Southgate, London N14 7AL *tel* 0181-886 1329. Criticism and assessment of poetry and serious fiction (including short stories). Suggestions for revision/development of work, advice about publication outlets. Special interest: poetry. Enquiries by phone or write. Sae essential.

Write on. . . (1989), 62 Kiln Lane, Oxford OX3 8EY *tel* (01865) 61169. *Contact:* Yvonne Newman. Writing seminars and holiday workshops. Freelance Open Learning writing.

Writerlink (1984), Bolsover House, 5 Clipstone Street, London W1P 7EB *tel* 0171-323 4323 *fax* 0171-323 0286. *Director:* Charles Dawes; *chief reader:* Paul Usiskin. Expert individual reports made and issued to authors by a team of readers widely experienced in publishing.

The Writers Advice Centre for Children's Books (1994), Palace Wharf, Rainville Road, London W6 9HN *tel/fax* 0181-874 7347. *Directors:* Louise Jordan,

Nancy Smith, Jane Baker. Editorial and marketing advice to children's writers; training; reading and consultancy service for children's book publishers/agents.

The Writers' Exchange (1977), 14 Yewdale, Clifton Green, Swinton, Manchester M27 8GN *tel* 0161-281 0544. *Secretary:* Peter Collins. Copywriting, ghost-writing and editorial services, including appraisal service for amateur writers preparing to submit material to literary agents/publishers. Offers 'constructive, objective evaluation service, particularly for those who cannot get past the standard rejection slip barrier, or who have had work rejected by publishers and need an impartial view of why it did not sell'; fee £5 per 1000 words. Novels, short stories, film, TV, radio and stage plays. Send sae for details.

Hans Zell, Publishing Consultant (1987), 11 Richmond Road, PO Box 56, Oxford OX1 2SJ *tel* (01865) 511428 *fax* (01865) 311534. Consultancies, project evaluations, market assessments, feasibility studies, research and surveys, funding proposals, freelance editorial work, commissioning, journals man-agement, exhibition services. Specialises in services to publishers and the book community in Third World countries and provides specific expertise in these areas.

Plotting through the characters

Characters who are too easily manipulable tend to be puppets – 'cardboard' as editors and reviewers label them – and will not grip your readers or engage their sympathy. Treat them as suspect. They will be nothing but a liability.

To take an example: you have perhaps decided to tell of a girl placed by her parents in a convent. If she is docile, dedicated and with a strong sense of vocation, you will have a story lacking in drama, since the conflict is likely to be minimal. If, however, she is a strong character with a rebellious spirit, who has perhaps been committed against her inclination, as was often the case at certain periods in history (she may have refused to marry the man selected for her, or have nipped out and made her own arrangements with resultant loss of 'honour' and marriageability), then you have only to stand back and watch the sparks fly! The docile girl, on the other hand, will become more interesting if, having thought she was suited to the religious life, she discovers too late that she is not. In either case, the interest of the story will hinge, not on what you may have decided about her fate, but on what she brings upon herself.

from *Writing Historical Fiction* by Rhona Martin (A & C Black, £8.99).
See order form on page 690.

Classified Index of Editorial, Literary and Production Services

Addresses for editorial, literary and production services start on page 490.

Complete Editorial, Literary and Book Production Services

'A Feature Factory' Editorial
Services
Academic File
Linda Auld Associates
Book Production Consultants
Brittan Design Partnership
Central Office of Information
Karyn Claridge Book
Production

D & N Publishing
Global Syndications
Graham-Cameron Publishing
Grahame & Grahame
Northern Writers Advisory
Services
Oxprint Design
Christopher Pick

Keith Povey Editorial Services
Anton Rippon Press Services
Small Print
Teamwork
Rita Winter Editorial Services
Wordwise

Advisory and Consultancy Services, Critical Assessments, Reports

Academic File
Advice and Criticism Service
Archaeological Consultants
Arkst Publishing Ltd
Authors Appraisal Service
Authors' Advisory Service
Blair Services
Bookwatch Ltd
Calderbridge Associates
Ingrid Cranfield
Lewis Esson Publishing
FJN Associates
James Wilson Flegg
Geo Group & Associates
C.N. Gilmore
Heath Associates
Rosemary Horstmann
E.J. Hunter

Indexing Specialists
JG Editorial
Miles Litvinoff
Duncan McAra
Manuscript Appraisals
M.C. Martinez
James Moore Associates
Susan Moore Editorial
Services
Paul H. Niekirk
Pageant Publishing
Penman Literary Service
Christopher Pick
Reading and Righting
S. Ribeiro Literary Services
Sandhurst Editorial
Consultants
Sandton Literary Agency

Science Unit
Scriptmate
Mrs Ellen Seager
Robert and Jane Songhurst
Teral Research Services
Gordon R. Wainwright
Caroline White
Joan Wilkins Associates
The Word Service
Wordwise
Write Line Critical Service
Writerlink
The Writers Advice Centre for
Children's Books
The Writers' Exchange
Hans Zell, Publishing
Consultant

Editing, Copy-editing, Proof-reading

Abbey Writing Services
Alpha Word Power
Lucia Alvarez de Toledo
Anvil Editorial Associates
Arkst Publishing Ltd
Aspect
Linda Auld Associates
Authors' Advisory Service
Richard A. Beck
Beswick Writing Services
Black Ace Book Production
Blair Services
Brooke Publications Ltd
Mrs D. Buckmaster
John Button
Calderbridge Associates
Combrógos

Ingrid Cranfield
David A. Cross
Margaret Crush
Meg and Stephen Davies
DOLPHIN ECS
Rosemary Dooley
Editorial/Visual Research
Dr Martin Edwards
Lewis Esson Publishing
First Edition Translations Ltd
FJN Associates
James Wilson Flegg
Freelance Editorial Services
C.N. Gilmore
Guildford Reading Services
Bernard Hawton
Heath Associates

E.J. Hunter
Indexing Specialists
Ken Jackson
JG Editorial
Hugh Lamb
Miles Litvinoff
Duncan McAra
McText
Manuscript Appraisals
Marlinoak
James Moore Associates
My Word!
Paul H. Niekirk
Geoffrey D. Palmer
Penman Literary Service
Phoenix 2
Christopher Pick

PJ Typecraft
Victoria Ramsay
Reading and Righting
S. Ribeiro Literary Services
Vernon Robinson Editorial
  Services
Sandhurst Editorial
  Consultants
Sandton Literary Agency
SciText
SeaStar Editorial Services

Serpentine Editorial
Joan Shannon Freelance
  Services
Christine Shuttleworth
Small Print
Roger Smithells Ltd, Editorial
  Services
Robert and Jane Songhurst
Mrs Gene M. Spencer
Strand Editorial Services
Lyn M. Taylor (UK)

Gordon R. Wainwright
Caroline White
David Winpenny
Rita Winter Editorial Services
The Word Service
Wordwise
Richard M. Wright
The Writers' Exchange
Hans Zell, Publishing
  Consultant

Design, Typing, Word Processing, DTP, Book Production

'A Feature Factory' Editorial
  Services
Alpha Word Power
Arioma Editorial Services
Aspect
Auteursbureau
Ayrshire Business Services
Black Ace Book Production
Books-in-Hand Ltd
Calderbridge Associates
Cambridge Language Services
Vanessa Charles
DOLPHIN ECS
First Edition Translations Ltd

FJN Associates
Christine Foley Secretarial
  Services
Shelagh Furness
Heath Associates
Hurst Village Publishing
JG Editorial
Leeds Postcards
Marlinoak
M.C. Martinez
My Word!
Oriental Languages Bureau
Pageant Publishing

Pages Editorial & Publishing
  Services
Penman Literary Service
Phoenix 2
PJ Typecraft
Sandhurst Editorial
  Consultants
SeaStar Editorial Services
Serpentine Editorial
Joan Shannon Freelance
  Services
I.R. Sinclair
Tecmedia Ltd

Research and/or Writing, Rewriting, Picture Research

'A Feature Factory' Editorial
  Services
Abbey Writing Services
Lucia Alvarez de Toledo
Anvil Editorial Associates
Archaeological Consultants
Arioma Editorial Services
Arkst Publishing Ltd
Aspect
Linda Auld Associates
Authors' Research Services
Laraine Bamrah
Beswick Writing Services
Blair Services
Bookwatch Ltd
Brooke Publications Ltd
Causeway Resources
Combrógos
Ingrid Cranfield
David A. Cross
Margaret Crush
Andrew Duncan
Editorial/Visual Research
Dr Martin Edwards

Lewis Esson Publishing
First Edition Translations Ltd
James Wilson Flegg
Shelagh Furness
Geo Group & Associates
Global Syndications
Heath Associates
Antony Hemans
The Information Bureau
Library Research Agency
Miles Litvinoff
Kenneth Lysons
Manuscript Appraisals
Marlinoak
Susan Moore Editorial
  Services
Murder Files
Elizabeth Murray
Paul H. Niekirk
Ormrod Research Services
Penman Literary Service
Phoenix 2
Christopher Pick
Picture Research Agency

Victoria Ramsay
Rich Research
Anton Rippon Press Services
Sandhurst Editorial
  Consultants
Sandton Literary Agency
Sarratt Information Services
SeaStar Editorial Services
Serpentine Editorial
Joan Shannon Freelance
  Services
I.R. Sinclair
Roger Smithells Ltd, Editorial
  Services
Robert and Jane Songhurst
Mrs Gene M. Spencer
Teral Research Services
Caroline White
David Winpenny
The Word Service
The Writers' Exchange
Hans Zell, Publishing
  Consultant

Indexing

Archaeological Consultants
Linda Auld Associates
Richard A. Beck
Ingrid Cranfield
Meg and Stephen Davies
First Edition Translations Ltd

Freelance Editorial Services
Society of Indexers
Indexing Specialists
Ken Jackson
Paul Nash
Geoffrey D. Palmer

Sandton Literary Agency
Sarratt Information Services
Christine Shuttleworth
Richard M. Wright
The Writers' Exchange

Translations

Lucia Alvarez de Toledo
Auteursbureau
Laraine Bamrah
Central Office of Information
Ingrid Cranfield
DOLPHIN ECS

First Edition Translations Ltd
James Wilson Flegg
Freelance Editorial Services
Library Research Agency
M.C. Martinez

James Moore Associates
Oriental Languages Bureau
Christine Shuttleworth
Small Print
Caroline White

Specialist Services

Archives

Murder Files

Hans Tasiemka Archives

John Vickers

Cartography, artwork, cartoons, puzzles

Creative Comics
Morley Adams

Reginald Piggott
Streetwise Town Plans Ltd

Cassettes, visual aids

Geo Group & Associates

Small Print

Contracts and copyright services

Roger Palmer Ltd

Freelance employment agency

etr

Interpreting

First Edition Translations Ltd

Lecture agents

Holland-Ford Associates

Sandton Literary Agency

Media and publicity services

Central Office of Information

Freelance Press Services

3 & 5 Promotion

Multimedia

Working Press

Tuition, lectures, conference services

Authors' Advisory Service
Copywriting One-to-One
David A. Cross
Rosemary Horstmann
Northgate Training

Reading and Righting
S. Ribeiro Literary Services
Mrs Ellen Seager
Gordon R. Wainwright
Joan Wilkins Associates

Working Press
Write on . . .
The Writers Advice Centre for
  Children's Books

Voice overs, subtitles

Lucia Alvarez de Toledo
First Edition Translations Ltd

Indexing

INDEXES – DEFINITION AND FUNCTION

An index is a detailed key to the contents of a document, in contrast to a contents list, which gives only the titles of the parts into which the document is divided (chapters, for example).

Precisely, an index is 'A systematic arrangement of entries designed to enable users to locate information in a document'. The document may be a book, a series of books, an issue of a periodical, a run of several volumes of a periodical, an audiotape, a map, a film, a picture, a computer disk, an object, or any other information-carrying artefact in print or non-print form.

The objective of an index is to guide enquirers to information on given subjects in a document by providing the terms of their choice (single words, phrases, abbreviations, acronyms, dates, names, and so on) in an appropriately organised list which refers them to specific locations using page, column, section, frame, figure, table, paragraph, line or other appropriate numbers.

An index differs from a catalogue, which is a record of the documents held in a particular collection, such as a library; though a catalogue may require an index, for example to guide searchers from subject words to class numbers.

A document may have separate indexes for different classes of heading, so that personal names are distinguished from subjects, for example, or a single index in which all classes of heading are interfiled.

INDEXERS THE PEOPLE

An index compiler needs:

- the ability to analyse the text on behalf of a wide range of users who may want to locate information on a particular topic; scan the index to assess the scope of the book; find out how particular themes or ideas are developed; return to passages they remember reading
- a good knowledge of the subject matter
- the ability to devise suitable terms expressing the concepts in the text concisely and precisely
- the ability to organise the entries in the index in the most appropriate and retrievable fashion
- a passion for accuracy.

THE SOCIETY OF INDEXERS

The Society of Indexers is a non-profit organisation founded in 1957 and is the only autonomous professional body for indexers in the UK. It is affiliated with the American Society of Indexers, the Australian Society of Indexers and the Indexing and Abstracting Society of Canada, and has close ties with The Library Association and the Society of Freelance Editors and Proofreaders.

The main objectives of the Society are to promote all types of indexing standards and techniques and the role of indexers in the organisation of knowledge; to provide, promote and recognise facilities for both the initial and the further training of indexers; to establish criteria for assessing indexing standards; and to conduct research and publish guidance, ideas and information about indexing. It seeks to establish good relationships between indexers, librarians, publishers and authors both to advance good indexing and to improve the role and well-being of indexers.

Services to indexers. The Society publishes a learned journal *The Indexer*, a newsletter and *Occasional Papers in Indexing*. Meetings are held regularly on a wide range of subjects while local and special interest groups provide the chance for members to meet to discuss common interests. A weekend conference is held every two years. All levels of training are supported by regular workshops held at various venues throughout the country.

Professional competence is recognised in two stages by the Society. Accredited Indexers who have completed the open-learning course qualification (see Training in indexing below) have shown theoretical competence in indexing while Registered Indexers have proved their experience and competence in practical indexing through an assessment procedure and admission to the Register of Indexers. The services of Registered Indexers are actively promoted by the Society while all trained and experienced members have the opportunity of an annual entry in *Indexers Available*, a directory published by the Society and distributed without charge to over 1000 publishers to help them find an indexer.

The Society sets annually a minimum recommended indexing rate (£11.00 per hour in 1996) and provides advice on the business side of indexing to its members.

Services to publishers and authors. Anyone who commissions indexes needs to be certain of engaging a professional indexer working to the highest standards and able to meet deadlines.

Indexers Available only lists members of the Society and gives basic contact details (name, address, etc.) and subject specialisms. Those accepted for listing need to fall into the following categories: Registered Indexers who have had their competence in practical indexing recognised by the Society; Accredited Indexers who have passed the Society's tests of technical competence; and others who have successfully completed two other recognised training courses.

Advice on the selection of indexers is available from the Registrar, who may also be able to suggest names of professionals able to undertake related tasks such as thesaurus construction, terminology control or database indexing. The Registrar will also advise on relations with indexers.

The Society co-operates with The Library Association in the award of the Wheatley Medal for an outstanding index.

Training in indexing. The Society's course is based on the principle of open learning with Units, tutorial support and formal tests all available separately so that individuals can learn in their own way and at their own pace. The Units cover five core subjects and contain practical exercises and self-administered tests. Members of the Society receive a substantial discount on the cost although anyone can purchase the Units. Only members of the Society can apply for the formal tests or for tutorial support.

Further information on the Society may be obtained by writing to The Secretary, Society of Indexers, 38 Rochester Road, London NW1 9JJ. Enquiries from publishers and authors seeking to commission an indexer should be made to The Registrar on 0181-940 4771.

FURTHER READING

British Standards Institution, *Recommendations for the preparation of indexes to books, periodicals and other documents*, BSI, 1988 (BS3700:1988)

British Standards Institution, *British Standard recommendations for examining documents, determining their subjects and selecting indexing terms*, BSI, 1984 (BS6529:1984)

Translation

The role of the translator in enabling books, plays, etc. to pass beyond national frontiers is receiving growing recognition. In view of the general increase of activity in this field, it is not surprising that many people with writing ability and a knowledge of languages should think of adopting freelance translating as a full- or part-time occupation. Some advice may be usefully given to such would-be translators.

The first difficulty the beginner will encounter is the unwillingness of publishers to entrust a translation to anyone who has not already established a reputation for sound work. The least the publisher will demand before commissioning a translation is a fairly lengthy specimen of the applicant's work, even if unpublished. The publisher cannot be expected to pay for a specimen sent in by a translator seeking work. If, on the other hand, a publisher specifically asks for a lengthy specimen of a commissioned book the firm will usually pay for this specimen at the current rate. Perhaps the best way would-be translators can begin is to select some book of the type which they feel competent and anxious to translate, ascertain from the foreign author or publisher that the English-language rights are still free, translate a substantial section of the book and then submit the book and their specimen translation to an appropriate publisher. If they are extremely lucky, this may result in a commission to translate the book. More likely, however – since publishers are generally very well informed about foreign books likely to interest them and are rarely open to a chance introduction – the publisher will reject the book as such. But publishers who are favourably impressed may commission a translation of some other book of a similar nature which they already have in mind.

In this connection it is important to stress that translators should confine themselves to subjects of which they possess an expert knowledge. In the case of non-fiction, they may have to cope with technical expressions not to be found in the dictionary and disaster may ensue if they are not fully conversant with the subject. The translation of fiction, on the other hand, demands different skills (e.g. in the writing of dialogue) and translators would be wise to ask themselves whether they possess these skills before taking steps to secure work of this nature.

Having obtained a commission to translate a book, the translator will be faced with negotiating terms. These vary considerably from publisher to publisher but for the commoner languages the advance payment should range from £55.00 upwards per thousand words. Translators should be able to arrange that the advance is on account of a royalty of $2\frac{1}{2}\%$ and a small share of the proceeds from secondary uses such as paperback reprint and American rights. However, some publishers avoid paying royalties to the translator even after reducing the royalties they pay to the original author. In the past it was common practice for translators to assign their copyright to the publisher outright, but this is no longer the rule. Most reputable publishers will now sign agreements specifying the rights they require in the translation and leaving the copyright in the translator's hands.

Advice regarding contracts for full-length works, copyright, Public Lending Right and other matters may be obtained from the Translators Association of the Society of Authors (see page 632). Translators of technical and commercial material are catered for by the Institute of Translation and Interpreting (see page 631).

Annual or biennial prizes are awarded for translations from German, Italian and French (see page 637). There is also a prize for translations from Portuguese.

Government Offices and Public Services

Enquiries, accompanied by a stamped addressed envelope, should be sent to the Public Relations Officer.

Advertising Standards Authority, 2 Torrington Place, London WC1E 7HW *tel* 0171-580 5555 *fax* 0171-631 3051.

AEA Technology, Harwell, Didcot, Oxon OX11 0RA *tel* (01235) 821111 *telex* 83135 ATOMHA G *fax* (01235) 432916.

Agriculture, Fisheries and Food, Ministry of, 3-8 Whitehall Place, London SW1A 2HH *Helpline* (01645) 335577 *tel* 0171-270 3000 *fax* 0171-270 8125.

Arts Council of England, 14 Great Peter Street, London SW1P 3NQ *tel* 0171-333 0100 *Library/enquiry line* 0171-973 6517 *fax* 0171-973 6590. For full details, see page 596.

Arts Council of Northern Ireland, 185 Stranmillis Road, Belfast BT9 5DU *tel* (01232) 381591 *fax* (01232) 661715.

Arts Council of Wales, 9 Museum Place, Cardiff CF1 3NX *tel* (01222) 394711 *fax* (01222) 221447.

Australian High Commission, Australia House, Strand, London WC2B 4LA *tel* 0171-379 4334 *telex* 27565 *fax* 0171-240 5333.

Austrian Embassy, 18 Belgrave Mews West, London SW1X 8HU *tel* 0171-235 3731 *telex* 28327 *fax* 0171-344 0292.

Bahamas High Commission, Bahamas House, 10 Chesterfield Street, London W1X 8AH *tel* 0171-408 4488 *telex* 892617 BAHREG G *fax* 0171-499 9937.

Bangladesh High Commission, 28 Queen's Gate, London SW7 5JA *tel* 0171-584 0081-4 *fax* 0171-225 2130.

The Bank of England, Threadneedle Street, London EC2R 8AH *tel* 0171-601 4444.

Barbados High Commission, 1 Great Russell Street, London WC1B 3JY *tel* 0171-631 4975 *fax* 0171-323 6872.

Royal Belgian Embassy, 103 Eaton Square, London SW1W 9AB *tel* 0171-470 3700 *telex* 22823 *fax* 0171-259 6213.

Bodleian Library, Oxford OX1 3BG *tel* (01865) 277000 *telex* 83656 *fax* (01865) 277182.

Bosnia-Hercegovina, Embassy of the Republic of, 40-41 Conduit Street, London W1R 9FB *tel* 0171-743 3758.

Botswana High Commission, 6 Stratford Place, London W1N 9AE *tel* 0171-499 0031.

British Broadcasting Corporation, Broadcasting House, London W1A 1AA *tel* 0171-580 4468.

British Coal, Hobart House, Grosvenor Place, London SW1X 7AE *tel* 0171-201 4141 *telex* 882161 CBHOB G *fax* 0171-201 4682.

The British Council, 10 Spring Gardens, London SW1A 2BN *tel* 0171-930 8466 *telex* 895220 BRICON G *fax* 0171-839 6347.

British Film Institute, 21 Stephen Street, London W1P 2LN *tel* 0171-255 1444 *telex* 27624 BFILDING *fax* 0171-436 7950.

The British Library, 96 Euston Road, London NW1 2DB   *tel* 0171-412 7111   *telex* 21462 BLREF G   *fax* 0171-412 7268.

British Library, Document Supply Centre, Boston Spa, Wetherby, West Yorkshire LS23 7BQ   *tel* Boston Spa (01937) 546000   *fax* (01937) 546333   *e-mail* dsc.customer.services@bl.uk

British Library Newspaper Library, Colindale Avenue, London NW9 5HE   *tel* 0171-412 7353   *fax* 0171-412 7379.

British Museum, Great Russell Street, London WC1B 3DG   *tel* 0171-636 1555   *fax* 0171-323 8118.

British Railways Board, Euston House, 24 Eversholt Street, PO Box 100, London NW1 1DZ   *tel* 0171-928 5151   *telex* 299431 BRHQLN G   *fax* 0171-922 6545.

British Standards Institution, Information Centre, 389 Chiswick High Road, Chiswick, London W4 4AL   *tel* 0181-996 7111   *fax* 0181-996 7048.

British Tourist Authority/English Tourist Board, Thames Tower, Black's Road, London W6 9EL   *tel* 0181-846 9000   *fax* 0181-563 0302.

The Broadcasting Complaints Commission, 7 The Sanctuary, London SW1P 3JS   *tel* 0171-233 0544   *fax* 0171-222 3172.

Broadcasting Standards Council, 7 The Sanctuary, London SW1P 3JS   *tel* 0171-233 0544   *fax* 0171-233 0397.

Bulgaria, Embassy of the Republic of, 186-188 Queen's Gate, London SW7 5HL   *tel* 0171-584 9400/9433, 0171-581 3144 (5 lines)   *fax* 0171-584 4948.

The Cabinet Office, 70 Whitehall, London SW1A 2AS   *tel* 0171-270 1234.

Cadw: Welsh Historic Monuments, Brunel House, 2 Fitzalan Road, Cardiff CF2 1UY   *tel* (01222) 500200   *fax* (01222) 500300.

Canadian High Commission, Cultural Affairs Section, MacDonald House, 1 Grosvenor Square, London W1X 0AB   *tel* 0171-258 6366   *fax* 0171-258 6322.

Central Office of Information, Hercules Road, London SE1 7DU   *tel* 0171-928 2345. In the UK conducts press, television, radio and poster advertising; produces booklets, leaflets, films, radio and television material, exhibitions and other visual material. It also prepares for publication by HMSO the annual *Britain: An Official Handbook* and the Aspects of Britain series of factual books on British affairs. For the Foreign and Commonwealth Office, COI supplies British information posts overseas with press, radio and television material, publications and briefing material, films, exhibitions and display and reading-room material.

Central Statistical Office, now part of **National Statistics, Office for,** Great George Street, London SW1P 3AQ   *tel* 0171-270 6363/6364.

Centre for Information on Language Teaching and Research (CILT), 20 Bedfordbury, Covent Garden, London WC2N 4LB   *tel* 0171-379 5101   *fax* 0171-379 5082. Supports the work of all professionals concerned with language teaching and learning throughout the UK, across every sector and stage of education. Offers a full conference programme, plus *free* on-site INSET for teachers, a complete range of publications and the CILT Teaching Resources Library with extensive IT and AV facilities. CILT also provides a comprehensive information service and knowledge of research and developmental activity.

College of Arms (or Heralds' College), Queen Victoria Street, London EC4V 4BT   *tel* 0171-248 2762   *fax* 0171-248 6448.

The Commonwealth Institute, Kensington High Street, London W8 6NQ   *tel* 0171-603 4535   *fax* 0171-602 7374. For full details, see page 606.

Copyright Tribunal, Room 4/6, Hazlitt House, 45 Southampton Buildings, London WC2A 1AR   *tel* 0171-438 4776   *fax* 0171-438 4780.

Countryside Commission, John Dower House, Crescent Place, Cheltenham, Glos. GL50 3RA   *tel* (01242) 521381   *fax* (01242) 584270.

Court of the Lord Lyon, HM New Register House, Edinburgh EH1 3YT   *tel* 0131-556 7255   *fax* 0131-557 2148.

Crafts Council, 44a Pentonville Road, Islington, London N1 9BY   *tel* 0171-278 7700   *fax* 0171-837 6891. Exhibition Galleries, Picture Library, Reference Library, Information Centre, Shop, Education Workshop, Cafe.

Croatia, Embassy of the Republic of, 21 Conway Street, London W1P 5HL   *tel* 0171-387 2022   *fax* 0171-387 3289.

Cyprus High Commission, 93 Park Street, London W1Y 4ET   *tel* 0171-499 8272   *fax* 0171-491 0691

Czech Republic, Embassy of the, 26 Kensington Palace Gardens, London W8 4QY   *tel* 0171-243 1115   *fax* 0171-727 9654.

Royal Danish Embassy, 55 Sloane Street, London SW1X 9SR   *tel* 0171-333 0200   *fax* 0171-333 0270.

Data Protection Registrar, Office of the, Wycliffe House, Water Lane, Wilmslow, Cheshire SK9 5AF   *tel (enquiries)* (01625) 545745   *(switchboard)* (01625) 545700   *fax* (01625) 524510.

Defence, Ministry of, Main Building, Whitehall, London SW1A 2HB   *tel* 0171-218 9000.

The Design Council, Haymarket House, 1 Oxendon Street, London SW1Y 4EE   *tel* 0171-208 2121   *fax* 0171-839 6033.

DTI: Department of Trade and Industry, 1 Victoria Street, London SW1H 0ET   *tel (general enquiries)* 0171-215 5000   *telex* 8813148 DTHQ G   *fax* 0171-222 2629   *Business in Europe* (0117) 944 4888   *The Innovation Enquiry Line* 0171-215 1217.

Economic and Social Research Council, Polaris House, North Star Avenue, Swindon, Wilts. SN2 1UJ   *tel* (01793) 413000   *fax* (01793) 413001.

Education and Employment, Department for, Sanctuary Buildings, Great Smith Street, London SW1P 3BT   *tel* 0171-925 5000 (main switchboard)   *public enquiries* 0171-925 5555.

Electricity Regulation Northern Ireland, Office of (OFFER NI), Brookmount Buildings, 42 Fountain Street, Belfast, Northern Ireland BT1 5EE   *tel* (01232) 311575   *fax* (01232) 311740.

Electricity Regulation, Office of, Hagley House, Hagley Road, Edgbaston, Birmingham B16 8QG   *tel* 0121-456 2100   *fax* 0121-456 4664.

Engineering and Physical Sciences Research Council, Polaris House, North Star Avenue, Swindon, Wilts. SN2 1ET   *tel* (01793) 444000   *fax* (01793) 444010.

English Heritage, 23 Savile Row, London W1X 1AB   *tel* 0171-973 3000   *fax* 0171-973 3001.

English Regional Arts Boards, 5 City Road, Winchester, Hants SO23 8SD   *tel* (01962) 851063   *fax* (01962) 842033. Representative body for the ten Regional Arts Boards in England; see page 625.

Environment, Department of the, 2 Marsham Street, London SW1P 3EB   *tel* 0171-276 3000.

Equal Opportunities Commission, Overseas House, Quay Street, Manchester M3 3HN   *tel* 0161-833 9244   *fax* 0161-835 1657.

The European Commission, Jean Monnet House, 8 Storey's Gate, London SW1P 3AT   *tel* 0171-973 1992   *fax* 0171-973 1907.

European Parliament, UK Office, 2 Queen Anne's Gate, London SW1H 9AA   *tel* 0171-227 4300   *fax* 0171-227 4302   *library fax* 0171-227 4301.

Fair Trading, Office of, Field House, 15-25 Bream's Buildings, London EC4A 1PR   *tel*   0171-242   2858   *fax*   0171-269   8800   *e-mail*   enquiries @oftuk.demon.co.uk

Finland, Embassy of, 38 Chesham Place, London SW1W 8HW   *tel* 0171-838 6200   *fax* 0171-235 3860 (general)/259 5602 (press and information).

Foreign and Commonwealth Office, King Charles Street, London SW1A 2AL   *tel* 0171-270 3000.

Forestry Commission, 231 Corstorphine Road, Edinburgh EH12 7AT   *tel* 0131-334 0303   *fax* 0131-334 4473.

French Embassy, 58 Knightsbridge, London SW1X 7JT   *tel* 0171-201 1000; *Cultural department:* 23 Cromwell Road, London SW7 2EL   *tel* 0171-838 2055.

Gambia High Commission, 57 Kensington Court, London W8 5DG   *tel* 0171-937 6316/7/8   *telex* 857911 GAMEXT G   *fax* 0171-937 9095.

Gas Supply, Office of, Stockley House, 130 Wilton Road, London SW1V 1LQ   *tel* 0171-828 0898   *fax* 0171-932 1600.

General Register Office, now part of the **National Statistics, Office for.**

Germany, Embassy of the Federal Republic of, 23 Belgrave Square, London SW1X 8PZ   *tel* 0171-824 1300   *fax* 0171-824 1435.

Ghana, High Commission for, 104 Highgate Hill, London N6 5HE   *tel* 0181-342 8686   *fax* 0181-342 8566.

Greece, Embassy of, Press and Information Office, 1A Holland Park, London W11 3TP   *tel* 0171-727 3071   *fax* 0171-727 8960.

Guyana High Commission, 3 Palace Court, Bayswater Road, London W2 4LP   *tel* 0171-229 7684   *fax* 0171-727 9809.

Hayward Gallery, Belvedere Road, London SE1 8XZ   *tel* 0171-928 3144   *fax* 0171-401 2664.

Health, Department of, Richmond House, 79 Whitehall, London SW1A 2NS   *tel* 0171-210 3000.

Historic Scotland, Longmore House, Salisbury Place, Edinburgh EH9 1SH   *tel* 0131-668 8600   *fax* 0131-668 8888.

HMSO Books, St Crispins, Duke Street, Norwich NR3 1PD. Enquiries: *tel* 0171-873 0011.

Home Office, Queen Anne's Gate, London SW1H 9AT   *tel* 0171-273 4000. *Communication directorate:* Director, communication: M.S.D. Granatt.

Housing Corporation, 149 Tottenham Court Road, London W1P 0BN   *tel* 0171-393 2000   *fax* 0171-393 2111.

Hungary, Embassy of the Republic of, 35 Eaton Place, London SW1X 8BY   *tel* 0171-235 4048/7191   *fax* 0171-823 1348.

Independent Television Commission, 33 Foley Street, London W1P 7LB   *tel* 0171-255 3000   *fax* 0171-306 7800.

India, High Commission of, Press & Information Wing, India House, Aldwych, London WC2B 4NA   *tel* 0171-836 8484 ext 147, 286, 327   *fax* 0171-836 4331.

Inland Revenue, Board of, Somerset House, London WC2R 1LB   *Library tel* 0171-438 6648   *fax* 0171-438 7562.

Ireland, Embassy of, 17 Grosvenor Place, London SW1X 7HR   *tel* 0171-235 2171   *fax* 0171-245 6961.

Israel, Embassy of, 2 Palace Green, Kensington, London W8 4QB   *tel* 0171-957 9500   *fax* 0171-957 9555.

Italian Embassy, 14 Three Kings Yard, Davies Street, London W1Y 2EH   *tel* 0171-312 2200   *fax* 0171-312 2230.

Jamaican High Commission, 1-2 Prince Consort Road, London SW7 2BZ   *tel* 0171-823 9911   *telex* 263304 JAMCOM G, 295510 JAMDEV G   *fax* 0171-589 5154.

Japan, Embassy of, 101-104 Piccadilly, London W1V 9FN   *tel* 0171-465 6500.

Kenya High Commission, 45 Portland Place, London W1N 4AS   *tel* 0171-636 2371   *telex* 262551   *fax* 0171-323 6717.

HM Land Registry, Lincoln's Inn Fields, London WC2A 3PH   *tel* 0171-917 8888   *fax* 0171-955 0110. *Head of information:* Eric Davies.

Law Commission, Conquest House, 37-38 John Street, Theobalds Road, London WC1N 2BQ   *tel* 0171-453 1220   *fax* 0171-453 1297. Covers England and Wales.

Law Commission, Scottish, 140 Causewayside, Edinburgh EH9 1PR   *tel* 0131-668 2131   *fax* 0131-662 4900.

The Legal Deposit Office, The British Library, Boston Spa, Wetherby, West Yorkshire LS23 7BY   *tel* (01937) 546267/546268   *fax* (01937) 546176.

Legal Services Ombudsman, Office of the, 22 Oxford Court, Oxford Street, Manchester M2 3WQ   *tel* 0161-236 9532   *fax* 0161-236 2651   *dx* 18569 MAN-CHESTER 7.

Lesotho, High Commission of the Kingdom of, 7 Chesham Place, Belgravia, London SW1 8HN   *tel* 0171-235 5686   *fax* 0171-235 5023.

London Museum—see Museum of London.

London Records Office, Corporation of, Guildhall, London EC2P 2EJ   *tel* 0171-332 1251   *fax* 0171-332 1119.

London Transport, 55 Broadway, London SW1H 0BD   *tel* 0171-222 5600 (administration), 0171-222 1234 (travel information)   *telex* 893633 LRTBDY G   *fax* 0171-222 5719.

Luxembourg, Embassy of, 27 Wilton Crescent, London SW1X 8SD   *tel* 0171-235 6961   *fax* 0171-235 9734.

Malawi High Commission, 33 Grosvenor Street, London W1X 0DE   *tel* 0171-491 4172/7   *telex* 263308   *fax* 0171-491 9916.

Malaysian High Commission, 45 Belgrave Square, London SW1X 8QT   *tel* 0171-235 8033   *telex* 262550   *fax* 0171-235 5161.

Malta High Commission, Malta House, 36-38 Piccadilly, London W1V 0PQ   *tel* 0171-292 4800   *fax* 0171-734 1831.

Mauritius, High Commission for the Republic of, 32-33 Elvaston Place, London SW7 5NW   *tel* 0171-581 0294/5   *fax* 0171-823 8437   *commercial section* 0171-225 3331   *fax* 0171-225 1580   *tourist information* 0171-584 3666   *fax* 0171-823 8437.

Medical Research Council, 20 Park Crescent, London W1N 4AL   *tel* 0171-636 5422   *fax* 0171-436 6179.

Monopolies and Mergers Commission, New Court, 48 Carey Street, London WC2A 2JT   *tel* 0171-324 1467/8   *fax* 0171-324 1400.

Museum of London, London Wall, London EC2Y 5HN   *tel* 0171-600 3699   *fax* 0171-600 1058. Comprises the collections of the London Museum and the Guildhall Museum.

Museum of Mankind (Ethnography Department of the British Museum), 6 Burlington Gardens, London W1X 2EX *tel* 0171-323 8043 (information)   *fax* 0171-323 8013.

Museum of the Moving Image, South Bank, Waterloo, London SE1 8XT   *tel* 0171-928 3535   *fax* 0171-815 1419.

National Audit Office, 157-197 Buckingham Palace Road, London SW1W 9SP   *tel* 0171-798 7000   *fax* 0171-828 3774   *e-mail* nao@gtnet.gov.uk; 22 Melville Street, Edinburgh EH3 7NS   *tel* 0131-244 2736   *fax* 0131-244 2721; Audit House, 23-24 Park Place, Cardiff CF1 3BA   *tel* (01222) 378661   *fax* (01222) 388415.

National Gallery, Trafalgar Square, London WC2N 5DN   *tel* 0171-839 3321   *general information tel* 0171-747 2885   *press office fax* 0171-930 4764.

National Maritime Museum, Greenwich, London SE10 9NF, including the Queen's House and the Old Royal Observatory   *tel* 0181-858 4422   *fax* 0181-312 6632.

National Savings, Department for, Marketing Division, Charles House, 375 Kensington High Street, London W14 8SD   *tel* 0171-605 9300   *fax* 0171-605 9432/9481.

National Statistics, Office for, St Catherine's House, 10 Kingsway, London WC2B 6JP   *tel* 0171-242 0262   *fax* 0171-396 2369.

The National Trust for Scotland, 5 Charlotte Square, Edinburgh EH2 4DU   *tel* 0131-226 5922   *fax* 0131-243 9501.

Natural Environment Research Council, Polaris House, North Star Avenue, Swindon, Wilts. SN2 1EU   *tel* (01793) 411500   *fax* (01793) 411501.

The Natural History Museum, Cromwell Road, London SW7 5BD   *tel* 0171-938 9123   *fax* 0171-938 8754.

Royal Netherlands Embassy, 38 Hyde Park Gate, London SW7 5DP   *tel* 0171-584 5040   *fax* 0171-581 3450; press and cultural affairs   *fax* 0171-581 0053.

New Zealand High Commission, New Zealand House, Haymarket, London SW1Y 4TQ   *tel* 0171-930 8422   *telex* 24368   *fax* 0171-839 4580.

Nigeria High Commission, Nigeria House, 9 Northumberland Avenue, London WC2N 5BX   *tel* 0171-839 1244   *fax* 0171-839 8746.

Northern Ireland Office, Whitehall, London SW1A 2AZ   *tel* 0171-210 3000; also Stormont Castle, Belfast, Northern Ireland BT4 3ST   *tel* (01232) 520700.

Northern Ireland Tourist Board, 59 North Street, Belfast, Northern Ireland BT1 1NB   *tel* (01232) 231221   *fax* (01232) 240960.

Royal Norwegian Embassy, 25 Belgrave Square, London SW1X 8QD   *tel* 0171-235 7151   *fax* 0171-245 6993.

Oftel—see **Telecommunications, Office of.**

OFWAT—see **Water Services, Office of.**

Ordnance Survey, Romsey Road, Maybush, Southampton SO16 4GU *tel* (01703) 792000 *press officer tel* (01703) 792635 *fax* (01703) 792452.

Particle Physics and Astronomy Research Council, Polaris House, North Star Avenue, Swindon, Wilts. SN2 1SZ *tel* (01793) 442000 *fax* (01793) 442002 *e-mail* pr_pus@pparc.ac.uk

Patent Office: *General enquiries:* (designs, patents, trade marks), Cardiff Road, Newport, Gwent NP9 1RH *tel* (0645) 500505; *Copyright enquiries:* Industrial Property and Policy Directorate, The Patent Office, Hazlitt House, 45 Southampton Buildings, Chancery Lane, London WC2A 1AR *tel* 0171-438 4777.

Pensions Ombudsman, The, 11 Belgrave Road, London SW1V 1RB *tel* 0171-834 9144 *fax* 0171-821 0065.

PLR Office, Bayheath House, Prince Regent Street, Stockton-on-Tees, Cleveland TS18 1DF *tel* (01642) 604699 *fax* (01642) 615641. Address enquiries to the Registrar of Public Lending Right.

Poland, Embassy of the Republic of, 47 Portland Place, London W1N 4JH *tel* 0171-580 4324 *telex* 265691 *fax* 0171-323 4018; *Polish Cultural Institute:* 34 Portland Place, London W1N 4HQ *tel* 0171-636 6032 *fax* 0171-637 2190.

Police Complaints Authority, 10 Great George Street, London SW1P 3AE *tel* 0171-273 6450 *fax* 0171-273 6401.

Population Census and Surveys, Office of—now **National Statistics, Office for.**

Portuguese Embassy, 11 Belgrave Square, London SW1X 8PP *tel* 0171-235 5331 *fax* 0171-245 1287.

Post Office Headquarters, 5th Floor, 148 Old Street, London EC1V 9HQ *tel* 0171-490 2888.

Privy Council Office, Whitehall, London SW1A 2AT *tel* 0171-270 3000.

Public Record Office, *Records of Government Departments and central courts of law:* Ruskin Avenue, Kew, Richmond, Surrey TW9 4DU *tel* 0181-876 3444 *fax* 0181-878 8905.

Public Service, Office of (OPS), Horse Guards Road, London SW1P 3AL; 70 Whitehall, London SW1A 2AS *tel* 0171-270 1234.

Public Trust Office, Stewart House, 24 Kingsway, London WC2B 6JX *tel* 0171-269 7000 *fax* 0171-831 0060 *dx* 37965 Kingsway.

Racial Equality, Commission for, Elliot House, 10-12 Allington Street, London SW1E 5EH *tel* 0171-828 7022 *fax* 0171-931 0429.

The Radio Authority, Holbrook House, 14 Great Queen Street, Holborn, London WC2B 5DG *tel* 0171-430 2724 *fax* 0171-405 7062.

Regional Arts Boards—see **English Regional Arts Boards.**

Romania, Embassy of, 4 Palace Green, London W8 4QD *tel* 0171-937 9666 *telex* 22232 ROMCOM G *fax* 0171-937 8069.

Royal Commission on the Ancient and Historical Monuments of Scotland, John Sinclair House, 16 Bernard Terrace, Edinburgh EH8 9NX *tel* 0131-662 1456 *fax* 0131-662 1477/1499.

Royal Commission on the Ancient and Historical Monuments of Wales, Crown Building, Plas Crug, Aberystwyth, Dyfed SY23 1NJ *tel* (01970) 621200 *fax* (01970) 627701.

Royal Commission on Historical Manuscripts, Quality House, Quality Court, Chancery Lane, London WC2A 1HP   *tel* 0171-242 1198   *fax* 0171-831 3550   *e-mail* nra@hmc.gov.uk   *WWW* http://www.hmc.gov.uk

Royal Commission on the Historical Monuments of England, National Monuments Record Centre, Kemble Drive, Swindon, Wilts. SN2 2GZ   *tel* (01793) 414700   *fax* (01793) 414707.

Royal Fine Art Commission, 7 St James's Square, London SW1Y 4JU   *tel* 0171-839 6537   *fax* 0171-839 8475.

Royal Fine Art Commission for Scotland, 9 Atholl Crescent, Edinburgh EH3 8HA   *tel* 0131-229 1109   *fax* 0131-229 6031.

Royal Mint, Llantrisant, Pontyclun, Mid-Glamorgan CF72 8YT   *tel* Llantrisant (01443) 222111.

Royal National Theatre, South Bank, London SE1 9PX   *tel* 0171-928 2033   *fax* 0171-620 1197.

Russian Federation, Embassy of the, 13 Kensington Palace Gardens, London W8 4QX   *tel* 0171-229 3628   *fax* 0171-727 8625.

Science and Technology, Office of, Department of Trade and Industry, Albany House, Petty France, London SW1H 9ST   *tel* 0171-271 2000.

Science Museum, Exhibition Road, South Kensington, London SW7 2DD   *tel* 0171-938 8000   *fax* 0171-938 8118. *Enquiries: Information Desk* 0171-938 8080/8008; *Press Office tel* 0171-938 8188/8181   *fax* 0171-938 8112.

Scotland, National Galleries of: National Gallery of Scotland, The Mound, Edinburgh EH2 2EL; Scottish National Portrait Gallery, 1 Queen Street, Edinburgh EH2 1JD; Scottish National Gallery of Modern Art, Belford Road, Edinburgh EH4 3DR   *information tel* 0131-556 8921.

Scotland, National Library of, George IV Bridge, Edinburgh EH1 1EW   *tel* 0131-226 4531   *fax* 0131-220 6662.

Scottish Natural Heritage, 12 Hope Terrace, Edinburgh EH9 2AS   *tel* 0131-447 4784   *press office fax* 0131-446 2279.

The Scottish Office, Dover House, Whitehall, London SW1A 2AU   *tel* 0171-270 3000.

The Scottish Office Information Directorate, New St Andrew's House, Edinburgh EH1 3TG   *tel* 0131-244 1111; and Dover House, Whitehall, London SW1A 2AU   *tel* 0171-270 6744.

Scottish Record Office, HM General Register House, Edinburgh EH1 3YY   *tel* 0131-535 1314   *fax* 0131-535 1360.

Scottish Tourist Board, Thistle House, Beechwood Park North, Inverness IV2 3ED   *tel* (01463) 716996   *fax* (01463) 717299.

Serpentine Gallery, Kensington Gardens, London W2 3XA   *tel* 0171-402 6075/0343   *fax* 0171-402 4103   *recorded information* 0171-723 9072. International exhibitions of modern and contemporary art.

Seychelles High Commission, 2nd Floor, Eros House, 111 Baker Street, London W1M 1FE   *tel* 0171-224 1660   *fax* 0171-487 5756.

Sierra Leone High Commission, 33 Portland Place, London W1N 3AG   *tel* 0171-636 6483-5   *fax* 0171-323 3159.

Singapore High Commission, 9 Wilton Crescent, London SW1X 8SA   *tel* 0171-235 8315   *telex* 51-262564 SHCIUK G   *fax* 0171-245 6583.

Slovak Republic, Embassy of the, 25 Kensington Palace Gardens, London W8 4QY   *tel* 0171-243 0803   *fax* 0171-727 5824.

Slovenia, Embassy of, Suite One, Cavendish Court, 11-15 Wigmore Street, London W1H 9LA   *tel* 0171-495 7775   *fax* 0171-495 7776.

Social Security, Department of, Richmond House, 79 Whitehall, London SW1A 2NS   *tel* 0171-210 3000. Contact Benefits Agency Overseas Benefits Directorate (OBD) for a query about benefits being paid abroad, and Contributions Agency International Services (IS) for queries about writing abroad and paying National Insurance contributions. Both OBD and IS are at: Department of Social Security, Longbenton, Newcastle upon Tyne NE98 1YX   *tel* 0191-213 5000.

South Africa, Republic of, South African High Commission, South Africa House, Trafalgar Square, London WC2N 5DP   *tel* 0171-451 7299   *fax* 0171-451 7283/ 7284.

Spanish Embassy, 24 Belgrave Square, London SW1X 8QA   *tel* 0171-235 5555   *fax* 0171-259 5392.

Sri Lanka, High Commission of the Democratic Socialist Republic of, 13 Hyde Park Gardens, London W2 2LU   *tel* 0171-262 1841   *fax* 0171-262 7970.

Swaziland High Commission, 20 Buckingham Gate, London SW1E 6LB   *tel* 0171-630 6611   *telex* 28853   *fax* 0171-630 6564.

Sweden, Embassy of, 11 Montagu Place, London W1H 2AL   *tel* 0171-724 2101   *fax* 0171-724 4174   *cultural section fax* 0171-917 6477.

Swiss Embassy, 16-18 Montagu Place, London W1H 2BQ   *tel* 0171-723 0701   *telex* 28212 AMSWIS G   *fax* 0171-724 7001.

Tanzania High Commission, 43 Hertford Street, London W1Y 8DB   *tel* 0171-499 8951   *telex* 262504 TANLON G   *fax* 0171-491 9321.

Tate Gallery, Millbank, London SW1P 4RG   *tel* 0171-887 8000   *fax* 0171-887 8007; Albert Dock, Liverpool L3 4BB   *tel* 0151-709 3223; Porthmeor Beach, St Ives, Cornwall TR26 1TG   *tel* (01736) 796226.

Telecommunications, Office of, 50 Ludgate Hill, London EC4M 7JJ   *tel* 0171-634 8700   *fax* 0171-634 8943.

Theatre Museum, National Museum of the Performing Arts, 1E Tavistock Street, London WC2E 7PA   *tel* 0171-836 7891   *fax* 0171-836 5148. See page 365 for reprographic services.

Transport, Department of, 76 Marsham Street, London SW1P 4DR   *tel* 0171-271 5000.

HM Treasury, Parliament Street, London SW1P 3AG   *tel* 0171-270 3000   *fax* 0171-270 5653.

Trinidad and Tobago High Commission, 42 Belgrave Square, London SW1X 8NT   *tel* 0171-245 9351   *fax* 0171-823 1065.

Trinity House, Corporation of, Tower Hill, London EC3N 4DH   *tel* 0171-480 6601   *telex* 987526 NAVAID G   *fax* 0171-480 7662. The General Lighthouse Authority for England, Wales and the Channel Islands and a Deep Sea Pilotage Authority.

Turkish Embassy, 43 Belgrave Square, London SW1X 8PA   *tel* 0171-393 0202   *telex* 884236 TURKEL G   *fax* 0171-393 0066; *Turkish Tourist Office:* 170-173 Piccadilly, London W1V 9DD   *tel* 0171-629 7771   *fax* 0171-491 0773.

Uganda High Commission, Uganda House, 58-59 Trafalgar Square, London WC2N 5DX   *tel* 0171-839 5783   *fax* 0171-839 8925.

United States Embassy, 24 Grosvenor Square, London W1A 1AE   *tel* 0171-499 9000.

Victoria and Albert Museum, South Kensington, London SW7 2RL   *tel* 0171-938 8500   *fax* 0171-938 8379.

Vocational Qualifications, National Council for, 222 Euston Road, London NW1 2BZ   *tel* 0171-387 9898   *fax* 0171-387 0978.

Wales, The National Library of, Aberystwyth, Dyfed SY23 3BU   *tel* (01970) 623816   *fax* (01970) 615709.

Wales Tourist Board, Brunel House, 2 Fitzalan Road, Cardiff CF2 1UY   *tel* (01222) 499909   *fax* (01222) 485031.

Water Services, Office of (OFWAT), Centre City Tower, 7 Hill Street, Birmingham B5 4UA   *tel* 0121-625 1300   *fax* 0121-625 1400.

Wellington Museum, Apsley House, 149 Piccadilly, Hyde Park Corner, London W1V 9FA   *tel* 0171-499 5676   *fax* 0171-493 6576. Open Tues-Sun, 11.00-17.00.

Welsh Office, Gwydyr House, Whitehall, London SW1A 2ER   *tel* 0171-270 0565   *fax* 0171-270 0577; and Cathays Park, Cardiff, CF1 3NQ   *tel* (01222) 825111   *fax* (01222) 823807.

West India Committee (The Caribbean), Nelson House, 8/9 Northumberland Street, London WC2N 5RA   *tel* 0171-976 1493   *fax* 0171-976 1541.

Yugoslavia, Embassy of the Federal Republic of, 5-7 Lexham Gardens, London W8 5JJ   *tel* 0171-370 6105   *telex* 928542   *fax* 0171-370 3838.

Zambia High Commission, 2 Palace Gate, Kensington, London W8 5NG   *tel* 0171-589 6655   *telex* 263544   *fax* 0171-581 1353.

Zimbabwe, High Commission of the Republic of, Zimbabwe House, 429 Strand, London WC2R 0SA   *tel* 0171-836 7755.

The names and addresses of many other public bodies can be found in *Whitaker's Almanack.*

Structure

When you read a professionally written article you will leave it with several distinct impressions in your mind: those impressions are there because the writer arranged the arguments and points in a particular order. This order lends weight to some important paragraphs and allows others of less value space further on in the article. You, the reader, absorbed the result of clever paragraphing without even realising it existed: that is one proof of skilful structure planning. In the same way, arranging paragraphs in relation to each other also needs key sentences inserted at the most meaningful points, drawing attention to important aspects of your theme where you wish to make them.

from *Writing for Magazines* by Jill Dick (A & C Black, £9.99).
See order form on page 690.

Publishing practice

Publishing Agreements

MICHAEL LEGAT

Any author, presented with so complex a document as a publisher's agreement, should read it carefully before signing, making sure that every clause is understood, and not taking anything for granted. Bear in mind that there is no such thing as a standard form. A given publisher's 'standard' contract may not only differ substantially from those of other publishers, but will often vary from author to author and from book to book. Don't be fooled into believing that it is a standard form because it appears to have been printed – each agreement can be individually produced on a word processor to give exactly that effect.

MAKE SURE THE AGREEMENT IS FAIR AND REASONABLE

You should be able to rely on your agent, if you have one, to check the agreement for you, or – if you are a member – you can get it vetted by the Society of Authors or the Writers' Guild of Great Britain. But if you are on your own, you must either go to one of the solicitors who specialise in publishing business (probably expensive) or Do It Yourself. In the latter case it will help to compare the contract you have been offered, clause by clause, with a typical Minimum Terms Agreement such as those printed in my own books, *An Author's Guide to Publishing* and *Understanding Publishers' Contracts*.

THE MINIMUM TERMS AGREEMENT

The MTA, developed jointly by the Society of Authors and the Writers' Guild, is signed by a publisher on the one hand and the Society and the Guild on the other. It is not an agreement between a publisher and an individual author. It commits the publisher to offering his or her authors terms which are at least as good as those in the MTA. The intention is that only members of the Society and Guild should be eligible for this special treatment, but in practice publishers who sign the agreement tend to offer its terms to all their authors. There is no standard MTA, and most signatory publishers have insisted on certain variations in the agreement; nevertheless, the more important basic principles have always been accepted. It must be pointed out that the MTA does not usually apply to books in which illustrations take up 40 per cent or more of the space, to specialist works on the visual arts in which illustrations fill 25 per cent or more of the space, to books involving three or more participants in royalties, or to technical books, manuals and reference books.

Since its origins in 1980 comparatively few publishers have signed a Minimum Terms Agreement, although the signatories include several major publishing houses. Some publishers have refused, claiming to treat their authors quite well enough already, while others say that each author and each book is so different that standard terms cannot be laid down. Nonetheless, the MTA has been a resounding success. Almost all non-signatory publishers have adopted some or all of its provisions, and even in the case of the excluded books mentioned above, the terms have tended to improve. All authors can now argue, from a position of some strength, that their own agreements should meet the MTA's standards.

THE PROVISIONS OF THE MTA

The MTA is a royalty agreement (usually the most satisfactory form for an author), and it lays down the minimum acceptable royalties on sales, and the levels at which the rate should rise. These royalties are expressed as percentages of the book's retail price, but can easily be adjusted to apply to royalties based on price received, a system to which a number of publishers are changing, increasing the percentages so that the author's earnings are not adversely affected. The MTA also covers the size of the advance (calculated in accordance with the expected initial print quantity and retail price), and recommended splits between publisher and author of moneys from the sale of subsidiary rights (including US and translation rights). However, it is not by any means concerned solely with money, but with fairness to the author in all clauses of a publishing agreement, special attention being paid to provisions designed to make the author/publisher relationship more of a partnership than it has often been in the past. While recognising the publisher's right to take final decisions on such matters as print quantity, publication date, retail price, jacket or cover design, wording of the blurb, promotion and publicity, and remaindering, the MTA insists that the author has a right to consultation (which should not be an empty formality, but should mean that serious consideration is given to his or her views), in all such cases. Also the author's approval must be sought for the sale of any subsidiary rights.

SOME ESSENTIAL CLAUSES IN A PUBLISHER'S AGREEMENT

Any publisher's agreement you sign should contain, in addition to acceptable financial terms, clauses covering the following points:

– clear definition of which rights you are licensing to the publisher. The publisher will normally require volume rights, but the agreement must specify whether such rights will apply in all languages (or perhaps only in English) and throughout the world (or only in an agreed list of territories). The duration of the publisher's licence should be spelt out; commonly this is for the period of copyright (previously the author's lifetime plus 50 years, but increased on 1 January 1996 to the author's lifetime plus 70 years upon implementation of 'the Term Directive' which harmonised copyright laws within the European Union), although some publishers now accept a shorter term. A list of those subsidiary rights of which control is granted to the publisher must be included (make sure that the splits of moneys earned from these rights are in accordance with, or approximate reasonably to, those in the MTA, especially in the currently growing areas of merchandising and electronic and multimedia publishing).
– commitment by the publisher to publication of the book by a specific date

(usually within a year or eighteen months from the delivery of the typescript). Avoid signing an agreement which is vague on this point, saying, for instance, only that the book will be published 'within a reasonable period'.

- confirmation that in all copies of the book the publisher will print a copyright notice in the author's name and a statement that the author has asserted his or her 'Right of Paternity' (the right to be identified as the author in future exploitation of the material in any form), and that a similar commitment will be required from any subsidiary licensee.
- clarification, if the book is to include a professionally prepared index or material the copyright of which does not belong to the author, of whether the author or the publisher will be responsible for the fees (or if costs are to be shared, in what proportions) and the clearance of permissions.
- acceptable accounting procedures. Most publishers divide the year into two six-month periods, accounting to the author, and paying any sums due, three months after the end of each period. Look askance at any less frequent accounting or longer delay after the royalty period. The publisher should also agree to pay the author the due share of any subsidiary moneys promptly on receipt, provided that the advance on the book has been earned.
- clear definition of the various conditions under which the agreement shall be terminated, with reversion of rights to the author.

CLAUSES TO QUESTION

You can question anything in a publisher's agreement before you sign it. Provided that you do so politely and are not just being difficult, the publisher should be prepared to answer every query, to explain, and where possible to meet your objections. Most publishing contracts are not designed to exploit the author unfairly, but you should watch out for the following points:

- it is unwise to accept a clause which allows the publisher to assign the rights in your book to another firm or person without your approval.
- the contract for a commissioned book often includes wording which alludes to the publisher's acceptance of the work, implying that there is no obligation to publish it if he or she deems it unacceptable. It may be understandable that the publisher wants an escape route in case the author turns in an inferior work, but he or she should be obliged to justify the rejection, and to give the author an opportunity to revise the work to bring it up to standard.
- some agreements prohibit the author from writing similar material for any other publisher. This may clearly affect the author's earning ability.
- don't agree to the publisher's right to edit your work without any requirement for him or her to obtain your approval of any changes made.
- while it is normal practice for an agreement to allow the publisher to pay a lower royalty on books which are sold at high trade discounts, the disappearance of the Net Book Agreement increases the likelihood of such sales, and you should therefore make sure the royalty rate on high discount sales is not unfairly low.
- the Society of Authors and the Writers' Guild are generally opposed to clauses giving the publisher the right to publish the author's next work, feeling that this privilege should be earned by the publisher's handling of the earlier book. If you accept an option clause, at least make sure that it leaves all terms for a future book to be agreed.

AGREEMENTS FOR JOINT AND MULTIPLE AUTHORSHIP

In the case of joint authorship (a work so written that the individual contributions of the authors cannot be readily separated), the first written agreement should be between the authors themselves, setting out the proportions in which any

moneys earned by the book will be split, specifying how the authors' responsibilities are to be shared, and especially laying down the procedure to be adopted
should the authors ever find themselves in dispute. The terms of any publishing
agreement which they sign (each author having an identical copy) should reflect
their joint understanding. The total earnings should not be less than would be
paid were the book by a single author, and the authors should have normal rights
of consultation.

In the case of multiple authorship (when the work of each contributor can be
clearly separated), each author is likely to have an individual contract, and may
not be aware of what terms are offered to the others involved. Because of the
possibility of disagreement between the authors, the publisher will probably offer
little in the way of consultation. All the individual author can do is to ensure that
the agreement appears to be fair in relation to the amount of work contributed,
and that the author's responsibilities indicated by the contract refer only to his
or her work.

OUTRIGHT SALE

As a general rule no author should agree to surrender his or her copyright to the
publisher, although this may be unavoidable in the case of a book with many
contributors, such as an encyclopaedia. Even then, give up your copyright with
great reluctance and only after an adequate explanation from the publisher of
why you should (and probably a substantial financial inducement). The agreement itself will probably be no more than a brief and unequivocal letter.

SUBSIDIES AND VANITY PUBLISHING

Few commercial publishers will be interested in publishing your book on a subsidy
basis (i.e. with a contribution from you towards costs), unless perhaps it is of a
serious, highly specialised nature, such as an academic monograph, when a
publisher who is well-established within that particular field will certainly behave
with probity and offer a fair contract. Vanity publishers, on the other hand, will
accept your book with enthusiasm, ask for 'a small contribution to production
costs' (which turns out to be a very substantial sum, not a penny of which you
are likely to see again), and will fail to achieve any sales for your book apart
from the copies which you yourself buy. If you want to put your own money into
the publication of your book, try self-publishing – you will be far better off than
going to a vanity house. How do you tell which are the vanity publishers? That's
easy – they're the ones who put advertisements in the papers saying things like,
'Authors Wanted!'. Regular publishers don't need to do that.

FURTHER READING

Clark, Charles (ed.), *Publishing Agreements: A Book of Precedents*, 4th edn,
    Butterworths, 1993 (5th edn, ready February 1997)
Flint, Michael F., *A User's Guide to Copyright*, 4th edn, Butterworths, 1995
Legat, Michael, *An Authors' Guide to Publishing*, 3rd edn, Robert Hale, 1991
Legat, Michael, *Understanding Publishers' Contracts*, Robert Hale, 1992
Unwin, Sir Stanley, *The Truth About Publishing*, 8th edn, Unwin Hyman, 1976,
    O.P.

Book Clubs

Artists' Choice (Quarterly), Artists' Choice Ltd, PO Box 3, Huntingdon, Cambs. PE18 0QX   *tel* (01832) 710201   *fax* (01832) 710488.

BCA, 87 Newman Street, London W1P 4EN   *tel* 0171-637 0341   *fax* 0171-291 3525.

Ancient & Medieval History Book Club	Home Computer Club
Arts Guild	The Literary Guild
Book of the Month Club	Military and Aviation Book Society
Children's Book of the Month Club	Music Direct
Classical Music Direct	Mystery & Thriller Guild
Executive World	The New Home & Garden Guild
Fantasy & SF	Quality Paperbacks Direct
History Guild	Railway Book Club
	World Books

Bookmarx Club (Quarterly), IS Books Ltd, 265 Seven Sisters Road, London N4 2DE   *tel* 0181-802 6145   *fax* 0181-802 3835.

Books for Children (Monthly), Time-Life UK, 4 Furzeground Way, Stockley Park, Middlesex UB11 1DP   *tel* 0181-606 3061   *fax* 0181-606 3099.

The Bookworm Club, Children's Club in Schools (6 p.a.), Heffers Booksellers, 20 Trinity Street, Cambridge CB2 3NG   *tel* (01223) 568650   *fax* (01223) 568591.

The British Psycho-Analytical Society Book Club (3 p.a.), The Institute of Psycho-Analysis, 63 New Cavendish Street, London W1M 7RD   *tel* 0171-580 4952   *fax* 0171-323 5312.

Cygnus Book Club (Monthly), PO Box 15, Llandeilo, Dyfed SA19 6YX   *tel* (01550) 777693/777701   *fax* (01550) 777569. Includes: psychology and self-help, diet, health and exercise, world religions, new economics and education, green issues, mythology, spirituality.

The Folio Society, 44 Eagle Street, London WC1R 4FS   *tel* 0171-400 4200   *fax* 0171-400 4242. *Showroom:* The Folio Gallery at Henry Sotheran, 2 Sackville Street, London W1X 1DD   *tel* 0171-629 6517.

Letterbox Library, Unit 2D, Leroy House, 436 Essex Road, London N1 3QP   *tel* 0171-226 1633   *fax* 0171-226 1768. Multicultural and non-sexist children's books. Quarterly catalogue and newsletter.

New Left Review Editions, 6 Meard Street, London W1V 3HR   *tel* 0171-734 8830   *fax* 0171-734 0059.

Poetry Book Society, Book House, 45 East Hill, London SW18 2QZ   *tel* 0181-870 8403   *fax* 0181-877 1615.

Pooh Corner Book Club, For all things Pooh, High Street, Hartfield, East Sussex TN7 4AE   *tel* (01892) 770453.

Readers Union Ltd, PO Box 6, Brunel House, Newton Abbot, Devon TQ12 2DW   *tel* (01626) 336424   *telex* 42904 BOOKS G   *fax* (01626) 664463/331374.

Country Sports Book Society	Gardeners Book Society
Craftsman Book Society	Needlecraft Book Society
Creative Living Book Club	Photographic Book Society
Equestrian Book Society	Ramblers and Climbers Book Society

The Red House Book Club (13 p.a.), Windrush Park, Witney, Oxon OX8 5YF   *tel* (01993) 771144   *fax* (01993) 776813.

The Red House School Book Club (2 per term), Windrush Park, Witney, Oxon OX8 5YF   *tel* (01993) 708225   *fax* (01993) 708159.

Scholastic Ltd, Villiers House, Clarendon Avenue, Leamington Spa, Warks. CV32 5PR   *tel* (01926) 887799   *fax* (01926) 883331.

The Softback Preview (Monthly), Time-Life UK, 4 Furzeground Way, Stockley Park, Middlesex UB11 1DP   *tel* 0181-606 3073   *fax* 0181-606 3099. *Publishing director:* Ms Chris Holifield.

The Women's Press Book Club (Quarterly), 34 Great Sutton Street, London EC1V 0DX   *tel* 0171-251 3007   *fax* 0171-608 1938.

'Right' and 'wrong' characters

'Wrong' characters are wallflowers at the party: they relate to no-one else, they don't spark off anybody, nobody wants to know their secrets (now that *defines* dull), and they suggest nothing interesting they can do either with or in opposition to the leading characters. If they are your leading characters, you're in trouble and must start again because you've gone wrong somewhere. This is fortunately a rare occurrence; far more commonly they are subsidiary characters and by their very uselessness declare their irrelevance to the story you're telling. Write them out.

'Right' characters are different, they sparkle with contradictions, they spark off all the other characters... Such characters are a joy and a pleasure and almost write the books they appear in. You collect them by living body and soul with your writing, thinking about your characters every moment that you can find, worrying at them like a dog at a bone for that last little scrap of interaction with the other characters and the reasons behind it. But beware, many 'overwritten' novels (a fatal description in editorial offices) result from the author's fascination with and pleasure in just such appealing characters; by all means write it all down but be prepared to murder your darlings ruthlessly if they hold up the forward momentum of the action.

You can't find out about the right and wrong characters without actually writing the story. It is impossible to find those characters you can or should do without except by creating them on paper at some considerable length. And, since they won't reveal themselves except in relevant action, you cannot do this in some dry description apart from the story you want to tell, you must do it in your novel. This is one advantage of the 'John Braine method' (see next chapter) of writing a complete first draft at high speed before coming back to refine character descriptions and plot outline prior to writing a completely new draft: all the dud characters can be eliminated in a draft you are already resigned to scrapping.

from *Writing a Thriller* by André Jute (A & C Black, £9.99).
See order form on page 690.

International Standard Book Numbering (ISBN)

The Standard Book Numbering (SBN) system was introduced in this country in 1967. It became the International Standard Book Numbering (ISBN) system three years later.

The overall administration of the international system is done from Berlin, by the International ISBN-Agentur, Staatsbibliothek Preussicher Kulturbesitz, Potsdamer Str 33, 10785 Berlin, Germany.

In this country the system is administered by the Standard Book Numbering Agency Ltd, 12 Dyott Street, London WC1A 1DF   *tel* 0171-420 6000   *fax* 0171-836 4342. The Agency was set up before the scheme became international, which is why that word does not appear in its title.

Over the years a number of misconceptions have grown up about ISBNs, and this article endeavours to put right some of these.

The Standard Book Numbering Agency gets a large number of telephone calls, many of which follow a common pattern. For instance:

Are they legal? Do we have to have them?

There is no legal requirement for a book to carry an ISBN. But it is useful to educational authorities, certain library suppliers, public libraries and some computer using distributors, and is now essential to booksellers using the tele-ordering system. The introduction of Public Lending Right has also made ISBNs of importance to authors.

I am about to publish a book. Must I deposit a copy with the ISBN Agency to obtain copyright?

No. Copyright is obtained by the simple act of publication. However, by law, a copy of every new book must be deposited at the Legal Deposit Office of the British Library, Boston Spa, Wetherby, West Yorkshire LS23 7BY. The Legal Deposit Office issues a receipt, and this has, in the past, proved useful when a dispute has arisen over the date of publication.

Titles deposited are catalogued by the British National Bibliography, which records ISBNs where available. Perhaps a confusion about copyright and ISBNs arises from this, but the ISBN, of itself, has nothing to do with copyright.

What are the fees for ISBNs?

No charge is made for the allocation of a publisher prefix. Publishers may ask the Agency to supply a computer print out of all the ISBNs available to the publisher, with check digits calculated. A small charge is made for this print out.

Are you a Government Department?

No. Our parent company pays taxes; we get no subsidy from anyone. In most other countries the costs *are* borne by the state, through the national library system which frequently administers the scheme overseas.

Do I need an ISBN for a Church Magazine?

No. But you may need an ISSN (International Standard Serial Number). These are obtainable from the UK National Serials Data Centre, The British Library, Boston Spa, Wetherby, West Yorkshire LS23 7BY.

Incidentally, a yearbook can have both an ISBN and an ISSN.

Should we have our own identifier? We do not consider ourselves within the English speaking group.

This comes from publishers with devolution in mind. Usually Welsh, less often Irish. The group system within the ISBN scheme is not quite so categoric as to be dictated by language considerations only. A group is defined as a 'language, geographic or other convenient area'. There is no strict logic applied, just pragmatism as to what is most *convenient* for trading purposes.

I want my book to reach as wide a market as possible. Should I have an ISBN?

The ISBN will not automatically sell a book. If the book, like that famous mousetrap, is a better one, the world will beat a path to its door. However, the ISBN will oil the wheels of distribution and it is therefore advisable to have one.

Will you supply an ISBN for a carton of assorted painting books?

No. In the words of the ISBN manual (available from the SBN agency at £4.50, cash with order), 'an ISBN identifies one title, or edition of a title, from one specific publisher, and is unique to that title or edition'. It is now additionally used to identify computer software and maps. It is not designed for a carton of assorted painting books.

How does a publisher get an ISBN?

If they have not had ISBNs before, publishers should contact the SBN Agency. Written answers are required to some basic questions.

Reproduced by kind permission of the Standard Book Numbering Agency Ltd.

The importance of age

Make particular note of birth dates so that, when writing, you can maintain consistency. This is particularly important when writing a story spanning a number of years, when it is essential that a character should remain at the right age throughout and not be, for instance, twenty-one at the start and thirty-one only five years later.

Noting birth dates will also help you to visualise their growth from childhood and through the progression of time. Even though you may not write of them retrospectively, or refer much to their childhood or youth, you will have a greater depth of feeling for them if you know exactly when they were born and what life was like throughout their formative years, all of which has inevitably left its mark on them.

from *Writing Popular Fiction* by Rona Randall (A & C Black, £7.99).
See order form on page 690.

Public Lending Right

Outline

Under the PLR system, payment is made from public funds to authors (writers, translators, illustrators and some editors/compilers) whose books are lent out from public libraries. Payment is made once a year, in February, and the amount authors receive is proportionate to the number of times (established from a sample) that their books were borrowed during the previous year (July to June).

The legislation

PLR was created, and its principles established, by the Public Lending Right Act 1979 (HMSO, 30p). The Act required the rules for the administration of PLR to be laid down by a scheme. That was done in the Public Lending Right Scheme 1982 (HMSO, £2.95), which includes details of transfer (assignment), transmission after death, renunciation, trusteeship, bankruptcy, etc. Amending orders made in 1983, 1984, 1988, 1989 and 1990 were consolidated in December 1990 (S.I. 2360, £3.90). Some further amendments affecting author eligibility came into effect in December 1991 (S.I. 2618, £1.00).

How the system works

From the applications he receives, the Registrar of PLR compiles a register of authors and books which is held on computer. A representative sample of book issues is recorded, consisting of all loans from selected public libraries. This is then multiplied in proportion to total library lending to produce, for each book, an estimate of its total annual loans throughout the country. Each year the computer compares the register with the estimated loans to discover how many loans are credited to each registered book for the calculation of PLR payments. The computer does this using code numbers – in most cases the ISBN printed in the book.

Parliament allocates a sum each year (£5,000,000 for 1996-97) for PLR. This Fund pays the administrative costs of PLR and reimburses local authorities for recording loans in the sample libraries. The remaining money is then divided by the total registered loan figure in order to work out how much can be paid for each estimated loan of a registered book.

Limits on payments

(1) *Bottom limit*. If all the registered interests in an author's books score so few loans that they would earn less than £1 in a year, no payment is due.
(2) *Top limit*. If the books of one registered author score so high that the author's PLR earnings for the year would exceed £6000, then only £6000 is paid. No author can earn more than £6000 in PLR in any one year.

Money that is not paid out because of these limits belongs to the Fund and increases the amounts paid that year to other authors.

The sample

The basic sample represents only public libraries (no academic, school, private or commercial libraries are included) and only loans made over the counter (not consultations of books on library premises). It follows that only those books which are loaned from public libraries can earn PLR and make an application worthwhile. However, the feasibility of extending PLR to reference books is currently under review.

The sample consists of the entire loans records for a year from libraries in thirty public library authorities spread through England, Scotland, Wales and Northern Ireland. Sample loans are about 4% of the national total. It is intended to change to a situation where all computerised sampling points in an authority contribute loans data ('multi-site' sampling). This change is being introduced gradually, and began in July 1991. The aim is to increase the sample without any significant increase in costs. In order to counteract sampling error, libraries in the sample change every two to three years. Loans are totalled every twelve months for the period 1 July to 30 June.

An author's entitlement to PLR depends, under the 1979 Act, on the loans accrued by his or her books in the sample. This figure is multiplied to produce regional and national estimated loans.

ISBNs

PLR depends on the use of code numbers to identify books lent and to correlate loans with entries on the register so that payment can be made. Principally the system uses the International Standard Book Number – the ISBN – which consists of ten digits and is usually printed with the publishing information on the back of the title page; it may also be on the back flap or back of the jacket or cover. Examples are: 0 10 541079 9 and 185036110x.

From July 1991 an ISBN was required for all new registrations. Different editions (for example, 1st, 2nd, hardcover, paperback, large print) of the same book have different ISBNs.

Authorship

In the PLR system the author of a book is the writer, illustrator, translator, compiler, editor or reviser. Authors must be named on the book's title page, or be able to prove authorship by some other means (e.g. receipt of royalties). The ownership of copyright (apart from crown copyright for which see below) has no bearing on PLR eligibility.

Co-authorship/illustrators

In the PLR system the authors of a book are those writers, translators, editors, compilers and illustrators as defined above. Authors must apply for registration before their books can earn PLR. There is no restriction on the number of authors who can register shares in any one book as long as they satisfy the eligibility criteria.

Applications from writers and/or illustrators

At least one must be eligible and they must jointly agree what share of PLR each will take. This agreement is necessary even if one or two are ineligible or do not wish to register for PLR. If they are not all eligible, those who are will receive a share(s) specified in the application. PLR can be any whole percentage. Illustrators and joint writers may only register more than 50% if justified by their actual contribution to the book. Detailed advice is available from the PLR office.

Applications from translators

Translators may apply, without reference to other authors, for a 30% fixed share (to be divided equally between joint translators).

Applications from editors and compilers

An editor or compiler may apply, either with others or without reference to them, to register a 20% share. Unless in receipt of royalties an editor must have written at least 10% of the book's contents or more than 10 pages of text in addition to normal editorial work. The share of joint editors/compilers is 20% in total to be divided equally. An application from an editor or compiler to register a greater percentage share must be accompanied by supporting documentary evidence of actual contribution.

Dead or missing co-authors

Where it is impossible to agree shares with a co-author because that person is dead or untraceable, then the surviving co-author or co-authors may submit an application without the dead or missing co-author, but must name the co-author and provide supporting evidence as to why that co-author has not agreed shares. The living co-author(s) will then be able to register a share in the book which will be 20% for the illustrator (or illustrators) and the residual percentage for the writer (or writers). If this percentage is to be divided between more than one writer or illustrator, then this will be in equal shares unless some other apportionment is requested and agreed by the Registrar.

Writers or illustrators may apply for a different percentage apportionment, and the Registrar will register different percentage shares if it is reasonable in relation to the authors' contribution to the particular book. Detailed advice and forms are available from the PLR Office.

The PLR Office keeps a file of missing authors (mostly illustrators) to help locate co-authors. Help is also available from publishers, the writers' organisations, and The Association of Illustrators, 1 Colville Place, London W1P 1HN.

Life and death

Authors can only be registered for PLR during their lifetime. However, for authors so registered, books can later be registered if first published within one year before their death or ten years afterwards. New versions of titles registered by the author can be registered posthumously.

Residential qualifications

Eligibility for PLR is restricted to authors who are resident in the United Kingdom or Germany. A resident in these countries (for PLR purposes) has his or her only or principal home there. The United Kingdom does not include the Channel Islands or the Isle of Man.

Eligible books

In the PLR system each separate edition of a book is registered and treated as a separate book.

A book is eligible for PLR registration provided that:
(1) it has an eligible author (or co-author);
(2) it is printed and bound (paperbacks counting as bound);
(3) copies of it have been put on sale (i.e. it is not a free handout and it has already been published);
(4) it is not a newspaper, magazine, journal or periodical;
(5) the authorship is personal (i.e. not a company or association) and the book is not crown copyright;
(6) it is not wholly or mainly a musical score;
(7) it has an ISBN.

Notification and payment

Every registered author receives from the Registrar an annual statement of estimated loans for each book and the PLR due.

SAMPLING ARRANGEMENTS

Libraries

To help minimise the unfairnesses that arise inevitably from a sampling system, the Scheme specifies the eight regions within which authorities and sampling points have to be designated and includes libraries of varying size. Part of the sample drops out by rotation each year to allow fresh libraries to be included.

The following library authorities have been designated for the year beginning 1 July 1996 (all are multi-site authorities). *Wales*: Clwyd/Denbighshire, Bridgend/Mid-Glamorgan, Newport; *Scotland*: Aberdeen, Angus, Edinburgh; *Northern Ireland*: W Education & Library Board, S Education & Library Board; *London*: Haringey, Kensington and Chelsea, Lewisham, Wandsworth; *Metropolitan Districts*: Kirklees, Liverpool, Manchester, Sandwell, Sunderland; *Counties S&E*: Berkshire, Cambridge, Hertfordshire, Northamptonshire, West Sussex; *Counties S&W*: Hereford & Worcester, Somerset, Staffordshire, Wiltshire; *Counties N*: Cumbria, Derbyshire, Leicestershire, West Yorkshire.

Participating local authorities are reimbursed on an actual cost basis for additional expenditure incurred in providing loans data to the PLR Office. The extra PLR work mostly consists of modifications to computer programs to accumulate data already held in the local authority computer and to produce a monthly magnetic tape to be sent to the PLR Office at Stockton-on-Tees.

SUMMARY OF THE THIRTEENTH YEAR'S RESULTS

Registration: authors

When registration closed for the thirteenth year (30 June 1995) the number of shares in books registered was 243,798 for 24,871 authors. This included 686 German authors.

Eligible loans

Of the 550.5 million estimated loans from UK libraries, 244 million belong to books on the PLR register. The loans credited to registered books – 44.3% of all library borrowings – qualify for payment. The remaining 55.7% of loans relate to books that are ineligible for various reasons, to books written by dead or foreign authors, and to books that have simply not been applied for.

Money and payments

PLR's administrative costs are deducted from the fund allocated to the Registrar annually by Parliament. Operating the Scheme this year cost £606,250 representing some 12.3% of the PLR fund. The Rate per Loan for 1995-96 remained at 2.00 pence and was calculated to distribute all the £4,329,750 available. The total of PLR distribution and costs is therefore the full £4,936,000 which the Government provided in 1995-96.

The numbers of authors in various payment categories are as follows:

		£
104	payments at	6,000 maximum
37	payments at	5,000-5,999
228	payments between	2,500-4,999
649	payments between	1,000-2,499
734	payments between	500-999
3,745	payments between	100-499
14,630	payments between	1-99
20,127	TOTAL	

There were also 4744 registered authors whose books earned them *nil* payment. As a result of the £6000 maximum payment rule some £544,290 became available for redistribution to other authors.

MOST BORROWED AUTHORS IN UK PUBLIC LIBRARIES

Based on PLR sample loans July 1994-June 1995. Includes all writers, both registered and unregistered, but not illustrators where the book has a separate writer. Writing names are used; pseudonyms have not been combined. (C) indicates a children's book author.

Authors with estimated loans over 1 million (5% of national loans)

Janet & Allan Ahlberg (C)	John Cunliffe (C)	Jack Higgins	Wilbur Smith
Enid Blyton (C)	Roald Dahl (C)	Ann M. Martin (C)	Danielle Steel
Agatha Christie	Dick Francis	Ellis Peters	Kate William (C)
Catherine Cookson	René Goscinny (C)	Ruth Rendell	

Authors with estimated loans over 500,000 (7% of national loans)

Jean & Gareth Adamson (C)	Josephine Cox	P.D. James	Claire Rayner
Ted Allbeury	Len Deighton	Penny Jordan	Miss Read
Virginia Andrews	Colin Dexter	Marie Joseph	Douglas Reeman
Evelyn Anthony	Elizabeth Ferrars	Carolyn Keene (C)	Tony Ross (C)
Jeffrey Archer	Colin Forbes	Lena Kennedy	Sidney Sheldon
Rev W. Awdry (C)	Helen Forrester	Stephen King	Mary Jane Staples
Tessa Barclay	Christine Marion Fraser	Dick King-Smith (C)	R.L. Stine (C)
Maeve Binchy	Iris Gower	Dean R. Koontz	Jessica Stirling
Emma Blair	James Herbert	Charlotte Lamb	Jamie Suzanne (C)
Barbara Taylor Bradford	Hergé (C)	Ed McBain	E.V. Thompson
Tony Bradman (C)	Georgette Heyer	Betty Neels	Joanna Trollope
John Burningham (C)	Eric Hill (C)	Pamela Oldfield (C)	Martin Waddell (C)
Mary Higgins Clark	Victoria Holt	Rosamunde Pilcher	Mary Wesley
Babette Cole (C)	Shirley Hughes (C)	Beatrix Potter (C)	Margaret Yorke
Bernard Cornwell	Pat Hutchins (C)	Terry Pratchett	

RECIPROCAL ARRANGEMENTS

In 1981-1982 reciprocal arrangements with West Germany were sought by British writers to help ensure that they did not lose the German PLR they had enjoyed since 1974. The German Scheme, although loan based, is very different in most other respects. Reciprocity was brought into effect in January 1985. Authors can apply for German PLR through the Authors' Licensing and Collecting Society. (Comparison of PLR schemes internationally and consideration of prospects for reciprocity are covered in *PLR in Practice*, John Sumsion, 2nd edn, 1991, £14.50 inc. UK postage, from the PLR Office.)

ADVISORY COMMITTEE

The PLR Advisory Committee advises the Secretary of State for National Heritage and the Registrar on matters concerning PLR. Its present chairman is Philip Ziegler.

FURTHER INFORMATION

PLR application forms, information and publications can be obtained from The Registrar, PLR Office, Bayheath House, Prince Regent Street, Stockton-on-Tees, Cleveland TS18 1DF   *tel* (01642) 604699   *fax* (01642) 615641. The Registrar publishes an Annual Review, obtainable from the PLR Office.

The Authors' Licensing and Collecting Society Ltd

ALCS was set up in 1977 to collect and distribute money to writers for payments which authors and other copyright holders are unable to collect individually.

ALCS is a company limited by guarantee (i.e. not having a share capital). It is run by members through a Council of Management on which the Society of Authors and Writers' Guild of Great Britain are represented.

ALCS is a member of CISAC (International Confederation of Authors and Composers Societies) and IFRRO (International Federation of Reprographic Rights Organisation) and through them maintains constant links with continental European and other overseas collecting societies.

ADMINISTRATION

The Council of Management has twelve members, all of whom are active writers. Four are elected by and from the Ordinary Members of ALCS, four are nominated by the Society of Authors and four by the Writers' Guild. The ALCS is served by the Secretary General and a small staff who manage the office and arrange the regular distributions.

POWER

On joining, members transfer to the Society the power to administer on their behalf specific rights which they are unable to exercise as individuals. Under the Society's constitution ALCS may administer (a) in the United Kingdom and the Republic of Ireland and (b) through its agreements in other Countries:

  lending right (not British PLR);
  reprographic (photocopying) right;
  cable transmission right;
  private recording right;
  off-air recording right;
  right of public reception of broadcasts;
  rental right;
  right of exploitation by electronic means or in electronic form.

Where such a right can be exercised by an individual, the Society does not normally intervene.

From time to time ALCS may add other rights by special Resolution of a General Meeting to reflect the development of technology.

DISTRIBUTIONS

Foreign PLR

ALCS makes annual distributions from the collecting society, VG WORT, in Germany. Further money is held in Germany on behalf of British writers who have not yet joined ALCS. Those eligible to receive German PLR through ALCS are:

  living British authors resident anywhere;
  heirs of British authors through successor membership;
  foreign writers resident in Britain.

Reprography

Set up in 1983 by ALCS together with the Publishers Licensing Society, the Copyright Licensing Agency (CLA) is now well-established and offers licences for reprography. ALCS is responsible for paying writers of books their share in any fees collected from such licences. (See the following article.)

Cable retransmission

ALCS collects fees for the cable retransmissions of the BBC television and radio signals in Belgium, The Netherlands and the Republic of Ireland, where it also collects fees for the retransmission of the ITV, C4 and S4C signals. ALCS also licenses and distributes fees for BBC World and BBC Prime and collects fees in other European countries for British writers whose works are cabled in neighbouring countries.

Educational off-air recording

ALCS is part of the Educational Recording Agency Ltd (ERA) set up to license educational establishments to record off-air under the provisions of the 1988 Copyright Act.

GENERAL

ALCS is represented on the British Copyright Council and the Secretary General is a member of the PLR Advisory Committee. ALCS maintains a watching brief on all matters affecting copyright both in Great Britain and abroad and is recognised internationally as expert on writers' collective rights. ALCS increasingly operates as a central international information exchange.

TO JOIN

The current subscription is £5.88 (incl. VAT), £5.00 for EC residents, £7.00 overseas. Application forms from: The Administration Manager, The Authors' Licensing and Collecting Society Ltd, 74 New Oxford Street, London WC1A 1EF   *tel* 0171-255 2034   *e-mail* alcs@alcs.co.uk

Members of the Society of Authors and the Writers' Guild have free membership of ALCS.

Tell it as it is

Encounters with creepy-crawlies, however unpleasant, shouldn't be omitted from your copy. Few places are perfect, and if a reader has a fear of spiders then obviously they would rather have advance warning. But things that creep, scud and scurry don't just occur in the jungles of this world. You are much more likely to be attacked by mosquitoes than by alligators in the Florida Everglades and I have encountered large land crabs scuttling around our hotel garden in Martinique. They – or their close relations – subsequently featured on the menu and, needless to say, in articles too.

from *Writing About Travel* by Morag Campbell (A & C Black, £7.99).
See order form on page 690.

The Copyright Licensing Agency Ltd (CLA)

The need to regulate copying
Over twenty years have passed since 1973, when interest groups in the UK started to prepare submissions to the government-appointed committee under the Hon. Mr Justice Whitford about ways of regulating copying from books, journals and periodicals. These interest groups, representing owners of copyright, were seeking both a mechanism of control and just recompense for authors and publishers while at the same time continuing to satisfy the reasonable demands of a modern information-driven society.

The CLA – what it is and what it does
When it was eventually published in 1977, the Whitford Report on Copyright and Designs Law suggested, as the best likely solution to the problem, a collective administration system for copying rights organised by the rightsholders themselves.

This recommendation spawned first the Wolfenden Committee that brought together representatives of authors' societies and publishers' associations, and then the de Freitas committee that hammered out and fashioned, with these two sometimes antagonistic groups, a mutually acceptable constitution for such a licensing body. The outcome was the formation of the Copyright Licensing Agency, CLA, in April 1982 and its incorporation in January 1983 as a non-profit making company limited by guarantee. The Agency, which is primarily concerned with licensing 'heavy user' groups, issued its first licence in May 1984.

CLA is 'owned' by the Authors' Licensing and Collecting Society (ALCS) and the Publishers Licensing Society (PLS) in that they are its members. ALCS's members are members of the Society of Authors (SoA) and the Writers' Guild of Great Britain (WGoGB) and several thousand individual members; and PLS's members are the Publishers Association (PA), the Periodical Publishers Association (PPA) and the Association of Learned and Professional Society Publishers (ALPSP). All are represented on CLA's board of twelve directors, six being ALCS nominations and six PLS nominations.

CLA has six main functions and these are:

- to obtain mandates from publishers and authors in association with ALCS and PLS
- to license users for copying extracts from books, journals and periodicals
- to collect fees from licensed users for such copying
- to implement a system of record-keeping sufficient to provide statistically acceptable information on which to calculate a fair apportionment of the distributable income
- to pay ALCS and PLS their correct shares of the distributable income and provide sufficient data to enable these societies to pay individual authors and publishers
- to institute such legal proceedings as may be necessary for the enforcement of the rights entrusted to the Agency

Licence to copy
CLA sees its principal licensing areas in the UK as being *education, government* and *industry*. Each of these broad categories has three or four sub-groups. In company with nearly all other Reprographic Rights Organisations (RROs) around the world, CLA started licensing in the general education sector. The first major development occurred in April 1986, when three-year voluntary

licensing agreements with the country's local education authorities (LEAs) came into effect; in April 1989 these licences were extended for a further three years; copying in all thirty thousand or so state colleges and schools is now covered by such licences. The Agency also licenses the independent education sector through its licensing scheme for independent schools.

With the general education sector (5 to 16 years) covered, CLA next turned its attention to higher and further education (HE & FE) and during 1989, after several years of negotiating, finalised arrangements whereby universities, polytechnics, independent colleges and language schools, etc. all became licensed from 1 January 1990. Three-year licences once again were agreed.

Having successfully negotiated the local education authority licences with a joint committee of representatives appointed by the Association of County Councils (ACC), the Association of Metropolitan Authorities (AMA) and the Convention of Scottish Local Authorities (CoSLA), CLA will try to license the non-LEA parts of local government in one fell swoop with a similar committee but expanded to include representatives of the Association of District Councils (ADC) and the Association of London Authorities (ALA).

It is the Agency's intention to deal with central government on a ministry by ministry basis, starting with the Department of Trade & Industry (DTI) as the sponsors of the Copyright, Designs and Patents Act 1988; the Department for Education (DfE), as educational institutions are already licensed; and the National Health Service (NHS) which, with 1.25 million employees, is the largest employer in Europe.

Public bodies, i.e. those organisations for which government ministers have some accountability (e.g. The British Council), may have to be dealt with in some non-collective manner.

Trade, industry, commerce and the professions present CLA with its greatest challenge because of their size and diversity. A first step has already been taken, however, with the setting up of a joint task force with the Confederation of British Industry (CBI). This CBI/CLA working party, chaired by an industrialist, is examining the best way or ways forward, concentrating initially on manufacturing industry, with particular emphasis on R&D-driven sectors such as pharmaceuticals, chemicals, engineering, electronics, aerospace and oil fuel.

Basically, CLA is a banking operation with legal overtones: it collects fees from licensed users in respect of acts of photocopying from books and serials and other copying such as microfiche printing and, after deducting its administration costs and any reserves or provisions the Board may decide, distributes the balance to ALCS and PLS for them to pay to authors and publishers.

CLA currently offers two basic services, that is, licences to copy, authorised by many individual owners of copyright, both of which offer the collective repertoire of copyright works mandated to CLA by those owners:

- a *collective user* service such as that made with the associations representing local education authorities for state colleges and schools
- a *transactional user* service for those institutions where a suitable representative organisation, such as an LEA, is unable or unwilling to provide the level of administrative support that a collective user scheme requires, e.g. implementation and supervision of a sampling system, single cheque payment, etc.

Both types of licence are valid for a specific period, usually two or three years.

Under a collective user arrangement the level of copying for a group of institutions is mutually agreed and a global fee set; this fee total is then apportioned by the organising body amongst its constituents and paid by them to CLA on presentation of the agency's invoice. With the transactional user scheme, fees are paid on a straight cost per copy-page basis; returns to CLA are made at regular, agreed intervals, and a self-billing system is used.

Who benefits?

Importantly, from the user community's standpoint, CLA indemnifies all licensees against any inadvertent infringement of copyright.

Right from the outset, the authors' representatives insisted first that writers should benefit individually and directly from the copying of their works and that the money should not go to authors' societies for 'social benefit' purposes, as is the case in some parts of the world. Secondly, they insisted that the individual authors' shares should be paid to them directly, and not through the accounting systems of their publishers.

Keeping records of copying

In order to fulfil these requirements CLA had to devise a title-based distribution system and a form of record-keeping suitable for a geographically spread, stratified and statistically sound sample of the licensees. Some form of itemised record-keeping, therefore, is necessary on the part of both categories of licence holders. With *collective user* licensing, a rotating sample of about 5% of institutions in each broad category is required to maintain records of their copying, which are returned to CLA at agreed intervals, where they are checked and analysed. *Transactional user* licensees are required to keep records of all their copying.

Controlled record-keeping is crucial to CLA because the statistical information extracted from these records of copying is used as the basis for making payments to copyright owners whose works have been copied.

Once a licence has been issued, it has been relatively simple, so far, to collect fees. It is quite another matter, however, to edit, process and analyse the returns of copying, and to calculate the correct amounts due to copyright owners.

On return to the Agency, the record-keeping forms, which are regarded and treated as strictly confidential documents, some of which are deemed to be personal data under the Data Protection Act 1984, are:

- checked by the licensing officer responsible to ensure that the conditions of the licence are being adhered to
- scrutinised by the data preparation department to validate the information being submitted, e.g. missing ISBN/ISSNs etc. are searched for
- keyed for computer analysis
- subjected to a final edit for data quality

The results are analysed and summaries produced showing pages copied, by ISBN/ISSN and by title, by author and by publisher. Apportionments are then calculated, statements produced and cheques drawn.

The existence of the International Standard Book Number (ISBN) and the International Standard Serial Number (ISSN) systems is a great benefit to CLA and makes the Agency's task that much easier than it would otherwise be.

Distribution of fees

The CLA Board decided that the first distribution to members would be £1.4 million (US$2.3 million) and would be paid in two parts: the first tranche of just over £500,000 in October 1987, and the balance of around £900,000 in March/April 1988. Thereafter, payments to rights owners would be made every six months. At the time of writing CLA has distributed over £40 million to members.

It must be emphasised that a CLA licence is not a carte blanche to copy without restrictions. The conditions are clearly set down and are required to be displayed alongside every copying machine within the control of the licensee. The wording of the notices may vary slightly depending on the category of the licensee, but the core message is always the same! CLA also produces various user guides for issue to employees, and there is a warning sticker that goes on top of machines to act as a reminder to copier users.

Reciprocal agreements with other countries

For CLA there is comfort in knowing that it is not alone in pioneering the collective administration of copying rights. Counterpart organisations to CLA now exist in nineteen other countries – Australia, Austria, Canada, Denmark, Finland, France, Germany, Iceland, Ireland, Italy, Japan, the Netherlands, New Zealand, Norway, South Africa, Spain, Sweden, Switzerland and the United States – nearly all of them in membership of IFRRO, the International Federation of Reproduction Rights Organisations. RROs are also presently being formed in Belgium and Israel.

Finally, the broader the repertoire an RRO can offer its licensees the better, and it is a priority of CLA to secure reciprocal agreements with counterpart organisations overseas, particularly those in English-speaking countries where UK books, journals and periodicals are being widely and extensively copied, and, equally, where much publishing in the English language takes place.

Administration

Critics of collecting societies say that they spend pounds to distribute pennies. From the start, this is a potential criticism of which the CLA directors were acutely conscious. As far back as November 1982 the board designate set down in its minutes that on no account were CLA's administration costs to exceed 20% of the fee income. The Agency has done much better than that: CLA's overhead is working out at about $12\frac{1}{2}\%$ of the fee income, and the Agency continually strives to reduce that level where possible. It is, however, in the business of handling large numbers of documents and processing a great deal of information, and to do so efficiently in this day and age a high degree of office automation is required and technological wizardry does not come cheap.

CLA's aim is to distribute as much as it can, as fast as it can, and as efficiently as it can. It believes that over £40 million, distributed between October 1987 and March 1995, speaks louder than any words, and demonstrates better than anything else the Agency's resolve to achieve its objectives.

Further information from The Secretary, The Copyright Licensing Agency Ltd, 90 Tottenham Court Road, London W1P 0LP *tel* 0171-436 5931 *fax* 0171-436 3986.

Copyright and libel

British Copyright Law

AMANDA L. MICHAELS MA
Barrister

INTRODUCTION

Copyright is a creature of statute. There have been a series of Copyright Acts over the years, gradually extending the scope of this area of the law so as to offer protection to the widening range of media used by writers and artists of all types.

On 1 August 1989, the Copyright Act 1956, previously the major Act in this field, was replaced by the Copyright, Designs and Patents Act 1988 ('the Act'). The Act restated the law of copyright, especially in so far as it related to the essentials of what may be protected as a copyright work and the nature of that protection. Section 172 of the Act in particular provided that mere changes of expression from the old law do not denote a substantive change in the law, whilst prior decisions may be referred to as an aid to the construction of the Act.

However, there was a good deal in the Act which was innovatory (see, for instance, the comments below on the new design right, and the repercussions upon infringement actions of section 51), as well as a number of provisions where one might well ask whether all that was intended was a change of expression from the old law, or whether a change of words implies a change of substance. Reference to Parliamentary debates as reported in Hansard may help to resolve such difficulties: see *Pepper* v. *Hart* [1993] AC 593.

Continuing effects of old law

There were complicated transitional provisions (in Schedule 1 to the Act) relating to pre-existing works and infringements, and reference will need to be made to these and to the old law for some years to come, as well as to numerous Orders in Council made under the Act. Users of this yearbook particularly need to note that forms of publishing and licensing agreements suitable for use under the old law will probably need revision in the light of the Act. In particular, old texts on the subject may not apply to new copyright works.

Further recent changes to the law

On 1 January 1996, further important changes were made to UK copyright law, upon the implementation of EC Directive 93/98 ('the Term Directive') by the Duration of Copyright and Rights in Performances Regulations 1995 (S.I. 1995 No. 3297). The Term Directive harmonised copyright laws throughout the European Union as to the period of copyright protection offered to various types of copyright work, with a view to avoiding distortions within the internal market. Rather than take away vested rights in any one state, the term was harmonised 'upwards' to meet the longest protection already offered in Germany. The end result is that the term of copyright in the UK and in some other countries has been extended from the 'life of the author plus 50 years' provided by the Berne Convention to life plus 70 years. Certain works may, as a result benefit from a 'revived' term of copyright protection in the UK and this may well make the task of deciding whether a work is still protected by copyright fraught with difficulty (see below). The Regulations also deal with what is to happen to a variety of existing rights (e.g. publishing contracts) in the works offered an extended term of protection.

In an article of this length, it is not possible to deal fully with all the changes in the law effected by the Act, nor indeed with all the complexities of this technical area of the law. The purpose of the article is rather to set out the basic principles of copyright protection, and to identify topics which may be of particular interest to readers of this yearbook.

WORKS CAPABLE OF COPYRIGHT PROTECTION

Copyright protection has always protected the *form* in which the artist/author has set out his or her inspiration, not the underlying idea. So, plots, artistic ideas, systems and themes cannot be protected by copyright. Whilst an idea remains no more than that, it can be protected only by the law relating to confidential information (contrast the cases of *Green* v. *Broadcasting Corp. of New Zealand* [1989] RPC 700: no copyright in 'format' of *Opportunity Knocks*, and *Fraser* v. *Thames TV Ltd* [1984] QB 44: plot of a projected TV series protected by law of confidence). The law of copyright prevents the copying of the material form in which the idea has been presented, or of a substantial part of it, measured in terms of quality, not quantity.

The Act therefore starts out, in section 1, by setting out a number of different categories of works which can be the subject of copyright protection. These are:

(a) original literary, dramatic, musical or artistic works,
(b) sound recordings, films, broadcasts or cable programmes, and
(c) typographical arrangements of published editions.

These works are further defined in sections 3 to 8. The definitions are not identical to those in the 1956 Act. A literary work, for instance, is defined as: 'any work, other than a dramatic or musical work, which is written, spoken or sung, and accordingly includes: (a) a table or compilation, and (b) a computer program.' A musical work means: 'a work consisting of music, exclusive of any words or action intended to be sung, spoken or performed with the music.' An artistic work means: '(a) a graphic work, photograph, sculpture or collage, irrespective of artistic quality, (b) a work of architecture being a building or model for a building, or (c) a work of artistic craftsmanship.'

The definitions of literary and musical works do not, however, contradict the basic rule that copyright protects the form (or the 'expression of the idea') and not the idea; works are not protected *before* being reduced into tangible form. Section 3 (2) specifically provides that no copyright shall subsist in a literary, musical or artistic work until it has been recorded in writing or otherwise.

On the other hand, all that is required to achieve copyright protection is to record the original work in any appropriate medium. Once that has been done, copyright will subsist in the work (assuming that the qualifying features set out below are present) without any formality of registration or otherwise. As long as the work is produced in some tangible form there is, for instance, no need for it to be published in any way for the protection to attach to it. (Please note, however, that although this lack of formality applies here and in most European countries, the law of the USA does differ – see article: **US Copyright**). The common idea that one must register a work at Stationers Hall, or send it to oneself or to, say, a bank, in a sealed envelope so as to obtain copyright protection is incorrect. All that this precaution may do is provide some proof in an infringement action (whether as plaintiff or defendant) of the date of creation and form of one's work.

ORIGINALITY

Section 1 provides that in order to gain copyright protection, literary, dramatic, artistic and musical works must be original. Similarly, there are provisions which exclude from copyright protection sound recordings or films which are mere copies of pre-existing sound recordings and films, broadcasts which infringe rights in another broadcast or cable programmes which consist of immediate retransmissions of broadcasts.

The test of originality may not be quite that expected by the layman. Just as the law protects the form, rather than the idea, originality relates to the 'expression of the thought', rather than to the thought itself. Thus, over a number of years, the courts have held that a work need not be original in the sense of showing innovative or cultural merit, but that it needs only to have been the product of skill and labour on the part of the author. This can be seen from various sections in the Act, for instance in the definition of certain artistic works, and in the fact that it offers copyright protection to works such as compilations (like football pools coupons or directories) and tables (including mathematical tables).

There may be considerable difficulty, at times, in deciding whether a work is of sufficient originality, or has original features, where there have been a series of similar designs or amendments of existing works. See *L.A. Gear Inc* v. *Hi-Tec Sports Plc* [1992] FSR 121. What is clear, though, is that merely making a 'slavish copy' of a drawing will not create an original work: see *Interlego AG* v. *Tyco Industries* [1989] AC 217.

On the other hand, 'works' comprising the titles of books or periodicals, or advertising slogans, which may have required a good deal of original thought, generally are not accorded copyright protection, because they are too short to be deemed literary works.

See, too, the limited protection given to drawings of a functional or engineering type in the sections on infringement and design right below.

QUALIFICATION

The Act is limited in its effects to the UK (and to colonies to which it may be extended by Order in Council). It is aimed primarily at protecting the works of British citizens, or works which were first published here. However, in line with the requirements of various international conventions to which the UK is a party, copyright protection in the UK is also accorded to the works of nationals of many foreign states which are also party to these conventions, as well as to works first published in those states, on a reciprocal basis.

The position is somewhat different where copyright in works of nationals of other member states of the European Union are concerned, as there is a principle of equal treatment which applies to copyright protection, so that protection must be offered to such works here: see *Phil Collins* v. *Imtrat Handelsgesellschaft mbH* (Case C92/92) [1993] 2 CMLR 773.

The importance of these rules mainly arises when one is trying to find out whether a pre-existing foreign work is protected by copyright here, for instance, if one wishes to make a film based upon a foreign novel. Within the confines of this article, all that can be said is that there have been numerous different Orders in Council regulating the position for most of the major countries of the world, including the other member states of the EU and the USA, and further Orders continue to be made, but that in every case it will be wise to check the position.

OWNERSHIP

The general rule is that a work will initially be owned by its author, the author being the creator of the work, or in the case of a film or sound recording, the person who makes the arrangements necessary for it to be made. The Term Directive (in common with certain other EC Directives) provided that the 'principal director' of a film shall be deemed to be its author or one of its authors.

One essential exception to the general rule is that the copyright in a work made by an employee in the course of his or her employment will belong to their employer, subject to any agreement to the contrary. However, this rule applies only to true employees, not to freelance designers, journalists, etc., and not even to nominally self-employed company directors. This obviously may lead to problems if the question of copyright ownership is not agreed (see discussion of assignments, below).

There can be joint authorship of a work where the work is produced by several people in such collaboration that the contribution of one is not distinct from the contribution of the other. Where two people collaborate to write a song, one producing the lyrics and the other the music, there will be two separate copyright works, the copyright in which will be owned by each of the authors separately. But where two people write a play, each rewriting what the other produces, there will be a joint work.

The importance of knowing whether the work is joint or not arises firstly in working out the duration of the copyright and secondly from the fact that joint works can only be exploited with the agreement of all the joint authors, so that all of them have to join in any licence, although each of them can sue for infringement without joining the other author(s) in the proceedings.

DURATION OF COPYRIGHT

As a result of the amendments brought into effect on 1 January 1996, copyright in literary, dramatic, musical or artistic works expires at the end of the period of 70 years from the end of the calendar year in which the author dies (new section 12(1)). Where there are joint authors (see ownership section above), then the 70 years runs from the year of the death of the last of them to die. If the author is unknown, there will be 70 years protection from the date the work was first made available to the public by being performed, etc.

The extended 70-year term also applies to films, and runs from the end of the calendar year in which the death occurs of the last to die of the principal director, the author of the screenplay, the author of the dialogue or the composer of any music especially created for the film (new section 13B). This could obviously be a nightmare to establish, and there are certain presumptions in section 66A which may help someone wishing to use material from an old film.

However, sound recordings are still protected by copyright for only 50 years from the year of making or release (new section 13A); similarly, broadcasts and cable programmes still get only 50 years protection. Computer generated works keep a 50-year term of protection.

The new longer term obviously applies without difficulty to works created after 1 January 1996. Nor is the extension of term especially hard to apply to works which were in copyright here on 31 December 1995, as the term will simply be extended for a further 20 years, and the owner of that extended copyright will be the person who owned it on 31 December 1995, unless that person had only a limited term of ownership, in which case the extra 20 years will be added on to the reversionary term (see paragraph 18 of the Regulations).

Where copyright had expired here, but the author died between 50 and 70 years ago, the position is more complicated. The Term Directive provided that if a work was protected by copyright anywhere in the European Union on 1 July 1995, then copyright protection should revive for it in any other state in which it had expired, until the end of the same 70-year period (this was given effect by paragraph 16(*d*) of the 1995 Regulations). This is not, unfortunately, simply a question of looking at the date of the author's death, since protection may not have been offered to a particular work even by Germany, the state offering the 70-year period of protection prior to the Directive, for other reasons, e.g. lack of originality according to German law. It might therefore be necessary to look at the position in the other states offering a longer term of protection, namely France and Spain.

Ownership of the revived term of copyright will belong to the person who was the owner of the copyright when the initial term expired, save that if that person died (or a company, etc., ceased to exist) before 1 January 1996, then the revived term will vest in the author or his personal representatives, and in the case of a film, in the principal director or his personal representatives (paragraph 19 of the Regulations).

The increased term offered to works of other EU nationals as a result of the Term Directive is *not* offered automatically to the nationals of other states, but will only apply where an equally long term is offered in their state of origin (new sub-sections 12(6), 13A(4) and 13B(7)).

Where acts are carried out in relation to such revived copyright works, pursuant to things done whilst they were in the public domain prior to such revival, certain protection from infringement is available (see paragraph 23 of the Regulations). A licence as of right may also be available, on giving notice and paying a royalty (see paragraph 24).

Finally, where one is dealing with a work made before the Act came into force, one needs to look at the law in force when it was made, as well as at the transitional provisions of the 1956 Act (for pre-1957 works) and/or of the Act (for pre-1989 works).

DEALING WITH COPYRIGHT WORKS: ASSIGNMENT AND LICENSING

As will be seen below, ownership of the copyright in a work confers upon the owner the exclusive right to deal with the work in a number of ways, and essentially stops all unauthorised exploitation of the work. Ownership of the copyright is capable of being separated from ownership of the material form in which the work is embodied, whether the transfer of the latter includes the former will depend upon the terms of any agreement or the circumstances. The sale of a copy of a book implies no sale of the copyright but a sale of a piece of sculpture might do so.

Copyright works can be exploited by their owners in two ways: the whole right in the work may be sold, with the owner retaining no interest in it (except, possibly, for payment by way of royalties); this is what is known as assignment. Alternatively, the owner may grant a licence to another to exploit the right, whilst retaining overall ownership. Agreements dealing with copyright should make it clear whether an assignment or a licence is being granted, and should clearly define the scope of any assignment or licence. The question of moral rights (see below) will also have to be considered by parties negotiating an assignment or licence.

An assignment must be in writing, signed by or on behalf of the assignor, but no other formality is required. One can make an assignment of future copyright (under section 91). Where the author of a projected work agrees in writing that he will assign the rights in a future work to another, the copyright vests in the assignee immediately upon the creation of the work, without further formalities. This facility may be used where works are commissioned from the author, as the specific provisions as to ownership of commissioned works which existed in the 1956 Act are not reproduced as such in the new Act, save in respect of works protected by the new design right (see below).

These rules do not, apparently, affect the common law as to beneficial interests in copyright. Essentially, where someone has been commissioned to create a work for another, in circumstances in which copyright will not vest automatically in the latter, and the court finds that it was the parties' mutual intention that the copyright should belong to the 'commissioner', it will hold that the 'commissioner' is the equitable or beneficial owner of the copyright, and the author will be obliged to assign the copyright to him. 'Commission' in this context means only to order a particular piece of work to be done: see *Apple Corps. Ltd.* v. *Cooper* [1993] FSR 286 (on the 1956 Act).

Licences do not need to take any form in particular, and may indeed be granted orally. However, an exclusive licence (i.e. one which excludes even the copyright owner himself from exploiting the work in the manner authorised by the licence) must be in writing, if the licensee is to enjoy rights in respect of infringements concurrent with those of the copyright owner.

Both assignments and licences can, and frequently do, split up the various rights contained within the copyright. So, for instance, a licence might be granted to one person to publish a novel in hardback and to another to publish in softback, a third person might be granted the film, television and video rights, and yet a fourth the right to translate the novel into other languages.

Assignments and licences may also confer rights according to territory, dividing the USA from the EU or different EU countries one from the other. Two comments must be made about this. Firstly, it must be appreciated that any such agreement would be dealing with a bundle of different national copyrights, as each country's law extends only to its own borders; each country's law on copyright protection, on licensing and on infringement may differ and will continue to do so even after the implementation of the Term Directive. Secondly, when seeking to divide rights between different territories of the EU there is a danger that one will infringe the competition rules of the EU (in the main Articles 30-36 and 85-86 of the Treaty of Rome). Professional advice should be taken to ensure that one is not in breach of these rules, which would render the parties liable to be fined, as well as making the agreement void in whole or in part.

Licences can also, of course, be of varying lengths. There is no need for a licence to be granted for the whole term of copyright; indeed this would be unusual, if not foolish. Well-drafted licences will provide for termination on breach, including the failure of the licensee to exploit the work properly, and on the bankruptcy or winding up of the licensee.

Copyright may be assigned by will, and where a bequest is given of an original document, etc. embodying an unpublished copyright work, the bequest will carry the copyright.

Any licence affecting a copyright work which subsisted on 31 December 1995 *and* was then for the full term of the copyright, shall continue to have effect during any extended term, subject to any agreement to the contrary (paragraph 21 of the Regulations).

INFRINGEMENT

Copyright is infringed by doing any of a number of specified acts in relation to the copyright work, without the authority of the owner. In all forms of infringement, it suffices if a substantial part of the original is used, and the question is one to be judged according to quality not quantity (see, e.g., *Ravenscroft* v. *Herbert* [1980] RPC 193). The form of infringement common to all forms of copyright works is that of copying. This means reproducing the work in any material form. It is important to note that primary infringement, such as copying, can be done innocently of any intention to infringe.

Infringement may occur where an existing work provides the inspiration for a later one, if copying results, e.g. by including edited extracts from a history book in a novel (*Ravenscroft* v. *Herbert*, see above) or using a photograph as the inspiration for a painting (*Baumann* v. *Fussell* [1978] RPC 485). Infringement will not necessarily be prevented merely by the application of significant new skill and labour by the infringer, nor by a change of medium.

In the case of a two-dimensional artistic work, reproduction can mean making a copy in three dimensions, and vice versa, although there is an important limitation on this general rule in section 51 of the Act, which provides that in the case of a 'design document or model' (defined as a record of a design of any aspect of the shape or configuration, internal or external, of the whole or part of an article, other than surface decoration) for something which is not itself an artistic work, it is no infringement to make an article to that design. This would appear to mean that whilst it would be an infringement to make an article from a design drawing for, say, a sculpture, it will not be an infringement of *copyright* to make a handbag from a copy of the design drawing therefor, or from a handbag which one has purchased. In order to protect such designs one will have to rely upon design right or upon a registered design (for both see below). However, under the transitional provisions, the right to rely upon copyright protection for any such designs made before the commencement of the new Act will continue until 1 August 1999 (see Schedule 1, para. 19) and see *Entec (Pollution Control) Ltd* v. *Abacus Mouldings* [1992] FSR 332.

Copying of a film, broadcast or cable programme can include making a copy of the whole or a substantial part of any image from it (see section 17(4)). This means that copying one frame of the film would be an infringement, as it was under the previous law (see *Spelling Goldberg Productions* v. *BPC* [1981] RPC 283).

Copying is generally proved by showing substantial similarities between the original and the alleged copy, plus an opportunity to copy. Surprisingly often, minor errors in the original are reproduced by an infringer.

Copying need not be direct, so that, for instance, where the copyright is in a fabric design, copying the material, without ever having seen the original drawing, will still be an infringement, as will 'reverse engineering' of industrial designs e.g. to make unlicensed spare parts (subject to any defence of implied licence: see *British Leyland Motor Corp* v. *Armstrong Patents Co Ltd* [1984] FSR 591).

Issuing copies of a work to the public when it has not previously been put into circulation in the UK is also an infringement of all types of work.

Other acts which may amount to an infringement depend upon the nature of the work. It will be an infringement of the copyright in a literary, dramatic or musical work to perform it in public, whether by live performance or by playing recordings. Similarly, it is an infringement of the copyright in a sound recording, film, broadcast or cable programme to play or show it in public.

One rather different form of infringement is to make an adaptation of a literary, dramatic or musical work. An adaptation includes, in the case of a literary work, a translation, in the case of a non-dramatic work, making a dramatic work of it, and in the case of a dramatic work, making a non-dramatic work of it. An adaptation of a musical work is a transcription or arrangement of it.

There are also a number of 'secondary' infringements. These consist not of making the infringing copies, but of dealing with them in some way. So, it is an infringement to import an infringing copy into the UK, and to possess in the course of business, or to sell, hire, offer for sale or hire, or distribute in the course of trade an infringing copy. However, none of these acts will be an infringement unless the alleged infringer knew or had reason to believe that the articles were infringing copies. Merely putting someone on notice of a dispute as to ownership of copyright will not, it seems, suffice to give him or her reason to believe in infringement for this purpose: *Hutchison Personal Communications* v. *Hook Advertising* [1995] FRS 365.

Other secondary infringements consist of permitting a place to be used for a public performance in which copyright is infringed and supplying apparatus to be used for infringing public performance, again, in each case, with safeguards for innocent acts.

EXCEPTIONS TO INFRINGEMENT

The Act provides a large number of exceptions to the rules on infringement, many of which are innovatory. They are far too numerous to be dealt with here in full, but they include: fair dealing with literary, dramatic, musical or artistic works for the purpose of research or private study; fair dealing for the purpose of criticism or review or reporting current events; incidental inclusion of a work in an artistic work, sound recording, film, broadcast or cable programme; various educational exceptions (see sections 32-36); various exceptions for libraries (see sections 37-44); various exceptions for public administration (see sections 45-50); dealing with a work where the author cannot be identified and the work seems likely to be out of copyright; public recitation, if accompanied by a sufficient acknowledgement; recording broadcasts or cable programmes at home for viewing at a more convenient time.

REMEDIES FOR INFRINGEMENT

The copyright owner has all the remedies offered to other owners of property. Usually the owner will want one or both of two things: firstly, to prevent the repetition or continuation of the infringement, and, secondly, compensation.

In almost all cases an injunction will be sought at trial, stopping the continuation of the infringement. A very useful remedy offered by the courts is the 'interlocutory injunction'. This is a form of interim relief, applied for at short notice, with a view to stopping damaging infringement at an early stage, without having to await the outcome of a full trial. Interlocutory injunctions are not always granted in copyright cases, but it is always worth considering the matter as soon as an infringement comes to notice, for delay in bringing an interlocutory application may be fatal to its success. Where an infringement is threatened, the courts will in appropriate cases make a 'quia timet' injunction to prevent the infringement ever taking place.

Financial compensation may be sought in one of two forms. Firstly, damages may be granted for infringement. These will usually be calculated upon evidence of the loss caused to the plaintiff, sometimes based upon loss of business, at others upon the basis of what would have been a proper licence fee had the defendant sought a licence for the acts complained of. Additional damages may be awarded in rare cases for flagrant infringements.

Damages will not be awarded for infringement where the infringer did not know, and had no reason to believe, that copyright subsisted in the work. This exception is of limited use to a defendant, though, in the usual situation where he had no actual knowledge of the copyright, but the work was of such a nature that he should have known that copyright would subsist in it.

The alternative to a claim for damages is a claim for an account of profits, that is, the profits made by the infringer by virtue of his illicit exploitation of the copyright. This is an equitable remedy, however, and is therefore discretionary.

A copyright owner may also apply for delivery up of infringing copies of his work (sections 99 and 113-15). Finally, there are various criminal offences relating to the making, importation, possession, sale, hire, distribution, etc. of infringing copies (see sections 107-110).

DESIGN RIGHT

Many industrial designs will now effectively be excluded from copyright protection, by reason of the provisions of section 51 of the Act, described above. Alternatively, they may have the term of their copyright protection limited to 25 years from first industrial exploitation, by section 52 of the Act. However, they may instead be protected by the new 'design right' created by sections 213-64 of the Act.

The protection of the new right will be given to original designs consisting of the shape or configuration (internal or external) of the whole or part of an article and not being merely 'surface decoration'. A design is not to be considered original if it was commonplace in the design field in question at the time of its creation. Nor will designs be protected if they consist of a method or principle of construction, or are dictated by the shape, etc. of an article to which the new article is to be connected or of which it is to form part, the so-called 'must-fit' and 'must-match' exclusions.

The new right will be granted to designs made by qualifying persons (in this part of the Act meaning UK and EU citizens or residents or others to whom the right may be extended) or commissioned by a qualifying person, or first marketed in the UK, another EU state or any other country to which the provision may be extended by Order in Council.

The design right lasts only 15 years from the end of the year in which it was first recorded or an article made to the design, or (if shorter) ten years from the end of the year in which articles made according to the design were first sold or hired out.

The designer will be the owner of the right, unless he or she made it in pursuance of a commission, in which case the commissioner will be the first owner of the right. The same rule applies as in copyright, that an employee's designs made in the course of his or her employment will belong to the employer.

The right given to the owner of a design right is the exclusive right to reproduce the design for commercial purposes. The rules as to assignments and licensing and as to infringement, both primary and secondary, are substantially similar to those described above in relation to copyright, as are the remedies available.

This new design right will co-exist with the scheme of registered designs of the *Registered Designs Act* 1949 (as amended by the Act), which provides a monopoly right renewable for up to 25 years in respect of designs which have been accepted on to a register. Registered designs must contain features which appeal to and are judged by the eye, unlike designs protected by the design right.

MORAL RIGHTS

Another new departure in the Act is the provision of 'moral rights', commonly known as the rights of 'paternity' and 'integrity'.

The right of 'paternity' is for the author of a copyright literary, dramatic, musical or artistic work, and the director of a copyright film, to be identified as the author/director in a number of different situations, largely whenever the work is published, performed or otherwise commercially exploited (section 77).

However, the right does not arise unless it has been 'asserted' by the author or director, by appropriate words in an assignment, or otherwise by an instrument in writing (section 78), or in the case of an artistic work by ensuring that the artist's name appears on the frame, etc. Writers should therefore aim to ensure that all copies of their works carry a clear assertion of their rights under this provision (see end).

There are exceptions to the right, in particular where the first ownership of the copyright vested in the author's or director's employer.

The right of 'integrity' is not to have one's work subjected to 'derogatory treatment'. This is defined as meaning an addition to, deletion from, alteration or adaptation of a work (save for a translation of a literary or dramatic work or an arrangement of a musical work involving no more than a change of key or register) which amounts to distortion or mutilation of the work or is otherwise prejudicial to the honour or reputation of the author/director.

Again, infringement of the right takes place when the maltreated work is published commercially or performed or exhibited in public. There are various exceptions set out in section 81 of the Act, in particular where the publication is in a newspaper, etc., and the work was made for inclusion therein or made available with the author's consent.

Where the copyright in the work vested first in the author's or director's employer, he has no right to 'integrity' unless he was identified at the time of the relevant act or was previously identified on published copies of the work.

These rights subsist for as long as the copyright in the work subsists.

A third moral right conferred by the Act is not to have a literary, dramatic, musical or artistic work falsely attributed to one as author, or to have a film falsely attributed to one as director, again where the work in question is published, publicly performed, etc. This right subsists until 20 years after a person's death.

None of these rights can be assigned during the person's lifetime, but all of them either pass on the person's death as directed by his will or fall into his residuary estate.

A fourth but rather different moral right is conferred by section 85. It gives a person who has commissioned the taking of photographs for private purposes a right to prevent copies of the work being issued to the public, etc.

The remedies for breach of these moral rights may again include damages and an injunction, although section 103(2) specifically foresees the granting of an injunction qualified by a right to the defendant to do the acts complained of, if subject to a suitable disclaimer.

Moral rights will be exercisable in relation to works in which the copyright has revived subject to any waiver or assertion of the right made before 1 January 1996 (see details as to who may exercise rights in paragraph 22 of the Regulations).

NOTICE

I, AMANDA LOUISE MICHAELS, hereby assert and give notice of my right under section 77 of the Copyright, Designs and Patents Act 1988 to be identified as the author of the foregoing article.

AMANDA MICHAELS

US Copyright

GAVIN McFARLANE LLM. PhD
Barrister at Titmuss Sainer Dechert

THE SYSTEM OF INTERNATIONAL COPYRIGHT

The international copyright conventions

There is no general principle of international copyright which provides a uniform code for the protection of right owners throughout the world. There are however two major international copyright conventions which lay down certain minimum standards for member states, in particular requiring member states to accord to right owners of other member states the same protection which is granted to their own nationals. One is the higher standard Berne Convention of 1886, the most recent revision of which was signed in Paris in 1971. The other is the Universal Copyright Convention signed in 1952 with lower minimum standards, and sponsored by Unesco. This also was most recently revised in Paris in 1971, jointly with the Berne Convention. To this latter Convention the United States has belonged since 1955. On 16 November 1988, the Government of the United States deposited its instrument of accession to the Paris Revision of the Berne Convention. The Convention entered into force as regards the United States on 1 March 1989. Together with certain new statutory provisions made in consequence of accession to Berne, this advances substantially the process of overhaul and modernisation of US copyright law which was begun in the 1970s.

Summary of the Universal Copyright Convention

(1) The fundamental intent is to accord reciprocally in each member state to nationals of all other member states the same protection as that member grants to its own nationals.
(2) The minimum term of protection is the life of the author and twenty-five years after his or her death (by contrast with the Berne Convention which demands a term of the life of the author and a post-mortem period of fifty years).
(3) Any national requirement as a condition of copyright of such formalities as deposit, registration, notice, payment, or manufacture or publication within that state shall be satisfied for all works first published outside its territory and of which the author is not one of its nationals if all copies bear the symbol © accompanied by the name of the copyright owner and the year of first publication.
(4) Publication for the purposes of the Universal Copyright Convention means the reproduction in tangible form and the general distribution to the public of copies of a work from which it can be read or otherwise visually perceived.
(5) The effect of American ratification of the Universal Copyright Convention on 16 September 1955 was to alter completely the nature of the protection granted by the United States to copyright works originating abroad. The previous policy of American domestic law had been extremely restrictive for foreign authors, particularly those writing in the English language. But in consequence of ratification American law was amended to exempt from many of these restrictions works published in other member states, or by nationals of other member states. Recent amendments have relaxed the position even further.

Effect on British copyright owners

The copyright statute of the United States having been brought into line with the requirements of the Universal Copyright Convention, compliance with the formalities required by American law is all that is needed to acquire protection for the work of a British author first published outside the United States. Even these formality requirements have been largely removed now that the United States has joined the Berne Convention, although caution is still required. The Berne Convention Implementation Act of 1988 makes statutory amendments to the way foreign works are now treated in US law. These are now inserted in the US codified law as Title 17 – The Copyright Act. 'Foreign works' are works having a country of origin other than the United States. The formalities which were for so long a considerable handicap for foreign copyright owners in the American system have now become optional, though not removed altogether. Indeed the new system provides incentives to encourage such foreign right owners to continue to comply with formalities on a voluntary basis.

SUMMARY OF UNITED STATES COPYRIGHT LAW

Introduction of new law

After many years of debate, the new Copyright Statute of the United States was passed on 19 October 1976. The greater part of its relevant provisions came into force on 1 January 1978. It has extended the range of copyright protection, and further eased the requirements whereby British authors can obtain copyright protection in America. New Public Law 100-568 of 31 October 1988 has made further amendments to the Copyright Statute which were necessary to enable ratification of the Berne Convention to take place. The problems which derived from the old system of common law copyright no longer now exist.

Works protected in American law

Works of authorship include the following categories:
(1) literary works;
Note: Computer programs are classified as literary works for the purposes of United States copyright. In *Whelan Associates Inc.* v. *Jaslow Dental Laboratory Inc.* (1987) F.S.R.1, it was held that the copyright of a computer program could be infringed even in the absence of copying of the literal code if the structure was part of the expression of the idea behind a program rather than the idea itself.
(2) musical works, including any accompanying words;
(3) dramatic works, including any accompanying music;
(4) pantomimes and choreographic works;
(5) pictorial, graphic and sculptural works;
(6) motion pictures and other audiovisual works – note: copyright in certain motion pictures has been extended by the North American Free Trade Agreement Information Act 1993;
(7) sound recordings, but copyright in sound recordings is not to include a right of public performance.
(8) architectural works: the design of a building as embodied in any tangible medium of expression, including a building, architectural plans or drawings. The Architectural Works Copyright Protections Act applies this protection to works created on or after 1 December 1990.

The rights of a copyright owner

(1) To reproduce the copyrighted work in copies or phonorecords;
(2) to prepare derivative works based upon the copyrighted work;
(3) to distribute copies or phonorecords of the copyrighted work to the public by sale or other transfer of ownership, or by rental, lease or lending;
(4) in the case of literary, musical, dramatic and choreographic works, pantomimes, and motion pictures and other audiovisual works, but NOT sound recordings, to perform the copyrighted work publicly;

(5) in the case of literary, musical, dramatic, and choreographic works, pantomimes, and pictorial, graphic, or sculptural works, including the individual images of a motion picture or other audiovisual work, to display the copyrighted work publicly.

(6) By the Record Rental Amendment Act 1984, s.109 of the Copyright Statute is amended. Now, unless authorised by the owners of copyright in the sound recording and the musical works thereon, the owner of a phonorecord may not, for direct or indirect commercial advantage, rent, lease or lend the phonorecord. A compulsory licence under s.115(c) includes the right of a maker of a phonorecord of non-dramatic musical work to distribute or authorise the distribution of the phonorecord by rental, lease, or lending, and an additional royalty is payable in respect of that. This modifies the 'first sale doctrine', which otherwise permits someone buying a copyright work to hire or sell a lawfully purchased copy to third parties without compensating the copyright owners, and without his or her consent.

(7) A further exception to the 'first sale doctrine' and s.109 of the Copyright Act is made by the Computer Software Rental Amendments Act. A similar restriction has been placed on the unauthorised rental, lease or lending of software, subject to certain limited exceptions. Both the phonecard and software exceptions to the first sale doctrine terminate on 1 October 1997.

(8) The Semiconductor Chip Protection Act 1984 adds to the Copyright Statute a new chapter on the protection of semiconductor chip products.

(9) The Visual Artists Rights Act 1990 has added moral rights to the various economic rights listed above. These moral rights are the right of integrity, and the right of attribution or paternity. A new category of 'work of visual art' is created, broadly paintings, drawings, prints and sculptures, with an upper limit of 200 copies. Works generally exploited in mass market copies such as books, newspapers, motion pictures and electronic information services are specifically excluded from these new moral rights provisions. Where they apply, they do so only in respect of works created on or after 1 June 1991, and to certain works previously created where title has not already been transferred by the author.

Manufacturing requirements

With effect from 1 July 1982, these ceased to have effect. Prior to 1 July 1982, the importation into or public distribution in the United States of a work consisting preponderantly of non-dramatic literary material that was in the English language and protected under American law was prohibited unless the portions consisting of such material had been manufactured in the United States or Canada. This provision did not apply where, on the date when importation was sought or public distribution in the United States was made, the author of any substantial part of such material was not a national of the United States or, if a national, had been domiciled outside the United States for a continuous period of at least one year immediately preceding that date.

Thus since 1 July 1982, there is no manufacturing requirement in respect of works of British authors. Certain interested groups in the United States still lobby for the restoration of the manufacturing clause in American law. Countries such as Britain will no doubt oppose this vigorously through diplomatic channels. With American ratification of the Berne Convention, the formalities previously required in relation to copyright notice, deposit and registration have been greatly modified.

Formalities: notice, deposit and registration

(1) Notice of copyright

Whenever a work protected by the American Copyright Statute is published in the United States or elsewhere by authority of the copyright owner, a notice of copyright should be placed on all publicly distributed copies. This should consist of (i) either the symbol © or the word 'Copyright' or the abbreviation 'Copr.' plus (ii) the year of first publication of the work, plus (iii) the name of the copyright owner. Since the Berne Amendments, both US and works of foreign origin which were first published in the US after 1 March 1989 without having notice of copyright placed on them will no longer be unprotected. However, notice will allow a right owner to bring an infringement action. In general, authors are advised to place copyright notices on their works, as this is a considerable deterrent to plagiarism. Damages may well be lower in a case where no notice of copyright was placed on the work.

(2) Deposit
The owner of copyright or the exclusive right of publication in a work published with notice of copyright in the United States should within three months of such publication deposit in the Copyright Office for the use or disposition of the Library of Congress two complete copies of the best edition of the work (or two records, if the work is a sound recording). Deposit is part of the administrative procedure of registration, and no longer mandatory.

(3) Registration
Registration for copyright in the United States is optional. However, any owner of copyright in a work first published outside the United States may register a work by making application to the Copyright Office with the appropriate fee, and by depositing one complete copy of the work. This requirement of deposit may be satisfied by using copies deposited for the Library of Congress. Whilst registration is still a requirement for works of US origin and from non-Berne countries, it is no longer necessary for foreign works from Berne countries. But as a matter of practice there are considerable advantages in any litigation where there has been registration. On the whole, it is advisable. The United States has interpreted the Berne Convention as allowing formalities which are not in themselves conditions for obtaining copyright protection, but which lead to improved protection.

Restoration of copyright

Works by non-US authors which lost copyright protection in the United States because of failure to comply with any of these provisions may have protection restored in certain circumstances. Works claiming restoration must still be in copyright in their country of origin. If a work succeeds in having copyright restored, it will last for the remainder of the period to which it would originally have been entitled in the United States.

Duration of copyright

An important change in the new American law is that in general, copyright in a work created on or after 1 January 1978 endures for a term of the life of the author, and a period of fifty years after the author's death. This brought the United States into line with most other advanced countries, and with the further amendments made by Public Law 100-568 of 31 October 1988 has enabled that government to ratify the higher standard Berne Convention. Copyright in a work created before 1 January 1978, but not published or copyrighted before then, subsists from 1 January 1978, and lasts for the life of the author and a post-mortem period of fifty years.

Any copyright, the first term of which under the previous law was still subsisting on 1 January 1978, shall endure for twenty-eight years from the date when it was originally secured, and the copyright proprietor or his or her representative may apply for a further term of forty-seven years within one year prior to the expiry of the original term. Until 1992, application for renewal and extension was required. Failure to do so produced disastrous results with some material of great merit passing into the public domain in error. However, by Public Law 102-307 enacted on 26 June 1992, there is no longer necessity to make a renewal registration in order to obtain the longer period of protection. Now renewal copyright vests automatically in the person entitled to renewal at the end of the 28th year of the original term of copyright.

The duration of any copyright, the renewal term of which was subsisting at any time between 31 December 1976 and 31 December 1977, or for which renewal registration was made between those dates, is extended to endure for a term of seventy-five years from the date copyright was originally secured.

These alterations are of great importance for owners of existing American copyrights.

All terms of copyright provided for by the sections referred to above run to the end of the calendar year in which they would otherwise expire.

Public performance

Under the previous American law the provisions relating to performance in public were less generous to right owners than those existing in United Kingdom copyright law. In particular, performance of a musical work was formerly only an infringement if it was 'for profit'. Moreover, the considerable American coin-operated record-playing machine industry (juke boxes) had obtained an exemption from being regarded as instruments of profit, and accordingly their owners did not have to pay royalties for the use of copyright musical works.

Now by the new law one of the exclusive rights of the copyright owner is, in the case of literary, musical, dramatic and choreographic works, pantomimes, and motion pictures and other audiovisual works, to perform the work publicly, without any requirement of such performance being 'for profit'. By Section 114 however, the exclusive rights of the owner of copyright in a sound recording are specifically stated not to include any right of public performance.

The position of coin-operated record players (juke boxes) is governed by the new Section 116A, inserted by Public Law 100-568 of 31 October 1988. It covers the position of negotiated licences. Limitations are placed on the exclusive right if licences are not negotiated.

These extensions of the scope of the right of public performance should augment the royalty income of authors, composers and publishers of musical works widely performed in the United States. All such right owners should ensure that their American interests are properly taken care of.

Mechanical right – alteration of the rate of royalty

Where sound recordings of a non-dramatic musical work have been distributed to the public in the United States with the authority of the copyright owner, any other person may, by following the provisions of the law, obtain a compulsory licence to make and distribute sound recordings of the work. This right is known in the United Kingdom as 'the mechanical right'. Notice must be served on the copyright owner, who is entitled to a royalty in respect of each of his or her works recorded of either two and three fourths cents or one half of one cent per minute of playing time or fraction thereof, whichever amount is the larger. Failure to serve or file the required notice forecloses the possibility of a compulsory licence and, in the absence of a negotiated licence, renders the making and distribution of such records actionable as acts of infringement.

Transfer of copyright

Under the previous American law copyright was regarded as indivisible, which meant that on the transfer of copyright, where it was intended that only film rights or some other such limited right be transferred, the entire copyright nevertheless had to be passed. This led to a cumbersome procedure whereby the author would assign the whole copyright to his or her publisher, who would return to the author by means of an exclusive licence those rights which it was not meant to transfer.

Now it is provided by Section 201(d) of the Copyright Statute that (1) the ownership of a copyright may be transferred in whole or in part by any means of conveyance or by operation of law, and may be bequeathed by will or pass as personal property by the applicable laws of intestate succession and (2) any of the exclusive rights comprised in a copyright (including any subdivision of any of the rights set out in *The rights of a copyright owner* above) may be transferred as provided in (1) above and owned separately. The owner of any particular exclusive right is entitled, to the extent of that right, to all the protection and remedies accorded to the copyright owner by that Statute. This removes the difficulties which existed under the previous law, and brings the position much closer to that existing in the copyright law of the United Kingdom.

Copyright Royalty Tribunal

A feature of the new United States law is the establishment of a Copyright Royalty Tribunal, with the purpose of making adjustments of reasonable copyright royalty rates in respect of the exercise of certain rights, mainly affecting the musical interests. The Tribunal consists of five commissioners appointed by the President with the advice and consent of the Senate for a term of seven years each. This body performs in the United States a function similar to the new Copyright Tribunal in the United Kingdom.

The new American law spells out the economic objectives which its Copyright Tribunal is to apply in calculating the relevant rates. These are:

(1) to maximise the availability of creative works to the public;
(2) to afford the copyright owner a fair return for his creative work and the copyright user a fair income under existing economic conditions;
(3) to reflect the relative roles of the copyright owner and the copyright user in the product made available to the public with respect to relative creative contribution, technological contribution, capital investment, cost, risk, and contribution to the opening of new markets for creative expression and media for their communication.
(4) to minimise any disruptive impact on the structure of the industries involved and on generally prevailing industry practices.

Every final determination of the Tribunal shall be published in the Federal Register. It shall state in detail the criteria that the Tribunal determined to be applicable to the particular proceeding, the various facts that it found relevant to its determination in that proceeding, and the specific reasons for its determination. Any final decision of the Tribunal in a proceeding may be appealed to the United States Court of Appeals by an aggrieved party, within thirty days after its publication in the Federal Register.

Fair use

One of the most controversial factors which held up the introduction of the new American copyright law for at least a decade was the extent to which a balance should be struck between the desire of copyright owners to benefit from their works by extending copyright protection as far as possible, and the pressure from users of copyright to obtain access to copyright material as cheaply as possible – if not completely freely. The new law provides by Section 107 that the fair use of a copyright work, including such use by reproduction in copies or on records, for purposes such as criticism, comment, news reporting, teaching (including multiple copies for classroom use), scholarship or research is not an infringement of copyright. In determining whether the use made of a work in any particular case is a fair use, the factors to be considered shall include:

(1) the purpose and character of the use, including whether such use is of a commercial nature or is for non-profit educational purposes;
(2) the nature of the copyrighted work;
(3) the amount and substantiality of the portion used in relation to the copyrighted work as a whole; and
(4) the effect of the use upon the potential market for or value of the copyrighted work.

It is not an infringement of copyright for a library or archive, or any of its employees acting within the scope of their employment, to reproduce or distribute no more than one copy of a work, if:

(1) the reproduction or distribution is made without any purpose of direct or indirect commercial advantage;
(2) the collections of the library or archive are either open to the public or available not only to researchers affiliated with the library or archive or with the institution of which it is a part, but also to other persons doing research in a specialised field; and
(3) the reproduction or distribution of the work includes a notice of copyright.

It is not generally an infringement of copyright if a performance or display of a work is given by instructors or pupils in the course of face to face teaching activities of a non-profit educational institution, in a classroom or similar place devoted to instruction.

Nor is it an infringement of copyright to give a performance of a non-dramatic literary or musical work or a dramatico-musical work of a religious nature in the course of services at a place of worship or other religious assembly.

It is also not an infringement of copyright to give a performance of a non-dramatic literary or musical work other than in a transmission to the public, without any purpose of direct or indirect commercial advantage and without payment of any fee for the performance to any of the performing artists, promoters or organisers if either (i) there is no direct or indirect admission charge or (ii) the proceeds, after deducting the reasonable costs of producing the performance, are used exclusively for educational, religious or charitable purposes and not for private financial gain. In this case the copyright owner has the right to serve notice of objection to the performance in a prescribed form.

Note the important decision of the Supreme Court in *Sony Corporation of America* v. *Universal City Studios.* (No. 81-1687, 52 USLW 4090.) This decided that the sale of video-recorders to the public does not amount to contributory infringement of the rights in films which are copied as a result of television broadcasts of them. (The practice known as time-switching.) Among other reasons for their decision advanced by the majority of the judges was their opinion that even unauthorised time-switching is legitimate fair use.

REMEDIES FOR COPYRIGHT OWNERS

Infringement of copyright

Copyright is infringed by anyone who violates any of the exclusive rights referred to in *The rights of a copyright owner* above, or who imports copies or records into the United States in violation of the law. The owner of copyright is entitled to institute an action for infringement so long as that infringement is committed while he or she is the owner of the right infringed. Previously, no action for infringement of copyright could be instituted until registration of the copyright claim had been made, but this requirement has been modified now that the United States has ratified the Berne Convention.

Injunctions

Any court having civil jurisdiction under the copyright law may grant interim and final injunctions on such terms as it may deem reasonable to prevent or restrain infringement of copyright. Such injunction may be served anywhere in the United States on the person named. An injunction is operative throughout the whole of the United States, and can be enforced by proceedings in contempt or otherwise by any American court which has jurisdiction over the infringer.

Impounding and disposition of infringing articles

At any time while a copyright action under American law is pending, the court may order the impounding on such terms as it considers reasonable of all copies or records claimed to have been made or used in violation of the copyright owner's exclusive rights; it may also order the impounding of all plates, moulds, matrices, masters, tapes, film negatives or other articles by means of which infringing copies or records may be reproduced. A court may order as part of a final judgement or decree the destruction or other disposition of all copies or records found to have been made or used in violation of the copyright owner's exclusive rights. It also has the power to order the destruction of all articles by means of which infringing copies or records were reproduced.

Damages and profits

An infringer of copyright is generally liable either for the copyright owner's actual damage and any additional profits made by the infringer, or for statutory damages.

(1) The copyright owner is entitled to recover the actual damages suffered by him or her as a result of the infringement, and in addition any profits of the infringer which are attributed to the infringement and are not taken into account in computing the actual damages. In establishing the infringer's profits, the copyright owner is only required to present proof of the infringer's gross revenue, and it is for the infringer to prove his or her deductible expenses and the elements of profit attributable to factors other than the copyright work.

(2) Except where the copyright owner has persuaded the court that the infringement was committed wilfully, the copyright owner may elect, at any time before final judgement is given, to recover, instead of actual damages and profits, an award of statutory damages for all infringements involved in the action in respect of any one work, which may be between $250 and $10,000 according to what the court considers justified.

(3) However, where the copyright owner satisfies the court that the infringement was committed wilfully, the court has the discretion to increase the award of statutory damages to not more than $50,000. Where the infringer succeeds in proving that he or she was not aware that and had no reason to believe that his or her acts constituted an infringement of copyright, the court has the discretion to reduce the award of statutory damages to not less than $100.

Costs: time limits

In any civil proceedings under American copyright law, the court has the discretion to allow the recovery of full costs by or against any party except the Government of the United States. It may also award a reasonable sum in respect of an attorney's fee.

No civil or criminal proceedings in respect of copyright law shall be permitted unless begun within three years after the claim or cause of action arose.

Criminal proceedings in respect of copyright

(1) Anyone who infringes a copyright wilfully and for purposes of commercial advantage and private financial gain shall be fined not more than $10,000 or imprisoned for not more than one year, or both. However, if the infringement relates to copyright in a sound recording or a film, the infringer is liable to a fine of not more than $25,000 or imprisonment for not more than one year or both on a first offence, which can be increased to a fine of up to $50,000 or imprisonment for not more than two years or both for a subsequent offence.

(2) Following a conviction for criminal infringement a court may in addition to these penalties order the forfeiture and destruction of all infringing copies and records, together with implements and equipment used in their manufacture.

(3) It is also an offence knowingly and with fraudulent intent to place on any article a notice of copyright or words of the same purport, or to import or distribute such copies. A fine is provided for this offence of not more than $2500. The fraudulent removal of a copyright notice also attracts the same maximum fine, as does the false representation of a material particular on an application for copyright representation.

Counterfeiting

By the Piracy and Counterfeiting Amendment Act 1982, pirates and counterfeiters of sound recordings and of motion pictures now face maximum penalties of up to five years imprisonment or fines of up to $250,000.

Colouring films

The United States Copyright Office has decided that adding colour to a black and white film may qualify for copyright protection whenever it amounts to more than a trivial change.

Satellite home viewers

The position of satellite home viewers is now controlled by the Satellite Home Viewer Act of 1988. (Title II of Public Law 100-667 of 16 November 1988.)

The Copyright Remedy Clarification Act has created s.511 of the Copyright Act, in order to rectify a situation which had developed in case law. By this, the component States of the Union, their agencies and employees are placed in the same position as private individuals and entities in relation to their liability for copyright infringement.

GENERAL OBSERVATIONS

The copyright law of the United States has been very greatly improved as a result of the new statute passed by Congress on 19 October 1976. (Title 17, United States Code.) Apart from lifting the general standards of protection for copyright owners to a much higher level than that which previously existed, it has on the whole shifted the balance of copyright protection in favour of the copyright owner and away from the copyright user in many of the areas where controversy existed. But most important for British and other non-American authors and publishers, it has gone a long way towards bringing American copyright law up to the same standards of international protection for non-national copyright proprietors which have long been offered by the United Kingdom and the other major countries, both in Europe and elsewhere in the English-speaking world. The ratification by the United States of the Berne Convention with effect from 1 March 1989 was an action which at that time put American copyright law on par with the protection offered by other major countries.

Libel

ANTONY WHITAKER
Legal Manager, Times Newspapers Ltd

What follows is an outline of the main principles of the law of libel, with special reference to points which appear most frequently to be misunderstood. But it is no more than that, and specific legal advice should be taken when practical problems arise. The law discussed is the law of England and Wales. Scotland has its own, albeit somewhat similar, rules. A summary of the main differences between the two systems appears at the end of this article.

At the time of going to press, a bill to reform, streamline and simplify certain aspects of this branch of the law was on its way through Parliament. It would be premature to forecast the precise form in which the proposed changes will eventually reach the statute-book, probably in early 1997, but it should be possible to cover them in the next edition.

LIBEL: LIABILITY TO PAY DAMAGES

English law draws a distinction between defamation published in permanent form and that which is not. The former is libel, the latter slander. 'Permanent form' includes writing, printing, drawings and photographs and radio and television broadcasts. It follows that it is the law of libel rather than slander which most concerns writers and artists professionally, and the slightly differing rules applicable to slander will not be mentioned in this article.

Publication of a libel can result in a civil action for damages, an injunction to prevent repetition and/or in certain cases a criminal prosecution against those responsible, who include the writer (or artist or photographer), the printers, the publishers, and the editor, if any, of the publication in which the libel appeared. Prosecutions are rare. Certain special rules apply to them and these will be explained below after a discussion of the question of civil liability, which in practice arises much more frequently.

Civil libel cases, for which legal aid is not available, are usually heard by a judge and jury, and it is the jury who decide the amount of any award, which is tax-free. It is not necessary for the plaintiff to prove that he or she has actually suffered any loss, because the law presumes damage. While the main purpose of a libel claim is to compensate the plaintiff for the injury to his or her reputation, a jury may give additional sums either as 'aggravated' damages, if it appears a defendant has behaved malevolently or spitefully, or as 'exemplary', or 'punitive', damages where a defendant hopes the economic advantages of publication will outweigh any sum awarded against them. Damages can also be 'nominal' if the libel complained of is trivial. It is generally very difficult to forecast the amounts juries are likely to award, though recent awards against newspapers have disclosed a tendency towards considerable generosity. The Court of Appeal now has power to reduce excessive awards of damages.

In an action for damages for libel, it is for the plaintiff to establish that the matter he or she complains of (1) has been published by the defendant, (2) refers to them, (3) is defamatory. If this is done, the plaintiff establishes a *prima facie* case. However, the defendant will escape liability if he or she can show he has a good defence. There are five defences to a libel action. They are Justification, Fair Comment, Privilege, S.4 of the Defamation Act, 1952, Apology, etc., under the Libel Acts, 1843 and 1845. A libel claim can also become barred under the Limitation Acts, as explained below. These matters must now be examined in detail.

THE PLAINTIFF'S CASE

(1) 'Published' in the legal sense means communicated to a person other than the plaintiff. Thus the legal sense is wider than the lay sense but includes it. It follows that the content of a book is published in the legal sense when the manuscript is first sent to the publishing firm just as much as it is when the book is later placed on sale to the public. Both types of publication are sufficient for the purpose of establishing liability for libel, but the law differentiates between them, since the scope of publication can properly be taken into account by the jury in considering the actual amount of damages to award.

(2) The plaintiff must also establish that the matter complained of refers to him or her. It is of course by no means necessary to mention a person's name before it is clear that he or she is referred to. Nicknames by which he or she is known or corruptions of his name are just two ways in which his or her identity can be indicated. There are more subtle methods. The sole question is whether the plaintiff is indicated to those who read the matter complained of. In some cases he or she will not be unless it is read in the light of facts known to the reader from other sources, but this is sufficient for the plaintiff's purpose. The test is purely objective and does not depend at all on whether the writer intended to refer to the plaintiff.

It is because it is impossible to establish reference to any individual that generalisations, broadly speaking, are not successfully actionable. To say boldly 'All lawyers are crooks' does not give any single lawyer a cause of action, because the statement does not point a finger at any individual. However, if anyone is named in conjunction with a generalisation, then it may lose its general character and become particular from the context. Again if one says 'One of the X Committee has been convicted of murder' and the X Committee consists of, say, four persons, it cannot be said that the statement is not actionable because no individual is indicated and it could be referring to any of the committee. This is precisely why it is actionable at the suit of each of them as suspicion has been cast on all.

(3) It is for the plaintiff to show that the matter complained of is defamatory. What is defamatory is decided by the jury except in the extreme cases where the judge rules that the words cannot bear a defamatory meaning. Various tests have been laid down for determining this. It is sufficient that any one test is satisfied. The basic tests are: (i) Does the matter complained of tend to lower the plaintiff in the estimation of society? (ii) Does it tend to bring him or her into hatred, ridicule, contempt, dislike or disesteem with society? (iii) Does it tend to make him shunned or avoided or cut off from society? The mere fact that what is published is inaccurate is not enough to involve liability; it is the adverse impact on the plaintiff's reputation that matters. For example, merely to overstate a person's income is not defamatory; but it will be if the context implies he has not fully declared it to the tax authorities.

'Society' means right-thinking members of society generally. It is by reference to such people that the above tests must be applied. A libel action against a newspaper which had stated that the police had taken a statement from the plaintiff failed, notwithstanding that the plaintiff gave evidence that his apparent assistance to the police (which he denied) had brought him into grave disrepute with the underworld. It was not by their wrongheaded standards that the matter fell to be judged.

Further, it is not necessary to imply that the plaintiff is at fault in some way in order to defame him. To say of a woman that she has been raped or of someone that he is insane, imputes to them no degree of blame, but nonetheless both statements are defamatory.

Sometimes a defamatory meaning is conveyed by words which on the face of them have no such meaning. 'But Brutus is an honourable man' is an example. If a jury finds that words are meant ironically they will consider this ironical sense when determining whether the words are defamatory. In deciding therefore whether or not the words are defamatory, the jury seek to discover what, without straining the words or putting a perverse construction on them, they will be understood to mean. In some cases this may differ substantially from their literal meaning.

Matter may also be defamatory by innuendo. Strictly so called, an innuendo is a meaning that words acquire by virtue of facts known to the reader but not stated in the passage complained of. Words, quite innocent on the face of them, may acquire a defamatory meaning when read in the light of these facts. For example, where a newspaper published a photograph of a man and a woman, with the caption that they had just announced their engagement, it was held to be defamatory of the man's wife since those who knew that she had cohabited with him were led to the belief that she had done so only as his mistress. The newspaper was unaware that the man was already married, but some of its readers were not.

DEFENCES TO A LIBEL ACTION

Justification

English law does not protect the reputation that a person either does not or should not possess. Stating the truth therefore does not incur liability, and the plea of justification – namely, that what is complained of is true in substance and in fact – is a complete answer to an action for damages. However, this defence is by no means to be undertaken lightly. For instance, to prove one instance of using bad language will be insufficient to justify the allegation that a person is 'foulmouthed'. It would be necessary to prove several instances, and the defendant is obliged in most cases to particularise in his pleadings giving details, dates and places. However, the requirement that the truth of every allegation must be proved is not absolute, and is qualified by the 'multiple charge – no worse off' defence. This applies where two or more distinct charges are levelled against a plaintiff, and some of what is said turns out to be inaccurate. If his reputation in the light of what is shown to be true is made no worse by the unprovable defamatory allegations – for example, mistaken accusations that a convicted pickpocket and car thief is also a shoplifter – the publisher will be safe. This is the extent of the law's recognition that some individuals are so disreputable as to be beyond redemption by awards of damages regardless of what is said about them. Subject to this, however, it is for the defendant to prove that what he or she has published is true, not for the plaintiff to disprove it, though if he can do so, so much the better for him.

One point requires special mention. It is insufficient for the defendant to prove that he has accurately repeated what a third person has written or said or that such statements have gone uncontradicted when made on occasions in the past. If X writes 'Y told me that Z is a liar', it is no defence to an action against X merely to prove that Y did say that. X has given currency to a defamatory statement concerning Z and has so made it his own. His only defence is to prove that Z is a liar by establishing a number of instances of Z's untruthfulness. Nor is it a defence to prove that the defendant genuinely believed what he or she published to be true. This might well be a complete answer in an action, other than a libel action, based on a false but non-defamatory statement. For such statements do not incur liability in the absence of fraud or malice, which, in this context, means a dishonest or otherwise improper motive. Bona fide belief, however, may be relevant to the assessment of damages, even in a libel action.

Special care should be taken in relation to references to a person's convictions, however accurately described. Since the Rehabilitation of Offenders Act, 1974, a person's convictions may become 'spent' and thereafter it may involve liability to refer to them. Reference to the Act and orders thereunder must be made in order to determine the position in any particular case.

Fair comment

It is a defence to prove that what is complained of is fair comment made in good faith and without malice on a matter of public interest.

'Fair' in this context means 'honest'. 'Fair comment' means therefore the expression of the writer's genuinely held opinion. It does not necessarily mean opinion with which the jury agree. Comment may therefore be quite extreme and still be 'fair' in the legal sense. However, if it is utterly perverse the jury may be led to think that no one could have genuinely held such views. In such a case the defence would fail, for the comment could not be honest. 'Malice' here includes the popular sense of personal spite, but covers any dishonest or improper motive.

The defence only applies when what is complained of is comment as distinct from a statement of fact. The line between comment and fact is notoriously difficult to draw in some cases. Comment means a statement of opinion. The facts on which comment is made must be stated together with the comment or be sufficiently indicated with it. This is merely another way of saying that it must be clear that the defamatory statement is one of opinion and not of fact, for which the only defence would be the onerous one of justification. The exact extent to which the facts commented on must be stated or referred to is a difficult question, but some help may be derived in answering it by considering the purpose of the rule, which is to enable the reader to exercise his own judgement and to agree or disagree with the comment. It is quite plain that it is not necessary to state every single detail of the facts. In one case it was sufficient merely to mention the name of one of the Press lords in an article about a newspaper though not one owned by him. He was so well known that to mention his name indicated the substratum of fact commented upon, namely his control of his group of newspapers. No universal rule can be laid down, except that, in general, the fuller the facts set out or referred to with the comment, the better. All these facts must be proved to be true subject, however, to the flexibility of the 'proportionate truth' rule. This means that the defence remains available even if, for example, only three out of five factual claims can be proved true, provided that these three are by themselves sufficient to sustain, and are proportionate to, the fairness of the comment. The impact of the two unproven claims would probably fall to be assessed in accordance with the 'multiple charge – no worse off' rule in justification, set out above.

The defence only applies where the matters commented on are of public interest, i.e. of legitimate concern to the public or a substantial section of it. Thus the conduct of national and local government, international affairs, the administration of justice, etc., are all matters of public interest, whereas other people's private affairs may very well not be, although they undoubtedly interest the public, or provoke curiosity.

In addition, matters of which criticism has been expressly or impliedly invited, such as publicly performed plays and published books, are a legitimate subject of comment. Criticism need not be confined merely to their artistic merit but equally may deal with the attitudes to life and the opinions therein expressed.

It is sometimes said that a man's moral character is never a proper subject of comment for the purpose of this defence. This is certainly true where it is a private individual who is concerned, and some authorities say it is the same in the case of a public figure even though his or her character may be relevant to his or her public life. Again, it may in some cases be exceeding the bounds of fair comment to impute a dishonourable motive to a person, as is frequently done by way of inference from facts. In general, the imputation is a dangerous and potentially expensive practice.

Privilege

In the public interest, certain occasions are privileged so that to make defamatory statements upon them does not incur liability. The following are privileged in any event: (i) fair, accurate, and contemporaneous reports of public judicial proceedings in England published in a newspaper, (ii) Parliamentary papers published by the direction of either House, or full republications thereof. The following are privileged provided publication is made only for the reason that the privilege is given and not for some wrongful or indirect motive: (i) fair and accurate but non-contemporaneous reports of public judicial proceedings in England, whether in a newspaper or not, (ii) extracts of Parliamentary papers, (iii) fair and accurate reports of Parliamentary proceedings, (iv) a fair and accurate report in a newspaper of the proceedings at any public meeting held in the United Kingdom. The meeting must be bona fide and lawfully held for a lawful purpose and for the furtherance or discussion of any matter of public concern. Admission to the meeting may be general or restricted. In the case of public meetings, the defence is not available, if it is proved that the defendant has been requested by the plaintiff to publish in the newspaper in which the original publication was made a reasonable letter or statement by way of explanation or contradiction, and has refused or neglected to do so, or has done so in a manner not adequate or not reasonable having regard to all the circumstances. This list of privileged occasions is by no means exhaustive, but they are those most commonly utilised.

S.4 of the Defamation Act, 1952

The defence provided by the above section is only available where the defamation is 'innocent'. As has been seen, liability for libel is in no way dependent on the existence of an intention to defame on the part of the defendant and the absence of such an intention does not mean that the defamation is 'innocent'.

Defamation is innocent if the publisher did not intend to publish the matter complained of about the plaintiff and did not know of circumstances by virtue of which it might be understood to refer to him, or, if the matter published was not defamatory on the face of it, if the publisher did not know of circumstances by virtue of which it might be understood to be defamatory. Further the publisher must have exercised all reasonable care in relation to the publication. If the publisher has published matter innocently, he or she should make an 'offer of amends' to the party aggrieved. This consists of an offer to publish a correction and apology and as far as practicable to inform others to whom the alleged libel has been distributed that the matter is said to be defamatory. If the offer of amends is accepted, it is a bar to further proceedings against the person making the offer. If rejected, the making of the offer affords a defence provided the defendant can prove that he did publish innocently and made the offer as soon as practicable after learning that the matter published was or might be defamatory. The offer must not have been withdrawn and must have been expressed to be for the purposes of the defence under S.4 and have been accompanied by an affidavit. It is vital that the offer should be made swiftly, but it is inadvisable to make it without professional advice owing to its technicality.

An example of the first type of innocent publication is where a reference to a person by name has been understood to refer to another person of the same name and this could not reasonably have been foreseen.

An example of the other type of innocent publication is the case referred to earlier in this article of the man pictured with 'his fiancée'. The publishers did not know that he was already married and that accordingly the picture and caption could be understood to be defamatory of his wife.

In practice all the conditions for a successful defence under this section are infrequently fulfilled.

Apology under the Libel Acts, 1843 and 1845

This defence is rarely utilised, since if any condition of it is not fulfilled, the plaintiff must succeed and the only question is the actual amount of damages. It only applies to actions in respect of libels in newspapers and periodicals. The defendant pleads that the libel was inserted without actual malice and without gross negligence and that before the action commenced or as soon afterwards as possible he inserted a full apology in the same newspaper, etc., or had offered to publish it in a newspaper, etc., of the plaintiff's choice, where the original newspaper is published at intervals greater than a week. Further a sum must be paid into court with this defence to compensate the plaintiff.

Apologies in general

Quite apart from the provisions concerning statutory apologies mentioned above, a swift and well publicised apology will always go some way towards assuaging injured feelings and help reduce an award of damages.

Limitation and death

In general, unless an action is started within three years of publication, a libel claim becomes 'statute-barred' through lapse of time. But successive and subsequent publications, such as the issue of later editions of the same book, or the sale of surplus copies of an old newspaper, can give rise to fresh claims.

Civil claims for libel cannot be brought on behalf of the dead. If an individual living plaintiff or defendant in a libel case dies before the jury gives their verdict, the action 'abates', i.e. comes to an end, so far as their involvement is concerned, and no rights arising out of it survive either for or against their personal representatives.

Insurance

For an author, the importance of at least an awareness of this branch of law lies first, in the fact that most book contracts contain a clause enabling the publisher to look to him should any libel claims result; and second, in the increasingly large awards of damages. It is therefore advisable to check what libel insurance a publisher carries, and whether it also covers the author who, if he or she is to have the benefit of it, should always alert the publisher to any potential risk. One company which offers libel insurance for authors is the Sun Alliance of 1 Leadenhall Street, London EC3V 1PP. Premiums start at £1000, and can be substantially higher if the book is tendentious or likely to be controversial. The company generally insists on the author obtaining, and paying for, a legal opinion first. Indemnity limits vary between £50,000 and £1 million, and the author is required to bear at least the first £5000, and 10 per cent of the remainder, of any loss. It is worth remembering that 'losses' include legal costs as well as damages, which they can often exceed. Libel insurance can also be obtained through a Lloyds broker.

CRIMINAL LIABILITY IN LIBEL AND RELATED AREAS

Whereas the object of a civil action is to obtain compensation for the wrong done or to prevent repetition, the object of criminal proceedings is to punish the wrongdoer by fine or imprisonment or both. There are four main types of writing which may provoke a prosecution:

(1) defamatory libel
(2) obscene publications
(3) sedition and incitement to racial hatred
(4) blasphemous libel

(1) The publication of defamatory matter is in certain circumstances a crime as well as a civil wrong. But whereas the principal object of civil proceedings will normally be to obtain compensation, the principal object of a criminal prosecution will be to secure punishment of the accused, for example by way of a fine. Prosecutions are not frequent, but there have been signs of late of a revival of interest. There are important differences between the rules applicable to criminal libel and its civil counterpart. For example, a criminal libel may be 'published' even though only communicated to the person defamed and may be found to have occurred even where the person defamed is dead, or where only a group of persons but no particular individual has been maligned. During election campaigns, it is an 'illegal practice' to publish false statements about the personal character or conduct of a candidate irrespective of whether they are also defamatory.

(2) It is an offence to publish obscene matter. By the Obscene Publications Act, 1959, matter is obscene if its effect is such as to tend to deprave and corrupt persons who are likely, having regard to all relevant circumstances, to read, see or hear it. 'To deprave and corrupt' is to be distinguished from 'to shock and disgust'. It is a defence to a prosecution to prove that publication of the matter in question is justified as being for the public good, on the ground that it is in the interests of science, literature, art or learning, or of other objects of general concern. Expert evidence may be given as to its literary, artistic, scientific or other merits. Playwrights, directors and producers should note that the Theatres Act, 1968, though designed to afford similar protection to stage productions, does not necessarily prevent prosecutions for indecency under other statutes.

(3) Writings which tend to destroy the peace of the realm may be prosecuted as being seditious or as amounting to incitement to racial hatred. Seditious writings include those which advocate reform by unconstitutional or violent means or incite contempt or hatred for the monarch or Parliament. These institutions may be criticised stringently, but not in a manner which is likely to lead to insurrection or civil commotion or indeed any physical force. Prosecutions are a rarity, but it should be remembered that writers of matter contemptuous of the House of Commons, though not prosecuted for seditious libel are, from time to time, punished by that House for breach of its privileges, although, if a full apology is made, it is often an end of the matter. The Public Order Act 1986 makes it an offence, irrespective of the author's or publisher's intention, to publish, or put on plays containing, threatening, abusive or insulting matter if hatred is likely to be stirred up against any racial group in Great Britain.

(4) Blasphemous libel consists in the vilification of the Christian religion or its ceremonies. Other religions are not protected. The offence lies essentially in the impact of what is said concerning, for instance, God, Christ, the Bible, the Book of Common Prayer, etc.; it is irrelevant that the publisher does not intend to shock or arouse resentment. While temperate and sober writings on religious

topics however anti-Christian in sentiment will not involve liability, if the discussion is 'so scurrilous and offensive as to pass the limit of decent controversy and to outrage any Christian feeling', it will.

MAIN DIFFERENCES BETWEEN ENGLISH AND SCOTTISH LAW

Much of the terminology of the Scots law of defamation differs from that of English law, and in certain minor respects the law itself is different. North of the border, libel and slander are virtually indistinguishable, both as to the nature of the wrongs and their consequences; and Scots law does not recognise the offence of criminal libel. Where individual English litigants enjoy absolute privilege for what they say in court, their Scottish counterparts have only qualified privilege. 'Exemplary', or 'punitive', damages are not awarded by the Scottish courts. Until recently, libel cases in Scotland were for the most part heard by judges sitting alone, but there is now a marked trend towards trial by jury, which has been accompanied by a significant increase in the levels of damages awarded.

Sales conference

Your editor will have been allocated perhaps half an hour to address the sales force at its biennial conference. In that time she will have to fire every representative there with enthusiasm for your book and all the others (maybe fifty in all) to be published in that season. The room will be filled with people from the UK, from other parts of the English-speaking world such as Australia, New Zealand and South Africa, and from places like Holland and Sweden where books in English are read, and they will be listening for two days on end to editors describing their hopes for the next Booker prize, the latest sex-and-shopping blockbuster, or handbooks for weight-lifting as well as weight-losing. It's like running a four-minute mile with only one chance to succeed. Sales Directors sometimes set an exercise for this trial of oratory. Reduce to one sentence the nature of the book, your reason for publishing it, the inducement for a bookseller to stock it!

from *Writing for Children* by Margaret Clark (A & C Black, £7.99).
See order form on page 690.

Finance

Income Tax for Writers and Artists

PETER VAINES FCA, ATII, *Barrister*
Partner, Brebner, Allen & Trapp
Chartered Accountants

This article is intended to explain the impact of taxation on writers and others engaged in similar activities. Despite attempts by many Governments to simplify our taxation system, the subject has become increasingly complicated and the following is an attempt to give a broad outline of the position. At the time of writing the proposals in the November 1995 Budget have been announced and these are reflected in this article.

HOW INCOME IS TAXED

(a) Generally

Authors are usually treated for tax purposes as carrying on a profession and are taxed in a similar fashion to other professional persons, i.e. as self-employed persons assessable under Schedule D. This article is directed to self-employed persons only, because if a writer is employed he or she will be subject to the rules of Schedule E where different considerations apply – substantially to his disadvantage. Attempts are often made by employed persons to shake off the status of 'employee' and to attain 'freelance' status so as to qualify for the advantages of Schedule D, such attempts meeting with varying degrees of success. The problems involved in making this transition are considerable and space does not permit a detailed explanation to be made here – proper advice is necessary if the difficulties are to be avoided.

Particular attention has been paid by the Inland Revenue to journalists and to those engaged in the entertainment industry with a view to reclassifying them as employees so that PAYE is deducted from their earnings. This blanket treatment has been extended to other areas and, although it is obviously open to challenge by individual taxpayers, it is always difficult to persuade the Inland Revenue to change their views.

There is no reason why employed people cannot carry on a freelance business in their spare time. Indeed, aspiring authors, painters, musicians, etc., often derive so little income from their craft that the financial security of an employment, perhaps in a different sphere of activity, is necessary. The existence of the employment is irrelevant to the taxation of the freelance earnings although it is most important not to confuse the income or expenditure of the employment with the income or expenditure of the self-employed activity. The Inland Revenue are aware of the advantages which can be derived by an individual having 'freelance' income from an organisation of which he or she is also an employee, and where such circumstances are contrived, it can be extremely difficult to convince an Inspector of Taxes that a genuine freelance activity is being carried on.

For those starting in business or commencing work on a freelance basis the Inland Revenue produce a very useful booklet entitled 'Starting in Business (IR28)', which is available from any tax office.

(b) Income

For income to be taxable it need not be substantial, nor even the author's only source of income; earnings from casual writing are also taxable but this can be an advantage, because occasional writers do not often make a profit from their writing. The expenses incurred in connection with writing may well exceed any income receivable and the resultant loss may then be used to reclaim tax paid on other income. There may be deducted from the income certain allowable expenses and capital allowances which are set out in more detail below. The possibility of a loss being used as a basis for a tax repayment is fully appreciated by the Inland Revenue who sometimes attempt to treat casual writing as a hobby so that any losses incurred cannot be used to reclaim tax; of course by the same token any income receivable would not be chargeable to tax. This treatment may sound attractive but it should be resisted vigorously because the Inland Revenue do not hesitate to change their mind when profits begin to arise. However, in the case of exceptional or non-recurring writing, such as the autobiography of a sports personality or the memoirs of a politician, it could be better to be treated as pursuing a hobby and not as a professional author. Sales of copyright can only be charged to capital gains tax (if at all) unless the recipient is a professional author.

(c) Royalties

Where the recipient is a professional author, a series of cases has laid down a clear principle that sales of copyright are taxable as income and not as capital receipts. Similarly, lump sums on account of, or in advance of royalties are also taxable as income in the year of receipt, subject to a claim for spreading relief (see below).

Copyright royalties are generally paid without deduction of Income Tax. However, if royalties are paid to a person who normally lives abroad, tax will be deducted by the payer or his agent at the time the payment is made unless arrangements are made with the Inland Revenue for payments to be made gross.

(d) Arts Council Grants

Persons in receipt of grants from the Arts Council or similar bodies will be concerned whether or not such grants are liable to Income Tax. The Inland Revenue have issued a Statement of Practice after detailed discussions with the Arts Council regarding the tax treatment of such awards. Grants and other receipts of a similar nature have now been divided into two categories – those which are to be treated by the Inland Revenue as chargeable to tax and those which are not. Category A awards are considered to be taxable and arise from the following:

(1) Direct or indirect musical, design or choreographic commissions and direct or indirect commission of sculpture and paintings for public sites.
(2) The Royalty Supplement Guarantee Scheme.
(3) The contract writers' scheme.

(4) Jazz bursaries.
(5) Translators' grants.
(6) Photographic awards and bursaries.
(7) Film and video awards and bursaries.
(8) Performance Art Awards.
(9) Art Publishing Grants.
(10) Grants to assist with a specific project or projects (such as the writing of a book) or to meet specific professional expenses such as a contribution towards copying expenses made to a composer or to an artist's studio expenses.

Awards made under category B are not chargeable to tax and are as follows:
(1) Bursaries to trainee directors.
(2) In-service bursaries for theatre directors.
(3) Bursaries for associate directors.
(4) Bursaries to people attending full-time courses in arts administration (the practical training course).
(5) In-service bursaries to theatre designers and bursaries to trainees on the theatre designers' scheme.
(6) In-service bursaries for administrators.
(7) Bursaries for actors and actresses.
(8) Bursaries for technicians and stage managers.
(9) Bursaries made to students attending the City University Arts Administration courses.
(10) Awards, known as the Buying Time Awards, made not to assist with a specific project or professional expenses but to maintain the recipient to enable him or her to take time off to develop his personal talents. These at present include the awards and bursaries known as the Theatre Writing Bursaries, awards and bursaries to composers, awards and bursaries to painters, sculptures and print makers, literature awards and bursaries.

This Statement of Practice has no legal force and is used merely to ease the administration of the tax system. It is open to anyone in receipt of a grant or award to disregard the agreed statement and challenge the Inland Revenue view on the merits of their particular case. However, it must be recognised that the Inland Revenue do not issue such statements lightly and any challenge to their view would almost certainly involve a lengthy and expensive action through the Courts.

The tax position of persons in receipt of literary prizes will generally follow a decision by the Special Commissioners in connection with the Whitbread Literary Award. In that case it was held that the prize was not part of the author's professional income and accordingly not chargeable to tax. The precise details are not available because decisions of the Special Commissioners were not, at that time, reported unless an appeal was made to the High Court and the Inland Revenue chose not to appeal against this decision. Elsewhere in this *Yearbook* will be found details of the many literary awards which are given each year and this decision is of considerable significance to the winners of each of these prizes. It would be unwise to assume that all such awards will be free of tax as the precise facts which were present in the case of the Whitbread award may not be repeated in another case; however it is clear that an author winning a prize has some very powerful arguments in his or her favour, should the Inland Revenue seek to charge tax on the award.

ALLOWABLE EXPENSES

To qualify as an allowable business expense, expenditure has to be laid out wholly and exclusively for business purposes. Strictly there must be no 'duality of purpose', which means that expenditure cannot be apportioned to reflect the private and business usage, e.g. food, clothing, telephone, travelling expenses, etc. However, the Inland Revenue do not usually interpret this principle strictly and are prepared to allow all reasonable expenses (including apportioned sums) where the amounts can be commercially justified. It should be noted carefully that the expenditure does not have to be 'necessary', it merely has to be incurred 'wholly and exclusively' for business purposes; naturally, however, expenditure of an outrageous and wholly unnecessary character might well give rise to a presumption that it was not really for business purposes. As with all things, some expenses are unquestionably allowable and some expenses are equally unquestionably not allowable – it is the grey area in between which gives rise to all the difficulties and the outcome invariably depends on negotiation with the Inland Revenue.

Great care should be taken when claiming a deduction for items where there is a 'duality of purpose' and negotiations should be conducted with more than usual care and courtesy – if provoked the Inspector of Taxes may well choose to allow nothing. An appeal is always possible although unlikely to succeed as a string of cases in the Courts has clearly demonstrated. An example is the case of *Caillebotte* v. *Quinn* where the taxpayer (who normally had lunch at home) sought to claim the excess cost of meals incurred because he was working a long way from his home. The taxpayer's arguments failed because he did not eat only in order to work, one of the reasons for his eating was in order to sustain his life; a duality of purpose therefore existed and no tax relief was due. Other cases have shown that expenditure on clothing can also be disallowed if it is the kind of clothing which is in everyday use, because clothing is worn not only to assist the pursuit of one's profession but also to accord with public decency. This duality of purpose may be sufficient to deny relief – even where the particular type of clothing is of a kind not otherwise worn by the taxpayer. In the case of *Mallalieu* v. *Drummond* a lady barrister failed to obtain a tax deduction for items of sombre clothing purchased specifically for wearing in Court. The House of Lords decided that a duality of purpose existed because clothing represented part of her needs as a human being.

Despite the above Inspectors of Taxes are not usually inflexible and the following expenses are among those generally allowed:

(a) Cost of all materials used up in the course of preparation of the work.

(b) Cost of typewriting and secretarial assistance, etc.; if this or other help is obtained from one's spouse then it is entirely proper for a deduction to be claimed for the amounts paid for the work. The amounts claimed must actually be paid to the spouse and should be at the market rate although some uplift can be made for unsocial hours, etc. Payments to a wife (or husband) are of course taxable in her (or his) hands and should therefore be most carefully considered. The wife's earnings may also be liable for National Insurance contributions and it is important to take care because otherwise you may find that these contributions may outweigh the tax savings.

(c) All expenditure on normal business items such as postage, stationery, telephone, fax and answering machines, agent's fees, accountancy charges, photography, subscriptions, periodicals, magazines, etc., may be claimed. The cost of daily papers should not be overlooked if these form part of research material. Visits to theatres, cinemas, etc., for research purposes may also be permissible (but not the cost relating to guests). Unfortunately expenditure on all types of business entertaining is specifically denied tax relief.

(d) If work is conducted at home, a deduction for 'use of home' is usually allowed providing the amount claimed is reasonable. If the claim is based on an appropriate proportion of the total costs of rent, light and heat, cleaning and maintenance, insurance, etc. (but not the Council Tax), care should be taken to ensure that no single room is used '*exclusively*' for business purposes, because this may result in the Capital Gains Tax exemption on the house as the only or main residence being partially forfeited. However, it would be a strange household where one room was in fact used exclusively for business purposes and for no other purpose whatsoever (e.g. storing personal bank statements and other private papers); the usual formula is to claim a deduction on the basis that most or all of the rooms in the house are used at one time or another for business purposes, thereby avoiding any suggestion that any part was used exclusively for business purposes.

(e) The appropriate business proportion of motor running expenses may also be claimed although what is the appropriate proportion will naturally depend on the particular circumstances of each case; it should be mentioned that the well-known scale benefits, whereby one is taxed according to the size and cost of the car, do not apply to self-employed persons.

(f) It has been long established that the cost of travelling from home to work (whether employed or self-employed) is not an allowable expense. However, if home is one's place of work then no expenditure under this heading is likely to be incurred and difficulties are unlikely to arise.

(g) Travelling and hotel expenses incurred for business purposes will normally be allowed but if any part could be construed as disguised holiday or pleasure expenditure, considerable thought would need to be given to the commercial reasons for the journey in order to justify the claim. The principle of 'duality of purpose' will always be a difficult hurdle in this connection – although not insurmountable.

(h) If a separate business bank account is maintained, any overdraft interest thereon will be an allowable expense. This is the *only* circumstance in which overdraft interest is allowed for tax purposes and care should be taken to avoid overdrafts in all other circumstances.

(i) Where capital allowances (see below) are claimed for a personal computer, television, video, CD or tape player, etc., used for business purposes an appropriate proportion of the costs of maintenance and repair of the equipment may also be claimed.

Clearly many other allowable items may be claimed in addition to those mentioned above. Wherever there is any reasonable business motive for some expenditure it should be claimed as a deduction although one should avoid an excess of imagination as this would naturally cause the Inspector of Taxes to doubt the genuineness of other expenses claimed.

The question is often raised whether the whole amount of an expense may be deducted or whether the VAT content must be excluded. Where VAT is reclaimed from the Customs and Excise (on the quarterly returns made by a registered person), the VAT element of the expense cannot be treated as an allowable deduction. Where the VAT is not reclaimed, the whole expense (inclusive of VAT) is allowable for Income Tax purposes.

CAPITAL ALLOWANCES

(a) Allowances

Where expenditure of a capital nature is incurred, it cannot be deducted from income as an expense – a separate and sometimes more valuable capital allowance being available instead. Capital allowances are given for many different types of expenditure, but authors and similar professional people are likely to claim only for 'plant and machinery'; this is a very wide expression which may include motor cars, computers and other business machines, televisions, CD, video and cassette players used for business purposes, books – and even a horse! Plant and machinery generally qualify for a 25% allowance in the year of purchase and 25% of the reducing balance in subsequent years. Where the useful life of an asset is expected to be short, it is possible to claim special treatment as a 'short life asset' enabling the allowances to be accelerated.

The reason these allowances can be more valuable than allowable expenses is that they may be wholly or partly disclaimed in any year that full benefit cannot be obtained – ordinary business expenses cannot be similarly disclaimed. Where, for example, the income of an author does not exceed her personal allowances, she would not be liable to tax and a claim for capital allowances would be wasted. If the capital allowances were to be disclaimed their benefit would be carried forward for use in subsequent years.

Careful planning with claims for capital allowances is therefore essential if maximum benefit is to be obtained.

As an alternative to capital allowances claims can be made on the 'renewals' basis whereby all renewals are treated as allowable deductions in the year; no allowance is obtained for the initial purchase, but the cost of replacement (excluding any improvement element) is allowed in full. This basis is no longer widely used, as it is considerably less advantageous than claiming capital allowances as described above.

Leasing is a popular method of acquiring fixed assets, and where cash is not available to enable an outright purchase to be made, assets may be leased over a period of time. Whilst leasing may have financial benefits in certain circumstances, in normal cases there is likely to be no *tax* advantage in leasing an asset where the alternative of outright purchase is available. Indeed, leasing can be a positive disadvantage in the case of motor cars with a new retail price of more than £12,000. If such a car is leased, only a proportion of the leasing charges will be tax deductible.

(b) Books

The question of whether the cost of books is eligible for tax relief has long been a source of difficulty. The annual cost of replacing books used for the purposes of one's professional activities (e.g. the annual cost of a new *Writers' & Artists' Yearbook*) has always been an allowable expense; the difficulty arose because the initial cost of reference books, etc. (for example when commencing one's profession) was treated as capital expenditure but no allowances were due as the books were not considered to be 'plant'. However, the matter was clarified by the case of *Munby* v. *Furlong* in which the Court of Appeal decided that the initial cost of law books purchased by a barrister was expenditure on 'plant' and eligible for capital allowances. This is clearly a most important decision, particularly relevant to any person who uses expensive books in the course of exercising his or her profession.

PENSION CONTRIBUTIONS

(a) Personal pensions

Where a self-employed person pays annual premiums under an approved personal pension policy, tax relief may now be obtained each year for the following amounts:

Age at 6/4/96	Maximum %
35 and under	17.5% (max) £14,385
36 – 45	20% (max) £16,440
46 – 50	25% (max) £20,550
51 – 55	30% (max) £24,660
56 – 60	35% (max) £28,770
61 and over	40% (max) £32,880

These figures do not apply to existing retirement annuity policies; these remain subject to the old limits which are unchanged.

These arrangements can be extremely advantageous in providing for a pension as premiums are usually paid when the income is high (and the tax relief is also high) and the pension (taxed as earned income when received) usually arises when the income is low and little tax is payable. The reduction in the rates of income tax to a maximum of 40% makes this decision a little more difficult because the tax advantages could go into reverse. When the pension is paid it could, if rates rise again, be taxed at a higher rate than the rate of tax relief at the moment. One would be deferring income in order to pay more tax on it later. However, this involves a large element of guesswork, and many people will be content simply with the long-term pension benefits.

(b) Class 4 National Insurance contributions

Allied to pensions is the payment of Class 4 National Insurance contributions, although no pension or other benefit is obtained by the contributions; the Class 4 contributions are designed solely to extract additional amounts from self-employed persons and are payable in addition to the normal Class 2 (self-employed) contributions. The rates are changed each year and for 1996/97 self-employed persons will be obliged to contribute 6% of their profits between the range £6860-£23,660 per annum, a maximum liability of £1008 for 1996/97. This amount is collected in conjunction with the Schedule D Income Tax liability and appears on the same assessment; the comments below regarding assessments, appeals and postponement apply equally to Class 4 contributions. Tax relief was available for one half of the Class 4 contributions, but this has been abolished for 1996/97.

SPREADING RELIEF

(a) Relief for copyright payments

Special provisions enable authors and similar persons who have been engaged on a literary, dramatic, musical or artistic work for a period of more than twelve months, to spread certain amounts received over two or three years depending on the time spent in preparing the work. If the author was engaged on the work for a period exceeding twelve months, the receipt may be spread backwards over two years; if the author was engaged on the work for more than 24 months, the receipt may be spread backwards over three years. (Analogous provisions apply to sums received for the sale of a painting, sculpture or other work of art.) The relief applies to:

a. lump sums received on the assignment of copyright, in whole or in part;
b. sums received on the grant of any interest in the copyright by licence;
c. non-returnable advances on account of royalties;
d. any receipts of or on account of royalties or any periodical sums received within two years of first publication.

A claim for spreading relief has to be made within eight years from 5 April following the date of first publication.

(b) Relief where copyright sold after ten years

Where copyright is assigned (or a licence in it is granted) more than ten years after the first publication of the work, then the amounts received can qualify for a different spreading relief. The assignment (or licence) must be for a period of more than two years and the receipt will be spread forward over the number of years for which the assignment (or licence) is granted – but with a maximum of six years. The relief is terminated by death, but there are provisions enabling the deceased author's personal representatives to re-spread the amounts if it is to the beneficiaries' advantage.

The above rules are arbitrary and cumbersome, only providing a limited measure of relief in special circumstances. The provisions can sometimes be helpful to repair matters when consideration of the tax position has been neglected, but invariably a better solution is found if the likely tax implications are considered fully in advance.

COLLECTION OF TAX

Assessments

In order to collect the tax which is due on the profits of authorship the Inland Revenue issue an assessment based on the income for the relevant period. Normally the income to be assessed will be that for the previous year (e.g. the 1996/97 assessment will be based on the accounts made up to some date in 1995/96 – perhaps 31 December 1995 or 5 April 1996). However, there are complicated rules for determining the income to be assessed in the years immediately after commencement, and in the years immediately prior to the discontinuance of the profession, and if for any reason there is a change in the date to which accounts are made up.

A new system for calculating tax assessments will come into effect for the tax year 1997/98. Under the new system, profits will not be taxed on the previous year basis but on the actual basis – that is to say, the profits for the accounting period ending in the year. This change causes an obvious problem in calculating the figures. If your accounts for the year ended 31 December 1996 were going to be assessed in 1997/98 on the preceding year basis but now will be based on the profits in the accounts ending in the current tax year, i.e. the profits for the year ended 31 December 1997, what happens to the 31 December 1996 profits? Are they tax free? The answer is nearly but not quite. What happens is that the year 1996/97 is designated the transitional year and the profits taxed in that year will be the average of the profits for the accounts that end in 1994/95 and 1995/96. This means that half of those profits will not be taxed. There is obviously a substantial opportunity for advantage here and there are special rules to prevent abuse.

When an assessment is received it should be examined carefully.

(a) If it is correct, the tax should be paid on the dates specified. Usually the tax is payable in two equal instalments, on 1 January in the year of assessment and on the following 1 July. If payment is delayed then interest may arise – see below.

(b) If the assessment is incorrect (for example, if it is estimated), then prompt action is required. An appeal must be lodged within 30 days of the date of issue of the assessment specifying the grounds of the appeal. An appeal form usually accompanies the notice of assessment. (If for some reason an appeal cannot be lodged within the 30 days the Inland Revenue are often prepared to accept a late appeal, but this is at their discretion and acceptance cannot be guaranteed.) If there is any tax charged on an incorrect assessment it cannot simply be forgotten, because it will become payable despite any appeal, unless an application for 'postponement' is also made. (This may be done by completing the other half of the appeal form.) Tax can be postponed only where there are grounds for believing that too much tax has been charged, and the Inspector of Taxes will agree to postpone tax only if these grounds are reasonable. The tax which is not postponed will usually be payable on the normal due dates. It is necessary to consider claims for postponement most carefully to ensure that approximately the correct amount of tax remains payable; otherwise an unfortunate (and expensive) charge to interest could arise. It is important to recognise that 'postponement' does not mean elimination; it simply means that payment of tax may be deferred, and after six months interest will start to run on any tax which has been postponed but which is ultimately found to be payable. As agreement of the final liability may take a long time, a large amount of interest can arise unless a reasonably accurate amount has been paid on time.

Interest

Interest is chargeable on overdue tax at a variable rate, which at the time of writing is 7% per annum. It does not rank for any tax relief, which can make the Inland Revenue an expensive source of credit. It can be very difficult to persuade the Inland Revenue to withdraw a charge to interest – even where the delay is their fault.

However, the Inland Revenue can also be obliged to pay interest at the same rate (known as repayment supplement) tax-free where repayments are delayed. The rules relating to repayment supplement are less beneficial and even more complicated than the rules for interest payable but they do exist and can be very welcome if a large repayment has been delayed for a long time.

Example

Author's accounts made up to 30 April 1995 showing profits of £10,000 giving rise to tax of (say) £1500.
Assessment issued in September 1996 for 1996/97 in an estimated figure of £15,000 – showing tax payable of £2500.

Appeal must be made within 30 days of issue.
Application for postponement must also be made within 30 days to postpone £1000 of the tax charged.
Tax therefore becomes payable thus:

1 Jan 1997	£750
1 July 1997	£750

(If no application for postponement were to be made £1250 would become payable on each of these dates. When the final liability is agreed the excess of £1000 would be refunded but that could take some time, and repayment supplement might not apply.)

Unfortunately life is never as simple as the above illustration would suggest, particularly this year (1996/97), the transitional year to the new current year basis of assessment; however, it serves to demonstrate the principle.

VALUE ADDED TAX

The activities of writers, painters, composers, etc., are all 'taxable supplies' within the scope of VAT and chargeable at the standard rate. (Zero rating which applies to publishers, booksellers, etc. on the supply of books does not extend to the work performed by writers.) Accordingly, authors are obliged to register for VAT if their income for the past twelve months exceeds £47,000 or if their income for the coming month will exceed that figure.

Delay in registering can be a most serious matter because if registration is not effected at the proper time, the Customs and Excise can (and invariably do) claim VAT from all the income received since the date on which registration should have been made. As no VAT would have been included in the amounts received during this period the amount claimed by the Customs and Excise must inevitably come straight from the pocket of the author.

The author may be entitled to seek reimbursement of the VAT from those whom he or she ought to have charged VAT but this is obviously a matter of some difficulty and may indeed damage his commercial relationships. Apart from these disadvantages there is also a penalty for late registration. The rules are extremely harsh and are imposed automatically even in cases of innocent error. It is therefore extremely important to monitor the income very carefully because if in any period of twelve months the income exceeds the £47,000 limit, the Customs and Excise must be notified within 30 days of the end of the period. Failure to do so will give rise to an automatic penalty. It should be emphasised that this is a penalty for failing to submit a form and has nothing to do with any real or potential loss of tax. Furthermore, whether the failure was innocent or deliberate will not matter. Only the existence of a 'reasonable excuse' will be a defence to the penalty. However, a reasonable excuse does not include ignorance, error, a lack of funds or reliance on any third party.

However it is possible to regard VAT registration as a privilege and not a penalty, because only VAT registered persons can reclaim VAT paid on their expenses such as stationery, telephone, professional fees, etc., even typewriters and other plant and machinery (excluding cars). However, many find that the administrative inconvenience – the cost of maintaining the necessary records and completing the necessary forms – more than outweighs the benefits to be gained from registration and prefer to stay outside the scope of VAT for as long as possible.

OVERSEAS MATTERS

The general observation may be made that self-employed persons resident and domiciled in the United Kingdom are not well treated with regard to their overseas work, being taxable on their worldwide income. It is important to emphasise that if fees are earned abroad, no tax saving can be achieved merely by keeping the money outside the country. Although exchange control regulations no longer exist to require repatriation of foreign earnings, such income remains taxable in the UK and must be disclosed to the Inland Revenue; the same applies to interest or other income arising on any investment of these earnings overseas. Accordingly whenever foreign earnings are likely to become substantial, prompt and effective action is required to limit the impact of UK and foreign taxation. In the case of non-resident authors it is important that arrangements concerning writing for publication in the UK, e.g. in newspapers, are undertaken with great care. A case concerning the wife of one of the great train robbers who provided detailed information for a series of articles in a Sunday newspaper is most instructive. Although she was acknowledged to be resident in Canada for all the relevant years, the income from the articles was treated as arising in this country and fully chargeable to UK tax.

The United Kingdom has double taxation agreements with many other countries and these agreements are designed to ensure that income arising in a foreign country is taxed either in that country or in the United Kingdom. Where a withholding tax is deducted from payments received from another country (or where tax is paid in full in the absence of a double taxation agreement), the amount of foreign tax paid can usually be set off against the related UK tax liability. Many successful authors can be found living in Eire because of the complete exemption from tax which attaches to works of cultural or artistic merit by persons who are resident there. However, such a step should only be contemplated having careful regard to all the other domestic and commercial considerations and specialist advice is essential if the exemption is to be obtained and kept; a careless breach of the conditions could cause the exemption to be withdrawn with catastrophic consequences.

COMPANIES

When an author becomes successful the prospect of paying tax at the higher rate may drive him or her to take hasty action such as the formation of companies, etc., which may not always be to his advantage. Indeed some authors seeing the exodus into tax exile of their more successful colleagues even form companies in low tax areas in the naive expectation of saving large amounts of tax. The Inland Revenue are fully aware of the opportunities and have extensive powers to charge tax and combat avoidance. Accordingly such action is just as likely to *increase* tax liabilities and generate other costs and should never be contemplated without expert advice; some very expensive mistakes are often made in this area which are not always able to be remedied.

To conduct one's business through the medium of a company can be a most effective method of mitigating tax liabilities, and providing it is done at the right time and under the right circumstances very substantial advantages can be derived. However, if done without due care and attention the intended advantages will simply evaporate. At the very least it is essential to ensure that the company's business is genuine and conducted properly with regard to the realities of the situation. If the author continues his or her activities unchanged, simply paying all the receipts from his work into a company's bank account, he cannot expect to persuade the Inland Revenue that it is the company and not himself who is entitled to, and should be assessed to tax on, that income. It must be strongly emphasised that many pitfalls exist which can easily eliminate all the tax benefits expected to arise by the formation of the company. For example, company directors are employees of the company and will be liable to pay much higher National Insurance contributions; the company must also pay the employer's proportion of the contribution and a total liability of over 20% of gross salary may arise. This compares most unfavourably with the position of a self-employed person. Moreover on the commencement of the company's business the individual's profession will cease and the Inland Revenue have the power to re-open earlier years' assessments to increase the liabilities for previous years; this is always a crucial factor in determining the best moment when the changeover to a company should take place.

No mention has been made above of personal reliefs and allowances (for example the single and married couples allowances, etc.); this is because these allowances and the rates of tax are subject to constant change and are always set out in detail in the explanatory notes which accompany the Tax Return. The annual Tax Return is an important document and should not be ignored because it is crucial to one's tax position. Indeed, it should be completed promptly with extreme care because the Inland Revenue treat failures to disclose income very harshly, invariably exacting interest and penalties – sometimes of substantial amounts. If filling in the Return is a source of difficulty or anxiety, comfort may be found in the Consumer Association's publication *Money Which? – Tax Saving Guide*; this is published in March of each year and includes much which is likely to be of interest and assistance.

Social Security Contributions

PETER ARROWSMITH FCA
National Insurance Consultant, Grant Thornton

In general, every individual who works in Great Britain either as an employee or as a self-employed person is liable to pay social security contributions. The law governing this subject is complicated and the following should only be regarded as a summary of the position.

All contributions are payable in respect of years ending on 5 April, the classes of contributions being as follows:

Class 1 These are payable by employees (primary contributions) and their employers (secondary contributions) and are based on earnings.

Class 1A Use of company car, and fuel, for private purposes.

Class 2 These are weekly flat rate contributions, payable by the self-employed.

Class 3 These are weekly flat rate contributions, payable on a voluntary basis in order to provide, or make up entitlement to, certain social security benefits.

Class 4 These are payable by the self-employed in respect of their trading or professional income and are based on earnings.

EMPLOYED OR SELF-EMPLOYED?

The question as to whether a person is employed under a contract *of* service and is thereby an employee liable to Class 1 contributions, or performs services (either solely or in partnership) under a contract *for* service and is thereby self-employed liable to Class 2 and Class 4 contributions, often has to be decided in practice. One of the best guides can be found in the case of *Market Investigations Limited* v. *Minister of Social Security* (1969 2 WLR 1) when Cooke J. remarked as follows:

'. . . the fundamental test to be applied is this: "Is the person who has engaged himself to perform these services performing them as a person in business on his own account?" If the answer to that question is "yes", then the contract is a contract for services. If the answer is "no", then the contract is a contract of service. No exhaustive list has been compiled and perhaps no exhaustive list can be compiled of the considerations which are relevant in determining that question, nor can strict rules be laid down as to the relative weight which the various considerations should carry in particular cases. The most that can be said is that control will no doubt always have to be considered, although it can no longer be regarded as the sole determining factor; and that factors which may be of importance are such matters as
—whether the man performing the services provides his own equipment,
—whether he hires his own helpers,
—what degree of financial risk he takes,
—what degree of responsibility for investment and management he has, and
—whether and how far he has an opportunity of profiting from sound management in the performance of his task.'

The above case was also considered as recently as November 1993 by the Court of Appeal in the case of *Hall* v. *Lorimer*. In this case a vision mixer with around 20 clients and with around 120-150 separate engagements per annum was held to be self-employed. This follows the, perhaps surprising, contention of the Inland Revenue that the taxpayer was an employee.

There have been three cases dealing with musicians, in relatively recent times, which provide further guidance on the question as to whether an individual is employed or self-employed.

Midland Sinfonia Concert Society Ltd v. *Secretary of State for Social Services* (1981 ICR 454): A musician, employed to play in an orchestra by separate invitation at irregular intervals and remunerated solely in respect of each occasion upon which he does play, is employed under a contract for services. He is therefore self-employed, not an employed earner, for the purposes of the Social Security Contributions and Benefits Act 1992, and the orchestra which engages him is not liable to pay National Insurance contributions in respect of his earnings.

Addison v. *London Philharmonic Orchestra Limited* (1981 ICR 261): This was an appeal to determine whether certain individuals were employees for the purposes of section 11(1) of the Employment Protection (Consolidation) Act 1978.

The Employment Appeal Tribunal upheld the decision of an industrial tribunal that an associate player and three additional or extra players of the London Philharmonic Orchestra were not employees under a contract of service, but were essentially freelance musicians carrying on their own business. The facts found by the industrial tribunal showed that, when playing for the orchestra, each appellant remained essentially a freelance musician, pursuing his or her own profession as an instrumentalist, with an individual reputation, and carrying on his or her own business, and they contributed their own skills and interpretative powers to the orchestra's performances as independent contractors.

Winfield v. *London Philharmonic Orchestra Limited* (ICR 1979, page 726): This case dealt with the question as to whether an individual was an employee within the meaning of section 30 of the Trade Union and Labour Relations Act 1974.

The following remarks by the appeal tribunal are of interest in relation to the status of musicians:

'. . . making music is an art, and the co-operation required for a performance of Berlioz's *Requiem* is dissimilar to that required between the manufacturer of concrete and the truck driver who takes the concrete where it is needed. . .

It took the view, as we think it was entitled on the material before it to do, that the company was simply machinery through which the members of the orchestra managed and controlled the orchestra's operation . . . In deciding whether you are in the presence of a contract of service or not, you look at the whole of the picture. This picture looks to us, as it looked to the industrial tribunal, like a co-operative of distinguished musicians running themselves with self and mutual discipline, and in no sense like a boss and his musician employees.'

Other recent cases have concerned a professional dancer and holiday camp entertainers (all of whom were regarded as employees). In two recent cases income from part-time lecturing was held to be from an employment.

Accordingly, if a person is regarded as an employee under the above rules, he or she will be liable to pay contributions even if his employment is casual, part time or temporary. Furthermore, if a person is an employee and also carries on a trade or profession either solely or in partnership, there will be a liability to more than one class of contributions (subject to certain maxima – see below).

Exceptions

There are certain exceptions to the above rules, those most relevant to artists and writers being:

(a) The employment of a wife by her husband, or vice versa, is disregarded for social security purposes unless it is for the purposes of a trade or profession (e.g. the employment of his wife by an author would not be disregarded and would result in a liability for contributions if her salary reached the minimum levels).

(b) The employment of certain relatives in a private dwelling house in which both employee and employer reside is disregarded for social security purposes provided the employment is not for the purposes of a trade or business carried on at those premises by the employer. This would cover the employment of a relative (as defined) as a housekeeper in a private residence.

(c) In general, lecturers, teachers and instructors engaged by an educational establishment to teach on at least four days in three consecutive months are regarded as employees, although this rule does not apply to fees received by persons giving public lectures.

Freelance film workers

As regards the status of workers in the film and allied industries, the Inland Revenue made the following announcement on 30 March 1983:

'The Inland Revenue has recently carried out a review of the employment status of workers engaged on "freelance" terms within the industry. Following this review there has been an extensive series of discussions with representative bodies in the industry, including Independent Programme Producers Association, British Film and Television Producers Association, Advertising Film and Video Tape Producers Association, National Association of Theatrical and Kine Employees, and Association of Cinematograph, Television and Allied Technicians.

'As a result of that review and the subsequent discussions, the Inland Revenue consider that a number of workers engaged on "freelance" terms within the industry are engaged as employees under contracts of service, either written or oral, and should be assessed under Schedule E. Many workers in the industry already pay employee's National Insurance contributions.

'The Inland Revenue, however, accept that a number of "freelance" workers in certain types of work within the industry are likely to be engaged under contracts for services, as people in self-employment, and should therefore be assessed under Schedule D. Any individual who does not agree with the Revenue's determination of his position has the normal right of appeal to the independent Income Tax Commissioners.'

There is a list of grades in the film industry in respect of which PAYE need not be deducted and who are regarded as self-employed for tax purposes.

Further information can be obtained from the March 1992 edition of the Inland Revenue guidance notes on the application of PAYE to casual and freelance staff in the film industry. In view of the Inland Revenue announcement that the same status will apply for PAYE and DSS purposes, no liability for employee's and employer's contributions should arise in the case of any of the grades mentioned above. However, in the film and TV industry this general rule has not always been followed in practice. In December 1992, after a long review, the DSS agreed that individuals working behind the camera and who have jobs on the Inland Revenue Schedule D list are self-employed for social security purposes. The Contributions Agency will accept claims for repayment of Class 1 contributions where persons were correctly to have been treated as self-employed. It was announced on 23 June 1995 that a provision had been included in the Pensions Bill to enable a self-employed person who had erroneously been charged Class 1 contributions to forego a refund of the employee's contributions and retain the right to earnings-related state pension entitlement and, if applicable, personal pension rebates. The provision does not prevent the 'employer' reclaiming the employer's portion of contributions. The individual's benefit position will be preserved provided that it is only the employer's contributions that are refunded. Individuals or employers wishing to seek refunds should write to The Contributions Agency Refunds Group, Employers Unit 4, Room 101E,

Benton Park Road, Longbenton, Newcastle upon Tyne NE98 1YX *tel* (06451) 54260 (local call rates apply).

There are special rules for, *inter alia*, personnel appearing before the camera, short engagements, payments to limited companies and payments to overseas personalities.

Artistes, performers and non-performers

From 6 April 1990 to 5 April 1996 artistes and performers (excluding established performers with 'reserved Schedule D status' and guest artistes engaged by opera companies) working under standard Equity contracts were treated as employees for income tax purposes so far as earnings from such employments were concerned. This brought the income tax treatment into line with that of social security, as it has been the view of the DSS for many years that the vast majority of performers are employees for social security contribution purposes because of the general conditions under which they usually work. However, from 6 April 1994 it is understood that the Inland Revenue accept that the earnings of many artistes should be assessed under Schedule D Case I. This does not, of itself, affect the social security position but the DSS has always acknowledged that there is some scope for self-employment for performers (especially 'act as known' engagements), and specific claims to self-employment are looked into in detail. Accordingly 'act as known' engagements will normally be treated as self-employment for both social security and income tax purposes.

The DSS does, however, permit subsistence allowances to be paid without liability to contributions, and special rules apply to travelling expenses.

The industry also uses standard agreements for the engagement of non-performers. The Inland Revenue has looked at some of these and concluded that some are normally contracts *for* services (self-employed) and others contracts *of* service (employed).

CLASS 1 CONTRIBUTIONS BY EMPLOYEES AND EMPLOYERS

As mentioned above, these are related to earnings, the amount payable depending upon whether the employer has applied for his employees to be 'contracted-out' of the State earnings-related pension scheme; such application can be made where the employer's own pension scheme provides a requisite level of benefits for his or her employees and their dependants.

Contributions are only payable once earnings exceed the lower earnings limit but are then due on *all* such earnings up to the upper earnings limit by employees ('primary contributions') but without an upper limit for employers ('secondary contributions'). Contributions are normally collected via the PAYE tax deduction machinery, and there are penalties for late submission of returns and for errors therein. From 19 April 1993, interest will be charged automatically on unpaid PAYE and social security contributions.

Employees liable to pay contributions

These are payable by any employee who is aged 16 years and over (even though he or she may still be at school) and who is paid an amount equal to, or exceeding, the lower earnings limit (see below). Nationality is irrelevant for contribution purposes and, subject to special rules covering employees not normally resident in Great Britain, Northern Ireland or the Isle of Man, or resident in EC countries or those with which there are reciprocal agreements, contributions must be paid whether the employee concerned is a British subject or not provided he is gainfully employed in Great Britain.

Employees exempt from liability to pay contributions

Persons over pensionable age (65 for men; 60 for women) are exempt from liability to pay primary contributions, even if they have not retired. However, the fact that an employee may be exempt from liability does not relieve an employer from liability to pay secondary contributions in respect of that employee.

Rate of employees' contributions

From 6 April 1996, the rate of employees' contributions, where the earnings are not less than the lower earnings limit, is 2% of earnings to the lower earnings limit and 10% of earnings between the lower and upper earnings limits (8.2% for contracted-out employments).

Certain married women who made appropriate elections before 12 May 1977 may be entitled to pay a reduced rate of 3.85%. However, they will have no entitlement to benefits in respect of these contributions.

Employers' contributions

All employers are liable to pay contributions on the gross earnings of employees. As mentioned above, an employer's liability is not reduced as a result of employees being exempted from, or being liable to pay only the (3.85%) reduced rate of, contributions.

For earnings paid on or after 6 April 1996 employers are liable at rates of 3%, 5%, 7% or 10.2% on earnings paid (without any upper earnings limit) depending upon the particular band into which the earnings fall (see below). The rate of contributions attributable to the band into which the earnings fall is applied to *all* those earnings and not merely to the earnings falling into that band. The above four rates of secondary contributions are reduced to zero%, 2%, 4% and 7.2% in respect of earnings above the lower earnings limit and up to and including the upper earnings limit for contracted-out employments from 6 April 1996.

The employer is responsible for the payment of both employees' and employer's contributions, but is entitled to deduct the employees' contributions from the earnings on which they are calculated. Effectively, therefore, the employee suffers a deduction in respect of his or her social security contributions in arriving at his weekly or monthly wage or salary. Special rules apply to company directors and persons employed through agencies.

Rates of Class 1 contributions and earnings limits from 6 April 1996

Earnings per week	Rates payable on all earnings			
	Not Contracted-out		Contracted-out	
	Employee	Employer	Employee	Employer
£		%		%
Below 61.00	—	—	—	—
61.00 – 109.99	2% to lower	3.0	2% to lower	*3.0/nil
110.00 – 154.99	earnings limit,	5.0	earnings limit,	*5.0/2.0
155.00 – 209.99	10% between	7.0	8.2% between	*7.0/4.0
210.00 – 455.00	lower and	10.2	lower and	*10.2/7.2
Over £455.00	upper earnings	10.2	upper earnings	†10.2/7.2
	limits		limits	

* The first figure is the rate to the lower earnings limit and the second is to all the excess.

† 10.2% to lower earnings limit and above upper earnings limit; 7.2% between these limits.

Items included in, or excluded from, earnings

Contributions are calculated on the basis of a person's gross earnings from his or her employment. This will normally be the figure shown on the tax deduction working sheet, except where the employee pays superannuation contributions and, from 6 April 1987, charitable gifts – these must be added back for the purposes of calculating Class 1 liability. Profit-related pay exempt from income tax is not exempt from social security contributions.

Earnings include salary, wages, overtime pay, commissions, bonuses, holiday pay, payments made while the employee is sick or absent from work, payments to cover travel between home and office, and payments under the statutory sick pay and statutory maternity pay schemes.

However, certain payments, some of which may be regarded as taxable income for income tax purposes, are ignored for social security purposes. These include certain gratuities paid other than by the employer, redundancy payments and most payments in lieu of notice, certain payments in kind, reimbursement of specific expenses incurred in the carrying out of the employment, benefits given on an individual basis for personal reasons (e.g. wedding and birthday presents), compensation for loss of office, and meal vouchers which can only be redeemed for food or drink.

DSS booklet CA 28 (April 1995) and its April 1996 supplement give a list of items to include in or exclude from earnings for Class 1 contribution purposes.

Maximum contributions

There is a limit to the total liability for social security contributions payable by a person who is employed in more than one employment, or is also self-employed or a partner.

Where only not contracted-out Class 1 contributions, or not contracted-out Class 1 and Class 2 contributions, are payable, the maximum contribution is limited to 53 primary Class 1 contributions at the maximum weekly non-contracted-out standard rate. For 1996/97 the maximum will thus be £2152.86.

However, where contracted-out Class 1 contributions are payable, the maximum primary Class 1 contributions payable for 1996/97 where all employments are contracted-out are £1776.98.

Where Class 4 contributions are payable in addition to Class 1 and/or Class 2 contributions, *the Class 4 contributions are restricted* so that they shall not exceed the excess of £1328.65 (i.e. 53 Class 2 contributions plus maximum Class 4 contributions) over the aggregate of the Class 1 and Class 2 contributions.

Miscellaneous rules

There are detailed rules covering a person with two or more employments; where a person receives a bonus or commission in addition to a regular wage or salary; and where a person is in receipt of holiday pay. From 6 April 1991 employers' social security contributions arise under Class 1A in respect of the private use of a company car, and of fuel provided for private use therein. The rate is currently 10.2%.

CLASS 2 CONTRIBUTIONS BY THE SELF-EMPLOYED

Rate

Class 2 contributions are payable at the weekly rate of £6.05 as from 6 April 1996.

Exemptions from Class 2 liability

These are as follows:

(1) A man over 65 or a woman over 60.
(2) A person who has not attained the age of 16.
(3) A married woman or, in certain cases, a widow who elected prior to 12 May 1977 not to pay Class 2 contributions.

(4) Persons with small earnings (see below).
(5) Persons not ordinarily self-employed (see below).

Small earnings

Any person who can show that his or her net self-employed earnings per his profit and loss account (as opposed to taxable profits):
(1) for the year of application are expected to be less than a specified limit (£3430 in the 1996/97 tax year); or
(2) for the year preceding the application were less than the limit specified for that year (£3260 for 1995/96) and there has been no material change of circumstances;
may apply for a certificate of exception from Class 2 contributions. Certificates of exception must be renewed in accordance with the instructions stated thereon. At the Secretary of State's discretion the certificate may commence up to 13 weeks before the date on which the application is made. Despite a certificate of exception being in force, a person who is self-employed is still entitled to pay Class 2 contributions if he or she wishes, in order to maintain entitlement to social security benefits.

Persons not ordinarily self-employed

Part-time self-employed activities as a writer or artist are disregarded for contribution purposes if the person concerned is not ordinarily employed in such activities and has a full-time job as an employee. There is no definition of 'ordinarily employed' for this purpose but the DSS regard a person who has a regular job and whose earnings from spare-time occupation are not expected to be more than £800 per annum as falling within this category. Persons qualifying for this relief do not require certificates of exception. It should be noted that many activities covered by this relief would probably also be eligible for relief under the small earnings rule (see above).

Method of payment

From April 1993, Class 2 contributions may be paid by monthly direct debit in arrears or by cheque, bank giro, etc. following receipt of a quarterly (in arrears) bill from DSS.

Overpaid contributions

If, following the payment of Class 2 contributions, it is found that the earnings are below the exception limit (e.g. the relevant accounts are prepared late), the Class 2 contributions that have been overpaid can be reclaimed for tax years 1988/89 onwards, provided a claim is made between 6 April and 31 December immediately following the end of the tax year.

CLASS 3 CONTRIBUTIONS

These are payable voluntarily, at the weekly rate of £5.95 per week from 6 April 1996, by persons aged 16 or over with a view to enabling them to qualify for a limited range of benefits if their contribution record is not otherwise sufficient. In general, Class 3 contributions can be paid by employees, the self-employed and the non employed.

Broadly speaking, no more than 52 Class 3 contributions are payable for any one tax year, and contributions are not payable after the end of the tax year in which the individual concerned reaches the age of 64 (59 for women).

Class 3 contributions may be paid in the same manner as Class 2 (see above) or by annual cheque in arrears.

CLASS 4 CONTRIBUTIONS BY THE SELF-EMPLOYED

Rate

In addition to Class 2 contributions, self-employed persons are liable to pay Class 4 contributions. These are calculated at the rate of 6% on the amount of profits or gains chargeable to income tax under Schedule D Case I or II which exceed £6860 per annum but which do not exceed £23,660 per annum for 1996/97. Thus the maximum Class 4 contribution is 6% of £16,800 – i.e. £1008.00 for 1996/97.

For the tax year 1996/97, Class 4 contributions are based on the income tax assessment for 1996/97 (for example, under the transitional income tax rules for self-assessment, the annual average of the profits for the two years ended 31 December 1996 – in the case of a long-established business) and so on for subsequent years.

The income tax assessment on which Class 4 contributions are calculated is after deducting capital allowances and losses, but before deducting personal tax allowances or retirement annuity or personal pension plan premiums.

Class 4 contributions produce no additional benefits, but were introduced to ensure that self-employed persons as a whole pay a fair share of the cost of pensions and other social security benefits without the self-employed who make only small profits having to pay excessively high flat rate contributions.

From 6 April 1996 no income tax relief is available for Class 4 contributions. Previously, half the liability attracted income tax relief.

Payment of contributions

In general, contributions are calculated and collected by the Inland Revenue together with the income tax under Schedule D Case I or II, and accordingly the contributions are due and payable at the same time as the income tax liability on the relevant profits. Under self-assessment, interim payments of Class 4 contributions will be payable at the same time as interim payments of tax.

Persons exempt from Class 4 contributions

The following persons are exempt from Class 4 contributions:
(1) Men over 65 and women over 60 at the commencement of the year of assessment (i.e. on 6 April).
(2) An individual not resident in the United Kingdom for income tax purposes in the year of assessment.
(3) Persons whose earnings are not 'immediately derived' from carrying on a trade, profession or vocation (for example, sleeping partners and, possibly, limited partners).
(4) A child under 16 on 6 April of the year of assessment.
(5) Persons not ordinarily self-employed (see above as for Class 2 contributions).

Calculation of liability for married persons and partnerships

Under independent taxation of husband and wife from 1990/91 onwards, each spouse is responsible for his or her Class 4 liability.

In partnerships, each partner's liability is calculated separately, and the Inland Revenue will normally collect each partner's Class 4 liability in the partnership name as is the case with the income tax liability of the partnership under Schedule D. If a partner also carries on another trade or profession, the profits of all such businesses are aggregated for the purposes of calculating his or her Class 4 liability; in these circumstances the Class 4 liability in respect of his share of partnership profits may be assessed separately and not in the partnership name.

When an assessment has become final and conclusive for the purposes of income tax, it is also final and conclusive for the purposes of calculating Class 4 liability.

SOURCES OF FURTHER INFORMATION

Further information can be obtained from the many booklets published by the Department of Social Security. These can be obtained from local offices – refer to telephone directory under 'Contributions Agency' in the first instance. Individuals resident abroad should address their enquiries to Contributions Agency, International Services, Newcastle upon Tyne NE98 1YX.

Social Security Benefits

K.D. BARTLETT FCA
Partner, Clark Whitehill

Social security benefits are quite difficult to understand. There are many leaflets produced by the Department of Social Security and this article is written to try to simplify some of the more usual benefits that are available under the Social Security Acts. It deliberately does not cover every aspect of the legislation but the references given should enable the relevant information to be easily traced. These references are to the leaflets issued by the Department of Social Security.

It is usual for only one periodical benefit to be payable at any one time. If the contribution conditions are satisfied for more than one benefit it is the larger benefit that is payable. Benefit rates shown below were those payable from week commencing 6 April 1996.

Employed persons (Category A or D contributors) are covered for all benefits. Certain married women and widows (Category B and E contributors) who elected to pay at the reduced rate receive only attendance allowance, guardian's allowance and industrial injuries benefits. Other benefits may be available dependent on their husbands' contributions.

Self-employed persons (Class 2 and Class 4 contributors) are covered for all benefits except earnings-related supplements, unemployment benefit, widow's and invalidity pensions, widowed mother's allowance and industrial injury benefits.

The major changes, which took place from the week beginning 6 April 1996, were:

- Contributory benefits, including retirement pension, rise by 3.9% in line with the Retail Price Index for September 1995.
- Income-related benefits rise by 3% in line with the September 1995 'ROSSI' index.
- A programme to restructure benefits for lone parents.

FAMILY BENEFITS

Child Benefits (CH 1)

Child benefit is payable for all children who are either under 16 or under 19 and receiving full-time education at a recognised educational establishment. The rate is £10.80 for the first or eldest child and £8.80 a week for each subsequent child. It is payable to the person who is responsible for the child but excludes foster parents or people exempt from UK tax. A higher benefit (£6.30 a week more) is payable for the first or only child in a one parent family.

Maternity Benefits

Help with maternity expenses is given to selected people from the social fund. To be eligible the claimant must be receiving income support or family credit. £100 is paid for each new or adopted baby reduced by the amount of any savings over £500 held by the claimant or his or her family. A payment can be obtained from the social fund for an adopted baby provided the child is not more than 12 months old when application is made. The claimant has three months to make the claim from when adoption has taken place.

Maternity Pay (NI 17A)

Statutory maternity pay (SMP) was introduced for female employees who leave employment because of pregnancy.

SMP is applicable to those who have worked for 26 weeks by the 15th week before the expected date of confinement. This 15th week is known as the qualifying week (QW). The other qualifying conditions are that the woman must:
(1) be pregnant at the 11th week before the expected week of confinement, or already have been confined;
(2) have stopped working for her employer wholly or partly because of pregnancy or confinement;
(3) have average earnings of not less than the lower earnings limit for the payment of National Insurance contributions which is in force during her QW;
(4) provide her employer with evidence of her expected week of confinement;
(5) provide her employer with notice of her maternity absence.

Rates of SMP

There is a higher and a lower rate. The higher rate of SMP is 90% of an employee's weekly earnings and is paid for the first six weeks for which there is entitlement to SMP. To be eligible for the higher rate, a woman must meet all the qualifying conditions and have been employed by the employer for a continuous period of at least two years (at between 8 and 16 hours a week). Her service must continue into the QW.

The lower rate of SMP is a set rate reviewed each year. The rate for the tax year beginning 6 April 1996 is £54.55 per week. It is paid for 18 weeks to those not entitled to the higher amount and for up to 12 weeks to those who receive the higher rate for the first six weeks.

SMP is taxable and also subject to National Insurance contributions. The gross amount of SMP and the employer's portion of National Insurance payable on the SMP can be recovered from the State by deducting the amounts from the amount normally due for PAYE and National Insurance deductions payable to the Collector of Taxes.

Guardian's Allowance (NI 14)

This is paid at the rate of £9.85 a week. For each subsequent child the rate of benefit is £11.15 a week to people who have taken orphans into their own family. Usually both of the child's parents must be dead and at least one of them must have satisfied a residence condition.

The allowance can only be paid to the person who is entitled to child benefit for the child (or to that person's spouse). It is not necessary to be the legal guardian. The claim should be made within three months of the date of entitlement.

DISABILITY LIVING ALLOWANCE

Disability living allowance (DLA) was introduced on 6 April 1992 and replaces attendance allowance for disabled people before they reach the age of 65. It has also replaced mobility allowance. Those who are disabled after reaching 65 may be able to claim attendance allowance. The case component is divided into three rates whereas the mobility allowance has two rates. The rate of benefit from 6 April 1996 is as follows:

Care Component

	Per week £
Higher rate (day and night, or terminally ill)	48.50
Middle rate (day or night)	32.40
Lower rate (if need some help during day, or over 16 and need help preparing a meal)	12.90

Mobility Component

Higher rate (unable or virtually unable to walk)	33.90
Lower rate (can walk but needs help when outside)	12.90

Attendance Allowance

Attendance allowance has been replaced by DLA from 6 April 1992 for those aged under 65. For those aged 65 or over, attendance allowance will continue to be paid.

The rate of benefit from 6 April 1996 is as follows:

	Per week £
Higher rate (day and night)	48.50
Lower rate (day or night)	32.40

The attendance allowance board decide whether, and for how long, a person is eligible for this allowance. Attendance allowance is not taxable.

BENEFITS FOR THE ILL OR UNEMPLOYED

Statutory Sick Pay (NI 27, NI 16, NI 244)

In the majority of cases the employer now has the responsibility of paying sick pay to its employees. The payment is dependent on satisfying various conditions in respect of periods of incapacity, periods of entitlement, qualifying days and rules on notification of absence. The rules are quite complicated and reference should be made to the relevant booklets for further clarification but the key points are:

(1) Payment is made by the employer.
(2) There is a possibility of two rates of payment dependent on the employee's gross average earnings.
(3) The employee must not be capable of work and must do no work on the day concerned.
(4) SSP is not usually payable for the first three working days.
(5) The maximum entitlement is 28 weeks in any period of incapacity.
(6) Notification must be made by the employer but this procedure must be within statutory guidelines.
(7) Payment can be withheld if notification of sickness is not given in due time.

From 6 April 1996 most employers will no longer be able to reclaim any SSP back. Small employers may, in certain circumstances, receive compensation called the New Relief Scheme which will help all employers faced with exceptionally high levels of sickness absence.

Sickness Benefit (DSS Leaflet NI 16)

The majority of illnesses are now covered by statutory sick pay and sickness benefit now only applies to those employees who are excluded from statutory sickness pay and the self-employed.

Sickness benefit is paid for up to 28 weeks for those who are off work. If a claimant is still ill after 28 weeks he or she is transferred to the long term benefit, invalidity benefit.

To be eligible for sickness benefit the claimant must have paid, in any one tax year ending before the calendar year in which the claim is made, Class I contributions on an amount of earnings at least 25 times the weekly lower earnings limit for that tax year (or the equivalent of Class 2 contributions for self-employed people).

There is another condition which must be satisfied in that the claimant must have paid, or been credited with, in the tax year ending before the benefit year in which he or she makes the claim, Class 1 contributions on an amount of earnings at least 50 times the weekly lower earnings limit for both the last two tax years (or the equivalent number of Class 2 contributions for self-employed people).

Incapacity Benefit (DS 700)

Incapacity benefit replaced sickness benefit and invalidity benefit. The contribution conditions haven't changed but a new medical test has been brought in which includes a comprehensive questionnaire. The rates from 6 April 1996 are:

	£
Long-term Incapacity Benefit	61.15
Short-term Incapacity Benefit	
Higher rate	54.55
Lower rate	46.15
Increase of Long-term Incapacity Benefit for age:	
Higher rate	12.90
Lower rate	6.45

Severe Disablement Allowance (NI 252)

This is a benefit for people under pensionable age who cannot work because of physical or mental ill health and do not have sufficient NI contributions to qualify for sickness or invalidity benefit. The basic allowance is £36.95 a week. There are increases of £21.95 a week for adult dependants and £11.15 for each child.

Invalid Care Allowance (NI 212)

This is a taxable benefit paid to people of working age who cannot take a job because they have to stay at home to look after a severely disabled person. The basic allowance is £36.60 per week. An extra £21.90 is paid for each adult dependant and £11.15 for each child.

Unemployment Benefit (NI 12)

In October 1996 unemployment benefit will be replaced by Jobseekers Allowance. This new allowance is payable for up to six months but the claimant must be available to work at least 40 hours a week. During the first 13 weeks of unemployment jobseekers can restrict their search to their usual occupation but afterwards they must look outside their normal occupation.

Persons over 18 should claim benefit from the Unemployment Benefit Office. Either a P45 or a note of their national insurance number should be produced. Persons under 18 should register for work at their local Youth Employment Office. Unemployment benefit is reduced, pound for pound, for those claimants over 55 years of age, whose pensions exceed £35.00 per week.

The standard rate of unemployment benefit is £48.25 for a single person and £29.75 for a wife or other adult dependant.

PENSIONS AND WIDOW'S BENEFITS (NP 23, NP 35, NP 31)

The state pension is divided into two parts – the basic pension, presently £61.15 per week for a single person or £97.75 per week for a married couple, and the State Earnings Related Pension Scheme, which will after it matures on the present basis pay a pension of 25% of revalued earnings between the lower and upper earnings limits.

The cost of the State Earnings Related Pension Scheme (SERPS) has been a major political consideration for some time. In order to reduce the long-term cost of the scheme, benefits will be reduced for those retiring or widowed after the year 2000. The benefits will be reduced as follows:

(1) The pension will be based on lifetime average earnings rather than the best 20 years as at present.

(2) The pension will be calculated on the basis of 20% of earnings between the lower and upper earnings limit rather than 25%. This will be phased in over ten years from the tax year 2000/2001.

(3) Presently all of a member's state earnings-related benefit is inherited by a surviving spouse. For deaths occurring after April 2000 this will be reduced to 50%.

Women paying standard rate contributions into the scheme are eligible for the same amount of pension as men but five years earlier, from age 60. If a woman stays at home to bring up her children or to look after a person receiving attendance allowance she can have her basic pension rights protected without paying contributions.

The widow's pension and widowed mother's allowance also consists of a basic pension and an additional earnings-related pension. The full amount of the additional pension applies only if the husband has contributed to the new scheme for at least 20 years.

Widow's Benefits

From 11 April 1988 there are three main widow's benefits:

(1) Widow's payment, which has replaced the widow's allowance which has been abolished;

(2) Widowed mother's allowance;

(3) Widow's pension.

Widow's payment

This is a new allowance, currently a lump sum payment of £1000 payable to widows who were bereaved on or after 11 April 1988. It is payable immediately on the death of the husband. Entitlement to this benefit is based on the late husband's contribution record but no payment will be made if the widow is living with another man as husband and wife at the date of death. The late husband must have actually paid contributions on earnings of at least 25 times the weekly or lower earnings limit for a given tax year in any tax year ending before his death (or ending before he reached pensionable age if he was over 65 when he died). The equivalent number of Class 2 or voluntary Class 3 contributions will be sufficient.

When claiming, the widow should complete the form on the back of the death certificate and send it to the local social security office. On receipt of this information the DSS will send the claimant a more detailed form (BD8) which, once completed, has to go back to the social security office. It is important to claim the benefit within twelve months of the husband's death.

Widowed mother's allowance (NP 45)

If a widow is left with children to look after she is entitled to a widowed mother's allowance provided that her late husband had paid sufficient national insurance contributions. These contributions are:

(a) 25 Class 1, 2 or 3 contributions before age 65 and before 6 April 1975; or
(b) contributions in any one tax year after 6 April 1975 on earnings of at least 25 times the weekly lower earnings limit for that year.

It is important that the widow is looking after either her own child or her husband's child and that the child is under 16 or, if between the age of 16 and 19, is continuing in full-time education.

The allowance stops immediately if the widow remarries and will be suspended if she lives with a man as his wife. From April 1996 the amounts payable are as follows:

	£
Basic allowance	61.15
Increase for each child	11.15

Where a husband's contributions only satisfied the first test above, the basic allowance may be payable at a reduced rate. This reduction does not alter the rate of an increase for a child.

Widow's pension (NP 45)

A widow who is over the age of 45 when her husband dies may be eligible for a widow's pension unless she is eligible for the widowed mother's allowance. In this situation the widow's pension becomes payable when the widowed mother's allowance ends, provided she is still under the age of 65. However, where a woman had been receiving widowed mother's allowance, she becomes entitled to a widow's pension if she is between the ages of 45 and 65 when the allowance ends, no matter what her age may have been when her husband died. Before 11 April 1988 a widow aged 40 or over could qualify for a widow's pension.

Qualification conditions

(a) The contributions conditions must be satisfied and these conditions are the same as those for the widowed mother's allowance above.
(b) The widow must not be receiving the widowed mother's allowance.
(c) When her husband died she was aged between 45 and 65 or she was entitled to widowed mother's allowance and is aged between 45 and 65 when her widowed mother's allowance finished.

Cessation of Widow's Pension

(a) Entitlement finishes if the widowed mother's allowance stops because she has remarried.
(b) Widow's pension must not be claimed when the payment of the widowed mother's allowance has been suspended because the widow is in pension or is living with a man as his wife.

From 11 April 1988 both the basic and additional pension are paid at a reduced rate if the widow was aged under 55:

(a) when her husband died, if she did not subsequently become entitled to widowed mother's allowance; or
(b) when her widowed mother's allowance ceased to be paid. The relevant rates from 6 April 1994 are as follows (the ages given in parentheses apply to women for whom widow's pension was payable before 11 April 1988):

Age related		£	Age related		(£)
Age 54	(49)	56.87	49	(44)	35.47
53	(48)	52.59	48	(43)	31.19
52	(47)	48.31	47	(42)	26.91
51	(46)	44.03	46	(41)	22.63
50	(45)	39.75	45	(40)	18.35

Funeral Expenses

The death grant was abolished from 6 April 1987. It has been replaced by a payment from the social fund where the claimant is in receipt of income support, family credit or housing benefit. The full cost of a reasonable funeral is paid, reduced by any savings over £500 held by the claimant or his family (£1000 for couples over 60).

FAMILY CREDIT

Family credit replaced family income supplement (FIS) with effect from 11 April 1988. Family credit is a tax-free benefit payable to families in Great Britain where:

(1) the claimant or partner is engaged in remunerative work for 16 hours or more per week; and

(2) there is at least one child under 16 in the family (or under 19 if in full-time education up to and including A level or OND standard) for whom the claimant and/or partner is responsible.

Entitlement to family credit is determined by comparing the family's normal income with a prescribed amount, known as the 'applicable amount'. The current applicable amount is £75.20. Eligible families fall into two income groups:

(i) those whose total income does not exceed the applicable amount. Such families will be entitled to the appropriate maximum amount of family credit payable; and

(ii) those whose total income does exceed the applicable amount but by an amount which still allows some entitlement. To determine eligibility, a prescribed percentage (currently 70%) of the excess income (over and above the applicable amount) is deducted from the appropriate maximum family credit. If there is an amount left (i.e. the figure is a plus sum of at least 50p) the family will be able to receive family credit equal to this amount, rounded to the nearest penny.

Maximum family credit benefit rates (from 6 April 1996)

Adult	£46.45
Child	
aged less than 11 years	£11.75
aged 11 to 15 years	£19.45
Young Person	
aged 16 to 17 years	£24.15
aged 18 years	£33.80

An award is normally made for a period of 26 weeks. Changes of circumstances during this period will not usually affect the award.

Capital and income

Families where the claimant and partner hold capital in excess of £8000 will not be entitled to family credit. The resources of a family taken into account as income for family credit are the aggregate of their normal net earnings and other income plus any tariff income. Certain payments are disregarded in the calculation of income. For those with capital of between £3000 and £8000, the rate of benefit will be affected. For every £250 (or part of £250) held in excess of £3000, a 'tariff' income of £1.00 will be added to the family's other income.

INCOME SUPPORT (SBI, SB20)

Income support has replaced supplementary benefit. It is usually only payable to eligible persons who are unemployed or people who work less than 16 hours a week. If a person or partner works for 16 hours or more on average per week in 'remunerative' work, then no income support is payable.

Income support gives financial assistance towards regular weekly needs only. Claimants with exceptional needs will now have to apply for payments (in the form of a loan or grant) from the social fund.

The person's income must be insufficient to bring him or her up to the designated minimum level of income, known as the 'applicable amount'. The applicable amount is made up of a 'basic' personal allowance plus 'additional' premiums for those with additional needs, e.g. pensioners. People who are entitled to income support and who have no income at all will be entitled to the appropriate applicable amount in full. Those who have an income will receive income support equal to the difference between their income and the appropriate applicable amount.

As with supplementary benefit, there is a limit to the amount of capital a person can hold before income support is affected. Those who have capital above £8000 are disqualified from receiving income support altogether. Capital up to £3000 is disregarded but savings between £3000 and £8000 affect income support in the same way as for family credit.

As in the case of supplementary benefit, eligibility for income support is, in most instances, dependent on the claimant being 'available for work'. Where a person is disqualified from receiving unemployment benefit (or would be if it were otherwise payable), for such reasons as being dismissed from his or her former job because of misconduct, entitlement to income support will also be affected.

GRANTS FROM LOCAL AUTHORITIES

Council Tax Benefit

Those who will be able to claim benefit are those who:

(1) are on a low income, or
(2) are in receipt of income support
(3) share the house with certain other persons who are receiving income support.

The maximum benefit entitlement for a liable person claiming will be 100% of the liability.

The above does not set out to cover every aspect of the Social Security Acts legislation. Further information can be obtained from the local office of the Department of Social Security or from Accountants Digest No. 333 published by the Institute of Chartered Accountants in England and Wales. Readers resident abroad who have queries should write to the Department's Overseas Branch, Newcastle upon Tyne NE98 1YX.

Societies, prizes and festivals

Societies, Associations and Clubs

Yr Academi Gymreig (Welsh Academy). *President:* Prof J.E. Caerwyn Williams; *chairman:* Nesta Wyn Jones; *director:* Dafydd Rogers, 3rd Floor, Mount Stuart House, Mount Stuart Square, The Docks, Cardiff CF1 6DQ *tel* (01222) 492064. Founded in 1959 to promote creative writing in the Welsh language, existing members elect new members on the basis of their contribution to Welsh literature or criticism. Publishes a literary magazine, *Taliesin*, books on Welsh literature and translations of modern European classics into Welsh; has recently published a new English/Welsh Dictionary.
English Language Section. *President:* Roland Mathias; *chairman:* Sally Roberts Jones; *director:* Kevin Thomas *tel* (01222) 492025 *fax* (01222) 492930. Founded in 1968 to provide a meeting point for writers in the English language who are of Welsh origin and/or take Wales as a main theme of their work. Membership open to all those deemed to have made a contribution to the literature of Wales, whether as writers, editors or critics. Associate membership is open to all interested individuals or organisations.

Acrylic Painters' Association, National (NAPA) (1985). *President:* Alwyn Crawshaw; *vice-president:* Dr Sally A. Bulgin; *director and founder:* Kenneth J. Hodgson, 134 Rake Lane, Wallasey, Wirral, Merseyside L45 1JW *tel* 0151-639 2980. Promotes interest in, and encourages excellence and innovation in, the work of painters in acrylic. Holds an annual exhibition at the Royal Birmingham Society of Artists Gallery; publishes an annual journal and a newsletter. *Full membership:* £16 p.a.; *associate membership:* £8 p.a.

Agricultural Journalists, Guild of. *President:* Drew Sloan; *chairman:* Victor Robertson; *hon. general secretary:* Don Gomery, Charmwood, 47 Court Meadow, Rotherfield, East Sussex TN6 3LQ *tel* (01892) 853187. Established to promote a high standard among journalists who specialise in agricultural matters and to assist them to increase their sources of information and technical knowledge.

Amateur Artists, Society of (1992), PO Box 50, Newark, Notts. NG23 5GY *tel* (01949) 844050 *fax* (01949) 844051. To inform, encourage and inspire everyone, whatever their ability, who wants to paint, and to promote friendship and companionship amongst fellow artists. Holds meetings and events at local level, organises painting holidays, workshops, local exhibitions and competitions, publishes newsletter *Paint* (Q.). *Initial membership fee:* £17.50, overseas £27.50.

American Correspondents, Association of. *President:* Lawrence Ingrassia, c/o Secretary, Sandra Marshall, Associated Press, 12 Norwich Street, London EC4A 1BP *tel* 0171-353 1515 ext 4202 *fax* 0171-936 2229.

American Publishers, Association of, Inc. (1970). *President:* Nicholas A. Veliotes; *executive vice president:* Thomas D. McKee, 71 Fifth Avenue, New York, NY 10003, USA *tel* 212-255-0200 *fax* 212-255-7007.

American Society of Composers, Authors and Publishers (1914), One Lincoln Plaza, New York, NY 10023 *tel* 212-621-6000 *fax* 212-721-0955. *President:* Marilyn Bergman. ASCAP is a membership association of over 50,000 writers and publishers, which protects its members' rights and those of affiliated foreign societies. It licenses and collects royalties for public performance of copyrighted music. *Annual membership fees:* writers $10.00, publishers $50.00.

American Society of Indexers (1968), PO Box 48267, Seattle, WA 98148-0267, USA *tel* 206-241-9196 *fax* 206-727-6430. Aims to improve the quality and standards of indexing and related areas of information science; acts as an advisory board on renumeration and qualifications of indexers and abstractors; defends and safeguards the professional interests of indexers. Holds meetings, seminars, workshops; provides bi-annual *The Indexer* and 6 p.a. newsletter, *Key Words. Annual membership fee:* $65, student $35, corporate $150.

Art and Design, National Society for Education in (1888), The Gatehouse, Corsham Court, Corsham, Wilts. SN13 0BZ *tel* (01249) 714825 *fax* (01249) 716138. *General secretary:* Dr John Steers NDD, ATC, DAE, PhD. Professional association of principals and lecturers in colleges and schools of art and of specialist art, craft and design teachers in other schools and colleges. Has representatives on National and Regional Committees concerned with Art and Design Education. Publication: *Journal of Art and Design Education* (3 p.a.), (Blackwells).

Art Club, New English, 17 Carlton House Terrace, London SW1Y 5BD *tel* 0171-930 6844 *fax* 0171-839 7830. *Hon. secretary:* William Bowyer RA, RWS, RP. For all those interested in the art of painting, and the promotion of fine arts. Open Annual Exhibition at Mall Galleries.

Artists, Federation of British, 17 Carlton House Terrace, London SW1Y 5BD *tel* 0171-930 6844 *fax* 0171-839 7830. Administers nine major National Art Societies at The Mall Galleries, The Mall, London SW1.

Artists, International Guild of, Ralston House, 41 Lister Street, Riverside Gardens, Ilkley, West Yorkshire LS29 9ET *tel* (01943) 609075. *Director:* Leslie Simpson FRSA. Organises four seasonal exhibitions per year for three national societies: Society of Miniaturists, British Society of Painters in Oils, Pastels & Acrylics and British Watercolour Society. Promotes these three societies in countries outside the British Isles.

Artists Agents, Society of, (1992) 144 Royal College Street, London NW1 0TA *tel* 0171-267 9661. *Contact:* Alison Eldred. Formed to promote professionalism in the industry and to forge closer links between clients and artists through an agreed set of guidelines. The Society believes in an ethical approach through proper terms and conditions, thereby protecting the interests of the artists and clients.

Artists in Ireland, Association of (1981), Arthouse, Temple Bar, Dublin 2, Republic of Ireland *tel* (01) 8740529 *fax* (01) 6771585. *Director:* Stella Coffey. To support and advise professional visual artists in Ireland, to promote the visual arts, to develop international exchanges of artists. Publishes *Art Bulletin* (6 p.a.). Published (1994) *Irish Visual Artists' Handbook*, available by mail £14 (incl. p&p). *Membership fee:* £25 p.a.

Artists, Royal Birmingham Society of, 69A New Street, Birmingham B2 4DU   *tel* 0121-643 3768. Society has its own galleries and rooms in the city centre. Members (RBSA) and Associates (ARBSA) are elected annually. Holds three Open Exhibitions: Oil & Sculpture (March), Watercolour & Crafts (May), Pastel & Drawing (November) – send sae for schedules, available six weeks prior to Exhibition. Also an Autumn Exhibition open to Members and Associates, and two Friends Exhibitions (January and July). Friends of the RBSA pay an annual subscription of £12, which entitles them to attend various functions and to submit work for the Annual Exhibitions.

Artists, Royal Society of British, 17 Carlton House Terrace, London SW1Y 5BD   *tel* 0171-930 6844   *fax* 0171-839 7830. *President:* Colin Hayes RA; *keeper:* Alfred Daniels. Incorporated by Royal Charter for the purpose of encouraging the study and practice of the arts of painting, sculpture and architectural designs. Annual Open Exhibition at the Mall Galleries, The Mall, London SW1.

Arts Boards—see **Regional Arts Boards.**

Arts Club (1863), 40 Dover Street, London W1X 3RB   *tel* 0171-499 8581   *fax* 0171-409 0913. *Secretary:* Jackie Downing. For all those connected with or interested in the arts.

The Arts Council/An Chomhairle Ealáion (1951), Literature Officer, 70 Merrion Square, Dublin 2, Republic of Ireland   *tel* (01) 6611840   *fax* (01) 6761302. The national agency which promotes the arts in Ireland, including literature in English and Irish.

Arts Council of England, 14 Great Peter Street, London SW1P 3NQ   *tel* 0171-333 0100. *Chairman:* Lord Gowrie; *secretary-general:* Mary Allen; *director of literature:* Alastair Niven. To develop and improve the knowledge, understanding and practice of the arts, and to increase their accessibility to the public throughout England. The arts with which the Council is mainly concerned are dance, drama, mime, literature, music and opera, the visual arts, including photography and documentary films and videos on the arts. Within literature, 15 annual writers' awards are awarded competitively (see also page 644). Subsidies are provided to literary organisations and magazines, and schemes include support for translation, writers' residencies in prisons, tours by authors and the promotion of literature in libraries and education.

Arts Council of Northern Ireland, 185 Stranmillis Road, Belfast BT9 5DU   *tel* (01232) 381591   *fax* (01232) 661715. *Chief executive:* Brian Ferran; *literature officer:* Ciaran Carson. Promotes and encourages the arts throughout Northern Ireland.

Arts Council of Wales, 9 Museum Place, Cardiff CF1 3NX   *tel* (01222) 394711   *fax* (01222) 221447. *Chairman:* Sir Richard Lloyd Jones KCB; *chief executive:* Emyr Jenkins; *literature director:* Tony Bianchi; *acting visual art director:* Isabel Hitchman; *craft director:* Roger Lefevre; *drama director:* Michael Baker; *dance director:* Maldwyn Pate; *music director:* Roy Bohana. Has departments for Music, Visual Art, Literature, Drama, Craft and Dance, and also runs the Oriel Gallery in Cardiff; undertakes this work in both the English and Welsh languages.
North Wales Regional Office, 10 Wellfield House, Bangor, Gwynedd LL57 1ER   *tel* (01248) 353248   *fax* (01248) 351077. *Director:* Sandra Wynne.
South East Wales Regional Office, Victoria Street, Cwmbran, Gwent NP44 3YT   *tel* (01633) 875075   *fax* (01633) 875389. *Acting director:* Nigel Emery.
West Wales Regional Office, 3 Red Street, Carmarthen, Dyfed SA31 1QL   *tel* (01267) 234248   *fax* (01267) 233084. *Director:* Carwyn Rogers.

Arts, Manufactures and Commerce, Royal Society for the encouragement of (RSA) (1754), 8 John Adam Street, London WC2N 6EZ *tel* 0171-930 5115 *fax* 0171-839 5805. *Chairman of council:* Prudence Leith OBE; *director:* Peter Cowling. With 20,000 Fellows, the RSA sustains a forum for people from all walks of life to come together to address issues, shape new ideas and stimulate action. It works through projects, award schemes and its lecture programme, the proceedings of which are recorded in the monthly *RSA Journal*.

Asian Affairs, Royal Society for (1901), 2 Belgrave Square, London SW1X 8PJ *tel* 0171-235 5122 *fax* 0171-259 6771. *President:* The Lord Denman CBE, MC, TD; *chairman of council:* Sir Donald Hawley KCMG, MBE; *secretary:* Mrs Helen McKeag. For the study of all Asia past and present; fortnightly lectures, etc.; library. Publishes *Asian Affairs*, 3 p.a., free to members. *Subscription:* £45 London, £35 more than 60 miles from London; other rates on application.

Aslib, The Association for Information Management (1924), Helen Rebera, Membership Manager, Information House, 20-24 Old Street, London EC1V 9AP *tel* 0171-253 4488 *fax* 0171-430 0514 *e-mail* aslib@aslib.co.uk Actively promotes best practice in the management of information resources. It represents its members and lobbies on all aspects of the management of and legislation concerning information at local, national and international levels. Aslib provides consultancy and information services, professional development training, conferences, specialist recruitment and the Aslib Internet Programme, and publishes primary and secondary journals, conference proceedings, directories and monographs.

The Jane Austen Society. *Secretary:* Mrs Susan McCartan, Carton House, Redwood Lane, Medstead, Alton, Hants GU34 5PE *tel* (01705) 475855 (answerphone) *fax* (01705) 788842 *e-mail* rosemary@sndc.demon.co.uk Founded in 1940 to promote interest in, and enjoyment of, Jane Austen's novels and letters. Eight branches in UK, and two overseas. *Membership:* UK from £10, life £150; overseas from £12, life £180.

Australia Council, PO Box 788, Strawberry Hills, NSW 2012, Australia *located at* 181 Lawson Street, Redfern, NSW 2016, Australia *tel* (02) 9950 9000 *fax* (02) 9950 9111. *Chairperson:* Hilary McPhee AM. Provides a broad range of support for the arts in Australia, embracing music, theatre, literature, visual arts, crafts, Aboriginal arts and community arts. It has seven major Funds: Literature, Visual Arts/Craft, Music, Theatre, Dance, Community Cultural Development, Major Organisations, as well as the Aboriginal and Torres Strait Islander Arts Board.

The Literature Fund, Australia Council, PO Box 788, Strawberry Hills, NSW 2012, Australia *tel* (02) 9950 9000 *fax* (02) 9950 9111. Because of its size and isolation and the competition its literature meets from other English-speaking countries, Australia has always needed to subsidise writing of creative and cultural significance. The Board's chief objective is the support of the writing of all forms of creative literature – novels, short stories, poetry, plays and literary non-fiction. It also assists with the publication of literary magazines, has a publishing subsidies programme, and initiates and supports projects of many kinds designed to promote Australian literature both within Australia and abroad.

Australian Publishers Association (APA), 89 Jones Street, Ultimo, NSW 2007, Australia *tel* (02) 281 9788 *fax* (02) 281 1073.

Australian Library and Information Association, PO Box E441, Queen Victoria Terrace, ACT 2600, Australia *tel* (06) 285 1877 *fax* (06) 282 2249. *Executive director:* Virginia Walsh. Aims to promote and improve the services of libraries and other information agencies; to improve the standard of library and information personnel and foster their professional interests; to represent the interests of members to governments, other organisations and the community; and to encourage people to contribute to the improvement of library and information services by supporting the association.

The Australian Society of Authors, PO Box 1566, Strawberry Hills, NSW 2012, Australia *located at* 98 Pitt Street, Redfern, NSW 2016, Australia *tel* (02) 9318 0877 *fax* (02) 9318 0530 *e-mail* asauthors@peg.pegasus.oz.au *Executive director:* Lynne Spender. Aims to represent and enhance author rights and interests, through providing information, contract advice, publications (newsletters and journals), representation in disputes. Also seminars, research and information on new issues and new directions in writing and publishing. *Joining fee:* $20; *annual membership:* full/associate $110, affiliate $70.

Australian Writers' Guild Ltd (1962), 60 Kellett Street, Kings Cross, NSW 2011, Australia *tel* (02) 357 7888 *fax* (02) 357 7776. *Executive officer:* Ms Chris Sharp. Professional association dedicated to promoting and protecting the professional interests of writers for stage, screen, television and radio. *Subscription:* full members: entrance fee $140, annual fee $150-$560 dependent on income from writing; associate members: entrance fee $70, annual fee $80.

Authors, The Society of, 84 Drayton Gardens, London SW10 9SB *tel* 0171-373 6642. *Chairman:* Simon Brett; *general secretary:* Mark Le Fanu. Founded in 1884 by Sir Walter Besant with the object of representing, assisting and protecting authors. A limited company and independent trade union, the Society's scope has been continuously extended; specialist associations have been created for translators, broadcasters, educational, medical and children's writers and illustrators (details are elsewhere in this Yearbook). Members are entitled to legal as well as general advice in connection with the marketing of their work, their contracts, their choice of a publisher, problems with publishers, broadcasting organisations, etc. *Subscription:* £70 (£65 by direct debit) p.a. with certain reductions available to authors under 35 or over 65. Full particulars of membership from the Society's offices. (See also article on page 637.)

Authors' Agents, The Association of (1974). *President:* Caroline Dawnay; *treasurer:* Brian Stone; *secretary:* Carol Heaton, 37 Goldhawk Road, London W12 8QQ *tel* 0181-749 0315 *fax* 0181-749 0318. Maintains a code of professional practice to which all members of the Association commit themselves; holds regular meetings to discuss matters of common professional interest; and provides a vehicle for representing the view of authors' agents in discussion of matters of common interest with other professional bodies.

Authors' Club (1891) (at the Arts Club), 40 Dover Street, London W1X 3RB *tel* 0171-499 8581 *fax* 0171-409 0913. *Secretary:* Ann Carter. Founded by Sir Walter Besant, the Authors' Club welcomes as members writers, publishers, critics, journalists, academics and anyone involved with literature. Administers the Authors' Club Best First Novel Award, Sir Banister Fletcher Award, Marsh Biography Award and the Marsh Award for Children's Literature in Translation. *Membership fee:* apply to secretary.

The Authors League of America, Inc. (1912), 330 West 42nd Street, New York, NY 10036, USA *tel* 212-564-8350 *fax* 212-564-8363. National membership organisation to promote the professional interest of authors and dramatists, procure satisfactory copyright legislation and treaties, guard freedom of expression and support fair tax treatment for writers.

Authors' Licensing and Collecting Society Ltd (ALCS), Isis House, 74 New Oxford Street, London WC1A 1EF *tel* 0171-255 2034 *fax* 0171-323 0486 *e-mail* alcs@alcs.co.uk Independent collecting society for the collective administration of literary and dramatic rights in the spheres of reprography, lending right (*not* British lending right), off-air and private recording and cable retransmission. *Membership:* £5.88 p.a. (inc. VAT) for UK residents, £5 for other EU residents, £7 for residents outside EU; open to authors, successor membership to authors' heirs. Free membership to members of the Society of Authors and the Writers' Guild of Great Britain. See **ALCS** article on page 534.

Authors' Representatives, Inc., Association of (1991), Ten Astor Place, 3rd Floor, New York, NY 10003, USA *tel* 212-353-3709.

Aviation Artists, The Guild of (incorporating the Society of Aviation Artists), The Bondway Business Centre, 71 Bondway, Vauxhall Cross, London SW8 1SQ *tel* 0171-735 0634. *President:* Michael Turner PGAvA; *secretary:* Hugo Trotter DFC. Formed in 1971 to promote aviation art through the organisation of exhibitions and meetings. Holds annual open exhibition in July in London; £1000 for 'Aviation Painting of the Year'. Quarterly members' journal. Associates £40, Members £55 (by invitation), non-exhibiting artists and friends £15.

BAPLA (British Association of Picture Libraries and Agencies) (1975). *Administrator:* Sarah Saunders. BAPLA, 18 Vine Hill, London EC1R 5DX *tel* 0171-713 1780 *fax* 0171-713 1211. BAPLA is the trade organisation representing the British picture library and agency industry, offering an impressive 300 million pictures. With 310 members, it is the largest organisation of its kind in the world, and offers a unique pool of material and expertise. The Association promotes the highest standards of professionalism and service in the loan and reproduction of pictures. No library or agency is admitted to membership unless it undertakes to abide by the code of practice. BAPLA vigilantly promotes the fact that pictures have a copyright, and that copyright has a commercial value.

BASCA (British Academy of Songwriters, Composers and Authors), 34 Hanway Street, London W1P 9DE *tel* 0171-436 2261 *fax* 0171-436 1913. *General secretary:* Amanda Harcourt. Europe's largest composer body. Represented on PRS and MCPS boards. Competitions. Quarterly magazine. Song for Europe. Presents Ivor Novello Awards.

The E.F. Benson Society (1984), 88 Tollington Park, London N4 3RA *tel* 0171-272 3375. *Secretary:* Allan Downend. To promote interest in the author E.F. Benson and the Benson family. Arranges annual literary evening, annual outing to Rye (July), talks on the Bensons and exhibitions. Archive includes the Austin Seckersen Collection, transcriptions of the Benson diaries and letters. Publishes postcards, anthologies of Benson's works and an annual journal, *The Dodo. Annual subscription:* £7.50 single, £8.50 two people at same address; £12.50 overseas.

E.F. Benson: The Tilling Society (1982), Martello Bookshop, 26 High Street, Rye, East Sussex TN31 7JJ *tel* (01797) 222242 *fax* (01797) 227335. *Secretaries:* Cynthia and Tony Reavell. To bring together enthusiasts for E.F. Benson and his Mapp & Lucia novels; annual gathering in Rye. Publishes two lengthy newsletters p.a. *Annual subscription:* £8, overseas £10; full starters membership (including all back newsletters) £20, overseas £24.

Bibliographical Society (1892), National Art Library, Victoria & Albert Museum, South Kensington, London SW7 2RL. *President:* P.C.G. Isaac; *hon. secretary:*

D. Pearson *tel* 0171-938 9655 *fax* 0171-938 8461. Acquisition and dissemination of information upon subjects connected with historical bibliography.

The Blackpool Art Society (1884), The Studio, Wilkinson Avenue, Blackpool FY3 9HB. *President:* Lynette Hodkinson; *hon. secretary:* Denise Fergyson, 29 Stafford Avenue, Poulton-le-Fylde, Lancs. FY6 8BJ *tel* (01253) 884645. Summer and autumn exhibition (members' work only). Studio meetings, practicals, lectures, etc., out-of-door sketching, workshops.

Book Packagers Association (1985), 93a Blenheim Crescent, London W11 2EQ *tel* 0171-221 9089. *Secretary:* Rosemary Pettit. Aims to represent the interests of book packagers; to exchange information at meetings and seminars; to provide services such as standard contracts and display/meeting facilities at book fairs. *Subscription:* £75-£150 p.a.

Book Trust (1925, as the National Book Council), Book House, 45 East Hill, Wandsworth, London SW18 2QZ *tel* 0181-870 9055 *fax* 0181-874-4790. *Patron:* HRH Prince Philip, Duke of Edinburgh; *chairman:* Richard Hoggart; *director:* Brian Perman. Book Trust exists to open up the world of books and reading to people of all ages and cultures. Its services include the Book Information Service, a unique, specialist information and research service for all queries on books and reading. Book Trust administers a number of literary prizes, including the Booker Prize; produces a wide range of books, pamphlets and leaflets designed to make books more easily accessible to the public.
Young Book Trust provides practical help and advice on all aspects of children's books and reading. The Children's Library houses a unique collection of every children's title published in the UK during the last two years. On joining, subscribers receive Bookfax, a folder full of information, regularly updated, on book prizes, costume characters, exhibitions, etc., plus author information, book week material and booklists. Young Book Trust produces a termly newsletter for its subscribers who include publishers, schools, libraries and booksellers. *Subscription:* £30 + VAT p.a.

Book Trust Scotland (1960), The Scottish Book Centre, 137 Dundee Street, Edinburgh EH11 1BG *tel* 0131-229 3663 *fax* 0131-228 4293. With a particular responsibility towards Scottish writing, and especially active in the field of children's writing, Book Trust Scotland exists to promote literature and reading, and aims to reach (and create) a wider reading public than has existed before. It also organises exhibitions, readings and storytellings, operates an extensive children's reference library available to everyone and administers literary prizes. Book Trust Scotland also publishes short biographies, literary guides and directories and advises other relevant art organisations.

Books Across the Sea, The English-Speaking Union of the Commonwealth, Dartmouth House, 37 Charles Street, London W1X 8AB *tel* 0171-493 3328 *fax* 0171-495 6108; The English Speaking Union of the United States, 16 East 69th Street, New York, NY 10021, USA *tel* 212-879-6800 *fax* 212-772-2886. World voluntary organisation devoted to the promotion of international understanding and friendship. Exchanges books regularly with its corresponding BAS Committees in New York, occasionally with Australia, Canada and New Zealand. The books are selected to reflect the life and culture of each country and the best of its recent publishing and writing. New selections are announced by bulletin, *The Ambassador Booklist.*

Booksellers Association of Great Britain and Ireland (1895), 272 Vauxhall Bridge Road, London SW1V 1BA *tel* 0171-834 5477 *fax* 0171-834 8812. *Chief executive:* T.E. Godfray.

The George Borrow Society (1991). *Hon. secretary:* Dr James H. Reading, The Gables, 112 Irchester Road, Rushden, Northants. NN10 9XQ *tel/fax* (01933) 312965. To promote knowledge of the life and works of George Borrow (1803-81), traveller and author. Bi-annual *Bulletin. Annual membership fee:* £8.

Botanical Artists, Society of (1985). *Founder president:* Suzanne Lucas FLS. PRMS. FPSBA; *hon. treasurer:* Pamela Davis; *hon. secretary:* Margaret Stevens; *executive secretary:* Mrs Pam Henderson, 1 Knapp Cottages, Wyke, Gillingham, Dorset SP8 4NQ *tel* (01747) 825718 (during exhibitions 0171-222 2723). Aims to encourage the art of botanical painting. Membership through selection. Annual Open Exhibition held, around Easter time, at The Westminster Gallery, Westminster Central Hall, Storey's Gate, London SW1H 9NH. Information and entrance forms available from the Executive Secretary from October, on receipt of sae. *Membership fee:* £35; lay members £20.

British Academy (1901), 20-21 Cornwall Terrace, London NW1 4QP *tel* 0171-487 5966 *telex* 2631947 *fax* 0171-224 3807 *e-mail* basec@britac.ac.uk *President:* Sir Keith Thomas; *vice-presidents:* Prof G.P.K. Beer, Prof P. Haggett CBE; *treasurer:* Mr J.S. Flemming; *foreign secretary:* Prof B.E. Supple; *publications secretary:* Prof D.E. Luscombe; *secretary:* P.W.H. Brown CBE. The British Academy is the national Academy for the humanities and social sciences. It is an independent and self-governing fellowship of scholars, elected for distinction and achievement in one or more branches of the academic disciplines that make up the humanities and social sciences. In the absence of a research council with responsibility for the humanities, the British Academy is now the principal channel outside the universities for the Government's support of advanced research in the humanities, and it receives a Parliamentary grant-in-aid to support its activities. These include a wide range of grant schemes for research at postdoctoral level, and the organisation of the national scheme for postgraduate awards in the humanities.

British Amateur Press Association (BAPA) (1890), Flat 36, Priory Park, Botanical Way, St Osyth, Essex CO16 8TE. *Secretary:* Mr L.E. Linford. A non-profit making, non-sectarian hobby organisation to 'promote the fellowship of amateur writers, artists, editors, printers, publishers and others, and to encourage them to edit, print and publish, *as a hobby*, magazines and newsletters, etc' by letterpress and other processes, including photocopiers and DTP/word-processors. Not an outlet for placing work commercially, only with other members in their private publications circulated within the association and friends. A fraternity providing contacts between amateur writers, poets, editors, artists, etc. Postal enquiries only, please send first class stamp.

British American Arts Association (BAAA), 116 Commercial Street, London E1 6NF *tel* 0171-247 5385 *fax* 0171-247 5256. *Director:* Jennifer Williams. A non-profit organisation working in the field of arts and education. BAAA conducts research, organises conferences, produces a quarterly newsletter and is part of an international network of arts and education organisations. As well as a specialised arts and education library, BAAA has a more general library holding information on opportunities for artists and performers both in the UK and abroad. BAAA is not a grant-giving organisation.

The British Council, 10 Spring Gardens, London SW1A 2BN *tel* 0171-930 8466 *telex* 8952201 BRICON G *fax* 0171-839 6347. *Chairman:* Sir Martin Jacomb; *director-general:* Sir John Hanson KCMG, CBE. The British Council promotes Britain abroad, by providing access to British ideas, talent and experience in education and training, books and the English language, information, the arts, the sciences and technology. The Council is an authority on teaching English as a second or foreign language and gives advice and information on curriculum, methodology, materials and testing through its Professional Services Division. It also promotes British literature overseas through writers' tours, academic visits, seminars and exhibitions. The Council works in 109 countries where it runs 185 libraries and resource centres and 94 teaching centres.

The Council's lending and reference libraries throughout the world stock material appropriate to the Council's priorities in individual countries. Where appropriate the libraries act as showcases for the latest British publications. They vary in size from small reference collections and information centres to comprehensive libraries equipped with reference works, CD-ROM, on-line facilities and a selection of British periodicals. Bibliographies of British books on special subjects are prepared on request.

The Council organises book and electronic publishing exhibitions for showing overseas, ranging from small specialist displays to larger exhibitions at major international book fairs such as Frankfurt.

The Council publishes a series of literary bibliographies, including *The Novel in Britain since 1970* and *Shakespeare*; *Contemporary Writers*, a series of over 30 pamphlets on modern British writers; and exhibitions on literary topics such as *Writers Abroad: British Travel Writing*. A catalogue is available on request, as is a catalogue of other publications, covering the arts, books, libraries and publishing, education and training, English language teaching and information for and about overseas students.

The Council acts as an agent of the Overseas Development Administration for book aid projects for developing countries. In 1994/95 the Council also supported over 1000 events in the visual arts, film and television, drama, literature, dance and music, ranging from the classical to the contemporary.

Further information about the work of the British Council is available from the Press and Public Relations Department at the headquarters in London or from British Council offices and libraries overseas.

British Film Institute (BFI), 21 Stephen Street, London W1P 2LN   *tel* 0171-255 1444   *telex* 27624   *fax* 0171-436 7950. *Director:* Wilf Stevenson; *head of press and corporate affairs:* Tony Slaughter. Established in 1933 by Royal Charter, the BFI is the UK national agency with responsibility for encouraging and preserving the arts of film and television. The BFI's aim is to ensure that the many audiences in the UK are offered access to the widest possible choice of cinema and television, so that their enjoyment is enhanced through a deeper understanding of the history and potential of these vital and popular art forms. The BFI's Library and Information Service contains the world's largest collection of published and unpublished material relating to film and television. *Annual membership:* £11.95; includes NFT monthly programmes. Library passes: £17.50 (members); £30 (non-members). Concessionary rates are available.

British Interactive Multimedia Association (BIMA) (1984), 6 Washingley Road, Folksworth, Peterborough PE7 3SY   *tel* (01733) 245700   *fax* (01733) 240020. *Secretary:* Jane Callaghan. BIMA was established to promote a wider understanding of the benefits of interactive multimedia to industry, government and education and to provide a regular forum for the exchange of views amongst members. Members come from the fields of application development, computer manufacturing, publishing, disk pressing, hardware distribution, programming and consultancy. Membership is open to any organisation or individual with an interest in multimedia. As well as regular monthly meetings, BIMA publishes a quarterly newsletter. *Membership:* commercial £650; institutional £300; individual £150.

Broadcasting Entertainment Cinematograph and Theatre Union, Writers Section (1946), 111 Wardour Street, London W1V 4AY *tel* 0171-437 8506 *fax* 0171-437 8268. *Supervisory official:* Marilyn Goodman; *general secretary:* R. Bolton. To defend the interests of writers in film, television and radio. By virtue of its industrial strength, the Union is able to help its writer members to secure favourable terms and conditions. In cases of disputes with employers, the Union can intervene in order to ensure an equitable settlement. Its production agreement with PACT lays down minimum terms for writers working in the documentary area.

Broadcasting Group, 84 Drayton Gardens, London SW10 9SB *tel* 0171-373 6642. Specialist group within the Society of Authors for radio and television writers and others involved in broadcasting.

The Brontë Society, Membership Secretary, Brontë Parsonage Museum, Haworth, Keighley, West Yorkshire BD22 8DR *tel* Haworth (01535) 642323 *fax* (01535) 647131. Examination, preservation, illustration of the memoirs and literary remains of the Brontë family; exhibitions of MSS and other subjects. Publishes: *The Transactions of the Brontë Society* (bi-annual) and *The Brontë Gazette* (bi-annual).

The Browning Society (1881, refounded 1969). *Secretary:* Mairi Calcraft-Rennie, Cherry Tree Cottage, Fyning Lane, Rogate, Petersfield, Hants GU31 5DQ *tel* (01730) 821666. Aims to widen the appreciation and understanding of the lives and poetry of Robert Browning and Elizabeth Barrett Browning, and other Victorian writers and poets. *Membership:* £10.

The John Buchan Society (1979). *Hon. secretary:* Russell Paterson, Limpsfield, 16 Ranfurly Road, Bridge of Weir, Renfrewshire PA11 3EL *tel* (01505) 613116. Promotes a wider understanding and appreciation of the life and works of John Buchan. Encourages publication of a complete annotated edition of Buchan's works, and supports the John Buchan Centre and Museum at Broughton, Borders. Holds regular meetings and social gatherings; produces a Newsletter and a Journal. *Subscription:* £10.00 p.a. full/overseas; other rates on application.

Byron Society (International) (1971), Byron House, 6 Gertrude Street, London SW10 0JN *tel* 0171-352 5112 *fax* 0171-352 1226. *Hon. director:* Mrs Elma Dangerfield OBE. To promote research into the life and works of Lord Byron by seminars, discussions, lectures and readings. Publishes *The Byron Journal* (annual, £5 + postage). *Subscription:* £18 p.a.

Cable Communications Association (1934), The Fifth Floor, Artillery House, Artillery Row, London SW1P 1RT *tel* 0171-222 2900 *fax* 0171-799 1471.

Randolph Caldecott Society (1983). *Secretary:* Kenn Oultram, Clatterwick Hall, Little Leigh, Northwich, Cheshire CW8 4RJ *tel* (01606) 891303 (office hours). To encourage an interest in the life and works of Randolph Caldecott, the Victorian artist, illustrator and sculptor. Meetings held in Chester. Newsletter (*Caldecott Sketch*) published bi-annually. *Subscription:* £7-£10 p.a.

Canada, Periodical Writers Association of (1976), 54 Wolseley Street, Toronto, Ontario M5T 1A5, Canada *tel* 416-504-1645 *fax* 416-703-0059. *Executive director:* Ruth Biderman.

Canada, Writers Guild of, 35 McCaul Street, 3rd Floor, Toronto, Ontario M5T 1V7, Canada *tel* 416-979-7907 *toll free* 1-800-567-9974 *fax* 416-979-9273. *Director of member & information services:* Sarah Dearing. To further the professional, creative and economic rights and interests of writers in radio, TV, film, video and all recorded media; to promote full freedom of expression and communication, and to oppose censorship unequivocally. *Annual membership fee:* $150, plus 2% of fees earned in the Guild's jurisdiction.

Canada, The Writers' Union of, 24 Ryerson Avenue, Toronto, Ontario M5T 2P3, Canada   *tel* 416-703-8982   *fax* 416-703-0826. *Chair:* Paul Quarrington.

Canadian Authors Association, PO Box 419, 27 Doxsee Avenue North, Campbellford, Ontario K0L 1L0, Canada   *tel* 705-653-0323   *fax* 705-653-0593. *President:* Cora Taylor; *administrator:* Alec McEachern.

Canadian Magazine Publishers Association (1989), 130 Spadina Avenue, Suite 202, Toronto, Ontario M5V 2L4, Canada   *tel* 416-504-0274   *fax* 416-504-0437. *President:* Catherine Keachie.

Canadian Poets, League of (1966), 54 Wolseley Street, 3rd Floor, Toronto, Ontario M5T 1A5, Canada   *tel* 416-504-1657   *fax* 416-703-0059. *Executive director:* Edita Petrauskaite. To promote the interests of poets and to advance Canadian poetry in Canada and abroad. Administers two annual awards; runs annual poetry competition; publishes a newsletter and the books *Poetry Markets for Canadians*, *Who's Who in The League of Canadian Poets*, *Poets in the Classroom* (teaching guide), *Vintage 94* (contest anthology).

Canadian Publishers, Association of (1976; formerly Independent Publishers Association 1971), 2 Gloucester Street, Suite 301, Toronto, Ontario M4Y 1L5, Canada   *tel* 416-413-4929   *fax* 416-413-4920. *Director:* Paul Davidson.

Canadian Publishers' Council, 250 Merton Street, Suite 203, Toronto, Ontario M4S 1B1, Canada *tel* 416-322-7011 *fax* 416-322-6999 *WWW* www.pubcouncil.ca *Executive director:* Jacqueline Hushion.

Careers Writers' Association (1980). *Chairman:* Catherine Avent OBE, 9 Temple Grove, London NW11 7UA   *tel* 0181-458 2546. Society for established writers on the inter-related topics of education, training and careers. Holds occasional meetings on subjects of interest to members, and circulates details of members to information providers. *Annual membership fee:* £15.

(Daresbury) Lewis Carroll Society (1970). *Secretary:* Kenn Oultram, Clatterwick Hall, Little Leigh, Northwich, Cheshire CW8 4RJ   *tel* (01606) 891303 (office hours). To encourage an interest in the life and works of Lewis Carroll, author of *Alice's Adventures*. Meetings at Carroll's birth village (Daresbury). Newsletter (*Stuff & Nonsense*) bi-annually. *Subscription:* £5 p.a.

The Lewis Carroll Society (1969). *Secretary:* Sarah Stanfield, Acorns, Dargate, Nr Faversham, Kent ME13 9HG. To promote interest in the life and works of Lewis Carroll (Revd Charles Lutwidge Dodgson) and to encourage research. Activities include regular meetings and publication of *Jabberwocky* quarterly and newsletter *Bandersnatch*. *Annual subscription:* ordinary £8 ($20); institutions £10 ($23); students and retired £5 ($15).

Cartoonists Club of Great Britain. *Secretary:* Terry Christien, 46 Strawberry Vale, Twickenham TW1 4SE   *tel* 0181-892 3621   *fax* 0181-891 5946. Aims to encourage social contact between members and endeavours to promote the professional standing and prestige of cartoonists. Fee on joining: full, provisional, or associate £30; thereafter annual fee £20.

The Chesterton Society (1974), 11 Lawrence Leys, Bloxham, Nr Banbury, Oxon OX15 4NU   *tel* (01295) 720869. To promote interest in the life and work of G.K. Chesterton and those associated with him or influenced by his writings. *Subscription:* £20 p.a., includes journal *The Chesterton Review* (Q.) and newsletters.

Children's Book Foundation—now **Young Book Trust**; see entry under **Book Trust.**

Children's Writers and Illustrators Group, 84 Drayton Gardens, London SW10 9SB *tel* 0171-373 6642. *Secretary:* Gareth Shannon. Subsidiary group for writers and illustrators of children's books, who are members of the Society of Authors.

Christian Literature, United Society for (1799), Robertson House, Leas Road, Guildford, Surrey GU1 4QW *tel* (01483) 577877 *fax* (01483) 301387. *President:* Lord Luke; *chairman:* John Clark; *general secretary:* Dr Alwyn Marriage. To aid Christian literature principally in developing countries and Eastern Europe.

Agatha Christie Society (1993). *Secretary:* Elaine Z. Wiltshire, PO Box 985, London SW1X 9XA. To promote communication between the fans of Agatha Christie and the various media who bring her works to the public. Publishes four newsletters p.a. *Annual subscription:* UK £12.50, Europe £15, USA $30, rest of world £15.

Civil Service Authors, Society of. *Secretary:* Mrs J.M. Hykin, 4 Top Street, Wing, nr Oakham, Rutland, Leics. LE15 8SE. Aims to encourage authorship by present and past members of the Civil Service (and some other public service bodies). Holds annual competitions for poetry, short stories, etc., open to members only, and annual 'Writer of the Year' award. The Society's magazine, *The Civil Service Author*, is free to members. *Annual subscription:* £12. Sae for enquiries.

The John Clare Society (1981), The Stables, 1a West Street, Helpston, Peterborough PE6 7DU *tel* (01733) 252678. Promotes a wider appreciation of the life and works of the poet John Clare. *Annual subscription:* UK individual £9.50; other rates (including overseas) on application.

Classical Association. *Secretary (branches):* Mrs Ann Hunt, 5 Grove Avenue, London N10 2AS; *secretary (council):* Dr M. Schofield, St John's College, Cambridge CB2 1TP. To promote and sustain interest in classical studies, to maintain their rightful position in universities and schools, and to give scholars and teachers opportunities for meeting and discussing their problems. Organises an annual conference lasting 3/4 days, in a university centre, and sponsors over 30 branches, which arrange programmes and lectures and discussions. *Annual subscription:* £3.00; life membership, for individuals only, £63.00.

The William Cobbett Society (1976). *Chairman:* Molly Townsend, Johnsons Farm, Sheet, Petersfield, Hants GU32 2BY *tel* (01730) 262060. To make the life and work of William Cobbett better known. *Subscription:* £8 p.a.

The Wilkie Collins Society (1981). *Chairman:* Andrew Gasson; *membership secretary:* Louise Marchant, 10A Tibberton Square, Islington, London N1 8SF. To promote interest in the life and works of Wilkie Collins. Publishes a newsletter, an occasional scholarly journal and reprints of Collins's lesser known works. *Annual subscription:* £7.50, USA $10.

Comedy Writers Association of Great Britain (1981). Ken Rock, 61 Parry Road, Wolverhampton WV11 2PS *tel/fax* (01902) 722729. Aims to develop and promote comedy writing in a professional and friendly way. *Annual membership:* £40.

Comhairle nan Leabhraichean (The Gaelic Books Council) (1968), Department of Celtic, University of Glasgow, Glasgow G12 8QQ *tel* 0141-330 5190. *Chairman:* Professor Donald MacAulay. Stimulates Scottish Gaelic publishing by awarding publication grants for new books, commissioning authors and providing editorial services and general assistance to writers and readers.

Comics Creators Guild (formerly **Society for Strip Illustration**), 7 Dilke Street, London SW3 4JE. Open to all those concerned with, or interested in, professional comics creation. Holds monthly meetings and publishes a monthly newsletter, *Comics Forum*, a Directory of Members' Work, Submission Guidelines for the major comics publishers, sample scripts for artists, a 'Guide to Contracts' and 'Getting Started in Comics', a beginners' guide to working in the industry.

The Commonwealth Institute (1893), Kensington High Street, London W8 6NQ   *tel* 0171-603 4535   *fax* 0171-602 7374. *Director general:* Stephen Cox. Promotes Commonwealth education and culture in Britain. The Commonwealth Galleries are due to reopen in 1997 after closure for essential building works and installation of new exhibitions. The Education Centre and Resource Centre continue to offer services to teachers and school groups, and facilities for commercial hire continue to be available.

Communicators in Business, The British Association of (1995), 3 Locks Yard, High Street, Sevenoaks, Kent TN13 1LT   *tel* (01732) 459331   *fax* (01732) 461757. Aims to be the market leader for those involved in corporate media management and practice by providing professional, authoritative, dynamic, supportive and innovative services.

Composers, The Association of Professional (1980), 34 Hanway Street, London W1P 9DE   *tel* 0171-436 0919   *fax* 0171-436 1913. *Administrator:* Rosemary Dixson. Furthers the collective interest of its members and informs and advises them on professional and artistic matters. Holds four general meetings p.a., and arranges a number of seminars and workshops. Publishes *The Composer's Guide to Music Publishing*, *Professional Composing* and a Newsletter (3 p.a.). *Annual subscription:* £30, plus 2% levy on PRS royalties amounting to c.£170.

The Composers' Guild of Great Britain, 34 Hanway Street, London W1P 9DE   *tel* 0171-436 0007   *fax* 0171-436 1913. Aims to represent and protect the professional interests of composers and to nurture the art of composition. It provides copyright and commissioning advice. Publications include *Composer News* and *First Performances*. *Annual subscription:* £30.00, associate membership £22.50. Further particulars obtainable from the General Secretary.

The Joseph Conrad Society (UK) (1973). *Chairman:* Keith Carabine; *president:* Philip Conrad; *secretary:* Hugh Epstein; *editor of The Conradian:* Andrew Roberts, Dept. of English, University of Dundee, Dundee DD1 4HW. Maintains close and friendly links with the Conrad family. Activities include an annual international conference; publication of *The Conradian* and a series of pamphlets; and maintenance of a study centre in London at the Polish Cultural Centre, 238-246 King Street, W6 0RF. Administers the Juliet McLauchlan Prize: £100 annual award for the winner of an essay competition.

Contemporary Arts, Institute of, The Mall, London SW1Y 5AH   *tel* 0171-930 0493   *fax* 0171-873 0051. Encourages collaboration between artforms, promotes experimental work and the mutual interchange of ideas and cultural practice at a national and international level. Produces diverse monthly programme of exhibitions, theatre, dance, music, literature, cinema, video, lectures, conferences, discussions. Open 1200-0100 Mon-Sat, 1200-2300 Sun. Various levels of membership available; open to the public with daypass £1.50.

Copyright Clearance Center, Inc. (1978), 222 Rosewood Drive, Danvers, MA 01923, USA   *tel* 508-750-8400   *fax* 508-750-4250. Operates a centralised photocopy authorisations and payment system in the US, serving photocopy users in their efforts to comply with the law, and foreign and domestic copyright owners in their efforts to protect their printed works. *Free registration* to rights holders.

Copyright Council, The British, Copyright House, 29-33 Berners Street, London W1P 4AA   *tel/fax* 0171-359 1895. *Chairman:* Maureen Duffy; *vice chairmen:* Rachel Duffield, Mark Le Fanu, Robert Montgomery; *secretary:* Geoffrey Adams; *treasurer:* Lord Brain. Aims to defend and foster the true principles of creators' copyright and their acceptance throughout the world, to bring together bodies representing all who are interested in the protection of such copyright, and to keep watch on any legal or other changes which may require an amendment of the law.

The Copyright Licensing Agency Ltd (1983), 90 Tottenham Court Road, London W1P 0LP   *tel* 0171-436 5931   *fax* 0171-436 3986. *Secretary:* Colin P. Hadley. CLA administers collectively photocopying and other copying rights that it is uneconomic for writers and publishers to administer for themselves. The Agency issues collective and transactional licences, and the fees it collects, after the deduction of its operating costs, are distributed at regular intervals to authors and publishers via their respective societies. See article on page 536.

Crime Writers' Association (1953), PO Box 10772, London N6 4SD. *Secretary:* Richard Grayson. For professional writers of crime novels, short stories, plays for stage, television and sound radio, or of serious works on crime. Associate membership open to publishers, journalists, booksellers specialising in crime literature. Publishes *Red Herrings* monthly (for members only).

The Critics' Circle (1913). *President:* Stephen Pettitt; *hon. general secretary:* Peter Hepple, 47 Bermondsey Street, London SE1 3XT   *tel* 0171-403 1818. Aims to promote the art of criticism, to uphold its integrity in practice, to foster and safeguard the professional interests of its members, to provide opportunities for social intercourse among them, and to support the advancement of the arts. Membership is by invitation of the Council. Such invitations are issued only to persons engaged professionally, regularly and substantially in the writing or broadcasting of criticism of drama, music, films, dance and the visual arts.

The Cromwell Association (1935), *Press liaison officer:* B. Denton, 10 Melrose Avenue, off Bants Lane, Northampton NN5 5PB   *tel/fax* (01604) 582516 during normal office hours, Mon.-Fri. Encourages the study of Oliver Cromwell and his times, holds academic lectures and meetings, publishes annual journal *Cromwelliana*. *Subscription:* £10 p.a.

Cyngor Llyfrau Cymru—see **Welsh Books Council.**

The Danish Publishers Association (Den Danske Forlaeggerforening) (1837), Købmagergade 11, DK 1150, Copenhagen K, Denmark   *tel* 33 15 66 88   *fax* 33 15 65 88. *Secretary:* Erik V. Krustrup.

The De Vere Society (1986), 8 Western Road, Henley-on-Thames, Oxon RG9 1JL   *tel* (01491) 576662   *fax* (01491) 579111. *Secretary:* Christopher H. Dams. Aims to seek, and if possible to establish, the truth concerning the authorship of the Shakespeare plays and poems and, in addition, to promote research into the life of Edward de Vere, 17th Earl of Oxford.

Design and Artists Copyright Society Ltd (DACS) (1983), Parchment House, 13 Northburgh Street, London EC1V 0AH   *tel* 0171-336 8811   *fax* 0171-336 8822. *Chief executive:* Rachel Duffield; *deputy chief executive:* Janet Ibbotson; *administrator:* Janet Tod. DACS is the British copyright and collecting society for the visual arts. It aims to protect and administer visual artists' copyright both nationally and internationally. DACS provides individual and blanket licences to users of artistic works in the UK. The Society also advises about copyright for visual creators, and pursues infringements where appropriate. *Life membership:* £25 (inc. VAT).

Designers, The Chartered Society of, First Floor, 32-38 Saffron Hill, London EC1N 8FH   *tel* 0171-831 9777   *fax* 0171-831 6277. *Director:* Brian Lymbery. Works to promote and regulate standards of competence, professional conduct and integrity, including representation on government and official bodies, design education and competitions. The services to members include general information, guidance on copyright and other professional issues, access to professional indemnity insurance and a credit-checking/debt collection service. Members may use the rooms available at the Society's headquarters. Activities in the regions are included in an extensive annual programme of events and training courses. The Society publishes a Code of Conduct, and has developed a Business and Design Programme to strengthen the links between designers and clients in business and industry.

Designers in Ireland, Society of (1972), 8 Merrion Square, Dublin 2, Republic of Ireland   *tel/fax* (01) 2841477. Irish design profession's representative body, covering every field of design. Details from the honorary secretary. *Full member:* £100 p.a.; *licentiate:* £45 p.a.

Dickens Fellowship (1902), The Dickens House, 48 Doughty Street, London WC1N 2LF   *tel* 0171-405 2127   *fax* 0171-831 5175. *Hon. secretary:* Edward G. Preston. Based in house occupied by Dickens 1837-9; publishes *The Dickensian*, 3 p.a. Membership rates and particulars on application.

Directory Publishers Association (1970). *Secretary:* Rosemary Pettit, 93a Blenheim Crescent, London W11 2EQ   *tel* 0171-221 9089. Maintains a code of professional practice; aims to raise the standard and professional status of UK directory publishing and to protect (and promote) the legal, statutory and common interests of directory publishers; provides for the exchange of technical, commercial and management information between members. *Subscription:* £100-£1000 p.a.

Sean Dorman Manuscript Society (1957), Cherry Trees, Crosemere Road, Cockshutt, Ellesmere, Shropshire SY12 0JP   *tel* (01939) 270293. *Director:* Mary Driver. Aims to provide mutual help among part-time writers in England, Scotland and Wales. Members regularly receive circulating manuscript parcels affording constructive criticism of their work and providing opportunities for technical and general discussion. *Subscription:* £6.50 p.a. Full details available on receipt of sae.

The Arthur Conan Doyle Society (1989). *Joint organisers:* Christopher Roden and Barbara Roden, Ashcroft, 2 Abbottsford Drive, Penyffordd, Chester CH4 0JG   *tel* (01244) 545210. Promotes the study of the life and works of Sir Arthur Conan Doyle. Publishes *ACD*, annual journal, *The Parish Magazine*, bi-annual newsletter and occasional reprints of Conan Doyle material. Major annual convention. *Subscription:* £15 p.a., overseas £16 p.a. (airmail extra).

Royal Dutch Publishers Association (Koninklijke Nederlandse Uitgeversbond), Keizersgracht 391, 1016 EJ Amsterdam, The Netherlands   *tel* (020) 626 77 36. *Secretary general:* R.M. Vrij.

Early English Text Society (1864). *Executive secretary:* R.F.S. Hamer, Christ Church, Oxford OX1 1DP; *hon. director:* Professor John Burrow. To bring unprinted early English literature within the reach of students in sound texts. *Annual subscription:* £15.

The Eckhart Society (1987), Summa, 22 Tippings Lane, Woodley, Reading, Berks. RG5 4RX   *tel* (01189) 690118. *Secretary:* Ashley Young. Aims to promote the understanding and appreciation of Eckhart's writings and their importance for Christian thought and practice; to facilitate scholarly research into Eckhart's life and works; and to promote the study of Eckhart's teaching as a contribution to inter-religious dialogue. *Membership:* £12.50 p.a.; £7.00 p.a. OAPs/students.

Editors, Association of British (1985). *Executive director:* Jock Gallagher, Broadvision, 49 Frederick Road, Edgbaston, Birmingham B15 1HN *tel* 0121-455 7949 *fax* 0121-454 6187. Independent organisation set up to study and enhance the practice of journalism in all media; to protect and promote the freedom of the media, in the UK and throughout the world; to consider common problems independent of any individual, group or interest. Publishes a quarterly journal, *British Editor. Annual subscription:* £50.

Edinburgh Bibliographical Society (1890), c/o Dept. of Special Collections, Edinburgh University Library, George Square, Edinburgh EH8 9LJ *tel* 0131-650 3412 *fax* 0131-650 6863. *Secretary:* M.C.T. Simpson; *treasurer:* E.D. Yeo. Encourages bibliographical activity through organising talks for members, particularly on bibliographical topics relating to Scotland, and visits to libraries. Also publishes *Transactions* (Bi-A., free to members) and other occasional publications. *Membership:* £7 p.a. (£5 p.a. for full-time students).

Educational Writers Group, 84 Drayton Gardens, London SW10 9SB *tel* 0171-373 6642. Specialist group within the membership of the Society of Authors.

The Eighteen Nineties Society. *Honorary secretary,* 97-D Brixton Road, London SW9 6EE *tel* 0171-582 4690. *Patron:* HRH Princess Michael of Kent; *president:* Countess of Longford CBE; *chairman:* Martyn Goff OBE; *secretary:* Dr G. Krishnamurti. Founded in 1963 as The Francis Thompson Society, it now embraces the entire artistic and literary scene of the 1890 decade. Holds exhibitions, lectures, poetry readings; publishes biographies of neglected authors and artists of the period; also check lists, bibliographies, etc. Its Journal appears periodically, and includes biographical, bibliographical and critical articles and book reviews.

The George Eliot Fellowship (1930). *President:* Jonathan G. Ouvry; *secretary:* Mrs K.M. Adams, 71 Stepping Stones Road, Coventry CV5 8JT *tel* (01203) 592231. Promotes an interest in the life and work of George Eliot and helps to extend her influence; arranges meetings; produces an annual magazine and a quarterly newsletter. *Annual subscription:* £8.

English Association, University of Leicester, University Road, Leicester LE1 7RH *tel* (0116) 252 3982 *fax* (0116) 252 2301. *Chairman:* Roger Knight; *secretary:* Helen Lucas. Aims to further knowledge, understanding and enjoyment of English literature and the English language, by working towards a fuller recognition of English as an essential element in education and in the community at large; by encouraging the study of English literature and language by means of conferences, lectures and publications; by fostering the discussion of methods of teaching English of all kinds; and by the establishment of local groups for the exchange of views and to work to further the status of English literature and language in the community.

English Regional Arts Boards—see **Regional Arts Boards.**

English Speaking Board (International) Ltd, 26A Princes Street, Southport PR8 1EQ *tel* (01704) 501730. *President:* Christabel Burniston MBE; *chairman:* Richard Ellis. Aims to foster all activities concerned with oral communication. The Board conducts examinations and training courses for teachers and students in schools and colleges where stress is on individual oral expression; also for those engaged in technical or industrial concerns, and for those using English as an acquired language. Members receive *Spoken English* (Mar/

Sept); articles are invited on any special aspect of spoken English. Members can purchase other ESB publications at reduced rates. Conference and AGM in the spring. *Membership:* individuals, £20 p.a., corporate £35 p.a.

The English-Speaking Union (1918), Dartmouth House, 37 Charles Street, London W1X 8AB   *tel* 0171-493 3328   *fax* 0171-495 6108. *Director-general:* Mrs Valerie Mitchell. Promotes international understanding through the English language. The ESU is an educational charity which sponsors scholarships and exchanges, educational programmes promoting the effective use of English, and a wide range of international and cultural events. Members contribute to our work across the world. *Annual membership fee:* various categories. See also **Books Across the Sea.**

European Broadcasting Union (1950), Ancienne Route 17, Case Postale 67, CH-1218 Grand Saconnex (Geneva), Switzerland   *tel* (22) 7172111   *telex* 415700 EBU CH   *fax* (22) 7172481. *Secretary-general:* Dr Jean-Bernard Münch. Supports and promotes co-operation between its members and broadcasting organisations world-wide; represents the interests of its members in programme, legal, technical and other fields. *Annual membership fee:* according to number of broadcasting licences or households equipped with radio and/or TV receivers.

European Publishers, Federation of (1967). *President:* John Clement; *secretary:* Mechthild von Alemann, 204 avenue de Tervuren, 1150 Brussels, Belgium   *tel* (2) 770 11 10   *fax* (2) 771 20 71. Represents the interests of European publishers on EU affairs; informs members on the development of EU policies which could affect the publishing industry; lobbies the Commission and the European Parliament on behalf of European book publishers.

Fabian Society, 11 Dartmouth Street, London SW1H 9BN   *tel* 0171-222 8877   *fax* 0171-976 7153. Membership organisation which serves as a forum for the discussion of democratic socialist ideas. Holds conferences and publishes pamphlets and *Fabian Review*, a bi-monthly journal. Individual membership £25 (£10.50 reduced rate), Library subscription £60.

Fantasy Society, The British (1971), 2 Harwood Street, Heaton Norris, Stockport SK4 1JJ   *tel* 0161-476 5368 (after 6 pm). *President:* Ramsey Campbell; *secretary:* Robert Parkinson. For devotees of fantasy, horror and related fields, in literature, art and the cinema. Publications include *British Fantasy Newsletter* (Bi-M.) featuring news and reviews and approx. four annual booklets, including: *Dark Horizons*; *Winter Chills*, an all-fiction publication; *Masters of Fantasy* on individual authors; and *Mystique*, containing fiction and non-fiction. There is a small-press library and an annual convention and fantasy awards sponsored by the Society. *Membership:* £17 p.a.

Federation Against Copyright Theft Ltd (FACT) (1982), 7 Victory Business Centre, Worton Road, Isleworth, Middlesex TW7 6ER   *tel* 0181-568 6646   *fax* 0181-560 6364. *Director general:* Reg Dixon; *Company secretary:* David Lowe. FACT aims to protect the interests of its members and others against infringement in the UK of copyright in cinematograph films, television programmes and all forms of audio-visual recording.

The Fine Art Trade Guild (1910), 16-18 Empress Place, London SW6 1TT   *tel* 0171-381 6616   *fax* 0171-381 2596. *Managing director:* Scott Siemers. Promotes the sale of fine art prints and picture framing in the UK and overseas markets; establishes and raises standards amongst members and communicates these to the buying public. The Guild publishes a number of directories and guides, and *Art Business Today*, the trade's longest established magazine.

FOCAL – Federation of Commercial AudioVisual Libraries Ltd (1985), PO Box 422, Harrow, Middlesex HA1 3YN *tel/fax* 0181-423 5853. *Administrator/ secretariat:* Anne Johnson.

The Folklore Society (1878), University College, Gower Street, London WC1E 6BT *tel* 0171-387 5894. *Hon. secretary:* Dr Juliette Wood. Collection, recording and study of folklore.

Foreign Press Association in London (1888). *President:* Hans Joachim Werbke; *secretaries:* Davina Crole and Catherine Flury. *Registered office:* 11 Carlton House Terrace, London SW1Y 5AJ *tel* 0171-930 0445 *fax* 0171-925 0469. Aims to promote the professional interests of its members. Full Membership open to overseas professional journalists residing in the UK; Associate Membership available for British press and freelance journalists. *Entrance fee:* £139.23; *annual subscription:* £107.51.

Français, Syndicat des Conseils Littéraires, c/o Agence Hoffman, 77 bd Saint-Michel, 75005 Paris, France *tel* (1) 43 26 56 94 *telex* 203605 Aghoff *fax* (1) 43 26 34 07.

Free Painters & Sculptors, Loggia Gallery and Sculpture Garden, 15 Buckingham Gate, London SW1E 6LB *tel* 0171-828 5963. Gallery hours: Mon.-Fri. 6-8 p.m., Sat.-Sun. 2-6 p.m. *Hon. secretary:* Philip Worth. Exhibits progressive work of all artistic allegiances and provides opportunities for FPS members to meet and discuss their work in either one-person or group shows.

Freelance Editors and Proofreaders, Society of (1988). *Office:* SFEP, 38 Rochester Road, London NW1 9JJ *tel* 0171-813 3113. Aims to promote high editorial standards and achieve recognition of its members' professional status, through local and national meetings, an annual conference, a monthly newsletter and a programme of reasonably priced workshops/training sessions. These sessions help newcomers to acquire basic skills, enable experienced editors to update their skills or broaden their competence, and also cover aspects of professional practice or business for the self-employed. An annual directory of members' services is available to publishers. The Society supports moves towards recognised standards of training and accreditation for editors and proofreaders; its own system of accreditation will come into operation during 1996. It has close links with Book House Training Centre and the Society of Indexers, is represented on the BSI Technical Committee dealing with copy preparation and proof correction (BS 5261), and works to foster good relations with all relevant bodies and organisations in the UK and worldwide.

Freelance Photographers, Bureau of (1965), Focus House, 497 Green Lanes, London N13 4BP *tel* 0181-882 3315 *fax* 0181-886 5174. *Chief executive:* John Tracy. To help the freelance photographer by providing information on markets, and free advisory service. Publishes monthly *Market Newsletter*. *Membership:* £40 p.a.

French Publishers' Association (Syndicat National de l'Edition), 35 rue Grégoire de Tours, 75279 Paris 06, France *tel* (1) 43 29 75 75/44 41 28 00 *fax* (1) 43 25 35 01.

The Gaelic Books Council—see Comhairle nan Leabhraichean.

The Gaskell Society (1985). *Hon. secretary:* Mrs Joan Leach, Far Yew Tree House, Over Tabley, Knutsford, Cheshire WA16 0HN *tel* (01565) 634668. Promotes and encourages the study and appreciation of the work and life of Elizabeth Cleghorn Gaskell. Holds regular meetings in Knutsford, London and Manchester, visits and residential conferences; produces an annual Journal and bi-annual Newsletters. *Subscription:* £7.00 p.a.

Gay Authors Workshop (1978), Kathryn Byrd, BM Box 5700, London WC1N
3XX   *tel* 0181-520 5223. To encourage writers who are lesbian, gay or bisexual.
Quarterly newsletter. *Membership:* £5.00; unwaged £2.00.

General Practitioners Writers Association (1985). *President:* Dr Robin Hull,
Jasmine Cottage, Hampton Lucy, Warwick CV35 8BE   *tel* (01789) 840509.
Aims to improve the writing by, for, from or about general medical practice.
Publishes *The GP Writer* (2 p.a.); register of members' writing interests is sent
to medical editors and publishers.

German Publishers' and Booksellers' Association (Börsenverein des Deutschen
Buchhandels e.V.), Postfach 100442, 60004 Frankfurt am Main, Germany   *tel*
(069) 13060   *telex* 413573 BUCHV D   *fax* (069) 1306201. *General manager:* Dr
Hans-Karl von Kupsch.

The Ghost Story Society (1988), *Organisers:* Barbara Roden and Christopher
Roden, Ashcroft, 2 Abbottsford Drive, Penyffordd, Chester CH4 0JG   *tel*
(01244) 545210. Devoted mainly to supernatural fiction in the literary tradition
of M.R. James, Walter de la Mare, Arthur Machen, Algernon Blackwood,
etc. Thrice-yearly magazine. *Membership:* £13.50 (£15/$25 overseas).

Gothic Association, The International (1991), Dept. of English Studies, University
of Stirling, Stirling FK9 4LA   *e-mail* gs1@stirling.ac.uk *Secretary treasurer:*
Glennis Byron. Promotes and encourages scholarly research into all periods
of Gothic fiction; publishes a quarterly newsletter, *The Monk*, and a journal,
Gothic, and organises conferences. *Annual subscription:* £10 (US$16), student/
unwaged £6 (US$8).

The Gothic Society (1990), Chatham House, Gosshill Road, Chislehurst, Kent
BR7 5NS   *tel* 0181-467 8475   *fax* 0181-295 1967. For the study of morbid,
macabre and black-hued themes: Mrs Radcliffe, Monk Lewis, Mary Shelley,
Sheridan Le Fanu, the Brontës, Bram Stoker, and many other writers and
artists in the horror-romance genre. Also publish new art and literature in the
same mood. Books, monographs and a quarterly magazine, *Udolpho. Annual
subscription:* £20, overseas £23 (£26 airmail).

Graphic Fine Art, Society of (1919), 15 Willow Way, Hatfield, Herts AL10 9QD.
President: Jean Canter. A fine art society holding an annual open exhibition.
Membership by election, requires work of high quality with an emphasis on
good drawing, whether by pen, pencil (with our without wash), watercolour,
pastel or any of the forms of print making.

Graphical, Paper & Media Union, Keys House, 63-67 Bromham Road, Bedford
MK40 2AG   *tel* (01234) 351521   *fax* (01234) 270580. *General secretary:* Tony
Dubbins. Trade union representing the interests of employees in the printing,
paper, publishing and allied industries.

The Greeting Card Association, 41 Links Drive, Elstree, Herts. WD6 3PP   *tel/
fax* 0181-236 0024. *Administrator:* Lesley Grace; *secretary:* Ray Cousins. Publishes *Greetings* (10 p.a.).

Guernsey Arts Council (1981), St James Concert and Assembly Hall, St Peter
Port, Guernsey, CI   *tel* (01481) 721902. *Secretary:* Angela Simon. Co-ordinates the organisations under the council's umbrella, presents artistic events,
sponsors reports, aims to bring about the creation of an arts centre in Guernsey
and to encourage all the arts in Guernsey, Alderney and Sark. *Membership
fee:* £5, under 18 £2.

The Neil Gunn Society (1985). *Secretary:* Mrs J. Campbell, 25 Newton Avenue,
Wick, Caithness KW1 5LJ   *tel* (01955) 602607. To promote the works of the
Scottish novelist, Neil Gunn; to research into the background of, and to

encourage discussion on and evaluation of, Gunn's work; to collect material related to his life and work; to provide a focal point for and help with any Gunn-related activity. *Annual membership fee:* £5.00 (students £2.00).

Hakluyt Society (1846), c/o The Map Library, The British Library, Great Russell Street, London WC1B 3DG *tel* (01986) 788359 *fax* (01986) 788181. *President:* Professor P.E.H. Hair; *hon. secretary:* Anthony P. Payne. Publication of original narratives of voyages, travels, naval expeditions, and other geographical records.

The Thomas Hardy Society Ltd (1967), PO Box 1438, Dorchester, Dorset DT1 1YH *tel* (01305) 251501. Publishes *The Thomas Hardy Journal* (3 p.a.). Biennial conference in Dorchester, 1996. *Subscription:* £12.00 (£15.00 overseas) p.a.

Harleian Society (1869), College of Arms, Queen Victoria Street, London EC4V 4BT. *Chairman:* J. Brooke-Little CVO, MA, FSA, Clarenceaux King of Arms; *secretary:* T.H.S. Duke, Chester Herald of Arms. Instituted for transcribing, printing and publishing the heraldic visitations of Counties, Parish Registers and any manuscripts relating to genealogy, family history and heraldry.

Heraldic Arts, Society of (1987), 46 Reigate Road, Reigate, Surrey RH2 0QN *tel* (01737) 242945. *Secretary:* John Ferguson ARCA, SHA, FRSA. Aims to serve the interests of heraldic artists, craftsmen, designers and writers, to provide a 'shop window' for their work, to obtain commissions on their behalf and to act as a forum for the exchange of information and ideas. Also offers an information service to the public. Candidates for admission as craft members should be artists or craftsmen whose work comprises a substantial element of heraldry and is of a sufficiently high standard to satisfy the requirements of the society's advisory council. *Associate membership:* £12 p.a.; *craft membership:* £17 p.a.

The Sherlock Holmes Society of London (1951). *President:* A.D. Howlett MA. LLB; *chairman:* Richard Lancelyn-Green; *general enquiries:* H.C. Owen, 64 Graham Road, Wimbledon, London SW19 3SS *tel* 0181-540 7657; *membership:* R.J. Ellis, 13 Crofton Avenue, Orpington, Kent BA6 8DU *tel* (01689) 811314. Aims to bring together those who have a common interest as readers and students of the literature of Sherlock Holmes, and to encourage the pursuit of knowledge of the public and private lives of Sherlock Holmes and Dr Watson. *Subscription*, including two issues of *The Sherlock Holmes Journal:* £12.50 p.a. UK/Europe, £16.50 Far East, US$27.50 Americas.

Hopkins Society (1990), c/o The Secretary, Arts Council of Wales, Library, Museum & Gallery, Earl Road, Mold CH7 1AP *tel* (01352) 758403 *fax* (01352) 700236. To promote and celebrate the work of the poet, Gerard Manley Hopkins, to inform members about the latest publications about Hopkins and to support educational projects concerning his work. Annual lecture held in North Wales in the spring; two Newsletters p.a. *Annual subscription:* £5.

Housman Society (1973), 80 New Road, Bromsgrove, Worcs. B60 2LA *tel* (01527) 874136 *fax* (01527) 837274. *Chairman:* Jim Page. Aims to foster interest in and promote knowledge of A.E. Housman, his sister Clemence and their brother Laurence. *Membership:* £7.50 p.a.

Hesketh Hubbard Art Society, 17 Carlton House Terrace, London SW1Y 5BD *tel* 0171-930 6844 *fax* 0171-839 7830. *President:* Simon Whittle. Weekly drawing workshops open to all.

Illustrators, The Association of (1973), First Floor, 32-38 Saffron Hill, London EC1N 8FN *tel* 0171-831 7377 *fax* 0171-831 6277. *Contact:* Stephanie Smith.

To support illustrators, promote illustration and encourage professional standards in the industry. Publishes monthly magazine; annual competition, Images – the Best of British Illustration: call for entries March/April.

Illustrators, Society of Architectural and Industrial (1975), PO Box 22, Stroud, Glos. GL5 3DH   *tel/fax* (01453) 882563. *Administrator:* Eric Monk. Professional body to represent all who practise architectural, industrial and technical illustration, including the related fields of model making and photography.

Independent Literary Agents Association, Inc.—merged in 1991 with **Society of Authors' Representatives, Inc.,** to become **Authors' Representatives, Inc., Association of.**

Independent Programme Producers Association—see **PACT.**

Indexers, Society of. *Secretary:* Mrs H.C. Troughton, 38 Rochester Road, London NW1 9JJ   *tel* 0171-916 7809. Aims to improve the standard of indexing, and to raise the status of indexers and to safeguard their interests. Maintains a Register of Indexers; acts as an advisory body on the qualifications and remuneration of indexers; publishes or communicates books, papers and notes on the subject of indexing; publishes and runs an open-learning indexing course, 'Training in Indexing'. The Society's journal, *The Indexer*, is sent free to members. *Annual subscription:* £25 (£30 overseas), corporate £35 (£40 overseas).

Indian Publishers, The Federation of, 18/1-C Institutional Area, J.N.U. Road, New Delhi 110067, India   *tel* 6964847, 6852263   *fax* 91-11-6864054.

Irish Book Publishers Association (Clé), Irish Writers' Centre, 19 Parnell Square, Dublin 1, Republic of Ireland   *tel* (01) 8729090   *fax* (01) 8722035. *President:* John Spillane.

The Irish Copyright Licensing Agency (1992), 19 Parnell Square, Dublin 1, Republic of Ireland   *tel* (01) 8729090   *fax* (01) 8722035. *Administrator:* Orla O'Sullivan. Licences schools and other users of copyright material to photocopy extracts of such material, and distributes the monies collected to the authors and publishers whose works have been copied.

Irish Playwrights, Society of (Cumann Drámadóirí na hÉireann) (1969), Irish Writers' Centre, 19 Parnell Square, Dublin 1, Republic of Ireland   *tel* (01) 8721302   *fax* (01) 8726282. *Secretary:* Vera O'Donovan. To safeguard the rights of Irish playwrights and to foster and promote Irish playwriting. *Annual subscription:* IR£25.

Irish Translators' Association (1986), Irish Writers' Centre, 19 Parnell Square, Dublin 1, Republic of Ireland   *tel* (01) 8721302   *fax* (01) 8726282. *Secretary:* Miriam Lee. Promotes translation in Ireland, the translation of Irish authors abroad and the practical training of translators, and promotes the interests of translators. Catalogues the works of translators in areas of Irish interest; secures the awarding of prizes and bursaries for translators; and maintains a detailed register of translators. *Annual membership:* Member £15, Professional Member £30.

Irish Writers' Union (Comhar na Scríbhneoirí) (1986), Irish Writers' Centre, 19 Parnell Square, Dublin 1, Republic of Ireland   *tel* (01) 8721302   *fax* (01) 8726282. *Secretary:* Sam McAughtry. The Union aims to advance the cause of writing as a profession, to achieve better remuneration and more favourable conditions for writers and to provide a means for the expression of the collective opinion of writers on matters affecting their profession.

The Richard Jefferies Society (1950), Eidsvoll, Bedwells Heath, Boars Hill, Oxford OX1 5JE   *tel* (01865) 735678. *President:* Andrew Rossabi BA (Cantab);

hon. secretary: Phyllis Treitel. Worldwide membership. Promotes interest in the life, works and associations of the naturalist and novelist, Richard Jefferies; helps to preserve buildings and memorials, and co-operates in the development of a Museum in his birthplace. Arranges regular meetings in Swindon, and occasionally elsewhere; organises outings and displays; publishes a Journal and Newsletter in spring and an Annual Report in September. *Annual subscription:* £5.

The Johnson Society, Johnson Birthplace Museum, Breadmarket Street, Lichfield, Staffs. WS13 6LG   *tel* (01543) 264972. *Hon. general secretary:* Norma Hooper. To encourage the study of the life and works of Dr Samuel Johnson; to preserve the memorials, associations, books, manuscripts, letters of Dr Johnson and his contemporaries; preservation of his birthplace.

Johnson Society of London (1928). *President:* The Revd Dr E.F. Carpenter KCVO; *secretary:* Mrs Zandra O'Donnell MA, 255 Baring Road, Grove Park, London SE12 0BQ   *tel* 0181-851 0173. To study the life and works of Dr Johnson, and to perpetuate his memory in the city of his adoption.

Journalists, The Chartered Institute of. *General secretary:* Christopher Underwood FCIJ, 2 Dock Offices, Surrey Quays Road, London SE16 2XU   *tel* 0171-252 1187   *fax* 0171-232 2302. The senior organisation of the profession, founded in 1884 and incorporated by Royal Charter in 1890. The Chartered Institute maintains an employment register and has accumulated funds for the assistance of members. A Freelance Division links editors and publishers with freelances and a Directory is published of freelance writers, with their specialisations. There are special sections for broadcasters, motoring correspondents and public relations practitioners. Occasional contributors to the media may qualify for election as Affiliates. *Subscription:* related to earnings – maximum £170, minimum £52.50; Affiliate £84.

Keats-Shelley Memorial Association (1903). *Hon. treasurer:* R.E. Cavaliero, 10 Lansdowne Road, Tunbridge Wells, Kent TN1 2NJ   *tel* (01892) 533452   *fax* (01892) 519142. *Patron:* HM Queen Elizabeth the Queen Mother; *chairman:* K.V. Prichard-Jones; *hon. secretary:* D.R. Leigh-Hunt. Owns and supports house in Rome where John Keats died, and celebrates the poets Keats, Shelley and Leigh Hunt. Occasional meetings; annual *Review* and progress reports. Subscription to 'Friends of the Keats-Shelley Memorial', minimum £10 p.a.

Kent and Sussex Poetry Society. *President:* Laurence Lerner; *chairman:* Clive Eastwood; *hon. secretary:* Mrs Doriel Hulse, Costens, Carpenters Lane, Hadlow, Kent TN11 0EY   *tel* (01732) 851404. Based in Tunbridge Wells, the society was formed in 1946 to create a greater interest in Poetry. Well-known poets address the Society, a Folio of members' work is produced and a full programme of recitals, discussions, competitions and readings is provided. See page 656 for details of Open Poetry Competition. *Annual subscription:* attending members £5.00; country members £3.00; students £1.00.

Kinematograph, Sound and Television Society, British (founded 1931, incorporated 1946), 63-71 Victoria House, Vernon Place, London WC1B 4DB   *tel* 0171-242 8400   *fax* 0171-405 3560. *Executive director:* Anne Fenton; *hon. secretary:* Ray Clipson. Aims to encourage technical and scientific progress in the industries of its title. Publishes technical information, arranges international conferences and exhibitions, lectures and demonstrations, and encourages the exchange of ideas. Monthly journals: *Image Technology*, *Images*; quarterly journal: *Cinema Technology*.

The Kipling Society. *Secretary:* Norman Entract, PO Box 68, Haslemere, Surrey GU27 2YR   *tel* (01428) 652709. Aims to honour and extend the influence of

Kipling, to assist in the study of Kipling's writings, to hold discussion-meetings, to publish a quarterly journal and to maintain a Kipling Reference Library. Membership details on application.

The Lancashire Authors' Association (1909). *President:* G.A. Wormleighton MBE, FCA; *general secretary:* Eric Holt, 5 Quakerfields, Westhoughton, Bolton BL5 2BJ *tel* (01942) 791390. 'For writers and lovers of Lancashire literature and history.' Publishes *The Record* (Q.). *Subscription:* £9.00 p.a.

The T.E. Lawrence Society (1985). PO Box 728, Oxford OX2 6YP. Promotes the memory of T.E. Lawrence and furthers knowledge by research into his life; publishes bi-annual *Journal* and quarterly *Newsletter. Subscription:* £14 p.a., overseas £18 p.a.

Learned and Professional Society Publishers, The Association of (1972). Aims to promote and develop the publishing activities of learned and professional organisations. Membership is open to professional and learned societies and allied organisations: details from the Secretary-General, Professor B.T. Donovan, 48 Kelsey Lane, Beckenham, Kent BR3 3NE *tel* 0181-658 0459.

Librarians, Association of Assistant (1895), c/o The Library Association, 7 Ridgmount Street, London WC1E 7AE. *President:* Patsy Heap BA. ALA; *hon. secretary:* Jean Bennett BA. Publishes bibliographical aids, the journal *Assistant Librarian*, works on librarianship; and runs educational courses.

The Library Association (1877), 7 Ridgmount Street, London WC1E 7AE *tel* 0171-636 7543 *fax* 0171-436 7218 *e-mail* info@la-hq.org.uk *Chief executive:* R. Shimmon FLA. For over a century, the Library Association has promoted and defended the interests of the Library and Information Service profession, those working within it and the people who use the services. The monthly journal, *The Library Association Record*, is distributed free to all members. *Subscription* varies according to income.

Limners, The Society of (1986). *Executive secretary:* Mrs C. Melmore, 104 Poverest Road, Orpington, Kent BR5 2DQ. *Founder/president:* Elizabeth Davys Wood PSLM, SWA. Aims to promote an interest in miniature painting (in any medium), calligraphy and heraldry and encourage their development to a high standard. New members are elected after the submission of four works of acceptable standard and guidelines are provided for new artists. Members receive up to four newsletters a year and two annual exhibitions are arranged. *Membership:* £20. Friends membership is open to non-exhibitors (£12 p.a.); Friends receive newsletters and invitations to exhibitions and seminar.

Linguists, Institute of, 24A Highbury Grove, London N5 2EA *tel* 0171-359 7445 *fax* 0171-354 0202. To provide language qualifications; to encourage Government and industry to develop the use of modern languages and encourage recognition of the status of professional linguists in all occupations; to promote the exchange and dissemination of information on matters of concern to linguists.

Literary Societies, Alliance of. *Secretary:* Bill Adams, 71 Stepping Stones Road, Coventry CV5 8JT *tel* (01203) 592231. Any literary society may affiliate and may attend the annual convention and receive an allocation of the official publication *Chapter One* (editor: Kenn Oultram, Clatterwick Hall, Little Leigh, Northwich, Cheshire CW8 4RJ *tel* (01606) 891303 office hours). Some financial assistance may be granted to small societies. *Subscription:* graded dependent upon size of society.

Literature, Royal Society of (1823), 1 Hyde Park Gardens, London W2 2LT *tel* 0171-723 5104 *fax* 0171-402 0199. *Chairman of Council:* John Mortimer CBE, QC, FRSL; *secretary:* Maggie Parham. For the advancement of literature by the holding of lectures, discussions, readings, and by publications. Administers the Dr Richards' Fund and the Royal Society of Literature Award, under the W.H. Heinemann Bequest and the Winifred Holtby Memorial Prize. *Subscription:* £25 p.a.

Little Presses, Association of (1966). *Co-ordinator:* Chris Jones, 86 Lytton Road, Oxford OX4 3NZ *tel* (01865) 718266. Loosely-knit association of individuals running little presses who have grouped together for mutual self-help, while retaining their right to operate autonomously. Publications include: Newsletter, *Poetry and Little Press Information*, *Catalogue of Little Press Books in Print*, *Getting Your Poetry Published*, *Publishing Yourself*. *Membership fee:* £12.50 p.a.

Little Theatre Guild of Great Britain. *Public relations officer:* Marjorie Havard, 19 Abbey Park Road, Great Grimsby DN32 0HJ *tel* (01472) 343424. Aims to promote closer co-operation amongst the little theatres constituting its membership; to act as co-ordinating and representative body on behalf of the little theatres; to maintain and advance the highest standards in the art of theatre; and to assist in encouraging the establishment of other little theatres. Yearbook available to non-members £5.00.

London Playwrights (formerly known as **The Playwrights' Co-operative**) (1978), 80 Lordsmead Road, London N1 6EY *tel* 0181-808 7622 or (01276) 65243 *fax* 0181-808 5323. Supports and encourages London playwrights who, having already written at least one script, want to move forward but need professional advice and contact. Offers story conferences, workshops, rehearsed readings and criticism. *Membership:* £20 p.a.

The Arthur Machen Society (1986), 19 Cross Street, Caerleon, Gwent NP6 1AF *tel* (01633) 422520 *fax* (01633) 421055. *Patron:* Julian Lloyd Webber; *president:* Barry Humphries; *secretary:* Rita Tait. Provides a forum for the exchange of ideas and information about Arthur Machen, novelist, and aims to bring his work before a new generation of readers. Publishes bi-annual journal *Avallaunius* and bi-annual newsletter *The Silurist*; hardback books, by and about Machen and his circle, and an audio-cassette tape. Relevant second-hand and small press booklist available. *Annual subscription:* £15 UK; £18 overseas and libraries; US$ account.

Marine Artists, Royal Society of, 17 Carlton House Terrace, London SW1Y 5BD *tel* 0171-930 6844 *fax* 0171-839 7830. *President:* Mark Myers. To promote and encourage marine painting. Open Annual Exhibition.

The Marlowe Society (1955). *Secretary:* Mrs Yolanda Hart, 5 Beaufield Gates, Three Gates Lane, Haslemere, Surrey GU27 2LN *tel* (01428) 641767. To extend appreciation and widen recognition of Christopher Marlowe (1564-93) as the foremost poet and dramatist preceding Shakespeare, whose development he influenced. Holds meetings, and visits Tudor stately homes, yeomen houses and farms, etc. *Annual subscription:* £7.50, concessions £5.

The John Masefield Society (1992). *Secretary:* Peter J.R. Carter, The Frith, Ledbury, Herefordshire HR8 1LW *tel* (01531) 633800. To stimulate interest in and public awareness and enjoyment of the life and works of the poet John Masefield. Holds a two-day annual festival, annual lecture and other, less formal, readings and gatherings; publishes an annual Journal and quarterly Newsletters. *Annual membership:* £5, overseas £10, family/institutions £8.

Mechanical-Copyright Protection Society Ltd (MCPS), Elgar House, 41 Streatham High Road, London SW16 1ER *tel* 0181-664 4400 *telex* 946792 MCPS G *fax* 0181-769 8792. *Chief executive:* Frans De Wit; *contact:* Corporate Communications Department. Founded in 1910, the Society grants licences for the use of copyright material by mechanical reproduction, be it sound, film, radio and television recordings, magnetic tape or videocassettes. Protection is world-wide, by virtue of its affiliations with other similar organisations and agencies. Membership of the Society is open to all music copyright owners, composers, lyric writers and publishers. No entrance fee or subscription.

The Media Society (1973). *Secretary:* Rodney Bennett-England, PO Box 124, East Rudham, Norfolk PE31 8TT   *tel* (01485) 528664   *fax* (01485) 528155. To promote and encourage collective and independent research into the standards, performance, organisation and economics of the media and hold regular discussions, debates, etc. on subjects of topical or special interest and concern to print and broadcast journalists and others working in or with the media. *Subscription:* £25 p.a.

Medical Journalists Association (1966), Barley Mow, 185 High Street, Stony Stratford, Milton Keynes MK11 1AP   *tel* (01908) 564623. *Chairman:* Michael Jeffries; *hon. secretary:* Gwen Yates. Aims to improve the quality and practice of health and medical journalism. Administers major awards for health and medical journalism and broadcasting. Publishes *The MJA Directory* and a newsletter, *MJA News. Membership fee:* £20 p.a.

Medical Writers Group, 84 Drayton Gardens, London SW10 9SB   *tel* 0171-373 6642. *Secretary:* Jacqueline Granger-Taylor. Specialist group within the membership of the Society of Authors giving contractual and legal advice. Also organises talks, day seminars covering many aspects of medical writing, and administers the medical prizes sponsored by the Royal Society of Medicine.

Miniature Painters, Sculptors and Gravers, Royal Society of (1895). *President:* Suzanne Lucas FLS, PRMS, FPSBA; *treasurer:* Alastair MacDonald; *hon. secretary:* Pauline Gyles. Membership is by selection and standard of work over a period of years (ARMS associate, RMS full member). Annual Open Exhibition in November in London, hand-in Sept/Oct; schedules available in July (send sae). Applications and enquiries to the *executive secretary:* Mrs Pam Henderson, 1 Knapp Cottages, Wyke, Gillingham, Dorset SP8 4NQ   *tel* (01747) 825718.

Miniaturists, British Society of (1895), *Director:* Leslie Simpson FRSA, Ralston House, 41 Lister Street, Riverside Gardens, Ilkley, West Yorkshire LS29 9ET   *tel* (01943) 609075. 'The world's oldest miniature society.' Holds two open exhibitions p.a. Membership by selection.

Miniaturists, The Hilliard Society of (1982). *The Executive Officer:* Mrs S.M. Burton, 15 Union Street, Wells, Somerset BA5 2PU   *tel* (01749) 674472   *fax* (01749) 672918. *President:* Commander G.W.G. Hunt, RMS, HS, MASF, RN. International society with approx. 300 members. Founded to increase knowledge and promote the art of miniature painting. Annual Exhibition held in May/June at Wells; seminars; Young People's Awards (11-19 years). Encourages Patron membership to keep collectors in touch with artists. Informative Newsletter includes technical section and news from miniature societies around the world.

William Morris Society (1955), Kelmscott House, 26 Upper Mall, London W6 9TA   *tel* 0181-741 3735. *Secretary:* Derek Baker. To spread knowledge of the life, work and ideas of William Morris; publishes *Newsletter* (Q.) and *Journal* (2 p.a.). Library and collections open to the public Thu and Sat, 2-5.

Motoring Artists, The Guild of (1986). *Administrator:* Roy Gardner FIMI, MIMgt, Woodlands, Welford Hill, Welford-on-Avon, Warwicks. CV37 8AE   *tel* (01789) 750618. To promote, publicise and develop motoring fine art; to build a recognised group of artists interested in motoring art, holding events and exchanging ideas and support; to hold motoring art exhibitions. *Annual membership fee:* £27.50, associate £22.50, friend £18.

Motoring Writers, The Guild of. General Secretary, 30 The Cravens, Smallfield, Surrey RH6 9QS *tel* (01342) 843294 *fax* (01342) 844093. To raise the standard of motoring journalism. For writers, broadcasters, photographers on matters of motoring, but who are not connected with the motor industry.

Music Publishers Association Ltd (1881), 3rd Floor, Strandgate, 18/20 York Buildings, London WC2N 6JU *tel* 0171-839 7779 *fax* 0171-839 7776. *Secretary:* P.J. Dadswell. The only trade organisation representing the UK music publishing industry; protects and promotes its members' interests in copyright, trade and related matters. A number of sub-committees and groups deal with particular interests. Details of subscriptions available on written request.

Musical Association, The Royal, Prof Julian Rushton, Department of Music, University of Leeds, Leeds LS2 9JT *tel* 0113-233 2579 *fax* 0113-233 2586.

Musicians, Incorporated Society of, 10 Stratford Place, London W1N 9AE *tel* 0171-629 4413 *fax* 0171-408 1538. *President:* 1996-7: Ian Partridge CBE; *chief executive:* Neil Hoyle. Professional body for musicians. Aims to promote the art of music; protect the interests and raise the standards of the musical profession; provide services, support and advice for its members. Publishes *Music Journal* (12 p.a.); Yearbook and three Registers of Specialists annually. *Subscription:* £76 p.a.

Musicians, The Worshipful Company of (1500), 2/4 Carey Lane, London EC2V 8AA *tel* 0171-600 4636 *fax* 0171-600 4392. *Clerk:* S.F.N. Waley.

Name Studies in Britain and Ireland, Society for. *Hon. secretary:* Miss Jennifer Scherr, c/o Queen's Building Library, University of Bristol, University Walk, Bristol BS8 1TR; *membership secretary:* Dr M. Higham, 22 Peel Park Avenue, Clitheroe, Lancs. BB7 1ET. Aims to advance, promote and support research into the place-names and personal names of Britain and Ireland and related regions by the collection, documentation and interpretation of such names; the publication of the material and the results of such research; the exchange of information between the various regions. Acts as a consultative body on Name Studies; publishes an annual journal, *Nomina*, and an occasional newsletter. *Subscription:* £15 p.a. (1996).

The National Small Press Centre (1992), Middlesex University, White Hart Lane, London N17 8HR. Provides a physical focus for small presses (independent self-publishers), and actively promotes small presses as a whole with exhibitions, talks, courses, workshops, conferences and Small Press fairs. Publishes *News from the Centre* (Bi-M.) and *Small Press Listings* (Q.). *Annual subscription:* from £6.

National Union of Journalists. Head Office: Acorn House, 314 Gray's Inn Road, London WC1X 8DP *tel* 0171-278 7916 *fax* 0171-837 8143 *e-mail* nuj@mcr1.poptel.org.uk Trade union for working journalists with 28,000 members and 147 branches throughout the UK and the Republic of Ireland, and in Paris, Brussels, Geneva and the Netherlands. It covers the newspaper press, news agencies and broadcasting, the major part of periodical and book publishing, and a number of public relations departments and consultancies, information services and Prestel-Viewdata services. Administers disputes, unemployment, benevolent and provident benefits. Official publications: *The Journalist, Freelance Directory, Freelance Fees Guide* and policy pamphlets.

New Science Fiction Alliance (NSFA) (1989), c/o Chris Reed, BBR, PO Box 625, Sheffield S1 3GY *Publicity officer:* Chris Reed. The NSFA is committed to supporting the work of new writers and artists by promoting independent and small press publications worldwide. It was founded by a group of independent publishers to give writers the opportunity to explore the small press and find the right market for their material. It offers a mail order service for magazines.

New Zealand, Book Publishers Association of, Inc., Box 101-271, North Shore Mail Centre, Auckland, New Zealand   *tel* (09) 444-4300   *fax* (09) 444-2030. *President:* Wendy Harrex.

New Zealand Copyright Council Inc., PO Box 5028, Wellington, New Zealand   *tel* (04) 472-4430   *fax* (04) 471-0765. *Chairman:* Bernard Darby; *secretary:* Tony Chance.

Newspaper Press Fund, Dickens House, 35 Wathen Road, Dorking, Surrey RH4 1JY   *tel* (01306) 887511. *Secretary:* P.W. Evans. For the relief of hardship amongst member journalists, their widows and dependants. Financial assistance and retirement housing are provided. Limited help is available for non-member journalists and their dependants.

The Newspaper Publishers Association Ltd, 34 Southwark Bridge Road, London SE1 9EU   *tel* 0171-928 6928   *fax* 0171-928 2067.

Newspaper Society, Bloomsbury House, 74-77 Great Russell Street, London WC1B 3DA   *tel* 0171-636 7014   *fax* 0171-631 5119   *AdDoc* DX35701 Bloomsbury   *e-mail* ns@newspapersoc.org.uk *Director:* Dugal Nisbet-Smith; *deputy director:* David Newell.

Oil Painters, Royal Institute of, 17 Carlton House Terrace, London SW1Y 5BD   *tel* 0171-930 6844   *fax* 0171-839 7830. *President:* Frederick Beckett. Promotes and encourages the art of painting in oils. Open Annual Exhibition.

Oils, Pastels and Acrylics, British Society of Painters in (1988), Ralston House, 41 Lister Street, Riverside Gardens, Ilkley, West Yorkshire LS29 9ET   *tel* (01943) 609075. *Director:* Leslie Simpson FRSA. Promotes interest and encourages high quality in the work of painters in these media. Holds two open exhibitions per annum. *Membership:* by selection.

The Orton Society (1994), 21 Brockenhurst Road, Croydon, Surrey CR0 7DR. *President:* Sue Townsend; *Chairman:* Bill Kelly. Aims to promote the life and work of Joe Orton and to draw him to the attention of future generations. *Membership:* £3.00 p.a.

Outdoor Writers' Guild (1980). *Secretary:* Terry Marsh, PO Box 520, Bamber Bridge, Preston, Lancs. PR5 8LF   *tel/fax* (01772) 696732. Aims to promote a high professional standard among writers who specialise in outdoor activities; represents members' interests to representative bodies in the outdoor leisure industry; circulates members with news of media opportunities; provides a forum for members to meet colleagues and others in the outdoor leisure industry. *Membership:* £35 p.a. plus £20 joining fee.

Wilfred Owen Association (1989), 17 Belmont, Shrewsbury SY1 1TE   *tel/fax* (01743) 235904. To commemorate the life and work of Wilfred Owen, and to encourage and enhance appreciation of his work. *Annual subscription:* £4 (£6 overseas); £10 groups/institutions; £2 senior citizens/students/unemployed.

PACT (Producers Alliance for Cinema and Television), Gordon House, Greencoat Place, London SW1P 1PH   *tel* 0171-233 6000   *fax* 0171-233 8935. *Contacts:* John Woodward (chief executive), David Alan Mills (membership officer). PACT serves the feature film and independent television production sector and is the UK contact point for co-production, co-finance partners and distributors.

Painter-Printmakers, Royal Society of (1880), Bankside Gallery, 48 Hopton Street, London SE1 9JH *tel* 0171-928 7521. *President:* Prof David L. Carpanini RBA, RWA, NEAC. Membership (RE) open to British and overseas artists. An election of Associates is held annually, and applications for the necesssary forms and particulars should be addressed to the Secretary. The Society organises workshops and lectures on original printmaking; holds one members' exhibition per year. Friends of the RE open to all those interested in artists' original printmaking.

Painters, Sculptors and Printmakers, National Society of (1930). *President:* Denis Baxter PNS, UA, FRSA; *hon. secretary:* Gwen Spencer, 122 Copse Hill, Wimbledon, London SW20 0NL *tel* 0181-946 7878. An annual exhibition in London representing all aspects of art for artists of every creed and outlook; Newsletter, 2 p.a. for members.

The Pastel Society (1899), 17 Carlton House Terrace, London SW1Y 5BD *tel* 0171-930 6844 *fax* 0171-839 7830. *President:* Thomas Coates. Pastel and drawings in pencil or chalk. Annual Exhibition open to all artists working in dry media. Members elected from approved candidates' list.

The Mervyn Peake Society (1975). *Hon. president:* Sebastian Peake; *chairman:* Brian Sibley; *secretary:* Frank Surry, 2 Mount Park Road, Ealing, London W5 2RP. Devoted to recording the life and works of Mervyn Peake; publishes a journal and newsletter. *Annual subscription:* £12 (UK and Europe); £10 students; £14 all other countries.

P.E.N., International. A world association of writers. *International president:* Ronald Harwood; *international secretary:* Alexandre Blokh, 9/10 Charterhouse Buildings, Goswell Road, London EC1M 7AT *tel* 0171-253 4308 *telegrams/cables* Lonpenclub, London EC1 *fax* 0171-253 5711; *English PEN Centre: president:* Josephine Pullein-Thompson MBE; *general secretary:* Gillian Vincent, 7 Dilke Street, London SW3 4JE *tel* 0171-352 6303 *fax* 0171-351 0220; *Scottish PEN Centre: president:* Paul H. Scott; *secretary:* Laura Fiorentini, 33 Drumsheugh Gardens, Edinburgh EH3 7RN *tel* 0131-225 1038; *Welsh PEN Centre: president:* Ned Thomas, University of Wales Press, Gwynneth Street, Cathays, Cardiff CF2 4YD *tel* (01222) 231919.

P.E.N. was founded in 1921 by C.A. Dawson Scott under the presidency of John Galsworthy, to promote friendship and understanding between writers and to defend freedom of expression within and between all nations. The initials P.E.N. stand for Poets, Playwrights, Editors, Essayists, Novelists – but membership is open to all writers of standing (including translators), whether men or women, without distinction of creed or race, who subscribe to these fundamental principles. P.E.N. takes no part in state or party politics. The International P.E.N. Writers in Prison Committee works on behalf of writers imprisoned for exercising their right to freedom of expression, a right implicit in the P.E.N. Charter to which all members subscribe. The International P.E.N. Translations and Linguistic Rights Committee strives to promote the translations of works by writers in the lesser-known languages and to defend those languages. The Writers for Peace Committee exists to find ways in which writers can work for peaceful co-existence in the world. The Women Writers' Committee works to promote women's writing and publishing in developing countries. International Congresses are held most years. The 62nd Congress was held in Fremantle, Western Australia in October 1995; the 63rd Congress will be held in Guadalajara, Mexico in November 1996.

Membership of any one Centre implies membership of all Centres; at present 126 autonomous Centres exist throughout the world. Membership of the English Centre is £30 p.a. for country and overseas members, £35 for London members. Associate membership is available for writers not yet eligible for full membership and for persons connected with literature. The English Centre has a programme of literary lectures, discussion, dinners and parties. A yearly *Writers' Day* is open to the public as are some literary lectures.

Please apply to the Scottish and Welsh Centres for information about their membership fees and activities.

The Penman Club (1950). *Secretary:* Mark Sorrell, 185 Daws Heath Road, Benfleet, Essex SS7 2TF   *tel* (01702) 557431. Writers' society offering criticism of members' work and general advice. Send sae for prospectus. *Membership fee:* £15 for first year, £8.25 p.a. thereafter.

Performing Right Society Ltd (1914), 29-33 Berners Street, London W1P 4AA   *tel* 0171-580 5544   *fax* 0171-631 4138. *Contact:* Public Affairs Department. An association of composers, authors and publishers of copyright musical works, established in 1914, to grant licences and collect royalties for the public performance, broadcasting and diffusion by cable of such works; also to restrain unauthorised use thereof. The Society is affiliated to the national societies of more than 30 other countries. All composers of musical works and authors of lyrics or poems which have been set to music are eligible for membership. An initial admission fee only is payable.

Periodical Publishers Association, Queens House, 28 Kingsway, London WC2B 6UN   *tel* 0171-379 6268   *fax* 0171-379 5661. *Chief executive:* Ian Lochs.

The Personal Managers' Association Ltd. *Liaison secretary:* Angela Adler, 1 Summer Road, East Molesey, Surrey KT8 9LX   *tel/fax* 0181-398 9796. Association of personal managers in the theatre, film and entertainment world generally.

Photographers, The Association of (1969). *Co-secretary:* Gwen Thomas, 9-10 Domingo Street, London EC1Y 0TA   *tel* 0171-608 1441   *fax* 0171-253 3007. To protect and promote the interests of fashion advertising and editorial photographers. *Annual subscription:* £72-£355, depending on turnover.

Photographers Association, Master, Hallmark House, 2 Beaumont Street, Darlington, Co. Durham DL1 5SZ   *tel* (01325) 356555   *fax* (01325) 357813. To promote and protect professional photographers. Members qualify for awards of Licentiate, Associate and Fellowship. *Subscription:* £82.00 p.a.

Photographic Society, The Royal (1853), The Octagon, Milsom Street, Bath BA1 1DN   *tel* (01225) 462841. Aims to promote the general advancement of photography and its applications; publishes *The Photographic Journal* (M.), £60 p.a., overseas £65 p.a. and *The Journal of Photographic Science* (Bi-M.), £89 p.a., overseas £99.

Photography, British Institute of Professional (founded 1901, incorporated 1921), Amwell End, Ware, Herts. SG12 9HN   *tel* (01920) 464011. To represent all who practise photography as a profession in any field; to improve the quality of photography; establish recognised examination qualifications and a high standard of conduct; to safeguard the interests of the public and the profession. Admission can be obtained either via examinations, or by submission of work and other information to the appropriate examining board. Fellows, Associates and Licentiates are entitled to the designation Incorporated Photographer or Incorporated Photographic Technician. Organises numerous meetings and conferences in various parts of the country throughout the year; publishes a monthly journal, *The Photographer*, and an annual Register of Members and *guide to buyers of photography*, plus various pamphlets and leaflets on professional photography.

Player-Playwrights (1948). *Secretary:* Peter Thompson, 9 Hillfield Park, London N10 3QT *tel* 0181-883 0371. Meets on Monday evenings at St Augustine's Church Hall, Queen's Gate, London SW1. The society reads, performs and discusses plays and scripts submitted by members, with a view to assisting the writers in improving and marketing their work. Newcomers and new acting members are always welcome. *Membership:* £5 p.a. (and £1 per attendance).

Playwrights Trust, New, Interchange Studios, Dalby Street, London NW5 3NQ *tel* 0171-284 2818 *fax* 0171-482 5292. *Executive director:* Jonathan Meth; *research director:* John Deeney. Research and development organisation for playwrights and aspiring playwrights, and those interested in developing and producing new work. Services include script-reading; information guides; writer/company Link Service; six-weekly *Newsletter*. *Subscription:* rates on application.

Poetry Book Society, Book House, 45 East Hill, London SW18 2QZ *tel* 0181-870 8403 *fax* 0181-877 1615. *Chairman:* Martyn Goff; *director:* Clare Brown. Foremost in getting books of new poetry to readers through *Choice* (Q.), offers, and 300-strong backlist which it sells at favourable rates to members. Publishes *Bulletin* (Q.) and holds quarterly readings at the Royal Festival Hall. Administers the T.S. Eliot Prize for the best collection of new poetry. Operates as a charitable Book Club with annual membership (£8, £30, £120) open to all.

Poetry Foundation, National (1981), 27 Mill Road, Fareham, Hants PO16 0TH *tel* (01329) 822218. Aims to provide a truly national poetry organisation which in turn provides advice, information and a magazine, all for a single low-cost fee, and to help poets have a book of their own poetry published at no additional cost, once they have sufficient poetry of a high enough standard. The Foundation also gives grants to deserving causes directly related to poetry and gives free advice on problems relating to book publication.

The Poetry Society (1909), 22 Betterton Street, London WC2H 9BU *tel* 0171-240 4810 *fax* 0171-240 4818. *Chairman:* Bill Swainson; *director:* Chris Meade. National membership body, open to all, to help poets and poetry thrive in Britain today. Publishes *Poetry Review* and *Poetry News* quarterly, has an information and imagination service, runs promotions and educational projects, and administers the annual National Poetry Competition and the biennial European Poetry Translation Prize.

The Polidori Society (1990). *President:* Franklin Bishop, Ebenezer House, 31 Ebenezer Street, Langley Mill, Notts. NG16 4DA. To promote appreciation of the life and works of John William Polidori MD (1795-1821), romantic poet, novelist, diarist, traveller, philosopher, essayist and tragedian. Author of the seminal *The Vampyre – A tale* (1819), thereby introducing into English literature the icon of the vampyre portrayed as an aristocrat and seducer. The Society celebrates the life of Polidori by way of an annual grand dinner and members receive newsletters, book offers and the opportunity to attend social events. Details of membership from the Secretary at the above address or *tel* 0181-994 5902 *fax* 0181-995 3275. International membership.

Portrait Painters, Royal Society of (1891), 17 Carlton House Terrace, London SW1Y 5BD *tel* 0171-930 6844 *fax* 0171-839 7830. *President:* Daphne Todd. Annual Exhibition when work may be submitted by non-members with a view to exhibition.

Portuguese Association of Publishers and Booksellers (Associação Portuguesa de Editores e Livreiros) (1939), Av. Estados Unidos da América, 97-6° Esq., Lisboa 1700, Portugal (1) *tel* 8489136 *fax* (1) 8489377.

Beatrix Potter Society (1980). *Chairman:* Judy Taylor; *secretary:* Marian Werner, 32 Etchingham Park Road, Finchley, London N3 2DT. Promotes the study and appreciation of the life and works of Beatrix Potter as author, artist, diarist, farmer and conservationist. *Subscription:* UK £7, overseas $US25, $Can27.50, $Aus30.

Press Agencies, National Association of (1983). *Administrator:* Jan Chambers, 41 Lansdowne Crescent, Leamington Spa, Warks. CV32 4PR   *tel* (01926) 424181   *fax* (01926) 424760. Trade association representing the interests of regional news and photographic agencies. *Annual subscription:* £250.

The Press Complaints Commission (1991), *Chairman:* The Rt Hon Lord Wakeham; *director:* Mark Bolland, 1 Salisbury Square, London EC4Y 8AE   *tel* 0171-353 1248   *Help-Line tel* 0171-353 3732   *fax* 0171-353 8355. Independent body founded to oversee self-regulation of the Press. Deals with complaints by the public about the contents and conduct of British newspapers and magazines and advises editors on journalistic ethics. Complaints must be about the failure of newspapers or magazines to follow the letter or spirit of a Code of Practice, drafted by newspaper and magazine editors, adopted by the industry and supervised by the Commission.

Private Libraries Association (1956), Ravelston, South View Road, Pinner, Middlesex HA5 3YD. *President:* Robin de Beaumont; *hon. editor:* David Chambers; *hon. secretary:* Frank Broomhead. International society of book collectors and private libraries. Publications include *Private Library* (Q.), annual *Private Press Books*, and other books on book collecting. *Subscription:* £25 p.a.

The Producers Association—see **PACT.**

The Publishers Association (1896), 19 Bedford Square, London WC1B 3HJ   *tel* 0171-580 6321   *telex* 267160 PUBASS G   *fax* 0171-636 5375. *Chief executive:* Clive Bradley; *director of International and Trade Divisions (BDC):* Ian Taylor; *director of educational and academic and professional publishing:* John Davies.

Publishers Association, International (1896), 3 avenue de Miremont, CH-1206 Geneva, Switzerland   *tel* (022) 346-30-18   *fax* (022) 347-57-17. *President:* Alain Gründ; *secretary-general:* J. Alexis Koutchoumow.

Publishers Guild, Independent (1962), 25 Cambridge Road, Hampton, Middlesex TW12 2JL   *tel* 0181-979 0250   *fax* 0181-979 6393. Full membership is open to new and established publishers and book packagers; supplier membership is available to specialists in fields allied to publishing (but not printers and binders). The Guild offers a forum for the exchange of ideas and information and represents the interests of its members. *Membership:* £75 (+ VAT) p.a.

Publishers Licensing Society Limited (1981), 90 Tottenham Court Road, London W1P 9HE   *tel* 0171-436 5931   *fax* 0171-436 3986. *Chairman:* Nicolas Thompson; *manager:* Caroline Elmslie. Aims to exercise and enforce on behalf of publishers the rights of copyright and other rights of a similar nature; to authorise the granting of licences for the making of reprographic copies of copyright works; and to receive and distribute to publisher copyright owners the sums received from licensed use. PLS intends to increase the range and repertoire of those mandated publishers including, specifically, seeking their authorisation for electro-storage of information and digital copying.

Publishers Publicity Circle (c. 1955). *Secretary:* Christina Thomas, 48 Crabtree Lane, London SW6 6LW   *tel/fax* 0171-385 3708. Enables all book publicists to meet and share information regularly. Monthly meetings provide a forum for press journalists, television and radio researchers and producers to meet publicists collectively. In conjunction with *Publishing News*, awards are presented for the best PR campaigns. Monthly newsletter includes recruitment advertising.

The Radclyffe International Philosophical Association (1955), BM-RIPhA, Old Gloucester Street, London WC1N 3XX. *President:* William Mann FRIPhA; *secretary general:* John Khasseyan FRIPhA. *Aims:* to dignify those achievements which might otherwise escape formal recognition; to promote the interests and talent of its members; to encourage their good fellowship; and to form a medium for the exchange of ideas between members. *Annual subscription:* £25.00 (Fellows, Members and Associates). Published authors and artists usually enter at Fellowship level.

The Radio Academy, PO Box 4SZ, London W1A 4SZ *tel* 0171-255 2010 *fax* 0171-255 2029 *e-mail* radacad.demon.co.uk *Director:* John Bradford. The Radio Academy is the professional association for those engaged in the UK radio industry. Over 1200 individual members and 30 corporate patrons. It organises conferences, seminars, debates, the annual UK Radio Festival and social events for members; publishes a monthly newsletter *Off Air*, and a twice-yearly magazine *Radio*. The Academy also has a number of Collegiate members and offers some practical training opportunities for students of radio.

Radio Producers, Independent Association of (1993), Essel House, 29 Foley Street, London W1P 7LB *tel* 0171-323 2770 *fax* 0171-436 0132. *Chair:* Sarah Dickinson; *vice-chair:* Simon Hughes *tel* 0171-278 6070. To protect and promote the interests of independent radio and audio producers and to promote the interests and advancement of the industry. *Membership fee:* £50 p.a.

Railway Artists, Guild of (1979). *Chief executive officer:* F.P. Hodges, 45 Dickins Road, Warwick CV34 5NS *tel* (01926) 499246. Aims to forge a link between artists depicting railway subjects and to give members a corporate identity; also stages railway art exhibitions and members' meetings.

Regional Arts Boards (RABs). Following a process of restructuring in 1990/91, a network of ten Regional Arts Boards now covers England. The RABs are autonomous, strategic bodies which work in partnership with local authorities and a wide variety of other sectors and organisations and are policy led. Legally, they are limited companies with charitable status. They are concerned with all the arts and crafts – visual, performing, media, published – and work at regional level as partners of the three national agencies which provide most of their funds: the Arts Council, the British Film Institute, the Crafts Council.

The Arts Council retains the national responsibility for funding and assessing the 'national companies', the symphony orchestras and a handful of other high profile clients. The building-based drama companies are mostly funded by the RABs. The overall planning system is becoming more 'integrated' with the principle of subsidiarity being increasingly applied to project and development work. The resources available to the RABs during 1995/96 total over £50 million.

English Regional Arts Boards is the representative body for the ten Regional Arts Boards in England. Its secretariat provides project management, services and information for the members and acts on their behalf in appropriate circumstances: 5 City Road, Winchester, Hants SO23 8SD *tel* (01962) 851063 *fax* (01962) 842033 *e-mail* christopher-gordon.erab@artsfbs.org.uk *Chief executive:* Christopher Gordon; *assistant:* Carolyn Nixson. The Welsh Regional Arts Associations have been integrated with the Arts Council of Wales (see page 596).

There are no regional arts boards in Scotland and all enquiries should be addressed to the Scottish Arts Council, 12 Manor Place, Edinburgh EH3 7DD   *tel* 0131-226 6051   *fax* 0131-225 9833.

East Midlands Arts Board (1969), Mountfields House, Epinal Way, Loughborough, Leics. LE11 0QE   *tel* (01509) 218292   *fax* (01509) 262214. *Chief executive:* John Buston; *literature officer:* Debbie Hicks. Derbyshire (excluding High Peak District), Leicestershire, Northamptonshire and Nottinghamshire.

Eastern Arts Board (1971), Cherry Hinton Hall, Cherry Hinton Road, Cambridge CB1 4DW   *tel* (01223) 215355   *fax* (01223) 248075. *Chief executive:* Lou Stein. Specialist officers for each art form. Bedfordshire, Cambridgeshire, Essex, Hertfordshire, Lincolnshire, Norfolk and Suffolk.

London Arts Board (1991), Elme House, 133 Long Acre, Covent Garden, London WC2E 9AF   *tel* 0171-240 1313   *fax* 0171-240 4580. *Principal literature officer:* John Hampson; *principal visual arts and crafts officer:* Holly Tebbutt. The area of the 32 London Boroughs and the Corporation of London.

North West Arts Board (1966), Manchester House, 22 Bridge Street, Manchester M3 3AB   *tel* 0161-834 6644   *fax* 0161-834 6969. *Chief executive:* Sue Harrison. Greater Manchester, Merseyside, High Peak District of Derbyshire, Lancashire and Cheshire.

Northern Arts (1961), 9-10 Osborne Terrace, Newcastle upon Tyne NE2 1NZ   *tel* 0191-281 6334   *fax* 0191-281 3276. *Chief executive:* Peter Hewitt; *head of published and broadcast arts:* Margaret O'Connor. Cumbria, Cleveland, Tyne and Wear, Northumberland and Durham.

South East Arts Board (1973), 10 Mount Ephraim, Tunbridge Wells, Kent TN4 8AS   *tel* (01892) 515210   *information dept. ext.* 205/206   *fax* (01892) 549383. *Chief executive:* Christopher Cooper; *literature officer:* Anne Downes (*ext.* 210/211). Covers Kent, Surrey, East Sussex and West Sussex. Information and publications list available.

South West Arts (1956), Bradninch Place, Gandy Street, Exeter, Devon EX4 3LS   *tel* (01392) 218188   *fax* (01392) 413554. *Chief executive:* Graham Long. Avon, Cornwall, Devon, Dorset (except Districts of Bournemouth, Christchurch and Poole), Gloucestershire, Somerset.

Southern Arts Board (1968), 13 St Clement Street, Winchester, Hants SO23 9DQ   *tel* (01962) 855099   *fax* (01962) 861186. *Executive director:* Sue Robertson; *literature officer:* Keiran Phelan. The arts development agency for Berkshire, Buckinghamshire, Hampshire, Isle of Wight, Oxfordshire, Wiltshire and South East Dorset.

West Midlands Arts Board (1971), 82 Granville Street, Birmingham B1 2LH   *tel* 0121-631 3121   *fax* 0121-643 7239. *Chief executive:* Michael Elliott. County of Hereford and Worcester, Shropshire, Staffordshire, Warwickshire and the Metropolitan West Midlands.

Yorkshire and Humberside Arts (1991). 21 Bond Street, Dewsbury, West Yorkshire WF13 1AX   *tel* (01924) 455555   *fax* (01924) 466522. *Literature officer:* Steve Dearden. North, South, West and East Yorkshire. Funds schemes and projects for the promotion of contemporary literature and writing activities. Provides grants for festivals, events, courses, residencies, publishing. Offers advice and information on various aspects of literature. Preliminary enquiry advised.

Ridley Art Society (1889), 37 James Street, Hounslow, Middlesex TW3 1SP   *tel* 0181-570 6419. *President:* Carel Weight CH, CBE, RA; *chairman:* Ernie Donagh. Represents a wide variety of attitudes towards the making of art. In recent years has sought to encourage young artists. At least one central London exhibition annually.

The Romantic Novelists' Association. *Chairman:* Elizabeth Buchan, 6 Franconia Road, London SW4 9HD *tel* 0171-720 3591; *hon. secretary:* Joyce Bell, Cobble Cottage, 129 New Street, Baddesley Ensor, Nr Atherstone, Warwickshire CV9 2DL *tel* (01827) 714776. To raise the prestige of Romantic Authorship. Open to romantic and historical novelists. See also under **Literary Awards.**

Royal Academy of Arts, Piccadilly, London W1V 0DS *tel* 0171-439 7438 *fax* 0171-434 0837. *President:* Sir Philip Dowson CBE; *keeper:* Leonard McComb RA; *treasurer:* Sir Philip Powell RA; *secretary:* Piers Rodgers. Academicians (RA) are elected from the most distinguished artists in the UK. Major loan exhibitions throughout the year with the Annual Summer Exhibition, June to August. Also runs art schools for 60 post-graduate students in painting and sculpture.

The Royal Literary Fund, 144 Temple Chambers, Temple Avenue, London EC4Y 0DA *tel* 0171-353 7150. *President:* His Honour Judge Stephen Tumim; *secretary:* Fiona Clark. Founded in 1790, the Fund is the oldest and largest charity serving literature, set up to help writers and their families who face hardship. It does not offer grants to writers who can earn their living in other ways, nor does it provide financial support for writing projects. But it sustains authors who have for one reason or another fallen on hard times – illness, family misfortune, or sheer loss of writing form. Applicants must have published work of approved literary merit, which may include important contributions to periodicals. The literary claim of every new applicant must be accepted by the General Committee before the question of need can be considered.

The Royal Society (1660), 6 Carlton House Terrace, London SW1Y 5AG *tel* 0171-839 5561 *telex* 917876 *fax* 0171-930 2170. *President:* Sir Aaron Klug OM, PRS; *treasurer:* Sir John H. Horlock FRS, F.Eng; *biological secretary:* Prof P. Lachmann FRS; *physical secretary:* Prof J.S. Rowlinson FRS, F.Eng; *foreign secretary:* Dr Anne L. McLaren DBE, FRS; *executive secretary:* Dr P.T. Warren. Promotion of the natural sciences (pure and applied).

The Ruskin Society of London (1985). *Hon. secretary:* Miss O.E. Forbes-Madden, 351 Woodstock Road, Oxford OX2 7NX *tel* (01865) 310987. To promote literary and biographical interest in John Ruskin and his contemporaries. The Society issues an annual *Ruskin Gazette* free to members. *Subscription:* £10 p.a.

The Dorothy L. Sayers Society (1976). *Chairman:* Christopher J. Dean, Rose Cottage, Malthouse Lane, Hurstpierpoint, West Sussex BN6 9JY *tel* (01273) 833444; *secretaries:* Lenelle Davis and Jasmine Simeone. To promote and encourage the study of the works of Dorothy L. Sayers; to collect relics and reminiscences about her and make them available to students and biographers; to hold an annual seminar and other meetings; to publish proceedings, pamphlets and a bi-monthly bulletin. *Annual subscription:* £9.

Science Fiction Association Ltd, The British (1958). *President:* Arthur C. Clarke; *membership secretary:* Alison Cook, 52 Woodhill Drive, Grove, Oxon OX12 0DF. For authors, publishers, booksellers and readers of science fiction, fantasy and allied genres. Publishes informal magazine, *Matrix*, of news and information, *Focus*, an amateur writers' magazine, *Vector*, a critical magazine and The Orbiter Service, a network of postal writers workshops (all enquiries to membership secretary).

Science Writers, Association of British, c/o British Association for the Advancement of Science, 23 Savile Row, London W1X 2NB   *tel* 0171-439 1205   *fax* 0171-973 3051. *Chairman:* Richard Stevenson; *administrator:* Barbara Drillsma. Association of science writers, editors, and radio, film and television producers concerned with the presentation and communication of science, technology and medicine. Aims to improve the standard of science writing and to assist its members in their work.

Scientific and Technical Communicators, The Institute of (1972), Kings Court, 2/16 Goodge Street, London W1P 1FF   *tel* 0171-436 4425   *fax* 0171-580 0747. *President:* Dave Griffiths; *executive secretary:* Jeannette Hobart. Professional body for those engaged in the communication of scientific and technical information. Aims to establish and maintain professional standards, to encourage and co-operate in professional training and to provide a source of information on, and to encourage research and development in, all aspects of scientific and technical communication. Publishes *The Communicator*, the official journal of the Institute, 4 p.a.

Scottish Academy, Royal (1826), The Mound, Edinburgh EH2 2EL   *tel* 0131-225 6671   *fax* 0131-225 2349. *President:* William J.L. Baillie PRSA; *secretary:* Ian McKenzie Smith RSA; *treasurer:* James Morris RSA. Academicians (RSA) and Associates (ARSA) and non-members may exhibit in the Annual Exhibition of Painting, Sculpture and Architecture, held approximately mid April to August; Festival Exhibition August/September. Other artists' societies' annual exhibitions, normally between October and January. Royal Scottish Academy Student Competition held in March.

Scottish Arts, 24 Rutland Square, Edinburgh EH1 2BW   *tel* 0131-229 1076. *Hon. secretary:* Colin J.M. Sutherland   *tel* 0131-229 8157. Art, literature, music. *Annual subscription:* Full £250.00, but various reductions.

Scottish Arts Council, 12 Manor Place, Edinburgh EH3 7DD   *tel* 0131-226 6051. *Chairman:* Dr William Brown; *director:* Seona Reid; *literature director:* Jenny Brown. Principal channel for government funding of the arts in Scotland, the Scottish Arts Council is funded by the Scottish Office. It aims to develop and improve the knowledge, understanding and practice of the arts, and to increase their accessibility throughout Scotland. It offers about 1300 grants a year to artists and arts organisations concerned with the visual arts, drama, dance and mime, literature, music, festivals, and traditional, ethnic and community arts.

Scottish History Society (1886), Department of History and Economic History, University of Aberdeen, King's College, Old Aberdeen AB9 2UB   *tel/fax* (01224) 272456. *Hon. secretary:* Steve Boardman PhD. The Society exists to publish documents illustrating the history of Scotland.

Scottish Literary Studies, Association for (1970), c/o Department of English, University of Aberdeen, Aberdeen AB9 2UB   *tel* (01224) 272634. *President:* Dr David Robb; *secretary:* Dorothy McMillan; *treasurer:* Prof David Hewitt; *publishing manager:* Catherine McInerney. Promotes the study, teaching and writing of Scottish literature and furthers the study of the languages of Scotland. Publishes annually an edited text of Scottish literature, an anthology of new Scottish writing and a series of academic journals, and a twice-yearly Newsletter. Also publishes *Scotnotes* – comprehensive study guides to major Scottish writers, and literary texts and commentary cassettes designed to assist the classroom teacher. *Annual membership:* individuals/schools £25, UK students £12.50, corporate £50.

Scottish Newspaper Publishers' Association, 48 Palmerston Place, Edinburgh EH12 5DE *tel* 0131-220 4353 *fax* 0131-220 4344. *President:* P. Cohen; *director:* J.B. Raeburn FCIS.

Scottish Publishers Association (1974), Scottish Book Centre, 137 Dundee Street, Edinburgh EH11 1BG *tel* 0131-228 6866 *fax* 0131-228 3220. *Director:* Lorraine Fannin; *administrator:* Neil Gowans; *marketing manager:* Susanne Gilmour.

Screenwriters Workshop, London (1983), 84 Wardour Street, London W1V 3LF *tel* 0171-434 0942. *Contact:* Anji Loman Field. Forum for contact, information and tuition, the LSW helps new and established writers work successfully in the film and TV industry, and organises a continuous programme of activities, events, courses and seminars, many of which are free/reduced to members and open to non-members at reasonable rates. *Annual subscription:* £25.

SCRIBO (1971), K. & P. Sylvester, Flat 1, 31 Hamilton Road, Bournemouth BH1 4EQ. A postal forum for novelists (published and unpublished), SCRIBO aims to give friendly, informed encouragement and help, to discuss all matters of interest to novelists and to offer criticism via MSS folios: crime/mystery, fantasy/sci-fi, mainstream/aga-saga, women's fiction and a literary MSS folio (mostly graduates writing serious novels). Send sae for details. No subscription.

Sculptors, Royal Society of British (RBS) (1904), 108 Old Brompton Road, London SW7 3RA *tel* 0171-373 8615 or 0171-244 8431 *fax* 0171-370 3721. *President:* Philomena Davidson Davis. Established to promote and advance the art and practice of sculpture,the RBS is now assisted in its endeavours by The Sculpture Company, its commissioning and event management arm. The Sculpture Company has a resource centre to assist corporate, municipal or private patrons to commission or purchase sculpture. The Sculpture Company also organises exhibitions, lectures and awards on behalf of the RBS and supports the RBS education policy and *Sculpture 108*, the RBS publication.

Shakespearean Authorship Trust. *Hon. secretary:* Dr D.W. Thomson Vessey, 26 Ouse Walk, Huntingdon, Cambs. PE18 6QL; *hon. treasurer:* John Silberrad, Dryads' Hall, Woodbury Hill, Loughton, Essex IG10 1JB. Promotes the advancement of learning with particular reference to the social, political and literary history of England in the sixteenth century and the authorship of the plays and poems commonly attributed to William Shakespeare. Subscribers receive copies of the Trust's publications, and are entitled to use its library. *Annual subscription:* £10.00.

The Shaw Society. *Secretary:* Toni Kanal, c/o 155A North View Road, London N8 7ED *tel* 0181-348 7411. Improvement and diffusion of knowledge of the life and works of Bernard Shaw and his circle. Meetings in London; annual festival at Ayot St Lawrence in July; publication: *The Shavian. Annual membership:* £9 ($15).

Singapore Book Publishers Association, c/o Chomen Publishers, 865 Mountbatten Road, 05-28/29 Katong Shopping Centre, Singapore 1543 *tel* (65) 3441495 *fax* (65) 3440180. *Hon. secretary:* Tan Wu Cheng.

Society of Authors—see **Authors, The Society of.**

Songwriters & Composers, The Guild of International, Sovereign House, 12 Trewartha Road, Praa Sands, Penzance, Cornwall TR20 9ST *tel* (01736) 762826 *fax* (01736) 763328. *Secretary:* Carole Ann Jones. Gives advice to members on contractual and copyright matters; assists with protection of members rights; assists with analysis of members' works; international collaboration register free to members; outlines requirements to record companies, publishers, artists. Publishes *Songwriting & Composing* (Q.). *Subscription:* £35 p.a. UK, £45 p.a. EU/overseas.

Songwriters, Composers and Authors, British Academy of—see **BASCA.**

South Africa, Publishers' Association of (PASA), PO Box 1001, 7990 Kalk Bay, South Africa   *tel* (021) 788-6470   *fax* (021) 788-6469.

South African Writers' Circle (1960). *Secretary:* Pat Lister, PO Box 10558, Marine Parade, Durban 4056, South Africa   *tel* (031) 307-5668. Aims to help and encourage all writers, new and experienced, in the art of writing. Publishes a monthly *Newsletter*, and runs competitions with prizes for the winners. *Annual subscription:* R50.

Spanish Publishers' Association, Federation of (Federación de Gremios de Editores de España), Juan Ramón Jiménez 45 9° Izda., 28036 Madrid, Spain   *tel* 350 91 05/03   *telex* 48457 FGEE E   *fax* 345 43 51. *President:* Pere Vicens; *secretary:* Ana Moltó Blasco.

SPREd – Society of Picture Researchers and Editors, 455 Finchley Road, London NW3 6HN   *tel* 0171-431 9886. Professional organisation of picture researchers and picture editors. Operates a freelance register service – details from Ruth Smith   *tel* (01727) 833676. See article on page 384.

Stationers and Newspaper Makers, Worshipful Company of (1557), Stationers' Hall, London EC4M 7DD   *tel* 0171-248 2934   *fax* 0171-489 1975. *Master:* R.F. Fullick; *clerk:* Brig. Denzil Sharp, AFC. One of the Livery Companies of the City of London. Connected with the printing, publishing, bookselling, newspaper and allied trades. Operates a Registry for those requiring proof of ownership of copyright. Written works or those on tape, record, video or computer disk can be registered.

Strip Illustration, Society for—now **Comics Creators Guild.**

Sussex Authors, The Society of (1969). *Secretary:* Michael Legat, Bookends, Lewes Road, Horsted Keynes, Haywards Heath, West Sussex RH17 7DP   *tel/fax* (01825) 790755. Aims to encourage social contact between members, and to promote interest in literature and authors. Membership open to writers living in Sussex who have had at least one book commercially published or who have worked extensively in journalism, radio, TV or the theatre. *Subscription:* £8 p.a.

Sussex Playwrights' Club (1935). Members' plays are read by local actors before an audience of Club members. The Club from time to time sponsors productions of members' plays by local drama companies. Non-writing members welcome. Details: Hon. Secretary, Sussex Playwrights' Club, 2 Princes Avenue, Hove, East Sussex BN3 4GD.

Swedish Publishers Association (Svenska Bokförläggareföreningen) (1843), Drottninggaten 97, 2 tr., 113 60 Stockholm, Sweden   *tel* 08-736 19 40   *fax* 08-736 19 44. *Secretary:* Kenth Muldin.

Television Society, Royal (1927), Holborn Hall, 100 Gray's Inn Road, London WC1X 8AL   *tel* 0171-430 1000   *fax* 0171-430 0924. *Executive director:* Michael Bunce; *membership secretary:* Lynda Gooderson. The Society is a unique, central, independent forum to debate the art, science and politics of television. Holds awards, conferences, dinners, lectures and workshops. *Annual membership:* £52.

The Tennyson Society (1960). *Secretary:* Kathleen Jefferson, Brayford House, Lucy Tower Street, Lincoln LN1 1XN   *tel* (01522) 552851   *fax* (01522) 552858   *e-mail* lincs.lib@dial.pipex.com Promotes the study and understanding of the life and work of the poet Alfred, Lord Tennyson and supports the Tennyson Research Centre in Lincoln; holds lectures, visits and seminars; publishes the *Tennyson Research Bulletin* (annual), Monographs and Occasional Papers; tapes/recordings available. *Annual membership:* £8, family £10, institutions £15.

Theatre Exchange, International. *Secretariat:* 19 Abbey Park Road, Grimsby DN32 0HJ *tel* (01472) 343424. To encourage, foster and promote exchanges of theatre; student, educational, adult, puppet theatre activities at international level. To organise international seminars, workshops, courses and conferences, and to collect and collate information of all types for national and international dissemination.

Theatre Research, The Society for. *Hon. secretaries:* Mrs Eileen Cottis and Miss Frances Dann, c/o The Theatre Museum, 1E Tavistock Street, London WC2E 7PA. Publishes annual volumes and journal, *Theatre Notebook*, holds lectures, runs enquiry service and makes research grants annually.

Theatre Writers' Union (1975), c/o GFTU, Central House, Upper Woburn Place, London WC1H 0HY *tel* 0181-673 6636. *Chair:* David Edgar; *administrator:* Suzy Gilmour. The only union devoted to the specific needs of those who write for live performance, and responsible for national standard agreements with management associations covering minimum pay and conditions for theatre writers. Members receive a quarterly newsletter, and are eligible for free professional and legal advice, support in disputes and copies of standard contracts; there is an active regional branch network. *Annual subscription:* based on writing income.

The Edward Thomas Fellowship (1980), Butler's Cottage, Halswell House, Goathurst, Nr Bridgwater, Somerset TA5 2DH *tel* (01278) 662856. *Hon. secretary:* Richard N. Emeny. To perpetuate the memory of Edward Thomas, poet and nature writer, foster an interest in his life and work, to assist in the preservation of places associated with him and to arrange events which extend fellowship amongst his admirers. *Annual subscription:* £5.00.

The Francis Thompson Society, now incorporated in **The Eighteen Nineties Society.**

The Tolkien Society (1969). *Secretary:* Annie Haward, Flat 6, 8 Staverton Road, Oxford, Oxon OX2 6XJ; *membership secretary:* Alan Reynolds, 40 Hunters Hill, High Wycombe, Bucks. HP13 7EW. Dedicated to promoting research into and educating the public in the life and works of Professor J.R.R. Tolkien. *Subscription:* UK £15; overseas rates on application.

Translation & Interpreting, The Institute of. The Secretary, 377 City Road, London EC1V 1NA *tel* 0171-713 7600 *fax* 0171-713 7650. Professional association for translators and interpreters, who have either passed translation or interpreting examinations in technical, scientific, commercial or social science fields, or can provide evidence of a similar degree of competence and experience gained by other specified means. Subscriber (non-qualified) and student membership also possible. A directory of members is available from the Institute office.

Translations Centre, International (1961), Schuttersveld 2, 2611 WE Delft, Netherlands *tel* (015) 214-22-42 *fax* (015) 215-85-35. *Director:* M. Risseeuw. A non-profit-making international awareness centre facilitating access to existing translations of scientific and technical literature in Western and other languages. ITC does not translate or commission translations of documents.

The Translators Association (1958), 84 Drayton Gardens, London SW10 9SB   *tel* 0171-373 6642. *Secretary:* Gordon Fielden. Specialist unit within the membership of the Society of Authors, exclusively concerned with the interests and special problems of translators into English whose work is published or performed commercially in Great Britain and English-speaking countries overseas. Members are entitled to general and legal advice on all questions connected with the marketing of their work, including remuneration and contractual arrangements with publishers, editors, broadcasting organisations. *Annual subscription:* £65 by direct debit, £70 by cheque – includes membership of the Society of Authors.

Travel Writers, The British Guild of. *Hon. secretary:* John Harrison, 90 Corringway, London W5 3HA   *tel* 0181-998 2223. Arranges meetings, discussions and visits for its members (who are all professional travel journalists) to help them encourage the public's interest in travel.

The Trollope Society (1987), 9A North Street, London SW4 0HN   *tel* 0171-720 6789. *Chairman:* John Letts. Aims to produce the first ever complete edition of the novels of Anthony Trollope (28 vols now available). *Membership fee:* ordinary (one year) £20, life £200.

The Turner Society (1975), BCM Box Turner, London WC1N 3XX. *Chairman:* Evelyn Joll. To foster a wider appreciation of all facets of Turner's work; to encourage exhibitions of his paintings, drawings and engravings. Publishes *Turner Society News. Subscriptions:* £10 p.a. (other rates on application).

Typographic Designers, Society of (1928). *President:* René Kerfante FSTD; *chair:* David Quay FSTD/Freda Sack FSTD; *hon. secretary:* Marilyn Sturgeon BA, FSTD, FCSD, Chapelfield Cottage, Randwick, Stroud, Glos. GL6 6HS   *tel* (01453) 759311   *fax* (01453) 759311. Advises and acts on matters of professional practice, provides a better understanding of the typographic craft and the rapidly changing technology in the graphic industries by lectures, discussions and through the journal *Typographic* and the Newsletter. Typographic students are encouraged to gain Licentiate membership of the Society, by entering the annual student assessment project.

Undeb Awduron Cymru (Union of Welsh Writers) (1975), Botacho Wyn, Nefyn, Gwynedd LL53 6HA   *tel* (01758) 720430. Aims to provide practical and inspirational help to writers in the Welsh language. Produces a newsletter/magazine (3 p.a.); meets at Aberystwyth (2 or 3 p.a.) and annually at the National Eisteddfod. *Annual subscription:* £5.

Visual Communication Association, International (IVCA) (1987), Bolsover House, 5-6 Clipstone Street, London W1P 8LD   *tel* 0171-580 0962   *fax* 0171-436 2606   *e-mail* 100434,1005@compuserve.com *Membership secretary:* Bridget Conneely. For those who use or supply visual communication. Aims to promote the industry and provide a collective voice; provides a range of services, publications and events to help existing and potential users to make the most of what video, film, multimedia and live events can offer their business. *Annual membership fee:* from £150.

Voice of the Listener & Viewer (1983), 101 King's Drive, Gravesend, Kent DA12 5BQ   *tel* (01474) 352835. *Chairman:* Jocelyn Hay; *administrative secretary:* Ann Leek. Independent association working to ensure independence, high standards and diversity in broadcasting in the UK. Membership open to all concerned about the future of public service broadcasting.

Wales, Arts Council of—see **Arts Council of Wales.**

Edgar Wallace Society (1969), Kohlbergsgracht 40, NL-6462 CD Kerkrade, The Netherlands. *Organiser:* Kai Jörg Hinz. To promote an interest in the life and work of Edgar Wallace through the *Crimson Circle* magazine (Q.). *Subscription:* Europe £10 p.a. (students/senior citizens £5), rest of world £15 (students/senior citizens £10).

The Walmsley Society (1985). *Secretary:* Fred Lane, April Cottage, 1 Brand Road, Hampden Park, Eastbourne, East Sussex BN22 9PX; *membership secretary:* Mrs Elizabeth Buckley, 21 The Crescent, Hipperholm, Halifax, West Yorkshire HX3 8NQ. Aims to promote and encourage an appreciation of the literary and artistic heritage left to us by Leo and J. Ulric Walmsley.

Water Colours, Royal Institute of Painters in (1831), 17 Carlton House Terrace, London SW1Y 5BD   *tel* 0171-930 6844   *fax* 0171-839 7830. *President:* Ronald Maddox. The Institute promotes the appreciation of watercolour painting in its traditional and contemporary forms, primarily by means of an annual exhibition at the Mall Galleries, London SW1 of members' and non-members' work and also by members' exhibitions at selected venues in Britain and abroad. Members elected from approved candidates' list.

Watercolour Society, British (1830). *Director:* Leslie Simpson, Ralston House, 41 Lister Street, Riverside Gardens, Ilkley, West Yorkshire LS29 9ET   *tel* (01943) 609075. Promotes the best in traditional watercolour painting. Holds two open exhibitions p.a. *Membership:* by selection.

Watercolour Society, Royal (1804), Bankside Gallery, 48 Hopton Street, London SE1 9JH   *tel* 0171-928 7521. *President:* Richard Seddon. Membership (RWS) open to British and overseas artists. An election of Associates is held annually, and applications for the necessary forms and particulars should be addressed to the Secretary. The Society gives lectures on watercolour paintings; organises residential/non-residential course; holds open exhibition in summer. Exhibitions: spring and autumn. Friends of the RWS open to all those interested in watercolour painting.

Mary Webb Society (1972). *Secretary:* Miss M. Austin, Tansy Cottage, Clunbury, Craven Arms SY7 0HF   *tel* (01588) 660565. To further an interest in the life and works of Mary Webb by meetings, lectures and excursions.

The H.G. Wells Society (1960). *Hon. membership secretary:* Mary Mayer, 75 Wellmeadow Road, Hither Green, London SE13 6TA   *tel* 0181-461 4583. Promotion of an active interest in and encouragement of an appreciation of the life, work and thought of H.G. Wells. Publishes *The Wellsian* (annually) and *The Newsletter* (bi-annually). *Subscription:* £12 p.a., corporate £18 p.a.

Welsh Books Council/Cyngor Llyfrau Cymru, Castell Brychan, Aberystwyth, Dyfed SY23 2JB   *tel* (01970) 624151   *fax* (01970) 625385. *Director:* Gwerfyl Pierce Jones. Founded in 1961 to promote Welsh-language and English-language books of Welsh interest. Editorial, design, marketing, distribution and children's books promotion services provided for publishers.

Welsh Union of Writers (1982). *Secretary:* John Harrison, 13 Richmond Road, Roath, Cardiff CF2 3AQ   *tel* (01222) 490303. Independent union open to persons born or working in Wales with at least one publication in a quality outlet, fiction, non-fiction or poetry. Lobbies for writing in Wales; represents members in disputes; annual conference; occasional events and publications. *Annual subscription:* £10 plus £5 joining fee. Associate membership now available for others with a committed interest in writing: £5 plus £5 joining fee.

Welsh Writers, Union of—see **Undeb Awduron Cymru.**

The West Country Writers' Association. *President:* Christopher Fry FRSL. DLitt; *chair:* The Dowager Lady Cottesloe; *hon. secretary:* Anne Double, Malvern View, Garway Hill, Orcop, Hereford HR2 8EZ   *tel* (01981) 580495. To foster love of literature in the West Country and to give authors an opportunity of meeting to exchange news and views. Holds Annual Weekend Congress and Regional Meetings. Newsletter (2 p.a.). Membership open to published authors. *Annual subscription:* £10.

West of England Academy, Royal (1844), Queens Road, Clifton, Bristol BS8 1PX *tel* (0117) 973 5129 *fax* (0117) 923 7874. *President:* Peter Thursby PRWA, FRBS; *Academy secretary:* Rachel Fear. Aims to further the interests of practising painters and sculptors. Holds art exhibitions and is a meeting place for artists and their work.

The Oscar Wilde Society (1990), 14 Syke Ings, Richings Park, Iver, Bucks. SL0 9ET *tel* (01753) 651782. *Secretary:* Rosemary McGlashon, 154 Derwent Road, Leighton Buzzard, Beds. LU7 7XT. To promote knowledge, appreciation and study of the life, personality and works of the writer and wit Oscar Wilde. Activities include exhibitions, readings, meetings and lectures. Issues to members a biannual journal, *The Wildean*, and a Newsletter (6 p.a.). *Annual membership:* £13, student/unwaged £11, overseas £16, household £18.

Wildlife Artists, Society of, 17 Carlton House Terrace, London SW1Y 5BD *tel* 0171-930 6844 *fax* 0171-839 7830. *President:* Bruce Pearson. To promote and encourage the art of wildlife painting and sculpture. Open Annual Exhibition.

Charles Williams Society (1975), 26 Village Road, Finchley, London N3 1TL *Secretary:* Mrs Gillian Lunn. To promote interest in Charles Williams' life and work and to make his writings more easily available.

The Henry Williamson Society (1980). *Chairman and general secretary:* Will Harris. All correspondence to *membership secretary:* Mrs Margaret Murphy, 16 Doran Drive, Redhill, Surrey RH1 6AX *tel* (01737) 763228. Aims to encourage a wider readership and greater understanding of the literary heritage left by Henry Williamson. Two meetings annually; also weekend activities. Publishes an annual journal. *Annual subscription:* £8.00; family, student and overseas rates available.

Women Artists, Society of (1855), Westminster Gallery, Westminster Central Hall, Storey's Gate, London SW1H 9NU. *President:* Barbara Tate. Annual Exhibition of painting, sculpture, etc. Open to all women.

Women in Publishing (1977), c/o J. Whitaker, 12 Dyott Street, London WC1A 1DF. Promotes the status of women within publishing; encourages networking and mutual support among women; provides a forum for the discussion of ideas, trends and subjects to women in the trade; offers practical training for career and personal development; supports and publicises women's achievements and successes. *Subscription:* £25 p.a.

Women Writers and Journalists, Society of (1894). *Secretary:* Jean Hawkes, 110 Whitehall Road, Chingford, London E4 6DW *tel* 0181-529 0886. For women writers: lectures, monthly lunch-time meetings; free literary advice for members. *The Woman Journalist* (3 p.a.) *Subscription:* town £25; country £21; overseas £15; joining fee £10.

Women Writers Network (1985), c/o Susan Kerr (information), 55 Burlington Lane, London W4 3ET *tel* 0181-994 0598; *membership secretary:* Cathy Smith, 23 Prospect Road, London NW2 2JU *tel* 0171-794 5861. London-based network serving both salaried and independent women writers from all disciplines, and providing a forum for the exchange of information, support and networking opportunities. Holds monthly meetings, workshops and publishes a newsletter and members' directory. Enclose A5 or A4 sae. *Annual membership:* £25.

Writers' Circles. Jill Dick, Oldacre, Horderns Park Road, Chapel-en-le-Frith, Derbyshire SK12 6SY *tel* (01298) 812305 *e-mail* jillie @cix.compulink.co.uk The *Directory of Writers' Circles*, containing addresses of several hundred writers' circles, guilds, workshops, literary clubs, societies and organisations, is published regularly. Copies of the 8th edition (£5 post free) are available from compiler/editor, Jill Dick.

Writers Guild of America (WGA), East Inc. (1954). *Executive director:* Mona Mangan, 555 West 57 Street, Suite 1230, New York, NY 10019, USA *tel* 212-767-7800. Represents writers in screen and television for collective bargaining. It oversees member services (pension and health) as well as educational and professional activities. *Membership:* 1½% of covered earnings p.a.

Writers Guild of America (WGA), West Inc. (1933). *Executive director:* Brian Walton, 7000 West 3rd Street, Los Angeles, CA 90048, USA *tel* 213-951-4000 *fax* 213-782-4800. Union representing and servicing writers in film, broadcast, cable and multimedia industries for purposes of collective bargaining, contract administration and other services, and functions to protect and advance the economic, professional and creative interests of writers. *Membership:* initiation $2500, quarterly $25, annually 1½% of income.

The Writers' Guild of Great Britain, 430 Edgware Road, London W2 1EH *tel* 0171-723 8074 *fax* 0171-706 2413. *General secretary:* Alison V. Gray. Founded in 1959 as the Screenwriters' Guild, now a trade union affiliated to the TUC, representing writers' interests in film, radio, television, theatre and publishing. Its scope extends into all areas of freelance writing and copyright protection and, where necessary, discusses at Government level policies on legislative matters affecting writers. The Guild's basic function is to negotiate minimum terms in those areas in which its members work. The Guild, by constitution non-political, employs a permanent secretariat and staff and is administered by an Executive Council of 26 members. There are also Regional Committees representing Scotland, Wales, the North and West of England. Full details of membership on request. (See also article on page 640.)

Writers in Oxford (1992), 7 London Place, Oxford OX4 1BD *tel* (01865) 251250. *Membership secretary:* Philip Pullman, 24 Templar Road, Oxford OX2 8LT. To promote valuable discussion and social meetings among all kinds of professional writers in and around Oxfordshire. Activities include: topical lunches and dinners, where subjects important to the writer are discussed; showcase evenings; parties. Quarterly newsletter, *The Oxford Writer. Annual subscription:* £15.

Writers' Postal Workshops and Folios. Writers' postal workshops and folios provide criticism, guidance, encouragement and support to both published and unpublished writers and enable regular contact to be made by post with others of similar interests. *The Cottage Guide to Writers' Postal Workshops* contains full details of postal workshops, folios and similar organisations and is published and updated regularly by Croftspun Publications. Price £2 post free from the compiler, Catherine M. Gill, Drakemyre Croft, Cairnorrie, Methlick, Ellon, Aberdeenshire AB41 0JN.

Yachting Journalists' Association (1969), 3 Friars Lane, Maldon, Essex CM9 6AG *tel* (01621) 855943 *fax* (01621) 852212. *Secretary:* Peter Cook. Aims to further the interests of yachting, sail and power, and yachting journalism. Organises the annual Yachtsman of the Year Awards, currently sponsored by BT. *Membership:* £30 p.a.

The Yorkshire Dialect Society (1897). *Hon. secretary:* Stanley Ellis, Farfields, Weeton, Leeds LS17 0AN. Aims to encourage interest in: dialect speech; the writing of dialect verse, prose and drama; the publication and circulation of dialect literature and the performance of dialect plays; the study of the origins and the history of dialect and kindred subjects – all dialects, not only of Yorkshire origin. Organises meetings; publishes annually *Transactions* and *The Summer Bulletin* free to members; list of other publications on request. *Annual subscription:* £6.

Young Book Trust—see **Book Trust.**

Young Publishers, Society of (1949). The Secretary, c/o 12 Dyott Street, London WC1A 1DF. Provides a lively forum for discussion on subjects relevant to its members in publishing. Membership open to anyone employed in publishing, printing, bookselling or allied trades with associate membership available to those over 35. Meetings held at the Publishers Association, usually on the last Wednesday of the month at 6.30 p.m. The SYP also organises social and other events. Please enclose an sae when writing.

Francis Brett Young Society (1979). *Secretary:* Mrs J. Pritchard, 52 Park Road, Hagley, Stourbridge, West Midlands DY9 0QF   *tel* (01562) 882973. To provide opportunities for members to meet, correspond, and to share the enjoyment of the author's works. Journal published 2 p.a. *Annual subscription:* £5.00 (individual), life membership £45 (other rates on application).

Recipe-writing

Although there is much more to food-writing than recipes alone, the art of creating and writing clear, usable recipes is a basic building block of most successful food-writing. If you have never written down a recipe before, you may think it is simple and straightforward. While the results should be both those things, achieving clarity in a recipe is a skill to be acquired.

Cookbooks, magazines and newspapers are filled with badly written and edited recipes. Some faults are glaringly obvious and should have been spotted before the recipe ever reached printed form. Common factual errors and omissions include: recipes which do not list all the ingredients that are used in the method; recipes which do not use all the ingredients listed; recipes which omit the cooking time or baking heat. Then there are problems of style and content: vagueness or inaccuracy in instructions; a skating over of problem areas; brevity when explanation is required; or badly ordered method.

from *Writing About Food* by Jenny Linford (A & C Black, £8.99).
See order form on page 690.

The Society of Authors

The Society of Authors is an independent trade union, representing writers' interests in all aspects of the writing profession, including publishing, broadcasting, TV and films, theatre and translation. Founded over a hundred years ago by Walter Besant, the Society now has more than 6000 members. It has a professional staff, responsible to a Management Committee of 12 authors and a Council (an advisory body meeting twice a year) consisting of 60 eminent writers. There are specialist groups within the Society to serve the particular needs of broadcasters, literary translators, educational writers, medical writers and children's writers and illustrators. There are also regional groups representing Scotland, the North of England and the Isle of Man.

WHAT THE SOCIETY DOES FOR MEMBERS

Through its permanent staff (including a solicitor), the Society is able to give its members a comprehensive personal and professional service covering the business aspects of authorship, including:

- providing information about agents, publishers, and others concerned with the book trade, journalism, broadcasting and the performing arts
- advising on negotiations, including the individual vetting of contracts, clause by clause, and assessing their terms both financial and otherwise
- taking up complaints on behalf of members on any issue concerned with the business of authorship
- pursuing legal actions for breach of contract, copyright infringement, and the non-payment of royalties and fees, when the risk and cost preclude individual action by a member and issues of general concern to the profession are at stake
- holding conferences, seminars, meetings and social occasions
- producing a comprehensive range of publications, free of charge to members, including the Society's quarterly journal, *The Author*, which has a twice yearly supplement, *The Electronic Author*. *Quick Guides* cover many aspects of the profession such as: copyright, publishing contracts, libel, income tax, VAT, authors' agents, permissions and the protection of titles. The Society also publishes a model translator/publisher agreement, *Guidelines for Academic Authors*, *Guidelines for Educational Writers*, *Guidelines for Medical Writers* and *Sell Your Writing*.

Members have access to:

- the Retirement Benefit Scheme
- Group Medical Insurance Schemes with both BUPA and the Bristol Contributory Welfare Association
- the Pension Fund (which offers discretionary pensions to a number of members)
- the Contingency Fund (which provides financial relief for authors or their dependents in sudden financial difficulties)
- automatic free membership of the Authors' Licensing and Collecting Society
- books at special rates
- membership of the Royal Over-Seas League at a discount
- use of the Society's photocopying machine at special rates.

The Society frequently secures improved conditions and better returns for members. It is common for members to report that, through the help and facilities offered, they have saved more, and sometimes substantially more, than their annual subscriptions (which are an allowable expense against income tax).

WHAT THE SOCIETY DOES FOR AUTHORS IN GENERAL

The Society lobbies Members of Parliament, Ministers and Government Departments on all issues of concern to writers. Recent issues have included the operation and funding of Public Lending Right, the threat of VAT on books, copyright legislation and European Community initiatives. Concessions have also been obtained under various Finance Acts.

The Society litigates in matters of importance to authors. For example, the Society backed Andrew Boyle when he won his appeal against the Inland Revenue's attempt to tax the Whitbread Award. It backed a number of members in proceedings against the BBC and Desmond Wilcox in connection with the publication of a book, *The Explorers*, and also in a High Court action over copyright infringement by *Coles Notes*.

The Society campaigns for better terms for writers. With the Writers' Guild, it has negotiated agreements with BBC Publications, Bloomsbury, Bodley Head, Jonathan Cape, Century, André Deutsch, Faber & Faber, Hamish Hamilton, HarperCollins, Hodder Headline, Hutchinson, Michael Joseph, Methuen, Penguin Books, Sinclair-Stevenson, Transworld and Viking. Other publishers are now being approached, and the campaign is active. The translators' section of the Society has also drawn up a minimum terms agreement for translators which has been adopted by Faber & Faber, and has been used on an individual basis by a number of other publishers.

The Society is recognised by the BBC for the purpose of negotiating rates for writers' contributions to radio drama, as well as for the broadcasting of published material. It was instrumental in setting up the Authors' Licensing and Collecting Society (ALCS), which collects and distributes fees from reprography and other methods whereby copyright material is exploited without direct payment to the originators.

The Society keeps in close touch with the Arts Councils, the Association of Authors' Agents, the British Council, the Broadcasting Entertainment Cinematograph and Theatre Union, the Institute of Translation and Interpreting, the Secretary of State for National Heritage, the National Union of Journalists, the Publishers Association and the Writers' Guild of Great Britain.

The Society is a member of the European Writers Congress, the British Copyright Council, the National Book Committee and the International Confederation of Societies of Authors and Composers (CISAC).

AWARDS ADMINISTERED BY THE SOCIETY

- two travel awards: the Somerset Maugham Awards and the Travelling Scholarships
- four prizes for novels: the Betty Trask Awards, the Encore Award, the McKitterick Prize and the Sagittarius Prize
- two poetry awards: the Eric Gregory Awards and the Cholmondeley Awards
- the Tom-Gallon Award for short story writers
- the Crompton Bequest for aiding financially the publication of selected original work
- the Authors' Foundation and Kathleen Blundell Trust, which are endowed with wide powers to support work in progress
- the Margaret Rhondda Award for women journalists

- the Scott Moncrieff Prize for translations from French
- the Schlegel-Tieck Prize for translations from German books published in Germany
- the Teixeira-Gomes Prize for translations from Portuguese
- the John Florio Prize for translations from Italian
- the Francis Head Bequest for assisting authors who, through physical mishap, are temporarily unable to maintain themselves or their families.

HOW TO JOIN

There are two categories of membership (admission to each being at the discretion of the Committee of Management):

Full Membership – those authors who have had a full-length work published, broadcast or performed commercially in the UK or have an established reputation in another medium.

Associate Membership – those authors who have had a full-length work accepted for publication, but not yet published; and those authors who have had occasional items broadcast or performed, or translations, articles, illustrations or short stories published.

Associate members pay the same annual subscription and are entitled to the same benefits as full members. The owner or administrator of a deceased author's copyrights can become a member on behalf of the author's estate.

The annual subscription (which is tax deductible under Schedule D) for full or associate membership of the Society is £70 (£65 by direct debit after the first year), and there are special joint membership terms for husband and wife. Authors under 35, who are not yet earning a significant income from their writing, may apply for membership at a lower subscription of £52. Authors over 65 may apply to pay at the reduced rate after their first year of membership.

Further information from The Society of Authors, 84 Drayton Gardens, London SW10 9SB   *tel* 0171-373 6642.

IN CONCLUSION

'When we begin working, we are so poor and so busy that we have neither the time nor the means to defend ourselves against the commercial organisations which exploit us. When we become famous, we become famous suddenly, passing at one bound from the state in which we are, as I have said, too poor to fight our own battles, to a state in which our time is so valuable that it is not worth our while wasting any of it on lawsuits and bad debts. We all, eminent and obscure alike, need the Authors' Society. We all owe it a share of our time, our means, our influence' *Bernard Shaw*

The Writers' Guild of Great Britain

The Writers' Guild of Great Britain is the writers' trade union, affiliated to the TUC, and representing writers' interests in film, radio, television, theatre and publishing. Formed in 1959 as the Screenwriters' Guild, the union gradually extended into all areas of freelance writing activity and copyright protection. In 1974 when book authors and stage dramatists became eligible for membership substantial numbers joined, and their interests are represented on the Executive Council. Apart from necessary dealings with Government and policies on legislative matters affecting writers, the Guild is, by constitution, non-political, has no involvement with any political party, and pays no political levy. The Guild employs a permanent secretariat and staff and is administered by an Executive Council of 26 members. There are also Regional Committees representing Scotland, Wales, the North and West of England.

The Guild comprises practising professional writers in all media, united in common concern for one another and regulating the conditions under which they work.

WHAT IT DOES

The Guild's basic function is to negotiate minimum terms in those areas in which its members work. Those agreements form the basis of the individual contracts signed by members.

Television

The Guild has national agreements with the BBC and the commercial companies regulating minimum fees and going rates, copyright licence, credit terms and conditions for television plays, series and serials, dramatisations and adaptations. One of the most important achievements in recent years has been the establishment of pension rights for Guild members only. The BBC pay an additional 7.5% of the going rate on the understanding that the Guild member pays 5% of his or her fee. ITV companies now pay an additional 8% and the writer 5%. The Guild Pension Fund amounts to well over £3 million at present.

In the late 1980s, comprehensive agreements were negotiated with the BBC and ITV to cover programme sales overseas and to cable and satellite stations. In addition, a special agreement was negotiated to cover the very successful serial *EastEnders*. In 1991, the first ever Light Entertainment Agreement was signed with the BBC. Most children's and educational drama has been similarly protected within the above industrial agreements. Rates of payment are updated from time to time.

Film

On 11 March 1985, an important agreement was signed with the two producer organisations: The British Film and Television Producers' Association and The Independent Programme Producers Association (now known as PACT, the Producers' Alliance for Cinema and Television). For the first time, there exists an industrial agreement which covers both independent television productions and independent film productions. Pension fund contributions have been negotiated for Guild members in the same way as for the BBC and ITV. The Agreement was comprehensively renegotiated and concluded in February 1992. The areas of participation have been improved and the money paid upfront is considerably more than it was in the past. The Guild is also drawing up guidelines for the use of dramatic material in multimedia.

Radio

The Guild has fought for and obtained a standard agreement with the BBC, establishing a fee structure which is annually reviewed. The current agreement includes a Code of Practice which is important for establishing good working conditions for the writer working for the BBC. In December 1985 the BBC agreed to extend the pension scheme already established for television writers to include radio writers. It was also agreed that all radio writers would be entitled to at least one attendance payment as of right. Again this brings the radio agreements more into line with the television agreements. In 1991 a comprehensive revision of the Agreement was undertaken and has been concluded.

Books

The Guild fought long, hard and successfully for the loans-based Public Lending Right to reimburse authors for books lent in libraries. This is now law and the Guild is constantly in touch with the Registrar of the scheme which is administered from offices in Stockton-on-Tees.

The Guild, together with its sister union the Society of Authors, has drawn up a draft Minimum Terms Book Agreement which has been widely circulated amongst publishers. In 1984, the unions achieved a significant breakthrough by signing agreements with two major publishers; negotiations were also opened with other publishers. The publishing agreements will, it is hoped, improve the relationship between writers and publishers and help to clarify what writers might reasonably expect from the exploitation of copyright in their works.

Agreements have now been signed with BBC Publications, Bloomsbury, Bodley Head, Jonathan Cape, Century, André Deutsch, Faber & Faber, Hamish Hamilton, HarperCollins, Hodder Headline, Hutchinson, Michael Joseph, Methuen, Penguin Books, Sinclair-Stevenson, Transworld and Viking. Negotiations are currently taking place with other leading publishers.

Theatre

In 1979, the Guild with its fellow union, the Theatre Writers' Union, negotiated the first ever industrial agreement for theatre writers. The Theatre National Committee Agreement covers the Royal Shakespeare Company, the Royal National Theatre Company and the English Stage Company. A new Agreement was concluded in April 1993.

On 2 June 1986, a new Agreement was signed with the Theatrical Management Association, covering some 95 provincial theatres. In 1991, negotiations opened for a comprehensive review of that agreement and were concluded in 1993.

In 1991, after many years of negotiation, an Agreement was concluded between the Guild and Theatre Writers' Union, and the Independent Theatre Council, which represents some 200 of the smaller and fringe theatres as well as educational, touring companies. The Agreement breaks new ground.

Only the West End is not covered by a union agreement.

Copies of all the above agreements are available to members and non-members at a small charge.

Miscellaneous

The Guild is in constant touch with Government and national institutions wherever and whenever the interests of writers are in question or are being discussed. The Guild has been holding cross party Parliamentary lobbies since 1989 with its fellow arts unions, Equity, the Musicians Union, the NUJ and BECTU. The

Guild and its fellow unions believe that it is important to keep in constant touch with all parties to ensure that the various art forms they represent are properly cared for. The Guild held a lobby under the auspices of the Creators Copyright Coalition, an umbrella group representing creators in newspapers and publishing, focusing on the threat to copyright posed by digital technology. Most recently the Guild has submitted amendments to the Broadcasting Bill and proposals to the Arts Council of England concerning a New Writing Fund.

Proposals for changes in the law on copyright were published in a draft Bill in August 1986. The Guild along with other organisations made important submissions on behalf of the Guild and writers in general. The new Act came into effect in 1989. Moral rights have been granted to writers for the first time.

Perhaps one of the closest working relationships the Guild has established is with its fellow arts unions, Equity and the Musicians Union. The three unions have agreed to work much more closely together where they share a common interest. Representatives of the three governing bodies meet on a quarterly basis.

Regular Craft Meetings are held by all the Guild's specialist committees. This gives Guild members the opportunity of meeting those who control, work within, or affect the sphere of writing within which they work.

Internationally, the Guild plays a leading role in the International Affiliation of Writers' Guilds, which includes the American Guilds East and West, the Canadian Guilds (French and English) and the Australian and New Zealand Guilds. When it is possible to make common cause, then the Guilds act accordingly.

The Guild takes a leading role in the European Writers' Congress. It has been represented at every Congress since 1981. That body is becoming increasingly important and successful. An initiative from the Writers' Guild of Great Britain saw the setting up of a Copyright Committee to protect writers' interests within the EU in particular and throughout Europe in general. With the harmonisation of Copyright Law, an opportunity has been seized to make representation directly to Brussels which could lead to an improvement for British writers.

The Guild in its day-to-day work takes up problems on behalf of individual members, gives advice on contracts, and helps with any problems which affect the lives of its members as professional writers.

The Guild publishes *The Writers' Newsletter* six times a year. This carries articles, letters and reports written by members.

MEMBERSHIP

Membership is by a points system. One major piece of work (a full-length book, an hour-long television or radio play, a feature film, etc.) entitles the author to Full Membership; lesser work helps to accumulate enough points for Full Membership, while Associate Membership may be enjoyed in the meantime. Importantly, previously unpublished, broadcast or performed writers can apply for membership when they receive their first contracts. The Guild's advice before signature can often be vital. Affiliate Membership is enjoyed by agents and other professional advisers.

The minimum subscription is £70 plus 1% of that part of an author's income earned from professional writing sources in the previous calendar year.

The Writers' Guild of Great Britain, 430 Edgware Road, London W2 1EH *tel* 0171-723 8074   *fax* 0171-706 2413.

Prizes and Awards

The following list provides details of many British prizes, competitions and awards, including grants, bursaries and fellowships, as well as details of major international prizes. In the UK, details of awards for novels, short stories and works of non-fiction, as they are offered, will be found in such journals as *The Author*. Book Trust publish the useful *Guide to Literary Prizes* (details available from Book Trust, Book House, 45 East Hill, Wandsworth, London SW18 2QZ *tel* 0181-870 9055).

J.R. Ackerley Prize for Autobiography

This prize, first awarded in 1982, is given annually for an outstanding work of literary autobiography written in English and published during the previous year by an author of British nationality or an author who has been a long-term resident in the UK. Books are nominated by the judges only. Information from P.E.N., 7 Dilke Street, Chelsea, London SW3 4JE *tel* 0171-352 6303 *fax* 0171-351 0220.

Acorn Award

Founded in 1989, this is an annual award of £250 to an author/illustrator who has published a book for younger children, fiction or poetry, in the preceding year. No application necessary; details from Nottinghamshire County Library Service, Glaisdale Parkway, Nottingham NG8 4GP *tel* (0115) 985 4203 or Dillons The Bookstore, 25 Wheelergate, Nottingham NG1 2NF *tel* (0115) 947 3531.

The Alexander Prize

The Alexander Prize (value £250) is awarded annually; closing date 1 November. Candidates must either be under the age of 35 or be registered for a higher degree now or within the last three years. They may choose their own subject for a paper, but they must submit their choice for approval to the Literary Director, Royal Historical Society, University College London, Gower Street, London WC1E 6BT *tel/fax* 0171-387 7532.

The Hans Christian Andersen Medals

The Hans Christian Andersen Medals are awarded every two years to a living author and an illustrator who by the outstanding value of their work are judged to have made a lasting contribution to literature for children and young people. Details from International Board on Books for Young People, Nonnenweg 12, Postfach, CH-4003 Basel, Switzerland *tel* 272 29 17 *fax* 272 27 57.

Aristeion Prizes

European Literary Prize

Founded in 1990, this annual award of 20,000 ecus is awarded for a single work, which may belong to any literary genre.

European Translation Prize

Founded in 1990, this annual award of 20,000 ecus is awarded to a translator for an outstanding translation of a significant work of contemporary European literature; the work may belong to any literary genre.

Candidates must be nationals of a member state of the European Union. Applications are not sought: nominations are made by an appointed authority from each member state and the winning titles are selected by a specially appointed jury of experts. Further details from Mrs Enrica Varese, DGX, D1 Cultural Action, rue de la Loi 102, 4/25, 1040 Brussels, Belgium *tel* (32) 2-299 94 19 *fax* (32) 2-299 92 83.

Rosemary Arthur Award

Founded in 1989, this is an annual award for a first book of poetry. The prize consists of the full cost of publishing the winner's book, £100 and an engraved clock. Full details from the National Poetry Foundation, 27 Mill Road, Fareham, Hants PO16 0TH   *tel* (01329) 822218.

The Arts Council/An Chomhairle Ealaíon, Ireland

Bursaries for Creative Writers

In 1995 awards totalling IR£79,000 were offered to creative writers of poetry, fiction and drama to enable them to concentrate on or complete writing projects. At least the same amount will be distributed in 1996. A limited number of literary non-fiction projects are also eligible.

Denis Devlin Memorial Award

This award, value IR£2000, is made triennially for the best book of poetry in the English language by an Irish citizen published in the preceding three years. The next award will be made in 1996.

Macaulay Fellowship

Fellowships, value IR£3500, are awarded once every three years to writers under 30 years of age (or in exceptional circumstances under 35 years) in order to help them to further their liberal education and careers. The cycle of awards is: Literature (1996), Visual Arts (1997), Music (1998).

The Marten Toonder Award

This award is given to an artist of recognised and established achievement on a rotating cycle as follows: Visual Arts (1996), Music (1997), Literature (1998). Candidates must be Irish-born (Northern Ireland is included). Value IR£3500.

An Duais don bhFilíocht i nGaeilge

This is Ireland's major award to Irish-language poetry; it is given triennially for the best book of Irish-language poetry published in the preceding three years. The next award will be made in 1996. Value IR£2000.

Travel Grants

Creative artists (including writers) may apply for assistance with travel grants to attend seminars, conferences, workshops, etc. Applications are assessed twice a year.

These literary awards are available only to Irish citizens, or to those who have been resident in Ireland for the previous five years. Further details may be obtained from The Arts Council (An Chomhairle Ealaíon), 70 Merrion Square, Dublin 2, Republic of Ireland   *tel* (01) 6611840   *fax* (01) 6761302.

Arts Council of England

Writers' Awards

The Arts Council gives annual bursaries to writers whose work is of outstanding quality. In 1996-97 there will be fifteen such awards. They will be offered only to already published authors who are writing works of poetry, fiction, autobiography, biography, literature for young people and drama (intended for publication). The value of each bursary is £7000. The closing date for applications is 30 September each year. Details are available from July onwards from the Literature Department, Arts Council of England, 14 Great Peter Street, London SW1P 3NQ   *tel* 0171-333 0100.

Translation Fund

This fund supports the publication of translated work. Any text suggested for support should already have secured a publisher by whom nominations should be made. Grants may be given for specimen chapters of a work in progress. Grants are occasionally given to initiatives outside publishing which support an appreciation of translation. The budget for 1996-97 is just over £100,000 and there are two deadline dates each year. Further information from Jilly Paver, Literature Officer, Arts Council of England, 14 Great Peter Street, London SW1P 3NQ *tel* 0171-333 0100.

The Arts Council of Wales Awards to Writers

Book of the Year Award
£3000 prize awarded to winners, in Welsh and English, and £1000 to four other short-listed authors for works of exceptional merit by Welsh authors (by birth or residence) published during the previous calendar year in the categories of poetry, fiction and creative non-fiction.

Bursaries and competitions
Bursaries totalling about £75,000 are awarded annually to authors writing in both Welsh and English. In addition, the Council organises occasional competitions.

For further details of the Arts Council of Wales' policies, write to the Literature Department, The Arts Council of Wales, Museum Place, Cardiff CF1 3NX *tel* (01222) 394711 *fax* (01222) 221447.

Arvon Foundation International Poetry Competition

This competition, founded in 1980, is awarded biennially for previously unpublished poems written in English. First prize £5000, plus at least £5000 in other cash prizes. Full details from Arvon Foundation Poetry Competition, Kilnhurst, Kilnhurst Road, Todmorden, Lancs. OL14 6AX *tel* (01706) 816582 *fax* (01706) 816359.

Author of the Year Award

Founded in 1993, £1000 is awarded annually, by vote of the members of the Booksellers Association, to the British or Irish author considered to have had the most impact during the previous year. Nomination takes place during November/December by the BA Membership in a postal ballot. Information available from Meryl Halls or Susannah Dann, Booksellers Association, 272 Vauxhall Bridge Road, London SW1V 1BA *tel* 0171-834 5477.

Authors' Club

Best First Novel Award
Instituted in 1954 by Lawrence Meynell, an award of £750 is presented, at a dinner held in the Club, to the author of the most promising first novel published in the UK during each year. Entries (one from each publisher's imprint) are accepted during October and November and must be full-length novels – short stories are not eligible.

Sir Banister Fletcher Award for Authors' Club
The late Sir Banister Fletcher, a former President of both the Authors' Club and the Royal Institute of British Architects instituted an annual prize 'for the book on architecture or the arts most deserving'. The award, first given in 1954, is made on the recommendation of the Professional Literature Committee of RIBA, to whom nominations for eligible titles (i.e. those written by British authors or those resident in the UK and published under a British imprint) should be submitted by the end of May of the year after publication. The prize of £750 is awarded by the Authors' Club during September.

Marsh Award for Children's Literature in Translation
Founded in 1995, this biennial award of £750 is given to a British translator of a book for children (aged 4-16) from a foreign language into English and published in the UK by a British publisher. Electronic books, and encyclopedias and other reference books, are not eligible.

Marsh Biography Award
Introduced for the years 1985-86, this major national biography prize of £3500 plus a trophy is presented every two years. Entries must be serious biographies written by British authors and published in the UK.

Details of all the above available from: Ann Carter, Secretary, Authors' Club, 40 Dover Street, London W1X 3RB   *tel* 0171-499 8581   *fax* 0171-409 0913.

The Authors' Foundation
Founded in 1984 to mark the centenary of the Society of Authors, the Foundation provides grants to published authors working on their next book. The aim is to provide funding (in addition to a proper advance) for research, travel or other necessary expenditure. Grants are available to novelists, poets and writers of non-fiction. Closing date: 30 April; an information sheet is available from the Society of Authors, 84 Drayton Gardens, London SW10 9SB.

BA/Bookseller Author of the Year
Founded in 1993, this annual award of £1000 is judged by members of the Booksellers Association of Great Britain and Ireland (4000 bookshops) in a postal ballot. Any living, British or Irish published writer is eligible and the award is given to the author judged to have had the most impact in the year. Further information from: The Booksellers Association of Great Britain and Ireland, 272 Vauxhall Bridge Road, London SW1V 1BA   *tel* 0171-834 5477   *fax* 0171-834 8812.

Verity Bargate Award
Created as a memorial to the founder of the Soho Theatre Company, this bi-annual award is made to the writer of a new and previously unperformed full length play. In addition to the cash prize of £1500, the winning play has normally gone on to a full production by the Soho Theatre Company. Accordingly, the chosen playwright is required to offer first option to produce the winning play to the Soho Theatre Company. It is also intended that emerging writers of interest – such as those whose plays are shortlisted – will be provided with workshop facilities to assist in their further development. For details on the submission of scripts and the closing date, send an sae to Verity Bargate Award, The Soho Theatre Company, 24 Mortimer Street, London W1N 7RD.

H.E. Bates Short Story Competition
This annual prize is awarded for a short story – maximum length 2000 words – to anyone resident in Great Britain. The first prize is for £200, other prizes to a total value of £150. Further details from the Events Team Office, Directorate of Environment Services, Cliftonville House, Bedford Road, Northampton NN4 7NR   *tel* (01604) 233500 ext 4243.

BBC Wildlife Magazine Awards for Nature Writing
BBC Wildlife Magazine awards prizes annually with the aim of reviving the art of nature writing, discovering and encouraging new essayists and focusing attention on those writers whose skills might otherwise be neglected. Entries accepted from professional or amateur writers, and from young writers aged 17 and under. For further information see *BBC Wildlife Magazine*, or send an sae to: BBC Wildlife Magazine, Broadcasting House, Whiteladies Road, Bristol BS8 2LR   *tel* (0117) 9738402   *fax* (0117) 9467075.

The Samuel Beckett Award
Founded in 1983, this award is open to residents of the UK and the Republic of Ireland for new dramatic writing, professionally performed. The provisions of the award are currently under review. Further information from: Editorial Department, Faber and Faber, 3 Queen Square, London WC1N 3AU.

The David Berry Prize

Candidates for the David Berry Prize may select any subject dealing with Scottish history within the reigns of James I to James VI inclusive, provided such subject has been previously submitted to and approved by the Council of the Royal Historical Society, University College London, Gower Street, London WC1E 6BT *tel/fax* 0171-387 7532. Next closing date: 31 October 1997. Value of prize: £250.

The Bisto Book of the Year Award

Founded in 1990, this award is given annually for any children's book in English or Irish by an author or illustrator born or resident in Ireland, and first published between 1 January and 31 December of each judging year. Overall winner receives IR£1500, plus three category winners receive IR£500 each. Closing date: 31 January. Details from: The Secretary, The Irish Children's Book Trust, the Irish Writers' Centre, 19 Parnell Square, Dublin 1, Republic of Ireland *tel* (01) 8721302 *fax* (01) 8726282.

The James Tait Black Memorial Prizes

Founded in memory of a partner in the publishing house of A. & C. Black, these prizes were instituted in 1918 and since 1979 have been supplemented by the Scottish Arts Council. Two prizes, of £3000 each, are awarded annually: one for the best biography or work of that nature, the other for the best novel, published during the calendar year. The adjudicator is the Professor of English Literature in the University of Edinburgh. Eligible novels and biographies are those written in English, originating with a British publisher, and usually first published in Britain in the year of the award. Both prizes may go to the same author; but neither to the same author a second time.

Publishers should submit a copy of any appropriate biography, or work of fiction, as early as possible with a note of the date of publication, marked 'James Tait Black Prize' to the Department of English Literature, David Hume Tower, George Square, Edinburgh EH8 9JX *tel* 0131-650 3619 *fax* 0131-650 6898. Closing date for submissions: 30 September.

The Kathleen Blundell Trust

The Trust provides awards to published writers under the age of 40 to assist them with their next book. Applications should be in the form of a letter sent to the Kathleen Blundell Trust at the Society of Authors (84 Drayton Gardens, London SW10 9SB), giving reasons for the application, and must be accompanied by a copy of the author's latest book. The author's work must 'contribute to the greater understanding of existing social and economic organisation'. Closing date: 30 April. Information sheet available from the Society of Authors.

The Boardman Tasker Prize

This annual prize of £2000, founded in 1983, is given for a work of fiction, non-fiction or poetry, the central theme of which is concerned with the mountain environment. Authors of any nationality are eligible but the work must be published or distributed in the UK. Entries from publishers only. Further details from Mrs Dorothy Boardman, 14 Pine Lodge, Dairyground Road, Bramhall, Stockport, Cheshire SK7 2HS.

Book of the Year

Founded in 1990, an annual award (1st IR£1500 + 3 at IR£500) to a writer or illustrator of children's books, born or currently living in Ireland. Details from: Irish Children's Book Trust, Irish Writers' Centre, 19 Parnell Square, Dublin 1, Republic of Ireland *tel* (01) 8721302 *fax* (01) 8726282.

The Booker Prize
This annual prize for fiction of £20,000, sponsored by Booker plc, is awarded to the best novel published each year, and is open to novels written in English by citizens of the British Commonwealth, Republic of Ireland and South Africa and published for the first time in the UK by a British publisher, although previous publication of a book outside the UK does not disqualify it. Entries only from UK publishers who may each submit not more than two novels with scheduled publication dates between 1 October of the previous year and 30 September of the current year, but the judges may also ask for other eligible novels to be submitted to them. In addition, publishers may submit one eligible title by authors who have been shortlisted or won the Booker Prize previously. Entry forms and further information from Book Trust, Book House, 45 East Hill, London SW18 2QZ   *tel* 0181-870 9055.

BP Conservation Book Prize
Established in 1987, the European Year of the Environment, for the best book on an environmental or conservation issue published in the UK in the year ending 31 December. Two awards – £5000 for an adult book and £2000 for a children's book – are sponsored by BP. Details and entry form from Book Trust, Book House, 45 East Hill, London SW18 2QZ   *tel* 0181-870 9055.

Alfred Bradley Bursary Award
Founded in 1992, this biennial bursary of £6000 (spread over two years, plus a full commission for a radio play) is awarded to a writer resident or born in the North of England who has had a small amount of work published or produced. The focus for the 1996-97 award is verse drama. The scheme also allows for a group of finalists to receive small bursaries and participate in workshops. Details from: BBC Radio Drama Department, BBC North, New Broadcasting House, Oxford Road, Manchester M60 1SJ   *tel* 0161-244 4251.

The Bridport Prize
Founded in 1980 (as the Bridport Arts Centre Creative Writing Competition), annual prizes are awarded for poetry and short stories – 1st £2500, 2nd £1000, 3rd £500 in both categories. Entries should be in English, original work, typed or clearly written, and never published, read on radio/television/stage or entered for any other current competition. Closing date: 30 June each year. Winning stories are read by leading London literary agent, without obligation. Details from the Competition Secretary, Arts Centre, South Street, Bridport, Dorset DT6 3NR   *tel* (01308) 427183   *fax* (01308) 424204.

Katharine Briggs Folklore Award
An award of £50 and an engraved goblet is given annually for a book in English, having its first, original and initial publication in the UK, which has made the most distinguished contribution to folklore studies. The term folklore studies is interpreted broadly to include all aspects of traditional and popular culture, narrative, belief, customs and folk arts. Details from the Convenor, The Folklore Society, University College London, Gower Street, London WC1E 6BT   *tel* 0171-387 5894.

British Academy Medals and Prizes
The Academy awards a number of medals and prizes for outstanding work in various fields of the humanities on the recommendation of specialist committees: Burkitt Medal for Biblical Studies; Derek Allen Prize (made annually in turn in musicology, numismatics and Celtic studies); Sir Israel Gollancz Prize (in English studies); Grahame Clark Medal for Prehistory; Kenyon Medal for Classical Studies; Rose Mary Crawshay Prize (for English literature); Serena Medal for Italian Studies.

The British Academy Research Awards

These are made annually (for Learned Societies or group research applications) and quarterly (for individual applications) to scholars conducting advanced academic research in the humanities and normally resident in the UK. Applications accepted for travel and maintenance expenses in connection with an approved programme of research; archaeology fieldwork; costs of preparation of research for publication; in special cases, aid to the publication of research. Details and application forms from The British Academy, 20-21 Cornwall Terrace, London NW1 4QP *tel* 0171-487 5966.

British Book Awards

These awards, founded in 1989, are presented annually. Major categories include Author of the Year, Publisher of the Year, Bookseller of the Year, and Children's Book of the Year. Further information from Merric Davidson, British Book Awards, Publishing News, 43 Museum Street, London WC1A 1LY *tel* 0171-404 0304 *fax* 0171-242 0762.

British Fantasy Awards

Founded in 1972, the members of the British Fantasy Society vote annually for the best novel, short fiction, artist, small press and anthology of the preceding year. A further award, the Committee Award, is decided separately. The awards take the form of a statuette. Closing date for nominations: end August each year. Details from Robert Parkinson, Secretary, The British Fantasy Society, 2 Harwood Street, Stockport SK4 1JJ.

The British Film Institute Michael Powell Book Award

The Award highlights the importance of film and television literature and is presented for books published in the UK dealing with film and television by a UK author. Details from Promotions Officer, Press Office, British Film Institute, 21 Stephen Street, London W1P 2LN *tel* 0171-255 1444.

Children's Book Award

Founded in 1980 by the Federation of Children's Book Groups, this award is given annually to authors of works of fiction for children published in the UK. Children participate in the judging of the award. 'Pick of the Year' booklist is published in conjunction with the award. Details from Jenny Blanch, 30 Senneleys Park Road, Northfield, Birmingham B31 1AL *tel* 0121-427 4860 *fax* 0121-643 3152.

Cholmondeley Award.

In 1965, the then Dowager Marchioness of Cholmondeley established these non-competitive awards, for which submissions are not required, for the benefit and encouragement of poets of any age, sex or nationality. Total value of awards about £8000. The scheme is administered by the Society of Authors.

Arthur C. Clarke Award

Founded in 1985, an annual award of £1000 (+ engraved bookend) is given for the best science fiction novel with first UK publication during the previous calendar year. Titles are submitted by publishers. Details from The Administrator, Paul Kincaid, 60 Bournemouth Road, Folkestone, Kent CT19 5AZ.

The Cló Iar-Chonnachta Literary Award

Founded in 1985, this award of £5000 is open to all writers in the Irish language. The subject of the award alternates from year to year; the 1997 prize is for Short Story Collection/Drama. Further information from: Cló Iar-Chonnachta (Publishing Company), Indreabhán, Conamara, Co. na Gaillimhe, Ireland *tel* (091) 593307.

The David Cohen British Literature Prize
This prize of £30,000, currently the largest in the UK, will be awarded every two years to a living writer, novelist, short story writer, poet, essayist or dramatist in recognition of a lifetime's substantial body of achievement. Work must be written primarily in English and the writer must be a British citizen. In addition, the Arts Council will make available an extra £10,000 to enable the winner to encourage reading or writing among younger people. No application needed; the choice of the winner is made by a distinguished jury on the basis of its collective reading. Further information from The Literature Department, Arts Council of England, 14 Great Peter Street, London SW1P 3NQ   *tel* 0171-333 0100.

Commonwealth Writers Prize
Sponsored by the Commonwealth Foundation, this annual award is for the best work of fiction in English by a citizen of the Commonwealth published in the year prior to the award. A prize of £10,000 is awarded for best entry and a prize of £3000 for best first published book, selected from eight regional winners who each receive prizes of £1000. Details and entry form available from The Commonwealth Foundation, Marlborough House, Pall Mall, London SW1Y 5HY   *tel* 0171-930 3783   *fax* 0171-839 8157.

The Catherine Cookson Fiction Prize
Instituted in 1992, this annual award of £10,000 is given for an unpublished novel (which is free of commitment), of at least 70,000 words in length, and which has some of the distinctive qualities of Catherine Cookson. Next closing date: 31 May. For further details, send an sae to The Catherine Cookson Fiction Prize, Transworld Publishers Ltd, 61-63 Uxbridge Road, London W5 5SA   *tel* 0181-579 2652.

The Duff Cooper Prize
Friends and admirers of Duff Cooper, first Viscount Norwich (1890-1954), contributed a sum of money which has been invested in a Trust Fund. The interest is devoted to an annual prize for a literary work in the field of biography, history, politics or poetry published in English or French by a recognised publisher during the previous twelve months. All communications should be sent to Artemis Cooper, 54 St Maur Road, London SW6 4DP   *tel* 0171-736 3729   *fax* 0171-731 7638.

County of Cardiff International Poetry Competition
Fourteen annual prizes totalling £5000 are awarded for unpublished poetry, written in English (1st prize £1000; 2nd £750; 3rd £500 and ten 4th prizes of £250 each. Wales Writers' Group prize £250). Next closing date: October 1996. Prize-giving in December 1996. Entry form and further details from: County of Cardiff International Poetry Competition, PO Box 438, Cardiff CF1 6YA.

The Rose Mary Crawshay Prizes
Founded in 1888, one or more Rose Mary Crawshay prizes are awarded each year to women of any nationality who, in the judgement of the Council of the British Academy, have written or published within the three calendar years immediately preceding the date of the award an historical or critical work of sufficient value on any subject connected with English literature, preference being given to a work regarding Byron, Shelley or Keats. Applications are not sought in this competition.

CWA Cartier Diamond Dagger
This award was first given in 1986 and is for outstanding contribution to the genre. Nominations not required. It is sponsored by Cartier in conjunction with the Crime Writers' Association, PO Box 10772, London N6 4SD.

CWA John Creasey Memorial Dagger
The award was founded in 1973 following the death of John Creasey, to commemorate his foundation of the Crime Writers' Association. It is given annually, for the best crime novel by an author who has not previously published a full-length work of fiction, by the Crime Writers' Association. Nominations by publishers only. PO Box 10772, London N6 4SD. Award sponsored by Chivers Press.

CWA Gold Dagger and Silver Dagger
Founded in 1955 and awarded annually for a crime novel published in the UK. Nominations by publishers only. Given by the Crime Writers' Association, PO Box 10772, London N6 4SD.

CWA Gold Dagger for Non-Fiction
Founded in 1977 and awarded annually for a non-fiction crime book to an author published in the UK. Nominations by publishers only. Chosen by four judges of different professions. Given by the Crime Writers' Association, PO Box 10772, London N6 4SD.

CWA Last Laugh Dagger
Founded in 1989 and awarded annually for the most amusing crime novel of the year. Nominations by publishers only.

CWA/The Macallan Short Story Dagger
Now sponsored by The Macallan, this award was instituted in 1993 for the best published short story of the year, to be submitted by publishers. Panels of judges vary from year to year and the winner receives a cheque and a Dagger lapel pin.

CWA Silver Dagger—for details see under CWA Gold Dagger.

DT Charitable Trust Awards
David Thomas Self-Publishing Awards
Established in 1993, these awards are given annually to anyone resident in the UK who has self-published a book during the calendar year preceding the award. The awards are in three categories – novel, non-fiction, poetry – with a prize of £250 in each category. Next closing date: 31 January 1996. Full details and entry form from Self-Publishing Awards, DT Charitable Trust, Writers News Ltd, PO Box 4, Nairn IV12 4HU   *tel* (01667) 454441.

DT Charitable Trust Open Poetry Competition
Established in 1994, this annual award is open to anyone aged over 16 and writing in the English language. Poems can be up to 60 lines; there are no other restrictions on form or subject. The prize is £1200 and the winner holds the Silver Cup for one year. Full details and entry form from Lorna Edwardson, *Writing Magazine*, PO Box 4, Nairn IV12 4HU   *tel* (01667) 454441.

The Rhys Davies Trust
The Trust aims to foster Welsh writing in English and offers financial assistance to English-language literary projects in Wales, directly or in association with other bodies. The Trust also supports the annual Rhys Davies Lecture at the University of Glamorgan. Details from Mr Meic Stephens, The Secretary, The Rhys Davies Trust, 10 Heol Don, Whitchurch. Cardiff CF4 2AU   *tel* (01222) 623359   *fax* (01222) 529202.

The Dillons First Fiction Award
Founded in 1995, this annual award of £5000 (and substantial promotion through Dillons stores) is given to the best first-time novelist whose work, originally written in English, was published in the UK in the calendar year of the award. Shortlist of six titles selected by panel of Dillons booksellers; winning novel chosen by panel of Dillons customers (selected through a

competition in the Dillons magazine). Full details from: Dillons Publicity, Royal House, Prince's Gate, Homer Road, Solihull B91 3QQ.

The T.S. Eliot Prize

Founded in 1993, an annual prize of £5000 is awarded to the best collection of new poetry published in the UK or the Republic of Ireland during the year. Apply, in autumn, to Poetry Book Society, Book House, 45 East Hill, London SW18 2QZ   *tel* 0181-870 8403.

Encore Award

This annual award of £7500 is for the best second novel of the year. The work submitted must be (a) a novel by one author who has had one (and only one) novel published previously, and (b) in the English language, first published in the UK. Closing date: 30 November. Details from The Society of Authors, 84 Drayton Gardens, London SW10 9SB   *tel* 0171-373 6642.

Esquire/Apple/Waterstone's Non Fiction Award

Established in 1993, this award is given for the best non-fiction title published in the UK in the preceding year. The award (winner £10,000, 5 runners up of £1000 each) is open to writers of all nationalities. Details from The Administrator, Esquire/Waterstone's Non Fiction Award, Esquire, 72 Broadwick Street, London W1V 2BP.

The European Poetry Translation Prize

Founded in 1983 a prize of £1000 is given every two years for a published volume of poetry which has been translated into English from a European language. Next award 1997. Funded by the Arts Council of England and administered by The Poetry Society, 22 Betterton Street, London WC2H 9BU.

Christopher Ewart-Biggs Memorial Prize

This prize of £4000 is awarded once every two years to the writer, of any nationality, whose work contributes most, in the opinion of the judges, to peace and understanding in Ireland; to closer ties between the peoples of Britain and Ireland; or to co-operation between the partners of the European Union. Eligible works must be published during the two years to 31 December 1996. Information from Secretary, Memorial Prize, Flat 3, 149 Hamilton Terrace, London NW8 9QS   *tel* 0171-624 1863.

The Geoffrey Faber Memorial Prize

Established in 1963 by Faber and Faber Ltd, as a memorial to the founder and first Chairman of the firm, an annual prize of £1000 is awarded in alternate years for a volume of verse and for a volume of prose fiction, first published originally in the UK during the two years preceding the year in which the award is given which is, in the opinion of the judges, of the greatest literary merit. Eligible writers must be not more than 40 years old at the date of publication of the book and a citizen of the UK and Colonies, of any other Commonwealth state or of the Republic of Ireland. There are three judges who are reviewers of poetry or fiction as the case may be; they are nominated each year by the literary editors of newspapers and magazines which regularly publish such reviews. Faber and Faber invite nominations from reviewers and literary editors. No submissions for the prize are to be made.

The Eleanor Farjeon Award

In 1965 the Children's Book Circle instituted an annual award to be given for distinguished services to children's books and to be known as the Eleanor Farjeon Award in memory of the much-loved children's writer. A prize of (minimum) £750 may be given to a librarian, teacher, author, artist, publisher, reviewer, television producer or any other person working with or for children through books. The award is sponsored by Books for Children.

Prudence Farmer Poetry Prize

This poetry prize was founded in 1974 and is awarded annually for the best poem printed during the previous year in the *New Statesman & Society*, Foundation House, Perseverance Works, 38 Kingsland Road, London E2 8DQ *tel* 0171-739 3211 *fax* 0171-739 9307 *e-mail* new-statesman @geo2.poptel.org.uk

The Fawcett Bookprize—'New Light on Women's Lives'

Founded in 1982, the Fawcett Bookprize is awarded annually to the book which does most to further our understanding of women's lives and experiences. The prize is awarded during early June, in London. Entries to be submitted by 31 December, for titles published in the previous year in Britain, Ireland and the Commonwealth. Details from the Administrative Officer, The Fawcett Society, Fifth Floor, 45 Beech Street, London EC2Y 8AD *tel* 0171-628 4441 *fax* 0171-628 2865.

The Kathleen Fidler Award

An annual award for an unpublished novel for children aged 8-12 years, to encourage authors new to writing for this age group. The work should be the author's first attempt to write for this age range. The winner will receive a cash prize of £1000 and the winning entry will be published. Administered by Book Trust Scotland. For details, send an sae to Book Trust Scotland, The Scottish Book Centre, 137 Dundee Street, Edinburgh EH11 1BG.

The John Florio Prize

This prize was established in 1963 under the auspices of the Society of Authors and its Translators Association to be awarded biennially for the best translation into English published by a British publisher during the previous two years. Only translations of Italian 20th-century works of literary merit and general interest will be considered. The work should be entered by the publisher and not by the individual translator. Details from the Secretary, The Translators Association, 84 Drayton Gardens, London SW10 9SB.

E.M. Forster Award

The distinguished English author, E.M. Forster, bequeathed the American publication rights and royalties of his posthumous novel *Maurice* to Christopher Isherwood, who transferred them to the American Academy of Arts and Letters (633 West 155th Street, New York, NY 10032, USA), for the establishment of an E.M. Forster Award, currently $12,500, to be given annually to an English writer for a stay in the United States. *Applications for this award are not accepted.*

Forward Poetry Prizes

Established in 1992, three prizes are awarded annually: 1) best collection of poetry published between 1 October and 30 September (£10,000); 2) best first collection of poetry published between 1 October and 30 September (£5000); and 3) best individual poem, published but not as part of a collection between 1 May 1996 and 30 April 1997 (£1000). All poems entered are also considered for inclusion in the *Forward Book of Poetry*, an annual anthology. Entries must be submitted by book publishers and editors of newspapers, periodicals and magazines in the UK and Eire. Individual entries from poets will not be accepted. Details from: Forward Poetry Prize Administrator, Colman Getty PR, Carrington House, 126-130 Regent Street, London W1R 5FE *tel* 0171-439 1783 *fax* 0171-439 1784.

Miles Franklin Literary Award

Founded in 1957, this annual award of $25,000 is for a novel or play first published in the preceding year, which presents Australian life in any of its phases. More than one entry may be submitted by each author; collaborations between two or more authors are eligible. Biographies, collections of short stories or children's books are not eligible. Closing date: approx. 31 January each year. Details from Arts Management, 180 Goulburn Street, Darlinghurst, NSW 2010, Australia   *tel* (02) 283 2066   *fax* (02) 264 8201.

The Lionel Gelber Prize

Established in 1989, this prize of $50,000 is given annually to the author of the winning book on the subject of international relations published in English or in English translation. Details from the Manager, The Lionel Gelber Prize, c/o Applause Communications, 398 Adelaide St. West, Suite 1007, Toronto, Ontario M5V 1S7, Canada   *tel* 416-504-7200   *fax* 416-504-5647   *e-mail* applause@idirect.com

The Glenfiddich Awards

Founded in 1970, awards are given annually to recognise excellence in writing, publishing and broadcasting relating to the subjects of food and drink. £800 is given per category (12 in all), together with a case of Glenfiddich Single Malt Scotch Whisky and an engraved quaich. The overall winner receives The Glenfiddich Trophy and an additional £3000. Details from The Glenfiddich Awards, 27 Fitzroy Square, London W1P 5HH   *tel* 0171-383 3024   *fax* 0171-383 4593.

E.C. Gregory Trust Fund

A number of substantial awards are made annually for the encouragement of young poets who can show that they are likely to benefit from an opportunity to give more time to writing. An eligible candidate must: (a) be a British subject by birth but *not* a national of Eire or any of the British dominions or colonies and be ordinarily resident in the UK or Northern Ireland; (b) be under the age of thirty at 31 March in the year of the Award (i.e. the year following submission); (c) submit for consideration a published or unpublished work of belles-lettres, poetry or drama poems (not more than 30 poems). Further details from, and entries (no later than 31 October) to the Society of Authors, 84 Drayton Gardens, London SW10 9SB.

The Guardian Children's Fiction Prize

The *Guardian*'s annual prize of £1500 for a work of children's fiction (usually for children over eight), published by a British or Commonwealth writer. The winning book is chosen by the Children's Book Editor together with a team of three or four other authors of children's books.

The Guardian Fiction Prize

The *Guardian*'s annual prize of £2000 for a work of fiction showing originality and promise published by a British or Commonwealth writer. The winning book will be chosen by the Literary Editor in conjunction with the *Guardian*'s regular reviewers of new fiction.

Guild Awards

Eighteen awards, covering radio, theatre, books, film and television, are awarded annually by the Writers' Guild of Great Britain. Nominations are made from works which have been published, performed or broadcast during the period 1 July to 30 June. The awards are presented in October each year. No nominations are required from the public.

The Hawthornden Prize

The Hawthornden Prize, for which books do not have to be specially submitted, is awarded annually to the author of what, in the opinion of the Committee, is the best work of imaginative literature published during the preceding calendar year by a British author. Details from The Administrator, 42a Hays Mews, Berkeley Square, London W1X 7RU.

Hawthornden Writers' Fellowships

Applications are invited from novelists, poets, dramatists and other creative writers whose work has already been published. Four-week fellowships are offered to those working on a current project. Details from The Administrator, Hawthornden Castle International Retreat for Writers, Hawthornden Castle, Lasswade, Midlothian EH18 1EG *tel* 0131-440 2180.

The Felicia Hemans Prize for Lyrical Poetry

This annual prize of books or money, open to past and present members and students of the University of Liverpool only, is awarded for a lyrical poem, the subject of which may be chosen by the competitor. Only one poem, either published or unpublished, may be submitted. The prize shall not be awarded more than once to the same competitor. Poems, endorsed 'Hemans Prize', must be sent to the Registrar, The University of Liverpool, PO Box 147, Liverpool L69 3BX *tel* 0151-794 2458 *fax* 0151-794 2454, on or before 1 May.

Heywood Hill Literary Prize

Established in 1995, an award of £10,000 is given annually to a person chosen for their lifetime's contribution to the enjoyment of books. No applications. Administration: Heywood Hill Booksellers, 10 Curzon Street, London SW1Y 7FJ.

David Higham Prize for Fiction

This prize of £1000 which was founded in 1975 is awarded annually to a citizen of the British Commonwealth, Republic of Ireland, South Africa or Pakistan for a first novel or book of short stories written in English and published during the current year. Publishers only may submit books. Entry forms from Book Trust, Book House, 45 East Hill, London SW18 2QZ *tel* 0181-870 9055.

William Hill Sports Book of the Year Award

Founded in 1989, this award is given annually in November for a book with a sporting theme (record books and listings excluded). Title must be in the English language, and published for the first time in the UK during the relevant calendar year. Total value of prize is £6000, including £5000 in cash. An award for the best cover design was introduced in 1991; value £500. Details from Graham Sharpe, William Hill Organisation, Greenside House, 50 Station Road, Wood Green, London N22 4TP *tel* 0181-918 3731.

The Calvin and Rose G. Hoffman Memorial Prize for Distinguished Publication on Christopher Marlowe

This annual prize of around £6500 is awarded to the best unpublished work that examines the life and works of Christopher Marlowe and the relationship between the works of Marlowe and Shakespeare. The adjudicator is Professor T. Craik, University of Durham. Closing date: 1 September. Applications to The Headmaster, The King's School, Canterbury, Kent CT1 2ES *tel* (01227) 595501 *fax* (01227) 595595.

Winifred Holtby Memorial Prize

Awarded for the best regional novel of the year written in the English language. The writer must be of British or Irish nationality, or a citizen of the Commonwealth. Translations, unless made by the author of the work, are not eligible for consideration. If in any year it is considered that no regional novel is of sufficient merit the prize (value £800) may be awarded to an author, qualified as aforesaid, of a literary work of non-fiction or poetry, concerning a regional subject. Novels published during the current year should be submitted by 31 October to The Royal Society of Literature, 1 Hyde Park Gardens, London W2 2LT.

The Richard Imison Memorial Award
Founded in 1993, this annual prize of £1000 is awarded to any new writer of radio drama first transmitted within the UK during the period 1 January-31 December 1996 by a writer new to radio. Entry form and details from: The Secretary, The Broadcasting Committee, The Society of Authors, 84 Drayton Gardens, London SW10 9SB *tel* 0171-373 6642.

The Independent/Scholastic Story of the Year Competition
Founded in 1993, prizes are awarded annually (£2000 winner, £500 each to runners up, £200 each to up to seven finalists, whose entries are published in the anthology) for the best short stories, of 1500-2500 words, for 6-9-year-old children. Full entry details are advertised in *The Independent* each spring (March-April).

International IMPAC Dublin Literary Award
Founded in 1995, an award of IR£100,000 will be presented annually to the work of fiction, written and published in the English language or written in a language other than English and published in English translation, which in the opinion of the judges is of high literary merit and constitutes a lasting contribution to world literature. Nominations accepted from library systems of major cities from all over the world, regardless of national origin of the author or the place of publication. Further details from: The International IMPAC Dublin Literary Award Office, Dublin City Public Libraries, Administrative Headquarters, Cumberland House, Fenian Street, Dublin 2, Republic of Ireland *tel* (01) 6619000 *fax* (01) 6761628 *e-mail* dublin.city.libs@iol.ie

International Playwriting Festival
Established in 1986, an annual competition for full-length plays which must be previously unperformed. Plays are accepted from all around the world and from both new and established writers. Deadline for entries: 4 July. Finalists are given a professionally directed and acted rehearsed reading in November (many winners have later had a full production). Details and entry form from: Warehouse Theatre, Dingwall Road, Croydon CR0 2NF *tel* 0181-681 1257 *fax* 0181-688 6699.

Irish Times Literary Prizes
Founded in 1989, these biennial prizes are awarded from nominations submitted by literary editors and critics. In 1997 the Irish Literature Prizes will be IR£5000 for each of three categories: fiction (novel, novella or collection of short stories); non-fictional prose (history, biography, autobiography, criticism, politics, sociological interest, travel, current affairs and belles-lettres); poetry (collection of works or long poem or sequence of poems or revised/updated edition of previously published selection or collection of a poet's work); work published in English and Irish. The International Fiction Prize will be IR£7500 for a work of fiction written in the English language and published in Ireland, the UK or the USA. For further information, please contact Gerard Cavanagh, Administrator *tel* (01) 6792022 *fax* (01) 6709383.

Jewish Quarterly Literary Prizes
Founded in 1977, prizes are awarded annually for a work of fiction (£4000) and non-fiction (£3000) which best stimulate an interest in and awareness of themes of Jewish concern among a wider reading public. Details from The Administrator, Jewish Quarterly, PO Box 2078, London W1A 1JR *tel* 0171-629 5004 *fax* 0171-629 5110.

Kent & Sussex Poetry Society Open Poetry Competition
Founded in 1985, this competition is open to all unpublished poems, no longer than 40 lines in length. Prizes: 1st £300, 2nd £100, 3rd £50, 4th five at £20. Closing date: 31 January. Entries, an entry fee of £2 per poem, the author's

name and address and a list of poems submitted, should be sent to: The
Organiser, 8 Edward Street, Southborough, Kent TN4 0HP.

Kraszna-Krausz Awards

Instituted in 1985, awards totalling £40,000 are made each year, alternating
annually between the best books on a) still photography: art and culture,
educational, photographic innovations; and b) moving picture media: culture,
business, techniques and technology. The prize in each category will be
awarded to the best book published in the preceding two years. Closing
date: 30 June each year. 1996 award = a). The Foundation is also open to
applications for grants concerned with the literature of photography. Details
from A.J. Mahoney, Kraszna-Krausz Foundation, c/o Winter-Taylors, Park
House, London Road, High Wycombe, Bucks. HP11 1BZ *tel* (01494)
450171.

The Lady Short Story Competition

Founded in 1993, the competition is open to anyone possessing a coupon from
the first October issue of *The Lady*. First prize is £1000. Subjects for short
stories change each year. Further information in the relevant issue – please do
not contact the magazine office directly in connection with the competition.
The Lady, 39-40 Bedford Street, London WC2E 9ER.

The Library Association

Carnegie Medal

Awarded annually for an outstanding book for children (fiction or non-fiction)
written in English and first published in the UK during the preceding year or
co-published elsewhere within a three-month time lapse. Recommendations
for the award are invited from members of the Library Association, who are
asked to submit a preliminary list of not more than two titles, accompanied by
a 50-word appraisal justifying the recommendation of each book. The award
is sponsored by Peters Library Service and selected by the Youth Libraries
Group of the Library Association.

Kate Greenaway Medal

Awarded annually for an outstanding illustrated book for children first published in the UK during the preceding year or co-published elsewhere within
a three-month time lapse. Recommendations for the award are invited from
members of the Library Association, who are asked to submit a preliminary
list of not more than two titles, accompanied by a 50-word appraisal justifying
the recommendation of each book. Books intended for older as well as younger
children are included, and reproduction will be taken into account. The award
is sponsored by Peters Library Service and selected by the Youth Libraries
Group of the Library Association.

The Library Association Reference Awards

The Besterman Medal

Awarded annually for an outstanding bibliography or guide to the literature
first published in the UK during the preceding year either in print or in
electronic form. Recommendations for the award are invited from members
of the Library Association, who are asked to submit a preliminary list of not
more than three titles, and submissions from publishers are welcome.

The McColvin Medal

Awarded annually for an outstanding reference work either in print or in
electronic form first published in the UK during the preceding year. Works
eligible for consideration are encyclopedias, general and special; dictionaries,
general and special; biographical dictionaries; annuals, yearbooks and directories; handbooks and compendia of data; atlases. Recommendations for the
award are invited from members of the Library Association, who are asked to

submit a preliminary list of not more than three titles, and submissions from publishers are welcome.

The Walford Award
Awarded annually to an individual who has made a sustained and continued contribution to the science and art of British bibliography over a period of years. The bibliographer's work can encompass effort in the history, classification and description of printed, written, audiovisual and machine readable materials. Recommendations may be made for the work of a living person or persons, or for an organisation. The award can be made to a British bibliographer or to a person or organisation working in the UK.

The Wheatley Medal
Awarded annually for an outstanding index published during the preceding three years. Printed indexes to any type of publication may be submitted for consideration, providing that the whole work, including the index, or the index alone has originated in the UK. Recommendations for the award are invited from members of the Library Association and the Society of Indexers, publishers and others. The final selection is made by a committee consisting of representatives of the Library Association Cataloguing and Indexing Group and the Society of Indexers.

The Lichfield Prize
Lichfield District Council's biennial prize of £5000 and the chance of publication, instituted in 1988, for the best novel based recognisably on the geographical area of Lichfield District, Staffordshire. Next closing date: 30 April 1997. Details from the Tourist Information Centre, Donegal House, Bore Street, Lichfield, Staffs. WS13 6NE   *tel* (01543) 252109   *fax* (01543) 417308.

The Livingstone Award for Travel
Founded in 1990, the award is open to any writer of a travel guide printed in the English language and published in the 12 months prior to closing date (31 August). The prize is £1000 plus an engraved goblet. Further details from: The Livingstone Award for Travel, PO Box 3821, London NW2 3DQ.

The London Short Story Competition
Founded in 1992, and open to adults resident in Greater London, this biennial competition awards 15 prizes of £200 each (plus publication in an anthology) for the best short stories about London. Next closing date: end November 1996. Entry form from London Arts Board, Elme House, 133 Long Acre, London WC2E 9AF   *tel* 0171-240 1313   *fax* 0171-240 4580.

The Sir William Lyons Award
This annual award (trophy, £1000 and two years' probationary membership of The Guild of Motoring Writers) was set up to encourage young people in automotive journalism, including broadcasting, and to foster interest in motoring and the motor industry through these media. Open to any person of British nationality resident in the UK under the age of 23, it consists of writing two essays and an interview with the Award Committee. Further details from the General Secretary, 30 The Cravens, Smallfield, Surrey RH6 9QS   *tel* (01342) 843294   *fax* (01342) 844093.

The Macallan/Scotland on Sunday Short Story Competition
Instituted in 1990, this annual prize (£6000; second prize £600; four runners up £100 each; publication in *Scotland on Sunday*) is awarded for the best short story, of less than 3000 words, written by a person born in Scotland, now living in Scotland or by a Scot living abroad. Details from The Administrator, The Macallan/Scotland on Sunday Short Story Competition, 20 North Bridge, Edinburgh EH1 1YT.

The McKitterick Prize
This annual award of £4000-£6000 was endowed by the late Tom McKitterick for first novels by authors over the age of 40. Closing date: 16 December, and the award is open to first published novels and unpublished typescripts. Full details from The Society of Authors, 84 Drayton Gardens, London SW10 9SB.

The Enid McLeod Literary Prize
This annual prize of £200 is given for a full-length work of literature which contributes most to Franco-British understanding. It must be written in English by a citizen of the UK, British Commonwealth, the Republic of Ireland, Pakistan, Bangladesh or South Africa, and first published in the UK. Further details from the Executive Secretary, Franco-British Society, Room 623, Linen Hall, 162-168 Regent Street, London W1R 5TB *tel/fax* 0171-734 0815.

The Macmillan Prize for a Children's Picture Book
Three prizes of £1000 (1st), £500 (2nd) and £250 (3rd) are awarded annually for children's book illustrations by art students in higher education establishments in the UK. Applications to Marketing Director, Macmillan Children's Books, 25 Eccleston Place, London SW1W 9NF.

Macmillan Silver Pen Award for Fiction
This award of £500 founded in 1969 and sponsored by Macmillan since 1986 is given annually for an outstanding collection of short stories written in English and published during the previous year by an author of British nationality or an author who has been a long-term resident in the UK. Books are nominated by members of the P.E.N. Executive Committee. Details from P.E.N., 7 Dilke Street, Chelsea, London SW3 4JE *tel* 0171-352 6303 *fax* 0171-351 0220.

The McVitie's Prize for Scottish Writer of the Year
Annual prize of £1000 to each of five shortlisted writers, and a further £9000 to the winner. Submissions include novels, volumes of short stories, poetry, biography, autobiography, journalism, science fiction and children's books as well as theatre, cinema, radio and television scripts. Open to writers who were born or have been resident in Scotland, who have Scottish parents, or who take Scotland as their inspiration. Closing date: 31 July for work first made public during the previous twelve months. Details from The McVitie's Prize, Book Trust Scotland, Scottish Book Centre, 137 Dundee Street, Edinburgh EH11 1BG *tel* 0131-229 3663 *fax* 0131-228 4293.

The Mail on Sunday–John Llewellyn Rhys Prize
This annual prize of £5000, inaugurated in memory of the writer John Llewellyn Rhys, is offered to the author of the most promising literary work of any kind published for the first time during the current year. The author must be a citizen of this country or the Commonwealth, and not have passed his or her 35th birthday by the date of the publication of the work submitted. Publishers only may submit books. Entry forms and further information from The Mail on Sunday–John Llewellyn Rhys Prize, c/o Book Trust, Book House, 45 East Hill, London SW18 2QZ *tel* 0181-870 9055.

The Kurt Maschler Award
This annual prize of £1000, founded in 1982, is awarded to a British author/artist or an author/artist (who has been resident in Britain for more than ten years) for a children's book in which text and illustrations are of excellence and enhance and balance each other. Details from Book Trust, Book House, 45 East Hill, London SW18 2QZ *tel* 0181-870 9055.

The Somerset Maugham Awards
These annual awards, totalling about £15,000, are to encourage young writers to travel. Mr Maugham urged that originality and promise should be the

touchstones: he did not wish the judges to 'play for safety' in their choice. A candidate must be a British subject by birth and ordinarily resident in the UK or Northern Ireland, must be under 35 years of age and must submit a published literary work in the English language, of which the candidate is the sole author. Poetry, fiction, non-fiction, belles-lettres or philosophy, but not dramatic works, are eligible. An information sheet is available from The Society of Authors, 84 Drayton Gardens, London SW10 9SB. Four, non-returnable copies of one published work should be submitted, and must be accompanied by a statement of the author's date and place of birth, and other published works. Closing date: 31 December.

MCA Book Prize

Founded in 1993, an annual main prize of £5000, and a Young Writers Award (under 35) of up to £2000, are given to books which contribute stimulating, original and progressive ideas on management issues. Authors must be British subjects domiciled in the UK. Next closing date: 15 November 1996. Details from: Andrea Livingstone, Administrator, MCA Book Prize, 122 Fawnbrake Avenue, London SE24 0BZ   *tel/fax* 0171-738 6701.

Meyer-Whitworth Award

Set up to help further the careers of UK contemporary playwrights who are not yet established, this award of £8000 is given annually for an English-language play which shows writing of individual quality and the promise of a developing new talent. Candidates will have had no more than two of their plays professionally produced. Nominated plays must have been produced professionally in the UK for the first time between 1 August and 31 July; next closing date: 30 August. Details from the Theatre Writing Section, Drama Department, Arts Council of England, 14 Great Peter Street, London SW1P 3NQ   *tel* 0171-333 0100 ext 431.

Mind Book of the Year/Allen Lane Award

This £1000 award, inaugurated in memory of Sir Allen Lane in 1981 and administered by Mind, the National Association for Mental Health, is given to the author of any book (fiction or non-fiction) published in the UK in the current year which outstandingly furthers public understanding of the prevention, causes, treatment or experience of mental health problems. Entries by 31 December. Details from Caroline Scott, Mind Publications, Granta House, 15-19 Broadway, Stratford, London E15 4BQ   *tel* 0181-519 2122   *fax* 0181-522 1725.

The Mother Goose Award

Sponsored by Books for Children, and open to all artists having published a first major book for children during the previous year, only books first published in Britain will be considered, including co-productions where the illustration originated in Britain. The award, presented annually in April, is a bronze egg together with a cheque for £1000. Recommendations for the award are invited from publishers and should be sent to each panel member, whose names and addresses are available from Books for Children, 4 Furzeground Way, Stockley Park, Middlesex UB11 1DP.

Shiva Naipaul Memorial Prize

This annual prize of £3000 was founded in 1985, and is given to an English language writer of any nationality under the age of 35 for an essay of not more than 4000 words describing a visit to a foreign place or people. Details from *The Spectator*, 56 Doughty Street, London WC1N 2LL.

The National Art Library Illustration Awards

These annual awards, sponsored by The Enid Linder Foundation, are given to practising book and magazine illustrators, for work first published in Great

Britain in the 12 months preceding the judging of the awards. Book covers, illustrations of a purely technical nature and photographs together with works produced as limited editions are excluded. Cover illustrations to magazines are eligible. Enquiries to The National Art Library, Victoria and Albert Museum, South Kensington, London SW7 2RL   *tel* 0171-938 8313 or to Dr Leo De Freitas   *tel/fax* (01295) 256110.

National Poetry Competition
One of Britain's major annual open poetry competitions. Prizes: 1st £4000, 2nd £1000, 3rd £500, ten runners up of £50. Maximum length 100 lines. Closing date: 30 October 1996. For rules and entry form send an sae to the Competition Organiser, The Poetry Society, 22 Betterton Street, London WC2H 9BU   *tel* 0171-240 4810   *fax* 0171-240 4818   *e-mail* poetrysoc @bbcnc.org.uk

Natural World Book of the Year Award
This £500 prize is awarded annually to the best book on British wildlife or the countryside by *Natural World*, the national magazine of The Wildlife Trusts. Submissions must be made by 1 September, and books must have been published between 1 October of the previous year and 30 September of the year of the award. Details from Natural World Book of the Year Award, 20 Upper Ground, London SE1 9PF   *tel* 0171-805 5555   *fax* 0171-805 5911.

The NCR Book Award for Non-Fiction
An annual award founded in 1987 and sponsored by NCR Ltd to stimulate more interest in non-fiction writing and publishing in the UK. The award carries a prize of £25,000, currently the highest non-fiction award available in the UK. Additionally, each shortlisted author receives a prize bringing the overall value to £35,000. Applications welcomed from publishers. Details from The Administrator, NCR Book Award, 206 Marylebone Road, London NW1 6LY   *tel* 0171-725 8325   *telex* 263931   *fax* 0171-724 6519.

The Nobel Prize in Literature
This is one of the awards stipulated in the will of the late Alfred Nobel, the Swedish scientist who invented dynamite. The awarding authority is the Swedish Academy, Box 2118, S-10313 Stockholm, Sweden   *tel* (08) 10-65-24 *fax* (08) 24-42-25. No direct application for a prize will, however, be taken into consideration. For authors writing in English it was bestowed upon Rudyard Kipling in 1907, W.B. Yeats in 1923, George Bernard Shaw in 1925, Sinclair Lewis in 1930, John Galsworthy in 1932, Eugene O'Neill in 1936, Pearl Buck in 1938, T.S. Eliot in 1948, William Faulkner in 1949, Bertrand Russell in 1950, Sir Winston Churchill in 1953, Ernest Hemingway in 1954, John Steinbeck in 1962, Samuel Beckett in 1969, Patrick White in 1973, Saul Bellow in 1976, William Golding in 1983, Wole Soyinka in 1986, Joseph Brodsky in 1987, Nadine Gordimer in 1991, Derek Walcott in 1992, Toni Morrison in 1993 and Seamus Heaney in 1995.

Northern Arts Writers' Awards
Up to £3000 is available annually to support previously published novelists, short story writers, poets and literary critics living in the Northern Arts region of Cleveland, Cumbria, Co Durham, Tyne & Wear and Northumberland. Details from Allison Wild, Published & Broadcast Arts Department, Northern Arts, 9-10 Osborne Terrace, Jesmond, Newcastle upon Tyne NE2 1NZ   *tel* 0191-281 6334.

Northern Short Story Competition
Founded in 1988, this competition (total prize money £500) is open to residents of the area covered by Northern Arts, North West Arts and Yorkshire and Humberside Arts Boards (see page 626). Stories may be on any subject, of no

more than 3000 words. Closing date: 30 June each year. Application form from Rosemary Jones, Short Story Competition, Arc Publications, Nanholme Mill, Shaw Wood Road, Todmorden, Lancs. OL14 6DY *tel* (01706) 812338 *fax* (01706) 818948.

Oak Tree Award

Founded in 1989, this is an annual award of £250 to an author/illustrator who has published a book for children aged 8-12 years old, fiction or poetry, in the preceding year. No application necessary; details from Nottinghamshire County Library Service, Glaisdale Parkway, Nottingham NG8 4GP *tel* (0115) 985 4203 or Dillons The Bookstore, 25 Wheelergate, Nottingham NG1 2NF *tel* (0115) 947 3531.

One Voice

Founded in 1992, this competition is open to all writers. Prizes are to the value of approximately £4000 and finalists' work will be performed and published. The Catrin Collier Random House Prize enables a writer in the Short Story section to spend a day with Catrin Collier and an editor from Random House and to attend a professional performance of the winning entries. There are three categories: Letter; Story; Monologue. Further information: One Voice, c/o Theatr Cwmtawe, Parc Ynysderw, Pontardawe, W. Glamorgan SA8 4EG *tel* (01792) 830111 *fax* (01792) 862020.

Oppenheim–John Downes Memorial Trust

Awards, varying from £50 to £1500 depending on need, are given each December (and only then) to deserving artists of any kind including writers, musicians, artists who are unable through poverty to pursue their vocation effectively. Applicants must be over 30 years of age and of British birth. Full details and application form from the Trust, c/o 36 Whitefriars Street, London EC4Y 8BH, enclosing sae.

Orange Prize for Fiction

This new award is for a full length novel written in English by a woman of any nationality and first published in the UK between 1 April 1996 and 31 March 1997. It is to be an annual award with a prize of £30,000. Orange Prize for Fiction, Book Trust, Book House, 45 East Hill, London SW18 2QZ *tel* 0181-870 9055 *fax* 0181-874 4790.

George Orwell Memorial Prize

Founded in 1993, two prizes of £1000 each are awarded in March each year – one for the best political book, and one for best political journalism, of the previous year giving equal merit to content and good style accessible to the general public. Next closing date: 20 January 1997 for work published in 1996. Full details from: The Literary Editor, *The Political Quarterly*, 8a Bellevue Terrace, Edinburgh EH7 4DT.

Catherine Pakenham Memorial Award

Young women journalists, or aspiring journalists (over 18 and under 25 years of age), resident in Britain, are eligible for this award, founded in 1970 in memory of Catherine Pakenham, who died in a car crash while working for the *Telegraph Magazine*. The award of £1000 is given for a non-fiction article between 750 and 2000 words long. Entry forms, available after 1 September, from: Michèle Marcus, Public Relations Dept, The Sunday Telegraph, 1 Canada Square, Canary Wharf, London E14 5DT *tel* 0171-538 6259 *fax* 0171-513 2512.

Peterloo Poets Open Poetry Competition

Founded in 1986 this annual competition sponsored by Marks & Spencer offers for 1997 a first prize of £3000 and five other prizes totalling £2100. Closing date for entries is 1 March 1997. Full details and rules of entry from Peterloo Poets, 2 Kelly Gardens, Calstock, Cornwall PL18 9SA.

The Portico Prize

Founded in 1985, this biennial prize of £2500 (next prize 1997) is awarded for a published work of general interest and literary merit set wholly or mainly in the North-West of England (Lancashire, Manchester, Liverpool, High Peak of Derbyshire, Cheshire and Cumbria). Information from Mrs Jo Francis, Librarian, Portico Library, 57 Mosley Street, Manchester M2 3HY *tel* 0161-236 6785.

Dennis Potter Play of the Year Award

Founded in 1994, this annual £10,000 development commission for a television play is awarded to a writer who has not previously had a single play or film produced on television, excepting short films under 30 minutes. Submissions accepted from an individual producer, a BBC producer or a production company. Next closing date: end September. Details from: Tessa Ross, Independents Commissioning Department, Drama, c/o Room D333, BBC Centre House, 56 Wood Lane, London W12 7SB.

The Mathew Prichard Award for Short Story Writing

Prizes (first £1000, two runner-up prizes of £250) are awarded annually in this open competition for original short stories in English of not more than 2500 words. Adjudication is organised in May each year by the South and Mid Wales Association of Writers. Next closing date: 1 March 1997. Details from The Competition Secretary, The Mathew Prichard Award, 95 Celyn Avenue, Lakeside, Cardiff CF2 6EL, on receipt of an sae.

Trevor Reese Memorial Prize

This prize of £1000 is awarded biennially, usually for a scholarly work by a single author in the field of Imperial and Commonwealth history. The next award (for a book published in 1995 or 1996) will be given in 1998. Details from The Seminar Secretary, Institute of Commonwealth Studies, 28 Russell Square, London WC1B 5DS.

The Margaret Rhondda Award

This award, first made in July 1968 on the tenth anniversary of Lady Rhondda's death, and afterwards every three years, is given to a woman writer as a grant-in-aid towards the expenses of a research project in journalism, in recognition of the service which women journalists give to the public through journalism. Closing date for next award 31 December 1998. Further details from The Society of Authors, 84 Drayton Gardens, London SW10 9SB.

The Rhône-Poulenc Prizes for Science Books

These prizes, established in 1987 by COPUS and the Science Museum and sponsored by Rhône-Poulenc, are awarded annually for the best popular science books for the non-specialist reader. Eligible books must be written in English and published for the first time in the UK in the year preceding the prize. The Rhône-Poulenc prize (£10,000) is for a book with a general readership; the Junior Prize (£10,000), is for a book written specifically for young people (under 14): publishers may enter any number of books for each prize. Entries may cover any aspect of science and technology, including biography and history, but books published as educational textbooks or for professional or specialist audiences are not eligible. A prize-winning author will be ineligible for another Rhône-Poulenc Prize for two years. Details from COPUS, c/o The Royal Society, 6 Carlton House Terrace, London SW1Y 5AG *tel* 0171-839 5561 *fax* 0171-451 2693.

Rhyme International Annual Poetry Competition
The only annual international competition exclusively devoted to rhymed poetry, it was founded as Rhyme Revival in collaboration with Coventry Chamber of Commerce in 1981. Total annual prizes average around £1000, divided into two classes, 'formal' and 'open'. Entry fee: £2.50 per poem, minimum £5; closing date: 30 September each year. Adjudicated by a different leading poet each year. Full details and entry forms from *Orbis Literary Magazine*, 199 The Long Shoot, Nuneaton, Warks. CV11 6JQ   *tel* (01203) 327440.

Romantic Novelists' Association Award
This annual award for the best romantic novel of the year is open to both members and non-members of the Romantic Novelists' Association, provided they are domiciled in the UK. Novels must be published between the previous 1 December and 30 November of the year of entry. Three copies of the novel are required. Entry forms and details after July from the Award Organiser, Mrs Jean Chapman, 3 Arnesby Lane, Peatling Magna, Leicester LE8 5UN   *tel/fax* (0116) 247 8330.

The **New Writers' Award** is for writers previously unpublished in the romantic novel field and who are probationary members of the Association. MSS are submitted each September under the New Writers' Scheme. All receive a critique. Any MSS which have passed through the Scheme and which are subsequently accepted for publication become eligible for the Award. Details from New Writers' Scheme Organiser, Hilary Johnson, 5 St Agnes Gate, Wendover, Bucks. HP22 6DP   *tel* (01296) 623260   *fax* (01296) 623601.

The Rooney Prize for Irish Literature
The Rooney Prize was set up in 1976 to encourage young Irish writing talent. The sum of IR£5000 is awarded annually to a different individual, who must be Irish, published in either Irish or English and under 40 years of age. The prize is non-competitive and there is no application procedure or entry form. Information from J.A. Sherwin, Strathin, Templecarrig, Delgany, Co. Wicklow, Republic of Ireland   *tel* (01) 287 4769   *fax* (01) 287 2595.

The Royal Society of Literature Award under the W.H. Heinemann Bequest
Set up to encourage the production of literary works of real worth, works in any branch of literature, originally written in the English language, may be submitted by their publishers for this annual award of £5000. Prose fiction is not excluded, but the Testator's intention was primarily to reward less remunerative classes of literature: poetry, criticism, biography, history, etc. The recipient of a Prize shall not be eligible again for five years. Entries by 31 October to the Royal Society of Literature, 1 Hyde Park Gardens, London W2 2LT   *tel* 0171-723 5104.

The Royal Society of Medicine Prizes
The Medical Writers Group of the Society of Authors administers the prizes sponsored by The Royal Society of Medicine. The closing date for submissions of medical textbooks, illustrated texts, atlases and electronic publications will be 30 June 1997. Further details from the Secretary, MWG, Society of Authors, 84 Drayton Gardens, London SW10 9SB.

The RTZ David Watt Memorial Prize
This £5000 prize, introduced in 1988 and organised, funded and administered by The RTZ Corporation plc, is awarded for outstanding written contributions towards the greater understanding of international and political issues. Those eligible for the prize are writers actively engaged in writing for newspapers and journals in the English language. Entries should comprise a published article in English of not more than 10,000 words. Closing date for entries and

nominations: end March. Details and entry forms from The Administrator, The RTZ David Watt Memorial Prize, The RTZ Corporation plc, 6 St James's Square, London SW1Y 4LD.

Runciman Award

Established in 1985 by the Anglo-Hellenic League for a work – fiction, non-fiction, biography, history or poetry – wholly, or mainly, about Greece or the Hellenic world. The annual £1800 prize is sponsored by the Onassis Foundation. To be eligible a work must be published in its first English edition in the UK. Details from Anglo-Hellenic League, Flat 4, 68 Elm Park Gardens, London SW10 9PB *tel* 0171-352 2676 *fax* 0171-351 5657.

Saga Prize

Founded in 1995, this annual award is eligible to black writers born in Great Britain or the Republic of Ireland who have a black African ancestor. Entrants submit an unpublished MS of a novel no longer than 80,000 words. The entry fee is £15.00 and the prize is £3000 plus publication by Virago Press. Applications to: Saga Prize, Book Trust, Book House, 45 East Hill, London SW18 2QZ *tel* 0181-870 9055.

The Ian St James Awards

Annual awards, founded in 1989 for writers of short stories: top prize £2000 and runner-up prizes of £200 each, plus publication in annual collection. The remaining 60 shortlisted writers are published throughout the year in the fiction magazine, *Acclaim*. Eligible writers must be 18 or over and not have had a novel or novella previously published. Entries must be in English but can come from anywhere in the world. Closing date: 30 April. Entry forms and further information from: The New Writers' Club, PO Box 101, Tunbridge Wells, Kent TN4 8YD *tel* (01892) 511322.

The Schlegel-Tieck Prize

This prize was established in 1964 under the auspices of the Society of Authors and its Translators Association to be awarded annually for the best translation published by a British publisher during the previous year. Only translations of German twentieth-century works of literary merit and general interest will be considered. The work should be entered by the publisher and not the individual translator. Details from the Secretary, The Translators Association, 84 Drayton Gardens, London SW10 9SB.

Scoop of the Year Award

Founded in 1990, and chosen by a panel of senior editors, this annual award of a bronze statuette is given for the reporting scoop of the year, appearing in either a newspaper or electronic media. Details from the Hon. Secretary, London Press Club, Dockmaster's House, Hertsmere Road, London E14 8JJ *tel* 0171-363 1010 *fax* 0171-538 9615.

The Scott Moncrieff Prize

This prize was established in 1964 under the auspices of the Society of Authors and its Translators Association to be awarded annually for the best translation published by a British publisher during the previous year. Only translations of French works of literary merit and general interest, first published in the last 150 years, will be considered. The work should be entered by the publisher and not the individual translator. Details from the Secretary, The Translators Association, 84 Drayton Gardens, London SW10 9SB.

The Scottish Arts Council

Writers Bursaries

A limited number of bursaries – of between £3000 and £8000 each – are offered to enable professional writers to devote more time to writing. Priority is given to writers of fiction and verse, but writers of literary non-fiction are also considered. Application normally open only to writers who have been living and working in Scotland for at least two years. Applications may be discussed with Jenny Brown, Literature Director, The Scottish Arts Council, 12 Manor Place, Edinburgh EH3 7DD   *tel* 0131-226 6051.

Book Awards
Five awards of £1000 each are made in both spring and autumn. Preference is given to literary fiction and verse, but literary non-fiction is also considered. Authors should be Scottish or resident in Scotland, but books of Scottish interest by other authors are eligible for consideration. Publishers should apply for further information to Shonagh Irvine, Literature Officer, The Scottish Arts Council, 12 Manor Place, Edinburgh EH3 7DD   *tel* 0131-226 6051.

The Scottish Book of the Year and Scottish First Book
Established in 1982 and 1988 respectively, these two annual awards (£5000 and £1500), sponsored by The Scotsman Publications Ltd, are open to any author of Scottish descent or living in Scotland, or for a book by anyone which deals with the work or life of a Scot or with a Scottish problem, event or situation. Nominations are made by literary editors of Scottish newspapers and periodicals. Details from The Saltire Society, 9 Fountain Close, 22 High Street, Edinburgh EH1 1TF   *tel* 0131-556 1836   *fax* 0131-557 1675.

The Seebohm Trophy – Age Concern Book of the Year
Founded in 1995, in memory of Frederic, Lord Seebohm, President of Age Concern, 1971-1989, an annual award is made to the author and publisher of a non-fiction title (published in the previous calendar year) which, in the opinion of the judges, is most successful in promoting the wellbeing and understanding of older people. The author receives £1000, the publisher the silver Seebohm Trophy. Application form available from Age Concern England, Astral House, 1268 London Road, London SW16 4ER   *tel* 0181-679 8000 ext 2353 and nominations must be received before the middle of May each year.

She Short Story Competition
Annual prizes, plus publication in *She* magazine, of the best short story of a maximum of 2500 words. Details of application announced in magazine, usually in a spring issue.

The Signal Poetry for Children Award
A prize of £100 is given annually for an outstanding book of poetry published for children in Britain and the Commonwealth during the previous year, whether single poem or anthology and regardless of country of original publication. Articles about the winning book are published in *Signal* each May. Not open to unpublished work. Further details from The Thimble Press, Lockwood, Station Road, South Woodchester, Stroud, Glos. GL5 5EQ.

The André Simon Memorial Fund Book Awards
Two awards, founded in 1978, are given annually, one each for the best new book on food and on drink (£2000 each), plus one Special Commendation of £1000 in either category. Closing date: 1 November each year. Details from Tessa Hayward, 5 Sion Hill Place, Bath BA1 5SJ   *tel* (01225) 336305.

Smarties Book Prize
Established in 1985 and sponsored by Nestlé Smarties, a prize (Gold Award) of £2500 is awarded to each of the three age category winners (0-5, 6-8 and 9-11 years). Runners-up (Silver Award) receive £1500 each, and third prize (Bronze Award) winners receive £500 each. Eligible books must be published in the UK in the 12 months ending 30 September of the year of presentation

and be a work of fiction or poetry for children written in English by a citizen or resident of the UK. Closing date for entries: 31 July of the year of presentation. Details from Book Trust, Book House, 45 East Hill, London SW18 2QZ *tel* 0181-870 9055.

The W.H. Smith Annual Literary Award

A prize of £10,000 is awarded annually to a Commonwealth author (including a citizen of the UK) whose book, written in English and published in the UK, within 12 months ending on 31 December preceding the date of the Award, in the opinion of the judges makes the most outstanding contribution to literature. Submissions are not accepted; the judges make their decision independently. Further details from W.H. Smith Group, Strand House, 7 Holbein Place, London SW1W 8NR *tel* 0171-824 5456 (direct line).

W.H. Smith Mind Boggling Books Award

Founded in 1993, an award of £5000 is made annually to the best paperback fiction title for children aged 9-12. The award is judged by children of the same age group.

W.H. Smith Thumping Good Read Award

Founded in 1992, an annual award of £5000 is presented to the best new fiction of the year. The award is judged by a panel of WHS customers.

W.H. Smith Young Writers' Competition

Founded in 1959, this competition with prize money totalling £7000 is open to anyone aged 16 or under on 28 February of year of entry. Any original writing (poetry, prose, short fiction, drama) is accepted but must not exceed 3500 words. Up to three entries may be made per person. Winners' work is published by Macmillan in a paperback book. Further information: Schools Projects Manager, W.H. Smith Group plc, Strand House, 7 Holbein Place, London SW1W 8NR *tel* 0171-824 5456.

Southern Arts Literature Prize

This prize is awarded annually on a rotating basis for a published novel, poetry collection, or work of literary non-fiction to writers living within the Southern Arts region. Prize: £1000 plus a craft commission to the value of £600. The 1996 award is for fiction. Closing date: 4 October. Details from The Literature Department, Southern Arts, 13 St Clement Street, Winchester, Hants SO23 9DQ *tel* (01962) 855099 *fax* (01962) 861186.

Stand Magazine Awards

Stand Magazine Short Story Competition

Founded in 1980, this biennial short story competition – prizes to the value of £2250 – is open to any writer for an original, untranslated story in English, not longer than 8000 words, not previously published, broadcast or under consideration elsewhere. Next competition opens September 1996 and closes March 1997. Entry forms available from June 1996 on receipt of a UK sae or 2 International Reply Coupons. Further details from Stand Magazine, 179 Wingrove Road, Newcastle upon Tyne NE4 9DA *tel/fax* 0191-273 3280.

Stand Poetry Competition

New international biennial competition with prizes to the value of £2500. Entrants may submit as many poems as they wish but each poem must be accompanied by a donation of at least £3.50/$7.50 for the first, and £3.00/$7.00 for each subsequent poem. Closing date: 30 June 1996. For further details and entry form send sae or two international reply coupons (abroad) to: *Stand* Magazine, 179 Wingrove Road, Newcastle upon Tyne NE4 9DA.

The Steinbeck Award

Founded in 1994, this annual award is given to a writer under 40 for a new work of fiction in English, written in the spirit of Steinbeck, e.g. a work dedicated to issues of poverty, race or political injustice. The award is £10,000, half of which goes to a charity of the winner's choice. Closing date: 1 March. Details from: William Heinemann, Michelin House, 81 Fulham Road, London SW3 6RB   *tel* 0171-581 9393   *fax* 0171-225 9095.

The James Stern Silver Pen Award for Non-Fiction

This award of £1000 founded in 1969 and sponsored by the Stern family since 1996 is given annually for an outstanding work of non-fiction written in English and published during the previous year by an author of British nationality or an author who has been a long-term resident in the UK. Books are nominated by members of the P.E.N. Executive Committee. Details from P.E.N., 7 Dilke Street, Chelsea, London SW3 4JE   *tel* 0171-352 6303   *fax* 0171-351 0220.

Reginald Taylor and Lord Fletcher Essay Competition

A prize of £300, in memory of E. Reginald Taylor FSA and of Lord Fletcher FSA, is awarded biennially for the best unpublished essay, not exceeding 7500 words, which shows *original research* on a subject of archaeological, art-historical or antiquarian interest within the period from the Roman era to AD 1830. The successful competitor may be invited to read the essay before the Association and the essay may be published in the Association's *Journal*. Competitors should notify the Hon. Editor in advance of the intended subject of their work. Next award: May 1997 and the essay should be submitted not later than 31 October 1996 to the Hon. Editor, Dr Martin Henig, British Archaeological Association, Institute of Archaeology, 36 Beaumont Street, Oxford OX1 2PG, enclosing an sae.

The Teixeira-Gomes Prize

Founded in 1990, this prize is awarded every three years for the best translation into English of a work by a Portuguese national. Any genre of book considered. Details from The Society of Authors, 84 Drayton Gardens, London SW10 9SB.

The Thomas Cook Travel Book Award

Established in 1980, an annual award is given to encourage the art of travel writing. Travel narrative books (150pp minimum) written in English and published between 1 January and 31 December of the preceding year are eligible. Further information from: Corporate Affairs, The Thomas Cook Group Ltd, 43 Berkeley Street, London W1A 1EB   *tel* 0171-499 4000.

Anne Tibble Poetry Competition

This annual prize is awarded for a poem, maximum length 20 lines, to anyone resident in Great Britain. The first prize is for £200; other prizes to a total value of £200. Further details from the Events Team Office, Directorate of Environment Services, Cliftonville House, Bedford Road, Northampton NN4 7NR   *tel* (01604) 233500 ext 4243.

The Times Educational Supplement Book Awards

There are two annual awards for the best books used in schools – Primary and Secondary categories. The books must be published in Britain or the Commonwealth. Details from The Literary Editor, The Times Educational Supplement, Admiral House, 66-68 East Smithfield, London E1 9XY   *tel* 0171-782 3000   *fax* 0171-782 3200.

Tir Na N-og Awards

Three annual awards to children's authors and illustrators, founded in 1976. (1) Best Welsh fiction, including short stories and picture books; (2) best Welsh non-fiction book of the year; (3) best English book with an authentic Welsh background. Total value of prize £3000. Details from: Welsh Books Council, Castell Brychan, Aberystwyth, Ceredigion SY23 2JB *tel* (01970) 624151 *fax* (01970) 625385.

The Tom-Gallon Trust
A biennial award is made to fiction writers of limited means who have had at least one short story accepted for publication. An award of £500 was made in 1995. Authors wishing to enter should send to the Secretary, The Society of Authors, 84 Drayton Gardens, SW10 9SB: (1) a list of their already published fiction, giving the name of the publisher or periodical in each case and the approximate date of publication; (2) one published or unpublished short story; (3) a brief statement of their financial position; (4) an undertaking that they intend to devote a substantial amount of time to the writing of fiction as soon as they are financially able to do so; (5) an sae for the return of the work submitted. Next closing date: 20 September 1998.

The Betty Trask Awards
These awards, through a generous bequest from Miss Betty Trask, are for the benefit of young authors under 35 and are given on the strength of a first novel (published or unpublished) of a romantic or traditional, rather than experimental, nature. It is expected that prizes totalling at least £25,000 will be presented each year. The winners are required to use the money for a period or periods of foreign travel. Full details from The Society of Authors, 84 Drayton Gardens, London SW10 9SB. Closing date: 31 January.

The Travelling Scholarships
These are non-competitive awards administered by the Society of Authors. Submissions are not required.

T.E. Utley Memorial Fund Award
Prizes of £2500 and two of £1500 will be awarded annually for an essay on a given subject. Details from Virginia Utley, 111 Sugden Road, London SW11 5ED *tel* 0171-228 3900.

'Charles Veillon' European Essay Prize
Launched in 1975, a prize of 20,000 Swiss francs is awarded annually to a European writer or essayist for essays offering a critical look at modern society's way of life and ideology. Details from: The Secretary, Charles Veillon Foundation, CH 1017 Lausanne, Switzerland *tel* (021) 701 41 47.

Edgar Wallace Award
Founded in 1990, and chosen by a panel of senior editors, this annual award of a silver inkstand is given for outstanding writing by a journalist. Details from the Hon. Secretary, London Press Club, Dockmaster's House, Hertsmere Road, London E14 8JJ *tel* 0171-363 1010 *fax* 0171-538 9615.

Wandsworth London Writers Competition
Open to writers of 16 years and over who live, work or study in the Greater London Area, awards are made annually in two classes, Poetry and Short Story, the prizes totalling £1000 in each class. Entries must be previously unpublished work. Judging is under the chairmanship of Martyn Goff, Chairman of Book Trust. Further details from Assistant Director of Leisure and Amenity Services (Libraries, Museum and Arts), Wandsworth Town Hall, High Street, London SW18 2PU *tel* 0181-871 7037 *fax* 0181-871 7630.

Whitbread Literary Awards
Judged in two stages and offering a total of £31,000 prize money open to five categories: Novel, First Novel, Children's Novel, Biography/Autobiography, Poetry, the winner in each category receives a Whitbread Nomination Award

of £2000. These five nominations are judged for the Whitbread Book of the Year, the overall winner receiving an additional £21,000. Writers must have lived in Great Britain and Ireland for three or more years. Submissions only from publishers. Closing date: mid July. Further details from The Booksellers Association, Minster House, 272 Vauxhall Bridge Road, London SW1V 1BA *tel* 0171-834 5477.

The Whitfield Prize

The Whitfield Prize (value £1000) is announced in July each year for the best work on a subject within a field of British history. It must be its author's first solely written history book, an original and scholarly work of historical research and have been published in the UK in the preceding calendar year. Three non-returnable copies of an eligible book should be submitted before 31 December to the Executive Secretary, Royal Historical Society, University College London, Gower Street, London WC1E 6BT *tel/fax* 0171-387 7532.

John Whiting Award

Founded in 1965, this prize of £6000 is given annually. Eligible to apply are any writers who have received during the previous two calendar years an award through the Arts Council new theatre writing schemes, or who have had a commission or premier production by a theatre company in receipt of an annual subsidy. Details from the Drama Director, Arts Council of England, 14 Great Peter Street, London SW1P 3NQ *tel* 0171-333 0100.

The Raymond Williams Community Publishing Prizes

Founded in 1990, these annual prizes are awarded to non-profit making publishers for work which offers outstanding imaginative and creative qualities and which exemplifies the values of ordinary people and their lives. First prize: £2000 to publisher, £1000 to writer/group, runner-up: £1500 to publisher, £500 to writer/group. Details from The Secretary, Literature Department, The Arts Council of England, 14 Great Peter Street, London SW1P 3NQ *tel* 0171-973 6442.

Write A Story for Children Competition

Founded in 1984, three prizes are awarded annually (1st £1000, 2nd £200, 3rd £100) for a short story for children, maximum 1000 words, by an unpublished writer of children's fiction. Write, enclosing an sae, for entry form to The Academy of Children's Writers, PO Box 95, Huntingdon, Cambs. PE17 5RL *tel* (01487) 832752.

Yorkshire Post Literary Awards

Yorkshire Post Book of the Year

A prize of £1200 is awarded annually for the Best Book, either fiction or non-fiction. Next closing date: 31 December.

Yorkshire Post Best First Work Award

A prize of £1000 for the Best First Work by a new author, either fiction or non-fiction. Next closing date: 31 December.

Yorkshire Post Art and Music Book Award

Prizes of £1000 each are given to authors whose books are judged to have contributed most to the understanding and appreciation of Art and of Music. Next closing date: 31 January.

Yorkshire Author of the Year Award

Prizes of £1000 are awarded for the Best Book of the Year, either fiction or non-fiction, by an author born in Yorkshire but not necessarily still a resident. Next closing date: 31 December.

In all cases, submissions are accepted only from publishers. For the first two listed above, authors should be British or resident in the UK; for the third, authors need not be British, nor residents. Submissions should be sent to: Margaret Brown, Yorkshire Post Literary Awards, Yorkshire Post Newspapers Ltd, PO Box 168, Wellington Street, Leeds LS1 1RF.

Young Writers' Festival: Write Your Play

Anyone aged 23 or under can submit a play on any subject. A selection of plays will be professionally presented by the Royal Court Theatre in the autumn of 1998, with the writers fully involved in rehearsal and production. This will be followed by a tour to the regions. Workshops are run by professional theatre practitioners and designed to help everyone attending to write a play. Closing date: June 1998. Further information: Young Writers' Festival, Royal Court Young People's Theatre, 309 Portobello Road, London W10 5TD *tel* 0181-960 4641 *fax* 0181-960 1434.

Copyright

For a start, it can be said, in simple terms, that as far as authors are concerned, copyright means effectively that anything original that any person writes, whether for publication or not, is automatically copyright as soon as it is written, whether the words appear on paper, or on a word processor disk or on a tape recorder or in any other tangible form, without necessarily being published; and it is protected by law, both in Britain and in almost all other countries of the world, against unauthorised use by any other person or organisation. This does not apply only to literary works, but to letters, notices and any other original writings. 'Original' in this context does not mean that the work must be innovative, unusual or even literate, let alone literary, but that it has not been copied from anyone else's work, and that the author has worked, however minimally, to produce it. The copyright in your shopping list belongs to you. But, please note, whatever it may be, the material is copyright only if it has been written down or recorded in some way. A speech is not copyright, unless the orator has put it in writing or recorded it on tape or disk.

from *The Writer's Rights* by Michael Legat (A & C Black, £8.99).
See order form on page 690.

Literature Festivals

There are hundreds of arts festivals held in the UK each year – too many to mention in this yearbook and many of which are not applicable specifically to writers. We give here a selection of literature festivals and general arts festivals which include literature events. Space constraints and the nature of an annual publication together determine that only brief details are given; contact festival organisers for a full programme of events.

Aldeburgh Poetry Festival, Aldeburgh Poetry Trust, Goldings, Goldings Lane, Leiston, Suffolk IP16 4EB   *tel* (01728) 830631   *fax* (01728) 832029. *Contact:* Michael Laskey (festival co-ordinator). The 8th annual international festival of contemporary poetry which, each year, has a chosen theme: 'Trust and Betrayal' in 1996. Includes readings, workshops, an open masterclass lecture and children's event. Festival prize for the year's best first collection. Writer in residence. BBC coverage from *The Bookworm*. Twenty poets including Fleur Adcock, Sharon Olds, Brian Patten, Charles Simic, Lemn Sissay. Takes place 1-3 November 1996.

Aspects Festival, North Down Borough Council, Town Hall, The Castle, Bangor, County Down BT20 4BT   *tel* (01247) 270371   *fax* (01247) 271370. *Contact:* Paula Clamp (arts officer). *Festival director:* Kenneth Irvine. An annual celebration of contemporary Irish writing with novelists, poets, playwrights and non-fiction writers. Includes readings, discussions, workshops and a children's day. Takes place in the autumn.

Ballymena Arts Festival, Ballymena Borough Council, Ardeevin, 80 Galgorm Road, Ballymena, County Antrim BT42 1AB   *tel* (01266) 44111   *fax* (01226) 46296. A general arts festival which includes literature events. Takes place 30 September-12 October 1996.

Bath Literature Festival, Bath Festivals Trust, Linley House, 1 Pierrepont Place, Bath BA1 1JY   *tel* (01225) 462231   *fax* (01225) 445551. *Contact:* Laurence Staig (programme director). An annual 9-day festival with leading guest writers. Includes readings, debates, discussions and workshops, and children's activities. Education and community programme includes author visits to schools and a children's writing competition. Each year has a chosen theme. Takes place in late February/early March.

Belfast Festival at Queen's, Festival House, 25 College Gardens, Belfast BT9 6BS   *tel* (01232) 667687   *fax* (01232) 663733. *Contact:* Rosie Turner (marketing manager). The largest annual arts event in Ireland. Includes literature events. Takes place 4-23 November 1996; programme available mid-September.

Birmingham Readers & Writers Festival, Festival Office, Central Library, Chamberlain Square, Birmingham B3 3HQ   *tel* 0121-235 4244   *fax* 0121-233 9702   *e-mail* readers.writers@dial.pipex.com *Festival director:* Jonathan Davidson. An annual 9-day festival which aims to promote the best in contemporary literature, both from within the city and internationally. Over 100 events are on offer: workshops, performances, talks, discussions, plus a special day of events for children. Leading guest writers and poets; poet in residence; BBC tie-ins. The festival runs the *Midlands Poetry Competition* and organises the *TSB Birmingham Children's Book Awards*. Takes place in May.

Book Now!, Leisure Service Department, London Borough of Richmond upon Thames, Langholm Lodge, 146 Petersham Road, Richmond, Surrey TW10 6UX *tel* 0181-332 0534 *fax* 0181-940 7568. *Contact:* Nigel Cutting (principal arts officer). An annual literature festival covering a broad range of subjects. Leading British guest writers and poets hold discussions, talks, debates and workshops and give readings. There are also exhibitions, storytelling sessions and a schools programme. Takes place throughout November.

Bournemouth International Festival, 2 Digby Chambers, Post Office Road, Bournemouth BH1 1BA *tel* (01202) 297327 *fax* (01202) 552510. An annual general arts festival with poetry a prominent aspect of the literature programme. The festival also encompasses a literary weekend with contributions from leading British writers. Takes place 10-25 May 1997; programme published end of February.

Brighton Festival, Brighton Festival Society Ltd, 21-22 Old Steine, Brighton BN1 1EL *tel* (01273) 713875 *fax* (01273) 622453. An annual general arts festival with a large literature programme. Leading guest writers cover a broad range of subjects in a diverse programme of events. Takes place in May; programme published end of February.

Broadstairs Dickens Festival, c/o Rooftops, 58 High Street, Broadstairs, Kent CT10 1JT *tel* (01843) 863453. *Contact:* Honorary Festival Organiser. An annual festival held annually since 1937 with a variety of events inspired by Dickens. Includes walks, talks, dramatic readings, and a festival play of a Dickens work. Takes place in June.

Cambridge Conference of Contemporary Poetry, c/o Ian Patterson, PO Box 940, King's College, Cambridge CB2 1ST *tel* (01223) 327455. An annual weekend of poetry readings, discussion and performance of international poetry from the more modernist end. Takes place in April.

Canterbury Festival, Festival Office, Christ Church Gate, The Precincts, Canterbury, Kent CT1 2EE *tel* (01227) 472820 *fax* (01227) 781830. An annual general arts festival with a literature programme and open poetry competition with £2000 in prizes. Takes place 12-26 October 1996; programme published in July.

Cardiff Literature Festival, The Welsh Academy, 3rd Floor, Mount Stuart House, Mount Stuart Square, Cardiff CF1 6DQ *tel* (01222) 492025 *fax* (01222) 492930. *Director:* Kevin Thomas. An annual festival with a programme of poetry readings, talks, discussions, debates, workshops and children's events. Takes place in spring 1997; dates to be confirmed.

Chaucer Festival, Chaucer Heritage Trust, 22 St Peter's Street, Canterbury, Kent CT1 2BQ *tel* (01227) 470379 *fax* (01227) 761416 or *tel/fax* 0171-229 0635. *Contact:* Philippe Wibrotte (manager and events organiser). An annual festival which includes commemoration services, theatre productions, exhibitions, readings, recitals, Chaucer site visits, medieval fairs, costumed cavalcades, educational programmes for schools. Takes place in London, Canterbury and the County of Kent in the Spring (Easter Chaucer Pilgrimage) and Summer (June-July).

Cheltenham Festival of Literature, Town Hall, Imperial Square, Cheltenham, Glos. GL50 1QA *tel* (01242) 521621 *fax* (01242) 573902. *Contact:* Sarah Smyth (festival organiser). An annual festival with a chosen theme each year; 1996 focuses on women's writing. Includes themed days with talks around one specific subject and 3-hour 'Write Away' sessions with a team of writing tutors (day themes for 1996 include women, comedy writing, science, gardening and art books). *Book It!* is a festival for children within the main festival. Takes place 11-20 October 1996; programme available in August.

Chichester Festivities, Canon Gate House, South Street, Chichester, West Sussex PO19 1PU   *tel* (01243) 785718   *fax* (01243) 528356. An annual general arts festival with a programme of literature events. Takes place in June/July; programme published in April.

City of London Festival, City Arts Trust, Bishopsgate Hall, 230 Bishopsgate, London EC2M 4QD   *tel* 0171-377 0540   *fax* 0171-377 1972. An annual general arts festival with a programme of literature events, including leading guest writers. Takes place in June/July for 3 weeks; programme published in April.

Durham Literature Festival, c/o Durham City Arts Ltd, Byland Lodge, Hawthorn Terrace, Durham DH1 4TD   *tel* (0191) 386 6111 ext. 338   *fax* (0191) 386 0625. *Contact:* Simon Thirsk or Paul Rubinstein (festival co-ordinators). A showcase for major international writers. This annual festival offers a wide range of events covering the finest literature and poetry to the best in popular fiction and children's writing. Readings and performances, talks, discussions and workshops for adults and children, with contributions from leading guest writers. Also a special day for aspiring writers and poets. Takes place in May/June.

Edinburgh Book Festival, Scottish Book Centre, 137 Dundee Street, Fountainbridge, Edinburgh EH11 1BG   *tel* 0131-228 5444   *fax* 0131-228 4333. *Director:* Jan Fairley; *assistant director:* Alison Plackitt. Biennial festival regarded as Europe's largest book event for the public. In addition to the displays of books, over 250 international writers contribute to the programme of events. Takes place 9-25 August 1997; programme details available in June. Runs concurrently with Edinburgh International Festival.

Edinburgh International Festival, 21 Market Street, Edinburgh EH1 1BW   *tel* 0131-226 4001   *fax* 0131-225 1173. An annual international general arts festival. Offers fewer literature events when the Edinburgh Book Festival is held. Takes place 10-30 August 1997; programme published in April.

Exeter Festival, Festival Office, Civic Centre, Exeter EX1 1JN   *tel* (01392) 265200   *fax* (01392) 265265. *Contact:* Gerri Bennett (city centre marketing officer). An annual general arts festival which includes a programme of literary evenings. Takes place in July; programme of events available in April.

Federation of Worker Writers and Community Publishers Festival of Writing, PO Box 540, Burslem, Stoke-on-Trent ST6 6DR   *tel/fax* (01782) 822327. The Federation was formed in 1976 to promote working-class writing as an alternative to establishment literature. An annual weekend festival of readings, workshops, discussions and an opportunity to meet writers from different communities. Takes place in April.

Female Eye National Festival of Women's Writing, Female Eye, Watersmead, Norwood Green Hill, Halifax, West Yorks. HX3 8QX   *tel/fax* (01274) 670181. Female Eye is a non-profit-making organisation set up to encourage and promote writing by women. Each year has a chosen theme and the festival comprises performance, writing workshops and discussion. The 1996/97 theme is the female muse and there will be three weekends in June, September and April, each with a separate emphasis on prose, poetry and drama.

Festival at the Edge, c/o The Old Salt House, Bower Yard, Ironbridge, Telford, Shropshire TF8 7JP   *tel* (01952) 883936. *Contact:* Genevieve Tudor. 'Tales at the Edge' story club hosts an annual weekend of storytelling, music, dance and song. Takes place on the second full weekend of July each year.

Grayshott Literary Festival, The Grayshott Bookshop, The Square, Grayshott, Hindhead, Surrey GU26 6LQ *tel* (01428) 604798. *Contact:* Julia Fry (arts co-ordinator) (01730) 234383 or John Owen Smith (01428) 712892. In the heart of Jane Austen country, an annual weekend festival of events to appreciate local literary history and contemporary writing. Takes place 20-22 September 1996.

Guildford Book Festival, c/o Arts Office, University of Surrey, Guildford GU2 5XH. *Contact:* Joan König (festival organiser). An annual festival with a chosen theme (1996 theme: 'Encounters'), with a programme of over 40 events at 12 different venues. Includes readings, literary lunches and dinners, discussions, performance poetry, writing competitions, a writer in residence, the annual University of Surrey Poetry Lecture and children's events. Takes place 18-27 October 1996.

Harrogate International Festival, The Festival Office, Royal Baths, Harrogate, North Yorks. HG1 2RR *tel* (01423) 562303 *fax* (01423) 521264. An annual international general arts festival which includes a programme of literary events. Takes place in July/August; programme available in May.

Hastings Poetry Festival, c/o Burdett Cottage, 4 Burdett Place, George Street, Hastings, East Sussex TN34 3ED *tel* (01424) 428855 *fax* (01424) 428855. *Contact:* Josephine Austin (organiser and editor of *First Time*). Started in 1968, this national festival is held at the Marina Pavilion, St Leonards on Sea. Includes the prize-giving of the *Hastings National Poetry Competition.* Poems are invited for consideration for the biannual *First Time* poetry magazine. Please include sae. Takes place 2-3 November 1996.

The Hay Festival, Festival Office, Hay-on-Wye HR3 5BX *tel* (01497) 821217 *fax* (01497) 821066. This annual festival aims to celebrate the best in writing and performance from around the world, to commission new work, and to promote and encourage young writers of excellence and potential. Over 100 events in 10 days with leading guest writers. Takes place in May/June; programme published mid-March.

Huddersfield Poetry Festival, The Word Hoard Ltd, 46-47 Byram Arcade, Westgate, Huddersfield HD1 1ND *tel* (01484) 452070. *Contact:* Dianne Darby. This annual festival consists of two seasons. The Spring season consists of readings at various locations. The Autumn season (spread over 3 weekends in September and October) also includes readings but is more participatory, with workshops leading to performances.

International Playwriting Festival, Warehouse Theatre, Dingwall Road, Croydon CR0 2NF *tel* 0181-681 1257 *fax* 0181-688 6699. *Contact:* Rose Marie Vernon. Organised by the Warehouse Theatre in Croydon, the festival includes performed excerpts from short-listed plays and workshops (see page 656).

Ilkley Literature Festival, Manor House, Ilkley, West Yorks. LS29 9DT *tel* (01943) 601210. *Director:* David Porter. Into its 23rd season, this annual festival has 3 seasons: Spring, Summer and Autumn. Includes readings, talks, lectures, workshops, story-telling, children's and family events; also accredited courses run in association with the University of Leeds in creative poetry writing, short story writing and understanding literature. Brings the best new and established writers from Britain and abroad. Takes place 18-21 October 1996; 7-9 March 1997.

King's Lynn Festival, 27-29 King Street, King's Lynn, Norfolk PE30 1HA *tel* (01553) 774725 *fax* (01553) 770591. *Contact:* Catherine Moore (press and marketing officer). An annual general arts festival with literature events featuring leading guest writers. Takes place in July.

Lancaster Literature Festival, 67 Church Street, Lancaster LA1 1ET *tel* (01524) 62166. *Contact:* Andrew Darby. This annual festival has a chosen theme each year and includes performances, readings, workshops, storytelling and children's events. In addition, there are literature events throughout the year on the last Thursday of every month. Takes place in October.

Leicestershire Literature Festival, Leicestershire Libraries and Information Service, County Hall, Glenfield, Leicester LE3 8SS *tel* 0116-265 7386 *fax* 0116-265 7370. *Contact:* Michael Maxwell. A biennial festival with a set theme each year. Includes readings, discussions, exhibitions, workshops and competitions, with contributions from leading guest writers. Date of next festival to be confirmed.

Lincolnshire Literature Festival, Education and Cultural Services Directorate, Lincolnshire County Council, County Offices, Lincoln LN1 1YL *tel* (01522) 552831. *Contact:* David Lambert (county arts development officer). A series of festivals throughout the year (March-June/July-October) focusing on specific genres, cultures and topical issues. Also a monthly series of literary events at Lincoln Central Library.

Norfolk and Norwich Festival, 16 Princes Street, Norwich NR3 1AE *tel* (01603) 614921 *fax* (01603) 632303. *Festival director:* Marcus Davey. A general arts festival with some literary events. Takes place 10-20 October 1996; programme published in June.

Off the Shelf Festival of Reading and Writing, c/o Sheffield Libraries and Information Services, Central Library, Surrey Street, Sheffield S1 1XZ *tel* 0114-273 6645 *fax* 0114-273 5009. *Contact:* Judith Adam. The festival comprises a wide range of events for adults and children, including writing workshops, talks, storytelling, drama sessions, illustration workshops and exhibitions. Takes place 19 October-2 November 1996; programme available in September.

Poetry International, Literature Department, Royal Festival Hall, London SE1 8XX *tel* 0171-921 0906 *fax* 0171-928 2049. *Contact:* Caroline Hughes. The biggest poetry festival in the British Isles, bringing together a wide range of poets from around the world. Includes readings, workshops, discussions and events for children. Poetry International is a biennial festival. Takes place over 10 days in October/November 1996.

Poets and Small Press Festival, Iron Press, 5 Marden Terrace, Cullercoats, North Shields, Tyne & Wear NE30 4PD *tel* 0191-2531901. *Contact:* Peter Mortimer. The festival celebrates the role that small presses have played in the current resurgence of poetry. Includes readings, performances, debates, live music and a magazine and book fair.

Royal Court Young Writers' Festival, The Royal Court Young People's Theatre, 309 Portobello Road, London W10 5TD *tel* 0181-960 4641. *Contact:* Dominic Tickell. Each festival targets a different area of the UK. Anyone up to the age of 23 can attend workshops at various locations within these areas. Promising plays which arise from the workshops are then developed and performed at the Royal Court's Theatre Upstairs and at venues in the participating area (see page 671).

Salisbury Festival, 75 New Street, Salisbury, Wiltshire SP1 2PH *tel* (01722) 323883 *fax* (01722) 410552. *Director:* Helen Marriage. An annual general arts festival with a literature programme of events. Each year has a chosen theme. Takes place in May/June; programme published in March.

Shots on the Page, Broadwords, Broadway Media Centre, 14 Broad Street, Nottingham NG1 3AL *tel* 0115-955 7171 *fax* 0115-952 6622. Taking place at the same time as the *Shots in the Dark* annual festival, this crime-writing convention is for writers and fans. Includes talks, workshops and discussions with leading guest writers.

The Torrington Literature Festival, The Plough Arts Centre, Fore Street, Torrington, Devon EX38 8HQ *tel* (01805) 622552 *fax* (01805) 624624. *Contact:* Anne Tattersall. The festival comprises workshops (including children's), readings, performances and exhibitions. Takes place 10-12 October 1996.

Warwick & Leamington Festival, Warwick Arts Society, Northgate, Warwick CV34 4JL *tel* (01926) 410747 *fax* (01926) 407606. *Festival director:* Richard Phillips. A music festival which includes some literature and poetry events: readings, performances and workshops. Takes place in first half of July.

Ways With Words Literature Festival, Droridge Farm, Dartington, Totnes, South Devon TQ9 6JQ *tel* (01803) 867311 *fax* (01803) 863688. *Contact:* Kay Dunbar. The festival includes readings, talks, interviews, discussions, seminars, workshops with leading guest writers. Literary weekends and writing courses also organised.

Wells Festival of Literature, Tower House, St Andrew Street, Wells, Somerset BA5 2UN *tel* (01749) 673385. This annual festival features leading guest writers and poets; includes writing workshops. Takes place in October.

Writearound: Cleveland's Annual Festival for Writers and Readers, c/o Cleveland Arts, 7-9 Eastbourne Road, Linthorpe, Middlesbrough, Cleveland TS5 6QS *tel* (01642) 812288 *fax* (01642) 813388. *Contact:* Mark Robinson. Writearound is an independent non-profit-making organisation dedicated to encouraging, promoting and developing literary activity on Teesside and surrounding areas, through an annual literary festival. A programme of events is offered throughout Cleveland, including workshops, performances, poetry, open readings and children's events. Takes place 11-20 October 1996.

Frequency of erotic scenes

Writing erotic prose is unlike most other kinds of writing in that there is a certain mechanical scenic repetitiveness about it: you must provide at least two sex scenes per chapter, or one every couple of thousand words or so, and it would certainly be a mistake to let much more than one thousand words of mere conventional narrative pass without either preparing for the next sex scene (by setting up some kind of sensuous location) or having something to say about the result (psychological or physiological) of the last one. This is rather like having to set up a dinner party scene every few pages – you had better have a good store of dishes in mind; however bright your imagination, you will need all the help you can get as far as language is concerned.

from *Writing Erotic Fiction* by Derek Parker (A & C Black, £8.99). See order form on page 690.

Index

Books in the 'Writing' series

___ Freelance writing for newspapers £9.99
___ Writing for children £7.99
___ Writing crime fiction, 2nd edn £9.99
___ Writing erotic fiction £8.99
___ Writing fantasy fiction £8.99
___ Writing about food £8.99
___ Writing historical fiction, 2nd edn £8.99
___ Writing horror fiction £8.99
___ Writing for magazines, 2nd edn Oct '96 .... £9.99
___ Writing a play, 2nd edn £8.99
___ Writing popular fiction £7.99
___ Writing for radio, 2nd edn £8.99
___ Writing for the teenage market £8.99
___ Writing for television, 2nd edn £9.99
___ Writing a thriller, 2nd edn £9.99
___ Writing about travel, 2nd edn £7.99

Other books for writers

___ Interviewing techniques for writers and researchers £7.99
___ Research for writers, 5th edn £13.99
___ Word power: a guide to creative writing, 2nd edn £9.99
___ The writer's rights £8.99

All these books can be read through your local bookshop. Just tick the titles you want and fill in the form below.
Prices and availability subject to change without notice.

Please return to A&C Black (Publishers) Ltd,
Dept WWA2, PO Box 19, Huntingdon, Cambs PE19 3SF   Tel (0)1480 212666 Fax (0)1480 405014

Send a cheque or postal order for the value of the book(s), adding the postage and packing (UK & Eire £1.00 and Europe 20% overseas)

Amount enclosed or debit my account.

OR please debit this amount from my Access/Visa/Amex (delete as appropriate)

Card number ☐☐☐☐ ☐☐☐☐ ☐☐☐☐ ☐☐☐☐

Amount _____ Expiry date ☐☐ / ☐☐

Signed _____

Name (please print) _____

Address _____

Postcode _____

Books in the 'Writing' series

_____	Freelance writing for newspapers	**£9.99**
_____	Writing for children	**£7.99**
_____	Writing crime fiction *2nd edn*	**£7.99**
_____	Writing erotic fiction	**£8.99**
_____	Writing fantasy fiction	**£8.99**
_____	Writing about food	**£8.99**
_____	Writing historical fiction *2nd edn*	**£8.99**
_____	Writing horror fiction	**£8.99**
_____	Writing for magazines *2nd edn Oct '96*	**£9.99**
_____	Writing a play *2nd edn*	**£8.99**
_____	Writing popular fiction	**£7.99**
_____	Writing for radio *2nd edn*	**£6.99**
_____	Writing for the teenage market	**£8.99**
_____	Writing for television *2nd edn*	**£9.99**
_____	Writing a thriller *2nd edn*	**£9.99**
_____	Writing about travel *2nd edn*	**£7.99**

Other books for writers

_____	Interviewing techniques for writers and researchers	**£7.99**
_____	Research for writers *5th edn*	**£11.99**
_____	Word power: a guide to creative writing *2nd edn*	**£9.99**
_____	The writer's rights	**£8.99**

All these books can be ordered through your local bookshop or direct from the publisher.
Tick the titles you want and fill in the form below.
Prices and availability subject to change without notice

Please return to **A&C Black (Publishers) Ltd,**
Dept YB97, PO Box 19, Huntingdon, Cambs, PE19 3SF   tel (01480) 212666 fax (01480) 405014

Send a cheque or postal order for the value of the book(s), adding (for postage and packing) 15% UK
and Eire; 20% overseas.
Airmail rates available on application.

OR please debit this amount from my Access\Visa Card (delete as appropriate)

Card number ☐☐☐☐☐☐☐☐☐☐☐☐☐☐☐☐☐☐

Amount ——————————   Expiry date ☐☐ ☐☐ ☐☐

Signed ——————————————————————————————

Name (please print) ——————————————————————————

Address ————————————————————————————————

——————————————————— Postcode ———————————————